WILLIAM SHAKESPEARE
1564-1616

A companion guide
to his life & achievements

WHO'S WHO IN SHAKESPEARE
The characters' proper names and sources of all the plays and poems

Gill Davies

SHELTER HARBOR PRESS
NEW YORK

This 2016 edition published by Shelter Harbor Press
by arrangement with Worth Press Ltd

Text Shakespeare Companion Guide: Gill Davies
Design: Jessica Moon

SHELTER HARBOR PRESS
603 W. 115th Street, Suite 163
New York, New York 10025

For sales, contact:
info@shelterharborpress.com

ISBN 978-1-62795-078-7

10 9 8 7 6 5 4 3 2 1

Printed in China.

CONTENTS

INTRODUCTION TO GENIUS

Born over four hundred and fifty years ago, the talented bard from Queen Elizabeth I's Merrie England is today the most read author in the world, drawing enthusiastic admiration from every age group, every nation, and every category of audience ever known. In Shakespeare's day when he was numbered among the actors on the stage, the plays were performed to boisterous audiences that included the groundlings, who paid just one penny to stand right in front of the stage. A line in his play *Henry VIII* describes, 'the youths that thunder at a playhouse, and fight for bitten apples'. This potential rabble included hecklers as well as loud, enthusiastic participants, shoving, manoeuvering and undoubtedly making eyes at the opposite sex as well as watching both the players and the antics of the back-stage crew. Meanwhile, the richer patrons relaxed in the covered galleries, paying perhaps half a crown each for their coveted seats. At the most prestigious end of the scale, the dramas were also presented at the courts of both Queen Elizabeth I and King James I of England.

So the plays had to appeal to a wide sweep of spectators – and still do so today. His works are truly international, with an estimated four billion copies sold over the ages. He is among the most translated authors in history, eclipsed only by the Bible. Ben Jonson stated, 'He was not of an age, but for all time!' and this most popular dramatist and poet certainly

Medley of Shakespeare's characters in
The Plays of Shakespeare by John Gilbert, 1849

told every kind of story. His comedies, tragedies and histories encompass all genres and topics – melodrama, fairy tales, adventure, horror, love stories, humour, burlesque, death, politics, war and romance. The stories transcend time and culture and are as powerful today as ever they were in the sixteenth and seventeenth centuries. They appeal to all while seeming personal, pertinent to every individual watching.

Full of twists of fate that add to the drama and climatic plots, the stories often incorporate magic and superstition, spells, fairies, witches and ghosts. They were penned at a time when witchcraft was taken very seriously; King James himself wrote a book about witches and demons. In sixteenth-century Europe, alchemists were still trying to transform matter into gold, people believed the stars and planets controlled their lives and Elizabeth I's astronomer, Dr John Dee, was trying to establish the language of the angels. The Age of Reason and Enlightenment (1620s–1780s) was still to emerge from medieval thinking – and modern science was in its infancy. The Americas had been discovered in 1492 so the Elizabethan Age saw much greater world exploration and the formation of colonies across the Atlantic. Now the stage was set for new ideas and concepts, but witches would continue to be hunted and burned, peaking in England with the cruel exploits of Witchfinder General, Matthew Hopkins between 1644 and 1647. The very last executions of convicted witches in Europe took place in the 1700s. So, although today we may be tempted to regard such characters as escapism or a dramatic device, they would have been accepted as real and potent by the audience of their day.

Most of the plays were based upon existing older stories. With the exception of *A Midsummer Night's Dream*, *Love's Labour's Lost* and *The Tempest*, which are entirely his original stories, Shakespeare unashamedly borrowed many of his plots and was inspired by stories in the Bible as well as the works of Geoffrey Chaucer (1340–1400), Plutarch (AD 46–120), the Roman poet Ovid (born 43 BC) and English historians like Raphael Holinshed (1529–80), among others. From such sources, Shakespeare went on to pen some of the most celebrated dramas ever known – but he also added to the language, inventing an amazing 1,700 new words and many catchphrases. Four centuries onward, Shakespeare's writings continue to enthrall and enrapture audiences, to inspire and thrill, not just at Stratford or in London's Globe theatre but in every corner of the globe. His works have been translated into more than 100 languages. But of course, it is not only the plays, but also his poetry and sonnets that form part of the Bard's prodigious output and, in fact, earned him serious attention and a not inconsiderable fortune. Shakespeare was not among those geniuses overlooked in his time. He was very much appreciated and of great renown while alive.

It is hoped that this highly illustrated book – teeming with images plus interesting and often surprising facts – manages in some way to encapsulate the glory of this amazing man, his life, his works, his language and legacy.

Gill Davies

Procession of Characters from Shakespeare Plays by unknown British artist

DISCOVERING THE MAN AND THE MYSTERIES

William Shakespeare was born in April 1564 and died on 23 April 1616, four hundred years ago. Shakespeare penned some of the most celebrated dramas ever enjoyed around the world. His words and phrases are widely recognized, but he also left in his wake a plethora of unsolved mysteries.

THE YOUNG SHAKESPEARE

In the sixteenth century, Stratford-upon-Avon in central England's Warwickshire was a centre for the marketing and distribution of sheep, tanning and the wool trade. Baby William Shakespeare put in his first appearance there as the son of glove-maker, leather-worker and wool merchant, John Shakespeare and his wife, Mary Arden, who came from a landowning family. The actual date of his birth remains uncertain but he was christened on 26 April 1564, so it is assumed he had been born a few days prior to that. His birthday is now generally accepted to be 23 April, the same day of the month on which he died.

One of eight children, young Shakespeare was probably educated at the local King Edward VI Grammar School in Stratford where he would have been taught basic reading and writing. There are no records remaining to support this but it is the most likely scenario.

First Folio (*Mr William Shakespeare's Comedies, Histories & Tragedies*), London 1623 (photographed by Andreas Praefcke)

Shakespeare's family circle
by an unknown German engraver, c.1890

At the young age of eighteen, he married Anne Hathaway. The daughter of a local yeoman farmer, she was some eight years older than young Will and evidently already pregnant when they were wed; their first child, Susanna, was born just six months after they took their vows. Some historians suggest that Will really wished to marry another Anne (Anne Whateley) but was forced into marriage because of Anne Hathaway's pregnancy – and was never entirely happy in the relationship, despite the fact that her family were both socially and financially well established and she would have been considered a 'good catch'. His dissatisfaction may have been one of the reasons he eventually set off to seek his fortune in London … but this is all speculation.

Meanwhile, in February 1585, the couple went on to have twins, Hamnet and Judith, named after some close friends of theirs.

WHAT DON'T WE KNOW? THE MYSTERY OF SEVEN LOST YEARS

Shakespeare disappears from historical records from 1585 to 1592. We know nothing of the Bard's life from the year his twin children were born until he appeared in London – without his family and working in the theatre. It was in 1592 that author Robert Greene referred to him in London as an 'upstart crow'. Nothing is known of what Shakespeare was doing in the seven years prior to that or where he was. Some surmise that the Bard fled Stratford after being caught poaching deer from the local squire, Thomas Lucy. Others suggest that he may have joined the players, Queen Elizabeth's Men, to replace one of their actors who had been killed in a fight. The company's tour included Stratford – and thus Shakespeare may have joined their troupe and found his way to London … but all this remains speculative. All we know for certain is that he left Stratford for the city at some point and would eventually make his name there as an actor and playwright.

During Shakespeare's time in London, back in Stratford his son sadly died when aged only eleven years, possibly having contracted bubonic plague – then an all-too-frequent occurrence. Shakespeare's marriage was not really functioning with his prolonged absence from home and he and Anne would live apart for some twenty years whilst he enthusiastically pursued his craft.

SUCCESS IN LONDON

The Bard gradually established his reputation as both an actor and a playwright, ultimately becoming a managing partner of the Lord Chamberlain's Company (renamed the King's Company when James I succeeded to the English throne). The company were involved with both the Globe and the Blackfriars theatres in Southwark, London, set close to the bustling River Thames.

By 1596, Shakespeare had moved to Bishopsgate into the parish of St. Helen's. By 1598 his name appeared at the top of a list of actors in a play written by Ben Jonson (*Every Man in His Humour*) and he was also listed as an actor in Jonson's *Sejanus: His Fall.* That very same year, Shakespeare's name began to appear on the title pages of his own plays.

This print of the original Old Globe theatre was created in 1642 by Wenceslaus Hollar. The label 'The Globe' has been superimposed; in the original drawing, the building was wrongly described as a venue for bear baiting!

Now Shakespeare's writing output would become prolific. From that point on he produced an average of two plays a year until around 1611. His hard work quickly paid dividends, and he seems to have prospered following the publication of his plays. All of his works proved highly successful and popular.

By 1597, he was sufficiently affluent to have purchased New Place, the second largest house in Stratford and, it is believed, a coat of arms for his father. The family crest was a yellow spear on a yellow shield, with the inscription *Non Sans Droit* (Not without right). The Bard made his greatest financial gain in 1605 when he purchased leases of real estate near Stratford. His investment of some £440 doubled in value and earned him £60 each year, the equivalent of many thousands of pounds today. Perhaps this extra income gave him the opportunity and time he needed to write consistently.

Over the years, his plays would mutate from histories and comedies to tragedies. As his reputation grew, the now-famous playwright was summoned to stage several of his plays at the royal court for Queen Elizabeth's entertainment … and then, later, they were performed before her successor, James I, an enthusiastic patron of Shakespeare's work. Shakespeare moved to live in more salubrious surroundings in Silver Street (now lost under the Barbican) and here he conceived some of his greatest tragedies including *Hamlet*, *Othello*, and *Macbeth*.

THE LATTER YEARS

During the latter five years of his life, Shakespeare returned to the Midlands, to New Place in Stratford. Albeit he may have visited Stratford during the Lenten theatre lulls each year, he returned to his family properly only in 1609. He revised his will on 25 March 1616, less than a month before he died, aged 52, on 23 April 1616.

He gave legacies to any future grandsons and, intriguingly, bequeathed his 'second-best bed' to his wife. Most of his estate was left to his eldest daughter, Susanna, who had married a prominent and distinguished physician named John Hall in June 1607. His will also named actors Richard Burbage, Henry Condell and John Hemminges, evidence of his long theatre involvement.

This pre-1616 image of Shakespeare sporting a hooped earring is named the Chandos Portrait after its owner, James Brydges, 1st Duke of Chandos.

HAVING THE LAST WORD

William Shakespeare was buried in Stratford's Holy Trinity Church. Written upon his tombstone is his own epitaph:

Good friend, for Jesus´ sake forbeare
To digg the dust enclosed here!
Blest be ye man that spares thes stones
And curst be he that moues [moves]
my bones.

Church of the Holy Trinity, Stratford-upon-Avon.

The statue of William Shakespeare in Leicester Square, London, UK, sculpted by Giovanni Fontana in 1874

FACTS, FIGURES and FRIVOLITY

- One of Shakespeare's relatives, William Arden, was arrested for plotting against Queen Elizabeth I, imprisoned in the Tower of London and executed.
- Shakespeare's father had a variety of jobs and at one point was actually paid to drink beer!
- Shakespeare probably acted in several of his own plays. There is evidence that he played Adam in *As You Like It* and the ghost in *Hamlet*.
- Shakespeare wore a gold hoop earring in his left ear – shown in the Chandos Portrait on page 13.
- Shakespeare's work was fully appreciated in his own time.
- An excellent businessman, he became a very wealthy man who owned several large properties.
- He formed a joint-stock company with his actors so took a share in the profits, as well as earning a fee for every play he wrote.
- Pestilence led to poetry! Because of the plague outbreak, all London playhouses were closed from 1592 to 1594. This was when Shakespeare began to write poetry.
- Shakespeare's only grandchild, Elizabeth, died childless in 1670 so he has no descendants.
- Shakespeare's Way is a long-distance footpath that traces a possible 234-kilometre (146-mile) route that the young Shakespeare might have walked to and from London.
- Only a few of his original signatures have survived and not a single one spells his name the way we know it today. Variations include:

Wm Shakspe, Willm Shaksp, Willm Shakspere,

William Shakespe, William Shakspere, William Shakspeare

THE PLAYS AND THE POETRY

The Bard's surviving works, including several collaborations, consist of at least 37 plays (the authorship of some others is still debated), 154 sonnets, two long narrative poems, and a few other poems.

At the time when Shakespeare was feverishly writing both poetry and plays, dramatists were not considered 'serious' authors; such stuff was for relaxed entertainment and the amusement of common folk. Poems, however, were aimed at the elite and were usually penned by such nobility as Sir Walter Raleigh and Sir Philip Sydney. The fact that William Shakespeare found success as a poet (rather than merely in the theatre) would have greatly helped his status. Moreover, when plague led to the closure of the London playhouses, this provided an opportunity for Shakespeare to explore other media.

Despite being from farming and yeoman stock, with a background and lack of formal education that might well have undermined his credibility as a serious author, ultimately Shakespeare's fine poems served to underline his abilities, his control of words and his wit. Here, indeed, was a writing force to be reckoned with. Moreover, their publication proved lucrative for the up-and-coming writer and actor.

Shakespeare performing before Queen Elizabeth and her court; an 1839 engraving

THE POEMS AND THE SONNETS

Between about 1592 and 1604, Shakespeare wrote four poems (*Venus and Adonis*, *The Rape of Lucrece, A Lover's Complaint* and *Funeral Elegy*) as well as creating his amazing collection of 154 sonnets. These were printed in quarto editions (small, inexpensive pamphlets) between 1593 and 1609.

Venus and Adonis, written in 1592–93, has a plot based upon passages from the *Metamorphoses* by the classical Roman poet Ovid Initially published and printed by a Stratford-upon-Avon contemporary of Shakespeare, Richard Field, this would become the most widely printed of the Bard's works during his lifetime. In the following year, 1594, Shakespeare published *The Rape of Lucrece*, again printed by Richard Field, but sold by the bookseller John Harrison the Elder from his shop at the sign of the White Greyhound in the churchyard of St Paul's. Both poems gave Shakespeare's reputation a boost and helped to upgrade his financial status, too.

Besides all this, of course, many of the plays contain verse format, superb poetry and entrancing songs, such as 'Where the Bee Sucks', 'Hark; Hark! the Lark' and 'Under the Greenwood Tree'.

Where the bee sucks, there suck I

Where the bee sucks, there suck I:
In a cowslip's bell I lie;
There I couch when owls do cry.
On the bat's back I do fly
After summer merrily.
Merrily, merrily shall I live now
Under the blossom that hangs on the bough.

Song from *The Tempest*, Act V, Scene 1

Sonnet 18:
Shall I compare thee to a summer's day?

Shall I compare thee to a summer's day?
Thou art more lovely and more temperate.
Rough winds do shake the darling buds of May,
And summer's lease hath all too short a date.
Sometime too hot the eye of heaven shines,
And often is his gold complexion dimmed;
And every fair from fair sometime declines,
By chance, or nature's changing course, untrimmed;
But thy eternal summer shall not fade,
Nor lose possession of that fair thou ow'st,
Nor shall death brag thou wand'rest in his shade,
When in eternal lines to Time thou grow'st.
  So long as men can breathe, or eyes can see,
  So long lives this, and this gives life to thee.

SONNETS

Probably the most popular verse form in Shakespeare's England, a sonnet has fourteen lines and a specific rhyme scheme. At some point in the early 1590s, Shakespeare began writing a compilation of sonnets, the first edition of which was printed in 1609, although some had appeared as early versions in the 1599 folio, *The Passionate Pilgrim*. His sonnets reflect upon love, beauty, mortality and time.

Sonnets 1–126 are concerned with a young, unnamed lord, the Fair Youth.

Sonnets 127–152 deal with with the poet's relationship to the Dark Lady, a mysterious mistress.

Sonnets 153–154 are poetic exercises dedicated to Cupid.

THE PLAYS

Shakespeare created his plays between about 1590 and 1614, and they began to be printed in cheap quarto editions in 1594. In 1623, *Mr. William Shakespeare's Comedies, Histories, & Tragedies* appeared in an expensive folio volume. This contained 36 plays and is now referred to as the First Folio. Happily, these printed editions ensured that Shakespeare's plays survived, and they have been used as the mainspring of Shakespearian scripts since the 1600s. Today both actors and directors owe their ability to still enjoy and perform these works to this foresighted preservation.

All the world's a stage

All the world's a stage,
And all the men and women merely players;
They have their exits and their entrances,
And one man in his time plays many parts,
His acts being seven ages. At first, the infant,
Mewling and puking in the nurse's arms.
Then the whining schoolboy, with his satchel
And shining morning face, creeping like snail
Unwillingly to school. And then the lover,
Sighing like furnace, with a woeful ballad
Made to his mistress' eyebrow. Then a soldier,
Full of strange oaths and bearded like the pard,
Jealous in honor, sudden and quick in quarrel,
Seeking the bubble reputation
Even in the cannon's mouth. And then the justice,
In fair round belly with good capon lined,
With eyes severe and beard of formal cut,
Full of wise saws and modern instances;
And so he plays his part. The sixth age shifts
Into the lean and slippered pantaloon,
With spectacles on nose and pouch on side;
His youthful hose, well saved, a world too wide
For his shrunk shank, and his big manly voice,
Turning again toward childish treble, pipes
And whistles in his sound. Last scene of all,
That ends this strange eventful history,
Is second childishness and mere oblivion,
Sans teeth, sans eyes, sans taste, sans everything.

From *As You Like It*, Act II, Scene 7

Wrestling scene from *As You Like It*
by Raymond Robert Reikes, 1892

SHAKESPEARE'S PLAYS

Henry VI, Part 1 (1589–92) (History)
Henry VI, Part 2 (1590–92) (History)
Henry VI, Part 3 (1590–93) (History)
Richard III (1592–93) (History)
The Comedy of Errors (1592–93) (Comedy)
Titus Andronicus (1593–94) (Tragedy)
The Taming of the Shrew (1593–94) (Comedy)
The Two Gentlemen of Verona (1594–95) (Comedy)
Love's Labour's Lost (1594–95) (Comedy)
Romeo and Juliet (1594–95) (Tragedy)
Richard II (1595–96) (History)
A Midsummer Night's Dream (1595–96) (Comedy)
King John (1596–97) (History)
The Merchant of Venice (1596–97) (Comedy)
Henry IV, Part 1 (1597–98) (History)
Henry IV, Part 2 (1597–98) (History)
Much Ado About Nothing (1598–99) (Comedy)
Henry V (1598–99) (History)
Julius Caesar (1599–1600) (Tragedy)
As You Like It (1599–1600) (Comedy)
Twelfth Night (1599–1600) (Comedy)
Hamlet (1600–01) (Tragedy)
The Merry Wives of Windsor (1600–01) (Comedy)
Troilus and Cressida (1601–02) (Comedy)
All's Well That Ends Well (1602–03) (Comedy)
Measure for Measure (1604–05) (Comedy)
Othello (1604–05) (Tragedy)
King Lear (1605–06) (Tragedy)
Macbeth (1605–06) (Tragedy)
Antony and Cleopatra (1606–07) (Tragedy)
Coriolanus (1607–08) (Tragedy)
Timon of Athens (1607–08) (Tragedy)
Pericles, Prince of Tyre (1608–09) (Comedy)
Cymbeline (1609–10) (Comedy)
The Winter's Tale (1610–11) (Comedy)
The Tempest (1611–12) (Comedy)
Henry VIII (1612–13) (History)

None of Shakespeare's original manuscripts have survived, so the printed texts of his plays are our only source of his original works. Eighteen of Shakespeare's plays had appeared in quarto editions by the time of his death in 1616, and another three plays were printed in quarto before 1642. The 1623 First Folio included most of those printed in quarto. The quarto editions are the texts closest to Shakespeare's time. Some are thought to preserve his working drafts (called his 'foul papers') and some his final 'fair' copies. Others may record versions remembered by actors who performed in the plays, and these include stage directions that add to our knowledge of Elizabethan and Jacobean staging practices.

Two works still disputed, or under joint authorship, are *The Two Noble Kinsmen* (1612–13) written with John Fletcher and *Edward III*, published anonymously in 1596 but possibly written by Shakespeare with Thomas Kyd.

Winter

When icicles hang by the wall
And Dick the shepherd blows his nail
And Tom bears logs into the hall,
And milk comes frozen home in pail,
When Blood is nipped and ways be foul,
Then nightly sings the staring owl,
Tu-who;
Tu-whit, tu-who: a merry note,
While greasy Joan doth keel the pot.

When all aloud the wind doth blow,
And coughing drowns the parson's saw,
And birds sit brooding in the snow,
And Marian's nose looks red and raw
When roasted crabs hiss in the bowl,
Then nightly sings the staring owl,
Tu-who;
Tu-whit, tu-who: a merry note,
While greasy Joan doth keel the pot.

From *Love's Labour's Lost* Act V, Scene 2

GALLERY OF MEMORABLE CHARACTERS

William Shakespeare's plays contain a total of 34,895 speeches spoken by 1,223 characters. Hamlet had the most to say by far with 1,495 lines but there were many other garrulous parts – the top sixteen are all male!

THE TOP TWENTY

1 Hamlet (*Hamlet*) 1,495
2 Richard III (*Richard III*) 1,171
3 Iago (*Othello*) 1,098
4 King Henry V (*Henry V*) 1,028
5 Coriolanus (*Coriolanus*) 897
6 Othello (*Othello*) 887
7 Timon (*Timon of Athens*) 865
8 Vincentio (*Measure for Measure*) 852
9 Mark Antony (*Antony and Cleopatra*) 851
10 King Lear (*King Lear*) 758
11 Richard II (*Richard II*) 758
12 Edward III (*Edward III*) 749
13 Marcus Brutus (*Julius Caesar*) 728
14 Titus Andronicus (*Titus Andronicus*) 723
15 Macbeth (*Macbeth*) 719
16 Leontes (*The Winter's Tale*) 692
17 Cleopatra (*Antony and Cleopatra*) 686
18 Rosalind (*As You Like It*) 677
19 Prospero (*The Tempest*) 674
20 Falstaff (*Henry IV, Part 2*) 637

Scene from A Midsummer Night's Dream.
Titania and Bottom by Edwin Landseer, 1851

SHAKESPEARE'S VILLAINS: THE LADIES

The Queen in *Cymbeline*
This unnamed lady pursues her ambitions with ruthless determination and murder.

Lady Macbeth in *Macbeth*
To advance her husband's position and attain her own ambitions, she urges and helps Macbeth to kill the king but eventually loses her sanity and commits suicide.

Regan in *King Lear*
Lear's ungrateful second daughter turns on her father most cruelly. She also ties his old friend, Gloucester, to a chair and then pulls out his eyes.

Tamora in *Titus Andronicus*
Queen of the Goths, Tamora seeks revenge for the death of her son, involving her lover, Aaron the Moor, in the violence and instructing her sons to rape and dismember Lavinia and to kill her husband. However (presaging Sweeney Todd), Tamore ends up unknowingly eating her sons baked within meat pies.

Ellen Terry plays Lady Macbeth, 1888

SHAKESPEARE'S VILLAINS: THE MEN

Angelo in *Measure for Measure*
With ruthless hypocrisy Angelo imprisons and executes people who conduct sexual affairs outside of marriage while bargaining with Isabella, a beautiful young nun, to save her brother's life only if she agrees to have sex with him.

Claudius in *Hamlet*
Claudius is Hamlet's uncle who has murdered his brother (Hamlet's father) in order to gain the throne and marry the queen. He also plots (but fails) to have Hamlet murdered.

Macbeth in *Macbeth*
Macbeth kills King Duncan and then embarks on a murderous career, killing (or ordering the murders of) all those who oppose him or threaten his success, including his close friend, Banquo, and Lady Macduff's young son.

Aaron the Moor in *Titus Andronicus*
Aaron the Moor is the lover of Tamora and helps her seek revenge on the Andronicus family. Enjoying violence, he instigates rape, mutilation and murder.

Richard III in *Richard III*
Richard III is a villain who addresses the audience directly and solicits their sympathy as he pursues his selfish motives and intent to attain the throne. He has his brother Clarence drowned in a great vat of wine, seduces Anne Neville and persuades her to marry him even though he has murdered her husband and her father, and also has two of his nephews beheaded.

Iago in *Othello*
Iago seems charming on the surface but is cruel, manipulative and sly. A veritable psychopath, he destroys the lives of those around him.

David Garrick as Richard III, c.1745

SHAKESPEARE'S MAJOR HEROES

All of Shakespeare's characters are complex, many full of self doubt, but courageous and compelling. Here are just a few of the many male celebrities that so capture our imagination:

Antony in *Antony and Cleopatra*

Brutus in *Julius Caesar*

Hamlet in *Hamlet*

Horatio in *Hamlet*

Orsino in *Twelfth Night*

Othello in *Othello*

Petruchio in *The Taming of the Shrew*

Prince Hal (and later Henry V) in *Henry IV, Parts 1* and *2* and *Henry V*

Prospero in *The Tempest*

Romeo in *Romeo and Juliet*

Oberon in *A Midsummer Night's Dream*

Orlando in *As You Like It*

King Lear in *King Lear*

Frank Robert Benson as Petruchio in *The Taming of the Shrew*, 1901

SHAKESPEARE'S WOMEN

In Elizabethan England many wives or daughters were regarded as possessions, often used to forge alliances between the rich and powerful and generally expected to give birth to heirs with as little fuss as possible. Notwithstanding this, Shakespeare created some amazingly strong female characters. Many disguised themselves as men to attain their ends although most, like Katherina in *The Taming of the Shrew*, ultimately seem to accept marriage and obedience to their husbands.

Cordelia in *King Lear*

A Cinderella character, dutiful daughter Cordelia loves her father but shows great courage when he banishes her. Ultimately, when he is also imprisoned, she comforts him but is eventually hanged.

Portia in *The Merchant of Venice*
Portia is a rich, beautiful, and intelligent heiress. Disguised as a famous young judge she delivers her decisions in court with wisdom, saving the life of Antonio and outwitting Shylock.

Lady Macbeth in *Macbeth*
As the play begins, Lady Macbeth has great power over her husband, Macbeth, as she encourages him to murder the king, Duncan.

Beatrice in *Much Ado About Nothing*
This feisty, highly intelligent feminist has contempt for men. She particularly dislikes Benedick, but the pair are tricked by their friends and eventually do fall in love.

Juliet in *Romeo and Juliet*
Headstrong, courageous and intelligent, Juliet is a mere fourteen years old when she meets and falls in love with Romeo and so refuses to marry the Count of Paris, despite his great anger. Her plan to take a drug that will make her appear lifeless misfires when Romeo discovers her and believes she really is dead.

Desdemona in *Othello*
Venetian beauty Desdemona elopes with Othello, but will ultimately be strangled by him when he is persuaded that she has been unfaithful. A strong, independent woman she is passionate, bold and much misunderstood.

Rosalind in *As You Like It*
Intelligent, quick-witted, and beautiful, Rosalind disguises herself as a shepherd as she aims to win the heart of someone who can match her qualities and strength. She proves a faithful friend and leader and a clever architect of her future, no matter how dangerous the route.

Viola in *Twelfth Night*
Shipwrecked and having lost her twin brother, Viola disguises herself as a man and secures a servant's post in the household of the Duke. Able to adapt and manipulate her circumstances, she achieves her desired outcome, which is to marry the Duke.

Margaret of Anjou in four history plays
A ruthless, ambitious, intelligent woman who dominates her husband King Henry VI.

Hermia in *A Midsummer Night's Dream*
Hermia is determined to control her own destiny, despite a potential death sentence or dismissal to a nunnery.

SHAKESPEARE'S AMAZING COUPLES

Romeo and **Juliet** *Romeo and Juliet*
Katherina and **Petruchio** *The Taming of the Shrew*
Macbeth and **Lady Macbeth** *Macbeth*
Othello and **Desdemona** *Othello*
Beatrice and **Benedick** *Much Ado About Nothing*
Titania and **Oberon** *A Midsummer Night's Dream*
Antony and **Cleopatra** *Antony and Cleopatra*
Hermia and **Lysander** *A Midsummer Night's Dream*
Lorenzo and **Jessica** *The Merchant of Venice*
Henry V and **Katherine** *Henry V*
Helena and **Demetrius** *A Midsummer Night's Dream*
Claudio and **Hero** *Much Ado About Nothing*
Sebastian and **Olivia** *Twelfth Night*
Orsino and **Viola** *Twelfth Night*
Orlando and **Rosalind** *As You Like It*
Ferdinand and **Miranda** *The Tempest*
Claudio and **Juliet** *Measure for Measure*
Oliver and **Celia** *As You Like It*
Silvia and **Valentine** *The Two Gentlemen of Verona*
Antipholus and **Adriana** *The Comedy of Errors*
Julia and **Proteus** *The Two Gentlemen of Verona*
Leontes and **Hermione** *The Winter's Tale*
Florizel and **Perdita** *The Winter's Tale*
Biron and **Rosaline** *Love's Labour's Lost*
Henry VIII and **Queen Katherine** *Henry VIII*
Henry VIII and **Anne Boleyn** *Henry VIII*

Romeo and Juliet
by Frank Dicksee, 1884

SHAKESPEARE'S COMIC CHARACTERS AND FOOLS

This fellow is wise enough to play the fool,
And to do that well craves a kind of wit.
Twelfth Night

Nick Bottom and the simple 'mechanicals' *A Midsummer Night's Dream*

Trinculo *The Tempest* (jester and domestic buffoon)

Launce and **Speed** *Two Gentlemen of Verona* (Speed is a clever, witty servant; Launce a simpleton)

Feste *Twelfth Night* (Olivia's domestic fool and jester)

Costard *Love's Labour's Lost* (country bumpkin fool)

Launcelot Gobbo *The Merchant of Venice* (a 'patch' and unofficial fool)

Touchstone *As You Like It* (domestic wise and natural fool)

Lavache *Alls Well That Ends Well* (domestic fool, bitter with dark wit)

The Fool *King Lear* (amusing, loyal and brutally honest)

Fool *Timon of Athens* (only nine lines to say but perceptive ones)

Thersites *Troilus and Cressida* (Greek slave who speaks his mind, insulting all with his cruel comments)

Clown *Othello* (makes exasperating lame jokes)

Pompey *Measure for Measure* (rogue, barman, long-winded but witty clown)

Autolycus *The Winter's Tale* (scheming peddler and pickpocket but likeable, an entertaining rogue)

Clown *The Winter's Tale* (dim-witted rustic buffoon)

Grumio *The Taming of the Shrew* (astute old servant and source of much comic relief)

Dromio of Syracuse and **Dromio** of Ephesus, *Comedy of Errors* (absurd and mischievous but dimwitted servants)

The Porter *Macbeth* (provides light comic relief as, drunk and sleepy, he interacts with the audience)

Cloten *Cymbaline* (coarse, stupid, bestial, arrogant and clumsy, this fool provides profound humour)

Falstaff *Henry IV, Part 1, Henry IV, Part 2, The Merry Wives of Windsor* (possibly the Bard's greatest comic role, a glutton and dupe but witty, harmless and kind. He invites affection and was liked by Queen Elizabeth I)

Dogberry *Much Ado About Nothing* (leader of a group of bumbling, ridiculous police watchmen who exhibit comic incompetence)

While not classic clowns or fools, great humour is also provided by:

Malvolio's posturing in *Twelfth Night*

Fluellen, the Welsh captain in *Henry V*

The Nurse in *Romeo and Juliet*

Polonius is long winded and ridiculous in *Hamlet*

Autolycus selling his wares by Charles Robert Leslie, 1836 (*The Winter's Tale*)

Ira Aldridge as Aaron in *Titus Andronicus* in 1852:
'He dies upon my scimetar's [sic] sharp point,
That touches this my first-born son and heir!'

John William Waterhouse's 1889 depiction of *Hamlet*'s Ophelia

Timon of Athens: Timon Laying Aside the Gold
by Johann Heinrich Ramberg, 1829

Theda Bara as Cleopatra in 1917

Cleopatra greets Antony in a 1906 drawing by A. M. Faulkner

Alan Roscoe and Theda Bara in *Cleopatra*, 1917

Falstaff in the Boar's Head Tavern, from *Henry IV, Part 1*, by an unknown artist, c.1840

Queen Katherine of France in H*enry V*, by Laura T. Alma-Tadema, 1888

Dame Ellen Terry as Katherine of Aragon in *Henry VIII* by unknown artist, 1892

Falstaff with a tankard and cup
by Eduard von Grützner, 1896

Falstaff and Prince Hal
by an unknown artist

Miranda – The Tempest
by John William Waterhouse, 1916

George Romney depicts *The Tempest* Act I, Scene 1 in an engraving published in 1797

Ferdinand, Prospero and Miranda in *The Tempest*
by an unknown artist

Edwin Booth as Hamlet, lithograph, 1873

Mignon Nevada as Ophelia, 1910

Hamlet's Vision by Pedro Américo, 1893

Sarah Bernhardt as Hamlet, 1885–1900 (photograph by James Lafayette)

Charles Albert Fechter as Hamlet, c.1872

Pascal Dagnan-Bouveret depicts Hamlet and the Gravediggers, 1883

Sir Herbert Beerbohm Tree (1853–1917) as William Shakespeare's Shylock in *The Merchant of Venice*, by Charles Buchel, 1914

Jessica by Sir Samuel Luke Fildes, 1888

The Merchant of Venice: *Portia and Shylock* by Thomas Sully, 1835

Shylock and Jessica by Maurycy Gottlieb, 1887, reworked by Lestat (Jan Mehlich)

Othello and Desdemona by Alexandre-Marie Colin, 1829

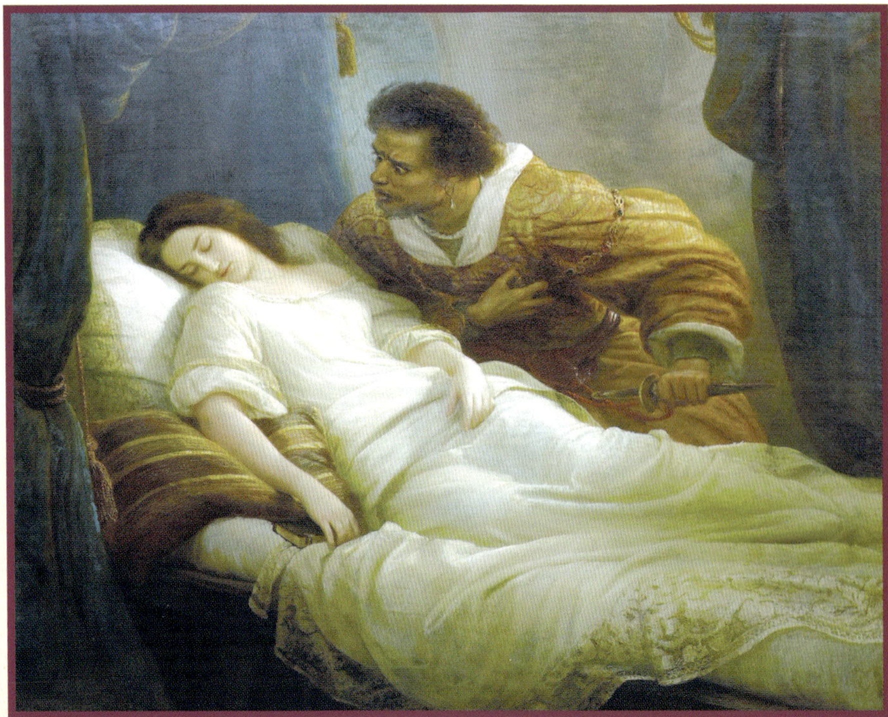

Othello and Desdemona by Christian Köhler, 1859

Edwin Booth as Iago, 1870

Paul Robeson as Othello, 1944

Othello Tells the Stories of His Adventures,
by Carl Ludwig Friedrich Becker, c.1880

Twelfth Night: Observed by the three tricksters Sir Toby Belch, Sir Andrew Aguecheek and Maria, Malvolio finds the fake love letter addressed to him

Twelfth Night: Viola and the Countess by Frederick Richard Pickersgill, 1859

Stipple engraving of Viola in *Twelfth Night:* by W. H. Mote, 1836

Orsino and Viola (from *Twelfth Night*) by
Frederick Richard Pickersgill, c.1850

Ludwig Devrient as King Lear, 1769

Király-Szacsvay Imre as King Lear, 1897, Budapest

King Lear, Act III by Benjamin West, 1788

King Lear and Cordelia by Benjamin West, 1793

Poster of Thomas W. Keene in *Macbeth*, c.1884

The Three Witches by Henry Fuseli, 1785

Lady Macbeth by George Cattermole, 1850

Sarah Siddons as Lady Macbeth by Robert Smirke, c.1790–1810

Macbeth and Banquo meet the Three Witches
by an unknown artist

Lobby card for the 1936 film of *Romeo and Juliet*

Romeo and Juliet's last kiss, depicted by Francesco Hayez, 1823

Juliet or *The Blue Necklace* by John William Waterhouse, 1898

Audrey, the country goatherd, in *As You Like It*,
depicted by Philip Richard Morris, 1888

The jester, Touchstone, falls in love with the simple-witted shepherdess, Audrey, in *As You Like It* (John Collier, 1892)

The Mock Marriage of Orlando and Rosalind, Walter Deverell's forest scene from *As You Like It*, 1853

Katherine and Petruchio, a watercolour
by James Dromgole Linton, c.1890

Kate and Petruchio in a production of
The Taming of the Shrew in Carmel, California (October 2003)

Katherina contemplates her empty plate in
The Taming of the Shrew by Edward Robert Hughes, 1898

The Reconciliation of Oberon and Titania
by Joseph Noel Paton, 1847

Titania and Bottom
by Henry Fuseli, c.1790

Tindřich Mošna as Thisbe in Prague, 1884

Jean Muir (Helena) and Olivia de Havilland (Hermia) in the 1935 film *A Midsummer Night's Dream*

Autolycus selling his wares in *The Winter's Tale* by John Cawse, c.1830

Perdita from *The Winter's Tale* by Anthony Frederick Augustus Sandys, 1866

PLACES IN HIS LIFE AND PLAYS

Shakespeare lived in both London and Stratford-upon-Avon so these two places are the focus of attention for those who wish to trace his steps but the Bard dreamed, imagined and wrote about many other parts of the then known world. The Americas were only just being explored by Europeans but North Africa and the Middle East provide settings for his plays as do many European nations, with Italy and Mediterranean sites clearly a great source of inspiration.

STRATFORD-UPON-AVON

Some 4.9 million visitors come to 800-year-old Stratford-upon-Avon each year to visit the places associated with Shakespeare – many also enjoying a performance at the Royal Shakespeare Theatre. The town has several Tudor timbered buildings including some beautiful historic houses and gardens directly linked with William Shakespeare and his family. William probably went to the King Edward VI Grammar School when he was seven and this is occasionally open to visitors. The church where he was baptized and eventually buried also attracts tourists and there are many walking tours and special events that celebrate the town's most famous son.

Shakespeare's birthplace in Henley Street, Stratford-upon-Avon

SHAKESPEARE'S BIRTHPLACE

William Shakespeare was born and spent his childhood years here, as well as the first five years of married life with Anne Hathaway. First opened to the public over 250 years ago, this intriguing place offers a chance to visualize the young Shakespeare at home, where his father ran a glove-making business. Well-known visitors have included Charles Dickens, John Keats, Walter Scott and Thomas Hardy. Today there is live theatre with costumed actors performing excerpts from the plays.

ANNE HATHAWAY'S COTTAGE

A delightful cottage and garden – the childhood home of William Shakespeare's wife.

HALL'S CROFT

This elegant house was the home of William's daughter, Susanna, and her wealthy husband, Dr John Hall, an eminent physician. Today it houses an intriguing collection of apothecaries' equipment and books in the doctor's consulting room, along with a first edition of his medical notes published in 1657. Its beautiful gardens include a walled garden, a herb garden and a rose garden.

NASH'S HOUSE

The well-preserved Tudor building was named after wealthy property-owner Thomas Nash, the first husband of Shakespeare's granddaughter. Its ground floor is furnished as in Nash's day.

Halls Croft, Stratford-upon-Avon

NEW PLACE

Next door to Nash's House can be seen the foundations of New Place – the second biggest house in Stratford at the time and where Shakespeare lived when he was not in London. He bought it in 1597 and would live there for his last nineteen years, enjoying his success as a writer and as a prominent citizen of Stratford-upon-Avon. Here he was at last reunited with his wife and family after so many years away in London, and he died in New Place in 1616. It is thought that here Shakespeare wrote some of his later works such as *The Tempest*.

MARY ARDEN'S FARM

This working, authentic Tudor farm dates back to the 1570s and was the childhood home of Shakespeare's mother.

SHAKESPEARE'S LONDON

Shakespeare spent most of his working life in London – the largest, richest English city and a vibrant port, busy with all classes of people, many of who were theatregoers. Between 1550 and 1600 the city's population rose from around 50,000 to over 200,000, and from 1567 to 1622, nine new outdoor playhouses were built. Wealthy traders, merchants, manufacturers and their apprentices and workers all enjoyed the theatre. By 1600, London's theatregoers may have numbered as many as 20,000 per week. Rich noblemen and royalty supported playhouses, often as patrons, giving financial and legal help. From 1603 to 1613, Shakespeare's company played at the court of King James about fifteen times per year.

London's crowded conditions encouraged several diseases including plague. There were no street lamps or police in thoroughfares ever busy with thieves, prostitutes and pickpockets. Places like Shoreditch and Cheapside attracted boisterous characters personified in Shakespeare's Falstaff. There were dancers, entertainers, bear pits, cockpits, musicians, bull-baiting and a social and ethnic mix that included Jews, Africans, Moroccans – some foreigners were former slaves liberated from Spanish galleys – maimed veterans from the war in Ireland, and countless hungry beggars.

LONDON THEATRES INCLUDED:

Blackfriars Blackfriars

Small, roofed, second-floor theatre, built 1596, pulled down 1655: with its paved auditorium and artificial lighting, Blackfriars catered to the wealthy, educated classes and became London's premier playhouse, charging five times more than the Globe and seating some 700 playgoers. King James I, a theatre enthusiast, became patron of the Lord Chamberlain's Men and, renamed the King's Men, they took on the lease of the Blackfriars from the Burbage theatrical family in 1608. The company performed there during the winter months while still spending its summer seasons at the Globe.

The Cockpit (reopened as **the Phoenix**) Drury Lane
Small, roofed theatre, constructed in the Cockpit around 1616–17, closed 1665.

The Curtain Moore-fields, Shoreditch, by the Theatre, north of London Wall
Unroofed, built 1576–77, pulled down about 1630: this London playhouse had the same structure as the Theatre but was slightly smaller. At times both theatres were under the same management. From 1597–98, the Curtain was the home of the Lord Chamberlain's Men, before they moved to the Globe in 1599. It was then used by many popular acting companies, including the Queen's Men and the Prince Charles' Company.

The Fortune (First) Golden Lane (later Red Cross Street), Cripplegate
Unroofed, square, built 1600, burnt down 1621.

The Fortune (Second) between Golden Lane and Whitecross Street
Unroofed, brick theatre, erected about 1623, closed 1649, but later used as a brewery.

The Globe Bankside
Unroofed, built 1598–99, burnt down 1613, rebuilt with a tiled roof 1614 on site of the first house, pulled down 1644: much of Shakespeare's wealth came from his holdings in the Globe, designed and constructed for the Lord Chamberlain's Men by Cuthbert Burbage, son of the theatre creator, and this was the primary home of Shakespeare's acting company from late 1599. *As You Like It* may have been written especially for the launch. In 1613, during a performance of *Henry VIII*, a misfired cannon set the Globe's thatched roof on fire and the whole theatre burned down, but it was quickly rebuilt with the addition of a tiled roof. Its open courtyard and three semicircular galleries could together hold more than 1,500 people.

The Hope Bankside
Unroofed theatre and bear-baiting arena, built 1614, pulled down 1656.

Newington Butts Lambeth
Unroofed theatre, built about 1586, pulled down around 1603: situated over a mile from the Thames, near an archery-training field. In 1594, the Lord Chamberlain's Men gave their earliest recorded performances of *Titus Andronicus*, *The Taming of the Shrew*, and Thomas Kyd's version of *Hamlet* here.

Paul's in the Choir Singing School (St Paul's)
The first roofed theatre, built about 1581, burnt down in the Great Fire, 1666.

ON LOCATION ...

Shakespeare set his plays in many varied settings:

All's Well That Ends Well
Rousillon (France), also Paris and Marseille (France) plus Florence (Italy)

Antony and Cleopatra
Alexandria (Egypt) and other parts of the Roman Empire

As You Like It
Forest of Arden (imaginary county that may be based on England's Warwickshire region and France's Ardennes forest)

The Comedy of Errors
Ephesus (Turkey)

Coriolanus
Rome, plus Corioli and Antium (Italy)

Cymbeline
Mythic pre-Christian Britain plus Italy

Hamlet
Elsinore Castle (Denmark)

Henry IV, Part 1
London (England) plus Wales

Henry IV, Part 2
London plus other UK locations

Henry V
London plus France and other UK locations

Henry VI, Part 1
London plus Orleans (France)

Henry VI, Part 2
London plus other UK locations

Henry VI, Part 3
London plus France

Henry VIII
London plus other UK locations

Julius Caesar
Rome (Italy), afterwards Sardis (in modern Turkey) and near Philippi (Macedonia, in modern Greece)

King John
London plus France

King Lear
Mythical pre-Christian Britain

Love's Labour's Lost
Navarre (Spain)

Macbeth
Inverness (Scotland) and other Scottish and British locations

Measure for Measure
Vienna (Austria)

The Merchant of Venice
Venice and Portia's home in fictional Belmont (Italy)

The Merry Wives of Windsor
Windsor (England)

A Midsummer Night's Dream
Athens, and a wood (Greece)

Much Ado About Nothing
Messina (Italy)

Othello
Venice (for first act) and a seaport in Cyprus

Pericles, Prince of Tyre
Tyre (Lebanon) plus various Mediterranean locations including Antioch (in modern Turkey)

Richard II
London and Wales

Richard III
London

Romeo and Juliet
Verona and Mantua (Italy)

The Taming of the Shrew
Padua and Petruchio's country home (Italy)

The Tempest
At sea, then a fictional island

Timon of Athens
Athens (Greece)

Titus Andronicus
Rome (Italy)

Troilus and Cressida
Troy (in modern Turkey)

Twelfth Night
Illyria (Western Balkans: the coasts of modern day Slovenia, Croatia, Montenegro and Albania)

Two Gentlemen of Verona
Verona (Italy)

The Two Noble Kinsmen
Athens plus Thebes (Greece)

The Winter's Tale
Sicily (Italy) plus Bohemia

The Swan Paris Garden, Southwark, south of the Thames
Unroofed, built 1595, pulled down about 1635: scholars argue over whether Shakespeare and his company, the Lord Chamberlain's Men, played there. The Swan is depicted in the only known contemporary drawing of an Elizabethan playhouse.

This 1596 sketch of the Swan was made
by Dutch traveller Johannes de Witt while visiting London

The Red Bull St. John Street, Clerkenwell
Unroofed, built about 1600, enlarged 1632, last used as a playhouse in 1663.

The Rose Bankside, Southwark
Small, unroofed theatre, built 1587–92: raised above an old rose garden by businessman and royal groom, Philip Henslowe. Playgoers were ferried across the Thames to see companies perform, including Lord Strange's Men (probably with Shakespeare acting) from 1592 to 1593 and the Admiral's Men (Shakespeare's chief rivals). During the 1593 plague the Rose closed down as nearly 11,000 Londoners died.

Salisbury Court Salisbury Court, Fleet Street
Roofed theatre, built 1629, dismantled 1649, last used in 1661, destroyed by the Great Fire in 1666.

The Theatre Moore-fields, Shoreditch
Unroofed, built 1576, pulled down 1598: first London playhouse built by actor and entrepreneur James Burbage. It was a vast, three-storey, polygonal, timber structure, open to all weathers and used primarily by Shakespeare's acting troupe, the Lord Chamberlain's Men.

Vere Street Vere Street, Clare Market
Oblong, roofed theatre, built in a tennis-court 1660, closed 1663.

Whitefriars near Salisbury Court, Fleet Street
Small, roofed theatre, built about 1603

WORDS AND PHRASES COINED BY SHAKESPEARE

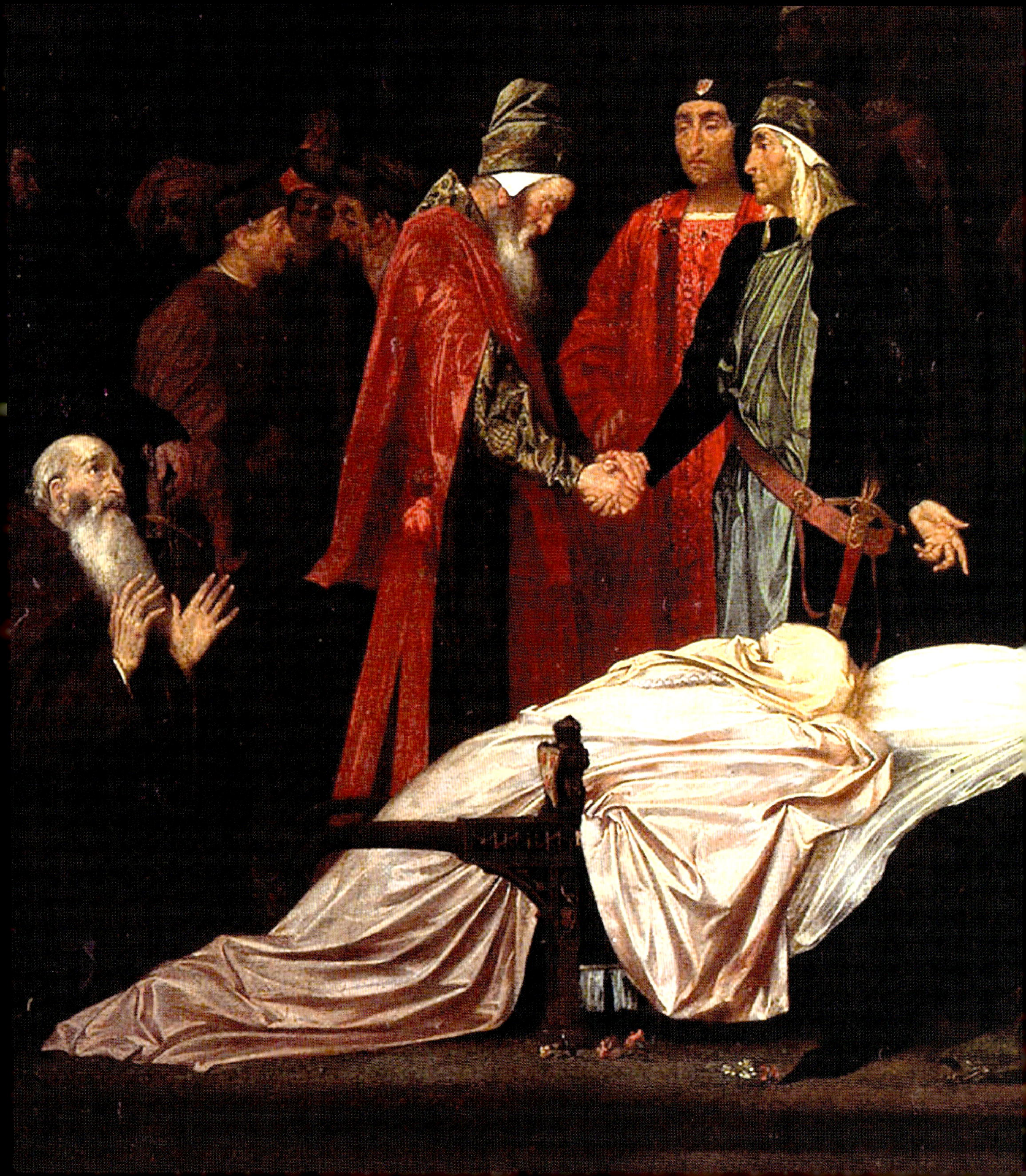

Mercutio's famous cry, 'A plague a' both your houses!' from *Romeo and Juliet* refers to the impact of family feuding that will ultimately lead to the death of the 'pair of star-crossed lovers' – yet another oft-quoted line from the same play.

Shakespeare invented more than 1,700 words by changing nouns into verbs and verbs into adjectives, adding prefixes and suffixes, connecting words never before used together and devising entirely original new words. Some scholars point out that Shakespeare might not have actually *created* certain words and phrases, but was the first to use them in written rather than spoken form.

SHAKESPEAREAN PHRASES IN COMMON USE:

A fool's paradise
A sorry sight
All corners of the world
All of a sudden
All one to me
All our yesterdays
All that glisters is not gold
As dead as a doornail
As good luck would have it
As merry as the day is long
As pure as the driven snow
At one fell swoop
Bag and baggage
Band of brothers
Bated breath
Beggar all description
Brave new world

Painted by Frederick Leighton 1853-55
The Reconciliation of the Montagues and Capulets over the Dead Bodies of Romeo and Juliet.

Break the ice
Breathed his last
Cold comfort
Dash to pieces
Dead as a doornail
Devil incarnate
Dog will have his day
Eaten me out of house and home
Elbow room
Faint hearted
Fair play
Fancy-free
For ever and a day
For goodness' sake
Foregone conclusion
Foul play
Full circle
Give the devil his due
Good riddance
Green-eyed monster
Heart of gold
Heart's content
High time
Hot-blooded
In a pickle
In my heart of hearts
In my mind's eye
In the twinkling of an eye
It smells to heaven
It was Greek to me
Itching palm
Kill with kindness
Knock knock! Who's there?
Laid on with a trowel
Laughing stock
Lie low
Lily-livered
Live long day
Love is blind
Make your hair stand on end
Melted into thin air
Midsummer madness
Milk of human kindness
More fool you
Murder most foul
Naked truth
Night owl
Not slept one wink
Off with his head
One fell swoop
Out of the jaws of death
Own flesh and blood
Parting is such sweet sorrow
Pitched battle
Play fast and loose
Pomp and circumstance
Pound of flesh
Primrose path
Refuse to budge an inch
Rhyme nor reason
Salad days
Seen better days
Send him packing
Set your teeth on edge
Short shrift
Sick at heart
Snail paced
Something in the wind
Sound and fury
Spotless reputation
Star crossed lovers
Stony hearted
That way madness lies
The be-all and the end-all
The course of true love never did run smooth
The game is up
The Queen's English
The slings and arrows of outrageous fortune
The world's my oyster
There's the rub
This is the short and the long of it
This sceptered isle
Time is out of joint
'Tis high time
To be or not to be
To thine own self be true
Too much of a good thing
Tower of strength
Truth will out
Under the greenwood tree
Up in arms
Vanish into thin air
We have seen better days
Wear my heart upon my sleeve
What the dickens
What's done is done
Wild goose chase

THE WORDSMITH

Whether or not he actually invented them, some of the words Shakespeare introduced to the English language are:

accommodation
addiction
advertising
aerial
amazement
apostrophe
arch-villain
arouse
assassination
auspicious
bandit
barefaced
baseless
beached
bedazzled
bedroom
belongings
besmirch
bloody
blushing
bump
buzzer
caked
castigate
cater
changeful
clangor
cold-blooded
cold-hearted
control (noun)
countless
courtship
critic
critical
dexterously
dishearten
dislocate
dwindle
eventful
exposure
eyeball
fashionable
fitful
frugal
generous
gloomy
gnarled
grovel
gust
hot-blooded
hurry
impartial
inaudible
inauspicious
indistinguishable
invulnerable
lapse
laughable
lonely
majestic
manager
misplaced
monumental
moonbeam
multitudinous
new-fangled
obscene
palmy
perusal
pious
premeditated
radiance
reliance
road
sanctimonious
scuffle
seamy
sportive
submerge
suspicious
swagger
uncomfortable
vaulting
watchdog

QUOTES AND EXTRACTS

First Witch: When shall we three meet again?
In thunder, lightning, or in rain?

Second Witch: When the hurly-burly's done,
When the battle's lost and won.

Third Witch: That will be ere the set of sun.

First Witch: Where the place?

Second Witch: Upon the heath.

Third Witch: There to meet with Macbeth.

Macbeth,
Act I, Scene 1

Shakespeare's plays and poetry encompass truths, wisdom, wit, emotion and succinct observations about human nature. Here follow some of the thoughts and moments of high drama encapsulated by this most quoted author.

HUMAN NATURE

'If you prick us, do we not bleed?
If you tickle us, do we not laugh?
If you poison us do we not die?
And if you wrong us, shall we not revenge?'

Shylock in *The Merchant of Venice*,
Act III, Scene 1

'We know what we are,
but know not what we may be.'

Ophelia in *Hamlet*, Act IV, Scene 5

'A fool thinks himself to be wise,
but a wise man knows himself to be a fool.'

Touchstone in *As You Like It*, Act V, Scene 1

'What a piece of work is a man, how noble in reason, how infinite in faculties … in action how like an angel, in apprehension how like a god.'

Hamlet in *Hamlet*, Act II, Scene 2

LOVE

'Love looks not with the eyes but with the mind.
And therefore is winged Cupid painted blind.'

Helena in *A Midsummer Night's Dream*,
Act I, Scene 1

The Three Witches or *The Weird Sisters*
by Henry Fuseli, c.1782

Hermia and Lysander in *A Midsummer Night's Dream*, depicted by John Simmons, 1870

'No sooner met but they looked, no sooner looked but they loved, no sooner loved, but they sighed …'
Rosalind in *As You Like It*, Act V, Scene 2

'The course of true love never did run smooth.'
Lysander in *A Midsummer Night's Dream*. Act I, Scene 2

'Love is blind, and lovers cannot see
The pretty follies that themselves commit …'
Jessica in *The Merchant of Venice*, Act II, Scene 6

'My bounty is as boundless as the sea,
My love as deep; the more I give to thee,
The more I have, for both are infinite.'
Juliet in *Romeo and Juliet*, Act II, Scene 2

THEATRE REFERENCES

'Life's but a walking shadow, a poor player, that struts and frets his hour upon the stage, and then is heard no more; it is a tale told by an idiot, full of sound and fury, signifying nothing.'
Macbeth in *Macbeth*, Act V, Scene 5

'All the world's a stage, and all the men and women merely players: they have their exits and their entrances; and one man in his time plays many parts, his acts being seven ages.'
Jaques in *As You Like It*, Act II, Scene 7

'Life's but a walking shadow, a poor player
That struts and frets his hour upon the stage
And then is heard no more: it is a tale
Told by an idiot, full of sound and fury …'
Macbeth in *Macbeth*, Act V, Scene 5

COURAGE AND VALOUR

'Once more unto the breach, dear friends,
once more;
Or close the wall up with our English dead.
In peace there's nothing so becomes a man
As modest stillness and humility;
But when the blast of war blows in our ears,
Then imitate the action of the tiger …'
Henry V in *Henry V*, Act III, Scene 1

'Advance our standards, set upon our foes
But screw your courage to the sticking place …'
Lady Macbeth in *Macbeth*, Act I, Scene 7

'The better part of valor is discretion, in the which better part I have saved my life.'
Falstaff in *Henry IV, Part 1*, Act V, Scene 4

DREAMS AND SLEEP

'We are such stuff
As dreams are made on, and our little life
Is rounded with a sleep.'
Prospero in *The Tempest,* Act IV, Scene 1

'If we shadows have offended,
Think but this and all is mended,
That you have but slumber'd here,

While these visions did appear.
And this weak and idle theme,
No more yielding but a dream …'

Puck in *A Midsummer Night's Dream*, Act V, Scene 1

'O sleep! O gentle sleep!
Nature's soft nurse, how have I frighted thee,
That thou no more wilt weigh my eyelids down
And steep my senses in forgetfulness?'

Henry IV in *Henry IV, Part 2*, Act III, Scene 1

DEATH

'… To die: to sleep;
No more; and by a sleep to say we end
The heart-ache and the thousand natural shocks
That flesh is heir to, 'tis a consummation
Devoutly to be wish'd. To die, to sleep;
To sleep: perchance to dream: ay, there's the rub;
For in that sleep of death what dreams may come
When we have shuffled off this mortal coil …'

Hamlet in *Hamlet*, Act III, Scene 1

Ariel by Louis Rhaed, late 1800s or early 1900s

'Alas, poor Yorick! I knew him, Horatio: a fellow
of infinite jest, of most excellent fancy:
He hath borne me on his back a thousand times;
and now, how abhorred in my imagination it is!
My gorge rims at it.
Here hung those lips that I have kissed
I know not how oft.
Where be your gibes now? Your gambols?
Your songs?
Your flashes of merriment, that were wont
to set the table on a roar?'

Hamlet in *Hamlet*, Act V, Scene 1

'When beggars die, there are no comets seen;
The heavens themselves blaze forth the death
of princes.'

Calpurnia in *Julius Caesar*, Act II, Scene 2

'Cowards die many times before their deaths;
The valiant never taste of death but once.'

Caesar in *Julius Caesar*, Act II, Scene 2

FLOWERS AND FAIRIES

'I know a bank where the wild thyme blows,
Where oxlips and the nodding violet grows,
Quite over-canopied with luscious woodbine,
With sweet musk-roses and with eglantine:
There sleeps Titania some time of the night,
Lull'd in these flowers with dances and delight;
And there the snake throws her enamell'd skin,
Weed wide enough to wrap a fairy in.'

Oberon in *A Midsummer Night's Dream*, Act II, Scene 1

'Ye elves of hills, brooks, standing lakes, and
groves;
And ye, that on the sands with printless foot
Do chase the ebbing Neptune, and do fly him
When he comes back –'

Prospero in *The Tempest*, Act V, Scene 1

SHAKESPEARE IN THE MEDIA

Mention must be made here of the Royal Shakespeare Company (RSC), a major British institution, based in Stratford-upon-Avon. The company produces around twenty plays a year at the Royal Shakespeare Theatre (a 1,060-seat thrust stage theatre), the Swan Theatre and the Courtyard Theatre plus playing regularly at various other venues in both the UK and abroad. In 2013 the company launched *Live from Stratford-upon-Avon*, a series of live screenings of its Shakespeare productions distributed globally and videos in the *Great Performances* series, showcasing stage performances.

SHAKESPEARE AT THE MOVIES

The earliest known movie production of a Shakespeare play was in 1900 and starred Sarah Bernhardt in *Le Duel d'Hamlet*, a French film that lasted just two minutes. William Shakespeare is the most filmed author in any language: to date the ever-growing list includes some 410 feature-length film and television versions of his plays. Not all are faithful to the original story and text, with several concentrating on plot rather than original dialogue. The Internet Movie Database gives Shakespeare

Royal Shakespeare Theatre, Waterside, Stratford-upon-Avon

Juliet's vigil over Romeo in the tomb (Beersheba Theatre, Israel), 2015

the writing credit for 1,088 films. *Hamlet* has been one of the most popular with more than 60 films and over 20 television adaptations.

The subject matter in Shakespeare's plots offers film-makers ambitious, power-hungry kings, queens, dukes and throne-seekers; forbidden romance; young men wild with love or jealousy; sibling rivalry; strong women showing their mettle; battles; death; mystery; secrets; happy and tragic endings.

RADIO AND TELEVISION

The first Shakespeare radio programme produced by the British Broadcasting Corporation (BBC) was on 16 February 1923 and ever since, all around the world, there have been countless adaptations although retelling the stories on radio has always needed imaginative adjustments to meet the medium's non-visual needs.

Canada boasts the first North American Shakespeare broadcast, with regular productions from the 1930s to the 1990s. The US had several broadcasts in the 1920s. The 1930s saw trailblazer Orson Welles, who worked enthusiastically within both radio and the stage, adapting many of his stage productions for the wireless, including *Hamlet, Romeo and Juliet, Richard III, Macbeth* and *Julius Caesar*. From 1936–38 Australia produced ninety-minute broadcasts that accrued excellent ratings.

In 1960, *An Age of Kings* was a UK serial adaptation of the eight sequential history plays that included the Wars of the Roses period (*Richard II, Henry IV, Parts 1 and 2, Henry V, Henry VI, Parts 1, 2 and 3* and *Richard III*). This ambitious series was a critical and commercial success in both the UK and North America. Nearly two decades

INSPIRATION!

Movies based on Shakespeare's plays (and their directors) include:

The Taming of the Shrew (1929) featuring Douglas Fairbanks and Mary Pickford

Romeo and Juliet (1935) by George Cukor

A Midsummer Night's Dream (1935) by Max Reinhardt and William Dieterle

Henry V (1945) by Laurence Olivier

Macbeth (1948) by Orson Welles

Hamlet (1948) by Laurence Olivier

Othello (1952) by Orson Welles

Julius Caesar (1953) by Joseph L Mankiewicz

Richard III (1955) by Laurence Olivier

Forbidden Planet (1956) by Fred M Wilcox (based on *The Tempest*)

Throne of Blood (1957) by Akira Kurosawa (based on *Macbeth*)

The Tempest (1960) (TV movie): Richard Burton, by George Schaefer

Hamlet (1964): Richard Burton by Bill Colleran and John Gielgud

Hamlet (1964) by Grigori Kozintsev

The Taming of the Shrew (1967): Elizabeth Taylor and Richard Burton, by Franco Zeffirelli

Romeo and Juliet (1968) by Franco Zeffirelli

King Lear (1971) by Peter Brook

King Lear (1971) by Grigori Kozintsev

Macbeth (1972) by Roman Polanski

Antony and Cleopatra (1974) (TV movie): Patrick Stewart and Ben Kingsley, by Jon Schofield

The Comedy of Errors (1978) (TV): Judi Dench and Francesca Annis, by Philip Casson and Trevor Nunn

Hamlet (1980) (TV): Derek Jacobi and Patrick Stewart, by Rodney Bennett

The Merry Wives of Windsor (1982) (TV): Ben Kingsley, by David Hugh Jones

The Tempest (1982) by Paul Mazursky

King Lear (1987) by Jean-Luc Godard

Henry V (1989) by Kenneth Branagh

Romeo and Juliet (1990) voice-overs: Francesca Annis, Vanessa Redgrave and Ben Kingsley, by Armando Acosta

Hamlet (1990): Mel Gibson, by Franco Zeffirelli

Prospero's Books (1991) by Peter Greenaway (based on *The Tempest*)

As You Like It (1992) by Christine Edzard

Much Ado about Nothing (1993) directed by Kenneth Branagh

Othello (1995) by Oliver Parker

Richard III (1995): Ian McKellen and Robert Downey Jr., by Richard Loncraine

Romeo and Juliet (1996): Leonardo DiCaprio and Claire Danes, by Baz Luhrmann

Hamlet (1996): Kenneth Branagh, Derek Jacobi, Julie Christie and Kate Winslet, by Kenneth Branagh

Twelfth Night (1996): Helena Bonham Carter, Nigel Hawthorne, Ben Kingsley, Imogen Stubbs and Mel Smith, by Trevor Nunn

10 Things I Hate About You (1999): Julia Stiles and Heather Ledger, by Gil Junger (based on *The Taming of the Shrew*)

A Midsummer's Night's Dream (1999): Calista Flockhart, Christian Bale and Michelle Pfeiffer, by Michael Hoffman

Love's Labour's Lost (2000) by Kenneth Branagh

Prospero and Caliban in the RSC 1993 production of *The Tempest* (Photograph by Bardolator21)

later, the BBC's television series *The Hollow Crown* filmed all 37 plays under Jonathan Miller's direction and with amazing performances including John Cleese as Petruchio and Derek Jacobi as Hamlet. Other television highlights have been Laurence Olivier's King Lear in 1983, plus interpretations of Macbeth by Ian McKellen and Patrick Stewart, and Judi Dench portraying Lady Macbeth.

ShakespeaRe-Told was a UK series by BBC television broadcast in 2005. In the same year *A Waste of Shame: The Mystery of Shakespeare and His Sonnets* was televised by the BBC, starring Rupert Graves; it explored the time when the Bard was writing his sonnets.

OTHER PRODUCTIONS

In the 1982 television series *Playing Shakespeare*, members of the RSC and other leading actors gave master classes by playing out scenes, reciting sonnets and giving commentaries. *The Shakespeare Sessions* was an American 2003 spin-off from this. *Looking for Richard* (1996), directed by Al Pacino, examined Shakespeare's influence on popular culture. It included extracts from *Richard III*.

In 2001 the website *Academia.edu* produced the *Themes of Shakespeare* series as short video documentaries, each considering a particular play's theme.

In Search of Shakespeare (2003) was a BBC documentary series of four episodes.

Slings and Arrows (Canada, 2003–06) was a Canadian television comedy-drama set in the fictional New Burbage Shakespeare Festival. It also had a Brazilian adaptation.

Elizabeth Rex (Canada, 2004) is a play by Timothy Findley about Shakespeare's interactions with Queen Elizabeth I and members of his cast on the night that her lover is to be executed.

In 2007 *Doctor Who*, the BBC children's science fiction series, introduced Shakespeare into an episode set in 1599 called *The Shakespeare Code*.

From 2011 to 2013 the BBC produced an online and YouTube programme *60-Second Shakespeare* suggesting ways to explore his themes and characters.

The Complete Works of William Shakespeare (Abridged) or *The Compleat Wrks of Wllm*

Shkspr (Abridged) by the Reduced Shakespeare Company is a stage comedy and movie, with all the plays performed (in comically shortened or amalgamated form) by only three actors.

Shakespeare also made cameo appearances in UK television comedy series *Blackadder* (launched 1983) and *Histeria!* the US animated series (from 1999).

The movie *Shakespeare in Love* (1998) explored Shakespeare's writing of *Romeo and Juliet* and fictional romance with a noblewoman.

ART

Many artists have been inspired by Shakespearean characters and scenes, including John Singer Sargent, Sir John Everett Millais, Sir Joseph Noel Paton, William Hogarth, Frederick Richard Pickersgill, Edwin Austin Abbey, Théodore Chassériа, Maurycy Gottlieb and William Morris.

LITERATURE

Books and plays inspired by Shakespeare's works include:

A Thousand Acres by Jane Smiley (*King Lear*)
Brave New World by Aldous Huxley (*The Tempest*)
Cakes and Ale by W. Somerset Maugham (*Twelfth Night*)
Dead Fathers Club by Matt Haig (*Hamlet*)
Fool by Christopher Moore (*King Lear*)
Love in Idleness by Amanda Craig (*A Midsummer Night's Dream*)
The Madness of Love: A Novel by Katharine Davies (*Twelfth Night*)
Moby Dick by Hermann Melville (*Macbeth/King Lear*)
My Name Is Will: A Novel of Sex, Drugs, and Shakespeare by Jess Winfield
The Black Prince by Iris Murdoch (*Hamlet*)
The Daughter of Time by Josephine Tey (*Richard III*)
The Dogs of War by Frederick Forsyth (*Julius Caesar*).
The Sandman, Vol. 3: Dream Country by Neil Gaiman (*A Midsummer Night's Dream*)
The Talented Mr. Ripley by Patricia Highsmith (*Macbeth*)
The Tragedy of Arthur by Arthur Phillips (*Hamlet, Henry IV, Parts 1* and *2*, *Henry V* and *Macbeth*)
Wise Children by Angela Carter (sets of twins and mistaken identities)

MUSIC, BALLET AND OPERA

Shakespeare's plays have inspired great music, epitomized in 1827 by 18-year-old Felix Mendelssohn's brilliant overture to a German production of *A Midsummer Night's Dream* – now one of the most frequently chosen wedding marches.

Hector Berlioz wrote a *King Lear* overture, used the death of Ophelia from *Hamlet* in a haunting women's chorus in Tristan and, in 1839, his symphony *Romeo et Juliette* arrived. In 1862, he wrote the opera *Beatrice et Benedict* based on *Much Ado About Nothing.*

The Enchanted Island is a pastiche of music by various baroque composers, including George Frideric Handel and Antonio Vivaldi, while Matthew Locke wrote music for John Dryden and William Davenant's version of *The Tempest*.

Ballets include:
A Midsummer Night's Dream by Felix Mendelssohn
The Dream by Frederic Ashton
The Moor's Pavane about Othello by Henry Purcell
Othello by Elliot Goldenthal
Romeo and Juliet: several versions including one by Sergei Prokofiev
The Winter's Tale by Joby Talbot

Operas:
The Merry Wives of Windsor by Carl Otto Ehrenfried Nicolai
Falstaff by Antonio Salieri
Otello by Gioachino Rossini
Giulietta e Romeo by Nicola Vaccai
Roméo et Juliette by Charles Gounod
Romeo und Julia by Heinrich Sutermeister
Der Sturm (The Tempest) by Frank Martin
The Tempest by Thomas Adès
A Midsummer Night's Dream by Benjamin Britten with libretto by Peter Pears
Antony and Cleopatra by Samuel Barber
Giuseppe Verdi wrote works based on *Macbeth, Othello* and *King Lear.*

SONGS AND MUSICALS

Songs include:
'Hark; Hark! the Lark'
Desdemona's 'Willow Song' from *Othello*.
'Come unto These Yellow Sands', 'Full Fathom Five' and 'Where the Bee Sucks' are

Ariel's songs from *The Tempest*.
Let us Garlands Bring a medley by Gerald Finzi contains:
'Come Away, Come Away, Death' (*Twelfth Night*)
'Who is Silvia?' (*Two Gentlemen of Verona*)
'Fear No More the Heat o' the Sun' (*Cymbeline*)
'O Mistress Mine' (*Twelfth Night*)
'It was a Lover and His Lass' (*As You Like It*)

Musicals include:
West Side Story – Romeo and Juliet
Kiss Me, Kate – Adaptation of *The Taming of the Shrew*; includes the song 'Brush up your Shakespeare'
The Boys from Syracuse – Comedy of Errors
The Lion King – Hamlet
Swingin' the Dream – A Midsummer Night's Dream (a jazz musical)
Two Gentlemen of Verona – rock music version
Play On! – Sets *Twelfth Night* in 1940s' Harlem and features Duke Ellington songs

A new musical version of *Romeo and Juliet* – complete with balcony scene – was *West Side Story*, introduced to the Broadway stage in 1957 and filmed in 1961 (Photo by Fred Fehl)

INTRIGUING FACTS AND FIGURES

There is so much that we do *not* know about Shakespeare himself. It is believed that he was born and died on the same date, 23 April which is also Saint George's Day … this national saint of England was called upon by Henry V in Shakespeare's play of that name: 'God for Harry, England, and Saint George!' Notwithstanding all the mysteries, however, there are many amazing facts that we *do* know about the Bard's achievements, the plays and his very special place in literature and theatre.

THE MAN

Nobody knows where Shakespeare was or what he did between 1585 and 1592. For seven years there are no records of his activities. Some historians think that he may have worked as a schoolteacher, studied law or crossed the channel to Europe. He may perhaps have joined an acting troupe that was passing through Stratford. One seventeenth-century account purports that he fled Stratford after being caught poaching deer.

Other historians believe that Shakespeare was bisexual, especially because of his writing about a 'Fair Youth', the beautiful young man referred to as a lover in the sonnets. Moreover the effeminate youth Henry Wriothesley, third Earl of Southampton and Baron of Titchfield, to whom Shakespeare dedicated

Shakespeare Before Thomas Lucy
by Thomas Brooks, 1861

his narrative poems *Venus and Adonis* and *The Rape of Lucrece*, was said to share quarters with a fellow officer whom he would 'hug in his arms and play wantonly with'.

The average life expectancy in Elizabethan England was only 35 years so when Shakespeare died aged 52, that would have been deemed a good innings.

Local gossip hinted that Shakespeare died from a fever after a drinking binge with fellow playwrights Ben Jonson and Michael Drayton. But, in fact, he had been sick for over a month before he dictated his shakily-signed will and finally succumbed. His depiction in the First Folio has outstanding shadings that suggest a thickening of the left temporal artery; he may well have had a cerebral haemorrhage.

Is this Shakespeare's 'Fair Youth'? Henry Wriothesley in the Tower of London in 1603, attributed to John de Critz.

The Chandos Portrait of Shakespeare (see page 12), attributed to artist John Taylor, is probably the only representation painted from life … here Shakespeare has a full beard, a receding hairline, loosened shirt-ties and a shiny gold hoop dangling from his left ear – then the latest trend, possibly because sailors wore a single gold earring to cover funeral costs in case they died abroad.

After Shakespeare's death there would undoubtedly have been a full inventory of his books and possessions but this was probably sent to London and destroyed in the Great Fire of 1666.

FAMILY AND FRIENDS

While Shakespeare's father John was a glove-maker, he also sold malt, corn and wool (as an illegal 'brogger', an unlicensed wool dealer) – and became the borough's official 'ale taster' responsible for inspecting and tasting bread and malt liquors and checking that weights, measures and prices were observed by innkeepers, publicans, butchers, bakers and traders. He also bought and leased out houses, served as both bailiff and alderman and was the chief magistrate of Stratford.

In the 1570s, John Shakespeare was either prosecuted (or threatened with this) four times for illegal trading in wool and money lending.

Shakespeare's father may not have been able to read or write. Certainly he always signed his name with a mark.

Will had four sisters (two Joans, Margaret and Anne) and three brothers (Gilbert, Richard and Edmund).

Shakespeare's son, Hamnet, died in 1596. His younger daughter Judith had three children, but all died before their mother and childless. His granddaughter Elizabeth, daughter of Shakespeare's first daughter Susanna, died childless in 1670, so the William Shakespeare line ended.

Will's wife Anne and their two daughters, Susanna and Judith, were probably illiterate, although Susanna could scrawl her signature.

THE PLAYS

There has always been great debate over whether Shakespeare was indeed the author of the plays that bear his name, and at least fifty writers including Edward de Vere, seventeenth Earl of Oxford, Christopher Marlowe, Mary Sidney Herbert and Sir Francis Bacon have been proposed as the real author.

Fellow playwright Ben Jonson said of the Bard: 'Whatsoever he [Shakespeare] penned, he never blotted out a line.'

Hamlet survives in three versions: a 1603 quarto (a printing size) of 2,200 lines, a 1604 quarto of 3,800 lines, and the First Folio edition of 1623 with 3,570 lines. Some scholars believe that the shortest quarto is most likely the one closest to the play that was first performed.

In one of Adolf Hitler's 1926 sketchbooks, there is a design for the staging of *Julius Caesar*.

There are fifteen suicides in Shakespeare's plays: Romeo and Juliet; Cassius, Brutus and his wife Portia in *Julius Caesar*; Mark Antony and Cleopatra; Charmian, Iras and Eros in *Antony and Cleopatra*; Ophelia in *Hamlet*; Lady Macbeth in *Macbeth*; Goneril in *King Lear* and Timon in *Timon of Athens*. Also, Othello stabs himself. In addition, in the play within a play in *A Midsummer Night's Dream*, Pyramus and Thisbe dispatch themselves!

A sheet of Park's Shakespeare characters with riddle clues (c.1840) for a children's game

Only two of his plays are written entirely in verse: *King John* and *Richard II*.

Shakespeare may have written some twenty plays that have disappeared.

Shakespeare's works contain the first-ever recordings of 2,035 English words.

Many of Shakespeare's plays are based on other authors' plays and poems. This was quite acceptable then, especially as the works concerned were generally from a rather earlier time.

Catherine the Great, Empress of Russia, wrote an adaptation of *The Merry Wives of Windsor*, renaming it *What it is to have Linen and Buck-baskets*.

Shakespeare penned about one-tenth of the most quotable quotations ever written or spoken in English.

The Comedy of Errors is Shakespeare's shortest play with 1,770 lines, lasting less than two hours … *Hamlet* is the longest with 4,042 lines and takes some four hours to perform.

Hamlet and *Much Ado about Nothing* have been translated into Klingon (the language of the alien warrior species in the television series *Star Trek*.

Shakespeare never actually published any of his plays. It was two of his fellow actors – John Hemminges and Henry Condell – who recorded and published 36 of them posthumously in 1623 in the First Folio.

King Lear was possibly rewritten to suit performances on an indoor stage when the King's Men moved to the Blackfriars Theatre.

The play *Double Falsehood*, published in 1728, may have been based on *Cardenio*, Shakespeare's lost play, known to have been performed by the King's Men in 1613.

A rival, Robert Greene, wrote, 'There is an upstart Crow, beautified with our feathers, that with his Tiger's heart wrapped in a Player's hide, supposes he is as well able to bombast out a blank verse as the best of you: and being an absolute Johannes fac totum, is in his own conceit the only Shake-scene in a country.'

Detail of *A Sculptor's Workshop, Stratford-upon-Avon – 1617* by Henry Wallis (c.1857) depicting Gerard Johnson carving the Stratford monument that is now in Stratford's Holy Trinity Church. Ben Jonson is showing the sculptor the 'Kesselstadt death mask' (supposedly of Shakespeare), which was discovered in a German shop in the eighteenth century.

THEATRE

In Shakespeare's time all actors were male. It was not until the Restoration that the first women appeared on the English stage.

Shakespeare performed small parts in his own plays, taking minor roles. He is listed as an actor on documents from 1592, 1598, 1603, and 1608.

All London theatres closed between 1592 and 1594 due to an outbreak of the plague. Shakespeare seized the opportunity to write poetry.

In Shakespeare's time, there were no curtains drawn across the stage and there was scant scenery, so playwrights used the actors to describe the setting as part of the performance, especially in the prologue, as in *Henry V*:

And let us, ciphers to this great accompt,
On your imaginary forces work.
Suppose within the girdle of these walls
Are now confined two mighty monarchies,
Whose high upreared and abutting fronts
The perilous narrow ocean parts asunder:
Piece out our imperfections with your thoughts;
Into a thousand parts divide on man,
And make imaginary puissance;
Think when we talk of horses, that you see them
Printing their proud hoofs i' the receiving earth;
For 'tis your thoughts that now must deck our kings,
Carry them here and there; jumping o'er times,
Turning the accomplishment of many years
Into an hour-glass: for the which supply,
Admit me Chorus to this history;
Who prologue-like your humble patience pray,
Gently to hear, kindly to judge, our play.

From *Henry V*

Elizabethan theatergoers could purchase apples and pears to eat during the play and these might well be thrown at any actors who failed to please.

ALSO OF INTEREST

The solar system's seventh planet, Uranus, has 27 known moons – all are named after characters from the works of Shakespeare or Alexander Pope. The first two found were called Titania and Oberon.

Due to the risk of a play being copied, actors were given their lines only once the play was in rehearsal. Sometimes a company member working as a backstage cue would whisper the lines shortly before an actor was due to speak!

Shakespeare's works contain more than 600 references to various types of birds, from sparrows and doves to swans and turkeys. In 1890 Eugene Schiffelin decided to import to America every species of bird mentioned in Shakespeare's works missing from the US. This included two flocks of 60 starlings released into New York's Central Park. The USA now boasts some 200 million starlings. This lustrous songbird makes just one Shakespearean appearance, in *Henry IV, Part 1*.

US President Abraham Lincoln, a lover of Shakespeare's works who often recited extracts, was assassinated by John Wilkes Booth – a renowned Shakespearean actor.

Poet John Keats kept a bust of Shakespeare beside him while he wrote, hoping to absorb some of the Bard's creativity.

'William Shakespeare' is an anagram of 'I am a weakish speller.'

Shakespeare is ever regarded as an Elizabethan playwright but, in fact, much of his finest work was produced during King James I's Jacobean reign.

Almost nothing is known about when his 154 sonnets were written, to whom they were addressed, or even if our present assembly is in the correct order. Although sonnets are often love poems, Shakespeare's can be somewhat bitter.

THE BARD'S TIMES AND TIMELINE

Official records are few and so a number of these dates are assumptions, especially those for Shakespeare's youth. But this timeline, nevertheless, does provide an overall guide to the pattern of his life and career.

In Stratford-upon-Avon, much about Shakespeare's life and times can be discovered. The Birthplace Trust was founded back in 1847 and has been impressing visitors ever since – including Thomas Hardy (who bought a copy of *Hamlet* from a local shop), John Keats, Charles Dickens, US president Theodore Roosevelt, Chinese premier Wen Jiabao and UK's Princess Diana. Today, the highest numbers of overseas visitors come from the USA, Australia, Germany, Canada, France, New Zealand, Asia, Netherlands, Spain, Russia, South Africa, Ireland, Italy and Belgium. All are eager to explore the story and background of this genius 'Swan of Avon', the nickname bestowed upon Shakespeare by his contemporary playwright, Ben Jonson.

Shakespeare at the Mermaid Tavern with his contemporaries

1560–1589

23 April, 1564 Birth
Birth of Shakespeare in Stratford-upon-Avon to glove-maker, leather-worker and wool merchant, John Shakespeare and wife, Mary Arden.

26 April, 1564 Baptism
William Shakespeare is christened at Holy Trinity Church in Stratford.

1569 School begins
Shakespeare possibly begins his schooldays at King's New School (or King Edward VI Grammar School).

1582
Shakespeare may have hoped to marry Anne Whateley (a marriage license was issued) but Anne Hathaway's pregnancy precluded this.

28 November, 1582 Marriage
A license to 'William Shagspere' and 'Ann Hathwey' formalizes the marriage of 18-year-old William to 26-year-old Anne Hathaway from Shottery.

26 May, 1583 Susanna arrives
Shakespeare's first child, a daughter, is born and baptized.

1585 Twins born
A son called Hamnet and a daughter, Judith, are named after Shakespeare's close friends, Hamnet and Judith Sadler.

1590–1599

c.1590 First Play
Shakespeare begins work as an actor in London. His first play *Henry VI, Part 1* is penned.

1592 Robert Greene's critique
Dramatist Greene refers to Shakespeare as an 'upstart crow', the first known mention of Shakespeare as a writer.

January 1593 Bubonic plague!
London playhouses close. Plague will kill some 5 percent of city residents. Will writes poetry and sonnets.

April 1593 Venus and Adonis
Shakespeare publishes his first long poem – dedicated to Henry Wriothesley, his patron.

Spring 1594 Theatres reopen
The plague abates. The Lord Chamberlain's Men, Shakespeare's troupe, become very popular and are often invited to perform for Queen Elizabeth I.

May 1594 The Rape of Lucrece
Shakespeare publishes his second epic poem *The Rape of Lucrece* and purchases shares in the Lord Chamberlain's Men.

11 August 1596 Hamnet dies
Shakespeare's son, Hamnet dies of unknown causes, aged 11.

May 1597 New Place
Shakespeare buys New Place, the second-largest house in Stratford.

1598 Francis Meres' review
Praise for Shakespeare's work; he has now become a noted playwright.

1599 Globe Theatre
The Chamberlain's Men will launch many of Shakespeare's most famous plays at the Globe, including *Julius Caesar* on 21st September.

1600–1609

1601 Hamlet
Shakespeare's father dies; this may have motivated him to write *Hamlet*.

1603 Change of monarch
A Midsummer Night's Dream is performed at Hampton Court for the pleasure of Queen Elizabeth who dies later that year.
King James ascends the throne. The Lord Chamberlain's Men become the King's Men and perform before the king eleven times in one year.

1603 Taking his bow
Shakespeare's last recorded acting role is in Ben Jonson's *Sejanus*.

1608 Blackfriars Theatre
The King's Men perform at Blackfriars theatre. Shakespeare's work becomes lighter with plays like *The Winter's Tale*.

1609 Sonnets
A collection of 154 of Shakespeare's sonnets is published.

1610–1619

c.1610–13 Back to Stratford
Shakespeare moves back to Stratford, rejoining his wife and now in closer contact with his two married daughters.

1612–14 The last plays
Shakespeare, with the King's Men playwright John Fletcher, writes *Henry VIII*, *The Two Noble Kinsmen* and *Cardenio*.

1613 The Globe burns down
The Globe theatre is set alight during a performance of *Henry VIII* and burns to the ground.

25 March, 1616 Will's will
Feeling ill, Shakespeare calls his lawyer to revise his will, leaving his second-best bed to his wife and £10 to the poor.

23 April 1616 The Bard dies
William Shakespeare leaves this mortal coil on his 52nd birthday.

25 April 1616 Funeral
Shakespeare's burial at Holy Trinity Church in Stratford is recorded in the Stratford Holy Church Register. His epitaph warns of a curse on anyone who disturbs his grave.

1619 Christmas at Court
Hamlet is performed as part of Christmas celebrations at court.

1620+

1623 Shakespeare's wife dies
Aged 67, Anne Hathaway dies and is buried beside her husband.

1623 First Folio published
Former colleagues in the King's Men collect 36 of Shakespeare's plays and publish them in the First Folio.

ALL AROUND THE WORLD

For more than 400 years William Shakespeare's words have intrigued, impressed and galvanized people from all round the globe. It is quite staggering to discover how the thoughts of one writer have travelled through all the nations, inspiring artists in every medium, and are now enjoyed in over eighty languages. At Shakespeare's Globe theatre in London, for example, about 20,000 high school students visit from Germany each year, plus many thousands more from the USA, Asia, South Africa – from all round the world.

Shakespeare's history plays were set firmly on British soil but the only comedy set in the UK is *The Merry Wives of Windsor*. Most of his settings offer a more exotic backdrop, flowing through Europe, Africa and the Middle East. His dramas encompass twelve countries, with cities in today's Italy offering the backdrop he seemed most to favour. Some plays are located in Asia and Africa, including the Middle East, the Levant and Egypt. Some unfold in imaginary places – *The Tempest*, for example (although its un-named Mediterranean island may well be Sicily). Many have central characters living or cast abroad on islands such as Cyprus.

A number of the plays are drawn from French or Italian origins, while ancient Greece and Rome also provided sources. The Bard must have researched a great deal, albeit some details are for dramatic effect rather than accuracy – such as the lion in *As You Like It*. He would have drawn upon local colour; London then was very

Shakespeare Garden in Central Park, New York, USA

cosmopolitan – a hotchpotch of religious refugees, foreign sailors, merchants and ambassadors – and explorers returning with news of amazing new lands recently discovered.

By the 1600s, adaptations of the Bard's works were already being acted by English companies in Poland, the German principalities and Baltic Gdansk. At the end of that century, Italy knew of his works and by about 1750 the plays had arrived in France and America. By 1854 even the Japanese were enjoying the popular *Tales from Shakespeare* adaptations for children written by Charles and Mary Lamb. Today Shakespeare is appreciated on a truly global scale. There has even been a life-size, ice-sculpted replica of the Globe theatre in Lapland.

As well as in English, Shakespeare's plays have been enacted – in one format or another – in languages as varied as British sign language, Chinese Mandarin and Cantonese, Turkish, German, Spanish, Korean, French, Italian, Japanese, Polish, Finnish, Russian, Dutch, Estonian, Czech, Hebrew, Ukrainian, Romanian, Arabic, Zulu, Klingon, Esperanto and Interlingua. In India they were first performed in English in Kolkota and Mumbai for employees of the East India Company; now there are Indian translations in Hindi, Gujarati, Urdu, Marathi, Punjabi and Bengali.

Macbeth, *The Merchant of Venice* and *Romeo and Juliet* are especially popular, with the last performed in 24 countries in the last decade. *Hamlet* is a special favourite and, over fifty years or so, has appeared in more than 75 languages. Possibly the first ever 'talkie movie' of a Shakespeare play was a 1935 version of *Hamlet* in Indian while one of the most popular Bollywood movies is *Angoor* (1982), based on *The Comedy of Errors*.

So the formula works, whoever or wherever audiences gather!

PLACES TO VISIT IN THE UK

The Royal Shakespeare Company sells more than half a million tickets a year for productions at their theatres in Stratford-upon-Avon, London and Newcastle – introducing some 50,000 people to a live Shakespeare performance for the first time each year. Visitors to Stratford can also tour the Royal Shakespeare and Swan Theatres by day – or learn about all the ghosts on an after-dark tour.

Also in or near Stratford:

Shakespeare's birthplace: Half-timbered, Tudor-style cottage, Elizabethan furnishings, garden, exhibition on Shakespeare's life.

Anne Hathaway's cottage: Home of Anne Hathaway, Shakespeare's wife: Tudor farmhouse, original furniture, beautiful gardens.

Hall's Croft: Home of Shakespeare's eldest daughter and her husband, Doctor Hall; 16th- and 17th-century paintings and furnishings, exhibition on medicine of that era.

Holy Trinity Church: Here the Bard was baptized in 1564. It is also home to

The room where Shakespeare was born

Shakespeare's grave and his monument, erected in 1621.

Mary Arden's farm, Wilmcote: His mother's timbered farmhouse with Shakespeare Countryside Museum, falconry displays, blacksmith's forge, and Tudor archery lessons.

Outside Stratford:

Shakespeare's Globe, London: Shakespeare's plays are performed from April to October in this restoration of Shakespeare's 16th-century Jacobean playhouse of which Shakespeare was a shareholder. Exhibition and tours available all year.

Poets' Corner, Westminster Abbey, London: Statue of William Shakespeare designed by William Kent and executed by Peter Scheemakers in 1740.

The Macbeth Trail, Scotland: A driving route includes Glamis Castle, Lumphanan (the Aberdeenshire village where Macbeth was killed in battle in 1057) and Cairn O'Mount (where Macbeth and his army crossed the Grampians

SHAKESPEARE IN THE USA

Lincoln Park, Chicago

In 1888, a large seated statue by William Ordway Partridge was unveiled.

Comedy and Tragedy: Touchstone the jester and Hamlet, Philadelphia

Created in 1926, these statues were designed by Alexander Stirling Calder.

New York's Puck Building, named after the character in *A Midsummer Night's Dream,* sports two gilded statues of the sprite, one on the northeast corner and one over the main entrance

Central Park, New York
As well as the Shakespeare Garden and annual festival, the park has a statue by John Quincy Adams Ward was erected in 1872, commissioned to celebrate the tricentenary of Shakespeare's birth. In 1986, a replica was made for the State Theater in Montgomery, Alabama, which has an annual Shakespeare Festival.

American Shakespeare Center; Blackfriars Playhouse, Staunton, Virginia
Explores Shakespeare's theatre, language, and humanity – and the English Renaissance stage through theatres, performance, exhibitions, and educational programmes. Features a re-creation of the Blackfriars Playhouse.

Library of Congress, Thomas Jefferson Building, Washington DC
An 1896 bronze statue of Shakespeare by Frederick William MacMonnies graces the reading-room gallery.

Folger Shakespeare Library, Washington DC
This research centre offers plays, concerts, literary readings, family activities, exhibitions and college programmes.

First Folio! The Book that Gave Us Shakespeare
A touring exhibition of multiple copies of the First Folio – published seven years after his death and saving for posterity eighteen of the Bard's plays.

Alabama Shakespeare Festival
Presents classical works, contemporary plays, musicals, and new works commissioned by the Festival's Southern Writers Project.

California Shakespeare Theater
An annual season of professional classic theatre runs from June to October at the Bruns Amphitheatre in Orinda, CA.

Cincinnati Shakespeare Festival
Produces the best of Shakespeare and the classics.

Colorado Shakespeare Festival
Peformances indoors and outdoors of classic plays of the past and potential future ones.

Georgia Shakespeare Festival
Professional repertory company performing Shakespeare and other enduring authors.
Idaho Shakespeare Festival
Founded in 1977, this repertory theatre company performs Shakespeare in an outdoor amphitheatre beside the Boise River.
Oregon Shakespeare Festival
Elizabethan, classic, and contemporary plays in three different theatres.
Philadelphia Shakespeare Festival
Dedicated to performing the works of the Bard.
Shakespeare Festival of Dallas
Professional productions offered free of charge at Samuell-Grand Park.
Texas Shakespeare Festival
Offers a programme of the world's dramatic literary masterpieces.
Utah Shakespearean Festival
Summer and fall seasons of classic and contemporary plays and musicals.

CANADA

Stratford Festival of Canada
A classical and contemporary repertoire, with special emphasis on the works of William Shakespeare.
Festival Theatre, Stratford Shakespeare Festival, Stratford, Ontario, Canada
Many Shakespeare events and a tin Shakespeare statue in the gardens.
Bard on the Beach Festival, Vanier Park, Vancouver, Canada
Two stages offer a programme of plays, talks and other celebrations of Shakespeare.
Canadian Adaptations of Shakespeare Project
An online resource exploring the many ways that Shakespeare's plays can be transformed and adapted in Canada. www.canadianshakespeares.ca

The statue of William Shakespeare in Chicago's Lincoln Park

EUROPE

Shakespeare Statue, Weimar, Germany
In 1904 a statue, designed by Otto Lessing, was raised showing Shakespeare seated and staring into the distance.

Shakespeare Statue, Elsinore, Denmark
Memorial statue by Louis Hasselriis commissioned to commemorate the 300th anniversary of the publication of *Hamlet* in 1603.

Elsinore Castle, Helsingør, Kronborg, Denmark
Castle turrets where Hamlet (and his father's ghost) prowled. *Hamlet* productions are often set within its walls, including performances by Laurence Olivier, Christopher Plummer, Derek Jacobi and Jude Law.

Juliet's Balcony, Verona, Italy
Tourist attractions in Verona include the Casa de Giulietta (Juliet's House), a fourteenth-century house and courtyard with a stone balcony (added much, much later) that evokes *Romeo and Juliet.*

Messina, Sicily, Italy
Shakespeare set *Much Ado About Nothing* in northeast Sicily.

Venice, Italy
Setting for *The Merchant of Venice*; the Italian city-state was a major commercial hub and a pivot of international trade in Shakespeare's time.

Mount Párnitha, Párnitha National Park, near Athens, Greece
One contender for the 'wood outside Athens' of *A Midsummer Night's Dream*; reached by cable car, it offers caves, gorges, peaks, trails and forest.

Juliet's balcony in Verona, Italy

ASIA

Shakespeare Country Park, Maruyama, northeast of Tokyo, Japan
Half-timbered cottages have been built around a village green, with stocks, maypole and windmill. The buildings include replicas of Shakespeare's birthplace and Mary Arden's house. An on-site theatre presents Shakespeare's plays in Japanese.

AUSTRALIA AND NEW ZEALAND

Shakespeare Memorial, Shakespeare Place, Sydney, Australia
Built in 1926 by Sir Bertram MacKennal and commissioned by the Shakespeare Society of New South Wales, this statue depicts Shakespeare bowing at the end of a performance, as well as Hamlet, Romeo, Juliet, Portia and Falstaff.

Australian Shakespeare Company, Arts Centre, Melbourne, Australia
Began by presenting Shakespeare *Under the Stars* in 1987; now hosts contemporary productions of Shakespeare's plays.

Bell Shakespeare, Millers Point, NSW, Australia
A theatre company dedicated to making Shakespeare accessible and relevant to modern Australia using Shakespeare's universal insights.

Australian and New Zealand Shakespeare Association (ANZSA)
Not-for-profit organization offering a forum for national and international scholarship in Shakespeare studies and performance. Its biennial conference attracts international speakers and delegates.

AFRICA

Corniche and Alexandria National Museum, Alexandria, Egypt
Reminders of *Antony and Cleopatra* abound, although her royal palace was destroyed by earthquakes and lies sunken in the ancient harbour.

HISTORY IN THE MAKING

Many of Shakespeare's history plays are set in England and include *King John* and *Henry VIII*, as well as those covering the turbulent Hundred Years War. The Wars of the Roses period is explored in two cycles: the first set, apparently written in the early 1590s, deals with the later part of the struggle and includes *Henry VI, Parts 1, 2* and *3* and *Richard III*. The second set, finished in 1599, covers *Richard II, Henry IV, Parts 1* and *2* and *Henry V*, with the young Prince Hal a favourite character.

Shakespeare also penned three Roman histories – *Julius Caesar, Coriolanus* and *Antony and Cleopatra* – while, of course, *Macbeth* is based upon a real Scottish king born about 1005, but who is regarded as a fair ruler, not the usurping tyrant Shakespeare depicts. Meanwhile, with Tudor Queen Elizabeth's blessing needed, Richard III is also shown as a far blacker character than was the real king killed at Bosworth Field, thus making way for the first Tudor sovereign, Elizabeth I's grandfather Henry VII.

Shakespeare wrote his plays in order to entertain rather than to educate. These are works of imagination, aiming to engage an audience. Nonetheless, they do convey very convincing historical characters and the times in which they lived. Shakespeare read history avidly and recognized the

The Meeting of Antony and Cleopatra by Lawrence Alma-Tadema, 1885

Richard, Duke of Gloucester, and the Lady Anne
by Edwin Austin Abbey, 1896

dramatic impact of strong, sympathetic or humorous characters and major historical events. His skill in storytelling has left a lasting impression and many of us today still associate characters like Julius Caesar, Cleopatra, Henry V and Richard III with their Shakespearean presentations, however much the truth has been adapted for dramatic ends.

Shakespeare's histories paint such vivid pictures of Roman or medieval life: politics, battles, bustling taverns, brothels, royal courts, prisons, death, torture, murder, passion and every possible emotion as the narrative is carried forward by a procession of royal figures or street beggars, engaging clowns, bawdy knights like Falstaff and brave soldiers that include women – such as Joan of Arc and Margaret of Anjou – marching in serried ranks through times long past.

George F Cooke as Richard III,
by Thomas Sully, 1811–12

The ghost of Julius Caesar in an engraving from 1892

BIBLIOGRAPHY AND FURTHER READING

Peter Ackroyd *Shakespeare: The Biography* Vintage, 2006

Alexander, Catherine M. S. *The Treasures of William Shakespeare: The Life, the Works, the Performances* Andre Deutsch Ltd, 2014

Bryson, Bill *Shakespeare: The World as a Stage* HarperCollins Publishers, 2007

Bullen, Arthur Henry *The Complete Works of William Shakespeare* CRW Publishing Ltd, 2005

Crystal, Ben *Shakespeare on Toast: Getting a Taste for the Bard* Icon Books, 2009

Greenblatt, Stephen *Will in the World: How Shakespeare Became Shakespeare* W.W. Norton & Company, 2004

Greer, Dr. Germaine *Shakespeare's Wife* Bloomsbury Publishing PLC, 2008

Hammerschmidt-Hummel, Hildegard *The Life and Times of William Shakespeare 1564–1616* Chaucer Press, 2007

Morgan, Jude *The Secret Life of William Shakespeare* St. Martin's Press, 2014

Orgel, Stephen *King Lear by William Shakespeare*, Penguin Putnam Inc., 2001.

Schoenbaum, Samuel *William Shakespeare: A Compact Documentary Life* Oxford University Press, 1987

Weis, René *Shakespeare Unbound* Henry Holt and Company, 2007

Wood, Michael *Shakespeare* Basic Books, 2003

Wood, Michael *In Search of Shakespeare* BBC Books, 2005

INDEX

WHO'S WHO IN SHAKESPEARE

A Dictionary of Characters and Proper Names

FRANCIS GRIFFIN STOKES

Here is the scroll of every man's name . . .

A Midsummer Night's Dream, i, 2

WORTH PRESS • LONDON

INTRODUCTION

'And one man in his time plays many parts . . .'

JAQUES in *As You Like It*

Who's Who in Shakespeare was originally published in 1909 and thus for over 100 years has been a highly reliable and almost certainly unique source of Shakesperean scholarship. William Shakespeare's output was prodigious. With his two epic poems, other poetry, 154 sonnets and 37 (or maybe more) plays, all with a fairly busy list of characters, the personalities inevitably add up to several thousand. The historical *dramatis personae* – so many kings, queens, princes, princesses, dukes, counts and nobles appear – account for a great number, but also throughout every play are the ordinary folk – local citizens, rogues, ruffians, clowns, innkeepers, watchmen and servants – who add greatly to the reality of the worlds into which Shakespeare leads us so admirably. There are also those who gain stature and renown in spite of humble origins. As Malvolio in *Twelfth Night* commented, 'Be not afraid of greatness: some are born great, some achieve greatness, and some have greatness thrust upon them.' Shakespeare depicts them all: the seekers of power like Macbeth or Richard III, and those who at times fear greatness and may become ineffective like Richard II and Hamlet.

This *Who's Who* offers an amazingly comprehensive and authoritative guide to all those individuals that people the pages of Shakespeare's complete works and strut stages in every nation of the world. Places are also included – for example, a glance at Greece, Ithaca, Italy, London, Venice, Verona or Athens will reveal a note about these countries and cities, detailing the plays in which they occur as well as brief quotes and references.

This is a prolific store of information but the clarity of its presentation makes it highly accessible and an invaluable guide to the wonderful array of Shakespeare's fascinating characters – the heroes, heroines, villains and audience-pleasers. There are many wise men, and even more fools – and wise fools, too. As the fool in *Twelfth Night* remarks, 'Better a witty fool than a foolish wit.' There are fairies, mythical or semi-mythical beings and legendary figures, as well as the conventional human characters. From Hamlet to Romeo and Juliet, Macbeth, Puck and Portia, Henry VIII, Julius Caesar and Cleopatra to old shepherds, many a soldier, gravediggers and tinkers, here is the world at large set upon a little stage for all to see as events and the passage of time work their magic.

'Let every man be master of his time.'

MACBETH in *Macbeth*

PREFACE

This dictionary is designed to treat the proper names in Shakespeare's plays and poems on a plan as comprehensive as that adopted for his general vocabulary in Alexander Schmidt's well-known *Shakespeare Lexicon* (3rd edn. 1902), and thus to furnish an aid to students which has hitherto been lacking.

In Schmidt's valuable book the signification of every word in the poet's vast vocabulary is discussed; but although the names of persons and places are formally recorded, as words they are summarily dismissed – usually in a line – as scarcely falling within the scope of the work.

The present dictionary, however, has a quite different aim, and consists of detailed articles, arranged in alphabetical order, not merely on the *dramatis personae*, but on every proper name, be its importance great or small, which occurs in the First Folio (1623), *Pericles*, and the poems generally attributed to Shakespeare.

The subjects dealt with may be classed under the following six heads: (i) characters recorded in, or based on, medieval history, such as Pandulf, Hotspur, Macbeth; (ii) Greek and Roman historical and legendary characters, such as Ulysses, Brutus, Cleopatra; (iii) purely fictitious characters, such as Ariel, Malvolio, Othello; (iv) persons mentioned, or alluded to, who do not figure as *dramatis personae*; (v) place-names; (vi) miscellaneous subjects, not comprised under any of the foregoing heads, such as festivals, seasons, planets, and the titles of books and tunes.

In the case of characters drawn from medieval history, their authentic biographies – so far as relevant – are sketched, their dramatic action in the plays is summarized, the dramatist's indebtedness to, and divergences from, Holinshed, Hall, and other chroniclers are noted, and attention is drawn, upon occasion, to the same characters when they appear in earlier non-Shakespearean plays.

A parallel plan is adopted in the case of the classical characters, Sir Thomas North's *Plutarch* being the equivalent of Holinshed's *Chronicles* as the main source in the historical plays, and Ovid – especially in his *Metamorphoses* – providing the chief storehouse of myth and legend.

Fictitious characters are similarly dealt with, so far as their dramatic action is concerned, and their prototypes, if any, in earlier plays and romances are indicated.

Personages – biblical, mythological, and historical – who, though not *dramatis personae*, are mentioned or alluded to are duly recorded.

All place-names appear, but only such details in connection with them as are strictly germane to the subject are given.

Certain personal names are also inserted which, although not occurring in the text, claim admission, since they are met with in the introductory pages of the First Folio and of the poems. It should be added that all important variations in the spelling of names occurring in the Quartos and Folios are noted.

Although the present work, as indicated by its title, is essentially a dictionary of proper names, this term is used in a liberal acceptation, and is not regarded as wholly excluding cognate adjectives – such as Cretan, Hyrcanian, Roman – or abstract nouns when denoting distinct personifications. Furthermore, under the titles of the plays succinct accounts of the sources, conjectural or undoubted, of their plots have been inserted, as well as notices of the early editions of those which appeared separately before 1623. Reference to such matters when they crop up in other articles is thus facilitated.

Brief illustrative comments by eminent critics have been occasionally appended to articles, where called for.

Genealogical tables illustrating the complex relationships of some of the ruling and noble houses existing at the time of the Wars of the Roses are given as Appendices.

In the seemingly inevitable absence of a universally received text, the choice of an edition to serve as a source of quotations presents some difficulty. But textual criticism does not lie within the province of this work, and the middle course has been adopted of following pretty closely the Cambridge reading, and indicating important variations, within brackets, where it seems desirable to do so.

The numbering of acts and scenes, however – and, where expedient, of lines – is that of the widely used 'Globe' edition, from which few modern editions substantially differ.

ABBREVIATED TITLES OF PLAYS AND POEMS

All's Well	*All's Well that Ends Well*
Ant. Cl.	*Anthony and Cleopatra*
A.Y.L.	*As You Like It*
Com. Err.	*The Comedy of Errors*
Cor.	*Coriolanus*
Cymb.	*Cymbeline*
F.P.C.	*First Part of the Contention* (early form of 2 *Hen. VI*)
Haml.	*Hamlet, Prince of Denmark*
1 (2) *Hen. IV*	*1st (2nd) Part of King Henry IV*
Hen. V	*The Life of King Henry V*
1 (2, 3) *Hen. VI*	*The 1st (2nd, 3rd) Part of King Henry VI*
Hen. VIII	*The Famous History of the Life of King Henry VIII*
John	*The Life and Death of King John*
Jul. C.	*Julius Caesar*
L.C.	*A Lover's Complaint*
Lear	*King Lear*
L.L.L.	*Love's Labour's Lost*
Lucr.	*The Rape of Lucrece*
Mach.	*Macbeth*
M. Ado	*Much Ado about Nothing*
M. for M.	*Measure for Measure*
M.N.D.	*A Midsummer Night's Dream*
M.V.	*The Merchant of Venice*
M.W.W.	*The Merry Wives of Windsor*
Oth.	*Othello, the Moor of Venice*
Per.	*Pericles*
P.P.	*The Passionate Pilgrim*
P.T.	*The Phoenix and the Turtle*
Rich. II	*The Tragedy of King Richard II*
Rich. III	*The Tragedy of King Richard III*
Rom. J.	*Romeo and Juliet*
Son.	*Sonnets*
Tam. Sh.	*The Taming of the Shrew*
T. And.	*Titus Andronicus*
Temp.	*The Tempest*
T.G.V.	*The Two Gentlemen of Verona*
Timon	*Timon of Athens*
T. Nt.	*Twelfth Night; or, What You Will*
Tr. Cr.	*Troilus and Cressida*
Tr. R.	*The Troublesome Raigne of King John* (groundwork of *King John*)
Tr. Tr.	*The True Tragedie* (early form of 3 *Hen. VI*)
V.A.	*Venus and Adonis*
Wint. T.	*The Winter's Tale*

GENERAL ABBREVIATIONS

acc.	according to
Ar.	Arabic
Arch. f. n. Sprachen	*Archiv für das Studium der neueren Sprachen* (Elberfeld, 1877)
Arg.	Argument (*Lucrece*)
A.-S.	Anglo-Saxon (Old English)
A.V.	Authorized Version (English Bible)
b.	born
Barante	Baron de Barante, *Histoire des Ducs de Bourgogne* (1824)
Boece	H. Boece, *Scotorum Historia* (1575)
B.-S.	W. G. Boswell-Stone, *Shakspere's Holinshed* (1896)
c.	approximately or about (Latin *circa*)
Camb.	Cambridge edition (1887)
Cap.	Edward Capell (1713–81); editor
Caxton	William Caxton, *Recuyell of the Historyes of Troye* (1474)
Chapman	George Chapman, *The Iliads of Homer* (1598–1611)
Chor.	Chorus
Chron. A. de Usk	*Chronicon Adae de Usk* (ed. Thompson, 1876)
Clar.	Clarendon Press edition (of certain plays)
Coke, *Instit.*	Sir Edward Coke, *Institutes of the Laws of England* (1628–44)
Coleridge	S. T. Coleridge, *Notes and Lectures* (1849)
Coleridge, Hartley	H. Coleridge, *Essays and Marginalia* (1851)

Collier MS.	J. P. Collier, *Notes and Emendations* (1853)
Conf. Amant.	John Gower, *Confessio Amantis* (ed. Morley, 1888)
conj.	conjecture
Cron. (or *Chr.*) *Hist.*	*The Cronicle History of Henry the Fifth* (early, imperfect, form of *Henry V*)
C.T.	*Canterbury Tales* (Chaucer)
d., dau.	daughter
D., Dss.	Duke, Duchess
Dan.	Danish
'Dares'	'Dares Phrygius', *De Excidio Trojae Historia* (Bonn, 1837)
'Dict. Cret.'	'Dictys Cretensis', *De Bello Trojano* (Bonn, 1835)
D.N.B.	*Dictionary of National Biography*
dim	diminutive
Douce	Francis Douce, *Illustrations of Shakespeare* (1807)
Dowden	Edward Dowden, *Shakespeare: His Mind and Art* (1875)
D.P., D.PP.	The character, -s in a play (Latin *Dramatis persona, -ae)*
Dyce	Alexander Dyce (1798–1869); editor
E.	Earl
e.d., e.s.	eldest daughter, son
ed., edn., edr.	edited by, edition, editor
Eden	Richard Eden, *The Decades of the Newe Worlde* (1555)
E.E.T.S.	Early English Text Society
Elmh.	Thomas de Elmham, *Vita et Gesta Henrici Quinti* (1727)
Evesham, Monach. de	*Monachi de Evesham Historia Vitae et Regni Ricardi II* (1729)
F, Ff	Folio, -s. Early editions of Shakespeare's plays were printed in a large size commonly known as folio, the smaller quarto size were used for later printings.
ff.	following
fl.	He or she flourished (Latin *floruit*)
Fordun	*Joannis de Fordun Scotichronicon* (ed. 1759)
Foxe	John Foxe, *Actes and Monuments* (1576)
F.Q.	E. Spenser, *The Faerie Queene* (1590–6)
Fr.	French
French	G. R. French, *Shakespeareana Genealogica* (1869)
Furness	*New Variorum Edition of Sh.*, ed. H. H. Furness and H. H. Furness, Jr
Ger.	German
Ger. Lib.	Tasso, *Gerusalemme Liberata* (Fairfax's translation, 1600)
Gk.	Greek
Golding's *Metam.*	Arthur Golding, *The XV Booke of P. Ouidius Naso* (1567)
Gow.	Gower (*Pericles*)
Grafton	R. Grafton, *A Chronicle of Englande* (1568)
g.s., g.g.s.	grandson, great-grandson
Hall	See article Hall, Edward.
Halliwell	J. O. Halliwell (afterwards Halliwell-Phillipps) (1820–89); editor
Harsnet	Samuel Harsnet, *Declaration of Egregious Popish Impostures* (1603)
Hazlitt	William Hazlitt, *Characters of Sh.'s Plays* (1817)
Herc. Oet.	M. Annaeus Seneca, *Hercules Oetaeus*
Hol.	See article Holinshed, Raphael
Hor.	Horace
Hunter	Jos. Hunter, *New Illustrations of Sh.* (1845)
Hygin. *Fab.*	C. Julius Hyginus, *Fabulae*
ib., ib. ib.	in the same source, -s (Latin *ibidem* the same)
Ind.	Induction
It.	Italian
Jameson	Anna B. Jameson, *Characteristics of Women* (1832)
Johnson	Samuel Johnson (1709–84); editor
Knight	Charles Knight (1791–1873); editor
l., ll.	line, lines
Lat.	Latin
Lee	Sir Sidney Lee, *Life of William Shakespeare* (1915)
Locrine	*The Tragedy of Locrine* (anonymous, 1595)
m.	married
Malone	Edm. Malone (1741–1812); editor and commentator
Minsheu	John Minsheu, *Guide into Tongues* (1617)
Mon.	Dante, *De Monarchia*
Monstrelet	*Chroniques d'Enguerrand de Monstrelet* (ed. Buchon)
mtd.	mentioned
N. and Q.	*Notes and Queries*
N.E.D.	*A New English Dictionary* (Oxford)
N.S.S.Tr.	*Transactions of the New Shakspere Society*
N.T.	New Testament
ob.	died (Latin *obiit*)

Overbury, *Char.*	Sir Thomas Overbury, *Characters* (1614)
perh.	perhaps
Pers.	Aulus Persius Flaccus, *Satires*
pfx.	prefix; *i.e.* name of character prefixed to speech
Phil.	M. Tullius Cicero, *Philippics*
Pliny, *Nat. Hist.*	(or *N.H.*) *The Naturall Historie of C. Plinius Secundus*, translated by P. Holland (1601)
Plut.	W. W. Skeat, *Shakespeare's Plutarch* (1875; page cited)
p.m.	the character is present but does not speak (Latin *persona muta*)
poet.	*poetice*, poetically
Pol. Verg.	*Polydori Vergilii Anglicae Historiae Libri XXVII* (1555)
Proc. Priv. Co.	*Proceedings . . . of the Privy Council* (ed. Nicolas, 1834–7)
Pss.	Princess
Q, Qq	Quarto, -s
q.v.	For further information see entry under this reference (literally 'which see', Latin *quod vide*).
Recuyell	William Caxton, *Recuyell of the Historyes of Troye* (1474)
rep.	repeated
Rotul. Parl.	*Rotuli Parliamentorum* (published by Record Commissioners)
Rowe	Nicholas Rowe (1674–1718); editor
St-Remy	*M moires de J. Lefevre, Seigneur de St-Remy* (ed. Buchon)
Sh.	William Shakespeare
Sh.	The plays in the First Folio, with *Pericles* and the Poems
Sh. Comm.	*Shakespeare Commentaries* (Gervinus)
Sh. Eng.	*Shakespeare's England* (Oxford, 1916)
Sh. Jahr.	*Jahrbücher d. deutschen Shakespeare Gesellschaft* (1894–1914)
sol.	in soliloquy
Sp.	Spanish
st. dir.	stage direction
Steevens	George Steevens (1736–1800); editor and commentator
Stevenson	*Letters and Papers illustrative of the Wars of the English in France* (ed. J. Stevenson)
Stow, *Annales*	John Stow, *Annales of England* (1605)
Stow, *Chron.*	John Stow, *English Chronicles*
Stow, *Survey*	John Stow, *Survey of London* (1603, ed. Morley)
s.v.	under the specified word (Latin *sub verbo*)
Theob.	Lewis Theobald (1688–1744); editor and commentator
T.L.S.	*The Times Literary Supplement*
Ulrici	Hermann Ulrici, *Ueber Sh.'s dramatische Kunst* (English translation, 1846)
Upton	John Upton, *Critical Observations on Sh.* (1746)
Val. Max.	Valerius Maximus, *De Factis Dictisque Memorabilibus Libri IX*
Var.	*Variorum* edition (of 1821, unless otherwise specified)
w.	wife
Walker	[W.] Sidney Walker, *Critical Examination of the Text of Sh.* (1860)
Warb.	William Warburton (1698–1779); editor
Wilh. Worc.	*Wilhelmi Worcestrii Annales Rerum Anglicarum* (ed. T. Hearne, 1774)
Wright	W. Aldis Wright, notes in Clarendon Press series

EXPLANATION OF SIGNS, ETC.

iii, 4	Act III, Scene 4.
iii, 4 (2)	Twice mentioned in iii, 4.
iii, 4]	The character takes part in the scene.
(iii, 4)	The character is merely referred to.
later	The character returns after quitting the stage.
p.m.	*persona muta*; the character is present, but does not speak.

Head-words in square brackets, *e.g.* [**Thyamis**], denote persons or places alluded to, but not mentioned by name, in *Sh.*

Numerals in parentheses after head-words are used to distinguish between persons or places of the same name, *e.g.* **Portia** (1), **Portia** (2).

Names of disguised characters are distinguished by quotation marks, *e.g.* 'Cesario' for Viola (*T.Nt.*).

A

Aaron. D.P. *T. And.* A Moor, beloved by Tamora. i, 1] *p.m.* ii, 1] (*sol.*) resolves 'to mount aloft with his 'imperial mistress'; checks & quarrel between her sons over Lavinia, and shows them how they may both work their will. ii, 3] conceals gold in the forest; hints to Tam. the fate of Bassianus and Lav., and gives her a 'fatal plotted scroll' for Saturninus. ii, 4] lures Quintus and Martius to the pit wherein lies the body of Bas.; later, brings Sat. to the spot, and unearths the gold, to confirm the letter fixing the murder of Bas. on the two young men. iii, 1] cuts off Titus' hand as a pretended sacrifice to save his sons. iv, 2] realizes that Tit. knows the truth; his infant by Tam. is brought to him to be slain, but he spares it, and kills the nurse; plans to exchange the babe for another. (iv, 4) mtd. v, 1] is led to Lucius with the babe in his arms, and, to save it, makes full confession. v, 3] is condemned to be set 'breast-deep in earth' and famished.

'The powerful sketch of Aaron is a good deal indebted to the Barabas of Marlowe... Both have a delight in evil spart from the pleasure anticipated from an end gained. They revel in it, like a virtuous egoist in the consciousness of virtue.' (A. Symons, *Introduction to Sh. Quarto Facsimiles* (Pretorius), No. 29, p. xi.)

Abbess. D.P. *Com. Err.* See AEMILIA (1).

Abel. Second son of Adam. 'Which blood, like sacrificing A.'s, cries, Even from the tongueless caverns of the earth' (*Rich. II*, i, 1; *cf.* Gen. iv, 10); 'This be Damascus, be thou cursed Cain, To slay thy brother A., if thou wilt' (*1 Hen. VI*, i, 3). *Cf.* Higden, *Polychronicon*, f. xii : 'Damascus is as moche as to say a shedynge of blood. For there Chaym slowe Abell and hidde hym in the sande'; also Mandeville (1725), p. 148: 'and in that place where Damascus was founded Kaym slew A. his brother.'

'The tomb of A.' is shown on a hill, Nebi-Abel, near Damascus. But the old Jewish tradition may find its source in the fact that the affix 'Abel' means a grassy spot.

Abergavenny, or **Aberga'ny, Lord.** See NEVILLE, GEORGE (1).

Abhorson. D.P. *M. for M.* An executioner. iv, 2] fears that the clown, as an assistant, would 'discredit our mystery.' iv, 3] summons Barnardine to execution.

Abradas. See BARGULUS.

Abraham. Originally 'Abram' (Gen. xvii, 5). Patriarch. 'A.'s bosom' the abode of the blessed (Luke xvi, 22).

'Holy A.' (*M.V.* i, 3); 'O father A.' (*ib. ib.*); 'the bosom of good old A.!' (*Rich. II*, iv, 1); 'the sons of Edward sleep in A.'s bosom' (*Rich. III*, iv, 3). See ARTHUR.

The form 'Abram' is used by Shylock (QqFf).

Abraham Cupid. 'Young A.C., he that shot so trim, When King Cophetua lov'd the beggar-maid' (*Rom. J.* ii, 1); in allusion to 'the blinded boy, that shoots so trim' of the ballad (Percy, *Reliques*, ed. Wheatley, i, 193).

'Abraham,' or 'Abram,' is the reading of QqFf, and has been explained as a mistake for 'auburn,' or as referring to Cupid's perpetual youth, or to his being a cheat – an 'Abraham-man.' But Upton (1746) held that 'Abram' is merely a printer's error for 'Adam,' and that the reference is to Adam Bell, an archer of proverbial skill. See ADAM (5).

Abram (1). See ABRAHAM.

Abram (2). D.P. *Rom. J.* Servant to Montague. i, 1] joins in a fray.

Absyrtus. Son of Aeëtes and brother of Medea. M., when pursued by her father, slew Ab. and scattered his body in pieces on the way, to delay Aeëtes (Ovid, *Trist.* iii, 9).

'Meet I an infant of the house of York, Into as many gobbets will I cut it As wild Medea young Ab. did' (2 *Hen. VI*, v, 2; 'Absirtis,' Ff).

Academe. Also 'Achademe' (QF1). Garden, near Athens, where Plato taught; hence a university, etc. 'Our court shall be a little A.' (*L.L.L.* i, 1); mtd., *ib.* iv, 3 (2).

Perh. in allusion to tho 'Philosophical Academy' of the 'Wizard' E. of Northumberland (1564–1632). Cf. *Sh. Eng.* i, 248.

Accost, Mary. Aguecheek, blundering, attributes this name to Maria; *T. Nt.* i, 3.

One of the fashionable terms of courtship in Sh.'s time, acc. Halliwell, who quotes various 'exploytes of good Accost' from *Sir Gyles Goosecap* (1606).

Acheron. One of the rivers of the infernal regions; sometimes the underworld itself; often, it would appear, regarded in *Sh.* as a lake.

'*Hecate*. At the pit of A. meet me' (*Macb.* iii, 5; this, Wright suggests, is merely a poetical name of 'some foul tarn' near Macbeth's castle); 'drooping fog as black as A.' (*M.N.D.* iii, 2; *cf.* Fairfax, *Ger. Lib.* ii, 2, 'A.'s darke shores'); 'I'll dive into the burning lake below, And pull her out of A. by the heels' (*T. And.* iv, 3).

The infernal 'lake' mtd. but not named: 'Pluto's damned lake' (2 *Hen. IV*, ii, 4); 'Descend to darkness and the burning lake' (2 *Hen. VI*, i, 4); 'Nero is an angler in the lake of darkness' (*Lear*, iii, 6). In all these cases the identification of the 'lake' with A. is merely conjectural.

Achilles. Son of Peleus and Thetis (*Tr. Cr.* iii, 3); chief hero of the Greeks in the Trojan War; he feared (as did all the Greeks save Menelaus) to meet Hector in single combat (Hom. *Il.* vii), but ultimately slew H. in revenge for the death of his friend Patroclus at H.'s hands (*Il.* xxii). According to a later tradition, Telephus, having been wounded by the spear of A., was cured by applying the rust of the same weapon (Ovid, *Rem. Am.* 48; *Metam.* xii, 112. 'Dict. Cret.'2,10). Achilles' love for Polyxena, which plays an important part in later traditions, is not mentioned in the Homeric poems.

'Hide thy head, A., here comes Hector in arms' (*L.L.L.* v, 2, l. 635); 'Whose smile and frown, like to A.'s spear, Is able with the change to kill and cure' (2 *Hen. VI*, v, 1; *cf.* Chaucer, *The Squire's Tale*, 1. 239).

D.P. *Tr. Cr.* (i, 3) he lies in his tent, and loves to hear Patroclus mimic the other chiefs; Ulysses schemes to 'crop' his pride. ii, 1] intervenes as Ajax is chastising Thersites; speaks scornfully of Hector's challenge to the Greeks. ii, 3] tolerates Thersites' jibes; retires to his tent, and sends word by Ulysses that he 'will not to the field.' iii, 3] as he stands at the entrance of his tent, the chiefs pass by him with ostentatious indifference; he is thereby perplexed; obtains converse with U., who tries to arouse his jealousy of Ajax, and warns him that his love for Polyxena is known; Ach. suddenly has 'a woman's longing' to see Hector in his 'weeds of peace'; sends word to Ajax to this effect. iv, 5] converses with H.; begs the heavens say 'in which part of his body Shall I destroy him'; challenges him to combat on the morrow. v, 1] receives a letter from Hecuba and 'a token' from Polyxena urging him to keep an oath that he has sworn; declares that he will obey this 'major vow'; invites Hector to his tent. (v, 4) mtd. v, 5] is roused to action by the death of Patroclus, whom he swears to avenge. v, 6] while his 'arms are out of use' encounters Hector, who bids him pause if he will; accepts H.'s courtesy, but exclaims 'anon thou shalt hear of me again.' v, 7] instructs his Myrmidons to fall on H. as soon as he is found. v, 8] gives the word to his Myrmidons, who attack the unarmed H. and kill him; drags H.'s body at his horse's tail. v, 9] is accorded the glory of having slain H.

In making Achilles a traitorous ally and a treacherous foe Sh. does but follow medieval tradition, for the Romancists always sided with the Trojans, as being ancestors of the Romans; but in attributing his 'awakening' to a desire to avenge Patroclus Sh. follows Homer and not Benoît de Sainte-More, who attributes it to jealousy of the exploits of Troilus.

The brawn and bulk of Achilles are strongly insisted on: 'large A., on his press'd bed lolling' (i, 3); 'broad A.' (*ib.*). (Caxton mentions his 'brodo sholdres.')

Achitophel, or **Ahitophel.** The Gilonite, who deserted David for Absalom (2 Sam. xv–xvii); hence a treacherous friend. Falstaff calls his mercer, who would not give him credit, 'a whoreson Ach.' (*2 Hen. IV*, i, 2).

Actaeon. Famous hunter, grandson of Cadmus, who saw Diana bathing with her nymphs, and was changed by her into a stag and torn to pieces by his hounds (Ovid, *Metam.* iii, 155 ff.); hence, in allusion to his horns, a cuckold.

'Like Sir A. he, with Ringwood [*q.v.*] at thy heels' (*M.W.W.* ii, 1); 'a secure and wilful A.' (*ib.* iii, 2). The story elaborated and applied, *T. And.* ii, 3. (Orsino alludes to the story, *T. Nt.* i, 1: 'That instant was I turn'd into a hart, And my desires like fell and cruel hounds E'er since pursue me.')

Actium. Promontory in Acarnania, at the entrance of the Ambracian Gulf, off which Octavius gained a naval victory over Antony and Cleopatra, 31 B.C. (*Plut.* pp. 213–6).

'The head of Actium' (*Ant. Cl.* iii, 7); the battle described, *ib.* iii, 10.

Adallas. 'King of Thracia,' an ally of Antony's (*Plut.* p. 207). Mtd. ('Adullas,' Ff), *Ant. Cl.* iii, 6.

Adam (1). The first man. 'A.'s sons are my brethren, and ... I hold it a sin to match in my kindred' (*M. Ado*, ii, 1, l. 66); 'endowed with all A. had left him before he transgressed' (*i.e.* all the world; *ib. ib.* l. 226); 'The moon was a month old, when A. was no more' (*L.L.L.* iv, 2); 'Had he been A., he had tempted Eve' (*ib.* v, 2, l. 322); 'old A.'s likeness' (*Rich. II*, iii, 4); 'the old days of goodman A.' (*1 Hen. IV*, ii, 4); 'in the state of innocency, A. fell' (*ib.* iii, 3); 'consideration ... whipped the offending A. out of him' (*Hen. V*, v, 1; *cf.* Gen. iii, 23–4); 'A. was a gardener' (*2 Hen. VI*, iv, 2); 'A.'s profession' (*Haml.* v, 1); 'the scripture says, A. digged' (*ib. ib.*; *cf.* Gen. iii, 23); '*Dro. S.* What, have you got the picture of old A. new apparelled? *Ant. S.* ... What A. dost thou mean? *Dro. S.* Not that A. that kept the Paradise, but that A. that keeps the prison' (*Com. Err.* iv, 3).

Adam (2). D.P. *A.Y.L.* 'An old servant of Sir Rowland de Boys, now following the fortunes of Orlando' (Rowe). i, 1] to him Or. discourses on his wrongs; he tries to stay the quarrel between Or. and his brother Oliver; is treated with contumely by the latter. ii, 3] urges Or. to flee from Oliver; presses on him the savings of a thrifty lifetime, and accompanies him in his flight. ii, 6] sinks exhausted by hunger and fatigue. ii, 7] is borne by Or. to the Duke's table.

The corresponding character in Lodge's *Rosalynde*, and in *The Tale of Gamelyn*, is Adam Spencer, or Adam the spencer – *i.e.* steward. There is a tradition that the part of A. was played by Sh. himself; *cf.* Lee, pp. 88, 462.

Adam (3). 'A. that keeps the prison' (*Com. Err.* iv, 3). Acc. some commentators, because his buff garments resembled the native 'buff' of A.

Adam (4). A servant; *Tam. Sh.* iv, 1, l. 139.

Adam (5). For 'Adam Bell,' a traditional archer of great skill (*cf.* Percy, *Reliques*, ed. Wheatley, i, 153). 'He that hits me, let him be clapped on the shoulder and called A.' (*M. Ado*, i, 1, l. 261).

Adam Cupid. See ABRAHAM CUPID.

Adon. For 'Adonis.' Mtd., *V. A.* 769; 'two A.s dead' (*ib.* 1070).

Adonis. To the myth of A. there is no allusion in the plays, the only mention of him being: 'A., painted by a running brook' (*Tam. Sh.* Ind. 2). Mtd. *Son.* liii. Named sixteen times in *Venus and Adonis* (*q.v.*), five times in *P.P.*

Adonis, Gardens of. 'Adonis horti' (κῆποι 'Αδώνιδος). In connection with the rites of Adonis these were baskets filled with earth, in which corn and flowers were sown and tended for eight days. The plants shot up quickly, but withered immediately, and were then thrown, symbolically, into running water. (Frazer, *Adonis, Attis, Osiris* (1914), i, 236 ff.; *cf.* Pliny, *Nat. Hist.* XIX, xix, 1.) This description, however, does not accord with the only allusion in *Sh.* to the G. of A.: 'Adonis' gardens That one day bloom'd and fruitful were the next' (*1 Hen. VI*, i, 6). It has been suggested that there is confusion here with the 'garden of Alcinous' (Hom. *Od.* vii); but the allegorical 'Garden of Adonis, far renowned by fame,' described in *The Faerie Queene* (1590), III, vi, as of surpassing fertility, and where 'there is continuall Spring, and harvest there Continuall, both meeting at one time,' suggests a more likely source of the discrepancy. *Cf.* also *Every Man out of his Humour* (1598), iv, 6.

Adramadio, Dun. Costard's perversion of 'Don Adriano de Armado' (*q.v.*); *L.L.L.* iv, 3, l. 199.

Adrian (1). D.P. *Temp.* 'A Lord' (Ff); 'the cockrel' (ii, 1); shipwrecked on Prospero's island with Alonso, King of Naples. ii, 1] praises the climate of the isle; converses with Gonzago. iii, 3] follows Alonso to save him from suicide. v, 1] *p.m.*

Adrian (2). D.P. *Cor.* ('A Volsce' in st. dirs. and pfxs.) iv, 3] on his way to Rome meets Nicanor (*q.v.*), a traitorous

Roman, and hears the welcome news of insurrections in the city and the banishment of Coriolanus; returns to Antium with N.

Adriana. D.P. *Com. Err.* Wife to Antipholus of Ephesus. ii, 1] perturbed at her husband's absence, she scorns the counsel of her sister, who advises patience and submission, is informed by Dromio that Ant. is 'stark mad,' since he demands 'his gold' and repudiates both wife and home; she is overcome with jealous fears, and speaks of a chain Ant. had promised her. ii, 2] meeting Ant. of Syracuse, reproaches him for his supposed faithlessness, but forgives him, and persuades him to come to dinner forthwith. (iv, 1) Dro. of Syracuse is sent to her. iv, 2] is dismayed on hearing that 'her husband' has been making love to her sister Luciana; is told by Dro. S. that 'his master' has been arrested for the price of a chain and requires money from his desk; she sends it. iv, 4] believing Ant. possessed, she brings 'a conjuror' to exorcize him; she is, to her amazement, accused of having shut her husband out of his house, and sent him no money; has Ant. bound as a lunatic and carried home; about to visit the goldsmith and pay for the chain, she flees in terror from Ant. S., who enters with drawn rapier. v, 1] meeting Ant. S. and Dro. S., urges the bystanders to seize them, and on their taking refuge in an abbey hard by explains to the abbess that her husband is out of his mind; is told that this must be due to her own shrewishness; clamours to have her husband restored to her; explains matters to the Duke; to her astonishment her husband enters from another quarter, as though 'borne about invisible'; finally, when the twin brothers both stand before her, she remains unable to distinguish between them.

The wife to Menaechmus of Epidamnus, in the *Menaechmi* of Plautus, is unnamed.

Adriano. See ARMADO.

Adriatic, *adj.* 'Were she as rough As are the swelling A. seas' (*Tam. Sh.* i, 2).

cf. 'inquieti Hadriae' (Hor. *Odes*, iii, 3).

Aeacides. Patronymic of descendants of Aeacus. 'Ae. was Ajax' (*Tam. Sh.* iii, 1); 'Aio te, Aeacida, Romanos vincere posse,' as an instance of ambiguous oracle (2 *Hen. VI*, i, 4).

Aedile, An. D.P. *Cor.* iii, 1] *p.m.* iii, 3] announces approach of Cor.; exults over his fall. iv, 2] *p.m.*

In iii, 1, several Aediles are present.

Aegeon. D.P. *Com. Err.* A merchant of Syracuse. i, 1] relates to the Duke how he came to Ephesus in quest of a lost son; is condemned to death for unlawfully landing at Eph., unless he can procure a ransom during the day. v, 1] on his way to execution recognizes his sons and also his lost wife Aemilia; is granted his life, without ransom.

The father of the twins in the *Menaechmi* of Plautus is Moschus.

Aegles. Properly 'Aegle.' A nymph, d. of Panopeus; 'Aegles, the nymph, was loved of Theseus' (*Plut.* p. 284). 'And make him with fair Ae. ['Eagles,' Ff] break his faith' (*M.N.D.* ii, 1).

The classical spelling was restored by Rowe.

[Aelian.] Claudius Aelianus. His *Varia Historia* (Eng. transln. 1576) yields a passage (xii, 23) which has been supposed to be the origin of Hamlet's 'sea of troubles' (*Haml.* iii, 1).

Aemilia (1). D.P. *Com. Err.* An abbess, long-lost wife of Aegeon. v, 1] refuses to give up Antipholus of Syracuse, who has taken refuge in her abbey; declares that if he is mad he has been made so by his scolding wife; later, recognizes her husband on his way to execution, and reveals that she is his wife, and mother of the twin Antipholuses; bids the Duke and the assembled company come to a feast in the abbey, 'And hear at large discoursed all our fortunes.'

'Abbess' in st. dirs. and pfxs. There is no corresponding character in the *Menaechmi* of Plautus.

Aemilia (2). See EMILIA (1).

Aemilius. D.P. *T. And.* A noble Roman. iv, 4] announces that the Goths, under Lucius Andronicus, are marching on Rome; is sent as an envoy to L. v, 1] delivers his message. v, 3] presents L. to the populace as emperor.

Aeneas. Trojan hero, son of Anchises and Venus; his wanderings after the capture of Troy are related in Virgil's *Aeneid* (see DIDO). For his rescue of Anchises see *Aen.* ii, 707 ff. On gems and coins he is usually represented as carrying his father on his shoulders, and leading his son, the little Ascanius (*q.v.*).

'What if he had said "widower Ae."?' (*Temp.* ii, 1); 'As did Ae. old Anchises bear, So bear I thee' (2 *Hen. VI*, v, 2); 'Ae., our great ancestor, Did from the flames of Troy ... The old Anchises bear' (*Jul. C.* i, 2); 'Dido and her Ae.' (*Ant. Cl.* iv, 14); 'false Ae.' (*Cymb.* iii, 4); 'To bid Ae. tell the tale twice o'er, How Troy was burnt' (*T. And.* iii, 2); 'Ae.'s tale to Dido' (*Haml.* ii, 2). Allusions: 'The wand'ring prince and Dido' (*T. And.* ii, 3); 'our ancestor, When with his solemn tongue he did discourse To love-sick Dido's sad attending ear' (*ib.* v, 3).

D.P. *Tr. Cr.* i, 1] is accompanied by Troilus to the field. i, 2] *p.m.* i, 3] with much ceremony greets Agamemnon, and delivers a chivalric challenge from Hector to the Grecian princes. iv, 1] exchanges 'the most despitefull'st gentle greeting' with Diomedes. iv, 2] informs Troilus that Cressida must be given up. iv, 4] follows Hector to the lists. iv, 5] is present at the combat between H. and Ajax. (v, 3) mtd. (v, 6) 'Ajax hath ta'en Ae.' v, 10] hears that H. is dead.

Aeolus. Ruler of the winds, which he keeps shut up 'in their brazen caves' (2 *Hen. VI*, iii, 2); *cf.* 'vasto antro' (Virg. *Aen.* i, 52–4), and, for 'brazen,' τεῖχος χάλκεον (Hom. *Od.* x).

Aesculapius. God of medicine, acc. post-Homeric tradition; hence, popularly, a physician. 'Ae. guide us' (*Per.* iii, 2); 'my Ae.' (*i.e.* Dr Caius; *M.W.W.* ii, 3).

The name of Ae. is not mtd. in Ovid ('Apolline nato,' *Metam.* xv, 639), but is used by Golding in his transln.: 'leech-craft had again Receiv'd by Aesculapius' meanes.'

Aeson. Father of Jason; made young again in his old age by Medea (Ovid, *Metam.* vii, 255 ff.). His rejuvenation by 'enchanted herbs' mtd. *M.V.* v, 1. ('Eson,' QqFf.)

Aesop, or **Esop.** *Fl. c.* 570 B.C. Reputed author of the fables bearing his name. 'Let Ae. fable in a winter's night' (3 *Hen. VI*, v, 5). The fable of the fox and the grapes alluded to, *All's Well*, ii, 1, ll. 73 ff.

A Latin version was a school-book in Sh.'s days. Cf. *Sh. Eng.* i, 232.

Aetna, or **Etna.** Volcano in Sicily. 'Now let hot Aetna cool in Sicily' (*T. And.* iii, 1); 'I will be thrown into Etna … ere I will leave her thus' (*M.W.W.* iii, 5); 'As smoke from Ae., that in air consumes' (*Lucr.* 1042).

Cf. Peele, *Garter*, l. 79.

Affection. Personified. 'Jealousy doth call himself A.'s sentinel' (*V.A.* 650); 'A. is my captain' (*Lucr.* 271).

Afric. (*a*) *Subst.*, Africa. 'I would they were in A.' (*Cymb.* i, 2); 'we put them on first in A.' (*Temp.* ii, 1); 'Not A. owns a serpent' (*Cor.* i, 8). (*b*) *Adj.*, African. 'Parch in A. sun' (*Tr. Cr.* i, 3).

Africa. 'I speak of A. and golden joys' (2 *Hen. IV*, v, 3).

African, *subst.* Native of Africa. 'Lose her to an A.' (*Temp.* ii, 1).

Agamemnon. Son (or grandson) of Atreus, and brother to Menelaus. King of Mycenae, and commander-in-chief of the Grecian expedition against Troy, but neither in Homeric nor medieval story is he personally of the supreme importance due to his office. '*Doll* [to Falstaff]. Thou art … worth five of A.' (2 *Hen. IV*, ii, 4); '*Flu.* The Duke of Exeter is as magnanimous as A.' (*Hen. V*, iii, 6); Menelaus (*q.v.*) mtd. as 'A.'s brother' (3 *Hen. VI*, ii, 2).

D.P. *Tr. Cr.* (i, 2) compared with Troilus. i, 3] as their leader, demands of the princes why they are downcast, since their long check before Troy is but a trial made of them by Jove; calls on Ulysses to speak; gives audience to Aeneas, as the bearer of a challenge from Hector, but at first does not reveal his identity; conducts Ae. to his tent. (ii, 1) reviled by Thersites. ii, 3] sends Patroclus to summon Achilles; discourses on pride; on Achilles refusing to come, suggests sending Ajax to him, but is dissuaded by Ulysses. iii, 3] consents to exchange Antenor for Cressida; at Ulysses' suggestion, ostentatiously ignores Achilles; is ironically termed by Achilles the 'six-or-seven-times-honour'd captain-general.' iv, 5] welcomes Cressida to the Grecian camp; presides at the lists. v, 1] does courtesy to Hector. v, 5] rehearses the losses of the Greeks, and urges them to renew the fight. v, 9] believes that, with the death of Hector, 'Troy is ours.'

[**Aganippus.**] See France, King of (*Lear*).

Agenor. Son of Poseidon and father of Europa (*q.v.*). 'Sweet beauty … Such as the daughter of A. had' (*Tam. Sh.* i, 1); *cf.* Ovid, *Fasti*, vi, 712.

Agincourt. Village in France, about 30 m. S.E. of Boulogne, where, on Oct. 25, 1415, Henry V gained a great victory over the French under the Constable d'Albret. The English numbered about 15,000 men and the French nearly 60,000. When the battle was over Henry 'desired of Montioie [French herald] to understand the name of the castell neere adjoining: when they had told him that it was called Agincourt, he said: "Then shall this conflict be called the battell of Agincourt" ' (*Hol.* iii, 555). Act IV of *Hen. V* deals with the conflict, but the name occurs only thrice in the text of the play, viz. i, Chor.; iv, Chor.; iv, 7.

Agrippa, M. Vipsanius (63–12 B.C.). One of the two chief friends of Octavius (*Plut.* p. 183); commanded the left wing for Oct. at Actium (*ib.* pp. 210, 212).

D.P. *Ant. Cl.* ii, 2] suggests to the triumvirs a marriage between Antony and Octavia; converses with Enobarbus on the charms and wiles of Cleopatra. ii, 4] sets out for Misenum. ii, 7] *p.m.* iii, 2] discusses Lepidus with Enobarbus; avers that Ant. is prone to tears. iii, 6] converses with Octavius. iv, 1] *p.m.* iv, 6] is ordered by Oct. 'to begin the fight.' iv, 7] retires before unexpected resistance. v, 1] extols the memory of Antony (Theob.; assigned to Dolabella, Ff).

Agrippa, Menenius. See Menenius.

[**Agrippina.**] Mother of Nero (*q.v.*). Her murder, by her son's orders, alluded to, *John*, v, 2; *Haml.* iii, 2, l. 412. *Cf.* Higden, *Polychronicon* (ed. Lumby), iv, 395.

Aguecheek, Sir Andrew. D.P. *T. Nt.* 'A foolish knight pretending to Olivia' (Rowe). i, 3] (is discussed by Sir Toby and Maria); is presented to M., who banters him; despairs of Olivia, but is persuaded by Sir T. to 'stay a month longer'; boasts of his accomplishments. ii, 3] carouses with Sir T. and Feste. ii, 5] witnesses Malvolio's discovery of the forged letter. iii, 1] meets 'Cesario,' and considers him 'a rare courtier.' iii, 2] tells Sir T. and Fabian that he has seen Olivia 'do favours to the Count's serving-man'; is persuaded to write a challenge to 'Cesario.' iii, 4] shows the challenge to Sir T. and Fab.; is terrified on learning from Sir T. that his opponent is a noted fencer; suggests offering him his horse to 'let the matter slip'; on 'C.'s' entrance, is assured by Sir T. that his opponent will not hurt him, and, unwillingly, draws; the duel is interrupted by the entrance of Antonio; upon 'C.'s' departure Sir A., now believing him a coward, resolves to pursue him 'and beat him.' iv, 1] meeting Sebastian, mistakes him for 'C.' and strikes him; is chastised by S. and threatens 'an action of battery' against him. v, 1] enters, 'with his head broke' (Rowe), and, seeing 'C.,' taxes him with the assault; offers to aid Sir T., who is drunk and wounded, but his help is rejected with scorn.

'A. is drawn with great propriety, but his character is, in a great measure, that of natural fatuity, and is therefore not the proper prey of a satirist' (Johnson, 1765). 'Always enjoying a joke, and never understanding it' (Halliwell, 1857). For a description of J. W. Dodd's famous impersonation of the character see C. Lamb, *Essays of Elia*, 'On Some of the Old Actors.'

Agueface (Ff). A perversion, by Sir Toby, of 'Aguecheek'; *T. Nt.* i, 3, l. 47 (restored by Dyce).

Ahenobarbus, Cn. Domitius. Served under Mark Antony against the Parthians; consul 32 B.C.; fled from Rome to Antony at Ephesus, where he found Cleopatra with him, and urged fruitlessly that she should be removed from the army; was offered the command by the soldiers, but in disgust deserted Ant. and went over to Octavius shortly before Actium; he was not present at that battle, but died shortly after joining Oct. Plutarch's account of Ah. is meagre (*Plut.* pp. 203, 209), and the clear-cut character of 'Enobarbus' is almost wholly the creation of Sh. ('Aenobarbus,' *Plut.*).

D.P. *Ant. Cl.* 'Enobarbus,' or 'Domitius' (iii, 5; iv, 2). i, 2] superintends the preparation of a 'banquet,' and declares that his 'fortune' will 'be – drunk to bed.' ii, 2] scorns the request of Lepidus that he should entreat Antony to gentle speech; interrupts the debate between the triumvirs, but is checked by Ant.; describes the first meeting of Ant. and Cl., and characterizes the latter. ii, 6] checks Pompey's indiscreet allusions to Cl.'s early adventures; exchanges compliments with him; informs Menas of Ant.'s marriage to Octavia. ii, 7] joins in the revelry on Pompey's galley. iii, 2] satirizes the hypocrisy of Octavius and Lepidus, and comments on Ant.'s alleged grief for Jul. Caesar. iii, 5] hears from Eros that Oct. has deposed Lep. iii, 7] urges Cl. not to join in the coming battle, advises Ant. to fight on land and not by sea. iii, 10] relates how his 'eyes did sicken' at beholding the flight of Cl. at Actium. iii, 13] casts the chief blame on Ant. and resolves to desert to Oct. iv, 2] is disconcerted by Ant.'s trustfulness. (iv, 5) his desertion is reported to Ant. iv, 6] is stricken with remorse. iv, 9] dies, with the words 'Oh, Antony!' upon his lips.

'Strong Enobarbe' (trisyllable), ii, 7; 'Domitian,' iv, 2, Ff.

'A soldier of the old Roman times; hard, bold, dryly humorous, without ceremony or compliment, upright and true towards friend and foe... His sound knowledge of human nature is sufficient to enable him to see through the whole inner web of his enigmatical master, but he is helpless in the web of the artful Cleopatra.' (Gervinus.) 'The fugitive once ruined by his flight and again redeemed by the death-agony of his dark and doomed repentance.' (Swinburne.)

Ajax. Son of Telamon (King of Salamis), and grandson of Aeacus; called A. Telamonius to distinguish him from Ajax son of Oïleus. Acc. Homer he was, next to Achilles, the most eminent of the Greeks. Later writers describe his discomfiture by Ulysses, which threw A. into a state of madness in which he slew the sheep of the Greek army, fancying they were his foes, and on recovering his senses slew himself. (For Sh.'s supposed acquaintance with the *Ajax* of Sophocles see J. C. Collins, *Studies in Sh.* (1904), pp. 63 ff.)

'This Love is as mad as A.: it kills sheep; it kills me, I a sheep' (*L.L.L.* iv, 3); a ribald pun made on the name, *ib.* v, 2, l. 582; 'Aeacides Was A., call'd so from his grandfather' (*Tam. Sh.* iii, l); 'like A. Telamonius, On sheep or oxen could I spend my fury' (2 *Hen. VI*, v, 1); 'the sevenfold shield of A.' (*Ant. Cl.* iv, 14); 'Thersites' body is as good as Ajax', When neither are alive' (*Cymb.* iv, 2); 'The Greeks ... did bury A. That slew himself' (*T. And.* i, 2); 'None of these rogues and cowards But A. is their fool [perh. 'a fool to them in bragging']' (*Lear*, ii, 2); contrasted with Ulysses, *Lucr.* 1394–8.

The shield of A., 'seven ox-hides within it quilted hard' (Chapman's *Iliads*, vii), is also mtd. by Ovid (*Metam.* xiii, 2): 'clipei dominus septemplicis Ajax.'

D.P. *Tr. Cr.* (i, 2) 'a lord of Trojan blood, nephew to Hector'; characterized by Alexander. (i, 3) Ulysses suggests that A. should, by craft, seem to be selected by lot to fight with Hector; U. styles A. 'blockish,' 'dull,' and 'brainless.' ii, 1] A. is reviled by Thersites, and beats him; hears of Hector's challenge to the Greeks. ii, 3] marvels at Achilles' pride, and. won over by the flattery of Ulysses, is ready to take his place. (iii, 3) Thersites describes A. as beside himself with 'vain glory' at the notion of fighting Hector. iv, 5] the combat begins, but is broken off on H.'s remembering their kinship (see Hesione). v, 1] in command of the guard. (v, 2) mtd. (v, 4) Ther. comments on A.'s pride. v, 5] A. seeks Troilus, to slay him. v, 6] overcomes Aeneas. v, 9] hears of Hector's death.

In depicting Ajax Sh. appears to have relied but little on medieval legend; the part A. plays toward Achilles seems borrowed direct from Homer; *cf.* P. Stapfer, *Sh. and Classical Antiquity* (1880), p. 224. See Ulysses.

Alarbus. D.P. *T. And.* Son to Tamora. i, 2] *p.m.*; is doomed to death, as a sacrifice to appease the 'groaning shadows' of Titus' sons.

Alban, St. First British martyr; put to death at Verulamium, A.D. 303. Mtd. 2 *Hen. VI*, ii, 1 (3), in connection with a pretended miracle wrought at his shrine. See Simpcox.

[**Albany** (1), or Albania.] A district of Britain.

Thus defined (*Hol.* i, 116): 'The third and last part of the Iland he [Brute] allotted unto Albanacte his yoongest sonne... This later parcell at the first, tooke the name of Albanactus, who called it Albania. But now a small portion onelie of the region (being under the regiment of a duke) reteineth the said denomination, the rest being called Scotland, of certeine Scots that came ouer from Ireland to inhabit in those quarters. It is diuided from Lhoegres [England] also by the Solue and the Firth, yet some doo note the Humber; so that Albania (as Brute left it) conteined all the north part of the Iland that is to be found beyond the aforesaid streame, vnto the point of Cathnesse.'

Albany (2). For 'Duke of A.' *Lear*, i, 1; iii, 1; iv, 3.

Albany, Duke of. D.P. *Lear*. Husband to Goneril. i, 1] is present when Lear parts his kingdom; interposes when the King threatens Kent's life. i, 4] declares his ignorance of what has enraged L. against Goneril; attempts to allay G.'s anger, and is scorned by her for his 'milky gentleness.' (ii, 1) mtd. (iii, 1) 'division' between him and Cornwall mtd. iv, 2] sternly rebukes his wife for her conduct to Lear, and with rising wrath declares that he can scarce restrain his hands from such a 'flend'; hears of the blinding of Gloucester, and vows 'to revenge his eyes.' (iv, 3) mtd. v, 1] (in the British camp) is irresolute as to resisting the invaders, seeing that the King is with them; is given a letter by Edgar (disguised). v, 3] praises Edmund's valour in the field, but demands his captives; on Edm. declaring that he had already disposed of them, reminds him that he is but a subject, and arrests him 'on capital treason'; tells Regan, bitterly, that her claim (to Edm.) is barred in the interest of 'the gilded serpent,' Goneril; challenges Edm., in the event of no one else appearing, to prove treason 'upon his person'; (Edgar presents himself and mortally wounds Edm.); Albany produces the paper proving Goneril's guilt; embraces Edg. and listens to his narrative; learns that the sisters are both dead, and declares that 'the judgment of the heavens touches us not with pity'; urges Edg. to hasten to the prison and save Lear and Cordelia if he can; is present when L. bears in C.'s body; declares that while L. lives he himself will exercise no sovereignty; requests Edg. and Kent to rule the State, and (Qq) speaks the final speech (which Ff give to Edgar).

In *Hol.* i, 12, the 'Duke of Albania' is named Maglanus. For a complete account of the changes rung upon the names of Lear's two elder daughters and their husbands in old versions of the story see W. Perrett, *Palaestra*, xxxv (Berlin, 1904).

Acc. *Hol.* Maglanus was slain in battle against Leir and Cordeilla.

Albany, Robert Stewart, Duke of. See Fife, Earl of.

Albemarle, or **Aumale.** (*Lat.* Alba Marla); a French town (Dept. Seine-Inf.), giving a title to an ancient countship and duchy. Also 'Aumerle' (*Sh.*) (*q.v.*).

Albemarle, Earl of. See Beauchamp, R.

Albion. Ancient name of Britain (Pliny, *N.H.* IV, xvi, 30). Also for 'England': 'That nook-shotten isle of A.' (*Hen. V*, iii, 5); 'A.'s wished coast' (*2 Hen. VI*, iii, 2); '*Q. Mar.* I was ... Great A.'s queen in former golden days' (*3 Hen. Vi*, iii, 3); 'Then shall the realm of A. Come to great confusion' (*Lear*, iii, 2).

Albret, Charles d'. Constable of France; natural son of Charles le Mauvais, King of Navarre. In command of the French at Agincourt, where he was mortally wounded (*Hol.* iii, 549, 555).

D.P. *Hen. V.* 'Constable,' or 'C. of France,' in st. dirs. and pfxs. ii, 4] warns the Dauphin that he is wholly mistaken in his estimate of Henry's character. iii, 5] expresses his contempt for the English. iii, 7] longs for the fray, but doubts the Dauphin's valour. iv, 2] anticipates an easy victory over 'yon poor and starved band.' iv, 5] admits defeat. (iv, 8) among the slain.

'Charles lord de la Broth,' *Hol.* iii, 555; 'Charles Delabreth,' Ff; 'De la brot,' Hall.

Alce. For 'Alice'; *Tam. Sh.* Ind. 2, FfQ.

Alcibiades. Son of Clinias (*c.* 450–404 B.C.). Though A. is a character of some importance in *Timon*, Sh. does not seem to have made much use of Plutarch's account of A. when depicting him. An interview of A. with Timon is mentioned (*Plut.* p. 296), and A.'s lack of money to pay his men (*ib.* p. 303), but his career as a whole is irrelevant to the play. 'A., the practical man, intended as an antithesis to the idealism of Timon, has none of his well-known characteristics' (P. Stapfer, *Sh. and Classical Antiquity* (1880), p. 259).

D.P. *Timon.* 'An Athenian captain.' i, 1, 2] is welcomed by Timon to a feast. ii, 2] *p.m.* iii, 5] craves pardon from the Senate for a friend who has slain a man in anger, but who has deserved well of the State; on being refused, retorts defiantly, and is sentenced to banishment; (*sol.*) plans revenge. (iii, 6) is exiled. iv, 3] encounters Timon in his cave; would fain aid him, but his offers are spurned; accepts gold from T. to pay his men. (v, 1) mtd. (v, 2) his attack is dreaded by the Senators. v, 5] enters Athens, and promises to take vengeance only on the personal foes of Timon and himself; pronounces a funeral oration on T.

'With less nobility of nature than Timon, Alcibiades has far more judgment, and is more moderate and more just in his hatred; this "complete soldier," as Gervinus calls him, "a man of coarse texture, in no way enthusiastic about the extreme end of things," and caring only for himself, has not the raging thirst for blood ... that consumes the generous philanthropist who has been completely maddened by the discovery that his dream of friendship was a delusion.' (P. Stapfer, *op. cit.* p. 241.)

Alcides. See Hercules.

Alecto. One of the Furies. 'Fell A.'s snake' (*2 Hen. IV*, v, 5). ('How doth A. whisper in mine ears' (*Tr. R.* I, 2).)

Pistol can scarcely be credited with an allusion to 'Gorgoneis Allecto infecta venenis' (Virg. *Aen.* vii, 341). See Furies.

Alençon. Former duchy of N. France; an appanage of the house of Valois.

Alençon, Duchess of. Margaret of Valois, sister to Francis I of France. Wolsey was alleged (*Hol.* iii, 906, following Polydore Vergil, p. 687) to have wished in the autumn of 1527 (Hall, p. 728) to arrange a marriage between her and Hen. VIII. At this date, however, she was already married to Henry of Navarre.

'*Wol*... the Duchess of A., the French King's sister: he shall marry her' (*Hen. VIII*, ii, 2; iii, 2).

Alençon, Duke of (fictitious). Katharine mentions having met Dumain at 'the Duke A.'s once,' and she is called 'heir of A.' (*L.L.L.* ii, 1).

'Alansoes,' or 'Alanzoes,' QFf.

Alençon, John I, Duke of (*ob.* 1415). Before Agincourt, *Hen. V*, iii, 5; his combat with Henry alluded to, *ib.* iv, 7; his 'glove,' *ib.* iv, 8; slain, *ib. ib.*

Henry was 'almost felled by the Duke of A.; yet with plaine strength he slue two of the dukes companie, and felled the duke himself; whome, when he would have yielded, the king's gard (contrarie to his mind) slue out of hand' (*Hol.* iii, 552).

Alençon, John II, Duke of. Son of John I, *ob.* 1476; present at Patay, *Hol.* iii, 601; at the relief of Orleans, *ib.* iii, 600.

D.P. *1 Hen. VI.* (i, 1) takes part with Charles against the English. i, 2] marvels at the 'courage and audacity' of the 'rawboned' English; suspects Joan of Arc to be a temptress. ii, 1] is accused of keeping imperfect watch. iii, 2] present at the capture of Rouen. iii, 3] eulogizes Joan. (iv, 1, 4, 6) mtd. iv, 7] *p.m.* v, 2] suggests marching to Paris. v, 4] advises Charles to make a truce, and 'break it when his pleasure serves.'

Mtd. 2 *Hen. VI*, i, 1, as being present at Margaret's espousals; cf. *Hol.* iii, 625, where the name is 'Alanson.'

Aleppo, or Haleb. Capital of province of the same name, to the N. of Syria; once a great emporium of trade between Europe and Asia. Tripoli and Scanderoon were the ports whence the caravan routes to Aleppo started. After a treaty with Turkey (1580) English ships began to sail to Tripoli, notably the *Tiger* (Martins, owner; Rickman, master). In 1583 Newbury and Fitch also sailed to Tripoli on a ship of the same name. See Tiger.

'Her husband's to Aleppo gone, master o' the Tiger' (*Macb.* i, 3); 'in Al. once, Where a malignant and a turban'd Turk Beat a Venetian' (*Oth.* v, 2).

Alexander (1), surnamed 'the Great.' Son of Philip II of Macedon (356–323 B.C.). A biography of the conqueror of Asia is included in Plutarch's *Lives*.

Impersonated by Nathaniel, the curate, in the masque of 'The Nine Worthies' (*L.L.L.* v, 2); he declares that 'When in the world I liv'd I was the world's commander'; spectators jestingly comment on his not fulfilling two characteristics of A. mentioned by Plutarch, viz. that his head inclined 'towards the left side' and that his body had 'a passing delightful savour' (*cf.* North (1595), *Alex.* p. 178). 'Great A. left his crown to the worthiest' (*Wint. T.* v, 1); 'Fathers that, like so many A.s, Have ... from morn till even fought' (*Hen. V*, iii, 1); Fluellen draws a parallel between 'A. the pig,' born in Macedon, and Henry 'born at Monmouth' (*ib.* iv, 7; see Cleitus); 'he sits in state, as a thing [statue] made for A.' (*Cor.* v, 4). Hamlet traces, in imagination, 'the noble dust of A.' till he finds it 'stopping a bung-hole' (*Haml.* v, 1).

Alexander (2). Son of Mark Antony and Cleopatra. 'Great Media, Parthia and Armenia He gave to A.' (*Ant. Cl.* iii, 6; cf. *Plut.* p. 202.)

Alexander (3). As a forename; see Iden.

Alexander (4). D.P. *Tr. Cr.* Servant to Cressida. i, 2] characterizes Ajax, and explains to C. the cause of Hector's wrath.

Man,' QFf. Pope omits the only sentence in which his name appears.

Alexandria. Capital of Egypt under the Ptolemies; principal residence of Cleopatra. Antony's revels at A. (*Ant. Cl.* i, 4; ii, 2); enthronement of Ant. and Cl. there (*ib.* iii, 6); Octavius at A. (*ib.* iii, 13); 'Through A. make a jolly march' (*ib.* iv, 8).

The following scenes of *Ant. Cl.* are laid there: i, 1, 2, 3, 5; ii, 5; iii, 3, 11, 13; iv, 1–15; v, 1, 2.

Alexandrian, *adj.* 'A. feast' (*Ant. Cl.* ii, 7); 'A. revels' (*ib.* v, 2).

Alexas. 'One of Cleopatra's ministers to win Antonius'; trusted by Ant. and sent by him on a mission to Herod; treacherously advised Herod to join Octavius; H., however, sent him in chains to his own country, where he was executed (*Plut.* p. 218).

D.P. *Ant. Cl.* i, 2] exchanges raillery with Charmian and Iras. i, 3] *p.m.*; is sent by Cl. to Ant. i, 5] brings Cl. a pearl as a gift from Ant. ii, 5] *p.m.*; is sent to glean information about Octavia. iii, 3] tells Cl. that Herod dare not look upon her but when she is pleased. iv, 2] *p.m.* (iv, 6) his treachery and its punishment related.

In iv, 4, Ff, 'Alex.' appears, as pfx., for 'Capt.' This is probably due to the same actor having assumed both characters. It is clear (iv, 6) that Alexas is not present.

Alice (1). D.P. *Hen. V.* Attendant on Pss. Katharine. iii, 4] gives K. a lesson in English. v, 2] acts as interpreter between K. and Hen. V.

'An old gentlewoman' in st. dir. iii, 4, Ff. The authenticity of iii, 4, is disputed.

Alice (2). As a forename. 'A. Shortcake,' 'A. Ford' (*qq.v.*). *Cf.* Sly's blunder, 'Alce Madam' (*Tam. Sh.* Ind. 2).

Aliena. Name assumed by Celia (*q.v.*) in disguise, *A.Y.L.* i, 3, as in Lodge's *Rosalynde*. For the pronunciation see *N.S.S. Tr.*, 1887–92, Pt. I, p. 168.

Alinda. See Celia.

Alisander. For 'Alexander'; *L.L.L.* v, 2 (6).

Allhallond Eve. The eve of All Saints. 'Was't not at Hallowmas, Master Froth? *Fro.* A. Eve' (*M. for M.* ii, 1).

All-hallowmas. The feast of All Saints (Nov. 1). 'All-hallowmas' (*M.W.W.* i, 1); Simple apparently confuses it with Holy Cross Day (Sept. 14), or Michaelmas with Martinmas.

All-hallown Summer. A season of fine weather in the late autumn (also 'St Martin's summer'), applied to Falstaff by Prince Hal, *1 Hen. IV*, i, 2.

[**All is True.**] A play, supposed to be identical with *Hen. VIII* (*q.v.*).

All Souls' Day. The festival (Nov. 2) on which Catholics offer prayers for the souls of the faithful deceased. '*Buck.* This is A.-S. day, fellow, is it not? *Sher.* It is, my lord. *Buck.* Why, then A.-S. day is my body's doomsday' (*Rich. III*, v, 1).

'Buckingham upon All soules daie ... was at Salisburie ... put to death' (*Hol.* iii, 744).

All's Well that Ends Well.

Publication. First published in the Folio of 1623 under the title 'All's Well, That Ends Well.' The acts, but not the scenes, are numbered.

Date of Composition. Uncertain; possibly completed *c.* 1602; criticism has detected two different styles in the play, corresponding to two periods of Sh.'s work. The Folio text has been held to be a version of an earlier draft. (But see R. Crompton Rhodes, *Sh.'s First Folio*, p. 101.)

Source of the Plot. A tale (xxxviii) in Painter's *Palace of Pleasure* (1566) which is derived from Boccaccio's *Decamerone* (Day iii, Nov. 9). The characters of the Countess, Parolles, Lafeu, and the Clown are Sh.'s own.

Almain. A German. Iago declares that an Englishman, as a toss-pot, 'sweats not to overthrow your A.' (*Oth.* ii, 1).

Alonso. D.P. *Temp.* King of Naples; an inveterate enemy of Prospero (i, 2), whose dukedom he had aided the usurper Antonio to seize, conditionally on its being held as a fief of Naples. i, 1] (on board ship) appeals to the boatswain; betakes himself to prayer. ii, 1] wrecked on Prospero's island, believes that his son Ferdinand has perished, and refuses comfort, iii, 3] is sternly rebuked by Ariel for his 'foul deed' against Pr.; is seized by remorse, and threatens suicide. v, 1] Pr. having revealed himself, Al. entreats pardon and makes reparation; joyfully assents to the union of his recovered son with Miranda.

The name, as well as 'Sebastian,' 'Anthonio,' 'Ferdinand,' and 'Gonzalo,' occurs in Eden's *History of Travaille*; see Setebos. Dryden makes Al. 'Duke of Savoy.'

Alphonso, Don. A gentleman; mtd. *T.G.V.* iv, 2.

Alps. European mountain range. 'Talking of the A. and Apennines' (*John*, i, 1); 'the frozen ridges of the A.' (*Rich. II*, i, 1); hardships endured by Antony while crossing the Alps, *Ant. Cl.* i, 4; (the range as a whole, treated as a sing. noun) 'the valleys, whose low vassal seat The A. doth spit and void his rheum on' (*Hen. V*, iii, 5).

For the grotesque metaphor in the last quotation *cf.* Hor. *Sat.* ii, 5, where M. Furius Bibaculus is ridiculed for attributing a similar origin to the snows – 'Juppiter hibernas cana nive conspuit Alpes.'

Althaea. Wife of Oeneus, King of Calydon, and mother of Meleager; was warned by the Fates that her son would die when a certain brand on the hearth should be consumed; she accordingly extinguished it and hid it; in after years, to avenge the death of her brothers at M.'s hands, she threw it into the fire, and her son died in agony (Ovid, *Metam.* viii, 445 ff.).

'Methinks, the realms of England, France, and Ireland Bear that proportion to my flesh and blood As did the fatal brand A. burn'd Unto the prince's heart of Calydon' (*2 Hen. VI*, i, 1). In the following passage A. is confused with Hecuba (*q.v.*): '*Page* [to Bardolph]. Away, you rascally A.'s dream, away! ... A. dream'd she was delivered of a firebrand, and therefore I call him her dream' (*2 Hen. IV*, ii, 2).

Alton. One of John Talbot's titles was Lord Verdun of A.' (*1 Hen. VI*, iv, 7).

Amaimon. A fiend 'reigning in the furthest regions of the East,' who, acc. R. Scot, *Discoverie of Witchcraft* (1584), xv, 2, could be bound at certain hours.

'[Glendower] gave A. the bastinado' (*1 Hen. IV*, ii, 4); 'A. sounds well; Lucifer, well ... the names of fiends' (*M.W.W.* ii, 2).

'Amamon' until changed by Capell; 'Amoimon' acc. Scot.

Amazon. One of a race of female warriors alleged by Herodotus to exist in Scythia. For the Battle of Theseus with the A.s see *Plut.* pp. 286–7.

'Pale-visaged maids Like A.s come tripping after drums' (*John*, v, 2); Hippolyta termed by Titania 'the bouncing A.' (*M.N.D.* ii, 1); 'thou [La Pucelle] art an A.' (*1 Hen. VI*, i, 2); 'Belike she [Q. Margaret] minds to play the A.' (*3 Hen. VI*, iv, 1). 'A mask of ladies as Amazons' is presented to Timon's guests (*Timon*, i, 2).

Amazonian, *adj.* Caius Marcius as a youth had 'an A. chin,' *i.e.* beardless (*Cor.* ii, 2); York compares Q. Margaret to 'an A. trull' (*3 Hen. VI*, i. 4).

Ambassadors, English. D.PP. *Haml.* 1st Amb. alone speaks. v, 2] announces the death of Rosencrantz and Guildenstern – but, seeing that the King is dead, deems it 'too late for thanks.'

Ambassadors of France. D.PP. *Hen. V* 1st Amb. alone speaks. i, 2] announces that, in reply to Henry's claim to 'certain dukedoms,' the Dauphin, 'in lieu,' sends a 'tun of treasure' – which proves to contain tennis balls (*Hol.* iii, 545, where 'Paris balles' are specified).

French (p. 116), quoting Rymer and Grafton, gives the names of the envoys, viz. Louis, Earl of Vendome, Bouratin, Abp. of Bourges, the Bp. of Lisieux, and the Lords of Ivry and Braquemont – the Abp. being the chief spokesman.

America. Mtd. *Com. Err.* iii, 2; 'one of the boldest anachronisms in Sh.' (Knight).

Amiens. D.P. *A.Y.L.* 'Lord attending upon the Duke in his Banishment' (Rowe). (ii, 1) mtd. by a courtier as 'my Lord of A.' ii, 5] sings 'Under the greenwood tree.' ii, 7] sings (presumably) 'Blow, blow, thou winter wind.' v, 4] *p.m.*

'Amiens is certainly to be considered as first and chief of the *Musical* characters in Sh.' (Roffe, *A Musical Triad*, etc. (1872), p. 21).

Amintas. See AMYNTAS.

Amphimachus. A Greek warrior. 'A. and Thoas, deadly hurt' (*Tr. Cr.* v, 5).

The death of Amphimachus at the hands of Hector is described in Hom. *Il.* xiii, 185 ff. 'Amphymacus' appears as the name of two Trojans and three Greeks in Caxton's *Recuyell*.

[**Amphion.**] Son of Zeus and Antiope, who raised the walls of Thebes by means of his magic lyre. *Cf.* Ovid, *Metam.* vi, 178: '[Niobe *loq.*] fidibusque mei commissa mariti Moenia.'

This seems to be alluded to, *Temp.* ii, 1: 'His word is more than the miraculous harp. He hath raised the wall, and houses too'; but Apollo's lyre, instrumental in building Troy (Ovid, *Her.* xvi, 180), may be meant.

Ampthill Castle. Six miles from Dunstable (*q.v.*); built by Lord Fanhope in the reign of Hen. VI, and became Crown property under Hen. VII. Katharine of Arragon was resident there when her divorce was pronounced (*Hol.* iii, 929), May 23, 1533.

'The Archbishop of Canterbury ... Held a late court at Dunstable, six miles off From A., where the Princess lay; to which She was often cited, but appear'd not' (*Hen. VIII*, iv, 1).

Amurath, or Murad. The name of five Sultans of Turkey. 'This is the English, not the Turkish Court; Not A. to A. succeeds, but Harry, Harry' (*2 Hen. IV*, v, 2, Q; 'Amurah,' Ff).

Murad I died in 1389, Murad II came to the throne in 1421, so that when Henry IV died (1413) only one Murad had reigned. When the play was written there had been three Sultans of the name (but no Murad ever succeeded a Murad). Amurath or Amarath is a character in *Solimon and Perseda* (1599).

Amyntas. 'King of Lycaonia and the Galatians' (*Plut.* p. 207); he was one of Mark Antony's adherents, but deserted to Octavius (*ib.* p. 209).

Mtd. *Ant. Cl.* iii, 6, somewhat confusedly. 'Amintas,' Ff.

Anchises. Father of Aeneas, whose rescue of Anch. from burning Troy is described by Virgil (*Aen.* ii, 721 ff.). Young Clifford carries the body of his father 'As did Aen. old Anch. bear' (*2 Hen. VI*, v, 2); Aen. asseverates 'by A.'s life' (*Tr. Cr.* iv, 1); Cassius rescued Caesar from the Tiber 'as Aen. our great ancestor Did from the flames of Troy upon his shoulder The old A. bear' (*Jul. C.* i, 2).

Ancus Marcius. Fourth king of Rome. Mtd. as 'Numa's daughter's son' (*Cor.* ii, 3). Cf. *Plut.* p. 1.

Andren, or **Andern, Vale of.** In Picardy; scene of the meeting between Henry VIII and Francis I, known as the Field of the Cloth of Gold (*Hol.* iii, 858).

'*Buck.* Those two lights of men Met in the vale of Andren. *Norf.* 'Twixt Guynes and Arde: I then was present' (*Hen. VIII*, i, 1).

Andrew (1). Name of a ship. 'See my wealthy A. docked in sand' (*M.V.* i, 1).

Perh. in allusion to the Genoese admiral and statesman Andrea Doria (1468–1560).

Andrew (2). As a forename, only of Aguecheek (*q.v.*).

Andrew (3). The pfx. of *M. Ado*, iv, 2,1.4, in QFf, instead of 'Dog.'; supposed to be a nickname (*quasi* 'Merry A.') of the actor Kemp (*q.v.*), who played Dogberry.

Andromache. Wife of Hector. Homer's description of their farewell meeting (*Iliad*, vi) supplies no hint for the medieval tradition (followed by Sh.) that the courteous Hector was rough only with his wife.

D.P. *Tr. Cr.* (i, 2) Hector in his anger chides her. v, 3] she passionately urges H. not to fight that day, since she has had ominous dreams; is harshly rebuffed.

Andronici, Family of the. 'Till all the A. be made away' (*T. And.* ii, 3); 'you sad A.,' (*ib.* v, 3); 'the poor remainder of A.' (*ib. ib.*).

The name is common in classical biography – accented on the 3rd syllable and not on the 2nd as in *Sh*.

Andronicus, Marcus. D.P. *T. And.* A Roman tribune, brother to Titus And. i, 1] announces that the people have adopted Titus as their candidate for the vacant throne; welcomes the victorious Titus, and bids him don the robe of candidature; on T. declining the honour, declares Saturninus emperor; takes part with Bassianus, who claims Lavinia as his bride; induces T. to consent to the burial of Mutius with his brethren. ii, 2] joins in the chase. ii, 5] discovers the violated and maimed Lav. iii, 1] brings her to T.; offers his own hand as a ransom for his nephews' lives; at the sight of their severed heads, cannot restrain his passionate grief. iii, 2] is rebuked by the distraught T. for killing a fly, and to soothe him declares it was 'black ... like to the empress' Moor.' iv, 2] instructs Lav. to write her woe upon the sand. iv, 3] humours his brother's insanity, and orders the arrows T. meant for the gods to be shot into the royal court. v, 2] is sent to invite Lucius to T.'s feast. v, 3] is present at the fatal repast; tells the people the motive of T.'s revenge, and hails Lucius as emperor.

Andronicus, Titus. D.P. *T. And.* A Roman general. i, 1] returns to Rome after his sixth victory over the Goths, bringing with him Tamora, their queen, as a captive; causes Alarbus, her son, to be slain, despite his mother's entreaties, as a sacrifice for his own dead sons, whom he commits to the ancestral tomb; is virtually offered the imperial crown, but waives the honour in favour of Saturninus, the late Emperor's son; consents, moreover, to the marriage of his daughter Lavinia to Sat.; on L. being claimed by Bassianus, the new Emperor's brother, and forcibly carried off, T. kills, in a rage, his own son Mutius, who tries to bar his pursuit; is scorned by the Emperor, who chooses Tam. for his bride. In the extremity of his wrath Titus at first refuses burial to Mutius, but relents; is received into the Emperor's favour, at Tamora's treacherous solicitation; invites Sat. to hunt with him on the morrow. ii, 2] greets Sat. and Tam. in the forest. ii, 4] suspicion of the murder of Bassianus having been thrown on Quintus and Martius, his sons, T. swears that they shall duly answer the charge. iii, 1] implores the judges to 'reverse the doom of death' passed upon his two sons; urges their brother Lucius to flee from Rome; the mutilated Lavinia is brought to him, and he is overcome with anguish; he is told that if he will sacrifice his hand his two sons shall be spared; he consents to the deprivation, but the hand, with his sons' heads, is brought back to him; urges Lucius to raise an avenging army of Goths. iii, 2] (at table in his own house) talks wildly, urging Lav. to suicide, and chiding his brother Marcus for killing a fly. iv, 1] learns that Lav. has been outraged, as well as maimed, by Tam.'s sons, and plans revenge. (iv, 2) sends 'weapons wrapt about with lines' to the criminals. iv, 3] in a fit of insanity, causes arrows to be shot into the Emperor's court, bearing messages for the gods; sends a 'clown' to Sat. with a letter in which a knife is wrapped. v, 2] is visited by Tam. and her two sons in the guise of 'Revenge,' 'Murder,' and 'Rapine'; they cunningly request Titus to invite Lucius to a banquet; recognizing them, T. assents, and, on Tam.'s departure, summons aid, and cutting the throats of her sons resolves to make a pasty of their heads. v, 3] Tam. and the Emperor come to the feast; T. places the grim dish upon the table; they partake of it; then, after killing Lav. 'and her shame,' T. tells his guests what they have eaten, and stabs Tam.; he is instantly killed by Sat.

Angelica. The Nurse (*q.v.*), D.P. *Rom. J.* '*Cap.* Look to the bak'd meats, good A.' (iv, 4).

Angelo (1). D.P. *M. for M.* 'Deputy in the Duke's absence.' i, 1] he is given full authority to act; withdraws to consult with his 'secondary,' Escalus, as to their respective powers. (i, 3) commits Claudio to prison on a charge of incontinence, (i, 4) the D. tells Friar Thomas that he has entrusted Ang., 'a man of stricture and firm abstinence,' with supreme authority, in order to enforce certain laws that had fallen into desuetude; he declares that 'Lord Ang... scarce confesses that his blood flows,' while Lucio (i, 5) says A. is a man whose 'blood is very snowbroth,' and urges Isabella to try to soften him in Claudio's case. ii, 1] Ang. protests against making ' a scarecrow of the law,' and, in spite of Escalus' pleas for leniency, condemns Claudio to execution; as for his own faults, he reminds E. that ' 'Tis one thing to be tempted ... Another thing to fall.' ii, 2] blames the Provost's hesitation, and reiterates his order that 'Claudio shall die tomorrow'; he sternly rejects all Isabella's pleas for mercy, and harps on the inflexibility of the law, but at length yields to the extent of bidding her come again on the morrow; (*sol.*) realizes the gravity of the temptation to which he is subjected – 'this virtuous maid subdues me quite. Ever till now, When men were fond, I smil'd and wondered how.' ii, 4] (*sol.*) he is torn asunder between his duty and his passion; on I.'s entrance he at first questions her as to whether, to save her brother's life, there might not be 'a charity in sin'; he then plainly asks her if she would forfeit her chastity to save her brother; tells her that he will spare Cl. if she will 'give me love'; on her indignantly replying that she will 'tell the world aloud What man thou art,' he coldly replies that none would believe her, and threatens torture as well as death to Cl. if she is obdurate. (iii, 1) A.'s former desertion of Mariana related. (iii, 2) his conduct discussed (iv, 2) orders the Provost to bring him Claudio's head 'by five.' (iv, 3) I. inveighs against his cruelty. iv, 4] (he has visited Mariana, believing her to be 1.); learning that the Duke is about to return, is struck by fear and remorse. v, 1] greets the Duke at the City Gate; is accused by I. of being a murderer and a violator, and is confronted by Mariana; declares he is the victim of 'some more mightier member That sets them on'; makes full confession, and begs for death; is commanded first to marry Mariana; later, is ordered to instant execution, but, on the appearance of Claudio unscathed, is pardoned.

The corresponding character in Cinthio's novel is named Juriste, and in Whetstone's *Promos and Cassandra* Promos. In Cinthio's tragedy, *Epitia*, Juriste has a sister named Angela – but Angelo is not an uncommon name in the dramatic literature of the early 17th cent.

'He seems to have a much greater passion for hypocrisy than for his mistress' (Hazlitt). 'The pardon and marriage of A. not merely baffles the strong indignant claim of justice ... but it is likewise degrading to the character of woman' (Coleridge).

Angelo (2). D.P. *Com. Err.* A goldsmith. iii, 1] is ordered to bring to Antipholus of Ephesus a necklace, which he has made for him. iii, 2] meeting Ant. of Syracuse, believes him to be jesting when he repudiates the order, and gives him the chain. iv, 1] as Ang. is being dunned for a debt, Ant. E., entering, bids him take the chain to Adriana and ask her for payment; Ang. declares that Ant. E. already has the chain, and, on being refused payment, has him arrested. (iv, 4) mtd. v, 1] assures his creditor of Ant. E.'s high repute, and on Ant. S.'s entering, wearing the chain, expostulates with him on his conduct; takes part in the *éclaircissement*.

Angelo (3). A naval officer; *Oth.* i, 3, l. 16.

Angers. On the Maine, formerly capital of Anjou. (In *Sh.* always 'Angiers,' following the *Tr. R.* and *Hol.*) The scene in *John*, ii, iii, is laid at, or near, A.

In error for 'Anjou' (Ff), *John*, ii, 1, ll. 152, 487.

Angiers (Angers), First Citizen of. D.P. *John.* ii, 1] declares that the citizens are loyal to the rightful king of England; after the combat avows that they cannot judge whether Philip or John is victor, and refuses to open the gates; suggests the marriage of Blanch of 'Spain' to the Dauphin as a basis of peace. (The *Tr. R.* is closely followed throughout.)

The First Citizen on his second appearance is designated 'Hubert' in Ff. Critics differ as to whether H. de Burgh is really intended, or whether there is an error due to the same actor taking both parts. H. does not appear in the corresponding scene of *Tr. R.*

Angleterre (*Fr.*). England. *Hen. V*, iii, 4 (2); iv, 4; v, 2.

Anglia (*Lat.*). England. 'Henricus, Rex Angliae' (*Hen. V*, v, 2).

Anglois (*Fr.*). English language. *Hen. V*, iii, 4 (3); v, 2.

Angus, George Douglas, 1st Earl of (*c.* 1380–1403). Taken prisoner at the Battle of Homildon, 1402 (*Hol.* ii, 254); the fact mtd. *1 Hen. IV*, i, 1.

Angus, Thane of. Created earl by Malcolm Canmore on his coronation (*Hol.* ii, 176).

D.P. *Macb.* i, 2] *p.m.* i, 3] informs Macbeth that the rebel Cawdor has been deprived of his thaneship. i, 4] *p.m.* i, 6] *p.m.* v, 2] comments on Macbeth's peril – M. must feel 'his title Hang loose about him, like a giant's robe Upon a dwarfish thief.' v, 4] *p.m.* v, 8] with the other thanes hails Malcolm king.

Anjou. A former province in the N.W. of France. By the marriage of Geoffrey Plantagenet, Count of A., with Matilda, heiress of Henry I, their son when he ascended the English throne as Henry II (1154) acquired Anjou. It fell as a prize of war to Philip Augustus of France (1205), was united to England for a few years under Hen. V and Hen. VI, and finally ceded by the latter (1444).

Anjou claimed for Arthur of Brittany, *John*, i, 1, ii, 1; offered as dowry to Blanch of Castile, *ib.* ii, 2 (2); claimed by Reignier, *1 Hen. VI*, i, 1, v, 3 (3); ceded, *2 Hen. VI*, i, 1 (4); 'sold' (*ib.* iv, 1).

In *John*, ii, 1, ll. 152, 487, 'Angiers' in error for 'Anjou' (Ff).

Anjou, René, Duke of (1434–80). Known as 'le bon Roi René'; second son of Louis II, Count of Provence, etc.; he 'named himselfe King of Sicill, Naples, and Jerusalem; having onlie the name and stile of those realmes, without anie penie, profit, or foot of possession' (*Hol.* iii, 624). His 2nd d., Margaret of Anjou, became queen of Henry VI. An interesting sketch of the Duke's character is given by Scott, *Anne of Geierstein*, ch. 29.

'René' appears variously, in *Sh.* and the *Chronicles*, as 'Reignier,' 'Reiner,' 'Reynold,' 'Reignard,' and 'Ranard.'

D.P. *1 Hen. VI.* (i, 1) reported to have joined the Dauphin. i, 2] proposes raising the siege of Orleans; despises the English, but soon has cause to admit their prowess; changes places with the Dauphin, in order to test the acumen of Joan of Arc; puts trust in her. i, 6] enters Orleans, in triumph, with Joan. ii, 1] flees with the rest when Talbot recaptures Orleans. (All the preceding scenes are unhistorical; R. was not at the siege of Orleans.) (iv, 4) mtd. v, 3] (his poverty mtd.); consents, through Suffolk, to Margaret's betrothal to Henry, provided that he may peaceably enjoy Maine and Anjou. v, 4] urges Charles to make peace. (v, 5) Suffolk boasts that M.'s father is a king.

Styled 'King of Naples, Sicilia and Jerusalem'; Gloucester comments that his 'large style Agrees not with the leanness of his purse' (*2 Hen. VI*, i, 1); pawns 'the Sicils and Jerusalem' to pay his daughter's ransom (*3 Hen. VI*, v, 7; *cf.* Hall, p. 301).

Anna. Daughter of Belus and sister to Dido, whom she greatly loved (Ovid, *Fasti*, iii, 559 ff.; Virg. *Aen.* iv). 'As dear As A. to the Queen of Carthage was' (*Tam. Sh.* i, 1).

Anne. As a forename. 'A. Page' (*M.W.W. saepe*); 'A. Bullen' (*Hen. VIII*, iii, 2); 'Lady A. [Anne B.]' (*ib.* iii, 2; iv, 1). For 'Anne Page,' *M.W.W. saepe*; for 'Anne Mortimer' (*q.v.*), 2 *Hen. VI*, ii, 2 (2).

Anne, Lady. D.P. *Rich. III.* See Neville, Anne.

[**Anne Beame.**] 'Here pitch our tents, even here in Bosworth field' (*Rich. III*, v, 3). 'He [Richard] marched to a place ... by a village called Bosworth, not farre from Leicester: and there he pitched his field on a hill called A.B.' (*Hol.* iii, 755).

Anne, St. Mother of the Virgin Mary. 'Yes, by St A.' (*T. Nt.* ii, 3; *Tam. Sh.* i, 1).

Why St A. should be invoked by Feste and Sly is not apparent. *Cf.* Furness, *T. Nt.* p. 126.

[**Anselm, Friar.**] Acc. Heywood, A. originated the prophecy that one whose name began with 'G' should succeed Edw. IV (Clar.). Attributed by Clarence to 'a wizard' (*Rich. III*, i, 1, l. 56; cf. *Hol.* iii, 703).

Anselme. 'County A.,' an invited guest; *Rom. J.* i, 2.

Antenor. In the *Iliad* one of the wisest of the Trojans, who advised the restoration of Helen to Menelaus. Acc. later writers his friendship for the Greeks led him to actual treachery against his own country; *cf.* 'Dictys Cretensis,' i, 11, iv, 22.

D.P. *Tr. Cr.* ('Anthenor,' QFf.) i, 2] Pandarus declares that 'he's one of the soundest judgments in Troy.' (iii, 1) mtd. among 'all the gallantry of Troy.' (iii, 3) held prisoner by the Gks.; Calchas asks that he should be exchanged for Cressida, since 'Troy holds him very dear.' (iv, 1) mtd. (iv, 2) the exchange is demurred to by Pandarus. iv, 3, 4] *p.m.*

The medieval belief that A. betrayed Troy is reflected in Dante, *Inf.* xxxii, where the name 'Antenora' is given to the division of Hell where traitors are punished. Acc. Lydgate, A. was an inveterate jester who always, however, preserved a grave countenance.

Antenorides. One of the gates of Troy; *Tr. Cr.* Prol. ('Antenonidus,' F1.) See Troy, Gates of.

Anthony and Cleopatra. (In F1: 'The Tragedie of Anthonie, and Cleopatra.' Except i, 1, the acts and scenes are not indicated.)

Date of Composition. It is almost universally agreed that this play was written in 1607 or 1608, much weight being attached to the fact that on May 20, 1608, 'A booke

Called Anthony and Cleopatra' was entered in the Stationers' Registers to 'Edward Blunt.' It cannot be regarded as absolutely certain that this entry refers to *Ant. Cl.*, but characteristics of the style and metre of the play accord well enough with the date in question.

Publication. So far as is known, no edition of the play appeared before its issue in the First Folio, 1623, and in recording the licence granted to Blount and Jaggard to print the hitherto unpublished plays of the First Folio the Stationers' Registers include *Anthonie and Cleopatra* among the tragedies 'not formerly entered to other men.' (It is not, however, clear why Blount sought a new licence for a play already assigned to him.)

Source of the Plot. The incidents, and much of the language, of the tragedy are derived from North's *Plutarch*, but 'the leading events and characters ... are, despite his liberal borrowings of phrase and fact, reincarnated in the crucible of the poet's imagination, so that they glow in his verse with an heroic and poetic glamour of which Plutarch gives faint conception' (Lee, p. 411). The following dramas on the subject of Cleopatra are anterior to *Ant. Cl.*: *Cleopatra*, by Giraldi Cinthio (*c.* 1540); *Cléopatre Captive*, by Estienne Jodelle (1552); *Marc Antoine*, by Robert Garnier (1578) (translated by the Countess of Pembroke, 1592); *Clépatre*, by Nicholas de Montreux (1594); *The Tragedie of Cleopatra*, by Samuel Daniel (1594) (frequently reprinted); and *The Tragicomoedie of the Virtuous Octavia*, by Samuel Brandon (1598). To none of these does it appear that Sh. had any indebtedness. (Sh.'s divergences from Plutarch's narrative are indicated in connection with the characters involved.)

'During his first three Acts Sh. merely paints the man and the woman who are to suffer and die in his two others; and for these portraits he has scraped together all his colour from the many such passages as are scattered through the earlier and longer portion of North's *Antonius*. But in the Fourth Act Sh. changes his method: he has no more need to gather and arrange. Rather the concentrated passion born of, and contained in, North's serried narrative, expands in his verse – nay, explodes from it – into those flashes of immortal speech which have given the Fourth Act of *Antony and Cleopatra* its place apart even in Shakespeare.' (G. Wyndham, *North's Plutarch* (1895), p. xciii.)

Anthropophagi. Cannibals. 'The cannibals that each other eat, the A.' (*Oth.* i, 3). ('Anthropophague,' F1.) See Scythian.

Two 16th-cent. instances of the word are given in *N.E.D.* It occurs several times in Pliny, *Nat. Hist.*

Anthropophaginian. Coined from the preceding, by the Host of the Garter, and applied to Falstaff. 'He'll speak like an A. unto thee' (*M.W.W.* iv, 5).

Antiates. Inhabitants of Antium (*q.v.*); cf. *Plut.* p. 9, etc. Mtd. *Cor.* i, 6 (2); iii, 3; v, 6.

Ff, in the first example, have 'Antients,' corrected by Pope.

Antigonus. D.P. *Wint. T.* One of the 'Foure Lords of Sicil(l)ia' (Ff). ii, 1] protests that the King must have been deceived by a villain, but that if Hermione has offended 'every dram of woman's flesh is false.' ii, 3] fails to exclude his wife (Paulina) from the King's presence; is declared by Leontes 'worthy to be hanged' for failing to stay P.'s tongue; professes that he will do anything to save the life of Hermione's infant, and is bidden to take it and expose it in some 'remote and desart place.' iii, 3] lands in Bohemia with the babe; relates (*sol.*) how Hermione had appeared to him in a prophetic vision; lays down the babe and flees, pursued by a bear; (his death is related). (v, 1) Paulina speaks of him as dead. (v, 2) 'torn to pieces with a bear.'

'A., King of the Jews,' is mtd. *Plut.* p. 184, in connection with M. Antony. There is no corresponding character in *Pandosto.*

Antioch. Capital of the Greek kingdom of Syria, situate on the Orontes, about 20 m. from the sea. 'The fairest [city] in all Syria' (*Per.* i, Prol.); its foundation ascribed to 'Antiochus the Great' (*ib. ib.*); mtd., *ib.* i, 1, 2, 3; a knight of A., *ib.* ii, 2.

The scene in *Per.* i, 1, is laid at A.

Antiochus. D.P. *Per.* King of Antioch ('A Tyrant of Greece,' F3). i, 1] presents his daughter to Pericles, and warns him that failure to expound the verses proposed to him will involve his death; on Per. finding the meaning of the riddle, viz. A.'s incest with his daughter, Ant. resolves to put him to death – 'He must not live to trumpet forth my infamy.' (i, 2) his ruthlessness. (i, 3) mtd. (ii, 4) his dreadful death. (iii, Gow.) mtd.

Cf. Chaucer, Group B, ll. 82 ff.

Antiochus, Daughter of. D.P. *Per.* (See Hesperides.) i, 1] she is presented to Pericles, who, solving the riddle of her shame, rejects her. (ii, 4) her death. (iii, Gow.) mtd.

Antiopa, or Antiope. An Amazon, vanquished by Theseus and afterward wedded to him (*Plut.* pp. 286–7). Oberon accuses Titania of making Th. break his faith with A., *M.N.D.* ii, 1.

Antipholus of Ephesus. D.P. *Com. Err.* (v, 1) son of Aegeon and twin-brother to Ant. of Syracuse (*q.v.*); was brought from Corinth to Ephesus by Duke Menaphon, uncle to Solinus, and has been for twenty years under the patronage of Sol., whom he has served as a soldier. iii, 1] is husband to Adriana; instructs Angelo, a goldsmith, about Adr.'s chain; chides his servant Dromio E. for telling him what seems a farrago of nonsense; invites Balthazar to dinner; finds his own door locked against him; in great wrath prepares to break it down, but is dissuaded by Balth.; resolves to dine with 'a wench of excellent discourse' instead, and to give her the chain he had intended for his wife. iv, 1] bids Dromio E. go and buy him a rope's end, wherewith to chastise his wife 'and her confederates'; complains that Ang. has not sent the chain as promised; is bewildered when Ang. declares that he already has the chain, and requires payment; is arrested for the debt, and is further amazed when Drom. S. informs him that a ship waits for him; sends Drom. S. to Adr. for a purse of ducats. iv, 4] Drom. E. brings him a rope, but no money; master and man are bound, and carried off as lunatics by Pinch, an exorcist, and his assistants, after passionately contradicting Adr.'s amazing asseverations. v, 1] entreats the Duke, whose life he saved in the wars, for justice against Adr. for locking him out of his house, and for imprisoning him and his servant in a vault, whence they have just escaped; the courtezan proves that he dined with her at the Porpentine; confronted with Aegeon, he declares that he never saw his father in his life; on the *imbroglio* being cleared up, offers to pay Aegeon's ransom.

In Ff Aemilia declares the age of the twins to be thirty-three. This seems to be an error, and was corrected by Theobald to twenty-five, for (i, 1) Ant. S. began to seek his brother at the age of eighteen, and (v, 1) this was 'seven years since.'

Ant. E. is the 'Antipholus surreptus' of the *Men aechmi* of Plautus.

Often 'Antipholis,' Ff. 'Corrupted from Antiphi lus' (Camb.). 'Antipholis Sereptus,' st. dir. ii, 1, Ff.

Antipholus of Syracuse. D.P. *Com. Err.* Son of Aegeon, and twin-brother to Ant. of Ephesus (*q.v.*). (i, 1) at the age of eighteen starts in quest of his long-lost brother. (v, 1) after seven years' travel arrives at Eph. i, 2] is warned that, in consequence of the feud between the two cities, he risks his life, or a heavy ransom, if he remains; sends his purse to the Centaur by his servant Dromio S.; encounters Drom. E., and is bewildered by his own servant, as it seems, denying all knowledge of the money and informing him that 'my mistress ... prays that you will hie you home to dinner'; beats Drom., and opines that he has fallen among cheats or sorcerers. ii, 2] finds his gold safe at the Centaur, but chastises his servant for flouting him; meets Adriana and Luciana (his brother's wife and sister-in-law); is rated by A. for deserting her; but on her softening, and begging him, as her husband, to return to their home, he acquiesces, but doubts whether he be 'sleeping or waking.' (iii, 1) feasts with the two ladies. iii, 2] woos Luciana, to her great confusion; is amused by his servant's recent experience, but thinks it high time that he were away from the abode of witches; a goldsmith forces a chain upon him, and proposes to call for his money at 'supper-time.' iv, 3] marvels that the townsfolk seem to know him; decides to embark on a ship sailing that night; a courtezan, unknown to him, demands either the chain he wears or the return of a ring he had of her at dinner; exclaiming 'Avaunt, thou witch!' he departs. iv, 4] entering with his sword drawn, gathers from the flight of the bystanders that the 'witches are afraid of swords'; orders Drom. 'to get our stuff a board' forthwith. v, 1] confronted by the goldsmith (who accuses him of denying his possession of the chain he wears), draws upon a merchant who confirms the charge; on the arrival of a clamorous crowd seeks safety with Drom. in an adjoining priory; the Abbess (his mother) leads them out to the Duke, and the *imbroglio* is disentangled.

The corresponding character in the *Menaechmi* of Plautus is Menaechmus Sosicles.

'Antipholis Erotes,' st. dir. i, 2, Ff; 'A. Errotis,' st. dir. ii, 2, F1; 'Antipolis Erotes,' *ib.* F2. Porh. for 'Errans' (Camb.).

Antipodes. (*a*) The region of the globe diametrically opposite to our own; (*b*) inhabitants thereof. 'I will go on the slightest errand now to the A.' (*M. Ado*, ii, 1); 'the moon May through the centre creep and so displease Her brother's noontide with the A.' (*M.N.D.* iii, 2); 'We should hold day with the A.' (*M.V.* v, 1); 'whilst we were wandering with the A.' (*Rich. II*, iii, 2); 'Thou art as opposite to every good As the A. are unto us' (*3 Hen. VI*, i, 4).

It is difficult to distinguish between (*a*) and (*b*), but the latter meaning was the commoner in Sh.'s days.

Antium. Ancient town of Latium, the modern Porto d'Anzio, on the Mediterranean, about 30 m. S. of Rome. A Volscian stronghold which finally became a Roman colony, 338 B.C. The scene of *Cor.* iv, 4, 5, and v, 6; Aufidius resides at A., *Cor.* iii, 1; 'A goodly city is this A.' (*ib.* iv, 4).

Antium, Citizen of. D.P. *Cor.* iv, 4] directs Coriolanus.

Antoniad. 'The admiral-galley of Cleopatra was called A., in the which there chanced a marvellous ill sign: swallows had bred under the poop ... and there came others ... and plucked down their nests' (*Plut.* p. 207).

'The A., the Egyptian admiral, With all their sixty, fly' (*Ant. Cl.* iii, 10; 'Thantoniad,' Ff).

The incident of swallows building in the ships (*ib.* iv, 12) is not connected especially with the A. by Sh.

Antonio (1). D.P. *T.G.V.* 'Father to Proteus' (F1). i, 3] following the advice of his (unnamed) brother, resolves to send P. to the imperial Court at Milan to consort with his equals and acquire accomplishments fitted to his birth; despite P.'s protests, orders him to start on the morrow. ('Anthonio,' Ff.)

Antonio (2). D.P. *M. V.* A merchant of Venice. i, 1] is dejected, but knows not why, and protests that anxiety about his ventures at sea is not the cause; assures Bassanio that his 'extremest means' are at his disposal if need be; on hearing that B. desires ready money in order to make an appearance befitting a suitor of the wealthy Portia, bids him 'try what my credit can in Venice do,' and promises to inquire 'where money is.' i, 3] joins B., who is bargaining with Shylock for a loan on Ant.'s security; discusses with S. the scriptural warrant for usury and observes that 'the devil can cite Scripture for his purpose'; bids S. lend the money not as to a friend, but to an enemy; reassures B., who would not have him put himself in the Jew's power; consents to sign a bond binding himself to forfeit a pound of his flesh 'if he should break his day.' ii, 6] bids Gratiano and the rest hasten to embark with Bassanio. (ii, 8) his parting with B. described. (iii, 1) rumours of the loss of his argosies are current. (iii, 2) their loss confirmed. iii, 3] appears in custody; attempts, fruitlessly, to compromise with S.; declares that he is resigned to his fate. (iii, 4) Lorenzo lauds him to Portia. iv, 1] appears before the court; expresses his willingness to suffer patiently; protests that it is lost labour to attempt to soften the Jew's heart – let Bassanio write his epitaph; bids B. tell Portia how he loved him to the end; on Shylock's conviction for plotting against the life of a citizen, A. is prepared to hold his share of the Jew's wealth in trust for Lorenzo and Jessica, but stipulates that S. should 'presently become a Christian.' v, 1] welcomed at Belmont; learns that three of his argosies 'are richly come to harbour.'

'He is affable, mild, and generous to all, without knowing their tricks and without sharing their mirth. ... His pleasure in their intercourse is passive, according to his universal apathy... Touched by no fault, but moved also by no virtue, he appears passionless, and almost an automaton.' (Gervinus, *Sh. Comm.* (1875), p. 238.)

Antonio (3). D.P. *M. Ado.* Brother to Leonato. i, 2] informs L. that he has heard that Don Pedro is about to propose marriage to L.'s daughter, Hero. ii, 1] trusts his niece will be ruled by her father; Ursula recognizes him, though masked, 'by the waggling of his head.' v, 1] attempts to give counsel to Leonato in his grief, but is rebuffed; denounces Claudio in unmeasured terms, and, old as he is, challenges 'Sir boy' to fight; later, hears Borachio's confession. v, 4] gives the masked Hero in marriage to Claudio.

In the st. dirs. of i, 2, QFf have merely 'an old man brother to Leonato.' Antonio's son is mtd. (i, 2, l. 1) and is possibly a D.P. in the scene (Johnson and Dyce).

Antonio (4). D.P. *T. Nt.* 'A sea-captain, friend to Sebastian' (Rowe). ii, 1] begs to be allowed to accompany Seb. as his servant; on learning that Seb. intends proceeding to Orsino's Court, resolves to follow him, though he has 'many enemies' there. iii, 3] joins Seb. in the city, and lends him his purse, but, fearing to be recognized, betakes himself to his inn. iii, 4] entering when 'Cesario' is about to fight with Aguecheek, mistakes 'C.' for Seb., and offers to take his place; is arrested 'at the suit of Count Orsino'; asks the supposed Seb. to return the purse, and is amazed and indignant when 'C.' disavows him; is led away in custody. v, 1] is brought before Or., and by him recognized as the hostile victor in a sea-fight; declares that he 'never yet was thief or pirate,' though Or.'s foe; adds that he was induced to enter the city by the 'witchcraft' of his affection for Seb. – for whom he again mistakes 'Cesario' standing by; on the entrance of Seb., realizes his error.

The spelling in Ff varies between 'Antonio' and 'Anthonio.'

Antonio (5). ('Anthonio,' Ff.) D.P. *Temp.* The usurping Duke of Milan. (i, 2) treacherously misusing the power vested in him by his brother Prospero, he had – twelve years before the opening of the play – made a league with Alonso, King of Naples, to whom he offered Milan as a fief conditionally on being himself recognized as its duke; he then admitted Neapolitan troops and caused Pr., with his little daughter, to be cast adrift. (Throughout the play Ant. is associated with Sebastian, the King's brother.) i, 1] during the storm Ant. and Seb. vituperate the mariners. ii, 1] after landing on the island they combine in deriding Gonzalo's attempts to divert the King's gloomy thoughts; Ariel having magically lulled to sleep all the King's party except Ant. and Seb., the former insidiously urges the latter to join him in murdering Alonso and Gonzalo; Seb. yields, with some reluctance; he pleads 'hereditary sloth,' but raises no moral objections to the crime; he dreads, however, pangs of conscience until reassured by his more unscrupulous associate; the conspirators' project is foiled by Ariel awaking Gon. in the nick of time. iii, 3] the conspirators plan a renewal of the attempt that night; they are denounced, together with the King, by Ar. in the form of a harpy, but, unlike Alonso, evince no sign of repentance. v, 1] they are led by Ar. within an enchanted circle, and confronted by Prospero himself; he sternly upbraids them, but accords them his forgiveness; they however remain sullen, manifest no contrition, and are sufficiently self-possessed to jest at the plight of Stephano and his comrades. See Sebastian.

Antonio (6). Eldest son of the Duke of Florence. D.P. *All's Well.* iii, 5] *p.m.*

Antonio (7). Petruchio's late father. *Tam. Sh.* i, 2 (2); 'a man well known throughout all Italy' (*ib.* ii, 1).

In i, 2, 'Butonio,' FfQ.

Antonius. For '(Mark) Antony.' *Jul. C.* i, 2 (rep.), 3; *Ant. Cl.* i, 1, ii, 2, iii, 1; 'Marcus A.' (*ib.* ii, 6).

Antonius, Lucius. Brother of Mark Antony. 'L. and Fulvia his [Antony's] wife fell out first between themselves, and afterward fell to open war with Caesar' (*Plut.* p. 178). These events referred to, *Ant. Cl.* i, 2.

Antonius, Marcus (*c.* 83–30 B.C.). Triumvir. The salient facts of his life, so far as they are relevant to the dramatic character of 'Mark Antony,' are as follows: In 44 B.C., being consul with Caesar, he offered the latter a kingly crown during the Lupercalia; after C.'s murder he delivered a funeral oration over the body, and, having obtained C.'s private papers from Calpurnia, read his will to the people; he speedily found a rival in the young Octavius (or Octavianus), the dictator's great-nephew. At the end of 44 Ant. received Cisalpine Gaul for his province, and proceeded thither, but found that Dec. Brutus, who had made Mutina his stronghold, refused to yield possession; Antony laid siege to the town, whereupon the Senate declared him a public enemy, and he was defeated in the spring of 43 before Mutina, and compelled to cross the Alps; there he was joined by Lepidus with a powerful army, and, Octavius having become reconciled to Ant., the three formed the Triumvirate, which lasted for five years. The personal enemies of each triumvir were proscribed, and among those who fell was Cicero (*q.v.*). In 42 Ant. and Oct. wholly defeated the republicans under Brutus and Cassius at Philippi, 'Asia' fell to Ant. as his share of the Roman world, and proceeding to Cilicia he met Cleopatra, by whose charms he was completely captivated and whom he followed to Egypt. In 41 his wife Fulvia (*q.v.*) and his brother L. Antonius made war on Octavius in Italy, but it terminated without involving the triumvirs in the contest. The death of Fulvia, shortly afterward, enabled Ant. to marry Octavia, sister to Octavius, and brought about a new reconciliation between the rivals. In 39 the triumvirs concluded peace with Sext. Pompeius, and in this and the following year Ventidius (*q.v.*) defeated the Parthians. In 37 the Triumvirate was renewed for five years. On returning to the East, Ant. sent back his wife to her brother, wholly surrendered himself to the fascinations of Cleopatra, and assumed the character of an Oriental monarch. Oct., thinking the time ripe for crushing his rival, made war on him, and defeated the fleet of Ant. and Cl. at Actium, 31 B.C. Ant. and Cl. fled to Alexandria, where the former shortly afterward put an end to his life.

D.P. *Jul. C.* i, 2] is present at the celebration of the Lupercalia, and is asked by Caesar to touch Calphurnia in his 'holy chase' (*Plut.* p. 96); Brutus speaks of his 'quick spirit'; is asked by Caesar his opinion of Cassius; is a lover of plays (*ib.* p. 161); is reported to have thrice offered Caesar a crown (*ib.* p. 96). (ii, 1) his assassination is proposed by Cassius, but vetoed by Brutus, on the ground that he is but 'a limb of Caesar' and therefore harmless 'when Caesar's head is off' (*ib.* p. 119). ii, 2] although he 'revels long o' nights,' attends early to escort Caesar to the Senate-house, with the conspirators. iii, 1] leaves the Senate-house shortly before the assassination of Caesar (*ib.* p. 118); is reported to have 'fled to his house amaz'd'; sends his servant to ask whether he may safely present himself to Brutus and 'be resolv'd' concerning Caesar's death; later, enters, and begs the conspirators to slay him; then, after shaking their bloodstained hands, he passionately laments over the mighty dead; begs permission to speak C.'s funeral oration; this is accorded by Brutus, despite a protest from Cassius; (*sol.*) apostrophizes the corpse, and predicts the 'domestic fury and fierce civil strife' that will ensue; receives a message from Octavius, and detains the messenger. iii, 2] pronounces a funeral oration over Caes., and so sways the passions and emotions of the populace that they are filled with fury against the murderers (*ib.* pp. 121–2); left alone, he exclaims, 'Mischief, thou art afoot, Take thou what course thou wilt!'; learns that Oct. has reached Rome, and resolves to join him. iv, 1] confers with Oct. and Lepidus; consents to the proscription of his own nephew (cf. *ib.* p. 169); in the absence of L., characterizes him as a 'barren-spirited fellow,' who must, nevertheless, be made use of by his colleagues. (iv, 3) mtd. v, 1] (at Philippi) disputes with Oct. on the conduct of the coming battle; parleys with the leaders of the foe, and reviles them as murderers and flatterers. (v, 3) is reported to have overthrown Cassius' legions. v, 4] directs that the prisoner Lucilius should be shown 'all kindness' (*ib.* p. 149). v, 5] pronounces a eulogy over the body of Brutus.

D.P. *Ant. Cl.* i, 1] declares his unbounded love for Cleopatra; is loath to listen to the news from Rome; is bantered by Cl. for his subservience to Fulvia and Octavius, but vows that he is hers alone. i, 2] hearing of the war stirred up by Ful. and his brother Lucius, and of the capture of Asia by Labienus, is struck by remorse at his 'dotage'; hears that Ful. is dead, and pays tribute to her as a 'great spirit'; determines to 'break off' from Cl.; converses with Enobarbus on the grave news he has just heard, and orders him to prepare for immediate departure from Egypt. i, 3] breaks the news to Cl., and with difficulty prevails on her to acknowledge the necessity of the step. (i, 4) his conduct discussed by Lep. and Oct.; his endurance of hardships in war referred to. (i, 5) he is named by Cl. 'the demi-Atlas of this Earth'; he sends her a pearl. (ii, 1) is hourly expected at Rome. ii, 2] confers with the other triumvirs; agrees to marry Octavia; (his first meeting with Cl. described). ii, 3] bids farewell to Octavia; is warned by a soothsayer to keep apart from Octavius, since his 'angel' is overpowered in his presence; sends Ventidius to Parthia. (ii, 4) mtd. (ii, 5) his marriage with Octavia reported to Cl. ii, 6] with the other triumvirs, parleys with Sext. Pompeius. ii, 7] takes part in the revels on Pompey's galley; discourses with the tipsy Lepidus on the wonders of Egypt. (iii, 1) Ventidius (*q.v.*) fears to arouse his envy. iii, 2] bids farewell to Octavius on taking from him his sister-in-law as a bride; (how he lamented over Caesar and Brutus). (iii, 3) mtd. iii, 4] comforts Octavia with regard to the imminent war with her brother. (iii, 5) sends for Enobarbus. (iii, 6) his enthronement in Alexandria, and desertion of Octavia. iii, 7] despite advice to the contrary, resolves to fight Octavius by sea. iii, 9] posts his land-forces at Actium. (iii, 10) his flight from the naval battle described. iii, 11] despairing, divides his treasure among his followers and dismisses them; on the entrance of Cl., gently reproaches her; sends an envoy to Octavius. (iii, 12) requests permission to live in Egypt, or in Athens as 'a private man.' iii, 13] resolves to challenge Octavius to single combat; later, finds Thidias kissing Cleopatra's hand, and in a fury orders him to be whipped; assails Cl. with unmeasured abuse; recovers himself, resolves to attack Oct. by land, but will first have one more 'gaudy night' with his captains. (iv, 1) his personal challenge refused by Oct. iv, 2] bids his 'good fellows' wait on him at what may be their last feast together; cheers them when they weep, having taken his words 'in too dolorous a sense.' iv, 4] is armed by Cl. and Eros; sets out to fight. iv, 5] hears that Enobarbus has deserted him, and directs that his treasure should be sent after him. (iv, 6) mtd. iv, 7] praises Scarus for his valour. iv, 8] rejoices with Cl. over the day's success in the field. (iv, 9) mtd. iv, 10] prepares for a naval engagement. iv, 12] about to watch the fight, is dismayed to see his men fraternizing with the foe; objurgates Cl. for betraying him; declares that 'the witch shall die.' (iv, 13) mtd. iv, 14] compares himself to the transient pageantry of a cloud, and accuses Cl. of packing 'cards with Caesar'; is told (falsely) that Cl. has died with his name upon her lips; bids Eros kill him, but E. falls on his own sword, and Ant. ineffectually tries to kill himself in the same manner; he learns that Cl. still lives, and is borne wounded to her. iv, 15] is drawn up with difficulty into the monument, and, after last words with Cl., dies – 'a Roman, by a Roman, Valiantly vanquished.' (v, 1) his sword is brought to Octavius, who laments over his 'mate in empire.' (v, 2) Cl. glorifies his greatness.

Macbeth says of Banquo that 'under him My genius is rebuked, as it is said Mark Antony's was by Caesar' (*Macb.* iii, 1; cf. *Ant. Cl.* ii, 3, *Plut.* p. 181); Fluellen thinks Pistol 'as valiant a man as M. A.' (*Hen. V*, iii, 6).

Antony (1). For 'Antonio' (D.P.); *M. Ado*, v, 1 (2).

Antony (2). Forename of Dull (D.P.), *L.L.L.* i, 1 (2); of Woodville, *Rich. III*, i, 1.

Antony (3). A servant; *Rom. J.* i, 5.

Antony and Cleopatra. See ANTHONY AND CLEOPATRA.

Antony, Duke of Brabant. See BRABANT, ANTONY, DUKE OF.

Apemantus. D.P. *Timon.* 'A churlish philosopher.' i, 1] in cynical banter shows himself easily the master of Timon and the rest of the company present. i, 2] sits apart at T.'s banquet; soliloquizes on human insincerity; pronounces an ironical grace; comments on the maskers; foresees T.'s ruin. ii, 2] enters with the Fool, whose buffoonery at the expense of those present he chimes in with (generally regarded as an interpolated passage). iv, 3] visits T. in the woods, advises T. to turn flatterer, and exclaims, 'I love thee better now than e'er I did'; his anger rises, and T. reviles and stones him; in departing, A. threatens to tell them in Athens that T. has gold, and 'thou wilt be throng'd to shortly.'

Apemantus is mtd. *Plut.* pp. 216–6 as a companion of Timon the misanthrope, because he was much like of his nature and condition.' For a suggested derivation from ἀπήμαντος ('unhurt', or 'without misery') see *Cornhill Magazine*, Feb. 1876. Frequently 'Apermantus' in F1. 'Thrasycles' in Lucian's *Dialogue*.

'The soul of Diogenes appears to have been seated on the lips of A. His lurking selfishness does not pass undetected amidst the grossness of his sarcasms and his contempt for the pretension of others.' (W. Hazlitt.)

Apennines. Mountain range in Italy. 'Talking of the Alps and Apennines' (*John*, i, 1).

In Golding's *Metam.* xv, 'the hill of Apennine.'

Apollo. Son of Zeus and Leto; one of the chief Greek divinities. He was regarded in several aspects, but principally as (*a*) the beautiful god of song and music; (*b*) the sun-god, in this case being usually distinguished by the epithet Phoebus (*q.v.*); and (*c*) the god of prophecy, especially in connection with his oracle at Delphi (*q.v.*). (For the favourite story of his pursuit of the nymph Daphne see that name.)

'The words of Mercury are harsh after the songs of A.' (*L.L.L.* v, 2); '[Helen] whose youth and freshness wrinkles A.'s' (*Tr. Cr.* ii, 2); 'the fiddler A.' (*ib.* iii, 3); (of Achilles' brain) 'A. knows,'Tis dry enough' (*ib.* i, 3); invoked, *T. And.* iv, 1; mtd., *ib.* iv, 4; 'A., perfect me in the characters!' (*Per.* iii, 2); 'by A.' (*Lear*, i, 1); 'the fire-robed god, Golden A., [became] a poor humble swain' (*Wint. T.* iv, 4); 'as bright A.'s lute strung with his hair' (*L.L.L.* iv, 3; not a classical allusion; a parallel passage occurs in Lyly's *Midas* (1592), IV, i, 13, ed. Bond, where Pan tells A.: 'Had thy lute been of lawrell, and the strings of Daphne's haire, thy tunes might have beene compared to my noates'); 'A. flies, and Daphne holds the chase' (*M.N.D.* ii, 1); 'And at that sight [Daphne bleeding] shall sad A. weep' (*Tam. Sh.* Ind. 2); 'Tell me, A., for thy Daphne's love' (*Tr. Cr.* i, 1). For the mission sent by Leontes to consult the oracle of A. see Delphos; cf. *Wint. T.* ii, 1, 3, iii, 1 (2), 2 (4), v, 1. As a Latin word: 'ad Apollinem' (*T. And.* iv, 3).

With ref. to Lear's invocation (*Lear*, i, 1) Malone observes (not very aptly) that acc. Geoffrey of Monmouth Lear's father, Bladud, was killed by falling on the temple of A. while trying to fly. The allusion in *Wint. T.* may be to A.'s keeping the flocks of Admetus (*cf.* Virg. *Georg.* iii, 2); it occurs in the parallel passage in *Pandosto*: 'A. a shepheard.'

Apollodorus. A Sicilian who helped to convey Cleopatra to Julius Caesar in a mattress, 'bound up together like a bundle with a great leather thong' (*Plut.* p. 86).

Pompey begins to refer to the adventure, but is checked by Enobarbus, *Ant. Cl.* ii, 6.

The name is spelt 'Appolodorus' in F1.

[**Apollonius.**] See Pericles.

[**Apolonius and Silla.**] A story in Barnabe Riche's *Farewell to Militarie Profession* (1581), which has been regarded as a source of *Twelfth Night* (*q.v.*).

Apothecary, An. D.P. *Rom. J.* v, 1] (the contents of his shop described by Romeo); driven by poverty, consents to supply R. with poison at the risk of his own life.

In *Romeus and Juliet* the apothecary is hanged. Bandello calls him Spolentino.

[**Appian,** or **Appianus.**] Roman historian. Conjectured to have been the source of Sh.'s account of Sextus Pompeius in *Ant. Cl.*

A version of A.'s *History* was published in 1578 by Henry Binniman, or Bynniman.

Apparitions, Three. D.PP. *Macb.* iv, 1] 1st, 'an armed head,' bids Macb. beware Macduff; 2nd, 'a bloody child,' declares that none of woman born shall harm Macb.; 3rd, 'a child crowned, with a tree in his hand,' declares that Macb. shall be unconquered until Birnam Wood shall come to Dunsinane.

Upton, *Crit. Observ. on Sh.* (1746), pointed out that the apparitions symbolize respectively Macbeth himself, Macduff, and Malcolm.

April, Month of. 'The A.'s in her [Octavia's] eyes: it is Love's spring' (*Ant. Cl.* iii, 2); 'O earth, I will befriend thee more with rain ... Than youthful A. shall with all his showers' (*T. And.* iii, 1); 'When well-apparell'd A. on the heel Of limping winter treads' (*Rom. J.* i, 2); 'banks ... Which spongy A. at thy hest betrims' (*Temp.* iv, 1); 'The uncertain glory of an A. day' (*T.G.V.* i, 3); 'he [Fenton] speaks holiday, he smells A. and May' (*M.W.W.* iii, 2); 'a day in A. never came so sweet, To show how costly summer was at hand' (*M.V.* ii, 9); 'men are A. when they woo, December when they wed' (*A.Y.L.* iv, 1); 'Flora Peering in A.'s front' (*Wint. T.* iv, 4); 'the first of A.' (given as the day of Queen Elinor's death, *John*, iv, 2); 'he will weep you an 'twere a man born in A.' (*Tr. Cr.* i, 2); 'she, whom the spital-house ... would cast the gorge at, this [gold] ... spices to the A. day again' (*Timon*, iv, 3); 'the fourscore of A.' (*Wint. T.* iv, 4); 'an A. daisy' (*Lucr.* 395); 'the lovely A. of her prime' (*Son.* iii); 'A.'s first-born flowers' (*ib.* xxi); 'proud-pied A.' (*ib.* xcviii; 'A. perfumes' (*ib.* civ); 'a storm ... 'twixt May and A.' (*L.C.* xv).

Aquilon, Aquilo. *Gk.* Βορέας (see Boreas); personification of the North Wind. 'Blow ... till thy sphered bias cheek Outswell the colic of puff'd A.' (*Tr. Cr.* iv, 5).

With reference to the cherub-like representatives of the winds in old maps.

Aquitain. Ancient division of S.W. France; of much importance in Anglo-French history, but only named in *Sh.* in connection with imaginary negotiations between 'Ferdinand' and the 'Princess of France.' *L.L.L.* i, 1; ii, 1(7).

Practically identical with Guienne (*q.v.*).

Arabia. 'In Ar. there is one tree, the phoenix' throne' (*Temp.* iii, 3); 'vasty wilds of Ar.' (*M.V.* ii, 7); 'perfumes of Ar.' (*Macb.* v,1); 'King Malchus of Ar.' (*Ant. Cl.* iii, 6); 'I would my son Were in Ar., and thy tribe before him,' *i.e.* in the desert (*Cor.* iv, 2; cf. *Cymb.* i, 2, l. 167, and *Macb.* iii, 4, l. 104).

Arabian. 'Ar. bird' (*i.e.* the phoenix; *Cymb.* i, 6, and *Ant. Cl.* iii, 2); gum of 'Ar. trees' (*Oth.* v, 2); 'sole Ar. tree' (*P.T.* ii).

[**Arachne.**] A Lydian maiden who challenged Athena to compete with her in weaving, and was changed by the goddess into a spider (Ovid, *Metam.* vi, 1 ff.; Virg. *Georg.* iv, 246). See Ariachne.

Arc. See Joan of Arc.

Archelaus. Descendant of A., the distinguished general of Mithridates; made king of Cappadocia, 34 B.C., by Mark Antony (Dion Cass. xlix, 32).

Mtd. as an ally of Ant., *Ant. Cl.* iii, 6 ('Archilaus,' Ff); cf. *Plut.* p. 207.

Archibald. *1 Hen. IV*, i, 1; see Douglas.

Archidamus. D.P. *Wint. T.* 'A Lord of Bohemia' (Ff). i, 1] dilates on the hospitality Polixenes and his train have met with in Sicily, and speaks of the coming visit of Leontes to Bohemia.

The name is probably taken from Plutarch, where it occurs frequently as that of a line of Spartan kings.

Arde. French town in Picardy, between which and the English town of Guynes lay the vale of Andren, where the Field of the Cloth of Gold was held; *Hen. VIII*, i, 1.

Ardea. Capital of the Rutuli, in Latium; besieged by the Tarquinii, *Lucr.* Arg., and II. 1, 1332; *cf.* Ovid, *Fasti*, ii, 721 ff.

Arden, Forest of. (*a*) A great forest (Ardennes = Arduenna Silva) anciently stretching from the Rhine to the Sambre; (*b*) an English forest lying in Warwickshire and the adjacent counties (described in the 13th Song of Drayton's *Polyolbion*); (*c*) the name of the locality in which the pastoral scenes of Lodge's *Rosalynde* and of *As You Like It* are laid. The introduction of an incongruous fauna and flora by both Lodge and Sh. tends to show that neither of them meant his forest to have an identifiable situation: in the words of Francois Victor Hugo, 'C'est le forêt vierge de la Muse,' and yet 'there are fifty places in England where with *As You Like It* in hand one might linger "from morn to dewy eve," and say, "Ay, now am I in Arden" ' (Lady Morgan, qtd. by C. Knight).

Named: *A.Y.L.* i, 1, 3; ii, 4.

Argier, Algiers. 'The foul witch Sycorax' (*q.v.*) banished thence; *Temp.* i, 2.

Arabic Al-Gezair, 'The Islands,' but perhaps a corruption of 'Caesarea'; spelt in many ways – Arger, Argel, Algel, etc. (*Cf.* S. Lane-Poole, *The Barbary Corsairs*, p. 13 *n.*)

Argus. A being with a hundred eyes, some of which were always awake (Ovid, *Metam.* i, 624); type of a watchful guardian. See HYDRA.

'One that will do the deed Though A. were her eunuch and her guard' (*L.L.L.* iii, 1); 'Lie not a night from home; watch me, like A.' (*M.V.* v, 1); Ajax is scornfully characterized as 'purblind A., all eyes and no sight' (*Tr. Cr.* i, 2).

Ariachne. A seemingly arbitrary variation of 'Arachne' (*q.v.*) to suit the metre. 'A point as subtle as Ariachne's broken woof to enter' (*Tr. Cr.* v, 2).

So Ff; 'Ariochna,' Q; 'Ariathna,' Steevens' copy of Q in Brit. Mus. Possibly Ariadne is meant.

Ariadne. Daughter of Minos; acc. one legend she, out of love for Theseus, enabled him by means of a string to find his way out of the Labyrinth, but was forsaken by him in the island of Naxos (*Plut.* pp. 283–4; Ovid, *Metam.* viii, 175, *Heroid.* 10).

'A lamentable part ... Ar. passioning For Theseus' perjury and unjust flight' (*T.G.V.* iv, 4); Oberon accuses Titania of making Th. break his vows with A., *M.N.D.* ii, 1.

Ariel. D.P. *Temp.* 'An ayrie spirit' (F1), who, on refusing to obey the witch Sycorax, being 'a spirit too delicate to act her earthy and abhorr'd commands,' was confined by her in a cloven pine, there to 'painfully remain a dozen years,' until released by the superior powers of Prospero. i, 2] A. relates how he has 'performed to point the tempest' which he had been instructed to raise, and how he dispersed Alonso's fleet, and 'flamed amazement' in the King's own ship, which moreover he had brought safely to harbour in a 'deep nook' of the island; warned by Pr. that 'there's more work' for him to perform, A. becomes 'moody,' and demands his promised liberty, but on being sternly rebuked by Pr. craves pardon, and is promised release after two days. A. then assumes invisibility, presenting, however, to Pr. (and to the audience) the aspect of a sea-nymph; later, re-enters, followed by Ferdinand, whom he has beguiled to Pr.'s cell with his music, ii, 1] he lulls to sleep the King and his train. with the exception of Antonio and Sebastian, but awakes Gonzalo in time to preserve his life and that of the King from these two conspirators. iii, 2] as an invisible taborer, sets the drunken trio – Stephano, Trinculo, and Caliban – at loggerheads, and (iv, 1) lures them into a 'filthy-mantled pool.' iii, 3] in the form of a harpy sternly denounces the 'three men of sin' – Alonso, Antonio, and Sebastian – for their treachery toward Pr., and exhorts them to repentance. iv, 1] assembles 'the rabble' of inferior spirits to enact a masque before Ferdinand and Miranda; hangs up 'glistering apparel' as a bait for Stephano and his companions, and with much zest sets on spirit-hounds to hunt them down. v, 1] is charged to lead Alonso and his train to Pr.'s cell; helps his master to don his ducal garments, and is sent to fetch successively the shipmaster and boatswain, and the drunken trio. A.'s final task before regaining his freedom is to ensure for the royal fleet a calm voyage homeward.

The name Ariel (*Heb.* 'lion of God') occurs twice in the O.T. – Isaiah xxix, 1 (Jerusalem); Ezra viii, 16 (man's name) – but its choice for a 'spirit of the air' is clearly independent of this etymology. 'Is there anything in nature from which Sh. caught the idea of this delicate and delightful being, with such childlike simplicity, yet with such preternatural powers? He is born neither of heaven nor of earth; but, as it were, between both, like a May-blossom kept suspended in air by the fanning breeze, which prevents it from falling to the ground, and only finally, and by compulsion, touching the earth. This reluctance of the Sylph to be under the command even of Prospero is kept up through the whole play, and in the exercise of his admirable judgment Sh. has availed himself of it, in order to give Ariel an interest in the event, looking forward to that moment when he was to gain his last and only reward – simple and eternal liberty.' (Coleridge, *Seven Lectures.*) The theory that A. was 'female' ('The Sex of Ariel,' *Athenæum*, Oct. 1, 1904) is refuted by A. himself in his first speech. *Cf.* 'his wings,' st, dir. iii, 4.

Aries. The Ram; constellation and sign of the zodiac. 'The Bull ... gave A. such a knock, That down fell both the Ram's horns in the court' (*T. And.* iv, 3).

Arion. Traditional inventor of dithyrambic poetry, and master on the cithara. While returning from Sicily to Corinth he was in danger of being murdered by the sailors for the sake of the valuable prizes he had won, but being permitted to play once more upon his cithara he attracted dolphins round the ship, and flinging himself into the sea was rescued on the back of one of them.

Sebastian, *T. Nt*, i, 2, is described as floating on a mast, 'like Arion on the dolphin's back' (printed 'Orion' until corrected by Pope).

A.'s adventure, first related by Herodotus (i, 24), is alluded to by Virgil, *Ecl.* viii, 56, but the story would be familiar to an Elizabethan audience as a classical commonplace.

Aristotle (384–322 B.C.). Greek philosopher, founder of the Peripatetic school. 'Let's be no stoicks ... or so devote to A.'s checks' (*Tam. Sh.* i, 1); 'young men, whom A. thought Unfit to hear moral philosophy' (*Tr. Cr.* ii, 2).

The passage in *Tr. Cr.* is based on the *Nicomachean Ethics*, i, 8, where A. states that 'political' philosophy is unsuited to young men. Bacon, *Advancement of Learning* (bk. ii), appears to make the same mistake as Sh. But it has been shown that, precisely in this connection, 'moral,' or its equivalent, occurs in contemporary English, French, and Italian works. See Lee, p. 653 *n*. The anachronism of Hector's quoting A. is, of course, a peculiarly daring one.

Armado, Don Adriano de. ('Adriana,' F1.) D.P. *L.L.L.* 'A fantastical Spaniard' (Rowe). (i, 1) Costard is committed to his custody. i, 2] converses with Moth, whose quickness of retort he resents; asks 'what great men have been in love?' and admits that he is enamoured of Jaquenetta; Jaq. on entering saucily banters him; Arm. resolves accordingly to write to her, and is 'for whole volumes in folio.' iii, 1] discourses with Moth, and praises that 'most acute juvenal'; sends for Costard and promises his freedom if he will convey a letter to Jaq. (iv, 1) the letter is read to the Princess; Boyet describes Arm. as 'a phantasm, a Monarcho' (*q.v.*). v, 1] Arm. tells the Curate and the Pedant that the King has entrusted him with the presentation of some 'show or pageant' to please the Princess. v, 2] he enacts Hector in the pageant of 'The Nine Worthies,' and is jeered by the courtiers; is told publicly by Costard that Jaq. is 'quick by him'; prepares to fight, when the proceedings are interrupted; departs with the words 'I will right myself like a soldier'; later, informs the King that he has 'vowed to Jaq. to hold the plough for her sweet love three years'; introduces the singers, and, their songs being ended, declares that 'the words of Mercury are harsh after the songs of Apollo.'

The name is spelled 'Armado' and 'Armatho' indifferently in the Ff. It has been argued by Fleay ('Sh. and Puritanism,' *Anglia*, 1884, vii, 223) that A. was intended as a caricature of John Lyly; Sir S. Lee, on the other hand, is not alone in maintaining that 'Sir Tophas, a "foolish braggart" in Lyly's play of Endimion (1591), was the father of Sh.'s character of Armado' (Lee, p. 105). It is to be observed that in most of the st. dirs. and pfxs. of the Ff Arm. is termed 'Braggart' – a stock character in Italian comedy. (It does not fall within our scope to discuss the alleged parody of 'Euphuism' in A.'s speeches; suffice it to remark that it is now widely acknowledged that the essential characteristics of 'Euphues' are scarcely recognizable in the Braggart's high-flown diction. *Cf.* Ward, *Eng. Dram. Lit.* i, 276.)

Armagnac. ('Arminack,' Ff.) A district of France, nearly equivalent to the Dept. of Gers. John IV, Count of A. ('Earl,' *Hol.* and *Sh.*) offered his d. in marriage to Hen. VI (1442) with 'great summes of monie' as dowry and other advantages (*Hol.* iii, 623).

The offer described, *1 Hen. VI*, v, 1; the E.'s wealth contrasted with the poverty of Margaret of Anjou's father, *ib.* v, 5.

Armatho. See ARMADO.

Armenia. Country lying between Asia Minor and the Caspian. Subject of contention between Octavius and Mark Antony, *Ant. Cl.* iii, 6; cf. *Plut.* p. 202.

Armin, Robert. Actor and dramatist; mtd. in 'The Names of the Principall Actors' pfxd. to F1. Probably succeeded Kemp as Dogberry.

For a supposed portrait of A. see *Sh. Eng.* ii, 263.

Arragon, Aragon. A former kingdom in the N.E. of Spain. Don Pedro (*q.v.*), D.P. *M. Ado*, was Prince of A. Mtd. *M. Ado*, i, 1; iii, 2.

Arragon, Prince of. D.P. *M. V.* Suitor to Portia. ii, 9] makes trial of the caskets; chooses the silver one, bearing the motto: 'Who chooseth me shall get as much as he deserves'; finds within it 'the portrait of a blinking idiot'; reads the accompanying verses, and retires with dignity.

In reply to critics who object to the repetition of two such similar episodes as the trial of the caskets by Morocco and Arragon, Furness, *Variorum Edn.* p. 113, points out the utility of this dramatic device in impressing upon the audience the sense of indefinite flight of time.

Artemidorus. 'Born in the isle of Gnidos, a doctor of rhetoric in the Greek tongue' (*Plut.* p. 99).

D.P. *Jul. C.* 'A. of Cnidos, a teacher of rhetoric.' ii, 3] (*sol.*) reads a paper which he intends to give to Caesar, warning him against the conspirators. iii, 1] vainly urges C. to peruse it.

Plutarch's account (p. 99) differs in detail from Sh.'s.

Arthur. For 'Abraham' (*q.v.*). 'He [Falstaff] is in A.'s bosom, if ever man went to A.'s bosom' (*Hen. V*, ii, 3).

Arthur, Duke, or **Count, of Brittany** (1187–1203). Posthumous son of Geoffrey Plantagenet, 3rd son of Henry II by his wife Constance of Brittany. By right of primogeniture A. had therefore a better title to the crown of England than his uncle John, who was Henry's youngest son, but Richard Coeur-de-lion's death-bed bequeathal of the crown to John was generally held in England to constitute the better claim. Philip II of France, for his own ends, supported A.'s pretensions to the French possessions of Richard I, with a tragic result to A., as unfolded in the play.

D.P. *John.* (i, 1) A.'s claims to England, Ireland, and four French provinces are presented to John (this is unhistorical, since no claim to England and Ireland was made on A.'s behalf). ii, 1] (before Angiers) A. is presented to 'Austria' and welcomes him, with 'a powerless hand' but a loving heart; is dismayed by the quarrel between Constance and the queen-mother Elinor, wishing he were in his grave, and exclaiming 'I am not worth this coil that's made for me'; A.'s French territories having been bestowed as a marriage portion on the Dauphin's bride, John promises to make him 'D. of Bretagne and E. of Richmond' (*Hol.*, iii, 161–2). iii, 1] witnesses his mother's frenzied outburst against Philip's perfidy and begs her to 'be content.' iii, 2] *p.m.*; is handed over to the keeping of Hubert. iv, 1] Hubert, by John's order, prepares to put out Arthur's eyes, but the boy by the pathos of his pleading turns him from his design (*Hol.* iii, 165). (iv, 2) his death is announced and contradicted. iv, 3] he leaps from the castle walls, in an attempt to escape, disguised as a ship-boy, but is killed by the fall.

A. is dramatically represented as much younger than he really was, for instead of being a mere child he was 16 years old at the time of his death; the timid gentleness of his disposition as portrayed by Sh. does not, moreover, accord with the accounts given of him in the *Chronicles*, where he is found besieging his grandmother in a tower (*Hol.* iii, 164) and making 'a presumptuous answer' to John when he sought to make terms with him (*Hol.* iii, 165). The story of his death as given by Holinshed (iii, 165) is as follows: 'Certeine it is that ... he was removed from Falais into the castell or tower of Rouen, out of the which there was not any that would confess that ever he saw him go alive. Some have written that as he assaied to have escaped out of prison, and prooving to clime over the wals of the castell, he fell into the river of Saine, and so was drowned. Others write that through verie greefe and langour he pined awaie, and died of naturall sicknesse. But some affirme that King John secretlie caused him to be murthered and made awaie, so as it is not throughlie agreed upon, in what sort he finished his daies; but verilie King John was had in great suspicion, whether worthilie or not, the Lord knoweth.'

Arthur, King. Legendary king of Britain. Falstaff sings a snatch of a ballad (Percy, *Reliques*, i): 'When A. first in court' (2 *Hen. IV*, ii, 4); 'A.'s show' (*ib.* iii, 2; see DAGONET).

Arthur, Prince (1486–1502). Eldest son of Hen. VII; married Katharine of Arragon 1501. 'Katharine ... princess dowager and widow to Prince A.' (*Hen. VIII*, iii, 2).

Artois. Former province of France, nearly corresponding to the Dept. of Pas-de-Calais; came into the possession of the Dukes of Burgundy in 1384. 'Redoubted Burgundy, By whose approach the regions of A... are friends to us' (*1 Hen. VI*, ii, 1).

[**Arundel, Thomas, Earl of** (1381–1415).] Son of Richard, 3rd E. of A. 'The E. of A.'s sonne, named Thomas, which was kept in the duke of Exeters house, escaped out of the realme' (*Hol.* iii, 496).

A line containing his name is assumed to be accidentally omitted in *Rich. II*, ii, I, after 1. 279, if the passage is to agree with the *Chronicle*.

Arviragus. D.P. *Cymb.* Supposed son to Belarius, disguised under the name of Cadwal (*q.v.*). (i, 1; iii, 3) as an infant was stolen, with his elder brother Guiderius, from his home. iii, 3] laments that when old they will have, in their ignorance, no subjects of discourse wherewith to wile away the freezing hours in their 'pinching cave.' iii, 6] is struck by the appearance of 'Fidele,' and will love him as a brother. iv, 2] declares that though he knows not why he loves the youth, he would rather see his father dead than 'F.'; vies with his brother in praise of him; on Cloten's approach departs with Belarius; on G.'s entrance with Cloten's head, wishes that he himself 'had done it'; enters the cave and returns with 'F.,' apparently dead in his arms; resolves to sweeten his sad grave with flowers, and is rebuked by his brother for 'wench-like words'; proposes to recite their mother's funeral dirge over 'F.' iv, 4] resolves to join the British force, and no longer to remain 'a poor unknown.' v, 2] takes part in the battle. v, 5] can be identified as Cymbeline's son by a 'curious mantle' in which he was wrapped as an infant; welcomes Posthumus as a brother.

Arv. is mtd. as one of the sons of Kymbeline, *Hol.* i, 32. The name occurs in Juvenal, *Sat.* iv, 127, as that of a British prince. The penultimate in Latin is short, but it is long in Cymb. iii, 3, l. 105, and v, 5, l. 427. Leland, in his *New Year's Gift to King Henry VIII*, speaks of 'the tyme of Kynge Arviragus, when S. Peter yet preached to the dispersed bretheren.' *Cf.* Ward, *Eng. Dram. Lit.* i, 171 *n*. The name 'Arveragus' occurs in Chaucer, *The Franklin's Tale*, 1. 808, etc. *Cf.* Spenser, *The Faerie Queene*, II, x, 51: 'For Arvirage his brothers [Kimbeline] place supplyde.' Malone points out that the name also occurs as that of 'the King of Venedocia' in a poem by Robt. Chester (*q.v.*) entitled *The Strange Birth ... and most unhappie Death of famous Arthur King of Brytaine* (1601).

Ascanius, or Iulus. Son of Aeneas. Acc. Virg. *Aen.* i, 657 ff., Cupid assumed the form of Ascanius, and nestled in Dido's arms while Aeneas began the story of the fall of Troy. The following passage seems due to an imperfect recollection of this incident;

'Witch me, as A. did, When he to madding Dido would unfold His father's acts, commenc'd in burning Troy' (2 *Hen. VI*, iii,2).

Ascapart. See BEVIS.

Ascension Day. 'Holy Thursday,' the fortieth day after Easter. Peter of Pomfret prophesied that John should yield up his crown 'ere the next A.-day at noon' (*John*, iv, 2); in *Tr. R.*, 'ere A.-D. Have brought the sun unto his usual height'; in *Hol.* iii, 180, 'at the feast of A.'; cf. *John*, v, 1.

Historically, the feast in 1213 fell on May 23, and John did homage to the Pope on May 15. Matthew Paris, to make this a fulfilment of Peter's prophecy, calls this the eve of Ascension Day. But during the whole of the reign A. Day never fell on May 16 (Wright).

Asher. Old form of 'Esher.' 'Asher, which was an house situat nigh unto Hampton Court, belonging to the Bishoprike of Winchester' (*Hol.* iii, 909).

Wolsey, on surrendering the Great Seal, was ordered to confine himself 'to Asher House, my Lord of Winchester's' (*Hen. VIII*, iii, 2).

Ashford. Town in Kent. 'John Cade of A.' (2 *Hen. VI*, iii, 1); '*Cade*. Where's Dick, the butcher of A.?' (*ib.* iv, 3).

Cade's connection with Ashford is not authenticated.

Ash Wednesday. Mtd. *M.V.* ii, 5; see BLACK MONDAY.

Asia. 'Furthest inch of A.' (*M. Ado*, ii, 1); 'pampered jades of A.' (2 *Hen. IV*, ii, 4; from Marlowe's *Tamburlaine*). For 'Asia Minor': 'roaming clean through the bounds of A.' (*Com. Err.* i, 1); 'Labienus ... hath with his Parthian force extended [seized] A.' (*Ant. Cl.* i, 2).

Asmath. For 'Asmodeus,' a fiend; *cf.* Tobit iii, 8; invoked by Margery Jourdain, 2 *Hen. VI*, i, 4. ('Askalon,' *F.P.C.*)

[**Aspall.**] See RUTLAND, TUTOR TO.

Aspley, William. Joint publisher of 2 *Hen. IV* (1600), *M. Ado* (1600), the *Sonnets* (1609), and the First Folio (1623).

Assyrian, *adj.* 'As swift as stones Enforced from the old A. slings' (*Hen. V*, iv, 7; acc. Theobald, an allusion to Judith ix, 7: 'The Assyrians ... trust to shield and bow and sling'); Falstaff jocularly addresses Pistol as 'base A. knight' (2 *Hen. IV*, v, 3).

Astraea. A divine maiden who dwelt on earth during the Golden Age, and then withdrew and was placed among the stars. The Dauphin addresses La Pucelle as 'Divinest creature, bright A.'s daughter' (*1 Hen. VI*, i, 6); 'Terras Astraea reliquit ... she's gone, she's fled' (*T. And.* iv, 3; *cf.* Ovid, *Metam.* i, 149).

'A.'s daughter' probably means 'a second A.'

Astringer, A gentle. Acc. st. dir. of F1, D.P. *All's Well.* v, 1] (at Marseilles) is asked by Helena to present a petition to the King; informs her that the King has started for Rousillon, but consents to take the paper. v, 3] presents the petition; later, brings in the Widow and Diana.

'A gentle astringer' would mean a noble acting as falconer to the King. But the reading in F2 is 'a gentle Astranger,' and in F3, 4, 'a gentleman, a stranger.' In the pfxs. 'Gent.' throughout.

[**Astyanax.**] Son of Hector and Andromache, to whom an allusion seems intended when Marcus refers to young Lucius as 'the Roman Hector's hope' (*T. And.* iv, 1).

[**Astynome.**] See Chryseis.

As You Like It.

Publication. Although 'As you like yt a booke' is entered in the Stationers' Registers of Aug. 4, 1600, 'to be staied,' no edition is known previous to the Folio of 1623. The acts and scenes are numbered.

Date of Composition. Not ascertained, but probably *c.* 1599. A line (iii, 5, l. 82) is quoted from Marlowe's *Hero and Leander* (1598).

Source of the Plot. Thos. Lodge's romance, *Rosalynde. Euphues Golden Legacie* (1590), the characters of Touchstone, Jaques, and Audrey being added by Sh. (*Rosalynde* is, in turn, partly based on *The Tale of Gamelyn* (*q.v.*), formerly attributed to Chaucer.)

For a comparison between *A.Y.L.* and *Rosalynde* see *N.S.S.Tr.*, 1882, Pt. II, p. 277, where the parallelisms are recorded by W. B. Stone.

Atalanta. Acc. one legend a maiden who was the most swift-footed of mortals; she was, however, outrun by her lover, who delayed her by a stratagem.

'You have a nimble wit; I think 'twas made of A.'s heels' (*A.Y.L.* iii, 2); 'A.'s better part, sad Lucretia's modesty' (*ib.* iii, 2). This allusion, after copious discussion, has not been satisfactorily explained. Golding's reference, 'Hard it is to tell Thee whether she in footemanshippe or beawty more excell' (*Metam.* p. 137 *a*), does not appear decisive.

For an account of the numerous suggestions made by commentators see Furness, *Var.* pp. 149–52.

Ate. A Gk. divinity inciting to rash actions, discord, and revenge. Not mtd. by Latin writers. (Elaborately described in *The Faerie Queene*, IV, i, 19–30; v, 203: 'mother of debate and all dissention,' 'hard by the gates of hell her dwelling is,' 'by infernall furies nourished.')

'You shall find her [Beatrice] the infernal A. in good apparel' (*M. Ado* ii, 1); 'An A. ['Ace', Ff], stirring him to blood and strife' (*John*, ii, 1); 'Caesar's spirit, raging for revenge, with A. by his side come hot from hell' (*Jul. C.* iii, 1); 'more A.s; more A.s; stir them on!' (*L.L.L.* v,2, l. 694).

Ate appears as D.P. in *Locrine*, an anonymous tragedy, 1595. Though Bk. IV of *The Faerie Queene* did not appear till 1598 the passage in *L.L.L.* may be a later addition.

Athenian. (*a*) *Adj. M.N.D.* i, 1 (2), ii, 2 (2), 3 (2), iii, 2 (3), iv, 1 (2), v, 1; *Tr. Cr.* Prol.; *Timon*, iv, 1, 3, v, 5.

(*b*) *Subst.*, native of Athens. *M.N.D.* iii, 2 (3), iv, 2; *Timon*, i, 1 (2), 2, iv, 1, v, 2 (2). (Lear to Edgar) 'Come, good A.' (*Lear, iii, 4*).

Athenian, An Old. *D.P. Timon.* i, 1] protests against his daughter's wedding Lucilius, but consents on Timon's endowing the latter.

Athens. Ancient capital of Attica. In *M.N.D.* and *Timon* the scene is laid throughout in Athens or its vicinity. The city is frequently mtd. in all the acts of these plays, the following being noteworthy instances: 'the ancient privilege of A.' (*M.N.D.* i, 1); 'the law of A.' (*ib. ib.*); 'A.'s gates' (*ib. ib.*); 'weeds of A.' (*ib.* ii, 3). 'The senators of A.' (*Timon*, i, 1); 'the wealth of A.' (*ib.* iii, 2); Alcibiades resolves to 'strike at A.' (*ib.* iii, 5); 'cursed A.' (*ib.* iv, 3); 'the commonwealth of A.' (*ib. ib.*), 'walls of A.' (*ib.* v, 2). For 'the Athenians': 'tell A… say to A.' (*ib. ib.*). 'Proud A.' (*ib.* v, 4); Antony 'purposeth to A.' (*Ant. Cl.* iii, 1); mtd., *ib.* iii, 6; Ant. would fain be 'a private man in A.' (*ib.* iii, 10); the Greek leaders at 'the port of A.' (*Tr. Cr.* Prol.).

[**Atherstone.**] Near Bosworth, where Richmond encamped before the battle. Rightly, the scene of *Rich. III*, v, 3, ll. 79–107. ('Aderston,' *Hol.* iii, 755.)

Atholl, or Athole, Earl of. See Stewart, Walter.

Atlas. A hero of conflicting myths, nearly all of which, however, represent him as bearing on his shoulders heaven, or earth, or both. Acc. Ovid, *Metam.* iv, 630 ff., he was changed into Mount Atlas by the aspect of the head of Medusa.

'Thou art no A. for so great a weight' (*3 Hen. VI*, v, 1); Cleopatra speaks of Antony as 'The demi-Atlas of this earth' (*Ant. Cl.* i, 5; 'demy Atlas,' Ff).

Atropos. One of the Fates (*q.v.*). '*Pist.* Come, A., I say' (2 *Hen. IV*, ii, 4).

Attendant. D.P. *M. Ado.* v, 3] present.

Attendant on Lord Chief Justice. D.P. 2 *Hen. IV.* i, 2] is ridiculed by Falstaff while attempting to address him.

Attendant on Mamillius. D.P. *Wint. T.* Not mtd. in 'The Names of the Actors' (Ff). ii, 3] reports on the child's sickness.

Aubrey. As a forename. 'Lord A. Vere' (*3 Hen. VI*, iii, 3).

[**Audley, Thomas** (1488–1544).] Baron A. of Walden; Lord Chancellor 1533–44, and present in that capacity in the coronation procession of Anne (Boleyn), *Hen. VIII*, iv, 1.

Audrey. D.P. *A. Y. L.* 'A country wench' (Rowe). iii, 3] is wooed by Touchstone, and, though perplexed by his pleasantries, accepts him. v, 1] is present when T. flouts her former lover William, whom she lightly dismisses; desires to be 'a woman of the world.' v, 3] listens to the page's song. v, 4] is presented to the Duke by T. as 'an illfavoured thing, sir, but mine own.'

Reduced from *A.S.* Aetheldryht (*cf.* Camden, *Remaines* (1629), p. 77). The name occurs in the parish register, 1603, of Aston-Cantlow, the birthplace of Sh.'s mother.

Aufidius, Tullus. A Volscian leader; described, *Plut.* p. 23, as one 'who for his riches, as also for his nobility and valiantness, was honoured among the Volscians as a king'; 'a marvellous private hate' existed between him and Caius Marcius, and after the latter had joined the Volscians 'it grieved him [Aufidius] to see his own reputation blemished through Martius' great fame and honour.' A.'s relations to Coriolanus as described by Plutarch are closely followed by Sh.; the insult to the body of Cor. is, however, not found in Plutarch, who relates that the Volscians paid him funeral honours.

D.P. *Cor.* (i, 1) Marcius declares him 'a lion That I am proud to hunt.' i, 2] Ant. announces to the Senate of Corioli that the Romans are in the field, and sets out against them.

(i, 3) Volumnia and Virgilia speak of him. (i, 4) M. learns that Aufldius is not within Corioli. (i, 5) M. determines to fight with A., 'my soul's hate.' (i, 6) mtd. i, 8] A. and M. defy one another, and fight, but Volscians come to A.'s aid. (i, 9) mtd. i, 10] yearns for a decisive combat with M. (ii, 1) his indecisive combat mtd. (iii, 1) retires to Antium, cursing the Volscians. (iv, 3) mtd. (iv, 4) Cor. appears before his house. iv, 5] Auf. bids 'a thousand welcomes' to Cor., recalls their former encounters, and offers him 'the one half of my commission.' (iv, 6) invades Roman territory with Cor. iv, 7] comments on Cor.'s popularity and success, but declares that, once Rome is conquered, 'then shortly art thou mine.' v, 2] is present when Menenius appeals to Cor. v, 3] when the ladies persuade him to spare Rome, rejoices to observe that Cor. sets his mercy and his honour 'at difference.' v, 5] inveighs against Cor.'s ingratitude and treachery, with those of his faction; accuses him before the lords of the City; joins the conspirators in killing Cor.; tramples upon the body, but is struck with remorse, and helps to bear the corpse away with martial honours.

In v, 5, the plural form 'Aufidiuses' occurs.

August, Month of. 'You sun-burn'd sicklemen of A. weary' (*Temp.* iv, 1); 'the tenth of A.' is given, *1 Hen. VI*, i, 1, as the date of the Battle of Patay (*q.v.*) (actually June 18,1429).

Augustus. First Roman emperor. See OCTAVIUS. Mtd. *Cymb.* ii, 4; iii, 5; v, 5. 'Aug. Caesar' (*ib.* iii, 1 (2), 5).

Aumerle, Duke of. See PLANTAGENET, EDWARD.

Aurelius. See LUCENTIO (1).

Aurora. Goddess of the dawn. 'A.'s harbinger' (*i.e.* Venus; *M.N.D.* iii, 2); 'A.'s bed' (*Rom. J.* i, 1).

Austria. See LYMOGES.

Austria, A Ruler of. Mtd. by the 'King of France' as 'our cousin Austria' (*All's Well*, i, 2).

Authority. Personified. 'The demi-god, A.' (*M. for M.* i, 3).

Autolycus (1). Son of Mercury and Chione; *cf.* Ovid, *Metam.* xi, 312, thus translated by Golding (1565): 'Now when shee full her tyme had gon, shee bare by Mercurye A sonne that hyght Awtolychus who provde a wyly pye, And such a fellow as in theft and filching had no peere.'

Autolycus (2). ('Autolicus,' Ff.) D.P. *Wint. T.* 'A rogue' (Ff). iv, 3] explains (*sol.*) that he was named A., 'who, being as I am, littered under Mercury, was likewise a snapper-up of unconsidered trifles'; feigning to have been robbed and beaten, 'by Autolycus,' picks the pockets of the Clown, who succours him. iv, 4] as a singing pedlar, visits the rustics' merry-making and disposes of his wares; later, congratulates himself on the ease with which he fleeced the rustics; is confronted by Camillo and Florizel and made to change garments with the latter; overhears the shepherd and his son planning to tell the King the truth about Perdita, and (now in the guise of a courtier) terrifles them by telling them that 'the shepherd and his son' are in danger of torture and death; receives gold from them to present their case at Court; resolves to befriend the Prince and be reinstated in his service. v, 2] (in Sicily) hears that Perdita's story has been divulged, and that the revelation will not be his; begs the now enriched shepherd and his son to commend him to Florizel.

As regards the character of A., it has been suggested that Sh. had in his recollection that singular production by Thomas Newbery, 'A booke in Englyshe metre of the great Marchaunte man called Diues Pragmaticus, very preaty for children to rede ... London ... 1563.' (This very curious tract, which is a riming list of articles for sale, was reprinted in 1910 from the unique copy in the John Rylands Library.)

Autumn, Season of. 'The childing A.' (*M.N.D.* ii, 1; *i.e.* 'fruitful,' see *N.E.D. s.v.*); breeding time for sheep, *M.V.* i, 3; time of thunder, *Tam. Sh.* i, 2; 'like to A.'s corn. Have we mow'd down' (*3 Hen. VI*, v, 7); 'a cloud in A.' (*Tr. Cr.* i, 2); 'an A. it was, that grew the more by reaping' (*Ant. Cl.* v, 2, Theobald's conj.; 'Anthony' in Ff); 'use his eyes ... for laying A.'s dust' (*Lear*, iv, 6; Qq only); 'teeming A.,' etc. (*Son.* xcvii); 'yellow A.' (*ib.* civ).

Referred to as 'fall of the leaf' (*Rich. II*, iii, 4).

Auvergne, Countess of. D.P. *1 Hen. VI.* (ii, 2) invites Talbot to her castle. ii, 3] having, as she supposes, made T. prisoner, taunts him with the meanness of his stature; when T. winds his horn and his men burst into the castle she acknowledges his power, and craves and receives pardon.

'May be intended for Mary, daughter of Godefroi d'Auvergne, wife of Bortrand III, Lord de la Tour' (French, p. 150). There is no foundation in the *Chronicles* for the lady's taunt.

B

B. 'Fair as a text B in a copy-book' (*L.L.L.* v, 2, l. 42). Collier MS. suggests 'R,' for 'Rosaline.'

Babylon. Ancient capital of Babylonia; in the Apocalypse, standing for the city of Anti-Christ. 'There dwelt a man in Babylon' (*T. Nt.* ii, 3); '[Falstaff] talked of the whore of B.' (*Hen. V*, ii, 3; *cf.* Rev. xvii, 1–5).

The first stanza of the song quoted by Sir Toby runs: 'There dwelt a man in B. Of reputation great by fame, He took a wife a faire woman, Susanna she was callde by name; A woman fair and vertuous; Lady, lady; Why should we not of her learn thus To live godly!' (Percy, *Reliques* (1765), i, 187). See also PABYLON.

Bacchanal. (*a*) A dance in honour of Bacchus. 'Dance now the Egyptian Bacchanals' (*Ant. Cl.* ii, 7). (*b*) A Bacchant, a votary of Bacchus. 'The tipsy Bacchanals' (*M.N.D.* v, 1).

Bacchus. God of Wine. In art usually of youthful beauty. 'Love's tongue proves dainty B. gross in taste' (*L.L.L.* iv, 3); 'Come, thou monarch of the vine, Plumpy B. with pink eyne' (*Ant. Cl.* ii, 7; here perh. confused with Silenus).

[Baginton]. See BAGOT.

Bagot, Sir William (*ob. c.* 1400). A minister of Richard II, one of the Council of the Realm during the King's absence in Ireland; committed to the Tower by Hen. IV.

Acc. *Hol.* he was hated by the commons as being one of those to whom Richard had 'farmed' the realm (iii, 492, 496), and on Bolingbroke's landing escaped to Chester and thence to Ireland (iii, 498); he later declared to Hen. IV, that the D. of Gloucester had been murdered by Richard's orders and that Aumerle was implicated in the matter.

D.P. *Rich. II.* i, 4; ii, 1] *p.m.* ii, 2] dreads the vengeance of the commons, and resolves to join the King in Ireland. iv, 1] accuses Aumerle, before Hen., of having brought about Gloucester's death and of treachery. (ii, 3) at Bristol. (iii, 2) mtd.

Bolingbroke, the night before the intended combat at Coventry, lodged at B.'s house at Baginton, Warwick (*Hol.* iii, 494).

Bajazet, Bayazid. Sultan of the 'Turks (1347–1403); son of Amurath I. 'Tongue, I must put you into a butter-woman's mouth and buy myself another of B.'s mule, if you prattle me into these perils' (*All's Well*, iv, 1, Ff).

Warburton's suggestion of 'mute' for 'mule' is accepted by many edrs., but Reed quotes S. Haynes, *Collection of State Papers* (1740), p. 369 (W. Maitland to Sec. Cecil, Aug. 9, 1561): 'the Philosopher, who for Themperor's Plesure tooke upon him to make a moyle speak.'

Balthasar (1). D.P. *M. Ado.* Attendant on Don Pedro. i, 1] *p.m.* ii, 1] converses, masked, with Margaret. ii, 3] apologizing for 'so bad a voice,' sings 'Sigh no more, ladies.'

It has been suggested, without much probability, that the name – which is the Gk. form of 'Belshazzar' (see Chaucer, *The Monkes Tale*, ll 14189 ff., ed. Tyrwhitt) – was adapted from 'Baltazarini,' a famous violinist and intendant of music to Catherine de Medici.

Balthasar (2). D.P. *Com. Err.* A merchant. iii, 1] is invited to dine with Antipholus of Ephesus, but dissuades him from breaking in when refused admittance to his house. (v, 1) mtd.

Balthasar (3). D.P. *M.V.* Servant to Portia. iii, 4] sent to fetch 'notes and garments' from Bellario. ('Balthaser,' F1.)

Balthasar (4). Name adopted by Portia, as 'a young doctor from Rome'; *M.V.* iv, 1. ('Balthazer,' Qq.)

Balthasar (5). D.P. *Rom. J.* Servant to Romeo. i, 1] *p.m.* v, 1] announces Juliet's (supposed) death to R. v, 3] accompanies R. to the tomb of the Capulets and leaves him there; tells Fr. Laurence that R. is in the vault; is discovered by the watch, and relates all he knows.

Balthazar. Variant of 'Balthasar.' (A character of the name appears in Kyd's *Spanish Tragedy*.)

Banbury. Town in Oxfordshire; one of the two routes from Stratford to London lay through B. '*Bardolph* [to Slender]. You Banbury cheese!' (*M.W.W.* i, 1).

Acc. T. Cogan, *The Haven of Helthe* (1584), B. cheese was the best kind of all; but Knight quotes *Jack Drum's Entertainment* (1601): 'you are like a Banbury cheese – nothing but paring.' Cf. *Sh. Eng.* i, 356–7.

Banister, or **Banaster, Humfrey.** Servant of Henry Stafford, D. of Buckingham, who, 'were it more for fear of life and losse of goods, or allured and prouoked by the auaricious desire of the thousand pounds [reward] ... bewraied his guest and master to John Mitton, then shiriffe of Shropshire' (*Hol.* iii, 744).

'Flying for succour to his servant Banister, Being distress'd, was by that wretch betray'd' (*Hen. VIII*, ii, 1).

Bangor, The Archd., or Dean, of. Northumberland, Hotspur, and Glendower 'by their deputies, in the house of the archdeacon of B., divided the realm amongst them' (*Hol.* iii, 521).

Acc. Mortimer, *1 Hen. IV*, iii, 1, the Archd. himself divided the map referred to in the 'tripartite indenture.' The scene of iii, 1, is laid in his house.

W. G. Boswell-Stone in the index to his *Shakspere's Holinshed* gives David Daron as the Archd.'s name.

[Bankes.] A Scottish showman, the wonderful performances of whose 'dancing horse.' Morocco, at the end of the 16th cent. are mtd. very frequently in the literature of the day. The only certain allusion in *Sh.*, however, is: 'how easy it is to put years to the word three, and study three years in two words, the dancing horse will tell you' (*L.L.L.* i, 2). Lafeu's exclamation, 'I'd give bay Curtal, and his furniture, my mouth no more were broken than these boys" (*All's Well*, ii, 3), may also refer to Morocco, who is variously described as bay and white.

The story that Bankes, with his horse, was burned as a witch, 'beyond the sea,' is now discredited. He seems to have settled down as a vintner in Cheapside and to have lived till 1637.

Banquo. Thane of Lochaber; an apparently fictitious personage, first met with, as well as his son Fleance, in Hector Boece's *Scotorum Historiae* (1527, Eng. transln. 1577). Acc. *Hol.* (after Boece) an ancestor of the house of Stewart. He was assailed by rebels while collecting funds for King Duncan; was sent with Macbeth against the rebels, who were defeated; held command in the King's army against Sweno, King of Norway; assisted in repelling another invasion; encountered 'three weird sisters'; by a jest on their prediction stirred up Macbeth's ambition; connived at M.'s murder of Duncan, but was slain by M., who was jealous of the prophecy that B. should be ancestor of a line of kings.

D.P. *Macb.* (i, 2) his bravery eulogized. i, 3] encounters the witches; after hearing their prophetic greetings to Macb., is told that he himself will be the ancestor of kings; suspects that the witches are nothing more than phantasms; on hearing that Macb. has become Thane of Cawdor, exclaims, 'What, can the devil speak true?'; on Macb.'s asking him, 'Do you not hope your children shall be kings?' deprecates reliance on 'the instruments of darkness'; confers with Ross and Angus. i, 4] is graciously welcomed by Duncan. i, 6] comments on the love of 'the temple-haunting martlet' for delicate air. ii, 1] by reason of evil dreams dreads to sleep; meets Macb. at midnight, and hands him a jewel for Lady M., from the King; consents to confer later with Macb. on the witches' predictions, and promises to follow his counsel so far as it is consistent with his allegiance. ii, 3] resolves to 'question this most bloody piece of work.' iii, 1] trusts that the prediction may be fulfilled as regards himself, but suspects M. of foul play; is welcomed as 'chief guest' by M. and his wife; announces his intention of riding out with his son that afternoon, but promises to fail not at the feast. (iii, 2) his coming murder hinted at. iii, 3] is attacked by three assassins and slain. iii, 4] failing not at the feast, his apparition appears to Macb., occupies a vacant chair, but soon vanishes; as M. is pledging 'our dear friend Banquo' the ghost again appears. (iii, 6) mtd. (iv, 1) 'blood-bolter'd,' his spirit appears to Macb. (v, 1) 'B.'s buried; he cannot come out on's grave.'

There has been much controversy as to whether the ghost of Banquo is intended to appear twice at the feast, or whether one of the apparitions is to be regarded as that of Duncan. It is noteworthy that neither the *exit* of the first apparition nor the entrance of the second is indicated in F1.

Baptista (1). Wife of the Duke in the play presented before Claudius; *Haml.* iii, 2.

Incorrectly used as a feminine name.

Baptista (2). As a masc. forename: 'B. Minola' (*q.v.*).

[**Bar.**] Former territory in Eastern France; capital Bar-le-Duc.

Bar, Duke of. Present at Agincourt, *Hen. V*, iii, 5; slain, 'Edward, Duke of B.' (*ib.* iv, 8). Cf. *Hol.* iii, 555.

Barabbas. See BARRABAS.

Barbara. Feminine name. Desdemona's 'mother had a maid call'd B.' (*Oth.* iv, 3).

'Barbary,' Qq; 'Barbarie,' F1 (once misprinted 'Brabarie'). Furness, *Var.* p. 276, notes that in New England the Christian name is still frequently so pronounced.

Barbary. The Saracen countries along the N. coast of Africa. Trading ships sent thither, *M.V.* iii, 2. The Barbary horse, or barb, a small but swift animal, was highly esteemed in Sh.'s days: a wager of 'six B. horses against six French swords' is mtd., *Haml.* v, 2 (2); 'a B. horse' (*Oth.* i, 1); 'Roan Barbary' is the name given by Sh. to Rich. II's favourite steed; Bolingbroke rode on 'Roan B.' on his coronation day, *Rich. II*, v, 5 (2).

A breed of pigeons from Barbary (known as 'the barb') is referred to, *A.Y.L.* iv, 1: 'more jealous than a B. cock-pigeon over his hen.' A guinea-fowl is probably referred to in: 'he will not swagger with a B. hen if her feathers turn back' (*2 Hen. IV*, ii, 4); 'In B.,' used to mystify the drawer, *1 Hen. IV*, ii, 4.

Barbason. Name of a fiend. 'Amaimon sounds well; ... B., well; yet they are ... the names of fiends' (*M.W.W.* ii, 2); '*Nym.* I am not B.; you cannot conjure me' (*Hen. V*, ii, 1).

'Marbas, alias Barbas, is a great president and appeareth in the form of a mightie lion; but at the commandment of a conjurer cometh up in the likeness of man, and answereth fullie as touching anything that is hidden' (R. Scot, *Discoverie of Witchcraft* (1584), p. 293).

[**Barcheston.**] See BARSON.

Bardolf, or **Bardolph.** Thomas B., 5th Baron (1368–1408). Joined Abp. Scrope's revolt against Hen. IV (*Hol.* iii, 529); mortally wounded at the Battle of Bramham Moor (*ib.* iii, 534).

D.P. *2 Hen, IV.* i, 1] bears to Northumberland the false news that Hotspur has been victorious at Shrewsbury; on learning the truth urges renewed efforts. i, 3] at a council of war advocates prudence and the postponement of operations until Northumberland's help is available. (iv, 4) mtd. as defeated.

It has been pointed out (*N.S.S.Tr.*, 1877–9, pp. 347–53) that Lord B. seems in *2 Hen. IV*, i, 1, to be confused with Sir John Umfreville (*q.v.*). As pfx. to 1. 161 ('This strained ...' etc.) – which is missing in Ff – Q has '*Umfr.*' Modern edns. restore this line, but give it to Travers. Comparing ll. 81–2 of i, 3, with i, 1, ll. 134–5, it would appear that Sh. originally did not intend Lord B. to appear in i,1 at all.

Bardolph. ('Bardol(l),' Qq.) D.P. *1 Hen. IV.* ii, 2] one of Falstaff's robber-band discomfited at Gadshill. ii, 4] admits to the Prince that he 'ran when the others ran'; announces the arrival of the Sheriff. iii, 3] is bantered by F. on 'the everlasting bonfire' of his face, and takes it in dudgeon; is sent by the Prince with a letter to Pr. John. iv, 2] is sent to precede F. into Coventry.

George Bardolf was the name of a Stratford contemporary of Sh.

D.P. *M.W.W.* i, 1] declares that Slender was drunk when he supposed himself robbed. i, 3] becomes tapster at the Garter. ii, 2] ushers in 'Master Brook.' iii, 5] officiates as tapster. iv, 3] tells the Host that 'the Germans desire three of his horses,' iv, 5] relates that the Germans have fled with the horses.

D.P. *2 Hen. IV.* (i, 2) Falstaff 'bought him in Paul's.' ii, 1] *p.m.* (termed by Quickly 'arrant malmsey-nose'). ii, 2] exchanges banter with the Page; hands a letter from Falstaff to the Prince, who questions him. ii, 4] (at the Boar's Head) helps to eject the obstreperous Pistol. iii, 2] announces Falstaff's arrival to Shallow; discusses the word 'accommodated'; is bribed to free two of the recruits. iv, 3] tells F. that the army is to be discharged.' v, 1] in attendance on F. v, 3] is hospitably entertained by Shallow; hears that 'the old King' is dead, and 'would not take a knighthood for his fortune.' v, 5] *p.m.*

D.P. *Hen. V.* Now 'a soldier in the King's army.' ii, 1] forcibly composes a quarrel between Nym and Pistol. ii, 3] hears the news of Falstaff's death, exclaims 'would I were with him, wheresome'er he is,' and prepares to depart for France, iii, 2] urges his comrades 'to the breach'; is characterized by the Boy. (iii, 6) having stolen a 'pax,' is condemned to be hanged; (his physiognomy described by Fluellen).

Acc. *Hol.* iii, 552, 'a souldieur took a pix out of a church,' and was hanged for the theft.

Bardylis. See BARGULUS.

Bare, George. See BARNES, GEORGE.

Bargulus 'This villain here, Being captain of a pinnace, threatens more than B., the strong Illyrian pirate' (*2 Hen, VI*, iv, 1).

The Illyrian chief Bardylis, or Bardyllis – who was said to have become ruler of Illyria – was famous for his equity in dividing the spoils. 'Bargulis ['Bargilius,' *Cod. Bern.* n. 104; 'Bardylis,' Orelli] Illyrius latro, de quo est apud Theopompum, magnas opes habuit' (Cicero, *De Off*, ii, 11; *cf.* Plut. *Pelop.* 26, *Pyrr.* 9).

The form 'Bargulus' is due to N. Grimald's translation of Cicero, *De Off.* (1558, 1574, 1588). Diodorus Siculus, xvi, 2, 4, calls him Βάρδυλις (In *The First Part of the Contention* the equivalent is Abradas, a name which seems to occur only in Greene's *Penelope's Web*; see *N.S.S.Tr.*, 1876, p. 249.)

Barkloughly. ('Barclowlie,' *Hol.* iii, 499.) Landing-place of Richard II on his return from Ireland; *Rich. II*, iii, 2.

Acc. *Monach. de Evesham Hist.* (1729), p. 142, 'Castrum de Hertlowli in Wallia,' which has been conjectured, with much probability, to be Harlech. Other chroniclers give Milford, or Pembroke, as R.'s landing-place.

Barnardine. D.P. *M. for M.* (iv, 2) 'a Bohemian' who has recently pleaded guilty to a charge of murder, on which he has been imprisoned for nine years; sunk in drunkenness, he is wholly unmoved by his impending fate; his immediate execution is ordered, and his head is to be taken to the Governor in lieu of Claudio's. iv, 3] is summoned to execution, but refuses to stir, since he has 'been drinking all night' and is 'not fitted for it'; is ordered to be placed 'in secret hold.' v, 1] *p.m.*; is pardoned by the Duke.

'The personification of the coarse, sensual nature of man which becomes inhuman, because humanity has withdrawn her training and guiding hand' (Ulrici, ii, 161). 'B.' as D.P. in *The Jew of Malta* is a friar.

Barnes, George. (Qq; 'Bare,' Ff.) A former acquaintance of Shallow's at Clement's Inn. 'Black G. B.' (2 *Hen. IV*, iii, 2).

Barnet. Town in Hertfordshire, 'in the meane waye betwene London and saynct Albones ... beyng tenne myle distaunt from bothe the tounes' (Hall, p. 295), where, on Apr. 14, 1471, a battle was fought between Yorkists and Lancastrians, resulting in the defeat of the latter, under Warwick 'the Kingmaker,' and the establishment of Edward IV on the throne.

'*Warw.* I will away towards B. presently, And bid thee battle, Edward, if thou dar'st' (*3 Hen. VI*, v, 1); '*K. Edw.* We having now the best at B. field' (*ib.* v, 3).

The scene of *3 Hen. VI*, v, 2, 3, is laid at, or near, B.

Barrabas, Barabas, or **Barabbas.** A robber and murderer, whose release from prison, instead of Christ's, was demanded by the Jews (Matt. xxvii, 16 ff.; Mark xv, 7 ff.; Luke xxiii, 18 ff.).

'*Shy.* Would any of the stock of Barrabas Had been her [Jessica's] husband rather than a Christian' (*M.V.* iv, 1).

The name is spelt thus by Tyndale and Coverdale. The Jew in Marlowe's *Jew of Malta* is 'Barabas,' the second syllable being always short.

Barson. Probably for 'Barcheston' near Stratford, which is, or was, thus pronounced. The name, as Barson, occurs on a monument there, mtd. in Dugdale's *Warwickshire*, p. 456. 'Barston' and 'Barton-on-the-Heath' have also been suggested; *cf.* French, p. 327. See PUFF.

Bartholomew. D.P. *Tam. Sh.* Ind. A page who enacts the wife of the 'noble lord' with whom Sly is assumed to be identical.

'Bartholmew,' FfQ. In *The Taming of A Shrew* merely 'Boy.' One of Sh.'s brothers-in-law was B. Hathaway.

[Bartholomew Fair.] Doll addresses Falstaff as 'Thou whoreson little, tidy Bartholomew boar-pig' (2 *Hen, IV*, ii, 4).

'A roasted pig in B. fair was a dainty to which Ben Jonson has several allusions, and thus it is used as a term of endearment to Falstaff' (C. Knight).

Bartholomew-tide. The season of St Bartholomew's Day (Aug. 24). 'Like flies at B.-tide, blind, though they have their eyes' (*Hen, V*, v, 2; of doubtful import).

[Barton-on-the-Heath.] See BARSON.

Basan, Bashan. District of Palestine famous for its breed of cattle. *Cf.* Psal. xxii, 12, lxviii, 15; Ezek. xxxix, 18; Amos iv, 1.

'*Ant.* O that I were upon the hill of B., to outroar The horned herd!' (*Ant. Cl.* iii, 13).

Basilisco. Character (a cowardly braggart) in *The Tragedie of Solimon and Perseda*, printed in 1599, and probably written in 1592. Piston, a buffoon, gets on B.'s back and pulls him down. B. cries 'Knight! good fellow, Knight, Knight!' to which P. replies, 'Knave! good fellow,' etc.

'*Lady F.*... thou most untoward knave. *Bast.* Knight, knight, good mother, Basilisco-like' (*John*, i, 1).

Cf. also Nashe's *Saffron Walden* (1596): 'He is such a vaine B ... and swarmeth in vile Canniball words.'

Basimecu. Ribald nonce-name (*baisez mon cul*) applied to the Dauphin by Cade (2 *Hen. VI*, iv, 7). See *Mod. Lang. Rev.* Jan. 1911, p. 96. *Cf.* Rabelais, *Pantag.* i, 10.

Basingstoke. Town in Hants; Henry IV at B., 2 *Hen. IV*. ii, 1.

Bassanio. D.P. *M. V.* Antonio's kinsman, suitor to Portia. i, 1] comments on Gratiano's loquacity; tells Antonio that he desires to pay 'the great debts' caused by his too lavish expenditure, and suggests that his friend might, by making a further advance, recover his previous loans; further admits that he would become a suitor of the wealthy heiress Portia, if he could but raise the necessary means; Ant. empowers him to use his credit 'to the uttermost' in raising a loan. (i, 2) mtd. i, 3] approaches Shylock with the view to obtaining 3000 ducats, on Ant.'s security; is present while S. bargains with Ant.; tries to deter Ant. from sealing the 'merry bond' suggested by the Jew. ii, 2] takes Launcelot Gobbo into his service; is willing that Gratiano should accompany him to Belmont, if he can curb his 'wild behaviour.' (ii, 5, 6) mtd. (ii, 8) parts with Ant. (ii, 9) approaches Belmont. iii, 2] presents himself as a suitor at Belmont; demurs to Portia's suggestion that he should wait 'some month or two' before making trial of the caskets, 'for,' he says, 'as I am, I live upon the rack'; since 'the world is still deceived by ornament' he chooses the casket of 'meagre lead' and finds within it 'fair Portia's counterfeit,' and a scroll proclaiming him the accepted suitor; scarcely believing his good fortune, asks P. to ratify it; is given a ring by her which he swears to part with only with his life; receives a letter from Ant. announcing that his ventures have all failed and that his bond to the Jew is forfeit; assured by P. that the debt shall be paid 'twenty times over' if need be, hastens away to relieve his friend. (iii, 3, 4, 5) mtd. iv, 1] (in the Court of Justice) expostulates with Shylock, and bids Ant. have good courage; tenders S. double the sum named in the bond; declares that to deliver Ant. from 'the devil' he would sacrifice even his wife; after the trial offers 'Balthasar' (Portia) 3000 ducats as a fee, but it is refused; 'Bal.' then asks him for his ring; Bass. offers, in lieu of it, 'the dearest ring in Venice'; 'Bal.' affects to be affronted, and, on his departing, Bass. sends Gratiano after him with the ring. (iv, 2) his ring delivered. v, 1] returns to Belmont; is welcomed by P.; she points out the absence of the ring, and accuses him of parting with it; Bass. pleads stress of circumstances, and protests that it was given to a 'civil doctor'; to his amazement it is restored to him.

For his view of 'the redemption by fiery trial' of 'a man utterly poor, ruined in his circumstances, inconsiderate, and extravagant at the expense of his friend,' see Gervinus, *Sh. Comm.* (1875), pp. 241–4.

Basset. D.P. *1 Hen. VI.* See VERNON.

Bassianus. D.P. *T. And.* Brother to Saturninus. i, 1] offers himself as a competitor for the throne. i, 2] solicits the aid of Titus in his candidature; carries off Lavinia as betrothed to him, though claimed by Sat.; later, justifies himself before Sat. (ii, 1) mtd. ii, 2] joins the royal hunting-party. ii, 3] rebukes Tamora for consorting with Aaron and threatens to inform Sat.; is slain by T.'s two sons. (ii, 4) his body is thrown into a pit. (v, 1) mtd.

The name is best known in history as that of the grandfather of Caracalla.

Bates, John. D.P. *Hen. V.* A soldier. iv, 1] converses before Agincourt with the King, whom he does not recognize.

Bates, or Bate, was a surname belonging to Stratford in Sh.'s days, as appears by the Records; *cf.* French, p. 327. In the *Chronicle Historie of Henry Fift* no names are given to 'The Three Soldiers.'

Bath. Town in Somerset; famous for its hot springs, resorted to by the Romans. Steevens considers that in *Son.* cliii, 1. 11, 'bath' should be 'Bath,' as being the name of the town.

[**Baucis.**] See PHILEMON (1).

Bawd. D.P. *Per.* Wife of Pander (*q.v.*). iv, 2] makes suggestions at which Marina stops her ears; instructs Boult to 'cry her through the market.' iv, 6] declares that M. would 'make a puritan of the devil'; introduces M. to Lysimachus; later, hands her to Boult.

It is now generally admitted that this revolting character is not the creation of Sh.

Baynard's Castle. So named after Ralph Baynard, a Norman nobleman, its founder. It was situated on the N. bank of the Thames, near Upper Thames Street, and rebuilt near its original site, in 1428, by Humphrey, D. of Gloucester. In 1446 it passed into the hands of Hen. VI, and from him to Richard, D. of York, who 'lodged there, as in his own house,' in 1457 (Stow, *Survey*, ed. Thoms, p. 25).

'*Glou.* Meet me within this hour at B.'s Castle' (*Rich. III*, iii, 5); the scene of *ib.* iii, 7, is laid there.

Bayonne, Bishop of. Jean de Bellay; alleged by Hen. VIII to have raised scruples in his mind concerning the legality of his marriage with Katharine, *Hen. VIII*, ii, 4; cf. *Hol.* iii, 907.

Sh. here follows an error of the *Chronicles*. De Grammont, Bp. of Tarbes, and not do Bellay, was officially credited with the comment; *cf.* Brewer, *Henry VIII*, ii, 163.

Bead. See BEDE.

Bear, The. The constellation Ursa Minor, containing the Pole Star. 'To cast water on the burning Bear, And quench the Guards [*q.v.*] of th' ever-fixed Pole' (*Oth.* ii, 1).

Beatrice. D.P. *M. Ado.* Daughter to Leonato. i, 1] makes eager inquiries about Benedick, who has returned from the wars; scoffs at him as nothing more than 'a valiant trencherman,' and pities his new friend Claudio 'if he have caught the Benedick'; on B.'s entrance, a smart 'skirmish of wits' ensues between them. ii, 1] discourses jestingly with her father on matrimony, but will not be wedded until men are made 'of some other metal than earth'; both being masked, she speaks disparagingly to B. about himself (B. takes her raillery to heart); later, on Hero's betrothal to Claudio, fears that she herself may 'cry heigh-ho for a husband,' but jestingly rejects Don Pedro, and declares that 'there was a star danced, and under that was I born.' ii, 3] 'against her will' bids Ben. come to dinner in discourteous terms (in which he finds 'a double meaning'). iii, 1] listens in hiding while Hero and Ursula dilate on her scornful coyness and pride, and on B.'s high qualities and love for her; (*sol.*) is amazed at the revelation, and exclaims 'Benedick, love on; I will requite thee.' (iii, 2) mtd. iii, 4] while Hero is being arrayed for her wedding, professes to be sick, and is prescribed 'Carduus Benedictus.' iv, 1] is present in the church when Hero is accused of faithlessness; weeping, declares she has been belied; tells B. that if he truly loves her, he must 'kill Claudio' for slandering her cousin. (v, 1) her alleged jibes against B. v, 2] engages in loving raillery with B. v, 4] they banter one another on the deception practised on them by their friends, but confronted by the love-sonnets addressed by each to the other, Beat. yields to Ben., 'upon great persuasion; and partly to save your life.'

For an analysis of this character, in the form of a letter to John Ruskin, see *On some of Sh.'s Female Characters*, by Helena Faucit (1887), pp. 211 ff.

Beauchamp, Richard, Earl of Warwick (1382–1439). E. of Albemarle 1422; Lord High Steward at the coronation of Hen. V. He fought vigorously against Glendower, and in the last year of Hen. was sent to make a treaty of peace with the regent Albany. By his second w., Isabel le Despencer, he had one d., Anne, who became the w. of Richard Neville, the 'E. of Warwick' in 2, *3 Hen. VI.* He was appointed Governor to Hen. VI and acted as Lt.-Governor in France and Normandy (1437–9). His splendid tomb is in St Mary's Church, Warwick.

D.P. *2 Hen. IV.* 'E. of Warwick.' iii, 1] bids the King not fear the Percies, and assures him that Glendower is dead. iv, 4] palliates the light conduct of Prince Henry; renders aid to the sorrowing King. v, 2] warns the Lord Chief Justice that the new King loves him not.

Glendower actually survived Henry. Historic time is but little observed in the play. In iii, 1, Henry addresses W. as 'cousin Nevil'; but this surname belongs to Warwick 'the King-maker,' his son-in-law (D.P. 2, *3 Hen. VI*).

D.P. *Hen. V.* i, 2] *p.m.* (iv, 3) mtd. as being at Agincourt. iv, 7] *p.m.*; is addressed by the King as 'good cousin W.' iv, 8] intervenes between Williams and Fluellen. v, 2] (at Troyes) *p.m.* (*Hol.* iii, 572).

W. was not at Agincourt, having returned to England after the capture of Harfleur.

D.P. *1 Hen. VI.* i, 1] *p.m.*; at the obsequies of Henry V (*Hol.* iii, 584). ii, 4] (in the Temple Gardens) declines to judge between Somerset (*q.v.*) and Richard Plantagenet, but plucks a white rose in token of his favouring the latter, and predicts the Wars of the Roses. iii, 1] deprecates the strife between Somerset and Bp. Beaufort; presents a petition to the King on behalf of Richard Plantagenet (*q.v.*). iv, 1] (at the coronation of Hen. VI in Paris; *Hol.* iii, 616) avers that the King 'thinks no harm' in wearing a red rose. v, 4] is present at the examination of La Pucelle, to whom he is implacable.

In the scene in the Temple Gardens W. is perh. confused with Richard Neville, the succeeding Earl.

Beaufort, Family of. See Appendix 1.

The name was given to John of Gaunt's illegitimate offspring by Cath. Swynford from the Castle of B., in Anjou, where they were born.

Beaufort, Edmund (1). 2nd D. of Somerset; younger brother of John B., 1st D. (*1 Hen. VI*). During his lieutenancy in France English power there was almost wholly lost; returning to England, he tried to carry on the government as a supporter of Hen. VI; imprisoned on York's becoming Protector; killed at the 1st Battle of St Albans, 1455. See BEAUFORT, JOHN (2).

Edmund B. was appointed 'to goo oure lieutenaunt into our duchie of Normandie' in Dec. 1447 (Stevenson, i, 477–8; B.-S. p. 251).

D.P. *2 Hen. VI.* i, 1] warns Buckingham against the 'haughty Cardinal.' i, 3] is appointed regent of France. (i, 4) a Spirit predicts that he will be in danger where 'castles' stand. iii, 1] announces that, in France, 'all is lost'; is taunted by York on his ill-success (*Hol.* iii, 612). iii, 2] present. iv, 9] is committed to the Tower to avert York's attack. v, 1] entering with Q. Margaret, orders York's arrest, but in vain. v, 2] is slain at St Albans by Richard Plantagenet (see CASTLE, THE).

Beaufort, Edmund (2) (*c.* 1438–71). Son of the preceding, styled 4th D. of Somerset on the death of his brother Henry, the 3rd D. (whose titles, however, were forfeited by attainder). Fought on the Lancastrian side at Tewkesbury and was executed after the battle.

D.P. *3 Hen. VI.* iv, 1] disapproving of the King's marriage to the Lady Grey, prepares to join Warwick. iv, 2] *p.m.*; joins W. iv, 3] is given custody of Edw. IV. iv, 6] resolves to send young Henry of Richmond to Brittany. v, 1] enters Coventry with his forces. v, 2] present at Barnet field. v, 4] with Q. Margaret at Tewkesbury. v, 5] a prisoner; sentenced to death.

The 'Somerset' of iv, 1, seems to be Henry Beaufort (2) (*q.v.*).

Beaufort, Henry (1) (*ob.* 1447). Bp. of Winchester; illegitimate son of John of Gaunt by Cath. Swynford; legitimized by Rich. II 1397; Bp. of Lincoln 1398; Bp. of Winchester 1404; Chancellor under Hen. V, and named by him guardian of the infant Hen. VI; nominated Cardinal-priest of St Eusebius 1426; crowned Hen. VI at Paris 1431; buried at Winchester. The dramatist's view of B.'s character seems largely influenced by Hall's account (p. 210): 'More noble of blood than notable in learning; haut in stomacke, and hygh in countenance; ryche above measure of all men and to fewe liberal; disdainfull to his kynne and dreadfull to his louers; preferrynge money before frendshippe ... his covetous insaciable, and hope of long lyfe, made hym bothe to forget God, his Prynce, and hymself, in his latter daies.'

D.P. *1 Hen. VI.* i, 1] eulogizes the dead King (Hen. V); is denounced by Gloucester as a hypocrite; (*sol.*) meditates removing the infant King from Eltham (cf. *Hol.* iii, 591). i, 3] in a violent altercation before the gates of the Tower is accused by Gl. of having 'contrived to murder' Hen. V (*ib.* 591); declares he will have Gl.'s head 'ere long.' iii, 1] is accused by Gl. of grievous misdeeds and of having laid a trap for his life at London Bridge (*ib.* 591); brings counter-charges against Gl. (*ib.* 595); after a conflict between his retainers and those of Gl., on the young King's mediation they agree to a truce, which B. (aside) declares he does not intend to keep. iv, 1] crowns Hen. VI at Paris (*ib.* 606). v, 1] as Cardinal, gives the papal legate an agreed sum for the Pope; declares that henceforth he will not 'be inferior to the proudest peer.' v, 4] presents Henry's conditions of peace to Charles (*ib.* 611).

D.P. *2 Hen. VI.* i, 1] after an altercation with Gl. hints to the nobles that Gl. will prove 'a dangerous protector' (*Hol.* iii, 626). i, 3] accuses Gl. of extortion. ii, 1] arranges a duel with Gl. (a grave charge against the Dss. of Gl. prevents the combat). (ii, 2) mtd. (ii, 4) characterized by the Dss. as 'impious B., that false priest.' iii, 1] is given the custody of Gl. at Bury; advocates his execution. iii, 2] hears of Gl.'s mysterious death. iii, 3] dies in terror (*cf.* Hall, p. 211 (historically, six weeks after Gl.).

The current pronunciation is illustrated by the spelling 'Bewford' (*F.P.O.* i, 1; ii, 4).

[**Beaufort, Henry** (2) (1436–64).] 3rd D. of Somerset; defeated Yorkists at 2nd Battle of St Albans; attainted 1461; pardoned by Edw. 1463; rejoined Margaret 1464; captured and executed at Hexham.

Alluded to, *3 Hen. VI*, v, 1, where Gloucester exclaims to Somerset: 'Two of thy name, both Dukes of S., have sold their lives unto the house of York' (viz. the 2nd and 3rd Dukes).

Beaufort, John (1) (1403–44). 1st D. of Somerset; g.s. of John of Gaunt; E. 1419; D. 1443; Captain-General in Normandy 1443. See following article.

Beaufort, John (2). D.P. *1 Hen. VI.* 'Earl, afterward Duke of Somerset.' ii, 4] in a bitter dispute with Richard Plantagenet, in the Temple Gardens, bids those present who side with him to pluck red roses; declares that Richard stands attainted, through the treason of his father, R., Earl of Cambridge; they part defiantly. iii, 1] deprecates the strife between the D. of Gloucester and the Bp. of Winchester. (iii, 4) mtd. iv, 1] (at Henry's coronation in Paris) renews his 'jarring discord' with York (Richard) before the King, who urges them to be friends, and gives York command of horse in France. (iv, 3) is denounced as a 'vile traitor' by York for not sending aid to Talbot. iv, 4] at first refuses to send reinforcements to Talbot, on the ground that the 'expedition was by York and T. too rashly plotted'; eventually consents to send aid. (iv, 7) mtd.

In this play two persons are confused under the title of 'Somerset.' The quarrel described took place between Richard Plantagenet and Edmund Beaufort, John's brother. A command in France was, however, given to John B. as mtd. (iv, 1) (though Hol. (iii, 619), following Hall, erroneously states that 'Edm., D. of Summerset' accompanied Richard in his campaign against Anjou). Richard (ii, 5) relates that the quarrel (ii, 4) took place on the day of 'Mortimer's' death (1425); he would then be only about 13 years old, while John Beaufort, whom he calls 'boy,' was some six years older.

Beaufort, Margaret (1443–1509). Countess of Richmond and Derby; mother of Hen. VII by her 1st husb. Edmund Tudor, E. of Richmond. Mtd. *Rich. III*, i, 3, l. 22, as wife of 'Lord Derby' (Thomas, Lord Stanley), who was her 3rd husband.

Beaufort, Thomas, Duke of Exeter (*ob.* 1427). Created D. of Exeter (for life) 1416; 3rd s. of John of Gaunt by his 2nd wife, Catherine Swynford, and therefore uncle to Henry V. As he was left in command at Harfleur, there is some doubt whether he took part in the Battle of Agincourt. Monstrelet (iii, 341) mentions him as present, and he may have left 'his lieutenant ... Sir John Fastolfe' in charge of Harfleur (*Hol.* iii, 550). He was one of the negotiators at Troyes (*ib.* 572) and was appointed a guardian of Henry VI (*ib.* 585).

D.P. *Hen. V.* i, 2] urges the King to 'rouse' himself against the French, and not to fear an attack by 'the weasel Scot'; announces that the Dauphin's 'tun of treasure' contains tennis-balls. ii, 2] arrests the conspirators, Cambridge, Scroop, and Grey. ii, 4] as ambassador from Henry, presents an ultimatum to Charles VI. iii, 1] (before Harfleur) *p.m.* iii, 3] is ordered to remain at Harfleur and 'fortify it strongly.' (iii, 6) his bravery at the bridge eulogized by Fluellen. iv, 3] (at Agincourt) remarks that the English are outnumbered; bids farewell to Salisbury. iv, 6] describes the death of Suffolk and York. iv, 7] with the King when the French herald presents himself after the battle. iv, 8] enumerates the prisoners. v, 2] (at Troyes) *p.m.*

D.P. *1 Hen. VI.* i, 1] (at the lying-in-state of Henry V) laments the King's death; hears evil tidings from France; as a 'special governor' of Henry VI, resolves to join him at Eltham. iii, 1] soliloquizes on the civil broils and on the prophecy that 'Henry born at Windsor should lose all.' iv, 1] (at the coronation of Henry VI in Paris) deprecates the strife between Somerset and York; soliloquizes on coming disaster. v, 1] recalls a prediction concerning Abp. Beaufort. v, 5] deprecates Henry's betrothal to Margaret of Anjou.

At the time of the coronation of Hen. VI in Paris Boaufort had been dead some five years; in Acts IV, V, the character must therefore be regarded as fictitious.

Beaumont, Earl of. Among the slain at Agincourt, *Hol.* iii, 555. Mtd. *Hen. V*, iii, 5; iv, 8. ('Gerard,' Qq.)

Not elsewhere mtd. 'Perhaps Henri II, Comte de Blamont (Mons. iii, 349) is meant' (B.-S. p. 510).

Beaumont, Henry, Baron. Joins Bolingbroke; *Rich. II.* ii, 2 (cf. *Hol.* iii, 498). ('Beaumond,' Ff.)

Bede, or **Bead.** Name of an impersonated fairy, suggestive of diminutive size; *M.W.W.* v, 5.

'Pede' in Qq, probably to represent Evans' pronunciation.

Bedford, Duke of. See John of Lancaster.

Bedlam. For 'Bethlehem,' in allusion to the Hospital of St Mary of Bethlehem, a priory, founded in 1247, and, before the dissolution of the monasteries, long known as a refuge for lunatics, being in 1547 incorporated as a royal foundation for that purpose. Its original situation was in Bishopsgate, the present building in Lambeth dating from 1815. Hence a lunatic, 'Tom o' Bedlam,' or Bedlam-beggar, denoting a discharged but usually half-witted mendicant holding a licence to beg, and wearing a tin badge on his left arm. 'B. beggars,' are characterized in *Lear*, ii, 3; 'melancholy, with a sigh like Tom of B.' (*Lear*, i, 2); 'To B. with him! is the man grown mad?' (*2 Hen. VI*, v, 1); '*K. John* [to Constance]. B., have done' (*John*, ii, 1, l. 183); '*Pist.* [to Fluellen]. Ha! Art thou B.?' (*Hen. V*, v, 1); 'Get the B. to lead him' (*Lear*, iii, 7). Attributively: 'the B. brain-sick Duchess' (*2 Hen. VI*, iii, 1).

Bel. Babylonian god; mtd. in the apocryphal book Bel and the Dragon. 'Like god B.'s priests in the old church-window' (*M. Ado*, iii, 3).

Belarius. D.P. *Cymb.* ('Bellarius,' Ff.) 'A banish'd Lord, disguised under the name of Morgan' (Rowe). iii, 3] tells his supposed sons that their life in a cave in Wales is nobler than that spent by courtiers; on their demurring, reminds them how, twenty years before, he had been unjustly banished by Cymbeline upon the perjured evidence of 'two villains'; (*sol.*) reflects that, though the young men little know that they are the sons of Cymb. stolen by him when he was exiled, their kingly nature peeps out. iii, 6] discovers 'Fidele' (Imogen) in the cave, and hospitably welcomes the 'fair youth.' iv, 2] recognizes Cloten as the King's son, and conceals himself, fearing 'an ambush'; is dismayed to learn that Guiderius has slain Cl.; (*sol.*) ponders over the instinct implanted in the 'princely boys'; laments over the supposed death of 'Fidele'; insists that Cl. shall be buried as befits his rank. iv, 4] dreads joining the British forces, lest he should be discovered; but on finding his 'sons' determined to fight, exclaims 'have with you, boys!' v, 2] they come to the rescue of the Britons when hard pressed. (v, 3) Posthumus describes how 'Morgan' and his two sons withstood, in a lane, the attack of the Romans, and by their exceeding valour retrieved the fortunes of the British. v, 5] is knighted after the battle by Cymb.; on the King's condemning Guid. to death for slaying Cl., declares himself to be the banished Belarius; Cymb. in wrath condemns him to death, but he startles the King with the 'blunt and saucy words': 'First pay me for the nursing of thy sons!' and thereupon confesses his crime – to be forgiven by Cymb. and greeted as a brother.

The warlike feat of B. and his sons seems founded on Holinshed's account (ii, 155) of the Battle of Loncarty, A.D. 976, and the repulse of the Danes by 'an husbandman ... named Hale' and his two sons, in a lane, where they stayed the flight of the Scots and turned defeat into victory.

Belch, Sir Toby. D.P. *T. Nt.* 'Uncle to Olivia' (Rowe). i, 3] makes light of Maria's warning that Olivia takes great exceptions to his ill hours; characterizes Aguecheek; presents him to Maria; ironically praises A.'s accomplishments. i, 5] informs Olivia, tipsily, that 'Cesario' is at the gate, ii, 3] carouses with A. and Feste; is chided by Malvolio; approves Maria's device for gulling the steward by 'some obscure epistles.' ii, 5] is a spectator of Mal.'s infatuated conduct on reading the forged letter. iii, 1] invites 'Cesario' to enter Olivia's house. iii, 2] incites A. to challenge 'C.' iii, 4] treats Mal. as one possessed, and suggests putting him in durance; reads A.'s challenge aloud; resolves to convey it to 'Cesario' by word of mouth; expatiates to 'C.' on A.'s 'strength and wrath,' but consents to inquire his cause of quarrel; brings back a report to A. and instils into him abject fear of 'C.'; insists on the duel taking place; considers 'C.' to be 'more of a coward than a hare.' iv, 1] meeting Sebastian, mistakes him for 'C.,' and draws upon him, but is checked by the entrance of Olivia. iv, 2] is present when 'Sir Topas' interviews Mal. in durance, but wishes 'we were well rid of this knavery.' v, 1] having been wounded by Seb., is led in, drunk, by Feste; expresses his scorn for A. (v, 1) it is announced by Feste that Sir T. is married to Maria.

The precise relationship supposed between Sir T. and Olivia is doubtful. Though he speaks of her as 'niece' she never speaks of him as 'uncle,' but 'cousin.' C. Knight suggested that the assumption that Sir T. was an Englishman whose sister had married O.'s father would account for the English name. (But this seems to be actualizing a fictitious character.)

Usually mtd. as 'Sir T.'; but as 'Toby' merely in ii, 5 (3); iv, 1; v, 1.

Belgia, Belgium. 'Where stood B., the Netherlands?' (*Com. Err.* iii, 2); 'Edward from B., With hasty Germans and blunt Hollanders, Hath pass'd ... through the narrow seas' (*3 Hen. VI*, iv, 8).

Bellario. 'A learned doctor' of Padua, and kinsman of Portia. *M.V.* iii, 4; iv, 1.

In iii, 4, 'Mantua' is given for 'Padua,' by an obvious slip, QqFf.

[Bellay, Jean de.] See Bayonne.

Bellona. Roman goddess of war, represented as sister or wife of Mars; mtd. *Hol.* iii, 567. Ross speaks of Macbeth as 'B.'s bridegroom' (*Macb.* i, 2).

Apparently alluded to, *1 Hen. IV*, iv, 1: 'And to the fire-eyed maid of smoky war ... will we offer them.'

Belman, or **Bellman.** Name of a hound; *Tam. Sh.* Ind. 1.

Cf. the hounds of Theseus, 'match'd in mouth like bells' (*M.N.D.* iv, 1).

Belmont. Portia's country-house, on the mainland near Venice. 'Her seat of B.' (*M.V.* i, 1). Mtd., ii, 2; iv, 1; v, l. The following scenes of the play are laid there: i, 2; ii, 1, 7, 9; iii, 2, 4, 5; v, 1.

Belmonte is the name given in *Il Pecorone* to the palace of the lady who is the equivalent of Portia.

Belzebub, or **Beelzebub.** 'The prince of the devils' (Matt. xii, 24). 'He holds B. at the stave's end' (*T. Nt.* v, 1); 'i' the name of B.' (*Macb.* ii, 3); 'as good a gentleman as the devil is, as Lucifer and B. himself' (*Hen. V*, iv, 7).

Benedick. D.P. *M. Ado.* 'A young lord of Padua.' i, 1] (is satirically characterized by Beatrice); on his return from the wars, is mercilessly bantered by her; praises her beauty, but deems her possessed with a fury; vows he will live a bachelor, but Don Pedro predicts that Cupid will make him 'quake for this shortly.' ii, 1] while both are masked, Beat. tells him that 'Signior B.' is 'the Prince's jester: a very dull fool'; later, he takes the imputation to heart; complains bitterly to Don P. that she is 'the infernal Ate in good apparel'; he would rather be commanded any service to the world's end 'than hold three words conference with the harpy.' ii, 3] (*sol.*) 'till all graces be in one woman, one woman shall not come in my grace'; conceals himself, but is observed by Don P. and the others; listens to a prearranged conversation in which Beat.'s supposed passion for him is dilated on; (*sol.*) is convinced by what he has heard, and vows that her love shall be requited; Beat. bids him come in to dinner, with a discourtesy in which he is fain to find 'a double meaning.' (iii, 1) his praises are sung in Beat.'s hearing. iii, 2] admits that he is not as he has been, but attributes the change to a toothache; draws apart with Leonato. (iii, 4) mtd. iv, 1] is present when Hero is falsely accused; is 'attired in wonder,' but believes Don John to be at the bottom of the villainy; Beat., confessing her love for Ben., bids him 'kill Claudio'; he is shocked at the suggestion, but finally consents to challenge him. v, 1] tells Cl. he is a villain, and challenges him; tells Don P. that he must discontinue his company, and declares that 'you have among you killed a sweet and innocent lady.' v, 2] persuades Margaret to summon Beat.; he declares to Beat. that he loves her against his will. v, 4] obtains Leonato's consent to marriage with his niece; after an exchange of banter with Beat., stops her mouth with a kiss; scorns the Prince's jests; proposes 'a dance ere we are married'; advises the Prince to follow his example.

At Beatrice's gibe that he is 'a jester,' he becomes 'perplexed and wounded, he takes counsel with himself as to whether his merry vein had really procured him this title. Pride of intellect is the strong point of his self-love ... it appears in him and becomes excitable and sensitive as soon as he is seriously reproached.' (Gervinus, *Sh. Comm.* (1875), p. 415.)

Benedictus. Humorously for 'Benedick'; *M. Ado*, iii, 4.

In allusion to the thistle, *Carduus Benedicius*, famed for its many virtues by the old herbalists. 'It strengtheneth all the principall parts of the bodie, it sharpeneth both the wit and the memorie, quickeneth all the senses, comforteth the stomach, procureth appetite' (T. Cogan, *The Haven of Health* (1584), xlvi).

Benfield, Robert. Mtd. as 'a principal actor' in F1.

Bennet, or **Benet.** As a forename. 'Sir B. Seely' (*Rich. II*, v, 6).

Bennet, St (St Benedict). Church dedicated to him mtd. 'The bells of St B.' (*T. Nt.* v, 1).

There were several churches dedicated to St B. in Sh.'s days. The allusion is perhaps to St Benet's, Paul's Wharf, opposite the Globe theatre (destroyed in the Great Fire) – or to an old rime now lost.

Bentii. Name of a commander; *All's Well*, iv, 3.

Bentivolii. Italian family. 'Vincentio, come of the B.' (*Tam. Sh.* i, 1).

Benvolio. D.P. *Rom. J.* Nephew to Montague, and friend to Romeo. i, 1] joins in a brawl between the rival factions; fights with Tybalt; explains the cause of the fray to Montague; converses sympathetically with Rom. on the latter's love for Rosaline. i, 2] advises him to go to Capulet's feast. i, 4] with the maskers. i, 5] with R. at Capulet's house. ii, 1] converses with Mercutio about R. ii, 4] converses. iii, 1] tries to check the fight between Merc. and Tyb.; bears out M., wounded; later, announces that M. is dead; describes the fatal fight to the Prince.

Bergamo. City of Northern Italy. 'He is a sailmaker in B.' (*Tam. Sh.* v, 1).

B. being far inland, the trade of sailmaker seems incongruous. The situation of the town between lakes Iseo and Como has been suggested as an explanation.

Bergomask. A dance of buffoons, so called from Bergamo (*q.v.*). 'A B. dance' (*M.N.D.* v, 1); 'But come, your B.' (*ib.* v, 1).

Berkeley (1), formerly Berkley. Town in Gloucestershire, between Bristol and Gloucester; B. Castle as a Norman fortress was founded soon after the Conquest; it was the scene of Edw. II's murder in 1327. York orders his men to be mustered at B., *Rich. II*, ii, 2; Hotspur refers to B. as the place 'where the madcap Duke his uncle kept' (*1 Hen. IV*, i, 3). ('Barkl(e)y,' Ff.)

Berkeley (2). D.P. *Rich. III*. i, 2] *p.m.*; in attendance on 'Lady Anne.' ('Barkley,' Ff.)

'He may be intended for one of the sons of James, 6th Lord B., who were Lancastrians' (French, p. 251).

Berkeley, Thomas, 5th Baron. D.P. *Rich. II*. 'Lord B.' ii, 3] demands, on behalf of the regent York, the cause of Bolingbroke's invasion.

Acc. *Hol.* iii, 498, the meeting of Bolingbroke and the D. of York took place in 'the church that stood without [Berkeley] castle'; Lord B.'s intervention is not mtd., but he was present. *Ob.* 1416, acc. French, p. 32; but acc. Clar. was living in 1417.

Bermoothes. See Bermudas.

Bermudas. Group of islands in the N. Atlantic, named from their discoverer, Juan Bermudez: formerly 'Bermoothes,' following the Spanish pronunciation.

Ariel sent by Prospero 'to fetch dew from the still-vexed Bermoothes' (*Temp*. i, 2).

For the connection of the Bermudas with the sources of the play see Tempest, The. The accounts of them brought back by early voyagers invariably represented them as constantly vexed by tempests. Other 17th-cent. forms are 'Bermoothas,' 'Barmotho,' and 'Burmoothes.'

Bernardo. D.P. *Haml.* An officer. i, 1] relieves Francisco on guard; begins to describe the apparition of the previous night to Horatio, when it comes again; he marks its resemblance to the late King. i, 2] with Hor. when he describes the ghost to Hamlet.

Berry, or **Berri, John, Duke of.** Uncle to Charles VI of France; the prevention by Rich. II of Bolingbroke's marriage to his daughter mtd. *Rich. II*, ii, 1, 1.167; cf. *Hol.* iii, 495. Present at councils of war held by the Dauphin and Charles VI upon the crossing of the Somme by Henry V (*Hol.* iii, 547, 552).

D.P. *Hen. V*. ii, 4] *p.m.* (at the council). (iii, 5) at Agincourt.

Berri, the ancient Biturica, a former government of Central France.

Bertram. D.P. *All's Well*. Count of Rousillon. i, 1] bids farewell to his mother on his departure for Paris to visit the King, to whom he is 'in ward' since his father's death; bids Helena 'be comfortable to my mother, your mistress.' i, 2] is presented to the King, who lauds his father's memory. ii, 1] is told he is too young to go to the wars, but is advised by Parolles to court the society of the other lords. ii, 3] is selected by Hel. as her husband; disdains her for her lowly birth, but yields to the King's command to marry her; later, declares to Par. his determination to send his bride home, and proceed to the wars to escape from his 'detested wife.' ii, 5] assures Lafeu that Par. is a valiant soldier; tells Hel. that ' 'twill be two days ere I see you,' and bids her adieu coldly; after her departure exclaims that he 'will never follow her.' iii, 3] is made general of Florentine horse. iii, 5] *p.m.*; (is pointed out by the Widow Capulet as the gallant Frenchman, who has been importunately wooing her daughter Diana). iii, 6] begins to distrust the valour of Par., who has acted as his messenger to Diana. iv, 2] in an interview with D. she prevails on him to give her the ring he is wearing, and promises him another ring when he visits her; (he visits Hel. by night and takes her for Diana). iv, 3] Hel.'s death is reported; B. remarks, lightly, that among sixteen businesses he has 'buried a wife and mourned for her'; he is present when Par. is brought in blindfolded, and witnesses his final discomfiture. v, 3] is brought before the King and asks pardon for his 'high-repented blames'; declares that the ring upon his finger (which he thinks was given him by Diana), was never Hel.'s; invents, on the spur of the moment, a story of how it had come into his possession at Florence; is suspected of having made away with H. and is taken away in custody; later, is confronted with Diana; declares her 'a common gamester of the camp'; at length admits that she has his 'monumental ring' (iv, 3), and that the ring which he wore on his first entrance was (as he believes) hers; on H.'s entrance he amazedly beseeches pardon, and declares that he will 'love her dearly, ever, ever dearly.'

'Seldom has a task so independent as the character of Bertram been left to the art of the actor; but still more seldom is the actor to be found who knows how to execute it. To Richard Burbage this part must have been a dainty feast.' (Gervinus, *Sh. Comm.* p. 186.) B.'s 'wilful stubbornness and youthful petulance' are noted by Hazlitt.

Berwick. Most northerly town in England; formerly regarded as neutral ground between Eng. and Scotland. The impostor Simpcox (*q.v.*) was born there, and was sentenced to be whipped thither from St Albans (*2 Hen. VI*, ii, 1). Henry is urged. to 'post amain' thither from Towton (*3 Hen. VI*, ii, 5; cf. *Hol.* iii, 665).

Bess. For 'Elizabeth' (Queen of Edw. IV); *3 Hen. VI*, v, 7.

Bessy. Feminine name. 'Come o'er the bourn, Bessy, to me' (*Lear*, iii, 6, song).

Malone points out that 'Bess' and 'Tom' were associates as vagabonds, and quotes *The Court of Conscience* (1607): 'Stowt roge and harlot counterfeited gomme; One calls herself poor *Besse* the other *Tom*.'

Best. 'B.'s son, the tanner of Wingham' (*2 Hen. VI*, iv, 2).

Wingham is a village 6 m. E. of Canterbury.

Best, The. Christ; see Judas Iscariot.

Bevis, George. D.P. *2 Hen. VI*. 'A follower of Jack Cade.' iv, 2] ingeniously predicts the fate of their foes at the hands of 'labouring men.' iv, 7] brings in Lord Say as prisoner.

Bevis of Hampton. A hero of English medieval romance. Among his exploits was the overthrow of a giant, Ascapart, whom he made his squire. 'That former fabulous story … got credit, That Bevis was believed' (*Hen. VIII*, i, 1).

In *2 Hen. VI*, ii, 3, some edrs. have introduced, after 'have at thee with a downright blow,' the words 'As Bevis of Southampton fell on Ascapart,' from the corresponding passage in *The Contention* (*q.v.*).

Bezonian, or **Besonian.** *2 Hen. IV*, v, 3; *2 Hen. VI*, iv, 1; although spelt with a capital, not a proper name.

It. *bisogno*, need; hence a worthless fellow.

Bianca (1). D.P. *Oth.* 'A curtezan' (Ff). iii, 4] chides Cassio for absenting himself; is asked by him to copy the work on a handkerchief which he has found in his chamber. iv, 1] in Othello's sight brings back the handkerchief to C., and in a fit of jealousy refuses to copy it. v, 1] finds C. lying wounded in the street, and admits that he supped with her that night.

There is no corresponding character in Cinthio's tale.

Bianca (2). D.P. *Tam. Sh.* Sister to Katharina and daughter to Baptista. i, 1] is forbidden by her father to receive any suitors until her elder sister is wedded; with apparent meekness retires to her studies. (i, 2) a tutor selected for her. ii, 1] she is bound, and struck, by Kath. iii, 1] is wooed by Lucentio and Hortensio, her pretended tutors. iii, 2] thinks that Kath., 'being mad herself,' is 'madly mated.' iv, 2] is affianced to Luc. (iv, 4) mtd. v, 1] asks pardon from her father for wedding Luc. without his consent. v, 2] (at Luc.'s banquet) refuses to return at her husband's bidding; later, calls Luc. a fool 'for laying on my duty.'

The corresponding character in *The Taming of A Shrew* is Philema, Alfonso's 2nd d., and in *I Suppositi* Polinesta, Damonio's only d.

Bible, The. Mtd. by name only once, viz. as 'Pible' by Sir Hugh Evans, *M.W.W.* ii, 2. See SCRIPTURE, HOLY WRIT, and GOD'S BOOK. The only book of the B. named in *Sh.* is Numbers (*q.v.*).

Direct Biblical references occur under the following headings: ABEL, ABRAHAM, ACHITOPHEL, ADAM, BARRABAS, BASAN, BEL, BELZEBUB, CAIN, CHRIST, DANIEL, DEBORAH, DIVES, EGYPT, EVE, GOLGOTHA, GOLIATH, HAGAR, HEROD, JACOB, JAPHET, JEPHTHAH, JEWRY, JEZEBEL, JOB, JOSHUA, JUDAS ISCARIOT, JUDAS MACCABAEUS, LABAN, LEGION, LEVIATHAN, LUCIFER, NAZARITE, NEBUCHADNEZZAR, NOAH, PHARAOH, PHILIP, PILATE, SAMSON, SATHAN, SHEBA, SOLOMON.

Sh. may have made use of any of the following English versions: the Great B. (1539); the Geneva B. (1560); the Bishops' B. (1568).

Biddy. Doubtfully a proper name (dim. of 'Bridget') in: 'Ay, Biddy, come with me' (*T. Nt.* iii, 4); perhaps a snatch of a song. In Ff 'I biddy,' etc., which may stand for 'I bid ye.'

Bigot, Lord. D.P. *John.* (iv, 2) mtd. iv, 3] with the E.s of Salisbury and Pembroke, discovers the body of Arthur and vows to avenge his death; accuses Hubert of having caused it. v, 2, 4, 7] *p.m.*

In *Tr. R.* (II, 3) variously named 'Earl B.,' 'Lord B.,' and (after *Hol.*) 'Richard, Earl of B.' Roger Bigot, 2nd E. of Norfolk, is perh. meant. In some edns. he is 'Robert B., E. of Norfolk'; but this name is unhistorical.

Billingsgate. Error for 'Basingstoke' (Q) 2 *Hen. IV*, ii, 1, l. 182.

Biondello. D.P. *Tam. Sh.* Servant to Lucentio. i, 1] enters, to find that his master and Tranio have exchanged attire, and is told that the former has killed a man in a quarrel. i, 2] attends the disguised Tr. ii, 1] *p.m.* iii, 2] describes the fantastic guise in which Petruchio is coming to his wedding. iv, 2] reports to Tr. the arrival of a Pedant. iv, 4] informs Luc. that 'the old priest at St Luke's Church' is at his command. v, 1] in attendance on Luc.; later, encounters Vincentio, whom, to his cost, he repudiates; later, flees on observing that Luc. and his father greet one another. v, 2] is sent to summon Bianca and Hortensio's wife, and reports their refusal to appear.

The name means 'fair-haired.' The corresponding character in *The Taming of A Shrew* is Catapie, Polidor's boy, and in *I Suppositi* Caprino, Erostrato's boy.

Birnam. ('Byrnam,' '-an,' '-ane,' Ff.) A hill about 12 m. from Dunsinane. Acc. *Hol*, ii, 174–6 (after Boece), Macbeth was told by 'a certeine witch in whom he had a great trust' that he would prove invincible until the wood of B. came to Dunsinane Castle. Malcolm's forces, resting in the wood, were ordered to conceal themselves with boughs before attacking Dunsinane. The prophecy uttered by an apparition, *Macb.* iv, 1; the stratagem adopted, *ib.* v, 4; mtd., *ib.* v, 2, 3, 5, 7.

A somewhat similar device adopted by the Kentishmen to deceive William the Conqueror is mtd. *Hol.* iii, 2. But the legend of the moving forest is an ancient one. Simrock, *Die Quellen des Shakespeare* (ii, 256, ed. 1870), refers to the story of King Grünewald, besieged in his castle until May-day, when the hostile army is seen approaching with green boughs, and the King's daughter knows that all is lost. This legend may be a myth typifying the vanquishing of the giant Winter by Spring. Halliwell cites from the Thornton MS. (Lincoln Cathedral) an account of a similar device employed by Alexander the Great against Darius. See Furness, *Macb.* p. 379.

Biron. D.P. *L.L.L.* Lord attending upon the King of Navarre. i, 1] demurs to the conditions of the oath of asceticism imposed by the King; declares that his 'study' will be how to evade the vow and argues that for any other purpose study is vain; reminds the King that the Princess of France is coming on an embassy; signs the 'schedule,' but predicts that 'these oaths and laws will prove an idle scorn.' ii, 1] exchanges raillery with the masked ladies attending the Princess. iii, 1] entrusts Costard with a sealed packet for Rosaline; comments (*sol.*) on finding himself Cupid's 'corporal of the field.' iv, 3] soliloquizes on the tyranny of love, and withdraws; observes the entrance of the King, Longaville, and Dumain successively, each of whom reads a love-sonnet, supposing himself alone; B. confronts the three lovers, and upbraids them for their folly, hardily asserting that he alone has kept his oath; Jaquenetta enters and hands the King B.'s letter to Rosaline; B.'s secret is discovered; he confesses all, and breaks into an impassioned eulogy of Ros.; he defends her dark complexion against the sportive disparagement of the others, eloquently maintains that their vow was 'flat treason against the kingly state of youth,' and expatiates on woman's eyes as the true subject of 'study,' and on the might and universality of Love – 'Let us once lose our oaths, to find ourselves ... It is religion to be thus forsworn'; his hearers yield to his arguments. v, 2] visits (with the King and courtiers, in Russian habits) the ladies, who are masked; woos the Princess in mistake for Ros.; on reentering in his proper attire, with the rest, finds that their disguise had been penetrated by the ladies, who banter them mercilessly; B., stung by R.'s raillery, bids her 'bruise me with scorn'; he will henceforth forswear 'taffeta phrases'; declares his love in plain words; discovers the trick by which he had been induced to pay his addresses to the Princess, and upbraids Boyet for his part in the plot; joins in jeering 'The Nine Worthies'; is sentenced by Ros. to spend the year which must elapse before their marriage in visiting hospitals and trying to make 'the pained impotent to smile.'

The name is 'Berowne' in F1, and in iv, 3, rimes with 'moon.' Marshal Biron, an officer of Henry IV of Navarre, at the time *L.L.L.* was written, was well known to Englishmen.

For an analysis of the character see W. Pater, *Appreciations* (1910), pp. 166 ff.

[Bithynia.] See BOHEMIA.

Black-Friars, Monastery of. Situated on the N. bank of the Thames. In the hall of B.-F. Wolsey and Campeggio sat 'to heare the cause of matrimonie betwixt' Henry VIII and Katharine of Arragon (*Hol.* iii, 907; Hall, p. 751).

The King appoints B.-F. as 'the most convenient place' (*Hen. VIII*, ii, 2); 'A hall in B.-F.' (*ib.* ii, 4, st. dir.) (Rowe).

The Blackfriars Theatre, in which toward the end of his life Sh. held a share, stood upon a part of the site of the monastery, and is still commemorated by 'Playhouse Yard,' E.C.

Blackheath. Heath S. of Greenwich. There Jack Cade assembled his forces (the scene of *2 Hen. VI*, iv, 2, 3 is laid there; cf. *Hol.* iii, 632), and there Henry V was met by the Mayor and many citizens of London on his return from Agincourt (*Hen. V*, v, Chor.; cf. *Hol.* iii, 556).

Blackmere, Lord Strange of. One of the titles of John Talbot, 1st E. of Shrewsbury; *1 Hen. VI*, iv, 7.

'The great Talbot was born at Blackmere, which derives its name from one of the three fine lakes in the neighbourhood of Whitechurch' (French, p. 132).

Black Monday. 'My nose fell a-bleeding on B.-M. last' (*M.V.* ii, 5).

Easter Monday was so called since Edw. III lay before Paris (1360), 'which day was full darke of mist and haile and so bitter cold that many men dyed on their horses with cold' (Stow, *Annales*, p. 264). But see Brand's *Pop. Antiq.* ed. Ellis (1813), i, 466 ff., and quot. (1700), *N.E.D.*

Black Prince, The. See EDWARD, PRINCE OF WALES.

[Blamont, Comte de.] See BEAUMONT, EARL OF.

Blanch. Name of a dog; *Lear*, iii, 6.

Blanch of Castile (*ob.* 1254). Niece to King John; d. of Alfonso VIII, King of Castile, and Eleanor, d. of Henry II (cf. *Hol.* iii, 161, 190).

D.P. *John.* ii, 1] lauds the memory of Coeur-de-lion; gives her hand to the Dauphin at her uncle's bidding. iii, 1] laments that on her wedding-day a war should break out, in which 'whoever wins, on that side shall I lose.' (iii, 4) mtd.

Historically, Blanch was betrothed to Lewis on May 23, 1200; she was not present at either of the interviews between John and Philip. From her were descended the royal houses of Valois, Bourbon, and Orleans, as well as Edward III of England. In ii, 1, l. 64, 'niece' has the not unusual sense of 'granddaughter.'

Blithild. A fictitious ancestress of Pepin, King of the Franks. 'Being descended of B., which was daughter to King Clothair' (*Hen. V*, i, 2; cf. *Hol.* iii, 545).

Blois. Medieval countship in France; Richard, Duke of York, laments its loss, *1 Hen. VI*, iv, 3.

Blomer. See BULMER.

Blount, Edward. Stationer; publisher of Chester's *Love's Martyr* (*q.v.*); his name appears on the title-page of the First Folio (1623) as one of its printers, and in the colophon as one of the four at whose 'charges' it was printed.

For a full discussion of E. B.'s activities see R. C. Rhodes, *Shakespeare's First Folio* (1923).

Blount, or Blunt, Sir James. Captain of Hammes Castle; g.g.s. of Sir Walter B. (*q.v.*). Cf. *Hol.* iii, 749.

D.P. *Rich. III.* (iv, 5) joins Richmond. v, 3] addressed as 'good Captain B.,' by Richmond, and sent on a message to Stanley.

Blount, or Blunt, Sir John. Governor of Calais; son of Sir Walter B. (*q.v.*).

D.P. *2 Hen. IV.* (i, 1) falsely reported slain at Shrewsbury with his father. iv, 3] *p.m.*; Coleville is given into his custody.

The name also occurs in the st. dirs. of iii, 1, Q1. Acc. French, p. 84, K.G. 1417 (1413, *D.N.B.*); *ob.* 1418.

Blount, or Blunt, Sir Thomas. Executed at Cirencester for conspiracy against Henry IV 1400 (*Hol.* iii, 514, 516). His execution reported, *Rich. II*, v, 6.

Blount, or Blunt, Sir Walter. One of John of Gaunt's executors; M.P. for Derbyshire; killed at Shrewsbury 1403.

D.P. *1 Hen. IV.* i, 1] brings from the field news of the victory of Homildon. i, 3] suggests to the King that Hotspur's hasty words concerning the prisoners might be overlooked. iii, 2] announces that the rebel forces have met at Shrewsbury. iv, 3] acts as an envoy from the King to the rebels under Hotspur (acc. *Hol.* iii, 523, the Abbot of Shrewsbury and a clerk of the Privy Seal were the envoys). (iv, 4) mtd. v, 1] *p.m.* v, 3] wearing the King's surcoat, is slain in combat by Douglas (cf. *Hol.* iii, 523). (v, 4) mtd.

[Blumer.] See BULMER.

Blunt. See BLOUNT.

[Boar's Head, The.] Famous tavern on the N. side of Eastcheap (*q.v.*), first mentioned in a lease dated 1537. It perished in the Great Fire and was rebuilt, but was finally demolished in 1831. The statue of William IV nearly marks its site.

The inn is not mtd. in the text of *Sh.*, but the scene is assumed to be laid there in *1 Hen. IV*, ii, 4, iii, 3, and *2 Hen. IV*, ii, 4.

Boatswain. D.P. *Temp.* i, 1] brusquely resents the interference of the King and courtiers during the storm. (i, 2) is, with the crew, 'under hatches stow'd.' v, 1] 'brought moping' to Prospero's cell.

Trincalo in Dryden's version.

Bocchus. King of Mauretania; erroneously stated (*Plut.* p. 207) to have sided with Antony, which is true of his brother Bogud (Dion Cass. xlviii, 45).

'Bocchus ['Bochus,' Ff] King of Libya ['Lybia,' Ff]' (*Ant. Cl.* iii, 6).

[Bogud.] See BOCCHUS.

Bohemia. An imaginary locality in which the scene of much of *The Winter's Tale*, and of Greene's *Pandosto* is laid. It possesses 'deserts' and a sea-coast (*Wint. T.* iii, 3), and no attempt is made to identify it with the European country so named, which is nowhere mtd. by Sh.

The following are the references to B. in *Wint. T.*: i, 1 (2); i, 2 (4); iii, 2; iii, 3 (2); iv, Chor.; iv, 2; iv, 3 (3); v, 1 (2). It is used for 'the King of B.' (Polixenes) in i, 1 (2); i, 2 (4); v, 1 (3); v, 2.

Much has been written on Sh.'s supposed geographical blunder, and Hanmer actually changed the name to 'Bithynia' throughout. It has, on the other hand, been argued that certain provinces on the coast of the Adriatic were at one time subject to Bohemia, and that Sh. (or rather, Greene) might have been aware of this. (For Ben Jonson's criticism see MARINER, A.)

Bohemian. (*a*) A native of Bohemia; (*b*) a gipsy, or vagabond, since the gipsies were thought to have come to Western Europe from, or through, Bohemia.

(*a*) Barnardine is 'a Bohemian born; but here nurst up and bred' (*M. for M.* iv, 2). (*b*) Host, ironically, terms Simple 'a Bohemian-Tartar' (*M.W.W.* iv, 5).

Bohun, Edmund. 'When I came hither, I was lord high constable And D. of Buckingham; now, poor Edmund Bohun' (*Hen. VIII*, ii, 1).

An error of Hall-Holinshed (*Hol.* iii, 865), followed by the dramatist. The D. of Buckingham was Edward Stafford (*q.v.*); Eleanor Bohun was an ancestress of his, and 'Edmund' was a known forename in the Stafford family; hence, perh., the mistake.

Bohun, Eleanor de. See GLOUCESTER, DUCHESS OF (1).

Bois. See BOYS.

Boleyn, or **Bullen, Anne.** Dau. of Sir Thos. B. (*q.v.*); a maid-of-honour to Queen Katharine; became mistress of Henry VIII after 1527; made Marchioness of Pembroke 1532, and was secretly married to Henry (*Hol.* iii, 929) 1533, and crowned queen. In the same year she gave birth to a daughter, Elizabeth. In 1536 her marriage was declared invalid, and she was executed.

Wolsey (*Hen. VIII*, 2) declares she was 'a spleeny Lutheran.' The name is spelt in *Hol.* 'Bullonge, 'Bullen,' and in Hall 'Bulleyn.'

D.P. *Hen. VIII.* i, 4] is present at an entertainment given by Wolsey; makes merry with Ld. Sands; on the King's entrance he is struck by her beauty and dances with her. ii, 3] in conversation with 'an old lady' she expresses her pity for Queen Katharine, and declares that she 'would not be a queen for all the world'; is informed by the Lord Ohamberlain that she has been made Marchioness of Pembroke, with an income of 'a thousand pound a year' (*Hol.* iii, 928); seems indifferent to the news. (iii, 2) Wolsey declares that Henry shall not marry her, but is told that 'in secrecy' he married her long ago, and that she is about to be crowned. iv, 1] *p.m.*; passes on her way to her coronation (*Hol.* iii, 933). (v, 1) the birth of her daughter announced.

[**Boleyn, George.**] Viscount Rochford; brother of Anne B.; a bearer of the canopy at the Princess Elizabeth's christening, *Hen. VIII*, v. 5; see NOBLEMEN, FOUR.

Executed for incest and treason 1536.

Boleyn, or **Bullen, Sir Thomas** (1497–1539). Father of Anne Boleyn (*q.v.*). 'Sir Thomas B.'s daughter – The Viscount Rochford' (*Hen. VIII*, i, 4; cf. *Hol.* iii, 908).

Historically, Sir T.B. did not become Viscount R. until 1525, whereas the entertainment described in the scene is supposed to take place before Buckingham's trial (1521).

Bolingbroke. A castle near Spilsby, Lincolnshire, where Henry IV was born, and whence he derived the cognomen by which he is often designated. 'Bolingbroke' alone is by far the commonest form in *Sh.*, and is frequent in *Rich. II*, *1 Hen. IV*, and *2 Hen. IV*. 'Harry B.' occurs *Rich. II*, iii, 3; *2 Hen. IV*, iv, 1. 'Henry B.,' *Rich. II*, iv, 1; *1 Hen. IV*, iii, 1; *2 Hen. VI*, ii, 2; also, ironically, 'King *B.*,' *Rich. II*, iii, 3. The more correct form, 'Henry of B.,' does not occur in *Sh.*

Also 'Bullingbrook,' 'Bullingbroke,' etc.

Bolingbroke, Roger. 'A cunning necromancer (as it was said),' arrested on the charge of conspiring with Eleanor Cobham (*q.v.*) to destroy Hen. VI by witchcraft, and executed at Tyburn (*Hol.* iii, 622–3). Acc. Hardyng, *Chronicle* (ed. 1812, p. 400), the necromancer's name was R. Oonly. (B.-S. p. 262).

D.P. *2 Hen. VI.* (1, 2) sent for by the Dss. of Gloucester. i, 4] attends the Dss. and, with incantations, raises a spirit that prophesies concerning the King and the Dukes of Suffolk and Somerset; is arrested. ii, 3] *p.m.*; sent to execution.

Bona (Bonne), Princess of Savoy. 3rd d. of Lewis, 1st D. of S. Acc. *Hol.* iii, 667, the E. of Warwick was sent to demand her hand on behalf of Edw. IV. The Princess was then at the French Court – her sister having married Lewis XI. The engagement was welcomed by all concerned, but Edw. in the meantime married Lady Grey, and Lewis 'was not well pleased to be thus dallied with.' (The Princess soon afterward married Galeazzo Maria Sforza, D. of Milan.)

D.P., *3 Hen. VI.* iii, 3] Warwick asks Lewis 'to grant That virtuous lady B., thy fair sister, To England's king in lawful marriage'; after hearing Q. Margaret's objections, L. consents; Bona admits that she looks on the proposal with favour; it is suddenly announced, by letter, that Edw. has married Lady Grey; B. longs to be revenged for the slight, and hopes Edw. may 'prove a widower shortly.' Mtd., *ib.* ii, 6, iv, 1(2), 3; *Rich. III*, iii, 7.

Bonville (and **Harington**), **William Bonville, Baron.** His heiress, Cicely, was married to Thomas Grey, Marq. of Dorset, son, by her 1st husb., of Elizabeth (whom Edw. IV made his queen); cf. *Hol.* iii, 668.

'*Clar.* [to K. Edw.]. Or else you would not have bestow'd the heir Of the Lord B. on your new wife's son' (*3 Hen. VI*, iv, 1).

Bonny Robin. Ballad alluded to; *Haml.* iv, 5, l. 187.

Cf. *Two Noble Kinsmen*, ii, 1. For the tune see Chappell's *Pop. Mus. of the Olden Time*, p. 234. 'Jolly Robin,' *T.Nt.* iv, 2, is a different song.

Book of Riddles, The. This book, with which Slender desired to refresh his wits before conversing with Anne Page (*M.W.W.* i, 1), is probably *The Booke of Merry Riddles, together with proper Questions and Witty Proverbs to make pleasant pastime*, etc., of which the edn. of 1629 is the earliest extant, but which is mtd. as early as 1575.

Book of Songs and Sonnets, The. This book, which Slender wishes he had 'rather than forty shillings' (*M.W.W.* i, 1), may well have been *Songes and Sonettes*, first publd. by R. Tottel, 1557, which had passed through eight edns. by 1587 and is now commonly cited as *Tottel's Miscellany*.

Borachio. D.P. *M. Ado.* A follower of Don John. i, 3] tells his master that Don Pedro intends to woo Hero and give her to Claudio. ii, 1] tells Cl. that Don P. is about to marry Hero himself that night. ii, 2] unfolds to Don John his scheme for making Hero appear faithless, and is promised a reward of a thousand ducats. iii, 3] tells Conrade how he has wooed Margaret that night 'by the name of Hero,' and how their 'amiable encounter' was watched by Cl. and others; Conr. and he are arrested by the watch. iv, 2] they are brought before Dogberry and his colleagues, and are sent bound to Leonato. v, 1] confesses that he courted 'Marg. in H.'s garments,' and was 'paid richly for the practice of it,' but exonerates Marg., who 'knew not what she did.'

Borachio, Sp., means a leathern wine-bottle. The fem. 'Borachia' occurs in Massinger's *A Very Woman*. No quite satisfactory explanation of the details of the trick devised by B. (ii, 2) has been given. Theobald's suggested reading of Borachio' for 'Claudio,' l. 45, seems to present the least difficulty.

Bordeaux, or **Bourdeaux.** Ancient commercial port of France on the R. Garonne; it formed part of the Duchy of Aquitaine, and shared its fortunes. The attack on B. by Talbot (*1 Hen. VI*, iv, 2, 5–7) is unhistorical, since the English party in the city opened its gates to him.

Richard II's birthplace, *Rich. II*, v, 6 ('Burdeaux'); 'a merchant's venture of B. stuff' (*2 Hen. IV*, ii, 4); the city summoned to surrender, *1 Hen. VI*. iv, 2 ('Burdeaux'); Talbot's danger at B., *ib.* iv, 3; 'France ... hath attach'd Our merchants' goods at B.' (*Hen. VIII*, i. 1; *cf.* Hall, pp. 632–3; 'Burdeaux,' F1).

The scene in *1 Hen. VI*, iv, 2, 5–7, is laid at or near B.

Boreas. The North Wind. 'Horrifer Boreas' (Ovid, *Metam.* i, 65); 'the ruffian B.' (*Tr. Cr.* i, 3).

Bosworth, or Market Bosworth. Town in Leicestershire, about 12 m. W. of Leicester. On a moor about 2 m. S. of the town was fought the final battle of the Wars of the Roses, in which Rich. III was slain (Aug. 22, 1485), the victorious E. of Richmond being crowned on the field as Hen. VII (*Hol.* iii, 760).

The scene in *Rich. III*, v, 3, 4, 5, is laid at B. Field, but the name is only once mtd. in the text (v, 3).

Bottom, Nick. D.P. *M.N.D.* A. weaver. i, 2] instructs Quince, the stage-manager, in his business; is allotted the part of Pyramus; yet his 'chief humour is for a tyrant'; would speak 'in a monstrous little voice' if allowed to play Thisbe; longs for the lion's part, in which he will roar so that the Duke will say 'let him roar again!' or, if it be preferred, 'as gently as any sucking dove.' iii, 1] at rehearsal, demurs to the use of a sword in the play, and the presence of a lion, as likely to affright the ladies – but devises remedies; overcomes the difficulty of introducing moonshine and a wall; recites the first speech of Pyr. and withdraws; re-enters with an ass's head, magically affixed by Puck; on his friends fleeing in terror, declares that it is 'a knavery of them to make him afeard'; sings to show he is undaunted; Titanic, awaking, declares she loves him; B. thinks she has 'little reason for that,' and wishes he had wit enough to get out of the wood; three attendant fairies are presented to him, whom he aptly addresses. iv, 1] he is caressed by Titania, and sets tasks to his attendants; mentions his taste in music and 'provender'; sleeps in T.'s arms; Puck disenchants him; he awakes, and muses on his strange dream – he will have a ballad written on it, and 'will sing it ... before the Duke.' iv, 2] rejoins his comrades, to their great delight; urges them to hurry on with their preparations for the play. v, 1] performs his part in the interlude, not without setting the Duke right on a point or two of the play.

The name has reference to the trade of a weaver, meaning a skein of thread or yarn (*cf.* 'beat me to death with a bottom of brown thread,' *Tam. Sh.* iv, 3); or, especially, the foundation on which skeins are wound, cf. *T. G. V.* iii, 2, l. 53.

'Bully Bottom, the epitome of all the conceited donkeys that ever strutted or straddled on this stage of the world' (C. Cowden-Clarke, *Sh. Char.* (1863), p. 97). 'As Romeo, the gentleman, is *the* unlucky man of Sh., so here does he exhibit Bottom, the blockhead, as *the* lucky man, as him on whom Fortune showers her favours beyond measure' (W. Maginn, *Sh. Papers* (1860), p. 122).

Bouchier, or **Bourchier, Thomas** (*c.* 1404–86). Successively Bp. of Worcester and Ely, and Abp. of Canterbury (1454); Cardinal 1473; was deputed to persuade the Queen-dowager to entrust her 2nd son Richard to the Protector; officiated at the coronation of Rich. III.

D.P. *Rich. III*. iii, 1] demurs to forcing the young D. of York from sanctuary, but in response to Buckingham's arguments consents to use persuasion; later, returns with York (cf. *Hol.* iii, 717).

B. had been nominated cardinal of St Cyriacus as early as 1464, or 1467. Acc. More, *Hist. of Rich. III*, it was the Abp. of York who undertook the mission to the Queen. See ROTHERHAM, THOMAS.

Bouciqualt, Lord. Jean de Meingre, 'Marshall of France' (*Hol.* iii, 549); present at Agincourt, where he was taken prisoner; 'he after died in England' (*ib.* iii, 555), 'being unable to pay the sum fixed for his ransom' (French, p. 121). Mtd., *Hen. V*, iii, 5; taken prisoner, *ib.* iv, 8.

'Bouciquall,' and 'Bouchiquald,' Ff.

Boult. D.P. *Per.* 'Servant to the Pander.' iv, 3] ordered to 'cry through the market' Marina's beauty. iv, 6] reports her invincible chastity; commends Lysimachus to her.

Bourbon, Admiral. See BOURBON, LEWIS.

Bourbon, John, Duke of. Uncle to Charles VI; succd. his father, Lewis the Good, in 1410. Taken prisoner at Agincourt (*Hol.* iii, 555) and conveyed to England, where he died (1433); buried at Christ-Church, Newgate Street.

D.P. *Hen. V.* iii, 5] declares that if they let the English depart 'unfought,' Frenchmen deserve to be scorned by the women-folk as fit merely to be dancing-masters. iv, 5] (at Agincourt) urges the nobles to follow him and die fighting. (iv, 8) is taken prisoner.

Bourbon, Lewis, Bastard of. Natural son of Charles, Duke of Bourbon, son of the preceding. The French King 'appointed the bastard of Burbon, admerell of France' to convoy 'Margaret and ... hir partakers' (*Hol.* iii, 675).

D.P. *3 Hen. VI*. iii, 3] *p.m.*; ordered, under the title of 'Lord Bourbon, our high admiral,' to 'waft over' the Lancastrians 'with our royal fleet.'

Also known as 'Louis, Comte de Rousillon.'

Boy (1). D.P. *Hen. V.* Attendant on Falstaff. ii, 1] summons Pistol to F., who is 'very ill'; cannot forbear a jest at Bardolph's expense. ii, 3] recalls some of F.'s sayings. iii, 2] (*sol.*) characterizes the 'three swashers,' his new masters. iv, 4] interprets between 'M. le Fer' and Pistol; deems the latter an even greater coward than his late comrades. (iv, 7) is left to guard the baggage, and is slain by the French.

Probably intended to be identical with the Page (*q.v.*) of *2 Hen. IV.*

Boy (2). D.P. *M. Ado.* ii, 3] sent on an errand by Benedick.

Boyet. D.P. *L.L.L.* A lord attending upon the Princess of France. ii, 1] reminds her of the importance of her embassy; is sent to inquire the King of Navarre's wishes; reports the King's approach; tells the courtiers the names of the masked ladies; gives reasons for believing the King to be enamoured of the Pss. iv, 1] at the Pss.'s command reads the love-letter written by Armado to Jaquenetta; exchanges raillery with Rosaline. v, 2] tells the Pss. that the King and his courtiers are about to visit her, in disguise; on their departure suggests that the ladies should change the favours by which they were distinguished when masked.

Where 'Boyet' ends a line (v, 2, l. 333) it rimes with 'debt.'

Boys, Sir Rowland de. (F1; 'Boyes,' F2, 3, 4; 'Bois,' Steevens.) '*Orl.* I am the youngest son of Sir R. de B.' (*A.Y.L.* i, 1; *ib.* i, 2).

'There were four generations in succession of lords of the manor of Weston-in-Arden, each of whom is called Sir Ernald de Bosco, or de Boys' (French, p. 316).

Brabant. A former duchy of the Netherlands, comprising the modern N. Brabant (Holland), with Antwerp and Brabant (Belgium). 'Did I not dance with you in Br. once?' (*L.L.L.* ii, 1).

Brabant, Antony, Duke of. D.P. *Hen. V.* ii, 4] *p.m.*; sent with other nobles to oppose the English invaders. iii, 5] *p.m.*; among the nobles addressed by Charles VI before Agincourt. (iv, 8) 'Anthony, D. of Br., The brother to the D. of Burgundy', among the slain. (Cf. *Hol.* iii, 555.)

Brabantio. D.P. *Oth.* A Venetian Senator, father to Desdemona. i, 1] is aroused at night by Iago and Roderigo; at first supposes that the disturbance is due to R.'s importunate courtship of Des., but on learning that she has fled from home sets out in pursuit of her with his servants. i, 2] meets Othello in the street, accuses him of having bewitched D., and hearing that the Duke is in council commands the Moor to be taken before him. i, 3] confronts O., before the Duke, and denounces him; asseverates that Desd. has been influenced by magical drugs, but, on her declaring that she is wedded to O. of her own free will, grudgingly bows to the inevitable; declines to receive Desd. during her husband's absence; warns O. that she may deceive him as she has deceived her father. (v, 2) his death, from grief, mtd.

Brabbler. Name of a dog. Thersites declares that Diomedes will but 'spend his mouth, and promise, like B. the hound' (*Tr. Cr.* v, 1).

A brabbler, or babbler, is a hound that gives tongue without having scent of the hare; cf. *Sh. Eng.* ii, 348.

Brackenbury. See BRAKENBURY.

Bracy, Sir John. '*Fal.* [to P. Henry]. Here was Sir J. B. from your father; you must to the court' (*1 Hen. IV*, ii, 4).

Not mtd. in *Hol.*, but the name is that of a former Worcestershire family; *cf.* French, p. 76. 'Braby' acc. Q4, 5, 6 Ff.

Brainford. See BRENTFORD.

Brakenbury, or **Brackenbury, Sir Robert** (*ob.* 1485). Constable of the Tower; refused to put the two Princes to death, but handed the keys to Sir James Tyrrel (*Hol.* iii, 734–5). Acc. Rymer, *Foed.* xii, 219, Sir R. B. was not Const. till 1483.

D.P. *Rich. III.* 'Sir R. B., Lieutenant of the Tower.' i, 1] has Clarence in his custody, and begs Gloucester to 'forbear his conference' with the Duke. i, 4] listens to C.'s narration of his dream; delivers Cl. into the hands of 'two murderers' on the royal warrant, and 'will not reason what is meant hereby.' iv, 1] by the King's orders refuses to allow Q. Elizabeth and other ladies to visit the Princes confined in the Tower. (v, 5) killed at Bosworth (*Hol.* iii, 759).

'Brokenbury,' Qq. In Ff Cl. relates his dream (i, 4) to 'a keeper,' B. not entering until Cl. sleeps. Cf. *N.S.S.Tr.*, 1875–6, pp. 69–70, where the matter is discussed by J. Spedding. In iv, 1, 'Lt.' for 'Br.,' QqFf.

Bramham Moor, Battle of. This defeat of Northumberland by the Sheriff of Yorkshire took place in 1408, but in *2 Hen. IV*, iv, 4, is, by implication, dated 1413.

Brandon. D.P. *Hen. VIII.* i, 1] with a Sergeant-at-arms arrests Buckingham and Abergavenny.

Acc. *Hol.* iii, 863, Sir Henry Marney made the arrest; Capell accordingly substituted his name. Perh. Sir Thos. B., Master of the King's Horse (*Hol.* iii, 801). (B.-S. p. 430 *n.*)

Brandon, Charles (*ob.* 1545). Created, by Hen. VIII, D. of Suffolk 1514; m. secretly Henry's sister, Mary (though his wife was living), by permission of the Pope; present at the Field of the Cloth of Gold; supported H.'s efforts to obtain divorce from Katharine of Arragon; made Steward of the royal household. The Duke presided over the commission of subsidies in Suffolk referred to, *Hen. VIII*, i, 2 (*Hol.* iii, 891); one of those deputed to demand the Great Seal from Wolsey (*Hol.* iii, 909).

D.P. *Hen. VIII.* 'Duke of Suffolk'; in attendance on Q. Katharine. i, 2] *p.m.* ii, 2] discusses the King's projected divorce, and Wolsey's arrogance; Suffolk 'neither loves nor fears' him; S. is denied an audience of the King. iii, 2] relates that Wolsey's letters to the Pope have fallen into the King's hands; states charges against W., and pronounces the King's pleasure. iv, 1] acts as High Steward at the coronation of Anne Boleyn (cf. *Hol.* iii, 933, 'for that daie'). v, 1] (plays primero with the King); is addressed by him as 'Charles.' v, 3] is present at the council when Cranmer is examined; recognizes the King's ring, and fears that they have set a 'dangerous stone a-rolling.' v, 5] at the christening of Elizabeth.

Brandon, Sir William. Father of Charles B., 1st D. of Suffolk; acc. *Hol.* iii, 759, he was slain by Rich. III at Bosworth, but a petition presented by B. in 1485 shows that this was not the case (*Rotuli Parl.* vi, 291), and Polydore Vergil (p. 563) merely states that Richard 'overthrew' the standard-bearer.

D.P. *Rich. III.* v, 3] *p.m.*; is ordered to bear Richmond's standard at Bosworth. (v, 5) reported killed (*cf.* B.-S. p. 419 *n.*).

Brecknock, Brecon. Town (and county) of S. Wales. Henry Stafford, D. of Buckingham, was lord of B., and Morton, Bp. of Ely, was committed to his custody there (*Hol.* iii, 736), where 'Ely Tower' still commemorates the fact.

'*Buck.* Let me ... be gone to B. while my fearful head is on!' (*Rich. III*, iv, 2).

Brentford. County town of Middlesex. '*Mrs Ford.* My maid's aunt, the fat woman of B.' (*M.W.W.* iv, 2); 'the wise woman of B.' (*ib.* iv, 5); 'the witch of B.' (*ib. ib.*). See GILLIAN.

Also 'Brainford' (QqFf) and 'Breyntford.'

Bretagne (1). Brittany (*q.v.*). 'Made his course again for B.' (*Rich. III*, iv, 4); 'long kept at B. at our mother's cost' (*ib.* v, 3). See also BRETAGNE, DUKES OF.

Variously spelt 'Brittaine,' 'Britain(e),' 'Britaigne,' etc.

Bretagne (2). (A) Breton (*q.v.*).

Bretagne, [Francis I], Duke of. Mtd. as present at Margaret of Anjou's espousals; *2 Hen. VI*, i, 1 (*Hol.* iii, 625).

[Bretagne, Francis II, Duke of.] His reception of the Earls of Richmond and Pembroke alluded to. *3 Hen. VI*, iv, 6; *Rich. III*, v, 3 (*Hol.* iii, 756).

Bretagne, [John V], Duke of. '[Bolingbroke] Furnished by the D. of Br. With eight tall ships' (*Rich. II*, ii, 1; cf. *Hol.* iii, 497).

Bretagne, [John VI], Duke of. At the council of war before Agincourt; *Hen. V*, ii, 4 (cf. *Hol.* iii, 552).

Breton. A native of Brittany (*q.v.*). Richard calls Richmond 'the Breton' from his having taken refuge in Brittany, *Rich. III*, iv, 3; 'a scum of Bretons' (*ib.* v, 3); 'these bastard Bretons' (*ib. ib.*). Also, attributively, 'the Br. navy is dispersed' (*ib.* iv, 4).

Variously spelt, in Qq and Ff, 'Brittaine,' 'Britain(e),' 'Brittain,' 'Britain,' and by certain late edrs., erroneously, 'Briton.'

Briarens. Son of Uranus and Gaea; a monster with a hundred arms (Hom. *Il.* i, 402), who secured victory for Zeus against the Titans. 'Centumgeminus Briareus' (Virg. *Aen.* vi, 287); 'him with the hundred hands' (Chapman, *Il.* i).

'He [Ajax] is a gouty Br., many hands and no use' (*Tr. Cr.* i, 2). 'Proud B,' (*Tr. R.* I, 4).

[Bridewell.] So called from the Well of St Bride, or St Bridget; a former royal palace, given to the Corporation of London as a workhouse, 1553, and afterward converted into a prison; not mtd. in *Sh.*, but the probable scene of the historical events described in *Hen. VIII*, i, 1, 2, 3, and iii; 'The Palace.'

Wolsey was ordered to 'repair unto the queen at Bridewell.' Accordingly, accompanied, as commanded, by Card. Campeius, he went 'unto B., directly to the queen's lodging' (Cavendish, *Life of Card. Wolsey*, edn. 2, pp. 225–7).

The name came to be used as a common noun, meaning a house of correction. The prison of B. was demolished in 1864.

Bridget. Fem. name, after a Celtic saint. 'When Mistress B. lost the handle of her fan' (*M.W.W.* ii, 2); 'Does B. paint still?' (*M. for M.* iii, 2); servant, mtd. *Com. Err.* iii, 1.

Bridgnorth. Town in Salop. Mtd. as the rendezvous of the royal forces before the Battle of Shrewsbury, *1 Hen. IV*, iii, 2 (2).

Bristol, City of. ('Bristow,' Ff.) Richard's adherents seek refuge in B. Castle, *Rich. II*, ii, 2; Bolingbroke proceeds thither, *ib.* ii, 3; the refugees surrender, and 'all of them at B. lost their heads' (*ib.* iii, 2; cf. *Hol.* iii, 498). The Abp. of York 'bears hard his brother's death at B.' (*1 Hen. IV*, i, 3); Rich., D. of York, prepares to sail thence for Ireland, *2 Hen. VI*, iii, 1.

Acc. Halliwell, the scene of *John*, v, 1, is laid at B.

Britain (1). Great Britain, or (in Arthurian romance) Brittany. 'They made B. India' (*Hen. VIII*, i, 1); 'Guinever of B.' (*L.L.L.* iv, 1). Frequently in *Cymb.*; 'our not-fearing B.' (ii, 4); 'B. is a world by itself' (iii, 1); mtd., i, 5, 7, ii, 4 (3), iii, 1 (3), 3, 4 (2), 5, v, 1, 2, 3, 4 (2), 5 (5).

Britain (2). For 'Briton' (*q.v.*).

British. 'B. crown' (*Cymb.* iii, 5); 'B. ensign' (*ib.* v, 5); 'I smell the blood of a B. man' (*Lear*, iii, 4); 'B. powers' (*ib.* iv, 4); 'B. party' (*ib.* iv, 6, Qq). See ENGLISH.

[Britomartis.] See DICTYNNA.

Briton. Native of Great Britain. Substituted by Theobald for 'Britain(e),' which is the sole form used in Ff, and occurs only in *Cymb.* i, 5, 7; iii, 1 (2), 5, 7; iv, 2, 4 (2); v, 3 (5), 5 (3). See BRETON.

Brittany, or **Britanny.** *Fr.* Bretagne (*q.v.*); the N.W. portion of France. 'A bay in B.' (*Rich. II*, ii, 1); 'to B. I'll cross the sea' (*3 Hen. VI*, ii, 6); 'we'll send him hence to B.' (*ib.* iv, 6); 'he shall to B.' (*ib. ib.*); 'Hoised sail and made away for B.' (*Rich. III*, iv, 4, l. 529; 'Brittaine,' QqFf).

In the above instances a trisyllable is metrically needed. In *Cymb.* i, 5, Ff also have 'Britanie (-y).'

Brittany, Duchess of. See CONSTANCE.

Brocas, Sir Bernard. Master of the Buckhounds to Rich. II; executed for conspiracy against Hen. IV 1400. ('Sir Leonard B.,' acc. *Hol.* iii, 516.)

His head sent to London, *Rich. II*, v, 6 ('Broccas,' QqFf).

Not to be confused with his father, of the same name (*ob.* 1395), who was Constable of Aquitaine and Chamberlain to Anne of Bohemia, Richard's queen (French, p. 52).

Brook, Master. Name assumed by Ford, *M.W.W.* (Qq; restored to the text by Pope); acc. Ff 'Broome,' which remained the stage-name for a century after Sh. See Johnson, *Lives of the Poets* (Life of Fenton).

'Tell him my name is Br.' (*M.W.W.* ii, 1); 'such Brooks are welcome to me that o'erflow such liquor' (*ib.* ii, 2); mtd., *ib.* iii, 5, iv, 4, v, 1, 5.

It is a suggestive fact that it was Henry Brooke, Lord Cobham, who objected to the use of his ancestor's name 'Oldcastle' (for 'Falstaff'), and his sensitiveness may have been deferred to in this instance also.

Brooke, Edward. Baron Cobham; summoned to Parliament as Lord C. of Kent 1445–60. Referred to as a 'speciall freend' of Rich., D. of York (*Hol.* iii, 637); and as joining a Yorkist force 1460 (*ib.* iii, 653).

'Lord C., with whom the Kentishmen will willingly rise' (*3 Hen. VI*, i, 2; rep.).

Brothers, Two, to Posthumus Leonatus. Appear to him in a vision; *Cymb.* v, 4. See LEONATUS.

Brownists. Members of a nonconformist sect founded by Robt. Browne *c.* 1550–1633. They aimed at a democratic form of Church Government without a distinct priesthood, and may be regarded as forerunners of the Independents. Many were banished, and emigrated to New England.

'I had as lief be a B. as a politician' (*T. Nt.* iii, 2).

Satirical allusions to the sect are not infrequent in contemporary literature. Browne himself seems to have been of a somewhat quarrelsome disposition, and boasted of having been imprisoned in thirty-two different jails.

[**Bruce, David.**] David II (1324–71), K. of Scotland; taken prisoner at Neville's Cross (Oct. 17, 1346) by the English under Philippa. He is represented in the anonymous play of *Edward III* (iv, 2) as having been taken to France by his captor, and handed over to the King; this unhistorical statement is reproduced, *Hen. V*, i, 2: 'the King of Scots; whom she did send to France,' etc.

Brundusium. Sea-port in Calabria. Used by Octavius as a harbour for his fleet before the Battle of Actium, *Ant. Cl.* iii, 7; cf. *Plut.* p. 208.

Brutus, Decius. In error for 'Decimus (Junius) Brutus (Albinus).' In this Sh. follows North's *Plutarch*, which in turn follows the 1st edn. of Amyot's transln. (corrected in 2nd edn.). Plutarch relates (p. 98) that Caesar had made him 'his next heir' and yet he 'was of the conspiracy.'

D.P. *Jul. C.* i, 2] *p.m.* (i, 3) mtd. among the conspirators. ii, 1] undertakes to bring Caes. to the Capitol. ii, 2] on finding that Caes. is unwilling to leave his home, in consequence of Calpurnia's dream, interprets it in a favourable sense, and informs Caes. that the Senate are resolved to offer him a crown (*Plut.* p. 98). (ii, 3) Artemidorus writes: 'D.B. loves thee not.' iii, 1] baffles Artem.; takes part in the murder; shakes hands with Antony. (iii, 3) the citizens resolve to burn his house.

Brutus, L. Junius (1). Roused the Romans to expel the Tarquins after the outraged Lucretia had stabbed herself. 'The ancient Romans made his statue of brass to be set up in the Capitol, with the images of the kings ... because he had valiantly put down the Tarquins from the kingdom of Rome' (*Plut.* p. 105). The story ran that he feigned idiocy to escape death at the hands of Tarquinius Superbus. 'As ... Lord Junius Brutus sware for Lucrece rape' (*T. And.* iv, 1); 'set this up with wax Upon old Brutus' statue' (*Jul. C.* i, 3); 'the outside of the Roman B., Covering discretion with a coat of folly' (*Hen. V*, ii, 4).

In *Lucr.* B. is described as plucking 'the knife from Lucrece' side,' throwing off his mask of folly, and vowing to 'revenge the death of this true wife' (ll. 1734, 1807–57).

Brutus, L. Junius (2). Acc. Plutarch (following Dionysius), a leader of the plebeians in their secession to Mons Sacer and chosen one of the first tribunes of the plebs; cf. *Plut.* p. 6.

D.P. *Cor.* 'Junius Brutus, a tribune of the people.' i, 1] (one of five tribunes); converses with Sicinius on Marcius' arrogance, and imputes a motive to him in serving under Cominius. ii, 1] receives Menenius' rebukes without impatience; later, inveighs against Marcius' pride. ii, 2] is present when Coriolanus is proposed as consul. ii, 3] chides the plebeians for not making their voices heard, and stirs them up to mutiny. iii, 1] has Cor. arrested, and orders him to be borne to the Tarpeian rock; he and his associates are driven off, but later they re-enter, 'with the rabble,' and he proposes to 'pursue him to his house.' iii, 3] instructs Sic. how to accuse Cor. iv, 2] seeks to evade Volumnia's reproaches. iv, 6] orders the bearer of ill news to be whipped; is dismayed to hear of the Volscian invasion under Cor. v, 1] urges Menenius to seek mercy for Rome from Cor.

Brutus, Marcus Junius. Joined Pompey on the breaking out of the Civil War, 49 B.C.; was pardoned and taken into favour by Jul. Caes. after the Battle of Pharsalia, 48 B.C.; was advanced to high honours, but was persuaded by Cassius to murder his benefactor, with the idea of re-establishing the republic. Joining Cassius, their united forces were opposed to those of Antony and Octavius. Two battles were fought near Philippi (*q.v.*), in the latter of which B. was defeated and killed himself.

Plutarch's narrative is closely followed by Sh.

D.P. *Jul. C.* i, 2] admits to Cass. that his mind is troubled; fears, from the shouting, that 'the people choose Caes. for their king'; is warned against the aim of Caesar's ambition, and promises to consider this weighty matter; learns from Casca what had occurred in the Forum; will confer with Cass. on the morrow; (Cass. resolves to throw in at B.'s windows 'writings all tending to the great opinion that Rome holds of his name'). (i, 3) Cass. believes 'three parts of him are ours already.' ii, 1] (*sol.*) although he has 'no personal cause to spurn at' Caes. 'it must be by his death'; finds a letter urging him to act; confers with the conspirators, and enters into the plot; refuses to reveal his secret to his wife; persuades C. Ligarius to conspire. ii, 2] is welcomed, with the other conspirators, by Caes. (ii, 3) Artemidorus would warn Caes. to beware of him. (ii, 4) Portia's anxiety for him. iii, 1] kisses Caesar's hand; is one of those that stab Caes., who, crying 'Et tu, Brute!' expires; seeks to allay the fears of the bystanders; bids Antony have no fear, seeing that the deed had been done in pity for Rome. iii, 2] speaking in the Forum, explains to the populace the reasons why Caes. suffered death; gives Ant. formal permission to make a funeral oration; (Br. is reported to have fled from Rome). (iii, 3) the mob proceed to burn his house. (iv, 1) is reported to be 'levying powers.' iv, 2] learns that Cass. has grievances against him; proposes a private conference with him. iv, 3] the two leaders quarrel, but are reconciled; Br. announces that Portia is dead; discusses the military situation and decides to meet the foe at Philippi; is visited by the ghost of Caes. v, 1] replies to Octavius' defiance; bids Cass. farewell before the battle. v, 2] orders an attack on Oct.'s wing. v, 3] finds Cass. dead; urges a renewal of the fight. v, 4] falsely reported a prisoner. v, 5] puts an end to his life; is eulogized by Ant. as 'the noblest Roman of them all.'

In 2 *Hen. VI*, iv, 1, Brutus is spoken of as Jul. C.'s bastard. This is based on a passage in *Plut.* p. 108, to the effect that Servilia, B.'s mother, was alleged to have been a mistress of Caesar's, so that the latter 'persuaded himself that he begat him.'

In *Ant. Cl.* ii, 6, the apparition of Caes. to Br. is mtd., and the latter is styled 'all-honoured, honest Roman Br.'; Antony's lament over him, *ib.* iii, 2; Ant. styles him 'mad B.' (*ib.* iii, 11).

Polonius, *Haml.* iii, 2, recalls having once played Caes.. 'I was killed i' the Capitol; Br. killed me'; 'Br.'s Portia' (*M. V.* i, 1).

Bryan, George. Mtd. as a 'principal actor' in F1.

Buckingham, County of. 'In B., Northampton and in Leicestershire' (*3 Hen. VI*, iv, 8).

Buckingham, Duke of (1). D.P. 2 *Hen. VI*, See STAFFORD, HUMPHREY.

Buckingham, Duke of (2). D.P. *Rich. III.* See STAFFORD, HENRY.

Buckingham Duke of (3). D.P. *Hen. VIII.* See STAFFORD, EDWARD.

Bucklersbury. Street leading out of Cheapside, consisting in Sh.'s time almost wholly of druggists' and herbalists' shops. Stow, in 1598, writes: 'the Peperers and Grocers of Sopers lane are now in Bucklesberrie, and other places dispersed.' John Sadler, who came to London later than Sh., and Rich. Quiney, both connections of Sh., sold drugs and groceries there. Cf. *Sh. Eng.* ii, 178.

'And smell like B. in simple time ' (*M.W.W.* iii, 3).

Bull, The. Sign of the zodiac. See TAURUS (1).

Bullcalf, Peter. D.P. *2 Hen. IV.* iii, 2] is taken as a recruit by Falstaff, but purchases his release. (Cf. *1 Hen. IV*, ii, 4, for the 'roaring' of a bull-calf.)

[**Bullen.**] See BOLEYN.

Bulmer, Sir William. Mtd. as having been retained by the D. of Buckingham after having been sworn servant to the King (*Hen. VIII*, i, 2; cf. *Hol.* iii, 855; Hall, p. 599).

'Blumer,' Ff; changed to 'Blomer' by Pope. The name appears as 'Bowmere,' *Lett. and Papers, Henry VIII*, iii, 494 (Wright).

Bunch of Grapes. Name of a room in a tavern; *M. for M.* ii, 1.

Burbage, Richard (*c.* 1567–1619). Mtd. (as 'Richard Burbadge') in 'The Names of the Principall Actors' pfxd. to F1. A famous tragedian; he impersonated Rich. III, Hamlet, Lear, and Othello.

[**Burbank, William.**] See PACE, RICHARD.

[**Burdet.**] See CROWN, THE.

Burgundy. A duchy of France. Mtd. *3 Hen. VI*, iv, 6; mtd., *Rich. III*, i, 4; 'milk of B.' (*Lear*, i, 1); 'waterish B.' (*ib. ib*). (Often 'Burgonie,' Ff.)

Burgundy, Duchess of. Mtd. as Edward's 'kind aunt,' *3 Hen. VI*, ii, 1 (unhistorical; the Dss. of B. of that date was only his distant connection).

Burgundy, Duke of (1). Fictitious. D.P. *Lear.* i, 1] declines to wed Cordelia when deprived of her dowry.

There is no corresponding character in *Leir*.

Burgundy, Duke of (2). Charles 'the Bold' (1467–77); son of D. Philip. Mtd. *3 Hen. VI*, iv, 6.

Burgundy, Duke of (3). John 'the Fearless' (1404–19); murdered at the bridge of Montereau at the instigation of Charles the Dauphin.

D.P. *Hen. V.* iii, 5] (at council of war) *p.m.*

Burgundy, Duke of (4). Philip 'the Good' (1419–67); son of D. John ('Count de Charolois' before his succession); his sister married the D. of Bedford; he was not present at Agincourt. Until 1435 Ph. was in alliance with England, and he became regent of France in 1429 – the 'fair persuasions' of Joan of Arc (*1 Hen. VI*, iii, 3) being unhistorical.

D.P. *Hen. V.* iii, 5] ('Charolois') *p.m.* (iv, 8) mtd. v, 2] (at Troyes) takes pride in having brought the Kings of England and France together, and pleads for peace to heal the wounds of France; later, jests with Henry on his wooing of Katharine; his peace proposals are agreed to (cf. *Hol.* iii, 569).

'Burgogne' in v, 2, F1.

D.P. *1 Hen. VI.* ii, 1] (before Orleans) with Talbot (*q.v.*), is addressed as 'Lord Regent'; inquires as to the Maid. ii, 2] within the town. iii, 2] (before Rouen) vows to enter the town or die; lauds Talbot for his gallant deeds. iii, 3] is 'vanquish'd' by the Maid's 'sugar'd' words, and throws in his lot with the French. iv, 7] pays respect to the bodies of Talbot and his son. v, 2] trusts that 'the ghost of Talbot' is not in the field. Mtd., iv, 1 (3), 4, 6.

Acc. Barante, Joan's appeal was made by letter.

Burton. On the Trent, Staffs. Mtd. by Hotspur in discussing the proposed partition of the kingdom with his two confederates, *1 Hen. IV*, iii, 1.

Burton Heath. 'Am not I Christopher Sly, old Sly's son of B.H.?' (*Tam. Sh.* Ind. 2).

Probably Barton-on-the-Heath, near Stratford. Sh.'s aunt, Joan Arden, married Edmund Lambert of B.; *cf.* French, p. 467, and Lee, p. 236.

Bury, Bury St Edmunds. See ST EDMUNDSBURY.

Bushy, Sir John. Speaker of the House of Commons 1394, etc.; appointed in 1398 as one of the 18 commissioners invested with the full powers of a parliament. He was one of Rich. II's chief favourites, and of him Holinshed (iii, 490) writes: 'Accompted to be an exceeding cruell man, ambitious, and covetous beyond measure.' He flattered the King with 'such strange names as were rather agreeable to the divine majestie of God, than to any earthlie potentate.' B. acted as spokesman and secretary of the King and Council in the proceedings with regard to Mowbray and Bolingbroke (*Hol.* iii, 494), and was believed to be one of those to whom the King had 'farmed' the realm (*ib.* iii, 496). Fearing the hostility of the Commons, after Bolingbroke's landing he rashly joined his friends at Bristol, where they were all seized, found guilty of treason, and executed, 1399 (*Hol.* iii, 498).

D.P. *Rich. II.* i, 4] brings Richard news of Gaunt's last illness. ii, 1] *p.m.*; is sent to summon the E. of Wiltshire. ii, 2] tries to console the Queen in her grief at Richard's departure; confers with Green and Bagot on their desperate straits; resolves to escape to Ireland. (ii, 3) reported at Bristol. iii, 1] (at Bristol) is condemned to death by Boling broke. (iii, 2) his execution announced (iii, 4) mtd.

Recorded in *D.N.B.* as Sir John Bussy.

Butler. Groom to Hotspur; mtd. *1 Hen. IV* ii, 3 (2).

[**Butler, James.**] See WILTSHIRE, EARL OF.

Butts, Sir William (*ob.* 1545). Physician to Hen. VIII and his Court. A firm friend to Cranmer and the Reformation, and highly regarded by the King for his professional skill.

D.P. *Hen. VIII.* v, 2] points out to the King that Cranmer is being insulted by prolonged exclusion from the council-chamber. *Cf.* Foxe, ii, 1759, where he is named 'Dr Buttes.'

B.'s portrait is prominent in the group of medical men, painted by Holbein, now preserved in the Barber-Surgeons' Court Room, Monkwell Street, E.C.

Byzantium. Constantinople (*q.v.*). Mtd. *Plut.* p. 123. '*Alcibiades* [pleading for his friend]. His service done At Lacedaemon and B. Were a sufficient briber for his life' (*Timon*, iii, 5).

The Athenians, led by Alcibiades, captured Byzantium 408 B.C.

C

C. Letter of the alphabet. 'These be her very C's' (*T. Nt.* ii, 5; rep.).

Cade, John (*ob.* 1450). The following is a synopsis of Holinshed's account of the rebel leader: 'A certain young man, of a goodly stature and right pregnant of wit' was enticed to assume the name of John Mortimer, cousin of the D. of York, though his name was John Cade (or Mend-all, an Irishman acc. the *Polychronicon*). His forces in a skirmish at Sevenoaks defeated a force under Sir Humphrey and Sir William Stafford and slew both these knights (June 18, 1450) – Cade then attiring himself in Sir Humphrey's brigandine; soon afterward Cade, encamping himself on Blackheath, demanded a conference of Henry VI, but the King fled to Kenilworth and left Lord Scales in command of the Tower; whereupon Cade entered Southwark, and made the White Hart his headquarters. The Mayor and citizens of London resolved to resist the rebels, but on July 2 Cade entered the city, and striking his sword on London Stone exclaimed 'Now is Mortimer Lord of this city!' Those of his old acquaintances who did not acknowledge his usurped surname he executed. In a fight on London Bridge Matthew Gough (*q.v.*), leader of the citizens, was slain, and on July 4 Lord Say and Sir James Cromer (*q.v.*) were executed by Cade's orders. After heavy fighting and losses on both sides the rebels were discouraged and soon afterward dispersed. Cade first 'fled into the wood country beside Lewes,' and then wandered about in disguise until 'one Alexander Iden [*q.v.*], esquire of Kent, found him in a garden, and there in his defence manfully slew the caitiff Cade and brought his dead body to London, whose head was set on London Bridge.'

It is to be observed, however, that several picturesque touches in the dramatist's picture of the rebellion are derived from Holinshed's record of the villeins' revolt in 1381, Among these details are: (*a*) the proposal to kill the lawyers (2 *Hen. VI*, iv, 2; cf. *Hol.* iii, 430–2); (*b*) the case of the Clerk of Chatham (*ib. ib.*; cf. *Hol.* iii, 436); (*c*) the destruction of the Savoy, etc. (*ib.* iv, 7; cf. *Hol.* iii, 431); (*d*) the destruction of the records (*ib. ib.*; cf. *Hol.* iii, 430).

D.P. 2 *Hen. VI.* (iii, 1) York has 'seduc'd a headstrong Kentishman, John Cade of Ashford, To make commotion, as full well he can, Under the title of John Mortimer'; Cade's marvellous prowess in Ireland is described, and his striking likeness, 'in face, in gait, in speech,' to John Mortimer is insisted on. iv, 2] Cade expounds his parentage to his followers, makes lavish promises, condemns the Clerk of Chatham, and knights himself. iv, 3] exclaims, 'This monument of the victory will I bear' (Humphrey Stafford's brigandine, acc. *Hol.* iii, 634). (iv, 4) Henry wishes to parley with him; Cade 'hath gotten London Bridge.' (iv, 5) mtd. iv, 6] strikes his staff on London Stone, iv, 7] orders the records to be burnt; condemns Lord Say and Sir James Cromer to death. iv, 8] his forces are dispersed by Buckingham and Clifford, and he takes to flight. iv, 10] is slain by Iden. (v, 1) his head is brought to Henry.

In *F.P.C.* iv, 2, Cade is termed 'the Diar of Ashford.' He strikes his sword, and not his staff, on London Stone. The actual circumstances of Cade's death are thus described by Ramsay (*Lanc. and York*, ii, 132); 'Eden, the new sheriff of Kent, rode after him and captured him by the roadside at Heathfield, after a scuffle in which C. was mortally wounded (12th July). He died in the cart as he was being brought to London.'

Cadmus. Son of Agenor. '*Hip.* I was with Hercules and C. once, When in a wood of Crete they bayed the bear ['boar,' conj.]' (*M.N.D.* iv, 1).

There is no classical foundation for the collocation of the names.

Cadwal. Name given to Arviragus, son of Cymbeline, by his supposed father Belarius. Cadwallon or Caedwalla (*ob.* 634) was King of North Wales. The name occurs (as Cadwallo) in *Hol.* i, 112. Malone's quotation, 'Cadual, King of Venedocia,' from R. Chester's *Arthur King of Brytaine* (1601), seems superfluous. (The name occurs: *Cymb.* iii, 3, 6; iv, 2 (4); v, 5.)

Cadwallader. A variant spelling of the name of at least four Welsh, or British, kings and princes: (*a*) Caedwalla (*ob.* 634), King of North Wales; (*b*) Cadwaladr Vendigaid, 'the Blessed' (*ob. c.* 664), who led the Northern Welsh against the Angles; (*c*) Caedwalla (*ob.* 689), King of Wessex; (*d*) Cadwaladr, son of Gruffudd, King of Gwynedd (*ob.* 1172).

The name used vaguely by Pistol: 'Not for Cadwallader and all his goats!' (*Hen. V*, v, 1; Schmidt, strangely, considers C. here to mean Wales).

Caelius. Leader of the left wing of Antony's fleet at Actium (*Plut.* p. 210). Mtd. *Ant. Cl.* iii, 7 ('Celius,' Ff).

Q. Caelius, a friend of M. Ant., was attacked by Cicero (*Phil.* xiii, 2, 12).

Caesar (1). The proper name used to denote 'emperor' or 'ruler.' 'Thou'rt an emperor, C., Keisar and Pheezer' (*M.W.W.* i, 3); 'No bending knee will call thee [Henry] C. now' (*3 Hen. VI*, iii, 1); 'she shall be sole victress, Caesar's Caesar' (*Rich. III*, iv, 4); 'Bassianus, C.'s son' (*T. And.* i, 1); 'a soldier fit to stand by C.' (*Oth.* ii, 3).

Caesar (2). For 'Octavius' (*q.v.*). *Ant. Cl.* passim; *Macb.* iii, 1; *Cymb.* iii, 1 (11), 7, v, 5 (2). See Augustus.

Caesar, Caius Julius (100–44 B.C.). Consul in 59; defeated Pompey at Pharsalia in 48, and Pompey's sons at Munda, on March 17, 45; thereupon he celebrated a triumph at Rome early in October, and on March 15, 44, was assassinated by the conspirators under Brutus and Cassius. The play of *Jul. C.* deals with the few months including the triumph and Caesar's death (Plutarch's narrative being closely followed throughout); Sh., moreover, has shortened the dramatic interval to one month, by making the triumph coincidentwith the Lupercalia (*q.v.*) (Feb. 15).

Caesar's fascination by Cleopatra took place when he pursued Pompey to Egypt (48 B.C.), and she had by him a son, Caesarion (*q.v.*). The 'thrasonical brag' (*A.Y.L.* v, 2) of 'Veni, vidi, vici' refers to his announcement of his victory over Pharnaces at Zela (47 B.C.); cf. *Cymb.* iii, 1, and 2 *Hen. IV*, iv, 3. Caesar's two invasions of Britain took place in 55 and 54; on the second occasion he crossed the Thames and put the Britons to tribute (cf. *Cymb.* ii, 4; iii, 1).

D.P. *Jul. C.* (i, 1) his triumph after defeating the sons of Pompey. i, 2] asks Antony to touch Calpurnia in the 'holy chase'; is bidden beware the Ides of March; (Cassius claims to have saved him from drowning; Caesar had 'a fever' in Spain); later, returns from the games with his train; characterizes Cassius, whom he deems dangerous; (Caesar's left ear is deaf); he has thrice refused the proffered crown. (i, 3) the Senate mean to make him king; 'he would not be a wolf, But that he sees the Romans are but sheep.' (ii, 1) his assassination determined on. ii, 2] is undismayed by the portents of the night, but is persuaded by his wife not to go to the Capitol; 'Decius' changes his resolve, telling him the Senate have concluded to give him 'this day a crown'; he greets the conspirators as friends. (ii, 3) Artemidorus prepares to warn him. (ii, 4) so also does a soothsayer. iii, 1] is warned that the Ides of March are 'not gone'; refuses to read Artemidorus' 'schedule'; refuses Metellus Cimber's petition; declares himself 'constant as the northern star'; is stabbed to death, crying 'Et tu, Brute! Then fall Caesar!' (iii, 2) his eulogy by Antony; his will. (iii, 3) mtd. (iv, 1) mtd. (iv, 3) his ghost appears to Brutus. (v, 1) his murder recalled. (v, 3) Brutus exclaims that Caesar 'is mighty yet! Thy spirit walks abroad, and turns our swords In our own proper entrails.' (v, 5) mtd.

C.'s deafness, and his rescue from drowning by Cassius, are the invention of Sh.

In *Ant. Cl.*: termed by Cl. 'broad-fronted C.,' perhaps in allusion to his baldness, i, 5; Cl.'s love for him, *ib.*; 'ghosted Brutus' at Philippi, ii, 6; 'grew fat' with feasting in Egypt, *ib.*; Cl. brought to him 'in a mattress' (cf. *Plut.* p. 86), *ib.*; Antony wept over him, iii, 2; termed 'father' of Octavius (*q.v.*), iii, 13; 'dead C.'s trencher' (*ib.*).

The references to Jul. C. in *Sh.*, other than in the Roman plays, are these: Escalus warns the clown, Pompey, that 'I will beat you to your tent, and prove a shrewd C. to you' (*M. for M.* ii, 1); and Lucio exclaims, 'How now, noble Pompey? What, at the wheels of C.?' (*ib.* iii, 2); 'C.'s thrasonical brag of "I came, saw, and overcame" ' (*A.Y.L.* v, 2); Holofernes compared to 'the pummel of C.'s faulchion' (*L.L.L.* v, 2); 'a disaster of war that C. himself could not have prevented' (*All's Well*, iii, 6); alleged founder of the Tower of London (*q.v.*), *Rich. II*, v, 1, and *Rich. III*, iii, 1; 'such a day ... came not ... till C.'s fortunes' (2 *Hen. IV*, i, 1); Henry V's reception by the Londoners compared with that of 'conquering C.' at Rome, *Hen. V*, v, Chor.; the soul of Henry V will make a more glorious star 'than Julius C.' (*1 Hen. VI*, i, 1); 'that proud insulting ship which C. and his fortune bare at once' (*ib.* i, 2; cf. *Plut.* p. 77); 'Brutus' bastard hand Stabb'd Jul. C.' (2 *Hen. VI*, iv, 1; see BRUTUS); his *Commentaries* (*q.v.*) referred to, *ib.* iv, 7; Q. Margaret refers to C.'s murder, *3 Hen. VI*, v, 5; Polonius 'did enact Julius Caesar; I was killed i' the Capitol' (*Haml.* iii, 2); he 'smil'd' at the Britons' lack of skill, but admitted their courage, *Cymb.* ii, 4.

Alluded to by Falstaff as 'the hook-nosed fellow of Rome' (2 *Hen. IV*, iv, 3). 'Caesars' coupled at random with 'Cannibals' (*i.e.* Hannibals) by Pistol, 2 *Hen. IV*, ii, 4.

For the play see pp. 129–30, **Julius Caesar**.

Caesarion. Son of Julius Caesar and Cleopatra, born 47 B.C.; executed by Octavius (Augustus) after his mother's death (*Plut.* pp. 87, 224).

In *Ant. Cl.* iii, 6, Octavius speaks of 'Caesarion, whom they call my father's son': this is explicable by the fact that Jul. Caes. had made Octavius his adopted son (*Plut.* p. 123) by his will. Cleopatra speaks of a hypothetical future child of hers as 'the next Caesarion' (*Ant. Cl.* iii, 13).

Cain. Eldest son of Adam, murderer of his brother Abel (*q.v.*).

'What was a month old at C.'s birth, that is not five weeks old as yet?' (*L.L.L.* iv, 2); 'Since the birth of C., the first male child' (*John*, iii, 4); 'With C. go wander through the shades of night' (Bolingbroke to Exton; *Rich. II*, v, 6; cf. Gen. iv, 12, 14); 'Let one spirit of the first-born C. reign in all bosoms' (2 *Hen. IV*, i, 1); 'cursed C.' (*1 Hen. VI*, i, 3); 'How the knave jowls it to the ground, as if it were C.'s jaw-bone, the first murderer' (*Haml.* v, 1; in allusion to the legend that C.'s weapon was the jaw-bone of an ass).

Cain-coloured. 'A little yellow beard; a C.-coloured beard ['cane-coloured,' Knight]' (*M.W.W.* i, 4). (C. and Judas were usually represented in the mystery plays with red or yellow beards.)

Caithness, Thane of. Ctd. earl by Malcolm Canmore at his coronation (*Hol.* ii, 176). 'These were the first earles that have beene heard of amongst the Scotishmen'.

D.P. *Macb.* v, 2] marches toward Dunsinane with the other thanes; comments on Macbeth's 'fury.' v, 8] with the other thanes hails Malc. king.

In Ff, as in *Hol.*, 'Cathnes.'

Caius (1). As a prenomen. 'C. Marcius' (*Cor.* passim); 'C. Cassius' (*Jul. C.* ii, 1; iii, 1; iv, 3; v, 3); 'C. Ligarius' (*Jul. C.* ii, 1, 2, 3; 'C. Marcellus' (*Ant. Cl.* ii, 6); 'C. Lucius' (*Cymb.* ii, 3, 4; v, 5).

Caius (2). D.P. *T. And.* Kinsman to Titus. iv, 3] *p.m.* v, 2] *p.m.*

Caius (3). Name assumed by the Earl of Kent, as a serving-man, *Lear*, v, 3: '*Lear* [to Kent]. Are you not Kent? *Kent.* The same, your servant Kent. Where is your servant Caius? *Lear*... He's dead and rotten. *Kent.* No, my good lord; I am the very man.'

Caius, Dr. D.P. *M.W.W.* A Frenchman. i, 4] finding that Evans is in love with Anne Page, sends him a challenge. ii, 3] awaits Evans' arrival; Justice Shallow forbids the encounter, and C. is conducted by the Host 'through Frogmore' to meet Anne. iii, 1] finds Evans waiting in vain for him near Frogmore; they agree to be avenged on the Host for his tricks. iii, 2] Mistress Page approves his visit to Anne. iii, 3] C. deprecates Ford's jealousy – 'it is not jealous in France.' iv, 2] *p.m.* iv, 5] tells the Host that the court knows nothing of 'the duke' who has cozened him. v, 3] plans to be wedded to Anne, with her mother's approval. v, 5] a boy is palmed off upon him in the forest, in Anne's disguise; *exit*, to 'raise all Windsor.'

It is a singular fact that Dr John Caius, who refounded Gonville Hall, Cambridge, in 1557, expressly excluded Welshmen from holding fellowships there.

Caius Ligarius. See LIGARIUS, QUINTUS.

Caius Lucius. D.P. *Cymb.* 'Ambassador from Rome' (Rowe); afterward general of the Roman forces. (ii, 3) his arrival as ambassador announced. (ii, 4) mtd. iii, 1] reminds Cymbeline that the tribute due to Rome has been of late intermitted; on Cymbeline's refusal to pay it, declares war against him 'in Caesar's name'; is personally treated with courtesy. iii, 5] bids farewell to Cymb., and is granted a conduct to Milford Haven. (iii, 7) is appointed proconsul, and general of the forces against Britain. iv, 2] (at Milford) receives news of his forces; listens to a soothsayer's auspicious vision; finds 'Fidele' lying unconscious and on his recovery questions him and takes him into his service. v, 2] during a skirmish with the British bids 'Fidele' save himself by flight. (v, 3) is made prisoner. v, 5] is brought before Cymb.; begs for 'Fidele's' life; expects 'F.' to do the like for him, but to his chagrin appears to be disdained by 'the boy'; is ultimately released; bids his soothsayer interpret the mystic scroll.

The name Lucius occurs in Holinshed as that of a British king (i, 51) and of a Roman captain (i, 91). The combination 'Caius Lucius' has been criticized as consisting of two prenomens. In st. dir. *Cymb.* iii, 1, Ff, the name is divided, 'Caius, Lucius.'

Calaber (Calabria), John of Anjou, Duke of. Present at the espousals of his sister, Margaret of Anjou, to Henry VI ('Calabre,' *Hol.* iii, 625). The fact mentioned, *2 Hen. VI*, i, 1.

'Certainly not "Calabria" ' (Schmidt, *s.v.*). This, however, is an error.

Calais. Sea-port of France on the Strait of Dover. From 1347, when it was captured by Edward III, to 1558, when it fell to the Duke of Guise, it was held by England. (In Ff 'Callis,' 'Callice,' following the English pronunciation.)

Thomas of Woodstock put to death at C. when Thomas Mowbray, D. of Norfolk, was Deputy of the town, *Rich. II*, iv, 1 (2); Mowbray accused of having appropriated money intended for the troops at C., *ib.* i, 1 (*Hol.* iii, 494); Nym and Bardolph in C. 'stole a fire-shovel' (*Hen. V*, iii, 2); Warwick appointed 'Lord of C.' (*3 Hen. VI*, i, 1); mtd. as a port of arrival from, and departure for, England (*Hen. V*, iii, 3, 6; iv, 8; v, Chor.); 'On towards C., ho!' (*John*, iii, 3); Fastolfe at C., *1 Hen. VI*, iv, 1; Henry VI to embark at C., *ib. ib.*

Calchas. Acc. Homer, son of Thestor, and the wisest soothsayer among the Greeks. 'Dares Phrygius' is the first writer who represents him as a Trojan who had gone over to the Greeks, since he foresaw the ruin of Troy. That he was the father of Cressida is the invention of Benoît de Sainte-More in *Le Roman de Troie*. See CRESSIDA.

D.P. *Tr. Cr.* 'A Trojan priest, taking part with the Greeks' (Rowe). iii, 3] enlarges on the sacrifice he has made in abandoning Troy, and begs that the Trojan prisoner Antenor may be exchanged for his daughter Cressida. (iv, 1) mtd. (iv, 5) a guest of Menelaus. (v, 1) mtd. v, 2] (before Calchas' tent) allows his daughter to come forth to Diomed.

Caliban. D.P. *Temp.* 'A salvage and deformed slave' (F1), offspring of the witch Sycorax (*q.v.*) and (i, 2) 'the devil himself.' Sycorax being dead, C. was found alone upon the enchanted island by Prospero, who at first treated him kindly and lodged him in his own cell (i, 2), but on seeking to violate Miranda's honour C. was 'stied' in a rock (*ib.*). i, 2] summoned by Prospero, C. enters with imprecations, objurgating his master for having filched the island from him; cowed by P.'s threats, he sullenly obeys. ii, 2] enters muttering curses on P., and bearing a bundle of wood; sees Trinculo approaching, and taking him for a tormenting spirit sent by P., lies down to escape notice; Trinculo creeps beneath C.'s cloak for shelter against an impending squall; Stephano enters and discovers the 'monster of the isle, with four legs'; C. is gradually reassured, and on being given sack to drink by Stephano swears to be his 'true subject'; overcome by his potations, and singing tipsily, he leads away his companions. iii, 2] becomes the devoted slave of St., who holds the bottle, but is irate with Tr., who derides him; unfolds his grudge against Prospero, and suggests murdering him when asleep. iv, 1] on reaching P.'s cell, C. urges his comrades to attack him forthwith, and is indignant when their attention is diverted by the gay apparel hung up by Ariel as a lure; as he is being laden with this 'trash,' spirits in the shape of hounds enter and chase the trio away. v, 1] C. humbles himself before P., and deems himself a 'thrice-double ass' to have taken Stephano for a god. (It is to be inferred that when the King's ship sets sail C. is once more left alone upon his island.)

'Caliban' is now generally regarded as a metathesis of 'Canibal' – the Indians (reputed man-eaters) seen by Columbus being 'Caribes Canibales' and their country 'Calibana.' It is noteworthy that the chapter in Florio's translation of Montaigne's *Essais* from which a distinct quotation is placed in the lips of Gonzalo (ii, 1) is headed 'The Caniballes.' Many fanciful derivations, however, have been suggested for the name – *e.g.* 'Calibia,' on the coast of Morocco; κελέβη (drinking-cup); and 'kalebon' (*Arab.* 'vile dog'). A notable anticipation of the conception occurs in *Tr. Cr.* iii, 3, where Thersites says of Ajax, 'He's grown a very land-fish, languageless, a monster.'

C.'s physical characteristics are still in dispute. On the one hand his fish-like appearance is insisted on, not merely by Stephano and Trinculo, but also by Antonio on seeing him for the first time (v, 1, 'one of them is plain fish,' but this may refer to his odour); on the other hand, he is sufficiently human to be classed by Miranda with Prospero and Ferdinand – F. being 'the third man' (i, 1) that she ever saw – yet sufficiently monstrous for her to remark later (iii, 1) to F. 'nor have I seen more that I may call men, than you … and my dear father.'

'The extent of C.'s ichthyological character will be determined from allusions in the play to be comparatively slight, perhaps restricted to the finny appearance of his arms. [But Trinculo does not say that C.'s arms are like fins, but that his fins are like arms (ii, 1), which has a different implication.] A misshapen man with this peculiarity would indicate a monster as unnatural as could with propriety be introduced as a dramatic character taking an active share in the action of the play. C. is certainly neither a Dagon nor a monkey, the two extremes which have been assigned to him by the critics.' (Halliwell, *Selected Notes on 'The Tempest'* (1868), p. 334.) See also *N.S.S. Tr.*, 1887–92, Pt. I, pp. 15*–16*.

Pictorially, C. is usually represented as of essentially human form. Fuseli gives him a diabolic face, but no fish-like characteristics. Kaulbach makes him wholly human, but gives him a cloak made of the skin of a conventional sea-monster. Modern illustrators have made him either a satyr, or a brawny and misshapen man with scaly or leaf-like appendages. (All represent him with 'forehead villainous low,' in spite of C.'s expressed aversion (iv, 1) to this deformity.)

Calipolis. A character (wife of the Moor, Muly Mahamet) in G. Peele's tragedy *The Battle of Alcazar* (1594). The line 'Feed then, and faint not, fair C.' (ii, 3) is parodied in Pistol's exclamation to the Hostess: 'Then, feed and be fat, my fair C.' (2 *Hen. IV*, ii, 4).

In Peele's play Muly Mahamet has robbed a lioness to feed his fainting wife; the phrase occurs twice.

Callice. See CALAIS.

Calphurnia. See CALPURNIA.

Calpurnia. Daughter of L. Calpurnius Piso; the last wife of Jul. Caes. (In *Plut.* also spelt 'Calphurnia.') For her ill dreams before the murder of Caes. see *Plut.* p. 98.

D.P. *Jul. C.* 'Calphurnia.' i, 2] is bidden to stand in Antony's way when he 'runs his course' and thus shake off her 'sterile curse' (cf. *Plut.* pp. 95–6). ii, 2] dreads the omens reported to her; her dream is interpreted favourably by 'Decius.'

In *Plut.* p. 98 it is related that Calpurnia dreamod that 'Caesar was slain, and that she had him in her arms'; he quotes Livy, however, as reporting that she dreamed that a pinnacle of their house was broken down. In *Plut.* p. 117 the cause of her anxiety is the inauspicious nature of the sacrifices. The dream of the statue spouting blood (*Jul. C.* ii, 2) seems Sh.'s invention.

Calydon. See ALTHAEA.

Cambio. Name assumed by Lucentio (*q.v.*) as a teacher of languages. *Tam. Sh.* ii, 1 (2); iv, 4 (3); v, 1 (2).

In *Tam. Sh.* iv, 4, 1, 62, 'Cambio' (Ff) is clearly an error for 'Biondello.'

Cambria. Wales. 'I am in C. at Milford Haven' (*Cymb.* iii, 2); 'in C. are we born' (*ib.* v, 5).

Cambridge, Earl of. See PLANTAGENET, RICHARD.

Cambyses. A character in the *Lamentable Tragedy mixed ful of pleasant mirth, conteyning the Life of Cambises King of Persia*, etc., by Thomas Preston, *c.* 1569. The language of the play, however, is not especially bombastic, as might be inferred from the only Shakespearean allusion to it. See Ward, *Eng. Dram. Lit.* i, 206.

'*Fal.* I must speak in passion, and I will do it in King C.'s vein' (*1 Hen. IV*, ii, 4).

Historically, Falstaff's allusion is not inappropriate. The furious temper of C., amounting at times to insanity, is referred to by Herodotus (bk. iii).

Camelot. The legendary place where King Arthur held his Court, and where the Round Table was. Its supposed situation is disputed. In *The History of King Arthur* it is, variously, placed in Somersetshire and identified with Winchester. Caxton in the *Mort d'Arthur* (1485) makes it a town in Wales. The only Shakespearean mention of it is: 'Goose, if I had you upon Sarum plain, I'd drive ye cackling home to Camelot' (*Lear*, ii, 2), a passage which has not been satisfactorily explained.

There is a village near Bath named Queen Camel; the bridge over the river Camel is styled 'Arthur's Bridge,' and a spring in the neighbourhood is 'Arthur's Well.'

Camillo. D.P. *Wint. T.* One of the 'Foure Lords of Sicil(l)ia' (Ff). i, 1] speaks of the affection 'rooted betwixt' Leontes and Polixenes and unimpaired by separation. i, 2] is questioned by the jealous Leontes with regard to Polixenes having protracted his visit at Hermione's request, and is reminded that he has acted almost as the King's confessor; defends himself against Leontes' random accusations of negligence, folly, and cowardice; protests against L.'s aspersions on the Queen; professes himself ready, as Polixenes' cupbearer, to poison him, provided that the Queen is absolved; (*sol.*) determines to flee rather than do the deed; divulges the whole situation to Polixenes, and urges him to escape secretly, offering to contrive the embarkation and accompany him to Bohemia. (ii, 1) their flight is made known to L., who speaks of C. as 'federary' with the Queen. (iii, 2) Camillo is declared 'a true subject' by the oracle, and his fidelity is acknowledged by L. iv, 1] (in Bohemia, after a lapse of sixteen years) having been sent for by Leontes, longs to return forthwith to his native land, but agrees to watch, with Polixenes, in disguise, the doings of Prince Florizel. iv, 3] admires the beauty of Perdita, the 'queen of curds and cream'; after seeking to turn Florizel from his purposed flight, plans the voyage of the Prince and Perd. to Sicily; resolves to tell Pol. of the elopement, in the hope that he may thus himself 'review Sicilia.' (v, 1) reaches Sicily. v, 2] learns who Perdita is; is present at the reunion of Leontes and Hermione; is affianced to Paulina at Leontes' request.

The name may have been suggested by Camillus, the subject of one of Plutarch's *Lives*. It is also the name of a character in Webster's *The White Devil* (1612).

The corresponding personage in Greene's *Pandosto* is Franion; Camillo's action in Act I follows the novel pretty closely, but in *Pandosto* Franion drops out of the story after his flight with Egistus (Polixenes).

[**Campeggio.**] See CAMPEIUS.

Campeius, Cardinal. Lorenzo Campeggio (1472–1539); papal legate; sent to England to hear, as Wolsey's coadjutor, the suit of Henry VIII for the divorce of Queen Katharine (1528–9). He was Bp. of Salisbury (1524–34), but was deprived of his bishopric by the King. Holinshed (iii, 906) speaks of him as 'Laurence Campeius, a preest cardinall, a man of great wit and experience.' That the legate departed clandestinely (*Hen. VIII*, iii, 2) is not borne out by Cavendish, who states that the Cardinal formally took leave of the King at Grafton Regis.

D.P. *Hen. VIII.* (ii, 1) his arrival announced. ii, 2] tenders to the King his commission from the Curia; converses with Wolsey about Dr Pace (*q.v.*). ii, 4] takes part in the trial of the Queen; comments on her 'obstinacy'; suggests the adjournment of the court, and that the Queen should 'call back her appeal' to the Pope. iii, 1] in an interview with the Queen, counsels her to rely upon Henry's loving protection. (iii, 2) Suffolk avers that he 'is stol'n away to Rome.'

Canary [Islands]. From Gran Canaria (lit. '[Isle] of Dogs'), one of the group. Hence (*a*) a wine, and (*b*) a dance.

(*a*) 2 *Hen. IV*, ii, 4, 1, 29; *M.W.W.* iii, 2, l. 89; *T. Nt.* i, 3, ll. 85, 88. (*b*) *L.L.L.* iii, 1, 1.12; *All's Well*, ii, 1, l. 77.

Cancer. Constellation, and fourth sign of the zodiac, entered by the sun at the summer solstice. 'Add more coals to C., when he burns With entertaining great Hyperion' (*Tr. Cr.* ii, 3).

Cf. 'But in the Crab did now bright Titan shine, And scorch'd with scalding beams the parching ground' (Fairfax, *Tasso* (1600), xiii, 52).

Candy. For 'Candia' (Crete). 'The Phoenix, and her fraught from Candy' (*T. Nt.* v, 1). See CRETE.

Canidius (L. Canidius Crassus). One of M. Antony's captains, 'a man of great estimation' (*Plut.* p. 191); was bribed by Cleopatra to become 'her spokesman' to Ant. (*ib.*p. 203); nevertheless he counselled Ant. to dismiss Cleopatra to Egypt, and to fight the main battle against Octavius by land (*ib.* p. 209); at Actium he commanded the land forces (*ib.* p. 210) and, after the battle, was ordered to return with his army into Asia; he, however, forsook his men, and brought word to Ant. that his land army was lost (*ib.* p. 216).

D.P. *Ant. Cl.* iii, 7] advises Ant. to fight by land, and is given command of the army. iii, 8] on learning the result of the sea-fight resolves to surrender. (iv, 6) is forgiven by Ant.

In F1 the name is nowhere correctly spelt: 'Camidias,' 'Camidius,' iii, 7, 8; 'Camindius,' iv, 6.

Canmore. See MALCOLM.

Canterbury. City in Kent. The shrine of St Thomas à Becket in C. Cathedral was an object of pilgrimage for several centuries until destroyed by Henry VIII. 'Pilgrims going to C. with rich offerings' (*1 Hen. IV*, i, 2). The Canterbury road was the highway between London and Dover through Rochester and C.

Acc. R. G. White, the scene of *John*, iv, 1, is laid at C.

Canterbury, Archbishops of. *John*, iii, 1, see LANGTON, STEPHEN. *Rich. II*, ii, 1, see ARUNDEL, THOMAS. D.P. *Hen. V*, see CHICHELEY, HENRY. *Hen. VIII*, ii, 4, see WARHAM, WILLIAM. D.P. *Hen. VIII*, see CRANMER, THOMAS.

[**Cantlow.**] See KEEPERS, TWO.

Capel. For 'Capulet.' 'Capel's monument' (*Rom. J.* v, 1; v, 3).

Caper, Master. A debtor; *M. for M.* iv, 3.

Capet, Hugh (Hugues). Founder of the Capetian dynasty in France; elected king by the feudal chiefs on the extinction of the direct line of Charlemagne by the death of Louis le Fainéant without issue (987), and thus became the real founder of the French monarchy.

The Abp. of Canterbury (*Hen. V*, i, 2) argues before Henry V that Hugh Capet 'usurp' d the crown of Charles the Duke of Lorraine,' and, 'to find his title with some shows of truth, Though in pure truth it was corrupt and naught,' claimed descent from Charlemagne through 'Lady Lingare' (*q.v.*).

This (unhistorical) statement follows *Hol.* iii, 546.

Caphis. D.P. *Timon.* A Senator's servant. ii, 1] is sent to importune Timon for repayment of a loan. ii, 2] (at T.'s house) converses with other servants on a like errand; presses T. for payment of 'certain dues'; is scorned by Apemantus.

The name occurs in Plutarch's *Sylla.* S. Walker suggests 'Capys.'

Capilet. Name of a horse. 'My horse, grey C.' (*T. Nt.* iii, 4).

Either for 'Capulet,' or dim. of 'caple,' a horse; *N.E.D. s.v.* 'Caple.'

Capitol, The. Capitolium; strictly speaking, the temple of Jupiter Opt. Max. at Rome, on the summit of the Mons Capitolinus. (The site is now partly occupied by the Pal. Caffarelli and the church of Ara Coeli.)

The Capitol was burnt down three times before its final rebuilding, in great magnificence, by Domitian. In the C. were kept the Sibylline books; there newly made consuls took their vows, and triumphant generals returned thanks to Jupiter. (The whole hill was sometimes called Capitolium.)

Sh. seems, on occasion, to regard the Tower of London as the English equivalent of the C.

Meeting-place of the Senate, *Cor.* i, 1; 'fane nor C.' (*ib.* i, 10); place of election of consul, *ib.* ii, 1; scene of *ib.* ii, 2; mtd., *ib.* ii, 3; 'not Romans ... though calved i' the porch of the C.' (*ib.* iii, 1); 'as far as doth the C. exceed The meanest house in Rome' (*ib.* iv, 2); mtd., *ib.* iv, 6; corner-stone of the C., *ib.* v, 4. Mtd., *Jul. C.* i, 1; conference of senators at the C., *ib.* i, 2; a lion, as a portent, in the C., *ib.* i, 3; to the E. of Brutus' house, *ib.* ii, 1; the heavens 'drizzled blood upon the C.' (*ib.* ii, 2); mtd., *ib.* ii, 4; scene of *ib.* iii, 1, 'before the C.'; 'the question of his [Caesar's] death is enrolled in the C.' (*ib.* iii, 2); 'I dwell by the C.' (*ib.* iii, 3); mtd., *ib.* iv, 1. Murder of Caesar erroneously placed in the C., *Ant. Cl.* ii, 6, and *Haml.* iii, 2; 'common as the stairs that mount the C.' (*Cymb.* i, 7); 'keep ... this passage to the C.' (*T. And.* i, 1); 'C. and senate's right' (*ib. ib.*); 'defender of this C.' (*ib.* i, 2); 'by the C. that we adore' (*Lucr.* 1835).

Cappadocia. District of Asia Minor. See ARCHELAUS.

Captain, A (1). D.P. *Haml.* iv, 4] explains to Hamlet the object of Fortinbras' expedition.

Captain, A (2). D.P. *T. And.* i, 2] announces the arrival of the victorious Titus.

Captain, A Roman. D.P. *Cymb.* iv, 2] tells Lucius that the legions have arrived at Milford, and that a body of 'Gentlemen of Italy,' under Iachimo, is on the way; uncovers the face of 'Fidele' who lies near, and reports that he lives.

Captain of a Band of Welshmen. D.P. *Rich. II.* ii, 4] refuses to tarry any longer for Richard, alleging the occurrence of portents forerunning the death of kings (*Hol.* iii, 496; not mentioned in 1st edn.).

Captains, Two British. D.PP. *Cymb.* v, 3] enter, conversing on the defeat of Lucius, and confront Posthumus, whom they make prisoner.

'Captaines,' Ff; 'British' added by Theobald.

Capucius. See CHAPUYS, EUSTACE.

Capulet. D.P. *Rom. J.* Head of the house of Capulet. i, 1] enters during a street brawl, and calls for his sword, but Lady Capulet checks him; is sternly rebuked by the Prince. i, 2] consents to Paris wooing Juliet; will hold feast that night. i, 5] welcomes his guests; forbids Tybalt openly to notice Romeo's presence. iii, 1] *p.m.* iii, 4] agrees to Paris' wedding Juliet 'on Thursday'; tells his wife to prepare Juliet. iii, 5] indulges in an outburst of fury at Juliet's refusal to wed Paris, and assails her with invectives – she may die in the streets ere he will acknowledge her. iv, 2, 4] earns the Nurse's epithet of 'cotquean.' iv, 5] laments the supposed death of Juliet – 'with my child my joys are buried.' v, 3] reaches the monument of the

Capulets, to find Juliet, Romeo, and Paris dead; is reconciled to Montague, and promises a rich tomb for Romeo.

Usually 'Capolet' in Q (except in Act I). In *Rhomeo and Julietta* named 'Anthonie' or 'Antonio.'

Capulet, Diana. See DIANA (2).

Capulet, Lady. D.P. *Rom. J.* Wife to Capulet. i, 1] deems a crutch more suitable for her husband than a sword. i, 3] tells Juliet that Paris seeks her hand in marriage, and favours the match. iii, 4] speaks of Juliet's sorrow at Tybalt's death. iii, 5] chides J. for excess of grief; declares she will have Romeo poisoned, and tells J. to prepare to be wedded to Paris; shows no pity for her daughter's anguish. iv, 2] prepares for Juliet's wedding. iv, 3] bids J. good-night. iv, 4] twits Capulet for having been 'a mouse-hunt' in his time. iv, 5] loudly laments Juliet's apparent death. v, 3] (at the Monument) 'this sight of death is as a bell, That warns my old age to a sepulchre.'

Capulet, Old Man, Kinsman to. D.P. *Rom. J.* i, 5] converses with Capulet, who calls him 'good cousin,' on the flight of time.

Capulets and Montagues. Described in *Rom. J.* as two rival families of Verona, whose feud is the cause of the tragedy. Historically, the Cappelletti (not a family name, but a nickname meaning 'shockheads') were the Guelfs of Cremona, and the Montecchi were the Ghibelline leaders at Verona. The names are coupled by Dante, *Purg.* vi, I. 106. See Toynbee, *Concise Dante Dictionary, s.vv.*

See *Rom. J.* i, 1; iii, 1 (2); iv, 1; v, 3.

In *Rhomeo and Julietta* 'Capellets' or 'Cap(p)elletts' and 'Montesches.' In *Romeus and Juliet* 'Capelet,' 'Capilet,' and 'Capel'; 'Montegew(e),' 'Montagew(e),' and 'Montague.'

Caputius. See CHAPUYS, EUSTACE.

Car, or Court, John de la. Carthusian monk, confessor to the D. of Buckingham; attached, *Hen. VIII*, i, 1. ('Court,' Warb.)

Another form of the name is 'Delacourt.' 'John de la Car *alias* de la Court' (*Hol.* iii, 863).

[Cardona, Timbreo de.] See CLAUDIO (1).

Carlisle, Bishop of. See MERKE, THOMAS.

Carnarvonshire. Mtd. as an unimportant county, *Hen. VIII*, ii, 3; 'For little England you'ld venture an emballing: I myself would for C., although there 'long'd No more to the crown but that.'

Carthage. Ancient city on the N. coast of Africa, traditionally founded by Dido; destroyed 146 B.C. The city of Tunis is about 10 m. from the site.

Adrian insists that 'Tunis was C.' (*Temp.* ii, 1); Dido 'the C. Queen' (*M.N.D.* i, 1); Dido at C., *M.V.* v, 1; 'the Queen of C.' (*Tam. Sh.* i, 1).

Casca, P. Servilius. Tribune; the first of the conspirators to stab Caesar; he fled from Rome and was deprived of his tribuneship. He fought at Philippi, and died soon afterward. Acc. *Plut.* p. 119, Casca 'strake Caesar upon the shoulder, but gave him no great wound,' whereupon Caesar seized him by the hand, and exclaimed, "O traitor Casca, what dost thou?" Casca on the other side cried in Greek and called his brother to help him.'

D.P. *Jul. C.* i, 2] as an eyewitness, tells Brutus and Cassius satirically how a crown was offered to Caesar and how he rejected it; declares that what Cicero said 'was Greek' to him; on his exit, is characterized by Cassius. i, 3] describes to Cicero, with much agitation, the recent portents; is persuaded by Cassius to join the conspiracy; speaks of Brutus' popularity. ii, 1] converses with Cinna; is easily swayed from his opinion that Cic. should be admitted to the plot. ii, 2] *p.m.*; is greeted by Caesar. (ii, 3) Artemidorus would warn Caes. against him. iii, 1] as arranged, is the first to stab Caesar; urges Brutus to 'go to the pulpit'; Antony shakes hands with 'valiant Casca'; later, A., in his oration, terms him 'envious C.' (v, 1) Ant. at Philippi declares that 'damned C., like a cur, behind Struck Caesar on the neck.'

'Caska,' Ff, ii, 2. The dramatic Casca is almost wholly the invention of Sh., Plutarch's references to him being meagre and colourless.

Cassado, Gregory de. Wolsey accused of sending a commission to Sir G. de C., to treat with the D. of Ferrara, without the King's knowledge; *Hen. VIII*, iii, 2 (cf. *Hol.* iii, 912, 'Sir Gregorie de Cassado, Knight').

Properly 'Casale,' or 'Cassalis,' as in the articles against Wolsey in Coke's *Instit.* iv, 8(3) (Clar.).

Cassalis. See CASSADO.

Cassandra. Daughter of Priam and Hecuba, gifted with prophetic powers; having offended Apollo, he punished her by causing her prophecies, although true, to be invariably disbelieved. In medieval traditions the main characteristics of C. are represented much as they are by Homer.

D.P. *Tr. Cr.* (i, 1) Pandarus speaks of her 'wit.' (i, 2) her laughter at a jest of Troilus'. ii, 2] she 'enters raving,' and cries out that Troy must perish if Helen is not restored; Hector is impressed by her warning, but Troilus scorns her as 'brainsick.' v, 3] passionately urges Hector not to fight that day; later, brings back Priam to add his entreaties; foresees Hector's death, and bids him farewell.

Cassibelan. *Fl.* 54 B.C.; better known as Cassivellaunus, the Latin form of the Welsh 'Caswallawn,' a British prince. He opposed Jul. Caesar's second invasion, but was defeated at a ford over the Thames, and submitted to Rome. *Cf.* Jul. Caes. *De Bello Gallico*, v, 22. Holinshed, however, cites early chronicles to the effect that Cassibelan defeated Caesar, and that the latter fled to Gaul, whereupon 'Cassibellane made a great feast in London, and there did sacrifice to the gods' (*Hol.* i, 30).

Mtd. as fighting against the Romans, *Cymb.* i, 1; referred to as Cymbeline's uncle, who was 'famous in Caesar's praises,' but had been compelled to grant Rome a tribute; how he nearly wrested Caesar's sword from him, and 'made Lud's Town with rejoicing fires bright' (*ib.* iii, 1).

In making Cymb. refuse tribute (iii, 1, l. 9) Sh. seems to follow *The Faerie Queene*, II, x, 50, rather than the *Chronicles*, where the refusal is made by Guiderius.

Cassio. D.P. *Oth.* 'An Honourable Lieutenant' (Ff). (i, 1) spoken of by Iago as 'a great arithmetician, one Michael Cassio, a Florentine'; Iago dilates on C.'s ignorance of the arts of war, yet Othello has chosen 'this counter-caster' as his lieutenant. i, 2] C. summons Oth. urgently to the Senate; affects surprise when informed that Oth. is married, and asks 'To who?' ii, 1] (in Cyprus) his ship has become separated from Othello's in a storm; C. gives a glowing description of Desdemona, and on her arrival greets her with respectful devotion; playfully greets Emilia, Iago's wife, with a kiss; Iago tells Roderigo that he believes Desd. loves Cas., and (*sol.*) professes misgivings as to his relations with Emilia. ii, 3] is led by Iago into praise of Desd.'s charms; later, is induced to join in a carousal, though he has 'very poor and unhappy brains for drinking'; later, while tipsy, assaults Roderigo and wounds Montano; is regretfully dismissed from his post by Oth.; deplores his own folly and the loss of his reputation; Iago persuades him to seek Desd.'s help in reinstating himself in the general's good graces. iii, 1] asks Emilia to gain access for him to Desd. iii, 3] pleads with Desd., in Emilia's presence, till she gives him 'warrant of his place'; (he had been Oth.'s constant comrade when Desd. was wooed); he is now suspected by Oth.; Iago resolves to leave Desd.'s handkerchief in C.'s lodging; Iago declares C. has given him proof of loving Desd. iii, 4] C. begs Desd. once more to urge his suit; gives the handkerchief found in his chamber to Bianca to copy; will visit her soon. iv, 1] is induced by Iago to admit, in Oth.'s hearing, that 'she' – meaning Bianca – 'loves me.' v, 1] is attacked in the street at night by Roderigo, whom he wounds; he is then in the darkness grievously wounded by Iago; Bianca enters and laments over him. v, 2] C. is borne, wounded, into the chamber where Desd. lies dead, and proves Iago's guilt; is given the command on Oth.'s death.

In Cinthio's tale the officer suspected of adultery with 'Disdemona' is unnamed and is referred to as 'un Capo di squadra.' His leg is completely severed, but he recovers and, has 'una gamba di legno' – a wooden leg.

Cassius (C. Cassius Longinus). Instigator of the plot against the life of Julius Caesar. Of uncertain parentage, he first becomes known in history as quaestor to Crassus in his unfortunate Parthian campaign (53 B.C.), and later as being himself victorious against the same enemy. As a supporter of the aristocratical party, he left Rome (49 B.C.), but surrendered to Caesar on the Hellespont and was received into favour by him. While Caes. was engaged in crushing his foes abroad, Cassius remained at Rome, and kept up a correspondence with Cicero. Honours were conferred upon him by the Dictator, but, animated by personal hatred and ambition, Cassius resolved to take his life, and for this end won over Brutus (*q.v.*) to his side. After the murder of Caes. Cassius at first remained in Rome, but soon found it prudent to withdraw, and was given, as praetor, the insignificant province of Cyrene instead of Syria, which had been promised him by Caes. Cassius accordingly determined to take possession of Syria by force, and declared war against Dolabella, to whom the province had been assigned. The Senate then veered round to the side of Cassius, and entrusted him with the command of the war against Dolabella, who was defeated. Cassius then attacked Rhodes and obtained thence an immense booty. In 42 B.C. he met Brutus at Sardis, and though they were on the point of coming to an open rupture they patched up a reconciliation and marched against the threatening forces of Antony and Octavius at Philippi (*q.v.*). In the battle which ensued C., ignorant that Brutus had repulsed Oct. and believing that all was lost, commanded his freedman Pindarus to slay him. Cassius was, in philosophy, a follower of Epicurus (*Plut.* pp. 100, 138), and (*ib.* p. 130) 'a hot, choleric, and cruel man, that would oftentimes be carried away from justice for gain; it was certainly thought that he made war, and put himself into sundry dangers, more to have absolute power and authority than to defend the liberty of his country.' Plutarch's account of C. is closely followed by Sh. throughout the play of *Jul. C.* In ii, 1, Cassius is called the brother of Brutus – having married Junia his sister (*Plut.* p. 110).

D.P. *Jul. C.* i, 2] privately sounds Brutus as to his changed demeanour toward his former friend; reassured on this point, offers to interpret the vague disquietude that oppresses Brutus, and to serve as a mirror in which he may view his thoughts; hearing Br. ejaculate that he fears 'the people choose Caesar for their king,' grasps the opportunity, and dilates on the tyranny exercised by the Dictator, and the human frailties to which, nevertheless, he is subject; reminds Br. of his patriot ancestor, Junius Brutus; (Caes., in passing, remarks that Cassius 'has a lean and hungry look ... such men are dangerous [*Plut.* p. 97]; he hears no music; seldom he smiles'); Cassius learns from Casca what happened when Caesar was offered a crown; resolves to enrol Casca as a conspirator; (*sol.*) will throw in at Brutus' windows papers, in various writings, hinting at what Rome expects of him. i, 3] meets Casca at midnight in the street; hails the portents, which dismay Casca, as warnings of great events; declares that he will take his own life if Caesar is made king; welcomes Casca as a fellow-conspirator; sends Cinna on certain errands; maintains that Brutus will join them on the morrow. ii, 1] (in Brutus' orchard) introduces the other conspirators to Br., and confers with him privately; suggests approaching Cicero; advises that Antony, whom he fears, should be slain with Caesar. (ii, 3) Artemidorus would fain warn Caesar against him. iii, 1] feigns to plead for Publius Cimber, on his knees, before Caesar; joins in the assassination; glories in the deed; has misgivings as to Antony; urges Br. not to allow Antony to speak to the people. iii, 2] while Br. makes his oration, leads off some of the citizens to address them elsewhere; (is reported to have fled from Rome). (iii, 3) the citizens prepare to burn his house down. (iv, 1) is reported to be 'levying powers' with Br. iv, 2] (near Sardis) greets Br., who, nevertheless, he declares has wronged him. iv, 3] (in Brutus' tent) upbraids Br. for having disregarded his appeal on behalf of Lucius Pella (*q.v.*); is accused by Br. of having 'an itching palm'; in his anger warns Br. that 'I may do that I shall be sorry for'; protests that he did not, as averred, deny Br. gold to pay his legions, and offers his breast to Br.'s dagger; Br. stifles his wrath, and the quarrel is composed; Cassius, on learning that Br. had just heard of Portia's death, exclaims, 'How scap'd I killing when I crossed you so?'; they pledge one another in a bowl of wine, and receive news from Rome of the proscription; Cassius urges dilatory tactics, but is overruled; bids Br. 'good night' in terms of warm affection. v, 1] (at Philippi) parleys defiantly with Antony and Octavius; admits to Messala that despite his Epicurean scepticism he is oppressed by recent portents; solemnly bids Br. 'an ever-lasting farewell.' v, 3] led erroneously to believe that all is lost, bids Pindarus slay him with the sword with which Caesar was stabbed; (Brutus exclaims over his body, 'The last of all the Romans, fare thee well!').

Cassius is twice mtd. in *Ant. Cl.*: 'What was't That mov'd pale C. to conspire?' (ii, 6); 'the lean and wrinkled C.' (iii, 11). Cf. *Plut.* p. 97, where Caesar says of C., 'I like not his pale looks.'

For a full analysis of the dramatic character see P. Stapfer, *Sh. and Clas. Antiq.* pp. 351–64.

[Cassivellaunus.] See CASSIBELAN.

Castalion. See CASTILIAN.

Castilian. *i.e.* a Spaniard, acc. Knight's conj.; applied to Caius by the Host as a pretended compliment, being really a term of reproach, *M.W.W.* ii, 3. ('Castalion-King-Urinal,' Ff.)

The phrase 'Castiliano vulgo' (*T.Nt.* i, 3) has given rise to much discussion, but has not been satisfactorily explained. *Cf.* 'Rivo Castiliano' (*Jew of Malta*, iv, 6).

Castle, The. 'An alehouse' paltry sign' at St Albans (*2 Hen. VI*, v, 2), under which the 2nd D. of Somerset was slain in accordance with a prophecy; cf. *2 Hen. VI*, i, 4, l. 70, and *Hol.* iii, 643. In *Chron. Rich. II*, etc. (Camden Society), p. 72, it is related that the D., dreading the prophecy, would not approach Windsor Castle.

Cataian. For 'Cathaian,' a man of Cathay (China); a term of reproach, the point of which is unascertained (cf. *N.E.D. s.v.*). Acc. Nares, 'a sharper, from the dexterous thieving of those people.'

'I will not believe such a C., though the priest ... commended him' (*M.W.W.* ii, 1), 'my lady's a C.' (*T. Nt.* ii, 3; 'Catayan,' Ff).

Furness, *Var.*, suggests that Sir Toby, who was in his cups, used the word at random by association with 'caterwauling,' just used by Maria.

Catesby, Sir William (*ob.* 1485). Lawyer, favourite of Richard III while D. of Gloucester; betrayed his first patron, Lord Hastings; Chancellor of the Exchequer 1483; Speaker of the H. of C. 1484; taken prisoner at Bosworth and beheaded. C. is 'the cat' in the traditional rime 'The Cat, the Rat, and Lovell our dog,' etc. (*Hol.* iii, 746).

D.P. *Rich. III.* i, 3] conveys a summons from the King. iii, 1] is instructed to sound Hastings, and, if possible, win him over to Gloucester's side. iii, 2] tells H. that Gl. aims at the crown, and that H.'s enemies, 'the kindred of the Queen,' are to be executed forthwith. (iii, 4) mtd. iii, 5] in attendance on Gl. (iii, 6) mtd. iii, 7] informs Buckingham and the citizens that Gloucester is engaged with 'two right reverend fathers'; later, announces that Gl. fears they 'mean no good to him'; later, returns as Gl. presents himself; joins in urging Gl. to accept the crown. iv, 2] is ordered to give out that Anne 'is sick and like to die.' iv, 3] tells Richard that Ely and Buckingham are in revolt. iv, 4] is sent to seek aid from the D. of Norfolk. v, 3] (at Bosworth) sent to summon Stanley. v, 4] aids Richard on the field.

(ii, 1) Ff, C. enters, but he is *p.m.*; (iii, 4) Theobald substituted 'C.' for 'Ratcliffe,' who was at Pomfret; (iv, 3) Ff have 'Ratcliffe' for 'C.'

Catling, Simon. D.P. *Rom. J.* iv, 5] 'first musician.'

The meaning of the word is 'lute-string,' but *Sh.* provides here the earliest instance (cf. *Tr. Cr.* iii, 3, l. 306).

Cato, Marcus Porcius (1) (95–46 B.C.). Conspicuous for his stern morality amidst the general profligacy of the age; after the Battle of Thapsus he put an end to his life rather than fall into the hands of Caesar (Plut. *Cato Minor*).

'C.'s daughter, Brutus' Portia' (*M.V.* i, 1); 'a soldier Even to C.'s wish' (*Cor.* i, 4; cf. *Plut.* p. 7; 'Calves,' Ff; 'Calvus,' Rowe); 'a woman [Portia] well reputed, C.'s daughter' (*Jul. C.* ii, 1); 'I did blame C. for the death Which he did give himself' (*ib.* v, 1).

The anachronism in *Cor.*, of making T. Lartius refer to Cato, is not Plutarch's, for the historian is speaking *in propria persona* in the parallel passage.

Cato, Marcus Porcius (2). Son of the above; after Caesar's death he attached himself to Brutus, his brother-in-law.

D.P. *Jul. C.* 'Young Cato.' v, 3] at Philippi. v, 4] falls, fighting gallantly.

[Catur, William.] See HORNER, THOMAS.

Caucasus. Range of mountains extending from the Caspian Sea to the Euxine. The scene of the torment of Prometheus (*q.v.*). 'The frosty C.' (*Rich. II*, i, 3); 'faster bound Than is Prometheus tied to C.' (*T. And.* ii, 1).

'Rigidique cacumine montis, Caucason appellant' (Ovid, *Metam.* viii, 799).

Cawdor. Castle and domain 5 1/2 m. S.W. of Nairn, which gave title to the Thane of C. 'The thane of C. being condemned at Fores of treason against the king committed; his lands, livings and offices were given of the king's liberalitie to Macbeth' (*Hol.* ii, 170). The earldom of C. was created in 1057.

The Thane of C. turns traitor and is condemned to death, *Macb.* i, 2; the witches hail Macb. as 'Thane of C.,' *ib.* i, 3; the execution of the former thane reported, *ib.* i, 4; Macb. is named C. by Duncan, *ib. ib.* Mtd., *ib.* i, 5, 6; ii, 2; iii, 1.

Macbeth's ignorance of the Thane of Cawdor's treason (i, 3) is explicable, since C. did not appear on the field of battle, but 'did line the rebel With hidden help and vantage' (i, 3).

Cedius. Greek warrior at the siege of Troy. 'The pashed corses of the kings Epistrophus and C.' (*Tr. Cr.* v, 5).

Cedeus, or Cedus, brother of Epistropus, is mentioned in Caxton's *Recuyell.*

Celia. D.P. *A. Y. L.* Only child of Frederick, the usurping Duke of Burgundy; throughout the play associated with her cousin Rosalind. (i, 1) 'never two ladies loved as they do.' i, 2] endeavours to console R., and, with her, witnesses the wrestling match. i, 3] intercedes with her father on R.'s behalf, and, failing in her endeavours, begs to share her banishment; plans, with her cousin, means of flight. ii, 4] disguised as 'Aliena,' shares R.'s hardships in Arden, and buys a cottage for their home. iii, 2] discovers Orlando's presence in the forest, and informs R. iii, 4] rallies her cousin on Or.'s supposed faithlessness. iii, 5] *p.m.* iv, 1] is present during the mock wooing of 'Ganymede' by Or. iv, 3] is present when the penitent Oliver relates how Or. was wounded in rescuing him. (v, 2) her engagement to Oliver (*q.v.*) is announced. v, 4] *p.m.*

The corresponding character in Lodge's *Rosalynde* is Alinda, who takes the name of 'Aliena,' and is married to Saladyne, who rescues her and her companions from a band of robbers.

Celo. For 'Coelum.' Used as a proper name: 'a jewel in the ear of C. the sky' (*L.L.L.* iv, 2; 'Caelo,' F3, 4).

Personified, Cicero, *De Nat. Deor.* iii, 17, 23.

Censorinus. 'C. also came of that family [Martians], that was so surnamed, because the people had chosen him Censor twice' (*Plut.* p. 1). In the rehearsal by Brutus (*Cor.* ii, 3) of the ancestors of Coriolanus, the disconnected line 'And nobly named so, twice being censor' occurs (Ff). Later editors have have amended the passage, introducing 'Censorinus' by sundry devices.

In the Camb. edn. (1892), vi, 353–5, twelve conjectural solutions of the difficulty are given.

Centaur, The. Name of an inn in Ephesus. *Com. Err.* i, 2; ii, 2; iv, 4; v, 1.

Centaurs. Mythical beings, half horses and half men; famous for their fight with the Lapithae at the marriage-feast of Perithous, described by Ovid (*Metam.* xii).

'The battle with the C.s' (*M.N.D.* v, 1); 'more stern and bloody than the C.s' feast' (*T. And.* v, 2); 'down from the waist they are C.s, Though women all above' (*Lear*, iv, 6).

A female centaur is described by Ovid, *Metam.* xii, 405 ff.

Cephalus. Beloved by Aurora; see SHAFALUS. An allusion to C. is seen by some commentators in *M.N.D.* iii, 2: 'I [Oberon] with the morning's love have oft made sport.' See TITHONUS.

Cerberus. A dog-like monster with three heads (Virg. *Aen.* vi, 417) who guarded the portal of Hades. Hercules seized him, and brought him to the upper world, but did not kill him (Ovid, *Metam.* vii, 413); Orpheus lulled him to sleep with his lyre, but *cf.* Virg. *Aen.* vi, 419 ff., where he is stupefied by the Sibyl.

'Hercules ... Whose club killed C. that three-headed Canus' (*L.L.L.* v, 2, QFf); '*Pist*... damn them with King C.' (2 *Hen. IV*, ii, 4); 'as full of envy ... as C. is at Proserpina's beauty' (*Tr. Cr.* ii, 1); 'full asleep, As C. at the Thracian poet's feet' (*T. And.* ii, 5).

Ceremony. Personified and apostrophized by the King; *Hen. V*, iv, 1, ll. 257 ff.

Ceres. Name given by the Romans to the goddess Demeter of the Greeks; protectress of agriculture and the fruits of the earth. 'Ceres' plenteous load' (2 *Hen. VI*, i, 2).

D.P. *Temp.* The part of C. is performed by a spirit in the masque presented by Prospero to Ferdinand and Miranda. iv, 1] she is summoned by Iris, declares she has forsworn the company of Venus, and promises the blessings of plenty to the young couple.

Acc. Ff, 'Ceres' blessing,' beginning 'Earth's increase,' etc., is sung by Juno, and the st. dir. is 'They sing' (Furness).

Cerimon. D.P. *Per.* 'A lord of Ephesus.' iii, 2] gives succour to shipwrecked mariners in his house; admits that it is his delight to use his medical knowledge, and his wealth, for the good of the needy; a chest is brought in which has been cast up by the sea; on opening it, he sees that Thaisa within it still lives, and takes measures for her recovery. iii, 4] gives Th. jewels and a letter found with her, and forwards her wish to become a votary of Diana. v, 3] relates to Pericles the story of Th.'s recovery. (Gower extols his 'learned charity.')

S. Walker conjectured that the name should be 'Chaeremon.'

Cesario. Name assumed by Viola (D.P. *T. Nt.*). In Curzio Gonzaga's *Gl' Inganni* (1592) the name assumed by the heroine is 'Cesare.' See TWELFTH NIGHT.

Cham. For 'Khan'; 'the great Cham' was a title especially applied to the Emperor of China. 'Under the dominion of the great Cham or Cane, Emperor of Tartaria' (Eden, *Treat. New Ind.* (Arber), p. 12). Benedick declares that he would rather 'fetch you a hair off the great C.'s beard' than converse with Beatrice (*M. Ado*, ii, 1).

Chamberlain, A. D.P. *1 Hen. IV.* ii, 1] tells Gadshill that wealthy travellers are on the point of setting out, and is promised 'a share in our purchase.'

For 'chamberlain,' in the sense of a waiter at an inn, see *N.E.D. s.v.*, where a quotation dated 1587 is given, in which the term is coupled with 'ostler.' (*Cf.* Milton, *On the University Carrier*, for a description of a ch.'s duties.)

Chamberlain, The Lord. D.P. *Hen. VIII.* i, 3] criticizes the Frenchified manners of the courtiers (*Hol.* iii, 850) with Lord Sands and Sir T. Lovell, whom he takes in his barge to Wolsey's supper, at which he is a controller. i, 4] (at York Place) acts as 'controller' at the entertainment; welcomes the masquers (*Hol.* iii, 922); presents Anne Boleyn to the King. ii, 2] laments Wolsey's arrogance. ii, 3] announces to Anne that she has been made Marchioness of Pembroke. iii, 2] confers with the nobles on Wolsey's impending overthrow; later, is struck with pity for the fallen Cardinal. v, 3] is present when Cranmer is brought before the Council. v, 4] rates the porters for admitting the rabble into the palace yard.

Historically, the Chamberlains during the period covered by the play were: (*a*) Charles Somerset, Earl of Worcester (1509–26), and (*b*) Lord Sands (*q.v.*) (1526–43).

Champ, Du. See DU CHAMP.

Champaigne. Ancient government of France; its loss (unhistorical) by England announced, *1 Hen. VI*, i, 1.

Chancellor, The Lord (1). D.P. *Hen. VIII.* See AUDLEY, THOMAS.

Chancellor, The Lord (2). D.P. *Hen. VIII.* v, 3] presides at meeting of the Council; formally accuses Cranmer of heresy; commits him to the Tower; is perturbed by C.'s production of the King's ring, and excuses himself to Henry. See WRIOTHESLEY, SIR THOMAS (2).

[Channel, English.] Referred to as 'the narrow seas.' *M.V.* ii, 8, iii, 1; *Hen. V*, ii, Chor.; *3 Hen. VI*, i, 1, iv, 8.

In *Sh.* always plural, though usually 'the narrow sea' in the 16th cent. But Hawkins, writing to Burghley, Nov. 30, 1593 (*Calendar of State Papers*, 1591–4, p. 389), speaks of 'the ships serving in the Narrow Seas' (Clar.).

Chanticleer. Proper name of the Cock in *Reynard the Fox*; used by Chaucer (*Nonne Pr. T.* 29), Caxton (*Reynard*), and Spenser (*F.Q.* I, ii, 1), 'My lungs began to crow like C.' (*A. Y. L.* ii, 7); 'the strain of strutting C.' (*Temp.* i, 2).

Chaos. The formless void out of which the cosmos, or orderly universe, was evolved. *Cf.* Ovid, *Metam.* i, 7. 'When I love thee not, Ch. is come again' (*Oth.* iii, 3).

Chaplain. *3 Hen. VI*, i, 3, l. 3; see RUTLAND, TUTOR TO.

Chapuys, Eustace. Ambassador to England from the Emperor Charles V 1536. When Katharine 'fell into hir last sicknesse' at Kimbolton 'Eustachius Caputius' was appointed by Henry to visit her 'and to doo his commendations to hir, and will hir to be of good comfort' (*Hol.* iii, 939).

D.P. *Hen. VIII.* ('Capuchius,' Ff.) iv, 2] performs his errand, as above, and is given a letter from K. to take to Henry.

Acc. *Calendar* (*Hen. VIII*), x, 59, Ch. himself asked leave to visit K., and was grudgingly permitted to do so.

Charbon. See POYSAM.

Charing Cross. A cross erected in Charing, a village near London, the last halt of the coffin of Queen Eleanor on its way to Westminster. (Demolished in 1647.)

'I have ... two razes of ginger to be delivered as far as C.C.' (*1 Hen. IV*, ii, 1).

Charity, St. 'By Gis and by St C.' (*Haml.* iv, 5). See GIS.

Cf. 'Ah, deare Lord! and sweet Saint C.' (Spenser, *Shep. Cal.*, Maye, l. 247 (1579)). 'Passio SS. Virginum Fidei, Spei et Caritatis, et Sophiae matris eorum. Edita in *Legenda Aurea* [ed. Colon, 1483] ff. 443–4' (*Analecta Bollandiana* (1886), tom. v, p. 322).

Charlemain. Charlemagne, King of the Franks, and Roman Emperor; mtd. *All's Well*, ii, 1, in connection with a tradition that he vainly tried to learn to write late in life.

The 'Charlemain' of *Hen. V*, i, 2, is not the Emperor, but Charles the Bald (875–7), son of the Emperor Lewis the Pious. The error is due to Holinshed (iii, 546).

Charles (1). D.P. *A.Y.L.* 'A wrestler, and servant to the usurping Duke Frederick' (Rowe). i, 1] brings news from the Court to Oliver de Bois, incidentally touching on the old Duke's banishment and the mutual love of Rosalind and Celia; urges that Oliver's brother, Orlando, should be dissuaded from wrestling with him on the morrow, but, on being assured that he is a dangerous villain, vows to 'give him his payment.' i, 2] is defeated by Orlando.

The wrestler in the *Tale of Gamelyn* is unnamed, as is the Norman Champion in Lodge's *Rosalynde*.

Charles (2). Father of 'Ferdinand, King of Navarre'; mtd. *L.L.L.* ii, 1.

Charles (3). For 'C. Brandon,' D. of Suffolk (*q.v.*); *Hen. VIII*, v, 1.

Charles V, Emperor (1500–58). Landed at Dover May 26, 1520, on a visit to Katharine of Arragon, who was sister to his mother Joanna, d. of Ferdinand and Isabella.

'Ch., the Emperor, Under pretence to see the Queen his aunt – For 'twas indeed his colour, but he came To whisper Wolsey – here makes visitation' (*Hen. VIII*, i, 1; cf. *Hol.* iii, 856).

Hol., following Polydore Vergil, proceeds to explain that the Emperor's chief motive was to prevent Henry's having an interview with the King of France, and that he bribed Wolsey heavily to bring to naught the amity between the two kings.

Charles VI (1368–1422). King of France; 'le Bien-aimé'; succd. his father Charles V in 1380; during his minority the Dukes of Anjou, Burgundy, and Berri acted as a council of regency. In 1392 Ch. became temporarily insane, and a struggle for power ensued between the D. of Burgundy and the D. of Orleans (brother of Ch.), which led to civil war between Burgundians and 'Armagnacs,' to the advantage of the former. After the invasion of France by the English and the Battle of Agincourt (1415) the Burgundians, supported by Queen Isabel (*q.v.*), made a treaty (1420) at Troyes with Henry V, which provided that the latter should become King of France after the death of Ch.; Henry, however, died first.

D.P. *Hen. V.* ii, 4] orders defensive measures against the English invaders; reminds his counsellors of the fatal issue of Cressy; receives the English ambassadors, and reserves his reply to their demands till the morrow (*Hol.* iii, 547, where it is stated that at this time Ch. 'was fallen into his old disease of frensie'). iii, 5] sends a herald to bid defiance to Henry (*Hol.* iii, 552). v, 2] (at Troyes) greets Henry and 'the English princes'; retires to discuss the proposed treaty; later, consents that Henry should be styled 'Heritier de France' (*Hol.* iii, 574), and gives him his d. Katharine in marriage. (Acc. *Hol.* iii, 572, the treaty of Troyes had been previously agreed to, and was only revised on Henry's arrival.)

Charles VII. King of France; proclaimed king in 1422 on the death of his father (*Hol.* iii, 585); his meeting with Joan of Arc is described at some length (*ib.* 600) and it is stated that he 'appointed hir a sufficient armie with absolute power to lead them'; hence (*ib.* 605) 'his dignitie abroad was foulie spotted in this point,' that he descended to 'dealing in divelish practises with misbeleevers and witches.' His presence at the espousals of the Princess Margaret is mtd. *2 Hen. VI*, i, 1 (*cf. Hol.* iii, 625).

D.P. *1 Hen. VI.* ('The Dauphin,' in the text, throughout the play.) (i, 1) 'The Dauphin Ch. is crowned king in Rheims.' i, 2] attacks the English before Orleans, but is driven back with loss; tests the pretensions of Joan of Arc, is convinced of her miraculous powers, and professes himself her 'prostrate thrall.' i, 5] *p.m.* i, 6] adulates Joan, and declares that he will divide his crown with her. ii, 1] expresses some doubt of Joan's infallibility. iii, 2] present at an unsuccessful attack on Rouen. iii, 3] makes a compact with the D. of Burgundy. (iv, 1, 4) mtd. iv, 7] shows respect to the bodies of the Talbots. (v, 1) mtd. v, 2] hears that the English are about to attack. (v, 3) is cursed by Joan. v, 4] after a parley, swears fealty to the crown of England. (v, 5) mtd.

Charles' Wain. A popular name for the principal stars of the Great Bear. 'Ch. W. is over the new chimney, and yet our horse is not packed' (*1 Hen. IV*, ii, 1). See URSA MAJOR.

Mtd. in Golding's *Metam.* xv.

Charmion. A waiting-woman to Cleopatra; declared by Octavius to be one of 'those that ruled all the affairs of Antonius' empire' (*Plut.* p. 206).

D.P. *Ant. Cl.* 'Charmian' ('Charmion' once in F1 (i, 5)). i, 2] has her hand read by a soothsayer; jests on the subject with her companions. i, 3] counsels Cleopatra to cross Antony in nothing. i, 5] reminds Cl. of her early love for Caesar. ii, 5] recalls a merry deceit once practised on Ant. (*Plut.* p. 178); intercedes for messenger; leads Cl. to her chamber. iii, 3] confirms Cl.'s confidence in the messenger. iii, 9] in attendance, iii, 11] *p.m.* iv, 2] *p.m.* iv, 4] in attendance. iv, 13] urges Cl. to betake herself to the Monument. iv, 15] succours her swooning mistress. v, 2] is sent on a whispered errand; later, is present at the death of Cl.; as she adjusts the dead Queen's diadem, the guards enter, whereupon she applies an asp, and dies (*Plut.* p. 227).

Charneco. Village in Portugal, near Lisbon; hence, probably, a wine made there. 'Here's a cup of Ch.' (2 *Hen. VI*, ii, 3).

Charolois, Charolais [Count of]. Mtd. as a French noble at Agincourt; *Hen. V*, iii, 5. ('Charaloyes,' Ff.) See BURGUNDY, PHILIP, DUKE OF.

Charon. Son of Erebus; ferried the shades of the dead across the rivers of the underworld (Virg. *Aen.* vi, 298–301). '*Tro*... O be thou, Pandarus, my Ch., And give me swift transportance to those fields' (*Tr. Cr.* iii, 2). 'That grim ferryman which poets write of' (*Rich. III*, i, 4). See STYX.

Chartreux. A monastery of the Carthusian order of monks; a 'Charterhouse.' 'A monk of the Ch.' (*Hen. VIII*, i, 1); attrib.: 'A Ch. friar, his confessor' (*ib.* i, 2). See HOPKINS.

Charybdis. See SCYLLA.

Chastity. Personified. 'Pure C. is rifled of her store' (*Lucr.* 692).

Chatham, Clerk of. See EMMANUEL. D.P. 2 *Hen. VI.* iv, 2] condemned by Cade to be hanged with 'pen and inkhorn about his neck' for the crime of being literate. 'Pennyinckhorne' (*F.P.C.*).

'Chartam,' F1; 'Chattam,' F2, 3, 4 French (p. 173) suggests that 'Chartham,' between Canterbury and Ashford, may be the place intended. Dick's comment that 'They use to write it [Emmanuel] on the top of letters' refers to the custom of heading official letters with this word, in its meaning of 'God with us.'

Chatillon. D.P. *John.* ('The Chattylion of France,' Ff; 'the Lord Chatillion,' or 'Shatillion,' *Tr. R.*) Ambassador from France to King John. i, 1] presents Philip's claim, on Arthur's behalf, to John's possessions. ii, 1] brings news to Ph. of J.'s invasion of France.

There is no reference to this embassy in the *Chronicles*, but 'Gervais de Chatillon' is mtd. as 'representative of the King of France' in a treaty between Philip Augustus and Richard I, made in 1194.

Châtillon, Jacques de. Admiral of France; summoned by Charles VI to his standard, *Hen. V*, iii, 5; slain at Agincourt, *ib.* iv, 8. Cf. *Hol.* iii, 552, 555.

'Lord of Dampier' (Soigneur de Dampierre) (*Hol.* iii, 555).

Cheapside. Street in London; centre of retail trade in the Middle Ages. '*Cade*. In Ch. shall my palfrey go to grass' (2 *Hen. VI*, iv, 2); '*Dick*. When shall we go to Ch., and take up commodities on our bills?' (*ib.* iv, 7).

Cheapside was famous for its goldsmiths' shops. In it also were situated the famous Mermaid and Mitre taverns.

Chertsey. Town on the Thames between London and Windsor. The body of Henry VI 'was conueied in a boat, without priest or clerke, torch or taper ... vnto the monasterie of Chertseie ... and there it was first buried' (*Hol.* iii, 690) on Ascension Day, 1471.

'Now towards Ch. with your holy load' (*Rich. III*, i, 2); 'After I have solemnly interr'd at Ch. monastery this noble king' (*ib. ib.*); mtd., *ib. ib.*

Cheshu. Fluellen's pronunciation of 'Jesu.' *Hen. V*, iii, 2 (3); iv, 1, 7.

Chester. Capital of Cheshire; mtd. 2 *Hen. IV*, i, 1.

Chester, Robert (*c.* 1566–*c.* 1640). A minor poet who published in 1601 a volume of verse in which *The Phoenix and the Turtle* (*q.v.*) appeared.

Chetas. See TROY, GATES OF.

Chichele, or Chicheley, Henry (*c.* 1362–1443). Abp. of Canterbury; founder of All Souls College, Oxford.

D.P. *Hen. V.* i, 1] tells the Bp. of Ely that the bill for largely disendowing the Church, nearly passed in the previous reign, has been revived; expatiates on the young King's wonderful reformation, and proposes to divert his attention from the bill by suggesting war with France (cf. *Hol.* iii, 545). i, 2] explains to the King that the Salic Law by no means bars his title to the crown of France (*ib. ib.*); promises an unexampled subsidy from the clergy (*Hol.* iii, 546); urges him not to fear the Scots (*ib. ib.*); compares the commonwealth to a hive of bees; urges immediate war.

The Abp.'s speech is cited by Holinshed (after Hall and Fabyan) as having been delivered at the parliamont held in Leicester (Apr. 30, 1414), but the scene is laid by Sh. in the presence-chamber of the King's palace in London. Acc. Stubbs (*Const. Hist.* iii, 83), Chichele was not present at Leicester as Abp. (The comparison of the bees is Sh.'s own.)

Child, Blackamoor. D.P. *T. And.* Son of Aaron and Tamora. iv, 2] is brought to A. to be slain, by T.'s command; A. preserves him. v, 1] with A. when he is captured; Lucius swears 'to nourish and bring him up.'

Childeric. King of the Franks; mtd. as deposed by Pepin, *Hen. V*, i, 2; cf. *Hol.* iii, 545.

Acc. A. Schmidt, 'Childeric' should be 'Chilperic'; but Childeric III was deposed by Pepin the Short A.D. 752; *cf.* L. Sergeant, *The Franks*, p. 205.

China. Country in Asia. Only found attributively in *Sh.*: 'They are not C.-dishes, but very good dishes' (*M. for M.* ii, 1, l. 97).

Cf. Florio, '*Porcellana* ... whereof they make C. dishes' (1598).

Chiron. D.P. *T. And.* Son to Tamora. i, 2] exclaims against the barbarity of Rome. ii, 1] contests the possession of Lavinia with his brother Demetrius, but listens to the evil counsel of Aaron the Moor. ii, 2] *p.m.* ii, 3] stabs Bassianus, and drags Lavinia away. ii, 5] scoffs at the now mutilated L. (iv, 1) L. writes his name on the sand. iv, 2] learns his mother's shame. iv, 4] *p.m.* v, 2] is killed by Titus. (v, 3) his flesh is served at table to Tamora.

The name is that of a centaur (Ovid, *Fasti.* v, 379 ff.) who was the toacher of Achilles.

Chitopher. Name of a commander; *All's Well*, iv, 3.

Chorus (1). D.P. *Hen. V.* Speaker of the prologue to each act. ('Prologue,' Ff.)

i] an apology for the impossibility of adequately representing 'so great an object' as war 'within the girdle of these walls'; the audience must call in the aid of imagination. ii] warlike preparations in England; a plot against the King's life by English nobles, instigated by the foe; change of scene, during the act, from Southampton to France notified. iii] passage of the Channel by the English host; the attempt of France to make peace having proved abortive, the siege of Harfleur has begun. iv] the contrasted behaviour of the opposing armies the night before Agincourt; the visit of 'the royal captain' to his men – 'a little touch of Harry in the night'; it is feared that 'the name of Agincourt' may be disgraced by the puny display upon the stage. v] the return of Henry to England (Nov. 1415); his reception in London; the visit of the Emperor (Sigismund) in 1416, 'in behalf of France'; spectators must transport their thoughts once more to France and suppose an interval (of some five years) to have elapsed.

An incidental allusion (v, Chor.) to the impending return of the Earl of Essex from Ireland is held to fix the date of the production of the play (1599).

Chorus (2). D.P. *Rom. J.* Between Acts I and II relates that Romeo and Juliet, now in love with one another, find means to meet.

Chrish. Fluellen's pronunciation of 'Christ'; *Hen. V*, iii, 2 (6).

Christ. 'The Anointed One,' a title of Jesus. 'Fought for Jesu Chr.' (*Rich. II*, iv, 1); 'gave ... his pure soul unto his captain Chr.' (*ib. ib.*); 'so Judas did to Chr.' (*ib. ib.*); 'the sepulchre of Chr.' (*1 Hen. IV*, i, 1); 'kingdoms that acknowledge Chr.' (*ib.* iii, 2); 'in the name of ... Chr.' (*Hen. V*, iv, 1); 'Christ's mother helps me' (*1 Hen. VI*, i, 2); 'you shall sup with Jesu Chr. tonight' (*2 Hen. VI*, v, 1); 'redemption By Chr.'s dear blood' (*Rich. III*, i, 4). Referred to: 'blessed Mary's son' (*Rich. II*, ii, 1); 'my Redeemer,' 'our dear Redeemer' (*Rich. III*, ii,1); 'our Saviour' (*Haml.* i, 1); 'that dread King' (*2 Hen. VI*, iii, 2, l. 154).

[**Christ Church.**] A college at Oxford, founded by Wolsey, 1525, as Cardinal College. 'Those twins of learning that he raised in you, Ipswich and Oxford! one of which fell with him ... The other, though unfinish'd, yet so famous, So excellent in art, and still so rising' (*Hen. VIII*, iv, 2).

Christendom. 'The civilized world,' or the world in general. 'The lyingest knave in C.' (*Tam. Sh.* Ind. 2; *2 Hen. VI*, ii, 1); 'all the kings of C.' (*John*, iii, 1); 'never a king's son in C.' (*1 Hen. IV*, i, 2); 'ne'er a king in C.' (*ib.* ii, 1); 'the states of C.' (*1 Hen. VI*, v, 4); 'the bluntest wooer in C.'(*3 Hen. VI*, iii, 2); 'the voice of C.' (*Hen. VIII*, ii, 2). Mtd., *Tam. Sh.* ii, 1; *Macb.* iv, 3; *John*, ii, 1; *1 Hen. IV*, iii, 1; *1 Hen. VI*, ii, 4; *Hen. VIII*, i, 3, iv, 2.

Christmas. As a winter season: 'at C. I no more desire a rose Than wish a snow in May's new-fangled mirth' (*L.L.L.* i, 1). As a time of merriment: 'a C. comedy' (*ib.* v, 2); 'a C. gambol' (*Tam. Sh.* Ind. 2).

'Ever 'gainst that season comes Wherein our Saviour's birth is celebrated ... no spirit dare stir abroad ... So hallow'd and so gracious is the time' (*Haml.* i, I).

Christopher. As a forename. 'Chr. Sly' (*Tam. Sh.* Ind.); 'Sir Chr. [Urswick]' (*Rich. III*, iv, 5).

Christophero. For 'Christopher'; *Tam. Sh.* Ind. 2.

[**Chryseis.**] Patronymic from 'Chryses'; Astynome, d. of Chryses, who was taken captive by Achilles, but, in the distribution of booty, given to Agamemnon, who had to restore her to her father to quell the wrath of Apollo (Hom. *Il.* i, 378; 'Dict. Cret.' ii, 17, 33, 47). See CRESSIDA.

Chus. A Jew, an acquaintance of Shylock; mtd. *M.V.* iii, 2.

'Cush' was the eldest son of Ham (Gen. x, 6; 1 Chron. i, 8).

Cicely. Feminine name. *Tam. Sh.* Ind. 2; *Com. Err.* iii, 1.

Cicero, Marcus Tullius. Roman philosopher, orator, and statesman, 106–43 B.C. During the year that elapsed after the murder of Julius Caesar he was at the height of his popularity and delivered his twelve 'Philippics,' but on the formation of the Triumvirate his name appeared in the list of the proscribed, and, after a vain attempt at escape, he was murdered near his villa at Formiae. 'A Roman sworder and banditto slave Murthered sweet Tully' (*2 Hen. VI*, iv, 1); Plutarch (North's transln. (1595), pp. 935–6) states that C. was killed by 'Herennius a centurion.' Of C.'s numerous writings only one is mtd. in *Sh.*, viz. 'Tully's *Orator*' (*T. And.* iv, 1).

D.P. *Jul. C.* i, 2] *p.m.*; in Caesar's train on the occasion of the Lupercalia; his 'ferret and ... fiery eyes' when 'cross'd in conference' mentioned by Brutus; is said to have spoken Greek to the populace. i, 3] listens to Casca's account of the recent prodigies, but makes light of them. (ii, 1) Brutus rejects the advice given him that Cic. should be sounded as to joining the conspiracy, on the ground that 'he will never follow anything that other men begin.' (iv, 3) his death announced.

Cicero's personal characteristics, as mentioned in the play, are Sh.'s invention. With regard to his speaking Greek, Plutarch relates that the plebeians 'commonly called him the Grecian, and scholer,' derisively (North, *ut supra*, p. 861).

Cicester, Cirencester. Town in Gloucestershire; reported burnt by rebels, *Rich. II*, v, 6. ('Ciceter,' QqFf; 'Circester' and 'Circiter' in *Hol.*)

Cilicia. Province in S.E. Asia Minor; assigned by Antony to Ptolemy, his son by Cleopatra, *Ant. Cl.* iii, 6; cf. *Plut.* p. 202. ('Silicia,' F1.)

Cimber, [L. Tillius]. One of the murderers of Julius Caesar. He was at first one of Caesar's warmest supporters, and was rewarded with the province of Bithynia; but for an unknown reason he joined the conspirators. On the fatal day Cimber pushed forward and presented a petition praying for his brother's return from exile. On Caesar's waving him back, he seized the Dictator's gown and drew him forward; this was the signal for the assassination. Plutarch calls him 'Tullius Cimber' (pp. 118–9), and 'Metellus Cimber' (p. 100), the latter name being adopted by Sh.

D.P. *Jul. C.* 'Metellus Cimber.' (i, 3) mtd. as being one of the conspirators. ii, 1] urges that Cicero should be asked to join them; suggests Caius Ligarius also, and is sent to fetch him. ii, 2] *p.m.*; is courteously addressed by Caes. (ii, 3) Artemidorus in his warning bids Caes. 'mark well M.C.' iii, 1] presents a petition to Caes., in favour of his 'banish'd brother,' shortly before the murder.

Cimber, Metellus. See CIMBER, L. TILLIUS.

Cimber, Publius. Brother of 'Metellus Cimber'; banished by Caesar, *Jul. C.* iii, 1. (The name seems to have been invented by Sh.)

Cimmerian. One of a race dwelling in what is now South Russia, which was fabled to be a place of perpetual darkness. Aaron, the Moor, is termed a 'swarth C.' (*T. And.* ii, 3), apparently in allusion to his complexion.

The word occurs in Peele, *Edw. I*, iv, 21.

Cinna (1). Acc. *Plut.* (p. 122), a poet, and one of Caesar's friends, who was torn to pieces by the mob under the belief that he was L. Cornelius Cinna the conspirator.

D.P. *Jul. C.* iii, 3] oppressed by an ominous dream, he is on his way to Caesar's funeral, when he encounters a mob, who, learning his name, take no heed of his protests, but kill him – 'for his bad verses,' as one of them exclaims.

It has been doubted whether this was C. Helvius Cinna, an eminent poet and a friend of Catullus. Suetonius and several other historians relate that 'Helvius Cinna' was killed as above described, but they do not refer to him as a poet, but as a tribune of the plebeians. Plutarch in another account of him, referring to his dream and his death (p. 102), merely speaks of him as 'one of Caesar's friends.'

Cinna, [L. Cornelius], the Younger. Was made praetor by Julius Caesar, but approved of his assassination. 'When another called C... began to accuse Caesar, they [the mob] ... marvellously reviled him' (*Plut.* p. 120).

D.P. *Jul. C.* i, 3] is commissioned by the conspirators to distribute papers. ii, 1] takes part in a meeting in Brutus' orchard. ii, 2] *p.m.* (ii, 3; paper) 'have an eye to C.' iii, 1] present at Caesar's death. (iii, 3) mtd.

'Cynna,' ii, 2, F1.

Cinque Ports. Sandwich, Dover, Hythe, Romney, and Hastings; their burgesses were styled 'barons.' 'Four [barons] of the C.-P.' bear a canopy over Anne (Boleyn) at her coronation, *Hen. VIII*, iv, 1; cf. *Hol.* iii, 933. Cf. *N.E.D. s.v.* 'baron.'

Circe. An enchantress who changed men to beasts by magical draughts from her cup (Hom. *Od.* x-xii; Ovid, *Metam.* xiv, 253 ff.).

'I think you all have drunk of C.'s cup' (*Com. Err.* v, 1); 'See how the ugly witch [Joan of Arc] doth bend her brows, As if, with C., she would change my shape' (*1 Hen. VI*, v, 3).

Citizen, First. D.P. *Rom. J.* iii, 1] detains Benvolio as a witness 'in the Prince's name.'

'First officer,' Capell.

Citizens, Several. D.PP. *Cor.* ii, 3; iv, 6.

Clare, St. St Clara, founder of the sisterhood of Les Clarisses, founded 1212; perh. alluded to in the following passage: 'A more strict restraint Upon the sisterhood, the votarists of St C.' (*M. for M.* i, 5).

A sisterhood of this order was established before 1350 at Rye (Sussex), a town visited by Sh.'s company in 1597.

Clarence, Dukes of. See George, Lionel, Thomas.

The origin of this ducal title is doubtful. It has been held to be derived from Κλαρέντζα *It.* Chiarenza, a port in Greece (which gave his title to the eldest son of the Prince of Achaia), and to have been introduced into England through Philippa, Edward III's queen. Other authorities derive it from Clare in Suffolk, which gives an earl's title to the British sovereign.

Clarence, Young Daughter of. D.P. *Rich. III.* See Plantagenet, Margaret.

Clarence, Young Son of. D.P. *Rich. III.* See Edward, Earl of Warwick.

Claribel. Daughter and heir of Alonso (D.P. *Temp.*), King of Naples; married unwillingly, for political reasons, to 'an African,' the King of Tunis. *Temp*, ii, 1; v, 1.

Claudio (1). D.P. *M. Ado.* 'A young lord of Florence.' i, 1] (has distinguished himself in the wars); becomes a guest of Leonato; on again seeing Hero, Leonato's daughter (he had previously 'look'd upon her with a soldier's eye'), falls in love with her; adopts the suggestion that Don Pedro should woo her in disguise during the revelling at night, and pass himself off as Cl. (i, 2) mtd. (i, 3) Don John is informed of 'the most exquisite Cl.'s' passion. ii, 1] Cl. learns from Don John that Don Pedro has wooed Hero for himself; this is confirmed by Benedick, by whom Cl. in his grief is compared to a 'poor hurt fowl'; later, Cl. learns from Don P. that all is well, and that Hero is won for him; the wedding is fixed for a week hence. (ii, 2) Don John and Borachio plot against the marriage. ii, 3] (Benedick describes how Cl. is metamorphosed by love); Cl. joins in the conversation designed to make Ben. believe Beatrice loves him. (iii, 1) mtd. iii, 2] banters Ben.; hears and credits the false accusation made against Hero by Don J., and vows to shame her 'in the congregation.' (iii, 3) witnesses the apparent confirmation of the slander. iv, 1] publicly, in the church, casts off Hero as a worthless woman and assails her with invective; (Beat. bids Benedick 'kill Claudio!'). (iv, 2) mtd. v, 1] Cl. is bitterly objurgated by Leonato and Antonio, who, though old, wish to fight him; is challenged by Ben.; hears Hero's exculpation by Borachio, who confesses all; Cl. is overcome with remorse; begs Leon. and Ant. to impose what penance they will upon him; is told that he must marry Leonato's niece. (v, 2) mtd. v, 3] performs a solemn rite at Hero's supposed tomb. v, 4] in wedding the 'niece,' finds her to be H. herself.

The corresponding character in Bandello's *Novella* is Timbreo di Cardona.

'With regard to Claudio's character, Sh. has so blended the elements in his nature – he has given such a good foundation of honour and self-reliance to his unstable mind and fickle youth – that we cannot, with all our disapprobation of his conduct, be doubtful as to his character. Changeable as he is, he continues stable in no choice of friends and loved ones, since he had never continuously tested them; at the slightest convulsion of events he is overpowered by first impressions, and he is without the strength of will to search to the bottom of things.' (Gervinus, *Sh. Comm.* (1875), pp. 413 ff.)

Clandio (2). D.P. *M. for M.* 'A young gentleman,' brother to Isabella. (i, 2) his arrest for intercourse with Juliet announced. i, 3] on his way to prison he asks his friend Lucio to implore Isabella to intercede for him with the Deputy (Angelo). (i, 5) his danger is explained to Isab. (ii, 1) his execution ordered 'by nine tomorrow morning,' (ii, 2) but postponed. (ii, 3, 4) mtd. iii, 1] the disguised Duke advises him to prepare for death; Isab. tells him that he can be saved at the price of her honour; at first he rejects the condition, then reflecting that 'Death is a fearful thing,' cries in despair, 'Sweet sister, let me live!' but she scornfully bids him die. (iii, 2) he is reported to be reconciled to his fate. iv, 2] is told that 'by eight tomorrow Thou must be made immortal'; (his execution three hours earlier is afterward commanded). (iv, 3) he is ordered by the Duke to be put 'in secret hold,' while the head of a pirate who has died is taken to Angelo. v, 1] he is brought before the Duke, and pardoned, but ordered to restore her he had wronged.

The equivalent character in Cinthio's *Novella* is Vico; he is actually executed.

Claudio (3), Mtd. as bearing letters from Hamlet; *Haml.* iv, 7.

Claudius (1). D.P. *Haml.* King of Denmark. i, 2] justifies his marriage while yet his brother's 'memory is green'; sends envoys to Norway; permits Laertes to return to France; deprecates Hamlet's 'obstinate condolement' for his father; rejoices at his 'fair reply.' (i, 5) the murder of Hamlet's father by Claudius related by the ghost of the former. ii, 2] Cl. instructs Rosencrantz and Guildenstern to probe the cause of Hamlet's 'transformation'; greets the envoys on their return from Norway; listens to Polonius' account of Hamlet's love for Ophelia. iii, 1] learns that H. is not 'forward to be sounded'; a chance remark by Polonius pricks his conscience; overhears a conversation between H. and Ophelia, and determines, for safety, to despatch the former to England. iii, 2] is present at the play selected by Hamlet, and is terror-stricken at the reproduction of his own crime. iii, 3] instructs Ros. and Guild, to escort Hamlet to England, with the secret intention (v, 2) that he should there be put to death; he is overwhelmed with remorse for his fratricide; he tries to pray, and is in imminent danger of being slain in the act by Hamlet. iv, 1] learns that H. has killed Polonius; his 'soul is full of discord, and dismay.' iv, 3] hastens H.'s departure; until H.'s death is announced he will know no joy. iv, 5] witnesses Ophelia's madness; is dismayed at the political consequences of Polonius' death; calms Laertes, who seeks to avenge his father, and declares he shall be satisfied. iv, 7] explains why he feared to proceed against H. as a murderer; learns that H. has returned; contrives with Laertes the means of H.'s death. v, 1] is present at the struggle of the two young men over Ophelia's grave. v, 2] makes them shake hands before the fencing-match; offers H. the poisoned cup, but fails to prevent the Queen drinking of it; (H., discovering the treachery, stabs him).

Not named in the text. In the st. dirs. of i, 2, in QqFf, 'Claudius King of Denmark.' The corresponding character in the *Historica Danica* of Saxo Grammaticus is Fengo, which becomes Fengon in *The Hystorie of Hamblet* (1608).

Claudius (2). D.P. *Jul. C.* 'Servant to Brutus.' iv, 3] in attendance on Br.; is ordered to lie down in the tent.

The name, or its equivalent 'Clodius,' occurs frequently in *Plutarch*.

[Cleandro.] See GREMIO.

Cleitus. A Macedonian who saved the life of Alexander the Great at Granicus, but was slain at a banquet by A., who was exasperated by his insolent language (Plutarch, *Alex.*).

'*Flu.* Alexander ... being a little intoxicates in his prains, did, in his ales and his angers, look you, kill his pest friend Cl.' (*Hen. V*, iv, 7).

'Clitus,' Qq; 'Clytus,' Ff.

Clement. As a forename; see PERKES.

[Clement VII.] Pope (Giulio de Medici); b.*c.* 1475; Pope 1523–34. The proceedings ending in the divorce of Henry VIII and Katharine of Arragon took place in his pontificate. Clement sent over Campeggio (*q.v.*) in 1528, and before his death pronounced the Queen's marriage valid (1534).

Sends Campeggio, *Hen. VIII*, ii, 2; Kath. appeals to the Pope, *ib.* ii, 4; Wolsey's letters to Clement fall into the King's hands, *ib.* iii, 2.

Clement's Inn. One of the eight, or nine, 'Inns of Chancery,' situated W. of the modern Law Courts in London. As Justice Shallow's abode in his Templar days, the Inn is referred to, 2 *Hen. IV*, iii, 2 (4).

'Clemham,' Q (once).

Cleomenes. D.P. *Wint. T.* ('Cleomines,' Ff.) A Sicilian lord. (ii, 1) is sent with Dion. by Leontes, to consult the oracle of Apollo. (ii, 3) they return to Sicily. iii, 1] he praises the climate of Delphos, and speaks of the mighty voice of the oracle. iii, 2] they present 'the seal'd-up oracle.' v, 1] Cl. urges Leontes to forget his long past faults, now redeemed; begs Paulina to refrain from further reminding the King of them; summons Florizel to greet L.

A Spartan king of the name is the subject of ono of Plutarch's *Lives*. In *Pandosto* six unnamed messengers are sent to Delphos.

Cleon. D.P. *Per.* Governor of Tarsus. i, 4] laments over the famine which has fallen upon Tarsus; on hearing of the arrival of Pericles' fleet, at first believes it to be hostile; on learning that it brings relief, invokes a curse on all who prove ungrateful to Pericles. (iii, 1) Per., in the storm, resolves to make for Tarsus and 'visit Cl.' iii, 3] Cl. invokes the vengeance of the gods on his wife and himself if they do not cherish the infant (Marina) entrusted to them. iv, 4] is struck with remorse at the (supposed) murder of Marina, but is upbraided by his wife Dionyza for cowardice; (appears in dumb show). (v, 1) 'cruel Cleon's' plot unfolded to P. (v, 2) 'inhospitable Cl.' (v, 3) his death described.

Stranguilio in *The Patterns of Painfull Adventures* (1576).

Cleopatra (69–30 B.C.). Daughter of Ptolemy Auletes, King of Egypt; succeeded to the throne on the death of her father (52 B.C.) conjointly with her brother Ptolemy, whom she was to marry. In 49 B.C. she was deposed by Pothinus and Achillas, Ptolemy's chief officers. Julius Caesar, arriving in Egypt soon after, replaced Cl. on the throne – an act which resulted in a war in which Ptolemy was defeated, and perished. For reasons of state, Cl. was then nominally married to another brother, also named Ptolemy, a mere boy, but lived openly with Caesar and accompanied him to Rome, where she remained until his death, 44 B.C. By him she had a son, Caesarion. After the death of Caesar she hurried back to Egypt, and, espousing the cause of the Triumvirate, assisted Dolabella with ships and men. Ill health and stormy weather served her as excuses for not coming to Ant.'s aid after Dola.'s defeat, but Ant. summoned her to Asia Minor, 41 B.C., to explain her conduct in not having efficiently supported the Triumvirate. On her arrival she completely captivated Ant. and became his mistress. Their connection was interrupted by his marriage with Octavia, but was renewed on his return from Italy, and again after his Parthian expedition. News of Octavia's having left Rome to join her husband led Cl. to exert her utmost influence over Ant., who became increasingly infatuated and ready to humour her every caprice. They posed as Isis and Osiris, and conferred the kingdoms of the world upon their children. Octavius, seeing his opportunity, declared war against Cl. The Battle of Actium was fought, 31 B.C., and in the midst of it Cl. fled with all her ships. Followed by Ant., she sought Alexandria, and seeing her position desperate entered into negotiations with Octavius, offering to make away with Antony. Shutting herself up in a mausoleum she had built, she caused a report of her death to be spread. Ant. thereupon stabbed himself. Failing to soften the heart of Octavius, and realizing that he intended to take her captive to Rome, Cl. put an end to her life by the poison of an asp.

D.P. *Ant. Cl.* i, 1] banters Antony on what she assumes to be his subservience to Fulvia and Octavius. i, 2] ostentatiously avoids a meeting with Ant. i, 3] on Ant.'s entrance declares she is 'sick and sullen'; bids A. depart to the wife to whom he has been false; on learning that Fulvia is dead, exclaims that A.'s callousness but shows how her own death would be received – let him weep for his wife and declare the tears are for 'Egypt'; after further bitter raillery her mood changes, she seeks forgiveness from A., and invokes victory for his sword, i, 5] laments A.'s absence and longs for tidings of him; eagerly questions Alexas (bearer of a pearl from A.) – 'what was he, sad or merry?'; resolves to send daily messengers to A.; rebukes Charmian for comparing Caesar to him. ii, 5] restlessly suggests one pastime after another, only to reject them; recalls past revelry with A. (*Plut.* p. 178); on the arrival of a messenger from Italy, Cl. plies him so eagerly with questions that he cannot deliver his tidings, but on learning that A. is 'married to Octavia' she hales the man up and down by the hair and threatens his life; recalling the man, who has escaped, she reiterates the question 'He is married?' only to be assured by the unwilling messenger that the news is true; bids him begone, but a moment after sends Alexas to inquire Octavia's age, appearance, and stature; bids her attendants lead her to her chamber. iii, 3] once more minutely questions the messenger, from whom she now receives gratifying replies; dismisses him with a gift. iii, 7] overrides the arguments of Enobarbus against her taking a personal part in Ant.'s campaign; on A.'s entrance reminds him she has 'sixty sails.' iii, 11] (after Actium) implores pardon from A., and is rewarded by a kiss. iii, 13] seeks, without effect, consolation from Enobarbus; listens to the message of Thyreus, an emissary from Octavius, and makes a submissive reply; is giving him her hand to kiss as Ant. enters (*Plut.* p. 218), and is furiously objurgated by A., whom, after he has spent his wrath upon Thyreus, she wins back into a mood of affection and hope. iv, 2] is present when A. addresses his officers on the morrow's battle (*Plut.* p. 219). iv, 4] helps to arm A. iv, 8] offers Scarus (*q.v.*), for his valour, a suit of golden armour. iv, 12] is assailed with invective by A., who is enraged at the defection of her fleet (*Plut.* p. 220). iv, 15] receives the dying Ant. in the Monument and listens to his last counsels (*Plut.* p. 221); after his death, on recovering from a momentary swoon, resolves on suicide. v, 2] listens through the gate to Octavius' terms as delivered by Proculeius (*Plut.* p. 222); on the entrance of the guard tries to stab herself, but is disarmed; exclaims that a 'ditch in Egypt' shall be her grave rather than that she will submit to Oct.; extols the greatness of Ant.; hears from Dolabella that Oct. means her to grace his triumph; on the entrance of Oct. kneels to him and expresses entire submission; renders him a 'brief' of her possessions, but is enraged with her treasurer for admitting that a part has been suppressed (*Plut.* p. 225); on the departure of Oct. sends Charmian on a secret errand; learns from Dolabella that Oct. intends to deport her and her children within three days (*Plut.* p. 226); dilates on the horrors of captivity; sends for her royal robe; is brought a basket containing asps (*Plut.* p. 227); dons her robe and crown, applies an asp, and dies (*Plut.* p. 228).

The following are references to Cleopatra in scenes in which she does not appear, or when she is absent from the stage: (i, 1) termed 'a strumpet' by Philo; (i, 2) Ant. bids the messenger 'name Cl. as she's call'd in Rome'; Enobarbus discusses her character with Ant., who would have 'left unseen a wonderful piece of work' if he had never seen her; (i, 4) 'the queen of Ptolemy'; (ii, 1) her 'witchcraft'; 'Egypt's widow'; (ii, 2) her first meeting with Ant. 'upon the river of Cydnus'; 'age cannot wither her nor custom stale Her infinite variety'; (iii, 6) enthroned, as the goddess Isis, in Alexandria; (iii, 10) her flight from Actium 'like a cow in June'; (iii, 13) 'a morsel cold upon Dead Caesar's trencher'; (iv, 8) 'great fairy'; (iv, 12) swallows build in the sails of her ship; (iv, 14) 'pack'd cards with Caesar.'

'C.'s majesty' attributed to Rosalind, *A.Y.L.* iii, 2; 'proud C., when she met hor Roman, And Cydnus swell'd above the banks,' subject of tapostry, *Cymb.* ii, 4.

Clifford, John de (*c.* 1435–61). 13th Baron Clifford; son of Thomas de C. (*q.v.*); at the head of an armed force demanded compensation at London for his father's death; joined the Yorkists 1459; fought against them at Wakefield; slain near Ferrybridge.

Hall (p. 251) relates that in ruthlessly stabbing the youthful Rutland after the Battle of Wakefield Clifford 'was accompted a tyraunt and no gentleman,' and further states that, according to one story, he set the Duke of York's head upon a pole, and decorating it with a paper crown took it to Margaret. He is called 'butcher,' 'cruel childkiller,' and 'treacherous coward' (*3 Hen. VI.* ii, 2).

D.P. *2 Hen. VI.* 'Young Clifford.' v, 1] taunts Richard with his deformity. v, 2] (at St Albans) enters, to find his father slain; vows to have no pity for the house of York.

D.P. *3 Hen. VI.* i, 1] (in the Parliament House) vows to support Henry, and thus avenge himself upon the slayer of his father. i, 3] (near Sandal Castle) ruthlessly stabs the young E. of Rutland despite his piteous entreaties. i, 4] claims the right of slaying the captive York, and is the first to stab him. ii, 2] urges the King to show no lenity to the Yorkists for his son's sake; advises him to quit the field before the coming battle; has a bitter altercation with Richard Plantagenet and Warwick. ii, 4] fights with Richard, but flees on the entrance of Warwick. ii, 6] dies of his wounds; (his head is sent to be placed over York Gates).

'The piteous moan that Rutland made When blackfaced Clifford shook his sword at him' (*Rich. III*, i, 2); '[a] deadly bloud-supper' (*Hol.* iii, 659).

Clifford, Thomas (1414–55). 12th Baron Clifford; attended Bedford in France; slain in the 1st Battle of St Albans. In *2 Hen. VI*, v, 2, he is called 'Clifford of Cumberland' (following *The First Part of the Contention*), but the title of E. of Cumberland was first conferred on his g.g.s. in 1525.

D.P. *2 Hen. VI.* 'Old Clifford.' iv, 8] appeals successfully to the rebels to forsake Cade and follow the King, warning them of the danger of a French invasion. iv, 9] announces the flight of Cade. v, 1] indignantly refuses to pay homage to York, whom he calls a traitor; bids defiance to the enemies of the King. v, 2] (at St Albans) is slain in combat with York.

In *3 Hen. VI*, i, 1, it is stated, in contradiction to the above, that Clifford was slain by 'common soldiers.'

Clifton, Sir John. Slain at Shrewsbury (*Hol.* iii, 523). 'Clifton' is mentioned as needing succour during the battle, *1 Hen. IV*, v, 4.

He was 'made banneret on the field' (French, p. 75).

Clitus. D.P. *Jul. C.* 'Servant to Brutus.' v, 5] is asked by Br. at Philippi to kill him, but 'would rather kill himself.'

Plutarch's account (p. 150) differs in certain details. 'Clytus,' Ff.

Cloten. D.P. *Cymb.* 'Son to the Queen by a former husband' (Rowe). (i, 1) is characterized as 'too bad for bad report.' (i, 2) 'draws on' Posthumus, but they are parted. i, 3] brags of the encounter. ii, 1] having lost a match at bowls, and 'broken the pate' of one who rebuked him for swearing, laments that his rank prevents him from fighting such 'jack-slaves'; hears of Iachimo's arrival, and resolves to 'win of him' at night. ii, 3] has been beaten at dice; arranges a serenade for Imogen; complains to his mother and the King that Im. 'vouchsafes no notice'; is given some hints on wooing her by the Queen; gains an interview with Im. and is rebuffed by her; takes greatly to heart Im.'s retort – stung by his abuse of Posthumus – that she would value P.'s 'meanest garment' more than a multitude of such men as Cl.; he vows vengeance. iii, 1] declares bluntly that Britain, being 'a world by itself, will pay no tribute to Rome'; tells Lucius that the arbitrament of war must decide all. (iii, 4) his love-suit has been to Imogen 'as fearful as a siege.' iii, 5] bids farewell to Lucius; finding that Im., whom he 'both loves and hates,' has fled to Milford, vows to kill Posthumus and force her in P.'s own garments, which he has obtained through Pisanio. iv, 1] (*sol.*) gloats over his coming revenge. iv, 2] is recognized by Belarius, and after an altercation with Guiderius is slain and beheaded by the latter; his headless body is taken for that of Posthumus by Imogen, and is buried by the Romans. (iv, 3, 4) mtd. (v, 5) the manner of his death made known to Cymbeline.

Cloten, or Clotenus, appears as a king of Cornwall and father of Malmucius (*Hol.* i, 15; 'Morgan' and 'Arviragus' occur on adjoining pages). Clotyn is a character in *Gorboduc* (*q.v.*).

'It is remarkable that though Cloten makes so poor a figure in love, he is described as assuming an air of consequence as the Queen's son in a council of state, and with all the absurdity of his person and manners, is not without shrewdness in his observations' (W. Hazlitt). The 'absurdity of his person' is scarcely compatible with Imogen's mistake. 'Cloten is a mere ass, without humour or even fun. Sh. has not another such. It is, however, a just and natural judgment upon the subtle witch, his mother, to have borne such a moon-calf. These amazing clever, wicked women gonerally produce Clotens.' (Hartley Coleridge.)

Clothair. *Lat.* Clotharius; name of three Merovingian kings. 'Blithhild [*q.v.*] which was daughter to King Clothair' (*Hen. V*, i, 2); 'counsellors to Pepin or Clotharius' (*Hen. VIII*, i, 3).

Clotharius. See CLOTHAIR.

Clowder. A hound; *Tam. Sh.* Ind. 1. See *Sh. Eng.* ii, 349.

Clown (1). D.P. *All's Well.* Servant to the Countess of Rousillon. i, 3] gives reasons why he would marry 'Isbel.' ii, 2] satirizes fashionable jargon. ii, 4] banters Parolles. iii, 2] 'has no mind to Isbel' since he has been at Court; later, announces that Bertram has 'run away.' iv, 5] jests on serving 'the black prince'; later, announces Bertram. v, 2] is called 'Monsieur Lavatch' (*q.v.*) by Parolles, whom he derides.

A typical domestic clown, whose duty it was ever to be ready to give a taste of his quality.

Clown (2). D.P. *Ant. Cl.* ('A countryman,' *Plut.* p. 227.) v, 2] 'a rural fellow'; brings an asp to Cleopatra in a basket of figs; enlarges on the properties of 'the worm.'

Clown (3). D.P. *M. for M.* A servant to Mistress Overdone, 'a poor widow's tapster.' ii, 1] defends himself volubly against Elbow's incoherent charge; is dismissed by Escalus, but warned to mend his ways. iv, 2] (in the prison) consents to assist the executioner. iv, 3] enumerates the prisoners; bids Bernardine 'rise and be hanged.'

In his examination declares his name to be Pompey Bum.

Clown (4). D.P. *Oth.* Servant to Othello. iii, 1] dismisses the musicians ordered to play before O.'s house. iii, 4] quibbles to his mistress.

'Intended to be an allowed, or domestic, fool in the service of Othello and Desdemona' (Douce, *Illust. Sh.* ii, 274).

Clown (5). D.P. *T. And.* iv, 3] entering with two pigeons destined as a gift for officials, is sent by Titus to present his pigeons and a petition to the Emperor. iv, 4] performs his errand and is ordered by Saturninus to be hanged.

Clown (6). D.P. *T. Nt.* See FESTE.

Clown (7). D.P. *Wint. T.* Son of Old Shepherd (reputed father of Perdita) (Ff). iii, 3] describes the wreck of the Sicilian bark and the killing of Antigonus by a bear; is shown the rescued babe (Perdita), and the treasure, by his father; proposes to bury whatever remains of Antig. there may be. iv, 3] encounters Autolycus and is befooled and robbed by him. iv, 4] is importuned by Mopsa to buy ballads from Aut.; later, advises his father to declare Perdita a changeling, to escape the King's wrath; meets Aut., who is in the guise of a courtier and who dilates on the tortures in store for 'the shepherd's son'; advises his father to bribe Aut. and is willing to remain with the latter as a hostage, but is ordered to proceed to the seashore. (v, 1) having been inveigled on Florizel's ship by Aut., is carried to Sicily. v, 2] (gives evidence of the death of Antigonus); now richly attired, gives himself airs as 'a gentleman born,' and is prepared to swear, if need be, that Aut. is 'as honest and true fellow as any in Bohemia.'

There is no corresponding character in Greene's *Pandosto*.

Clowns, Two. D.PP. *Haml.* (Grave-diggers.) v, 1] while digging Ophelia's grave they dispute on the 'crowner's quest law' of suicide; 1st. Cl. chops logic with Hamlet and points out Yorick's skull.

Clytus. See CLEITUS and CLITUS.

Cneius. See POMPEIUS, CN.

Cobham, Baron. See BROOKE, EDWARD, and OLDCASTLE, SIR JOHN.

Cobham, Eleanor, Duchess of Gloucester (*ob. c.* 1446). Originally mistress, and afterward wife, of Humphrey, D. of Gl. 'Accused of treason [1441]; for that she by sorcerie and inchantment intended to destroie the King, to the intent to advance her husband to the throne' (*Hol.* iii, 622), the means adopted being the usual consuming of a waxen image. (This charge is not alluded to in the play.) Sentenced to imprisonment in the Isle of Man, after doing penance in London (*ib.* 623).

D.P. *2 Hen. VI.* i, 2] urges the Duke to aim at the crown with her aid; makes light of the Duke's ominous dream, and relates one of her own; is sternly rebuked by the Duke for her ambition; bribes the priest, Hume, to confer with certain necromancers. i, 3] receives a box on the ear from Q. Margaret, and vows vengeance (historically, M. was not crowned until 4 years after the disgrace of the Duchess). i, 4] is present at a conjuration and is arrested. ii, 3] is sentenced to penance and banishment. ii, 4] while doing penance, meets the Duke; reproaches him for permitting her disgrace, and warns him of his coming fall; yields herself submissively to the custody of Sir John Stanley (*q.v.*).

Cobham, Lord. *3 Hen. VI*, i, 2. See Brooke, Edward.

Cobham, Reginald, Lord C. of Sterborough. Married the widow of Sir John Arundel, brother of Abp. Arundel. Mtd. among Bolingbroke's adherents: 'Rainold, Lord Cobham, that late broke from the Duke of Exeter' (*Rich. II*, ii, 1).

'Rainold,' Q1Q2; 'Raynold,' Q3Q4; 'Rainald,' Ff; 'Raynald,' Q5; 'Reignold,' Capell. Acc. the text, it would appear that it was Lord Cobham who broke from the D. of Exeter; but acc. *Hol.* iii, 496, it was Thos. Arundel (*q.v.*), and it seems probable that a line is lost.

Cobloaf. Name applied to Thersites by Ajax; *Tr. Cr.* ii, 1.

Defined by Minsheu, *Ductor Ling.* (1617), as 'a little loafe made with a round head' (*N.E.D.*).

Cobweb. D.P. *M.N.D.* A fairy. iii, 1] attends on Bottom, at Titania's bidding. iv, 1] is sent for a honey-bag.

Cock-pit, The. A theatre in Drury Lane, once used for cock-fighting and afterward named the Phoenix. Mtd. in the Epistle 'To the great Variety of Readers' prefixed to the First Folio.

Cocytus. In the underworld; the river of wailing. 'As hateful as C.'s misty mouth' (*T. And.* ii, 4).

Cf. *Locrine*, iii, 6; iv, 4.

Coeur-de-lion. Richard I (*q.v.*). Thus named: *John*, i, 1 (4), ii, 1; *1 Hen. VI*, iii, 2. ('Cordelion,' Ff.)

Coint, Francis, Esquire. Sailed from Brittany with Bolingbroke, (*Hol.* iii, 497). Mtd. *Rich. II*, ii, 1. ('Coines,' Qq; 'Quoint,' Ff.)

French (p. 50) suggests that the name is perhaps an error for 'Point,' and equivalent to 'Poyntz,' or 'Poins' (*q.v.*).

Colbrand. A gigantic Danish champion who plays a part in the early English romance of *Guy of Warwick*; he was slain by Guy in the presence of King Athelstan, who was besieged in Winchester by Anlaf the Dane. See Ellis, *Spec. of Early Eng. Metrical Romances*, ii, 1–94.

'C. the giant, that same mighty man?' (*John*, i, 1); 'I am not Samson, nor Sir Guy, nor C., To mow 'em down before me' (*Hen. VIII*, v, 4).

Colchos, Colchis. Country of Asia, S. of the Caucasus; famed in Greek mythology as the land whence Jason and the Argonauts carried away the golden fleece (Ovid, *Metam.* vii).

Portia's 'sunny locks Hang on her temples like a golden fleece; Which makes her seat of Belmont Colchos' strand, And many Jasons come in quest of her' (*M.V.* i, 1); 'We are the Jasons, we have won the fleece' (*ib.* iii, 2).

The spelling 'Colchos' was not unusual in the 16th cent.

Coldspur. Nonce-name, as correlative of 'Hotspur.' 'Said he young Harry Percy's spur was cold? Of Hotspur, Coldspur?' (*2 Hen. IV*, i, 1).

Colebrook, Colnbrook. Village near Slough; mtd. *M.W.W.* iv, 5, as one of the places where the hosts had been 'cozened ... of horses and money.'

Colevile, Sir John. Mtd. ('Sir John Collevill of the Dale') as executed at Durham for conspiracy, while Henry IV was marching against the Percies (*Hol.* iii, 530).

D.P. *2 Hen. IV.* iv, 3] surrenders to Falstaff in Gualtree Forest; is termed by his captor 'a most furious Knight and valorous enemy,' and by Prince John 'a famous rebel'; is sent to York for execution.

French (p. 89) specifies three writs of Hen. IV–V in which the name occurs. 'Collevile,' Ff; a trisyllable.

Collatinus, or Collatine. L. Tarquinius Collatinus; son of Egerius, governor of Collatia. He was married to Lucretia (*q.v.*) and on her death was made first consul with Junius Brutus. But the very name of the Tarquins had become so hateful to the people that C. resigned his office, and was succeeded by P. Valerius (*q.v.*).

His praise of his wife, *Lucr.* Arg. and 11.9 ff.; his valour and fame, *ib.* 105 ff.; is summoned to Collatia, *ib.* 1583 ff.; his lamentation over his wife's death, *ib.* 1772 ff.

The form 'Collatine' occurs 24 times, 'Collatinus' 5 times.

Collatium. For 'Collatia,' an ancient town of the Sabines, near Rome, of which L. Tarquinius Collatinus (*q.v.*) was governor; scene of the violation and death of Lucretia. *Lucr.* Arg. and Il. 4, 50.

The name is correctly given in Painter's *Palace of Pleasure*.

[**Collere.**] See Fortinbras (1).

Colme, St. See Inchcolme.

Colme-kill. The island of Iona, one of the Hebrides, acc. *Hol.* ii, 170, burial-place of almost every ancient king of Scotland. 'C., The sacred store-house of his predecessors, And guardian of their bones' (*Macb.* ii, 4).

More properly Icolmkill, contracted from Hii-Colum-kille, 'the island of Columba of the cell.'

'Colmes hill,' F2, 3, 4'

Colnbrook. See Colebrook.

Colossus, The (of Rhodes). A gigantic statue of the Sun, 'wrought by Chares of Lyndus ... it carried seventie cubits in height' (Pliny, *Nat. Hist.* XXIV, vii; Holland's transln. p. 495). '[Julius Caesar] doth bestride the narrow world Like a C.' (*Jul. C.* i, 2).

'C.-wise' (*Tr. Cr.* v, 5).

Comagene, Commagene. District in the N.E. of Syria on the Euphrates; remained independent, under Seleucid kings, after the annexation of Syria by Pompey. A Roman province A.D. 17–38, and again in A.D. 73. Mtd. *Plut.* pp. 182, 207 ('Commagena,' 'Comagena').

'Mithridates, King of C.' (*Ant. Cl.* iii, 6; 'Comageat,' Ff), mtd. among the adherents of Antony.

Comedy of Errors, The.

PUBLICATION. First appeared in the Folio of 1623, as 'The Comedie of Errors.' The acts, but not the scenes (except initial ones), are numbered. Acc. R. C. Rhodes, *Sh.'s First Folio* (1923), pp. 130–1, the text was produced by assembling the various parts of the players.

DATE OF COMPOSITION. Uncertain, but probably *c.* 1591. An allusion to France 'making war against her heir' (iii, 2, l. 125) clearly alludes to the civil war of 1589–94. It is mtd. by Meres (*Palladis Tamia*) 1598.

SOURCES OF THE PLOT. The primary source is the *Menaechmi* of Plautus – the second pair of twins, the two Dromios, being introduced by Sh. No English translation of the *Menaechmi* was published before 1594, but the translator, W.[illiam] W.[arner], explicitly states that his MS. had been shown to 'his private friends.' A play now lost, entitled *The Historie of Error*, had, moreover, been acted in 1576. Scene 1 of Act III may be founded on the *Amphitruo* of Plautus.

Comfect, Count. Nonce-name applied by Beatrice to Claudio; *M. Ado*, iv, 1.

It is uncertain whether 'comfect' is used in the sense of 'comfit,' or as an adjective, meaning 'fictitious.' (Perhaps with the double meaning.)

Cominius. Roman consul; acc. *Plut.* pp. 7, 9–11, he laid siege to Corioli, and leaving part of the army in camp, under T. Lartius, marched against a relieving force of Volscians; the campaign having proved successful, largely owing to the valour of Caius Marcius, Cominius offered him a tenth part of the spoils, with 'a goodly horse,' and conferred on him the surname of Coriolanus.

D.P. *Cor.* i, 1] is given command against the Volscians. i, 6] having himself 'fought at disadvantage,' receives from C. Marcius an account of the capture of Corioli. i, 9] offers rewards (as above) to C. Marcius, and pardons a Volscian at his request. ii, 1] returns to Rome, giving all the honour to Cor. ii, 2] pronounces a eulogy on Cor. before the Senate. iii, 1] accompanies Cor. when the tribunes intercept him on his way to the Forum; deprecates the folly of the plebeians, but induces Cor. to retire before 'odds beyond arithmetic.' iii, 2] advises Cor. either to proceed to the Forum and 'answer mildly,' or remain away. iii, 3] attempts to reason with the mob. iv, 1] proposes to follow Cor. into exile. iv, 6] tells the tribunes, with bitter scorn, that Cor. is coming to 'shake your Rome about your ears.' v, 1] sorrowfully relates that his mission to Cor. has been wholly unavailing.

Commagene. See COMAGENE.

Commentaries, The. *C. Julii Caesaris Commentarii*; mtd. with reference to Caesar's remark (lib. v, cap. 15): 'Ex his omnibus longe sunt humanissimi, qui Cantium incolunt,' *2 Hen. VI*, iv, 7; see KENT.

Translated by A. Golding (1565); there is a verbal ooinoidence between the English passage referred to and G.'s rendering.

Commodity. Personified by the Bastard, *John*, ii, 1, in the sense of political or personal expediency.

Concolinel. Of undetermined meaning; perhaps the name of an air, or the burden of a song; *L.L.L.* iii, 1.

Among suggested solutions are: 'Quand Colinelle,' 'Cantat Ital., 'Can cailin gheal,' 'Caoin Cuillenain,' 'Do'n colleen alwin' (the last three being Irish); *cf.* 'Calen o custure me' (*Hen. V*, iv, 4).

Condell, or **Cundell, Henry** (*ob.* 1627). Mtd. as a 'principal actor' in F1, of which he was co-editor. A lifelong friend of Sh. Church-warden of St Mary Aldermanbury in 1618. Co-signatory with Heminge of 'The Dedicatorie Epistle' to F1.

Conrade. D.P. *M. Ado*. Follower of Don John. i, 3] urges Don J. to dissimulate his sullen humour, and suggests that he should 'make use' of his discontent; promises to aid him 'to the death.' iii, 3] is informed by Borachio of the deception practised by him on Claudio; they are both arrested by the watch. iv, 2] is examined in the prison; calls Verges a coxcomb and Dogberry an ass. v, 1] *p.m.* Described as 'born under Saturn' (i, 3).

Conscience. Personified by Launcelot; *M.V.* ii, 2.

Conspirators with Aufidius. D.PP. *Cor.* v, 5] urge A. to slay Coriolanus; take part in his murder.

Three of them have speaking parts.

Constance, Duchess of Brittany (*ob.* 1201). Dau. of Conan le Petit, D. of Brittany and E. of Richmond (Yorks). She married successively (*a*) Geoffrey Plantagenet, 4th son of Henry II (1181), (*b*) Randulph de Blundeville, E. of Chester (1187), (*c*) Guy, Viscount of Thouars, and was mother, by her 1st husb., of Arthur, D. of Brittany, whom she entrusted to the care of Philip Augustus (*Hol.* iii, 158).

D.P. *John.* (i, 1) mtd. ii, 1] indignantly asserts Arthur's legitimacy, and bitterly reproaches his grandmother, Queen Elinor, for her injustice toward him. (ii, 2) mtd. iii, 1] learns with dismay that Blanch of Castile, dowered with provinces which are Arthur's by right, is betrothed to the Dauphin; on the entrance of John and Philip she curses the wedding-day, accuses Ph. of perjury, and pours scorn on 'Austria' for deserting her; when the papal legate pronounces excommunication on John she begs that her curse may be joined with the anathema of Rome; urges Philip to break with England; (C.'s reference to herself as a 'widow, husbandless,' is unhistorical, for at the time she was Guy's wife). iii, 4] enters Philip's tent in an agony of grief at Arthur's capture, and with impassioned eloquence invokes the 'carrion monster,' Death; yet she fears that Ar. will be so changed by his sorrows that 'when I meet him in the court of heaven, I shall not know him.' (iv, 2) the death of C., 'in a frenzy,' three days before that of Elinor, is announced. (Historically, she died three years before the queen-mother.)

The character has been very fully discussed by critics: see Mrs Jameson, *Characteristics of Women* (1836), ii, 213 ff.; T. Campbell, *Life of Mrs Siddons* (1834), i, 211 ff.; G. Fletcher, *Studies in Sh.* (1847), pp. 10 ff.; Gervinus, *Sh. Comm.* (1875), pp. 358 ff.; F.S. Boas, *Sh. and his Predecessors* (1896), pp. 244 ff.

Constantine, 'the Great.' Roman Emperor (306–37). Mtd. *1 Hen. VI*, i, 2. See HELENA, ST.

Constantinople. 'Go to C. and take the Turk by the beard' (*Hen. V*, v, 2).

Historically, C. did not pass into the hands of the Turks until 31 years after Henry V died. See also BYZANTIUM.

Contention, The. Abbreviated title of the play on which *2 Hen. VI* was based; in full: 'The First part of the Contention betwixt the two famous Houses of Yorke and Lancaster, with the death of the good Duke Humphrey; And the banishment and death of the Duke of Suffolke, and the Tragicall end of the proud Cardinall of Winchester, with the notable Rebellion of Iacke Cade: And the Duke of Yorkes first claime unto the crowne,' published in 1594 by Thomas Millington.

For a discussion of the vexed questions (*a*) whether *The Contention* and *The True Tragedie* (*q.v.*) are early drafts or imperfect transcripts of 2, *3 Hen. VI*; (*b*) whether Sh. had any hand in writing the two first-named plays; and (*c*) what other writers may be their authors, wholly or in part, see *N.S.S. Tr.*, 1876, Pt. II, pp. 219 ff.

Cooke, Alexander. Mtd. as a 'principal actor' in F1.

Cophetua. The king in the ballad of 'King C. and the Beggar-maid,' inserted in Percy's *Reliques* (see Wheatley's edn., i, 193) from Rich. Johnson's *Crown Garland of Goulden Roses* (1612).

'When King C. loved the beggar-maid' (*Rom. J.* ii, 1); Falstaff applies the name to himself, *2 Hen. IV*, v, 3 ('Couitha,' Ff; 'Couetua,' Q); the story is enlarged upon by Armado in a letter, *L.L.L.* iv, 1, where the beggar-maid's name is given as Zenelophon (*q.v.*) instead of Penelophon as in the ballad: 'What is thy name, faire maid? quoth he; Penelophon, O King, quoth she.'

The ballad is also alluded to, *L.L.L.* i, 2, and *Rich. II*, v, 3 ('our scene is ... now changed to "The Beggar and the King." ').

'Cophetua' occurs as an error for 'Caveto,' *Hen. V*, ii, 3, Qq.

Copperspur. A prisoner; *M. for M.* iv, 3.

Corambis. The name of Polonius in the First Quarto of Hamlet (1603). See CORAMBUS (2).

Corambus (1). A military commander, mtd. by Parolles; *All's Well*, iv, 3.

[**Corambus** (2).] The name of Polonius in the early German play on the subject of Hamlet, which is supposed to have been introduced into Germany by English players in 1603. (*Cf.* A. Cohn, *Sh. in Germany*.)

Cordelia. Daughter to Leir, King of Britain; the name is spelt 'Cordeilla' in *Hol.*, 'Cordella' in the older *King Leir*, 'Cordell' in *A Mirour for Magistrates*, and 'Cordelia' in *The Faerie Queene*, II, x, 29.

D.P. *Lear*. 'Cordelia, daughter of Lear.' i, 1] is wooed by 'the Princes, France and Burgundy'; Lear demands which of his daughters loves him most; after Goneril's reply, C. murmurs, aside, that she can but 'Love and be silent'; after Regan has exuberantly vowed her affection, C. is directly interrogated by Lear, and replies 'I love your Majesty according to my bond; no more nor less'; in answer to L.'s indignant warning, she declares that if she gives 'all' her love to her father, her husband's claim, should she marry, would be unsatisfied; L., enraged, declares her disinherited; Burgundy resigns his claim 'in such conditions'; on France demanding to hear the nature of her offence, C. entreats her father to make it known that 'no vicious blot' in her has caused his displeasure, and, on France's learning that her fault is but 'a tardiness in nature Which often leaves the history unspoke That it intends to do,' claims her as his bride; she scornfully bids farewell to her sisters and departs with France. (i, 4) L. speaks of her 'most small fault.' (ii, 2) Kent receives a letter from her. (iii, 1) she is reported to be at Dover with a French force. (iv, 3) her sorrow and indignation at L.'s brutal treatment by her sisters described (scene omitted in Ff). iv, 4] (in the French camp) C. sends out 'a century' to seek for L., who is wandering in madness; hears of the approach of 'the British powers.' iv, 7] converses with Kent and a Doctor as she watches by the side of her sleeping father; marvels at her sisters' cruelty to him; Lear on awaking takes her for 'a soul in bliss'; as he comes to himself he tells her that, unlike her sisters, she has some cause for not loving him – but she cries, 'No cause, no cause!' (v, 1) Edmund vows that in defeat she shall be shown no mercy. v, 2] *p.m.* v, 3] is made prisoner, and taken away guarded; (a reprieve arriving too late, she is hanged in prison); Lear enters with Cordelia dead in his arms.

Acc. Holinshed, after L.'s death 'Cordeilla ... was admitted Q. and supreme governesse of Britaine in the yeere of the world 3155 ... Uzia was then reigning in Juda, and Jeroboam over Israell. This Cordeilla ... ruled the land of Britaine right worthilie during the space of five yeeres, in which meane time hir husband [Aganippus] died, and then ... hir two nephews Margan and Cunedag, sonnes to her aforesaid sisters ... levied warre against hir ... and finally took hir prisoner, and laid hir fast in ward, wherewith she tooke suche griefe, being a woman of manlie courage, and despairing to recover libertie, there she slue hirselfe.'

Acc. *The Faerie Queene* (1590), II, x, 27, 'her selfe she hong.' The old drama *King Leir* ends with the departure of Cordella to France after a victory in England. Acc. the ballad in Percy's *Reliques*, she 'was in the battel slain.' In *A Mirour for Magistrates* (1586) Cordell tells her own story.

Coridon. See CORYDON and CORIN (1).

Corin (1). D.P. *A. Y. L.* An old (ii, 4, l. 25) shepherd. ii, 4] receives the confidences of the lovesick Silvius; informs Rosalind and Celia that he can purchase a cottage and pasture for them. iii, 2] discusses with Touchstone the relative advantages of Court and country life. iii, 4] offers to conduct the ladies to the spot where Silvius is wooing Phebe. iii, 5] *p.m.* v, 1] summons Touchstone.

The equivalent character in Lodge's *Rosalynde* is Coridon.

Corin (2). Conventional name of a shepherd. 'In the shape of C., sate all day, Playing on pipes of corn, and versing love To amorous Phillida' (*M.N.D.* ii, 1).

In *Tottel's Miscellany* (1557), ed. Arber, p. 138, we have 'Harpelus complaynt of Phillidaes loue bestowed on Corin.'

Corinth. Maritime city of Greece. Mtd., *Com. Err.* i, 1 (3); 'rude fishermen of C.' (*ib.* v, 1); mtd., *ib. ib.*; 'would we could see you at C.' (*Timon*, ii, 2; in allusion to its profligacy).

Corinthian. An inhabitant of Corinth; hence, 'a gay, licentious man' (*N.E.D.*), from the proverbial licentiousness of ancient C.

'*P. Hen.* I am ... a C., a lad of mettle, a good boy' (*1 Hen. IV*, ii, 4).

Coriolanus, Caius (or **Cn.**) **Marcius.** A legendary Roman hero, who received his surname from his valour at the capture of Corioli (*q.v.*). His haughtiness toward the plebeians led to his exile, and he thereupon, in command of a Volscian army, advanced on Rome, as far as the Cluilian fosse. He rejected all proposals for peace made by the Romans, but at length yielded to the entreaties of the matrons headed by his mother and wife. Returning to the country of the Volscians, he was, according to one account, immediately put to death by them. See CORIOLANUS, THE TRAGEDY OF.

D.P. *Cor.* ('Marcius,' or 'Caius Marcius,' in st. dirs. and pfxs. until the middle of i, 9; thenceforward 'Coriolanus.' In i, 9, ll. 65, 67, and ii, 1, l. 155, 'Marcus,' or 'Martius,' stands first in Ff.) i, 1] (the wrath of the citizens is aroused against him for being a 'dog to the commonalty'); he is loading the citizens with contumely when it is announced that 'the Volsces are in arms'; he rejoices that he will have the opportunity of meeting his inveterate foe Tullus Aufidius, and consents to serve under Cominius; (his motives discussed by the Tribunes). (i, 2) Aufidius declares that Cor. is hated at Rome. (i, 3) his valour recalled by his mother. i, 4] curses his men when they are repulsed at Corioli; pursues the Volscians, alone; later, while fighting, though wounded, he is succoured by Titus Lartius. i, 5] hastens to join Cominius, leaving Lartius in charge at Corioli. i, 6] prepares to attack Aufidius with a picked body of troops. i, 8] fights with Aufidius, but the combat is interrupted by Volscians. i, 9] is hailed, by acclamation, 'Coriolanus'; desires that favour should be shown to a Volscian who had befriended him. (i, 10) Aufidius longs to meet him once more. ii, 1] (Cor.'s many wounds); he returns as victor to Rome; (discussed by the Tribunes). ii, 2] is nominated to the consulship. ii, 3] presents himself 'in a gown of humility' for the approval of the citizens; (his ancestry described). iii, 1] on his way to the Forum is stopped by the Tribunes; a tumult ensues, and Cor. is persuaded to withdraw in the face of 'odds beyond arithmetic.' iii, 2] consents, on the advice of his mother and Cominius, but sorely against the grain, to speak the citizens fair in 'the market-place.' iii, 3] is accused by the Tribunes of seeking 'tyrannical power' and is sentenced to banishment; defies and denounces the citizens, and exclaims 'I banish you!' iv, 1] bids farewell to his friends at the gate of the city. (iv, 3) news of his banishment is spread. iv, 4] Cor. reaches the house of Aufidius. iv, 5] the serving-men fail to eject him; he reveals himself to Aufidius, who greets him eagerly as an ally. (iv, 6) his invasion becomes known at Rome. (iv, 7) Aufidius becomes jealous of him. (v, 1) Cor.'s rejection of Cominius as an envoy. v, 2] he rebuffs Menenius. v, 3] yields to the entreaties of his wife and mother. (v, 4) his attitude described by Menenius. (v, 5) mtd. v, 6] is accused of treachery by Aufidius and slain by the conspirators.

'This Martius' natural wit and great heart did marvellously stir up his courage to do and attempt notable acts. But on the other side, for lack of education, he was so choleric and impatient, that he would yield to no living creature: which made him churlish, uncivil, and altogether unfit for any man's conversation. Yet men marvelling much at his constancy, that he was never overcome with pleasure nor money, and how he would endure easily all manner of pains and travails: thereupon they well liked and commended his stoutness and temperancy. But for all that they could not be acquainted with him, as one citizen useth to be with another in the city: his behaviour was so unpleasant to them by reason of a certain insolent and stern manner he had, which, because he was too lordly, was disliked... Moreover he did so exercise his body to hardness and all kind of activity, that he was very swift in running, strong in wrestling, and mighty in griping, so that no man could ever cast him.' (*Plut.* p. 2.)

The action of Coriolanus in the tragedy follows Plutarch in its main incidents, but events follow one another in a different order, and the dramatic details are often of a composite origin.

Mtd. *T. And.* iv, 4: 'Lucius ... threats, in course of this revenge, to do As much as ever Cor. did.'

Coriolanus, The Tragedy of.
PUBLICATION. First appeared in the Folio of 1623, with title as above: the acts, but not the scenes, are indicated.

DATE OF COMPOSITION. Considerations of style and metre have induced the majority of critics to place this play after *Ant. Cl.* and about 1609. Direct evidence, external or internal, is lacking, except, perhaps, the phrase 'He lurch'd all swords of the garland' (*Cor.* ii, 2), which seems to be satirized by Ben Jonson in *The Silent Woman* (v, 1), produced in 1609. But the phrase may have been a current one.

SOURCE OF THE PLOT. Mainly the life of Coriolanus in North's *Plutarch*, though the story, derived from Livy, had appeared in Painter's *Palace of Pleasure*. The characterization is largely Sh.'s own.

'The text abounds with errors' (Camb. edn.); *cf.* R. C. Rhodes, *Sh.'s First Folio* (1923), pp. 133–4.

Corioli. Town in Latium, capital of the Volsci; from its capture (493 B. C.) Caius Marcius was surnamed 'Coriolanus' (Livy, ii, 33 ff.). ('Corioles,' *Plut.* pp. 7–11.)

The scene is laid in or near Corioli: *Cor.* i, 2, 4, 5–10. Warlike preparations at C., *ib.* i, 2; mtd., *ib.* i, 3; sally from C., *ib.* i, 6; Caius Marcius gains a surname thence, *ib.* i, 9; mtd., *ib.* ii, 1 (3), 2 (2); the deeds of C. Marcius before C. recalled, *ib.* iv, 5; mtd., *ib.* v, 3; 'like an eagle in a dove-cote, I Flutter'd your Volscians in C.' (*ib.* v, 5).

The following forms are met with in Ff: 'Corioles' (usually), 'Coriolus,' 'Carioles,' 'Cariolus,' 'Corialus' (in st. dirs.). The crucial line, 'Let us alone to guard Corioli' (i, 2), shows that the second syllable is accented.

Cornelia (1). Mother of the Gracchi, who devoted herself to the training of her sons (Plut. *Ti. Gracch.* and *C. Gracch.*). 'Cornelia never with more care Read to her sons than she hath read to thee' (*T. And.* iv, 1).

Cornelia (2). Name of a midwife; *T. And.* iv, 2.

Cornelius (1). D.P. *Cymb.* 'A doctor, servant to the Queen' (Rowe). i, 6] gives at her request a box of 'poisonous compounds' to the Queen, but tries to dissuade her from making trial of them; explains (aside) that the drug will produce but 'a show of death.' v, 5] announces the Queen's death to Cymbeline and relates her dying confession (see QUEEN TO CYMB.); reveals the true nature of the drug he compounded for her.

The name may be derived from Cornelius Celsus, the famous writer on medicine who lived at the beginning of the Christian era, and whose *De Medicina* had appeared in many edns. by the end of the 16th cent.; or from the physician Cornelius, who cured Charles V of gout.

Cornelius (2). D.P. *Haml.* A courtier. i, 2] sent on a embassage to the King of Norway. ii, 2] *p.m.*

The companion of Voltimand (*q.v.*), but an almost negligible character. 'Cornelia,' Q1.

Cornish, *adj.* See LE ROY.

Cornwall, Duke of. D.P. *Lear*. Husband to Regan. i, 1] present when Lear parts his kingdom; interposes when the King threatens Kent's life. ii, 1] arrives at Gloucester's castle; hears of Edgar's supposed plot against Gl. and declares that the bastard Edmund 'shall be ours. Natures of such deep trust we shall much need.' ii, 2] breaks in upon the fight between Oswald and Kent; comments on the latter's 'saucy roughness' and orders him to be put in the stocks. ii, 4] rebukes Lear for his imprecations on Goneril; agrees with his wife's suggestion that the castle doors should be shut against L. (iii, 1) mtd. iii, 5] is given a letter by Edm., supposed to prove Gl.'s treason; tells Edm. to seek out his father, 'and thou shalt find a dearer father in my love.' iii, 7] orders Gl., brought in pinioned, to be bound to a chair; questions him as to communications with France; tears out his eyes, but is wounded by a servant who tries to defend the Earl. (iv, 2) dies of the wound. (iv, 3, 7) mtd.

In Holinshed the 'D. of Cornwal,' Henninus, is slain in battle against Leir and Cordeilla; in *A Mirour for Magistrates* (1586) Regan's husband is Prince Maglaurus, and in *The Faerie Queene*, Bk. II, Maglan, King of Scots; in *King Leir* 'the king of Cornwall' is Gonorill's husband and is put to flight by Leir's forces.

For a full record of the discrepancies of early versions of the story with regard to the daughters' marriages see W. Perrett, *Palaestra*, xxxv (Berlin, 1904).

Corydon. Conventional name for a shepherd, used by Theocritus, Virgil, and Spenser. 'Poor Coridon must live alone' (*P.P.* 18). See CORIN (1).

Cosmo. Commander mtd. by Parolles; *All's Well*, iv, 3.

Costard. D.P. *L.L.L.* 'A clown' (Rowe). i, 1] is brought in custody before the King on the charge of consorting with a woman (Jaquenetta), and is sentenced to a week's fast on bran and water. i, 2] is placed under Armado's care. iii, 1] is set free by Ar. on condition that he bears a letter from him to Jaquenetta; is also entrusted by Biron with a letter for Rosaline. iv, 1] hands Armado's letter to Ros. iv, 2] shows B.'s letter to the curate and is advised to take it to the King. iv, 3] lets B.'s letter fall into the King's hands. v, 1] is delighted at Moth's banter. v, 2] begs leave to present 'The Pageant of the Nine Worthies' before the King; assumes the part of Pompey; publicly exhorts Armado to 'play the honest Trojan' by Jaquenetta; takes part in the final songs. See POMPEY THE GREAT.

'The clown in the play is a mere country fellow' (Douce, *Illust. Sh.* (1807), i, 247). Longaville, however (i, 1), looks forward to C.'s providing them with sport – perhaps as a butt. A costard is a large apple, hence, jocularly, the head; Moth plays on the double meaning (iii, 1).

Cotswold. Variously spelt; the C. Hills in Gloucestershire, noted for coursing meetings and games in Sh.'s time.

'I heard say that he [greyhound] was outrun on Cotsall' (*M.W.W.* i, 1); 'What a weary way from Ravenspurgh to C. ['Cotshall,' Qq; 'Cotshold,' Ff] will be found' (*Rich. II*, ii, 3); 'Will Squele a C. ['Cotsole,' Qq; 'Cotsal,' Ff] man' (*2 Hen. IV*, iii, 2).

For an account of the 'Cotsall Games,' held near Chipping Campden, *cf.* Gosse, *Seventeenth-Century Studies*.

Cotus. Servant to Aufidius; mtd. *Cor.* iv, 5.

The name is unknown in classical literature; perh. for 'Cotys,' which is of frequent occurrence.

Counter-gate (not strictly a proper name). Any one of the prisons for debtors in London and Southwark was called a 'counter,' later 'compter.' 'Thou mightest as well say I [Falstaff] love to walk by the C.; which is as hateful to me as the reek of a lime-kiln' (*M.W.W.* iii, 3).

Also punningly alluded to: *Com. Err.* iv, 2, ll. 37–9; *2 Hen. IV*, i, 2, ll. 102–3.

Court, Alexander. D.P. *Hen. V*. One of the soldiers with whom the King converses incognito. iv, 1] points out the dawn.

'Court' was a well-known name in Stratford in Sh.'s day, and in the records is several times associated with that of Sh. *Cf.* French, pp. 327–8.

Court, John de la. See CAR.

Courtenay, Sir Edward. Ctd. E. of Devonshire 1485; *ob.* 1509; see COURTENAY, PETER. In Ff (*Rich. III.* iv, 4) 'Courteney,' after *Hol.* ('William,' Qq.)

[**Courtenay, Peter.**] Bp. of Exeter 1478; attainted for rebellion 1484; sought refuge in Brittany, and returned with Richmond; Keeper of the Privy Seal to Hen. VII 1485; Bp. of Winchester 1487; *ob.* 1492.

'Sir Edw. C., and the haughty prelate Bishop of Ex., his brother ... are in arms' (*Rich. III*, iv, 4).

Sh. follows *Hol.* iii, 743, in making the Bp. brother, instead of cousin, of Sir E. C.

Courtezan, A. D.P. *Com. Err.* (ii, 1) described by Ant. E. as 'of excellent discourse; pretty and witty; wild, and, yet too, gentle.' iv, 3] meeting Ant. S. (whom she mistakes for Ant. E.) demands from him the chain he wears, or the return of the ring he had from her at dinner; (*sol.*) resolves to tell his wife what has befallen. iv, 4] accompanies Adriana and others when Ant. E. is bound and borne away as a madman. v, 1] her ring is restored to her by Ant. E.

Erotium in Plautus' *Menaechmi*.

Coventry. City in Warwickshire; the place appointed for the trial by battle between Bolingbroke and Mowbray (*Rich. II*, i, 1, 2 (2); the scene of i, 3, is laid there).

Falstaff refuses to march through C. with his ragged company, *1 Hen. IV*, iv, 2; mtd., *2 Hen. IV*, iv, 1; Edward IV plans to meet Warwick at C., *3 Hen. VI*, iv, 8 (3); the scene of *ib.* v, 1, is laid there (*cf.* Hall, p. 293, where we are told that the King 'pytched his filde' in a plain by the city, but Warwick 'kept hym selfe close within the walles').

Coventry, John. See MAYOR (2).

Cowly, or **Cowley, Richard.** Actor; friend of Sh. and the creator of 'Verges'; his name is given in F1 among the principal actors.

In QFf 'Couley' occurs for 'Verg.' in the pfx. of iv, 2, ll. 2, 62, 63 (also in 1. 67, prob. in mistake for 'Con.').

Cox. For 'Cock's,' *i.e.* 'God's'; *All's Well*, v, 2.

Crab. Name of Launce's dog; he is 'the sourest-natured dog that lives' (*T.G.V.* ii, 3); his master suffers for him, *ib.* iv, 4.

Cranmer, Thomas (1489–1556). Abp. of Canterbury; supported the opinion that Henry VIII's marriage with Katharine of Arragon was invalid; as Abp., pronounced Anne Boleyn's marriage to the King lawful. He was sent on an embassy to Rome (Foxe, ii, 1754); crowned Anne

Boleyn (*Hol.* iii, 933); saved from the hostility of the Council by Henry's interposition (Foxe, ii, 1759); godfather to Elizabeth (*Hol.* iii, 934).

Of Cranmer's disposition Foxe (ii, 1756) writes: 'It came into a common proverbe: "Do unto my Lord of Canterburie displeasure or a shrewd turne, and then you may be sure to have him your friend whiles he lyveth." '

D.P. *Hen. VIII.* (ii, 4) the King yearns for the return of his 'learn'd and well-beloved servant Cranmer,' who was absent on an embassy. (iii, 2) his return announced, 'in his opinions' (which he had sent in advance); Norfolk terms him 'a worthy fellow, and has ta'en much pain In the King's business'; Wolsey terms him an arch heretic, who 'hath crawl'd into the favour of the King And is his oracle'; he is installed Abp. (iv, 1) he crowns Anne. v, 1] is graciously received by Henry, to whom he confides his fears, and by whom he is reassured and given a ring. v, 2] is discourteously refused admission to the council-chamber. v, 3] defends himself before the Council when charged with heresy; is ordered to the Tower; produces the ring; the King honours him before the Council. v, 5] is godfather to the infant Princess Elizabeth, and pronounces over her an oration prophetic of her future greatness.

C.'s trial (v, 3) is antedated by the dramatist some ten years.

Crassus. An officer of Vincentio's; mtd., *M. for M.* iv, 5.

Crassus, M. Licinius. Surnamed 'Dives.' Defeated by the Parthians, 53 B.C., and slain. See PACORUS.

[**Crécy.**] See CRESSY.

Cressida. Daughter of Calchas. Not mentioned in 'Dictys Cretensis,' and figuring in 'Dares Phrygius' (see TROY) only as (Briseida) the captive of Achilles, 'sweet and gentle with modesty of heart.' As a character of romance, C. first assumed prominence in *Le Roman de Troie* of Benoft de Sainte-More, who, while emphasizing her beauty, embellishes 'Dares'' account by the pregnant suggestion that 'her wit was quick and ready,' and 'her heart was changeable.' Sh., independently realizing, as it seems, the dramatic possibilities of this aspect of Cressida, turned the 'widow' of Boccaccio and Chaucer into a girlish coquette, thus rendering less unaccountable her heartless fickleness.

The name, which seems founded on Chryseis (*q.v.*), or Briseis, is spelt in many ways by Chaucer, and appears as 'Briséida' in Benoît's poem, and 'Griseide' in Boccaccio' *Filostrato*.

'In Chaucer, Cr. is represented as a grave, sober, considerate personage ... who has an alternate eye to her character, her interest, and her pleasure' (W. Hazlitt).

'I would play Lord Pandarus ... to bring a Cressida to this Troylus' (*T. Nt.* iii, 1); 'C. was a beggar' (*ib. ib.*; the allusion here is to a passage in a poem by Robt. Henryson (once thought to be Chaucer's), entitled *The Testament of Cresseid*, in which the gods pronounce this sentence on her; 'This sall thow go begging fra hous to hous, With cop and clapper lyke ane lazarous'); 'the lazar kite of Cressid's kind' (*Hen. V*, ii, 1) seems due to the same source. In the two following passages the form 'Cressid' also occurs: 'Troilus ... sigh'd his soul towards the Grecian tents, Where C. lay that night' (*M.V.* v, 1); 'C.'s uncle' (*All's Well*, ii, 1).

D.P. *Tr. Cr.* 'Daughter to Calchas.' (i, 1) Troilus dilates to Pandarus on his love for her, and on her supposed 'stubbornness.' i, 2] in bantering converse with her uncle, Cr. affects to despise Troilus, but afterward (*sol.*) admits that though she loves him, yet she 'holds off,' from sheer coquetry. (iii, 1) mtd. iii, 2] Pandarus brings about a meeting between her and Tr.; she declares that if she prove faithless to him let it become a proverb: 'As false as Cressid.' (iii, 3) the Greeks agree to take Cr. in return for the prisoner Antenor. (iv, 1) Diomed comes to fetch her. iv, 2] passionately refuses to be severed from her lover. iv, 4] gives Tr. a glove, and receives from him a sleeve. iv, 5] arrives in the Grecian camp; all the chiefs (except Ulysses) salute her with a kiss, which she gaily accepts, not without witty retorts; (Ulysses characterizes her bitterly). v, 2] Troilus and Ulysses witness, unseen, an interview between Diomedes and Cr., and see her give D. the sleeve she had received from Tr.; the latter exclaims: 'O Cressid! O false Cressid! false, false, false! Let all untruths stand by thy stained name, And they'll seem glorious.' (v, 5) Diomed sends her Tr.'s horse, whose master he has overthrown.

Cressy, Crécy. A village about 30 m. N.W. of Amiens, where Edward III and the Black Prince routed a greatly superior French army under Philip VI, Aug. 26, 1346.

Charles VI, before Agincourt, reminds his council of that fatal day, *Hen. V*, ii, 4; the battle alluded to by Abp. Chichele, *ib.* i, 2.

Cretan. Pertaining to Crete, whither Europa (*q. v.*) was conveyed by Jupiter. 'When with his knees he [Jove] kissed the Cr. strand' (*Tam. Sh.* i, 1).

Crete, Candia. Island in the Mediterranean, long the abode of Daedalus (*q.v.*). Cretan hounds are mentioned by Ovid. 'When in a wood of Cr. they bay'd the bear' (*M.N.D.* iv, 1); 'a cry more tuneable Was never holla'd to ... in Cr.' (*ib. ib.*). '*Pist.* O hound of Cr.!' (*Hen. V*, ii, 1); '*Tal.* Then follow thou thy desperate sire of Cr., Thou Icarus' (*1 Hen. VI*, iv, 6); 'What a peevish fool was that of Cr., That taught his son the office of a fowl' (*3 Hen. VI*, v, 6).

Cricket. An impersonated fairy. 'C., to Windsor chimneys shalt thou leap' (*M.W.W.* v, 5).

The equivalent in Qq is 'Peane' – perh. for 'Bean.' C. is the name of a fairy in Lyly's *The Maides Metamorphosis*.

Crier, A. D.P. *Hen. VIII.* ii, 4] summons Henry and Katharine before the court at Blackfriars (*Hol.* iii, 907).

Crispin, St, and **St Crispian** (**Crispinus** and **Crispianus**). Two brothers martyred at Augusta Suessionum (Soissons) *c.*287. As Crispin worked at shoemaking he became the patron saint of shoemakers.

The Battle of Agincourt was fought on 'the flue and twentith of October in the yeare 1415, being then fridale and the feast of Crispine and Crispinian' (*Hol.* iii, 552). The day is thus diversely mentioned in *Hen. V*, iv, 3: 'Crispian'; 'the feast of Crispian'; 'St Crispian'; 'Crispin's day'; 'Crispian Crispian'; 'St Crispin's day'; and (iv, 7) 'the day of Crispin Crispianus.'

Cromer, Sir James. See FIENNES. 'Break into his [Lord Say's] son-in-law's house, Sir James Cr., and strike off his head' (*2 Hen. VI*, iv, 7).

'There is great discrepancy in the statement of authors respecting the connection between the families of Say and Cromer' (French, p. 164).

Cromwell, Lord, of Wingfield. One of the titles of John Talbot (*q.v.*); *1 Hen. VI*, iv, 7.

Cromwell, Thomas (*c.* 1485–1540). Of obscure parentage; after an adventurous youth, chiefly spent on the Continent, he gained the favour of Wolsey, and was made collector of the revenues of the see of York; in 1525 as one of the commissioners to inquire into the state of the smaller monasteries (*Hol.* iii, 913) he carried out his duties with great harshness; Privy Councillor 1531; Master of the Jewels 1532 (*ib.* 929); Henry's Secretary and Master of the Rolls 1534; active in bringing about the dissolution of the smaller monasteries. (Ctd. E. of Essex 1540; beheaded, on a charge of treason, in the same year.)

D.P. *Hen. VIII.* 'Cromwell, servant to Wolsey.' iii, 2] informs Wolsey that he delivered 'the packet' into the King's own hands; later, condoles with W. upon the disastrous results of the wrong packet having been sent to the King, and announces the promotion of More and Cranmer, and Henry's secret marriage to Anne Boleyn; sorrowfully bids his master farewell. (iv, 1) his appointment as Master of the Jewel-house mtd.; is 'in much esteem with the King.' (v, 1) made Master of the Rolls and King's Secretary. v, 3] acts as secretary to the Council; checks the Bp. of Winchester for being 'too sharp' against Cranmer; Gardiner retorts that Cromwell favours 'this new sect' (Foxe, ii, 1759); Cromwell lauds Cranmer's honesty.

Cromwell was not actually a member of the Council until after Wolsey's death. Of him Foxe (ii, 1159) writes: 'In this worthy and noble person … iii. things especially are to bee considered, to wytte, florishyng authoritie, excellyng wysedome, and fervent zeale to Christ and to his Gospell.'

Crosby Place. (Also 'C. House,' Ff.) Formerly in Bishopsgate, built in 1466 by Sir John C. 'Richard, D. of Gloucester … was lodged in this house' (Stow, *Survey*, ed. Thoms, p. 65). The Hall, a fine specimen of medieval domestic architecture, survived the Great Fire, and after many vicissitudes was pulled down to be re-erected in Cheyne Walk, Chelsea.

Gloucester tells Lady Anne to 'repair to C. Place,' where he will join her later, *Rich. III*, i, 2; he similarly instructs the murderers of Clarence, *ib.* i, 3, and Catesby, *ib.* iii, 1.

Crosse, Samuel. Mtd. as a 'principal actor' in F1 ('Samuell').

Crown, The. Sign of a shop in Cheapside. Acc. Hall (p. 369), a merchant named Burdet, who dwelt at the sign of the Crown, was executed in the reign of Edward IV for having declared that he would make his son 'inheritor of the Crown.'

Gloucester tells Buckingham to stir up the wrath of the citizens by relating this incident at the Guildhall, *Rich. III*, iii, 5.

Hall adds that in his time the sign was changed to the 'floure de luse, over agaynst soper lane.'

Cumberland. A district formerly including C., Westmoreland, and part of Strathclyde. King Duncan named Malcolm, his elder son, Prince of C., 'as it were thereby to appoint him his successor in the Kingdome, immediatlie after his decease' (*Hol.* ii, 170). The fact mtd. *Macb.* i, 4.

For 'Clifford of Cumberland' see CLIFFORD, THOS.

[**Cunobelinus.**] See CYMBELINE.

Cupid. Amor or Cupido, the Roman equivalent of the Greek Eros, 'god of love.' The C. of the epigrammatists and erotic poets is, however, rather a poetic conception than a mythological entity; in this aspect he is son of Venus; he bears arrows in a golden quiver — some golden, which arouse love, others tipped with lead, which produce aversion; he has, moreover, golden wings, which give him birdlike powers of flight, and his eyes are often covered, so that he acts blindly. He is represented by artists of post-classical times as a little boy. Among things sacred to him are the ram, the cock, and the hare.

His bow and arrows: 'C.'s bow' (*V.A.* 581); 'If C. have not spent all his quiver in Venice' (*M. Ado*, i, 1); 'he challenged C. at the flight' (*ib. ib.*); 'C. is no longer an archer' (*ib.* ii, 1); 'little C.'s crafty arrow' (*ib.* iii, 1); 'some C. kills with arrows, some with traps' (*ib. ib.*); 'he hath cut C.'s bowstring, and the little hangman [*i.e.* rogue] dare not shoot at him' (*ib.* iii, 2); 'I swear by C.'s strongest bow, by his best arrow with the golden head' (*M.N.D.* i, 1); 'young C.'s fiery shaft' (*ib.* ii, 2); 'the bolt of C. (*ib. ib.*); 'hit with C.'s archery' (*ib.* iii, 2); 'C.'s buttshaft is too hard for Hercules' club' (*L.L.L.* i, 2); 'proceed, sweet C., thou hast thump'd him with thy bird-bolt under the left pap' (*ib.* iv, 3); 'C.'s arrow' (*Rom. J.* i, 1).

His wings and flight: 'Flying between the cold moon and the Earth, C. all armed' (*M.N.D.* ii, 2); 'From C.'s shoulder pluck his painted wings' (*Tr. Cr.* iii, 2); 'borrow C.'s wings and soar' (*Rom. J.* i, 4); 'therefore hath the wind-swift C. wings' (*ib.* ii, 5); 'feather'd C.!' (*Oth.* i, 3).

His blindness: 'Hang me up … for the sign of blind C.' (*M. Ado*, i, 1); 'Love looks not with the eyes, but with the mind, And therefore is wing'd C. painted blind' (*M.N.D.* i, 1); 'Christendoms that blinking C. gossips' (*All's Well*, i, 1); 'do thy worst, blind C., I'll not love' (*Lear*, iv, 6); 'we'll have no C. hoodwinked with a scarf' (*Rom. J.* i, 4).

Miscellaneous: 'One of C.'s carriers' (*M.W.W.* ii, 2); 'now is C. a child of conscience' (*ib.* v, 5); 'to tell us C. is a good hare-finder' (*M. Ado*, i, 1); 'C. is a knavish lad' (*M.N.D.* iii, 2); 'C.'s flower' (*ib.* iv, 1); 'I should out-swear C.' (*L.L.L.* i, 2); 'he [Boyet] is C.'s grandfather' (*ib.* ii, 1); 'a plague that C. will impose' (*ib.* iii, 1); 'guards on wanton C.'s hose' (*ib.* iv, 3); 'Saint C., then! to the field' (*ib. ib.*); 'he [C.] hath been five thousand years a boy' (*ib.* v, 2); 'Saint Dennis to Saint C.' (*ib. ib.*); 'C. himself would blush' (*M.V.* ii, 6); 'quick C.'s post' (*ib.* ii, 9); 'C. have mercy!' (*A.Y.L.* i, 3); 'C. hath clapp'd him o' the shoulder' (*ib.* iv, 1); 'the brains of my C.'s knocked out' (*All's Well*, iii, 2); 'Oh, C., C., C.!' (*Tr. Cr.* iii, 1); 'in all C.'s pageant there is presented no monster' (*ib.* iii, 2); 'C. grant all tongue-tied maidens here Bed, chamber [etc.]' (*ib.* iii, 2); 'weak, wanton C.' (*ib.* iii, 3); 'boys, like smiling C.s' (*Ant. Cl.* ii, 2); 'two winking C.s of silver' (*Cymb.* ii, 4); 'young C.'s tables' (*ib.* iii, 2); 'slain in C.'s wars' (*Per.* i, 1); his brand, *Son.* cliii.

Characterized, at length, by Biron, *L.L.L.* iii, 1; by Rosalind, *A.Y.L.* iv, 1; by Ceres, *Temp.* iv, 1.

D.P. *Timon.* i, 2] speaks a short prologue, and ushers in the mask of 'Amazons.'

Curan. D.P. *Lear.* A courtier. ii, 1] hints to Edmund that war is imminent between the Dukes.

Curio. D.P. *T. Nt.* i, 1] in attendance on Orsino. i, 4] *p.m.* ii, 4] mentions 'Feste the Jester,' and is sent to summon him.

Curtal. Name of a horse. 'I'll give bay C. and his furniture' (*All's Well*, ii, 3).

A curtal is a horse with his tail docked.

Curtis. D.P. *Tam. Sh.* Servant to Petruchio. iv, 1] seeks the news from Grumio while he makes a fire; later, reports that Petruchio is 'making a sermon of continency' to Katharine.

The name ('Curteys') was that of a Stratford family (1607). 'Cortese' has been conjectured.

Cut. Name of a horse; 'beat C.'s saddle; ... the poor jade is wrung in the withers' (*1 Hen. IV*, ii, 1).

Prob., specifically, a horse with a docked tail – or gelded.

Cyclops. Acc. Virgilian legend, one of a race of one-eyed (lit. round-eyed) giants (Cyclopes) who aided Vulcan in making armour and weapons for the gods (*Georg.* iv, 170; *Aen.* viii, 416 ff.). The word is sometimes regarded as the plu. of a sing. 'Cyclop.' 'Big-boned men framed of the Cyclops' size' (*T. And.* iv, 3); 'never did the Cyclops' hammers fall On Mars's armour...with less remorse' (*Haml.* ii, 2).

Cydnus. River of Cilicia; the scene of Cleopatra's first meeting with Mark Antony (*Plut.* p. 174). 'She purs'd up his heart upon the river of C.' (*Ant. Cl.* ii, 2; 'Sidnis,' F1); 'I am again for C.' (*ib.* v, 2; 'Cidrus,' Ff); 'C. swell'd above the banks' (*Cymb.* ii, 4; 'Sidnus,' F1; 'Cidnus,' F2, 3, 4).

Cymbeline.

Publication. No edition of *Cymb.*, so far as is known, appeared before its publication in the Folio of 1623, in which it occupies the last place. No list of *dramatis personae* is affixed, but the acts and scenes are indicated throughout. Title: 'The Tragedie of Cymbeline'; but 'Cymbeline King of Britaine' in the 'Catalogue' of plays.

Dates of Composition and Production. That *Cymbeline* was first produced not later than 1610–11 is certain from the fact that the astrologer Dr Simon Forman in his MS. *Book of Plaies and Notes thereof [etc.]*, in which the latest entry is May 15,1611, mentions having seen a performance of the play, and gives a convincing synopsis of the plot. Commentators, however, have to some extent differed as to the date, anterior to this, at which it was written. Of relevant internal evidence there is next to none, except that afforded by the important points of metre, and style in its widest sense; a consideration of these has led most critics to fix 1609–10 as the most probable date of composition. The 'Vision' of (v, 4) is generally held to be an interpolation of later date. Its authenticity has been defended by Knight, Ward, Fletcher, and others, but Sir S. Lee (p. 425) terms it 'pitiful mummery which may be assigned to an incompetent coadjutor.' See Furness, *Var.* pp. 374–9.

Sources of The Plot. The complex plot of *Cymb.* is resolvable into three distinct elements: (*a*) the quasi-historical background, based on the quarrels of Britain, under King Cymbeline, with Rome; (*b*) the main romantic story of Imogen; (*c*) the minor plot, depending on the kidnapping of the King's sons by Belarius.

(*a*) For the 'national' part of the play Sh. seems to have relied wholly on Holinshed's *Chronicles*, in which are to be found not only historical details, but many of the personal names introduced.

(*b*) The story of Imogen and her husband's wager is generally admitted to be derived from Boccaccio's *Decamerone*, Day ii, Nov. 3, the details of which are closely followed, including the discovery of the 'birthmark' and the device of concealment in a chest. It has been held that Sh. might have been indebted to the second tale in a miscellany bearing the name of *Westward for Smelts* [*etc.*], alleged to have been published in 1603, but of which no edition earlier than 1620 is known. But *Cymb.* is far more closely connected with Boccaccio's tale than with the English story; suffice it to say that the important incidents of the 'chest' and the 'birthmark' are wanting in the latter.

(*c*) The story of Belarius and his revenge on the King is believed to be of Sh.'s own invention.

Cymbeline. A Shakespearean character assumed to be equivalent to the historical Cunobelinus. But there is 'nothing but the name in common between the historical and the poetical king, for the plot of Cymbeline is only partially derived from the legendary history of Cunobelinus that Sh. found in Holinshed ... and even that has no claim to historic truth' (*D.N.B.*). The only trust-worthy information about Cunobelin is derived from coins and from the historians Suetonius and Dion Cassius (Evans, *Coins of the Ancient Britons*; Suet. *Caligula*, xliv; Dion Cassius, lx, 20–1). He appears to have been the son of Cassivelaunus (or Tasciovanus); his capital was Colchester, and he died about A.D. 43. The expedition sent against Britain by Claudius did not land until after his death. It was opposed by the late King's sons, Togodumnus and Caractacus. See Boswell-Stone, *Sh. Hol.* p. 6.

Holinshed's brief account may be thus summarized: Kymbeline or Cimbeline, son of Theomantius (or Tenantius) came to the throne 33 B.C., and was *persona grata* to Augustus (*Cymb.* iii, 1). He died about A.D. 2, and left two sons, Guiderius and Arviragus. Whether Britain paid tribute to Rome during C.'s reign seems doubtful, but there was amity between the two peoples. Upon the death of his father, Guiderius rebelled against Rome (*Hol.* i, 32–3). *Cf.* Spenser, *F.Q.* II, x, 50.

D.P. *Cymb.* 'King of Britain' (Rowe). (i, 1) he is reported to be in great wrath, since his daughter Imogen has wedded a poor gentleman (Posthumus) instead of his stepson, Cloten, for whom she was intended; the kidnapping of his two infant sons twenty years before is mtd. i, 2] banishes Posthumus with contumely; vituperates Imogen for her choice; chides the Queen for allowing them to meet, ii, 3] hears that Caius Lucius, the Roman ambassador, has arrived 'on angry purpose,' but will receive him courteously. iii, 1] yielding to the Queen's persuasion, he refuses tribute to Rome, but tells Lucius that he is personally welcome, and reminds him that 'thy Caesar knighted me' (*Hol.* i, 32). iii, 5] bids farewell to Lucius as an honoured enemy, and gives him safe conduct to Milford; in speaking of the coming war, he is led to inquire for Imogen, and learns that she is missing; ('he rages, none dare come about him'). iv, 3] grieves over his wife's 'madness,' and Cloten's absence; hears that the Roman legions have landed, and is 'amazed with matter.' (v, 4) mtd. v, 5] (after the battle) honours Belarius and his sons'; the death-bed confession of the 'delicate fiend,' his queen, is related to him; tells Lucius that the slaughter of the captives is demanded; is struck by the 'familiar favour' of 'Fidele' and grants him any boon he may ask; speaks privately with him; commands Iachimo to tell his tale; learns who 'Fidele' is, and exclaims: 'the gods do mean to strike me To death with mortal joy'; orders Guiderius to be executed for killing Cloten; learns that the two supposed sons of Belarius are his own; pardons all the prisoners; resolves, though victorious, to pay tribute to Rome; will celebrate the peace in Lud's Town.

Cynthia. An epithet of Diana; hence the moon (Ovid). 'This by the eye of C. hath she vowed' (*Per.* ii, 5); 'Yon grey... 'Tis but the pale reflex of C.'s brow' (*Rom. J.* iii, 5); 'C. for shame obscures her silver shine' (*V.A.* 728).

Cyprus. Island in the Mediterranean; made a Roman province 58 B.C.; became a 'protectorate' of the republic of Venice in 1471, and was then garrisoned by Venetian troops. In 1570 the island was attacked by the Turks, and in the following year became a part of Selim II's dominions. Famagusta, the principal seaport, surrendered after a stubborn defence. (The action of *Othello*, therefore, must be referred to a period earlier than 1571.)

Cleopatra made 'absolute queen' of C. by Antony, *Ant. Cl.* iii, 6; Iago has seen service at C., *Oth.* i, 1; news received thence at Venice, *ib.* i, 2; a Turkish fleet reported bearing up to it; its importance to the Turks, *ib.* i, 3; Othello ordered to defend C. against the 'mighty preparation' of the Turks, *ib. ib.*; Othello welcomed there, *ib.* ii, 1; 'this warlike isle' (*ib.* ii, 2). Mtd., iii, 1, 4; iv, 1.

Cyrus. See Thomyris.

Cytherea. An epithet of Venus; hence the goddess. 'Violets ... sweeter than ... C.'s breath' (*Wint. T.* iv, 4); 'C. all in sedges hid' (*Tam. Sh.* Ind. 2); 'C., how bravely thou becom'st thy bed' (*Cymb.* ii, 2); mtd., *P.P.* 4, 6.

D

Daedalus. See Icarus.

Dagonet. '*Shal.* I was then Sir D. in Arthur's show' (*2 Hen. IV*, iii, 2).

'Prince Arthur's Knights' were primarily a fraternity of archers, described by Rich. Mulcaster in a tract (1581), entitled *The Friendly and Frank Fellowship of Prince Arthur's Knights in and about the City of London*. It appears from this that members of the society personated characters in Arthurian Romance, and 'Dagonet,' being the king's fool, might with propriety fall to Shallow. The justice's interest in archery is shown by his comments, in the same scene, on 'old Double's' skill. See Mile End.

A bequest of 20s. to be spent in Mile End for the Knights of the Round Table is cited in *Archaeologia*, xxxix, 34 *n*.

Daintry. See Daventry.

Dalmatians. People of Dalmatia, on the E. coast of the Adriatic. They were defeated, 39 B.C., by Asinius Pollio, and finally subdued, 23 B.C., by Statilius Taurus. A revolt, in which they joined the Pannonians, was quelled by Tiberius A.D. 9. Holinshed (i, 32) states that Augustus was diverted from his intention of invading Britain by the rebellion of the 'Pannonians, which inhabited the countrie now called Hungarie, and the Dalmatians whom we now call Saluons.' This revolt mtd. *Cymb.* iii, 1; iii, 7.

Damascus. See Abel.

Damon. A Pythagorean who, having offered his life for that of his associate Pythias, became a type of the faithful friend (Val. Max. iv, 7, Ext. 1). Hamlet apostrophizes Horatio as 'Damon dear' in verse, *Haml.* iii, 2.

Damon and Pithias, a play by Richard Edwardes, was printed in 1571.

[**Danae.**] Perh. alluded to, *Rom. J.* i, 1, l. 220: 'She will not ... ope her lap to saint-seducing gold.'

Dancer, A. D.P. *2 Hen. IV* (Pope). Speaks the Epilogue, and hints at a continuation of the story. ('Epilogue,' QFf.)

Dane. Native of Denmark. 'If there be here German, or D... let him speak to me' (*All's Well*, iv, 2); 'king, father, royal D.' (*Haml.* i, 4); 'Hamlet the D.' (*ib.* v, 1); 'damned D., drink off this potion' (*ib.* v, 2); 'more an antique Roman than a D.' (*ib. ib.*). The drinking powers of the English compared with those of the Danes, *Oth.* ii, 3.

Dane, The. For 'King of Denmark.' 'Liegemen to the D.' (*Haml.* i, 1); 'you cannot speak of reason to the D., And lose your voice' (*ib.* i, 2).

Danger. Personified. '*Caesar.* Danger knows full well That Caesar is more dangerous ous than he: We are two lions litter'd in one day, And I the elder and more terrible' (*Jul. C.* ii, 2); '[the artisans] are all in uproar, and Danger serves among them' (*Hen. VIII*, i, 2).

'Danger is often personified in our old poets' (Knight).

Daniel. Hebrew prophet of the Chaldean period, who in the apocryphal History of Susanna is represented, though but a youth (v, 45), as confounding the guilty elders by examining them separately. *Cf.* Ezekiel xxviii, 3; Daniel vi, 3.

Shylock apostrophizes Portia as 'a Daniel come to judgment. Yea, a Daniel! O wise young judge, how I do honour thee!' (*M.V.* iv, 1) – a phrase which Gratiano jeeringly reiterates upon the Jew's discomfiture.

Danish. Pertaining to Denmark. Claudius refers to England having been wounded by the D. sword, *Haml.* iv, 3; 'the D. king' (*ib.* iv, 4); Gertrude speaks of the rabble as 'false D. dogs' (*ib.* iv, 5); 'D. seal' (*ib.* v, 2); 'the French bet against the D.' (*ib. ib.*).

Danskers. Danes. 'Inquire ... what D. are in Paris' (*Haml.* ii, 1).

The only instance quoted of the English use of the word in *N.E.D.*

Daphne. Daughter of Peneus; when pursued by Apollo, she prayed for aid to Tellus, and was changed into a laurel (Ovid, *Metam.* i, 525 ff.).

'The story shall be changed, Apollo flies, and D. holds the chase' (*M.N.D.* ii, 1); 'Tell me, Apollo, for thy D.'s love' (*Tr. Cr.* i, 1); 'D. roaming through a thorny wood, Scratching her legs that one shall swear she bleeds' (*Tam. Sh.* Ind. 2; *cf.* Ovid, *Metam.* i, 508: 'indignave laedi Crura notent sentes').

Dardan. (*a*) *Subst.*, for 'Dardania' (*poet.* for 'Troy,' frequent in Virgil). 'From the strand of Dardan, where they fought' (*Lucr.* 1436).

(*b*) *Adj.*, 'Trojan,' from Dardanus, the mythical ancestor of the Trojans. 'Dardan plains' (*Tr. Cr.* Prol.). See also TROY, GATES OF.

Dardanian. Same as 'Dardan' (*adj.*). 'The D. wives ... come forth to view The issue of the exploit' (*M.V.* iii, 2; *i.e.* the rescue of Hesione (*q.v.*)).

Dardanius. D.P. *Jul. C.* 'Servant to Brutus.' v, 5] is asked by Br. to kill him.

'Dardanus,' *Plut.* p. 150.

Darius. King of Persia (521–485 B.C.). 'The rich jewell'd coffer of D.' (*1 Hen. VI*, i, 6).

Cf. Puttenham, *Arte of English Poesie* (1589), i, 8: 'In what price the noble poemes of *Homer* were holden with *Alexander* the great, in so much as euery night they were layd vnder his pillow, and by day were carried in the rich iewell cofer of *Darius* lately before vanquished by him in battaile.' (Steevens conjectured that 'jewel-coffer' should be read in *Sh.*)

Datchet. Village near Windsor. 'Go take up these clothes ... carry them to the laundress in D.-mead' (*M.W.W.* iii, 3); '*Fal.* Being thus crammed in the basket [I was carried] to D.-lane' (*ib.* iii, 5). See next article.

Datchet Lane. That part of the road leading to D. nearest to the town of Windsor. For the supposed scene of Falstaff's immersion (Hog Hole) see Tighe and Davis, *Annals of Windsor* (1858), i, 680.

Datchet Mead. *M.W.W.* iii, 3.

Dauphin, The. ('Dolphin,' Ff.) Title of the eldest son of the King of France (1349–1830). The last lord of Dauphiny, on ceding the province to Philip of Valois, made it a condition that the title of Dauphin should be perpetuated in the manner indicated. Dauphiny was so named from the crest (three dolphins) of its lords.

The Dauphins figuring as D.PP. in *Sh.* are: (*a*) Lewis, son of Philip Augustus (*John*) (but the title is here an anachronism). See LEWIS (1). (*b*) Lewis, son of Charles VI (*Hen. V*); unnamed, and mtd. only as 'the D.' (during the reign of Henry V three sons of Charles VI – Lewis, John, and Charles – bore the title in rapid succession). See LEWIS (2). (*c*) Charles, son of Charles VI (*1 Hen. VI*); really King when the play opens, but called Dauphin until crowned at Rheims (1429). See CHARLES VII.

References in other plays: 'Till France be won into the D.'s hands' (*2 Hen. VI*, i, 3; cf. *Hol.* iii, 612); mtd. insultingly by Cade, *ib.* iv, 7; 'Henry the Fifth, who made the D. and the French to stoop' (*3 Hen. VI*, i, 1); 'Made the D. stoop' (*ib.* ii, 2).

Daventry. Or 'Daintry,' as commonly pronounced; a town in Northamptonshire. 'The red-nose inn-keeper of Daventry [or 'Dauintry']' (*1 Hen. IV*, iv, 2); '*War.* Where is the post that came from Montague? *2 Mess.* By this at Daintry' (*3 Hen. VI*, v, 1).

[David, II.] See BRUCE, DAVID.

[David, John.] See HORNER, THOMAS.

Davy (1). For 'David': 'St Davy's Day,' *i.e.* March 1 (*Hen. V*, iv, 1; v, 1). As a forename: 'D. Gam' (*q.v.*).

Davy (2). D.P. *2 Hen. IV*. Servant to Shallow. v, 1] is bid prepare for his master's guests, and finds it difficult to gain Shallow's attention for domestic business. v, 3] busies himself in serving the guests and plying them with wine; hopes to see London once ere he dies.

Known as a surname in Stratford in 1579 (Halliwell).

Death. Personified. 'The sudden hand of D. close up mine eye' (*L.L.L.* v, 2, l. 825); 'not D. himself, In mortal fury half so peremptory' (*John*, ii, 1); 'the rotten car-case of old D.' (*ib. ib.*); 'keeps D. his court and there the antic sits' (*Rich. II*, iii, 2); 'goodman D., goodman bones!' (*2 Hen. IV*, v, 4); 'Thou antic D., which laugh'st us here to scorn' (*1 Hen. VI*, iv, 7); 'an ugly monster' (*Cymb.* v, 3); 'Hard-favoured tyrant, ugly, meagre, lean, Hateful divorce of love ... grim-grinning, earth's worm,' etc. (*V.A.* 931 ff.); 'D.'s ebon dart' (*ib.* 948); 'not to blame' (*ib.* 992); 'Sweet D.' (*ib.* 997); 'with D. she humbly doth insinuate' (*ib.* 1012); mtd., *Son.* vi (2); 'that churl D.' (*ib.* xxxii).

In *M. V.* ii, 7, l. 63, a skull is intended.

Deborah. Prophetess and judge of Israel, who incited, and accompanied, Barak to attack Sisera (Judges iv–v). 'Thou [Joan of Arc] ... fightest with the sword of D.' (*1 Hen. VI*, i, 2).

December, Month of. Sir Toby, *T. Nt.* ii, 3, sings a snatch of a lost song beginning 'O! the twelfth day of D.'; Beatrice exceeds Hero in beauty 'as the first day of May doth the last of D.' (*M. Ado*, i, 1); 'men are April when they woo, D. when they wed' (*A.Y.L.* iv, 1); Florizel 'makes a July's day short as D.' (*Wint. T.* i, 2); 'wallow naked in D. snow' (*Rich. II*, i, 3); 'when we shall hear The rain and wind beat dark D.' (*Cymb.* iii, 3); 'old D.'s bareness' (*Son.* xcvii).

Decimus. See BRUTUS, DECIUS.

Decius. For 'Decius Brutus' (*q.v.*). *Jul. C.* ii, 1, 2 (2); iii, 3.

Decretas. See DERCETAS.

Deep-vow. A debtor; *M. for M.* iv, 3.

Deformed. Mistaken for a personal name by the watchmen. *M. Ado*, iii, 3; v, 1.

Deiphobus. Son of Priam; acc. post-Homeric tradition, he married Helen on the death of Paris, and was slain and mutilated by Menelaus ('Dict. Cret.' 1, 10; 5,12).

D.P. *Tr. Cr.* (i, 2; iii, 1) mtd. iv, 1] announces Aeneas. (iv, 2) mtd. iv, 3] *p.m.* iv, 4] present.

Delabret(h). See ALBRET, CHARLES D'.

Delacourt. See CAR.

Delphos, Island of. For 'Delphi' (accusative form), in Phocis, famous for its oracle of Apollo. The oracle consulted as to Hermione's guilt, *Wint. T.* ii, 1, 3; iii, 2.

In Greene's *Dorastus and Fawnia* Bellaria (Hermione) begs the King 'to send sixe of his noble men whome he best trusted, to the Isle of Delphos, there to enquire of the oracle of Apollo,' and after a voyage of three weeks they arrive at the island.

Chaucer, *The Franklin's Tale*, l. 1077, mentions Apollo's temple in 'Delphos.' (Milton, *On the Nativity*, uses the same form.)

Demetrius (1). D.P. *Ant. Cl.* 'Friend and follower of Antony' (Rowe). i, 1] regrets that A. 'approves the common liar' at Rome.

The name is mtd. in *Plut.* p. 144, as that of 'one of Cassius' men.'

Demetrius (2). D.P. *M.N.D.* i, 1] urges Lysander to abandon his 'crazed title' to Hermia; is accused by Lys. of having 'won the soul' of Helena. ii, 2] seeking for the runaways (Lys. and Herm.) he is followed by Hel., whom he roughly upbraids and would leave 'to the mercy of wild beasts'; but he fails to shake her off. ii, 3] escapes from her. iii, 2] is accused by Herm. of having slain Lys. in his sleep; rebuts the charge, and on her flight lies down for repose; Oberon touches his eyes with magic love-juice; awaking, Dem. sees Hel. and, disregarding the presence of Lys. wooes her with amorous hyperbole; bids Lys. keep his Hermia, for his heart 'to Helen is home returned'; angry words pass between the rivals, and they seek a place for combat; led astray by Puck, Dem. fails to find his rival and lies down to sleep till dawn. iv, 1] he awakes, still under the influence of the charm, and assures Egeus that his fancy for Herm. has 'melted as the snow,' and vows to be true for evermore to his first love Helena; feels a passing doubt whether he is yet awake. v, 1] ridicules the performance of the Interlude.

E. Tiessen, *Arch. f. n. Sprachen* (1877), lviii, 4, with reference to Lysander's remark: 'Oh how fit a word is that vile name to perish on my sword,' gravely suggests that there is an allusion 'to meat which is stuck on a spit.' (See Furness, *Var. M.N.D.* p. 110.)

Demetrius (3). D.P. *T. And.* Son to Tamora. i, 1] urges his mother to seek revenge on Rome. ii, 1] quarrels with his younger brother Chiron, his rival for Lavinia; yields to Aaron's advice that they should work their will on L. ii, 2] present with the royal hunting-party. ii, 3] stabs Bassianus, at Tamora's instigation; bids T. view, 'as unrelenting flint,' Lavinia's tears; (Lav. is violated and mutilated by the brothers). ii, 5] Demetrius derides their victim. (iv, 1) he is accused by Lav., who writes his name in the sand. iv, 2] receives weapons from Titus, with a scroll; is eager to kill Tamora's child by Aaron, but, dissuaded by A., condones the Queen's shame. iv, 4] *p.m.* v, 2] disguised as 'Murther,' visits Titus; is slain by him. (v, 3) mtd.

Denmark. Occurs only in *Haml.* (*a*) For 'King of D.' 'The majesty of buried D.' (i, 1); 'look like a friend on D.' (i, 2); 'D.'s health' (v, 2). (*b*) Country or people of D. Mtd., i, 2 (3); 'main voice of D.' (i, 3); 'Something is rotten in the state of D.' (i, 4); 'the whole ear of D.' (i, 5); 'royal bed of D.' (*ib.*); mtd., *ib.* (2); 'D.'s a prison' (ii, 2); mtd., *ib.* (3), iii, 2, iv, 5, v, 1, 2 (2).

Dennis. D.P. *A.Y.L.* 'Servant to Oliver' (Rowe). i, 1] in attendance.

Dennis, St, or **St Denis.** Apostle to the Gauls; beheaded, according to tradition, at Paris; patron saint of France. 'Saint D. to Saint Cupid' (*L.L.L.* v, 2); invoked, *Hen. V*, v, 2, and *1 Hen. VI*, iii, 2; 'St D. and St George' (*Hen. V*, v, 2).

Denny, Lady. See Lady, An Old.

Denny, Sir Anthony (1501–49). Groom of the Stole to Henry VIII, and Privy Councillor; knighted Sept. 30, 1544. (Acc. French, p. 267, he died in 1547.)

D.P. *Hen. VIII.* v, 1] conducts Abp. Cranmer to the King's presence.

This incident is recorded by Foxe, *Actes and Monumentes (1576), ii, 1759. Foxe, in turn, used a Life of Cranmer* written by Ralph Morice, the Abp.'s secretary, who calls Sir Anthony 'Mr Deny.'

De Oratore. A work by Cicero; see Cicero, Marcus Tullius.

Derby. Mtd. in the text only in Bolingbroke's title: 'Harry of Hereford, Lancaster, and Derby' (*Rich. II*, i, 3). In *Hol.* iii, 429, 'Henrie of Lancaster, Duke of Hereford' only. 'E. of Derby' was Henry's earliest title.

Derby, 1st Earl of. See Stanley, Thomas.

Deroetas. ('Decretas,' except in one pfx., until altered by Pope.) D.P. *Ant. Cl.* iv, 14] resolves to inform Octavius of Antony's death. v, 1] brings Ant.'s blood-stained sword to Oct.

Plutarch's narrative (*Plut.* p. 222) is closely followed, but the name there given is Dercetaeus.

Desdemona. D.P. *Oth.* 'Wife to Othello' (F1). (i, 1) her father is informed that she has eloped with Oth. (Roderigo having previously solicited her hand). (i, 2) Brabantio believes she must have been constrained to yield to Oth. by magic arts. i, 3] Othello declares before the Senate that 'she lov'd me for the dangers I had pass'd; And I lov'd her that she did pity them'; she is accorded leave to accompany him to the war; Brabantio warns Oth. that 'she has deceiv'd her father, and may thee'; (Iago tells Roderigo that she will soon tire of the Moor). ii, 1] she arrives in Cyprus; is welcomed by Cassio; exchanges raillery with Iago; affectionately greets Oth. ii, 3] present. (iii, 1) mtd. iii, 3] promises Cassio to use the utmost importunity in persuading Oth. to receive him again into favour; she pleads for him, and Oth. declares that he will deny her nothing; (suspicions are instilled into Oth.'s mind by Iago); later, D. lends Oth. her handkerchief to bind his brow; (he drops it, and it is picked up by Iago's wife). iii, 4] she is distressed at the loss of her handkerchief; reminds Oth. of his promise with regard to Cassio, but he persists in demanding the handkerchief (which Iago has declared he saw in Cassio's possession); she is bewildered by his fury, and on Cassio's entry tells him that 'my advocation is not now in tune'; Emilia warns her that Oth. is jealous. iv, 1] D. greets her kinsman Lodovico, and, on expressing joy that Oth. is ordered home and Cassio appointed his deputy, is struck by Oth. and assailed with frantic invective. iv, 2] is utterly dismayed by Othello's open accusation of faithlessness, and cries, 'What ignorant sin have I committed?'; stunned by the charge, she seeks advice and consolation from Iago and his wife. iv, 3] is ordered to her chamber by Oth.; converses sadly with Emilia, who attends her, and sings a ballad with the burden 'Willow, willow!' (v, 1) Roderigo's gifts for her stolen by Iago. v, 2] vainly protesting against Othello's furious accusations, is smothered by him, and after reviving for a moment, dies – her last words, spoken to Emilia, being 'Commend me to my kind lord: O, farewell!'

The precise supposed manner of Desdemona's death has caused much controversy, and remains a mystery. For a full account of various medical theories and for the difficulties presented by the stage tradition that Othello stabs her after an ineffectual attempt at suffocation see Furness, *Var. Oth.* pp. 302–7. The name occurs in the shortened form 'Desdemon' (in F1) in the following instances: iii, 1, l. 6; iii, 3, l. 55; iv, 2, 1, 41; v, 2, ll. 29, 204, 281. Knight's suggestion that this is an abbreviation 'of familiar tenderness' does not appear tenable.

In Cinthio's *Novella* the 'virtuosa Donna, di maravigliosa bellazza' is Disdomona. She is murdered by the Moor and the Ensign, who despatch her with a stocking filled with sand, and then pull down the ceiling of the chamber to make her death appear accidental.

The Greek original of the name is undoubtedly Δυσδαίμων 'unfortunate,' or 'ill-starred.' 'We may go further ... and say it is merely a variation of δυσδαιμονία "ill-starredness." She is not only unhappy, she is unhappiness itself.' (Hales, *Notes and Essays* (1884), p. 112.)

Desire. Personified. 'Now quick Desire hath caught the yielding prey' (*V.A.* 547, 703 ff.); 'out of the shot and danger of Desire' (*Haml.* i, 3).

Despenser, Thomas le, Earl of Gloucester (1373–1400). 'Thomas lord Spenser, late earle of Glocester,' joined the Abbot of Westminster's conspiracy (*Hol.* iii, 514); beheaded at Bristol (*ib.* iii, 516; 'Hugh' in text, 'Thomas' in margin, acc. Walsingham).

'I have to London sent the heads of Salisbury, Spencer,' etc. (*Rich. II*, v, 6).

This is the reading of Ff; Qq have 'Oxford, Salisbury,' by an error.

Destiny. The goddess of destiny; in plu., the Fates (*q.v.*). *Sing.*: 'Think you I bear the shears of D.?' (*John*, iv, 2). *Plu.*: 'According to the fates and D.s and such odd sayings' (*M.V.* ii, 2); 'as the D.s decree (*A.Y.L.* i, 2); 'those branches by the D.s cut' (*Rich. II*, i, 2); 'by the D.s to be avoided' (*3 Hen. VI*, ii, 1); 'or D.s do cut his thread of life' (*Per.* i, 2); 'she bribed the D.s' (*V.A.* 733); 'the D.s will curse thee' (*ib.* 945).

Deucalion. Son of Prometheus; with his wife Pyrrha, alone of mortals saved from the flood sent by Jupiter. The human race was regenerated from stones cast on the ground by D. and P. (Ovid, *Metam.* i, 313–415).

'No, not our kin, far [farther] than D. off' (*Wint. T.* iv, 4); 'Worth all your predecessors since D.' (*Cor.* ii, 1). The flood alluded to, *Jul. C.* i, 2, l. 152.

Deus. *Lat.* 'Laus deo, bone intelligo' (*L.L.L.* v, 1); (plu.) 'dii faciant' (*3 Hen. VI*, i, 3).

Devil, The. The supreme spirit of evil. (*a*) *In proverbial expressions:* 'He must needs go that the d. drives' (*All's Well*, i, 3); 'he must have a long spoon that must eat with the d.' (*Com. Err.* iv, 3); 'give the d. his due' (*1 Hen. IV*, i, 2; *Hen. V*, iii, 7); 'the d. rides upon a fiddle-stick' (*1 Hen. IV*, ii, 4); 'Tell truth and shame the d. (*1 Hen. IV*, iii, 1); 'a pox of the d.' (*Hen. V*, iii, 7).

(*b*) *Characteristics:* haughty, *1 Hen. VI*, i, 1; a niggard, *Hen. VIII*, i, 1; 'hath power to assume a pleasing shape' (*Haml.* ii, 2); 'the d.'s horn' (*M. for M.* ii, 4); 'the eternal d.' (*Jul. C.* i, 2); father of Caliban, *Temp.* i, 2; 'mortal eyes cannot endure the d.' (*Rich. III*, i, 2).

(*c*) *In imprecations and expletives: Temp.* ii, 2, iii, 2; *M.W.W.* ii, 1; *Rich. II*, v, 5; *1 Hen. IV*, i, 3; *2 Hen. IV*, ii, 4; *Hen. V*, ii, 1; *Rich. III*, iv, 3; *Hen. VIII*, i, 1, 3; *Tr. Cr.* iv, 2, v, 8; *Haml.* v, 1; *M.V.* iv, 1; *A.Y.L.* iii, 2; *All's Well*, iv, 1; *Tam. Sh.* iv, 3; *Cymb.* ii, 3; *Rom. J.* ii, 4, iii, 1.

(*d*) *Miscellaneous:* 'The d. can cite Scripture for his purpose' (*M.V.* i, 3, in allusion to Matt. iv, 4, 6); 'Pork ... the habitation your prophet the Nazarite conjured the d. into' (*M.V.* i, 3, in allusion to Luke viii, 26 ff.); 'let me say "amen" betimes, lest the d. cross my prayer' (*ib.* iii, 1); 'the black prince, sir, *alias*, the prince of darkness; *alias*, the d.' (*All's Well*, iv, 5); 'the d. knew not what he did when he made man politic' (*Timon*, iii, 3); 'the d. himself will not eat a woman ... a woman is a dish for the gods if the d. dress her not' (*Ant. Cl.* v, 2); 'make a puritan of the d.' (*Per.* iv, 6); 'the d. will make a grandsire of you' (*Oth.* i, 1); 'hypocrisy against the d.' (*ib.* iv, 1); 'the d. their virtue tempts' (*ib. ib.*).

In the phrase 'the devil and his dam': *Tam. Sh.* i, 1, iii, 2; *Com. Err.* iv, 3; *John*, ii, 1; *1 Hen. VI*, i, 5; *T. And.* iv, 2; *Oth.* iv, 1. His disciples, *Hen. VIII*, v, 3. His writ, *2 Hen. VI*, i, 4. His grace, *1 Hen. VI*, v, 3. His illusions, *Hen. VIII*, i, 2. His book, *2 Hen. IV*, ii, 2. The d. 'speaks in' Prospero, *Temp.* v, 1; 'the d. himself hath not such a name [as cuckold]' (*M.W.W.* ii, 2); 'the d. that guides him' (*ib.* iii, 5); 'the d. guide his cudgel' (*ib.* iv, 2); 'now shall the d. be shamed' (*ib. ib.*); 'if the d. have him not in fee-simple' (*ib. ib.*); 'I think the d. will not have me [Falstaff] damned' (*ib.* v, 5); 'that ever the d. could have made you our delight' (*ib. ib.*); 'let him be the d. an he will' (*T. Nt.* i, 5); 'if you were the d., you are fair' (*ib. ib.*); 'an you speak ill of the d., how he [Malvolio] takes it to heart' (*ib.* iii, 4); 'empty trunks, o'erflourished by the d.' (*ib. ib.*); 'gentle ones that will use the d. himself with courtesy' (*ib.* iv, 2); 'ah, ha! to the d... adieu, goodman D.' (*ib. ib.* song); 'he's the very d. incardinate' (*ib.* v, 1); 'What, can the d. speak true ?' (*Macb.* i, 3); 'that which might appal the d.' (*ib.* iii, 4); 'would not betray the d. to his fellow' (*ib.* iv, 3); 'the d. damn thee black' (*ib.* v, 3); 'The d. himself could not pronounce a title More hateful' (*ib.* v, 7); 'as faithfully as I deny the d.' (*John*, i, 1); 'the d. tempts thee' (*ib.* iii, 1); 'thou wert better gall the d.' (*ib.* iv, 3); 'you shall think the d. is come from hell' (*ib. ib.*); 'the d. that told me I did well' (*Rich. II*, v, 5); 'how agrees the d. and thee' (*1 Hen. IV*, i, 2); 'keeping thy word with the d.' (*ib. ib.*); 'cozening the d.' (*ib. ib.*); 'he durst as well have met the d. alone' (*ib.* i, 3); 'if the d. come and roar them' (*ib. ib.*); 'as the d. would have it' (*ib.* ii, 4); Glendower 'swore the d. his true liegeman' (*1 Hen. IV*, ii, 4); 'if that the d. and mischance look big' (*ib.* iv, 1); 'as lief hear the d. as a drum' (*ib.* iv, 2); 'there is a good angel about him, but the d. outbids him' (*2 Hen.IV*, ii, 4); 'a' once said the d. would have him about women' (*Hen. V*, ii, 3); 'make a moral of the d. himself' (*ib.* iv, 1); 'the d. take order now' (*ib.* iv, 5); 'the d. was in arms' (*1 Hen. VI*, i, 1); 'there's two of you; the d. make a third' (*2 Hen. VI*, iii, 2); 'no friends but the plain d.' (*Rich. III*, i, 2); 'take the d. in thy mind' (*ib.* i, 4); 'the d. and my rage' (*ib. ib.*); '*Q. Eliz.* Shall I be tempted of the d. thus? *K. Rich.* Ay, if the d. tempt thee to do good' (*ib.* iv, 4); 'the d. was amongst 'em' (*Hen. VIII*, v, 4); 'an the d. come to him, it's all one' (*Tr. Cr.* i, 2); 'we do sugar o'er The d. himself' (*Haml.* iii, 1); 'let the d. wear black' (*ib.* iii, 2); 'curb the d.' (*ib.* iii, 4); 'He's the d.' (*Cor.* i, 10); 'disdains thee and the d. alike' (*Cymb.* i, 7); 'will not serve God if the d. bid you' (*Oth.* i, 1); 'to look on the d.' (*ib.* ii, 1); 'cannon ... like the d.' (*ib.* iii, 4); 'in the d.'s teeth' (*ib. ib.*); 'the d. their virtue tempts' (*ib.* iv, 1);

'if the d. Have given thee proofs for sin' (*M. for M.* iii, 2); 'you bid me seek redemption of the d.' (*ib.* v, 1); 'let the d. be sometime honoured' (*ib. ib.*); 'O, ... some quillets, how to cheat the d.' (*L.L.L.* iv, 3); 'if the d. be within [the casket]' (*M.V.* i, 2); Shylock declared to be 'the very d. incarnate' (*ib.* ii, 2); 'if the d. may be her judge' (*ib.* iii, 1); 'unless the d. himself turn Jew' (*ib. ib.*); 'the d. himself will have no shepherds' (*A.Y.L.* iii, 2); 'though the d. lead the measure' (*All's Well,* ii, 1); 'the d. it is that's thy master' (*ib.* ii, 3); 'at once both the office of God and the d.' (*ib.* v, 2).

'Diable,' *M.W.W.* i, 4, iii, 1; *Hen. V,* iv, 5. 'Diablo,' *Oth.* ii, 3.

Devonshire. Forces under the Courtenays reported in D.; *Rich. III,* iv, 4 (*Hol.* iii, 743).

Dew, Seigneur. Pistol's error for 'Dieu'; *Hen. V,* iv, 4.

Diable, Diablo. See Devil, The.

Diana (1). An Italian divinity identified by the Romans with the Greek Artemis. Regarded in many aspects, but especially as the goddess of chastity, the immortal huntress, and the moon-goddess. Her priests and priestesses were bound by strict vows of chastity. As a huntress she was attended by troops of nymphs. The Ephesian 'Diana,' in whose honour the famous temple was erected at Ephesus (*q.v.*) was a totally distinct divinity. See also Dictynna.

(*a*) 'Dian.' '*Claudio* [to Hero]. You seem to me as D. in her orb, As chaste as is the bud ere it be blown' (*M. Ado,* iv, 1); 'D.'s bud' (*M.N.D.* iv, 1; probably the *agnus castus, cf.* Chaucer, *The Flower and the Leaf,* II. 472–5: 'In her [D.'s] hond the braunch she beareth this, That *agnus castus* men call properly'); Katharina compared to D., *Tam. Sh.* ii, 1 (3); 'modest D. circled with her nymphs' (*3 Hen. VI,* iv, 8); 'the consecrated snow That lies on D.'s lap' (*Timon,* iv, 3); 'chaste as the icicle That's curdied by the frost from purest snow, And hangs on D.'s temple' (*Cor.* v, 3); 'the chimneypiece Chaste D.' (*Cymb.* ii, 4); 'my mother seem'd The D. of that time' (*ib.* ii, 5); 'as D. had dreams' (*ib.* v, 5); Tamora ironically compared to D., *T. And.* ii, 3 (2) (see Actaeon); 'she hath D.'s wit' (*Rom. J.* i, 1); 'as fresh as D.'s visage' (*Oth.* iii, 3); 'vail to her mistress D.' (*Per.* iv, Gow.); 'celestial D., goddess argentine' (*ib.* v, 1, 1.250; *cf.* 'argentea ... Cynthia,' Ovid, *Her.* xviii, 71); 'as D. bid' (*ib.* v, 2, Gow.); 'Hail, D.!' 'immortal D.' (*ib.* v, 3); 'make modest D. cloudy and forlorn' (*V.A.* 725); 'a maid of D.'s' (*Son.* cliii).

(*b*)'Diana.' 'D.'s lip is not more smooth and rubious' (*T. Nt.* i, 4); 'on D.'s altar to protest For aye austerity and single life' (*M.N.D.* i, 1); 'I will die as chaste as D.' (*M.V.* i, 2); 'wake D. with a hymn' (*ib.* v, 1; as the moon-goddess, see Endymion); 'he hath bought a pair of cast ['chast,' F2, 3, 4] lips of D.' (*A.Y.L.* iii, 4); 'I will weep for nothing, like D. in the fountain' (*ib.* iv, 1; probably with reference to some particular image); 'let us be D.'s foresters, gentlemen of the shade, minions of the moon [*i.e.* nocturnal robbers]' (*1 Hen. IV,* i, 2); 'By all D.'s waiting-women yond, And by herself' (*Tr. Cr.* v, 2); 'live like D.'s priest' (*Cymb.* i, 7; cf. *Per.* v, 1, l. 243); 'makes D.'s rangers false themselves (*ib.* ii, 3; meaning Imogen's attendants); 'twelve moons more she'll wear D.'s livery' (*Per.* ii, 5); mtd., *ib.* ii, 3, 4; invoked by Marina, *ib.* iv, 3; 'D.'s altar,' 'D.'s temple,' 'pure D.' (*ib.* v, 3).

D.P. *Per.* v, 1] appearing 'as in a vision,' instructs Pericles to proceed to Ephesus.

In *All's Well,* i, 3, l. 106, 'Diana no' was inserted by Theobald.

'The thrice-crowned queen of night' (*A.Y.L.* iii, 2) seems to allude to Hecate-Diana-Luna (Ovid, *Her.* xii, 79; *Metam.* vii, 177).

Diana (2). D.P. *All's Well.* Daughter to a Widow of Florence; signs herself (v, 3) 'Diana Capulet.' iii, 5] is warned against the advances of the 'French earl' (Bertram); tells Helena that 'the Count Rousillon' has deserted his wife; points out Bertram admiringly, but wishes 'he were honester'; considers Parolles 'a vile rascal.' (iii, 7) referred to by Bertram as 'wondrous cold.' iv, 2] grants an interview to B.; chides him for neglecting his wife; obtains a ring from his finger as a loan; seems to yield to his wooing, and consents to being visited by him that night. (iv, 3) Parolles' sonnet to her read; (Helena takes D.'s place secretly at night). iv, 4] declares herself ready to endure much on Helena's behalf. v, 1] (at Marseilles) *p.m.* v, 3] presents herself before the King as 'a wretched Florentine,' and declares that she is affianced to Bertram; B. scoffs at her as 'a fond and desperate creature'; she produces his ring and mentions that the ring she gave him resembled that on the King's finger; refuses to explain how she obtained the latter ring, and is committed to prison; on the entrance of Helena the *dénouement* takes place.

'Capilet,' v, 3, Ff.

Dick (1). Familiar abbreviation of 'Richard.' 'Didst see D. surgeon?' (*T. Nt.* v, 1); 'D. the shepherd' (*L.L.L.* v, 2); 'Tom, D. and Francis' (*1 Hen. IV,* ii, 4); Prince Edward addresses Richard, Duke of Gloucester, as 'misshapen D.' (*3 Hen. VI,* v, 5). Used, like 'Jack' (*q.v.*), to mean 'a fellow': 'some trencher-knight, some D.' (*L.L.L.* v, 2); 'to beg of Hob and D.' (*Cor.* ii, 3).

Dick (2). D.P. 2 *Hen. VI.* 'D. the butcher of Ashford.' iv, 2] scoffs (aside) at Cade's boasts; would fain 'kill all the lawyers'; demands Lord Say's head. iv, 3] is praised for his valour by Cade; proposes to break open the gaols. iv, 6] announces 'an army ... in Smithfield.' iv, 7] is prominent in support of Cade. Not named as 'of Ashford' in *F.P.C.*

Dickens. Apparently a euphemism for 'devil,' the earliest known instance being *M.W.W.* iii, 2, l. 10; but, as a dim. of 'Dick,' 'Dickin' or 'Dickon' was in use long before. There is no evidence of its derivation from 'devilkin' as has been suggested. See *N.E.D. s.v.*

Dickon. For 'Richard.' 'D. thy master is bought and sold' (*Rich. III,* v, 3). See Jockey.

Dicky. For 'Richard.' 'That valiant crookback prodigy, D. your boy' (*3 Hen. VI,* i, 4).

Dictynna. Properly a surname of Britomartis, a Cretan divinity of hunters and fishermen; later identified with Diana, as the moon-goddess and huntress; *cf.* Ovid, *Metam.* ii, 441, 'Ecce suo comitata choro Dictynna ... et caede superba ferarum,' translated by Golding: 'D. garded with her traine, and proud of killing deere' (ii, 21). Pedantically used by Holofernes: 'Dictynna, goodman Dull,' etc. (*L.L.L.* iv, 2).

The word puzzled the printers, for we have in Qq and Ff 'Dictissima,' 'dictisima,' 'dictima,' and 'dictinna.' The correct form was restored by Rowe.

Dido. Daughter of Belus, King of Tyre. She married her uncle Acerbas, and upon his murder by her brother Pygmalion she fled to Africa and founded Carthage. Having vowed eternal fidelity to her late husband, she stabbed herself to escape marriage with a neighbouring king. Virgil, however, makes D. a contemporary of Aeneas, with whom she falls in love; on being deserted by him she immolates herself on a funeral pyre.

'Widow D.' (*Temp.* i, 1); 'stood D. with a willow in her hand Upon the wild sea banks' (*M.V.* v, 1; *cf.* Ovid, *Her.* vii); 'madding D.' (2 *Hen. VI*, iii, 2); 'D. and her Aeneas' (*Ant. Cl.* iv, 12); 'the wand'ring prince and D.' (*T. And.* ii, 3); 'love-sick D.' (*ib.* v, 3); 'to his lady ... D. a dowdy' (*Rom. J.* ii, 4); 'Aeneas' tale to D.' (*Haml.* ii, 2); ('that fire which burn'd the Carthage queen,' *M.N.D.* i, 1).

The amours of Dido and Aeneas are dilated upon in Marlowe and Nashe's *Dido, Queen of Carthage* (1593).

Dieu. *Fr.* God. 'D. vous garde' (*T. Nt.* iii, 1); 'O seigneur D.' (*Hen. V*, iii, 4; iv, 4); 'la grace de D.' (*ib.* iii, 4); 'O D. vivant' (*ib.* iii, 5); 'D. de batailles' (*ib. ib.*); 'l'amour de D.' (*ib.* iv, 4); 'O bon D.' (*ib.* v, 2); 'Mort D.' (2 *Hen. VI*, i, 1). See DEW.

Digges, Leonard (1588–1635). Author of commendatory verses pfxd. to F1, and the 'Poems' (1640).

Dighton, John. One of the murderers of the Princes in the Tower; suborned by Tyrrel, whose horsekeeper he was, 'a big, broad, square and strong knave' (*Hol.* iii, 735). He 'lyved at Caleys long after, no lesse disdayned and hated then pointed at, and there dyed in great misery' (Hall, p. 379).

He is described, *Rich. III*, iv, 3, as overcome by remorse.

Diomedes (1). Son of Tydeus; acc. Homeric legend the bravest Greek next to Achilles; he fought against Hector and Aeneas, and even against Aphrodite and Ares. The story of his love for Cressida belongs wholly to medieval romance.

D.P. *Tr. Cr.* ii, 3] joins in persuading Ajax to accept Hector's challenge. iii, 3] is sent to Troy to fetch Cressida – 'a burden Which I am proud to bear.' iv, 1] exchanges defiant compliments with Aeneas; inveighs against Helen. (iv, 2) mtd. iv, 3] *p.m.* iv, 4] Cressida is given into his keeping – 'she shall be prized,' but not at Troilus' bidding. iv, 5] presents C. to the Greeks; later, acts as 'second' to Ajax. v, 1] Thersites characterizes him as 'a false-hearted rogue,' and suspects his loyalty. v, 2] his interview with Cressida, in which she gives him Troilus' sleeve, is overheard by the latter, who vows vengeance. (v, 3) mtd. v, 4] fights with Tr. v, 5] sends Cressida Troilus' horse, since he has 'chastis'd the amorous Trojan.' v, 6] again fights with Tr. v, 10] present.

Chaucer relates that Cressida gave D. 'the fair bay steed The which she ones won of Troilus,' and that 'when through the body hurt was Diomed of Troilus, then wept she many a tear.'

The form 'Diomed' is used everywhere in the text of *Tr. Cr.* except once in iv, 2.

Mtd. in connection with Rhesus (*q.v.*), *3 Hen. VI*, iv, 2.

Diomedes (2). 'A secretary' bidden by the dying Antony 'to bring him' to Cleopatra (*Plut.* p. 221).

D.P. *Ant. Cl.* ('Diomed,' except in st. dir. of iv, 14.) iv, 14] tells Ant. that Cl. is not dead. iv, 15] brings Cl. news of Ant.

Dion. D.P. *Wint. T.* A Sicilian lord. (ii, 1) is sent with Cleomenes by Leontes to consult the oracle of Apollo. (ii, 3) they return. iii, 1] D. speaks of the solemnity of the sacrifice to the god; trusts the result will be favourable to Hermione. iii, 2] presents, with C., the 'sealed-up oracle'; urges Leontes to marry again. See CLEOMENES.

Dion, tyrant of Syraouse, is the subject of one of Plutarch's *Lives*.

Dionyza. D.P. *Per.* Wife to Cleon. i, 4] laments, with her husband, the famine prevailing at Tarsus. iii, 3] accepts the charge of the infant Marina. (iv, Gow.) resolves, out of envy, to murder the child. iv, 1] instructs Leonine to do the deed; urges Marina, for her health's sake, to 'walk with Leonine.' iv, 4] believing Marina and her would-be murderer to be both dead, combats Cleon's fears of discovery; he compares her to a harpy 'with angel's face' and 'eagle's talons.' (iv, Gow.) composes a flattering epitaph for Marina. (v, 3) is burnt, with Cleon, in their palace by the enraged citizens.

'Dionysia' in 'The Actors Names,' F3. Variously spelt 'Dyoniza,' 'Dioniza,' 'Dionisia,' 'Dionisa,' Qq. The accepted form is due to Malone.

'Dionisiades' in *The Patterne of Painefull Adventures*

Dis. Name sometimes given to Pluto, and hence to the underworld ('atri janua Ditis,' Virg. *Aen.* vi, 127; see PLUTO); 'Dusky D.' (*Temp.* iv, 1); 'D.'s waggon' (*Wint. T.* iv, 3; *cf.* Ovid, *Metam.* v, 385 ff.; 'Dysses,' 'Disses,' Ff).

Disdain, Lady. Nonce-name applied to Beatrice by Benedick. 'Dear Lady D.' (*M. Ado*, i, 1).

Dives. The rich man in the parable of D. and Lazarus (Luke xvi, 19–31). 'D. that lived in purple' (*1 Hen. IV*, iii, 3). Alluded to, 2 *Hen. IV*, i, 2: 'let him be damned like the glutton! May his tongue be hotter!' (Luke xvi, 24).

Dizy. A debtor; *M. for M.* iv, 3. ('Dizie,' F1.)

'Dicey,' Steevens, conj.

Dobbin. (Variation of 'Robin,' dim. of 'Robert.') Name of a horse, *M. V.* ii, 2.

Doctor, English. D.P. *Macb.* iv, 3] announces that the King is about to touch for 'the evil.'

It is generally agreed that this irrelevant incident was introduced in compliment to James I, who prided himself on possessing Edward the Confessor's healing power. To this a reference in *Hol.* (i, 195) lay at hand: 'He [Edward] used to helpe those that were vexed with ... the king's evill, and left that virtue as it were a portion of inheritance unto his successors.'

Doctor of Physic. D.P. *Macb.* 'A Scotch Doctor' (Rowe). v, 1] witnesses the Queen's somnambulism and suspects her secret; 'Go to,' he whispers, 'you have known what you should not.' v, 3] tells Macbeth that his wife's malady is mental and must be selfcured; longs to be clear away from Dunsinane.

Dogberry. D.P. *M. Ado.* 'A constable.' iii, 3] 'charges' the watch, and warns them that there will be 'a great coil' at Leonato's house that night. iii, 5] after much circumlocution inadvertently allows Verges to inform Leonato that the watch had taken a couple of 'arrant knaves'; prepares 'to examination' the culprits. iv, 2] assists at the examination of Borachio and Conrade; is scoffed at by the latter, and laments that the Sexton is not present to 'write him down an ass.' v, 1] presents Bor. and Con. bound; struggles to formulate a charge against them to Don Pedro; after B.'s confession, informs Leonato that C. has further committed an offence, 'which indeed is not under black and white'; having been rewarded by L., departs, with a profusion of grotesque valedictions.

'Dogberry' is the berry of the wild cornel, the wood of which is used for skewers. In iv, 2, QFf have 'Keeper' and 'Andrews' respectively, as pfxs. to two of D.'s speeches. The former seems to be a mistake for 'Kemp,' *i.e.* William Kemp, the comedian who played the part, 'Andrew,' or 'Merry Andrew,' being a nickname for the same actor.

There is a tradition, mtd. by Aubrey, that Sh. met the prototype of D. at Grendon Underwood, near Buckingham.

Dog-days. The hottest days of the year; vaguely associated with the heliacal rising of the greater or lesser dog-star (Sirius or Procyon). 'Twenty of the dog-days now reign in 's nose' (*Hen. VIII*, v, 4, l. 43).

Dolabella, P. Cornelius. Son of the notorious consul of the same name. 'He sent her [Cleopatra] word secretly ... that Caesar determined to take his journey through Syria, and that within three days he would send her away before with her children' (*Plut.* p. 226).

D.P. *Ant. Cl.* iii, 12] derides Antony's choice of 'so poor a pinion of his wing' (Euphronius) as messenger. v, 1] sent on a message. v, 2] tells Cl. that Octavius intends to lead her in triumph; later, adds that she has but three more days in Egypt.

In v, 1, several speeches are allotted to D. in Ff which are now given to Agrippa (D. having left the stage). Spelt 'Dollabella' several times in Ff.

Doll. Abbreviation of 'Dorothy.' Applied only to D. Tearsheet (*q.v.*), except once (*Hen. V*, v, 1), where Pistol speaks of Mistress Quickly ('Nell,' ii, 1) as 'my Doll,' perhaps as a term of endearment. This reading, common to Qq and Ff, was changed by Capell to 'Nell.'

The matter has been discussed at length by B. Nicholson, *N.S.S.Tr.*, 1880–2, pp. 209–11.

Dolphin (1). 'D. my boy, boy, sessa!' (*Lear*, iii, 4, F1); supposed by Steevens and others to be a fragment of an old ballad. Farmer cites: 'Od's my life! I am not allied to the sculler yet; he shall be Dauphin my boy' (*Bartholomew Fair*, v, 3).

Dolphin (2). See DAUPHIN.

Dolphin, Sir Guichard. 'Great Master of France,' slain at Agincourt, *Hen. V*, iv, 8 (following *Hol.* iii, 555, 'Sir Guischard D.').

It has been conjectured that Sh., unhistorically, brought the Dauphin to the field of Agincourt by confusion with Sir G. D. See A. Daniel, *Parallel Texts of Hen. V* (New Sh. Society), p. xiii.

'Gwigzard, Dolphin,' Qq.

Dolphin-chamber. Name of a room in an inn; *2 Hen. IV*, ii, 1.

Domitius. See AHENOBARBUS.

Donalbain, or **Donald Bane.** Son of Duncan, King of Scots. Acc. *Hol.* ii, 171, he fled to Cumberland, and thence to Ireland, for fear of Macbeth: became King 1093.

D.P. *Macb.* i, 2, 4, 6] *p.m.* (ii, 2) 'lies i' the second chamber' on the night of Duncan's murder. ii, 3] learns that the King is dead; fears for his life, and, on his brother Malcolm's proposing flight to England, determines to seek Ireland, so that 'our separated fortune shall keep us both the safer.' (ii, 4) his flight arouses suspicion, (iii, 6) and is commented on. (v, 2) reported 'not with his brother.'

Doncaster. Bolingbroke there made oath that he did but claim his rightful inheritance (*Hol.* iii, 498; cf. *Rich. II*, ii, 3). 'You swore to us, And you did swear that oath at D.' (*1 Hen. IV*, v, 1; rep.). ('Dancaster' also, Qq.)

Doomsday. The Day of Judgment. 'I'll prove her fair, or talk till D.' (*L.L.L.* iv, 3); 'If she lives till D., she'll burn a week longer than the whole world' (*Com. Err.* iii, 2); 'the moon was sick almost to D. with eclipse' (*Haml.* i, 1); '*Ros.* The world's grown honest. *Ham.* Then is D. near' (*ib.* ii, 2); 'the houses that he [gravemaker] makes last till D.' (*ib.* v, 1); 'Men ... cry out and run An it were D.' (*Jul. C.* iii, 1); 'I'll give thee leave to play till D.' (*Ant. Cl.* v, 2).

In the following passages D. means the day of death, and is scarcely a proper name: 'D. is near: die all, die merrily' (*1 Hen. IV*, iv, 3); 'All Souls' Day is my body's D.' (*Rich. III*, v, 1); 'What less than D. is the Prince's doom?' (*Rom. J.* iii, 3); 'their stolen marriage-day was Tybalt's D.' (*ib.* v, 3).

Doorkeeper of Council-chamber. D.P. *Hen. VIII.* ('Keeper,' Ff.) v, 2] by order, refuses admittance to Cranmer. v, 3] admits C.

[**Dorastus.**] See FLORIZEL.

Dorcas. D.P. *Wint. T.* 'A shepherdess' (Ff). iv, 3] gives flowers to Perdita; joins in rustic raillery and shows jealousy of Mopsa; takes part in a song.

Doreus. A Greek taken prisoner before Troy; *Tr. Cr.* v, 5.

Mtd. as a Gk. king, Caxton, *Recuyell.*

Doricles. Name assumed by Florizel; *Wint. T.* iv, 3.

A similar name occurs in Virg. *Aen.* v, 620, 'Fit Beroe, Tmarii conjunx longaeva Dorycli.'

Dorothy (1). 'Doll [Tearsheet],' *2 Hen. VI*, ii, 4 (2); twice addressed as 'Mistress Dorothy' by Pistol.

Dorothy (2). A serving-woman of Imogen's; *Cymb.* ii, 3.

Dorset, Marquess of (1). (*Rich. III*); see GREY, THOMAS.

Dorset, Marquess of (2). (*Hen. VIII*); see GREY, HENRY.

Dorsetshire. Richmond reported off the coast of D., *Rich. III*, iv, 4. The attempt to induce Richmond to land near Poole is related at some length, *Hol.* iii, 744–5.

Dotchet. For 'Datchet'; *M.W.W.* iii, 3, F1, 2, 3.

Double. An archer eulogized by Shallow, who laments his death; *2 Hen. IV*, iii, 2 (2).

With regard to the merits of 'Old Double's' performance see *Sh. Eng.* ii, 383.

Douglas, Archibald. 4th E. of Douglas (*c.*1369–1424); taken prisoner at Milfield by the E. of March and Hotspur; fought on Hotspur's side at Shrewsbury, where he was again made prisoner; he was ransomed five years later. Slain at Verneuil.

Acc. *Hol.* iii, 520, 'Archembald earle Douglas' was taken prisoner at Homildon (*q.v.*) and in the fight lost an eye; the Percies offered him 'Berwike and a part of Northumberland' if he would aid them (*ib.* 522); at Shrewsbury he directed his attack against Henry IV in person, and slew four knights accoutred like the King; he was captured, and released without ransom (*ib.* 522–3).

Characterized by Falstaff (*1 Hen. IV*, ii, 4) as 'that sprightly Scot of Scots ... that runs a' horseback up a hill perpendicular.' See Scot.

D.P. *1 Hen. IV.* (i, 1) 'discomfited' at Homildon. (i, 3) suggested to Hotspur as an ally. (ii, 3, 4) mtd. (iii, 2) lauded by the King as pre-eminent among soldiers. iv, 1] gives stout-hearted counsel before the Battle of Shrewsbury. iv, 3] advises an attack at night. (iv, 4; v, 1) mtd. v, 2] conveys a message of defiance to the King. v, 3] slays Blunt, believing him to be the King. v, 4] fights with the King, and has him at an advantage, but Prince Hal rescues his father; Douglas fights with Falstaff, who feigns death. (v, 5) for his valour, D. is set free, ransomless.

'The King before the Douglas' rage Stoop'd his anointed head as low as death' (*2 Hen. IV*, Ind.; cf. *Hol.* iii, 523); 'both the Blunts killed by the hand of Douglas,' 'the noble D.,' 'D. is living,' 'the bloody D., whose well-labouring sword Had three times slain the appearance of the King' (*ib.* i, 1).

Douglas, George. See Angus, 1st Earl of.

Dover. Port in Kent; the castle of Dover was held by Hubert de Burgh against the French (1216). It is announced to John that 'All Kent hath yielded; nothing there holds out But D. Castle' (*John*, v, 1); the French ambassadors ordered to be 'safely brought to D.' (*1 Hen. VI*, v, 1); Lear's friends at D., *Lear*, iii, 1; the King borne in a litter thither, *ib.* iii, 6; the fact admitted by Gloucester, *ib.* iii, 7 (4); Gloucester makes his way thither; cliff at D., *ib.* iv, 1 (3).

The scene of *Lear*, iv, 3, 4, 6, 7, and v, 1, 2, 3, is laid near D.; also of *2 Hen. VI*, iv, 1.

Acc. Halliwell, the scene of *John*, iv, 1, 2, is also laid at Dover.

Dowland, John (*c.* 1563–*c.* 1626). Lutenist. 'Dowland to thee is dear, whose heavenly touch Upon the lute doth ravish human sense' (*P.P.* 8).

Downs, The. See Goodwins.

Dowsabel. (*Douce et belle.*) Name applied by Dromio of Syracuse, *Com. Err.* iv, 1, to Adriana's fat kitchen-wench, who, mistaking him for his brother, declares he is affianced to her; Dro. S. compares her to a terrestrial globe, *ib.* iii, 2.

The cook in the *Menaechmi* of Plautus is named Cylindrus.

Dragon's Tail, The. The descending node of the moon's orbit. 'My father compounded with my mother under the Dragon's tail, and my nativity was under Ursa Major' (*Lear*, i, 2).

When this node, of varying position, 'joined with the evil planets, their malice, or the evil intended thereby, was doubled, and trebled, or extremely augmented' (*Sh. Eng.* i, 459).

Dread. Personified. 'Sable Night, mother of D. and Fear' (*Lucr.* 117).

Droeshout, Martin. Engraver of the portrait of Sh. prefixed to the First Folio (1623) – the words 'Martin Droeshout sculpsit London' appearing in the margin. D. was only about fifteen years old when Sh. died, and was by no means practised in his art (in which he never attained note) in 1623. *Cf.* Lee, *Life of Sh.* pp. 528 ff.

Dromio of Ephesus. D.P. *Com. Err.* Twin brother to D. of Syracuse, and servant to Antipholus of Eph. i, 2] meeting Ant. S., mistakes him for his master, and urges him to return home for dinner; is accordingly cuffed. ii, 1] tells his mistress that his master must be mad, since he demands certain money from him, and denies having a wife or house; Dro. E. is again sent to fetch his master. iii, 1] in attendance on Ant. E.; assists his master in trying to gain admission to his house. iv, 1] is sent by Ant. E. to buy 'a rope's end.' iv, 4] returns with the rope, but is beaten by his master, who mistakes him for Dromio S., whom he has ordered to fetch a sum of money; is certified to be mad, as well as his master, and they are carried bound to a 'dark room.' v, 1] is liberated by his master's efforts; is confronted by Dromio S. and, the 'error' being cleared up, exclaims 'Methinks, you are my glass and not my brother!'

There is no corresponding character in the *Menaechmi* of Plautus.

Dromio of Syracuse. D.P. *Com. Err.* Twin brother to D. of Ephesus, and servant to Antipholus of Syr. i, 2] is sent to the Centaur with his master's money. ii, 2] is amazed at being beaten by his master for faults which he cannot comprehend; gives proof of his quality as a jester; accompanies his master to Adriana's house, and is ordered to 'keep the gate.' iii, 1] in his capacity as porter flouts, from within, his brother and Ant. E., who wish to force the door. iii, 2] relates how he was claimed in marriage by Adriana's kitchen-wench. iv, 1] tells Ant. E., whom he takes for his master, that a ship awaits him; is sent to fetch a purse from Adriana. iv, 2] tells Adriana that 'his master' is arrested, and is given the purse. iv, 3] gives Ant. S. the purse, and reminds him that the ship 'puts forth tonight'; his master thinks him 'distract'; urges Ant. S. not to give his chain to the courtezan who claims it, since she may be a fiend. iv, 4] takes courage, and suggests staying longer in Ephesus, since the folk give them gold for nothing. v, 1] seeks refuge in a priory with his master; is brought before the Duke; is confronted with his brother, and learns the solution of the mystery.

The equivalent character in the *Menaechmi* of Plautus is Messenio; but he has no brother.

'Dromio Siracusia,' st. dir. ii, 2, F1, and st. dir. iii, 2, Ff.

Dropheir. Prisoner; *M. for M.* iv, 3.

Drum, Tom. '*Lafeu* [to Parolles]. Good T. D., lend me a handkercher' (*All's Well*, v, 3).

The phrase 'Tom [or 'Jack'] D.'s entertainment' meant 'a good drubbing.' In Marston's *Jack D.'s Entertainment* (1601) J.D. is a servant who is continually baffled in his knavish tricks.

Du Champ, Richard. A random name attributed by Imogen to the dead man she supposes to be Posthumus; *Cymb.* iv, 2, l. 377.

Duff. For 'Macduff'; *Macb.* ii, 3. Changed to 'Macduff' by Pope and some succeeding edrs.

Duke of Milan. D.P. *T.G.V.* 'Duke, father to Silvia' (F1). ii, 4] tells Valentine that Proteus has arrived at Court, and questions him about his friend. (ii, 6) has destined Silvia for Thurio. iii, 1] learns from Proteus that Valentine is about to elope with Silvia, and is informed of the means (a rope-ladder) by which she is to escape; intercepts Val. as he hurries by, and tells him that Silvia has offended him by her disobedience; he further declares that he contemplates marrying again, and asks Val.'s advice as to the best mode of wooing the coy lady of his affections; after artful questioning he discovers on Val.'s person a letter for Silvia and the rope ladder he is going to use; orders Val. instantly to leave Milan on pain of death. iii, 2] tells Proteus that Silvia is pining for Val., and bids P. slander his friend and urge her to marry Thurio. v, 2] bids P. and Thurio follow him in pursuit of Silvia. v, 4] on finding that Th. is ready tamely to resign S., declares that Valentine deserves her, and pardons the outlaws with whom Val. is in company.

Duke Senior. D.P. *A.Y.L.* 'Duke of Burgundy' (Rowe). (i, 1) banished by his younger brother, who has usurped the dukedom, he has betaken himself to the Forest of Arden, with a few 'loving lords' and 'a many merry men, where they fleet the time carelessly, as they did in the golden world.' ii, 1] expatiates to his comrades on the sweetness of their present life. ii, 7] rebukes Jaques, and receives Orlando courteously, despite his unmannerly intrusion. v, 4] though not recognizing 'Ganymede' as Rosalind, observes in him 'some lively touches of my daughter's favour'; promises 'G.' to bestow his daughter upon Orlando if she can be produced, and, when R. appears in her proper garb, ratifies his consent to the marriage.

By some error, which has caused much discussion among commentators, the Duke (always 'Duke Senior' in st. dirs. and pfxs.) is spoken of as 'Frederick' in i, 2, whereas in v, 4, that name is given to the usurper. The equivalent character in Lodge's *Rosalynde* is Gerismond, King of France. See As You Like It.

Dull. D.P. *L.L.L.* A constable. i, 1] brings Costard, in custody, before the King. i, 2] hands C. over to Armado's keeping. iv, 2] resists the attempts of Holofernes and Nathaniel to abash him. v, 1] listens in silence to the discussion concerning the pageant of 'The Nine Worthies,' but finally offers to dance, or tabor, on the occasion.

Dull's forename is Anthony, as appears from Armado's letter (i, 1). 'Is not Antony Dull Antony Munday, the stage-plotter, but not stage-plotter, but not stage-actor, the informer against the seminary-priests, the conceited Antonio Balladino of Jonson, who could sing his ballads to his tabor or act as constable in detecting state plots?' (F. G. Fleay, 'Sh. and Puritanism,' *Anglia* (1884), vii, 224). (But Fleay is concerned to prove that the 'Worthies' in *L.L.L.* represent the six 'Anti-Martinist' writers of the day.)

Dumain (1). D.P. *L.L.L.* 'A Lord attending upon the King in his Retirement' (Rowe). i, 1] accepts with enthusiasm the vow of asceticism proposed by the King. ii, 1] speaks of Katharine ('Rosaline,' all early edns.) as a 'gallant lady.' iv, 3] thinking himself alone, reads a sonnet addressed to his mistress; is rebuked by Longaville. v, 2] (sends gloves and verses to K.); as 'a Muscovite,' addresses in error the masked Maria; derides 'the Worthies'; promises to serve K. 'true and faithfully' until their marriage a year hence.

The name of the Duc de Maine was familiar in England in connection with Henry of Navarre. The name rimes with 'pain' (iv, 3) and 'twain' (v, 2).

Dumain (2). D.P. *All's Well.* See Lords, Two.

Dumb, Master. 'Our minister' (2 *Hen. IV*, ii, 4) (the adj. was applied to ministers who read homilies instead of preaching).

Dumbleton. A mercer who refused Falstaff credit; 2 *Hen. IV*, i, 2.

Juliana de D. and John de D. are both mentioned in early Stratford records (French, p. 326).

'Dombledon,' Ff; 'Dommelton,' Q. The form given above is due to Malone. Other conjectures are 'Double-done' and 'Double-down.'

Duncan I. King of Scots (*ob.* 1040). A summary of Holinshed's account of Duncan, which was derived from Hector Boece's story, is subjoined. It must be premised, however, that the scanty records of more authentic history give but slight confirmation of Boece's picturesque narrative.

Duncan was the son of Crinan, Abbot of Dunkeld, and his wife Beatrice, daughter of Malcolm II. He was 'soft and gentle of nature,' and remiss in punishing offenders; hence, taking advantage of his weakness, many 'misruled persons' began to raise seditions. In particular, one Macdowald called D. 'a faint-hearted milksop,' and summoning to his aid men from the Western Isles, as well as 'kernes and gallowglasses' from Ireland, assembled a formidable force and defeated a royal army sent against him. Duncan, realizing his own 'small skill in warlike affairs,' accordingly sought help from his cousin Macbeth and Banquo, Lord of Lochquhaber, who wholly defeated the rebels. Soon after, Sweno, King of Norway, invaded Scotland, but was overthrown by the King with the aid of the same powerful auxiliaries, as was a Danish force sent by Canute to avenge Sweno's defeat. Some time after, D. made his elder son, Malcolm, Prince of Cumberland, 'as it were thereby to appoint him his successor.' This seemed to deprive Macb. of all hope of the crown (of which he had a prospect, since 'by the old laws of the realm ... if he that should succeed were not of able age to take the charge upon himself, he that was next of blood to him should be admitted'). Macbeth accordingly, with Banquo's connivance, murdered the King at Inverness (or Botgosuane) in the sixth year of his reign. Duncan was buried at Elgin, and five or six years later the body was removed to Colmkill. Historically, Duncan seems to have been a young man when he was murdered, but Lady Macbeth (*Macb.* v, 1) refers to him as aged.

D.P. *Macb.* i, 2] hears of Macdonwald's defeat by 'our captains' Macbeth and Banquo, and also of Sweno's surrender to the former, on whom he confers the thaneship of the traitor Cawdor. i, 4] thanks Macb. and Banq. for their services; states his intention of making his son Malcolm Prince of Cumberland; bids the thanes meet him at Inverness. (i, 5) Lady Macbeth learns that he comes 'tonight.' i, 6] reaches Macbeth's castle, and approves its 'pleasant seat'; is welcomed by 'our honour'd hostess.' (i, 7) his meekness commented on by Macbeth; his murder planned. (ii, 1) is murdered in his sleep by Macbeth. (ii, 2) Lady Macbeth declares that he resembled her father as he slept. (ii, 3) the murder discovered. (ii, 4) madness of his horses; his burial. (iii, 1) 'the gracious D.' (iii, 2) 'after life's fitful fever he sleeps well.' (iii, 4) mtd. (iii, 6) his sons.

[Dunne-marle Castle.] See Macduff, Lady.

Dunois, John, Count of. Illegitimate son of Louis, Duke of Orleans, by Marie D'Engheim, wife of his chamberlain, Albert, Lord of Cawny. Legitimated in 1439. He was an eminent soldier, and is called by Monstrelet 'one of the most eloquent men in all France.' He directed the sallies made by Joan of Arc from Orleans, where he was in sole command.

D.P. *1 Hen. VI*. 'The Bastard of Orleans.' i, 2] announces that he has brought with him 'a holy maid,' who will deliver France; later, returns with Joan of Arc. ii, 1] escapes from Orleans when it is surprised by Talbot. iii, 2] (at Rouen) observes Joan's signal torch. iii, 3] is present when Burgundy joins Charles. iv, 7] proposes to hack the bodies of the two Talbots in pieces. v, 4] *p.m.*

It has been suggested that the 'choice' made by Philip Faulconbridge (*q.v.*), as described in *John*, was founded on that made by the young Dunois, who declared that he would rather be regarded as the son of the Duke of Orleans than of that 'coward Cauni' (Hall); see B.-S. *Sh. Hol.* pp. 48–9.

Dunsinane. Hill about 7 N.E. of Perth; now Dunsinnan. Acc. *Hol.* ii, 174–5, Macbeth ordered the thanes to superintend, in turn, the building of a castle on its summit; Macduff refused, and incurred Macbeth's anger. Macb. took refuge in the castle when attacked by Siward and Malcolm. Macb. is unconquerable until Birnam Wood come to D., *Macb.* iv, 1; 'Great D. he strongly fortifies' (*ib.* v, 2). Mtd., v, 3, 4, 5, 7.

Dunsmore. The E. of Oxford with his forces at D.; *3 Hen. VI*, v, 1. D. Heath is 4 m. S.W. of Rugby.

Dunstable. Town in Bedfordshire on the highway from London to Chester. In D. Priory Cranmer, with four bishops 'and divers other learned men,' held the court which pronounced the decree of divorce between Henry VIII and Katharine of Arragon (*Hol.* iii, 929). See Ampthill Castle.

'D., six miles off From Ampthill, where the Princess lay' (*Hen. VIII*, iv, 1).

Dutch. (*a*) *Adj.*, pertaining to Germany, or Holland. 'Half stewed in grease, like a D. dish' (*M.W.W.* iii, 5). See Fleming.

(*b*) *Used as a subst.*: 'If there be here German, or Dane, low Dutch ... let him speak to me' (*All's Well*, iv, 1).

Dutchet Mead. For 'Datchet M.'; *M.W.W.* iii, 3, F4.

Dutchman. A 'German,' or, specifically, an inhabitant of the Netherlands.

'You will hang like an icicle on a D.'s beard' (*T. Nt.* iii, 2; perhaps with reference to an account of the Arctic voyage of William Barentz, entered for publication, in English, in 1598); 'A Dutchman today, a Frenchman tomorrow' (*M. Ado*, iii, 2; 'a German' occurs in the same speech); Maria (*L.L.L.* v, 2, l. 247), punning on the name of Longavile, exclaims, 'Veal, quoth the D. Is not "veal" a calf?' (where it is doubtful whether 'veal' stands for the German *viel*, or is meant for a foreign perversion of 'well'); 'Lustig, as the D. says' (*All's Well*, ii, 3).

Dutchman, A. D.P. *Cymb.* (in Ff only). i, 5] *p.m.*

E

E., Cap. Pfx., for 'Second Lord.' *All's Well*, iii, 6; iv, 3, Ff.

E., Lord. Pfx., for 'Second Lord.' *All's Well*, i, 2; iv, 1, Ff.

The initials 'E' and 'G' (*q.v.*) are probably those of actors. Among the 'Names of the Principall Actors,' prefixed to the First Folio, 'Goughe,' 'Gilburne,' and 'Ecclestone' occur. For an attempt to unravel the confusion attached to these initials see Camb. edn. iii, 260.

Earth, The. The terrestrial globe, as a whole. 'The sun gazing upon the E.' (*Com. Err.* i, 1); 'flying between the cold moon and the E.' (*M.N.D.* ii, 1); '*Ceres*. My bosky acres ... Rich scarf to my proud earth' (*Temp.* iv, 1, l. 82); 'I'll put a girdle round about the E.' (*M.N.D.* ii, 1); 'This whole E. may be bored, and that the moon May through the centre creep' (*ib.* iii, 2).

With especial reference to its central position in accordance with the Ptolemaic system: 'True as earth to the centre' (*Tr. Cr.* iii, 2).

In the following passages it is referred to as 'the centre': 'The Centre is not big enough to bear A schoolboy's top' (*Wint. T.* ii, 1); 'the heavens themselves, the planets, and this centre' (*Tr. Cr.* i, 3); cf. *Haml.* ii, 2, l.159.

The earth personified: 'the old beldam E.' (*1 Hen. IV*, iii, 1); 'our grandam E.' (*ib. ib.*); 'the E.'s a thief' (*Timon*, iv, 3); 'the E. that's nature's mother' (*Rom. J.* ii, 3).

Although the Copernican system was widely known, and accepted by scientific men, in Sh.'s lifetime, it is not recognized in his writings.

East, The. The eastern region (*a*) of the sky, (*b*) of the world. (References to the cardinal point, and the adjectival use of the word, are omitted.)

(*a*) The morn 'dapples the drowsy E. with spots of grey' (*M. Ado*, v, 3); 'shine comforts from the E.' (*M.N.D.* iii, 2); 'the first opening of the gorgeous E.' (*L.L.L.* iv, 3); 'Behold another day break in the E.' (*John*, v, 4); 'see us rising in our throne, the E.' (*Rich. II*, iii, 2); 'the fiery portal of the E.' (*ib.* iii, 3); 'begins his golden progress in the E.' (*1 Hen. IV*, iii, 1); 'darkness breaks within the E.' (*Rich. III* v, 3); '[the sun] should have braved the E. an hour ago' (*ib. ib.*); 'the golden window of the E.' (*Rom. J.* i, 1); 'in the farthest E.' (*ib. ib.*); 'it is the E. and Juliet is the sun' (*ib.* ii, 2); 'the severing clouds in yonder E.' (*ib.* iii, 5); 'grey cheeks of the E.' (*Son.* cxxxii).

(*b*) 'And the rich E. to boot' (*Macb.* iv, 3); 'all the E. shall call her mistress' (*Ant. Cl.* i, 5); 'in the E. my pleasure lies' (*ib.* ii, 3); 'the beds i' th' E. are soft' (*ib.* ii, 6); 'I may wander from E. to occident' (*Cymb.* iv, 2); 'to lash the rascals ... even from the E. to the West' (*Oth.* iv, 2).

Eastcheap. Street in London, E. of Gracechurch Street; in it was situated the famous Boar's Head Tavern (*q.v.*); it is mentioned by Lydgate as a street of cooks' shops, and Stow states that in his days it was 'a flesh-market of butchers' as well as a centre for those who 'sold victuals ready dressed of all sorts.'

Mtd., *1 Hen. IV*, i, 2; 'When I am King ... I shall command all the good lads in E.' (*ib.* ii, 4); mtd., *ib. ib.*; 'a poor widow of E.' (*2 Hen. IV*, ii, 1); 'where sups he [Falstaff]? ... At the old place, my lord, in E.' (*ib.* ii, 2).

Easter, Festival of. 'Didst thou not fall out with a tailor for wearing his new doublet before E.?' (*Rom. J.* iii, 1).

The Battle of Barnet (*q.v.*) was fought on Easter Day.

Ebrew. For 'Hebrew' (*adj.*). 'A Jew else, an Ebrew Jew' (*1 Hen. IV*, ii, 4).

Ecclestone, William. Mtd. as a 'principal actor' in F1.

Echo (1). A nymph transformed by Juno into an echo (Ovid, *Metam.* iii, 393 ff.). Distinctly personified only once in *Sh.*: 'Else would I tear the cave where E. lies, And make her airy tongue more hoarse than mine' (*Rom. J.* ii, 2). 'Babling' is Golding's transln. of 'vocalis [nymphe],' *Metam.* iii, 357; cf. *T. And.* ii, 3, l.17.

Echo (2). Name of a hound; *Tam. Sh.* Ind. 1.

Eden. Garden of E. '[England] this other E., demi-paradise' (*Rich. II*, ii, 1).

Eden, A. See IDEN.

Edgar. D.P. *Lear*. Son to Gloucester. (i, 1) is about a year older than Edmund. i, 2] (Edm. tells Gl. that Edg. has designs on his father's life, and produces a forged letter); Edm. advises Edg. to flee from his father's wrath. ii, 1] Edg. is forced into a pretended fight with Edm. and takes to flight. ii, 3] (*sol.*) resolves to disguise himself as a 'Bedlam beggar.' iii, 4] as 'poor Tom,' joins Lear on the heath, and takes shelter with him from the storm. iii, 6] his tears 'mar his counterfeiting.' (iii, 7) Gl. realizes that 'Edg. was abused.' iv, 1] wandering alone, meets the blinded Gl. and consents to lead him to Dover cliff. iv, 6] assures Gl. that he has reached the verge of the cliff; assuming another character, describes the supposed fall of Gl. from the summit unhurt; witnesses the meeting between Gl. and Lear; in the guise of a peasant, kills Goneril's steward, and takes from the body a letter from his mistress to Edmund. (iv, 7) reported to be in Germany. v, 1] gives the letter to Albany. v, 2] awaits, with Gl., the issue of the battle. v, 3] takes up Edmund's challenge, and mortally wounds him in single combat; discloses himself; is present at the death of Lear.

Edgar is faintly foreshadowed in Sir Philip Sidney's *Arcadia* (bk. ii) as 'the kind sonne' of the 'Paphlagonian unkinde king,' but, as seen in *Lear*, is wholly Sh.'s creation. 'To play this character a man must be "every inch an actor." He changes his part at least six different times. At first he is Edgar, then poor Tom; then ... he falls somewhat out of his assumed part; after this he describes the immeasurable depth of the pretended cliff, ... then he is the dweller on the sea-shore; then ... he is again another beggar, and before the steward he becomes changed into a peasant; in the lists with Edmund he is an unknown champion, and finally he is himself again.' (Gervinus, *Sh. Commentaries* (1875), p. 635.) Regan (ii, 1) speaks of Edg. as Lear's 'godson' – an anachronism.

Edmund. D.P. *Lear*. Natural son of Gloucester. i, 1] is presented to Kent by his father. i, 2] (*sol.*) vows to oust his legitimate brother, Edgar; with apparent unwillingness shows his father a (forged) letter from Edg., hinting at Gloucester's death; pretends to excuse Edg., as having written the letter to test his brother; (*sol.*) derides the claims of astrology; tells Edg. that Gl. is offended with him, and advises him to go armed; (*sol.*) scoffs at Edgar's 'foolish honesty.' ii, 1] hears of discussions between Cornwall and Albany; advises Edg. to escape, since he is suspected on all sides; after a mock fight, wounds himself, and tells Gl. that he has been attacked by Edg. (who has fled), and that Edg. tried to persuade him to kill his father; Gl. exclaims, 'Loyal and natural boy, I'll work the means To make thee capable'; Edm. is commended by Regan and Cornwall. ii, 2] present. iii, 3] Gl. confides to him that he is loyal to Lear, and will at any risk support him; Edm. (*sol.*) vows to betray his father. iii, 5] gives Corn. a secret letter received by Gl.; Corn. declares that 'True or false, it hath made thee Earl of Gl.' iii, 7] is sent from Gl.'s castle with Goneril, since the revenge to be taken on Gl. is 'not fit for your beholding.' iv, 2] on reaching Goneril's castle is dismissed by her with a kiss, which 'if it durst speak, would stretch thy spirits up into the air.' (iv, 5) Regan vainly tries to obtain from its bearer an important letter from Gon. to Edm. (iv, 6) the letter is read by Edg., who finds in it 'a plot upon her virtuous husband's life; and the exchange, my brother!' v, 1] assures Regan that he is but a friend to Gon.; later, admits (*sol.*) that 'to both these sisters have I sworn my love'; determines that Lear and Cordelia 'shall never see' the pardon Albany intends for them. v, 3] commits Lear and Cor. to prison, and sends after them an officer with a note, the deadly purport of which he hints; Albany arrests Edm. 'on capital treason'; Edm. claims judicial combat; fights with Edg., and is mortally wounded; exclaims, as he recognizes his brother, 'the wheel is come full circle; I am here'; before his death learns that Regan and Goneril are dead, by murder and suicide; in his last moments means to do 'some good ... despite of mine own nature,' and sends 'a token of reprieve' for Cordelia to the prison – too late.

In the story of 'the Paphlagonian unkinde king' (Sidney's *Arcadia*, bk. ii, pp. 133–8, ed. 1598), from which the Gloucester underplot is believed to be derived, the 'unlawfull and unnaturall sonne' is unnamed.

Edmund. As a forename. 'E. Beaufort,' 'E. Mortimer' 'E. Bohun' (*qq.v.*).

Edmund of Langley. See LANGLEY, EDMUND DE.

Edward. As a forename. 'Sir E. Courteney,' 'E., D. of Bar' (*qq.v.*). See also NED and YEDWARD.

Edward (*ob.* 1066). King of the English; called 'The Confessor'; crowned on Easter Day, 1043. The 'Feast of St Edward' is Oct. 13; acc. *Hol.* iii, 541, Henry V 'was taken with his last sickenesse' while praying at St Edward's shrine (at Westminster).

'Saint Edward the son of Ethelred ... received Malcolme [Canmore] by way of most friendly entertainment' (*Hol.* ii, 171; *Macb.* iii, 6, 'most pious E.'); Malcolm 'purchased such favor at King E.'s hands' that Siward was appointed to help him (*Hol.* ii, 175; *Macb.* iii, 6); his curing of 'the king's evil'

(*Hol.* i, 195; *Macb.* iv, 3); 'Edward Confessor's crown' used at the coronation of Anne Boleyn, *Hen. VIII*, iv, 1 ('the archbishop set the crowne of Saint Edward on hir head,' *Hol.* iii, 933).

'As has been thought, he [Edward] was inspired with the gift of prophesie, and also to have had the gift of healing infirmities and diseases. He vsed to helpe those that were vexed with the disease, commonlie called the kings euill, and left that vertue as it were a portion of inheritance vnto his successors the kings of this realme.' (*Hol.* i, 195.)

Edward III (1312–77). King of England; eldest son of Edward II; married Philippa of Hainault; paid homage to Philip VI for his French fiefs; planned the strategy which led to the victory of Crécy by the English under the command of the Black Prince (*q.v.*).

'E.'s seven sons ... were as seven vials of his sacred blood' (the Duchess of Gloucester discoursing on their fate and fortunes; *Rich. II*, i, 2 (2)); his family referred to, *ib.* ii, 1 (4); a portentous thrice-repeated flow of the Thames, 'no ebb between,' is declared by Clarence to have occurred 'before That our great grandsire, E., sick'd and died' (*2 Hen. IV*, iv, 4); Chichele refers to 'certain dukedoms' to which Henry V was entitled through E., 'his great-grandfather' (*Hen. V*, i, 1; cf. *Hol.* iii, 545), and bids the King 'go ... to your great grandsire's tomb, from whom you claim; invoke his warlike spirit' (*ib.* i, 2); mtd., *ib. ib.*; at Crécy 'on mountain standing, Up in the air, crown'd with the golden sun,' E. watched the Black Prince's victory, *ib.* ii, 4 ('aloft on a windmill hill,' *Hol.* iii, 372); prowess of the English in his reign, *1 Hen. VI*, i, 2; mtd., *ib.* ii, 4; his descendants, *ib.* ii, 5 (2), and *2 Hen. VI*, ii, 2 (3).

Edward IV (1442–83). King of England; son of Richard, D. of York (1, 2, *3 Hen. VI*). During his father's lifetime known as E. of March. He was attainted as a Yorkist (1459), but, returning with the Earls of Salisbury and Warwick, defeated the army of Henry VI at Northampton (1460). In 1461 he won the Battle of Mortimer's Cross, and, although Warwick was beaten a fortnight later at the 2nd Battle of St Albans, Edw. very shortly afterward, taking advantage of a reaction against Q. Margaret, entered London and was acclaimed king. The defeats of Margaret at Hedgeley Moor and Hexham (1464), and the capture of King Henry (1465), seated Edw. firmly on the throne.

The new King's licentious life, however, and his marriage (at first secret) with Elizabeth Woodville (*q.v.*), imperilled his popularity and aroused the animosity of Warwick and many other nobles. Warwick crossed to France, made friends with Margaret, and in 1470 landed in England. Edw. thereupon fled to Flanders, but returning after six months utterly defeated Warwick at Barnet (Easter Day, 1471) where 'the King-maker' was slain. The war ended by Edw.'s victory over Margaret at Tewkesbury, about three weeks later. Two crimes which stained Edw.'s name were the cruel murder of the young Prince Edw., and the private execution of his brother, George, D. of Clarence, in the Tower.

More's description of Edw. (*Hol.* iii, 711) is as follows: 'He was a goodlie personage, and princelie to behold, of heart couragious, politike in counsell, in adversitie nothing abashed, in prosperitie rather joifull than proud, in peace just and mercifull, in warre sharpe and fierce, in the field bold and hardie, and natheless no further (than wisdome would) adventurous; whose warres who so well considered, he shall no lesse commend his wisdome where he voided, than his manhood where he vanquished. He was of visage lovelie, of bodie mightie, strong, and cleane made: howbeit, in his latter daies, with over liberall diet, somewhat corpulent and boorelie, and natheless not uncomelie. He was of youth greatlie given to fleshlie wantonnesse.'

D.P. *2 Hen. VI.* 'Edward Plantagenet, son to the D. of York.' v, 1] with his father before the 1st Battle of St Albans.

He was then 13 years old, but, acc. *Hol.* iii, 639, he was believed to be at the time approaching London 'with a great armie of Marchmen.'

D.P. *3 Hen. VI.* 'Edward, E. of March, afterwards King Edward IV.' i, 1] claims to have slain, or grievously wounded, the D. of Buckingham; bids his father crown himself. i, 2] with his father at Sandal Castle. ii, 1] while discussing with his brother the doubtful fate of their father, sees the prodigy of three suns in the sky (*Hol.* iii, 600); receives news of his father's death on the field; Warwick acclaims him as Duke of York, and urges him to raise a Welsh force. ii, 2] demands the crown, and reviles Q. Margaret. ii, 3] (at Towton) after a repulse (actually a preliminary skirmish at Ferrybridge) resolves to make a final effort. ii, 6] (at Towton) is victor; creates his brothers, Richard and George, Dukes of Gloucester and Clarence respectively. iii, 2] offers marriage to Lady Grey (*Hol.* iii, 726); orders Henry VI to be conveyed to the Tower. iv, 1] defends his choice of a bride to his brothers (*ib. ib.*); learns that in consequence of his affront to the Lady Bona (*q.v.*) Warwick has sworn to dethrone him. iv, 3] is seized in his tent, near Warwick, by W. and Clarence, his crown is forcibly removed, and he is led away prisoner. iv, 5] with the aid of Gloucester and Hastings escapes from Middleham Castle (*Hol.* iii, 673). iv, 7] having returned with an army from Burgundy, obtains admission to York by declaring that he demands it only as its Duke (Hall, pp. 291–2); on the representation of his friends discards the pretence, and once more declares himself King (*Hol.* iii, 688). v, 1] (before Coventry) is denied admission by Warwick, who is joined by Oxford, Montague, and Somerset successively (Hall, p. 295); Edward is joined by Clarence, and they march toward Barnet. v, 2] (at Barnet) brings in Warwick, wounded. v, 3] as a victor, resolves to march against Q. Margaret at Tewkesbury. v, 4] (near Tewkesbury) heads his army. v, 5] after the battle, is the first to stab Prince Edward (acc. *Hol.* iii, 688, merely thrust him roughly aside), but directs that Q. Margaret's life should be spared. v, 7] seated on his throne, bids his brothers salute his infant son, and orders Q. Margaret to be deported to France.

D.P. *Rich. III.* ii, 1] is 'led in sick'; tries to procure amity between the contending parties at Court; mourns over the too hasty death of Clarence at his 'first order,' and laments that none of his nobles had pleaded for his life ('oh infortunate brother, for whose life none would make sute,' *Hol.* iii, 703). (ii, 2) Q. Elizabeth laments her husband's death.

Edward V (1470–83). King of England; e.s. of Edward IV by his queen, Elizabeth (Woodville); succeeded to the crown 1483; brought from Wales, where he was justiciar, to London by his uncle Gloucester; sent to the Tower; deposed by an assembly of Lords and Commons on the alleged ground that his mother's marriage was invalid, and murdered in the Tower, together with his brother the D. of York, by Gloucester's orders.

The account of the smothering of the two Princes by Dighton and Forrest (*qq.v.*) at the instance of Tyrrel (*q.v.*), as given in *Hol.* iii, 735, is followed by Sh. Of their burial the chronicler relates that at first they were buried 'at the staire foot, meetlie deepe in the ground, under a great heape of stones,' but that afterward 'a priest of Sir Robert Brakenberies tooke up the bodies againe, and secretlie interred them in such place, as, by the occasion of his death, which onlie knew it, could never since come to light.' In 1674 some bones were found below the stairs leading to the White Tower chapel, and were interred in Westminster Abbey as those of the two Princes.

D.P. *Rich. III.* (ii, 2) Buckingham advises that 'the young prince be fetch'd' from Ludlow, 'with some little train.' (ii, 3) his accession discussed by citizens. (ii, 4) his arrival in London awaited by his mother. iii, 1] is welcomed by Buckingham and the Lord Mayor; demurs to lodging in the Tower, and inquires as to its history; greets his brother; he fears 'no uncles dead, ... an if they live' hopes he need not fear; proceeds to the Tower. (iii, 5) rumours of his illegitimacy spread by Richard. (iv, 1) his relatives denied access to him. (iv, 2) his murder planned, and (iv, 3) described by Tyrrel, who professes to be ignorant where they are buried. (v, 3) the ghosts of Edward V and his brother appear to Richard before Bosworth.

Edward [VI]. 'Two E. shovel-boards, that cost me two shilling and two pence apiece' (*M.W.W.* i, 1); *i.e.* shillings of the reign, used for the game alluded to.

Cf. *2 Hen. IV*, ii, 4, l. 205. The smoother the coin the better adapted it was for the game.

Edward, Earl of Warwick (1475–99). E.s. of George, D. of Clarence; brought up by his aunt, Anne, Duchess of Gloucester. (His personation by Simnel and ultimate tragic fate are here irrelevant.)

D.P. *Rich. III.* 'A young son of Clarence.' ii, 2] laments his father's death, and is loth to believe his 'good uncle Gloucester' the cause. (iii, 5) G. determines to imprison him. (iv, 2) 'the boy is foolish.' (iv, 3) 'pent up close.'

After his imprisonment by Hen. VII 'he could not discern a goose from a capon' (*Hol.* iii, 787); he was imprisoned at Sheriff Hutton Castle, Yorks (Hall, *Henry VII*, p. 422).

Edward, Prince of Wales (1330–76). E.s. of Edward III; known as the Black Prince; permitted the honour of leading the victorious English at Crécy, where he seems to have been clad in black armour.

'In war was never lion raged more fierce, In peace was never gentle lamb more mild' (*Rich. II*, ii, 1); mtd. by Abp. Chichele as Henry V's 'great uncle ... Edward the Black Prince,' who defeated the French at Crécy, 'whiles his most mighty father on a hill Stood smiling to behold his lion's whelp Forage in blood of French nobility' (*Hen. V*, i, 2); Charles VI recalls the defeat of the French 'by the hand Of that black name E., Black Prince of Wales' (*ib.* ii, 4); mtd. by Fluellen, *ib.* iv, 7; eldest son of Edward III, 'died before his father' (*2 Hen. VI*, ii, 2).

The D. of York (Edmund of Langley) reminds Bolingbroke of the time when 'brave Gaunt, thy father, and myself Rescued the Black Prince, that young Mars of men, From forth the ranks of many thousand French' (*Rich. II*, ii, 3), but no historical foundation for this statement is known.

The Clown, *All's Well*, iv, 5, jests on the 'great prince' who 'has an English name ... the black prince, sir, *alias* the prince of darkness.'

Edward, Prince of Wales (1453–71). Only s. of Henry VI; knighted by the King 1461 (after the 2nd Battle of St Albans); taken by his mother, Q. Margaret, into France 1462; took refuge in Lorraine; returned to England, and was taken prisoner and slain at Tewkesbury.

D.P. *3 Hen. VI.* i, 1] protests against being disinherited by his father; declares that he will not see the King again until he returns 'with victory from the field'; departs with Q. Margaret. ii, 2] is knighted by Henry before York. ii, 5] (at Towton) urges Henry to flee. iii, 3] (with Q. Margaret at the French Court) pledges himself to wed Warwick's daughter. (iv, 6) is summoned from France by Henry. v, 4] (at Tewkesbury) shares his mother's 'valiant spirit,' despite misfortunes. v, 5] is made prisoner; boldly calls King Edward a traitor, and reviles 'lascivious Edward,' 'perjur'd George,' and 'misshapen Dick'; is stabbed to death by the three brothers.

Mtd. as husband of 'Warwick's youngest ['eldest,' in *3 Hen. VI*, iii, 3] daughter' (*Rich. III*, i, 1); Anne Neville (*q.v.*) laments him as her slaughtered husband, *ib.* i, 2; Richard's share in his death, *ib. ib.*; his death referred to by Margaret, *ib.* i, 3 (3); appears in Clarence's dream, *ib.* i, 4; referred to by Anne, *ib.* iv, 1, and by Q. Margaret, *ib.* iv, 4 (2); his ghost appears to Richard at Bosworth, *ib.* v, 3.

Some discrepancy exists in the *Chronicles* as to the precise manner of Edward's death. In *Hol.* iii, 688 (following Hall), it is stated that he was slain by Clarence, Gloucester, Dorset, and Hastings; in a Cottonian MS. quoted by Buck, *Hist. of Life and Reign of Richard III*, p. 81, it is stated that Gloucester 'onely of all the great persons stood still and drew not his sword'; in Warkworth's *Chronicle* (Camden Society, No. 10, p. 18) the Prince is merely related to have been 'slayne in the field.'

In *Rich. III*, i, 4, Clarence appears as the murderer, while in i, 2, Richard, after declaring that the deed was King Edward's, appears to accept Anne's accusation against himself.

Egeus. D.P. *M.N.D.* 'An Athenian lord' (Rowe). i, 1] lays a complaint before Theseus against his daughter Hermia, in that, 'bewitched' by Lysander, she refuses to wed Demetrius; he claims the 'privilege of Athens' to dispose of her as he thinks fit. iv, 1] recognizes Hermia asleep in the wood, near Lysander; begs 'the law upon his head,' but Theseus 'overbears his will.' See PHILOSTRATE.

The spelling of F2, 'Egaeus,' confirms the pronunciation indicated metrically.

[Egistus.] See POLIXENES.

Eglamour. D.P. *T.G.V.* 'Agent for Silvia in her escape' (F1). (i, 2) 'a knight well-spoken, neat and fine.' iv, 3] is appealed to by Sil., as one who has loved and lost, and now vows chastity, to escort her secretly to Mantua; he consents 'at any cost.' v, 1] meets her, as agreed. (v, 2) Thurio vows vengeance on him. (v, 3) is separated from Silvia and pursued by outlaws. ('Eglamore' in st. dir. iv, 3, Ff.)

C. and M. Lamb (*Tales from Sh.*) speak of E. as 'a worthy old gentleman'; but it is nowhere hinted that he is elderly, and the outlaws explicitly refer to him as 'nimble-footed' (v, 3). It may be doubted whether 'Sir E.' of i, 2, is intended to be identical with Silvia's escort. (Sir Eglamour, or Eglamore, was one of the Knights of the Round Table in Arthurian legend, and a dragon-slayer.)

Egypt (1). Country of E. 'Sees Helen's beauty in a brow of E.' (*M.N.D.* v, 1); (*cf.* Cleopatra 'with Phoebus' amorous pinches black' (*Ant. Cl.* i, 5)). 'I'll rail against all the first-born of E.' (*A.Y.L.* ii, 5; *cf.* Exod. xi, 5); 'would not be a queen ... for all the mud in E.' (*Hen. VIII*, ii, 3).

In *Ant. Cl.* mtd. 37 times (in no instance qualified by an epithet): i, 1, 5 (4); ii, 1 (2), 2 (6), 3 (3), 5 (2), 6, 7; iii, 3, 6, 8, 9 (2), 10 (2); iv, 1, 10, 12, 13 (2); v, 2 (5).

Egypt (2). For 'King of Egypt,' *i.e.* Ptolemy XII (*q.v.*). Cleopatra is called 'E.'s widow' by Pompey, *Ant. Cl.* ii, 1.

Egypt (3). For 'Queen of Egypt,' *i.e.* Cleopatra. '*Cleo.* I would I had thy inches, thou should'st know There were a heart in E.' (*Ant. Cl.* i, 3); 'say the tears belong to E.' (*ib. ib.*); 'the firm Roman to great E. sends This treasure of an oyster' (*ib.* i, 5); 'whither hast thou led me, E.?' (*ib.* iii, 11); 'E., thou knewst too well My heart was to thy rudder tied' (*ib. ib.*); 'I made these wars for E.' (*ib.* iv, 14); 'I am dying, E.' (*ib.* iv, 15); 'Royal E., Empress' (*ib. ib.*); 'rise, E.' (*ib.* v, 2).

Egyptian. (*a*) *Subst.*, native of Egypt. 'Thou art more puzzled than the E,s in their fog' (*T. Nt.* iv, 2; *cf.* Exod. x, 21–3); 'an E. That had nine hours lien dead, Who was by good appliance recovered' (*Per.* iii, 2); 'that handkerchief did an E. to my mother give' (*Oth.* iii, 4; perhaps, here, 'a gypsy'); 'rare E. [Cleopatra]' (*Ant. Cl.* ii, 2); 'Let the E.s And the Phoenicians go a ducking' (*ib.* iii, 7); 'my brave E.s' (*ib.* iii, 11); 'this foul E. [Cleopatra]' (*ib.* iv, 12).

(*b*) *Adj.* 'E. thief' (*T. Nt.* v, 1; see THYAMIS); 'these strong E. fetters I must break' (*Ant. Cl.* i, 2); 'he will to his E. dish again [Cleopatra]' (*ib.* ii, 6); 'E. Bacchanals' (*ib.* ii, 7); 'E. admiral' (*ib.* iii, 10; see ANTONIAD); 'an E. puppet [Iras]' (*ib.* v, 2).

Egyptian, An. D.P. *Ant. Cl.* v, 1] brings a message from Cleopatra to Octavius. ('Messenger,' Capell.)

Acc. J. Hunter, Cleopatra herself is the 'poor Egyptian' referred to by the messenger.

Elbe. River of Europe. Mtd. as a boundary of the 'Salique land' (*Hen. V*, i, 2). ('Elue,' Ff.)

Elbow. D.P. *M. for M.* 'A simple constable.' ii, 1] brings the Clown, Pompey, before the deputies, and makes an incoherent charge against him; Elbow, who has been 'seven years and a half' a constable, boasts that he undertakes other men's duties, 'as they are chosen, ... for some piece of money.' iii, 2] explains to the (disguised) Duke the reason for his again arresting Pompey.

Eleanor, Queen. See ELINOR.

Elephant, The. Name of an inn. *T. Nt.* iii, 3; iv, 3.

'The E.' or 'E. and Castle,' was a well-known sign in London in Sh.'s days.

Elinor, or **Eleanor** (*c.* 1122–1204). Mother to King John; daughter and heir to William X, D. of Aquitaine; married Lewis VII of France 1137, but was divorced (*John*, ii, 1, l. 125), and married Henry Plantagenet (Henry II of England) 1152, bringing her French possessions as dowry. By Henry she became mother of Richard (Coeur-de-lion), Geoffrey (father of Arthur), John, Eleanor (wife of Alfonso VIII of Castile), and other children. She took the veil two years before her death, which took place at Fontevrault in 1204.

D.P. *John.* i, 1] warns John against the ambition of Constance (*q.v.*) on her son Arthur's behalf (*Hol.* iii, 158); acknowledges Philip Faulconbridge as grandson. ii, 1] has an angry altercation with Const., and declares that she can produce a will that bars Arthur's title (*Hol.* iii, 155–6). iii, 1] is present when the ban of excommunication is pronounced against John; protests against Philip's consequent defection. iii, 3] bids farewell to John on his departure from England. (iv, 2) her death is announced as having taken place three days after that of Const. (historically, it was three years later).

Holinshed, after attributing John's accession to the queen-mother's efforts, adds that she was much honoured and loved by the nobility, and 'being bent to prefer hir son Iohn, left no stone vnturned to establish him in the throne ...'; moreover, she 'was sore against hir nephue Arthur, rather mooued thereto by enuie conceiued against his mother, than upon any just occasion given in the behalfe of the child, for that she saw, if he were king, how his mother Constance would looke to beare most rule within the realme of England, till hir sonne should come to lawfull age, to gouerne of himselfe' (iii, 158).

'Few women have had less justice done them in history than Eleanor. I do not speak of her moral qualities ... but of her remarkable political power and her great influence not only in her husband's states, but in Europe generally; of her great energy ... both in early youth and in extreme old age, there can be no question.' (Stubbs, Pref. to *Hist. Coll. of Walter of Coventry*, vol. ii, p. xxviii.)

Elizabeth (1). Queen of Edward IV (*c.* 1437–92); d. of Sir Richard Woodville (Earl Rivers); married Sir John Grey (killed at St Albans 1461), and three years later was privately married to Edward IV. After the King's death she took sanctuary at Westminster, but was persuaded to give up the young D. of York; her marriage with Edward was declared invalid by Parliament in 1484.

D.P. *3 Hen. VI.* 'Lady Grey.' iii, 2] petitions Edward IV for the lands seized from her husband after his death at St Albans; he consents, on condition that she becomes his mistress (*Hol.* iii, 726); on her refusal he exclaims, 'Answer no more, for thou shalt be my queen.' iv, 1] on the King's brothers raising objections to the match, she urges that her descent was not ignoble, and that meaner than herself 'have had like fortune'; Edward reassures her. iv, 4] the King having been made prisoner, she resolves to seek sanctuary (*Hol.* iii, 677), to save the unborn 'heir of Edward's right.' v, 7] *p.m.* (Ff); her infant son is presented to his uncles.

D.P. *Rich. III.* 'Elizabeth, Queen of King Edward IV.' i, 3] defends herself against Gloucester's accusations of favouring her kinsfolk, and exclaims 'I had rather be a country servant-maid Than a great queen, with this condition'; listens to Q. Margaret's denunciations, and hears herself termed a 'poor painted queen,' ensnared in a 'deadly web.' ii, 1] is present at the apparent reconciliation of her kinsmen with their foes. ii, 2] her lamentations over the King's death are echoed by the Duchess of York's for Clarence. ii, 4] hears of the imprisonment of Rivers and Grey, and resolves to take sanctuary (*Hol.* iii, 715), exclaiming, 'I see, as in a map, the end of all.' iv, 1] is denied access to her sons in the Tower; learns that Richard is king. iv, 4] laments the death of her sons; would fain learn from Q. Margaret how to curse her enemies; after a bitter logomachy with Richard, is persuaded into a promise that she will win her daughter to be his queen, and receives from him a parting kiss; (when she has gone he declares her a 'relenting fool, and shallow, changing woman').

The accusation cf afflicting him by her witchcraft made against her by Richard (*Rich. III*, iii, 4) is based on *Hol.* iii, 722. Elizabeth's mother was Jacquetta of Luxemburg, widow of John of Lancaster, D. of Bedford – hence her claim to noble birth (*Rich. III*, iv, 1). Buckingham (iii, 7, l. 184) speaks of her as 'mother of a many children' ('sons,' Ff); she had three by her first husband.

Elizabeth (2). E.d. to Edward IV (1465–1503); her marriage with the Dauphin was made a condition of peace between England and France, 1475, but was not carried out; she was promised in marriage to Henry of Richmond, then an exile, and is said to have received an offer of marriage from Richard III; married Henry VII in 1486.

'*Rich.* I must be married to my brother's daughter, Or else my kingdom stands on brittle glass' (*Rich. III*, iv, 2); 'I know the Breton Richmond aims at young Elizabeth' (*ib.* iv, 3; *Hol.* iii, 750–1); the Queen consents to the marriage, *ib.* iv, 5; 'let Richmond and E... conjoin together' (*ib.* v, 4).

Elizabeth (3). Queen of England (1533–1603). Only child of Henry VIII and Anne Boleyn. Her birth announced to Henry, *Hen. VIII*, v, 1; her christening procession, *ib.* v, 5; Cranmer's prophetic panegyric, *ib. ib.*

E. was born on Sept. 7, 1533, and baptized three days later. The only allusion to E. in the other plays seems to be 'the fair vestal throned by the west,' etc., of *M.N.D.* ii, 1.

Elizium (Ff). Elysium, abode of the blest in the lower world; *cf.* Virg. *Aen.* vi, 542, 744, *et al.* The spelling of Ff is that common in the 17th cent. (*N.E.D*). 'Rest as ... A blessed soul doth in E.' (*T.G.V.* ii, 7); 'My brother he is in E.' (*T. Nt.* i, 2); 'all night sleeps in E.' (*Hen. V*, iv, 1); 'sweet E.' (2 *Hen. VI*, iii, 2); 'Poor shadows of E., hence, and rest Upon your never-withering banks of flowers' (*Cymb.* v, 4). Metaph.: 'a crown within whose circuit is E.' (3 *Hen. VI*, i, 2); 'to clip E.' (*V.A.* 600). Alluded to: 'give me swift transportance to those fields Where I may wallow in the lily beds Propos'd for the deserver' (*Tr. Cr.* iii, 2); 'where souls do couch on flowers' (*Ant. Cl.* iv, 14).

For the flowers of E., *cf.* Virg. *Aen.* vi, 883.

Ellen. Daughter of Silence and god-daughter of Shallow. 'Alas! a black ouzel' (2 *Hen. IV*, iii, 2; i.e. a brunette).

Elsinore. *Dan.* Helsingör; a Danish seaport, on the Sound, birthplace of Saxo Grammaticus; it contains the fortress of Kronberg (1580). The scene of *Haml.* is laid at E. throughout. Mtd. *Haml.* i, 2; ii, 2 (3). ('Elsenoure' and 'Elsanoure,' Q1.)

The beetling cliff (i, 4, l. 70) is imaginary. The coast is low.

Eltham. Town in Kent, between Greenwich and Dartford; near it are the remains of El. Palace, a royal residence from Henry III to Henry VIII. Acc. *Hol.* iii, 591, Beaufort planned to remove the young King from E. to Windsor some four years after his accession as Henry VI.

The infant Prince Henry at E. ('Eltam,' Ff) when Henry V died, *1 Hen. VI*, i, 1; the palace mtd. as 'E.-place,' *ib.* iii, 1.

[**Elue.**] See Elbe.

Ely, Bishop of (1). D.P. *Hen. V.* See Fordham, John.

Ely, Bishop of (2). D.P. *Rich. III.* See Morton, John.

Ely, Bishop of (3). *Hen. VIII.* See West, Nicolas.

Ely House. The palace of the bishops of Ely in Holborn, where Ely Place still marks the site. The Chapel, dedicated to St Ethelreda, escaped the fire of 1666.

John of Gaunt lies sick there, *Rich. II*, i, 4; his death takes place there, *ib.* ii, 1; (Glou. to Ely) 'when I was last in Holborn, I saw good strawberries in your garden there' (*Rich. III*, iii, 4).

The date of the council referred to in the last quotation was, acc. *Hol.* iii, 722, Friday, June 13. 'After a little talking with them he [the Protector] said unto the bishop of Elie: "My lord, you have verie good strawberies at your garden in Holborn, I require you to let us have a messe of them." ... And therewithall in all the hast he sent his seruant for a messe of strawberies.' *Cf.* More, *Hist. Rich. III*, p. 45.

[**Elysium.**] See Elizium.

Ember Eve. The vigil of an Ember Day, occurring at four seasons of the year.

'*Gower.* It hath been sung at festivals, On ember-eves, and holy-days' (*Per.* i, 1; 'holy-ales,' acc. Steevens' generally accepted conjecture).

Emilia (1). D.P. *Oth.* 'Aemilia, Wife to Iago' (Ff). ii, 1] arrives at Cyprus with Iago; Cassio kisses her by way of greeting; she bickers lightly with her husband; (Iago, *sol.*, professes to doubt her faithfulness). iii, 1] assures Cas. that Othello and Desdemona will do their best to save him from the probable consequences of his tipsy brawl, and gains access for him to Des. iii, 3] is present when Des. promises Cas. to be 'solicitor' on his behalf, and when she eagerly pleads his cause to Oth. iii, 4] declares that she knows not where Desdemona's lost handkerchief is; views with grave concern Othello's rising jealousy. iv, 2] is closely examined by Oth. concerning Des., and will 'lay down her soul in stake' that the latter is faithful; later, re-enters with Des., and is ordered to guard the door without; after the interview between Oth. and Des. is given money by the former as he departs, and is charged to keep secrecy; tenderly seeks Desdemona's confidence; later, returns with Iago, and passionately inveighs against the unknown 'villainous knave' who has poisoned Othello's heart – she adds to Iago that 'some such squire he was That ... made you to suspect me with the Moor.' iv, 3] converses with Des. as she prepares her for rest, and speaks lightly of wifely frailty. v, 1] is sent to tell Oth. and Des. that Cassio is wounded. v, 2] is admitted, and finds Desdemona dying; learns that Iago is the villain who has brought about the murder; despises and defies Oth. as a dolt 'as ignorant as dirt'; admits that she found the fatal handkerchief and gave it to her husband; is stabbed by Iago, and dies by her 'mistress' side.'

In Cinthio's *Novella* the wife of 'the Ensign' is 'a young, and fair, and virtuous lady; and ... was much loved by Disdemona, who spent the greater part of every day with her' (in Cyprus). She takes no part in the action of the story, but 'was privy to the whole,' and after the Ensign's death narrates the events.

'Emilia in this play is a perfect portrait from common life, a masterpiece in the Flemish style' (Mrs Jameson, *Char. of Women* (1833), ii, 43).

'Her death and dying song upon Desdemona's chastity is an expiatory repentance at her grave, which is scarcely surpassed by the Moor's grand and calm retaliation upon himself' (Gervinus, *Sh. Comm.* (1875), p. 544).

Emilia (2). D.P. *Wint. T.* 'A Lady' in 'Names of the Actors' (Ff). ii, 2] tells Paulina that a daughter has been born to Hermione in prison, and enters into the design of showing the babe to Leontes.

Emmanuel. The Clerk of Chatham (*q.v.*).

Emperors. (*a*) Of the Roman Empire. Two only are named in *Sh.* – Augustus and Nero (*qq.v.*) (Saturninus, *T. And.*, is fictitious).

(*b*) Of Emperors of the West (after 1155, of the Holy Roman Empire). The following are mtd. or alluded to in *Sh.*: Charlemagne, Lewis the Pious, Sigismund, Charles V (*qq.v.*).

The 'emperor' of *T.G.V.* (i, 3; ii, 4) is indefinite, but he is represented as holding his Court at Milan.

W. G. Boswell-Stone, *Sh. Hol.* p. 50, has suggested that the Emperor to whom Sir Robert Faulconbridge was sent on an embassy (*John*, i, 1, l. 99) might be intended for Henry VI or Otto IV, though this would make Philip Faul. only some 10 years old at the period of the scene.

Enceladus. Son of Tartarus and Gaea, one of the giants who made war upon the gods (Virg. *Aen.* iv, 179; Ovid, *Amor.* iii, 12, 27). According to one account he was brother to Typhon (*q.v.*).

'Not E., With all his threat'ning band of Typhon's brood, ... Shall seize this prey out of his father's hands' (*T. And.* iv, 2).

C. Crawford (*Sh. Jahrbuch*, xxxvi, 115) compares: 'As if the God of War ... Had been in arms against Enceladus' (G. Peele, *The Honour of the Garter* (1593), l. 46).

Endymion. A beautiful youth, who, acc. one legend, was beloved by Selene (the Moon), and visited by her while he slumbered on Mount Latmus (Ovid, *Ars Am.* iii, 83; *Trist.* ii, 299).

'Peace, how the moon sleeps with E., And would not be awaked' (*M.V.* v, 1, QqFf).

England. See also ALBION. (*a*) In the non-historical plays, regarded as a foreign country. 'In E... when they will not give a doit to relieve a lame beggar, they will lay out ten to see a dead Indian' (*Temp.* ii, 2); 'the bed of Ware, in E.' (*T.Nt.* iii, 2); 'the young baron of E.' (*M.V.* i, 2); an argosy from Venice for E., *ib.* i, 3; coin 'called an angel in E.' (*ib.* ii, 7); mtd., *ib.* iii, 2; 'old Robin Hood of E.' (*A.Y.L.* i, 1); in the fat kitchen-wench, regarded as a globe, Dro. S. guessed E. 'stood in her chin, by the salt rheum that ran between France and it' (*Com. Err.* iii, 2); ambassadors from E. to Denmark, *Haml.* v, 2 (4); 'in E., where indeed they are most potent in potting ... oh sweet E.' (*Oth.* ii, 3).

b) In the Histories the references are very numerous. The following are noteworthy: 'Hedged in with the main' (*John*, ii, 1); the Bastard's exhortation to E. to be true to itself, *ib.* v, 7; Gaunt's eulogy of 'this sceptred isle,' *Rich. II*, ii, 1; in danger from the Scots, *Hen. V*, i, 2; 'breeds very valiant creatures' (*ib.* iii, 7); 'E. all Olivers and Rowlands bred' (*1 Hen. VI*, 1, 2); 'E. is safe if true within itself' (*3 Hen. VI*, iv, 1). 'Little E.,' see PEMBROKESHIRE.

In *Macb.* mtd. only with reference to the flight thither of Malcolm (*q.v.*).

(*c*) For 'king of England.' 'E... Hath put himself in arms' (*John*, ii, 1, l. 56); 'E., thou hast not saved one drop of blood' (*ib. ib.* 1. 341); 'Blanch Is niece to E.' (*ib. ib.*); 'and bloody E. into E. gone' (*ib.* iii, 4, l. 8); 'Harry E.' (*Hen. V*, iii, 5); 'E. shall repent his folly' (*ib.* iii, 6); 'brother E.' (*ib.* v, 2); 'gracious E.' (*Macb.* iv, 3, ll. 43, 189).

English. (*a*) *Subst.* (i) English language. 'He hath ... translated her will, out of honesty into E.' (*M.W.W.* i, 3); 'old abusing of ... the king's E.' (*ib.* i, 4); 'one that makes fritters of E.' (*ib.* v, 5); 'I [Portia] have a poor pennyworth in the E.' (*M.V.* i, 2); etc.

(ii) Englishmen. 'These E. and their discipline' (*John*, ii, 1); 'our lusty E.' (*ib.* ii, 2); 'abounding valour in our E.' (*Hen. V*, iv, 3); etc. At the Field of the Cloth of Gold, *Hen. VIII*, i, 1; 'Your Dane, your German ... are nothing to your E. [in drinking]' (*Oth.* ii, 2).

(*b*) *Adj.* Frequent in the Histories. In the other plays: 'E. tongue' (*M.W.W.* ii, 3); 'list of an E. kersey' (*M. for M.* ii, 2); 'has ed the drum before the E. tragedians' (*All's Well*, iv, 3); 'has an E. name' (*ib.* iv, 3; *i.e.* the Black Prince); 'E. tailor' (*Macb.* ii, 3); 'E. Court' (*ib.* iii, 6); 'E. power' (*ib.* v, 2); 'E. epicures' (*ib.* v, 3); 'E. force' (*ib. ib.*).

Englishman. *Sing.*: Evans so styled, *M.W.W.* ii, 3; the 'Scottish lord ... borrowed a box of the ear of the E.' (*M.V.* i, 2); Melun's 'grandsire was an E.' (*ib.* v, 4); 'Where ever E. durst set his foot' (*Rich. II*, i, 1); 'a trueborn E. [Bolingbroke]' (*ib.* i, 3); Q. Kath. doubts that any E. 'dare give her counsel,' *Hen. VIII*, iii, 1; drinking powers of 'your E.,' *Oth.* ii, 3; etc.

Plu.: 'slaughtered E.' (*Rich. II*, iii, 3); we shall have each a hundred E.' (*Hen. V*, iii, 7); etc.

Englishwoman. 'The Princess is the better E.' (*Hen. V*, v, 2).

Enobarbus. See AHENOBARBUS.

Envy. Personified. 'Devil E. say amen' (*Tr. Cr.* ii, 3); 'lean-faced E. in her loathsome cave' (2 *Hen. VI*, iii, 2, l. 315); 'that monster E.' (*Per.* iv, Gow.).

Ephesian. A boon companion; probably a mere imitation of 'Corinthian' (*q.v.*). '*P. Hen.* Where sups he [Falstaff]? ... What company? *Page*. Ephesians, my lord; of the old church' (2 *Hen. IV*, ii, 2); 'It is thine host, thine E. calls' (*M.W.W.* iv, 5).

Ephess. For 'Ephesus'; *Per.* iv, Gow. (Steevens, conj.).

Ephesus. Chief of the Ionian cities on the coast of Asia Minor. Near it stood the Temple of Diana, originally built in the 6th cent. B.C. See DIANA.

The scene of *Com. Err.* is wholly laid at E. Mtd. i, 1 (5); ii, 2; iv, 1, 4.

The scene of *Per.* iii, 2, 4, and v, 3, is also laid at E., v, 3, being at the Temple of Diana.

Epicurean, *adj.* 'E. rascal' (*M.W.W.* ii, 2); 'E. cooks' (*Ant. Cl.* ii, 1) – the accent being on the third syllable.

Epicurism. 'E. and lust' (*Lear*, i, 4).

Epicurus. Greek philosopher, 342–270 B.C., founder of a philosophical school which regarded happiness – in the sense of peace of mind – as the *summum bonum*, and virtue as the chief means to happiness. The gods, they held, had no interest in, or influence on, mankind. The idea that 'Epicurism' implied sensual indulgence was a widespread and not unnatural error.

Cassius, before Philippi, says: 'You know that I held Epicurus strong And his opinion: now I change my mind,

And partly credit things that do presage' (*Jul. C.* v, 1; cf. *Plut.* p. 100: 'It is also reported that Cassius (though otherwise he did favour the doctrine of E.) beholding the image of Pompey ... he did softly call upon it to aid him').

Epidamium. See Epidamnum.

Epidamnum. For 'Epidamnus,' the modern Durazzo, scene of the *Menaechmi* of Plautus; thus in the Eng. transln., 1595.

Aegeon often made 'prosperous voyages' from Syracuse to E., *Com. Err.* i, 1; Ant. Syr. is advised to declare that he is of E., *ib.* i, 2; a ship is ready to sail from Ephesus to E., *ib.* iv, 1; Aemilia rescued by men of E., *ib.* v, 1. ('Epidamium,' Ff.)

Epidarus. Probably a misprint (F1) for 'Epidamnum.' *Com. Err.* i, 1, l. 94; cf. *ib.* v, 1.

Epilogue. See Dancer, A.

Epistrophus. Three personages so named are mentioned in *Iliad*, bk. ii. It was 'Epistropus, kynge of the regne of Eliane' who brought the Sagittary (*q.v.*) to Troy (Caxton, *Recuyell*); there was also a Greek 'Epicropus,' or Epistropus, 'kynge of Focyden' (*ib.*).

Agamemnon (*Tr. Cr.* v, 5) laments 'the pashed corses of the Kings E. and Cedius [*q.v.*].'

Ercles. Bottom's perversion of 'Hercules' (*q.v.*); *M.N.D.* i, 2.

'Ercles' vein' may allude to a play entitled *Hercules*, produced in 1595. *Cf.* Ward, *Eng. Dram. Lit.* i, 193 *n.* The form 'Hercles occurs in Studley's transln. of Soneca's *Here. Oct.*

Erebus. 'Darkness,' son of Chaos; hence, the gloomy region through which the shades pass to Hades. 'Not E. himself were dim enough to hide thee' (*Jul. C.* ii, 1); 'dark as E.' (*M.V.* v, 1); (Pistol) 'E. and tortures vile' (*2 Hen. IV*, ii, 4).

Erinnys. A Fury (*q.v.*); the reading adopted, instead of 'entrance,' by Steevens and other edrs., in. 'No more the thirsty entrance of this soil Shall daub her lips with her own children's blood' (*1 Hen. IV*, i, 1).

Ermengare. ('Ermengard,' *Hol.* iii, 546.) Daughter of Charles, Duke of Lorraine, and ancestress of Lewis IX of France through his grandmother, 'that fair queen Isabel' (of Flanders); *Hen. V*, i, 2.

Eros. An attendant of M. Antony, by whom he was 'loved and trusted much' (*Plut.* p. 221).

D.P. *Ant. Cl.* iii, 5] converses with Enobarbus. iii, 11] (after Actium) entreats Ant. to recognize Cleopatra's presence. iv, 4] assists Ant. to arm. iv, 5] announces the defection of Enobarbus. iv, 7] (at Alexandria) exclaims that the foe is beaten. (iv, 12) Antony calls for him. iv, 14] is reminded by Ant. that he is sworn to slay his master when commanded, but, when bidden to keep his vow, kills himself.

'The freedman transfigured by a death more fair than freedom through the glory of the greatness of his faith' (Swinburne, *A Study of Sh.* (1880), p. 189).

Erpingham, Sir Thomas (1357–1428). Sailed with Bolingbroke from Brittany (*Hol.* iii, 497); made K.G. (1400), Chamberlain of the Household, and Warden of the Cinque Ports. At Agincourt, before the English 'went an old knight, Sir T. E... with a warder in his hand' (*Hol.* iii, 554). The 'Erpingham Gate' at Norwich was built by him. Mtd. as an adherent of Bol., *Rich. II*, ii, 1.

D.P. *Hen. V.* iv, 1] lends his cloak to the King; later, tells the King that his nobles seek him; 'a good old commander and a most kind gentleman.' ('Sir John E.,' Ff.)

Error. Personified. 'O hateful E., Melancholy's child,' etc. (*Jul. C.* v, 3).

Escalus (1). D.P. *M. for M.* 'An ancient Lord.' i, 1] is appointed by the Duke, Vincentio, as secondary' to Angelo, who is to be V.'s deputy during his absence; suggests to Angelo that they should discuss their respective powers. ii, 1] deprecates A.'s severity toward Claudio; deals with Elbow's charges against Froth and Pompey. iii, 2] sends Mistress Overdone to jail; converses with 'Friar Lodowick' (the disguised Duke), and declares that he has done his best to save Claudio's life. iv, 4] discusses with Ang. Vincentio's letter announcing his approaching return. v, 1] welcomes V.; examines V., who has resumed his disguise, and condemns him to prison; is amazed when Angelo's villainy is unmasked; is thanked for his 'much goodness' by the Duke.

Escalus (2). Prince of Verona. D.P. *Rom. J.* i, 1] intervenes during a fray between the Montagues and Capulets, and threatens death to the heads of the houses, 'If ever you disturb our streets again.' iii, 1] banishes Romeo for killing Tybalt in combat. v, 3] enters the churchyard in the early morning to find Romeo, Juliet, and his kinsman Paris dead; investigates the tragedy and declares that 'Some shall be pardon'd, and some punished.'

So named in A. Brooke's *Romeus and Juliet* (1562); 'Signor Escala' or 'Lord Bartholomew of Escala' in Painter's *Palace of Pleasure* (1567), ii. 'Eskalos' in st. dirs. i, 1, QqFf. (From the Della Scala, or Scaliger, family of Verona.)

Escalus (3). A soldier; mtd. *All's Well*, iii, 5.

Escanes. D.P. *Per.* A lord of Tyre. i, 3] *p.m.* ii, 4] is informed of the death of Antiochus. (iv, 4, Gow.) governs Tyre in the absence of Helicanus.

Eschines in Wilkins' novel.

Eson. See Aeson.

Esop. See Aesop.

Essex, County of. 'Thy southern power of Essex, Norfolk, Suffolk' (*3 Hen. VI*, i, 1).

[Essex, Earl of (1).] See Chorus (1).

Essex, Earl of (2). See Fitzpeter, G. 'Essex' as a personal name nowhere occurs in the text of *Sh.*, but only in the st. dirs. and pfxs. of *John*, i, 1.

Eternal, The. The Deity. 'By penitence the Eternal's wrath's appeased' (*T.G.V.* v, 4).

Ethiop, Ethiope, or **Aethiop.** (*a*) *Subst.* The same as 'Ethiopian' (*q.v.*). 'Silvia ... shows Julia but a swarthy E.' (*T.G.V.* ii, 6); 'I'll hold my mind, were she an E.' (*M. Ado*, v, 4); (Lysander to Hermia) 'Away, you E.' (*M.N.D.* iii, 2); 'And E.s of their sweet complexion crack' (*L.L.L.* iv, 3); 'Thou for whom Jove would swear Juno but an E. were' (*ib. ib.* and *P.P.* xvii); 'upon his shield is a black E.' (*Per.* ii, 2); 'rich jewel in an E.'s ear' (*Rom. J.* i, 5).

(*b*) *Adj.* 'E. words, blacker in their effect Than in their countenance' (*A.Y.L.* iv, 3).

Ethiopian, *subst.* In the general sense of a person with a dark skin; a 'blackamoor,' or even a brunette. 'White as ... E.'s tooth, or the fan'd snow' (*Wint. T.* iv, 4); used at random, to mean foreigner: (Host to Caius) 'Is he dead, my E.?' (*M.W.W.* ii, 3).

In *Sh.* usually 'Ethiop' (*q.v.*). The low esteem in which a 'brunette' complexion was held in Sh.'s days is well illustrated by the banter to which Biron is exposed (*L.L.L.* iv, 3); see also Ellen.

Eton. Village on the Thames, opposite Windsor. The marriage of Slender to Anne Page is planned to take place at E., *M.W.W.* iv, 4, 6, v, 5; a 'slough of mire' beyond E. mtd., *ib.* iv, 5.

Eton College was not founded until 1440.

[**Eugenius IV.**] Pope (Gabriel Condolmieri); b. 1383; Pope 1431–47. Recommends peace between England and France, *1 Hen. VI*, v, 1.

Euphrates. River; mtd. *Ant. Cl.* i, 2.

Accented on the first syllable, as usual in Elizabethan poetry.

Euphronius. 'And because they [Antony and Cleopatra] had no other men of estimation about them, for that some were fled, and those that remained they did not greatly trust, they were enforced to send E., the schoolmaster of their children' (*Plut.* pp. 217–18).

D.P. *Ant. Cl.* 'Ambassador,' until named by Capell. (iii, 11) *Antony*. 'We sent our schoolmaster; is he come back?' iii, 12] (Dolabella speaks scornfully of him); delivers message from Ant. and Cl. to Octavius. iii, 13] again acts as envoy.

Euriphile. Nurse to Cymbeline's two infant sons, whom, at the instigation of her husband Belarius, she stole. Guiderius and Arviragus 'every day do honour to her grave' (*Cymb.* iii, 3); they propose to lay 'Fidele' in the grave 'by good Eu. our mother' (*ib.* iv, 2); her crime related by Belarius, *ib.* v, 5.

The nearest classical name seems to be Eriphyle, wife of Amphiaraus (Hom. *Od.* xi, 326).

Europa. Daughter of Agenor. Jupiter, in the form of a bull, swam with her to Crete (Ovid, *Metam.* ii, 833 ff.). The story referred to, *M. Ado*, v, 4; 'Jove, thou wast a bull for thy Eu.' (*M.W.W.* v, 5); 'the daughter of Agenor ... That made great Jove to humble him to her hand' (*Tam. Sh.* i, 1).

Europe, Continent of. Sebastian chides Alonso for not having blessed 'our E.' with his daughter, *Temp.* ii, 1; 'no Court in E. is too good for thee [Hermione]' (*Wint. T.* ii, 2); 'the dearest chandler's in E.' (*1 Hen. IV*, iii, 3); 'John, with my brothers and sisters; and Sir John with all E.' (*2 Hen. IV*, ii, 2); 'the most active fellow in E.' (*ib.* iv, 3); 'were it the mistress-court of mighty E.' (*Hen. V*, ii, 4); Orleans' steed is 'the best horse of E.' (*ib.* iii, 7); Bedford's soldiers will 'make all E. quake' (*1 Hen. VI*, i, 1); the D. of York was 'the flower of E. for his chivalry' (*3 Hen. VI*, ii, 1); Imogen would not lose her jewel 'for a revenue of any king's in E.' (*Cymb.* ii, 3).

Evans, Sir Hugh. D.P. *M.W.W.* A Welsh parson. i, 1] tries to allay Shallow's anger against Falstaff; suggests Slender as a suitor for Anne Page. i, 2] sends a letter to Quickly. iii, 1] has been challenged by Dr Caius, and awaits his coming with much 'trempling of mind'; the fight is prevented, and the two opponents agree to be revenged on the Host, who has tricked them. iii, 2] *p.m.* iii, 3] chides Ford's jealousy. iv, 1] examines Page's son in Latin. iv, 2] again chides Ford; detects 'a great peard' under the witch's muffler. iv, 4] takes counsel with the others about discomfiting Falstaff. iv, 5] derides the Host for having been 'cozened' by Germans. v, 4] with the 'fairies' in the park. v, 5] disguised as a satyr, aids in tormenting Falstaff; Fal. declares he 'makes fritters of English,' but Evans loads him with abuse.

The name occurs in the Stratford records (1585) (French).

Eve. The first woman. 'Our grandmother' (*L.L.L.* i, 1); 'E.'s legacy' (*T.G.V.* iii, 1); 'E.'s daughters' (*M.W.W.* iv, 2); 'piece of E.'s flesh' (*T. Nt.* i, 5); 'what E., what serpent, hath suggested thee To make a second fall?' (*Rich. II*, iii, 4); 'Had he been Adam, he had tempted E.' (*L.L.L.* v, 2); 'E.'s apple' (*Son.* xciii).

Everlasting, The. Title of the Deity. 'O ... that the E. had not fixed His canon 'gainst self-slaughter' (*Haml.* i, 2).

Exeter, Bishop of. See Courtenay, Peter.

Exeter, City of. See Rougemont.

Exeter, Duke of. See Holland.

Exeter, Mayor of. Shows the Duke of Gloucester the castle; *Rich. III*, iv, 2. See Rougemont.

G. is received by 'the major and his brethren' (*Hol.* iii, 746).

Expectation. Personified; *Hen. V*, ii, Chor.

Exton, Sir Piers. Probably related to Sir Nicholas E., Mayor of London 1395, a virulent opponent of Richard II.

D.P. *Rich. II.* 'Sir Pierce of Exton.' v, 4] hearing Bolingbroke say 'Have I no friend will rid me of this living fear,' resolves to slay Richard at Pomfret (*Hol.* iii, 517). v, 5] (forbids the sewer to taste R.'s food); strikes down R., who has made a desperate resistance; is overcome by remorse. v, 6] brings the body to Bol., who, though he wished Richard dead, 'hates the murderer,' and bids him 'wander with Cain through endless night.'

Holinshed's account is closely followed, but v, 6, is Sh.'s own conception.

F

Fabian. D.P. *T.Nt.* 'Servant to Olivia' (Rowe). ii, 5] gives his reason for wishing to put Malvolio to shame; relishes M.'s infatuation over the forged letter. iii, 2] incites Aguecheek to challenge 'Cesario.' iii, 4] joins in baiting Mal.; criticizes A.'s challenge; warns 'Cesario' of A.'s skill in fence; stigmatizes 'C.' as a coward. iv, 1] *p.m.* v, 1] begs Feste, without avail, to show him Malvolio's letter; afterward, reads it aloud at Olivia's request; admits his share in the device set upon Mal. and unfolds the plot.

Fabian, though he 'addresses the two knights with the respectful "you" of an inferior' (Furness), can scarcely be regarded as much below them in rank. Sir Toby calls him 'Signior' (ii, 5; iii, 4), and Fabian addresses the knight as 'man' (ii, 5); 'Cesario' appeals to him as an equal in the matter of the duel (iii, 4), and he speaks to Olivia of her kinsman as 'Toby' (v, 1).

In *Gl' Ingannati* Lelia assumes in disguise the name of Fabio; hence, perhaps, 'Fabian' (Hunter).

Fairy. D.P. *M.N.D.* An attendant on Titania. ii, 1] describes to Puck the duties of a servant of the Fairy Queen; listens to P.'s account of the quarrel between Oberon and Titania, and of his own mischievous pranks.

Falconbridge (1). 'The young baron of England,' suitor to Portia. 'He is a proper man's picture, but, alas, who can converse with a dumbshow?' (*M.V.* i, 2) – for 'he hath neither Latin, French, nor Italian.'

Thus in mod. edns.; 'Fauconbridge,' Ff.

Falconbridge (2). A naval commander. 'Stern F. commands the narrow seas' (*3 Hen. VI*, i, 1).

Acc. Hall, p. 301, at some time before 1471, 'one Thomas Nevel, bastard son to Thomas [vere, William] lord Fauconbridge,' was appointed by Warwick 'to be Vyce-admirall of the sea,' to watch the straits of Dover, and intercept any friends of Edward IV.

Falconbridge (3). The spelling of 'Faulconbridge' adopted throughout in *John* by Dyce and other mod. edrs.

Falconbridge, Lord of. A title of John Talbot, E. of Shrewsbury; *1 Hen. VI*, iv, 7.

'Faulconbrige' in R. Crompton's *Mansion of Magnanimitie* (1599), E.4 (B.-S.).

Falstaff, Sir John. D.P. *1 Hen. IV.* i, 2] in bantering converse with Prince Hal, discusses the future course of events when that 'sweet wag' is king; at Poins' suggestion agrees to join in waylaying travellers, at Gadshill, early on the morrow. ii, 2] Poins removes his horse; F., on hearing that the travellers number 'eight, or ten,' fears lest they should 'rob us,' but in the encounter overcomes and robs them; while sharing the booty with Peto, Bardolph, and Gadshill, they are set upon by the Prince and Poins in disguise; F.'s companions instantly flee and he, 'after a blow or two, runs away too [Qq, om. Ff], leaving the booty behind.' ii, 4] accuses the Prince and Poins of being cowards, and brags of his exploits against an ever growing number of 'men in buckram'; on the trick being revealed, excuses himself on the ground that 'the lion will not touch the true prince'; is despatched to 'send packing' a messenger from the Court (Sir John Bracy); later, announces an outbreak of rebellion in the North; in the *rôle* of the King, advises 'Harry' to 'keep with' Falstaff, and 'the rest banish'; in turn, posing as the Prince, defends his own character; hearing that the Sheriff is at the door, hides himself behind the arras and falls asleep; the Prince and Poins search his pockets and find nothing but tavern bills. iii, 3] Falstaff banters Bardolph on his red face; complains that he has had his pocket picked, and thereupon objurgates the hostess, to whom he owes money; the Prince composes the quarrel, and tells F. that he has procured him 'a charge of foot.' iv, 2] will not march through Coventry with his soldiers, of whom he is ashamed and whom he calls 'a hundred and fifty battered prodigals' – but 'good for powder,' as he explains to the Prince. v, 1] (before Shrewsbury) soliloquizes on 'honour.' v, 3] (during the battle) declares that not three of his men are left alive; jests with the Prince; exclaims (*sol.*) 'give me life: which if I can save, so; if not, honour comes unlook'd for, and there's an end.' v, 4] fights with Douglas, and falls as though killed; the Prince exclaims 'I could have better spar'd a better man'; F., left alone, rises, stabs the body of Hotspur lying near, and takes it on his back; declares that he fought with Percy 'a long hour by Shrewsbury clock'; looks for advancement.

D.P. *2 Hen. IV.* i, 2] in an ill humour with his page and his mercer, meets the Lord Chief Justice, who severely admonishes him but is baffled in the encounter of wits that follows; Falstaff concludes by asking the L.C.J. to lend him a thousand pound 'to furnish him forth' for his expedition to the North. ii, 1] is on the point of being arrested 'at the suit of Mistress Quickly,' when the L.C.J. enters, and after some inquiry bids F. 'satisfy the poor woman'; F. wheedles the hostess into making a further loan; asks 'Master Gower' to dine or sup with him; seizes the opportunity of a final gibe at the L.C.J. (ii, 2) sends letter to Prince Hal. ii, 4] expels Pistol for brawling; is conversing amicably with Doll Tearsheet when the Prince and Poins enter, disguised as drawers, but are speedily detected by Falstaff; a summons to the North arrives in hot haste and he bids farewell with the rest. iii, 1] visits Justice Shallow and selects recruits; (*sol.*) sees to the bottom of Shallow, and resolves 'to make him a philosopher's two stones.' iv, 3] takes prisoner 'Colevile of the dale'; (*sol.*) dilates on the virtues of sack; resolves to revisit Shallow. v, 1] is welcomed by Shallow, and (*sol.*) resolves to make him a source of laughter for the Prince. (v, 2) the L.C.J. warned to 'speak him fair.' v, 3] is carousing with the justices when news of Henry IV's death arrives; he declares that he is 'fortune's steward,' now that Prince Hal is king. v, 5] is sternly repudiated by the new King, but is granted an allowance 'for competence of life'; still expresses some hope of advancement; is committed to the Fleet. (Epil.) mtd.

Hen. V. (ii, 1) his illness reported. (ii, 3) the manner of his death related by Mistress Quickly. (iv, 7) mtd. by Fluellen.

In *The Famous Victories of Henry V* there occurs the character of Sir John Oldcastle (*q.v.*), familiarly spoken of as 'Jockey.' As Knight remarks, he 'is a low worthless fellow, without a single spark of wit or humour to relieve his grovelling profligacy.' Moreover he has only thirty lines in the play, and there is no allusion to his being fat. Nevertheless Malone and others regarded him as the prototype of Falstaff.

D.P. *M.W.W.* i, 1] is accused by Shallow of killing his deer, and other misdemeanours; admits them, and also breaking Slender's head; Page invites F. and his followers to dinner, and 'to drink down all unkindness.' i, 3] F. dismisses Bardolph from his service; Pistol and Nym refusing to carry his letters to Mrs Page and Mrs Ford, Falstaff entrusts them to his page Robin. (ii, 1) the 'merry wives' plan his discomfiture; Pistol and Nym arouse the suspicions of their husbands. ii, 2] Falstaff dismisses Pistol; Quickly conveys messages to him from the wives; Ford, as 'Master Brook,' appeals to him for assistance in wooing Mistress Ford, and gives him money; Falstaff tells 'Brook' that he already has an appointment with her. (iii, 2) mtd. iii, 3] is saved from discovery in Ford's house by being carried away in a 'buckbasket.' (iii, 4) mtd. iii, 5] describes how he was 'thrown into the Thames.' iv, 2] escapes from Ford's house in the guise of 'Mother Prat,' but receives a drubbing from Ford. (iv, 4) the wives and their husbands plan to make 'public sport' of him. iv, 5] converses with Simple; (*sol.*) laments his own discomfiture; Quickly brings him a letter. (iv, 6) mtd. v, 1] bids 'Brook' be at Herne's oak about midnight, when he 'shall see wonders'; relates how he was beaten by Ford. (v, 3) mtd. V, 5] disguised as Herne the Hunter, he greets the wives in Windsor Forest; a crowd of pretended fairies pinch and deride him; he admits that he has been overreached, and is 'dejected'; is invited to accompany them all 'and laugh this sport o'er by a country fire.'

Much fruitless discussion has taken place as to the chronological position of the *M.W.W.* relatively to the historical plays in which F. appears. The F. of the *M.W.W.* is not the F. of *Henry IV*. 'Here the knight is fatuous, his genius deserts him; the never-defeated hangs his head before two country dames; the buck-basket, the drench of Thames water, the blows of Ford's cudgel are reprisals too coarse upon the most inimitable of jesters' (E. Dowden, *Shakspere*, p. 105). See FENTON.

Fame, Lady. Fame personified as a spreader of false reports. '*Bene.* I have played the part of Lady Fame' (*M. Ado*, ii, 1).

Famine. Personified. 'At his [Henry V's] heels (Leash'd in like hounds) should F., Sword, and Fire Crouch for employment' (*Hen. V*, i, Chor.).

In a speech by the King (*Hol.* iii, 567) Famine is called the meekest of Bellona's handmaidens, by whom he will punish Rouen.

[Famous Victories, The.] See HENRY THE FYFT, THE FAMOUS VICTORIES OF.

Fang. D.P. *2 Hen. IV*. A sheriff's officer. ii, 1] attempts to arrest Falstaff at the suit of the Hostess. ('Phang,' Q.)

Fastolfe, Sir John (*c.* 1378–1459). Of his career discrepant accounts have been given; he is thus referred to by Holinshed: At the siege of Orleans, Bedford appointed 'the Lord Talbot, Sir John Fastolfe, and diverse other right valiant capteins' to assist the E. of Suffolk (iii, 599); 'from this battell [Patay] departed without anie stroke striken Sir John Fastolfe; the same yeare for his valiantness elected into the Order of the Garter' (iii, 601); 'for doubt of misdealing' at Patay, Bedford took from Sir J. F. 'the image of Saint George, and his garter; though afterward, by meanes of good freends, and apparent causes of good excuse, the same were to him again delivered against the mind of the lord Talbot' (iii, 601).

Apart from Holinshed's account, on which the dramatist relied, it is known that F. fought valiantly at Agincourt; was regent of Normandy, and was victorious at 'the Battle of the Herrings' (1429); he was also friend of the writer of most of the 'Paston letters.' It appears that he was educated as a page in the household of Thomas Mowbray – a fact relevant to his identification with 'Falstaff' (*q.v.*), as is also his bequeathal, among other property, of the Boar's Head, in Southwark, to Magdalen College, Oxford; *cf.* French, pp. 136–8.

D.P. *1 Hen. VI.* ('Falstaffe,' Ff.) (i, 1) his cowardice before Orleans. (i, 4) Talbot's rage against him. iii, 2] shamelessly deserts Talbot before Rouen. iv, 1] brings a letter from the D. of Burgundy to the King; Talbot tears the garter from 'the craven's leg,' and denounces him for cowardice at Patay (*q.v.*); the King decrees his banishment.

Monstrelet, *Chroniques* (ed. Buchon), v, 230, states that the restoration of the Gartor to Fastolfe caused 'grand débat' between him and Talbot, after the latter's release from captivity (B.-S. *Sh. Hol.* p. 229*n.*).

Fates, The. Moirae, or Parcae; Atropos, Lachesis, and Clotho, regarded either as symbolizing 'fate' in the strict sense of the word, or as divinities presiding over the duration of human life. They are represented as spinning, and cutting, the thread of life. Atropos alone is named in *Sh.*

In some instances the personification of fate is indistinct, but in the following passages it is manifest: 'Phibbus' car shall ... make and mar the foolish Fates' (*M.N.D.* i, 2); 'till the Fates me kill' (*ib.* v, 1); 'O Fates, come, come: cut thread and thrum' (*ib. ib.*); 'according to the Fates and Destinies and such odd sayings' (*M.V.* ii, 2); 'Oh, the Fates!' (*Wint. T.* iv, 4); 'Hapless Aegeon, whom the Fates have mark'd To bear the extremity of dire mishap!' (*Com. Err.* i, 1); 'the Fates with traitors do contrive' (*Jul. C.* ii, 3); 'Fates, we will know your pleasures' (*Jul. C.* iii, 1, l. 98); 'the strict Fates' (*Per.* iii, 3); 'nurses are not the Fates' (*ib.* iv, 3).

Alluded to as 'sisters three': *M.N.D.* v, 1; *M.V.* ii, 2. *Cf.* 'the fatall sisters,' Spenser, *Shepheards Calender*, Nov.

Father that has Killed his Son. D.P. *3 Hen. VI.* ii, 5] (at the Battle of Towton) discovers whom he has slain, and bitterly laments the deed, in the presence of King Henry, who bewails this 'more than common grief.' See TOWTON.

Fauconberg, Earl. Among the French slain at Agincourt (*Hol.* iii, 555). 'Faulconbridge' and 'Fauconbridge' (Ff), *Hen. V*, iii, 5; iv, 8. ('Waleren, Count of Fauquembergue,' B.-S. *Sh. Hol.* p. 516.)

Fauconbridge. The spelling of 'Faulconbridge' in *Tr. R.* ('Fawconbridge' in title of Part I).

See also FALCONBRIDGE (1).

Faulconbridge, Jaques. A French Lord; mtd. *L.L.L.* ii, 1 (2). 'Fauconbridge,' once in F1, 2.

Faulconbridge, Lady. Mother of Philip F., by Richard Coeur-de-lion. Historically otherwise unknown, though it has been asserted that she was a lady of Poitou (French, p. 21).

D.P. *John.* i, 1] admits Philip's parentage.

'Lady Margaret' in *Tr. R.*, where she is present throughout the discussion between the brothers and even takes part in it.

Faulconbridge, Philip. Natural son of Richard I; identified by Steevens and others with Falcasius de Brente or Breauté (*ob. c.* 1228), who was ranked among the great barons, was a 'disposer' in King John's will, and was high in favour with Henry III. Holinshed (iii, 160) refers to him thus: 'Philip, bastard son to King Richard ... killed the vicomte of Limoges, in revenge of his father's death.' Philip's 'choice' (*John*, i, 1) seems founded on the case of Dunois, the Bastard of Orleans, as related by Hall. But the dramatic character is essentially Sh.'s creation.

D.P. *John*. ('Bastard' in pfxs. and st. dirs. after i, 1, l. 138.) i, 1] appears with his brother Robert before the King and claims his inheritance; Robert resists the claim on the ground that Ph. is illegitimate; the latter preferring to be 'reputed son of Coeur-de-lion,' gladly resigns his patrimony, with the approval of John, who dubs him 'Sir Richard and Plantagenet'; he soliloquizes satirically on his 'new-made honour,' and, on the entrance of his mother, induces her to admit his true parentage. ii, 1] (before Angiers) tries to pick a quarrel with Lymoges; urges John and Philip to unite in attacking the town; makes merry over the First Citizen's speech; soliloquizes on 'Commodity.' iii, 1] assails Lymoges with reiterated jibes. iii, 2] enters with the head of L., whom he has slain. iii, 3] is sent on a mission to England to 'shake the bags of hoarding abbots.' iv, 2] brings Peter of Pomfret to the King; warns the latter against the disaffected nobles. iv, 3] enters, to summon Salisbury and the others to the King, just as they discover Arthur's body; denounces the supposed murder; averts the vengeance of the nobles from Hubert, but on their departure tells him that he is 'damned beyond the reach of mercy' if he did the deed, or consented to it; bids him pick up the body; is convinced of Hubert's innocence, and meditates on the 'vast confusion' imminent at home. v, 1] tells John that the Dauphin has landed and that Arthur is dead; urges the King to be 'great in act,' and grieves to hear that he has placed himself in the hands of the papal legate. v, 2] presents himself before Pandulph and the Dauphin, and hurls defiance at the latter. (v, 3) advises John to leave the battlefield. v, 6] is told by Hubert that the King has been poisoned; reveals, on his part, that half his forces have been overwhelmed by the tide on 'these Lincoln washes.' v, 7] is present at John's death; does homage to Henry; declares that England can withstand a hostile world, if it 'to itself do rest but true.'

'Faulconbridge' throughout in F1; 'Fauconbridge' in *Tr. R.* The disputed question as to the source of the name is discussed very fully by Furness, *John*, pp. 6–9.

In *Tr. R.* Philip lays Limoges' lion-skin at Blanch's feet, and is accepted as her knight. This may explain P.'s animosity toward the Dauphin, expressed by his outburst, 'Vile lout,' etc. (ii, 1). In iii, 2, he is addressed by John as 'Philip'; this seems an oversight.

Faulconbridge, Sir Robert. Supposed father to Philip and Robt. F.; knighted on the field by Coeur-de-lion; sent on an embassy to Germany; *John*, i, 1. (Without historical warrant.)

In the play *Look About You* (1600) Lady F.'s husband is Sir Richard.' (This play deals with the intrigue between Lady F. and Coeur-de-lion.) Acc. *Tr. R.*, Sir R. was knighted at the siege of Acon (Acre).

Faulconbridge, Robert. D.P. *John*. i, 1] claims his late father's estate on the ground of the illegitimacy of his elder brother, Philip F. (*q.v.*).

Faustus, Johann. A necromancer, friend of Paracelsus and Cornelius Agrippa, who became identified with an early legend of a man who sold his soul to the devil.

The story of Faust appeared in a *Volksbuch* published at Frankfort-on-the-Main in 1587, and was soon afterward translated into English as *The History of the Damnable Life and Deserved Death of Dr John Faustus*. Marlowe's famous play on the subject appeared about 1588.

Bardolph describes the 'cozeners' as riding away 'like three German devils, three Doctor Faustuses' (*M.W.W.* iv, 5).

[Fawnia.] See PERDITA.

Fear. Personified. 'Thy angel becomes a Fear' (*Ant. Cl.* ii, 3; disputed); 'Night, mother of Dread and F.' (*Lucr.* 117); 'honest F... Doth too too oft betake him to retire' (*ib.* 175).

February. As a cold and stormy month. 'Such a F. face, So full of frost, of storm and cloudiness?' (*M. Ado*, v, 4).

Feeble, Francis. D.P. *2 Hen. IV*. 'A woman's tailor.' iii, 2] is taken as a recruit by Falstaff.

[Fengon.] See HORVENDILE.

Fenton. D.P. *M.W.W.* i, 4] seeks to enlist Mistress Quickly as an ally in his wooing of Anne Page. (iii, 2) Page objects to him, because although 'he speaks holiday' and 'smells April and May' he is a 'gentleman of no having,' and 'has kept company with the wild Prince and Poins.' iii, 4] Fenton admits to Anne that at first he wooed her for her father's wealth; but he now loves her for herself alone; he is rebuffed by Page; sends A. a ring, by Quickly. iv, 6] enlists the host's assistance in his scheme for secretly marrying Anne. v, 5] during the baiting of Falstaff by the 'fairies,' steals away with A.; returns with his bride; they are forgiven.

Gervinus, who considers that the period of the comedy is to be placed just before the death of Henry IV, sees in Fenton's reformation 'a counterpart in private life to the metamorphosis of the Prince himself' (*Sh. Comm.* (1875), p. 379). Fenton and Falstaff display no knowledge of each other; but they are never together on the stage – except in v, 5, which is irrelevant. 'Geffray Fenton' translated several books produced by Vautrollier, publisher of North's *Plutarch*, who was succeeded by Sh.'s friend T. Field, The name was also well known as that of Edward F. (*ob.* 1603), a noted navigator who sailed with Frobisher and served against the Armada.

[Ferando.] See PETRUCHIO.

Ferdinand (1). D.P. *L.L.L.* 'King of Navarre' (Rowe). i, 1] reminds his lords of their vow of asceticism, and combats Biron's objections; when reminded that 'the French King's daughter' is about to arrive 'in embassy,' admits that his decree prohibiting the approach of a woman to the Court must be suspended; characterizes Armado; deals with Ar.'s charge against Costard. ii, 1] welcomes the Princess; opens negotiations with her on affairs of state and apologizes for not admitting her within his gates. iv, 3] reads aloud (overheard by Biron) an ode expressing his love for the Princess, and drops it, in the hope it may reach her; steps aside upon the entrance of the lovesick

Longaville; listens also to Dumain as he reads, in supposed solitude, his ode to Maria; taxes both the lords with their 'guilty rimes,' but admits his own guilt when Biron 'steps forth to whip hypocrisy'; the discovery of B.'s letter to Rosaline having betrayed the writer, the King forgives him, but jestingly criticizes his lady's dark complexion. v, 2] together with his lords, all disguised as Muscovites, presents himself to the Princess and her ladies; mistakes the masked Rosaline for her mistress; on finding that they are 'drybeaten with pure scoff,' departs with his lords, soon to return in their proper habits; (after enduring the shafts of the ladies' wit, they discover how they have been deceived); witnesses the pageant of 'The Nine Worthies'; the Princess, hearing of her father's death, resolves on immediate departure; the King urges, 'Now, at the latest minute of the hour, grant us your loves,' but is condemned to wait 'a twelvemonth and a day.'

There is no king of Navarre of the name known in history; Monstrelet, however, relates (*Chronicles*, Johnes' transln. (1810), i, 108) that Charles, King of N., made a compact with France by which certain lands were exchanged on 200,000 crowns being paid to Navarre – a transaction resembling that mtd. (ii, 1).

Ferdinand (2). D.P. *Temp.* 'Son to the King of Naples' (F1). (ii, 1) when the King's ship is driven upon Prospero's island he swims ashore and is separated from his companions. i, 1] *p.m.* i, 2] led by Ariel's mysterious music to Pr.'s cell, he meets Miranda, and the two characters are henceforth associated. (iii, 3) mtd. See MIRANDA. In st. dir. i, 1, 'Ferdinando.'

Ferdinand (3). Mtd. by Petruchio as a 'cousin'; *Tam. Sh.* iv, 1.

Ferdinand V of Spain (II of Arragon and Sicily, III of Naples) (1452–1516). Mtd. by Queen Katharine: 'F. my father, King of Spain, was reckon'd one The wisest prince that there had reign'd by many A year before' (*Hen. VIII*, ii, 4; cf. *Hol.* iii, 907).

[**Fernandine.**] See JAQUES (4).

Ferrara. Former Duchy in the N.E. of Italy. One of the articles exhibited against Wolsey was that he had sent a commission to conclude a league between the King and the Duke of F. without Henry's knowledge (*Hol.* iii, 912; Hall, p. 767). The article quoted, *Hen. VIII*, iii, 2.

Ferrers, Baron. Sir W. Devereux, K.G., who married the heiress of the 6th Baron F. of Chartley. Mtd. as slain at Bosworth Field ('Ferris,' QqFf), *Rich. III*, v, 5. Cf. *Hol.* iii, 759, 'Walter lord Ferrers of Chartleie.'

Ferrers of Groby, Baron. See GREY, JOHN.

Feste. D.P. *T.Nt.* ('Clown' in prefixes). 'Clown, servant to Olivia' (Rowe); mtd. by name (iii, 4) as 'a fool that the Lady O.'s father took much delight in.' i, 5] exchanges banter with Maria; by permission, 'proves' his mistress 'a fool'; is scorned as 'a barren rascal' by Malvolio; discusses the stages of drunkenness. ii, 3] carouses with Sir Toby and Aguecheek; sings 'O mistress mine'; treats Malvolio with contempt. ii, 4] sings 'Come away, death,' before Orsino. iii, 1] jests with 'Cesario,' by whom he is sent with a message to Olivia. iv, 1] falls to cross-purposes with Sebastian, whom he mistakes for 'Cesario.' iv, 2] is disguised as 'Sir Topas,' and interrogates, in an assumed voice, Malvolio, who is in durance as a lunatic; on singing in his own voice, is appealed to by M. and consents to fetch him 'light and paper and ink.' v, 1] refuses to hand Fabian M.'s letter; gives Orsino a taste of his quality as jester; leads in Sir Toby, who is drunk and wounded; delivers M.'s letter to Olivia; begins to read it in an extravagant manner, but is checked; admits to the indignant M. that 'Sir Topas' was the erstwhile 'barren rascal' – thus 'the whirligig of time brings in his revenges.'

The name is perhaps from the It. *festeggiante* (C. C. Clarke).

'No other of Sh.'s fools is so conscious of his superiority as this one... He is fit for anything; he lives with each after his own fashion, knowing their weaknesses, considering their nature, carefully adapting himself to the mood of the moment.' (Gervinus, *Sh. Comm.* (1875), p. 438.) 'The contrast most fully worked out is that between the fool by profession and the involuntary fools, Malvolio, Sir Andrew, and Sir Toby. While the latter, in their own conceit and foolishness, unconsciously draw the cap and bells over their own ears, the former, in his self-adopted mental garb of motley colours, moves with inimitable adroitness, and pins the lappets of his wit to the back of all the other characters. (H. Ulrici, *Sh. Dram. Art*, ii, 7; cited by Furness, *Var.*)

Fidele. Name assumed by Imogen when disguised as a boy; *Cymb.* iii, 6. 'Thy name well fits thy faith; thy faith thy name' (*ib.* iv, 2); mtd., v, 5. See IMOGEN.

Field, Nathaniel (1587–1633). Actor and dramatist; mtd., as Nathan Field, in 'The Names of the Principall Actors' pfxd. to F1. There is a portrait of Field at Dulwich.

[**Field of the Cloth of Gold.**] See FRANCIS I.

Fiends. D.PP. *1 Hen. VI.* v, 3] they are summoned by Joan of Arc, who offers them her body and soul to help her, but they reply only by ominous gestures. See JOAN OF ARC.

Fiennes, James. Baron Say and Sele; *ob.* 1450; Lord Treasurer 1449; 'sequestered' for consenting to the cession of Anjou and Maine (*Hol.* iii, 632); accused of extortion, he was confined in the Tower, and handed over by the Governor to Jack Cade, who 'caused his head to be stricken off, and pitched it on a high pole,' which was carried before him through the streets. Cade next 'apprehended Sir James Cromer, then sheriffe of Kent, and sonne in law to the said Lord Saie; causing him likewise ... to be beheaded and his head fixed to a pole; and with these two heads this bloudie wretch entered into the city againe, and ... caused them in every street to kisse together' (*ib.* iii, 632).

D.P. *2 Hen. VI.* 'Lord Say.' iv, 4] the King warns him that Cade has sworn to have his head. iv, 7] is brought before C. and accused of 'giving up Normandy' and causing 'printing to be used'; argues in his own defence and pleads in vain for mercy; (he is treated as described above).

The allusion to printing is, of course, an anachronism.

Fife. District in Scotland, N. of the Firth of Forth. Acc. *Hol.* ii, 170, a Danish force landed at Kingcorne (Kinghorn in Fife). 'From F., great king, Where the Norweyan banners flout the sky' (*Macb.* i, 2); Macduff retires thither, *ib.* ii, 4.

Fife, Murdoch Stewart, Earl of (*ob.* 1425). He also had the title of E. of Menteith; taken prisoner by Hotspur at

Homildon, and delivered to Henry IV (*Hol.* ii, 254, and iii, 520). (Holinshed makes 'Menteith' another person, and Sh. follows him, *1 Hen. IV*, i, 1.) Murdoch S. was the son of Robert S., 1st D. of Albany and regent of Scotland, and not of Douglas, as would appear from: 'Of prisoners, Hotspur took Mordake the Earl of Fife, and eldest son To beaten Douglas' (*1 Hen. IV*, i, 1), Sh. having been misled by the faulty punctuation in *Hol.* iii, 520: 'M. Earl of F., son to the Governour[,] Archembald earle Douglas'; again, *Hen. IV*, i, 3, he is erroneously referred to as 'the Douglas' son.' 'One Mordake,' mtd. by Falstaff, *1 Hen. IV*, ii, 4; mtd. *ib.* iv, 4.

Fife, Thane of. Macduff (*q.v.*).

Finsbury. A London district, reclaimed from the marsh of Moorfields in the 16th cent. Pleasure fairs were held there, and booths for amusements and shows were erected.

Hotspur says to Lady Percy: 'you swear like a comfit-maker's wife ... And giv'st such sarcenet surety for thy oaths, As if thou never walk'dst further than F.' (*1 Hen. IV*, iii, 1; an anachronism).

Fire. Personified. 'At his [Henry V's] heels (Leash'd in like hounds) should Famine, Sword, and Fire Crouch for employment' (*Hen. V*, i, Chor.).

Mtd. as one of Bellona's handmaids in a speech attributed to Henry (*Hol.* iii, 567), the others being Famine and Blood.

Fish Street. In London; leading to St Magnus (*q.v.*). Cade cries, 'Up Fish-street! down St Magnus corner! ... throw them into the Thames' (*2 Hen. VI*, iv, 8).

Anciently known as Bridgestreete (Stow); one of the places authorized for the retail sale of fish.

[**Fitton, Mary.**] Maid of honour to Q. Elizabeth; mistress of William Herbert (*q.v.*), 3rd E. of Pembroke.

It has been conjectured that she was the 'dark lady' of Sh.'s sonnets. The discovery of two apparently well-authenticated portraits of Mary F. at Arbury, showing a lady of fair complexion and grey eyes, has dealt a severe blow to this theory. See Lady Newdegate-Newdigate's *Gossip from a Muniment Room* (1897).

Fitz-Alan, Thomas (1381–1415). E. of Arundel and Surrey; one of the first Knights of the Bath created by Henry IV; procured the execution of Scrope and Mowbray.

D.P. *2 Hen. IV*, iii, 1] enters with Warwick; *p.m.*

In 'The Actors Names,' F1, 'Surrey of the king's partie.'

Fitz-Alan, William. E. of Arundel and Surrey; *ob.* 1544; mtd. as 'the E. of Surrey,' *Hen. VIII*, iv, 1, in the coronation procession of Anne (Boleyn), bearing 'the rod of silver with the dove' (in *Hol.* iii,' 933, termed 'the earle of Arundell,' bearing the ivory dove).

Fitzgerald, Gerald. See KILDARE.

[**Fitz-James, Sir John** (*c.* 1470–*c.* 1542).] Mtd. as 'the King's attorney' (*Hen. VIII*, ii, 1, l. 15).

Fitzpeter, Geoffrey. Earl of Essex (*ob.* 1213); appointed Chief Justiciar by Richard I 1198; ennobled by John 1199.

D.P. *John.* i, 1] presents the disputants, Robt. Faulconbridge and his brother, to the King.

In *Tr. R.* Sheriff 'whispers the Earl of Sals, in the ear,' and as Essex speaks only three lines in *John*, i, 1, and does not reappear, Fleay has suggested that the name is introduced by mere inadvertence for 'Salisbury.' The name, however, appears in the st. dir. of i, 1, and Furness points out that 'Essex' did not fall into disgrace with Elizabeth until 1599, so there would be no reason for the omission of the character.

Fitz-Walter, Walter Fitz-Walter, 5th Baron (*c.* 1368–1407).

D.P. *Rich. II.* ('Fitzwater(s),' QqFf.) iv, 1] throws down his gage to Aumerle, whom he accuses of boasting of having caused Gloucester's death; passionately gives the lie to Surrey, who supports Aumerle (*Hol.* iii, 512). v, 6] announces that he has sent the heads of two traitors to London.

The pronunciation of 'Walter' as 'Water' is illustrated *2 Hen. VI*, iv, 1. Surrey calls him 'boy' (*Rich. II*, iv, 1), but he was thirty-one at the time.

[**Fitzwilliam, Thomas.**] The Recorder who rehearsed Buckingham's speech to the citizens; *Rich, III*, iii, 7.

'A sad man, and an honest, which was so new come into that office, that he never had spoken to the people before' (*Hol.* iii, 730).

Flaminius. D.P. *Timon.* Servant to Timon. ii, 2] is sent by T. to borrow money from Lucullus. iii, 1] is welcomed by L., who thinks he bears a gift; L. on learning the truth tries to bribe him, but Fl. throws down the money, and (*sol.*) invokes curses on L. as a false friend. iii, 4] tries to prevent his master from meeting the creditors' messengers.

In ii, 2, l. 185, Ff read 'Flavius,' and he is unnamed in the st. dir.

Fleay, *N.S.S. Tr.*, 1874, Pt. I, p. 147, points out that Flaminius and Servilius only appear in parts of the play which he holds to be non-Shakespearean. Wright (Camb. edn.) remarks that Fl. and Ser. may be regarded rather as gentlemen-in-waiting than menials.

Flanders. An ancient countship, now divided between Belgium, France, and Holland, Edward IV is urged to flee 'To Lynn, ... and ship from thence to Flanders' (*3 Hen. VI*, iv, 5; cf. *Hol.* iii, 675); Wolsey is accused of having secretly taken the Great Seal with him to F., *Hen. VIII*, iii, 2 (*Hol.* iii, 912).

Flavins (1). A tribune, who, with his colleague Marullus (*Plut.* p. 96), pulled down the crowned images of Caesar which had been set up in Rome, and committed to prison those who saluted Caesar as king. They were accordingly deprived of their tribuneships.

D.P. *Jul. C.* i, 1] bids the 'commoners,' who are making holiday, go to their homes; and proposes to 'disrobe the images.' (i, 2) Mar. and Fl. 'for pulling scarfs off Caesar's images, are put to silence.' See MARULLUS.

Flavius (2). Acc. *Plut.* p. 150, 'captain of the pioners' to Brutus.

D.P. *Jul. C.* v, 3] *p.m.* ('Flavio,' F1); is addressed by Brutus. v, 4] *p.m.* (mtd. in st. dirs. of Ff).

Flavius (3). An officer urgently summoned by the Duke; *M. for M.* iv, 5.

Flavius (4). D.P. *Timon.* Steward to T. i, 2] is dismayed at his lord's profusion. ii, 2] Timon demands of him the cause of his creditors' clamorous demands; Fl. lays bare the desperate state of T.'s finances, and warns him that it is useless to rely upon his friends. iii, 4] scorns the creditors' servants; is amazed at being told to 'let in the tide of knaves once more.' iv, 2] shares the last of his wealth among his fellow-servants; moralizes on T.'s strange fate – 'undone by goodness.' iv, 3] visits his master in the woods; is at first repudiated, but soon acknowledged as the 'one honest man,' yet 'more honest than wise'; is offered gold, and bidden to flee ere T. curses him. v, 2] conducts two senators to T.'s cave.

'Steward' (*q.v.*) in Ff, where (ii, 2) 'Flavius' occurs, in error, for 'Flaminius' (*q.v.*). 'Laches' in the anonymous *Timon*.

Fleance. A fictitious ancestor of the house of Stewart; Holinshed (ii, 172), following Boece, makes him son of Banquo, and relates that he escaped when, with his father, he was murderously attacked on returning from a supper at Macbeth's castle, and 'fled to Wales to avoid further peril.'

D.P. *Macb.* ii, 1] in attendance on Banquo. (iii, 1, 2) mtd. iii, 3] *p.m.*; escapes from the assassins. (iii, 4) his escape reported to Macbeth. (iii, 6) Lennox ironically suggests that he killed his father.

Fleet, The. Ancient prison in London, formerly standing on the E. side of the Fleet Brook; destroyed in the Great Fire, rebuilt, but demolished in 1846. A debtors' prison as early as 1290, and used for political offenders until 1641.

Falstaff and his companions committed to the Fl., *2 Hen. IV*, v, 5.

Fleming. An inhabitant of Flanders (*q.v.*). 'I will rather trust a F. with my butter [not in Qq], ... than my wife with herself' (*M.W.W.* ii, 2). *Cf.* 'half stewed in grease, like a Dutch dish' (*ib.* iii, 5). ('They [fasting days] are of a Flemish breed ... for they raven up more butter than all the days of the week beside' (*Every Man in his Humour*, iii, 2).)

Flemish. Pertaining to Flanders. Mistress Page speaks of Falstaff as 'a Flemish drunkard' (*M.W.W.* ii, 1). Elizabethan Englishmen accused the folk of the Low Countries of having taught them habits of drinking to excess; *cf.* Sir John Smythe, *Discourses* (1590).

The noted traveller Fynes Moryson (1566–1630) declared that 'In our time some ... Commanders from the warres of Netherland brought in the custome of the Germans large garaussing [carousing].' See *Sh. Eng.* i, 16.

Flibbertigibbet. ('Fliberdegibek,' Q1.) A fiend mtd. by Edgar. 'He begins at curfew, and walks at first cock; he gives the web and the pin,' etc. (*Lear*, iii, 4). See STIBERDIGEBIT.

'Fleberdigibet' was one of the 'foure deuils of the round, or Morrice' (S. Harsnet, *Declaration of Egregious Popish Impostures* (1603), p. 49). Cotgrave, *Dictionarie* (1611), gives: '*Coquette:* a pratling, or proud gossip, a titifill, a fiebergebit' (*N.E.D.*).

Flint. Sea-port on the estuary of the R. Dee; the castle was built by Edward I.

Acc. *Hol.* iii, 499, Richard II, on reaching Wales from Ireland, 'got him to the castell of Conwaie,' but in the marginal note it is stated that he 'stealeth awaie from his armie and taketh the castell of Flint.' The date of his arrival at Flint Castle is given as 'mondaie, the eighteenth of August 1399' and it is further stated that on the following day Bolingbroke led his forces to Flint. The narrative of the Frenchman Creton, who was in Richard's train, states that Richard was decoyed from Conway to Flint and fell into an ambush on the way (*Archaeologia*, xx, 129–149). But as to whether the meeting of Richard and Bolingbroke took place at Conway or Flint the chroniclers differ, the Monk of Evesham giving the former.

'*K. Rich.* Go to Flint Castle: there I'll pine away' (*Rich. II*, iii, 2); the meeting of Richard and Bolingbroke takes place at Fl., *ib.* iii, 3.

Flora. Roman goddess of spring and flowers; *cf.* Ovid, *Fasti*, v, 183 ff. 'No shepherdess, but Fl. Peering in April's front' (*Wint. T.* iv, 4). *Cf.* 'Shee seemed to be the goddesse Fl. her selfe for beauty' (*Pandosto*).

Florence. Capital of Tuscany. For 'Duke of Florence': *All's Well*, i, 2. Mtd., *ib.* iii, 2; iv, 3 (2); v, 3 (2). 'Vincentio's son, brought up in Fl.' (*Tam. Sh.* i, 1); 'I have bills ... by exchange from Fl.' (*ib.* iv, 2). 'Marcus Luccicos ... in Fl.' (*Oth.* i, 3).

Florence, Duke of. D.P. *All's Well*, iii, 1] marvels that 'our cousin France' will not give aid. iii, 3] appoints Bertram 'general of our horse.' (iv, 3) mtd.

'The only dispensable personage' (K. Elze, *Essays on Sh.* (1874), p. 144).

Florentine. (a) A native of Florence. 'The F.s and Senoys' (*All's Well*, i, 2); 'a troop of F.s' (*ib.* iii, 6); mtd., *ib.* v, 3 (2); (Claudio) 'a young F.' (*M. Ado*, i, 1); 'some F.' (*Tam. Sh.* i, 1); (Cassio) 'a F.' (*Oth.* i, 1); 'a F. [not Iago]' (*ib.* iii, 1).

(*b*) Duke of Florence. *All's Well*, i, 2; iv, 1, 3.

Florentius. 'Be she as foul as was F.'s love' (*Tam. Sh.* i, 2); referring to Florent, a young knight who bound himself to marry 'a lothly wommanysh figure,' on condition that she gave him the key of a riddle, on the solution of which his life depended (Gower, *Conf. Amant.* i, 1407–1861).

[Florio, John (*c.* 1553–1625).] Author of *The Worlde of Wordes*, an Italian-English Dictionary (1598); translator of Montaigne's *Essaies* (1603); supposed by Warburton, Farmer, and Steevens to be the original of Holofernes (*q.v.*). This theory has, however, been strongly opposed by Malone and other critics, since Florio was a *protégé* of Southampton's. See MONTAIGNE.

Florizel. D.P. *Wint. T.* Only son to Polixenes, King of Bohemia; at the opening of the play some four years old. (i, 2) his father's love for him described; (sixteen years elapse). (iv, Chor.) named. (iv, 1) his amour suspected. (iv, 2) mtd. iv, 3] woos Perdita, supposed daughter of a shepherd, in the name of Doricles, but reveals his identity to her and declares that his royal birth shall be no obstacle to their union; is enchanted by her grace as hostess of the day, and dances with her; in the presence of Polixenes (who is disguised) plights his troth to Perdita, but insists that their nuptials must be kept secret from his father; Polixenes, revealing himself, denounces him, and declares that his son shall be debarred from succession if he persists in his intention; after his father's departure, Fl. resolves to flee with Perdita, and is persuaded by the old courtier Camillo to sail for Sicily; exchanges attire with Autolycus and hastens to the seashore. v, 1] reaching Sicily, presents Perdita to Leontes, the King, and avers that she is a Libyan princess; learns that Polixenes has also arrived in

Sicily, and fears that Camillo has betrayed them; bids Perdita be of good cheer. (v, 2) P.'s identity as the lost daughter of Leontes is discovered. v, 3] *p.m.*; is present at the reunion of Leontes and his queen and is declared by the King trothplight to Perdita, heiress of Sicily.

The equivalent character in Greene's *Pandosto* is Dorastus, who, on landing in Bohemia, styles himself Meleagrus 'a gentleman of Trapalonia,' and is imprisoned by the King until, on the arrival of ambassadors from Sicily, the truth comes out. 'Don Florisel' is the hero of the ninth book of the *Amadis* romances (attributed to Don Feliciano de Silva, Burgos, 1535); as a shepherd he woos a princess disguised as a shepherdess. No English version of this is known, but a French version by C. Colet (1564), with woodcuts, is extant.

Fluellen. D.P. *Hen. V.* 'An officer in King Henry's army.' iii, 2] is sent for 'to the mines'; expresses his disapproval of their construction, as 'not according to the disciplines of the wars,' and declares that their director, Macmorris, 'is an ass'; on M.'s entrance, disputes with him, and they are coming to blows when 'the town sounds a parley.' iii, 6] commends the Duke of Exeter's bravery 'at the pridge'; listens to Pistol's plea on Bardolph's behalf, but replies that 'discipline ought to be used'; is enlightened as to Pistol's character; reports Exeter's gallant deeds to the King. iv, 1] (before Agincourt) rebukes Gower for unduly raising his voice. iv, 7] (after Agincourt) draws a parallel between Henry and Alexander the Great; congratulates the King on his Welsh blood; declares that Williams will be a craven if he does not strike, according to his vow, the man whom he sees with his glove in his cap; on W.'s departure, Fl. is given a glove, to stick in his own cap, which Henry declares is Alençon's, and adds that if any man challenge it he is 'an enemy to our person.' iv, 8] Fl. meets Williams, who, seeing the glove, forthwith strikes him; Fl. exclaims that W. is a traitor, and prepares to apprehend him, when the King enters and the jest is unfolded; Fl. offers W. a shilling 'to mend his shoes'; glories in the overthrow of the enemy, but when reproved by Henry acknowledges that God 'did us great good.' v, 1] makes Pistol eat the leek he had derided.

'Fluellen' ('Flewellen,' Qq), equivalent to the Welsh 'Llewelyn,' was a Stratford name; William Fluellan (as well as John Shackspere and George Bardolfe) appears as 'a recusant,' and 'not coming to church,' in 1592, acc. the Commissioners' Certificate. Anne Fl. was also a contemporary (French, p. 328). *Cf.* Carter, *Sh.: Puritan and Recusant*, p. 163.

Flute, Francis. Bellows-mender. D.P. *M.N.D.* i, 2] is allotted the part of Thisbe in the Interlude, though he has 'a beard coming.' iii, 1] rehearses his part. iv, 2] laments Bottom's disappearance. v, 1] enacts his part. (In error, for 'Snout,' 1. 157, Qq.)

'In Ben Jonson's *Masque of Pan's Anniversary* a man of the same profession is introduced' (Steevens). Furness, *Var.*, points out that there is no ground for Steevens' conjecture that the bellows of organs are especially alluded to.

Foix, Earl of. ('Loys,' 'Foyes,' Ff.) Slain at Agincourt. *Hen. V*, iii, 5; iv, 8. (*Hol.* iii, 555, 'Fois'; the present form is due to Capell.)

Fontibell. Fem. name; *All's Well*, iv, 2.

Fool (1). D.P. *Lear.* i, 4] ('hath much pined away' since Cordelia went to France); is greeted by Lear as 'my pretty knave'; jests keenly on L.'s folly in giving away his realm; is termed by Goneril 'your alllicens'd fool'; lingering after L.'s departure, is bidden by Gon. to follow him. i, 5] attemps to amuse L., who pays but little heed to his jests. ii, 4] converses sententiously with Kent, who is in the stocks. iii, 2] with Lear in the storm; exclaims, 'In; ask thy daughter's blessing; here's a night pities neither wise men nor fools'; L. asks tenderly, 'How dost, my boy? Art cold?'; 'speaks a prophecy.' iii, 4] is terrified by finding 'Poor Tom' in the hovel, but is reassured by Kent, who gives him his hand; checks L. who is throwing off his clothes – 'Nuncle, 'tis a naughty night to swim in!' iii, 6] present at L.'s imaginary trial of his daughters; his last words are: 'And I'll go to bed at noon.' (The meaning of L.'s cry, 'And my poor fool is hang'd!' (v, 3) is disputed; it may, or may not, refer to Cordelia; see Furness, *Var.* pp. 345–7.)

Critics have differed profoundly as to the age and personal characteristics of the Fool. There seems, however, to be much justice in the view which regards him as young, sensitive, timid, loyal, and loving. Macready (*Diaries*, Jan. 5–6, 1838) notes, with regard to the part: 'I have no hope of it, and think that at the last we shall be obliged to dispense with it. ... Bartley observed that a woman should play it. I caught at the idea, and instantly exclaimed: "Miss P. Horton is the very person!" '

'The most noteworthy point in him, and the real key to his character, lies in that, while his heart is slowly breaking, he never speaks, nor even appears so much as even to think, of his own suffering. He seems, indeed, quite unconscious of it. His anguish is purely the anguish of sympathy.' (Hudson, *The Tragedy of King Lear* (1879).)

'[The Fool's] well-timed levity comes in to break the continuity of feeling when it can no longer be borne, and to bring into play again the fibres of the heart just as they are growing rigid from overstrained excitement' (W. Hazlitt).

Fool (2). D.P. *Timon.* ii, 2] his professional banter of the creditors' servants pleases Apemantus.

'The fool in this play is a very obscure and insignificant character. Dr Johnson's conjecture that he belongs to one of Alcibiades's mistresses is extremely probable.' (Douce, *Ill. Sh.* ii, 73.) The passage is regarded as non-Shakespearean (*N.S.S.Tr.*, 1874, p. 132).

Ford. D.P. *M.W.W.* A gentleman dwelling at Windsor (called 'Frank' by his wife). ii, 1] is told by Pistol that Falstaff is in love with Mrs Ford; has his suspicions, notwithstanding Pistol's character; decides to visit Falstaff in the name of 'Brook' (*q.v.*). ii, 2] as 'Brook,' bribes Falstaff to 'lay an amiable siege' to Mrs Ford; (*sol.*) vows to detect his wife and 'be revenged on Fal.' iii, 2] meets Mrs Page with Falstaff's page; bids his friends come and dine with him, and he will show them 'a monster.' iii, 3] fails to find Falstaff in his house, and is rebuked for his jealousy. iii, 5] Fal. has another visit from 'Brook,' who learns that Fal. escaped in a basket. iv, 2] again fails to detect Fal., and is jeered for his suspicions, but beats 'Mother Prat,' who is Fal. in disguise. iv, 4] (has been informed of the trick played on him); Fal. repents of his jealousy. v, 1] Fal. tells 'B.' that he 'shall see wonders' in the park that night. v, 5] derides Falstaff; demands the return of his money; in the end forgives him.

The name is found in the records of both Stratford and Windsor in the 16th cent. (Halliwell).

Ford, Mistress. D.P. *M.W.W.* (Named 'Alice,' ii, 1.) i, 1] *p.m.*; is saluted by Falstaff. ii, 1] discusses with Mrs Page the (identical) letters they have received from Fal.; resolves to discomfit him, but plans to punish at the same time her husband for his baseless jealousy. (ii, 2) Quickly declares that 'the sweet woman leads an ill life with' Ford; the latter takes steps to test her fidelity. iii, 3] in concert with Mrs P. she encourages Fal.; is interrupted by Mrs P. and they pack off the panic-stricken knight in a buck-basket; Mrs F. knows not 'which pleases her better, that her husband is deceived, or Sir John.' iv, 2] again receives Fal., and after terrifying him persuades him to escape in disguise as 'the fat woman of Brentford'; lays a trap for her husband in the shape of another buck-basket, and rejoices in giving him a lesson. iv, 4] contrives with the others a public discomfiture for Falstaff. v, 3] on the way to the park. v, 5] plays her part in befooling Sir John.

[**Fordham, John.**] Bp. of Durham 1382; transferred to Ely 1388; *ob.* 1425.

D.P. *Hen. V.* 'Bp. of Ely.' i, 1] converses with Abp. Chichele (*q.v.*), on the advisability of urging the King to make war on France. i, 2] encourages Henry to emulate the gallant deeds of his ancestors.

There are no historical grounds for thus associating him with the Abp.

Fores, Forres. A town 12 m. W. of Elgin. Acc. Holinshed (ii, 149), King Duff was bewitched 'by a sort of witches dwelling in a towne of Murrey land, called F.'; Macbeth and Banquo met the three strange women as they journeyed toward F. (ii, 170); Duff was murdered at F. Castle (ii, 150).

Mtd. *Macb.* i, 3. The following scenes of the play are laid by various edrs. at, or near, F.: i, 1, 2, 3; iii, 1, 2, 3, 4. ('Soris,' i, 3, Ff.)

Forester, A. D.P. *L.L.L.* iv, 1] points out to the Princess 'a stand' where she 'may make the fairest shoot'; is sorely perplexed by her wilful misunderstanding of his remarks.

[**Forres.**] See FORES.

Forrest, Miles. One of the murderers of the two Princes in the Tower, 'one of the foure that kept them, a fellow fleshed in murther before time' (*Hol.* iii, 735). More (*Workes*, p. 69) relates of him that he subsequently 'pecemele rotted away.' His account of the murder quoted by Tyrrel, *Rich. III*, iv, 3.

Forthright. 'The tilter'; prisoner for debt, *M. for M.* iv, 3. ('Forthlight,' Ff.)

Fortinbras (1). King of Norway. Slain in single combat by Hamlet, King of Denmark, and thereby forfeited his lands to the victor; *Haml.* i, 1.

In *The Hystorie of Hamblet*, Collere, King of Norway, is thus slain by Horvendile.

Fortinbras (2). D.P. *Haml.* Prince of Norway, son of the preceding. (i, 1) prepares to recover by force the lands lost by his father, (i, 2) having already 'pestered' Claudius for them, (ii, 2) is checked by his uncle, Norway, and sets out against 'the Polack.' iv, 4] asks leave to pass through Denmark. (v, 1) mtd. v, 2] finds Hamlet, his mother, and his uncle slain; gives orders for their obsequies; announces his rights in Denmark.

Fortune. Often, as by the Romans, personified in *Sh.* as a divinity, her emblem being a wheel, symbolical of vicissitude. The personification is often indistinct, but in the following instances is explicit. The explanation of F. being called 'a housewife,' as in three examples below, seems to be that the latter word had come to be used opprobriously (usually in the form 'hussy') for a loose and fickle wench.

'Let me rail so high That the false housewife F. break her wheel' (*Ant. Cl.* iv, 15); '*Pist.* Doth F. play the huswife with me now?' (*Hen. V*, v, 1); '*Cel.* Let us sit and mock the good housewife F. from her wheel, that her gifts may henceforth be bestowed equally. *Ros.* ... the bountiful blind woman doth most mistake in her gifts to women' (*A.Y.L.* i, 2); 'Rail'd on Lady F. in good terms' (*ib.* ii, 7); 'F., she said, was no goddess' (*All's Well*, i, 3); 'Well, if F. be a woman, she's a good wench for this year' (*M.V.* ii, 2); 'Oh, giglet F.!' (*Cymb.* iii, 1); 'F., that arrant whore, Ne'er turns the key to the poor' (*Lear*, ii, 4); 'F., on his damned quarrel smiling, showed like a rebel's whore' (*Macb.* i, 2); 'O Lady F.' (*Wint. T.* iv, 4); 'ordered by Lady F.' (*Per.* iv, 4); 'On F.'s cap we are not the very button,' etc. (*Haml.* ii, 2); 'Out, thou strumpet, F.! All you gods ... break all the spokes and fellies from her wheel, And bowl the round nave down from the hill of heaven' (*ib. ib.*); the Painter and the Poet discuss the representation of F. by their respective arts, *Timon*, i, 1; 'a slave, whom F.'s tender arm With favour never clasp'd' (*ib.* iv, 3); 'Now the fair goddess, F., fall deep in love with thee' (*Cor.* i, 5); '*Pist.* Giddy F.'s furious, fickle wheel, that goddess blind, that stands upon the rolling, restless stone – – *Flu.* ... F. is painted blind, with a muffler before her eyes, to signify to you that F. is blind; and she is painted also with a wheel, to signify ... that she is turning, and inconstant, and mutability, and variation; and her foot ... is fixed upon a spherical stone, which rolls' (*Hen. V*, iii, 6); 'When F. means to men most good, She looks upon them with a threatening eye' (*John*, iii, 4, l. 119); 'her humorous ladyship' (*ib.* iii, 1, l. 119). Characterized, 2 *Hen. IV*, iv, 4, ll. 103 ff.

'Love and F. be my gods' (*Lucr.* 351); 'F.'s wheel' (*ib.* 952); *Son*, cxi, cxxiv; *P.P.* xviii, xxi (2).

For F.'s wheel *cf.* Ovid, *Pont.* ii, 3, 56; Chaucer, *Fortune*, l. 46; Gower, *Conf. Amant.* i, 2624. For her blindness *cf.* Pliny, *Nat. Hist.* II, v, 7.

Foyes. See FOIX.

France, Country of. Includes, in the Histories, portions held from time to time by England. The word frequently denotes 'King of F.,' but in many cases the ruler and his realm can scarcely be discriminated.

(*a*) In the Comedies:

Falstaff, flattering Mrs Ford, exclaims, 'Let the Court of F. show me such another' (*M.W.W.* iii, 3); jealousy is 'no de fashion of F.' (*ib. ib.*). Mtd. indefinitely, in connection with the 'Princess of France' (D.P.), *L.L.L.* ii, 1 (2); iv, 1 (3), 3; v, 2. 'He bought ... his round hose in F.' (*M.V.* i, 2); 'the stubbornest young fellow of F.' (*A.Y.L.* i, 1); 'royal blood of F.' (*All's Well*, ii, 1); 'F. is a dog-hole ... F. is a stable' (*ib.* ii, 3); mtd., *ib.* iii, 2, 5 (2), iv, 3 (4), 5, v, 1. In *Com. Err.* iii, 2, where the kitchen-wench is compared to a globe, F. stands 'in her forehead; arm'd and reverted, making war against her heir' – an allusion, it is believed, to the War of the League (1589–93).

(*b*) In the Histories:

John: mtd., i, 1 (6), ii, 1 (10), 2 (12), iii, 1 (12), iv, 1, 2 (3), 3; 'prince of F.' (v, 2).

Rich. II: Mowbray in F., i, 1; Richard's queen flees to F., v, 1.

1 Hen. IV: mtd., iii, 2.

2 Hen. IV: an attack on F. contemplated, v, 5; 'Katharine of F.' (Epil.).

Hen. V: 'the vasty fields of F.' (i, Chor.); mtd., i, 1 (2); Henry determines to invade F., i, 2; mtd., ii, Chor. (2), 1 (2); Henry sails for F., ii, 2; mtd., ii, 3; Henry lays claim to the crown of F.' ii, 4; mtd., iii, Chor.; 'les seigneurs de F.' (iii, 4); mtd., iii, 5 (3), 6, 7, iv, 1, 2, 3 (3), 7 (2), 8 (4), v, Chor. (2); 'malady of F.' (v, 1); 'fertile F.' (v, 2); mtd., *ib.* (13), Epil.

1 Hen. VI: mtd., i, 1 (6), 2, 4, 6 (4), ii, 1, 2 (2); Talbot, 'the scourge of F.' (ii, 3); Henry to be 'crown'd in F.' (iii, 1); mtd., *ib.*; 'base muleteers of F.' (iii, 2); mtd., *ib.* (5); 'fertile F.,' 'the pining malady of F.' (iii, 3); mtd., *ib.* (6), iii, 4, iv, 1 (4), 3 (4), 4, 5; 'rage of F.,' 'peasant boys of F.' (iv, 6); mtd., iv, 7 (3), v, 1 (3), 2 (2), 3 (5), 4 (2), 5 (2).

2 Hen. VI: 'F., his [Henry V's] true inheritance,' 'monuments of conquer'd F.,' 'F. will be lost ere long' (i, 1); mtd., i, 1 (2), 3 (4), ii, 2, iii, 1 (8), 2, iv, 1 (2), 7 (3), 8 (3); 'the fleur-de-luce of F.' (v, 1).

3 Hen. VI: mtd., i, 1 (2); 'many a battle have I won in F.' (i, 2); 'she-wolf of F., but worse than wolves in F.' (i, 4); mtd., ii, 2 (2), 6 (2), iii, 1, 3 (9); ' 'tis better using F. than trusting F.' (iv, 1); mtd., iv, 1 (4), 6, v, 2, 4, 7 (2).

Rich. III: 'I'll win our ancient right in F. again' (iii, 1); mtd., iii, 5, 7 (3), iv, 4 (2); 'these overweening rags of F. [Richmond's troops]' (v, 3).

Hen. VIII: mtd., i, 1 (4), 2 (2); 'the spells of F. should juggle Men into such strange mysteries [new fashions],' 'remnants Of fool and feather that they got in F.' (i, 3).

(*c*) In the Tragedies :

Cymb.: mtd., i, 5 (3), 7.

Lear (besides when meaning 'King of F.'): mtd., i, 1 (3), 4; iii, 1 (2), 5, 7 (2); iv, 3 (2), 7.

Haml.: mtd., i, 2 (2), 3; iv, 5; v, 2.

France, King of (1). D.P. *All's Well.* (i, 1) he suffers from a seemingly incurable malady. i, 2] refuses aid to the Florentines, but permits his gentlemen to volunteer in their service; welcomes Bertram to Court, and eulogizes his late father; laments the death of the famous physician Gerard. ii, 1] bids farewell to the lords proceeding to the war; is with difficulty persuaded by Helena to try her father's remedy, but only on condition that she forfeits her life if it fails, and that she shall have the husband of her choice if it succeeds. ii, 3] (he is cured); confirms Helena's choice of Bertram as her husband; severely censures B.'s unwillingness to marry her, and commands him to take her; promises to ennoble and enrich Helena. v, 3] laments the (supposed) death of Helena; pardons Bertram, and sanctions his marriage to Lafeu's daughter; recognizes on B.'s finger a ring he had given to Helena, and takes it back, adding that she had promised either to give it freely to B., as her husband, or send it to the King 'upon her great disaster'; reads a petition from Diana Capulet, craving redress for the (alleged) wrong Bertram had done her; is perplexed by Diana's declaring that the ring was hers; on Helena's entrance all is made plain; the King speaks the Epilogue.

France, King of (2). D.P. *Lear.* i, 1] on learning that the D. of Burgundy declines to wed Cordelia without a dowry, eagerly claims her as his queen. (i, 2) departs with her, 'in choler.' (iii, 1) prepares to invade Britain. (iv, 3) having led an army into Britain, returns to France on hearing of dangers at home, leaving his forces under a Marshal.

In *Hol.* i, 12, 'one of the princes of Gallia ... whose name was Aganippus' (so also in Percy's *Reliques*); in *The Faerie Queene*, Bk. II, 'Aganip of Celtia'; in *King Leir* 'the Gallian King' is unnamed.

Frances. See FRANCIS (1).

Francia. *Lat.* France. 'Et haeres Franciae' (*Hen. V*, v, 2).

Francis (1). As a forename. 'F. Seacole' (*M. Ado*, iii, 5); 'F. Flute' (*M.N.D.* i, 2); 'F. Quoint' (*Rich. II*, ii, 1); 'F. Pickbone' (2 *Hen. IV*, iii, 2); 'F. Feeble' (*ib. ib.*); 'O marry me to one F.' (Costard, misinterpreting the meaning of 'infranchise') (*L.L.L.* iii, 1; Capell changed this to 'Frances'). See FRANK.

Francis (2). D.P. *1 Hen. IV.* A drawer at the (Boar's Head) tavern. ii, 4] is bewildered by the conflicting demands of Prince Henry and Poins.

[**Francis I** (1494–1547).] King of France. His meeting with Henry VIII at the Field of the Cloth of Gold (1530) described, *Hen. VIII*, i, 1; attaches the goods of English merchants, *ib. ib.* (*Hol.* iii, 872).

Francis, Friar. D.P. *M. Ado.* iv, 1] prepares to solemnize the marriage of Claudio and Hero, but is bidden to stand aside by Cl.; on H.'s recovery from her swoon, after the departure of her accusers, Friar F. asserts his firm belief in her innocence; suggests that it shall be published 'that she is dead indeed,' and predicts that Cl. will be overcome with remorse. v, 4] is present to officiate at the wedding of Cl. to the masked bride, and promises later to 'tell you largely of fair Hero's death.' ('A Friar,' st. dirs. and pfxs.)

Francis, St, of Assisi (1182–1226). Italian monk, founder of the order of the Franciscans. Invoked by Friar Laurence (a 'holy Franciscan friar,' *Rom. J.* v, 2), *Rom. J.* ii, 3; v, 3.

Francis, The St. Name of hostel for pilgrims, at Florence; *All's Well*, iii, 5.

Francisca. D.P. *M. for M.* A nun. i, 5] explains the rules of the sisterhood to Isabella.

Francisco (1). D.P. *Temp.* Lord in attendance on Alonso, King of Naples; shipwrecked with him. ii, 1] attempts to reassure the King as to his son's safety by describing the vigour of his swimming. iii, 3] witnesses the magical banquet. v, 1] *p.m.*

H. Staunton has suggested (*Athenæum*, Nov. 16, 1872) that Fr. is Antonio's son, alluded to by Ferdinand (i, 2).

Francisco (2). '*Host* [to Dr Caius]. Is he dead, my Fr. ?' (*M.W.W.* ii, 3).

In Q, 'Françoyes,' i.e. Frenchman.

Francisco (3). D.P. *Haml.* A soldier. i, 1] is relieved at his post by Bernardo.

'A sentinel,' Q1.

François. *Fr.* French language. 'Le F. que vous parlez' (*Hen. V*, v, 2).

[Franion.] See CAMILLO.

Frank. As a forename. Mistress Ford addresses her husband as 'sweet F.' (*M.W.W.* ii, 1).

Frankfort. Frankfurt-am-Main, city in Hesse-Nassau; the fairs held there in the 16th cent. were among the most important in Europe; it was a great centre of Jewish commercial activity.

'A diamond gone, cost me [Shylock] two thousand ducats in F.' (*M.V.* iii, 1).

Frateretto. Name of a fiend. 'F. calls me' (*Lear*, iii, 6).

Fr. was one of the 'four deuils of the round, or Morrice, whom Sara in her fits, tuned together, in measure and sweet cadence' (Harsnet, p. 49).

Frederick (1). D.P. *A.Y.L.* 'Brother to the Duke, and usurper of his dukedom' (Rowe). i, 2] urges his niece and daughter to dissuade Orlando from encountering Charles, the wrestler; is displeased on learning Or.'s parentage. i, 3] mistrusts Rosalind and commands her to leave the Court within ten days, ii, 2] learns of the flight of R. and Celia. iii, 1] hears of Or.'s flight, and orders Oliver to bring his brother back, living or dead, within a twelvemonth. (v, 4) whilst leading 'a mighty power' against the rightful Duke, is converted 'both from his enterprise and from the world,' and yields up the dukedom. See DUKE SENIOR.

Torismond, the equivalent character in Lodge's *Rosalynde*, is slain in battle.

Frederick (2). 'The great soldier'; brother of Mariana (D.P. *M. for M.*), lost at sea; *M. for M.* iii, 1 (2).

Free-town. Villafranca, a town in the province of Verona, about 10 m. from the city. 'Old F., our common judgment place' (*Rom. J.* i, 1).

It is noteworthy that whereas it appears as Villa Franca in Painter's *Palace of Pleasure* (1567), it is Freetown in A. Brooke's *Romeus and Juliet* (1562).

French. (*a*) French language. 'The English baron knows neither Latin, F., nor Italian' (*M.V.* i, 2); 'speak it in F.' (*Rich. II*, v, 3); 'the chopping F.' (*ib. ib.*); 'ask me this slave in F.' (*Hen. V*, iv, 4); 'the F. for fer' (*ib. ib.*); mtd., *ib.* v, 5 (5); 'he can speak F., and therefore he is a traitor' (2 *Hen. VI*, iv, 2).

(*b*) People of France. 'Our F. lack language to deny' (*All's Well*, ii, 1); 'boys of ice ... the F. ne'er got them' (*ib.* ii, 3); 'Italian or F.' (*ib.* iv, 1); 'I've served against the F.' (*Haml.* iv, 7). Mtd. in the historical plays, *passim.*

Frenchman. (*a*) *Sing. M.W.W.* ii, 1; *M. Ado*, iii, 2; *M.V.* i, 2, ii, 8; *All's Well*, iii, 5, iv, 3, 5; *Hen. V*, i, 1; *1 Hen. VI*, iii, 3, iv, 7; 2 *Hen. VI*, iv, 8; *Cymb.* i, 7 (2); *Haml.* iv, 7. (In no case qualified by an adj.)

(*b*) *Plu.* 'Worthy Frenchmen' (*All's Well*, ii, 1); 'dastard F.' (*1 Hen. VI*, i, 4). Mtd., *All's Well*, iv, 2; *John*, ii, 1, 2; *Hen. V*, iii, 6; *1 Hen. VI*, i, 4 (2), ii, 1, 2, iv, 6, 7 (2), v, 3, 4, 5; 2 *Hen. VI*, i, 1, iv, 2.

Frenchmen, Two. D.PP. *All's Well.* iii, 1] offer their services to the Duke of Florence.

Frenchwoman. 'Proud F.' (2 *Hen. VI*, i, 3); 'false F.' (*3 Hen. VI*, i, 4).

In each case Q. Margaret.

Friday. (As a fast-day.) 'The Duke ... would eat mutton F.s' (*M. for M.* iii, 2); '*Ros.* Yes, faith, will I [love thee] F.s, Saturdays and all' (*A.Y.L.* iv, 1); 'She [Cressida] would be as fair on F. as Helen is on Sunday' (*Tr. Cr.* i, 1).

See also GOOD FRIDAY.

Frith, Mary. See MALL.

Frogmore. A farm-house, or perhaps a hamlet, in Sh.'s time, near Windsor. 'In a field near F.' Sir Hugh Evans waited for his adversary Dr Caius; and in a neighbouring farm-house was Anne Page 'a feasting' (*M.W.W.* ii, 3; iii, 1).

Froissart, Jean. Famous chronicler, born at Valenciennes, *c.* 1337; his *Chronique de France, d'Angleterre, d'Écosse et d'Espagne* relates the chief events from 1325 to 1400, and was one of the earliest books printed. In his youth he was secretary to Edward III's queen, and he shows little or no animus against the English. Alençon mentions that F., 'a countryman of ours' ('Froysard,' Ff), records that the Englishmen of the time of Edw. III were all 'Olivers and Rowlands' (*1 Hen. VI*, i, 2).

Froth. D.P. *M. for M.* 'A foolish gentleman.' ii, 1] is incoherently charged with a nebulous offence by Elbow; is dismissed with a caution not to consort with tapsters.

Fulvia. Widow of P. Clodius, married to M. Antony; a masterful woman but 'somewhat sour and crooked of condition.' In Ant.'s absence she first quarrelled with his brother Lucius, and afterward joined him in attacking Octavius. She died at Sicyon. (*Plut.* pp. 162, 178–9.)

'F. perchance is angry' (*Ant. Cl.* i, 1); 'F.'s process' (*ib. ib.*); 'when shrill-tongued F. scolds' (*ib. ib.*); her proceedings in A.'s absence, *ib.* i, 2; 'rail thou in F.'s phrase' (*ib. ib.*); her death, *ib. ib.*; Cl. comments on A.'s treatment of F., *ib.* i, 3; her attack on Oct., *ib.* ii, 2.

Furies. (*Lat.* Furiae, *Gk.* Erinyes); the Avenging Deities, Alecto (*q.v.*), Megaera, and Tisiphone. Among the crimes which they chiefly punished were murder and perjury. See also ERINNYS. In a general sense 'fiends,' in *Sh.*

'Approach, ye F. fell' (*M.N.D.* v, 1); 'he ... talked of Satan and of limbo and of furies' (*All's Well*, v, 3); 'Shall good news be baffled? Then, Pistol, lay thy head in F.'s lap' (2 *Hen. IV*, v, 3); 'false, fleeting, perjured Clarence, that stabb'd me ... Seize on him, F., take him to your torments!' (*Rich. III*, i, 4). (Benedick declares Beatrice is 'possessed by a fury,' *M. Ado*, i, 1.)

Furnival, Lord (of Sheffield). One of Talbot's titles; *1 Hen. VI*, iv, 7. See TALBOT, JOHN.

T. held the barony of F. through his wife Maud Neville, whose mother was Joan F., an heiress.

Fury. Dog's name; *Temp.* iv, 1.

G

G. See Anselm, Friar.

G., Cap. Pfx., for 'First Lord.' *All's Well*, iii, 6; iv, 3, in Ff. See E., Cap.

G., Lord. Pfx., for 'First Lord.' *All's Well*, i, 2; ii, 1, in Ff. See E., Lord.

Gabriel (1). A servant of Petruchio's. His 'pumps were all unpink'd i' the heel' (*Tam. Sh.* iv, 1).

Gabriel (2). In the st. dirs. of *3 Hen. VI*, i, 2, for 'Enter messenger' Ff have 'Enter Gabriel.' This is probably the name of an actor. 'Gabriel Spencer' was killed in a duel by Ben Jonson (1598), and 'Gabriel' is also mtd. by Heywood, *Apologie for Actors* (1612), as of posthumous reputation.

Gadshill (1). D.P. *1 Hen. IV.* (i, 2) acts as a spy upon travellers from Rochester for the benefit of Falstaff and his comrades. ii, 1] learns that a wealthy franklin is about to journey to London; boasts that he thieves in good company, and can defy justice. ii, 2] joins the robbers, and is hailed as 'our setter.' ii, 4] backs Falstaff in bragging to the Prince of the imaginary exploits of F.'s party.

Gadshill (2). A place to the W. of Rochester notorious for robberies, before the time of Sh. A ballad entitled 'The Robbery at Gadshill' is entered in the books of the Stationers' Company under the date 1558. Poins directs his band to be 'early at G.,' *1 Hen. IV*, i, 2; 'the road by G.' is the scene of Falstaff's discomfiture, *ib.* ii, 2. Mtd., *ib.* iii, 3; *2 Hen. IV*, i, 2, ii, 4.

Galathe. In medieval romance, Hector's horse; a gift from the fairy Morgana, acc. Benoît de Sainte-More, *Roman de Troie*, l. 7990. 'He [Hector] mounted upon his horse galathe that was one of the moste grete and strengest horse in the world' (Caxton, *Recuyell of the Histories of Troye*, f. 288).

'Now here he [Hector] fights on Galathe his horse' (*Tr. Cr.* v, 5).

Galen. Claudius Galenus (A.D. 130–*c.* 200). Celebrated physician, born at Pergamum; he practised in Rome and became physician to the Emperors Marcus Aurelius and L. Verus. His authentic works are very numerous, and he was regarded as the supreme authority on medicine as late as the 16th cent.

'*Host* [to Caius]. What says my ... G.?' (*M.W.W.* ii, 3); 'he has no more knowledge in ... G.' (*ib.* iii, 1); 'To be relinquished ... both of G. and Paracelsus' (*All's Well*, ii, 3); 'I have read the cause of his effects in G.' (*2 Hen. IV*, i, 2); 'the most sovereign prescription in G. is but empirictic' (*Cor.* ii, 1; his mention here being, of course, an anachronism).

Gallia. *Lat.* France; see also Guallia. 'You [Henry V] shall make all G. shake' (*Hen. V*, i, 2); 'the pride of G.' (*1 Hen. VI*, iv, 6); '[Talbot] England's glory, G.'s wonder' (*ib.* iv, 7); mtd., *3 Hen. VI*, v, 3; 'from G. I cross'd the seas' (*Cymb.* i, 7); mtd., *ib.* ii, 4, iii, 5, 7 (2), iv, 2, 3.

Gallian. *Adj.* French. '*Charles.* I am possess'd With more than half the G. territories' (*1 Hen. VI*, v, 4); 'Monsieur, that ... loves a G. girl at home' (*Cymb.* i, 7).

Galloway. A former division of S.W. Scotland, giving name to a breed of horses. '*Pist.* Thrust him downstairs! know we not Galloway nags?' (*2 Hen. IV*, ii, 4).

'There is a certain race of little horses in Scotland, called Galway Nagges, which I have seen hunt the Buck and Stagge exceedingly well' (Gervase Markham, quoted, *Sh. Eng.* ii, 410).

Cf. 'upon a G. right free, well pac'd' (*Tr. R. II*, 6).

Gallowglass. An Irish soldier armed with an axe; not a proper name, but often printed with an initial capital.

'Gallowgrosses,' *Macb.* i, 2, F1.

Gallus. D.P. *Ant. Cl.* 'A friend to Caesar' (Rowe). v, 1] *p.m.*; is sent as an emissary, with Proculeius, to Cleopatra in the Monument. v, 2] *p.m.* (Ff). The part played in this scene by G., according to later edns., is founded on the following extract from *Plut.* p. 223:

'After he [Proculeius] had viewed the place very well, he came and reported her answer unto Caesar; who immediately sent Gallus to speak once again with her, and bad him purposely hold him in talk, while Proc. set up a ladder ... and came down into the monument with two of his men, hard by the gate where Cl. stood to hear what Gallus said unto her.'

Gam, David. The nickname ('Squinting David') of a Welshman whose real name was Davydd ap Llewelyn. Mentioned as slain at Agincourt, *Hen. V*, iv, 8 (cf. *Hol.* iii, 555, 'Davie Gamme esquire').

It is related in Raleigh's *History of the World*, p. 451, that Llewelyn, who had followed Henry with only three archers, on being sent to reconnoitre the enemy, replied that 'there are enow to be killed, enow to be taken prisoners, and enow to run away.' It has been very plausibly suggested that David was the original of Fluellen.

[Gamelyn, Tale of.] A poem of unknown authorship added to Chaucer's *Canterbury Tales* by Urry (1721). Its Shakespearean interest lies in the fact that Lodge's *Rosalynde* is largely derived from it, and that some critics have urged that *A.Y.L.* shows direct borrowings from *Gamelyn*.

See *N.S.S. Tr.*, 1882, Pt.II, pp. 277–93; *Shakespeare Jahrbuch*, vi, 226 ff.; and a conspectus of all opinions in Furness, *Var.* pp. 310 ff.

Ganymede. In Greek mythology, the most beautiful of mortals; according to one legend, he was carried away by Jove in the form of an eagle, to become his cup-bearer.

The name assumed by Rosalind when in male attire – following Lodge's *Rosalynde*.

'*Ros.* I'll have no worse a name than Jove's own page; and therefore look you call me G.' (*A.Y.L.* i, 3). Mtd., *ib.* iii, 2; iv, 3; v, 2.

Hence may have arisen the absurd stage custom of attiring Ros. in a page's costume.

Gaoler (1). D.P. *Com. Err.* i, 1] takes Aegeon into custody.

Gaoler (2). D.P. *M.V.* iii, 3] has custody of Antonio.

Gaoler (3). D.P. *Wint. T.* ii, 2] refuses to conduct Paulina to Hermione, but summons Emilia, and consents to let the infant Perdita be carried forth.

'Keeper' in many edns., since Paulina thus refers to him.

Gaolers, Two. D.PP. *Cymb.* v, 4] conduct Posthumus to his prison; later, 1st G. dilates to Posthumus on the advantages of being hanged, and thus freed from all anxieties; is amazed at P.'s alacrity in going, as it seems, to his doom – 'unless a man should marry a gallows and beget young gibbets, I never saw one so prone.'

Gar. A perversion of 'God' frequently used by Dr Caius (*M.W.W.*) in expletives.

Gardiner, Stephen (*c.* 1483–1555). Bp. of Winchester 1531; after Wolsey's fall he acted as secretary to Hen. VIII (*Hol.* iii, 907); was member of the court which decreed Katharine's divorce; opposed Cromwell and Cranmer, and lost the King's favour for a while. (His subsequent career is irrelevant.) Of him Foxe (ii, 1679) writes: 'In his owne opinion and conceite flatterynge him selfe to muche; in wit craftie and subtile; towards his superiour flattering and faire spoken; to his inferiours fierce; against his equal stout and envious … And as touching divinitie, he was so variable waveryng with tyme, that no constant censure can be geuen what to make of hym.'

D.P. *Hen. VIII.* ii, 2] is summoned by the King as his new secretary; professes to be subservient to Wolsey. (iv, 1) takes part in the coronation procession as the new Bp. of Winchester. v, 1] in converse with Sir Thos. Lovell (*q.v.*) declares that 'it will ne'er be well' until the Queen (Anne), Cromwell, and Cranmer 'sleep in their graves'; confides that Cranmer is to be brought before the Council as a heretic. v, 3] (at the Council) accuses Cranmer of being a sectary, and announces his committal to the Tower; adulates the King upon his entrance, and is told that he was 'ever good at sudden commendations'; is compelled to embrace Cranmer.

Gargantua. A folk-giant of Northern France long before his fame was spread by Rabelais' great romance (*cf.* F. G. Stokes, *Hours with Rabelais* (1905), Introd. pp. xvii–xviii). Chap-book histories of the giant were popular in England in the 16th cent., and an Elizabethan translation of a part of 'Rabelais,' now lost, seems to have been current.

'You must borrow me Gargantua's mouth first; 'tis a word too great for this age's size' (*A.Y.L.* iii, 2).

The spelling was changed to 'Garagantua' by Pope and many succeeding edrs.

Gargrave, Sir Thomas. Mortally wounded, with the Earl of Salisbury, by a cannon-shot at the siege of Orleans (*Hol.* iii, 599).

D.P. *1 Hen. VI.* i, 4] as above. ('Gargrave' is situated in Yorkshire. Another Sir T. G. was speaker of the Council of the North in 1559.)

Garmombles. In the First Quarto of *M.W.W.* (iv, 5) 'cosen Garmombles' appears for 'cozen Germans.' This seems a burlesque perversion of 'Mömpelgard.' In 1592 Frederick, Duke of Würtemberg, travelling under the name of Count M., had been allowed by the Queen's government to requisition posthorses for his return journey without payment. This gave much offence to the innkeepers of the locality; hence the Host's grievance against the 'Duke of Jamany.' The Duke's *Journal* was publd. in 1602.

It has been ingeniously suggested, by Daniel, that Caius and Evans, in revenge for having been fooled by the Host, induced Nym and Bardolph to personate the Germans and steal his horses. This, of course, could not be gathered by the audience from the play as it stands, but is consistent with its details.

Garter, The. Name of a former inn in Windsor, near the White Hart, and perhaps where the present Star and Garter stands. *Cf.* Tighe and Davis, *Annals of Windsor*, i, 673 *n.* Mtd., *M.W.W.* i, 1, 3; ii, 1; iii, 1; v, 5. ('Gater,' i, 1, Ff.)

Garter King of Arms. See WRIOTHESLEY, SIR THOMAS (1).

Gascoigne, Sir William (*c.* 1350–1419). Attorney to Henry of Hereford on his banishment; Chief Justice of the King's Bench 1400; raised forces against the Percies 1403; was superseded as L.C.J. soon after the accession of Henry V.

Holinshed (iii, 543) relates that when Henry V came to the throne he called to mind that he had once 'with his fist stricken the cheefe justice for sending one of his minions (upon desert) to prison' and was thereupon 'commanded to ward' himself. This story first appeared in Sir Thomas Elyot's *Governour* (1531); E., however, represents the Prince as only threatening the judge. Stow (*Annales*, pp. 557–8) follows Elyot. Mr Solly Flood, in the *Transactions of the Royal Hist. Soc.*, 1886, has examined the evidence, and shows that the story originated in certain 'verba grossa et acerba' uttered by the first Prince of Wales near the end of the reign of Edward I, against an officer of the court.

D.P. *2 Hen. IV.* 'Lord Chief Justice of the King's Bench.' i, 2] attempts to reprove Falstaff, but is baffled by F.'s retorts; F. tells him that 'for the box of the ear the Prince gave you, he gave it like a rude prince, and you took it like a sensible lord'; he refuses to lend F. 'a penny.' ii, 1] listens to the Hostess's complaint against F., and orders him to make amends; attempts to abash F., but with ill success. v, 2] fears the worst on the accession of Henry V, but resolves that he will not crave pardon; gravely exculpates himself to the King, and is graciously confirmed in his office. v, 5] chides F. for addressing the King, and orders him to the Fleet.

Gaul. France. '*Host.* Peace, I say, Guallia and G.; French and Welsh' (*M.W.W.* iii, 1; 'gawle and gawlia,' Qq).

Gaunt, John of. See JOHN OF GAUNT.

Gawsey, Sir Nicholas. '*P. Hen.* Sir N. G. hath for succour sent. … *K. Hen.* I'll to Sir N. G.' (*1 Hen. IV*, v, 4). Sir Nich. Gausell was slain at Shrewsbury (*Hol.* iii, 523). French, p. 74, suggests that the name should be 'Goushill,' of Hoveringham, Notts.

Geffrey. See GEOFFREY.

General of the French Forces. D.P. *1 Hen. VI.* iv, 2] (before Bordeaux) parleys with Talbot, and warns him solemnly of the deadly dangers which encompass him. (The scene is unhistorical.)

Genoa. City of Italy. Scene of Jessica's reported extravagance, *M.V.* iii, 1; mtd., *Tam. Sh.* iv, 4.

'Genowa' in *M.V.* F1, 2, 3; 'Geneva,' F4.

Gentleman (1). D.P. *All's Well.* v, 3] in attendance on the King.

Gentleman (2). D.P. *Cymb.* French G., 'Friend to Philario' (Rowe). i, 5] reminds Posthumus that they previously met at Orleans, where a dispute arose over the merits of 'our country-mistresses.'

Gentleman (3). D.P. *Haml.* iv, 5] announces that Laertes, at the head of a rabble, has broken into the palace.

Gentleman (4). Attending on the Chief Justice. D.P. *2 Hen. IV.* 'Attendant.' i, 2] tells the C.J. that Falstaff has 'done good service at Shrewsbury'; addresses F., but is treated by him as a beggar, to his great indignation.

The same character probably appears, as *p.m.*, in ii, 1, where the C.J. is 'attended.'

Gentlemen, Three. D.PP. *Hen. VIII.* ii, 1] two of them converse on Buckingham's trial, and on the rumoured divorce of Henry and Q. Kath. iv, 1] while watching the coronation procession of Anne, they are joined by a friend who describes the ceremony in the Abbey; they all discuss State affairs.

Gentlemen, Two (1). D.PP. *Cymb.* i, 1] conversing in the gardens of the palace, the one relates to the other the cause of the King's present displeasure, and incidentally the early history of most of the protagonists in the play. (Their description as 'Two G. of Cymbeline's Court' is questionable, for the second is ignorant of the most notorious facts connected with the royal family.)

Gentlemen, Two (2). D.PP. *2 Hen. VI.* iv, 1] are captured with Suffolk, but ransom their lives; 1st G. advises S. to plead for his life; remains, to bear the Duke's body to the King.

Gentlemen, Two (3). D.PP. *M. for M.* In the 'Names of the Actors' (F1), Lucio being described as 'a fantastic,' his friends follow as 'Two other like Gentlemen.' i, 2] they indulge in light banter with L. and Mistress Overdone, and hear of Claudio's arrest. i, 3] *pp.m.*

Gentlewoman (1). D.P. *Cor.* i, 3] announces her mistress, Valeria.

Gentlewoman (2). D.P. *Macb.* v, 1] describes to the Doctor the Queen's somnambulism, but refuses to reveal what she has heard her say; comments on the words and action of the Queen as she enters.

Geoffrey or **Geffrey** (Ff). Fourth son of Henry II, b. 1158; married Constance, d. of Conan, Count of Brittany, 1181; accidentally killed at Paris 1186. His son Arthur was born posthumously. See ARTHUR and CONSTANCE.

'*K. Philip* [to K. John]. Geffrey was thy elder brother born, And this his son; England was G.'s right And this is G.'s' (*John*, ii, 1); mtd., *ib.* i, 1, iii, 4, iv, 1.

George. As a forename. 'If his name be G., I'll call him Peter' (*John*, i, 1). See also the following surnames: BARE, PAGE, SEACOAL, STANLEY.

George, Duke of Clarence (1449–78). S. of Richard, D. of York (1411–60) and brother to Edward IV. Married Isabella, d. of the E. of Warwick, 1469 (*Hol.* iii, 671; cf. *Rich. III*, i, 3, l. 135), and made Edw. IV prisoner at Edgcot; again, after escaping to France, invaded the kingdom with Warwick and caused the flight of Edw.; disapproved of Henry's restoration and deserted at Coventry to Edw.; fought on his side at Barnet and Tewkesbury; quarrelled with his brother Gloucester; charged with treason against Edw., he was put to death in the Tower; the manner of his death is uncertain.

D.P. *3 Hen. VI.* 'George, afterwards Duke of Clarence.' (i, 4) 'the lusty George.' (ii, 1) arrives in England from Burgundy. ii, 2] bids defiance to Q. Margaret. ii, 3] (at Towton) urges a renewal of the fight. ii, 6] is made D. of Clarence on the field. iii, 2] witnesses the wooing of Lady Grey by the King (Edward IV). (iii, 3) his defection from Edw. mtd. iv, 1] opposes the King's marriage; declares he will wed Warwick's younger daughter. iv, 2] joins Warwick's forces. iv, 3] *p.m.* iv, 6] is made Protector by Henry, jointly with Warwick. (iv, 7) 'froward C.' iv, 8] is charged with raising forces 'in Suffolk, Norfolk, and in Kent.' v, 1] rejoins Edward and bids defiance to Warwick at Coventry. v, 3] with King Edward at Barnet. v, 4] *p.m.*; Margaret styles him 'a quicksand of deceit.' v, 5] joins in the murder of young Prince Edward. (v, 6) Gloucester (*sol.*) declares that his 'turn is next.' v, 7] kisses the infant prince; is given orders to send Q. Margaret to France.

George was, actually, only twelve years old when he was made D. of Clarence. An attempt was made, after the Battle of Wakefield, to arrange a match between Clarence and the heiress of Burgundy (ii, 2). This was one of the rumoured reasons for his death (*Hol.* iii, 703).

D.P. *Rich. III.* i, 1] is committed to the Tower, 'for my name of George begins with G' (*Hol.* iii, 703); Gloucester assures him that 'I will deliver you.' (i, 3) the Queen (Elizabeth) declares that she has been his 'earnest advocate.' i, 4] relates a terrible dream; after eloquently pleading for his life, is stabbed to death by two murderers. (ii, 1) his murder is announced to Edward by Gloucester; E. recalls how Clarence succoured him at Tewkesbury. (ii, 2) his mother and children lament his death. (iii, i, 5; iv, 2, 3, 4) mtd. (v, 3) his ghost appears to Richard at Bosworth.

In i, 4, Cl. accuses himself of being Prince Edward's murderer; but in i, 2, Gloucester declares the deed was his own. More, Fabyan, Hall, and Stow agree in stating that Cl. was drowned in a butt of Malmsey (Malvoisie). i, 4, is due solely to Sh.

George, St. The patron saint of England since the reign of Edward III; formerly supposed to have been a Cappadocian, martyred in 303. St G. was said to have aided the Crusaders against the Saracens at Antioch, 1089. His most notable legendary feat was his victory over the dragon. But the identity of St George of the Eastern Church (the St G. of England) with the unscrupulous G. of Cappadocia is more than doubtful.

'St G. that swinged the dragon' (*John*, ii, 1); 'mine innocency and St G. to thrive' (*Rich. II*, i, 3); 'between St Denis and St G.' (*Hen. V*, v, 2); 'to keep our great St G.'s feast' (*1 Hen. VI*, i, 1). Used as a battle-cry, *Hen. V*, iii, 1; *1 Hen. VI*, iv, 2; *3 Hen. VI*, ii, 1, 2, iv, 2, v, 1; *Rich. III*, v, 3. 'The noble order of St G.' (*1 Hen. VI*, iv, 7); 'by St G.' (*Tam. Sh.* ii, 1); 'St G.'s half-cheek in a brooch' (*L.L.L.* v, 2, l. 620).

Gerard de Narbon. See NARBON, G. DE.

German. (*a*) *Subst.*, native of Germany. 'The G.s desire ... three of your horses' (*M.W.W.* iv, 3); 'the G.s are honest men' (*ib.* iv, 5); 'A G. from the waist down, all slops' (*M. Ado*, iii, 2); 'the young G., the Duke of Saxony's nephew' (*M.V.* i, 2); 'if there be here G., or Dane' (*All's Well*, iv, 2); 'hasty G.s' (*3 Hen. VI*, iv, 8); 'your G. ... nothing to your English in drinking' (*Oth.* ii, 2).

(*b*) *Adj.* 'Three G. devils' (*M.W.W.* iv, 5); 'G. clock' ['cloak,' QqF1] ... never going aright' (*L.L.L.* iii, 1); 'G. hunting in waterwork' (*2 Hen. IV*, i, 2); 'G. women' held in disdain, *Hen. V*, i, 2; 'full-acorned boar, a G. one' (*Cymb.* ii, 4, Rowe; 'a Jarmen on,' Ff).

Germany. 'I think he bought ... his bonnet in G.' (*M.V.* i, 2); Sir Robt. Faulconbridge sent thither on an embassy, *John*, i, 1; 'the land Salique lies in G.' and is 'in G. call'd Meisen' (*Hen. V*, i, 2); recent insurrections in 'Upper G.' instanced, *Hen. VIII*, v, 3; 'Edgar ... is with the E. of Kent in G.' (*Lear*, iv, 7).

[**Gernutus.**] Name of the Jew in the ballad (Percy, *Reliques* (1765), i, 191) which has been regarded as the immediate source of the 'bond story' in *M.V.*

Gertrude. D.P. *Haml.* Queen of Denmark and mother to Hamlet. i, 2] deprecates H.'s excessive grief for his father, and begs him to remain in Denmark. (i, 5) the ghost of Hamlet's father speaks of her as his 'most seeming-virtuous queen,' and bids H. 'leave her to heaven.' ii, 2] she begs Rosencrantz and Guildenstern to visit her 'too much changed son'; listens to Polonius' suggestion that Hamlet's madness is due to his love for Ophelia, and remarks 'it may be, very like.' iii, 1] questions Ros. and Guil.; trusts that Oph. will bring H. 'to his wonted way again.' iii, 2] present at the play enacted before the Court. iii, 4] begins to rebuke H. for his conduct, when she is suddenly assailed by him with reproaches; cries for help, and witnesses the death of Polonius at H.'s hand; is dismayed at H.'s denunciations – his 'words like daggers enter in mine ears'; she is amazed at the converse of H. with the ghost, invisible to her; H.'s words have 'cleft her heart in twain'; she promises not to breathe what H. has said. iv, 1] relates how H. 'mad as the sea and wind,' has slain Polonius. iv, 5] is witness of Ophelia's madness and the vengeful wrath of Laertes. iv, 7] describes Oph.'s death. v, 1] present at Oph.'s funeral. v, 2] drinks, unawares, of the poisoned cup and dies.

In *The Hystorie of Hamblet* the corresponding personage is Geruth, d. of Roderick, chief king of Denmark. See HORVENDILE and FENGON.

[**Geruth.**] See GERTRUDE.

Ghost of Hamlet's Father. D.P. *Haml.* i, 1] *p.m.*; (has already been twice seen); appears, and is adjured to speak by Horatio, without avail. (i, 2) its appearance is described to Hamlet. i, 4] beckons to Haml., who follows it. i, 5] reveals to H. the facts of his father's murder, and bids him revenge it; later, while unseen, bids Horatio and Marcellus swear to secrecy. iii, 4] unseen by the Queen, appears to Hamlet, and would whet his 'almost blunted purpose.'

Ghosts. The following are the apparitions of the dead which appear as D.PP. in *Sh.*

In *Rich. III*: the ghosts of Prince Edward; Henry VI; Clarence; Rivers, Grey, and Vaughan; Hastings; Edward V and Richard, D. of York; Lady Anne and Buckingham, who all address Richard and Richmond while they sleep (v, 3), bidding the former 'despair and die.'

In *Macb.*: Banquo (*q.v.*), and perhaps Duncan, appear to M. (iii, 6).

In *Haml.*: the ghost of Hamlet's father (i, 1, 4, 5; iii, 4).

In *Cymb.*: the father, mother, and brothers of Posthumus appear to the latter in a dream.

In *Jul. C.*: the 'Ghost of Caesar,' acc. st. dirs. (iv, 3) appears to Brutus; but the apparition declares itself to be B.'s 'evil spirit,' and in *Plut.* (p. 103) it is 'a horrible vision of a man of wonderful greatness and dreadful look.'

Gib. In the phrase 'gib cat,' an abbrn. of 'Gilbert.' Chaucer in *Rom. of the Rose* (i, 6204) translates 'Thibert le cas' as 'Gibbe, our cat.' Not used as a proper name in Sh.: 'melancholy as a gib cat' (*1 Hen. IV*, i, 2); 'a bat, a gib' (*Haml.* iii, 4, l. 187).

Gilbert. As a forename. 'Sir G. Talbot' (*Rich. III*, iv, 5); 'Sir G. Peck' (*Hen. VIII*, i, 1; ii, 1).

Gilburne or **Gilborne, Samuel.** Mtd. as a 'principal actor' in F1.

Gill. See JILL.

Gilliams. Servant of Hotspur's; *1 Hen. IV*, ii, 3.

Gillian (1). A servant; *Com. Err.* iii, 1.

Gillian (2). In *M.W.W.* iv, 2, Qq give, for 'the fat woman of Brentford,' 'Gillian of Brainford' (twice), and, later, 'the wise woman of B.' A tract, by R. Copeland, entitled *Jyl of Breyntford's Testament*, relates to this notorious contemporary character.

Cf. Dekker and Webster, *Westward Ho*: 'I doubt the old hag Gillian of Brainford has bewitched me.'

Ginn. Perh. for 'Jenny'; a servant, *Com. Err.* iii, 1, l. 31. ('Jen' in some mod. edns.)

[**Girondo.**] See JOHN, DON.

Gis. 'By Gis, and by Saint Charity' (Ophelia, singing; *Haml.* iv, 5).

Variously supposed to be for 'Cis' (Cicely); or 'St Gislen'; or, more probably, for 'Jesus.' It is noticeable that 'by Gis' and 'for St Charity' both occur in *Tr. R.* I, xi. (See CHARITY, ST.)

Gisors. See GUYSORS.

Glamis, Thane of. Acc. *Hol.* ii, 168, 170, a title descending to Macbeth on the death of his father. See SINEL. 'By Sinel's death I know I am thane of Gl.' (*Macb.* i, 3); 'Gl. thou art' (*ib.* i, 5); 'Gl. hath murder'd sleep' (*ib.* ii, 2); 'king, Cawdor, Gl., all' (*ib.* iii, 1).

Glamis Castle. In Strathmore, Scotland; seat of the Earls of Strathmore and Kinghorne.

Properly pronounced as a monosyllable, riming with 'alms.' Traditionally, the scene of Duncan's murder. Cf. *Letters of T. Gray* (1912), iii, 83–7.

Glansdale, Sir William (also Gladesdale, or Glasdale). (*a*) Entrusted with the keeping of 'the tower and bulworke' at the siege of Orleans, and (*b*) present when Salisbury was mortally wounded (*Hol.* iii, 599).

D.P. *1 Hen. VI.* i, 4] as above (*b*).

'Glacidas' in the French historians. In Southey's *Joan of Arc*, bk. vii, he figures somewhat conspicuously as 'Gladdisdale.'

Glendower, Owen (Owain ap Gruffydd) (*c.* 1359–*c.* 1416). Lord of Glendower (Glyndwr); claimed descent from Llewelyn, last Prince of Wales; was educated in London, and served with Rich. II against the Scots; he also served under Bolingbroke, but on B.'s accession, as Henry IV, Gl. headed a Welsh rebellion against him, and posed as Prince of Wales; this defection was largely due to the seizure by Lord Grey of Ruthin of part of his lands. In 1402 Owen captured Lord Grey and Sir Edmund Mortimer (*Hol.* iii, 520), but released the latter, after making him his son-in-law (*ib.* 521). About three years later Glendower formed an alliance with Mortimer and Northumberland, which was brought to naught at the Battle of

Shrewsbury, in the absence of Owen; after a long period of desultory warfare he seems to have been received into favour by the King, but his end is unknown. The statement (*2 Hen. VI*, ii, 2) that Owen kept Mortimer 'in captivity till he died,' seems founded on a confusion of Mortimer with Earl Grey of Ruthin.

The first allusion to Glendower in *Sh.* occurs in *Rich. II*, iii, 1, where Bolingbroke exclaims to his adherents: 'Come, lords, away, To fight with Gl. ['Glendoure,' Ff] and his complices.' (Theobald suspected this passage to be an interpolation, for this expedition against Gl. was not undertaken until the second year of Henry's reign.) The account of the portents which occurred at Owen's birth, *1 Hen. IV*, iii, 1, is without authority in the *Chronicles*, but the claim made by Gl., *1 Hen. IV*, iii, 1, to have thrice sent Henry 'weather-beaten back' to England, is founded on *Hol.* iii, 520, where it is stated that the King was driven from Wales by foul weather, caused '(as was thought), by art magike.' The meeting of Gl., Mortimer, and Hotspur, at Bangor, and the intended partition of the kingdom is related in *Hol.* iii, 521, where the prophecy, derided by Hotspur, concerning the mole, the dragon, and the lion is also mentioned. In 1405 the French sent aid to Gl. under 'one of the marshals of France, called Montmorancie' (*Hol.* iii, 531), and burnt the suburbs of Worcester, but retired into Wales on the King's approach.

D.P. *1 Hen. IV.* (i, 3) his combat with Mortimer described by Hotspur. (ii, 3) mtd. (ii, 4) characterized by Falstaff. iii, 1] (at Bangor) in conference with Mortimer and Hotspur; greets the latter as cousin; boasts of the wondrous portents that occurred at his birth, and of his magical powers, but is derided by Hotspur; his share of the kingdom is to be 'All westward, Wales beyond the Severn shore'; bickers with Hotspur over the boundaries shown on the map; speaks of his accomplishments when young and at the English Court; later, returns with the ladies; professes magically to produce the accompaniment to his daughter's song. (iv, 1) 'cannot draw his power these fourteen days.' (iv, 4) 'over-rul'd by prophecies.' (v, 5) mtd.

The King has to provide a power against Gl., *2 Hen. IV*, i, 3; Glendower's death is announced, *ib.* iii, 1.

[**Globe Theatre.**] Referred to as 'this wooden O' (*Hen. V*, i, Chor.).

Situated on Bankside; first erected out of the dismantled fabric of 'The Theatre' 1599; burnt down in 1613 during a performance of *All is True* (*q.v.*), and reopened in the following year. Sh. had a considerable pecunisry interest in the theatre from its opening until his death. The quotation refers to the circular, or octagonal, form then usual for such buildings.

Gloucester (variants of the name). 'In the Folio this name is printed Gloucester, or Glocester, in the st. dirs. and pfxs.; Gloster, sometimes Glouster, in the text; in either case, with very few exceptions. The distinction is least observed, perhaps, in *Lear*.' (W. S. Walker, *Sh. Vers.* p. 236.)

Gloucester, City of. Supposed to be referred to in *Lear*, i, 5: '*Lear.* Go you before to Gl. with these letters... If your diligence be not speedy, I shall be there afore you.'

Sh.'s company of players are recorded to have visited Gl. three times (Lee, pp. 81, 82 n.).

Gloucester, County of. 'In the county of Gl.' (*M.W.W.* i, 1). See GLOUCESTERSHIRE.

Gloucester. Edmund (D.P. *Lear*) is thus named by Goneril. *Lear*, iv, 2 (2), v, 3; cf. *ib.* iii, 5: '*Corn.* True or false, it hath made thee E. of Gl.'

Gloucester, Duchess of (1). Eleanor de Bohun (*ob.* 1399), e.d. of the last Earl of Hereford; married Thomas of Woodstock, D. of Gloucester, who was (probably) murdered at Calais in 1397.

D.P. *Rich. II.* i, 2] urges Gaunt to avenge his brother's death; entrusts him with a message for Edmund of Langley. (ii, 2) news of her death brought to Edmund.

Gloucester, Duchess of (2). See COBHAM, ELEANOR.

Gloucester, Duke of (1). See HUMPHREY.

Gloucester, Duke of (2). See RICHARD.

Gloucester, Duke of (3). See THOMAS OF WOODSTOCK.

Gloucester, Earl of. D.P. *Lear*. i, 1] presents his illegitimate son, Edmund, to Kent; is sent by the King to 'attend the lords of France and Burgundy'; later, presents them. i, 2] is allowed to read a letter, apparently from Edgar to Edmund, which hints at plotting their father's death; is overcome with horror at his son's seeming treachery; deems the recent eclipses to have been portents of dread events; begs Edmund to 'find out this villain.' ii, 1] (at his castle) is led to believe that Edgar had been lying in wait to murder him, and had been baffled only by the interposition of Edmund; Regan arrives, and to her Gl. unfolds his sorrow; she tells him that his advice is needed on a weighty matter. ii, 2] Gl. demurs to the disguised Kent being put in the stocks for brawling, since he is the King's messenger. ii, 4] tells Lear that Regan and Cornwall 'deny to speak' with him; later, returns with them; later, reports that Lear has 'in high rage' fled into the night. iii, 3] confides to Edmund that he has just received a letter, and that in the coming troubles they 'must incline to the King.' iii, 4] finds Lear and his companions on the heath, and leads them to shelter. (iii, 5) he is betrayed by Edm. iii, 6] conveys the King to shelter; later, finding that L. is in danger, helps to convey him toward Dover. iii, 7] is bound and questioned by Regan and Cornwall; is blinded, and thrust out of the castle. iv, 1] led by an old man, he meets Edgar (disguised), and begs the apparently crazy beggar to conduct him to Dover cliff. (iv, 2) Albany hears of his blinding. (iv, 5) Edm. is sent, 'to dispatch his nighted life.' iv, 6] guided by Edg., he approaches Dover cliff; believing that he is casting himself from the verge, he falls prostrate; Edg., in a changed voice, assures him that he has been miraculously preserved in his fall; Lear enters, in madness; Gl. recognizes the voice, and attempts to converse with the King; Gl. is in danger of being arrested by Oswald, but is rescued by Edg.; longs to be mad, with Lear. (iv, 7) mtd. v, 2] Edg. urges him from the field of battle when the day is lost.

The story of Gloucester is derived from Sidney's *Arcadia* (ii, 133–8, ed. 1598), where is related the history of 'The Paphlagonian unkinde king, and his kind sonne.'

Gloucestershire. 'As well as I love any woman in Gl.' (*M.W.W.* iii, 4); 'I'll make the best in Gl. know on't' (*ib.* v, 5); 'I am stranger here in Gl.' (*Rich. II*, ii, 3); 'our town of Cicester in Gl.' (*ib.* v, 6); Hotspur cannot recall the name of Berkeley, 'in Gl.,' *1 Hen. IV*, i, 3; Prince Henry's order to 'march through Gl.' (*ib.* iii, 2); Falstaff desires to pass through Gl., to visit Shallow, *2 Hen. IV*, iv, 3 (2).

[**Goap.**] See NORTH.

Gobbo, Launcelot. D.P. *M.V.* 'The clown,' servant to Shylock. ii, 2] is perplexed whether to quit his master's service or not; eventually yields to 'the fiend' and resolves to 'run'; meeting his purblind father, at first mystifies him, but soon reveals himself and persuades the old man to offer 'a dish of doves,' intended for the Jew, to Bassanio; is taken into the service of B., who tells him Shylock has already 'preferred' him. ii, 3] bids farewell to Jessica. ii, 4] brings Lorenzo a letter from J. ii, 5] brings Shylock an invitation to sup with Bassanio; the Jew explains that he parts with him as a 'drone.' iii, 5] (at Belmont) attends on Jessica and Lorenzo; shows them 'the wealth of his wit.' v, 1] announces that Bassanio is at hand.

Merely 'Launcelot,' except when first mtd., and in QqFf 'Launcelet' invariably.

Gobbo, Old. Father to Launcelot G. D.P. *M.V.* ii, 2] being 'sand-blind,' and not recognizing his son, inquires of him the way to 'Master Jew's'; is told that 'young master L.' has 'gone to heaven,' but is ultimately undeceived; on Bassanio's entrance tries to curry favour with him by offering him a 'dish of doves' he had intended for Shylock.

The family name of G., 'hunchback,' still exists in Venice. The *Gobbo di Rialto* is a stone figure supporting the pillar from which the laws of Venice were proclaimed. By a typographical freak the name is spelled 'Iobbe' six times in succession (*M. V.* ii, 2) in Q2F1, 2, 3.

Goche, Matthew. See GOUGH.

God. Name of the Deity. By an Act of Parliament, 3 James I, c. 21 (1605), entitled 'An Act to restrain the abuses of Players,' it was enacted that 'any person or persons who ... shall in any Stage-play, Enterlude, S[h]ew, May-game, or Pageant, jestingly or prophanely speak, or use the holy Name of God, or of Jesus Christ, or of the Holy Ghost, or of the Trinity, which are not to be spoken, but with fear and reverence, shall forfeit for every such offence by him or them committed, ten pounds.'

It would seem that this Act was held to prohibit not merely the profane or light use of the sacred name, but its use in even a grave and solemn context. In order to be on the safe side, therefore, it appears to have been eliminated from the prompt-books, the word 'heaven' usually taking its place; traces of the omission are sometimes seen in the pronoun following, *e.g.* 'this in the name of Heaven, I promise ... the which if He be pleased,' etc. (*1 Hen. IV*, iii, 2, Ff).

From the following seven plays the name is absent: *Temp.*, *T.G.V.*, *M. for M.*, *Wint. T.*, *Timon*, *Jul. C.*, *Cymb.*, all having been first published in F1.

The number of times the name occurs in each of the remaining plays (based on edns. in which readings from Qq occur) is indicated in parentheses: *Ant. Cl.* (1); *Tr. Cr.* (1); *Lear* (1); *Cor.* (2); *M.W.W.* (2); *Per.* (3); *M.N.D.* (5); *Oth.* (5); *T. And.* (6); *John* (7); *Com. Err.* (13); *Macb.* (14); *T. Nt.* (14); *Tam. Sh.* (18); *M.V.* (18); *A.Y.L.* (19); *All's Well* (20); *1 Hen. VI* (22); *L.L.L.* (26); *Haml.* (26); *Rom. J.* (30); *3 Hen. VI* (31); *Hen. VIII* (32); *1 Hen. IV* (46); *2 Hen. IV* (50; in both Parts mostly cancelled in F1); *2 Hen. VI* (57); *M. Ado* (60); *Hen. V* (61); *Rich. II* (62); *Rich. III* (103).

Equivalent phrases; 'King of Heaven' (*Rich. III*, i, 2); 'King of Kings' (*ib.* i, 4, ii, 1; *1 Hen. VI*, i, 1); 'High All-seer' (*ib.* v, 1); 'Lord of Hosts' (*1 Hen. VI*, i, 1); 'The Eternal' (*q.v.*); 'The Highest' (*All's Well*, iv, 2); 'The Everlasting' (*q.v.*); as Father of Christ, *2 Hen. VI*, iii, 2, I. 154.

God's Book. The Bible. 'Dame Eleanor Cobham ... Receive the sentence of the law, for sins Such as by God's book are adjudg'd to death' (*2 Hen. VI*, ii, 3).

Cf. Exod. xxii, 18, and Levit. xx, 27, on the penalty of witchcraft.

Golden Age, The. The first of the four ages of mankind, described by Ovid (*Metam.* i, 89 ff.); a period of innocence, peace, and abundance.

Mtd., *A.Y.L.* i, 1; *Temp.* ii, 1; *Lucr.* 60.

Golgotha. (Aramaean, 'a skull'); scene of the Crucifixion. 'Memorize another G.' (*Macb.* i, 2); 'this land be call'd the field of G., and dead men's skulls' (*Rich. II*, iv, 1).

The last phrase occurs in the Genevan version of the N.T. (Matt. xxvii, 33); 'place of a skull' in A.V.

Golias. See GOLIATH.

Goliath. The giant of Gath, the staff of whose spear 'was like a weaver's beam' (1 Sam. xvii, 7). 'I fear not G. with a weaver's beam' (*M.W.W.* v, 1; 'Goliah,' Ff); 'Samsons and Goliases' (*1 Hen. VI*, i, 2).

Goneril. D.P. *Lear*. The King's eldest daughter, wife to the D. of Albany. i, 1] professes ineffable love to Lear, and is given a third of his kingdom; bids farewell to Cordelia with a sneer at her being received 'at fortune's alms' by France (in Qq this speech is given to Regan); converses with her sister on L.'s growing infirmity and 'waywardness.' i, 3] orders her steward, Oswald, to see that L. is treated with negligence and disrespect. i, 4] upbraids her father for permitting riotous conduct on the part of his train, whom she calls a 'disorder'd rabble'; treats with disdain his impassioned curse; points out to Albany the impolicy of allowing L. to keep a hundred knights, and sends a letter, by Oswald, to her sister urging her to co-operate. ii, 4] reaches Gloucester's castle and supports Regan, whom she meets there, in refusing to harbour L. with any train whatever; when L. departs in the storm, declares that he is himself to blame, and urges Gloucester to 'entreat him by no means to stay.' (iii, 4) mtd. (iii, 6) Lear 'arraigns' her, in his madness. iii, 7] she suggests that the eyes of 'the traitor Gloucester' should be plucked out; departs, in Edmund's company, before the deed is done, iv, 2] on reaching home, learns that her husband has turned against her; she speaks of him as a coward, and dismisses Edm. with a passionate kiss; is rebuked by Albany for her barbarity to L. and retorts that he is a 'milk-liver'd man'; as their quarrel grows, a messenger arrives to announce that Gl. has been blinded and that Cornwall is dead; receives a letter from Regan; fears that her sister, now a widow, may prove a rival to her in Edmund's love. (iv, 6) her love-letter to Edm., urging him to kill her husband, falls into Edgar's hands. v, 1] (in the British camp) would 'rather lose the battle' than yield Edm. to Regan. v, 3] (after the battle) has an altercation with Regan, who claims Edm. as her lord and to whom Gon. has caused poison to be administered; witnesses the death of Edm. in combat with Edgar, and exclaims that he was not 'vanquish'd' but 'beguil'd'; on being confronted with her own letter by Albany, departs with the words 'the laws are mine not thine'; (it is announced that she has stabbed herself).

The name is spelt 'Gonorill' in *Leir* and *The Faerie Que ne* . Bk. II; 'Gonorilla' in *Holinshed*; 'Gonerell' in *A Mirror for Magistrates* (1586). For a full account of the variant forms in ancient versions of the story see W. Perrett, *Palaestra*, xxxv (Berlin, 1904). In Percy's *Reliques* 'Gonorell' is Leir's second daughter.

Gongarian. Pistol calls Bardolph a 'base Gongarian wight' (*M.W.W.* i, 3), acc. Qq, 'Hungarian' in Ff. The former was favoured by Steevens, who quotes 'O base Gongarian, wilt thou the distaff wield?' from 'an old play,' the name of which he had lost.

Gonzago. The character enacted by the 'Player King' before Claudius; *Haml.* ii, 2. 'Can you play the Murder of G.?' (*Haml.* ii, 2); 'His name's G.: the story is extant, and written in very choice Italian: you shall see anon how the murderer gets the love of G.'s wife' (*ib.* iii, 2).

'Albertus,' Q1.

Gonzalo. D.P. *Temp.* 'An honest old counsellor' (F1) in the train of the King of Naples. (i, 2) twelve years before the opening of the play he had been deputed to superintend the casting adrift of Prospero and his infant daughter, yet he had earned the gratitude of the banished Duke by providing him, 'out of his charity,' with many necessaries, and, above all, with the books which Pr. prized above his dukedom. i, 1] is undismayed by the storm; insists that the boatswain is born to be hanged. (i, 2) his services to Pr. ii, 1] attempts to console Alonso in his misfortune, and seeks to divert the King's thoughts by describing a Utopian commonwealth to be established on the island; treats with dignified indifference the ridicule of Antonio and Sebastian; having fallen asleep, is awakened by Ariel just in time to avert the murderous design of Ant. and Seb. iii, 3] when an illusory banquet is presented by spirits to the royal party he discusses the apparition as being strange but not supernatural, and when the 'three men of sin' flee frenzied from the spot he urges those 'of suppler joints' to follow and save them, v, 1] is brought, with Alonso and his train, before Pr., by whom he is affectionately greeted; invokes a blessing on Ferdinand and Miranda; humorously reminds the boatswain of his prediction.

G.'s sketch of a Utopian commonwealth closely follows a passage in Florio's translation of Montaigne's *Essais*, i, 30. In Dryden's version G. is 'a nobleman of Savoy.'

Good Friday. As a fast-day. Philip Faulconbridge declares that his supposed father 'might have eat his part in' him on G.F. 'and ne'er broke his fast' (*John*, i, 1); Poins suggests that Falstaff sold his soul on G.F. for wine and 'a cold capon's leg' (*1 Hen. IV*, i, 2).

Goodman, John. 'My lord cardinal's man'; *2 Hen. VI*, i, 3.

Goodrig, Goodrich (Herefordshire). One of the titles of John Talbot, Earl of Shrewsbury, was Lord Talbot of Goodrig; *1 Hen. VI*, iv, 7.

Goodwins, The, or **Goodwin Sands.** Dangerous shoals lying about 5 m. E. of Kent, from which they are separated by a roadstead called the Downs.

'The G. I think they call the place; a very dangerous flat and fatal' (*M.V.* iii, 1); 'wreck'd on G. sands' (*John*, v, 3); 'Sunk on G. sands' (*ib.* v, 5). ('Our pinnace anchors in the Downs,' *2 Hen. VI*, iv, 1.)

Gorboduc. ('Gorbodack,' '-e,' Ff.) Mythical King of Britain; he divided his realm, during his lifetime, between his two sons Ferrex and Porrex, and gives the title to the first English Tragedy, *Gorboduc*, by Thos. Norton and Thos. Sackville (publd. 1564).

'The old hermit of Prague ... very wittily said to the niece of King G., "That that is, is," ' (*T. Nt.* iv, 2). (No attempt at elucidating the 'niece' has been made.) See PRAGUE.

Gordian. 'The G. knot of it he will unloose' (*Hen. V*, i, 1); 'as slippery as the G. knot was hard' (*Cymb.* ii, 2). See following article.

[**Gordius.**] A peasant who became King of Phrygia. The pole of the waggon in which he first arrived at Telmissus was fastened to the yoke by a knot, and an oracle declared that whoever should untie this should be lord of Asia. Alexander the Great cut the knot with his sword.

Gorgon. The Gorgon Medusa, who alone of the three Gorgons was mortal. She was originally a beautiful maiden, but, her hair having been changed into serpents by Athena, her aspect became so frightful that all who beheld her were turned into stone (Ovid, *Metam.* v, 189 ff.).

'Approach the chamber, and destroy your sight with a new G.' (*Macb.* ii, 3); 'painted one way like a G., The other way's a Mars' (*Ant. Cl.* ii, 5).

[**Gorson.**] See NORTH.

Goth (1). D.P. *T.And.* v, 1] brings in Aaron with his child in his arms.

Goth (2). D.P. *T. And.* v, 1] announces a messenger from Rome. See also LORD, ROMAN.

Goths (1). A German people, a division of whom, the Visigoths, under their king Alaric, took and plundered Rome A.D. 410, and afterward settled permanently in the S.W. of Gaul.

Touchstone, *A.Y.L.* iii, 3, remarks: 'I am here with thee, and thy goats, as ... Ovid was among the Goths,' a jest which would be pointless if G. was not pronounced 'gotes.' In Wil. Thomas' *Historye of Italye* (1561), f. 86, 'against the gotes'; and, f. 201, 'King of the Goti.'

'Tamora, the Queen of the G., when G. were G.' (*T. And.* i, 2); 'Queen of G.' (*ib.* ii, 1); 'warlike G.' (*ib. ib.*); 'lascivious G.' (*ib.* ii, 3); Lucius sets out to the G., *ib.* iii, 1; 'traitorous G.' (*ib.* iv, 1); mtd., *ib.* iv, 2; 'join with the G.' (*ib.* iv, 3); the G. advance on Rome, *ib.* iv, 4; mtd., *ib.* v, 2 (4).

Goths (2). D.PP. *T. And.* v, 1] declare their fidelity to Lucius. v, 3] they attend Titus' banquet.

Gough, or **Goche, Matthew.** 'A man of great wit and much experience in feats of chivalrie' (*Hol.* iii, 635); he was sent by Talbot to spy out the condition of the French at Le Mans and 'Well sped his business' (*ib.* iii, 598).

D.P. *2 Hen. VI.* (iv, 5) is appointed to command the Londoners against Cade. iv, 7] *p.m.*; is slain at Smithfield.

Historically, G. fell at London Bridge (*Hol.* iii, 635).

Goughe, Robert. Mtd. as a 'principal actor' in F1.

Governor of Paris. D.P. *1 Hen. VI.* iv, 1] *p.m.*; the oath of fealty administered to him at the coronation of Henry VI.

Not mentioned in the Chronicles by name. Historically, John of Luxembourg was appointed Governor by the Duke of Bedford when Paris was captured (French. p. 148).

Gower (1). D.P. *2 Hen. IV.* 'Master G.' ii, 1] brings tidings to the Chief Justice from the King.

It has been suggested that this is intended for the poet, John G. (*q.v.*); but he became blind in 1400 and died 1408. The name of G. would be familiar to Sh. as that of a connection of his friend Ant. Nash.

Gower (2). D.P. *Hen. V.* An officer in the King's army ('Captain G.'). iii, 2] summons Fluellen 'to the mines'; interposes between Fl. and Macmorris. iii, 6] exposes Pistol's true character to Fl. iv, 1] (before Agincourt) is bidden by Fl. to 'speak lower.' iv, 7] listens to Fl.'s parallel between Henry V and 'Alexander the Pig.' (iv, 7) is eulogized by Fl. before the King. iv, 8] present when Williams (*q.v.*) strikes Fl. v, 1] present when Fl. makes Pistol eat the leek, and tells the latter that he deserves his 'Welsh correction.'

It is doubtful whether Fl.'s 'dear friend' is the same as the preceding character; yet an acquaintance of Falstaff's might well have recognized Pistol. The name does not appear in 'the roll of Agincourt.' For the incident of iv, 1, cf. *Hol.* iii, 552. (See GOWER (1).)

Gower, John (*c.* 1325–1408). Poet; his only English poem is the *Confessio Amantis*, containing many stories derived from Ovid and medieval sources.

D.P. *Per.* He acts as Chorus, speaking a Prologue to each act, and also an Epilogue; he also interpolates a descriptive speech in iv, 3, standing before Marina's monument, and another at the Temple of Diana at Ephesus. Two-thirds of these speeches are in the metre of the *Confessio Amantis*, and since much of the story is derived from the same source, the suitability of 'old Gower' for the part of Chorus is obvious.

Grace. Suggested as a fem. name; *Wint. T.* i, 2, l. 99.

Grace, A. One of the three Charites: Euphrosyne, Aglaia, and Thalia.

Pandarus, on seeing Troilus, exclaims: 'had I a sister were a grace, or a daughter a goddess, he should take his choice' (*Tr. Cr.* i, 2); 'more grace than boy' (*T.G.V.* v, 4, l. 166); doubtfully in *Per.* i, 1, l. 13; 'with the garment of a G., The naked fiend he covered' (*L.C.* 315).

[**Grammont, De.**] See BAYONNE.

Grandpré. D.P. *Hen. V* ('the erle of Grandpree,' *Hol.* iii, 555). (iii, 5) mtd. (iii, 7) 'a valiant and most expert gentleman.' iv, 2] (before Agincourt) enlarges on the miserable condition of 'yon island carrions,' the English army. (iv, 8) one of the slain.

Acc. Monstrelet and St-Remy, 'Count G.'; acc. Elmham, 'The earl of Grauntpre' (Sir H. Nicolas, *The Battle of Agincourt* (1832)). 'Grand Pree,' Ff.

Gratiano (1). D.P. *M.V.* Friend to Antonio and Bassanio. i, 1] on A.'s comparing the world to a stage, exclaims 'let me play the fool'; volubly urges A. to cast off his melancholy nor assume wisdom in the garb of silence; (Bassanio remarks that he 'speaks an infinite deal of nothing'). ii, 2] begs to accompany B. to Belmont, promising to behave demurely on the occasion – 'but I bar tonight.' ii, 4] is told by Lorenzo of his projected elopement with Jessica. ii, 6] awaits L. outside Shylock's house; reflects that all things are 'with more spirit chased than enjoy'd'; is eager to embark that night.' (ii, 8) mtd. iii, 2] (at Belmont) wishes B. and Portia all joy; announces his own engagement to Nerissa. iv, 1] (at the trial) declares that Shylock's 'currish spirit' once 'govern'd a wolf'; exults over the Jew's discomfiture. iv, 2] conveys Bassanio's ring to 'Balthasar' (Portia). v, 1] (at Belmont) has given his ring to 'the judge's clerk' (Nerissa); defends himself when taxed by N. with having given the ring to a woman; believes for a moment that N. has been faithless; the *imbroglio* is cleared up.

Gratiano (2). D.P. *Oth.* Brother to Brabantio. v, 1] has been seeking for Cassio, and finds him lying wounded in the street at night; realizes that a body lying near is that of his acquaintance Roderigo. v, 2] finds Desdemona murdered; relates that her father had died of grief at his daughter's marriage; prevents Oth. from leaving the chamber; declares that torments will open Iago's lips; witnesses Othello's self-inflicted death; is bidden by Lodovico to take possession of the Moor's fortune.

Gratii. Name of a commander; *All's Well*, iv, 3.

Grave-diggers (*Haml*). See CLOWNS, Two.

Graymalkin. Name of a cat; *Macb.* i, 1. 'Malkin,' dim. of Matilda; *cf.* Chaucer, Group B, 1. 30.

Gray's Inn. One of the Inns of Court, formerly paying a ground rent to the Lords Gray of Wilton. In its Hall, dating from 1556, *The Comedy of Errors* was acted in December 1594.

Justice Shallow, in his student days, fought with Stockfish (*q.v.*) 'behind Gray's Inn' (*2 Hen. IV*, iii, 2).

Grecian. (*a*) *Subst.*, a Greek. Mtd., *All's Well*, i, 3; *Tr. Cr.* i, 3, ii, 2 (2), iv, 1, 4 (3), 5 (2), v, 3, 4 (2).

(*b*) *Adj.* 'G. tents' (*M.V.* v, 1; *Tr. Cr.* i, 3, iv, 5); 'G. club' (*A.Y.L.* iv, 1); 'G. dames,' 'G. host' (*Tr. Cr.* i, 3); 'G. queen' (*ib.* ii, 2); 'G. lords,' 'G. army' (*ib.* iii, 3); 'G. Diomed' (*ib.* iv, 2); 'G. sentinels,' 'G. youths' (*ib.* iv, 4); 'hand is G.,' 'G. blood,' 'G. cause' (*ib.* iv, 5); 'G. part' (*ib.* v, 9); 'G. swords' (*Cor.* i, 3); 'G. tires' (*Son.* liii).

Greece. 'Hector of G.' (*M.W.W.* ii, 3); 'old John Naps of G.' (*Tam. Sh.* Ind. 2; see NAPS, JOHN); 'furthest G.' (*Com. Err.* i, 1); mtd., *1 Hen. VI*, v, 1; 'Helen of G.' (*3 Hen. VI*, ii, 2); 'isles of G.' (*Tr. Cr.* Prol.); mtd., *ib.* i, 2, 3 (2); 'plague of G.' (*ib.* ii, 1 (2)); mtd., *ib.* iv, 1, 4, 5; *Cor.* iii, 1 (2); 'Gods of G.' (*Per.* i, 4); 'country of G.' (*ib.* ii, 1).

Greek. (*a*) *Subst.* (i) Gk. language. 'Cunning in G.' (*Tam. Sh.* ii, 1); 'he spoke G. ... it was G. to me' (*Jul. C.* i, 2).

(ii) Native of Greece. 'Trojan G.s' (*2 Hen. IV*, ii, 4); 'the G.s that would have entered Troy' (*3 Hen. VI*, ii, 1); 'yet unbruised G.s' (*Tr. Cr.* Prol.); 'the G.s are strong' (*ib.* i, 1); 'a merry G.' (*ib.* i, 2; iv, 4); 'valiant G.' (*ib.* iv, 1, 3); 'sweet honey G.,' 'sweet G.' (*ib.* v, 2); 'strawy G.s' (*ib.* v, 5); 'cogging G.s' (*ib.* v, 6); 'subtle G.s' (*T. And.* v, 3); 'foolish G.' (*T. Nt.* iv, 1); 'the G.s' (*Lucr.* 1384, 1402, 1470). Mtd., *Tr. Cr.* i, 1, 2 (2), 3 (4), ii, 2 (5), iii, 3, iv, 1 (2), 4, 5 (3), v, 1 (2), 2 (2), 3, 4, 6, 9; *Cymb.* iv, 2; *T. And.* i, 2; *Haml.* ii, 2.

The phrase 'a merry G.' was proverbial. Mathew Merygreeke is a character in *Ralph Roister Doister*.

(*b*) *Adj.* 'A G. invocation' (*A.Y.L.* ii, 5); 'G. books' (*Tam. Sh.* ii, 1). Occurs: *Tr. Cr.* Prol.; iv, 5 (3).

Greek, A. D.P. *Tr. Cr.* v, 6] enters 'in sumptuous armour,' but flees from Hector, who will 'hunt him for his hide.'

Greekish, *adj.* 'G. ears' (*Tr. Cr.* i, 3, in Q only); 'G. heads' (*ib. ib.*); 'G. sinews' (*ib.* iii, 1); 'G. girls' (*ib.* iii, 3); 'G. member,' 'G. youth,' 'G. embassy' (*ib.* iv, 5); 'G. wine' (*ib.* v, 1); 'G. villain' (*ib.* v, 4).

Green, Sir Henry, of Drayton (*ob.* 1399). An adherent of Richard II; alleged to have been one of those to whom the realm was 'farmed' (*Hol.* iii, 496); present at York's council of war; fled to Bristol, and was there executed (*ib.* iii, 498).

D.P. *Rich. II.* i, 4] advises prompt measures against the Irish rebels. ii, 1] p.m. ii, 2] informs the Queen of Bolingbroke's landing; resolves to flee to Bristol. iii, 1] receives his sentence defiantly. (iii, 2) his execution announced. (iii, 4) mtd.

Green Sleeves. Name of a popular ballad and tune, twice mtd. in *M.W.W.* Mrs Ford says that Falstaff's words and disposition no more 'keep place together than the hundredth psalm to the tune of G.-S.' (ii, 1); and F. exclaims 'let it thunder to the tune of G.-S.' (v, 5).

This tune is still extant, and was introduced into *The Beggar's Opera*, set to the song, 'Since laws were made for every degree.'

It would appear that the original words of the song were of a scandalous character, and a pamphlet entitled *Reprehension against Green Sleeves*, by W. Elderton, was entered at Stationers' Hall in 1581, as also was *Greene Sleeves moralised to the Scripture*.

Greenwich, Town of. The D. of Buckingham was accused of having spoken traitorous words, 'at east G. in the county of Kent ... unto Charles Knevet' (*Hol.* iii, 864). The fact mtd. *Hen. VIII*, i, 2.

Gregory (1). D.P. *Tam. Sh.* A servant. iv, 1] in attendance.

Gregory (2). D.P. *Rom. J.* A servant of the Capulets. i, 1] is ready to quarrel with servants of the Montagues when he sees aid at hand.

Gregory de Casale. See Cassado.

Gregory, St. Several saints of this name are recorded in the Calendar; the attribution of 'St G.'s well' (*T.G.V.* iv, 2) is therefore indeterminate.

Gregory, Turk. See Turk Gregory.

Gremio. D.P. *Tam. Sh.* A suitor to Bianca. (ii, 1) elderly and wealthy. i, 1] agrees with his rival, Hortensio, to help 'Baptista's eldest daughter to a husband' and thus clear the way for Bianca's marriage. i, 2] secures 'Cambio' (*i.e.* Lucentio, who is disguised and unknown to him) as a tutor for Bianca; is introduced to Petruchio and learns that he will woo Katharina; finds that 'Lucentio' (*i.e.* Tranio) is also a suitor to Bianca. ii, 1] presents 'Cambio' to Bi.'s father; later, hears that Petruchio has made a match with Kath.; dilates to Baptista on the rich dower he can give his wife, but is 'outvied' by Tranio (posing as Lucentio). iii, 2] describes Petruchio's 'mad marriage.' (iv, 4) mtd. v, 1] witnesses the unmasking of the false Vincentio; laments that his 'cake is dough.' v, 2] is a guest at Lucentio's banquet.

The corresponding character in *I Suppositi* is Cleandro, an elderly Doctor of Laws, suitor to Polinesta.

Grey, Elizabeth. See Elizabeth (1).

Grey, Henry (*ob.* 1554). 3rd Marq. of Dorset; g.g.s. of Elizabeth Woodville (queen of Edw. IV), and father of Lady Jane Grey. He carried the sceptre at the coronation of Anne (Boleyn), *Hen. VIII*, iv, 1.

Grey, John (1432–61). 8th Baron Ferrers of Groby, usually styled 'Sir John'; 1st husb. of Elizabeth Woodville (*q.v.*); killed at the 2nd Battle of St Albans.

Erroneously referred to, *3 Hen. VI*, iii, 2, Ff, as 'Sir Richard G.' (following *Tr. Tr.*), and declared to have lost his life 'in the quarrel of the house of York,' whereas Sir John G. was a Lancastrian. In *Rich. III*, i, 3, l. 128, Elizabeth's husband is correctly described as 'factious for the house of Lancaster.' His lands were seized by Edward IV after Towton.

Sir John G. had a brother Richard, of no historical importance, with whom he may have been confused by the dramatist.

Grey, Lord. See Grey, Sir Richard (1).

Grey, Sir Richard (1) (*ob.* 1483). Styled Lord Richard G. by Sir T. More; youngest son of Elizabeth Woodville by her 1st husb., Sir John G. Arrested at Stony Stratford, on his way to London with Edw. V, on the charge of plotting to seize supreme power, and executed at Pontefract (*Hol.* iii, 715).

D.P. *Rich. III.* 'Lord Grey,' son to Elizabeth, King Edward IV's queen. i, 3] bids his mother be of good cheer; (remains silent while Gloucester upbraids her). ii, 1] *p.m.* (Gl. professes to be reconciled to him). (ii, 4) 'sent to Pomfret.' (iii, 2) mtd. iii, 3] is led to execution; 'Margaret's curse is fallen' on him. (iv, 4; v, 1) mtd. (v, 3) his ghost appears to Richard at Bosworth Field.

Grey, Sir Richard (2). See Grey, John.

Grey, Sir Thomas, of Heton, Northumberland. 2nd son of Sir Thos. G., Constable of Norham Castle; executed for conspiracy against Henry V, Aug. 2, 1415. 'The said Sir T. G. (as some write) was of the king's prime councell' (*Hol.* iii, 548).

D.P. *Hen. V.* (ii, Chor.) mtd. as having been bribed by France. ii, 2] advises the King not to pardon a prisoner who had 'railed' against him; is handed a paper disclosing Henry's knowledge of his guilt; appeals for mercy, but acknowledges the justice of the sentence.

Grey, Thomas. E.s. of Elizabeth Woodville (*q.v.*) by her first marriage; ctd. by Edward IV E. of Huntingdon (1471) and Marq. of Dorset (1475); fought for Edw. at Tewkesbury; joined Richmond in France, but did not return with him to England. Married the heiress of Lord Bonville and Harington (*q.v.*), *3 Hen. VI*, iv, 1.

D.P. *Rich. III.* 'Marq. of Dorset.' i, 3] is reminded by Q. Margaret that his 'fire-new stamp of honour is scarce current' (actually some eight years old). ii, 1] at K. Edward's bidding embraces Hastings (cf. *Hol.* iii, 713). ii, 2] bids his mother beware of ingratitude to heaven. iv, 1] *p.m.*; is advised to join Richmond (*Hol.* iii, 743). (iv, 2) his flight reported to Richard. (iv, 4) said to be in arms in Yorkshire (this refers to Buckingham's rebellion, 1483, Dorset having been in sanctuary before he escaped to Brittany (*Hol.* iii, 743)).

Grief. Personified. *T. Nt.* ii, 4, l. 17 (Malone); 'to pay G. must of poor Patience borrow' (*Oth.* i, 3); 'G. hath two tongues' (*V.A.* 100).

Partial personifications of G. are frequent, but in such cases as 'forefather G.' (*Rich. II*, ii, 2) a metaphorical use of the first word rather than a personification of the second is suggested.

Griffith. 'Gentleman usher' to Katharine of Arragon, as he is termed in *Sh.*; he was really named Griffin Richardes, and was her receiver-general. Cavendish, *Life of Wolsey*, p. 217, says that the Queen, departing from the trial of her marriage, leant 'as she was wont always to do, upon the arm of her General Receiver, called Master Griffith.'

D.P. *Hen. VIII.* ii, 4] in attendance on Kath. at the trial. iv, 2] (at Kimbolton) he describes Wolsey's last hours to Kath., and, begging leave to 'speak his good,' pronounces a measured eulogy upon the Cardinal; Kath. declares that after her death she would wish no other herald than G., to keep her 'honour from corruption'; G. remains while K. sleeps and dreams; ushers in Capucius.

Grindstone, Susan. A friend of one of Capulet's servants; *Rom. J.* i, 5.

Grissel, Griselda. Heroine of a famous medieval tale; a type of wifely submission and patience. The tale first assumed literary form in Boccaccio's *Decameron*. In English the most important version of the story is that in Chaucer's *Clerkes Tale*.

For patience she will prove a second Grissel' (*Tam. Sh.* ii, 1, FfQ).

[**Gruffydd, Owain ap.**] See Glendower.

Grumio. D.P. *Tam. Sh.* Described (i, 2) as Petruchio's 'ancient, trusty, pleasant servant.' i, 2] mistaking his master's humour, has his ears pulled for jocosely misinterpreting his orders; Hortensio interposes on his behalf, and Gr. characterizes Petruchio without restraint. iii, 2] in attendance, 'a very monster in apparel.' iv, 1] cold and weary, reaches P.'s house, and urges the other servants to make ready for the arrival of P. and his bride; relates their mishaps on the way; makes excuses to P. for his fellow-servants' unreadiness. iv, 3] tantalizes Katharina by suggesting dishes for her, and then raising objections to them; in opposition to the tailor, hotly repudiates responsibility for the fashion of K.'s dress. v, 1] *p.m.*; in attendance. v, 2] *p.m.*; is sent to summon K.

The name is that of a character in the *Mostellaria* of Plautus, but W. S. Walker suggests that it is 'a misreading of Grunnio in the old Timon.' The corresponding character in *The Taming of A Shrew* is Sander (perhaps the actor's name), servant to Ferando.

[**Gruoch.**] See Macbeth, Lady.

Guallia. *Lat.* Wallia; Wales. Mine host of 'the Garter' thus adjures Caius and Evans: 'Peace, I say, Guallia and Gaul; French and Welsh' (*M.W.W.* iii, 1; Farmer's conj.).

'Gawle and gawlia,' Qq; 'Gallia and Gaule,' Ff.

Gualtier. *Fr.* form of 'Walter.' When the D. of Suffolk learns that he has been captured by Walter Whitmore (*q.v.*) he attempts to avert the prophecy that he should die by 'water' (Walter) by urging that 'Thy name is G., being rightly sounded' (2 *Hen. VI*, iv, 1).

Gualtree Forest. Galtres forest, N. of the city of York, of great extent. The scene of 2 *Hen. IV*, iv, 1, 2, 3, is laid there.

Guards, The. The stars *b* and *g* of the constellation Ursa Minor (which contains the Pole Star); they were formerly much used in navigation. See Bear, The.

'Seems to cast water on the burning Bear, And quench the Guards of th' ever-fixed Pole' (*Oth.* ii, 1).

The word 'Guards' in this connection is the equivalent of the Spanish *guardas*, meaning 'signals.' See *Sh. Eng.* (1916), i, 453, for early references.

Guiana. Country of South America. Sir Walter Raleigh returned thence in 1596, and in the same year there was published his *The Discoverie of the large, rich and beautiful Empyre of G., with a relation of the great and golden citie of Manoa which the Spanyards call El Dorado*, etc.

'She [Mrs Page] is a region in G., all gold and bounty' (*M.W.W.* i, 3). See Vienna.

Guichard. As a forename. 'Sir G. Dolphin' (*q.v.*).

Guiderius. D.P. *Cymb.* Supposed son to Belarius, disguised under the name of Polydore (*q.v.*). (i, 1; iii, 3) at the age of three he was stolen, with his younger brother Arviragus, from his home. iii, 3] is dissatisfied with the 'quiet life' they spend in Belarius' cave, which he speaks of as 'a cell of ignorance.' iii, 6] is struck by the beauty of 'Fidele' – 'were you a woman, youth, I should woo hard.' iv, 2] vies with his brother in praises of 'Fidele'; meets Cloten, and after a hot altercation with him, they 'fight and *exeunt*'; later, G. returns with Cloten's head; argues to Belarius, who is dismayed at the act, that 'the law protects not us, then why should we be tender?'; (G. throws Cl.'s head into the stream); rebukes his brother for 'wench-like words' over 'Fidele' (supposed dead), yet 'cannot sing' for grief; helps to perform 'F.'s' obsequies. iv, 4] persuades Belarius to join, with his 'sons,' the British army. v, 2] takes part in the battle. v, 5] confesses to Cymbeline that he slew Cloten, and is doomed to die; he is identified by a birthmark, after Belarius has told his story.

Guiderius is mtd. as one of the sons of Kymbeline, *Hol.* i, 32. The name seems to be a Latinization of the well-known Welsh 'Gwydyr.'

Guienne. A former French province, approximately equivalent to the valley of the R. Garonne. With Gascony it formed 'Aquitania,' of which Guienne is a derivative. It is declared to be lost (*1 Hen. VI*, i, 1) in 1422, but as a matter of fact remained an English possession till 1451.

Guildenstern. D.P. *Haml.* See Rosencrantz.

Guildford, or **Guilford, Richard.** A gentleman of Kent, who helped to raise a company of troops in support of Buckingham's rebellion 1483 (*Hol.* iii, 743, 'Gilford').

'In Kent the Guildfords are in arms … and still their power increaseth' (*Rich. III*, iv, 4, l. 505).

Guildford, Sir Henry (1489–1532). Master of the Horse and Comptroller of the Household to Hen. VIII; a fast friend of Wolsey's.

D.P. *Hen. VIII.* (i, 3) mtd. i, 4] as a 'comptroller,' welcomes Wolsey's lady guests. ('Guilford,' Ff.)

Guildhall. London; originally built, in 1411–31, as a court for the magistrates and corporation of the city. Buckingham made a speech there in 1483 accusing Edward IV of harsh and tyrannical conduct to the citizens; cf. *Rich. III*, iii, 5.

Guiltian. A military commander; *All's Well*, iv, 3.

'Julian' has been conjectured by S. Walker.

Guines. See GUYNES.

Guinover. Guinevere, wife to King Arthur. Her name was 'proverbial in Sh.'s time, and any flaunting person was called after her, the name also being used jocularly or in contempt' (Halliwell).

'When Queen G. of Britain was a little wench' (*L.L.L.* iv, 1).

Guischard. See GUICHARD.

Gurney, James. D.P. *John*. 'Servant to Lady Faulconbridge' (Rowe). i, 1] in attendance. ('Gournie,' F1.)

The only character added by Sh. to the old play. (Gurney, or Gourney, is the name of an ancient English family.) Succeeding edrs. have followed Rowe in designating G. as 'servant,' but Furness (*Var.*) points out that Philip and he address one another familiarly, and seem 'on easy terms of friendship,' and that G. is 'merely acting as escort to Lady F.'

Guy, Sir. The legendary 'Sir Guy, of Warwick,' hero of one of the earliest English metrical romances. His last great feat was the slaying of the giant Colbrand (*q.v.*), after which he retired to a hermitage at 'Guy's Cliff,' near Warwick. Mtd. *Hen. VIII*, v, 4.

Guyana. See VIENNA.

Guynes, Guines. Dept. Pas-de-Calais, France; 7 m. S. of Calais; held by England, 14th–16th centuries. Mtd. *Hen. VIII*, i, 1; see ANDREN.

Guysors, Gisors. Dept. of Eure, France; the ancient capital of the Norman Vexin. Its now ruined castle was built by Henry I of England. Reported as lost to England (*1 Hen. VI*, i, 1) in 1422; historically, it was surrendered in 1449.

H

Haberdasher. D.P. *Tam. Sh.* iv, 3] brings a cap for Katharina, which is rejected by Petruchio.

There is a similar character in *The Taming of A Shrew*.

Hacket, Cicely. 'The woman's maid of the house'; *Tam. Sh.* Ind. 2. See HACKET, M.

Hacket, Marian. 'The fat ale-wife of Wincot'; *Tam. Sh.* Ind. 2.

'On Nov. 21, 1591, Sara H., the daughter of Robert H., was baptized in Quinton Church' (Lee, p. 237). 'The name of H. is still [1868] found in the neighbourhood of Stratford' (French, p. 320). See WINCOT.

Hagar. Concubine of Abraham, and mother of Ishmael (Gen. xvi). 'That fool of H.'s offspring' (*i.e.* Launcelot Gobbo) (*M.V.* ii, 5).

Perhaps in allusion to Ishmael's 'mocking' (Gen. xxi, 9).

Hal. Abbr. of 'Henry,' invariably used by Falstaff, and twice by Poins, in addressing Prince Henry. *1 Hen. IV*, i, 2, ii, 2, 4, iii, 3, iv, 2, v, 1, 3, 4; *2 Hen. IV*, ii, 4, v, 5.

Half-can. Name of a prisoner. 'Wild H. that stabbed Pots' (*M. for M.* iv, 3).

Half-moon. Name of a room in the (Boar's Head) tavern; *1 Hen. IV*, ii, 4.

[**Hall, Edward** (*ob.* 1547).] Historian. His *Vnion of the two noble and illustre famelies of Lancastre and Yorke*, etc., was published, with additions by R. Grafton, in 1550. This was prohibited by Queen Mary, and no new edn. appeared until 1809, to which edn. the page references in the present work are made (following W. G. Boswell-Stone's *Shakspere's Holinshed*).

Hall was freely quoted or paraphrased by Holinshed, and in all such cases Hol., rather than Hall, was probably the dramatist's immediate authority. (Also 'Halle.')

Hallowmas. For 'All-hallowmas' (*q.v.*). 'To speak puling, like a beggar at H.' (*T.G.V.* ii, 1); 'Was't not at H., Master Froth? *Froth*. Allhallond Eve' (*M. for M.* ii, 1); 'like H. or short'st of day' (*Rich. II*, v, 1; 'Hollowmas,' QqFf).

Nov. 1 was in Sh.'s time ten days nearer the winter solstice than now (Clar.).

Hamlet. (In F1: 'The Tragedie of Hamlet, Prince of Denmarke.' Only i, 1, 2, 3, and ii, 1, 2, are indicated.)

PUBLICATION. In the Stationers' Registers, under date July 26, 1602, there appears: 'A booke called the Revenge of Hamlett Prince [of] Denmarke, as yt was lateli acted by the Lord Chamberleyne his servantes'; this was entered to I.R. (probably James Roberts).

In 1603 there was published 'The Tragicall Historie of Hamlet Prince of Denmarke By William Shake-speare, ... printed for N.L. and Iohn Trundell.' This, according to one theory, is 'an imperfect reproduction of the play, printed from a manuscript surreptitiously obtained' (Camb. edrs.). At any rate this edn., known as Q1, contains in fact little more than half of the play as given in Q2, which appeared in 1604, and claims on its title-page to be 'Newly imprinted and enlarged to almost as much againe as it was, according to the true and perfect Coppie ... Printed by I.R. for N.L.'

Q3, published in 1605, is practically a reissue of Q2. It was followed by Q4 (1611) and Q5 (undated); these are of minor importance.

The text of the Folio of 1623 is not derived from any of the Quartos 'but from an independent MS.' (Camb. edrs.); it contains passages occurring in none of the Qq, and, on the other hand, omits passages found in Qq.

The text in modern edns. is, practically, based on a collation of Q2 and F1.

SOURCES OF THE PLOT. The story of Hamlet first appeared in the *Historia Danica* of Saxo Grammaticus, written about A.D. 1200. This was first printed (in Paris) in 1514, and was transferred to the *Histoires Tragiques* of Pierre de Belleforest (1570). A translation of this into English was published, but the earliest edition known, entitled *The Hystorie of Hamblet*, is dated 1608.

It is now generally believed that an old play, now lost, on the subject of Hamlet, was the basis on which Shakespeare worked; this early play, as it would appear from references by Nashe and Lodge (*c.* 1587 and 1596), had been performed in England as early as 1587, and has been attributed to Thomas Kyd. Henslowe, in his *Diary*, notes a performance in 1594.

Hamlet. D.P. *Haml.* Prince of Denmark, son to the former and nephew to the present King. (i, 1) Horatio suggests that he should be informed of the apparition. i, 2] Hamlet consents to remain in Denmark instead of returning to Wittenberg; (*sol.*) comments bitterly on his mother's too early second marriage; hears of the ghost from eye-witnesses, and promises to join them at 'the platform' that night. (i, 3) Ophelia is warned by her father and brother against his advances. i, 4] sees the ghost and follows its beckoning. i, 5] learns from the ghost that his father had been murdered by his uncle; administers an oath of secrecy to Horatio and Marcellus. (ii, 1) Ophelia describes H.'s seeming madness. ii, 2] (Rosencrantz and Guildenstern are urged by Claudius to discover what ails H.; Polonius declares that H. is mad through love for Ophelia); H. converses satirically with Pol.; parries Ros. and Guild.'s questions; learns that a company of players have arrived; converses with the First Player, and requests him to play *The Murder of Gonzago* with an addition of 'some dozen or sixteen lines'; (*sol.*) broods over his own lethargy, but trusts 'to catch the conscience of the King' by means of the play. iii, 1] (*sol.*) meditates on suicide; converses wildly with Oph., who deems him 'blasted with ecstasy.' iii, 2] instructs the Players; confides his scheme to Horatio; marks the King's confusion at the performance of the play, and is convinced of his guilt; is summouned by the Queen; converses derisively with Ros. and Guild.; (*sol.*) resolves to 'speak daggers' to his mother, 'but use none.' iii, 3] (Claudius resolves to send Hamlet to England, to his death); H. will not kill Claudius 'now he is praying,' for his own father was murdered 'with all his crimes broad blown.' iii, 4] has audience with his mother; kills Polonius, who is in hiding behind the arras, taking him for the King; sternly reproaches his mother; sees and speaks to the ghost, who is invisible to the Queen; urges the latter to repentance. (iv, 1) (the slaying of Polonius is made known to the King). iv, 2] Hamlet refuses to tell Ros. and Guild. where he has hidden the body. iv, 3] prepares to set out for England. iv, 4] converses with a Norwegian captain; (*sol.*) reviles himself for his indecision. (iv, 6) returns from his projected voyage to England. (iv, 7) announces, by letter, his return. v, 1] enters, with Horatio, the graveyard where Ophelia's grave is being dug; converses with the diggers, and moralizes on death; grapples with Laertes in the grave, and declares that he loved Oph. more than could 'forty thousand brothers.' v, 2] relates to Horatio his discovery of the plot against his life and how he sent Ros. and Guild. to their death; receives a challenge to fence with Laertes; in the bout which ensues he is wounded by L.'s poisoned rapier, but wounds him with it in turn; realizing the plot, he pierces the King fatally with the poisoned weapon and dies himself in Horatio's arms.

In *The Hystorie of Hamblet* H.'s father and uncle are respectively Horvendile and Fengon (the Horvendillus and Fengo of Saxo Grammaticus), while in the original story Hamlet becomes King of Denmark, marries two wives, is betrayed by one of them into the power of Wiglerus, his maternal uncle, and is finally slain in battle. In the Quarto of 1603 H.'s madness is much less ambiguously stated than in that of 1604.

Literature dealing with Hamlet as *dramatis persona* rivals in bulk and psychological minuteness that devoted to many an historical personage. The point on which criticism has mainly fastened is the 'inconsistency' supposed to be displayed by Hamlet in the course of the tragedy. This has been attributed to Sh.'s having sought to blend into dramatic unity several incongruous sources; but it is also possible that it was this very incongruity which suggested to the dramatist the portrayal of a mind swayed hither and thither by contending aims and emotions, and led him to depict it with so subtle an insight as to afford an inexhaustible subject of discussion by succeeding generations.

Hammes, Castle of. Near Calais. There John de Vere, 13th E. of Oxford, was confined for ten years (1474–84). (Acc. *Hol.* iii, 693, 'by the space of twelve yeeres.') '*K. Edw.* Away with Oxford to Hammes Castle straight' (*3 Hen. VI*, v, 5; 'Hawes,' QqFf).

Well known in modern times as the place of imprisonment of Louis Napoleon (1840–6).

Hampton. Southampton (*q.v.*); Cambridge and his fellow conspirators had sworn to kill Henry V at H., *Hen. V*, ii, 2. 'Suppose that you have seen The well-appointed King at H. pier' (*ib.* iii, Chor.; thus corrected by Theobald; 'Dover' in Ff).

Hannibal. Famous Carthaginian general, b. 247 B.C. The name used abusively (perh. for 'Cannibal') by the constable Elbow: 'O thou wicked H.' (*M. for M.* ii, 1); 'this Hector far surmounted H.' (*L.L.L.* v, 2); Talbot says, of La Pucelle, that 'A witch, by fear, not force, like H., Drives back our troops, and conquers as she lists' (*1 Hen. VI*, i, 5; referring to H.'s stratagem of affixing lighted twigs to the horns of cattle, Livy, xxii, 16).

On the other hand, 'Cannibal' is used for 'Hannibal,' *2 Hen. IV*, ii, 4: 'Compare with Caesars and with Cannibals.' (*Cf.* 'Would have me turn Hannibal, and eat my own flesh and blood!' *Every Man in his Humour*, iii, 2.)

Harcourt. D.P. *2 Hen. IV.* 'Of the King's party.' iv, 4] announces the victory gained by the sheriff of Yorkshire. See ROKEBY.

There is no authority for this incident in the *Chronicles*. The Harcourts of Stanton, Oxon, were porsonages of some importance during the reign.

Harfleur. A port of Northern France, near the mouth of the Seine. ('Harflew,' Ff; 'Harflue,' *Hol.*) In 1415 Hen. V laid siege to it, mines being laid under the direction of the D. of Gloucester, and counter-mining resorted to by the defenders (*Hol.* iii, 549–50); its surrender was demanded, but a few days' grace was accorded, in which the inhabitants applied in vain for help from the Dauphin; finally 'the souldiors were ransomed, and the town sacked, to the great gain of the Englishmen' (*ib.* iii, 550); the D. of Exeter, with Sir John Fastolfe as his lieutenant, was made captain of the town (*ib. ib.*).

The English fleet sails for H., which is invested, *Hen. V*, iii, Chor.; the town surrenders to Henry, and is occupied by the D. of Exeter, who is ordered 'to fortify it strongly against the French' (*ib.* iii, 3); mtd., *ib.* iii, 5; its loss explained by the French, *ib.* iii, 6; cf. *Hol.* iii, 550.

Harfleur, Governor of. D.P. *Hen. V.* iii, 3] surrenders the town to Henry.

Jean, Lord D'Estouteville, was in command when H. was first invested, but Raoul, Sieur de Gaucourt, joined him with 300 men later, and is spoken of by Lydgate as the Governor: 'The Lord G… was capteyn in that place.'

Harford-west, Haverfordwest. Town in Pembrokeshire. Richmond, landing on the northern shore of Milford Haven, on the next day 'at the sunne rising, remooved to Hereford west' (*Hol.* iii, 753; 'harfford west,' Hall, *Rich. III*, p. 410).

'*Stan.* Where is princely Richmond now? *Chris.* At Pembroke, or at Harford-west in Wales' (*Rich. III*, iv, 5; so Q1; 'Hertford West,' Ff).

[**Harington.**] See BONVILLE.

[**Harlech.**] See BARKLOUGHLY.

Harpier. Apparently the name of a 'familiar.' 'H. cries, " 'Tis time, 'tis time" ' (*Macb.* iv, 1).

Altered by Pope to 'Harper'; according to Steevens, an error for 'Harpy'; perh. the Hebrew *habar*, 'incantare,' mtd. in R. Scot's *Discoverie of Witchcraft*, xii, 1, may be the origin of the word (Clar.).

Harry. Dim. of 'Henry.' (i) *Used alone.* (α) For 'Henry of Bolingbroke' (Henry IV). Mtd., *Rich. II*, i, 1, 3 (3), ii, 1 (2); 'in that Jerusalem shall H. die' (*2 Hen. IV*, iv, 4); the two 'Harrys' (Hen. IV, Hen. V) named together, *ib.* v, 2 (3).

(*b*)For 'Henry Percy' ('Hotspur'). Mtd., *Rich. II*, iii, 3; 'then would I have his H., and he mine' (*1 Hen. IV*, i, 1); thus named by Lady Percy, *ib.* ii, 3 (3), 4; mtd., *ib.* iv, 1; 'lord H.' (*ib.* iv, 4); mtd., *ib.* v, 2; mtd., *2 Hen. IV*, ii, 3 (2).

(*c*) For 'Henry of Monmouth' (Henry V). 'My young H.' (*1 Hen. IV*, i, 1); Falstaff, impersonating the King, substitutes 'Harry' for his usual 'Hal,' *ib.* ii, 4; mtd., *ib.* iii, 2 (6); 'young H. with his beaver on' (*ib.* iv, 1); 'H. to H.' (*ib. ib.*); mtd., *ib.* v, 3, 4 (2), 5; mtd., *2 Hen. IV*, Ind., i, 1, 2, ii, 1, 2, iv, 3, 4 (4); the two H.s, *ib.* v, 2 (3); 'H.'s happy life' (*ib. ib.*); mtd., *ib.* v, 3 (2); 'warlike H.' (*Hen. V*, i, Chor.); mtd., *ib.* ii, Chor., 4 (2), iii, Chor., 1, 6, 7; 'a little touch of H. in the night' (*ib.* iv, Chor.); 'noble H.' (*ib.* iv, 1); 'H. le Roy' (*ib. ib.*); mtd., *ib.* iv, 3(3), 7, v, Chor. (2), 2 (2).

(*d*) For 'Henry VI.' Mtd., *1 Hen. VI*, iv, 2; mtd., *3 Hen. VI*, iii, 1; 'holy H.' (*Rich. III*, iv, 4); mtd., *ib.* v, 3 (2).

(ii) *As a forename.* 'H. Hereford' (*Rich. II*, i, 3; ii, 1); 'H. Bolingbroke' (*ib.* iii, 3 (2); *2 Hen. IV*, iv, 1); 'H. Percy' (*Rich. II*, ii, 3; *1 Hen. IV*, i, 1, 3 (3), ii, 3, iv, 4, v, 4 (2); *2 Hen. IV*, i, 1); 'H. Monmouth' (*1 Hen. IV*, v, 2, 4; *2 Hen. IV*, Ind., i, 1, 3; *Hen. V*, iv, 7 (2); 'H. England' (*Hen. V*, iii, 5); 'Sir H. Guildford' (*Hen. VIII*, i, 4).

(iii) *Attrib.* 'H. ten shillings' (*2 Hen. IV*, iii, 2).

Harvey. A name used for 'Bardolph' in QqFf, *1 Hen. IV*, i, 2, l. 182. See ROSSILL.

[**Hastings.**] See PURSUIVANT.

Hastings, Sir Ralph. Took part in Abp. Scrope's rebellion. In *Hol.* iii, 529–30, he is called 'Lord Hastings,' but in *Rotuli Parl.* iii, 604, he is 'Ralph Hastings, Chivaler.' Acc. Hume his life was spared.

D.P. *2 Hen. IV.* 'Lord Hastings' (Ff). i, 3] discusses, with Scrope and others, the relative strength of the rebel and royal forces. iv, 1] (in Gualtree forest) discusses the terms of peace. iv, 2] reports dispersal of the rebel forces; is arrested. (iv, 4) his capture announced to the King.

Hastings, William (*c.* 1430–83). Baron Hastings of Ashby-de-la-Zouch; ennobled as a zealous Yorkist by Edward IV; held many important offices, including that of Lord Chamberlain (*Rich. III*, i, 1, l. 77); helped the King to escape to Holland in 1470; acted for him in his absence, and gained Clarence as an ally; fought at Barnet and Tewkesbury; on the accession of Edward V declined Gloucester's overtures, and was beheaded.

Hastings, though a foe to the Woodvilles, was firmly attached to the children of Edward IV. Stow characterizes him as 'a good knight and gentle, but somewhat dissolute of living.'

Clarence's sneer (*3 Hen. VI*, iv, 1) that Hastings deserves 'the heir of Lord Hungerford,' is based on an error of the dramatist (see HUNGERFORD, SIR T.). The allegation (*Hol.* iii, 688) that H. was accessory to the murder of Prince Edward (son of Henry VI) is alluded to, *Rich. III*, i, 3, l. 211.

D.P. *3 Hen. VI.* iv, 1] deprecates seeking aid from France. iv, 3] *p.m.*; escapes when Edward IV is captured by Warwick. iv, 5] aids Edward to escape from Middleham Castle (cf. *Hol.* iii, 675). (iv, 6) mtd. iv, 7] 'persuades' the Mayor to open gates of York to Edward. v, 7] *p.m.*; in attendance on Edward.

D.P. *Rich. III.* i, 1] has been released from prison; is greeted as 'lord chamberlain' (*Hol.* iii, 713). i, 3] his imprisonment imputed to Q. Elizabeth; (stood by when Prince Edward was murdered); Gloucester deems him 'a simple gull.' ii, 1] at the King's bidding is reconciled to the Woodvilles (*Hol.* iii, 713). ii, 2] present. iii, 1] announces that the Queen has 'taken sanctuary' with the D. of York; later, returns with the latter; (Catesby is sent to sound him as to 'how he doth stand affected' to Gl.). iii, 2] receives a grave warning from Lord Stanley (*Hol.* iii, 723); tells Catesby that he will never bar his 'master's heirs in true descent' (*Hol.* iii, 722); proceeds toward the Tower, where he will 'stay dinner.' (iii, 3) mtd. iii, 4] (at the coronation council) is flattered by Gloucester, who afterward suddenly turns on him and condemns him to death (*Hol.* iii, 722–3). (iii, 5) his head brought to Gl. (iii, 6) his indictment (*Hol.* iii, 724). (iv, 2, 4; v, 1) mtd. (v, 3) his ghost appears to Richard.

Hatfield. See WILLIAM OF HATFIELD.

Haverfordwest. See HARFORD-WEST.

[**Haughmond Hill.**] Near the battlefield of Shrewsbury. Referred to as 'yon busky hill' (*1 Hen. IV*, v, 1).

Headborough. D.P. *M. Ado* (st. dir. of iii, 5, in QFf). Cf. *Tam. Sh.* Ind. 1, l. 11; for 'thirdborough,' in Ff. See VERGES.

Heart's Ease. Name of a song, or tune. '*Pet.* O, an you will have me live, play "Heart's Ease" … play me some merry dump' (*Rom. J.* iv, 5).

'Heart's Ease' is mtd. in the old English comedy of *Misogonus*. written as early as 1560 (see Ward, *Eng. Dram. Lit.* i, 259).

Heaven. The word occurs some 800 times in *Sh.* Examples of its various uses are subjoined.

(i) *For the Deity.* 'H.' is often substituted in Ff for 'God' (*q.v.*) in Qq. 'H., from thy endless goodness send prosperous life ... to ... Elizabeth' (*Hen. VIII*, v, 5; *cf.* 'God of his infinite goodnesse send,' etc., *Hol.* iii, 934); 'H. forgive my sins' (*M.W.W.* iii, 3); and in asseverations and invocations *passim*.

(ii) *The sky, the wellkin.* (*a*) *Sing.* 'Blue of h.'s own tinct' (*Cymb.* ii, 2); 'the grey vault of h.' (2 *Hen. IV*, ii, 3). With especial reference to the starry sphere of the Ptolemaic system: 'the axletree On which h. rides' (*Tr. Cr.* i, 3); 'The floor of h. Is thick inlaid with patines of bright gold' (*M.V.* v, 1). (*b*) *Plu.* 'I never saw the h.s so dim by day' (*Wint. T.* iii, 3); 'he holp the h.s to rain' (*Lear*, iii, 7).

(iii) *The abode of the departed souls of the righteous.* 'If not in h., you'll surely sup in hell' (2 *Hen. VI*, v, 1); 'a knell That summons thee to h. or to hell' (*Macb.* ii, 1); 'now she [Helena] sings in h.' (*All's Well*, iv, 3); 'I know his soul's in h.' (*T. Nt.* i, 5); etc.

(iv) *In plu., the celestial powers.* 'The h.s continue their loves' (*Wint. T.* i, 1); 'as h.s forfend' (*ib.* iv, 3); 'h.s keep him from these beasts' (*Temp.* ii, 1); 'h.s and honour be witness' (2 *Hen. VI*, iv, 8).

In the following passages 'h.' is followed by a plu. pronoun, and is equivalent to the foregoing: 'But h. hath pleased it so ... that I must be their scourge and minister' (*Haml.* iii, 4, l. 173); 'Put we our quarrel to the will of h., Who, when they see the hours ripe,' etc. (*Rich. II*, i, 2; Walker, *Crit. Exam.* ii, 110, gives similar instances from other dramatists).

(v) *Metaph.* 'The h. of her brow' (*L.L.L.* iv, 3); 'a h. on earth I have won' (*All's Well*, iv, 2); 'h. is here, Where Juliet lives' (*Rom. J.* iii, 3).

Hebrew. Jew (*subst.*). 'Thou are an H., a Jew, and not worth the name of a Christian' (*T.G.V.* ii, 5); 'this H. will turn Christian' (*M.V.* i, 3); 'a wealthy H.' (*ib. ib.*).

Hecate. A mysterious divinity, by early Greek writers identified with several goddesses, including Demeter, Artemis, and Persephone. Later, she is the spectral ruler of demons and phantoms. In works of art often represented as a three-headed monster; *cf.* Ovid, *Metam.* vii, 194, 'triceps Hecate,' where Golding interpolates: 'of whom the witches holde As of their goddesse.'

'Triple H.'s team' (*M.N.D.* v, 2); 'pale H.'s offerings' (*Macb.* ii, 1); 'black H.'s summons' (*ib.* iii, 2); 'that railing H. [Joan of Arc]' (*1 Hen. VI*, iii, 2); 'the mysteries of H. and the night' (*Lear*, i, 1); 'with H.'s ban thrice blasted' (*Haml.* iii, 2). A dissyllable except in *Hen. VI*.

D.P. *Macb.* iii, 5] chides the witches for taking it upon themselves 'to trade and traffic with Macb.'; bids them meet her on the morrow. iv, 1] commends their enchantments.

The 'superfluous interposition' (Lee, p. 397) of H. in the witch scenes has been attributed to another hand, possibly T. Middleton, in whose play *The Witch* (1610) she figures conspicuously. Steevens, who discovered the MS. of *The Witch*, contended that it preceded *Macbeth*; but it is now generally admitted that R. Scot's *Discoverie of Witchcraft* could have provided materials for the incantation scenes in each play.

Hector. Eldest son of Priam and Hecuba; 'the light and hope of the Trojans' (Virg. *Aen.* ii, 281). Acc. Homer, Hector was wounded by Ajax and cured by Apollo; in an encounter with Patroclus he at first gave way, but was encouraged by the god, and, returning, slew his opponent. He was chased thrice round Troy by Achilles, but at last, making a stand, was slain by Ach., who dragged his body behind his chariot. In medieval romance H. was regarded as 'the flower of chivalry,' in accordance with the Trojan sympathies of the Middle Ages, and this view is followed by Sh.

Host calls Falstaff 'bully H.' (*M.W.W.* i, 3), and Caius 'H. of Greece' (*ib.* ii, 3); 'valiant ... as H.' (*M. Ado*, ii, 3). Hector is one of the Nine Worthies (*q.v.*), and is represented by Armado, *L.L.L.* v, 2 (14). (A remark made by Dumain on the occasion, 'Hector's a greyhound,' seems to imply that it was the name of a dog.) 'As valorous as H. of Troy' (*2 Hen. IV*, iv, 4); 'A second H. for his grim aspect' (*1 Hen. VI*, ii, 3); '*Hen.* [to Warwick]. Farewell, my H. and my Troy's true hope' (*3 Hen. VI*, iv, 8); 'the breasts of Hecuba, When she did suckle H., look'd not lovelier Than H.'s forehead when it spit forth blood At Grecian sword' (*Cor.* i, 3); 'Roman H.'s hope' (*T. And.* iv, 1; see Astyanax); mtd., *Lucr.* 1430, 1486.

In plu.: 'You have shown all Hectors' (*Ant. Cl.* iv, 8). Alluded to: 'the hope of Troy' (*3 Hen. VI*, ii, 1).

D.P. *Tr. Cr.* (i, 1) mtd. i, 2] *p.m.*; Pandarus eulogizes him. (i, 3; ii, 1) his challenge to the Greeks. ii, 2] he advocates the restoration of Helen to Menelaus, but yields to the opposite opinion of his 'spritely brethren.' (iii, 1) Helen proud to unarm him. (iii, 3) mtd. (iv, 4) his trumpet heard. iv, 5] fights with Ajax, but, remembering their kinship, they desist; H. converses with the Grecian chiefs; on the morrow he will fight Achilles. v, 1] rests in the Greek camp. (v, 2) mtd. v, 3] rebukes his wife and Cassandra, who would persuade him not to take the field, but bids Troilus not 'fight today'; Priam begs him to 'come back,' and Cassandra has a prophetic vision of his death, but he persists. v, 4] spares Thersites. v, 6] meets Achilles, but they do not fight; pursues a sumptuously armed Greek. (v, 7) the Myrmidons instructed to kill him. v, 9] puts off his helmet and shield, and is slain. (v, 10) his death announced. (v, 11) Troilus laments him.

'The distinguishing feature in Hector's character, as pourtrayed in medieval tradition, was his possession of a wisdom and moderation equal to the prowess of his arm ... A thousand proofs might be given of the ancient popularity of Hector and of Troy, but it will be sufficient here to single out one that shall carry conviction with it; in the pack of cards still used in France, in which each court-card bears a name, we see Hector figuring by the side of Launcelot.' (P. Stapfer, *Sh. and Clas. Ant.* (1880), pp. 211, 213.)

Hecuba. Wife of Priam, and mother of Hector, Polydorus, Paris, and other children. After the fall of Troy, ace. 'Dictys Cretensis,' she uttered such invectives against the Greeks that they put her to death.

'Queen H.' (*Tr. Cr.* i, 2; v, 1); laughed, *ib.* i, 2; 'H. on knees' (*ib.* v, 3); sees visions, *ib. ib.*; Cassandra foresees her anguish, *ib. ib.*; who shall tell her of Hector's death? *ib.* v, 11; 'the breasts of H., When she did suckle Hector' (*Cor.* i, 3); 'all curses madded H. gave the Greeks' (*Cymb.* iv, 2); 'H. of Troy ran mad through sorrow' (*T. And.* iv, 1); her grief and terror at the capture of Troy, *Haml.* ii, 2; 'What's H. to him, or he to H., that he should weep for her?' (*ib. ib.*). 'The gods that arm'd the Queen of Troy With opportunity of sharp revenge Upon the Thracian tyrant [Polymestor] in his tent' (*T. And.* i, 1; *cf.* Ovid, *Metam.* xiii, 432 ff.; Euripides, *Hecuba*; Virg. *Aen.* iii, 49); 'despairing H.' (*Lucr.* 1447); mtd., *ib.* 1485.

For H.'s extreme grief see Ovid, *Metam.* xiii, 439–575.

Helen (1). For 'Helena' (D.P.). *M.N.D.* i, 1; ii, 3; iii, 2 (3); iv, 1.

Helen (2). For 'Helena' (D.P.). *All's Well*, i, 1, 3 (7); ii, 2, 3, 5; v, 3 (5). ('Hellen,' usually, in st. dirs. Ff.)

Helen (3). For 'St Helena' (*q.v.*).

Helen (4). D.P. *Cymb.* Waiting-woman to Imogen. ('Helene,' F1, 2; 'Lady' in st. dir. and pfxs.) ii, 2] is directed to retire, and call Im. 'by four o'th' clock.'

Helen (5). Daughter of Jupiter and Leda, and wife of Menelaus; her abduction by Paris led to the Trojan War; held to be of surpassing beauty. 'H.'s cheek, but not her ['his,' Ff] heart' (*A.Y.L.* iii, 2); 'H. of thy noble thoughts [*i.e.* Doll Tearsheet]' (*2 Hen. IV*, v, 5); 'H. of Greece was fairer far than thou [Q. Margaret]' (*3 Hen. VI*, ii, 2); 'the lover ... Sees H.'s beauty in a brow of Egypt' (*M.N.D.* v, 1); 'to his [Romeo's] lady ... H. and Hero, hildings' (*Rom. J.* ii, 4); mtd., *Son.* liii, *Lucr.* 1369.

D.P. *Tr. Cr.* (Prol.) 'with wanton Paris sleeps.' (i, 1) compared with Cressida by Pandarus. (i, 2) jests on a white hair on Troilus' chin. (ii, 1) 'the eye of H.'s needle.' (ii, 2) her restoration to the Greeks discussed. iii, 1] is described as 'the mortal Venus, the heart-blood of beauty, love's invisible soul'; importunes Pandarus to sing a love-song. (iv, 1) characterized with bitterness by Diomede. (iv, 5) mtd.

Allusions: 'Fair Leda's daughter had a thousand wooers' (*Tam. Sh.* i, 2); confused, by Flute, with Hero, *M.N.D.* v, 1, l. 199.

Helena (1). D.P. *All's Well.* ('Helen,' except in st. dirs. and once in i, 1.) A gentlewoman protected by the Countess of Rousillon. i, 1] her grief at Bertram's departure is mistaken for excess of sorrow for her father's death; (*sol.*) compares B. to 'a bright particular star ... he is so above me'; lightly discusses maidenhood with Parolles, and banters him on his lack of valour; (*sol.*) forms a plan for furthering her hopes. i, 3] her love for Bertram becomes known to the Countess; interrogated by the latter, she confesses that, though she is conscious of her lowlier birth, she loves B.; the Countess approves her design of going to Paris and making trial in the King's case of the remedy inherited from her father. ii, 1] is permitted to attempt the King's cure on pain of death if she fails, but with permission to choose a courtier for her husband if she succeeds. (ii, 2) the Countess sends her a letter. ii, 3] the remedy avails, and H. chooses Bertram for her husband; he takes her on compulsion, but vows to flee from her. ii, 4] she is informed that Bertram is called away by 'serious business.' ii, 5] she is bidden by B. to go home, whither he will follow her. iii, 2] having read Bertram's cruel letter, resolves to flee from Rousillon secretly. iii, 5] in the guise of a pilgrim reaches Florence; sees B. with the army; is hospitably received by a widow. iii, 7] persuades the widow to let her assume the character of her daughter Diana, of whom B. is enamoured, and take her place at night. (iv, 3) H.'s death is announced. iv, 4] she resolves to seek the King at Marseilles. v, 1] (at M.) learns that the King has departed for Rousillon; sends him a petition and follows it. v, 3] in the King's presence, her story having been unfolded, she is acknowledged by Bertram as his beloved wife.

In Boccaccio's novel the corresponding character is Giglietta di Narbona, a wealthy lady. She deliberately devises the artifice which in Helena's case is suggested by mere chance.

Helena (2). D.P. *M.N.D.* i, 1] admits her envy of Hermia, with whom Demetrius, false to his vows, is now in love; is entrusted with the secret of Hermia's projected flight with Lysander; muses on the blindness and the fickleness of love; resolves to betray the lovers to Dem. ii, 1] follows Dem. in his pursuit of Herm. through the wood; exclaims that he draws her heart as doth the magnet steel, and that though he spurn her she will follow him; despite threats she will 'make a heaven of hell.' ii, 2] in pursuit of Dem. finds Lys. asleep; he awakes, under the influence of a love-charm, is instantly enamoured of her, and declares he will kill Dem.; she bids him be content with Hermia's love, but he persists in his wooing; she rebukes him for mocking her with feigned love. iii, 2] she is still being courted by Lys. when Dem. awakes and also assails her with extravagant protestations of love; believing that they conspire to deride her, she exclaims that if they were men they 'would not use a gentle lady so'; Herm. enters, and Hel. believes that she too has joined in the plot; she reminds Herm. of their early friendship – how they 'grew together like a double cherry' – and yet now Herm. is pitiless and ready, with the rest, 'to make mouths upon her' when she turns her back; she begs the young men not to let Herm. – whom she has stung to fury – hurt her, and promises to 'bear her folly' back quietly to Athens; still fearing Hermia, 'who though she be but little she is fierce,' flees in dismay. iv, 1] awaking, finds the love of Dem. restored to her, but dreads lest she should have found him 'like a jewel, mine own and not mine own.' v, 1] *p.m.*

Helena (3). A guest. 'The lively H.' (*Rom. J.* i, 2).

Helena, St. Wife of Constantius Chlorus and mother of Constantine the Great. She is said to have discovered the true Cross, at Jerusalem, and in honour of this founded there the Church of the Holy Sepulchre. Joan of Arc is declared greater than 'Helen, the mother of great Constantine' (*1 Hen. VI*, i, 2).

Helenus. Son of Priam; acc. Homer, a skilful augur; as a warrior he fought against, and was wounded by, Menelaus (*Il.* vi, 76; vii, 44; xii, 94). The many later traditions about H. are not relevant. (Mtd. Virg. *Aen.* iii, 345 ff.; Ovid, *Metam.* xv, 438.)

D.P. *Tr. Cr.* i, 2] *p.m.*; passes by; Pandarus remarks that 'he'll fight indifferent well' and 'is a priest.' ii, 2] favours the giving up of Helen to the Greeks; is reproached by Troilus as a faint-hearted priest. (iii, 1) mtd. among 'all the gallantry of Troy.'

Helias. See Troy, Gates of.

Helicane. For 'Helicanus' (*q.v.*). *Per.* ii, Gow., 4 (4). (Also spelt 'Helicon,' 'Hellicon,' 'Hellican,' Qq.)

Helicanus. D.P. *Per.* A lord of Tyre. i, 2] disdains to flatter Pericles, and advises him to travel, and avoid Antiochus for a while. i, 3] announces P.'s departure. (ii, Gow.) he watches over P.'s safety. ii, 4] is offered the crown by the nobles, but defers acceptance for a year. v, 1] in attendance on Pericles' ship; receives Lysimachus and explains to him the cause of P.'s 'distemperature'; is present when Marina is made known to P. v, 2] *p.m.* v, 3] is presented to Thaisa; (Gower characterizes him as 'A figure of truth, of faith, of loyalty').

Helicons. Used by Pistol for 'Muses.' 'Shall dunghill curs confront the Helicons?' (2 *Hen. IV*, v, 3).

It is not necessary to suppose that P. meant 'Heliconides.'

Hell. The infernal regions, regarded as (i) the place of departed spirits (*Gk.* Hades); (ii) the place of torment for devils and the wicked (*Lat.* Tartarus). Hence, metaph., anguish.

(*a*) *In the Greek and Roman Plays.* 'A h. of pain' (*Tr. Cr.* iv, 1); 'as hideously ['tediously,' Q] as h.' (*ib.* iv, 2); 'by h. and h.'s torments' (*ib.* v, 2). 'Am I in earth, in heaven or in h.?' (*Com. Err.* ii, 2); 'in Tartar limbo, worse than h.' (*ib.* iv, 2); 'one [an officer] that ... carries poor souls to h.' (*ib. ib.*). 'Would thou wert shipp'd to h.' (*T. And.* i, 2); 'an ever-burning h.' (*ib.* iii, 1); 'revenge from h.' (*ib.* iv, 3); 'there is no justice in earth nor h.' (*ib. ib.*); 'would I were a devil To live and burn in everlasting fire, So I might have thy company in h.' (*ib.* v, 1); 'could not all h. afford you such a devil' (*ib.* v, 2); 'Pluto and h.!' (*Cor.* i, 4); 'the fires in the lowest h.' (*ib.* iii, 3; *cf.* Deut. xxxii, 22); 'Would I might go to h. among the rogues' (*Jul. C.* i, 2); 'Ate ... come hot from h.' (*ib.* iii, 1). 'When my good stars have shot their fires Into the abysm of h.' (*Ant. Cl.* iii, 13, I. 147). 'H. only danceth at so harsh a chime' (*Per.* i, 1); 'surges which wash both heaven and h.' (*ib.* iii, 1); 'the paind'st fiend in h.' (*ib.* iv, 6).

(*b*) *In the Comedies.* 'The one he chides to h.' (*Wint. T.* iv, 3); 'black is the badge of h.' (*L.L.L.* iv, 3); 'fiend of h. [Kath.]' (*Tam. Sh.* i, 1); who would be so foolish as 'to be married to h.'? (*ib. ib.*); 'lead apes in h.' (*ib.* ii, 1); 'H. is empty, and all the devils are here!' (*Temp.* i, 2); 'a pond as deep as h.' (*M. for M.* iii, 1); 'the cunning livery of h.' (*ib. ib.*); 'if I could go to h. for an eternal moment or so' (*M.W.W.* ii, 1); 'I am damned in h.' (*ib.* ii, 2); 'see the h. of having a false woman' (*ib. ib.*); 'lest the oil that is in me should set h. on fire' (*ib.* v, 5); 'given ourselves without scruple to h.' (*ib. ib.*). 'O, h., to choose love by another's eye!' (*M.N.D.* i, 1); 'he hath turned a heaven into h.,' 'make a heaven of h.' (*ib.* ii, 2); 'O, hell!' (*ib.* iii, 2); 'more devils than vast h. can hold' (*ib.* v, 1). Beatrice speaks of 'leading apes to h.' (*M. Ado*, ii, 1); 'I think his soul is in h.' (*T. Nt.* i, 5); 'if all the devils in h. be drawn in little and Legion himself possessed him' (*ib.* iii, 4); 'a fiend like thee [Cesario] might bear my soul to h.' (*ib. ib.*); Malvolio declares his chamber as dark as ignorance or h., *ib.* iv, 2 (2); 'our house is h.' (*M.V.* ii, 3); 'O, hell!' (*ib.* ii, 7).

(*c*) *In the Tragedies.* 'There's h., there's darkness, there's the sulphurous pit' (*Lear*, iv, 6); 'the dunnest smoke of h.' (*Macb.* i, 5); 'a knell That summons thee to heaven or to h.' (*ib.* ii, 1); 'this place is too cold for h.' (*ib. ii, 3); 'the legions of horrid h.'* (*ib.* iv, 3); 'pour the sweet milk of concord into h.' (*ib. ib.*); 'H. is murky' (*ib.* v, 1); 'a hotter name than any is in h.' (*ib.* v, 7). 'As I hate h.' (*Rom. J.* i, 1); 'dismal h.' (*ib.* iii, 2); 'what hadst thou to do in h.' (*ib. ib.*); 'h. itself' (*ib.* iii, 3); 'the damned use that word ['banished'] in h.' (*ib. ib.*). 'Practices of cunning h.' (*Oth.* i, 3); 'all the tribe of h.,' 'h. and night' (*ib. ib.*); 'as low as h.'s from heaven' (*ib. ib.*); 'Divinity of h.' (*ib.* ii, 3); 'arise, black vengeance, from the hollow h. ['cell,' Q]' (*ib.* iii, 3); 'the spite of h.' (*ib.* iv, 1); 'false as h.' (*ib.* iv, 2); 'grim as h.,' 'you, mistress, that ... keep the gate of h.,' 'h. gnaw his bones' (*ib. ib.*); 'gone to burning h.' (*ib.* v, 2); 'beneath all depth in h.' (*ib. ib.*). 'All the plagues of h.' (*Cymb.* i, 7); 'h. is here [in Iachimo's breast]' (*ib.* ii, 2); 'all the fiends of h.' (*ib.* ii, 4); 'another stain as big as h. can hold' (*ib. ib.*); 'all faults that h. knows' (*ib.* ii, 5). 'Though h. itself should gape' (*Haml.* i, 2); 'blasts from h.' (*ib.* i, 4); 'and shall I [with heaven and earth] couple h.?' (*ib.* i, 5); 'loosed out of h. to speak of horrors' (*ib.* ii, 1); 'prompted to my revenge by heaven and h.' (*ib.* ii, 2); 'the witching time of night When ... h. itself breathes out contagion' (*ib.* iii, 2); 'that his soul may be as damned and black As h. whereto it goes' (*ib.* iii, 3); 'rebellious h., If thou canst mutine in a matron's bones' (*ib.* iii, 4); 'To h., allegiance!' (*ib.* iv, 5); 'h. itself she turns to favour' (*ib. ib.*).

(*d*) *In the English Historical Plays.* 'I'll send his soul to h.' (*John*, i, 1); 'Make work upon ourselves for heaven or h.' (*ib.* ii, 2); 'h. lose a soul' (*ib.* iii, 1); (drums, etc.) 'clamours of h.' (*ib. ib.*); 'you think the devil is come from h.' (*ib.* iv, 3); 'so ugly a fiend of h.,' 'Let h. want pains enough to torture me' (*ib. ib.*); 'within me is a h.' (*ib.* v, 7). 'The pains of h.' (*Rich. II*, iii, 1); 'terrible h. make war Upon their spotted souls' (*ib.* iii, 2); 'marks thee out for h.' (*ib.* iv, 1); 'thou art damned to h.,' 'Fiend, thou tormentest me ere I come to h.' (*ib. ib.*); 'Go thou and fill another room in h.' (*ib.* v, 5); 'this deed is chronicled in h.' (*ib. ib.*). 'What hole in h. were hot enough for him?' (*1 Hen. IV*, i, 2); 'he wisheth you in h.' (*ib.* iii, 1); 'She's in h. already, and burns' (2 *Hen. IV*, ii, 4). 'If h. and treason hold their promises' (*Hen. V*, ii, Chor.); 'hath got the voice in h. for excellence' (*ib.* ii, 2); 'would I were with him [Falstaff] ... either in heaven or in h.' (*ib.* ii, 3); 'with conscience wide as h.' (*ib.* iii, 3); 'horrid night, the child of h.' (*ib.* iv, 1); 'All h. shall stir for this' (*ib.* v, 1). 'Hundreds he sent to h.' (*1 Hen. VI*, i, 1); 'can you suffer h. so to prevail' (*ib.* i, 5); 'the help of h.' (*ib.* ii, 1); 'a fiend of h.' (*ib. ib.*); 'h. our prison is' (*i.e.* no prisoners are spared) (*ib.* iv, 7); 'h. [is] too strong for me to buckle with' (*ib.* v, 3); 'thou foul accursed minister of h. [Joan of Arc]' (*ib.* v, 4); 'what is wedlock forced but a h.?' (*ib.* v, 5). 'To think upon my pomp shall be my h.' (2 *Hen. VI*, ii, 4); 'some black storm Shall blow ten thousand souls to heaven or h.' (*ib.* iii, 1); 'send thy soul to h.' (*ib.* iii, 2); 'the foul terrors in dark-seated h.' (*ib. ib.*); 'the hags of h.' (*ib.* iv, 1); 'in despite the devils and h.' (*ib.* iv, 8); 'thrust thy soul to h.' (*ib.* iv, 10); 'you'll surely sup in h.' (*ib.* v, 1); 'O war, thou son of h.' (*ib.* v, 2). 'I live in h.' (*3 Hen. VI*, i, 3); 'for his hoarding went to h.' (*ib.* ii, 2); Richard will 'account the world but h.' till he is king, *ib.* iii, 2; (Rich. to Hen.) 'Down, down to h., and say I sent thee thither !' (*ib.* v, 6); 'let h. make crook'd my mind' (*ib. ib.*). 'Thou [Richard] dreadful minister of h.' (*Rich. III*, i, 2); 'thou hast made the happy earth thy h.,' 'thou unfit for any place but h.' (*ib. ib.*); 'hie thee to h. for shame' (*ib.* i, 3); 'a hell of ugly devils,' 'son of h.,' 'Sin, death, and h. have set their mark on him' (*ib. ib.*); 'I [Clarence] could not believe but that I was in h.' (*ib.* i, 4); 'from the reach of h.' (*ib.* iv, 1); 'h.'s black intelligencer' (*ib.* iv, 4); 'h. burns' (for Rich.), 'to make earth my h.,' 'So long as h., and Richard, likes of it' (*ib. ib.*); 'hand in hand to h.' (*ib.* v, 3). (Wolsey's pride) 'if not from h. the devil is a niggard' (*Hen. VIII*, i, 1); 'he begins a new h. in himself' (*ib. ib.*); 'black As if besmear'd in h.' (*ib.* i, 2).

Followed by plu. pronoun: *Rich. III*, iv, 4, l. 71. 'A h. of time' (*Son.* cxx).

Hellen. For 'Helena,' or 'Helen.' *All's Well*, st. dirs. i, 3; ii, 1; v, 3, Ff.

Hellespont. Straits of the Dardanelles, connecting the Propontis (Sea of Marmora) with the Aegean Sea. See HERO (2).

'How young Leander cross'd the H... And yet you never swam the H.' (*T.G.V.* i, 1); 'He [Leander] ... went but forth to wash him in the H., and ... was drowned' (*A.Y.L.* iv, 1); 'Like to the Pontick sea, Whose icy current ... keeps due on To the Propontick and the H.' (*Oth.* iii, 3, l. 453).

'And the sea Pontus evermore floweth and runneth out into Propontis, but the sea never retireth backe againe within Pontus' (Holland's *Pliny* (1601), bk. ii, ch. 97).

Hemminge, John (*ob.* 1630). Mtd., as 'John Hemmings,' in 'The Names of the Principall Actors' pfxd. to F1, of which he was a coeditor. He is said to have been the original Falstaff.

Also 'Heming,' 'Heminges,' 'Heminge' (Dedication).

[**Henninus.**] See CORNWALL, DUKE OF.

Henricus (*Lat.*). Henry; *Hen. V*, v, 2, l. 470.

Henry. As a forename; see PIMPERNELL, PERCY, SCROOP, GUILDFORD.

Henry, Prince (1207–72). Son to King John, afterward King Henry III.

D.P. *John.* (v, 6) procures pardon for the rebel nobles. v, 7] announces his father's approaching end; is present at his death, and gives directions for his burial. (Historically, he was at the time barely ten years old.)

Henry IV (1367–1413). King of England ; son of John of Gaunt; called H. of Bolingbroke, or simply B. (*q.v.*), from his birthplace; in early life he was styled E. of Derby; he married (*a*) Mary de Bohun, heiress of Hereford (1380); and (*b*) Joan, d. of Charles of Navarre and widow of John de Montfort, D. of Brittany (1402). Henry's Shakespearean story begins with his banishment in 1398. In the following year he landed in Yorkshire, marched to Bristol, met Richard II at Flint, took him to London, and was 'elected' to the throne; after an unsuccessful attack on Welsh rebels he defeated the Percies at Shrewsbury (1403) and subdued the revolt of Northumberland and Scrope in 1405; he died at Westminster and was buried at Canterbury.

Holinshed (iii, 541), citing Hall, observes that H. did not die of leprosy, 'as foolish friers imagined; but a verie apoplexie' (cf. *2 Hen. IV*, i, 2, l. 123).

D.P. *Rich. II.* (In st. dirs. variously, 'Bolingbroke,' 'Bullingbroke,' 'Hereford,' 'Duke of H.,' and 'King.') i, 1] accuses Mowbray, before Richard, of being a traitor; throws down his gage; accuses M. of embezzlement, of being a leader in plots for the past 18 years, and of murdering Gloucester; refuses to withdraw his gage; is commanded to attend a judicial combat at Coventry. i, 3] enters the lists; salutes the King and his friends; the combat is forbidden by the King; B. is condemned to exile for ten years, and submits to the decree; takes oath not to plot against the King or be reconciled to Mowbray; urges M. to confess his guilt; his exile is reduced to six years; he speaks of its bitterness, but declares that where'er he wanders he will remain 'a true-born Englishman.' (ii, 1) his intended marriage prevented; he sails from Brittany. (ii, 2) reaches Ravenspurgh. ii, 3] nears Berkeley, with Northumberland; greets Harry Percy and other lords; declares to the D. of York that he comes merely to claim his patrimony; persuades Y. to accompany him to Bristol. iii, 1] condemns Bushy and Green to death; sends greetings to the Queen; speaks of and expedition against Glendower (historically, not undertaken until two years later). iii, 3] sends Northumberland to Richard to declare B.'s allegiance and his willingness to lay down his arms if his exile is repealed and his possessions are restored; kneels before the King, professes loyalty, but assents when Richard says 'do we must what force will have us do'; sets out with R. for London. (iii, 4) the completeness of his triumph. iv, 1] presides at the parliament at Westminster, and controls the disputants; on hearing from York that Richard will abdicate, declares that he will 'ascend the regal throne'; commands R. to be brought before the parliaments; presses R. to declare his willing abdication; treats R. with courtesy, but commits him to the Tower; names a day for his own coronation. v, 3] inquires about his 'unthrifty son'; receives Aumerle's confession of conspiracy, and after hearing York's accusation of his own son, and the Duchess's entreaties, pardons the offender. v, 6] hears of the defeat of the rebels under the Abbot of Westminster; declares to Exton, who brings in R.'s body, that he hates 'the murtherer, loves him murthered'; and resolves to purge his own guilt by making a voyage to the Holy Land.

D.P. *1 Hen. IV.* i, 1] is about to start with an expedition to the Holy Land when news comes that Mortimer has been defeated and captured by Glendower; this is followed by tidings of Hotspur's victory at Homildon; the King sorrowfully compares Hotspur with his 'young Harry.' i, 3] angrily dismisses Worcester for his lack of respect; peremptorily orders Hotspur forthwith to send him the prisoners taken at Homildon. iii, 2] sternly reproves Prince Henry for losing his 'princely privilege With vile participation'; instances his own politic conduct before he seized the throne (*Hol.* iii, 539); is touched by the Prince's contrition, and gives him a command against the northern rebels. v, 1] (at Shrewsbury) makes, through Worcester, an offer of pardon, upon conditions, to the rebels (*Hol.* iii, 523). v, 4] fights with Douglas and is rescued by Prince Henry (*ib. ib.*). v, 5] condemns the rebels to death.

D.P. *2 Hen. IV.* iii, 1] outworn with sleeplessness, he receives news of Northumberland's forces; again longs to go to the Holy Land. iv, 4] (in the Jerusalem chamber) converses with his two sons Humphrey and Thomas concerning their brother Henry; hears of the total defeat of the northern rebels; swoons. iv, 5] (lying on a bed) falls asleep and is watched by Prince Henry; the Prince, believing him dead, takes the crown with him from the room (*Hol.* iii, 541); the King, awaking, misses it; he sends for the Prince and bitterly reproaches him for his unfilial haste; after hearing the Prince's self-exculpation, forgives him, and gives him grave advice; desires to be borne to the Jerusalem chamber (*ib.*) in fulfilment of a prophecy. (v, 2) his death announced.

Acc. *Hol.* iii, 541, Prince Henry had good reason for believing his father to be dead, for the attendants had 'covered his face with a linnen cloth.'

For the plays see pp. 108–9, **Henry the Fourth, The First Part of** and **Henry the Fourth, The Second Part of.**

Henry V (1387–1422). King of England; e.s. of Henry IV; born at Monmouth. The chief events of his life recorded in *Holinshed* and referred to in *Sh*. are as follows: Deserted by his guardian, Worcester (*Hol.* iii, 522; *1 Hen. IV*, ii, 4, l. 392); suspected by his father (*Hol.* iii, 539; *1 Hen. IV*, iii, 2; for his youthful escapades *vide infra* and GASCOIGNE); fights 'like a lustie yoong gentleman' at Shrewsbury (*Hol.* iii, 523; 1*Hen. IV*, V, 2, 3, 4); as king, chooses for counsellors 'men of gravitie, wit, and high policie' (*Hol.* iii, 543; *2 Hen. IV*, V, 2), and 'determined to put on him the shape of a new man' (*Hol. ib.*; *2 Hen. IV*, v, 5); sends a defiant answer to the Dauphin's 'disdaineful ambassage' (*Hol.* iii, 545; *Hen. V*, i, 2); punishes the treason of Cambridge and his associates (*Hol.* iii, 548; *Hen. V*, ii, 2); besieges and captures Harfleur (*Hol.* iii, 549–50; *Hen. V*, iii, 2, 3); gains the victory of Agincourt (*Hol.* iii, 552–3; *Hen. V*, iii, 7–iv, 8). (Reference to the second French campaign, between Agincourt and the Treaty of Troyes, is omitted in the play.) Henry is affianced to 'the ladie Katharine' (*Hol.* iii, 572; *Hen. V*, v, 2).

The King died at Bois de Vincennes and was buried at Westminster.

In *Rich. II*, V, 3, Bolingbroke inquires for his 'unthrifty son,' refers to his 'loose companions,' but sees 'some sparks of better hope.'

D.P. *1 Hen. IV*. 'Henry, Prince of Wales.' i, 2] plans with Poins to 'be a madcap' and play a jest upon Falstaff; (*sol.*) reflects that when he throws off his 'loose behaviour,' his reformation will 'show more goodly.' (i, 3) Hotspur 'would have him poisoned with a pot of ale.' ii, 2] with Poins, attacks Falstaff and his companions in the dark, and carries off their stolen booty. ii, 4] plays a trick on the drawer; reveals to Falstaff the true story of Gadshill; assuming the character of his father, vituperates Fal. iii, 2] is chided by the King; offers a plea in extenuation; is given a command and vows to meet Hotspur in combat. iii, 3] tells Falstaff he has procured him 'a charge of foot.' (iv, 1) his martial appearance described to Hotspur by Vernon. iv, 2] bids Fal. hasten to Shrewsbury. v, 1] (at Shrewsbury) challenges Hotspur to meet him in single combat. (v, 2) Vernon delivers the challenge and praises the Prince. v, 3] banters Fal. v, 4] is wounded, but will not retire; later, rescues the King; fights with Hotspur and kills him; pronounces a eulogy over the body; humours Falstaff's deception. v, 5] spares Douglas' life, for his bravery.

Acc. *Hol.* iii, 523, the Prince was 'hurt in the face with an arrow.' He was only 16 at the Battle of Shrewsbury and was 23 years younger than Hotspur, who was killed by an unknown hand.

D.P. *2 Hen. IV*. 'Henry, Prince of Wales'; 'King' in v, 2, 5. (i, 1) his death falsely reported. (i, 2, 3; ii, 1) mtd. ii, 2] speaks to Poins, with humorous bitterness, of a certain sense of disgrace in his companionship; reads a letter from Falstaff warning him against Poins; they resolve to play Fal. a trick. ii, 4] disguised as drawers, they listen to Fal.'s conversation; Fal. detects them; the Prince hears that the King is at Westminster, feels 'much to blame,' and leaves the tavern. (iv, 4) the King discourses to Clarence and Thomas about their brother's character. iv, 5] Henry watches by the bedside of his father; believes him dead, and reverently takes the crown with him from the room; he is recalled and rebuked by the King; declares his innocence of any unworthy motives, and is forgiven. v, 2] as king, honours the Chief Justice for his uprightness. (v, 3) his accession announced to Falstaff. v, 5] riding in state, is accosted by Fal., but tells him he 'knows him not,' gives him a solemn warning, and commits him to the custody of the C.J.

Holinshed's colourless account of the levity of the Prince's youth is as follows (iii, 539): 'Indeed he was youthfullie given, growne to audacitie, and had chosen him companions agreeable to his age; with whome he spent the time in such recreations exercises and delights as he fansied.' But Stow (*Annales*, p. 557), writing in 1605, is much more explicit, and relates that 'he lived somewhat insolently, insomuch that, whilest his father lived, being accompanied by some of his yong Lords and gentlemen, he would waite in disguised aray for his own receivers, and distresse them of their money,' afterward giving them discharge for it and rewarding those that had made the stoutest resistance. Cf. *1 Hen.IV*, ii, 4, l. 599.

D.P. *Hen. V*. (i, Chor.) 'warlike Harry.' (i, 1) his 'reformation' dilated on by the Abp. of Canterbury; his talents eulogized. i, 2] consults the Abp. as to his claim to France and is urged to enforce his rights (*Hol.* iii, 545–6); receives the French Ambassadors, and in reply to the Dauphin's insulting message bids them take back a rejoinder of defiance and grave warning (cf. *Hol.* iii, 545, where it is related that the King was at the time 'at Killingworth' and that his answer was sent in writing). ii, 2] sternly inveighs against the treason of Scroop, Cambridge, and Grey, and condemns them to death (*Hol.* iii, 548). (ii, 4) his character is discussed at the French council. iii, 1] at the siege of Harfleur; urges his men to the attack. iii, 3] receives the submission of Harfleur and enters the town. iii, 6] confirms Exeter's sentence on Bardolph; in reply to a defiant message from the French, after a few boastful words – 'Forgive me, God, That I do brag thus' – declares his fixed determination not to shun a battle (cf. *Hol.* iii, 552). iv, 1] passes among his troops, in disguise, during the night; reasons with them on kingly responsibility; (*sol.*) meditates on the sorrows of greatness, and on 'the fault My father made in compassing the crown!'; prays for divine pardon. iv, 3] gives a stirring address to his 'band of brothers' – 'from this day to the ending of the world' shall the 'feast of Crispian' be remembered; sends a proud answer to the French, who insolently suggest his payment of a ransom. iv, 6] gives orders for the killing of the prisoners (cf. *Hol.* iii, 554, 'contrarie to his accustomed gentlenes'). iv,7] converses with Fluellen and gives him 'Alençon's glove' (see WILLIAMS). iv, 8] receives an account of the losses on each side. v, 2] Henry meets the French Court at Troyes; left alone with the Princess Katharine, he woos her with the aid of her gentlewoman as interpreter; on the return of the Court, peace is agreed to, and Henry and Katharine are formally betrothed.

1 Hen. VI. (i, 1) Henry's funeral in Westminster Abbey; his eulogy by the nobles. (ii, 5) mtd.

For the play see p. 109, **Henry the Fifth.**

Few characters in *Sh.* have met with more divergent criticism than Henry V. It is, however, difficult in many cases to gather whether it is the man, as depicted, who is censured, or Sh. for so depicting him. Extracts from Hall's account of the King, as reproduced in *Hol.* iii, 583, are subjoined: 'A prince whome all men loued, and of none disdained; a capteine against whome fortune never frowned, nor mischance once spurned; … he left no offense unpunished, nor freendship unrewarded ; a terror to rebels… In strength and nimbleness of bodie from his youth few to him comparable; for in wrestling, leaping, and running, no man well able to compare [cf. *Hen. V*, ii, ll. 142 ff.] … so manfull of mind as never seene to quinch at a wound, or to smart at the paine. … Everie honest person was permitted to come to him, sitting at meale; where either secretlie or openlie to declare his mind… Wantonnesse of life and thirst in avarice had he quite quenched in him… For bountifulnesse and liberalitie, no man more free, gentle, and franke.'

Henry VI (1421–71). King of England. Only child of Henry V and Katharine of France; born at Windsor, and succeeded to the throne at the age of nine months ('In infant bands crown'd king,' *Hen. V*, Epil.). His uncle Humphrey, D. of Gloucester, was appointed Protector (controlled by a council), and another uncle, John, D. of Bedford, ruled over France. Rich. Beauchamp, E. of Warwick, acted as the King's tutor. (In 1424 the English gained a great victory over Charles VII of France at Verneuil, but from this date their power slowly dwindled.) In 1429 Henry was crowned at Westminster, and in 1430 at Paris; he opened Parliament in 1432. The influence of Joan of Arc in France (1429–31) provided a dramatic episode during this period. Disputes between Gloucester and his uncle Card. Beaufort (Bp. of Winchester) were rife during the King's minority, and the Queen, Margaret of Anjou, whom Henry married in 1445, supported Beaufort, and succeeded in having Gloucester arrested for high treason (1447). A few days later Gl. was found dead in his bed. Beaufort only survived his nephew six weeks, and after his death trouble succeeded trouble. In 1448 Maine was surrendered to France; two years later a serious rising under Jack Cade was quelled with some difficulty, and in 1453, after the loss of Guienne, the King became temporarily insane. Richard, D. of York, now began to lay claim openly to the throne, and, meeting with strong support, he became Protector in 1454, during another mental eclipse of the King, on whose recovery he refused to relinquish his power. Hostilities ensued, and on May 22, 1455, was fought the first Battle of St Albans, in which the Yorkists were victorious, the D. of Somerset (the Queen's trusted minister) was slain, and Henry captured. The King became again mentally incapacitated, and on his recovery made vain attempts to reconcile the opposing parties of York and the Queen. Margaret, for her part, put herself at the head of the Lancastrian forces and sought victory during twenty years. In 1461 Edward (e.s. of York) after the Battle of Towton was proclaimed King, as Edw. IV, and in 1465 Henry was committed to the Tower. In 1470 Henry was restored to the throne by the E. of Warwick, but six months later he was again a prisoner, and after the fatal Battle of Tewkesbury (May 4, 1471), in which the Queen was captured, and Edward, Prince of Wales, slain, Henry was murdered in the Tower. (For a synopsis of the great struggle see Wars of the Roses.)

Holinshed (iii, 690) relates that the corpse was borne with due ceremony to St Paul's, where it 'in presence of the beholders did bleed'; thence it was carried to the Blackfriars, 'and bled there likewise,' and finally was conveyed in a boat to Chertsey and there first buried.

The three plays bearing the name of Henry VI deal with all periods of the reign, but chronological accuracy is throughout made subservient to dramatic expediency.

Of Henry, Hall writes (p. 303): '[He] was of stature goodly, of body slender … his face beautiful, in ye which continually was resydent the bountie of mynde wyth whych he was inwardly endued. He dyd abhorre of hys owne nature al the vices, as wel of the body as of the soule; Besyde thys, pacyence was so radicate in his harte that of all the injuries to him committed (which were no small nombre) he never asked vengeaunce nor punishment… .' Holinshed (iii, 691) adds that he was 'wholie given to praier, reading of scriptures, and almesdeeds.'

D.P. *1 Hen. VI*. iii, 1] adjures (*aet.* 5) with 'sighs and tears,' his 'uncles' of Gloucester and of Winchester to be at peace with one another (the truce was actually arranged by arbitrators, *Hol.* iii, 595); creates Richard Plantagenet D. of York. iii, 4] compliments Talbot, and creates him E. of Shrewsbury (not until 1442). iv, 1] is crowned at Paris (1430); banishes Fastolfe (*q.v.*); hears that the D. of Burgundy has revolted, and bids Talbot march against him; entreats York and Somerset to compose their strife; makes the former regent in France, but accepts as a badge 'a red rose.' v, 1] makes peace with France and accepts the d. of the 'E. of Armagnac' (*q.v.*) in marriage (1442). v, 5] gives audience to Suffolk, who expatiates on the beauty and virtues of Margaret of Anjou (*Hol.* iii, 625); despite Gloucester's expostulations, bids Suffolk 'post to France,' and 'procure that Lady M. do vouchsafe to come … to England' (1442).

D.P. *2 Hen. VI*. i, 1] welcomes his bride, escorted from France by the Marq. of Suffolk, whom he makes a duke; approves the terms of the marriage treaty. i, 3] (his wife deems him more fit to be a pope than a king); he leaves high state matters to the Queen's decision; appoints a day for judicial combat in a case of alleged treason. ii, 1] makes pious reflections, but fails to check bitter quarrels between the nobles; is impressed by the alleged miraculous cure of a blind man, but witnesses his discomfiture; learns that the Dss. of Gloucester is charged with treasonable practices. ii, 3] pronounces sentence on the Dss, and her confederates; dismisses the D. of Gloucester from his Protectorship; witnesses the judicial combat. iii, 1] (at Bury St Edmund's) expresses his belief in Gloucester's innocence; after hearing Gl.'s accusers, 'bewails his case.' iii, 2] swoons on hearing that Gl. has been found dead in his bed; regards Suffolk with abhorrence, and suspects the truth; on hearing of the tumult of the commonalty, sends them word that Suffolk shall be banished; rebukes the Queen for pleading for him. iii, 3] is present at Card. Beaufort's death, bids him raise his hand as a 'signal of his hope,' but B. dies 'and makes no sign.' iv, 4] proposes to parley with Cade ; flees to Kenilworth. iv, 9] pardons the surrendered rebels; learns that York has landed with an Irish army. v, 1] is assured by York that he seeks but to overthrow Somerset; knights Iden ; reproaches Salisbury for his disloyalty. v, 2] during the Battle of St Albans, flees to London.

The King's flight from St Albans is unhistorical. He remained there until the next day, when he accompanied York to London.

D.P. *3 Hen. VI*. i, 1] entering, with his adherents, the Parliament House where York has seated himself upon the throne (*Hol.* iii, 655), he restrains the more ardent of his supporters, who wish to fight the matter out on the spot, and by expostulations and arguments tries to prove his superior title to the throne; finally proposes that the crown should be his during his lifetime and then revert to the House of York (this was actually determined by Parliament in 1460); his three chief followers despise and desert him, as a 'degenerate king'; he laments thus disinheriting his son; piteously tries to exculpate himself to the Queen and the Prince ; resolves to write to the three defecting lords, 'and entreat them fair.' ii, 2] before York (unhistorical); the sight of York's head on the battlements (*Hol.* iii, 659) 'irks his very soul'; at the Queen's bidding, dubs his son a knight (actually, after the 2nd Battle of St Albans) and bids him 'draw his sword in right'; makes a feeble attempt to stem the mutual defiance of Yorkists and Lancastrians. ii, 5] at Towton, having been 'chid from the battle,' eloquently moralizes (*sol.*) on the superior happiness of a peasant's life, and bitterly laments the horrors of war presented to his eyes; is induced to flee from the field to Berwick (*Hol.* iii, 665). iii, 1] while in disguise is overheard, by two keepers, soliloquizing on state affairs; they tax him with being the deposed King, and he submits himself to them ('he was knowne and taken of one Cantlow,' *Hol.* iii, 667). iv, 6] after Edward's defeat at Warwick, is released from the Tower (1470) and makes Warwick and Clarence joint Protectors (*Hol.* iii, 678); lays his hand on the head of young Henry, E. of Richmond (1471), and predicts that he will wear a crown (*Hol.* iii, 678). iv, 8] hears that Edward has invaded England; reflects that the mildness of his own rule must have gained him the love of his subjects; is seized by the enemy and borne back to the Tower (*cf.* Hall, p. 295). v, 6] is stabbed by Gloucester in the Tower (May 21,1471), after predicting that thousands would rue the hour when his murderer was born.

Acc. More, as quoted by Hall (p. 343), 'Richard slewe in the towre kynge Henry the sixt; saiynge : "now is there no heire male of kynge Edwarde the thirde but wee of the house of Yorke!" whyche murder was doen without kynge Edward his assent; which would have appointed that bocherly office too some other rather than to hys owne brother.'

For the plays see pp. 109, **Henry the Sixth, The First Part of, Henry the Sixth, The Second Part of, Henry the Sixth, The Third Part of.**

Henry VII (1457–1509). King of England. Son of Edmund Tudor, E. of Richmond, and Margaret Beaufort, d. of John of Gaunt. He took refuge in Brittany during the reign of Edward IV, landed at Milford Haven in 1485, and in the same year defeated and slew Richard III at Bosworth and was crowned.

Acc. *Hol.* iii, 757, he was 'so formed and decorated with all gifts and lineaments of nature, that he seemed more an angelicall creature, than a terrestriall personage.

D.P. *3 Hen. VI.* 'Henry, E. of Richmond, a youth.' iv, 6] *p.m.*; Henry VI predicts that the 'pretty lad' will wear a crown and 'prove our country's bliss' (cf. *Hol.* iii, 678).

D.P. *Rich. III.* (iv, 1, 2) Dorset flees to him for safety; a prophecy that he should be king (cf. *3 Hen. VI*, iv, 6, ll. 65 ff.). (iv, 3) the Bp. of Ely joins him. (iv, 4) sets sail for England. (iv, 5) in Wales. v, 2] at Bosworth Field. v, 3] makes plans for the battle; when asleep is encouraged by the ghosts of Richard's victims; makes an oration to his soldiers. v, 5] slays Richard in fight; later, the crown is placed upon his head by Derby, and he prays for 'this fair land's peace' under the united roses.

Acc. *Hol.* iii, 759, Richard 'manfullie fighting in the middle of his enimies, was slaine,' and (*ib.* iii, 706) the crown 'was found amongst the spoile in the field.' Henry's attempted junction with Buckingham, and his landing at Milford (iv, 5) were really separated by an interval of 2 years (1483–5).

Lord Stanley speaks of 'Richmond' as 'my son' (*Rich. III*, iv, 2, l. 50); actually stepson, Lord S. having married the Lady Margaret.

Henry VIII (1491–1547). King of England; 2nd s. of Hen. VII. The following dates are those relevant to the drama, which, although entitled 'The Famous History of the Life of Henry VIII,' actually deals only with episodes of the period 1520–36, with not a few chronological liberties. Henry's meeting with Francis I at the Field of the Cloth of Gold took place in 1520; in 1527 the King began to treat with the Pope for the purpose of obtaining a divorce from Katharine of Arragon; in 1529 a commission met to hear the case, without result; in the same year Wolsey was dismissed and was succeeded as the King's adviser by Cromwell; Henry consulted various European universities in 1530, and in 1533 Anne Boleyn, whom he had secretly married, was crowned as queen.

D.P. *Hen. VIII.* (i, 1) the Field of the Cloth of Gold described (*Hol.* iii, 858). i, 2] listens to Q. Katharine's representations of the 'exactions imposed by Wolsey'; orders pardon to be sent to every man who has resisted the 'commission' (*Hol.* iii, 892); listens to the accusation against Buckingham made by Knyvet (*Hol.* iii, 862); orders B. to be arrested. i, 4] attends a great entertainment given by Wolsey (*Hol.* iii, 921–2), and is attracted by Anne Boleyn, with whom he dances. ii, 2] dismisses Norfolk and Suffolk brusquely from his presence, but graciously receives Wolsey and Campeius; declares that his conscience is troubled about the validity of his marriage with Kath. (ii, 3) makes Anne Boleyn Marchioness of Pembroke (*Hol.* iii, 928). ii, 4] attends the session of the divorce commission at Blackfriars (*Hol.* iii, 907); declares Kath. to be 'the queen of earthly queens,' but explains the grave scruples of conscience which impel him to divorce her; distrusts 'these cardinals' and resolves to be guided by Cranmer. iii, 2] papers revealing Wolsey's avarice fall into his hands (see RUTHALL); he points out to W. how deeply indebted he should feel for the royal favour, hands him the papers, and bids him read them, 'and then to breakfast with What appetite you have.' v, 1] converses with Cranmer, and gives him a ring to use in an emergency (Foxe, ii, 1759); hears of the birth of a daughter (Queen Elizabeth). v, 3] enters the council chamber, and rates the members roundly for their insulting treatment of Cranmer (Foxe, ii, 1760). v, 5] is present at the christening of Elizabeth.

For the play see p. 109, **Henry the Eighth**

Henry the Fourth, The First Part of. (In F1: 'The First Part of Henry the Fourth, with the Life and Death of Henry Sirnamed Hot-spurre.' The acts and scenes are numbered.)

PUBLICATION. On Feb. 25, 1597–8, a licence was granted to Andrew Wise for the publication of 'The Historye of Henry the iiijth with his battaile of Shrewsburye against Henry Hottspurre of the Northe with the conceipted mirthe of Sir John Ffalstoffe.' Soon afterward a quarto appeared bearing the title: 'The History of Henrie the Fovrth; With the battell at Shrewsburie, betweene the King and Lord Henry Percy, surnamed Henrie Hotspur of the North. With the humorous conceits of Sir John Falstaffe [etc.] Printed by P.S. for Andrew Wise,' 1598.

In 1599 a second edn. 'Newly corrected by W. Shakespeare' appeared, and was followed by further edns. in 1604, 1608, 1613, 1622, and later. The text in the First Folio of 1623 follows that of 1613 substantially.

SOURCES. The *Chronicles* of Holinshed, with some references to *The Famous Victories* (*q.v.*), and perh. to Stow, p. 557.

Henry the Fourth, The Second Part of. (In F1: 'The Second Part of Henry the Fourth, Containing his Death: and the Coronation of King Henry the Fift.' The acts and scenes are numbered.)

PUBLICATION. First appeared, in quarto, with this title-page: 'The Second part of Henrie the fourth, continuing to his death, and coronation of Henrie the fift. With the humours of Sir John Falstaffe, and swaggering. Pistoll... Written by William Shakespeare. London. Printed by V. S. for Andrew Wise, and William Aspley. 1600.' (There are two different impressions of this, marked by the omission of iii, 1, in some copies.)

The play as published in the Folio of 1623 contains important passages not printed in Q.

DATE OF COMPOSITION. Probably 1597–8, or about a year later than *1 Hen. IV*.

SOURCES. Holinshed's *Chronicles*, and *The Famous Victories* (*q.v.*), the important comicscenes being Sh.'s own, but seemingly suggested by faint analogies in the old play. (Stow, pp. 557–8, is also drawn upon.)

Henry the Fifth. (In F1: 'The Life of Henry the Fift.' The acts, but not the scenes, are numbered.)

PUBLICATION. This play, in its complete form, first appeared in the Folio of 1623. In the Stationers' Registers, under date Aug. 4, 1600, there occurs the note: 'Henry the ffift, a booke, to be staied,' but in the same year a truncated and perverted version of the play was piratically produced, by T. Millington and J. Busby, probably from shorthand notes. This quarto bears the title: 'The Cronicle History of Henry the fift, With his battell fought at Agin Court in France. Together with Auntient Pistoll,' etc., and contains less than half the play as we now know it. Two similar editions followed, dated 1602 and 1608 (the latter being probably a falsification for 1619).

DATES OF COMPOSITION AND PRODUCTION First performed early in 1599, probably at the Globe theatre, alluded to as 'this wooden O' in the Prologue of Act I. In the Prologue of Act V there is a clear allusion to the (expected) victorious return of Essex from his Irish expedition in the summer of 1599. On the other hand, the play is not mentioned by Meres (1598); 1598–9 is therefore the generally accepted date of its composition.

SOURCES. Holinshed's *Chronicles*, and the old play *The Famous Victories of Henrye the Fyft* (*q.v.*). The main divergencies from *Hol.* are noted under the appropriate headings.

It is now generally admitted that the text of the Folio is not an expansion of the quarto 'Chronicle History,' but that the latter is a poor abridgment of a much fuller text, which may reasonably be supposed practically identical with that of the Folio. The matter is very fully dealt with in P.A. Daniel's *Parallel Texts* of the play, publd. by the New Sh. Society; *cf.* also the Society's *Transactions*, 1880–6, p. 77.

Henrye the Fyft, The Famous Victories of. A popular old play, produced not later than 1588, since Richard Tarleton, who performed the part in it of Derrick, the clown, died in that year. In a crudely farcical spirit the horseplay of Prince Hal, Sir John Oldcastle, and their associates is dwelt upon, while the Prince's premature seizure of the crown, his martial deeds as king, and his courtship of Katharine all enter into the somewhat disjointed plot. 'Sh. was not blind to the hints of the old drama, but he touched its comic scenes with a magic of his own, and summoned out of its dust and ashes the radiance of his inimitable Falstaff' (Lee, p. 241). See also Ward, *Eng. Dram. Lit.* i, 222–3.

The play was acted by the Queen's players between 1588 and 1595, and was published in 1594. (See OLDCASTLE and FALSTAFF.)

Henry the Sixth, The First Part of. First published in the Folio of 1623; the acts and scenes are indicated. From references in Henslowe's *Diary* it appears that this play was frequently performed in the years 1591–3 and was exceedingly popular. The only parts allotted to Shakespeare by modern criticism are, with more or less probability, ii, 4, 5; iv, 5, 6, 7; v, 3. Holinshed is the basis of the historical portions, but chronology is recklessly disregarded. The play lacks unity, and consists of a series of loosely connected scenes. Gervinus argues that the new matter introduced by Sh. into *1 Hen. VI* was designed to prepare the way for 2, 3, *Hen. VI*, which he had already planned.

Henry the Sixth, The Second Part of. (In F1: 'The second Part of Henry the Sixt, with the death of the Good Duke Humfrey.' After i, 1, the acts and scenes are not indicated.)

First published in its present form in the Folio of 1623. In round numbers 1300 lines are either identical with, or obviously altered from, *The Contention* (*q.v.*), 700 lines of the latter play are omitted, and 1700 new lines are introduced. (The Simpcox episode is derived from More, Grafton, or Foxe.)

Henry the Sixth, The Third Part of. (In F1: 'The third Part of Henry the Sixt, with the death of the Duke of Yorke.' After i, 1, the acts and scenes are not indicated.)

First published in its present form in the Folio of 1623. In round numbers 1900 lines are identical with, or similar to, passages in *The True Tragedie* (*q.v.*), while 1000 new lines are added; there are no omissions.

Henry the Eighth.

PUBLICATION. First printed in the Folio of 1623 as 'The Famous History of the Life of King Henry the Eight.' The acts and scenes are numbered.

PRODUCTION. Appears to have been first acted as 'a new Play, called *All is True*' (cf. *Hen. VIII*, Prol. 1. 9), 1613. During its performance at the Globe the playhouse was set on fire, and burned to the ground, by 'certain cannons being shot off' at the entry of the King to 'a Masque at the Cardinal Wolsey's House' (i, 4). The identity of *All is True* and *Hen. VIII* has been disputed, but is now generally accepted.

AUTHORSHIP. Criticism has now decided, with reasonable certainty, that the play is the work of Sh. and John Fletcher in collaboration, the share of the former being: i, 1, 2;

ii, 3, 4; iii, 2 (to Henry's exit); v, 1 (partly). The intervention of a third hand, perhaps Massinger's, has also been suggested. (See *N.S.S. Tr.*,

Franion 1874, Pt. I, Appendix.)

SOURCES. Holinshed's *Chronicles* is closely followed, which, in turn, is indebted to George Cavendish's *Life of Wolsey*, Hall, and Stow. Foxe, *Actes and Monuments*, seems to be independently used in Act V.

CHRONOLOGY. The play begins soon after the Field of the Cloth of Gold, held in 1520, and ends with the christening of Elizabeth. But the historical sequence of events is arbitrarily altered.

The true dates of the following scenes are placed in brackets: i, 4 (1526, or later); ii, 1 (1521); ii, 2 (1528); ii, 3 (1532); ii, 4 (1529); iv, 1 (1533); iv, 2 (1536); v, i, 2, 3 (*c.* 1544); v, 4, 5 (1533).

Henton. See HOPKINS.

[**Heraclitus** of Ephesus.] Known, from his melancholy disposition, as 'the weeping philosopher.' Alluded to by Portia, who says of the County Palatine: 'I fear he will prove the weeping philosopher when he grows old' (*M.V.* i, 2).

Heraclitus is referred to by Cicero, *Tusc. Disp.* 5, 36, 105 – a work which had been translated by John Dolman in 1561.

Herald (1). D.P. *Hen. V.* iv, 8] brings a roll of those killed on both sides at Agincourt.

The three heralds present were John Ashwel!, 'Lancaster,' John Wroxworth, 'Guienne,' and John Kitteby, 'Ireland,' Kings at Arms (Weever, *Anc. Fun. Mon.*).

Herald (2). D.P. *2 Hen. VI.* ii, 4] summons the D. of Gloucester to 'his majesty's parliament, holden at Bury the first of this next month.'

This parliament did not meet until Feb. 10, 1447, some six years after the disgrace of the Duchess of Gl.

Herald (3). D.P. *Lear.* v, 3] summons to the combat any man who maintains that Edmund is a traitor.

Herald (4). D.P. *Oth.* ii, 2] declares a 'triumph' in honour of the destruction of the Turkish fleet, and of Othello's nuptials.

Herald, Roman. D.P. *Cor.* ii, 1] proclaims that Caius Marcius has merited the surname of Coriolanus.

Heralds. D.PP. *1 Hen. VI.* i, 1] *pp.m.*; officiate at the funeral of Henry V.

Herbert, Philip (1584–1650). E. of Montgomery (1605) and 4th E. of Pembroke (1630). To him and his brother William (*q.v.*) the First Folio was dedicated. P.H. is referred to as 'Gentleman of his Maiesties Bed-Chamber.'

Herbert, Sir Walter. Described by More as a person of great influence among the Welsh. He is mtd. (*Hol.* iii, 753) as having with Rice ap Thomas (*q.v.*) been at first prepared to resist Richmond's advance.

D.P. *Rich. III.* (iv, 5) reported, as 'a renowned soldier,' to be with Richmond. v, 2] at Tamworth. v, 3] at Bosworth.

Herbert, Sir William (*ob.* 1469). Yorkist; fought for Edward IV, and on the attainder of Jasper Tudor (*q.v.*) was made Earl of Pembroke (1468) (*Hol.* iii, 667) and guardian to Henry (afterward Henry VII); executed after his defeat and capture at Hedgecote.

D.P. *3 Hen. VI.* 'Earl of Pembroke.' iv, 1] *p.m.*; is bidden by the King 'Go levy men, and make prepare for war.' (iv, 3) Warwick speaks of his impending fight 'with P. and his fellows.'

Herbert, William (1580–1630). 3rd E. of Pembroke; fell into disgrace at Court for an intrigue with Mary Fitton (*q.v.*); he was a patron of Ben Jonson and other authors, and to him, as Lord Chamberlain, and to his brother, Philip, E. of Montgomery, the editors of the First Folio dedicated that volume.

The theory that Lord Pembroke is the 'Mr W. H.' associated with the *Sonnets* cannot here be examined at length: suffice it to say that the solitary piece of direct evidence of any association between Sh. and the Earl is contained in the following passage from the Dedication to the Folio: 'Since your L.L. have been pleas'd to thinke these trifles something, heeretofore; and have prosequuted both them, and their Authour living, with so much favour: we hope that ... you will use the like indulgence towards them, you have done unto their parent.'

It is clear that this need not be interpreted as implying any personal relations between Sh. and the Earls. See also W. H., MR.

Hercules. Son of Jupiter; as 'Heracles,' the most famous hero of Greek myth. Of the numberless legends associated with H. the following are alluded to in *Sh.*: (*a*) his strangling two snakes in his cradle (Ovid, *Her.* ix, 21; *Metam.* ix, 67); (*b*) his 'twelve labours,' imposed by Eurystheus, including the seizure of Cerberus (*q.v.*), fetching the golden apples from the Hesperides (*q.v.*), slaying Hydra (*q.v.*) and the Nemean lion (*q.v.*); (*c*) his rescue of Hesione (*q.v.*). For the death of H. see NESSUS and LICHAS. The hero's redoubtable club – *clava Herculis* – was proverbial. According to one tradition, H. became servant to Omphale, and changed attire with her.

'She [Beatrice] would have made H. have turned spit, yea, and have cleft his club to make the fire, too' (*M. Ado*, ii, 1); 'I will undertake one of H.'s labours' (*ib. ib.*); 'like the shaven H. in the ... tapestry' (*ib.* iii, 3; possibly intended for Samson; *cf.* Judges xvi, 17, 19); 'Valiant as H.' (*ib.* iv, 1); Moth mentions H. as a great man who had been in love, *L.L.L.* i, 2; 'Cupid's butt-shaft is too hard for H.'s club' (*ib. ib.*); 'To see great H. whipping a gig' (*ib.* iv, 3); 'For valour is not Love a H., Still climbing trees in the Hesperides?' (*ib. ib.*); Moth is entrusted with the part of H., 'in minority... strangling a snake' (*ib.* v, 1); 'H... whose club killed Cerberus ... And when he was a babe ... did strangle serpents' (*ib.* v, 2); 'If you had been the wife of H., six of his labours you'ld have done' (*Cor.* iv, 1); 'As H. did shake down mellow fruit' (*ib.* iv, 6); 'by H.' (*Ant. Cl.* iii, 7); ' 'Tis the god H., whom Antony lov'd' (*ib.* iv, 3; perhaps for 'Bacchus'); 'Not H. could have knock'd out his brains, for he had none' (*Cymb.* iv, 2); 'the brawns of H.' (*ib. ib.*); 'no more like my father Than I to H.' (*Haml.* i, 2); 'H. and his load too' (*ib.* ii, 2; supposed by Steevens to refer to the sign of the Globe theatre); 'Let H. himself do what he may' (*ib.* v, 1); 'Now, H. be thy speed, young man !' (*A.Y.L.* i, 2); 'as strong as H.' (*All's Well*, iv, 3); 'as valiant as H.' (*1 Hen. IV*, ii, 4); the Countess of Auvergne thought to 'have seen some H.' instead of the 'writhled shrimp' Talbot, *1 Hen. VI*, ii, 3; 'But H. himself must yield to odds' (*3 Hen. VI*, ii, 1); 'H. and Lichas [*q.v.*]' (*M.V.* ii, 1); 'the beards of H. and Mars' (*ib.* iii, 2); 'Go, H.!' (*ib. ib.*); Host addresses Falstaff as 'Bully H.' (*M.W.W.* i, 3); '*Hip.* I was with H. and Cadmus once, When in a wood of Crete they bay'd the bear' (*M.N.D.* iv, 1); '*Thes.* ... my kinsman H.' (*ib.* v, 1); 'leave that labour to great H., And let it be more than Alcides' twelve' (*Tam. Sh.* i, 2).

In the following passages the name Alcides is alone used: 'Nor great A... shall seize this prey' (*T. And.* iv, 2); 'The shirt of Nessus is upon me, teach me, A., thou my ancestor, thy rage' (*Ant. Cl.* iv, 12); 'the great A. of the field [Talbot]' (*1 Hen. VI*, iv, 7); 'A. beaten by his page' (*M.V.* ii, 1); 'young A. when he did redeem The virgin tribute' (*ib.* iii, 2); 'let that labour be more than A.'s twelve' (*Tam. Sh.* i, 2); 'As sightly ... as great A.'s shows ['shooes,' F1] upon an ass' (*John*, ii, 1; if 'shows' is the correct reading the skin of the Nemean lion seems referred to).

The jealous hatred of Juno for H. seems alluded to, *All's Well*, iii, 4: 'His [Bertram's] taken labours bid him me forgive; I, his despiteful Juno sent him forth,' etc.

Herford. (For 'H.,' 'Harry H.,' 'Harry of H.,' 'D. of H.,' 'E. of H.,' see HENRY IV.) The earldom of H. promised to Buckingham by Gloucester, *Rich. III*, iii, 1, iv, 2 (see BUCKINGHAM, DUKE OF (2)); one of the titles of Edward Stafford (*q.v.*), *Hen. VIII*, i, 1.

Hereford, Earl of. Buckingham (*Rich. III*, iii, 1; iv, 2) importunes Richard for this title, but it is not conferred. In *Hen. VIII*, i, 1, l. 200, Buckingham (son of the preceding) is styled 'E. of Hertford' in Ff, but 'Hereford' in *Hol.*

In *2 Hen. IV*, iv, 1, l. 131, Bolingbroke is wrongly entitled Earl of H., instead of Duke of H.; cf. *Rich. II*, i, 3, l. 21.

Herefordshire. Mortimer leads men of H. against Glendower; *1 Hen. IV*, i, 1 (*Hol.* iii, 520).

[Hereford West.] See HARFORD-WEST.

[Herennins.] See CICERO.

Hermes. The Greek equivalent of Mercury (*q.v.*). His having charmed Argus to sleep with the flute of Pan (Ovid, *Metam.* i, 676 ff., thus translated by Golding: 'He play'd upon his merrie Pipe to cause his watching eyes To fall a sleepe') seems referred to in *Hen. V*, iii, 7, where the Dauphin says of his horse: 'The basest horn of his hoof is more musical than the pipe of H.'

Hermia. D.P. *M.N.D.* Daughter of Egeus. i, 1] is charged by her father, before Theseus, with resisting his will in refusing to wed Demetrius; is warned that the penalty of disobedience is either death or perpetual virginity, but persists in her refusal; agrees with her lover Lysander to meet him in a wood the next night; reveals their plan to her friend Helena. ii, 2] wearied by their wanderings in the wood, the lovers lie down to rest; Herm. awakes to find herself alone. iii, 2] enters, followed by Demetrius, who is compelled by a love-charm to protest his adoration of her; accuses him of having slain Lys. and heaps bitter reproaches on him; later, discovers Lys. with Hel., and knowing nothing of his enchantment is amazed at his professions of love for her friend, and at Helena's reproaches; clings to Lys. but is harshly repulsed; turns upon Helena in a rage, and, calling her a 'thief of love' and a 'painted maypole,' threatens her with personal violence; later, lies down to sleep. iv, 1] awakes bewildered, to find Lys. restored to her, and to hear Theseus overrule her father and command two weddings to be celebrated with his own. v, 1] *p.m.*

The name appears to be of Sh.'s invention. Hartley Coleridge (*Essays*, etc. (1851), ii, 138) considers that 'one defect there may be. Perhaps the distress of Hermia and Helena, arising from Puck's blundering application of Love-in-Idleness, is too serious, too real for so fantastic a source. Yet their altercation is so very, very beautiful, so girlish, so loveable that one cannot wish it away.' F. J. Furnivall, *Introd. to Leopold Sh.* (1877), xxvi, compares 'the vixen Hermia' with Adriana in *Com. Err.*

Hermione. D.P. *Wint. T.* 'Queene to Leontes' (F1). i, 2] in accordance with her husband's bidding, urges Polixenes to prolong his stay at the Sicilian Court; she is successful, and accompanies her guest to the garden, incurring the jealousy of Leontes. ii, 1] as she listens to the prattle of her little son Mamillius, Leontes enters, and furiously taxes her with faithlessness, a charge which she repels with pathetic dignity; she is committed to prison. (ii, 2) in prison she gives birth to a daughter (Perdita). (iii, 1) mtd. iii, 2] she is charged before a court of justice with high treason and adultery; with calm and noble bearing she defends herself in words of queenly eloquence, and appeals to the oracle of Apollo; it declares her guiltless; on hearing of her son's death she swoons, and is believed to have expired. (iii, 3) appears in a dream to Antigonus. (v, 1) lives secretly in Paulina's house for sixteen years. (v, 2) a lifelike statue of her is reported to exist. v, 3] she poses as the statue, descends from the pedestal, and is reunited to the repentant Leontes and the daughter she believed to have perished in infancy.

The name of the corresponding character in *Pandosto* is Bellaria, who, however, really dies of shock, and it is her husband who sinks into a deathlike swoon.

The name is that of the beautiful daughter of Menelans (Hom. *Od.* iv, 14; *Il.* iii, 175); it also occurs as that of a male character in *The rare Triumphs of Love and Fortune* (1589). Ruskin sees in it an allusion to ἕρμα, a pillar (*Mun. Pulv.* (1872), p. 127). *Cf.* also Chaucer, Group B, l. 66.

Hartley Coleridge (*Essays*, etc. (1851), ii, 148), compares Hermione to Marie Antoinette, and W. W. Lloyd (Singer, ed. ii (1856), 131) to Alcestis. H. N. Hudson (*Introduction* to the play (1880)), considers that 'We can scarce call Hermione sweet or gentle, though she is both; she is a *noble* woman – one whom, even in her greatest anguish, we hardly *dare* to pity. ... As she acts the part of a statue in the play, so she has a statue-like calmness and firmness of soul. A certain austere and solid sweetness pervades her whole demeanour, and seems, as it were, the essential form of her life.'

Herne. It appears that there was a tradition in Windsor that a keeper, named H., hung himself on an oak, and afterward haunted the spot; but, apart from *Sh.*, there is no reference to the story earlier than the 18th cent.

The Quarto of *M.W.W.* (iv, 4) merely states that since 'Horne' died women frightened their children by saying that he 'walks in the shape of a great stag'; but the Folio makes him a more formidable spectre, with powers of evil-doing, and treats the story as an early legend.

'H.'s oak' (*M.W.W.* iv, 4, 6; v, 1, 3, 5).

In MS. *Bib. Reg.* 17 C, xvi (Brit. Mus.) the name of 'Rycharde Horne, yeoman' occurs among those of the 'hunters which he examyned and have confessed' unlawful hunting (Halliwell). On 'H.'s oak' see Tighe and Davis, *Annals of Windsor* (1858).

Hero (1). D.P. *M. Ado.* Daughter to Leonato. i, 1] is present at the arrival of Don Pedro and his train; in her absence Claudio confides to Benedick that she is 'the sweetest lady that ever I looked on,' and afterward converses with Don P. on the same subject; Don P. proposes to woo Hero in disguise at the coming revels, and pass himself off as Claudio. (i, 3) Borachio informs Don John of the scheme. ii, 1] Hero converses playfully with Don P., who is masked; (Don J. tells Cl., whom he takes for Benedick, that Don P. is wooing Hero for himself); Don P. announces that Hero is won for Cl.; and later, Hero declares that she 'will do any modest office' to help her cousin Beatrice to a good husband. (ii, 2) Borachio unfolds to Don J. a plot against Hero. (ii, 3) mtd. iii, 1] H. purposely praises Benedick to her gentlewoman, and dilates on his supposed love for Beatrice, where they can be overheard by the latter. (iii, 2) Don J. tells Cl. that he will give him plain proof of Hero's disloyalty. (iii, 3) Borachio relates how he made Cl. and his friends believe that Hero had been conversing with him at her window. iii, 4] H. is arrayed for the wedding. iv, 1] is publicly accused by Claudio of faithlessness, and swoons in the church; declares her innocence to Friar Francis; Leonato agrees, on the friar's suggestion, that a report of Hero's death should be spread abroad. (iv, 2) the sexton voices the common report that 'Hero was in this manner accused, in this very manner refused, and upon the grief of this suddenly died.' (v, 1) the plot against her revealed. (v, 2) the fact announced to Beatrice. (v, 3) Claudio hangs a scroll upon Hero's supposed tomb, celebrating her virtue and her wrongs. v, 4] she is presented, masked, to Cl., as the new wife selected for him by Leonato, and, revealing herself, is reunited to her lover.

The corresponding character in Bandello's novel is Fenicia, in *The Faerie Queene* Claribell, and in Ariosto Ginevra. See MUCH ADO ABOUT NOTHING. Lady Martin, *Sh.'s Female Characters* (1887), p. 308, finds Hero 'somewhat characterless and over-gentle.' 'With a heart tender and foreboding, she fascinates even when she is mute by the overpowering impression of her chaste, modest nature' (Gervinus, *Sh. Comm.* (1876), p. 408).

Hero (2). A priestess of Aphrodite, in Sestos, for love of whom Leander (*q.v.*) of Abydos nightly swam the Hellespont, guided by a light upon her tower. He was at last drowned in a storm, and Hero threw herself into the sea (Ovid, *Her.* xviii, xix; *Trist.* iii, 10).

'A ladder ... to scale another H.'s tower' (*T.G.V.* iii, 1); the story humorously perverted by Rosalind, *A.Y.L.* iv, 1; 'Helen and Hero' compared to Bomeo's lady, *Rom. J.* ii, 4.

Herod the Great. Made King of Judaea by Mark Antony; confirmed in his possession of the throne by Octavius 31 B.C. According to Josephus, Cleopatra went to Judaea, and having tried, unsuccessfully, to captivate Herod by her charms, was in danger of being put to death by him.

'H. of Jewry' (*Ant. Cl.* i, 2); 'that H.'s head I'll have' (*ib.* iii, 3); aids Antony, *ib.* iii, 6 (*Plut.* p. 207); revolts from Ant. to Octavius, *ib.* iv, 6 (*Plut.* pp. 216, 218); his 'massacre of the innocents' alluded to, *Hen. V*, iii, 3.

In the mystery plays Herod figured prominently as a raging and bloodthirsty tyrant; hence: 'What a H. of Jewry is this' (*M.W.W.* ii, 1); 'it out-Herods H.' (*Haml.* iii, 2).

[**Hertford, Earl of.**] See HEREFORD, E. OF.

[**Hertford West.**] See HARFORD-WEST.

[**Hertlowli.**] See BARKLOUGHLY.

[**Hesione.**] Daughter of Laomedon, King of Troy, and therefore sister of Priam. She was chained to a rock by her father to be devoured, as a propitiatory sacrifice, by a sea-monster, but was rescued by Hercules, at the price of certain horses promised him by Laomedon (Ovid, *Metam.* xi, 211 ff.).

'With much more love Than young Alcides, when he did redeem The virgin tribute paid by howling Troy To the sea-monster' (*M.V.* iii, 2).

Acc. 'Dares Phrygius,' Hesione was given as a slave to Telamon (father of Ajax), by whom she became the mother of Teucer. The combat between Hector and Ajax is interrupted by Hector's reminding A. that he is 'my father's sister's son, a cousin-german to great Priam's seed' (*Tr. Cr.* iv, 5; more precisely, Hesione would be Hector's aunt and Ajax's stepmother); 'And for an old aunt, whom the Greeks held captive, He brought a Grecian queen ... why keep we her?' (*Tr. Cr.* ii, 2); in 'Dares Phryg.' the rape of Helen is represented as a just revenge on the part of the Trojans, from whom the Greeks had stolen Hesione.

Hesperia. See HISPERIA.

Hesperides (1). Strictly, the daughters of Hesperus, who guarded, with the aid of a dragon, a garden in the Isles of the Blest in which grew golden apples. Hence the garden itself, or the islands; *cf.* Greene, *Frier Bacon and Frier Bongay* (1594): 'the garden cal'd H.'

'Still climbing trees in the H.' (*L.L.L.* iv, 3); 'Before thee stands this fair H., With golden fruit, but dangerous to be touch'd; For deathlike dragons here affright thee hard' (*Per.* i, 1).

Hesperides (2). In 'The Actors names' appended to *Pericles* in F3, 4, the 'Daughter to Antiochus' is called 'Hesperides.' This seems a mere error due to a misunderstanding of the passage (*Per.* i, 1) given above. Rowe perpetuated the mistake by inserting 'Enter H.' as a st. dir. in i, 1.

Hesperus. The evening star (Ovid, *Metam.* v, 441). 'Ere twice ... Moist H. hath quench'd her sleepy lamp' (*All's Well*, ii, 1).

'His' in mod. edns.

Hibocrates. See HIPPOCRATES.

Hiems. See HYEMS.

Highest, The. The Deity; *All's Well*, iv, 2.

[**Hildebrand.**] See TURK GREGORY.

Hill, The. *i.e.* Stinchcombe Hill near Dursley, Gloucestershire, still so termed locally. 'Clement Perkes of the hill' (2 *Hen. IV*, v, 1). See PERKES.

Hinckley. Town on the border of Leicestershire, to the N.E. of Coventry. 'H. fair' (2 *Hen. IV*, v, 1).

'Hunkley,' Q. Perh. for 'Henley-in-Arden' (French, p. 91).

Hipparchus. A freedman 'who was had in great estimation about Antonius' (*Plut.* p. 213). After having had Thyreus whipped, Ant. sent word to Octavius, 'thou hast H., one of my enfranchised bondmen ... hang him if thou wilt' (*ib.* p. 218). Plutarch's account is closely followed in *Ant. Cl.* iii, 13.

Hippocrates. The most famous physician of antiquity. The name distorted by Evans: 'He [Dr Caius] has no more knowledge in Hibocrates and Galen' (*M.W.W.* iii, 1).

Hippolita. See HIPPOLYTE.

Hippolyte. Ἱππολύτη, Queen of the Amazons and sister to Antiope. Traditions concerning her are conflicting. 'This historiographer [Clidemus] calleth the Amazon which Theseus married, Hippolyta and not Antiopa' (*Plut.* p. 288).

D.P. *M.N.D.* 'Hippolita, Princess of the Amazons, betrothed to Theseus' (Rowe). i, 1] declares that the four days before the nuptials 'will quickly steep themselves in night.' iv, 1] is reminded by the music of the hounds how, with Hercules and Cadmus, she once heard them bay the bear in Crete. v, 1] comments on the wondrous story of the past night; is unwilling to be a spectator of the clowns' Interlude, since she loves not 'to see wretchedness o'ercharged'; nevertheless criticizes the performance with some acerbity.

Hiren, Irene. 'Have we not H. here?' (2 *Hen. IV*, ii, 4). This phrase occurs in *Eastward Hoe* (by Chapman and others), 1605, in Dekker's *Satiromastix*, and other 17th-cent. works. In *The Merie Conceited Jests of George Peele* (Dyce, *Greene and Peele* (1861), p. 616) under the heading 'How George read a Playbook to a Gentleman,' we are told that the gentleman 'had George invited to half-a-score sheets of paper; whose Christianly pen had writ the word *Finis* to the famous play of *The Turkish Mahamet and Hyrin the fair Greek*, in Italian called a curtezan,' etc. No such play is known to have been published. Grosart believes 'the gentleman' to be W. Barksted, an actor, whose poem *Hiren or the faire Greeke* appeared in 1611.

Pistol may use the word for 'iron,' *i.e.* his sword.

Hirtius. Roman consul (43 B.C.); defeated Antony beneath the walls of Mutina, but was killed in the action (*Plut.* p. 167 ('Hircius'); *ib.* p. 234).

Mtd. *Ant. Cl.* i, 4 ('Hiraius,' F1, 2, 3).

Hisperia. Name of an attendant of Rosalind and Celia; *A.Y.L.* ii, 2 (arbitrarily changed by Warburton to 'Hesperia').

Hob. A diminutive of 'Robin, or 'Robert.' A familiar name of a clown or rustic; *cf.* Minsheu: 'A Quintaine ... a game ... where Jac and Tom, Die, Hob, and Will, strive for the gay garland.'

'Why ... should I stand here, To beg of Hob and Dick ...?' (*Cor.* ii, 3).

Hobbididence. Name of a fiend. 'H., prince of dumbness' (*Lear*, iv, 1). See HOPPEDANCE.

'Hobbididen,' Pope; 'Hobbididdance,' Capell.

Hobgoblin. Originally the name of a fiend; *cf.* R. Scot, *Discoverie of Witchcraft* (1584) (bk. vii, ch. 2, p. 105, ed. Nicholson): 'And know you this ... that heretofore Robin Goodfellow, and Hob-goblin were as terrible, and also credible to the people as hags and witches be now.' By Sh. identified with Robin Goodfellow.

'*Fairy* [to Puck]. You are that shrewd and knavish spirit Called Robin Goodfellow ... Those that Hobgoblin call you, and sweet Puck, you do their work' (*M.N.D.* ii, 1); 'Crier H., make the fairy oyes' (*M.W.W.* v, 5).

Holborn. A district of London, so called from the 'Hole Bourne,' or Fleet Brook, running through it. Mtd. *Rich. III*, iii, 4; see ELY HOUSE.

[**Holinshed, Raphael.**] Chronicler (*ob. c.* 1580). The first edition of his *Chronicles* appeared in two folio vols., 1577. 'The Firste volume' contains: 'The Description of Britayne' (by William Harrison); 'The Historie of Englande' to the Norman Conquest (by Hol.); 'The Description of Scotlande' (by Harrison, after Boece); 'The Historie of Scotlande' (by Hol.), to 1571; 'The Historie of Irelande to 1509' (by Hol., continued to 1547 by R. Stanyhurst, who also prefixed a Description of Ir.); 'The Laste volume' contains: 'The Chronicles of Englande from William Conquerour untill this present tyme ... by Raphaell Holinshed.'

A second edn. appeared in 1587, in three vols., with additions by J. Stow, R. Stanyhurst, J. Hooker, F. Thynne, A. Fleming, and others, but with the omission of certain passages expunged by order of the Privy Council.

These passages are restored in the mod. edn. of 1807–8 (6 vols., 4to), which is, however, rearranged.

Refs. in the present work are to the edn. of 1587, which is that quoted in *Shakspere's Holinshed*, by W. G. Boswell-Stone (1896), and was, moreover, probably the edn. made use of by the dramatist in the historical plays.

Holland, Henry (1447–73). D. of Exeter; only son of John H., 2nd E. of Huntingdon (*q.v.*); m. Anne, sister to Edward IV, but remained faithful to Henry VI, and was present at the battles of Wakefield (*Hol.* iii, 659), Towton, and Barnet (Hall, p. 295). He was attainted by Edw. IV, and died in poverty 1473.

D.P. *3 Hen. VI.* i, 1] at the Parliament House is addressed as 'cousin of Exeter' by Henry; bids York descend from the throne, where he has seated himself; admits to Henry that York appears to him 'lawful king,' but advises reconciliation. ii, 5] (at Towton) persuades the King to escape with him from the field (*Hol.* iii, 665). iv, 8] fears that Edward will seduce Henry's men; is present when H. is seized.

Acc. *Hol.* iii, 632, E.'s ship intercepted Suffolk (2 *Hen. VI*, iv, 1); but he is termed 'Constable of the Tower,' and this points to confusion with his father.

Holland, Hugh (*ob.* 1633). Writer of sonnet pfxd. to F1 'Upon the Lines and Life of the Famous Scenike Poet, Master William Shakespeare.'

Holland, John (1) (*c.* 1352–1400). E. of Huntingdon; son of Thomas H., Earl of Kent, and Joan Plantagenet; half-brother to Richard II; cr. E. of H. 1387, and D. of Exeter 1397, but was deprived of his dukedom 1399 (*Hol.* iii, 513); he married Elizabeth, sister of Bolingbroke, who terms him, ironically, 'our trusty brother-in-law' (*Rich. II*, v, 3); executed, 1400, for conspiring against Hen. IV. 'Harry Duke of Hereford, Reignold Lord Cobham, That late broke from the Duke of Exeter' (*Rich. II*, ii, 1).

It is supposed that an intermediate line, mentioning Thomas Fitz-Alan (son and heir of Richard, E. of Arundel) is here lost. Fitz-Alan actually escaped from 'Exeter's custody' and joined Bolingbroke (*Hol.* iii, 496).

Holland, John (2) (1395–1447). Earl of Huntingdon and Duke of Exeter; present at Troyes (*Hol.* iii, 572); and at the coronation of Henry VI in Paris (*ib.* iii, 606).

D.P. *Hen. V.* 'Huntington.' v, 2] (at Troyes) *p.m.*; is addressed by Henry.

Holland, John (3). D.P. *2 Hen. VI*. 'A follower of Jack Cade.' iv, 2] is urged to join the rebels; agrees, without enthusiasm. iv, 7] makes sarcastic comments (aside) on Cade's promises.

Holland, Thomas. See SURREY, DUKE OF.

Hollander. A Dutchman. 'Hasty Germans, and blunt Hollanders' (*3 Hen. VI*, iv, 8); 'your swag-bellied H.' (*Oth*, ii, 2); 'He [the Englishman] gives your H. a vomit, ere the next pottle can be fill'd' (*ib. ib.*).

'Since we had to doe in the quarrell of the Netherlands ... the custom of drinking ... was brought over to England, wherein let the Dutch be their owne judges, if we equall them not; yes I think rather excell them' (Peacham, *Compleat Gentleman* (1622), p. 193).

Hollowmas. See HALLOWMAS.

Holmedon. See HOMILDON HILL.

Holofernes. D.P. *L.L.L.* A schoolmaster. iv, 2] speaks of the deer killed by the Princess, and composes an alliterative epitaph thereon; criticizes Biron's sonnet. v, 1] discusses Don Armado with Nathaniel; is bantered by Moth; suggests presenting 'The Nine Worthies' before the Princess. v, 2] appears as Judas Maccabaeus (*q.v.*) in the 'pageant.'

Warburton supposed John Florio, a teacher of Italian in London, and author of a dictionary entitled *A World of Wordes* (1598), to be satirized as H. Others have suggested Richard Mulcastor, or Thos. Hunt, Sh.'s own schoolmaster, as the original. Fleay considers H. to stand for Bp. Cooper (see DULL). But 'the pedant' was a stock character in Italian comedy, and it is noteworthy that in the st. dirs. and pfxs. of the earliest edns. 'Pedant' occurs for 'Hol.' in most cases. Gargantua's first teacher was Master Tubal H. The character is called 'Sir H.' (v, 1), apparently being confused with the curate, Sir Nathaniel (*q.v.*). Nathaniel and Holifernes Pippo are schoolboys in J. Marston's *What You Will* (1607).

Holyrood Day. Otherwise 'Holy-Cross day,' and 'Rood-day'; a festival observed on Sept. 14 in commemoration of the exaltation of the holy cross after its recovery from the Persians by Heraclius, A.D. 628. 'On H. Day, the gallant Hotspur there, Young Harry Percy and brave Archibald, ... At Holmedon met' (*1 Hen. IV*, i, 1).

Acc. *Hol.* ii, 254, the battle was fought 'on the Rood day in harvest in the yeare 1403 upon a Tuesday.'

Holy Writ. The Bible (*q.v.*). 'So Holy Writ in babes hath judgment shown, When judges have been babes' (*All's Well*, ii, 1; *cf.* Matt. xxi, 15, 16); 'I clothe my naked villainy With old odd ends stolen out of Holy Writ' (*Rich. III*, i, 3; Gloucester having just alluded to Matt. v, 44); 'confirmations strong As proofs of Holy Writ' (*Oth.* iii, 3).

Homildon Hill. Near Wooler, Northumberland, scene of defeat of the Scots, under Earl Douglas, by the English under Henry Percy ('Hotapur') and the exiled E. of March, Sept. 1402. The battle is described in *Hol.* iii, 520, and the account is closely followed by Sh., *1 Hen. IV*, i, 1. Mtd., *ib.* i, 3; v, 3. ('Holmedon' in *Sh.*; a dissyllable.)

Hoodman. Name given to the person blindfolded in the game of blindman's buff. Applied to the blindfolded Parolles: 'Hoodman comes' (*All's Well*, iv, 3).

Hopdance. ('Hoppedance,' Qq.) Name of a fiend. 'H. cries in Tom's belly for two white herring' (*Lear*, iii, 6).

'Hoberdidance' was one of the 'four deuils of the round or Morrice' (Harsnet, p. 49).

Hopkins, Nicholas. A Carthusian monk, sometime confessor to the Duke of Buckingham (*Hol.* iii, 862). In July 1517 H. prophesied 'that before Christmas next there should be a change, and that the duke should have the rule and government of all England' (*ib.* iii, 864). At Buckingham's trial H. was produced as a witness, and is described (*ib.* iii, 865) as 'the monke of the priorie of the Charterhouse beside Bath which ... had induced the duke to treason with his false forged prophecies.'

Mtd., *Hen. VIII*, i, 1; 'a chartreux friar, His confessor; who fed him every minute With words of sovereignty' (*ib.* i, 2); 'that devil-monk, H.' (*ib.* ii, 1).

In Ff his forename is given as 'Michaell'; 'Nicholas' was restored by Theobald.

In two instances (i, 2) his name is given as 'Henton' in Ff – evidently from a misunderstanding of 'a monke of an house of the Chartreux order beside Bristow, called Henton' (*Hol.* iii, 862).

Horace. Quintus Horatius Flaccus, Roman poet, 65–8 B.C. 'As H. says in his ... ' (unfinished sentence) (*L.L.L.* iv, 2). For 'the works of H.': '*Demet.* ... Integer vitae, scelerisque purus, Non eget Mauri jaculis nec arcu. *Chi.* O, 'tis a verse in H.; I know it well, I read it in the grammar long ago. *Aaron.* Ay, just a verse in H.' (*T. And.* iv, 2; Hor. *Odes*, i, 22). See LILY.

The *Satires*, *Ars Poetica*, and *Epistles* were Englished in 1566–7, by T. Drant, but the *Odes* were not translated in Sh.'s lifetime. (Selections, by Sir Thos. Hawkins, appeared in 1625.)

Horatio. D.P. *Haml.* Friend to Hamlet. i, 1] joins the watch, and on the appearance of the ghost addresses it, without result; is convinced that it is the spirit of the late King; relates to the officers the threat offered by young Fortinbras to Denmark; again tries to make the ghost speak to him, and resolves to relate all to Hamlet. i, 2] describes the apparition to H. i, 4] accompanies H. to 'the platform'; vainly tries to prevent him from following the ghost. i, 5] is bewildered by Hamlet's account of what had passed, but swears secrecy. iii, 2] Hamlet tells him how he will test the King by means of a play; Horatio is convinced of the King's guilt. iv, 5] witnesses Ophelia's madness, and is ordered to watch her. iv, 6] learns that Hamlet has returned to Denmark, having defeated a plot against him. v, 1] converses with Hamlet in the graveyard; witnesses the encounter between H. and Laertes. v, 2] learns the nature of the plot from which Hamlet had escaped; deprecates H.'s acceptance of Laertes' challenge; witnesses the fatal duel; receives Hamlet's last injunctions; prepares to relate all the tragic story to Fortinbras.

Horatio is the name of the murdered son of Hieronimo in Kyd's *Spanish Tragedie* (1594).

'Horatio is indeed just as little an energetic character as Hamlet; ... but Horatio is a man of perfect calmness of mind, schooled to bear suffering and to take with equal thanks fortune's buffets and rewards; he is a hero of endurance, one of those blessed ones on whom Hamlet might look with envy, "whose blood and judgment are so well co-mingled, That they are not a pipe for fortune's finger To sound what stop she please." ' (Gorvinus, *Sh. Comm.* (1875), p. 563.)

[Horne.] See Herne.

Horner, Thomas. D.P. 2 *Hen. VI.* 'An armourer.' i, 3] is accused, by his servant, of treason; a day is appointed for a judicial combat between them. ii, 3] he is defeated, and dies confessing his guilt.

Acc. Stow (p. 635), the armourer's name was William Catur, and the servant's John David. 'Catur, on entering the lists intoxicated, was killed by his servant, who being afterwards convicted of felony, confessed the falsehood of the charge against his unhappy master' (Noorthouck, *Hist. of London* (1773), p. 94).

The combat took place at Smithfield in 1446, and Catur's head was sot up on London Bridge.

[Hornsey.] Richard D. of Gloucester was received by the Lord Mayor and Sheriffs (May 4, 1483), 'reverentile at Harnesie' (*Hol.* iii, 716): in 'London' acc. *Rich. III*, iii, 1, l. 1.

Horror. Personified. 'The brow Of bragging H.' (*John*, v, 1); 'H.'s head' (*Oth.* iii, 3).

Hortensio. D.P. *Tam. Sh.* 'A suitor to Bianca.' i, 1] agrees with his rival Gremio to help the shrewish Katharina Minola to a husband, and thus set her sister Bianca free to wed. i, 2] welcomes Petruchio to his house; explains the situation, and finding Petr. eager to woo the wealthy Kath., arranges to accompany him to Minola's house in the guise of a teacher of music; informs Gremio that their design prospers; ascertains that Tranio (posing as Lucentio) is also a suitor for Bianca. ii, 1] is introduced to Minola as 'Licio,' a musician; is sent to teach Kath.; later, returns 'with his head broken,' and describes his ill-treatment. iii, 1] after a squabble with her other tutor (Lucentio), woos Bianca under pretence of a music lesson; suspects B. to be a flirt, iii, 2] *p.m.* iv, 2] seeing Lucentio making love to B., forswears her, and declares he will marry a wealthy widow who looks kindly on him. iv, 3] witnesses Petruchio's rejection of K.'s new cap and gown; consoles the tailor. iv, 5] believes he has been taught by Petr. how to manage his widow. v, 2] (at Lucentio's feast) finds, after all, that 'his widow,' now his wife, scorns to obey him.

The corresponding character in *The Taming of A Shrew* is Polidor, a student at Athens, friend to Aurelius and suitor to Emelia.

Hortensius. D.P. *Timon.* Servant to one of Timon's creditors. iii, 4] waits for money from T., but it is 'against his heart'; deems T. mad.

The name (which, as in the case of the other servants, is probably that of his master) occurs, as well as that of Timon, in Plutarch's *Life of Marcus Antonius.* 'Hortensis' in 'The Actors Names' (F1).

[Horvendile.] In *The Hystorie of Hamblet*, Governor of the province of Ditmarse, who was father of Hamblet by Geruth, d. of the chief King of Denmark. He was treacherously slain, at a banquet, by his brother Fengon, who married Geruth.

'Horvendillus' in Saxo Grammaticus.

Host. D.P. *T.G.V.* 'Host where Julia lodges' (F1). iv, 2] escorts 'Sebastian' (Julia) to hear the serenade before Silvia's house; tells 'Seb.' that Proteus loves Sil. 'out of all nick,' and that he lies at his house.

Host of the Garter Inn. D.P. *M.W.W.* (i, 1) mtd. i, 3] accepts Bardolph as Tapster. ii, 1] agrees to aid Ford in approaching Falstaff in disguise. ii, 3] eggs on Caius to fight with Evans. iii, 1] C. and E. resolve to be revenged on him for flouting them. iii, 2] suggests Fenton as a suitor for Anne Page. iv, 3] tells Bardolph that 'the Germans' may hire three of his horses. iv, 5] hears that the Germans have run away with the horses, 'like three Doctor Faustuses'; Caius and Evans tell him he has been 'cozened'; he raises a hue and cry. iv, 6] his 'mind is heavy,' but on Fenton's offering him gold to cover his loss, he listens to F.'s confidences and agrees to help him.

Though not explicitly stated, it may be inferred that the loss of the Host's horses was due to Evans and Caius with Bardolph's aid. 'The simple men, who cannot even speak English,' cheat the 'boaster, full of mockery and tricks' (Gervinus, *Sh. Comm.* (1875), p. 384).

Hostess. D.P. *Tam. Sh.* Ind. 1] rates Sly for his delinquencies.

In *The Taming of A Shrew* the corresponding character is 'A Tapster.'

Hostilius. One of 'Three Strangers'; *Timon*, iii, 2.

Hotspur. See Percy, Henry (2).

Hour, Humphrey. ('Houre,' Qq; 'Hower,' Ff.) Of unknown signification. The Duchess of York asks her son Richard what 'comfortable hour ... ever graced me in thy company?' to which he replies 'Faith, none, but Humphrey H., that call'd your grace To breakfast once forth of my company' (*Rich. III*, iv, 4).

The phrase 'to dine with Duke Humphrey,' meaning to fast, seems irrelevant. Malone suggested that it was 'used in ludicrous language for "hour," like "Tom Troth" for Truth.' The spelling of Ff suggests a personal name, and may prove the key to the mystery.

Howard, John (*c.* 1430–85). Created 1st D. of Norfolk (of the H. family) 1483, and earlmarshal, by Richard III; commanded vanguard at Bosworth (*Hol.* iii, 755), and was there slain (*ib.* iii, 759). Before the battle he was warned by 'this rime upon his gate' (*ib. ib.*):

Iacke of Norffolke be not too bold,
For Dikon thy maister is bought and sold.

D.P. *Rich. III.* v, 3] commands the van; the rime. v, 4] *p.m.*; is slain.

Acc. French, p. 222, Norfolk in a combat with the E. of Oxford lost his beaver, and his face being thus exposed was struck by an arrow from one of Richmond's archers.

Howard, Lord Thomas. S. of Thomas H., 2nd D. of Norfolk, and Agnes Tilney; a bearer of the canopy at the Princess Elizabeth's christening, *Hen. VIII*, v, 5; see Noblemen, Four.

Howard, Thomas (1) (1443–1524). 2nd D. of Norfolk of the house of Howard; son of John H., 1st D. (*q.v.*); fought for Edw. IV at Barnet; made E. of Surrey 1483; fought for Rich. III at Bosworth; was a strong opponent of Wolsey's foreign policy; presided as Lord High Steward at the trial of Buckingham (1521); died at Framlingham. His eldest d. was wife to Sir Thos. Boleyn and mother of Anne B.

D.P. *Rich. III.* 'Earl of Surrey.' v, 3] before Bosworth, is rallied by Richard on looking sad (Ff; not mtd. Qq); placed in command with his father.

'Ouer this battell was capteine, John duke of Norffolke, with whome was Thomas earle of Surrie, his sonne' (*Hol.* iii, 755).

D.P. *Hen. VIII.* i, 1] describes, as an eyewitness, the Field of the Cloth of Gold (as a fact, he was in England at the time); repeatedly warns Buckingham against the malice and 'potency' of Wolsey. i, 2] attends Queen Katharine; supports her charge against Wolsey of unduly taxing the people. ii, 2] comments bitterly on W.'s efforts to obtain the Queen's divorce; attempts to have audience of Henry, but is rebuffed on Wolsey's entrance. iii, 2] shows that W.'s power is tottering; considers Cranmer 'a worthy fellow'; witnesses W.'s perturbation and mentions it to the King; later, demands the Great Seal from W., and, on his refusing to give it up, bids farewell to 'my little good lord cardinal.'

Wolsey was disgraced in 1529; 'Norfolk's' presence in the last scene is therefore an anachronism; the 'E. of Surrey' in the same scene would then be actually D. of Norfolk, having succeeded his father in 1524.

Howard, Thomas (2). E. of Surrey, and 3rd D. of Norfolk of the house of Howard (1473–1554); e.s. of Thos. H. (1) (*q.v.*); in high command at Flodden; Lord-Lieutenant of Ireland 1520; a strong opponent of Wolsey, and incited Hen. VIII against him. Married, as his 2nd wife, Buckingham's daughter Elizabeth Stafford.

D.P. *Hen. VIII.* (ii, 1) succeeds the E. of Kildare as 'deputy of Ireland'; Buckingham mtd. as his 'father.' iii, 2] is eager to revenge Buckingham's fate on Wolsey and rejoices to hear of the Cardinal's impending discomfiture; later, bitterly attacks Wol. for sending him out of the country before Buckingham's trial (*Hol.* iii, 855), and instances his other acts of arrogance and ruthless ambition. v, 3] present at a council. v, 5] mtd. as 'D. of Norfolk' in the christening procession of Elizabeth (*Hol.* iii, 934), 'with his marshal's staff.'

'Surrey's' presence in iii, 2, and v, 3, with the D. of Norfolk, is an anachronism. (See preceding article.)

Howard, William. Lord Howard of Effingham (*c.* 1510–73); e.s. of Thomas H., 2nd D. of Norfolk. Present at coronation of Anne Boleyn, as 'deputie to his [half] brother the duke of Norfolk marshall of England' (*Hol.* iii, 931), who was in France.

In *Hen. VIII*, iv, 1, the Duke himself is represented as present. Lord Howard was also at the christening of Princess Elizabeth (*Hol.* iii, 934; *Hen. VIII*, v, 5); see Noblemen, Four.

[**Hoyle's Mouth.**] A cave near Tenby, supposed to have been the original cave of Belarius (*q.v.*). From the high ground above it, known as the Ridgeway, a glimpse of Milford Haven (*q.v.*) may be caught.

Hubert de Burgh. Statesman; the most powerful English subject in the reigns of John and Henry III. Envoy to Portugal 1200; Chamberlain 1201; adherent of the King at Runnymede 1215, and made Justiciar the same year; became regent for Henry III in 1219; Earl of Kent 1227; *ob.* 1243. Holinshed's account (iii, 165) of the relations between Hubert and Arthur is to the effect that John, acting under advice, 'appointed certeine persons' to go to Falaise, 'where A. was kept in prison, under the charge of H. de B., and there to put out Arthur's eyes, but that H. delivered him, believing that John had spoken in haste and would repent his orders. To prevent, however, an attempt at rescue, he caused a report of A.'s death to be widely spread abroad. In 1216, on the Dauphin's landing, John left Dover Castle in the keeping of H. de B., 'a man of notable prowesse and valiancie' (*Hol.* iii, 191; cf. *John*, v, 1). The wreck of the Dauphin's 'great supply' on the Goodwins (*John*, v, 3) may be a reminiscence of the defeat of the French fleet by H. de B., 1217. The dramatic Hubert is a personage quite inferior in rank and importance to the powerful noble for whom he stands.

D.P. *John.* ii, 1] (speeches now attributed to the First Citizen are in Ff allotted to 'Hub.'). iii, 2] *p.m.*; is entrusted with the custody of Arthur. iii, 3] accepts the King's murderous suggestions as to A., and replies, 'he shall not live.' iv, 1] prepares to blind Arthur, but is prevailed upon by his entreaties to change his purpose. iv, 2] confers apart with John; leads away Peter of Pomfret; later, describes to J. the portent of the five moons (*Hol.* iii, 163); warns the King that there is widespread indignation at A.'s supposed death; on being reproached for having acted too hastily, tells John that A. still lives. iv, 3] ignorant that A. is really dead, tells the disaffected nobles that he is alive; on being confronted by the corpse exclaims: 'I loved him, and will weep My date of life out for his sweet life's loss'; bears away the body. (v, 1) mtd. v, 3] greets the sick King on the field of battle. v, 6] tells the Bastard that the King has been poisoned.

It is noteworthy that, although 'Hubert de Burgh' frequently occurs in the st. dirs. of *Tr. R.*, in Ff 'de Burgh' is never mentioned.

Hugh. As a forename. 'H. Evans,' 'H. Oatcake,' 'H. Capet,' 'H. Mortimer,' 'H. Rebeck' (*qq.v.*).

Hume, John. A priest; arraigned for having plotted to bewitch the King (*Hol.* iii, 622), but pardoned (*ib.* iii, 623). Acc. Fabian, *New Chronicles* (p. 614), H. was chaplain to the Dss. of Gloucester. The name is often spelt 'Hun,' also 'Hum' (riming with 'Mum'); cf. *2 Hen. VI*, i, 2.

D.P. *2 Hen. VI.* i, 2] tells the Dss. of Gloucester that he has procured necromancers who will raise a spirit for her to question; (*sol.*) has been suborned by Suffolk and Beaufort 'to undermine the Dss.' i, 4] leads the necromancers to the Dss. ii, 3] *p.m.*; sentenced by the King to be hanged.

Humfrey. See Sinklo.

Humphrey. As a forename. 'H. Stafford,' 'H. Hour' (*qq.v.*).

Humphrey, Duke of Gloucester (1391–1447). Youngest son of Henry IV; created D. of Gloucester in 1414 by his brother, Henry V. The following is a summary of Holinshed's account of him, so far as it is relevant to the plays in which he appears; He directed the mines at the siege of Harfleur (*Hol.* iii, 549); accompanied Henry to Troyes (*ib.* 572); was present at the King's deathbed, and by his behest became Protector of England (*ib.* 583). In 1425 dissension broke out between him and his uncle Henry Beaufort, Bp. of Winchester (*ib.* 590), and by Beaufort's orders Gl. was forcibly prevented from entering the Tower, whereupon he accused B. of having plotted the murder of Henry V when Prince of Wales. Open strife arose in London between the adherents of the Duke and the Bp. (*ib.* 591), but at length a truce was arranged between them (*ib.* 595). He acted as Lieutenant of England during the coronation of Henry VI in Paris, and is characterized as 'an upright ... governor ... loving to the poor commons, and beloved of them again; learned, wise ... void of pride and ambition' (*ib.* 627); he was 'much against' the King's marriage (*ib.* 624), and by the Queen's 'procurement, divers noble men' having conspired against him, he was accused of misappropriating public money, and of other offences (*ib.* 627). He resigned his protectorate (1429) and was deprived of power (*ib.* 626). He bore his troubles patiently, and was arrested at Bury St Edmunds by the High Constable of England. His defence proved of no avail, and he was found dead in his bed, 'but all indifferent persons might well understand that he died of some violent death' (*ib.* 627).

D.P. *2 Hen. IV.* 'Prince Humphrey.' iv, 4] is questioned by his father concerning his brother Henry; comments on portents of the times; is summoned by his dying father. v, 2] condoles with the Lord Chief Justice on losing a friend in Henry IV.

D.P. *Hen. V.* i, 2] (in the presence) *p.m.* iii, 1] (before Harfleur) *p.m.* (iii, 2) according to Gower, is given 'the order of the siege' of Harfleur, but is 'altogether directed by' Macmorris. iii, 6] (the eve of Agincourt) hopes the enemy 'will not come upon us now.' iv, 1] is sent by the King to summon 'the princes.' iv, 3] in the English camp. iv, 7] comments on Mountjoy's demeanour. iv, 8] *p.m.* v, 2] (at Troyes) *p.m.*

D.P. *1 Hen. VI.* i, 1] (at the lying in state of Henry V) eulogizes the late King; accuses the Bp. of Winchester (Beaufort) of desiring a weak monarch, and of irreligion; hears 'sad tidings' from France; departs to proclaim young Henry king after visiting the Tower. i, 3] is refused admittance to the Tower by Beaufort's orders; bitterly objurgates B., who arrives with his adherents; (a fight ensues between the two parties, which is quelled by the Mayor). (ii, 4) mtd. iii, 1] Gl. has a bitter altercation with Beaufort, whom he denounces in unmeasured terms; he quells a further encounter between their retainers; unwillingly gives his hand to B. in token of 'a truce'; advises the King to be crowned in France. iii, 4] in Paris, with the King. iv, 1] is present at the coronation as 'lord Protector'; reads Burgundy's letter announcing his defection; checks the strife between two 'presumptuous vassals.' v, 1] advocates the marriage of Henry with the daughter of the E. of Armagnac. v, 5] opposes the King's projected marriage with Margaret of Anjou.

D.P. *2 Hen. VI.* i, 1] breaks down in attempting to read the articles of peace with France; passionately addresses the peers on the shameful surrender of Maine and Anjou; (in his absence, Beaufort declares he is aiming at the crown, while Salisbury eulogizes 'good Duke Humphrey' as 'a noble gentleman'). i, 2] relates an ominous dream to his wife, and chides her for ambition. i, 3] is accused of malfeasance as Protector; later, proposes York as regent in France, ii, 1] agrees to fight a duel with Beaufort; detects the imposture of Simpcox (*q.v.*); learns, to his dismay, that the Dss. is accused of witchcraft. ii, 3] is present when sentence is pronounced against his wife; yields up his staff of office to the King. ii, 4] sees his wife do penance; bids her have patience; makes light of her warning; begs that she may be well treated. iii, 1] is arrested of high treason; speaks vigorously in his own defence, and is removed in custody. (iii, 2) his death is announced; he is lamented by the King; his body is shown upon a bed, with signs of having been strangled.

'[He] was found dead in his bed, and his bodie shewed to the lords and commons, as though he had died of a palsie, or of an imposteme' (*Hol.* iii, 627). In *The Contention* the st. dir. runs: 'Then the Curtaines being drawn, Duke H. is discovered in his bed, and two men lying on his brest and smothering him.'

Hundred Merry Tales, The. A collection of stories, printed (1526) by John Rastell, and edited (1866) by H. Oesterley from the unique copy preserved at Göttingen.

Mtd. *M. Ado*, ii, 1. Coupled with 'The Book of Riddles' (*q.v.*) in *Cyvile and Uncyvile Lyfe* (1579); cf. *Sh. Eng.* i, 35.

Hungarian, *adj.* Pertaining to Hungary. Only occurs in Pistol's random phrase, 'O base Hungarian wight' (*M.W.W.* i, 3) addressed to Bardolph (Ff). See GONGARIAN.

As a subst., probably with an allusion to 'hungry': 'the middle aile of St Paul's is much frequented at noon, with a company of hungarians, not walking so much for recreation as need' (Lupton, 'London,' *Harl. Misc.* ix, 314).

Hungary, Kingdom of. A King of H. mtd.; *M. for M.* i, 2.

Hungerford, Sir Thomas. E.s. of the 3rd Baron H.; executed (1469) as a supporter of Warwick. Clarence ironically remarks that 'lord Hastings well deserves To have the heir of the lord Hungerford' (*3 Hen. VI*, iv, 1).

The heiress in question was married to Edward, Lord Hastings, son of the Hastings of the play.

Hungerford, Sir Walter. 1st Baron H. (*ob. 1449); present at Agincourt and the siege of Rouen (1418). Acc. to Henrici Quinti Ang. Reg. Gesta*, p. 47, cited by Boswell-Stone (p. 190), it was he who uttered the wish for more troops attributed to Westmoreland, *Hen. V*, iv, 3. Taken prisoner at Patay, *1 Hen. VI*, i, 1 (*Hol.* iii, 601).

Huntingdon, Earl of. See GREY, THOMAS, and HOLLAND, JOHN.

Huntsman. D.P. *3 Hen. VI.* iv, 5] unwillingly accompanies Edward IV in his flight.

Huntsmen, Two. D.PP. *Tam. Sh.* Ind. 1] in attendance on their lord when Sly is discovered.

[Huon.] See OBERON.

[Hussey, Sir John], Baron Hussey (*c.* 1466–1537). A bearerof the canopy at the christening ceremony of Princess Elizabeth; *Hen. VIII*, v, 5. See NOBLEMEN, FOUR.

'The lord Husee' (*Hol.* iii, 934). His identity is, however, doubtful.

Hybla. A locality in Sicily, famous for its wild thyme and bees (Pliny, *Nat. Hist.* XI, xiii, 13; Ovid, *Trist.* V, xiii, 22; *Are Amat.* iii, 150).

'*Fal.* Is not my hostess ... a most sweet wench? *P. Hen.* As the honey of H.' (*1 Hen. IV*, i, 2); 'But for your words, they rob the H. bees, And leave them honeyless' (*Jul. C.* v, 1).

Hydra. A monster which ravaged Lernae, near Argos. It had numerous heads, of which one was immortal. Hercules cut off its heads, but two sprang up for each one he severed. At last he burnt all the heads except the immortal one, which he buried. *Cf.* Ovid, *Metam.* ix, 70 ff.

'Another King! They grow like H.'s heads!' (*1 Hen. IV*, v, 4; with reference to the many-headed multitude'): 'have you thus Given H. here to choose an officer' (*Cor.* iii, 1); 'had I as many mouths as H. such an answer would stop them all'

(*Oth.* ii, 3). Attrib.: 'The parcels and particulars of our grief ... whereon this H. son of war is born: Whose dangerous eyes may well be charmed asleep' (2 *Hen. IV*, iv, 2; apparently here confused with Argus).

Hydra-headed. 'H.-headed wilfulness' (*Hen. V*, i, 1).

Hyems, Hiems. Personification of Winter. 'And on old Hyems chin ['thin,' or 'chill,' conj.] and icy crown, An odorous chaplet of sweet summer buds Is as in mockery set' (*M.N.D.* ii, 1); 'This side is Hiems, Winter' (*L.L.L.* v, 2).

'Et glacialis Hiems canos hirsuta capillos' (Ovid, *Metam.* ii, 30); 'Inde senilis Hiems tremulo venit horrida passu, Aut spoliata suos, aut, quos habet, alba capillos' (*ib.* xv, 212–13).

For the controversy with reference to the reading in *M.N.D.* see Furness, Var.

Hymen. God of marriage; a personification of the bridal song, represented as a handsome youth bearing a torch.

'As H.'s lamp[s] shall light you' (*Temp.* iv, 1); 'no bed-rite shall be paid Till H.'s torch be lighted' (*ib. ib.*); 'and H. now with luckier issue speeds' (*M. Ado*, v, 3); (gold) 'thou bright defiler Of H.'s purest bed' (*Timon*, iv, 3); 'H. hath brought the bride to bed' (*Per.* iii, Gow.); 'H. did our hands unite' (*Haml.* iii, 2).

D.P. *A.Y.L.* 'A person presenting H.' (Capell). v, 4] conducts Rosalind and Celia to the Duke, singing, 'Good Duke receive thy daughter, H. from Heaven brought her,' etc., and addresses the four couples about to be married, concluding with another song in honour of 'H., god of every town.'

'Rosalind is imagined by the rest of the company to be brought by enchantment, and is therefore introduced by a supposed aeriel being in the character of H.' (Johnson). 'Sh. is not answerable for one absurdity in the conduct of the masque, that must lye at his editor's doors who, by bringing in H. *in propria persona* makes Rosalind a magician indeed' (Capell). C. further suggests that H. 'had some Loves in his train,' as chorus.

Hymenaeus. Hymen (*q.v.*). 'And tapers burn so bright and everything In readiness for H. stand' (*T. And.* i, 1).

Hyperion. A Titan, father of Helios; *cf.* Ovid, *Metam.* iv, 192, where the sun is addressed as 'Hyperione nate'; hence (from the patronymic Hyperionion), the sun-god, or the sun himself.

The early riser helps 'H. to his horse' (*Hen. V.* iv, 1); 'add more coals to Cancer when he burns With entertaining great H.' (*Tr. Cr.* ii, 3); 'whereon H.'s quickening fire doth shine' (*Timon*, iv, 3); 'Even from H.'s rising in the east Until his very downfall in the sea' (*T. And.* v, 2); Hamlet declares that his father was, compared to Claudius, 'H. to a satyr' (*Haml.* i, 2); 'H.'s curls' (*ib.* iii, 4).

Sh., as well as Chapman (and Keats), places the accent on the antepenultimate.

Hyrcan. For 'Hyrcanian.' 'Hyrcan tiger' (*Macb.* iii, 4).

Hyrcania. Province of the ancient Persian Empire, S. and S.E. of the Caspian. 'Tigers of H.' (*3 Hen. VI*, i, 4). *Cf.* 'Tygres are bred in H.' (Pliny, *N.H.* VIII, xviii, 25, Holland's transln. (1601)); Virg. *Aen*, iv, 367.

Hyrcanian, *adj.* Pertaining to Hyrcania. 'H. deserts' (*M.V.* ii, 7); 'the H. beast' (*Haml.* ii, 2).

I

I. As an initial, for 'J' invariably, QqF1 The differentiation between the two letters began about 1630. The retention of 'I' in 'Iago' is noticeable.

I., B. Signature of verses 'To the Reader' pfxd. to the First Folio; *i.e.* 'Ben Jonson.'

Iachimo. D.P. *Cymb.* 'Friend to Philario' (Rowe). i, 5] discusses Posthumus, whom he has seen in Britain, and whose prestige he considers has been enhanced by 'marrying his king's daughter'; on the entrance of Posthumus, falls into a dispute with him as to the merits and virtue of his 'unparagoned mistress' (Imogen), and finally wagers ten thousand ducats against P.'s diamond ring that he will undermine her honour. i, 7] arriving in Britain, he is presented to Imogen, and hands her a commendatory letter from Posthumus; in conversation with Imogen, hints at the levity and lax morals of P. and urges her to 'be reveng'd'; finding that he has gone too far, he declares that his words were but a test of her 'affiance,' and that in truth Posthumus is 'a holy witch'; being forgiven, he asks Imogen to stow in her room for the night a trunk containing valuable gifts for the Emperor. ii, 2] emerging from the trunk at midnight, he notes all the contents of the chamber, and takes from Imogen's arm her bracelet; in so doing observes 'a mole cinque-spotted' on her breast: reenters the trunk. ii, 4] returning to Rome, he convinces Posthumus by the evidence he is able to produce, that he has won the wager. (ii, 5) 'this yellow Iachimo.' (iii, 4) Imogen thinks he may have, after all, reported truly to her. (iv, 2) commands an invading Roman force in Britain; is termed 'Sienna's brother.' v, 2] is disarmed by Posthumus in single combat; fears that his remorse for accusing Imogen 'takes off his manhood.' (v, 4) 'slight thing of Italy.' v, 5] is brought as a prisoner before Cymbeline; is compelled to relate the means by which he became possessed of Posthumus' ring; is finally forgiven by P. with the words, 'Live, and deal with others better.'

The name is a variant of Giacomo, from Jacobus (James). It should properly be accented on the penultimate.

'Base as he is, we must, however, beware of making him still baser. Want of faith in human goodness is not innate in him, but acquired from his never having met with virtuous men. A mere glance of Imogen shews him what he has never seen… Repulsed by her, and ashamed, he feels neither hatred nor ill-will against her, but admiration alone.' His conscience is awakened, and 'the speedy confession of his sin shews him crushed with remorse worthy of pardon.' (Gervinus, *Sh. Comm.* (1862), ii, 276; cancelled in 2nd edn.)

Iago. D.P. *Oth.* 'A villaine' (F1). Othello's 'ancient,' or ensign. i, 1] is incensed at the promotion of Cassio, over his head, to be 'lieutenant'; yet he resolves to follow Oth., 'to serve my turn upon him'; with Roderigo tells Brabantio that Desdemona, his daughter, has eloped with Oth.; indicates where Oth. may be found, but thinks it politic himself to join the Moor. i, 2] tells Oth. that Roderigo has aroused Brabantio; on R.'s appearance, feigns to challenge him. i, 3] is sent to conduct Desdemona to the Senate; Oth., on his departure, entrusts D. to Iago's care, bidding him bring her to Cyprus; Iago urges Rod. 'to put money in his purse' and join him in seeking revenge upon Oth.; (*sol.*) recalls a rumour of an intrigue between Oth. and his wife Emilia; devises a 'double knavery' by which he will be revenged at once on Cassio and Othello. ii, 1] arrives in Cyprus with Desdemona and his wife; exchanges banter on womankind with D.; persuades Rod. that D. is in love with Cassio, and instructs him to pick a quarrel with C. that night; (*sol.*) elaborates his scheme, and, with 'the motive-hunting of a motiveless malignity' (Coleridge), inflames himself with jealousy against both Oth. and Cas. ii, 3] incites Cassio to drink to excess, and tells Montano that intemperance is C.'s prevailing vice; brings about a fight between Cassio and Montano; gives a misleading account of the transaction, but professes to exonerate C.; persuades C. to seek pardon from Oth. by the mediation of Desdemona; (*sol.*) ironically absolves himself from villainy, but adds that 'out of her own goodness' he will 'make the net That shall enmesh them all'; urges Rod. to have patience. iii, 1] sends his wife to Cassio. iii, 2] is given instructions by Oth. iii, 3] enables Oth. to observe Desd. and Cassio in conversation; gradually lights a flame of suspicion in Oth.'s heart; later, obtains D.'s handkerchief from Emilia, and determines to drop it 'in Cassio's lodging'; by cumulative suggestions stirs Oth. into a frenzy of jealousy. iii, 4] encourages Cassio to importune Desd. for her aid; expresses surprise at hearing that Oth. is 'angry.' iv, 1] works upon Oth.'s emotions until the Moor 'falls, in a trance'; on his recovery, Iago contrives to converse with Cassio on the subject of Bianca in the hearing of Oth., who supposes Desdemona to be referred to; urges Oth. to strangle his wife; hints to Lodovico that Oth.'s mind is unbalanced. iv, 2] expresses surprise and sorrow to Desd. at Othello's having reviled her, but assures her that 'all things shall be well'; finds that Rod. begins to suspect that the gifts of jewels entrusted to him for Desd. had been kept by him; resolves to be rid of R. and urges him to kill Cassio that night. v, 1] places Rod. in a suitable position for attacking C. in the dark; during the encounter which follows, I. covertly wounds C. and slips away; later, returns and despatches the wounded Rod.; expresses solicitude for Cassio, and has him borne away; professes to believe Bianca accessory to the crime. v, 2] Iago stabs his wife, who exposes his villainy in accusing Desd.; later, °to speak a word 'from this time forth'; his 'censure,' under torture, is left to the Governor.

In Cinthio's *Novella* the corresponding character is unnamed, and is simply 'the Ensign' ('1' Alfieri'). He is handsome, but depraved ('di bellissima presenza, ma della piu scelerata natura'), and falls in love with Disdemona; he obtains the fatal handkerchief while D. is caressing his little daughter. The actual murderer of Disdemona is the Ensign himself, who uses a sand-bag; he is aided by her husband; the Ensign dies from the effects of the rack.

Iago's statement (i, 3) that he had 'look'd upon the world for four times seven years' has been understood to mean that this time had elapsed since he arrived at years of discretion, and actors have represented him as about forty. *Cf.* Furness, *Var.* p. 81.

'The character of Iago is one of the supererogations of Sh.'s genius. Some persons, more nice than wise, have thought this whole character unnatural, because his villainy is *without a sufficient motive*. Sh., who was as good a philosopher as he was poet, thought otherwise. He knew that the love of power, which is another name for the love of mischief, is natural to man.' (W. Hazlitt.) 'The character of I. is so conducted, that he is from the first scene to the last hated and despised' (Dr Johnson). See Macaulay, *Edin. Rev.*, 1827, xlv, 272.

Icarus. Son of Daedalus. Minos having confined them in Crete by seizing all the ships on the coast, D., in order to escape, contrived wings for his son Icarus and himself. D. flew safely over the Aegean, but Ic. soared too high, and, the wax by which his wings were attached being melted by the sun, he fell into the sea and was drowned (Ovid, *Metam.* viii, 183 ff.).

'Then follow thou thy desperate sire of Crete, Thou Icarus' (Talbot to his son; *1 Hen. VI*, iv, 6); 'There died My Icarus, my blossom, in his pride' (*ib.* iv, 7).

'*Glo.* Why, what a peevish fool was that of Crete, That taught his son the office of a fowl; And yet, for all his wings, the fool was drowned. *K. Hen.* I, Daedalus; my poor boy, Icarus; Thy father, Minos, that denied our course; The sun that sear'd the wings of my sweet boy, Thy brother Edward; and thyself, the sea, Whose envious gulf did swallow up his life' (*3 Hen. VI*, v, 6). ('Wings To soar with peril after Ic.,' *Tr. R.* I, 2.)

Iceland. Dogs imported from I. were favourites as ladies' pets in Sh.'s days; *cf.* W. Harrison, *Description of England* (1807), III, vii, 389: 'Besides these also we have sholts or curs, daily brought out of I., and much made of among us because of their sauciness and quarrelling.'

(Pistol to Nym) 'Pish for thee, Iceland dog! thou prick-ear'd cur of Iceland!' (*Hen. V*, ii, 1).

Iden, or Eden, Alexander. Acc. *Hol.* iii, 635, 'a gentleman of Kent, named Alexander Eden, awaited so his time, that he took the said Cade in a garden in Sussex, so that there he was slain at Hothfield'; Hall (p. 222) states that a price having been put on Cade's head, 'many sought for hym, but few espied hym, til one (A. Iden), esquire of Kent, found hym in a garden and there in hys defence manfully slew the caitife' (see Cade). French, p. 169, quotes Rymer's *Foedera*, where is given the writ 28 Henry VI, dated July 15, 1450: 'The reward of mil. marc. [1000 marks] paid to A.I., Sheriff of our said co. of Kent.'

D.P. *2 Hen. VI*. 'A Kentish gentleman.' iv, 10] while strolling in his garden, is suddenly threatened by an apparent robber; is unwilling 'to combat a poor famish'd man,' but is compelled to do so, and kills him; learning from his dying words that he is Cade, resolves to carry his head to the King. v, 1] does so, and is rewarded by a thousand marks and a knighthood.

In iv, 10, a certain discrepancy is observable, in that though Iden is accompanied by servants they drop out of the scene, and he drags away the body himself. A monument near Heathfield marks the spot where C. was arrested, the road being known as 'Cade Street' (Lewis, *Topog. Dict.*). The name is spelt 'Eyden' in *F.P.C.*, where he bids his servants stand aside, since 'it never shall be saide whilst the world doth stand that Alexander Eyden an Esquire of Kent tooke oddes to combat with a famisht man' (iv, 10).

[**Iliad, The.**] George Chapman translated the *Shield of Achilles* and bks. i, ii, vii–xi, in 1598, completing the work in 1611. (See Troilus and Cressida.

Ilias. See Hellas.

Ilium, or Ilion. (*a*) A name of the city of Troy, from its founder Ilus, son of Tros, frequent in Latin poets; (*b*) also, in medieval romance, the palace of Priam: 'In the most apparaunt place of the cyte, vpon a roche the king Pryant dide do make hys ryche palays that was named Ylyon, that was one of the rycheste palays and stronge that euer was in the world' (Caxton, *Recuyell of the Historyes of Troye*, f. 253 *verso*); *cf.* 'A une part font Ylion De Troie le mestre danjon ... sor une roche tote entiere' (Benoît de Sainte-More, *Le Roman de Troie*, l. 3929); also, 'the noble tour of Ilioun That of the citee was the chief dungeoun' (Chaucer, *Legend of Fair Women* (Dido)).

It is not always possible to distinguish between the two meanings, but both seem to occur in *Sh.*

'Hector ... the heir of Ilion' (*L.L.L.* v, 2); 'then senseless Ilium ... with flaming top Stoops to his base' (*Haml.* ii, 2); (Troilus, of Cressida) 'between our Ilium and where she resides Let it be called the wild and wandering flood' (*Tr. Cr.* i, 1); (Pandarus to Cressida) 'was Hector armed and gone ere ye came to Ilium?' (*ib.* i, 2); 'Troy must not be, nor goodly Ilion stand' (*ib.* ii, 2); 'thy life shall be as safe As Priam is in Ilion' (*ib.* iv, 4); 'Did in great Ilion thus translate him to me' (*ib.* iv, 5); '*Hect.* ... Since first I saw yourself In Ilion, on your Greekish embassy' (*ib. ib.*); 'So Ilion, fall thou; now, Troy, sink down' (*ib.* v, 9); 'cloud-kissing Ilion' (*Lucr.* 1370); mtd., *ib.* 1524.

Illyria. A somewhat indefinite region, always comprising, however, the E. coast of the Adriatic. The action of *T. Nt.* takes place in Illyria, but of 'local colour' there is none. Mtd. *T. Nt.* i, 2, 3 (4), 5; iii, 4; iv, 1, 2.

Illyrian, *adj.* 'The strong I. pirate' (*2 Hen. VI*, iv, 1). See Bargulus.

Imogen. D.P. *Cymb.* 'Daughter to Cymbeline by a former Queen' (Rowe). (i, 1) she has dared to marry, without the royal permission, 'a poor but worthy gentleman' (Posthumus); her husband is under sentence of banishment. i, 2] mistrusts the Queen although granted, by her, time for a few parting words with Posthumus; gives P. a ring, and receives from him a bracelet; defends herself under Cymberline's bitter reproaches; learns with indignation that Cloten had drawn upon Posthumus; Pisanio, her husband's devoted retainer, remains with her. i, 4] she listens to Pisanio's account of Posthumus' embarkation; laments that her father broke in upon them while she had yet 'most pretty things to say,' and ere she could give her husband 'that parting kiss ... set Betwixt two charming words.' i, 7] is lamenting her fate, when the Roman Iachimo is ushered in with a letter from Posth.; is amazed at the account she receives from Iach. of P.'s levity of speech and conduct; demands from Iach. why he pities her; Iach. assumes indignation at her lord's disloyalty, and she murmurs sorrowfully 'I fear he has forgot Britain'; on Iachimo's urging her to 'be reveng'd,' and hinting at the means, she indignantly bids him leave her presence and cries in vain for Pisanio to dismiss him; Iach. immediately changes his tactics, and declares that all he has said was but a trial whether she were worthy of one who 'sits among men like a descended god'; Imogen, in relief, exclaims 'you make amends,' forgives him for all he has said, and consents to receive in her chamber on his behalf a trunk containing a rich 'present for the Emperor.' (ii, 1) mtd. as 'divine Imogen.' ii, 2] after reading, falls asleep; Iach. emerging from the trunk takes her bracelet, and notes the features of the room and a mole upon her breast. ii, 3] she tells Cloten, the Queen's son, who has supplied morning music beneath her window, that he lays 'out too much pains for purchasing but trouble'; to Cloten's importunity she replies with some asperity, for which she apologizes; but on his maligning Posthumus she retorts with scorn and contempt; misses, with dismay, her bracelet. iii, 2] receives a letter from Posthumus inviting her to meet him at Milford Haven, and cries, 'O for a horse with wings; resolves instantly to set out, attired as a franklin's wife, under Pisanio's escort. iii, 4] (near Milford Haven) is perplexed at Pisanio's strange manner; reads the letter he sadly hands to her, in which Post. accuses her of infidelity and orders Pi. to kill her; in utter despair bids the retainer 'strike'; on Pisanio's refusing, would fain slay herself, but is checked by the thought of the divine prohibition of self-slaughter; Pi. explains that he has planned to report her to Posthumus as dead, and advises her to don 'doublet and hose,' and present herself to Lucius the Roman ambassador, who is about to land; at parting he gives her the drug which the Queen gave him, and which is supposed to be a sovran remedy against all disorders. (iii, 5) her flight is discovered; Cloten sets out in pursuit. iii, 6] faint with hunger, Imogen enters the cave of Belarius; as she is partaking of food which she finds there, B. and his two supposed sons (Imogen's brothers) enter; she assumes the name 'Fidele,' and is warmly welcomed. iv, 2] one day, falling sick, she remains in the cave, while her hosts go hunting, and takes the drug, which throws her into a deathlike trance; she is believed to be dead, and her brothers perform her obsequies and cover her with flowers; awaking, she finds beside her the headless corpse of Cloten (who has been slain by Guiderius), and believes it to be the body of Posthumus; after a passionate lamentation, falls prostrate on the body; she is thus discovered by Lucius and his officers, and is taken to be his attendant. (iv, 3) Pisanio is perplexed by her silence. (v, 1) her supposed death lamented by Posthumus. (v, 3, 4) mtd. v, 5] Cymbeline vaguely recognizes her among the Roman prisoners; bids 'Fidele' ask freedom for any prisoner she will; she refuses to name Lucius, and converses privately with Cymbeline; she demands that Iachimo shall divulge whence he had the ring he wears; he confesses all; she springs toward Posthumus, during his passionate outburst, but he strikes 'Fidele' down; Pisanio reveals her identity, and she is restored to her husband, and greets her long-lost brothers; nor does she forget her 'good master' Lucius in her joy.

It seems probable that the name Imogen originated in a printer's error for Innogen (*q.v.*), the name given by Simon Forman in an account of a performance of the play (about 1611). In Layamon's *Brute*, the name of the wife of Brute, King of Britain, is Ignogen. See Innogen.

'What Sh. intends us to see in Imogen is made plain by the impression she is described as producing on all who came in contact with her – strangers as well as those who have seen her grow up at her father's Court. She is of royal nature as well as of royal blood – too noble to know that she is noble. A grand and patient faithfulness is at the root of her character. Yet she can be angry, vehement, passionate, upon occasion. With a being of so fine and sensitive an organization how could it be otherwise?' (Lady Martin, *Sh.'s Fem. Char.* (1887), p. 171.)

'Of all Sh.'s women she is perhaps the most tender and the most artless' (W. Hazlitt, *Char. of Sh.'s Plays*). 'The very crown and flower of all her father's daughters, – I do not speak here of her human father, but of her divine – woman above all Sh.'s women is Imogen... I am, therefore, something more than fain to close my book upon the name of the woman best beloved in all the world of song and all the tide of time; upon the name of Sh.'s Imogen.' (A.C. Swinburne, *A Study of Sh.* (1880), p. 227.)

[Inchcolm.] 'St Columba's Island,' in the Firth of Forth, on which are remains of an abbey. 'Nor would we deign him [Sweno] burial of his men Till he disbursed, at Saint Colme's inch, Ten thousand dollars to our general use' (*Macb.* i, 2). Cf. *Hol.* ii, 170. See Sweno.

Inde. Poetical form of 'India.' 'Savages and men of I.' (*Temp.* ii, 2); 'a rude and savage man of I.' (*L.L.L.* iv, 3); 'east to western I.' (*A.Y.L.* iii, 2).

India. Anciently, and down to the 16th cent., denoting the whole of S.E. Asia and the Indian Archipelago.

'My nettle ['mettle,' Ff] of I.' (*T. Nt* ii, 5); 'the farthest steep of I.' (*M.N.D.* ii, 2); 'Lisbon, Barbary and I.' (*M.V.* iii, 2); 'mines of I.' (*1 Hen. IV*, iii, 1); 'Made Britain, I.: every man... Showed like a mine' (*Hen. VIII*, i, 1); 'her bed is I.; there she lies, a pearl' (*Tr. Cr.* i, 1); 'I had gone barefoot to I.' (*ib.* i, 2). See Inde, Indies.

Indian. (*a*) *Subst.*, an inhabitant of India, or of the Indies. 'When they will not give a doit to relieve a lame Beggar, they will lay out ten to see a dead I.' (*Temp.* ii, 2); 'Have we some strange I... come to Court?' (*Hen. VIII*, v, 3); 'like the base I. ['Iudean,' F1], threw a pearl away' (*Oth.* v, 2).

(*b*) *Adj.*, pertaining to India or the Indies. 'Stolen from an I. King' (*M.N.D.* ii, 1); 'the spiced I. air' (*ib.* ii, 2); 'I. boy' (*ib.* iii, 2); 'Scarf veiling an I. beauty' (*M.V.* iii, 2); 'diamonds and I. stones' (*3 Hen. VI*, iii, 1).

Indian-like, *adv.* 'Indian-like ... I adore the sun, that looks upon his worshipper, But knows of him no more' (*All's Well*, i, 3).

Indies, East and West. 'The East I.' was practically identified with 'India' (*q.v.*); 'the West I.' meant not only the islands now so called, but the adjacent mainland of America, Columbus having supposed that he had reached the Eastern coast of Asia. Richard Eden's *Historye of Travayle in the East and West Indies*, etc., was publd. in 1577.

'They [Mistress Page and Mistress Ford] shall be my East and West I., and I will trade to them both' (*M.W.W.* i, 3); 'he does smile his face into more lines than is in the new map with the augmentation of the I.' (*T. Nt.* iii, 2; believed to refer to the first English map of the world, on Mercator's projection, by E. Wright, publd. 1600, and noteworthy for its conspicuous display of 'rhumb-lines'); 'an argosy bound ... to the I.' (*M.V.* i, 3); 'Where America, the I.? *Dro. S.* Oh, Sir, upon her nose, all o'er embellished with rubies, carbuncles ... declaring their rich aspect to the hot breath of Spain' (*Com. Err.* iii, 2); 'our king has all the I. in his arms ... when he strains that lady' (*Hen. VIII*, iv, 1).

Inger. See LINGARE.

Ingratitude. Personified. 'I., thou marblehearted fiend, More hideous when thou show'st thee in a child Than the sea-monster' (*Lear*, i, 4).

Iniquity. Part played by the dramatic 'Vice' (*q.v.*). 'Like the formal vice, I.' (*Rich. III*, iii, 1); 'this... grey iniquity' (*1 Hen. IV*, ii, 4).

The 'Vice' played many parts, besides 'Iniquity' – such as 'Fraud,' 'Covetousness,' 'Sin,' 'Desire, 'Vanity.' See *Rich. III*, Clar. edn. p. 175.

Innocent [III]. Pope (Lotario de' Conti di Segni ed Anagni); b. 1161; Pope 1198–1216. Acc. *Hol.*, on the refusal by John to accept Stephen Langton (*q.v.*) as Abp. of Canterbury, Innocent threatened to lay the kingdom under an interdict, and sent Pandulph (*q.v.*) to bring the King into submission; on the refusal of the latter to yield, Innocent urged 'the French king to make warre upon him, as a person for his wickedness excommunicated' (*Hol.* iii, 170, 175). On John 'utterlie despairing in his matters,' and submitting to papal authority, the Pope took him under his protection and defended his cause against the barons 'verie pithilie' (*Hol.* iii, 191–2).

The story as related in the *Tr. R.* is closely followed in *John*, i, 1; iii, 1; v, 1. The Pope is twice named (iii, 1) as in *Tr. R.*

The historic dates are: the interdict 1208; excommunication of John 1209; John's submission 1213.

Innogen. The st. dir. at the opening of *M. Ado*, QqFf, is: 'Enter Leonato, governor of Messina, Innogen his wife,' etc. (also, unnamed, in ii, 1). There is no allusion in the play to such a character, and the name is omitted by Theobald and later edrs.

The name occurs as that of the wife of Brute, the first ruler of Britain, *Hol.* i, 8 ('Inogene' in *The Faerie Queene*, II, x, 13). See IMOGEN.

Inverness. County town of I.shire; made the seat of a royal castle by Malcolm Canmore. 'At Envernes, or (as some say) at Botgosuane,' Macbeth slew Duncan (*Hol.* ii, 170). The scene of Act I, Scenes 5, 6, 7, and Act II of *Macb.*, acc. mod. edns.

Duncan bids the nobles meet him at I., *Macb.* i, 4 ('Envernes,' Ff).

Io. A maiden beloved of Jupiter and changed on account of Juno's jealousy into a white cow. 'We'll show thee Io as she was a maid, And how she was beguiled and surprised' (*Tam. Sh.* Ind. 2).

The allusion is somewhat vague; the beguilement of Io was effected in darkness: 'Cum deus inducta latas caligine terras Occuluit tenuitque fugam rapuitque pudorem' (Ovid, *Metam.* i, 599 ff.). It has, however, been suggested that Correggio's painting of Io had been seen by Sh. himself at Milan. See K. Elzo, *Essays on Sh.* (1874), p. 291.

[Iona.] See COLME-KILL.

Ionia. District on the W. coast of Asia Minor. Labienus is declared to have led his forces as far as Ionia, *Ant. Cl.* i, 2. (Cf. *Plut.* p. 178.)

Ionian Sea. *Ionium Mare*, the sea between Italy and Greece S. of the Adriatic. 'The sea *Ionium*' (*Plut.* p. 208). Mtd. *Ant. Cl.* iii, 7: 'Is it not strange... That from Tarentum and Brundusium, He could so quickly cut the Ionian Sea, And take in Toryne?'

Ipswich. County town of Suffolk; birthplace of Wolsey, where a gateway of his projected college still remains. 'I'll ... cry down this Ipswich fellow's insolence' (*Hen. VIII*, i, 1); 'those twins of learning that he raised in you, Ipswich and Oxford' (*ib.* iv, 2).

Iras. 'A woman of Cleopatra's bed-chamber, that frizzed her hair and dressed her head' (*Plut.* p. 206); her death, *ib.* p. 227.

D.P. *Ant. Cl.* i, 2] is told by a soothsayer that her fortune and Charmian's are alike; bandies jests with her companions. i, 3, 5; ii, 5; iii, 3] *p.m.* iii, 9] entreats Cl. to speak to Ant. iii, 11; iv, 2, 11] *p.m.* iv, 13] laments over her swooning mistress. v, 2] vows that she will never grace a Roman triumph; fetches Cl.'s crown and robe; falls dead before the Queen.

Commentators variously attribute the death of Iras to three causes: grief or the bite of an asp. either with or without her consent. Plut. merely states that she was found dead at Cl.'s feet.

Ireland. Donalbain seeks refuge there (and is 'tenderly cherished by the king of that land,' *Hol.* ii, 171), *Macb.* ii, 3, iii, 1; claimed for Arthur of Brittany (unhistorical, following *Tr. R.*), *John*, i, 1, ii, 1; Richard II sets out thither to put down a rebellion (this expedition took place in April 1399, to avenge the death of the E. of March), *Rich. II*, i, 4, ii, 1 (2), 2 (4); 'a kerne of Ir.' (*Hen. V*, iii, 7); impending return of Robt. Devereux, E. of Essex, from Ir. (Sept. 1599) alluded to, *ib.* v, Chor.; 'Ir. is thine [Katharine's]' (*ib.* v, 2); 'brother York, thy acts in Ir., In bringing them to civil discipline' (the success of Richard, D. of York, in pacifying the Irish is mtd. *Hol.* iii, 629) (*2 Hen. VI*, i, 1); 'Whiles I [Richard, D. of York] in Ir. nourish a mighty band ... In Ir. have I seen this stubborn Cade Oppose himself against a troop of kernes' (*ib.* iii, 1); 'The D. of York is newly come from Ir. with a puissant... power Of gallowglasses and stoutkernes' (*ib.* iv, 9); mtd., *ib.* v, 1; (Edw. IV) 'lord of Ir.' (*3 Hen. VI*, iv, 7); prophecy by 'a Bard of Ir.' (*Rich. III*, iv, 2); (Gerald Fitz-Gerald, 9th E. of Kildare) 'deputy of Ir.' (*Hen. VIII*, ii, 1); (Thos. Howard, E. of Surrey) 'deputy' (*ib.* iii, 2); 'bogs of Ir.' (*Com. Err.* iii, 2).

Iris. In Greek mythology, messenger of the gods; originally a personification of the rainbow. 'What is the matter. That this distempered messenger of wet, The manycoloured Ir. rounds thine eye?' (*All's Well, i, 3); 'an Ir. that shalt find thee out'* (*2 Hen. VI*, iii, 2); 'His crest that prouder than blue Ir. bends' (*Tr. Cr.* i, 3).

D.P. *Temp.* iv, 1] the part of Ir. performed by a spirit in the masque presented by Ariel and his fellows; as Juno's 'many-colour'd messenger,' she summons the other spirits.

Cf. Ovid, *Metam.* i, 270: 'Nuntia Junonis varios induta colores.'

Irish. (*a*) *Subst.*, Irish language. 'I had rather hear ... my brach howl in Ir.' (*1 Hen. IV*, iii, 1).

(*b*) *Adj.* 'I was never so be-rimed since Pythagoras' time, that I was an Ir. rat' (in allusion to the extermination of vermin by magical 'rimes') (*A.Y.L.* iii, 2); 'the howling of Ir. wolves against the moon' (*ib.* v, 2); 'Ir. wars' (*Rich. II*, i, 4, ii, 1 (2); *1 Hen. IV*, iv, 3, v, 1); 'Ir. expedition (*ib.* i, 3).

Irishman. 'I will rather trust an Irishman with my aqua-vitae bottle' (*M.W.W.* ii, 2); 'an Irishman' (*i.e.* Macmorris; *Hen. V*, iii, 2); 'try your hap against the Irishmen' (*2 Hen. VI*, iii, 1).

Isabel. See ISABELLA.

Isabella, or **Isabeau, of Bavaria** (1370–1435). Wife of Charles VI of France.

D.P. *Hen. V.* 'Isabel, Queen of France.' (i, 2) mtd. v, 2] is present at the meeting between the Kings of France and England to settle terms of peace; greets Henry and his nobles; retires with the Princes to discuss the treaty; later, invokes a blessing on the marriage of Henry and her daughter Katharine.

The presence of Is. at Troyes (May 1420) as well as at a previous meeting at Meulan (May 1419) is mtd. *Hol.* iii, 569, 572. Hallam, for reasons irrelevant to the play, speaks of Is. as 'the most infamous of women.'

Isabella. D.P. *M. for M.* 'Sister to Claudio.' i, 5] as a novice at the nunnery of St Clare, wishes the rule yet stricter; is entreated by Lucio to intercede with Lord Angelo for her brother's life. ii, 2] accompanied by Lucio, appeals to Ang.; is easily discouraged, but, urged by Lucio, entreats with greater ardour; at length is bid to 'come again tomorrow.' ii, 4] Ang. offers to spare Cl. at the price of Isabella's honour; she replies that it were better Cl. should die at once 'than that a sister, by redeeming him, should die for ever'; on Angelo's declaring his passion for herself, she threatens to expose him; Ang. scorns the threat. iii, 1] visits Cl. in prison; tells him the price at which alone he can be saved; Cl., after a moment's hesitation, entreats her to sacrifice her honour; she indignantly refuses; the (disguised) Duke imparts to her the plan by which both her chastity and her brother's life may be saved. iv, 1] tells the Duke that she has made an assignation with Ang. that night; (Mariana agrees to personate her). iv, 3] she is told that Cl. has nevertheless been executed, but is instructed how to be revenged on 'most damned Angelo.' iv, 6] converses with Mariana on the unmasking of Ang. v, 1] kneels before the Duke and begs for justice at his hand; denounces Ang. and dilates on his guilt; she is 'carried off guarded'; later, is induced by Mariana to plead for Angelo's life; Claudio is revealed alive, and the Duke seeks Isabella's hand in marriage. (Usually 'Isabel' in the text.)

The corresponding character in Cinthio's novel is Epitia, and in Whetstone's play and tale Cassandra; in each case the heroine sacrifices her virtue and marries the villain. Whetstone represents the story as having been reported to him by a Madam Isabella.

Isbel. The clown's sweetheart in *All's Well.* Mtd. i, 3; iii, 2. A mere mispronunciation of 'Isabel.'

Iscariot. Surname of Judas, the betrayer of Christ (Luke xxii, 3). '*Hol.* Judas I am. *Dum.* A Judas! *Hol.* Not Iscariot, sir' (*L.L.L.* v, 2); *cf.* John xiv, 22. See JUDAS ISCARIOT.

Isidore. One of Timon's creditors. 'To Isidore he owes nine thousand' (*Timon*, ii, 1); Isidore's servant is addressed by his master's name, *ib.* ii, 2.

Isis. One of the chief Egyptian divinities; her worship became popular among the Romans under the Empire.

Invoked by Charmian, *Ant. Cl.* i, 2 (3); 'by Isis' (*ib.* i, 5); invoked by Charmian, *ib.* iii, 3 (2); Cleopatra appeared 'in th' abiliments of the goddess Isis' (*ib.* iii, 6; cf. *Plut.* p. 202).

Israel. The Hebrew nation. 'O Jephthah, judge of Israel' (*Haml.* ii, 2). See JEPHTHAH.

Italian. (i) *Subst.* (*a*) A native of Italy. 'There's an It. come' (*Cymb.* ii, 1; rep.); 'false It.' (*ib.* iii, 2). (*b*) Italian language. 'Neither French nor It.' (*M.V.* i, 2); 'It., or French' (*All's Well*, iv, 1); 'very choice It.' (*Haml.* iii, 2).

(ii) *Adj.*, pertaining to Italy. 'It. fields' (*All's Well*, ii, 3); 'fox' (*Tam. Sh.* ii, 1); 'priest' (*John*, iii, 1); 'gentry' (*Cymb.* v, 1); 'weeds' (*ib. ib.*); 'brain' (*ib.* v, 5); 'fiend' (*ib. ib.*).

Italy. 'Bought his doublet in I.' (*M.V.* i, 2); 'girls of It.' (*All's Well*, ii, 1); 'the pleasant garden of great It.' (*Tam. Sh.* i, 1); 'proud It.' (*Rich. II*, ii, 1); 'the shes of It.' (*Cymb.* i, 4); 'drug-damned It.' (*ib.* iii, 4); 'some jay of It.' (*ib. ib.*). Mtd., *Temp.* ii, 1; *M. Ado*, iii, 1 (2), v, 1; *M.V.* ii, 2, iii, 2; *All's Well*, ii, 1, 3; *Tam. Sh.* ii, 1; *Rich. II*, iv, 1; *Cor.* v, 3 (2); *Jul. C.* i, 3, iii, 1; *Ant. Cl.* i, 2, 3, 4, ii, 5, iii, 5; *Cymb.* i, 5 (2), iii, 4, iv, 2, 3, v, 4, 5; *Rom. J.* iii, 1.

The meaning of 'higher It.' (*All's Well*, ii, 1) is undetermined. It has been variously explained as: (*a*) Upper It.; (*b*) It. bordering on the Adriatic; (*c*) It. more exalted than France; (*d*) the noblest of the Italians.

The question of the supposed travels of Sh. in Italy is discussed by K. Elze, *Essays on Sh.* (1874), pp. 262 ff.

Ithaca. Island in the Ionian Sea; the home of Ulysses, where his wife Penelope awaited his return. Ulysses is addressed as 'prince of It.' (*Tr. Cr.* i, 3); the yarn spun by Penelope 'did but fill It. full of moths' (*Cor.* i, 3).

[**Ixion.**] Condemned, as a punishment for his impious ingratitude to Zeus, to be bound to a wheel for ever revolving in the air. Perhaps alluded to: 'I am bound upon a wheel of fire' (*Lear*, iv, 7).

J

Jack. Personal name and general appellative; *Fr.* Jacques; came to be regarded as a dim. of John. (*a*) used as a term of contempt. 'The flouting J.' (*M. Ado*, i, 1); 'braggarts, J.s, milksops' (*ib.* v, 1); 'bragging J.s' (*M.V.* iii, 4); 'twangling J.' (*Tam. Sh.* ii, 1); 'a swearing J.' (*ib. ib.*); 'J. priest' (*M.W.W.* i, 4; ii, 3); 'J. of Caesar's' (*Ant. Cl.* iii, 13, 11.93,103; applied to Thidias); 'your fairy ... has played the J. with us' (*Temp.* iv, 1; either Jack-o'-lantern, or knave); 'if I be not J. Falstaff, then am I a J.' (*1 Hen. IV*, v, 4); 'the Prince is a J.' (*ib.* iii, 3); 'sly, insinuating J.s' (*Rich. III*, i, 3); 'Since every J. became a gentleman, There's many a gentle person made a J.' (*ib. ib.*); 'a J. guardant' (*Cor.* v, 2; 'Jack in office'); 'twenty such J.s' (*Rom. J.* ii, 4).

(*b*) Merely as a familiar appellation. 'Thou [Benvolio] art as hot a J. in thy mood as any in Italy' (*Rom. J.* iii, 1); 'hang him, J.' (*ib.* iv, 5).

(*c*) As a forename. 'J. Rugby,' 'J. Falstaff,' 'J. Cade' (*qq.v.*).

(*d*) Jack and Jill, generally, for man and woman. 'J. shall have Jill' (*M.N.D.* iii, 2); 'J. hath not Jill' (*L.L.L.* v, 2, l. 885).

(*e*) 'J., boy! ho, boy!' (*Tam. Sh.* iv, 1; a round or part-song).

(*z*) Phrases. 'Jack o' the clock,' a mechanical figure for striking the hours: *Rich. II*, v, 5; *Rich. III*, iv, 2. 'Jack-a-Lent,' a puppet to throw sticks at: 'little J.-a-Lent' (*M.W.W.* iii, 3); 'see now, how wit may be made a J.-a-Lent' (*ib.* v, 5). 'I will not be J. out of office' (*1 Hen. VI*, i, 1).

Jacob (1). For '(St) James.' 'The child is a year and a quarter old come Philip and Jacob' (*M. for M.* iii, 2; *i.e.* SS. Philip and James's Day, May 1).

Jacob (2). The patriarch. The artifice by which J. obtained the better part of Laban's flocks (Gen. xxx, 25 ff.) is expatiated on by Shylock, *M.V.* i, 3; Shylock swears 'by Jacob's staff' (*ib.* ii, 5).

'J.'s staff' meant a pilgrim's staff, and is often supposed to refer to St James (Jacobus), as patron of pilgrims; but an allusion to the patriarch's staff, with which he 'passed over this Jordan' (Gen. xxxii, 10), seems apter, especially in the mouth of a Jew.

Jaggard, Isaac. Son of Wm. J. (*q.v.*); his name appears on the title-page of the First Folio (1623) as one of its printers.

Jaggard, William. Published *The Passionate-Pilgrim* 1599; his name occurs in the colophon of the First Folio (1623) as one of the four at whose 'charges' it was printed. See R. C. Rhodes, *Sh.'s First Folio* (1923), pp. 33–51.

Jamany. For 'Germany'; *M.W.W.* iv, 5.

James. As a forename; see Blount, Cromer, Gurney, Soundpost, Tyrrel.

[**James I.**] King of England (James VI of Scotland); 1566–1625. Son of Mary Queen of Scots and Lord Darnley. Eulogized by Cranmer in exalted terms, *Hen. VIII*, v, 5.

See Henry the Eighth. For indications of the influence of the accession of James I on dramatic details see Macbeth, The Tragedy of.

Jamy (1). D.P. *Hen. V.* A 'Scots Captain'; in King Henry's army. (iii, 2) in Fluellen's opinion 'Captain James' was a 'marvellous falorous gentleman ... and of great expedition and knowledge in th' aunchient wars.' iii, 2] would fain hear Fluellen and Macmorris discuss the Roman wars.

Jamy (2). For 'James.' 'Nay, by Saint J.' (*Tam. Sh.* iii, 2).

Jane. As a forename. 'J. Smile' (*A. Y. L.* ii, 4); 'J. Nightwork' (*2 Hen. IV*, iii, 2).

January. As a cold and stormy month. '*Leon.* You will never run mad, niece. *Beat.* No, not till a hot J.' (*M. Ado*, i, 1); 'blasts of J.' (*Wint. T.* iv, 3).

Janus. Roman god of 'beginnings.' To him Numa dedicated a passage with two gates, opened in time of war and closed in time of peace. J. was often represented with a two-faced head.

'By two-headed J., Nature hath framed strange fellows in her time' (*M.V.* i, 1); 'By J.' (*Oth.* i, 2).

Japhet. Son of Noah; regarded as ancestor of Europeans. '*Prince.* Nay, they will be kin to us, or they will fetch it from J.' (*2 Hen. IV*, ii, 2).

Jaquenetta. D.P. *L.L.L.* A country wench. (i, 1) found by Armado in company with Costard. i, 2] saucily parries A.'s avowal of love. (iii, 1) A. sends her a letter. (iv, 1) mtd. iv, 2] begs Nathaniel to read A.'s verses to her. iv, 3] hands the 'treasonable' letter to the King. (v, 2) Costard declares that she has been seduced by Armado.

'The lofty gravity, with which the Spaniard proclaims his passion for the stolid Jaquenetta, is a curious anticipation, – though the absurdity takes a different form, – of Don Quixote and his Dulcinea' (W. J. Courthope, *Hist. of Eng. Poetry* (1903), IV, ii, 40).

Jaques (1). As a forename. 'J. Chatillon' (*Hen. V*, iii, 5) ('J. of Ch.,' *ib.* iv, 8); 'J. Faulconbridge' (*L.L.L.* ii, 1).

Jaques (2). A commander mtd, by Parolles; *All's Well*, iv, 3.

Jaques (3). D.P. *A. Y. L.* Lord attending upon the banished Duke of Burgundy. (ii, 1) his moralization upon a wounded stag described by a courtier. ii, 5] listens to Amiens' song, and adds a verse to it. ii, 7] tells how he 'met a fool i' the forest,' and is 'ambitious for a motley coat' himself, that he might lash human folly; compares the world to a stage and describes the 'seven ages' of man. iii, 2] bandies raillery with Orlando in the forest. iii, 3] overhears Touchstone's wooing of Audrey, and dissuades him from being married 'under a bush, like a beggar.' iv, 1] meets 'Ganymede,' and boasts of his melancholy, but is mercilessly bantered by the 'pretty youth.' iv, 2] suggests a reward for the slayer of the deer. v, 4] draws out Touchstone's humour before the Duke, and shows appreciation of 'the motley-minded gentleman'; on learning that Frederick had 'put on a religious life,' expresses his intention of joining him, and departs.

There is no corresponding character in Lodge's *Rosalynde*. The pronunciation of the name has been much discussed:

French, p. 317, points out that as a known Warwickshire name it is pronounced 'Jakes'; (a jest in Harington's *Metamorphosis of Ajax* (1576), p. 17, confirms this). On the other hand, the only line of the play in which its metrical value can be estimated makes it a dissyllable (presumably 'Jaq-wes') – 'the melancholy J.' (ii, 1). It is noteworthy that the common noun 'jakes is spelt 'jaques' in *Lear*, ii, 2, Qq.

The name occurs as a dissyllable in R. Greene's *Frier Bacon and Frier Bongay* (1589): 'What is thy judgment, Jacques Vandermast?'

'Jaques is the only purely contemplative character in *Sh.* He thinks and does nothing. His whole occupation is to amuse his mind, and he is totally regardless of his body and his fortunes. He is the prince of philosophical idlers.' (W. Hazlitt, *Char.* of Sh.'s Plays (1817), p. 306.)

'The fact is J. has always been taken for what he professes to be, – a moralist; but looked at as the Duke demonstrates him to be, and as Sh. has subtly drawn him, he is a mere lip-deep moralizer, a dealer in moral precepts, a morality-monger' (C. and M. V. Cowden-Clarke, note in edn. of 1864).

Jaques (4). D.P. *A. Y. L.* Younger brother to Oliver and second son of Sir Rowland de Bois. (i, 1) treated justly by his brother Oliver. v, 4] as 'Second Brother,' describes Duke Frederick's conversion.

The identity of his name (only once mentioned) with Jaques (3) has been regarded as an inadvertence. The corresponding character in Lodge's *Rosalynde* is Fernandine.

Jaques, St. St James, apostle, known as St J. the Great, to distinguish him from St J. the Less, author of the Epistle of James. The shrine of St J. at Santiago de Compostela, in Galicia (Spain), was one of the chief resorts of pilgrims in the Middle Ages.

'I am St J.'s pilgrim' (*All's Well*, iii, 4); Helena is bound 'to St J. le grand' (*ib.* iii, 5), and meets other penitents 'to great St J. bound' (*ib. ib.*); 'her pretence is a pilgrimage to St J. le grand' (*ib.* iv, 3).

Jarteer. Caius' pronunciation of 'Garter.' *M.W.W.* i, 4; iii, 1; iv, 5. ('Jarterre, Theob.)

Jason. See COLCHOS.

Jealousy. Personified. 'J., that sour, unwelcome guest' (*V.A.* 449); 'J. Doth call himself Affection's sentinel' (*ib.* 649); 'this carry-tale, dissentious J.' (*ib.* 657).

Jean, Maître. See MASTER-GUNNER.

Jen. Fem. name; abbr. of 'Jenny,' *Com. Err.* iii, 1.

Jenny. Dim. of 'Jane.' 'Vengeance of J.'s case' (*M.W.W.* iv, 1). ('Ginyes,' Ff.)

Jephthah. Judge of Israel, who sacrificed his daughter in fulfilment of a rash vow (Judges xi, 30 ff.).

Hamlet quotes a ballad on the subject (included in the 2nd and later edns. of Percy's *Reliques*), and applies the name of J. to Polonius, inasmuch as 'He had one fair daughter and no more, The which he loved passing well' (*Haml.* ii, 2). 'To keep that oath were more impiety Than J.'s, when he sacrificed his daughter' (*3 Hen. VI*, v, 1).

'Jepha,' *Haml.* Q1; 'Jephah,' *3 Hen. VI*, F1, 2; 'Jepthah,' *ib.* F3, 4.

Jeronimy. The phrase 'Go by! J.' was used in popular slang, derisively (Camb.). In *Tam. Sh.* Ind. 1, it appears (Ff) as 'go by S. Ieronimie.'

The allusion is to the character of Hieronymo in *The Spanish Tragedy*. The introduction of 'S.' may be a mere error of the press, or an intentional absurdity.

Jerusalem. Faulconbridge advises John and Philip to join in attacking Angiers, 'Like the mutines of J.'; acc. Malone, this refers to the temporary alliance of the mutually hostile factions in J., when it was besieged by Titus, as described in *A Compendious and Most Marvellous History of the Latter Times of the Jews Common-Weale*, etc., by Joseph Ben Gorion, translated by Peter Morwyng, 1575. See *John*, ii, 1.

In consequence of the Percies' rebellion, Henry IV 'must neglect our holy purpose to J.' (*1 Hen. IV*, i, 1); Henry desires, when dying, to be borne to a chamber 'call'd J.,' thus fulfilling a prophecy that 'I should not die but in J.' (*2 Hen. IV*, iv, 5). (The J.-Chamber is situated at the S.W. corner of Westminster Abbey; it dates from *c.* 1376, and was the Abbot's private withdrawing room, but little of its original features remain. It probably derived its name from the tapestry with which it was hung.)

Used in the sense of Paradise, or Heaven, *3 Hen. VI*, v, 5: 'So part we sadly in this troublous world, To meet with joy in sweet J.' For the title 'King of J.' see REIGNIER.

Jessica. D.P. *M.V.* Daughter to Shylock. ii, 3] bids farewell to the servant Launcelot Gobbo, and gives him a letter for her lover Lorenzo; resolves to become a Christian on her marriage with Lor. ii, 5] is warned by her father not to gaze into the street at masquers, and to keep shut the doors of the house; as he departs she murmurs, 'I have a father, you a daughter lost.' ii, 6] disguised in boy's clothes, prepares to accompany Lor. as his torch-bearer; gives her lover a casket, and 'gilds' herself with more ducats before leaving her home. (ii, 8) is seen with Lor. in a gondola. (iii, 1) her extravagance at Genoa reported to her father. iii, 2] is welcomed, with Lor., at Belmont; avows that she heard Shylock say 'That he would rather have Antonio's flesh than twenty times' the sum due. iii, 4] is left, with Lor., in charge of Belmont, during Portia's absence. iii, 5] good-humouredly parries Launcelot's raillery; eulogizes Portia as incomparable. v, 1] in sportive alternation with Lorenzo praises the beauty of the night; avows that she is never merry when she hears sweet music.

(Named 'Mistress Lorenza,' v, 1, Ff2, 3, 4.)

Acc. K. Elze, *Essays*, p. 282, the name is from 'Iscah' (Gen. xi, 29), which in Matthewe's Bible (1549) is 'Jesca'; 'Ιεσχά in the Septuagint. The Hebrew 'Jiscah' means 'a spy.'

'Jessica is a very faithful picture of a love-inclined young woman; betraying the Oriental warmth of her race, together with their craftiness. But she is not to be taken as a true sample of a Jewish daughter, for among no people are the ties of domestic life held more sacred than among the Hebrews.' (Thos. Campbell, *Dram. Wks. of Sh.* (1838), p. xxxv.) Cf. *Heine on Sh.* (1895), pp. 125 ff.

Jesu. This form of the name 'Jesus,' very frequent in the Prayer Book, 'is used in the oblique cases, or with the optative mood, or in exclamations. The only exception in *Sh.* to this usage is in *3 Hen. VI*, v, 6: "O, Jesus bless us, he is born with teeth" ' (Clar.). Also *1 Hen. IV* ii, 2, in Qq.

'Norfolk fought for Jesu Christ, in glorious Christian field' (*Rich. II*, iv, 1); 'you shall sup with Jesu Christ tonight' (*2 Hen. VI*, v, 1; *i.e.* die, in allusion to Luke xxiii, 43). In exclamations and invocations: *Rich. II*, v, 2; *1 Hen. IV*, ii, 2, 4, iii, 3; *2 Hen. IV*, ii, 4; *2 Hen. VI*, i, 1, 2, 3; *Rich. III*, i, 3, v, 3; *Rom. J.* ii, 4, 5. 'Jeshu,' *M.W.W.* v, 5.

Jesus. See JESU.

Jeweller, A. D.P. *Timon.* i, 1] sells T. a jewel.

Jewry. For 'Judaea' (which does not occur in *Sh.*). 'Herod of J.' (*M.W.W.* ii, 1; *Ant. Cl.* i, 2; iii, 3, 6); 'stubborn J.' (*Rich. II*, ii, 1); 'wives of J.' (*Hen. V*, iii, 3); Alexas 'went to J.' (*Ant. Cl.* iv, 6).

Jezebel. Wife of Ahab, King of Israel. Used as a random term of abuse by Aguecheek – 'fie on him, Jezebel' (*T. Nt.* ii, 5; 'Jezabel,' F1).

Jill, or Gill. Fem. name, used generically for a young woman; the correlative of 'Jack.' 'Jack shall have Jill, nought shall go ill' (*M.N.D.* iii, 2); 'our wooing doth not end like an old play; Jack hath not Jill' (*L.L.L.* v, 2); ('be the jacks fair within, and the jills fair without,' *Tam, Sh.* iv, 1).

In the last quotation a pun is intended, the words meaning drinking-vessels. The name is abbreviated from Jillian or Gillian, a corruption of Julia or Juliana. Steevens cites: 'All shalbe well, Iacke shall have Gill: Nay, nay, Gill is wedded to Wyll' (Heywood, *Epigrammes upon Proverbes* (1567)). *Cf.* also Skelton's *Magnyfycence*, ed. Dyce, i, 234 (Staunton).

Joan. Feminine name. 'Al'ce Madam, or Joan Madam?' (*Tam. Sh.* Ind. 2); especially denoting a woman of humble rank: 'Some men must love my lady and some Joan' (*L.L.L.* iii, 1); 'When shall you see me ... groan for Joan ['love,' conj.]?' (*ib.* iv, 3); 'while greasy J. doth keel the pot' (*ib.* v, 2); 'now can I make any J. a lady' (*John*, i, 1).

Name of a hawk: 'Ten to one old J. had not gone' (2 *Hen. VI*, ii, 1).

Also spelt 'Jone' or 'Joane.'

Joan of Arc, Jeanne D'Arc, or Darc. Called also La Pucelle, and The Maid of Orleans (1412–31). The national heroine of France; daughter of a peasant proprietor at Domremy. Prompted by what she deemed supernatural voices, and encouraged by an ancient prophecy, she presented herself before the Dauphin and was given command of an army. She raised the siege of Orleans by the English in May 1429; won the Battle of Patay a month later, and was captured May 24, 1430, while defending Compiègne against the D. of Burgundy, who sold her to his allies the English. She was burned at the stake as a heretic, at Rouen, May 30, 1431.

Sh. has been severely blamed for the brutal travesty of the heroine's character presented in *1 Hen. VI.* To this accusation two replies can be made: first, that the scene describing Joan's trial is almost universally acknowledged to be non-Shakespearean; and secondly that the dramatist simply adopted, without inquiry, the view of the Chronicles to which he had access. Extracts from Holinshed's narrative are appended:

At the time of the siege of Orleans there was presented to Charles 'a yoong wench of an eighteene yeeres old, called Ione Are,' daughter of a poor shepherd. 'Of favour she was counted likesome, of person stronglie made and manlie, of courage great, hardie and stout withall.' She was of devout behaviour, and 'the name of Jesus in hir mouth about all hir businesses.' On the way to Charles's Court she found at Fierbois, in Touraine, 'among old iron,' a finely engraved sword with which she afterward fought. When presented, she picked out the Dauphin from a number of 'gale lords' among whom he stood, and after a long private interview with him was entrusted with 'a sufficient armie with absolute power to lead them.' (*Hol.* iii, 600.)

On her being handed over to the English, the Regent caused an examination to be made into 'hir life and beleefe ... Wherein found though a virgin, yet first, shamefullie rejecting hir sex abominablie in acts and apparell, to have counterfeit mankind, and then, all damnablie faithlesse, to be a pernicious instrument to hostilitie and bloudshed in divelish witchcraft and sorcerie.' She was accordingly sentenced to imprisonment for life, on humble confession and making oath of reformation. She, however, relapsed, and after an ineffectual attempt to gain delay by declaring herself with child, was condemned and executed. The chronicler justifies her sentence on the ground of 'hir execrable abhominations,' and blames Charles for making use of a sorceress. (*Hol.* iii, 604–5.)

Joan's denial of her father at the trial seems to be an invention of the dramatist. Her interview with the fiends (v, 3) seems based on Holinshed's reference to 'hir campestrall conversation with wicked spirits, whome ... she uttered to be our Ladie, saint Katharine, and saint Anne' (*Hol.* iii, 604).

D.P. *1 Hen. VI.* i, 2] when brought before Charles, is not deceived by the substitution of Reignier for the Dauphin; relates to the latter her miraculous call; gives proof of her powers by overcoming Charles in combat with her famous sword; rejects the Dauphin's amorous advances; undertakes to raise the siege that night. (i, 4) the arrival of the 'holy prophetess' is announced to Talbot. i, 5] Joan fights indecisively with T. i, 6] enters Orleans; Charles exclaims, 'Joan la Pucelle shall be France's saint.' ii, 1] blames the 'improvident soldiers' for letting the English into the town. (ii, 2) sneeringly referred to by Talbot. iii, 2] enters Rouen by a stratagem and admits the French; derides the English from the walls; Talbot reviles her in turn; the French are routed. iii, 3] Burgundy, by force of her eloquence, or, as he suggests, because 'she hath bewitched me,' is seduced from his alliance with the English. iv, 7] comments on the 'silly stately style' of Talbot's titles; grants the bodies of T. and his son to Sir William Lucy. v, 2] declares that 'Of all base passions, fear is most accurs'd.' v, 3] for victory offers her body and soul to the fiends who were her familiar spirits, but they forsake her; she is taken prisoner. v, 4] when brought to trial repudiates her father, and declares she is 'issued from the progeny of kings'; declares she is with child, and accuses Alençon and Reignier; is taken to execution, uttering imprecations upon the English.

Job. Hero of the Book of Job; a type of poverty (Job i, 21). Falstaff is declared to be 'as poor as J.' (*M.W.W.* v, 5); F. says the same of himself, 2 *Hen. IV*, i, 2.

Jockey (1). Or 'Jocky,' for 'Jack.' The warning couplet addressed to John, Duke of Norfolk, is given thus, *Hol.* iii, 759: 'Iacke of Norffolke be not too bold, For Dikon thy master is bought and sold,' but 'Iacke' becomes 'Jockey' in *Sh.*

[**Jockey** (2).] See FALSTAFF.

John (1). D.P. *M.W.W.* iii, 3] one of the servants who carries out Falstaff in the buckbasket. iv, 2] assists.

John (2). As a forename; see Bates, Cade, Court, de la Court, Falstaff, Fastolfe, Goodman, Grey, Hume, Montgomery, Mortimer, Naps, Norbery, Ramston, Rugby, Southwell, Stanley, Talbot.

John (3). For 'Little John,' or John Nailor, one of Robin Hood's legendary band. '*Fal.* What say you, Scarlet and John?' (*M.W.W.* i, 1); '*Sil.* [sings]. And Robin Hood, Scarlet and John' (2 *Hen. IV*, v, 3).

John (*c.* 1167–1216). King of England; youngest son of Henry II and Elinor of Aquitaine; nominated as successor to the throne by his brother Richard I on his death-bed. Crowned May 27, 1199. The barons of Anjou, Maine, and Touraine, however, acknowledged the claims of Arthur of Brittany, son of John's elder brother Geoffrey. Elinor, the queen-mother, secured Aquitaine for J., and in 1200 he made terms with Philip II of France and married his niece Blanch to Philip's son Lewis. John's treatment of Arthur and his quarrel with the Pope – which are the features of his reign with which the play is chiefly concerned – are sketched below. The chaotic chronology of the drama almost defies elucidation, but the notes interpolated in the subjoined synopsis of the *rôle* of 'John' supply the most important corrections.

D.P. *John.* i, 1] gives audience to an envoy from Philip of France; in response to his demands threatens instant war, but dismisses him courteously; declares that the 'abbeys and priories' shall pay for the expedition; adjudicates in the appeal of Robt. Faulconbridge against his brother Philip, and knights the latter (there is no historical authority for any part of this scene). ii, 1] (before Angiers) confronts Philip, and offers peace on condition that his rights are undisputed; on Ph.'s asserting Arthur's claims, bids him defiance; assures Ar. that if he will submit he shall receive more at his uncle's hands than France can ever give; demands admission within the city walls of Angiers, but is refused; prepares to do battle with the French; later, after an inconclusive engagement, again demands admission to the city; accepts the Bastard's suggestion that the two kings shall unite in attacking 'the peevish town'; agrees to the proposal that all differences shall be composed by the marriage of his niece Blanch to the Dauphin; bestows on her as dowry five provinces and 30,000 marks (cf. *Hol.* iii, 161); offers to make Arthur Duke of Brittany and Earl of Richmond, and trusts the young Prince's mother, Constance, may be thus placated (this scene is also unhistorical; the meeting between the kings in 1199 did not take place at Angiers, and the betrothal was arranged in 1200; Angiers was, as a matter of fact, taken by Elinor in 1199 and again by John in 1206 (*Hol.* iii, 158, 170). iii, 1] the papal legate, Pandulph, 'religiously demands' why John forcibly keeps Stephen Langton, the Pope's nominee, from the see of Canterbury (*Hol.* iii, 170); J. defiantly replies that he admits the authority of 'no Italian priest,' and that all friends of the Pope shall be his foes; Pandulph pronounces him 'excommunicate'; on Philip's refusal to side with him, J. declares that France shall rue the hour, and departs 'burn'd up with inflaming wrath' (the excommunication of J. was actually pronounced in 1209, and his deposition by the Pope in 1212; meanwhile in 1211, at Northampton, Pandulph had threatened J. with the consequences of his contumacy (*Hol.* iii, 175)). iii, 2] gives Arthur into Hubert's charge. iii, 3] promises Arthur that he will be as dear to him as a father; sends Faulconbridge to England to 'shake the bags of hoarding abbots'; tells his 'good friend' Hubert de Burgh (*q.v.*), privately, that he is 'almost ashamed to say what good respect' he has of him, that he longs to pour his thoughts into his bosom at a fitting season, and at last whispers that 'you young boy' is 'a very serpent in my way ... Thou art his keeper'; on Hubert's acquiescing in J.'s dark and murderous hints, the King exclaims, 'I could be merry now,' and bids farewell to Elinor and Arthur (acc. *Hol.* iii, 165, Arthur, who had tried to take his grandmother prisoner, far from meeting his uncle's advances, 'made a presumptuous answer' and demanded all Coeur-de-lion's possessions, whereupon John confined him at Falaise). iv, 2] in response to the expostulations of the nobles on his second coronation (*Hol.* iii, 165) and his treatment of Arthur, offers to commit Ar. to their direction; after a whispered colloquy with Hubert, announces that Arthur is dead; on the wrathful departure of the nobles John avows his repentance; he is told that the French have landed and that Elinor and Constance are dead; orders Peter of Pomfret (*q.v.*) to be hanged on Ascension Day; bids Faulconbridge hasten to the disaffected nobles; is told of the portent of 'the five moons' (*Hol.* iii, 163); bitterly expostulates with Hubert for taking him at his word with regard to Arthur (*Hol.* iii, 165) and is amazed to learn that 'young Ar. is alive'; bids H. tell the nobles this with all haste. v, 1] makes submission to the Pope, and receives his crown again from Pandulph (*Hol.* iii, 177); admits that there was truth in Peter's prophecy (*Hol.* iii, 180); learns that Arthur is really dead; is urged by the Bastard to make peace with the French. v, 3] is counselled 'to leave the field,' and, being sick, resolves to be taken to the abbey at Swinstead (unhistorical). v, 7] (in the abbey garden) dies of poison, in great agony (the King actually died at Newark – acc. one account, of an ague, aggravated by a surfeit of raw peaches and new cider; but others say he was poisoned by a monk at Swineshead Abbey, for threatening to make corn dearer (*Hol.* iii, 194)). (v, 7) his burial at Worcester ordered.

'Verelie, whosoever shall consider the course of the historie written of this prince, he shall find, that he hath beene little beholden to the writers of that time in which he lived; for scarslie can they affoord him a good word, except when the trueth inforceth them to come out with it as it were against their willes. The occasion whereof (as some thinke) was, for that he was no great freend to the clergie... Certeinlie it should seeme the man had a princelie heart in him, and wanted nothing but faithfull subjects to have assisted him in revenging such wrongs as were doone and offered by the French king and others. Moreover, the pride and pretended authoritie of the cleargie he could not well abide, when they went about to wrest out of his hands the prerogative of his princelie rule and government. True it is that to mainteine his warres ... he was constreined to make all the shift he could devise to recover monie, and, bicause he pinched their purses they conceived no small hatred against him.' (*Hol.* iii, 196.)

Acc. *Tr. R.* II, 6, the name of the monk who murdered John was Thomas.

For the play see pp. 132–3, **King John**.

John, Don. D.P. *M. Ado*. Bastard brother of Don Pedro. i, 1] replies to Leonato's hearty welcome: 'I am not of many words, but I thank you.' i, 3] admits to Conrade that he is 'a plain dealing villain,' and refuses to 'sing in his cage'; resolves to be avenged on Claudio, who 'hath all the glory of my overthrow.' ii, 1] informs Claudio (when masked) that Don Pedro 'is enamoured on Hero.' ii, 2] listens to Borachio's scheme for making it appear that Hero is disloyal to C., and promises him a thousand ducats to carry it out. iii, 2] offers to prove Hero's guilt to C. that night. (iii, 3, 4) mtd. iv, 1] is present at C.'s repudiation of Hero, and tells the 'pretty lady' that he is sorry for her 'much misgovernment.' (iv,2) mtd. (v, 1) Borachio confesses that Don John 'incensed' him to slander Hero. (v, 2) his flight announced. (v, 4) he is captured; Benedick declares he will devise brave punishments for him.

Spoken of as 'Count J.' (ii, 1), 'Prince J.' by Dogberry (iv, 2), and 'J. the Bastard' (iv, 1). The partly equivalent character in Bandello's *Novella* is Girondo, who, however, is a rival for the hand of Fenicia (Hero) and not instigated by Don John's mere moody longing for revenge.

John, Friar. A Franciscan. D.P. *Rom. J.* v, 2] having been sent with a letter to Romeo (iv, 1) by Friar Laurence, relates that he was unable to deliver it.

In *Rhomeo and Julietta* the messenger is Friar Anselme. In Bandello's tale Anselmo.

John of Gaunt, Duke of Lancaster (1340–99). So named from Ghent or Gand, his birthplace; 4th son of Edw. III; father of Henry Bolingbroke by his first wife Blanche, d. of Henry Plantagenet, Duke of Lancaster. See Appendix 1.

D.P. *Rich. II.* i, 1] according to his bond, brings his son Henry Hereford (Bolingbroke) before the King to 'make good his appeal' against Mowbray, Duke of Norfolk (*Hol.* iii, 493); ineffectually bids his son throw down Norfolk's gage. i, 2] urged by the Duchess of Gl. to avenge his brother Gloucester's death, he declares that 'Heaven's is the quarrel,' and that he will not lift an arm against 'heaven's substitute,' the King (*Hol.* iii, 489). i. 3] attends the lists at Coventry; invokes the favour of heaven upon Hereford; thanks the King for shortening his son's exile; excuses himself for having, as councillor, assented to his banishment (*Hol.* iii, 489). ii, 1] feeling his death approaching, longs to give 'wholesome counsel' to Richard, who may listen to his dying words; passionately laments that England, 'this blessed plot … this dear dear land,' which was wont to conquer others, is now 'leased out – like to a tenement or pelting farm,' and 'hath made a shameful conquest of itself'; on Richard's entrance, grimly plays upon the name of 'Gaunt' – gaunt he is from watching over 'sleeping England,' and by fasting from the sight of his banished son; solemnly warns the King that it is he who lies 'in reputation sick,' that 'a thousand flatterers sit within' the compass of his crown, and that since he has leased the realm (*Hol.* iii, 496) he has become 'landlord of England' and not King; bitterly upbraids Richard for the murder of Gloucester, and is borne off, to die, by his attendants.

The account of Gaunt's death is due wholly to Sh.; Holinshed merely states that he died 'at the Bishop of Elie's place in Holborne.' Falstaff twice jests on 'Gaunt': *1 Hen. IV*, ii, 2; *2 Hen. IV*, iii, 2. Other refs. to J. of G. are: *1 Hen. IV*. v, 1; *1 Hen. VI*, ii, 5; *2 Hen. VI*. ii, 2; *3 Hen. VI*, i, 1, iii, 3.

John of Lancaster, Prince (1389–1435). 3rd son of Henry IV; Constable of England; K.G.; created Duke of Bedford 1414; lieutenant of England during Henry V's first expedition, 1415; and again in 1421; joined the King in France 1419; Regent of France 1422; married Philip of Burgundy's sister, Anne, 1423; successfully commanded in France until the raising of the siege of Orleans, 1429; caused Joan of Arc to be burnt as a witch at Rouen, 1431; died and was buried at Rouen.

The incidents of his career are treated with considerable freedom by the dramatist. Bedford remained in England during the Agincourt campaign and was neither present at the battle nor at Harfleur. He died peaceably after the execution of Joan of Arc, and not before, as represented. The *Chronicles* are not responsible for these discrepancies.

D.P. *1 Hen. IV*. 'Prince John of Lancaster.' v, 1] (before Shrewsbury) *p.m.* v, 4] after the battle Prince Henry declares that 'full bravely hast thou flesh'd Thy maiden sword.' v, 5] is sent, with Westmoreland, against the northern rebels (*Hol.* iii, 529).

D.P. *2 Hen. IV*. 'Prince John of Lancaster.' (i, 1) falsely reported defeated. (iv, 1) Westmoreland speaks of him as 'our general.' iv, 2] sternly rebukes Abp. Scrope for having employed 'the countenance and grace of Heaven' in rebellion against 'Heaven's substitute,' the King; promises redress of grievances if Scrope will dismiss his forces; the rebels having dispersed, Prince J. reminds the leaders that although he promised redress he did not promise to spare traitors, and sends them to execution (*Hol.* iii, 529–30). iv, 3] meets Falstaff with Colevile (*q.v.*) as his prisoner, and condemns the latter to death; promises to speak better of F. than he deserves. iv, 4] visits his dying father (*Hol.* iii, 583). v, 2] warns the Chief Justice that he cannot expect favour from the new King. v, 5] joyfully anticipates war with France.

In i, 3, named 'Duke of L.,' but this title belonged to the Prince of Wales; moreover Sir Robt. Waterton (*q.v.*), and not Prince John, was Westmoreland's colleague against Northumberland (*Hol.* iii, 524).

D.P. *Hen. V*. 'Duke of Bedford, brother to the King.' i, 2] *p.m.* ii, 2] comments on Henry's knowledge of Scrope's plot. iii, 1] (at Harfleur) *p.m.* iv, 1] (at Agincourt) *p.m*; saluted by H. as 'brother Bedford.' iv, 3] bids farewell to Salisbury before the battle. v, 2] (at Troyes) *p.m.*

Bedford was not present at Henry's marriage.

D.P. *1 Hen. VI*. 'Duke of Bedford, uncle to the King and Regent of France.' i, 1] mourns over the dead King (Henry V); prays that the kingdom may be saved from 'civil broils'; hears evil news of losses in France; as regent (*Hol.* iii, 583), resolves instantly to proceed thither; further hears that Talbot is a prisoner, and Orleans besieged – but, with ten thousand men, he will 'make all Europe quake.' (i, 4) mtd. ii, 1] captures Orleans by surprise. ii, 2] (in Orleans) orders the attack to cease. iii, 2] (before Rouen) is 'brought in sick, in a chair' though urged to seek safety, witnesses his 'enemies' overthrow,' and dies; is eulogized by Talbot.

His policy and vigilance commemorated, *2 Hen. VI*, i, 1.

John, St. Substituted in Ff (*Rich. III*, i, 1, l. 138) for 'St Paul' (*q.v.*).

John, Sir. D.P. *Rich. III*. A priest. iii, 2] greets Hastings, and receives a whispered (Q) confidence; cf. *Hol.* iii, 723.

John the Bastard. For 'Don John,' D.P. *M. Ado* (*q.v.*).

John, The Life and Death of King. See King John.

Jonson, Ben. See I., B.

Joseph. A servant; *Tam. Sh.* iv, 1.

Joshua. Mtd. as one of 'The Nine Worthies'; *L.L.L.* v, 1.

Jourdain, Margaret. Acc. Hall: 'Margerie Iourdayne, surnamed the witch of Eye; to whose charge it was laied yt thei [*i.e.* M. J. and her associates] at the request of the duchesse [of Gloucester] had devised an image of waxe representing the kyng, which by their sorcerie a litle and litle consumed ... and so to brying hym to death'; for this she was condemned to be burnt at Smithfield. Acc. Rymer (Henry VI, May 9, 1433), she had previously been accused of sorcery, but escaped with a light punishment.

D.P. *2 Hen. VI.* 'Margery Jourdain, a witch.' i, 4] assists in raising a spirit, and is arrested. ii, 3] 'the witch at Smithfield shall be burn'd to ashes'; is led to execution.

Jove. See Jupiter.

Judas Iscariot. The betrayer of Christ; there was a common legend that he hanged himself on an elder-tree: 'Faste by, is zit the Tree of Eldre, that Judas henge him self upon' (Mandeville, ed. 1725, p. 112). Represented in painting and tapestry with red hair. (See also Iscariot.)

'A kissing traitor' (*L.L.L.* v, 2); 'Judas was hanged on an elder' (*ib. ib.*); '*Ros.* This very hair is of the dissembling colour. *Cel.* Something browner than Judas's: marry, his kisses are J.'s own children' (*A.Y.L.* iii, 4); Richard calls the friends who, he supposed, had deserted him, 'Three Judases, each one thrice worse than Judas' (*Rich. II*, iii, 2); 'Did they not sometime cry "all hail!" to me? So Judas did to Christ' (*ib.* iv, 1); Gloucester, kissing the infant Prince, says, aside, 'so Judas kissed his master' (*3 Hen. VI*, v, 7).

Alluded to, *Wint. T.* i, 2, as '[he] that did betray the Best.'

'Let their beards be of J.'s own colour' (Kyd, *The Spanish Tragedy* (1599)).

Judas Maccabaeus (*ob.* 161 B.C.). Jewish warrior who waged a successful war, in defence of his religion, against Antiochus Epiphanes. Mentioned as one of 'The Nine Worthies,' *L.L.L.* v, 1 ('Machabeus,' Ff); the part is enacted by Holofernes, who protests that he is 'not Iscariot' and is bantered by the courtiers.

Jug. 'The old nickname for Joan' (Halliwell); 'a vulgar form of "Jane" ' (Moberly). 'Whoop, Jug, I love thee' (*Lear*, i, 4).

Jule. For 'Juliet'; *Rom. J.* i, 3 (2).

[**Julia.**] Mother of Mark Antony; referred to, *Ant. Cl.* ii, 6: 'your mother came to Sicily.'

Julia. D.P. *T.G.V.* 'Beloved of Proteus' (F1). (i, 1) mtd. i, 2] discusses her suitors with Lucetta; is given a letter (from Prot.) by L., which had been handed to the latter, in error, instead of to her mistress; J. returns it to L., with a show of anger; L. drops it, and J. tears it to pieces; on L.'s departing, J. picks up the fragments and kisses those on which she finds passionate phrases. (i, 3) sends a consenting letter to Protcus. ii, 2] in bidding P. farewell, they exchange rings. (ii, 4) P.'s love for her mentioned to Silvia. (ii, 5) mtd. (ii, 6) is held by P. to be 'a swarthy Ethiope' compared with Silvia, ii, 7] in spite of Lucetta's attempts to dissuade her, resolves to follow Proteus to Milan, disguised as a page. iv, 2] takes up her abode at an inn in Milan; overhears P.'s courtship of Silvia. iv, 4] in the name of 'Sebastian' enters the service of P. as his page; is told to take a ring (her own) to Silvia, and ask, in exchange, her portrait; receives the latter, but Sil. rejects the ring indignantly; 'Sebastian' describes the neglected Julia, and enlists Silvia's sympathy for her; (*sol.*) criticizes the portrait. v, 2] expresses (aside) her contempt for Thurio when Proteus banters him; prepares to follow P. in his pursuit of Silvia. v, 4] on Valentine's offering to yield Silvia to Proteus, swoons, and on recovering, shows both the rings, and reveals her identity; is restored to Proteus.

Felismena in Montemayor's story, and Philomena in the old play. See Two Gentlemen of Vhrona, The.

Juliet (1). D.P. *Rom. J.* Daughter to Capulet. i, 3] learns from her mother that Paris seeks her hand, and that the match is approved of. i,5] meets Romeo, who is masked, at her father's feast, and falls in love with him; learns that he is a Montague and therefore a foe to the family. ii, 2] in a soliloquy at her window by night she betrays her feelings to the listening Romeo; they become affianced, and resolve on immediate marriage. ii, 5] learns from the nurse that she must hasten to Friar Laurence's cell, there to be wedded. ii, 6] meets R. and the Friar at the cell. iii, 2] learns that Tybalt has been slain by R., who is therefore banished; sends her ring to R., and bids him 'come to take his last farewell.' iii, 5] bids R. farewell in the early morning; dissimulates her love in her mother's presence; learns, to her horror, that her wedding with Paris is arranged, and is furiously vituperated by her father for her refusal to submit. iv, 1] visiting Friar Laurence, meets Paris, and answers his importunate questions evasively; is advised by the Friar to 'give consent to marry Paris,' but is promised a potion which will throw her into a deathlike trance for 'two-and-forty hours'; meanwhile Romeo should be summoned from Mantua. iv, 2] professes obedience to her father's wishes. iv, 3] drinks the potion. (iv, 5) is discovered apparently dead in her bed. v, 3] awakes in the family monument; finds Romeo lying dead beside the tomb; stabs herself.

Juliet (2). D.P. *M. for M.* 'Beloved of Claudio,' and with child by him. i, 2] *p.m.* (i, 4) is spoken of by Isabella as 'my cousin ... adoptedly.' (ii, 2) 'the groaning J... is very near her hour.' ii, 3] assures the supposed Friar Lodowick of her penitence; admits that her sin is heavier than Claudio's, whose condemnation she hears of with horror. (ii, 4) mtd. v, 1] *p.m.* (Claudio is bidden by the Duke to restore her that he wronged).

Julietta. For 'Juliet'; *M. for M.* i, 2.

Julius Caesar.

Publication. First appeared in the Folio of 1623, with the title, 'The Tragedie of Iulius Caesar.' The acts, but not the scenes, are numbered.

Date of Composition and Production. Internal evidence seems to indicate 1600–1 as the most probable date of the composition of this tragedy. In a description of Mortimer in Drayton's *Barons' Wars* (1603) there is a passage recalling Antony's eulogy of Brutus (v, 5, ll. 68–75), and it is noteworthy that this does not occur in *Mortimeriados* (1596), the earlier form of Drayton's poem.

SOURCES OF THE PLOT. Plutarch's *Lives* of Antony, Brutus, and Caesar furnish all the historical materials for the play, but it has been suggested that Appian's *Civil Wars* (ii, 137–47) supplied hints for the great speeches of Brutus and Antony. Several earlier plays relating to Caesar had been acted in England, but they are now lost.

July, Month of. 'The sixth of July' (the date of an imaginary letter, being old Midsummer Day, as suitable to 'Midsummer madness'; *M. Ado*, i, 1); 'makes a July's day short as December' (*Wint. T.* i, 2); 'clear as founts in July when We see each grain of gravel' (*Hen. VIII*, i, 1).

In the last two instances the accent is on the first syllable.

June, Month of. 'If there come a hot June' (*1 Hen. IV*, ii, 4); 'as the cuckoo in June, heard not regarded' (*ib.* iii, 2); 'like a cow in J., Hoists sails ['tail,' Staunton's conj.] and flies' (*Ant. Cl.* iii, 10); 'three hot J.s' (*Son.* civ).

Juno. Queen of heaven, sister and wife of Jupiter; guardian of women and protectress of marriage.

'Thou for whom Jove would swear J. but an Ethiope were' (*L.L.L.* iv, 3; *P.P.* xvii); 'J. have mercy!' (*Tr. Cr.* i, 2); 'O Juno!' (*Ant. Cl.* iii, 11); 'great J.'s power' (*ib.* iv, 15); 'great J.' (*Cymb.* iii, 4); 'as J. had been sick' (*ib.* iv, 2); 'with J. chide' (*ib.* v, 4); 'by J., I swear' (*Lear*, ii, 4); 'for the love of J.' (*Cor.* ii, 1); 'I, his despiteful J.' (*All's Well*, iii, 4); 'J.-like' (*Cor.* iv, 2); 'queen of marriage' (*Per.* ii, 3); her pace, *ib.* v, 1; her swans, *A.Y.L.* i, 3; wedding, her crown, *ib.* v, 4; her eyelids, *Wint. T.* iv, 3. Alluded to; 'the jealous queen of heaven' (*Cor.* v, 3, l. 46).

D.P. *Temp.* iv, 1] represented by a spirit in Prospero's masque; in a song grants her blessing to the lovers. See CERES.

Jupiter, or **Jove.** Chief of the Roman gods, equivalent to the Greek Zeus; especially regarded as lord of the heavens, and ruler of storms, thunder, and lightning. Legends represent him as visiting Leda in the form of a swan, and, as a bull, carrying off Europa to Crete. The oak was sacred to him, and the eagle one of his attributes.

(*a*) *Jupiter*. 'If J. Should from yond cloud speak divine things' (*Cor.* iv, 5); 'J. forbid, and say in thunder' (*Tr. Cr.* ii, 3); (Menenius, throwing up his cap) 'take my cap, J., and I thank thee' (*Cor.* ii, 1); 'your letter [fastened to an arrow] is with J. by this' (*T. And.* iv, 3; rep.); 'J. is yonder, dealing life' (of Hector, sparing his foes; *Tr. Cr.* iv, 5); 'J. became a bull' (*Wint. T.* iv, 3); 'You were also, J., a swan' (*M.W.W.* v, 5); 'the goodly transformation of J. there [Menelaus] ... the bull, the primitive statue ... of cuckolds' (*Tr. Cr.* v, 1); 'the wife of J. [Juno]' (*Temp.* iv, 1); 'wert thou the son of J.' (*Cymb.* ii, 3); 'the J. of men' (*Ant. Cl.* iii, 2); 'great J. upon his eagle' (*Cymb.* v, 5); 'temple of great J.' (*ib. ib.*); 'J. be praised' (*Cymb.* v, 3). Invoked; 'O, J.!' (*A.Y.L.* ii, 4; *Cor.* i, 3; *Tr. Cr.* i, 2); 'O most gentle J.' (*al.* 'pulpiter'; *A.Y.L.* iii, 2). In adjuration: 'By Jupiter' (*Cor.* i, 9; *Ant. Cl.* ii, 2; *Cymb.* ii, 4, iii, 5, 6; *Lear*, i, 1, ii, 4); 'J.' (*Tr. Cr.* i, 2).

D.P. *Cymb.* v, 4] descends in thunder and lightning, sitting on an eagle, and rebukes the ghosts of the parents and brothers of Posthumus for their lack of faith; declares that the woes of P. are nearly at an end, and leaves on his breast a tablet inscribed with oracular words.

(*b*) *Jove*. 'J.'s great attributes' (*All's Well*, iv, 2); 'J.'s thunder' (*Wint. T.* iii, 1); 'J.'s spreading tree' (*3 Hen. VI*, v, 2); 'J. for his power to thunder' (*Cor.* iii, 1); 'J.'s lightnings' (*Temp.* i, 2; *L.L.L.* iv, 2; *P.P.* v); 'J. that thunders' (*Ant. Cl.* iii, 11); 'J.'s dread clamours' (thunder; *Oth.* iii, 3); 'Could great men thunder As J. himself does, J. would ne'er be quiet' (*M. for M.* ii, 2); 'She makes a shower of rain as well as J.' (*Ant. Cl.* i, 2); 'When J. will hang ... his poison in the thick air' (*Timon*, iv, 3); 'From a god to a bull ... it was J.'s case' (*2 Hen. IV*, ii, 2); 'J., thou wast a bull for thy Europa ... a swan for the love of Leda' (*M.W.W.* v, 5; rep.); 'Europa did at lusty J.' (*M. Ado.* v, 4; rep.); 'J.'s tree' (*A.Y.L.* iii, 2); 'J.'s bird, the Roman eagle' (*Cymb.* iv, 2); 'J.'s stout oak' (*Temp.* v, 1); 'J. sometimes went disguised' (*2 Hen. VI*, iv, 1; rep.) (from *The Contention*); 'J. multipotent' (*Tr. Cr.* iv, 5); 'J.'s statue' (*Cor.* ii, 1); 'J.'s own book' (*ib.* iii, 1); 'supreme J.' (*ib.* v, 3); 'the earthly J.' (*Ant. Cl.* ii, 7); 'the J. of power' (*ib.* iii, 4); 'high-judging J.' (*Lear*, ii, 4); 'she is sport for J.' (*Oth.* ii, 3); 'the embracements even of J. himself' (*Per.* i, 1); 'within the house is J.' (referring to the story of Baucis and Philemon; *M. Ado*, ii, 1); (also) 'J. in a thatched house' (*A.Y.L.* iii, 3); (Europa) 'that made great J. to humble him' (*Tam. Sh.* i, 1); 'If J. stray, who dares say J. doth ill?' (*Per.* i, 1); 'at lovers' perjuries ... J. laughs' (*Rom. J.* ii, 2); 'this realm dismantled was Of J. himself' (*Haml.* iii, 2); 'J. in heaven' (*T. And.* iv, 3); 'here's to J.' (*ib.* iv, 4); 'J. knows' (*Cymb.* iv, 2); 'front of J. himself' (*Haml.* iii, 4); 'A Jove' (*Ant. Cl.* iv, 6; *Hen. V*, ii, 4); 'by J.'s side' (*Ant. Cl.* iv, 13); 'my King, my J.!' (*2 Hen. IV*, v, 5); 'J.'s Mercury' (*Rich. III*, iv, 3); 'great J.' (*Tr. Cr.* i, 3); 'J.'s accord' (*ib. ib.*); 'fly like chidden Mercury from J.' (*Tr. Cr.* ii, 2); 'J. the king' (*ib.* ii, 3); 'to J. [*al.* 'love'] I have abandoned Troy' (*ib.* iii, 3).

Invoked and mtd.: *T. Nt.* i, 5, ii, 5, iii, 1; *Tr. Cr.* ii, 2, iii, 3, iv, 1, v, 2; *A.Y.L.* i, 3, ii, 4 (rep.); *Cymb.* ii, 4, iii, 3, 6; *T. And.* ii, 3, iv, 1; *M.N.D.* v, 1; *Wint. T.* ii, 3, iv, 4; *Oth.* ii, 1. As equivalent of 'God'; 'J.'s doing' (*T. Nt.* iii, 4; rep.); 'J. blesses thee' (*ib.* iv, 2); 'I beseech J. on my knees' (*2 Hen. VI*, iv, 10); mtd., *V.A.* 1015, *Lucr.* 568, *P.P.* vi, xvii (2). 'By J.' (*L.L.L.* v, 2; *All's Well*, v, 3; *Hen. V*, iv, 3; *Tr. Cr.* v, 2 (rep.); *Cor.* iii, 1 (rep.); *Per.* ii, 3). Latin: 'ad Jovem' (*T. And.* iv, 3).

'J.'s own book' (*Cor.* iii, 1, l. 293) seems an allusion to Malachi iii, 16, or Exodus xxxii, 32 (Clar.).

Justice. Personified. 'If J. had her right' (*Rich. II*, ii, 1, l. 227); 'almost persuade J. to break her sword' (*Oth.* v, 2, l. 17); 'thou look'st modest as J.' (*Per.* v, 1, l. 122); 'J. is feasting while the widow weeps' (*Lucr.* 906).

Justitia, as the goddess of justice, appears in Aulus Gellius, *Noct. Att.* xiv, 4.

Justice, A. D.P. *M. for M.* ii, 1] accepts Escalus' invitation to dinner after a sitting of the court; comments on Angelo's severity.

K

Kate. Abbr. of 'Katharine.' 'None of us cared for K.' (*Temp.* ii, 2); 'K. Keepdown' (*M. for M.* iii, 2); 'divine K.' (*L.L.L.* iv, 3).

For 'Katharina,' the shrew: *Tam. Sh.* ii, 1 (8); iii, 2 (5); iv, 1 (6), 3 (6), 5 (3); v, 1 (3), 2 (3).

For 'Lady Percy' (*q.v.*): *1 Hen. IV*, ii, 3 (7); iii, 1 (3).

For 'Katharine of Valois': *Hen. V*, v, 2 (28).

For 'Katharine of Arragon': *Hen. VIII*, ii, 4.

Hence 'Kated,' *i.e.* 'matched with K.' (*Tam. Sh.* iii, 2); 'Kate-Hall,' nonce-name, *ib.* ii, 1.

Petruchio plays upon the word: 'dainties all are cates' (*Tam. Sh.* ii, 1); and, 'bring you from a wild K. [cat] to a K. Conformable as other household K.s' (*ib. ib.*).

Katharina. D.P. *Tam. Sh.* 'The shrew'; d. to Baptista Minola. i, 1] she spurns the suitors suggested by her father, and derides her sister Bianca. (i, 2) Petruchio resolves to woo her in spite of her shrewishness. ii, 1] with threats and violence she bids Bianca name her favoured suitor; (breaks Hortensio's lute over his head); later, in spite of her attempts to rebuff Petr., she is boisterously wooed by him, and assured that they are to be married 'on Sunday.' iii, 2] fears that, after all, the 'mad-brain rudesby' will play her false; later (after the wedding), is compelled to depart before 'the bridal dinner.' iv, 1] arrives at Petruchio's countryhouse; is sent supperless to bed. iv, 3] entreats Grumio to get her some food, but is saucily bantered; is denied the cap and gown she had set her heart on; starts, with Petr., for Padua. iv, 5] is so 'tamed' that she consents to call the moon the sun, and an old man a maiden, at Petruchio's bidding. v, 1] witnesses, with Petr., the unmasking of the false Vincentio. v, 2] at a 'banquet' in Lucentio's house, exchanges banter with 'Hortensio's widow'; later, proves her complete wifely obedience, and discourses sagely on the duty of wives.

The corresponding character in *The Taming of A Shrew* is Kate, Alfonso's eldest daughter.

Sh. 'indicates the tragedy that occurs when a manly spirit is born into a woman's body. Katharina is vexed and plagued by forced submission to a father who cannot see her merit, and by jealousy of a gentle useless sister. She, who is entirely honest, sees the brainless Bianca, whom no amount of schooling will make even passably honest, preferred before her. Lastly, she is humbled into the state of submissive wifely falsehood by a boor who cares only for his own will, her flesh, and her money.' (J. Masefield, *Shakespeare*, p. 108.)

Katharine. D.P. *L.L.L.* Lady attending on the Princess of France. ii, 1] characterizes Dumain. iv, 1] *p.m.* v, 2] receives verses and gloves from Dumain; recalls the death of her sister through love; when masked, exchanges banter with Longaville; promises Du. that in a year, 'if I have much love, I'll give you some.'

In the early edns. there is much confusion between the pfxs. 'Ros.' and 'Kat.'

Katharine of Arragon (1485–1536). Dau. of Ferdinand and Isabella of Spain; married, in 1501, to Arthur, Prince of Wales (aged 15), who died the next year. In 1509 she married Henry VIII, being five years older than her husband. Her first four children died in their infancy (*Hen. VIII*, ii, 4), and the only surviving child of the marriage was Mary, who became queen. In 1520 she was visited by her nephew Charles V (*Hen. VIII*, i, 1). The King, about 1526, determined to divorce Katharine, on the plea that 'the marriage with his brother's wife' had 'crept too near his conscience' (*Hen. VIII*, ii, 2), but really with the object of marrying Anne Boleyn. In 1529 Katharine appeared before the legislative court under Card. Campeggio, and in open court before the King (*Hen. VIII*, ii, 4); she withdrew to Bishop's Hatfield in 1532, and her marriage was declared null, by Cranmer, in 1533, but was pronounced valid by the Pope in the following year; she died after a long illness, and was buried in Peterborough Abbey.

D.P. *Hen. VIII.* (i, 1) mtd. as the Emperor's aunt. i, 2] calls the King's attention to the grievous taxes attributed to Wolsey; is present at Knyvet's examination. (ii, 1) her separation from the King rumoured (*Hol.* iii, 897). (ii, 2) she is to be allowed scholars 'to argue for her' (*Hol.* iii, 907). (ii, 3) Anne Boleyn pities her. ii, 4] she pleads her cause before the King in open court, and accuses Wolsey of being her enemy (*Hol.* iii, 908). iii, 1] in an interview with Wolsey and Campeggio she scornfully rejects their advice that she should, without a struggle, consent to be deprived of her queenhood. (iv, 1) reported to be at Kimbolton after her marriage had been declared null. iv, 2] is informed by her gentleman-usher of the death of Wolsey, and discusses his character; falling asleep, a vision appears to her; on awaking she receives Capucius (*Hol.* iii, 939), ambassador from the Emperor, and entrusts him with a farewell letter to Henry containing her last requests (*ib. ib.*); she gives instructions regarding her obsequies, and is led out, to die.

Acc. Calendar (*Hen. VIII*), x, 59, Capucius left Kimbolton two days before K.'s death.

Katharine of Valois. Dau. of Charles VI of France and his wife Isabel of Bavaria; b. in Paris, Oct. 27, 1401; m. Henry V (1420), and by him became mother of Henry VI. Five or six years after the death of Henry V she privately married Owen Tudor, one of Henry's esquires, and their eldest son Edmund, by his marriage with Margaret Beaufort, became father of Henry VII. K. died in obscurity at Bermondsey Abbey, Jan. 3, 1437.

In the Epilogue to *2 Hen. IV* a promise is given that 'our humble author' will 'make you merry with fair K. of France.'

D.P. *Hen. V.* (iii, Chor.) is offered to Henry V in marriage. iii, 4] receives a lesson in English from her attendant Alice. v, 2] is wooed and won by Henry V, Alice serving as interpreter.

Acc. *Hol.* iii, 572, Henry 'went to visit the French king, the queene and the lady K. [at Troyes], whome he found in Saint Peter's church where was a very ioious meeting betwixt them,' and there they were affianced.

Keech. 'Goodwife K., the butcher's wife' (*2 Hen. IV*, ii, 1).

Buckingham refers to Wolsey as 'a keech,' *i.e.* a lump of fat, in allusion to his father having been a butcher, *Hen. VIII*, i. 1.

Keepdown, Kate. Mtd. as wronged by Lucio; *M. for M.* iii, 2.

Keeper. The pfx, of *M. Ado*, iv, 2, l. 1, QFf; perhaps a misprint for 'Kemp' (*q.v.*), who played Dogberry.

Keepers, Mortimer's. D.PP. *1 Hen. VI.* ii, 5] in attendance.

Keepers, Two. D.PP. *3 Hen. VI.* iii, 1] they are awaiting the approach of the deer when King Henry enters; he is disguised, but '1 Keep.' recognizes him; they declare they are Edward's subjects, and lead him away.

Styled 'deer-stealers' by Hazlitt. Acc. *Hol.* iii, 667, he was recognized by 'one Cantlow.'

Kemp, William. A comic actor and jigdancer; succeeded Richard Tarleton in popularity; acted with Richard Burbage and Sh. before Q. Elizabeth in 1594. Played the parts of Peter and Dogberry, 'Kemp' being given for 'P.' in *Rom. J.* iv, 5, l. 100, Q2, 3, and for 'D.' in *M. Ado*, iv, 2. While one of Lord Leicester's servants, Kemp visited Germany and Elsinore, as leader of the company. He was one of the seven original lessees of the Globe theatre.

Mtd., as 'William Kempt,' in 'The Names of the Principall Actors' pfxd. to the First Folio.

Kendal. Town in Westmoreland; cloth made there was famous in Sh.'s days. Falstaff complains of having been attacked by 'knaves in Kendal-green' (*1 Hen. IV*, ii, 4) – the livery of Robin Hood and his men.

'Bateman of Kendal gave us Kendal-green' (T. Heywood, *Robert, Earl of Huntingdon* (1601)).

Kenilworth. Formerly also 'Killingworth,' a town 5 m. N. of Warwick, with a famous castle, founded *c.* 1120, the property of the crown from Hen. IV to Elizabeth.

During Cade's rebellion Hen. VI fled to 'Killingworth,' *2 Hen. VI*, iv, 4; cf. *Hol.* iii, 634. This is the only mention of K. in the text of *Sh.*, but the 'Princely Pleasures' presented before Eliz. at K., in 1575, by the E. of Leicester, to whom the castle had been granted in 1562, have been regarded, on slender evidence, as alluded to in *M.N.D.* ii, 1, ll. 148 ff.

Kent, County of. Mtd., *John*, iv, 2, v, 1; *1 Hen. IV*, ii, 1; *2 Hen. VI*, iv, 1, 2, 7 (3), 10 (2), v, 1; *3 Hen. VI*, i, 1, iv, 8; *Rich. III*, iv, 4; its inhabitants characterized by Julius Caesar, *2 Hen. VI*, iv, 7; (*cf.* 'of all the inhabitants of this isle the civilist are the Kentish folke,' Golding's transln. of the *Commentaries* (*q.v.*), v, 15).

Kent, Earl of. D.P. *Lear*. i, 1] converses with Gloucester on Lear's intentions, and is made acquainted with Gl.'s bastard son Edmund; expostulates with Lear on his disowning Cordelia, and, on rebuking him unsparingly for his folly, is banished. i, 4] disguised as a serving-man, enters L.'s service, under the name (v, 3) of 'Caius'; trips up the heels of Albany's steward Oswald, who is insolent. i, 5] is sent by L. 'to Gloucester,' with a letter for Regan. (ii, 4) delivers the letter, and is ordered to follow Regan and Cornwall to Gloucester's castle. ii, 2] picks a quarrel with Oswald, and beats him; bluntly defends his conduct before Corn. and Reg. and is put in the stocks; (*sol.*) longs for daylight that he may read a letter which he has received from Cordelia. ii, 4] explains to Lear how he came to be stocked; is released on L.'s demand. iii, 1] meets a gentleman of L.'s train, at night; learns that L. is exposed to the storm; relates that 'there is division' between the Dukes and that French forces have landed; bids the gentleman convey a ring to Cordelia, then at Dover, and hence learn who the giver is; they part to seek the King. iii, 2] lighting upon Lear and the Fool, offers to conduct them to a hovel hard by. iii, 4] reaches the hovel within which 'Poor Tom' (Edgar) is couching; urges L. to seek shelter in Gloucester's castle. iii, 6] (in an outbuilding) tries to allay the King's rising frenzy, and on Lear's falling asleep helps to bear him out. iv, 3] (near Dover) meeting L.'s gentleman, learns from him Cordelia's wrath and grief at her sister's treatment of their father, and the condition of the latter (scene omitted in Ff). iv, 7] is fervently thanked by Cordelia, with whom he watches the sleeping King; prepares for the imminent battle. v, 3] (his impassioned revelation of himself to Edgar is described by the latter); is present when L. bears in Cordelia's corpse, and tries to make the King comprehend that he is his former servant; witnesses Lear's death; Kent's final words are: 'My master calls me, I must not say no' (acc. F2, 3, 4, he dies upon the stage, but QqF1 give no such direction).

In the old play of *Leir* the character which is in some respects the prototype of Kent is named Perillus.

Kent, Thomas Holland, Duke of Surrey and 3rd Earl of. See Surrey, Duke of.

Kentish, *adj.* 'These K. rebels' (*2 Hen. VI*, iv, 4; rep.).

Kentishman. 'A headstrong K., John Cade' (*2 Hen. VI*, iii, 1); (plu.) 'the Kentishmen will willingly rise' (*3 Hen. VI*, i, 2).

The Yorkist sympathies of the Kentish men are referred to, *Hol.* iii, 653.

Ketly, Sir Richard. Mtd. among the slain at Agincourt; *Hen. V*, iv, 8.

'Kikelie,' *Hol.* iii, 555; 'Kighley' (after Keighly in Yorks), French, p. 121; 'Kykelley,' Nicolas, *Agincourt*, 2nd edn. p. 369.

Kildare, Gerald Fitzgerald, 9th Earl of (1487–1534). Having offended Wolsey, the Cardinal 'accused him to the king, of that he had not borne himself uprightlie in his office in Ireland,' whereupon 'he was committed to prison' (*Hol.* iii, 855). 'K.'s attainder, then deputy of Ireland' (*Hen. VIII*, ii, 1).

Kimbolton Castle. In Hunts, about 10 m. W. of Huntingdon, now the seat of the Duke of Manchester. Scene of the death of Katharine of Arragon. The room in which she died remains intact, and relics of the Queen are preserved there. (In *Hol.* iii, 939, 'Kimbalton.')

'She was divorced, ... Since which she was removed to K. ['Kymmalton,' F1, 2], Where she remains now sick' (*Hen. VIII*, iv, 1). The next scene, in which the 'vision' of the dying Queen is presented, is laid at K. Castle.

King John.

Publication. First appeared in the Folio of 1623, with the title: 'The life and death of King John.' The acts and scenes are numbered throughout.

Date of Composition. Uncertain, but the limits 1593–6 are favoured by the great majority of critics. The play is mtd. by Meres in his *Palladis Tamia* (1598) (though it is possible that the older drama, *The Troublesome Raigne of John*, may be there referred to). Apart from evidences based on style, the three following points have been held to bear upon the date:

(*a*) a resemblance of a passage (ii, 1, ll. 155–66) to seven lines in a play entitled *The Famous History of Thomas Stukeley* (*c.* 1596); (*b*) the death of Sh.'s son Hamnet (1596), and the supposed reflection of the father's sorrow in Constance's grief for Arthur; (*c*) Chatillon's description (ii, 1, ll. 74–9) of the English forces, as inspired by the grand fleet sent against Spain in 1596.

Source. The older play, *The Troublesome Raigne* (*q.v.*) already referred to, which, in its turn, rests on Holinshed's *Chronicles*.

Knight. D.P. *Lear.* i, 4] tells L. of the disrespect shown him by Goneril and her retainers. ('Servant,' Qq.)

Knyvet, or **Knevet, Charles.** Surveyor to the Duke of Buckingham. Buckingham's tenants complained to the Duke of K.'s conduct, and he was dismissed from his office; whereupon, out of revenge and hope of reward, he laid information against the Duke which led to his fall (*Hol.* iii, 856, 862–3).

D.P. *Hen. VIII.* i, 2] summoned before the King, he declares that Buckingham aimed at the throne, being induced to do so by the prophecy of the friar Hopkins (*q.v.*), and that B. had even threatened to assassinate the King.

Acc. Grafton, K. was a 'cosyn' of the Duke's. *Cf.* French, p. 272, and Sir H.N. Nicolas, *Testamenta Vetusta*, ii, 547.

L

Laban. Uncle to the patriarch Jacob; outwitted by J. in the division of their flocks (Gen. xxx). The circumstances dilated on by Shylock, *M.V.* i, 3.

Labeo. (Common as a Roman name.) Mtd. *Plut.* p. 150, as 'lieutenant of pioners'; slain at Philippi. 'Labeo and Flavius, set our battles on' (*Jul. C.* v, 3).

In Ff 'Labio,' following the erroneous spelling in *Plut.*

Labienus, Q. Son of T. Labienus. He joined the party of Brutus and Cassius after the murder of Caesar, and was entrusted by Orodes, the Parthian king, with a large army. 'L... Hath with his Parthian force Extended Asia; from Euphrates his conquering banner shook' (*Ant. Cl.* i, 2; almost *verbatim* from *Plut.* p. 178).

Lacedaemon. Or Sparta (*q.v.*); the chief city of Laconia. 'To L. did my land extend' (*Timon*, ii, 2); (Alcibiades pleading for his friend) 'his service done at L. and Byzantium Were a sufficient briber for his life' (*ib*, iii, 5).

[**Laches.**] See Flavius (4).

Lackbeard, Lord. Nonce-name applied by Benedick to Claudio; *M. Ado*, v, 1, referring to his youth.

Lacy, Family of. '*Cade.* My father was a Mortimer ... my wife descended of the Lacies ... Therefore am I of an honourable house' (2 *Hen. VI*, iv, 2).

Walter de Lacy, 1st Baron L., is said to have fought at Hastings; 'Lacy' was also the family name of Earls of Lincoln, and of Ulster.

Ladies. D.PP. *Cymb.* Attending on the Queen. i, 5] are sent to gather flowers, and return with them.

Ladies, Two. D.PP. *Wint. T.* ii, 1] encourage Mamillius' prattle; he refers to them as 'yon crickets.'

Lady (1). Perh. name of a hound; *1 Hen. IV*, iii, 1, l. 240. Cf. *Lear*, i, 4, l. 125 (a doubtful passage).

Lady (2). D.P. *Rich. II.* Attending on the Queen. iii, 4] suggests diversions to her mistress, to dispel care.

Historically, the chief lady of the Queen's household at the time was either Lady de Couey (g.d. of Edw. III) or Eleanor Holland, widow of the 4th E. of March. See French, p. 48.

Lady, An Old. D.P. *Hen. VIII.* Friend to Anne Boleyn. ii, 3] discusses Q. Katharine's divorce with Anne; rallies A. for declaring that she 'would not be queen'; hints that A. may be a duchess, and is present when her promotion to the rank of marchioness is intimated. v, 1] announces to Henry the birth of a daughter, and, to her chagrin, is given only a hundred marks.

It is not explicitly stated that the 'Old Lady' of Act I is the same as that of Act II, but, as Steevens tartly remarks, 'this, I suppose, is the same old cat that appears with Anne Boleyn.' In modern representations she has been named, without warrant, 'Lady Denny' (Sir Anthony D.'smother, presumably).

Laenas, Popillius. A senator who unwittingly dismayed the conspirators by privately conversing with Caesar in the Senate-house shortly before C. was murdered (Appian, *Bell. Civ.* ii, 115–6; *Plut.* p. 118).

D.P. *Jul. C.* 'Popilius Lena, a senator.' iii, 1] (as related above). ('Popilius Laena' in *Plut.*)

Laertes (1). Father of Ulysses (Ovid, *Her.* i, 97 ff.; *Metam.* xiii, 48). 'Wise L.'s son' (*T. And.* i, 1).

Laertes (2). D.P. *Haml.* Son to Polonius. i, 2] obtains permission from the King to visit France. i, 3] in parting from his sister, Ophelia, warns her against giving credence to Hamlet's professions of love; is given counsel on conduct by his father. (ii, 1) Polonius instructs Reynaldo to spy on him in Paris. iv, 5] returns to Denmark; is hailed as king by the rabble; forces his way into the royal presence, and demands vengeance for his father's death; witnesses his sister's madness. iv, 7] hears from the King that all his woes are due to Hamlet; H.'s sudden return is announced, and the King and Laertes plan his death; L. hears of Ophelia's death. v, 1] at Ophelia's funeral L. inveighs against her burial in 'ground unsanctified'; has a furious encounter with Hamlet in her grave, but they are parted. v, 2] in a fencing-match with H. wounds him with a poisoned rapier, and in turn is pierced by it; dies, confessing his treachery.

'Leartes,' Q1.

La Far. 'The marshal of France' (*Lear*, iv, 3). (The scene is omitted in Ff.)

Lafeu. D.P. *All's Well.* An old lord. i, 1] attends to conduct Bertram to the royal Court; informs the Countess of the King's malady, and learns Helena's parentage. i, 2] *p.m.*; escorts Bertram. ii, 1] presents Helena to the King, as 'Doctor She.' ii, 3] in dilating on the King's wonderful cure, is continually interrupted by Parolles; is amazed at the 'boys of ice' in Helena's presence; quarrels with, and scorns, Parolles; re-enters, and declares, that if he 'were but two hours younger,' he would beat him. ii, 5] in P.'s presence, warns Bertram against him. (iii, 6) his 'smoking' of Parolles mtd. (iv, 3) mtd. iv, 5] tells the Countess that the marriage of Bertram to his daughter is favoured by the King, and announces that his Majesty is at hand. v, 2] listens to Parolles' entreaties, gives him a 'quart d'écu' and tells him that, although a fool and a knave, he shall eat. v, 3] speaks to the King of the treasure, in Helena, which Bertram has lost; rejoices at the approaching marriage of B. and his daughter; observes the King's ring on B.'s finger; is present at the *dénouement*.

See MAUDLIN. There is no corresponding character in Boccaccio's story. Steevens suggests 'Lefeu.'

'The valiant old lord L. is ... raised above the prejudice of distinction of rank, and places virtue and merit above nobility and blood' (Gervinus, *Sh. Comm.* (1875), p. 181).

Lakin. For 'Ladykin' (dim.), the Virgin Mary; in the phrase 'By our Lakin,' contracted to 'Berlaken,' 'Berlakin.' *Temp.* iii, 3; *M.N.D.* iii, 1.

Lambert, St. 'St L.'s Day,' *i.e.* Sept. 17 (*Rich. II*, i, 1). (The actual date fixed for the combat is doubtful.)

Lammas Eve. July 31, the day before Lammas. 'Come L.-eve at night she [Juliet] shall be fourteen' (*Rom. J.* i, 3).

Lammas (from A.S. *half-maesse*, 'loaf mass'), originally a harvest festival.

Lammas-tide. The season of Lammas. 'How long is it now To L-tide?' (*Rom. J.* i, 3).

Lamond. A Norman, mentioned by the King as a horseman of supreme skill, who had praised Laertes' swordmanship; *Haml.* iv, 7.

'Lamord,' Qq; 'Lamound,' Ff.

[**Lampedusa.**] Island in the Mediterranean, E. of Tunis; held by Jos. Hunter (*Disquisition*, etc. (1839); *New Illustrations*, etc. (1845) to be the scene of *The Tempest*.

Lamprius. Mtd. in the initial st. dir., *Ant. Cl.* i, 2, but is not a speaking character. The name suggests a reminiscence of Lampryas, Plutarch's grandfather, who is credited with repeating a story of Antony's extravagance (*Plut.* p. 176).

Lancaster. For 'John of Gaunt': *Rich. II*, i, 1; ii, 1. For 'Bolingbroke': *ib.* ii, 3. For 'Lord John of Lancaster': *1 Hen. IV*, v, 4; *2 Hen. IV*, i, 1. For 'Henry VI': *2 Hen. VI*, i, 1.

Lancaster, House of. The descendants of John of Gaunt, D. of Lancaster. The house held the crown during the reigns of Hen. IV, Hen. V, and Hen. VI.

The house explicitly mtd.: *1 Hen. VI*, ii, 5; *2 Hen. VI*, i, ii, 2 (2); *3 Hen. VI*, ii, 1, iii, 3; *Rich. III*, i, 2, 3, 4, v, 3. See Appendix 2.

Langley, Edmund de. 1st D. of York (1341–1402). Born and died at King's Langley, Herts; 5th s. of Edw. III, by Philippa of Hainault; member of Council of Regency on the accession of Rich. II; regent during the King's absence, Sept. 1394 and Sept. 1396. 'Being verelie a man of gentle nature, [he] wished that the state of the common-wealth might have beene redressed without losse of any mans life, or other cruell dealing' (*Hol.* iii, 464).

D.P. *Rich. II.* ii, 1] warns the dying Gaunt that his counsel will be wasted upon Richard, and advises him to 'deal mildly with his youth'; begs R. to forgive Gaunt's reproaches; dwells on the patience with which he himself has endured the ill-doings of his sovereign, whom he contrasts with the Black Prince; urges R. not to seize Hereford's rights, and departs with a grave warning (*Hol.* iii, 496). ii, 2] being 'weak with age,' is distraught under the burden of his responsibility as regent; hears of the death of the Dss. of Gloucester (*ib.* 514); gives confused and contradictory orders. ii, 3] bitterly upbraids Bolingbroke for his 'gross rebellion,' and laments that his palsied arm cannot chastise him; is mollified by B.'s words, and consents to accompany him to Bristol (*ib.* 498). iii, 1] (at Bristol) sends message from Bol. to the Queen. iii, 3] reproves Northumberland for speaking with disrespect of Richard; on R.'s appearance, is filled with pity 'that any harm should stain so fair a show.' iv, 1] announces R.'s abdication, and hails B. as Henry the Fourth. v, 2] describes to his wife the entrance of Bol. and Richard into London; detects his son Rutland (Aumerle) in possession of a treasonable document (*ib.* 514), and, despite the entreaties of the Dss., hurries away to lay it before Bol. v, 3] reaching Windsor, finds that Rutland has anticipated him (*ib.*), and is closely followed by the Dss., whose entreaties prevail against his denunciation of his son. v, 6] *p.m.*; is present when Richard's body is brought to Henry.

'Duke of York,' or 'York,' in pfxs. and st. dirs. Mtd. as founder of the house of York, *1 Hen. VI*, ii, 5; *2 Hen. VI*, ii, 2 (2).

His presence at Berkeley noted, *1 Hen. IV*, i, 3.

Langton, Stephen (*ob.* 1228). Abp. of Canterbury and cardinal. On the death of Abp. Fitzwalter (1205) King John nominated John Gray, Bp. of Norwich, in his place; the Pope (Innocent III), however, quashed the election, and ordered 'the moonkes of Canterburie ... to choose one Stephan L. the cardinall of S. Chrysogon an Englishman borne,' whom John at first rejected (*Hol.* iii, 171) on account of his French sympathies. The legate Pandulph formally demands why John by force keeps 'S.L., chosen Archbishop of Canterbury, from that holy see?' (*John*, iii, 1).

[**Laomedon.**] Father of Priam. Alluded to by Nestor in speaking to Hector: 'I knew thy grandsire, And once fought with him: he was a soldier good' (*Tr. Cr.* iv, 5).

Lapland. Famous for its wizards from early times. 'For practice of witchcraft and sorcery they [the Lapps] pass all the nations in the world' (Giles Fletcher, *Of the Russe Common Wealth* (1591)).

'These are but imaginary wiles, And Lapland sorcerers inhabit here' (*Com. Err.* iv, 3). Warburton also conjectured 'Lapland' for 'Poland,' *ib.* iii, 2, l. 100.

Lartius, Titus. Mtd. *Plut.* p. 7 ('T. Latius,' in error), as 'one of the valiantest men the Romans had at that time'; in command of the besiegers' camp at Corioli.

D.P. *Cor.* i, 1] declares that rather than not follow Cominius to the wars he will 'lean upon one crutch and fight with t'other.' (i, 2, 3) mtd. i, 4] (before Corioli) wins Marcius' horse in a wager; eulogizes M.'s valour, and leads a rescue party. i, 5] is given charge of the captured city. (i, 6) mtd. i, 7] proceeds to the Roman camp. i, 9] is left in command at Corioli. ii, 1] *p.m.* (ii, 2) mtd. iii, 1] relates that Aufidius has retired to Antium, burning for his revenge on Coriolanus.

Mtd. as 'Titus,' i, 4, 5, 9. 'Lucius' (i, 1, l. 233) in Ff.

[**Lasco, Albert a.**] See PALATINE.

Latin. (*a*) *Subst.*, Latin language. Slender takes Bardolph's jargon for L., *M.W.W.* i, 1; Evans examines William in L., *ib.* iv, 1; Falconbridge 'hath neither L., French nor Italian' (*M.V.* i, 2); 'A priest that lacks L. ... sleeps easily because he cannot study' (*A.Y.L.* iii, 2); 'no matter what he 'leges in L.' (*Tam. Sh.* i, 2); King Henry's style 'in L.' (*Hen. V*, v, 2); Cade condemns Lord Say for speaking L., *2 Hen. VI*, iv, 7; Katharine begs Wolsey not to speak in L., *Hen. VIII*, iii, 1.

(*b*) *Adj.* 'Remuneration! O, that's the L. word for three farthings' (*L.L.L.* iii, 1).

Launce. D.P. *T.G.V.* 'A clownish servant to Proteus' (F1). ii, 3] is enlarging on the callous behaviour of his dog Crab, when he is urgently summoned to join his master. ii, 5] meets Speed at Milan; they exchange banter about their masters' love-affairs, and repair to an ale-house. iii, 1] Launce cons a 'catlog' of his own sweetheart's 'conditions'; inveigles Speed into a lengthy discussion of the pros and cons of the matter, and then mischievously informs him that his master has all the time been awaiting him. (iv, 2) mtd. iv, 4] rates Crab for his bad manners; confesses that he lost the 'little jewel' of a dog, destined by Proteus as a present for Silvia, and offered Crab in lieu of it; is sent packing by Pr. to find 'the jewel.'

Laura. The lady (prob. Laure de Noves) celebrated by Petrarch in his *Canzoniere*. 'L. to his [Romeo's] lady, was but a kitchenwench; marry, she had a better love to berime her' (*Rom. J.* ii, 4).

Laurence, Friar (1). Mtd. as recognizing Silvia and Eglamour, 'as he in penance wandered through the forest' (*T.G.V.* v, 2).

Laurence, Friar (2). D.P. *Rom. J.* A Franciscan. ii, 3] is gathering herbs, and meditating on their virtues, when Romeo enters, tells him how his love for Rosaline has been transferred to Juliet, and begs him to marry them that very day; Friar L. deprecates such fickleness and haste, but consents, with the object of ending the feud between the families. (ii, 4, 5) the wedding is to take place at 'Friar L.'s cell.' ii, 6] receives the couple at his cell to wed them. (iii, 2) keeps Romeo in hiding there. iii, 3] tells R. that he is sentenced to banishment; seeks to moderate his passionate grief; dissuades him from suicide and advises him to have one parting interview with Juliet. (iii, 5) mtd. iv, 1] Paris dismays him by declaring that he must be wedded to J. 'on Thursday'; confers with J. on her desperate dilemma; tells her that he can supply her with 'a sleeping potion' (v, 3) which will make her appear as one dead for forty-two hours, during which time she may be laid in the ancestral vault; meanwhile he will send a message to Romeo in exile. (iv, 2) mtd. iv, 5] on reaching Capulet's house, ostensibly to conduct the bride to church, finds her an apparent corpse; administers formal consolation, and follows the funeral procession. v, 2] finds that his message to Romeo has failed in delivery; resolves to be at hand when J. awakes. v, 3] finds R. lying dead in the vault; urges J., now awakened, to seek refuge in 'a sisterhood of holy nuns'; dares stay no longer; later, returns in custody, and relates the whole story to the Prince.

Lavatch. Name by which the clown is addressed by Parolles; *All's Well*, v, 2. ('Levatch,' F3, 4.)

Probably for 'la vache.'

Lavinia. D.P. *T. And.* Daughter to Titus Andronicus. i, 1] welcomes Titus on his return as a victor, and mourns her brethren slain; Saturninus declares he will make her his empress; she acquiesces in his 'princely courtesy' to Tamora; she is suddenly claimed as his betrothed by Bassianus, and forcibly borne away. (ii, 1) Demetrius and Chiron become rivals for her; Aaron advises them to outrage her. ii, 2] she joins in the imperial hunting party. ii, 3] she discovers Tamora in Aaron's company, and scornfully reviles her; is dragged away by T.'s two sons to be violated. ii, 5] is brought back by Dem. and Chir., deprived of hands and tongue; she is thus discovered by Marcus. iii, 1] is brought to Titus. iii, 2] at Titus' banquet (not in Q). iv, 1] by the aid of the boy Lucius, she directs attention to 'the tale of Philomel' in Ovid; writes on the ground the names of her violators. v, 2] aids in the slaying of Dem. and Chir. v, 3] her father kills her, exclaiming, 'Die, die, Lavinia, and thy shame with thee!'

'I can never read [ii, 3] without amazement at the folly of the author, who, requiring in the nature of things to win our sympathy for his afflicted heroine, fills her mouth with the grossest and vilest insults against Tamora – so gross, so vile, so unwomanly, that her punishment becomes something of a retribution instead of being wholly a brutality' (A. Symons, *Introd. to Sh. Quarto Facsimiles* (Pretorius), No. 29, p. xii).

Lawrence (St), Pountney, or **Poultney.** A church, and college, formerly standing to the S. of Cannon Street; destroyed in the Great Fire. So named from its benefactor, Sir John de Poultnay, Mayor of London (*ob.* 1349).

The parish mtd. *Hen. VIII*, i, 2; ('saint Laurence Poultnie,' *Hol.* iii, 864).

Lawyer, A. D.P. *1 Hen. VI.* ii, 4] present when the red and white roses are plucked.

Lazarus. The beggar in the parable of 'The rich man and L.' (Luke xvi, 20). 'Ragged as L.' (*1 Hen. IV*, iv, 2).

Leah. Shylock's deceased wife; *M.V.* iii, 1.

Leander, of Abydos. See Hero (2). 'How young L. cross'd the Hellespont' (*T.G.V.* i, 1); his scaling of Hero's tower, *ib.* iii, 1; 'L. the good swimmer' (*M. Ado*, v, 2); according to Rosalind, 'was taken with the cramp' (*A.Y.L.* iv, 1).

Lear. D.P. *Lear*. 'King of Britain.' i, 1] announces that he has divided his kingdom into three parts, and purposes to allot them to his daughters; he bids them show by their answers who loves him most; the protestations of the two elder daughters satisfy him, but the youngest, Cordelia, infuriates him by refusing to compete with her sisters; in a rage L. disinherits her, and, on Kent expostulating with him, condemns him to exile; offers Cordelia to 'Burgundy' without a dower; on his refusal, resigns her to 'France,' 'without our grace, our love, our benison.' (i, 3) Goneril complains that day and night the 'idle old man' wrongs her; she bids the steward show negligence to him. i, 4] L. takes Kent (disguised) into his service; is made aware of the disrespect shown him by Goneril's domestics; converses with the Fool; is brusquely desired by Gon. to diminish his train; in a fury, he decides to make his home with Regan, and inveighs against Goneril's ingratitude; later, finding that fifty of his followers have been dismissed, threatens G. with 'the woundings of a father's curse.' i, 5] while awaiting his horses, converses unheedfully with the Fool, and prays heaven he may not grow mad. ii, 4] arrived at Gloucester's castle, he is enraged to find 'Caius' (Kent) in the stocks; is surprised that he is not received by Regan and Cornwall; goes to seek them; later, returns with Gloucester, who has tried to soothe L. by excuses for Reg. and Corn., they are 'sick' or 'weary'; L. tries to check his own wrath by considering that the excuse may be true, but is again aroused by seeing 'Caius' still in the stocks; on Regan's entry he describes Goneril's unkindness, but R. makes excuses for her sister; he kneels to her, but is chided for 'unsightly tricks'; he appeals piteously to R., who shall 'never have his curse'; Goneril arrives, and the two sisters coldly argue that if he visits them it must be without attendants; L., with a piteous appeal to heaven for patience, followed by an incoherent vow of vengeance on the 'unnatural hags,' rushes out into the night, crying, 'O fool, I shall go mad!' iii, 2] (in storm and darkness, upon a health) L. invokes the elements to destroy mankind – yet he himself is 'a man more sinn'd against than sinning'; Kent leads him to a hovel. iii, 4] (at the door of the hovel) L. declares that the storm is nothing compared to the tempest in his mind, but fears that hitherto he has 'ta'en too little care' concerning 'houseless poverty'; Edgar enters in the assumed character of a madman, and in discoursing with him L.'s wits begin to wander; he is led away by Gloucester. iii, 6] L. becomes insane, and holds a mock trial of his daughters; he sleeps, and is borne away. (iv, 4) he is reported to be 'mad as the vex'd sea,' and to be wandering, crowned with flowers; Cordelia sends to seek him. iv, 6] L. in his fantastic dress encounters the blinded Gloucester; he rages against women, and the hypocrisy of mankind; he fancies himself a prisoner, and escapes, running. iv, 7] he sleeps, watched by Cordelia and others; on awaking his wits return, but he fears he is not in his perfect mind. v, 2] *p.m.*'; a prisoner. v, 3] declares that in prison Cordelia and he will 'sing like birds i' the cage'; they are taken away guarded; later, L. returns with Cordelia dead in his arms; he watches, in an agony, for signs of life in the corpse; his mind loses its grasp of realities, and after a final flicker of reason he expires.

'The Lear of Sh. cannot be acted. The contemptible machinery by which they mimic the storm … is not more inadequate to represent the horrors of the real elements than any actor can be to represent Lear; they might more easily propose to personate the Satan of Milton upon a stage, or one of Michael Angelo's terrible figures. The greatness of Lear is not in corporal dimension, but in intellectual: the explosions of his passion are terrible as a volcano, they are storms turning up and disclosing to the bottom that sea, his mind, with all its vast riches. It is his mind which is laid bare. On the stage we see nothing but corporal infirmities and weakness … while we read it, we see not Lear, but we are Lear.' (C. Lamb.)

Lear, King. (In F1: 'The Tragedie of King Lear.' The acts and scenes are indicated.)

PUBLICATION. In the Stationers' Registers, under date May 14, 1594, there appears, entered to Edward White, 'The moste famous Chronicle historye of Leire Kinge of England and his Three Daughters.' Nothing more is known of this book, which may or may not have been a play. On May 8, 1605, there is entered to Simon Stafford 'a booke called "the Tragecall historie of Kinge Leir and his Three Daughters, &c." as it was latelie Acted.' This was published in 1605 under the title of 'The True Chronicle History of King Leir … As it hath bene divers and sundry times lately acted,' etc. This is not Sh.'s play. In 1608 there appeared: 'M. William Shak-speare: His True Chronicle Historie of the life and death of King Lear and his three daughters,' etc., published by Nath. Butter, 'at the signe of the Pide Bull,' and in the same year another edition, also by Butter (but without place of publication). There has been much discussion as to the priority of these two quartos, which are not identical. The text of *Lear* in the Folio of 1623 seems based on a revised copy of the play. But while Qq contain about 220 lines not in Ff, the latter contain only some 50 not in Qq. The usual modern text is a combination of QqFf.

DATE OF COMPOSITION AND PRODUCTION. The Stationers' Registers prove that the play was produced not later than Dec. 26, 1606. Internal evidence seems to show that it was written not earlier than 1603: Harsnet's book (see below) is dated 1603; notable eclipses of sun and moon occurred in Oct. 1605 (see *Lear*, i, 2, l. 98); and in the old rime 'I smell the blood of an Englishman' 'British' is substituted (iii, 4, l. 175), pointing to the union of 1604.

SOURCES OF THE PLOT. The secondary plot of Gloucester and his sons is manifestly derived from the story related in Sidney's *Arcadia* (1590), bk. ii, c. 10. The main plot is of ancient origin. It may be reasonably supposed that Sh. made use of some or all of the following published works: (*a*) the old play of *King Leir*; (*b*) Holinshed; (*c*) W. Warner's *Albion's England* (1586), iii, 14; (*d*) *The Mirror for Magistrates* (1587); (*e*) Harsnet's *Declaration of Popish Impostures* (1603), in the 'mad scenes'; (*z*) *The Faerie Queene* (1590), II, x, 27–32.

For an elaborate discussion of the pedigree of the story see W. Perrett, *Palaestra*, xxxv (Borlin, 1904).

Le Beau. D.P. *A.Y.L.* ('Le Beu,' Ff, except once.) A courtier attending on Duke Frederick. i, 2] describes the prowess of Charles, the wrestler, to Rosalind and Celia; presents Orlando to them; advises Or. to leave the Court.

Le Bon. A French lord, suitor to Portia. 'God made him, and therefore let him pass for a man' (*M.V.* i, 2).

'Le Bon,' Capell; 'Boun' or 'Boune,' QqFf.

Leda. Dau. of Thestius; she was visited by Jupiter in the form of a swan, and brought forth two eggs, from one of which issued Helen, who, after being wooed by many princely suitors, became wife of Menelaus (Ovid, *Her.* xvii, 55).

'Jupiter [became] a swan for the love of Leda' (*M.W.W.* v, 5); 'Fair L.'s daughter had a thousand wooers' (*Tam. Sh.* i, 2, l. 244).

[Le Despencer, Isabel.] See BEAUCHAMP, R.

Le Fer, Monsieur. D.P. *Hen. V.* 'French soldier' in st. dirs. and pfxs. iv, 4] is taken prisoner by Pistol, who extorts a ransom from him.

Legion. Used as the name of a devil; *cf.* Mark v, 9. 'If L. himself possest him' (*T. Nt.* iii, 4).

Leicester, Town of. Near the centre of Britain, *Rich. III*, v, 2; 'safe in L. town' (*ib.* v, 5); Wolsey's death at L. Abbey, *Hen. VIII*, iv, 2.

Leicestershire. Mtd. *3 Hen. VI*, iv, 8.

[Leir.] A legendary British king (son of Bladud, and contemporary with Joash, King of Judah), whose story as related by Geoffrey of Monmouth (*ob.* 1154) is, practically, the ultimate source of *Lear*. Geoffrey's *Historia Britonum* is based on Nennius (*fl.* 796) and a lost Breton collection of legends. See LEAR, KING.

Lena. See LAENAS.

Lenox, or **Lennox.** Scottish thane, made Earl of L. ('Leuenox') by Malcolm Canmore in 1057 (*Hol.* ii, 176).

D.P. *Macb.* i, 2] in attendance on Duncan. i, 4, 6] *p.m.* ii, 3] describes the portents which occurred on the night of Duncan's murder; visits D.'s chamber with Macbeth; later, describes the condition in which the attendants were found. iii, 1] *p.m.* iii, 4] attends Macbeth at the banquet; indicates as vacant the seat in which M. sees the form of Banquo. iii, 6] in terms of bitter irony hints his suspicions of Macb. iv, 1] informs Macb. of Macduff's flight. v, 2] in the field before Dunsinane. v, 4] *p.m.* v, 7] *p.m.* (not mtd. in Ff).

The spelling 'Lennox' was first introduced by Dyce.

Lent. Annual Christian fast of forty days. 'The licence to kill beasts during L. was one of the ancient modes of favouritism' (Knight).

'What's a joint of mutton or two in a whole L.?' (*2 Hen. IV*, ii, 4); 'The L. shall be as long again as it is; and thou shalt have a licence to kill for a hundred lacking one' (*2 Hen. VI*, iv, 3); 'an old hare hoar Is very good meat in L.' (*Rom. J.* ii, 4).

Lenten, *adj.* 'A good l. answer' (*T. Nt.* i, 5); 'a l. pie' (*Rom. J.* ii, 4); 'l. entertainment' (*Haml.* ii, 2).

[Leo X.] Pope (Giovanni de' Medici); b. 1475; Pope 1513–22. During his pontificate Wolsey was created cardinal. Suffolk says of Wolsey: 'I leave him to him that made him proud, the Pope' (*Hen. VIII*, ii, 2). Since Gardiner had then been appointed secretary (1529), the existing Pope was Clement VII (*q.v.*).

Leonardo. D.P. *M.V.* Servant to Bassanio. ii, 2] in attendance.

'Leonato,' Ff, in st. dir.

Leonato. D.P. *M. Ado.* Governor of Messina. i, 1] welcomes Don Pedro and his train to M. i, 2] hears that Don P. is in love with his d. Hero. (i, 3) mtd. ii, 1] warns his niece Beatrice against being 'shrewd,' if she hopes to be married; accepts Claudio as Hero's suitor; discusses the chances of Beatrice's marriage. (ii, 2) mtd. ii, 3] speaks of Beatrice's (supposed) love for Benedick in the latter's hearing. iii, 2] is privately consulted by Benedick. (iii, 3) mtd. iii, 5] tries vainly to gather the purport of Dogberry's report. iv, 1] hears Claudio's public accusation against Hero, and, believing it, reviles her; is persuaded by Friar Francis that the charge may be false, and vows, in that case, vengeance against those who have made it. (iv, 2) mtd. v, 1] is convinced that 'Hero is belied'; challenges Claudio, but seeks to pacify his brother Antonio; later, listens to Borachio's confession; insists that Claudio shall marry Hero's 'cousin.' (v, 3) mtd. v, 4] concerts the mode of Hero's reappearance; later, presents Hero, veiled, to Claudio and explains the deception.

In Bandello's *Novella*, the corresponding character is Lionato de' Lionati, a gentleman of Messina.

Leonatus. The 'sur-addition' granted to the name of Sicilius, father of Posthumus (see LEONATUS, POSTHUMUS), in recognition of his valour. In plu.: 'put the strength o' th' Leonati in me' (*Cymb.* v, 1); 'the two young L.' (*ib.* v, 4, vision, st. dir.); 'thrown from Leonati [Ff] seat' (*ib. ib.*, vision).

Leonatus, Posthumus. D.P. *Cymb.* 'A Gentleman in love with the Princess [Imogen] and privately married to her' (Rowe). (i, 1) the posthumous son of Sicilius (*q.v.*), taken under Cymbeline's protection, and brought up by him as a virtuous and accomplished gentleman, but on his unauthorized marriage with Imogen being discovered, he is sentenced to banishment. i, 2] in bidding farewell to Imogen, receives a diamond ring from her and gives her a bracelet; will proceed to Rome and reside with Philario, an old comrade of his father; is denounced by Cymb. and departs. i, 5] (at Rome) is led into wagering his ring against ten thousand ducats that Iachimo cannot undermine Imogen's fidelity. (i, 7) Iachimo traduces his character to Imogen, but retracts. (ii, 1) termed by Cloten 'a banish'd rascal.' ii, 4] predicts war between Rome and Britain; is induced to believe that Iachimo has won his wager, and would tear Imogen 'limb-meal.' ii, 5] (*sol.*) utters an unmeasured invective against women. (iii, 2) sends a letter to Pisanio bidding him to kill Imogen. (iii, 4) his letter is read by Im. (iii, 5) Cloten, with a view to murdering him, procures a suit of his garments. (iii, 6; iv, 1) mtd. (iv, 2) Cloten's headless corpse is mourned over as that of Posthumus by Imogen. v, 1] has received from Pisanio a token of Imogen's death; blames Pi. for taking him at his word; deems himself but an instrument of the gods; resolves to assume the garb of a peasant, and fight for his country. v, 2] 'vanquisheth and disarmeth Iachimo, and then leaves him' (Ff); aids Belarius (*q.v.*); 'they rescue Cymbeline.' v, 3] describes the fight; is taken prisoner, as a Roman. v, 4] (in prison) meditates on repentance; has a vision in his sleep; on awaking finds a mysterious tablet upon his breast; is led out to the King. v, 5] after hearing Iachimo's confession, exclaims to Cymb.: 'I am Posthumus that kill'd thy daughter!'; thinking Imogen to be a 'scornful page,' strikes her to the ground; learns the truth, and, as Imogen hangs upon his neck, cries, 'Hang there like fruit, my soul, Till the tree dies!'; forgives Iachimo; learns that he is himself the 'lion's whelp' of the prophetic scroll.

As a Latin adj. the penultimate of 'Posthumus' is short, but the name is accented on the second syllable in *Sh.* with two doubtful exceptions, viz.: i, 1, l. 52, and iv, 2, l. 200. 'Leonatus' is used throughout for 'P.,' wherever the metre calls for it.

Leonatus, Posthumus, Mother of. Appears to him in a vision; *Cymb.* v, 4.

Leonine. D.P. *Per.* 'A murtherer, servant to Dionisia' (Q1). (iv, Gow.) 'L. a murderer.' iv, 1] is ordered by his mistress to kill Marina, and is about to do the deed, when he is scared away by pirates. iv, 2] resolves to declare that he killed her. (iv, 3) mtd. (iv, 4) poisoned by Dionyza.

'Theophilus, Stranguilio's villaine' in *The Patterne of Painefull Adventures* (1576).

Leontes. D.P. *Wint. T.* King of Sicilia. (i, 1) friend of Polixenes from their childhood. i, 2] fruitlessly urges P. to prolong his visit; bids Hermione try to persuade him;

she succeeds, and L., after muttering 'at my request, he would not,' declares, 'thou never spokest to better purpose'; fancies that he observes undue familiarity between Pol. and Herm.; torments himself in questioning his little son; on the withdrawal of P. and H. he lashes himself into furious jealousy; confides his suspicions to Camillo, who refuses to mistrust the Queen; L. orders Cam. to poison Polixenes. ii, 1] hears of the escape of Pol. and Cam.; orders Mamillius to be taken from his mother, and, taxing the latter with unfaithfulness, cries, 'Away with her, to prison'; defends his conduct before his lords; has despatched messengers to the oracle of Apollo. ii, 3] hears that Mamillius is sick; on Paulina bringing him Hermione's newly born infant, orders it, in great wrath, to be 'consum'd with fire,' and afterward – softening somewhat – commands Antigonus to expose it in 'some remote and desart place'; learns that the messengers have returned from Delphos. iii, 2] presides at the trial of Hermione; finds that the oracle declares H. blameless, but scorns the god's reply; the death of Mamillius is announced to him; he recognizes the anger of Apollo; Paulina tells him that the Queen is dead; overcome by remorse and in deep penitence, L. is led away. (iv, Chor.) lives in seclusion. (iv, 4) Camillo assures Florizel that L. will welcome him. v, 1] L. is urged by his courtiers to wed again; Paulina makes him swear never to marry save by her 'free leave'; Florizel and Perdita are presented to him; he hears of Polixenes' arrival. (v, 2) Perdita's identity is revealed to him. v, 3] visits the supposed statue of Hermione, and is reunited to his lost Queen.

In Greene's *Pandosto* the corresponding character is Pandosto, King of Bohemia. A slip of the pen made by Steevens in 1778, to the effect that Egistus was 'Leontes,' has been perpetuated for more than a century (Furness). It may be observed that Steevena' error was perhaps due to the fact that in the novel the Kings of Bohemia and Sicilia change places as husband and supposed lover.

Leopard's Head. See LUBBAR'S HEAD.

Lepidus, M. Aemilius. Praetor 49 B.C.; consul with Caesar, 46. Being near Rome, with troops, at the time of Caesar's assassination, he was able to render efficient aid to M. Antony. He was made Pontifex Maximus (44) and repaired to his provinces in Gaul and Spain. He received Ant. after his defeat at Mutina (43); Octavius soon joined them, and the Triumvirate was formed (Oct. 43). After Philippi L. received Africa as his province. He aided Octavius against Sext. Pompeius (36), but, on endeavouring to obtain Sicily for himself, was deprived of all power and retired to Circeii, being allowed, however, keep the dignity of Pont. Max. He died 13 B.C. (References to Plutarch's account of L., so far as they are relevant, are given below.)

D.P. *Jul. C.* iii, 1] (present at Caesar's assassination) *p.m.* (iii, 2) meets Octavius 'at Caesar's house' (*Plut.* p. 101). iv, 1] consents, as triumvir, to his brother's proscription (*Plut.* p. 169); (Ant. describes him as 'a slight unmeritable man'; Oct. declares him to be a 'valiant soldier'). (iv, 3)mtd.

D.P. *Ant. Cl.* i, 4] in conference with Oct., condones the faults of Ant. (ii, 1) Pompey's opinion of his relation to the other triumvirs. ii, 2] desires Ant. to be entreated 'to soft and gentle speech'; tries to check a rising dispute between Ant. and Oct. ii, 4] converses with Maecenas and Agrippa. ii, 6] present at negotiations with Pompey. ii, 7] becomes helplessly drunk at P.'s banquet. iii, 2] bids Octavius farewell. (iii, 5) 'the poor third is up.' (iii, 6) Oct. on his deposition (*Plut.* p. 202).

Le Roy. Pistol mistakes 'Le roi' for this surname. 'A Cornish name: art thou of Cornish crew?' (*Hen. V*, iv, 1).

Lestrale, Earl of. French noble; mtd. at the council before Agincourt, *Hen. V*, iii, 5; among the slain, *ib.* iv, 8.

The name is given as 'Lestrake,' *Hol.* iii, 555; Harleian MS. 782, f. 48 *verso* (quoted in Nicolas's *Agincourt*, edn. 2, p. 367), also mentions him as 'The Countie de Lestrake' (B.-S. p. 522).

Lethe. River in the underworld, a draught from which conferred on the shades forgetfulness of the past (Ovid, *Pont.* ii, 4; *Trist.* iv, 1); *cf.* Milton, *Par. Lost*, ii, 583 ff. Immersion in L. is non-classical.

'Soft and delicate L.' (*Ant. Cl.* ii, 7); 'L. wharf' (*Haml.* i, 5); 'Let fancy still my sense in L. steep' (*T.Nt.* iv, 1); 'May this be wash'd in L., and forgotten?' (2 *Hen. IV*, v, 2); 'in the L. of thy angry soul Thou drown the sad remembrance' (*Rich. III*, iv, 4, l. 250).

In 'crimson'd in thy lethe' (*Jul. C.* iii, 1) the word possibly means 'death,' Lat. *letum* (improp. *lethum*), *and, if so, would seem to have been coined by Sh. Heywood, The Iron Age*, ii, 3, speaks of Troy as 'extinct in lethe,' but this is doubtfully parallel. Pope in *Jul. C.* reads 'death' (dethe). With a capital in F2, 3, 4.

Leviathan. Not strictly a proper name; the monster described in the Book of Job: 'Canst thou draw out l. with a hook? ... Will he make a convenant with thee?' (Job xli, 1, 4). Henry warns the citizens of Harfleur that it would be as bootless to tell the soldiers to refrain from pillage 'as send precepts to the L. To come ashore' (*Hen. V*, iii, 3); Puck is ordered to return, 'Ere the L. can swim a league' (*M.N.D.* ii, 1).

'The margins of the Bibles in Sh.'s days explained L. as a whale' (Wright).

Lewis (1) (1187–1226). Son of Philip II of France by his wife Isabel of Hainault; married Blanch of Castile, niece of King John (1202). By invitation of the disaffected nobles landed at Stonor, in Kent (1216) (*Hol.* iii, 191), but, lacking support, returned to France the following year. Succeeded to the French throne as Lewis VIII (1223). See DAUPHIN, THE.

D.P. *John.* 'The Dauphin.' ii, 1] bids Arthur welcome 'Austria' at Angiers; is betrothed to Blanch (*Hol.* iii, 161). iii, 1] in spite of his bride's pleadings resolves to take up arms against John. iii, 4] is persuaded by Pandulph to invade England. v, 2] (in his camp at St Edmundsbury) reminds the nobles of their solemn pledge and encourages the wavering Salisbury; though informed by Pandulph ('Gualo,' *Hol.* iii, 192), that John has made submission to Rome, refuses to abandon his enterprise. v, 5] hears that the nobles have deserted him and that his supplies are sunk on the Goodwins.

There is no historical evidence that Lewis was ever at Bury St Edmunds (*q.v.*). The sinking of the 'supply' seems to be an echo of the destruction of the French fleet in the Channel by Hubert de Burgh (*Hol.* iii, 201).

The attribution of the opening speeches of ii, 1, to Philip rather than to Lewis has commended itself to many commentators.

Lewis (2). Eldest son of Charles VI of France; *ob.* 1415, shortly after the Battle of Agincourt, at which he was not present (*Hol.* iii, 552). The story of his derisively sending tennis balls to Henry V (*Hen. V*, i, 2) is thus referred to by Holinshed: 'Whilest … the king laie at Killingworth there came to him from Charles [*sic*] Dolphin of France certeine ambassadors, that brought with them a barrell of Paris balles; which from their maister they presented to him for a token that was taken in verie ill part, as sent in scorne, to signifie, that it was more meet for the king to passe the time with such childish exercise, than to attempt any worthie exploit.' L. presided at the council held to devise measures of defence against the invading English (*Hol.* iii, 547), since 'his father was fallen into his old disease of frensie'; nevertheless he refused aid to Harfleur when it was sorely needed (*Hol.* iii, 550).

D.P. *Hen. V.* 'The Dauphin.' ii, 4] counsels making due preparations to repel the English invasion, but disdains Henry V as a vain and giddy youth; boasts to the English ambassadors of having sent the Paris balls to H. iii, 5] is eager to attack the despised foe, but is commanded by his father to 'stay with us in Rouen.' iii, 7] (the night before Agincourt) brags of the merits of his horse and of the execution he will do on the morrow. iv, 2] is confident of the result of the battle. iv, 5] is overcome with shame at the defeat of the French, and exclaims 'let's stab ourselves.'

Lewis X. In error for 'Lewis IX.' 'King L. also, the tenth, otherwise called Saint L.' (*Hen. V*, i, 2; following *Hol.* iii, 546).

Lewis XI (1423–83). King of France (1461–83); e.s. of Charles VII; during his reign Burgundy, Artois, and Provence were added to the French kingdom. Lewis was first cousin to both Henry VI and Q. Margaret, on his father's and mother's side respectively. He supported Warwick in his quarrel with Edward (IV), but on the victory of the latter made peace with him at Pecquigny (1475). The character of Lewis is best known to English readers as depicted in *Quentin Durward*.

Holinshed (iii, 665) states that Q. Margaret 'did obteine of the yoong French king … that all hir husband's friends, and those of the Lancastriall band,' should have free access into any part of France, to the exclusion 'of the contrarie faction'; Warwick's mission to Lewis is related, *Hol.* iii, 667.

D.P. *3 Hen. VI.* (ii, 6) Warwick impresses on Edward the importance of 'having France thy friend.' iii, 3] receives Q. Margaret and bids her sit by his side; promises her his help; receives Warwick as an envoy from Edward (IV); after hearing Margaret and Oxford in opposition to Edward's proposed match with the Lady Bona, confers with Warwick alone; agrees conditionally to the proposal; learns with indignation that Edward has married 'Lady Grey' and offers five thousand men under Warwick and Oxford for the invasion of England; adding, 'I long till Edward fall by war's mischance.' (iv, 1) L.'s enmity discussed by Edward in council. (v, 7) receives 'the Sicils and Jerusalem' in pawn from Reignier (*q.v.*). Mtd., *Rich. III*, iii, 7, l. 182.

Libya. Λιβύη; anciently denoting Africa in general, or Africa excluding Egypt and Ethiopia.

Florizel declares Perdita 'came from L.' *Wint. T.* v, 1 ('Libia,' 'Lybia,' Ff); 'Were his [Achilles'] brain as barren as banks of L.' (*Tr. Cr.* i, 3); 'Bocchus, King of L.' (*Ant. Cl.* iii, 6; 'Lybia,' Ff).

Lichas. The attendant of Hercules, who brought his master the poisoned shirt, and was hurled by him into the sea (Ovid, *Metam.* ix, 155, etc.).

'If H. and L. play at dice … the greater throw May turn by fortune from the weaker hand' (*M.V.* ii, 1); 'teach me, Alcides … thy rage: Let me lodge L. on the horns o' the moon' (*Ant. Cl.* iv, 12; Warburton compares Seneca, *Hercules Oetaeus*, iii, 817: 'In astra missus fertur, et nubes vago Spargit cruore'). ('Licas,' Ff.)

Licia. For 'Lycia,' a district in Asia Minor, between Caria and Pamphylia, prominently mtd. in the *Iliad*. In the title of the 2nd edn. of *Tr. Cr.* Pandarus is referred to as 'Prince of L.'

Licio. Name assumed by Hortensio (D.P.). *Tam. Sh.* ii, 1; iii, 1, 2; iv, 2 (3).

'Lisio,' iv, 2, FfQ.

Lieutenant of the Tower (1). D.P. *3 Hen. VI.* iv, 6] his apology to King Henry for having been obliged to keep him in ward is very graciously received.

The liberation of the King took place in Oct. 1470. French (p. 201) suggests that this officer was John Tiptoft, E. of Worcester; but this is very doubtful.

Lieutenant of the Tower (2). D.P. *3 Hen. VI.* v, 6] *p.m.*; in attendance on the night of Henry's murder.

John Sutton, Baron Dudley, seems to have been Constable in May 1471, and may be intended; see French, *ut eupra.*

Lieutenant to Aufidius. D.P. *Cor.* iv, 7] arouses A.'s jealousy against Coriolanus.

Ligarius, Quintus. Fought at Thapsus on the side of Pompey; was taken prisoner and banished by Caesar. Cicero made a speech in his defence, which is still extant, and Caesar pardoned him. Ligarius, however, joined the conspirators who murdered Caesar. He is called 'Caius L.' in *Plut.* (p. 113), and this error is followed by Sh.

D.P. *Jul. C.* 'Caius L.' ii, 1] Metellus reminds the conspirators that 'Caius Ligarius doth bear Caesar hard,' and is desired by Brutus 'to send him but hither'; Ligarius enters, though 'a sick man,' and eagerly joins in the plot. ii, 2] Caes. condoles with him on his ague. (ii, 3) Artemidorus desires to warn Caesar that he has 'wronged C. L.' (Ligarius is not mtd. as present at the assassination).

Light o' Love. Name of a dance tune. 'Goes without a burden; do you sing it, and I'll dance it' (*M. Ado*, iii, 4); cf. *T.G.V.* v, 1, 2.

'Strictly a ballet, to be sung and danced' (Chappell, *Pop. Mus. of the Olden Time*, pp. 222–4).

[**Lily**, or **Lyly, William** (*c.* 1468–1522).] Grammarian; his elementary works on Latin grammar for more than three centuries formed the basis of Latin teaching in English schools. A passage from Horace twice given by Lyly is quoted, *T. And.* iv, 2, with the comment 'I read it in the grammar long ago'; William's examination, *M.W.W.* iv, 1, is based on the first two pages. 'Homo is a common name' (*1 Hen. IV*, ii, 1), 'diluculo surgere,' etc. (*T. Nt.* ii, 3), and 'vir sapit,' etc. (*L.L.L.* iv, 2) are all found in the grammar, while 'redime to captum,' etc. (*Tam. Sh.* i, 1) is a reading of a passage in Terence (*Eun.* i, 1) peculiar to Lyly. Other probable references occur; see *Sh. Eng.* i, 230–2.

Limander. Apparently a blunder of Bottom's for 'Leander'; *M.N.D.* v, 1.

Limbo. Limbus Patrum, 'the borderland' (of hell), where the spirits of the righteous who were born before Christ's death were confined until the descent into hell; identified with the 'prison' of 1 Pet. iii, 18–20.

As a cant term for a prison: 'I have some of them in L. Patrum' (*Hen. VIII*, v, 4). As an equivalent of 'hell': 'talked of Satan, and of L., and of furies' (*All's Well*, v, 3); 'Tartar L., worse than hell' (*Com. Err.* iv, 2); 'as far from help as L. is from bliss' (*T. And.* iii, 1, l. 149).

Limehouse. A parish on the Thames, forming part of Stepney till 1730. Probably so named from its lime-kilns, or 'lyme oasts.' Only occurs in the phrase 'limbs of L.' *i.e.* riotous frequenters of the theatre, *Hen. VIII*, v, 4.

The suggestion of certain early commentators that L. was notorious for the quarrels between various religious sects, having places of worship there, is unsubstantiated.

Lincoln Washes. The Wash, and adjoining flats. Philip the Bastard laments that 'these Lincoln-Washes [Ff] have devoured' half his forces (*John*, v, 6).

'The king hasted forward till he came to Wellestreme sands, where passing the washes he lost a great part of his armie' (*Hol.* iii, 194).

Lincoln, Bishop of. See LONGLAND, JOHN.

Lincolnshire. Attrib.: 'As melancholy as ... the drone of a L. bagpipe' (*1 Hen. IV*, i, 2).

'At a Christmas time ... amongst all the pleasures provided, a noyse of minstrells and a L. bagpipe was prepared' (R. Armin, *A Nest of Ninnies* (1608)) (Malone). (Steevens believed the term to be used metaphorically for the croak of a frog.)

Lingare. ('Lingard,' *Hol.* iii, 546.) Supposed ancestress of Hugh Capet. 'L., daughter to Charlemaine' (*Hen. V*, i, 2).

'Inger,' Qq.

Lion. See SNUG.

Lionel of Antwerp. 1st D. of Clarence (1338–68); 3rd s. of Edw. III; married (*a*) Elizabeth de Burgh, (*b*) Violante, d. of Galeazzo Visconti, lord of Pavia. His g.g.d., Anne Mortimer, married Richard, E. of Cambridge. Richard Plantagenet's 'grandfather was L. Duke of Clarence,' third son to Edw. III, *1 Hen. VI*, ii, 4; 'Mortimer' claims to be 'derived' from him, *ib.* ii, 5; York claims the crown through him, *2 Hen. VI*, ii, 2; Cade claims descent from him, *ib.* iv, 2, 4.

Lipsbury. '*Kent* [in the guise of a churl, to Oswald]. If I had thee in Lipsbury pinfold, I would make thee care for me' (*Lear*, ii, 2). No place of the name is known, and the allusion remains unexplained. Nares, however, suggests that the phrase simply means 'the teeth.'

Lisbon. Capital of Portugal; mtd., as a place of trade, *M.V.* iii, 2.

Lisle, Lord (*ob.* 1453). Son of John Talbot, E. of Shrewsbury (*q.v.*). Killed by his father's side at Castillon – not at Bordeaux, as related in *1 Hen. VI*.

D.P. *1 Hen. VI*. 'John Talbot.' (iv, 3) travels to join his father, whom he has not seen for seven years. iv, 5] (before Bordeaux) his father urges him to flee, that 'part of thy father may be saved in thee,' but he refuses. iv, 6] hemmed in by the foe, is again urged to escape, in order to preserve the house, but again declares that rather will he 'die at Talbot's foot.' (iv, 7) his corpse is borne in; Joan of Arc declares that he disdained to fight with her. Cf. *Hol.* iii, 640.

The E. of Shrewsbury was succeeded by his son John, who was killed at the Battle of Northampton (1460).

Livia (1). Wife of Octavius (Augustus) (*Plut.* p. 226). 'Some nobler token I have kept apart For L.' (*Ant. Cl.* v, 2).

Livia (2). A guest; mtd. *Rom. J.* i, 2.

Lodovico. D.P. *Oth.* 'Kinsman to Brabantio.' iv, 1] hands despatches to Othello from the Venetian Senate, recalling him; reproaches Oth., who, in the height of his passion, strikes Desdemona in his presence; converses with Iago on Oth.'s apparent madness. iv, 3] withdraws with Oth., after an interview; (Desd. thinks him 'a proper man'). v, 1] finds Cassio lying wounded, and is present when Roderigo is stabbed by Iago. v, 2] produces letters found in R.'s pocket revealing Iago's plot; announces Othello's supersession by Cassio, and orders him to be put under arrest; on Othello's stabbing himself, tells the 'Spartan dog,' Iago, that all is his work, and bids the governor put the 'hellish villain' to torture.

There is no corresponding character in Cinthio's novel.

Lodowick. A commander mtd. by Parolles; *All's Well*, iv, 3.

Lodowick, Friar. Name assumed by Vincentio in disguise; *M. for M.* v, 1.

Lodovico, *It.* form of Lewis; *Ger.* Ludwig.

Lombard Street. See LUMBERT STREET.

Lombardy. A district formerly comprising most of the great plain of N. Italy. 'Fruitful L., The pleasant garden of great Italy' (*Tam. Sh.* i, 1).

London. Occurs only in the Histories; *cf.* 'Lud.' The Dauphin welcomed in L., *John*, v, 1; Richard II enters L. as a prisoner, *Rich. II*, iii, 3, 4, v, 2; L. streets, *ib.* v, 5; heads of rebels sent thither, *ib.* v, 6; traders riding thither with fat purses, *1 Hen. IV*, i, 2; 'L. road,' in Kent (*ib.* ii, 1); 'proud L.' (*2 Hen. IV*, i, 3); Davy hopes to see L. ere he die, *ib.* v, 3; 'would I were in an alehouse in L.' (*Hen. V*, iii, 2); L.'s greeting to the victorious Henry, *ib.* v, Chor.; in times of riot, *1 Hen. VI*, iii, 1; Cade's forces march thither, *2 Hen. VI*, iv, 3; Hen. loved in L., *ib.* v, 2.

London Bridge. The only bridge across the Thames at London until Westminster Bridge was built (1738). In the 15th cent. it formed a street, with houses on each side; in 1503 the houses on the N. side were burnt (as also in 1632 and 1666). It was finally demolished in 1758, the houses having been removed about seventy years before. The heads of traitors were exposed, at first over the drawbridge (which occupied one of the arches to admit of the passage of ships), and later over the bridge gate at Southwark.

(D. of Gloucester to Bp. of Winchester) 'Thou laid'st a trap to take my life ... at L.B.' (*1 Hen. VI*, iii, 1; cf. *Hol.* iii, 591); 'Jack Cade hath gotten L.B.' (*2 Hen. VI*, iv, 4); '*Cade*. Go and set L.B. on fire' (*ib.* iv, 6; for the fighting on this occasion see *Hol.* iii, 635).

Referred to as 'the bridge,' *Rich. III*, iii, 2, l. 72.

Londoners. *Hen. VIII*, i, 2, l. 154: 'What was the speech among the L. concerning the French journey.'

London Stone. A block of colitic limestone built into the S. wall of St Swithin's Church, Cannon Street, in 1798, after other removals. Probably a Roman milestone from which distances along the great roads were measured.

Jack Cade 'entred into London, cut the ropes of the drawbridge, and strooke his sword on London stone, saying "Now is Mortimer Lord of this city" ' (*Hol.* iii, 634).

The episode mtd., *2 Hen. VI*, iv, 6, where it is added that Cade sat on the stone to issue orders. [**Long, Henry.**] Sheriff of Wiltshire in 1483. D.P. *Rich. III*. v, 1] conducts Buckingham to execution.

Historically, Buckingham was betrayed to John Mitton, Sheriff of Shropshire.

Longaville. D.P. *L.L.L.* A lord attending upon the King of Navarre. i, 1] readily consents to take the oath of asceticism proposed by the King. ii, 1] considers Maria 'a most sweet lady.' iv, 3] believing himself alone, reads a sonnet addressed to his mistress, in which he argues that since she is a goddess, and not a woman, he is not perjured – and that even if he breaks his oath it is through no fault of his; he is overheard and rebuked by the King. (v, 2) sends verses and pearls to Maria. v, 2] disguised as a Russian, exchanges banter with the masked Katharine, whom he mistakes for M.; later, in his proper habit, joins in jeering Holofernes and Armado; is willing to wait patiently during a twelvemonth for Maria.

Both the spelling and pronunciation of the name were unsettled. It is 'Longavill' and 'Longavile' in the early edns. – riming respectively with 'ill' and 'mile' – but Katharine (v, 2, l. 273) puns on it as 'Longa-veal.' The modern form is due to Pope, but 'Longueville' is the historical original.

Longespé, William de, Earl of Salisbury (*ob.* 1226). Natural son of Henry II and 'Fair Rosamund'; married the heiress of William, Earl of Salisbury, and succeeded to his father in-law's title: served in the 3rd Crusade; joined the army of the Dauphin (*Hol.* iii, 192), but returned to his allegiance under Henry III. Doubtfully identical with:

D.P. *John*. (In the *Tr. R.* called 'Thomas Plantaginet, Earle of S.') i, 1] *p.m.* iii, 1] acts as an emissary to Constance from John. iv, 2] protests against the King's second coronation, and suspects foul play with regard to Arthur. iv, 3] informs Pembroke that he has been in communication with the Dauphin; discovers Arthur's body; vows to avenge the apparent murder, and accuses Hubert of the deed; sets out to join the Dauphin. v, 2] declares that it grieves his soul to join in the revolt. v, 4] on hearing Melun's revelations, resolves to submit to John. v, 7] is present at the King's death, and offers homage to Prince Henry.

The corresponding character in *Tr. R.* is not 'Earl of Salisbury,' but merely 'Thomas of Lancaster.' 'Longsword' is, however, clearly intended.

[**Longland, John** (1473–1547).] Bp. of Lincoln; confessor to Henry VIII; denied the legality of Henry's marriage to Katharine of Arragon (*Hol.* iii, 906).

D.P. *Hen. VIII*. ii, 4] (at the court held at Blackfriars) admits that he counselled the King to obtain a divorce from Katharine.

Long Lane. Name of a road; *Tam. Sh.* iv, 3.

Longsword, W. See LONGESPÉ.

Loraine. See LORRAINE.

Lord, A (1). D.P. *All's Well*. iii, 1] in attendance on the Duke of Florence.

Lord, A (2). D.P. *L.L.L.* ii, 1] in attendance.

Lord, A (3). D.P. *Rich. II*. iv, 1] challenges Aumerle (Qq, omitted in Ff).

Lord, A (4). D.P. *Tam. Sh.* Ind. 1] returning from the chase, finds Sly, a tinker, lying on the ground in a drunken sleep; directs that Sly should be borne to the fairest chamber in his house, and be told on awaking that he is really a lord who has long been lunatic; instructs a company of players to perform a play that night; orders his page to feign to be the supposed lord's wife. Ind. 2] disguised as a servant, on Sly's awaking, entreats him to cast off his strange lunacy, and assures him that his every command shall be obeyed.

In *The Taming of A Shrew*, st. dir., 'a nobleman'; he tells Sly that his name is Simon.

Lord, A (5). D.P. *Macb.* iii, 6] describes to Lenox the kindly reception of Malcolm and Macduff at the English Court, and the refusal of the latter to obey Macb.'s summons.

It is probable that this unnamed character is either Angus or Ross.

Lord, British. D.P. *Cymb.* v, 3] Posthumus describes to him the valiant action of Belarius and his two 'sons.'

'Britaine Lord,' Ff.

Lord, First (1). D.P. *A. Y. L.* Attendant on Duke Senior. ii, 1] recounts Jaques' soliloquy on the wounded stag.

Lord, First (2). D.P. *A. Y. L.* Attendant on Duke Frederick. ii, 2] reports Celia's flight.

Lord, Roman. D.P. *T. And.* v, 3] begs Lucius to relate the tragic tale of Titus to the nobles. (Thus in Qq; in Ff 'Goth.')

Lord, Scottish. Suitor to Portia. 'He borrowed a box of the ear of the Englishman' (*M.V.* i, 2, Qq).

'The other lord' (Ff); probably altered in the acting copies to avoid giving offence to James I.

Lord, Second. D.P. *A. Y. L.* Attendant on D. Frederick. ii, 2] reports Hisperia's conjecture about her mistress.

Lord, Sicilian. D.P. *Wint. T.* ii, 1] informs Leontes of the escape of Polixenes and Camillo; would stake his life that 'the Queen is spotless.' ii, 3] beseeches Leontes to spare the infant (Perdita). iii, 2] in attendance when the oracle of Apollo is read; rebukes Paulina for her boldness of speech.

Not distinguished from 'other Lords' in 'The Names of the Actors' (Ff).

'The character of this speaker is delineated with so much moral beauty throughout ... that in the play of any other dramatist it would assume name and shape as a person of importance' (Cowden-Clarke).

Lord, The. Used to denote God, or Christ. (Frequent, especially in exclamations and invocations, without the article.)

In 'for the L.'s sake' (*M. for M.* iv, 3; referring to the begging of alms by prisoners); 'the L.'s anointed temple' (*Macb.* ii, 3; cf. *Rich. III*, iv, 4); 'L. have mercy,' 'the L.'s tokens' (*L.L.L.* v, 2; in allusion to the plague); 'O Lord, sir' (*All's Well*, ii, 2 (8); in derision of a cant phrase); 'in the bowels of the L.' (*Hen. V*, ii, 4); etc.

Lords. Attendant on Cymbeline. D.PP. *Cymb.* iii, 5] are instructed to escort Lucius.

Lords, Several. D.PP. *All's Well.* ii, 3] are presented to Helena for her to make 'frank election' from.

Lords, Two (1). D.PP. *All's Well.* ii, 1] urge Bertram to accompany them to the wars. iii, 6] concert the discomfiture of Parolles. iv, 1] (1st Lord only) superintends the seizure of P. iv, 3] they discuss Bertram's conduct; listen to P.'s scandalous accusations against them.

It appears, from iv, 3, that the Lords are brothers, named Dumain.

Lords, Two (2). D.PP. *Cymb.* i, 2] the 1st flatters Cloten on the result of his encounter with Posthumus, and belittles Imogen's good sense; the 2nd, in a series of asides, derides Cl. and his companion. ii, 1] the 1st consoles Cl. with regard to a quarrel at bowls, and tells him an Italian stranger has come to Court; the 2nd sneers covertly as before, and soliloquizes on Imogen's sad fate.

Lorenza. Name applied to Jessica; *M.V.* v, 1, l. 42, in Ff2, 3, 4. (Prob. a printer's error perpetuated.)

Lorenzo. D.P. *M.V.* 'In love with Jessica.' i, 1] complains, jestingly, that Gratiano never lets him speak. ii, 4] plans, with his friends, a masque as a farewell entertainment for Bassanio; receives a letter from Jessica, and thereupon declares that he is 'provided of a torchbearer' for the masque; confides to Gratiano his plan of elopement with J. that night. ii, 6] receives a casket from J., and, accompanied by Salarino, hastens away with her. (ii, 8) his escape with J. in a gondola reported. iii, 2] arrives at Belmont with J., having been induced by Salerio to turn aside thither; they are welcomed by Portia. iii, 4] dilates to P. on Antonio's merits; is desired by P. to undertake 'the husbandry and manage' of Belmont during her absence. iii, 5] (at Belmont) is too hungry to relish Launcelot's jesting; listens to J.'s eulogy of Portia, and humorously applies it to himself. v, 1] in sportive alternation with J. lauds the moonlight night and its associations; hears that Portia is close at hand; summons the musicians; dilates on the glory of the heavens and on 'the sweet power of music'; welcomes P. home. Mtd., ii, 2, 3; iv, 1, 2.

L. finds no friends among the critics. 'As for Lorenzo, he is an accomplice in a most infamous burglary, and under Prussian laws he would have been condemned to fifteen years in the penitentiary, and to be branded, and to stand in the pillory, for all his sensibility to the alluring charms, not only of stolen ducats and jewels, but of moonlit landscapes and of music' (Heine, *Sämmtliche Werke* (1856), v, 325; transld. Furness, *Var.*).

Lorraine, or **Loraine.** Charles, D. of L., mtd. *Hen. V*, i, 2 (2), as being 'sole heir male ... of Charles the Great'; cf. *Hol.* iii, 546.

Louis. See Lewis.

Louvre. A castle in Paris of the kings of France from the 13th cent. (The existing building was begun in 1541.) 'He'll make your Paris L. shake for it' (*Hen. V*, ii, 4); 'An English courtier may be wise, And never see the L.' (*Hen. VIII*, i, 3).

Love. Personified. (*a*) *Masc.* (for 'Cupid'). 'L. is your master, for he masters you' (*T.G.V.* i, 1); 'a mighty lord' (*ib.* ii, 4); 'the boy L. is perjur'd everywhere,' etc. (*M.N.D.* i, 1); 'lord L.' (*M.V.* ii, 9); 'L.'s keen arrows' (*A.Y.L.* iii, 5); 'L., no god that would not extend his might' (*All's Well*, i, 3); 'imperial L., that god most high' (ii, 3); 'L. so gentle in his view' (*Rom. J.* i, 1); 'L.'s weak childish bow' (*ib. ib.*); 'L. keeps his revels' (*V.A.* 123); mtd., *ib.* 243–6; 'L.'s golden arrow' (*ib.* 947); 'L. is a babe' (*Son.* cxv); 'thou blind fool L.' (*ib.* cxxxvii); 'L. is too young to know what conscience is' (*ib.* cli).

(*b*) *Fem.* (for 'Venus'). 'Forerun fair L., strewing her way with flowers' (*L.L.L.* iv, 3); 'the love of L. and her soft hours' (*Ant. Cl.* i, 1; doubtful); Venus thus named, *V.A.* 814; 'L. lacked a dwelling and made him her place' (*L.C.* 82).

(*c*) Indeterminate. 'When L. speaks,' etc. (*L.L.L.* iv, 3); 'L. is a spirit all compact of fire' (*V.A.* 149); 'L.'s eyes' (*ib.* 632); 'L. to heaven is fled,' etc. (*ib.* 803 ff.); 'L. and Fortune be my gods' (*Lucr.* 351); 'L.'s own hand' (*Son.* cxlv); 'O, cunning L.' etc. (*ib.* cxlviii).

Love, Monsieur. Nonce-name applied to Claudio by Benedick; *M. Ado*, ii, 3, l. 38.

Love, Signior. Nonce-name applied to Orlando by Jaques; *A.Y.L.* iii, 2, l. 310.

Lovel, Sir Francis (1454–*c.* 1487). 9th Baron L. of Tichmarsh, Northants; Viscount L. 1483. Chamberlain to Rich. III. He was 'Lovell our dog' of Collingbourne's rimes, an allusion which the writer thus explained: 'Lord Lovel barkt and byt whom Richard would, Whom I therefore did rightly terme a dog.'

D.P. *Rich. III.* 'Lord Lovel.' iii, 4] with Ratcliffe, he takes Hastings into custody. iii, 5] brings in the head of H.; is sent to Dr Shaw.

There is a story that after the Battle of Stoke (1487) L. escaped and took refuge at Minster-Lovel, Oxfordshire, where a skeleton, presumed to be his, was found about 1708 with indications that he had been starved to death (French, p. 231).

Lovell, Sir Thomas (*ob.* 1524). Speaker of the House of Commons; fought for Richmond at Bosworth; made Chancellor of the Exchequer for life 1485; President of the Council 1502; Constable of the Tower 1509. Mtd. (*Rich. III*, iv, 4) as being under arms with Marq. Dorset; but it appears (B.-S. p. 403) that this statement (*Hol.* iii, 743) is due to a mistranslation of Polydore Vergil (p. 551), and that the name should here be 'Rowell.'

D.P. *Hen. VIII.* i, 2] in council; his head declared to have been in danger. i, 3] converses on the extravagance of 'our travell'd gallants,' and its remedy. i, 4] superintends Wolsey's banquet to the King. ii, 1] conducts Buckingham, after his trial, 'to the water side,' thence to be conveyed to the Tower (acc. *Hol.* iii, 763, Sir T.L. landed him at the Temple stairs). iii, 2; v, 1] in attendance.

Lover's Complaint, A. A poem of 343 lines bearing this title was appended by Thorpe to his 1609 edn. of the *Sonnets*. Its style is generally regarded as un-Shakespearean. Its authorship has been fully discussed by J. W. Mackail, in the English Association's *Essays and Studies* for 1912, and by Sir S. Lee in his introduction to the Clar. Press facsimile of the *Sonnets*.

Its subject is the pathetic lament of a girl who has been deceived by her lover.

Love's Labour's Lost.
PUBLICATION. 'A pleasant Conceited Comedie called, Loues labors lost. As it was presented before her Highnes this last Chistmas. Newly corrected and augmented By W. Shakespere,' was published by C. Burby, 1598, in quarto. An earlier edn. seems indicated, but none is extant. The Folio text of 1623 closely copies the Q, correcting a few of its very numerous errors; the acts, but not the scenes, are numbered.

DATE OF COMPOSITION. Not ascertained; but the play is widely held to be Sh.'s earliest dramatic production. The most direct evidence on the subject is afforded by a poem entitled *Alba*, by R.[obert] T.[ofte], 1598, beginning: 'Love's Labor Lost, I once did see a Play, Ycleped so,' a phrase that seems to imply a considerable lapse of time since the production.

TITLE. 'Loues labors lost,' Q; 'Loues Labour's lost,' F1; 'Loues Labour's lost,' F2; 'Love's Labour's lost,' F2 onward; 'Loue labors lost,' Meres; 'Loues Labour lost,' F1 in Catalogue of the plays.

SOURCE OF THE PLOT. Appears to be entirely Sh.'s invention. Details of characterization and dialogue are reminiscent of John Lyly's *Endimion*. (See ARMADO, MOTH, HOLOFERNES.) Act V, Scene 2, may allude to the visit of a Russian embassy to Elizabeth in 1584.

[**Love labours wonne.**] A play attributed to Sh. by F. Meres in his *Palladis Tamia* (1598). Has been identified with *All's Well* and *Tam. Sh.*

Love's Martyr. See PHOENIX AND THE TURTLE, THE.

Lowine, John. Mtd. as 'a principal actor' in F1.

Lubbar's Head. Quickly's perversion of 'Leopard's Head,' an inn in Lombard Street *2 Hen. IV*, ii, 1. ('Lubbers,' Q.)

Lucchese. See LUCCICOS.

Luccicos, Marcus. *Oth.* i, 3; 'most probably a Greek soldier of Cyprus, an Estradiot, one who from his local knowledge was able to give the Duke information' (Knight).

Unnecessarily changed to 'Lucchese' by Capell.

Luce. D.P. *Com. Err.* Servant to Adriana. iii, 1] refuses admission to her master, supposing him to be already within.

Lucentio (1). D.P. *Tam. Sh.* Son to Vincentio. i, 1] arrives at Padua with his servant Tranio, to pursue his studies; overhears a discussion between Baptista Minola, his daughters, and their suitors, and falls in love, at first sight, with the younger sister, Bianca; in order to gain access to Bi. (who is to live in seclusion until her sister is married), resolves that Tranio shall pose as his master while he himself will act the part of a tutor (under the name 'Cambio'). i, 2] is engaged by Gremio to act as tutor to Bi., and promises to use his position to plead for his patron. ii, 1] is accepted by Baptista, on Gremio's recommendation, as a tutor in languages for Bi. iii, 1] makes love to Bi. under pretence of teaching her Latin; wrangles with the music-master (Hortensio in disguise). iii, 2] briefly discusses plans with Tranio. iv, 2] is rid of Hortensio as a rival; agrees to Tr.'s scheme of passing off a Pedant as Vincentio. iv, 4] is informed that 'the old priest at Saint Luke's church' is at his command at all hours. v, 1] flees to the church with Bi.; later, meets Vincentio, acknowledges him as father, and admits to Baptista that he and Bi. are married. v, 2] presides at a banquet in his own house; loses a wager with Petruchio on the relative obedience of their wives, and concludes that it is 'a harsh hearing, when women are froward.'

The corresponding character in *The Taming of A Shrew* is Aurelius, s. to Jerobel and suitor to Philema, and in *I Suppositi* Eostrato, s. to Filogono and suitor to Polinesta.

Lucentio (2). A person mtd. by Capulet; *Rom. J.* i, 5.

Lucetta. D.P. *T.G.V.* 'Waiting-woman to Julia' (F1). i, 2] declares Proteus to be the best of all her mistress's suitors, and excuses his reticence; produces a letter from him for J. which had been handed to her by 'Valentine's page'; (J. refuses to take it); later, L. drops the letter, and, having thus again attracted J.'s attention to it, hands it to her; J. tears it, and dismisses her; later, L. is told that she may now take up the papers if she will (J. having already picked out the fragments containing tell-tale phrases). ii, 7] consulted as to her mistress's contemplated journey to Milan, seeks in vain to discourage her; is entrusted by J. with the disposal of all that is hers during her absence.

Luciana. D.P. *Com. Err.* 'Sister to Adriana.' ii, 1] counsels her sister to be patient, and not to fret at her husband's absence, ii, 2] deprecates her brother-in-law's apparent neglect. iii, 2] meets Ant. Syr. and gently chides him for his supposed neglect of her sister; is amazed when he declares his love for herself alone. iv, 2] tells Adriana what has happened. iv, 4] is present when her brother-in-law is bound as a lunatic. v, 1] defends her sister against Aemilia's aspersions, and advices the former to appeal to the Duke.

There is no corresponding character in the *Menaechmi* of Plautus.

Lucianus. D.P. *Haml.* A character in the play presented before Claudius, *Haml.* iii, 2; he pours poison in the ear of the sleeping Gonzago.

Lucifer. 'The day-star'; name applied to Satan, from an erroneous interpretation of Isaiah xiv, 12, 'How art thou fallen from heaven, O Lucifer, son of the morning!' which really refers to the King of Babylon. *Cf.* Chaucer, *C. T.*, Group B, l. 3194: 'O Lu.! brightest of angels alle.'

'L. take all!' (*M.W.W.* i, 3); 'Thou art more deep damn'd than Prince L.' (*John*, iv, 3); 'Glendower made L. cuckold' (*1 Hen. IV*, ii, 4); 'Bardolph's face is L.'s privy-kitchen' (*2 Hen. IV*, ii, 4); 'though he be as good a gentleman as L. and Belzebub' (*Hen. V*, iv, 7; cf. *Lear*, iii, 4); 'He falls like L., Never to hope again' (*Hen. VIII*, iii, 2, l. 371).

Lucilius (1). D.P. *Timon.* 'Servant to Timon.' i, 1] he is enabled by his master's munificence to wed the maiden of his choice.

Lucilius (2). 'One of Brutus' friends,' who later became faithful to Antony (*Plut.* p. 214).

D.P. *Jul. C.* 'A friend to Brutus and Cassius.' iv, 2] informs Br. that he has observed a lack of geniality in C.'s manner; is sent with orders to the commanders. iv, 3] *p.m.* v, 1] converses apart with Brutus. v, 3] *p.m* v, 4] on being made prisoner at Philippi, declares that he is Br., and offers his captors money to kill him; Antony recognizes him, and bids his soldiers treat him with all courtesy; tells Ant. that, dead or alive, Br. will be found 'like himself.' v, 5] on the discovery of the body of Br. exclaims, 'thou hast proved Lucilius' saying true' (cf. *Plut.* p. 149).

Lucillius. Mtd. in the initial st. dir., *Ant. Cl.* i, 2, but is not a speaking character. The only known bearer of the name is an epigrammatist of the Anthology; perhaps a mere variant of 'Lucilius.'

Lucina. 'She who brings to light'; a surname of both Juno and Diana; the goddess of childbirth.

'L. lent me not her aid, but took me in my throes' (*Cymb.* v, 4); 'at whose conception (till L. reign'd) Nature this dowry gave' (*Per.* i, 1); 'L., O divinest patroness, and midwife, gentle To those that cry by night' (*ib.* iii, 1).

Lucio (1). D.P. *M. for M.* i, 2] while engaging in ribald raillery with two friends, is concerned to hear that his friend Claudio is arrested. i, 3] meets Cl. in custody, and consents to ask Isabella to intercede for her brother to the Deputy. i, 5] visits Is., and lays Claudio's case before her. ii, 2] escorts Is. to Angelo; repeatedly encourages her to press her petition with more warmth. iii, 2] refuses to bail Pompey; in converse with 'friar Lodowick' (the disguised Duke), reprobates Angelo's severity; declares he was an 'inward' of the Duke, who was 'a shy fellow' and a libertine, and is challenged by 'the friar' to make good his accusation if the Duke returns. v, 1] frequently interrupts the Duke's examination of Isabella and Mariana; declares that 'a meddling friar' spoke ill of the Duke in his absence; later, is confronted with the Duke in his friar's habit, and reiterates his charges; the Duke reveals his identity and condemns him to marry a woman he has wronged; but 'marrying a punk,' L. declares, is 'pressing to death, whipping and hanging.'

In the 'Names of the Actors' given in F1, L. is described as 'a fantastic.' Sir T. Overbury, *Char.* (1613), defines the term: 'A Phantastique, An improvident young Gallant.' The complex character of L. has been diversely interpreted by critics. Dissolute, callous, impudent; yet witty, capable of sincero friendship, and imperturbable even when condemned to death, he cannot be curtly dismissed as the 'infamous slanderer and liar' of Gervinus; rather is he 'both vicious and voluptuous through frivolity ... without being intentionally wicked' (Ulrici, ii, 161).

Lucio (2). Name of an invited guest; *Rom. J.* i, 2.

Lucius (1). D.P. *Timon.* 'A lord, and flatterer of T.' i, 2] presents T. with four horses; mtd. as being likely to lend T. money. iii, 2] is asked for a loan, but regrets his inability to comply; discusses Timon's difficulties.

Lucius (2). D.P. *Timon.* Servant of Lucius (1). iii, 4] applies, fruitlessly, to T. for payment of the debt due to his master.

He is addressed as Lucius, being, in common with the other servants, known by his master's name.

Lucius (3). D.P. *Jul. C.* 'Servant to Brutus.' ii, 1] brings Br. a paper found near his window; consults a calendar; admits the conspirators; falls asleep; is aroused, and admits Ligarius. ii, 4] is sent on a vague errand to Br. by Portia. iv, 2] *p.m.* iv, 3] brings Br. wine; sleeps while the ghost of Caesar appears to Brutus.

Lucius (4). For 'Lucius Antonius' (*q.v.*); *Ant. Cl.* i, 2.

Lucius (5). For 'Caius Lucius' (*q.v.*). *Cymb.* iii, 4, 5, 7; v, 3. For Lucius, a British king, see Spenser, *F.Q.* II, x, 53.

Lucius (6). D.P. *T. And.* 'Son to Titus Andronicus.' i, 2] demands 'the proudest prisoner of the Goths' as a sacrifice for the *manes* of his brothers; later, reports the immolation of Alarbus; aids Bassianus in carrying off Lavinia; laments over his brother Mutius, slain by Titus; later, asks pardon of Saturninus. ii, 2, 4] *p.m.* iii, 1] resolves to flee to the Goths and lead a power against Saturninus. v, 1] addresses his army of Goths; offers to spare Aaron's child if the Moor will divulge the truth; welcomes the envoy from Rome. v, 3] kills Saturninus; is hailed emperor; gives orders for the bestowal of the bodies of the dead and the punishment of the Moor.

Lucius (7). D.P. *T. And.* A boy, son to Lucius (6). iii, 2] would see his aunt, Lavinia, made merry. iv, 1] fears that Lavinia, who pursues him with his books, is mad; finds that she wishes to indicate a passage in Ovid; vows to avenge her when he is a man. iv, 2] presents a bundle of arrows, from Titus, to the sons of Tamora. iv, 3] *p.m.*; shoots arrows in the air at Titus' bidding. v, 3] laments his grandfather's death.

'Young L.' in st. dirs.

Lucius Antonius. Brother of Mark Antony; consul 41 B.C. In Antony's absence, instigated by Fulvia (*q.v.*), he made war on Octavius (*Plut.* p. 178). Mtd. *nt. Cl.* i, 2; ii, 2.

Lucrece, [The Rape of].

Publication. In the Stationers' Registers, under date May 1594, there is 'Entred to Master Harrison, senior, under hand of Master Cawood Warden, a book intituled the Ravyshement of Lucrece.' In the same year there appeared: 'Lucrece. Printed by Richard Field, for John Harrison, and are to be sold at the signe of the white Greyhound in Paules Church-yard. 1594.' The poem contains 1855 lines in seven-line stanzas, 'rime-royal.' Editions followed in 1598, 1600, 1607, 1616, and later.

Sources. The tragic story of Lucrece lay ready to Sh.'s hand in Ovid, *Fasti*, ii (not translated before 1640); in Livy, i, 57–59 (freely translated in Painter's *Palace of Pleasure*), in Lydgate's *Fall of Princes*, in Gower's *Confessio Amantis*, and in Chaucer's *Legend of Good Women.* Echoes of S. Daniel's *Complaint of Rosamond* and of Lodge's *Scilla* have also been remarked in the poem (see Lee, *Life of Sh.* pp. 146–7).

The dedication to Lord Southampton is written in a more intimate style than that of *Venus and Adonis*, to the same nobleman, and this is followed by an 'Argument,' presumably written by Sh. himself, and remarkable as his only existing non-dramatic prose composition (apart from the Dedications).

Lucrece. A shortened form of 'Lucretia,' wife of L. Tarquinius Collatinus; her violation by Sextus Tarquinius and subsequent suicide were said to have led to the establishment of the Roman republic. L. became a type of chastity, and it appears that her portrait was common on signet-rings. The story of L. was the subject of Sh.'s second poem, publd. 1594.

Malvolio recognizes the impression of Olivia's signet, being 'her L., with which she uses to seal' (*T. Nt.* ii, 5); 'silence, like a Lucrece knife, with bloodless stroke my heart doth gore' (*ib. ib.*); 'she [Katharina] will prove ... Roman L. for her chastity' (*Tam. Sh.* ii, 1); 'L. was not more chaste than this Lavinia' (*T. And.* ii, 1); 'swear with me, as ... Lord Junius Brutus sware for L.'s rape' (*ib.* iv, 1). The name occurs 34 times in *Lucr.*

Lucretia. 'Sad L.'s modesty' (*A. Y. L.* iii, 2; 'Lucrecia,' F1); *Lucr.* 317, 510.

Lucretius. Sp. Lucr. Tricipitinus, father of Lucretia (*q.v.*); *cf.* Livy, i, 58. His lamentation over his daughter, *Lucr.* 1732 ff., 1751–73, 1800.

Lucullus. D.P. *Timon.* 'A lord, and a flatterer of Timon.' i, 2] sends T. a gift of greyhounds. (ii, 2) is applied to by T., who has just come from hunting with him, for a loan. iii, 1] greets the servant Flaminius, believing that he brings a gift; on learning that he comes to solicit a loan for Timon, animadverts on T.'s profusion, and offers Fl. a bribe to say that he saw him not. (iii, 1, 3) his refusal bruited abroad. (iii, 4) among those bidden to a feast by Timon.

The name occurs in *Plut.* pp. 45, 51.

Lucy, Elizabeth. Dr Shaw (*q.v.*) declared publicly that 'the children of king Edward the fourth were never lawfullie begotten; forsomuch as the King (leaving his verie wife dame Elizabeth Lucie) was never lawfullie married unto the queene their mother' (*Hol.* iii, 729).

This 'contract with Lady Lucy' referred to by Buckingham, *Rich. III*, iii, 7.

[**Lucy, Sir Thomas** (1532–1600).] Inherited the great Warwickshire estate of Charlecote; adopted the puritanical tenets of his teacher John Foxe, and is traditionally believed to have prosecuted Sh. for deer-stealing.

He is undoubtedly the original of Justice Shallow (2 *Hen. IV* and *M.W.W.*), the 'dozen white luces' in Shallow's coat of arms being an obvious allusion to the 'Gules, three luces haurient Argent' borne by the Lucy family. (See French, p. 90.)

Falstaff's reference to Shallow as 'the old pike' (2 *Hen. IV*, iii, 2) is also explicable, since a 'luce' is a full-grown pike (Lee, p. 35).

Lucy, Sir William. D.P. *1 Hen. VI.* iv, 3] urgently entreats York to come to the aid of Talbot, who is 'hemm'd about with grim destruction'; learns that this is impossible, since the 'vile traitor Somerset' has not sent his horsemen; (*sol.*) deplores that sedition bids fair to cause the loss of what 'our scarcecold conqueror,' Henry V, won. iv, 4] taxes Somerset, in bitter words, with neglecting to send aid to Talbot until it is too late. iv, 7] demands from the Dauphin the bodies of Talbot and the other slain nobles, with such a 'proud commanding spirit' that La Pucelle suggests he is 'old Talbot's ghost.'

This character has no historical basis; a Sir W.L. was, however, Sheriff of Warwickshire thrice during the reign of Hen. VI, and was ancestor to Sir Thos. L. (*q.v.*). In iv, 3, 'Mes.' or '2. Mes.' in Ff.

Lud. A mythical king of Britain, whose reign 'began 72 B.C.,' and who so greatly enlarged Troinovant 'that it was called Caerlud, that is to say Luds town; and after by corruption of speech it was named London' (*Hol.* i, 23). The name seems to survive in 'Ludgate.'

Thrice mentioned in *Cymb.* (iii, 1; iv, 2; v, 5).

Ludlow. Situated on the Welsh Marches, was selected as a place of residence for the youthful Edward, Prince of Wales (Edw. V); he was there in charge of Earl Rivers (*Hol.* iii, 714).

'Forthwith from L. the young Prince he fetch'd' (*Rich. III*, ii, 2).

In this scene Ludlow is again twice mtd. but Ff have 'London' in error (ll. 142, 154).

Luke, St. 'I will ... to St L.'s; there' at the moated grange, resides ... Mariana, (*M. for M.* iii, 1); 'the old priest at St L.'s church' (*Tam. Sh.* iv, 4).

Lumbert Street. Quickly's perversion of 'Lombard St.'; 2 *Hen. IV*, ii, 1 (Q; 'Lombard,' Ff).

Luna. Name of the moon. 'A title to Phoebe, to L., to the moon' (*L.L.L.* iv, 2). ('Like to L. in a sad eclipse,' *Tr. R.* II, 2).

Lupercal. A grotto in the Palatine Hill, where, according to tradition, the she-wolf suckled Romulus and Remus. Sh., however, uses the word for 'Lupercalia' (*q.v.*). *Jul. C.* i, 1; iii, 2.

It seems unnecessary to assume that Sh. thought the L. was a hill, since the phrase 'on the L.' (*Jul. C.* iii, 2) may simply mean 'on the feast of L.'

[**Lupercalia.**] A very ancient Roman festival, older than the legend of Romulus and Remus, named from the shepherds' divinity Lupercus, or Inuus. In early times it was accompanied by a human sacrifice, for which that of goats and a dog was substituted later. The celebrants ran round the old boundaries of the Palatine, striking all they met with thongs cut from the skins of the victims. Antony is mentioned as a celebrant (*Plut.* pp. 95, 163).

'Forget not in your speed, Antonius, To touch Calpurnia; for our elders say, The barren, touched in this holy chase, Shake off their sterile curse' (*Jul. C.* i, 2).

'Gentlewomen go also of purpose ... and do put forth their hands to be stricken ... persuading themselves that ... being barren, ... it will make them to conceive with child' (*Plut.* p. 93; *cf.* p. 163).

Lust. Personified. 'Love to heaven is fled, since sweating L. on earth usurped his name,' etc. (*V.A.* 793 ff.); 'L. and Murder wake to stain and kill' (*Lucr.* 168); 'school where L. shall learn' (*ib.* 617); mtd., *ib.* 693, 705; mtd., *Haml.* i, 5.

Lutheran. A follower of Luther; a Protestant. Wolsey speaks (aside) of Anne Boleyn as a 'spleeny L.' (*Hen. VIII*, iii, 2); *cf.* Foxe, ii, 1023, but the term itself is not used.

Luxury. Personified. 'The devil L., with his fat rump and potato finger' (*Tr. Cr.* v, 2).

Lybia. *Ant. Cl.* iii, 6 (for 'Libya,' following North's *Plutarch*); a Greek name for Africa in general, or excluding Egypt and Ethiopia. See LYDIA. 'As barren as banks of L.' (*Tr. Cr.* i, 3); 'Boc[c]hus the King of L.' (*Ant. Cl.* iii, 6; cf. *Plut.* p. 207); mtd., *Wint. T.* v, 1 (2).

Lycaonia. District of Asia Minor, forming the S.E. part of Phrygia. See AMYNTAS. Mtd. ('Licoania,' Ff) *Ant. Cl.* iii, 6.

Lychorida. D.P. *Per.* 'Nurse to Marina.' iii, Gow.] takes part in the dumb show. iii, 1] brings his new-born infant to Pericles and tells him that the Queen is dead. iii, 3] (at Tharsus) *p.m.*; is given charge of her 'little mistress.' (v, 11) Marina's 'good nurse.'

The accusative of 'Lycoris', a feminine name occurring in Ovid (*Ars Amat.* iii, 537; *Trist.* ii, 445, etc.) and Virgil (*Ecl.* x, 2). 'Lycorida' in G. Wilkins' novel of *Pericles*.

Lycia. See LICIA.

Lycurgus. Famous Spartan lawgiver. Menenius tells the two tribunes of the people that he 'cannot call them Lycurguses' (*Cor.* ii, 1).

Lydia. Λυδία, a district of Asia Minor between Mysia and Caria. The banner of Labienus shook 'from Syria to L., and to Ionia' (*Ant. Cl.* i, 2; cf. *Plut.* p. 178); 'of lower Syria, Cyprus, L., absolute queen' (*ib.* iii, 6).

Conjecturally changed to 'Lybia' by Upton.

Lyly, W. See Lily.

Lymoges. D.P. *John.* ('Austria' in pfxs. and st. dirs.) Duke of Austria. ii, 1] is welcomed by the Dauphin and Prince Arthur before Angiers, and promises his aid to the latter, who forgives him 'Coeur-de-lion's death'; is represented as wearing a lion's skin taken from Richard, a fact which forms the basis of bitter gibes from the lips of Philip the Bastard, by whom he is insulted and threatened. iii, 1] is denounced by Constance for deserting the cause of her son Arthur, and is checked by the Bastard's ribald mockery whenever he essays to speak. (iii, 2) the Bastard enters with the head of Lymoges, whom he has slain in combat.

In this character, Sh., following the *Tr. R.*, confuses two historical personages – Vidomar, Viscount of Limoges (in besieging whose castle Coeur-de-Lion was mortally wounded), and Leopold V, first Archduke of Austria, who imprisoned Richard on his return from the 3rd Crusade. Leopold had been dead for four years. Holinshed (iii, 160) merely says that 'Philip, bastard sonne to King Richard ... killed the viscount of Limoges in revenge of his father's death.'

The name is a dactyl in the only place where it occurs in the text (iii, 1), as in the *Tr. R.*

Lynn. King's Lynn, formerly a famous port on the Great Ouse, near the Wash. It is proposed that Edward IV should escape to Lynn and thence take ship to Flanders, *3 Hen. VI*, iv, 5 ('Lyn,' Ff). 'He [Edward] passed the Washes in great jeopardie, and comming to Lin found there an English ship,' etc. (*Hol.* iii, 675).

Lysander. D.P. *M.N.D.* i, 1] asserts his claim to Hermia's hand in the presence of Theseus; accuses Demetrius, his rival, of inconstancy; laments that 'the course of true love never did run smooth'; suggests to Herm. that she should escape from her father's house the next night and meet him in a wood; unfolds to Helena their intention. ii, 3] wandering in the wood with Herm., they lie down for repose, and soon fall asleep; Puck applies magic love-juice to his eyes; Lys. awaking beholds Hel. and is instantly enamoured of her, but she departs, believing his protestations to be scorn and mockery; turning to the sleeping Herm. he exclaims that he loathes and hates her. iii, 2] enters with Hel., whom he continues to woo passionately; tells Dem. that he gladly yields up to him his part in Hermia's love; falls to hot words with D. and heaps insulting epithets on Herm. when she clings to him; reiterates that he hates her, and flouts her as a 'dwarf'; departs to fight with D.; is led up and down in vain pursuit of his rival; sleeps, and Puck applies a counter-charm to his eyes. iv, 1] aroused by huntsmen's horns, he awakes, to find Herm. near him; is oblivious of what had happened during his enchantment, and all his love for Herm. is restored. v, 1] reads to Theseus a 'brief' of sports devised for the evening (acc. to Qq, this is read by Th. himself); comments on the performance of the Interlude.

Lysander, the Spartan general, is mtd. *Plut.* p. 303, in a passage utilized in *Timon*, iv, 3.

Lysimachus. D.P. *Per.* Governor of Mitylene. iv, 6] on learning that Marina, whom he supposed to be a courtesan, is a virtuous maiden, gives her gold, and promises to befriend her. (v, Gow.) mtd. v, 1] visits Pericles' vessel; finding him speechless with grief, sends for Marina to arouse him. v, 2] is thanked by Pericles for his noble conduct. v, 3] (at the temple of Diana) *p.m.*

The name of L., King of Thrace, occurs frequently in Plut. *Demetr.*

M

M., I. The signature of verses 'To the memorie of M. W. Shake-speare,' pfxd. to F1. Probably James Mabbe; or Jasper Mayne.

Mab, Queen. The first mention in literature of Queen M. 'the fairies midwife,' is that contained in the elaborate description of her by Mercutio, *Rom. J.* i, 4. Keightley suggested that the name was a corruption of 'Habundia,' who, according to Heywood, ruled the fairies. But W.J. Thoms, *Three Notelets* (1865), quotes Beauford, *Antient Topography of Ireland*, to show that 'Mahb' was the chief of Irish fairies. ('Mab' in Welsh signifies a male infant.) For the adoption of Mab as a fairy queen by Jonson and Drayton see *Sh. Eng.* i, 538.

Macard. See MERCADE.

Macbeth. King of Scots. Acc. Holinshed (ii, 168, 170–6), son of Sinel, Thane of Glamis, and Doada, daughter of Malcolm II; valiant, but somewhat cruel of nature; blamed King Duncan's lenity and slackness in punishing offenders; was sent with Banquo to subdue the rebel Macdowald; commanded the van in the campaign against Sweno of Norway; defeated, with Banquo, the forces sent by Canute; granted burial to their dead, at Inchcolm, on payment of a great sum; soon after, with Banquo, met three women in strange apparel, 'resembling creatures of the elder world,' who respectively hailed him as Thane of Glamis, Thane of Cawdor, and the future King of Scotland; it was also prophesied that B. should be the progenitor of a line of kings; the matter was made a mutual jest of by Macb. and B.; the Thane of Cawdor was condemned of treason, and his thanedom conferred on Macb., who began later to scheme how he might seize the throne, but hesitated; he was, however, egged on by his ambitious wife, and murdered Duncan at Inverness, with Banquo's connivance; was made king; governed equitably for ten years; remembering the prediction, devised the death of Banquo and his son Fleance, and caused them to be attacked by murderers without his castle; B. was slain, but F. escaped; after this nothing prospered with Macb., and, in dread for his own life, he built a strong castle on Dunsinane, ordering the thanes to superintend the work, and was offended with Macduff, who refused; learnt of certain wizards that he should beware of Macduff; was told by a witch that he 'cannot be slain by any man born of a woman, nor vanquished until Birnam wood comes to Dunsinane'; had a spy in every noble's house; entered Macduff's castle, without resistance, and caused all the inmates to be slain; withdrew to Dunsinane; was advised to flee to the Isles, but relied on the prophecies; witnessed the apparent advance of Birnam wood; escaped from Dunsinane; was killed, at Lunfannaine (Lumphanan) by Macduff (*q.v.*).

Holinshed's account, derived mainly from Boece, and Wyntoun's *Cronykil of Scotland*, is wholly untrustworthy. Macb. was Maormor (Great Steward) of Moray, and reigned as king for 17 years (1040–57); he was not killed in the battle against Siward, but escaped, and was slain three years later.

D.P. *Macb.* i, 3] encounters, with Banquo, three witches, who predict his future dignities; learns that he has become Thane of Cawdor. i, 4] professes homage to Duncan, and is bidden to receive him at Inverness; learns that Malcolm has been named Prince of Cumberland; harbours dark designs. i, 5] tells his wife that 'Duncan comes here tonight'; listens to her murderous suggestions. i, 7] soliloquizes on the projected crime, and resolves to 'proceed no further in this business'; his wavering will is overborne by his wife's arguments, and he 'screws his courage to the sticking-place.' ii, 1] meets Banquo in the court-yard of the castle and receives from him a diamond, as a gift to Lady Macb. from Duncan, who has retired to rest; Banq. refers to the weird sisters, and M. gives him, obscurely, an opportunity of hinting his inmost thoughts; left alone, Macb. is confronted by a visionary dagger which, after eluding his grasp, appears bloodstained; he soliloquizes on night; the ringing of a bell 'invites' him to the commission of the crime. ii, 2] (having murdered the sleeping King) rejoins his wife and tells her the deed is done; is affected by the 'sorry sight' of his bloodstained hands; relates how he heard a voice cry 'Sleep no more. Macbeth hath murdered sleep!' ; refuses to return to Duncan's chamber to smear the grooms with blood; upon his wife's departure on this errand, is disturbed by a knocking, and is again struck with horror at his tell-tale hands; is urged by his wife to retire; wishes that the knocking could awake Duncan. ii, 3] greets Macduff and Lenox; the former departs to visit the King, and on his return with tidings of the murder Macb. rushes from the stage with L.; later, Macb. confirms the news, and 'repents him' that he had killed both the grooms in a pardonable access of fury; proposes that the nobles should forthwith 'meet i' the hall together.' iii, 1] enters, as king; greets Banquo, and bids him be present without fail at a 'solemn supper' that night; ascertains that B. rides forth that afternoon; dismisses the Court; bids an attendant summon two men who wait at the gate; soliloquizes on the need of ridding himself of B.; on the entrance of the men incites them to take vengeance for fancied wrongs done them by B., and explains that he needs the 'absence' of B. and his son. iii, 2] in conference with his wife, admits his mental torments, and envies Duncan at peace in the grave; bids her behave with flattering courtesy to Banquo, but hints that 'a deed of dreadful note' will be done ere night, of which she must yet remain in ignorance. iii, 4] welcomes his guests to a banquet; learns from the murderers that, though Banquo is slain, Fleance has escaped; expresses regret to the guests at Banquo's absence; sees the form of B. seated in his place; is appalled at the vision, but on its disappearance apologizes for his 'strange infirmity' and drinks 'to our dear friend Banquo, whom we miss'; the ghost reenters, and Macb. is again overcome with horror, 'take any shape but that, and my firm nerves Shall never tremble'; the ghost disappears, and Macb. marvels that others can 'behold such sights' unmoved; left alone with his wife, ponders the saw that 'blood will have blood'; has become aware that 'Macduff denies his person at our great bidding'; resolves to visit the weird sisters, and reflects that he is too deeply involved in crime to draw back. iv, 1] visits the witches in their cave; is told that he need not put his questions into words; is warned against Macduff and assured by successive apparitions that 'none of woman born Shall harm' him, and that he shall be unconquered till Birnam wood come to Dunsinane; demands 'shall Banquo's issue ever Reign in this kingdom?' and is answered by an apparition of eight kings followed by 'the blood-boltered Banquo'; learning from Lenox that 'Macduff is fled to England,' resolves to surprise his castle and put its inmates to the sword. v, 3] learns that the English force approaches Dunsinane; calls for his armour; converses with a Doctor on the Queen's condition, and asks, 'Canst thou not minister to a mind diseased?'; prepares to meet the foe. v, 5] is told that the Queen is dead and that Birnam wood is approaching the castle; resolves to die with harness on his back. v, 7] slays young Siward in single combat. v, 8] encounters Macduff, who was not 'of woman born'; (is slain and decapitated by Macduff).

Commentators differ with regard to the apparitions seen by Macbeth at the banquet (iii, 4), some holding that Banquo and Duncan both appear. The st. dirs. in Ff are indecisive on the point.

An interesting discussion on Macb.'s personal courage, throwing light on other aspects of his character, is contained in Thomas Whateley's *Remarks on some Chars. of Sh.* (1785), and the *Answer* to this by J. P. Kemble.

'We can conceive a common actor to play Richard III tolerably well; we can conceive no one to play Macb. properly, or to look like a man that had encountered the Weird Sisters' (W. Hazlitt).

Macbeth, Lady. Wife of Macbeth, afterward Queen. Her name, Gruoch, occurs in a charter granted to the Culdees of a monastery on Loch Leven by 'Machbet filius Finlach ... et Gruoch filia Bodhe, Rex et Regina Scotorum.' Bodhe, her father, was eldest son of Kenneth IV, King of Scots; she therefore had a better right to the throne than Duncan. She was twice married: (*a*) to Kilcomgain, Thane of Moray (by whom she had a son, Lulach, who succeeded Macbeth on the throne); (*b*) to Macbeth.

Holinshed's only allusion to her is as follows (ii, 170): 'the words of the three weird sisters also ... greatly encouraged him hereunto, but speciallie his wife lay sore upon him to attempt the thing, as she that was verie ambitious, burning in unquenchable desire to beare the name of a queene.' But the part played by Lady M. in the murder of Duncan is more closely paralleled by that of Donwald's wife in the murder of King Duff (*Hol.* ii, 150): it is at her instigation that the King is murdered, while a guest at Forres Castle, by four of Donwald's servants – the victim's two chamberlains having been made drunk at a 'reare supper' prepared by the lady herself.

D.P. *Macb.* i, 5] reads letter from Macbeth relating the weird sisters' prediction; soliloquizes on M.'s weakness of character, and her own resolution; is informed that 'the King comes here tonight' and that Macb. is close at hand; in soliloquy invokes those spirits who are 'murthering ministers' to stop up in her all 'passage to remorse'; welcomes her husband; on hearing that Duncan purposes to depart on the morrow, exclaims, 'O, never shall sun that morrow see'; demands that Macb. 'shall put This night's great business into my despatch.' i, 6] welcomes Duncan to the castle. i, 7] finding that Macb. vacillates – 'letting I dare not wait upon I would' – urges him to take courage, and unfolds her murderous scheme. ii, 2] awaits the return of Macb. from Duncan's chamber, where 'had he not resembled My father as he slept, I had done't'; (she has drugged the 'possets' of the grooms and laid their daggers ready); on her husband's entrance strives to abate his horror and agitation; on his refusing to revisit the scene of the murder, she takes the dagger, wherewith to smear the sleeping grooms; on her return, shows her bloodstained hands and scoffs at M.'s 'white' heart; hears knocking, and urges him to prepare for events – 'Be not lost so poorly in your thoughts.' ii, 3] enters as though seeking the cause of the commotion in the castle; after listening to a description of Duncan as he lies, is carried out in a swoon – real or feigned. iii, 1] welcomes, as queen, the 'chief guest,' Banquo. iii, 2] seeks to wean her husband from his gloomy and remorseful thoughts; urges him to be 'bright and jovial' at the coming banquet. iii, 4] urges Macb. to perform his ceremonial duties at the feast; on his being unnerved at the apparition of Banquo, excuses him to the guests: 'The fit is momentary ... Feed, and regard him not'; tries to shame him into exerting self-control; after the second apparition once more seeks to soothe the company, but, seeing that it is in vain, hurriedly dismisses them; on being left alone with her husband has no other counsel for him than to seek 'the season of all natures, sleep.' v, 1] in the presence of a Doctor and a Gentlewoman, she enters a room in Dunsinane Castle walking in her sleep and rubbing her hands; the broken sentences that fall from her lips refer to the murder of Duncan and Lady Macduff – the sight and smell of blood upon her hands that 'all the perfumes of Arabia will not sweeten' – the murder of Banquo – and the knocking at the gate after the King's death. (v, 3) the Doctor tells Macbeth that the Queen's sickness is mental rather than physical. (v, 5) her death is announced. (v, 8) it is related that she died 'by self and violent hands.'

For Mrs Siddons' account of the terror which seized her on first studying the part, at night, see Campbell's *Life of Mrs Siddons*, ii, 35.

Macbeth, The Tragedy of.

Publication. That this tragedy was not published until it was included in the First Folio of 1623 is clear from the fact that in the books of the Stationers' Company it is registered, by Blount and Jaggard, Nov. 8, 1623, as 'not formerly entered to other men.' As published in the First Folio, the acts and scenes are all indicated, but there is no list of *dramatis personae*. It is regarded by the Cambridge editors as 'one of the worst printed of all the plays, especially as regards the metre, and not a few passages are hopelessly corrupt.' Some of the more obvious blunders are such as might be expected to arise in dictation to an amanuensis or a compositor. *Macbeth* is the shortest of all the plays, and 'it is possible that it survives only in an abbreviated acting version' (Lee, *Life of Sh.* p. 395).

Dates of Composition and Production. James VI of Scotland ascended the English throne, as James I, in March 1603, and it seems very probable that the choice of a Scottish subject was suggested to Sh. by this event. Nor is this inference without internal evidence in its support: (*a*) the apparition of the kings to Macbeth (iv, 1), some of whom 'two-fold balls and treble sceptres carry' contains a clear allusion to the union of the three kingdoms under one head, and (less certainly) to the two coronations of James; (*b*) the unblemished character attributed by the dramatist to Banquo – notwithstanding that, according to Holinshed, he was Macbeth's accomplice in Duncan's murder – could not fail to be pleasing to a king who prided himself on descent from that mythical founder of the house of Stewart; (*c*) the reference to the 'touching' by the royal hand for the cure of the 'king's evil' (iv, 3) – which is quite unconnected with the progress of the plot – is readily explicable as a compliment to James, who was proud to think that he had inherited the powers of Edward the Confessor, and frequently 'touched' during his progresses; (*d*) the introduction of the supernatural element of the three witches – though it is true that this is to some extent involved in the original story – could not fail to appeal to the royal author of the *Demonologie*.

A piece of internal evidence which has been held of importance in fixing the date of the play is the reiterated allusion by the Porter (ii, 3) to 'an equivocator, that could swear in both the scales against either scale.' This has been widely held to point to the doctrine of 'equivocation' avowed by the Jesuit Henry Garnet at his trial for being concerned in the Gunpowder Plot, in 1606. It must, however, be observed that the famous scene of 'the knocking at the gate,' in which the Porter appears, has been regarded by certain critics as an interpolation made at a later date, though that it is from Sh.'s pen is now hardly disputed.

That *Macbeth* was produced not later than Apr. 20, 1610, we have distinct external evidence. Dr Simon Forman, physician and astrologer, of Lambeth (who died in 1611), left a MS. entitled 'A Booke of Plaies, and Notes thereof for common Pollicie.' In this he describes a performance of a play called 'Macbeth' at the Globe theatre, which he witnessed on the date mentioned, and the details given by him prove indubitably that the play in question was substantially that which has come down to us. But Forman nowhere implies that the tragedy was a new production. Finally, it is not irrelevant to note that in July 1606 the King of Denmark came to England on a visit to his sister, Queen Anne, and the production of a play containing so much of personal interest to James would have been highly appropriate during the 'revellings' which, we are told, then took place at the Court. The brevity of the play, it may be added, would render it a suitable one for performance on an occasion of the kind. Consideration of the evidence briefly cited above, and of other points of minor importance, has led the great majority of critics to adopt 1605–6 as the most probable date of the composition of *Macbeth*, and the results of metrical analysis harmonize well enough with this conclusion.

Sources of the Plot. The historical, or rather, legendary, incidents of Macbeth's career are related in the *Scotorum Historiae* of Hector Boece (Boethius), who drew his information from the *Scotichronicon* of Joannes de Fordun – adding copious embellishments. On Boece, or perhaps on the translation of his work (1541) by John Bellenden, Holinshed based his account of Macbeth, and Sh. relied for the historical framework of his play solely on Holinshed – freely adapting, however, details of the (earlier) murder of King Duffe to the murder of Duncan, which is merely mentioned in the Chronicle. We are here concerned only to indicate the immediate sources of the tragedy, but it may be added that the incident of 'the moving forest' and the prophecy that 'none of a woman born' should prevail against the hero have been traced to earlier legends (see Birnam). Inferiority of style and certain inconsistencies have led to interpolations by other hands being suspected in i, 2, where the 'bleeding sergeant' appears; while in ii, 5, it is generally admitted that Hecate (*q.v.*) seems an unnecessary and incongruous character. Undoubted resemblances, however, in the supernatural scenes to certain passages in T. Middleton's *The Witch* (*c.* 1610) are in all probability due to 'conveyance' on Middleton's part. Banquo's ghost is jestingly alluded to in Beaumont and Fletcher's *Knight of the Burning Pestle* (1611). A ballad of *Macdobeth* was registered in 1596, and that there was an earlier play on the same subject seems probable from a highly depreciatory passage in *A Nine Days Wonder* (1600) by the comic actor William Kempe; but concerning this play nothing further is known.

'For two-thirds of a century, before Garrick's time, *Macbeth* had been worse than banished from the stage: for it had been acted with D'Avenant's alterations, in which every original beauty was either awkwardly disguised or arbitrarily omitted. Yet so ignorant were Englishmen, that *The Tatler* quotes Sh.'s *Macbeth* from D'Avenant's alteration of it; and when Quin heard of Garrick's intention to restore the original, he asked in astonishment, "Have I not all this time been acting Sh.'s play!" ' (T. Campbell, *Life of Mrs Siddons* (1834), ii, 7.)

Maccabaeus, Judas. Son of Mattathias, who succeeded his father as leader of the Judeans in their struggle against the Syrians. He reconsecrated the temple 164 B.C.

One of 'The Nine Worthies' (*q.v.*), a masque to be presented before the Court, *L.L.L.* v, 1; the character is presented by Holofernes, who can proceed no farther than 'Judas I am, ycliped Machabeus' (Ff), so mercilessly is he bantered by the audience, *ib.* v, 2.

Macdonwald. 'The merciless M.' slain by Macbeth; *Macb.* i, 2. Perhaps a confusion of two names. The rebel who was defeated by Macbeth (and slew himself) was, acc. *Hol.* ii, 168, 'Macdowald'; while the murderer of King Duff was 'Donwald' (*Hol.* ii, 150).

Macduff. Thane, or Earl, of Fife; eighth in descent from the great chieftain Mac Duff, who had been granted by Kenneth II all the land lying between the Firths of Tay and Forth.

Acc. *Hol.* ii, 174–6, he gave offence to King Macbeth by refusing to superintend the building of Dunsinane Castle; resolved to flee to England and stir up Malcolm Canmore to claim the Scottish crown; heard that his wife and children had been murdered by Macb.; related to Malcolm Macb.'s cruelty; was perturbed by Malc.'s self-accusations, until undeceived; urged the Scottish nobles to support Male. against Macb.; by favour of Edward the Confessor secured the aid of Siward, Earl of Northumberland, with 10,000 men; in battle near Dunsinane pursued Macb., and on the latter boasting that he is unconquerable 'by any born of a woman,' replied that he was 'ripped from his mother's womb,' and forthwith slew him; was confirmed in his earldom by Malcolm.

D.P. *Macb.* i, 6] *p.m.* ii, 3] visits Macbeth's castle at dawn, by Duncan's behest, and finds the King murdered; alarms the household. ii, 4] relates to Ross the events that followed D.'s murder. (iv, 1) Macb. is warned against him. iv, 3] is bewildered by Malcolm's feigned self-accusations; hears of the murder of his own wife and children; vows vengeance on Macbeth, 'this fiend of Scotland.' (v, 1) the murder of his wife recalled. v, 4, 6] with Malcolm's army. v, 7] meets Macb. in single combat; later, enters with Macb.'s head; hails Malcolm King of Scotland.

'Duff,' ii, 3, l. 87, Ff.

Macduff, Lady. Wife to Macduff (*q.v.*). Acc. *Hol.* ii, 174, was murdered, together with her children, by Macbeth's orders, though no resistance had been offered to the entrance of his forces into the castle.

D.P. *Macb.* iv, 2] complains to her kinsman Ross that her husband has deserted her in a time of danger; humours the precocious prattle of her little son; is warned of impending danger; on the entrance of the murderers, who stab the boy, flees in horror, and is pursued.

The traditional scene of the murder is Dunne-marle Castle, in Perthshire.

Macduff, Son of. D.P. *Macb.* 'Boy, son to M.' (Rowe). ('Son' in pfxs.) iv, 2] prattles about his father, whom he will not believe to be dead, and about the punishment of traitors; on the entrance of the murderers, gives the lie to one who calls his father a traitor, is stabbed, and, calling on his mother to escape, dies.

Macedon. Macedonia. An ancient government of vague extent in the S.E. of Europe. Alexander the Great was born at Pella, the capital of M.

Fluellen draws 'comparisons' between Macedon and Monmouth, since 'the situations is both alike,' each possesses a river, and 'there is salmons in both' (*Hen. V*, iv, 7); Thaisa's father was 'a prince of M.' (*Per.* ii, 2).

Machabeus. See MACCABAEUS.

Machiavelli, Niccolo (1469–1527). Italian patriot, diplomatist, and author. In his work *Il Principe*, designed for the private perusal of the Medici, with whom he wished to ingratiate himself, he maintained that the worst and most treacherous acts of the ruler are justified in combating wickedness on the part of the governed. Hence he became regarded as the incarnation of diabolical cunning in state affairs. '*Host.* Am I politic, am I subtle? am I a M.?' (*M.W.W.* iii, 1); 'Alençon! that notorious M.!' (*1 Hen. VI*, v, 4); '*Glo.* I can ... set the murtherous M. to school' (*3 Hen. VI*, iii, 2).

In an Eng. form ('Machi(a)vel,' etc.) throughout. Great interest was taken in M., as a personification of unscrupulous policy, by the Elizabethans. He speaks the Prologue to Marlowe's *Jew of Malta*. The references to M. in *Sh.* are anachronisms.

Macmorris. D.P. *Hen. V.* 'An Irishman,' officer in King Henry's army. iii, 2] enters into an acrimonious dispute with Fluellen on 'the disciplines of war.'

The management of the mines at the siege of Harfleur, which is given to M. in the play, was really in the hands of 'Master Giles' (French, p. 105). An account of the mining and countermining is given in *Hol.* iii. 549–50.

Madeira. Wine of M.; mtd. *1 Hen. IV*, i, 2.

Madonna. Applied by Feste to Olivia, in the sense merely of 'Madam.' *T. Nt.* i, 5 (7); v, 1.

Maecenas, C. Cilnius. One of the two 'chief friends' of Octavius (*Plut.* p. 183). (Later, famed as a literary patron.)

D.P. *Ant. Cl.* ii, 2] tries to compose the differences between the triumvirs; converses with Enobarbus on Cleopatra's power over Ant. ii, 4] prepares to set out for Misenum. ii, 6, 7] *p.m.* iii, 6] in council with Octavius; sympathizes with Octavia. iv, 1] advises Octavius to give Ant. 'no breath.' v, 1] comments on the dead Antony. v, 2] *p.m.*

'Mecenas' in Ff (except once in F4); then 'Mecaenas,' after Rowe. The correct form is only given in modern edns. (Ff give 'Menas' in the st. dir. of v, 1, but 'Mec.' as a pfx.)

[**Maglanus.**] See ALBANY, DUKE OF.

[**Maglaurus.**] See CORNWALL, DUKE OF.

Magnificoes of Venice. D.PP. *M.V.* iv, 1] *pp.m.*; present in court.

'Stalketh stately by, As if he wore some great M.' (Spenser, *Mother Hubberd*, l. 665).

Magnus, St. The original church of St M. the Martyr stood at the head of old London Bridge; it was destroyed in the Great Fire. '*Cade.* Down St M. corner ... throw them into Thames' (*2 Hen. VI*, iv, 8). ('Magnes,' Ff.)

'For som time, the Londoners were beaten backe to Saint Magnus Corner' (*Hol.* iii, 635).

Mahomet, Mohammed. Founder of Islam. 'Was M. inspired with a dove?' (*1 Hen. VI*, i, 2).

The story of M. training a dove to feed with wheat out of his ear, so as to appear whispering to him, is mentioned in Raleigh's *Hist. of the World*, I, i, 6.

Mahu. See MODO.

Maidenhead. Town in Berks. 'All the hosts of Readins, of Maidenhead' (*M.W.W.* iv, 5).

Maine. A former province of Northern France, S. of Normandy; united to Anjou 1110; became an English possession 1154; conquered by Philip Augustus of France 1204; passed again to England for a few years under Hen. V and Hen. VI, and was ceded by the latter to France.

Claimed for Arthur, *John*, i, 1, ii, 1; lost to England, *1 Hen. VI*, iv, 3; claimed by Reignier, *ib.* v, 3; ceded to France, *2 Hen. VI*, i, 1, iv, 1, 2, 7.

Malchus. (A title, meaning 'king.') King of Arabia Petraea ('Manchus,' *Plut.* p. 207). Mtd. ('Manchus,' Ff) *Ant. Cl.* iii, 6.

Malcolm. Surnamed Canmore, or Caenmohr, 'great-head'; elder son of Duncan I, King of Scots. Acc. *Hol.* ii, 170–1, 174–6, on being made Prince of Cumberland, Malc. fled thither to escape the enmity of Macbeth (1039); took refuge with Edward the Confessor; on hearing Macduff's account of Macb.'s barbarities, at first accused himself of lust, avarice, and dissimulation, to test his informant, but afterward undeceived him, and promised his aid; obtained the support of Earl Siward, his maternal uncle; ordered his men to conceal themselves with branches plucked from Birnam Wood; received Macb.'s head from Macduff; crowned at Scone 1057; instituted earldoms for the first time in Scotland.

D.P. *Macb.* i, 2] in attendance on Duncan. i, 4] reports Cawdor's execution. i, 6] *p.m.* ii, 3] after Duncan's murder resolves to flee to England to escape Macbeth's 'murtherous shaft.' (ii, 4) takes flight. (iii, 6) ironically suggested as Duncan's murderer. iv, 3] accuses himself to Macduff of many vices, testing him; undeceives Macd.; describes the cure of 'the king's evil'; reports that Siward is coming to their aid; listens to Ross's relation of the murder of Macduff's family, and urges Macd. to revenge. (v, 2) leads the English forces. (v, 3) scorned by Macbeth. v, 4] orders his men to conceal themselves with boughs. v, 6] prepares for battle. v, 7] receives Macb.'s head; is hailed king; makes his thanes and kinsmen earls, and bids them attend his coronation.

Mall, Mistress. 'Are they like to take the dust like Mistress M.'s picture?' (*T. Nt.* i, 3).

Usually supposed to refer to Mary Frith, 'Mall [or Moll] Cutpurse,' a notorious adventuress, but the allusion remains obscure.

'Mall' was a common dim. of 'Mary,' *cf.* 'Mall, Meg and Marian' (*Temp.* ii, 2).

Moll Cutpurse was the 'Roaring Girl' of Middleton and Dekkor. See Dyce, *Middleton*, ii, 429–31, for many references; also C. Whibley, in *Sh. Eng.* ii, 501.

Mallecho. '*Haml.* Marry, this is miching Mallecho; it means mischief' (*Haml.* iii, 2; 'Mallico,' Qq; 'Malicho,' Ff).

Capell conjectured that 'Malhecho' in the Spanish drama corresponded to the 'Iniquity' of the old English moralities (Clar.).

Malvolio. D.P. *T.Nt.* 'A fantastical steward to Olivia' (Rowe). i, 5] disparages Feste as 'a barren rascal'; informs Olivia that Orsino's emissary (whom he describes) refuses to leave her door; later, is sent after 'Cesario' with a ring from his mistress. ii, 2] meets 'C.,' and after some parley throws the ring at his feet. ii, 3] upbraids Sir Toby and his companions for their noisy carousals, and is bantered by the revellers. ii, 5] soliloquizes on his ambitious dreams, in the hearing of Sir T. and the rest; picks up and reads their forged letter, which he believes to be from Olivia; in deep infatuation expresses his resolve to fulfil all its absurd injunctions. (iii, 2) 'yond gull M. is turned heathen.' iii, 4] fantastically attired, presents himself before his mistress, with quaint gestures; quotes to her from the letter, and soliloquizes on the supposed success of his wooing; on the entrance of Sir Toby, Fabian, and Maria, treats them haughtily, but is met with derision, and departs in great wrath. iv, 2] having been confined, as a lunatic, in a dark room, is questioned from without by 'Sir Topas' (*i.e.* Feste); afterward appeals to the undisguised F. – entreating him to fetch writing materials and a light, and protesting his perfect sanity. v, 1] presents himself before Olivia, and, showing her the forged letter, taxes her with having made him a 'most notorious geck and gull'; finally departs with the words, 'I'll be revenged on the whole pack of you.'

Farmer's suggestion (1767) that the name is a mere transposition of 'Malivolo' is generally accepted. Hunter (1845) considers, however, 'Malevolti,' the assumed name of the writer of a madrigal prefixed to *Gl'Ingannati*, to be the source. See Twelfth Night. *Cf.* also 'Benvolio,' D.P. *Rom. J.*

For Charles Lamb's subtle analysis of the character, and his account of Bensley's conception of the part, see *Essays of Elia*, 'On Some of the Old Actors.'

Mamillius. D.P. *Wint. T.* 'Yong Prince of Sicillia' (F1). (i, 1) is eulogized as 'a gentleman of the greatest promise,' and 'a gallant child.' i, 2] after being strangely questioned by his father, who is distraught with jealousy, he is dismissed to play. ii, 1] diverts the attendant ladies with sprightly banter; prepares to tell a 'sad tale' of a man who 'dwelt by a churchyard,' when Leontes enters, and in his wrath orders the boy to be taken from his mother. (iii, 2) it is announced that he has died 'with mere conceit, and fear Of the Queen's speed.'

'Mamillus' (F1, 2) in 'Names of the Actors.' The young son of the Queen in *Pandosto* is Garinter; he dies suddenly, but the cause is not hinted.

Manningtree. Town in Essex. 'That roasted M. ox with the pudding in his belly [Falstaff]' (*1 Hen. IV*, ii, 4).

Fairs were held at M. and moralities were acted there. *Cf.* T. Dekker, *Newes from Hell*: 'you shall ... drink more in two days than all M. does at a Whitsun Ale.'

Mantua. Situated on an island in the Mincio; former capital of the duchy of M.

The scene of *T.G.V.* iv, 1, v, 3, 4, is laid near M.; mtd., iv, 1, 3, v, 2; 'Licio, born in M.' (*Tam. Sh.* ii, 1); ' 'Tis death for any one in Mantua to come to Padua' (*ib.* iv, 2); the abode of Romeo in exile; the scene of *Rom. J.* v, 1, is laid there; 'my lord and you were then at M.' (*Rom. J.* i, 3); Romeo advised to escape thither, *ib.* iii, 3 (2); R. sets out thither, *ib.* iii, 5 (2); mtd., *ib.* iv, 1 (2); 'a poison now, Whose sale is present death in M.' (*ib.* v, 1); mtd., *ib.* v, 2 (3), 3.

Mantuanus, Baptista Spagnolo (1448–1516). A native of Mantua. His *Eclogues* formed a very popular school-book in the 16th cent. (*cf.* T. S. Baynes, *Shakespeare Studies* (1896), p. 184). The extravagant value placed on the works of Mantuanus is satirized in the *Epistolae Obscurorum Virorum* (ed. F. G. Stokes (1909), p. 162), where 'Wilhelmus Lamp' exclaims: 'Quid curo illum paganum [Virgil]? Nos volumus ire ad Carmelitas et videre Baptistam Mantuanum qui in duplo est melior quam Virgillus!' (Prescribed as a text-book in the statutes of St Paul's, St Bees, and Durham.)

'*Hol.* "Fauste, precor, gelida quando pecus omne sub umbra Ruminat," and so forth. Ah, good old Mantuan! I may speak of thee as the traveller doth of Venice; "Venetia, Venetia, Chi non ti vede non ti pretia." Old Mantuan, old Mantuan, who understandeth thee not, loves thee not' (*L.L.L.* iv, 2, Q). In Q the Latin is much garbled. See Vinegia.

The quotation is the beginning of the first Eclogue. The works of Mantuanus have recently been edited by W.P. Mustard (Baltimore, 1911).

Marcade. See Mercade.

Marcellus. D.P. *Haml.* 'An officer.' i, 1] having twice seen the apparition, brings Horatio to the 'platform' to convince him of the truth of his account; on the appearance of the ghost, bids H. speak to it; inquires the reason of the warlike preparations pressed on day and night; on the reappearance of the ghost, strikes at it 'with his partisan'; comments on its vanishing at cock-crow. i, 2] takes part in the relation of the circumstances to Hamlet. i, 4] (on the platform) tries to prevent Hamlet from obeying the ghost's summons; follows him. i, 5] takes an oath of secrecy.

R. Crompton Rhodes (*Sh.'s First Folio* (1923), pp. 74 ff.) contends that the *Hamlet* of 1603 was printed from the prompt-book of the actor who played Marcellus and Voltimand.

Marcellus, Caius Claudius. Consul 51 B.C.; first husband of Octavia, sister to Octavius (Augustus). Cf. *Plut.* p. 179. 'Octavia ... was the wife of C. Marcellus' (*Ant. Cl.* ii, 6).

March, Earls of. The first five Earls of M. in the English peerage were: (*a*) Roger (IV) de Mortimer (*c.* 1287–1330); (*b*) Roger (V) de M. (*c.* 1327–60); (*c*) Edmund (II) de M. (1351–81); (*d*) Roger (VI) de M. (1374–98); (*e*) Edmund (IV) de M. (1391–1425), heir presumptive to the throne in succession to his father.

The following are the references to Earls of M., as such, in the Histories:

'Glendower, Whose daughter, as we hear, the Earl of March Hath lately married' (*1 Hen. IV*, i, 3; an error, following *Hol.* iii, 521; Glendower's son-in-law was Sir Edmund M., brother to Roger (VI)). Hotspur declares that Henry IV 'suffer'd his kinsman March ... to be engaged in Wales' (*ib.* iv, 3; the same error). 'You, son Harry, will towards Wales, To fight with Glendower and the Earl of M.' (*ib.* v, 5; the same error). 'Philippe, a daughter of Lionel, D. of Clarence Who married Edmund Mortimer, E. of March' (*2 Hen. VI*, ii, 2; this was the 3rd Earl). 'Roger, E. of March' mentioned as father to Anne Mortimer, *ib. ib.*

Henry VI mentions that York's g.f. was 'Roger Mortimer, E. of March' (*3 Hen. VI*, i, 1); Edward, afterward Edward IV, is spoken of as 'Earl of March' (*ib.* ii, 1).

See also MORTIMER, LORD, OF SCOTLAND, and Appendix 4.

March, Month of. 'Daffodils, that ... take the winds of M. with beauty' (*Wint. T.* iv, 3); 'worse than the sun in M., This praise doth nourish agues' (*1 Hen. IV*, iv, 1); Caesar bidden beware the Ides of M., *i.e.* the 15th of the month, *Jul. C.* i, 2 (3) (cf. *Plut.* p. 98); 'is not tomorrow ... the Ides of M.? ... Sir, M. is wasted fourteen days' (*ib.* ii, 1); 'the Ides of M. are come' (*ib.* iii, 1); 'remember M., the Ides of M. remember' (*ib.* iv, 3); mtd. by Brutus, *ib.* v, 1; 'A very forward M.-chick' (*M. Ado*, i, 3).

Marcians. The ancestors of Coriolanus (*q.v.*). 'The noble house o' the Marcians' (*Cor.* ii, 3).

Marcius (1). The *nomen* of C. (or Cn.) Marcius Coriolanus (*q.v.*), traditionally descended from King Ancus Marcius.

Marcius (2). D.P. *Cor.* Son to Coriolanus. v, 3] accompanies the Roman matrons when they entreat C. to spare Rome; exclaims 'I'll run away till I am bigger, but then I'll fight.'

Plut. merely refers to the presence of C.'s children.

Marcus. (*a*) As a *prenomen*. 'M. Brutus' (*Jul. C.* iii, 1; iv, 3); 'M. Cato' (*ib.* v, 4); 'M. Antonius' (*Ant. Cl.* ii, 6); 'M. Crassus' (*ib.* iii, 1 (2)); 'M. Octavius' (*ib.* iii, 7); 'M. Justeius' (*ib. ib.*); 'M. Andronicus' (D.P. *T. And.*) (*b*) As a Christian name. 'M. Lucchese [*q.v.*]' (*Oth.* i, 3). (*c*) Used alone. 'My cousin M.' (*Cor.* v, 6).

Marcus Justeius. A leader of the centre of Antony's fleet at Actium (*Plut.* p. 210). Mtd. *Ant. Cl.* iii, 7.

'Justeus,' F1; 'Justius,' F2, 3, 4.

Marcus Octavius. A leader of the centre of Antony's fleet at Actium (*Plut.* p. 210). Mtd. *Ant. Cl.* iii, 7.

[**Marcus Phaonius.**] A friend of Cato, who, on hearing a loud altercation between Brutus and Cassius, counterfeited a crazy philosopher, and forcing his way into their presence, recited mockingly 'the verses which old Nestor said in Homer; "My lords, I pray you hearken both to me, For I have seen mo years than suchie three," ' whereupon Cassius 'fell a-laughing at him,' and the quarrel came to an end (*Plut.* pp. 134–5).

D.P. *Jul. C.* 'A Poet.' iv, 3] as above.

Mardian. An eunuch, attendant on Cleopatra (*Plut.* p. 206). D.P. *Ant. Cl.* i, 5] is contemptuously questioned by Cl. ii, 5] in attendance. iv, 13] *p.m.*; is sent by Cl. to Ant. to tell him she has slain herself. iv, 14] graphically describes the supposed event.

Margarelon. D.P. *Tr. Cr.* 'A bastard son of Priam' (Theob.). (v, 5) 'bastard M. Hath Doreus prisoner.' v, 7] challenges Thersites to fight, but Th. replies that one bastard should not fight another.

'Bastard' in st. dir. and pfxs. (QFf); 'Margareton,' Caxton, *Recuyell*; 'Margarteton,' Lydgate.

Margaret. D.P. *M. Ado.* Gentlewoman attending on Hero. ii, 1] exchanges raillery with Balthasar at the masked dance. (ii, 2) mtd. by Borachio in connection with his plot. iii, 1] is sent to summon Beatrice. (iii, 2) mtd. (iii, 3) the part she took in the deception of Claudio described by Bor. iii, 4] discusses apparel with Hero and jests upon her coming marriage; indulges in licensed raillery with Beat. – prescribing her 'Carduus Benedictus,' *i.e.* Benedick, for her malady. (v, 1) her deception mtd. v, 2] after holding her own in raillery with Benedick, consents to summon Beat. v, 4] *p.m.* (omitted by Steevens) mtd. by Beat.

Margaret of Anjou (1430–82). Daughter of René (Reignier) (*q.v.*) of Anjou; married by proxy at Nancy, 1445, to Henry VI, and crowned at Westminster the same year; strove to ally the King and herself with the Beaufort-Suffolk party, who had brought about the marriage; on Suffolk's fall, relied on Somerset, whom she liberated from prison in 1450; failed to be made regent during Henry's incompetency; became the bitter opponent of York; was defeated at St Albans (1455), when Somerset was killed and York became Protector; after Henry's defeat at Northampton sought refuge in Wales and Scotland; won a victory at Wakefield (1460), and (over Warwick) at St Albans (1461); on her defeat at Towton fled to Scotland, and afterward went to France and appealed to Lewis XI; landed with an army at Weymouth (1471); was defeated and made prisoner at Tewkesbury, where her son was killed; imprisoned for five years; then sent to France (1475), where she died in poverty.

Shakespeare is generally held not to be responsible for the dramatic, and largely unhistorical, character of Margaret in 1, 2, *3 Hen. VI.* For the (fictitious) narrative of her intrigue with Suffolk, see POLE, WILLIAM DE LA.

Ace, the chroniclers, Margaret 'excelled all other, as well in beautie and favour as in wit and policie; and was of stomach and courage more like to a man than a woman'; she was 'desirous of glory and covetous of honour ... of white and wiliness she lacked nothing,' yet 'often tyme, when she was vehement and fully bent in a matter, she was sodainly, lyke a wethercocke, mutable, and turning' (Hall, p. 208; *Hol.* iii, 625–6).

D.P. *1 Hen. VI.* v, 3] after the capture of Joan of Arc, 'Lady Margaret' becomes Suffolk's prisoner; she asks what ransom she must pay, but can obtain no direct answer from the enamoured Earl; at length S. undertakes to make her

'Henry's queen' and negotiates with her father on the matter; S. kisses her in parting. (v, 5) Henry, on the strength of Suffolk's glowing description, resolves to marry her; S. resolves to rule the realm through her. (Founded on a brief mention of the marriage, *Hol.* iii, 238.)

D.P. *2 Hen. VI.* i, 1] is presented to Henry, and hailed as 'Queen Margaret' (*Hol.* iii, 625). (i, 2) mtd. i, 3] speaks scornfully of H., as more fitted to be Pope than King (cf. *Hol.* iii, 626); is infuriated with the Dss. of Gloucester, who dèrides her poverty; demands the Duke's dismissal; strikes the Dss. ii, 1] (at the royal hawking party) is checked by H. for rebuking Gloucester; learns that the Dss. is accused of witchcraft. ii, 3] on G.'s resigning his staff, feels at last a queen. iii, 1] warns H. against G., whose changed demeanour she notes; plans, with Suffolk and Beaufort, G.'s death. iii, 2] on witnessing Henry's grief at G.'s death passionately inveighs against the King for caring more for G. than for her; pleads for Suffolk, and plainly shows her love for him – in his exile he will 'take her heart with him.' (iv, 1) mtd. iv, 4] mourns bitterly over Suffolk's head. iv, 9] *p.m.* v, 1] is reviled by York as 'outcast of Naples, England's bloody scourge!' v, 2] (at St Albans) declares that Henry will neither 'fight nor fly'; urges him to flee with her to London.

D.P. *3 Hen. VI.* i, 1] denounces Henry as a 'timorous wretch,' for disinheriting their son; declares that she will 'divorce herself' until this wrong is righted; departs to join her army (*Hol.* iii, 659). i, 4] reviles the captured York at Wakefield; places a paper crown upon his head (*ib.*); stabs him with her own hand. ii, 2] welcomes Henry to the city of York; bids him knight their son; reviles her foes; is called by Edward (of York) a 'shameless callet.' ii, 5] (at the Battle of Towton) seeing that the day is lost, urges Henry to flee. (ii, 6) 'captain Margaret.' (iii, 1) mtd. iii, 3] (in France) pleads her cause before King Lewis, and obtains a promise of his aid (*Hol.* iii, 665); warns L. against consenting to the marriage of the Lady Bona to Edward IV; calls Warwick 'proud setter-up and puller-down of kings,' but on Edward's faithlessness, and Warwick's consequent defection from him, becoming known, gladly enlists W.'s aid, and will follow him to England (*Hol.* iii, 674–5). (iv, 1) her plans reported to Edward. (iv, 6) mtd. v, 4] (at Tewkesbury) seeks to imbue her adherents with new courage. v, 5] is made prisoner; swoons at seeing her son killed; recovering, reviles his murderers. (v, 7) is ransomed by her father, and dismissed to France (Hall, p. 301).

In iii, 2, l. 26, 'Nell' is given for 'Margaret,' apparently by mistake; so also is 'Elianor' or 'Elinor' in ll. 79, 100, 120.

D.P. *Rich. III.* (i, 2) mtd. i, 3] overhears the altercation between Richard and Q. Elizabeth; then, revealing herself, recites the crimes of the house of York; invokes terrible curses on all its members, and especially on Richard; exonerates Buckingham, but warns him of his fate. (iii, 3, 4) her curse recalled. (iv, 1) Q. Elizabeth dreads it. iv, 4] joins Q. Elizabeth and the Dss. of York in reciting their woes, and in calling down imprecations on Richard, 'hell's black intelligencer.' (v, 1) Buckingham remembers her prophecy.

In this play Margaret must be regarded as a fictitious character, since she never returned to England after 1475, and died in 1482 before the actual date of iv, 4.

God's 'judgment is embodied in the fearful Margaret and her curses, in which the avenging spirit utters its terrible decree. With striking glaringness, distinctness, and intensity, Sh. has pronounced, repeated, and accomplished these imprecations.' (Gervinus, *Sh. Comm.* (1875), p. 276.)

Margery. For 'Margaret.' Name used at random by Leontes, *Wint. T.* ii, 3; wife of old Gobbo, *M.V.* ii, 2; mtd., *Temp.* ii, 2, song; 'M. Jourdain' (*2 Hen. VI*, i, 2).

Maria (1). D.P. *L.L.L.* Lady attending on the Princess of France. ii, 1] characterizes Longaville; exchanges raillery with Boyet. iv, 1] comments on the banter between Boyet and Rosaline. (iv, 3) Longaville's sonnet to her. v, 2] receives a letter and gift from Longaville; is wooed, when masked, by Dumain; promises to wed L. 'at the twelvemonth's end.'

Maria (2). D.P. *T. Nt.* 'Olivia's woman (Rowe). i, 3] warns Sir Toby that Olivia disapproves of his 'ill hours'; discusses Aguecheek's character, and, on his entrance, banters him. i, 5] exchanges raillery with Feste; announces that 'Cesario' is at the gate; is present during the first part of the interview between Ol. and 'C.' ii, 3] warns Sir T. and his boon companions that Malvolio has been ordered to turn them out of doors; later, unfolds her plan of deceiving the steward. ii, 5] throws down a forged letter on the garden-walk; re-enters to learn the result of the plot. iii, 1] *p.m.* iii, 2] describes to Sir T. and his companions Mal.'s absurd dress and demeanour. iii, 4] tells Ol. that she believes Mal., who approaches, is 'tainted in's wits'; joins her mistress in interrogating Mal.; re-enters with Sir T. and Fabian; they all treat Mal. as one possessed. iv, 2] gives Feste his disguise and listens to his conversation with Mal. in durance. (v, 1) Feste announces that Sir T. has wedded her.

The wit, vivacity, and small stature of Maria are everywhere emphasized: 'as witty a piece of Eve's flesh as any in Illyria' (i, 5); 'some mollification for your giant, sweet lady' (*ib.*); 'Good night, Penthesilea' (ii, 4); 'She's a beagle, true bred' (*ib.*); 'Here comes the little villain' (ii, 5). 'Thou most excellent devil of wit!' (*ib.*); 'Look where the youngest wren of nine ['mine,' Ff] comes!' (iii, 2). Called 'marian' (ii, 3).

Marian. For 'Maria' (D.P.); *T. Nt.* ii, 3. As a feminine name: 'M. and Margery' (*Temp.* ii, 2); 'M.'s nose looks red' (*L.L.L.* v, 2); name of a servant, *Com. Err.* iii, 1. As a forename: 'M. Hacket' (*q.v.*).

Marian, Maid. Robin Hood's sweetheart in the ballads; one of the chief characters in the May-games; represented by a man who indulged in gross buffoonery. 'For womanhood, Maid Marian may be the deputy's wife of the ward to thee' (*1 Hen. IV*, iii, 3).

See *Sh. Eng.* ii, 430 ff.

Mariana (1). D.P. *M. for M.* 'Betrothed to Angelo' (F1). (iii, 1) affianced to Angelo, but rejected by him in consequence of the loss of her marriage-dowry; she leads a secluded life in a 'moated grange.' iv, 1] greets the Duke; later, consents to personate Isabella at her trysting-place with Angelo. iv, 6] converses with Is. v, 1] veiled, she accompanies Is. to meet the Duke; she unveils, and tells her story; the Duke at first feigns to disbelieve her, but afterward commands Angelo to marry her; later, she intercedes for A.'s life, which is spared.

The introduction of this character, by which the most repellant feature of Cinthio's tale is removed, is due to Sh.

Mariana (2). D.P. *All's Well*. A friend of Diana's mother. iii, 5] warns Diana against the suggestions of Parolles.

Mariana (3). See MARINA.

Marina. D.P. *Per.* Daughter to Pericles and Thaisa. (iii, 1) she is born at sea; Pericles resolves to leave the babe at Tharsus. iii, 3] she is left as an infant in the care of Cleon and Dionyza. (iv, Gow.) has grown up and incurred the jealous hatred of D. iv, 1] is about to be murdered, by D.'s orders, when she is carried away by pirates. (iv, 2) mtd. iv, 3] is sold by the pirates to the keepers of a *lupanar*; in her despair calls on Diana to aid her. (iv, 4) a monument is erected over her pretended tomb at Tharsus. iv, 6] appeals successfully to the virtue and generosity of the Governor, who gives her gold by which she purchases her release. (v, Gow.) she pays for her freedom by teaching feminine accomplishments. v, 1] recovers Pericles from his 'distemperature'; they are made known to each other. v, 2] *p.m.*; mtd. by Gower. v, 3] (at Ephesus) is made known to her mother, at the temple of Diana.

In Gower's *Confessio Amantis* Apollonius' d. is Thaise, and in Twine's novel Tarsia. In the title of the 1st edn. of *Pericles* the name is 'Mariana,' as in iv, 3.

Mariner, A. D.P. *Wint. T.* iii, 3] lands Antigonus and the infant Perdita on the coast of Bohemia, and is glad to be 'rid of the business.' (v, 2) his bark is wrecked and all the crew perish.

Drummond of Hawthornden relates that Ben Jonson, in 1619, animadverted on Sh.'s having 'in a play brought in a number of men saying they had suffered shipwreck in Bohemia, wher ther is no sea neer by some 100 miles'; this seems an imperfect reminiscence of the play.

Mark. For 'Marcus,' used only before 'Anthony' or 'Anthony.'

Marle, Robert de Bar, Count of. Fought bravely at Agincourt, where he was killed (*Hol.* iii, 554–5). Mtd. among the slain, *Hen. V*, iv, 8 ('Verton,' Qq).

[**Marlowe, Christopher** (*c.* 1564–93).] Poet and dramatist. Alluded to as 'Dead shepherd' (*A.Y.L.* iii, 5, l. 82) – line 72 of his paraphrase of the *Hero and Leander* of Musaeus being quoted.

[**Marney, Sir Henry.**] See BRANDON.

Mars (1). Roman god of war; sometimes represented as gigantic, bearded, and of ferocious aspect, sometimes as a youthful but powerful figure, clad in splendid armour. *Durus, torvus, cruentus, ferus, ferox, bellicus*, are epithets of M. in Virgil, Horace, and Ovid. Acc. one legend he was father of Cupid by Venus.

'This Hotspur, M. in swathing clothes' (*1 Hen. IV*, iii, 2); 'the mailed M. shall on his altar sit Up to the ears in blood' (*ib.* iv, 1); 'assume the part of M.' (*Hen. V*, i, Chor.); 'Big M. seems bankrupt in theirw'by M. his gauntlet' (noted as an 'untraded oath') (*ib.* iv, 5); 'by great M., the captain of us all' (*ib. ib.*); 'the forge that stithied M. his helm' (*ib. ib.*); 'in characters as red as M. his heart Inflam'd with Venus' (*ib.* v, 2); 'the hand of M. Beckoning with fiery truncheon' (*ib.* v, 3); 'thou valiant M. [gold]' (*Timon*, iv, 3); 'now M., I prithee, make us quick in work' (*Cor.* i, 4); 'Why, thou M. [Coriolanus]' (*ib.* iv, 5); 'as if he were son and heir to M.' (*ib. ib.*); 'Hear'st thou M.?' (*ib.* v, 5); 'his goodly eyes [Antony's] Have glowed like plated M.' (*Ant. Cl.* i, 1); 'What Venus did with M.' (*ib.* i, 5; cf. *P.P.* xi); 'speak as loud as M.' (*ib.* ii, 2); 'painted one way like a Gorgon, T'other way he's a M.' (*ib.* ii, 5); 'with M. fall out, with Juno chide' (*Cymb.* v, 4); 'M.'s armour, forged for proof eterne' (*Haml.* ii, 2); 'an eye like M., to threaten and command' (*ib.* iii, 4); 'M.'s hot minion [Venus]' (*Temp.* iv, 1); 'Thou art the M. of male-contents' (*M.W.W.* i, 3); 'the armipotent M.' (*L.L.L.* v, 2); 'the beards of Hercules and frowning M.' (*M.V.* iii, 2); 'M. dote on you for his novices' (*All's Well*, ii, 1); 'M.'s fiery steed' (*ib.* ii, 3); 'Great M., I put myself into thy file' (*ib.* 160 iii, 3); 'my heart hath the fear of M. before it' (*ib.* iv, 1); 'this seat of M. [England]' (*Rich. II*, ii, 1); 'the black Prince, that young M. of men' (*ib.* ii, 3). *Lat.* 'ad Martem' (*T. And.* iv, 3). Mtd., *Son.* lv.

Mars (2). Planet. The irregular, and at times retrograde, apparent motion of M. perplexed astronomers from very early days. Astrologically, M. was 'choleric and flery, a lover of slaughter and quarrels.'

Helena banters Parolles, who boasts that he was born under M., and suggests that it must have been 'when he was retrograde ... you go so much backward when you fight' (*All's Well*, i, 1); 'M. his true moving, even as in the heavens So in the earth, to this day is not known' (*1 Hen. VI*, i, 2).

Kepler's *De Motibus Stellae Martis* was published in 1609.

Marseilles. Chief sea-port of France, on the Mediterranean. The scene is laid there in *All's Well*, v, 1. 'His grace is at M.' (*All's Well*, iv, 4); 'his highness comes post from M.' (*ib. ib.*); 'An argosy ... lying in M. road' (*Tam. Sh.* ii, 1; 'Marcellus,' 'Marsellis,' FfQ).

The metre requires a trisyllable in the first and third instances; the second passage is prose. In *All's Well*, iv, 4, 5, 'Marcellae' and 'Marcellus' respectively (F1).

Marshal. D.P. *Per.* ii, 3] officiates at a banquet.

'Martiall,' QqF3; 'Martial,' F4.

Marshal, The Lord. D.P. *Rich. II.* i, 3] officiates in the lists at Coventry. See SURREY, DUKE OF.

Marshalsea. One of five gaols in Southwark; originally the prison of the court of the Knight Marshal; later used as a debtors' prison, and demolished in 1856. 'I'll find A M. shall hold ye play these two months' (*Hen. VIII*, v, 4).

Martext, Sir Oliver. D.P. *A. Y. L.* 'A country curate' (Rowe). iii, 3] is prepared to marry Touchstone and Audrey in the forest, but is checked by Jaques; in departing, he exclaims, 'ne'er a fantastical knave of them all shall flout me out of my calling.'

T. speaks of him (iii, 3) as 'the vicar of the next village.'

Martin, St. 'Expect St M.'s summer, halcyon days' (*1 Hen. VI*, i, 2), *i.e.* a spell of fine weather at about the date of St Martin's Day (Nov. 11).

Martino, Signor. An invited guest; *Rom. J.* i, 2.

Martius. D.P. *T. And.* 'Son to Titus Andronicus.' i, 2] fears that Titus 'is not with himself' in refusing burial to Mutius. ii, 2] *p.m.* ii, 3] is enticed by Aaron into the pit where lies the body of Bassianus; is accused, with his brother, of having murdered B. iii, 1] *p.m.*; the brothers are led to execution.

Martlemas. For 'Martinmas,' feast of St Martin (Nov. 11). Poins speaks of Falstaff as 'the M.' (*2 Hen. IV*, ii, 2), perh. in allusion to 'St Martin's Summer' (*q.v.*), or to 'M. beef,' fattened by that date (*cf.* Macaulay, *Hist. of Eng.* (1871), i, 154).

Marullus. (See FLAVIUS (1).) D.P. *Jul. C.* i, 1] with Flavius; chides the commoners bitterly for their ingratitude to Pompey's memory; bids them run to their houses; doubts whether the images may be 'disrobed' on a festival.

'Murellus' and 'Murrellus,' in early edns., until corrected by Theobald.

Mary (1). The Virgin Mary. The marriage of the Dauphin Lewis with Blanch of Castile at 'Saint M.'s chapel' (*John*, ii, 1); 'blessed M.'s son' (*Rich. II*, ii, 1); 'by holy M.' (*Hen. VIII*, v, 2).

Referred to as 'God's mother' (*1 Hen. VI*, i, 2; *2 Hen. VI*, ii, 1; *3 Hen. VI*, iii, 2); 'God's holy mother' (*Rich. III*, i, 3); 'God's blest mother' (*Hen. VIII*, v, 1); 'Christ's mother' (*1 Hen. VI*, i, 2); 'the holy mother of our Lord' (*Rich. III*, iii, 7).

Mary (2). Daughter of Henry VIII and Katharine of Arragon, afterward queen. Her projected marriage with the D. of Orleans, second son of Francis I, mtd. *Hen. VIII*, ii, 4.

Mary (3). For 'Maria' (D.P.). *T. Nt.* i, 3, 5; ii, 3.

Mary, St. See MARY (1).

Masham. 'My kind Lord of M.' (*Hen. V*, ii, 2). See SCROPE, LORD.

Master (of a ship). D.P. *2 Hen. VI.* iv, 1] he, as well as his mate, is allotted a prisoner, and gains a thousand crowns as ransom.

The master was the navigating officer of the vessel, which being 'a ship of warre' (*Hol.* iii, 632) had also a captain.

Master-Gunner, of Orleans, and his son. D.PP. *1 Hen. VI.* i, 4] tells his son to watch, during his absence ('at dinner,' *Hol.*) for any sign of the English at their spy-hole in the bridge-tower, and bring him word. His son fires the gun himself, and mortally wounds Salisbury and Gargrave.

Substantially, as related in *Hol.* iii, 599. The name of the M.-G. is, traditionally, Maître Jean.

Master's-mate. D.P. *2 Hen. VI.* iv, 1] see MASTER.

Matthew. As a forename. 'M. Gough' (*2 Hen. VI*, iv, 4).

Maud. A servant; *Com. Err.* iii, 1, l. 31. (Dim. of 'Magdalen.')

Maudlin. Daughter of Lafeu (D.P. *All's Well*); named only once (v, 3).

Lafeu tells the Countess that, 'in the minority of both of them,' the King had suggested a marriage between M. and Bertram (iv, 5); the King, believing Helena to be dead, reminds Lafeu of the fact, and declares that 'then we shall have a match' (v, 3); B. on being sounded by the King upon the subject, replies (*ib. ib.*) with an ambiguity which has not been satisfactorily resolved by commentators; see K. Elze, *Essays on Sh.* (1874), pp. 134–7.

Mauri. *Lat.*, gen. of 'Maurus.' In quotn., *T. And.* iv, 2, 'Non eget Mauri jaculis' (Hor. *Odes*, i, 22).

Mauritania. Land of the Moors; mtd. at random, by Iago, *Oth.* iv, 2.

May, Month of. Chiefly in its aspect as a period of Nature's renascence.

'Master Fenton ... smells April and M.' (*M.W.W.* iii, 2); the first of M. contrasted with the last of December, *M. Ado*, i, 1; 'His M. of youth' (*ib.* v, 1); to 'wish a snow in M.'s new-fangled shows' (*L.L.L.* i, 1; doubtful reading); 'Love, whose month is ever M.' (*ib.* iv, 3, Q); 'Maids are M. when they are maids, but the sky changes when they are wives' (*A.Y.L.* iv, 1); 'She came adorned hither like sweet M., Sent back like Hallowmas' (*Rich. II*, v, 1); 'As full of spirit as the month of M.' (*1 Hen. IV*, iv, 1); a date, *2 Hen. VI*, i, 1; 'Spring up ... an't were a nettle against M.' (*Tr. Cr.* i, 2); 'her smiles and tears Were like a wetter M.' (*Lear*, iv, 3; Warb. conj.); 'as flush as M.' (*Haml.* iii, 3); 'O rose of M.' (*ib.* iv, 5). The three following quotations refer to the celebration of May-day (*q.v.*): 'More matter for a M. morning' (*T. Nt.* iii, 4); 'to do observance for a morn of M.' (*M.N.D.* i, 1); 'to observe the rite of M.' (*ib.* iv, 1). 'Darling buds of M.' (*Son.* xviii); 'storm ... 'twixt M. and April' (*L.C.* 102); mtd., *P.P.* xvii, xxi.

May-day. The celebration of the first of May is of immemorial antiquity, and it was doubtless a just suspicion of the 'pagan' origin of the festival that induced the Puritans, toward the end of the 16th cent., to denounce the popular pastimes connected with its celebration. Stubbs in his *Anatomie of Abuses* (1585) declares that 'the superintendent and lord' over the sports was 'Sathan, Prince of Hell,' and terms the Maypole 'a stinking idol,' round which folk danced, 'as the heathen people did at the dedication of the Idols.' Far otherwise was the view taken by Chaucer (*Knight's Tale*) of the 'observance' due to May, and Stow relates how our ancestors went out 'into the sweet meadows and green woods, there to rejoice their spirits with the beauty and savour of sweet flowers, and with the harmony of the birds praising God in their kind.' The only specific allusions to May-day revelries in *Sh.* are connected with the Morris-dancers, including the rider of the hobby-horse, and the representatives of Robin Hood (*q.v.*) and his band, not forgetting Maid Marian (*q.v.*).

'As fit as ... a morris for May-day' (*All's Well*, ii, 2); 'as much impossible ... as 'tis to make 'em sleep On May-day morning' (*Hen. VIII*, v, 4).

May-morn. The morning of May-day. 'In the very May-morn of his youth' (*Hen. V*, i, 2).

Mayor, or **Lord Mayor, of London.** (*a*) To greet Henry V on his return from France, 'the mayor and all his brethren in best sort ... Go forth and fetch their conquering Caesar in' (*Hen. V*, v, Chor.).

Cf. *Hol.* iii, 556: 'The mayor of London, and the aldermen, apparelled in orient grained scarlet, and foure hundred commoners ... met the king on Blackheath' (1415).

(*b*) D.P. *1 Hen. VI.* i, 3] quells the riot between Gloucester's and the Bp. of Winchester's adherents, threatening to 'call for clubs.' iii, 1] complains to the King that in consequence of the broils between the partisans of the Duke and the Bp. the citizens have to shut their shops.

The Lord Mayor at this date (1425) was John Coventry. (The title of 'Lord Mayor' was first granted by Edw. III, in 1354.)

(*c*) Cade 'will have the mayor's sword borne before him' (2 *Hen. VI*, iv, 3); the Mayor begs for reinforcements from the Tower, *ib.* iv, 5.

(*d*) D.P. *Rich. III.* iii, 1] greets Prince Edward on his entrance into London. iii, 5] agrees that Hastings has justly met his death, and offers to impress the citizens with the fact. iii, 7] entreats Gloucester to assume the crown.

This Lord Mayor was Sir Edmund Shaw, or Shaa, brother to Dr Shaw (*q.v.*).

(*e*) Is commanded to suppress rumours about the King's divorce, *Hen. VIII*, ii, 1.

'Sir Thomas Seimour,' acc. *Hol.* iii, 897.

(*z*) D.P. *Hen. VIII.* v, 5] present at the baptism of Elizabeth; is thanked by the King; *p.m.*

The Lord Mayor at the time was Sir Stephen Pecocke (*Hol.* iii, 934). Presumably also present at the coronation of Anne Boleyn, but not named in *Hol.*

Measure for Measure.

PUBLICATION. First printed in the Folio of 1623. The acts and scenes are numbered. (A comma after the first word in title.) A list of *dramatis personae* is given.

DATE OF COMPOSITION. Uncertain, but generally held to be *c.* 1603. It was performed at Whitehall in the winter of 1604. The known aversion of James I to crowds, leading to somewhat ungracious behaviour on his part when he entered England in 1603, is perhaps apologetically touched on in i, 1, ll. 68–73, and ii, 4, ll. 24–9.

SOURCES OF THE PLOT. The basis of the plot is a tale by Giraldi Cinthio (*Hecatommithi*, viii, 5). This was dramatized as *Promos and Cassandra* (1578) by George Whetstone, who also introduced it as a prose tale into his *Heptameron of Civill Discourses* (1582). Sh., by the invention of the character of Mariana, deprived the original plot of its most repulsive element.

W. Pater, *Appreciations* (1910), p. 183, points out that the title 'expressly suggests the subject of *poetical justice*.'

Mede. 'The kings of M. and Lycaonia' (*Ant. Cl.* iii, 6). In the corresponding passage, *Plut.* p. 207, 'the king of Medes,' and in *Plut.* p. 199, 'the king of the Medes.'

Medea. Daughter of Aeetes, famous for her skill in magic. See ABSYRTUS and AESON. 'In such a night M. gather'd the enchanted herbs That did renew old Aeson' (*M.V.* v, 1); 'into as many gobbets will I cut it As wild M. young Absyrtus did' (2 *Hen. VI*, v, 2).

Media. A country of Asia, above Persia; one of the chief provinces of the ancient persian Empire. 'Spur through M., Mesopotamia' (*Ant. Cl.* iii, 1; *Plut.* p. 185); 'Great M.' conferred by Antony on his son Alexander, *ib.* iii, 6 (*Plut.* p. 202).

Mediterranean, *adj.* ('Mediterranian,' Ff.) 'Upon the M. flote' (*Temp.* i, 2).

Mediterraneum. ('Mediteranium,' Ff.) 'The salt wave of the M.' (*L.L.L.* v, 1).

[Medusa.] See GORGON.

Meg. Dim. of 'Margaret.' 'Mall, Meg and Marian' (*Temp.* ii, 2); Page addresses his wife by the name, *M.W.W.* ii, 1; 'Help to dress me, good coz, good M., good Ursula' (*M. Ado*, iii, 4); Queen Margaret so addressed by Henry, 2 *Hen. VI*, iii, 2.

Meisen, Meissen. In Saxony. Now the place of manufacture of 'Dresden' china. 'Which Salique ...'twixt Elbe and Sala, is at this day in Germany called M.' (*Hen. V*, i, 2).

Melancholy. Personified; *M.N.D.* i, 1, l. 16.

Melancholy, Monsieur. Nonce-name applied by Orlando to Jaques; *A.Y.L.* iii, 2, l. 311.

Meleager. See ALTHAEA.

[Meleagrus.] See FLORIZEL.

Melford. Better known as Long Melford, a small town in Suffolk, on the Stour, about 3 m. N. of Sudbury. In the 15th cent. of some importance for its cloth. There are three ancient mansions in the vicinity, formerly belonging to the families of Clopton, Cordell, and Martyn. A petition 'against the Duke of Suffolk for enclosing the commons of M.,' presented to Q. Margaret, 2 *Hen. VI*, i, 3.

'Long Melford,' *F.P.C.* Trouble arising from 'enclosures' was a cause of Kett's rebellion in 1549, Cf. *Sh. Eng.* i, 365.

Melun. D.P. *John.* ('Mel(l)oone,' Ff.) A French lord. (iv, 3) brings letter to Salisbury from 'the cardinal.' v, 2] *p.m.*; is entrusted with the draft of the agreement between Lewis and the barons. v, 4] is brought, mortally wounded, to the disaffected barons, and advises them to make their peace with John, since Lewis has treacherously determined to execute them in the event of his being victorious. (v, 5) his death announced.

Acc. *Hol.* iii, 193, this confession was made by 'the viscount of Melune, a French man' not on the battlefield, but in London, where he had fallen sick. A 'Count de M.' is mtd. in the treaty, dated 1194, between France and England. See CHATILLON. M.'s claim that his 'grandsire was an Englishman' (*John*, v, 4) is not found in the Chronicles, but *verbatim* in the *Tr. R.*

Robert de Melun, Bp. of Hereford (1163–6), was a chief opponent of Becket, and was called 'Episcopus Anglorum sapientissimus' (French, p. 18).

Memphis. An important city of ancient Egypt; near its site stand the great pyramids of Ghizeh. See RHODOPE. 'A statelier pyramis to her I'll rear than Rhodope's, or Memphis' (*1 Hen. VI*, i, 6).

Capell suggested 'Rhodope's of M.'

Menaphon. 'Duke'; mtd., as 'that famous warrior,' and 'most renowned uncle' of Solinus, *Com. Err.* v, 1.

The name of a character in Marlowe's *Tamerlaine* (Part I), and title of a work by R. Greene.

Menas. A freedman of Sext. Pompeius; given command of a fleet, 40 B.C., against Antony and Octavius (who were at that time reconciled). He tried to prevent his master from making peace with Ant. and Oct., and at a banquet given by Sextus on his galley suggested cutting one of the cables, putting to sea, and despatching both his rivals (Dion Cass. xlviii, 30, 36–8; *Plut.* p. 180).

D.P. *Ant. Cl.* (i, 4) a 'famous pirate.' ii, 1] informs Pompey that Oct. and Lepidus have joined forces. ii, 6] converses with Enobarbus, who reminds him that he had 'been a great thief by sea'; comments on Antony's marriage with Octavia. ii, 7] makes the proposal to Pompey mtd. above, but is told that he should have done the deed without imparting his intention. (iii, 2) mtd.

The appearance of M. in v, 1, is generally regarded as an error for 'Mecenas.'

[Mend-all.] See Cade, John.

Menecrates. A freedman of Sextus Pompeius, sent in command of a squadron against Menas the renegade. He threw himself overboard to escape capture by Menas (Dion Cass. xlviii, 46). Acc. *Plut.* p. 180, Menas and Menecrates were 'two notable pirates' who scoured the seas on behalf of Sext. Pomp. See Menas.

D.P. *Ant. Cl.* (i, 4) a 'famous pirate.' ii, 1] comments on the efficacy of prayer to the gods.

There is some difficulty in disentangling the speeches of Menecrates and Menas. Johnson remarks: 'I know not why Menecrates appears, Menas can do all without him.'

Menelaus. King of Lacedaemon and husband of Helen. In the Homeric poems he is represented as a man of few words, courageous, but mild and hospitable. Henry VI is compared to M. by Edward IV (*3 Hen. VI*, ii, 2) as being wronged by his wife.

D.P. *Tr. Cr.* 'Brother to Agamemnon.' (prol.) mtd. (i, 1) wounds Paris. i, 3] announces Aeneas. iii, 3] greets Achilles scornfully. (iv, 1) mtd. iv, 5] greets Cressida, and exchanges raillery with her; (Calchas lodges in his tent). v, 1] present. v, 8] fights with Paris. v, 10] *p.m.*

Menenius (Lanatus) Agrippa. Consul 503 B.C.; famous for having mediated between the patricians and the plebeians on the occasion of the secession of the latter to the Sacred Mount, 493 B.C. (Livy, ii, 16, 32, 33).

D.P. *Cor.* ('Menenius' alone, except once in i, 1.) i, 1] reasons with the plebeians, and relates the fable of 'the belly and the members'; learns from Marcius that tribunes have been appointed. ii, 1] upbraids the tribunes as 'a brace of unmeriting, proud, violent, testy magistrates, *alias* fools'; rejoices to hear that Marcius has returned, wounded but victorious – 'I will make my very house reel tonight'; greets Marcius with 'a hundred thousand welcomes,' but warns him that there are some in Rome who bear him no good will. ii, 2] bids Cominius rehearse the valorous deeds of Coriolanus; chides the tribunes for intruding their grievances at such a moment; informs Cor. that the Senate has made him consul, and bids him appeal to the people for their suffrages in due form. ii, 3] conducts Cor. to the place where he is to stand as candidate, and begs him to address the plebeians 'in wholesome manner'; later, escorts him toward the Senatehouse. iii, 1] vainly urges Cor. to be 'calm' when confronted by the tribunes on his way to the forum; after the resulting tumult has been allayed, M. persuades the tribunes to 'proceed by process.' iii, 2] begs Cor. to answer 'mildly' at the coming trial. iii, 3] asks the citizens to overlook any soldier-like roughness in Cor.'s words; tries in vain to check his outbursts. iv, 1] bids Cor. farewell. iv, 2] is escorting Volumnia and Virgilia, when they meet the tribunes. iv, 6] learns that Cor. is marching upon Rome; reproaches the citizens for their folly and cowardice, and gleefully predicts their fate. v, 1] undertakes to plead with Cor., after the general has dined. v, 2] is rebuffed by Cor., but given a letter. v, 4] predicts that as Cor. would not listen to him neither will he to his wife and mother; learns that 'the ladies have prevail'd.'

The dramatic character of Menenius is Sh.'s creation. Apart from the well-known 'fable' the only hint Sh. has worked upon is Plutarch's remark (p. 6) that M. was one 'of the pleasantest old men' in the Senate.

Menon. Greek warrior; acc. Caxton, *Recuyell*, a cousin of Achilles. Mtd. as overcome by Polydamas, *Tr. Cr.* v, 5.

A name of frequent occurrence in Plutarch.

Menteith. See Fife, Earl of.

Menteith, Thane of. Adherent of Malcolm Canmore, at whose coronation he was created earl (*Hol.* ii, 176).

D.P. *Macb.* v, 2] converses with the other thanes before Dunsinane. v, 4] points out Birnam wood to Siward. v, 8] joins in acclaiming Malcolm as king.

'Menteth' (following *Hol.*) in all edns. before Dyce.

Mephostophilus. An evil spirit in the prose *History of the Damnable Life and Deserved Death of Dr John Faustus* (*c.* 1589). Applied as a random term of abuse by Pistol to Slender: 'How now, M.?' (*M.W.W.* i, 1).

'Mephostophiles' in *The Second Report of Doctor John Faustus* (1594); in Marlowe's *Faustus* the name is variously spelt.

Mercade. D.P. *L.L.L.* A 'lord attending on the Princess of France' (Rowe). v, 2] announces to the Princess the death of her father.

Misprinted 'Macard' by Rowe – an error perpetuated by five succeeding edrs.; 'Marcade,' Q and Ff; the present form was first given by Capell. Perh. a trisyllable (v, 2, l. 724).

Mercatio. A suitor of Julia, who thinks 'well of his wealth; but of himself, so so' (*T.G.V.* i, 2).

'Mercutio,' Coll. MS.

Merchant (1). D.P. *Com. Err.* 'A friend to Antipholus of Syracuse.' i, 2] warns Ant. S. of the danger he runs at Ephesus, where Syracusans are proscribed; hands him a purse of which he had the care.

Merchant (2). D.P. *Com. Err.* iv, 1] demands a debt from Angelo, a goldsmith, and, on Angelo's failing to obtain money for a chain from Ant. E., has Ant. arrested. „ 1] encounters Ant. S. (whom he believes to be Ant. E.), wearing Angelo's chain; high words ensue, and they draw; is told his opponent is mad, and desists; later, when Ant. E. appears, swears that he is the man on whom he drew sword.

Merchant (3). D.P. *Timon.* i, 1] converses.

Merchant of Venice, The.

Publication. In 1598 a licence to publish 'The Marchant of Venyce or otherwise called the Jewe of Venyce,' was granted to James Roberts. By permission of Roberts, however, a second licence was obtained by Thomas Heyes, who published the play in quarto in 1600 under the title: 'The most excellent Historie of the Merchant of Venice. With the extreame crueltie of Shylocke the Iewe towards the sayd Merchant, in cutting a just pound of his flesh: and the obtayning of Portia by the choyse of three chests. As it has beene diuers times acted by the Lord Chamberlaine his Seruants. Written by William Shakespeare.'

Another quarto exists, also dated 1600, but this has been shown to have been really issued in 1619 by Thomas Pavier. (See A. W. Pollard, *Sh.'s Fight with the Pirates* (1920).) The text in the Folio of 1623 follows that of Heyes' Quarto, with a few alterations. The acts, but not the scenes, are numbered.

Date of Composition. Not ascertained, but probably *c.*1595. Mentioned by Meres in 1598. Acc. Henslowe's *Diary*, 'The Venesyon Comodey' was performed several times in 1594, but it is very doubtfully identical with *M.V.*

Sources of the Plot. The story of 'the pound of flesh' is related in *Il Pecorone* by 'Ser Giovanni Fiorentino,' written in the 14th cent. and published in 1558. Of this no English translation existed. The name of Belmonte and the incident of the ring (*M.V.* v, 1) also occur in this. This story of the pound of flesh is of ancient Eastern origin, being included in the *Mahábhárata*, and is given briefly in the *Gesta Romanorum*.

The story of the caskets is found in the Greek romance of *Barlaam and Josaphat* (*c.* 800), and thence descended to the English translation of the *Golden Legend* of Jacobus de Voragine, printed by Wynkyn de Worde in 1527. The same story occurs in a very suggestive form in the *Gesta Romanorum*, and in Boccaccio's *Decamerone* (x, 1).

It appears, moreover, that a play, now lost, in which the two plots were blended, had been produced before 1579; for Stephen Gosson in *The Schoole of Abuse*, published in that year (Arber, p. 40), speaks with approval of 'The Jew ... showne at the Bull, ... representing the greedinesse of worldly chusers, and bloody minds of Usurers.'

Sir S. Lee has pointed out that the trial and execution of Roderigo Lopez, the Queen's Jewish physician, in 1594 (*Life of Sh.* (1915), p. 133 and *n.*) may have directed Sh.'s attention to the Jews. The play of *The Three Ladies of London* by R.[obert] W.[ilson] contains anticipations of certain passages in *M.V.* (*ib.* p. 132).

The incident of the elopement of Jessica, and her theft of jewels, has been traced (Dunlop, *Hist. of Fiction* (1854), p. 254) to the 14th tale of Massuccio di Salerno (*c.* 1470).

The influence of Marlowe's *Jew of Malta* on *M.V.* has been discussed by K. Elze, *Sh. Jahrbuch*, vi, 133, and Sir A. W. Ward, *Hist. Eng. Dram. Lit.* (1875), i, 188.

Mercurial. Pertaining to Mercury (1). 'His foot M.' (*Cymb.* iv, 2).

Mercury (1). Roman god of commerce and gain, later identified with the Greek Hermes, whose attributes were all transferred to M. Hence he was regarded as the herald of the gods; the inventor of the syrinx, or pipe; the god of persuasive eloquence, endowed with the qualities even of fraud and perjury and an inclination for theft. His attributes are a winged hat, winged sandals, and a staff (*caduceus*), also winged and adorned with ribbons or serpents. See Hermes.

'Now M. indue them with leasing' (*T. Nt.* i, 5); 'Rise from the ground, like feathered M.' (*1 Hen. IV*, iv, 1); 'your first order ... a wing'd M. did bear' (*Rich. III*, ii, 1); 'then fiery expedition be my wing, Jove's M.' (*ib.* iv, 3); 'strong-wing'd M.' (*Ant. Cl.* iv, 15); M. set feathers to thy heels' (*John*, iv, 2); (the knights) 'with winged heels, as English M.s' (*Hen. V*, ii, Chor.); 'My good she M.' (Falstaff to Quickly, as a messenger; *M.W.W.* ii, 2); 'the words of M. are harsh after the songs of Apollo' (*L.L.L.* v, 2); 'M., lose all the serpentine craft of thy caduceus' (*Tr. Cr.* ii, 3); 'the herald M.' (*Haml.* iii, 4); nvoked, *T. And.* iv, 1; mtd., *ib.* iv, 3, 4; 'fly like chidden M. from Jove' (*Tr. Cr.* ii, 2; *cf.* Marlowe's *Hero and Leander*, i, but the origin of the episode is unknown).

Mercury (2). Planet; its astrological influence is illustrated by the remark of Autolycus that he was 'littered under M.' (*Wint. T.* iv, 2), and hence a pilferer.

Mercutio. D.P. *Rom. J.* Kinsman to the Prince, and friend to Romeo. (i, 2) invited to Capulet's feast. i, 4] urges Romeo to join the maskers; describes 'Queen Mab.' ii, 1] jests with Benvolio on Romeo's passion. ii, 4] characterizes Tybalt as a punctilious duellist; banters Romeo, on his falling in love, and also that 'ancient lady,' Juliet's nurse. iii, 1] is mortally wounded by Tybalt, who picks a quarrel with him – his hurt 'is not so deep as a well, nor so wide as a church door; but 'tis enough, 'twill serve'; (the manner in which he received his wound is described by Benvolio). (v, 3) mtd.

'Wit ever wakeful, fancy busy and procreative as an insect, courage, an easy mind that, without cares of its own, is at once disposed to laugh away those of others, and yet to be interested in them – these and all congenial qualities, melting into the common *copula* of them all, the man of rank and the gentleman, with all its excellencies and all its weaknesses, constitute the character of Mercutio!' (S.T. Coleridge). 'One of the most mercurial and spirited of the productions of Sh.'s comic muse' (W. Hazlitt).

[Merke, Thomas (*ob.* 1409).] A Benedictine monk of Westminster; made Bp. of Carlisle in 1397. As a faithful adherent of Rich. II, he was committed to the Tower, 1400, but was released and pardoned by Hen. IV on account of his high character. He afterward acted as episcopal deputy to the Bp. of Winchester.

D.P. *Rich. II.* Bp. of Carlisle ('Carlile,' Ff). iii, 2] *p.m.*; returns with Richard from Ireland. iii, 3] *p.m.*; with Rich. in Wales. iv, 1] solemnly protests against Bolingbroke's usurpation, and predicts future civil war as its consequence; is committed to the custody of the Abbot of Westminster 'till his day of trial'; the Abbot hints to him that a plot is afoot. v, 6] is brought before Bol. for sentence, as a conspirator, but is pardoned by the King for the 'high sparks of honour' seen in him.

Sh. has antedated the Bp.'s speech (iv, 1), which was not delivered on the occasion of Richard's deposition (Sept. 30), but on Oct. 22. Acc. *Hol.* iii, 516, the Bp. died shortly after being pardoned, 'more through feare than force of sickness'; but this is an error.

Merlin, or Myrddin Emrys. A legendary prophet and enchanter, variously associated with Wales, Scotland, Cornwall, and Brittany; acc. one tradition, he flourished at the time of the Saxon invasion. He is an important figure in Malory's *Morte d'Arthur*, and is frequently mentioned by Spenser.

'The dreamer M. and his prophecies' (*1 Hen. IV*, iii, 1); 'this prophecy M. shall make; for I live before his time' (*Lear, iii, 2*), *for, acc. Hol.* i, 12, Leir lived 'at what time Joas reigned in Juda.'

Merops. Husband of Clymene, the mother of Phaëthon (*q.v.*). 'Why, Phaëton, for thou art M.'s son, wilt thou aspire?' (*T.G.V.* iii, 1).

Cf. 'Ph., mistrusting silly Merops for his sire' (*Tr. R.* (1591), I, 1).

Merriman. Name of a hound; *Tam. Sh.* Ind. 1.

Still survives as a dog's name; *cf. Sh. Eng.* ii, 349.

Merry Wives of Windsor, The.

Publication. First printed in an imperfect form in 1602 (Q1), probably from notes hastily taken down in shorthand. The text in the Folio of 1623 omits several speeches found in Q, but adds so many new passages that it is nearly twice as long as the latter. The acts and scenes are numbered. A second edn. of Q1 was published in 1619 (Q2).

DATE OF COMPOSITION. There is a tradition, handed down by Dennis and Rowe, that Sh. wrote *M.W.W.* in a fortnight, at the bidding of Queen Elizabeth, who desired to see Falstaff in love. At any rate, the play closely followed 1, 2 *Hen. IV*, and is usually dated *c.* 1599. (See GARMOMBLES.)

M.W.W. is noteworthy as being written entirely in prose.

SOURCES OF THE PLOT. A tale in Tarleton's *Newes out of Purgatorie* (1590) adapted from Straparola's *Notti*, iv, 4; a tale in 'Ser Giovanni Fiorentino's' *Il Pecorone*, i, 2; and the Fishwife's tale of Brainford in *Westward for Smelts* – all may have supplied hints for the scenes of intrigue and jealousy.

R.C. Rhodes, *Sh.'s First Folio* (1923), pp. 97 ff., gives reasons for believing the text of F1 to have been 'assembled' from a collection of players' parts.

Mesopotamia. Country between the Euphrates and the Tigris; mtd. *Ant. Cl.* iii, 1. ('Mesapotamia,' Ff.)

Messala, or **Messalla.** M. Valerius Messalla Corvinus; a member of a distinguished family of the Valeria *gens*; he fought on the republican side at Philippi, but was pardoned by the triumvirs, and became a friend of Augustus, and one of his chief generals.

D.P. *Jul. C.* 'Friend to Brutus and Cassius.' iv, 3] converses with Bru. and Cas. on the proscription, and announces the death of Portia. v, 1] (before Philippi) to him Cassius declares that he is compelled against his will 'to set upon one battle all our liberties' (*Plut.* p. 139). v, 2] *p.m.*; bears orders on the field. v, 3] as he relates to Titinius the success of Brutus against Octavius, he sees the body of Cassius lying hard by, and laments that 'Mistrust of good success hath done this deed'; departs to tell Brutus, and returns with him to the spot. v, 5] enters as prisoner; commends Strato (*q.v.*) to Octavius (*Plut.* p. 151).

Messaline. An unknown locality. '*Seb.* My father was that Sebastian of M., whom I know you have heard of' (*T. Nt.* ii, 1); '*Seb.* What country-man? ... *Vio.* Of M.' (*ib.* v, 1).

'Metelin,' Hanmer; 'Mitylene,' Capell.

Messengers. The following D.PP., thus described in st. dirs., appear:

In *Cymb.* iii, 5] announces that Imogen is missing. ('Attendant' in mod. edns.)

In *Macb.* iv, 2] urges Lady Macduff to flee from imminent danger. v, 5] tells Macb. that Birnam wood 'began to move.'

In *M. Ado.* i, 1] announces the impending arrival of Don Pedro and his train; eulogizes Benedick. iii, 5] summons Leonato. v, 4] announces flight of Don John.

In *T. And.* iii, 1] brings back the hand of Titus, which he had sacrificed to save his sons, together with their heads.

Messengers, Three. D.PP. *1 Hen. VI.* i, 1] M. 1 announces loss of territories in France and blames the apathy and dissensions of the nobles; M. 2 announces the crowning of Charles; M. 3, the defeat of Talbot.

[**Messenio.**] See DROMIO OF SYRACUSE.

Messina. Capital of the province of M., in Sicily. Scene of *Much Ado About Nothing*, and of Bandello's novel from which the plot was derived. Mtd., *M. Ado*, i, 1; iii, 5; iv, 2; v, 1, 4.

Metamorphoses. One of the principal works of Ovid (*q.v.*); in use as a school-book, and widely known from Arthur Golding's translation (1567), of which the seventh edition appeared in 1597. Lavinia (*T. And.* iv, 1), trying to indicate the wrong done to her, seeks the aid of a copy of the M. belonging to the boy Lucius. ('Metamorphosis,' QqFf.)

Metellus. For 'Metellus Cimber.' *Jul. C.* ii, 1 (2), 2; iii, 1. See CIMBER, M.

Mexico. Commercial intercourse with M. mtd.: 'He hath a third argosy at Mexico' (*M.V.* i, 3); 'What, not one hit? ... from M... .?' (*ib.* iii, 2).

Michael. As a forename. 'M. Hopkins' (*Hen. VIII*, i, 1); for 'M. Cassio,' *Oth.* ii, 3 (3).

Michael. D.P. *2 Hen. VI.* 'A follower of Jack Cade.' iv, 2] announces, in terror, the approach of the Staffords (*q.v.*).

Michael, St, Order of. *1 Hen. VI*, iv, 7.

Michael, Sir. D.P. *1 Hen. IV.* A friend to Abp. Scrope. ('Gentleman' in st. dirs. and pfxs.) iv, 4] is entrusted with a sealed missive; assures the Abp. that their forces are strong and ready. (Spelt in five ways, QqFf.)

French (p. 66) suggests that the Abp.'s chaplain is intended, 'Sir' being a common clerical prefix.

Michaelmas. The festival of St Michael and All Angels (Sept. 29). 'A fortnight afore M.' (*M.W.W.* i, 1; see ALLHALLOWMAS); mtd., *1 Hen. IV*, ii, 4.

Midas. King of Phrygia. Bacchus granted his request that everything he touched should be turned into gold, and M. was consequently in danger of starvation until the god took back his favour (Ovid, *Metam.* xi, 102 ff.).

'Thou gaudy gold, Hard food for M.' (*M.V.* iii, 2).

[**Middleham Castle.**] Edw. IV, when taken prisoner by Warwick, is sent thither. 'See that forthwith Duke Edward be convey'd Unto my brother, Archbishop of York' (*3 Hen. VI*, iv, 3); see NEVILLE, GEORGE.

Midsummer. The period of the summer solstice, or, specifically, the Feast of St John Baptist, June 24. The proverbial phrase 'M. madness' appears to refer to the wild revelry once associated with M. Eve throughout Europe; but Halliwell quotes: 'He wyll waxe madde this mydsommer moone if you take nat good hede on hym' (Palsgrave (1852), p. 775). See JULY, MONTH OF.

Rosalind avows that Leander was drown'd on 'a hot M. night' (*A.Y.L.* iv, 1); 'gorgeous as the sun at M.' (*1 Hen. IV*, iv, 1); Olivia declares that Malvolio's strange behaviour is 'mere M. madness' (*T. Nt.* iii, 4).

Midsummer Night's Dream, A. (In F1: 'A Midsommer Nights Dreame.' The acts, but not the scenes, are numbered.)

PUBLICATION. The Stationers' Registers, under the date Oct. 8, 1600, note that 'A booke called A mydsommer nightes Dreame' was entered to 'Thomas ffyssher,' and in the same year Fisher published 'A Midsommer nights dreame. As it hath beene sundry times publickely acted, by ... the Lord Chamberlaine his seruants. Written by William Shakespeare. Imprinted at London, for Thomas Fisher.' This is known as the First Quarto, or Fisher's Quarto. But, also bearing the date 1600, there was published another edition (unregistered) printed by James Roberts. This is the Second, or Roberts', Quarto. Critics have differed as to which is really the first edition. Roberts' is the more carefully printed, and seems to be the copy used by the printers of F1. (*Cf.* Pollard, *Sh. Folios and Quartos* (1909), pp. 81 ff.)

DATE OF COMPOSITION. The play is mentioned by Meres in his *Palladis Tamia* (1598), and the majority of critics, relying on various points of internal evidence, fix the date of its composition between 1594 and 1596; but no item of such evidence has been universally accepted as crucial.

SOURCES OF THE PLOT. The scheme of the comedy as a whole is due entirely to Sh.'s invention. The wedding of Theseus and Hippolyta may be derived from Plutarch and Chaucer's *Knight's Tale*. The story of Pyramus and Thisbe had been familiarly known for centuries. (For supposed prototypes of Puck and Oberon, see those headings.)

The main points of internal evidence of the date of the play, alluded to above, are these: (*a*) Titania's account of the perverted seasons caused by her quarrel with Oberon, which is supposed to be based on extremely bad weather in 1593–4; (*b*) supposed allusions to Spenser's *Faerie Queene*, the first volume of which, however, had appeared in 1590; (*c*) the mention (v, 1) of 'The thrice three Muses, mourning for the death Of learning, late deceas'd in beggary,' which has been supposed to refer to the death of Robt. Greene, in 1592, or to *The Teares of the Muses* by Spenser (1591); (*d*) that the play was written on the occasion of some noble marriage – but as to what marriage critics differ widely.

Milan. Chief city of Lombardy; one of the Imperial residences as far back as Diocletian. See Bryce, *Holy Rom. Emp.* (1904), p. 6*n*. Gian Galeazzo Visconti, in 1395, bought the title of duke from the Emperor. Several Emperors were crowned with the Iron Crown at M., and used to hold their Court there – a fact alluded to, *T.G.V.* i, 3.

Frequently mentioned in *Temp.*: i, 2 (*saepe*); ii, 1 (3); iii, 3; v, 1 (*saepe*), Prospero being 'the rightful Duke of M.' (Spelt 'Millaine' in Ff throughout.) Thrice used for 'Duke of M.': 'absolute M.' (*Temp.* i, 2); 'I was sometime M.' (*ib.* v, 1); 'was M. thrust from M.' (*ib. ib.*).

'The Duchess of M.'s gown' (*M. Ado*, iii, 4). 'Pandulph, of fair M. cardinal' (*John*, iii, 1); (Bast. to Pand.) 'my holy lord of M.' (*ib.* v, 2).

Proteus 'embarks' from Verona to M., *T.G.V.* i, 1; mtd., *ib.* ii, 5, iv, 1. (The scene is laid at M. in ii, 1, 4–6; iii; iv, 2–4; v, 1, 2.)

In Ff 'Padua' occurs in ii, 5, l. 1, and 'Verona' in iii, 1, l. 81 and v, 4, l. 129, in lieu of 'Milan,' which is substituted in some modern edns. But 'these inaccuracies are interesting as showing that Sh. had written the whole of the play before he had finally determined where the scene was to be laid' (Camb.).

Milan, Duke of. See DUKE OF MILAN.

Mile End. E. of Whitechapel, formerly a drilling ground of London train-bands. Mile End Green was a favourite ground for archers, and there 'The Fellowship of Prince Arthur's Knights' held their meetings. Henry VIII is recorded to have personally attended one of the contests at Mile End in 1583. (See DAGONET.

Shallow recalls the 'little quiver fellow' he saw at Mile End Green when he was 'Sir Dagonet in Arthur's show' (*2 Hen. IV*, iii, 2); Parolles declares that 'Dumain' had been an officer at a place called Mile-end, 'to instruct for doubling of files' (*All's Well*, iv, 3), *i.e.* elementary drill.

Milford Haven, or **Milford.** In Pembrokeshire. Richmond landed there in Aug. 1485, two years after his first unsuccessful attempt to join Buckingham. 'The Earl of Richmond Is with a mighty power landed at M.' (*Rich. III*, iv, 4).

'He is at M.-H. ... how far it is To this same blessed M.' (*Cymb.* iii, 2); Pisanio instructed to kill Imogen at M.-H., *ib.* iii, 4; Lucius given safe conduct to M.-H., *ib.* iii, 5; mtd. by Cloten, *ib. ib.*; 'M., when from the mountain-top Pisanio show'd thee Thou wast within a ken' (*ib.* iii, 6); '*Bel.* Whither bound? *Imo.* To M.-H.' (*ib. ib.*); 'he embark'd at M.' (*ib. ib.*); mountains near to M., *ib.* v, 5.

Miller, Yead. *i.e.* 'Ned the miller'; *M.W.W.* i, 1.

Milo, Milon. Of Crotona; a famous athlete. He was said to have carried 'a heifer of four years old' through the Stadium at Olympia. 'Bull-bearing M.' (*Tr. Cr.* ii, 3).

Minerva. Roman goddess of wisdom, and patroness of arts and trades. 'Hark! ... thou mayst hear M. speak' (*Tam. Sh.* i, 1); 'The shrine of Venus or straight-pight M.' (*Cymb.* v, 5).

The last epithet is of doubtful meaning. It has been explained as 'erect,' or as a translation of *succincta*.

Minola, Baptista. D.P. *Tam. Sh.* A rich gentleman of Padua, father to Katharina and Bianca. i, 1] informs Bianca's suitors that he will not consent to her being married before her elder sister; asks the suitors whether they know of fitting tutors for his daughters. (i, 2) 'an affable and courteous gentleman.' ii, 1] protects B. from Kath.'s violence; greets the two tutors, 'Licio' and 'Cambio'; also Tranio, supposing him to be Lucentio; accepts Petruchio as a suitor for Kath. iii, 2] awaits with impatience P.'s arrival on the wedding-day; when he comes, urges him to change his fantastic attire; later, provides a wedding feast, though bride and groom are absent. iv, 4] is deceived by the Pedant, posing as Vincentio, and consents to the marriage of Bi. and Luc. v, 1] learns that he has been deceived, and goes 'to sound the depth of this knavery.' v, 2] is present at Luc.'s banquet, and is amazed to find that Petr. has effectually tamed the shrew.

Named Alfonso in *The Taming of A Shrew*, and Damonio, a merchant of Ferrara, in *I Suppositi*.

Minola, Katharina. See KATHARINA.

Minos. King of Crete; mtd. (*3 Hen. VI*, v, 6) as having 'denied the course' to Dae dalus and Icarus (*qq.v.*).

Minotaur. A monster, half man and half bull, confined in a labyrinth in Crete. 'Thou mayst not wander in that labyrinth; There Minotaurs and ugly treasons lurk' (*1 Hen. VI*, v, 3).

Miranda. D.P. *Temp.* Daughter to Prospero. (i, 2) cast with her father on a desolate island, when an infant; about fifteen years old when the play opens. i, 2] having witnessed the wreck of the King's ship, is overcome with pity for the 'poor souls' she supposes to have perished, until reassured by her father; listens to Pr.'s story of his life, and is afterward thrown into a slumber; upon her awaking, Caliban enters, and M. reproaches the 'abhorred slave' for his ingratitude, reminding him that she had pitied and instructed him. (By some edrs., however, this speech is given to Pr.) Upon the entrance of Ferdinand, M. at first takes him for a spirit, since 'nothing natural I ever saw so noble'; F. addresses her as 'the goddess on whom these airs attend,' and marvels to hear her speak his own language; heedless of Prospero's assumed wrath, F. disdains to conceal his admiration for M., and offers to make her 'Queen of Naples'; Pr., however, in spite of M.'s urgent entreaties, casts a spell upon him and leads him away to bondage. iii, 1] F. is engaged in carrying logs, when M. enters and offers to bear his burden for him; they converse; F. learns M.'s name and passionately eulogizes one 'so perfect and so peerless'; M. replies, 'I would not wish any companion in the world but you,' yet fears that, forgetful of her father's precepts, she prattles 'something too wildly'; F. presses his suit and at length M., while lamenting her own 'unworthiness,' exclaims 'I am your wife if you will marry me'; the lovers part 'till half an hour hence.' iv, 1] is present when Pr. accepts F. as his son-in-law; witnesses the magical masque presented by Ariel and his fellows. v, 1] F. and M. are suddenly revealed, while playing at chess, to the penitent Alonso and his train; amazed at the novel spectacle, she exclaims, 'How beauteous mankind is! O brave new world that has such people in't!' She is joyfully accepted by Alonso as his daughter. See FERDINAND and CALIBAN.

In Dryden's version of *The Tempest* Miranda is given a sister, named Dorinda.

'How finely is the true Shakespearian scene contrasted with Dryden's vulgar alteration of it, in which a mere ludicrous psychological experiment, as it were, is tried – displaying nothing but indelicacy without passion... The whole courting scene, indeed, is a masterpiece; and the first dawn of disobedience in the mind of Miranda to the command of her father is very finely drawn.' (S. T. Coleridge.) 'The courtship between Ferdinand and Miranda is one of the chief beauties of the play. It is the very purity of love.' (W. Hazlitt.)

Misanthropos. Name applied to himself by Timon. 'I am M., and hate mankind' (*Timon*, iv, 3).

'Timon, surnamed Misanthropos (as who would say, *loup-garou*, or the man-hater)' (*Plut.* p. 296).

Misenum. Now Punta di Miseno, promontory N.W. of the Bay of Naples. The fleet of Sextus Pompeius reported to lie near it, *Ant. Cl.* ii, 2.

'Mount-Mesena,' Ff; 'Misenum,' Rowe; 'Misenus,' Johnson; 'Mount of Misena,' *Plut.* p. 180.

Mithridates. King of Commagene; ally of Antony (*Plut.* p. 207); otherwise unknown. Mtd. *Ant. Cl.* iii, 6.

Mitigation, Madam. Nonce-name applied to Mistress Overdone; *M. for M.* i, 2.

[Mitton, John.] See LONG, HENRY.

Mitylene. Chief town of the island of Lesbos. Three scenes of *Pericles* (iv, 3, 5, 6) are laid in M. Mtd. *Per.* iv, 3, 4, 6; v, 1 (4), 3 (2). ('Metaline,' F3) See MESSALINE.

Mockwater, Mounseer. Nonce-name applied by the host to Dr Caius (probably in allusion to his profession). '*Caius.* Mockvater! Vat is dat? *Host*... in our English tongue, is valour, bully' (*M.W.W.* ii, 3).

Modena (Mutina). Town in Gallia Cisalpina; the consuls Hirtius and Pansa slain near it, 43 B.C. (*Plut.* pp. 167–8). Mtd. *Ant. Cl.* i, 4 ('Medena,' Ff).

Modo. '*Edg.* The prince of darkness is a gentleman; Modo he is called and Mahu' (*Lear*, iii, 4); 'Five fiends have been in poor Tom at once; ... Mahu of stealing; Modo of murder' (*ib.* iv, 1).

These names of fiends occur in Harsnet's *Declaration*. We are there informed that 'Modo, Master Maynies devill, was a graund commaunder, Muster-maister over the Captaines of the seaven deadly sinnes,' while of 'Captaine Maho, Saras devil' we learn that he was 'generall Dictator of hell; and yet for good manners sake, he was contented of his good nature to make shew, that himselfe was under the check of Modu' (cap. x, p. 50).

Mahu (Mohu) is perhaps adapted from 'Mahound.'

[Mömpelgard.] See GARMOMBLES.

Monarcho. A more or less insane Italian, who suffered from what would now be called 'megalomania.' In Scot's *Discoverie of Witchcraft* (1584), p. 54, we are told that 'the Italian whom we called here in England the Monarch,' supposed that all the ships that arrived in port belonged to him; in Nash's *Have with you to Saffron Walden* (1596) (p. 112, ed. Grosart) he is referred to as 'Monarcha, the Italian, that ware crownes on his shooes,' while in Thos. Churchyard's *Chance* (1580), 'The Phantasticall Monarkes Epitaphe' characterizes him at some length.

Armado is referred to as 'A Phantasme, a Monarcho' (*L.L.L.* iv, 1); Helena (*All's Well*, i, 1) doubtless refers to him when to Parolles' 'Save you, fair queen,' she replies 'And you, monarch.'

Monday. M. night contrasted with Tuesday morning, as illustrating a sudden change, *M. Ado*, v, 1; *1 Hen. IV*, i, 2. Mtd., *M. Ado*, ii, 1; *Rom. J.* iii, 4 (2); *Haml.* ii, 2.

For Monday (Black), see BLACK MONDAY.

Monmouth. For 'Harry M.' (*q.v.*); *2 Hen. IV*, ii, 3.

Monmouth. Town on the Wye; birthplace of Henry V. Fluellen draws a comparison between M. and Macedon, as the respective birthplaces of Henry and Alexander the Great, *Hen. V*, iv, 7, adding, 'I'll tell you, there is goot men porn at M.' A prophecy that 'Henry, born at M., should win all' quoted, *1 Hen. VI*, iii, 1. ('Monmoth,' Q.)

Monmouth, Harry (or **Henry**). E.s. of Henry IV; succeeded his father as Henry V (*q.v.*), so named from his birthplace. 'Harry': mtd., *1 Hen. IV*, v, 2, 4; *2 Hen. IV*, Ind., i, 1, 3; *Hen.V*, iv, 7. 'Henry,' *1 Hen. VI*, ii, 5.

Montacute, Baron. See POLE, HENRY.

Montacute, or **Montague, John de.** 3rd E. of Salisbury (*c.*1350–1400).

The following is a summary of Holinshed's account of him: As a trusted adherent of Richard II, he was sent by the King to France, to prevent Bolingbroke's marriage with the Duke of Berry's daughter (*Hol.* iii, 495; *Rich. II*, ii, 1); he accompanied Richard to Ireland, but was sent back to assemble an army in Wales to await the King's return; this he did, but a rumour of Richard's death led to the dispersal of the force (*Hol.* iii, 499); he was present at the meeting of Rich. and Bolingbroke (*ib.* iii, 501), joined the Abbot of Westminster's plot against Henry IV (*ib.* iii, 514), and, after marching on Windsor, retreated to Cirencester, where he was beheaded by the townspeople (Jan. 7, 1400).

D.P. *Rich. II.* ii, 4] vainly entreats the Welshmen to stay yet one more day for Richard; fears the King's case is desperate. iii, 2] informs Richard of the dispersal of the Welshmen. iii, 3] *p.m.*; is present at the meeting of Bolingbroke and Richard. (v, 6) his head is sent to London.

Montacute, or **Montague, Thomas de.** 4th E. of Salisbury (1388–1428). S. of the preceding; succd. 1409; m. Eleanor Holland, d. of Thomas H., 2nd E. of Kent. Their d. Alice m. Richard Neville (E. of Salisbury), 3rd s. of Ralph, E. of Westmoreland (cf. *Hen. V*, iv, 3). He was prominent in the French wars of Henry V, and was made E. of Perche (1419); he was one of the negotiators of Henry's marriage with Katharine of Valois (*Hol.* iii, 572); he was present at their betrothal (*ib. ib.*), and at the King's death (*ib.* iii, 583). 'Prompt in counsell and of courage invincible' (*ib.* iii, 598); mortally wounded at Orleans (*ib.* iii, 599).

D.P. *Hen. V.* 'E. of Salisbury.' iv, 3] bids adieu to his friends before Agincourt; Bedford says of him, 'He is as full of valour as of kindness; Princely in both'; later, announces that the attack of the French is imminent.

For his presence at Agincourt, see Nicolas, *Agincourt*, p. 373.

D.P. *1 Hen. VI.* i, 4] (before Orleans) welcomes Talbot on his release from captivity; is slain by a cannon-shot.

Historically, he died at Meung of the wound received at Tourelles.

Montague. D.P. *Rom. J.* 'Head of a house, at variance with the house of Capulet.' i, 1] enters while a fray is in progress between partisans of both houses; is commanded by the Prince to attend at the judgment-place; inquires the origin of the quarrel; deplores the melancholy humour of his son Romeo, the cause of which is unknown to him. iii, 1] defends Romeo's conduct in killing Tybalt. v, 3] announces his wife's death; finds Romeo dead; will raise a statue 'in pure gold' to Juliet.

Montague, Lady. D.P. *Rom. J.* i, 1] restrains her aged husband from taking part in the fray. iii, 1] *p.m.*

Montague, Marquess of. See NEVILLE, JOHN.

Montagues. Family of M., or their partisans. 'House of the M.s' (*Rom. J.* i, 1); 'I hate ... all M.s' (*ib. ib.*); 'down with the M.s' (*ib. ib.*); 'if you be not of the house of the M.s' (*ib.* i, 2); 'raise up the M.s' (*ib.* v, 3); 'A Montague' (*Rom. J.* i, 5 (3); ii, 2). See CAPULETS AND MONTAGUES.

[**Montaigne, Michel Eyquem de** (1533–92).] French essayist. His *Essayes* were Englished by John Florio (*q.v.*), and printed in 1603, but are known to have been seen in MS. in 1600. Gonzalo's speech, *Temp.* ii, 1, ll. 147–155, is almost identical with a passage in ch. xxx of Florio. The indebtedness of Sh. to M. has been much discussed. See Philarête Charles, *L'Angleterre au XV me Siècle* (1846); J. Feis, *Sh. and Montaigne* (1884); and J. M. Robertson, *Montaigne and Sh.* (1909).

Montano. D.P. *Oth.* 'Governour of Cyprus' (F1); 'Though M.'s rank in Cyprus cannot be exactly ascertained, yet, from many circumstances, we are sure he had not the powers with which Othello was subsequently invested' (Steevens). (i, 3) sends a despatch to the Venetian Senate, and is styled their 'trusty and most valiant servitor.' ii, 1] awaits with anxiety the arrival of Othello at Cyprus during a tempest; mentions having served under Oth.; converses with Cassio. ii, 3] is present when Cas. becomes tipsy, and thinks that Oth. should be 'put in mind' of his lieutenant's infirmity; Cas. returns, in pursuit of Roderigo, and in the brawl which follows wounds Montano; M. explains the cause of the conflict to Oth. v, 2] with others, enters the chamber after Desdemona's death; pursues Iago.

It is noteworthy that in ii, 1, M. greets neither Desd. nor Oth., yet his 'exit' is not provided for.

Montferrat, Marquis of. Mtd. as a friend of Bassanio; *M.V.* i, 2 ('Mountferrat,' F1).

M. was a marquisate in N.W. Italy; made a duchy, and united to Mantua, 1536.

Montgomery, Earl of. See HERBERT, PHILIP.

Montgomery, Sir John. See next article.

Montgomery, Sir Thomas. Acc. *Hol.* iii, 680, Sir T. M. and Sir Thos. Burgh joined Edw. IV at Nottingham with forces, and 'boldlie affirming to him that they would serve no man but a king' induced him to proclaim himself as such. In *Sh.* the name is 'Sir John M.,' and the place York.

D.P. *3 Hen. VI.* iv, 7] arrives at York 'to help King Edward'; on hearing that Edw. only claims the dukedom, is about to march away indignantly, but becomes Edw.'s eager champion on his boldly claiming the crown. ('Mountgomery' F1.)

Sir John M., brother of Sir Thos. M., was a Lancastrian, and was beheaded by Edward IV.

Montjoy. Not a proper name, but a title of the chief French herald – 'Mountjoy king at armes' (*Hol.* iii, 552).

D.P. *Hen. V.* (iii, 5) mtd. iii, 6] conveys a formal message of defiance from his king to Henry, receives his reply, and departs with a reward (*Hol.* iii, 552). iv, 3] is sent by the Constable of France to ask Henry what ransom he would offer. iv, 7] after the battle, craves leave to bury the dead; admits defeat; tells Henry that the name of the neighbouring castle is Agincourt (*Hol.* iii, 555).

The bearer of the Constable's message (iv, 3) is not named by Holinshed. Acc. H. the incident of iv, 7, took place 'in the morning' of the next day.

Moon, The. (See CYNTHIA, DIANA, DICTYNNA, ENDYMION, PHOEBE.)

Ruler of the tides: 'the moist star Upon whose influence Neptune's empire stands' (*Haml.* i, 1, l. 118); 'governess of floods' (*M.N.D.* ii, 1, l. 103); *Wint. T.* i, 2, l. 427.

Cause of dew: 'upon the corner of the m. There hangs a vaporous drop,' etc. (*Macb.* ii, 1).

'*La lumière cendrée*' alluded to: 2 *Hen. IV*, iv, 3, ll. 56–9.

Eclipses and portents: Macb. iv, 1, l. 28; *Lear*, i, 2 (2); *Rich. II*, ii, 4; *Oth.* v, 2; *Son.* xxxv, cvii. Five moons seen, *John*, iv, 2.

A cause of lunacy: 'She comes more nearer earth than she was wont, And makes men mad' (*Oth.* v, 2, l. 110).

Controlled by magic: Temp. v, 1; *Lear*, ii, 1, l. 41.

Borrowed light: Tr. Cr. v, 1; *Timon*, iv, 3 (3).

Influence of m.'s age: T. Nt. i, 5, l. 211; *M for M.* iii, 1, l. 24.

Distance of (in hyperbole): 'billow kiss the m.' (*Per.* iii, 1); 'a mile beyond the m.' (*T. And.* iv, 3); 'scarr'd the m. with splinters' (*Cor.* iv, 5); 'boring the m. with her mainmast' (*Wint. T.* iii, 3).

Horns of: Ant. Cl. iv, 10; *Cor.* i, 1.

Changes of: Oth. iii, 3; *M.N.D.* i, 1; *Lear*, v, 3; *Rom. J.* ii, 2.

Man in the m.: Temp. ii, 2 (2); *M.N.D.* v, 1.

Influence on vegetation: Tr. Cr. iii, 2, l. 184.

Patron of robbers: 1 Hen. IV, i, 2 (4).

Rosaline compared to the m., *L.L.L.* v, 2, ll. 203 ff. Dogs and wolves bay the m., *A.Y.L.* v, 3; *Jul. C.* iv, 3; *M.N.D.* v, 1, l. 379 (disputed). 'Glimpses of the m.' (*Haml.* i, 4).

'Watery': *Rom. J.* i, 4; *Wint. T.* i, 2; *M.N.D.* ii, 2, iii, 1; *Rich. III*, ii, 2. 'Cold': *M.N.D.* i, 1; ii, 1. 'Silver': *M.N.D.* i, 1; *L.L.L.* iv, 3; *Lucr.* 371.

Moonshine. See Starveling.

Moor, The (1). A Moorish woman; mtd. *M.V.* iii, 5.

Moor, The (2). For 'Aaron' (D.P.). *T. And.* iii, 2; iv, 2, 3.

Moor, The (3). Othello; frequently referred to thus throughout the tragedy.

Moorditch. 'A ditch which encompassed that part of the old London Wall fronting Finsbury and Moorfields' (H.B. Wheatley, *Lond. Past and Present* (1891)). Knight says that the citizens avoided it 'as amongst the melancholy places in which the pestilence continually lurked.'

'*P. Hen.* What say'st thou ... to the melancholy of M.? *Fal.* Thou hast the most unsavoury similes' (*1 Hen. IV*, i, 2).

Moorfields. A moor or fen without the city to the N., first drained in 1527; laid out in walks 1606. It became famous for its cudgelplayers and popular amusements. *Cf.* Wheatley, *ut sup.* There, too, the trainbands were exercised.

'Is this M. to muster in?' cries the Porter to the jostling crowd at the christening of Elizabeth (*Hen. VIII*, v, 4).

Mopsa. D.P. *Wint. T.* 'A shepherdess' (Ff). iv, 4] joins in rustic raillery; loves 'a ballad in print'; takes part in song.

In Greene's *Pandosto* Mopsa is the name of the old shepherd's wife.

Moray. See Murray.

Mordake. For 'Murdoch.' *1 Hen. IV*, i, 1; ii, 4; iv, 4. See Fife, Earl of.

More, Sir Thomas (1478–1535). His appointment as Lord Chancellor in Wolsey's place (1529) announced to the latter, *Hen. VIII*, iii, 2; cf. *Hol.* iii, 910.

Morgan (1). A man to whom Parolles has made confession, supposing him to be a friar; *All's Well*, iv, 3.

Morgan (2). Name assumed by Belarius (D.P. *Cymb.*). 'Myself, Belarius, that am Morgan called' (*Cymb.* iii, 3); mtd., *ib.* v, 5.

Furness has pointed out that the name occurs thrice in Harrison's *Description of Britain*, in close proximity with that of Cloten (*q.v.*). The name means 'seaborn,' and a Greek rendering of it is well known as that of the heresiarch Pelagius.

[**Morice, Ralph.**] See Denny, Sir A.

Morisco. A morris-dancer. 'I have seen ... Cade ... caper upright like a wild M., Shaking the bloody darts as he his bells' (*2 Hen. VI*, iii, 1).

Morn. Morning, personified. 'The greyeyed m. smiles on the frowning night' (*Rom. J.* ii, 3); 'the m., in russet mantle clad, Walks o'er the dew of yon high eastward hill' (*Haml.* i, 1).

Morning. Personified. (Fem.) 'modest as M. when she coldly eyes The youthful Phoebus' (*Tr. Cr.* i, 3); (masc.) 'his celestial face,' etc. (*Son.* xxxiii).

[**Morocco.**] Name of performing horse. See Bankes.

Morocco, Prince of. D.P. *M.V.* ii, 1] presents himself as suitor to Portia; speaks of his complexion as 'the shadow'd livery of the burnish'd sun'; vaunts his own courage; is told that his hazard shall be made 'after dinner.' ii, 7] arguing that 'never so rich a gem Was set in worse than gold,' chooses the golden casket, and finds within it 'a carrion death'; bids Portia adieu, saying 'I have too grieved a heart To take a tedious leave.'

In ii, 1, 'Morochus,' QqF1, 'Morochius,' F1, 2, 3; ii, 7, 'Morrocho,' QqFf.

Mortimer, Anne. Daughter of Roger (VI), 4th E. of March; m. Richard, E. of Cambridge, and was the mother of Richard Plantagenet, Duke of York, who, through her, claimed the throne; *2 Hen. VI*, ii, 2. See Appendix 4.

Mortimer, Edmund. 5th E. of March (1391–1424); son of Roger M., 4th Earl; recognized as heir presumptive by Rich. II; on the Lancastrian revolution was kept under surveillance, but honourably treated; became a fast friend of Hen. V, and fought at Agincourt; Lieutenant of Ireland 1423; died of plague 1424.

D.P. *1 Hen. VI.* ii, 5] 'brought in a chair by two keepers'; speaks of himself as being in the last stage of decrepitude from old age and long imprisonment 'within a loathsome dungeon'; in an interview with his 'nephew,' Richard Plantagenet, relates the history of the Mortimers and advises him to be wary in dealing with the 'strong-fixed' house of Lancaster; is borne out to die.

This scene seems founded on a confusion between the 5th Earl of March and his uncle Sir Edmund Mortimer – the 'Lord Mortimer' (erroneously) of *1 Hen. IV.* The dramatist was doubtless misled by *Hol.* iii, 520, where Glendower's prisoner is called 'earle of March,' and *Hol.* iii, 589, where it is erroneously stated that 'Edmund Mortimer, the last Earle of M.' had long 'beene restrained from his libertie, and finallie waxed lame,' and that his inheritance descended to the lord Richard Plantagenet.' See Appendix 4. Or, possibly, confused with Sir John M., the Earl's cousin (Hall, p. 128), who had been imprisoned in the Tower, but escaped in 1422 (B.-S. p. 219).

Mortimer, Sir Edmund (1376–*c.* 1409). Uncle to the preceding (*q.v.*), with whom he is confused in *Hol.* and *Sh.* He was taken prisoner by Glendower, but became his adherent and married his daughter. Killed at the siege of Harlech.

D.P. *1 Hen. IV*, under the erroneous title of 'Earl of March.' (i, 1) his capture by Glendower related. (i, 3) Hotspur defends M.'s conduct to Henry IV, demands his ransom, and will train a starling 'to speak nothing but Mortimer'; 'lord M.' (ii, 3) Lady Percy speaks of him as 'my brother M.' iii, 1] discusses the division of the kingdom with Hotspur and Glendower; deprecates Hotspur's derisive treatment of G.; his wife can speak no English, he no Welsh.

Mortimer, Lady. Dau. of Owen Glendower; married Sir Edmund M., whom Glendower had taken prisoner.

D.P. *1 Hen. IV.* Erroneously represented as wife of 'Lord Mortimer.' iii, 1] she can speak no English, and her husband knows no Welsh; she sings a Welsh song.

Doubts have been thrown on this marriage of Glendower's daughter, but the following passage from *Mon. de Evesham Hist. Vit. et Regn. Ricards II* (ed. Hearne), p. 182 (quoted, B.-S. p. 135), is explicit 'Eodem anno 1402 Dominus Edmundus Mortimer ... filiam praedicti Owyni Glyndore desponsavit maxima cum solemnitate, et (sicut vulgariter dicitur) conversus est totaliter ad Wallicos.'

Mortimer, Lord, 'of Scotland.' Named as having 'sent word, that Douglas, and the English rebels, met' (*1 Hen. IV*, iii, 2). There was no Scottish 'Lord Mortimer'; the noble here mtd. is George of Dunbar, E. of the March (of Scotland), being confused with the English E. of March (Mortimer). The mistake is not Holinshed's, but the historian does not explicitly distinguish the two earldoms.

The Earl was one of the victorious commanders at Homildon, and was instrumental in saving the King's life at Shrewsbury.

Mortimer, Sir Hugh. See MORTIMER, SIR JOHN.

Mortimer, Sir John. Acc. Courtenay, an illegitimate son of Anne Mortimer, as was his brother Sir Hugh; they fell at Wakefield.

D.P. *3 Hen. VI.* i, 2] Richard, D. of York, addresses them as 'mine uncles.' (Cf. *Hol.* iii, 659, 'his two bastard uncles.')

Other authorities make them illegitimate sons of York's maternal grandfather, Roger Mortimer, E. of March.

[**Mortimer's Cross.**] Situated about 5 m. N.W. of Leominster; scene of a battle, Feb. 2, 1461, at which Edward, Earl of March (Edw. IV), defeated the Lancastrians. The battle is not described in *Sh.*, but the portent of 'three suns' which appeared at the time, is related, *3 Hen. VI*, ii, 1 ('M.C.' does not occur in the text, but is found in the st. dirs. of modern edns.).

Morton. D.P. *2 Hen. IV.* A retainer of the Earl of Northumberland. i, 1] describes the disastrous Battle of Shrewsbury; but tries to hearten his master by bringing him tidings that the Abp. of York, with 'well-appointed powers ... Turns insurrection to religion.'

'Travers and Morton are both the names of good families, such as would send their sons to learn the duties of chivalry as pages and esquires ... in the establishments of great barons and prelates' (French, p. 89).

Morton, John (*c.* 1420–1500). Bp. of Ely. In 1483 he was arrested and imprisoned in the Tower, whence he was handed to the custody of Buckingham at Brecknock (*q.v.*), where he encouraged the Duke to revolt; he then escaped to Flanders, and returning home in 1485 was made Abp. of Canterbury, Lord Chancellor, and cardinal. He probably collaborated with Sir Thos. More in his *History of Richard III*, in which the incident of the strawberries (*infra*) is mentioned.

D.P. *Rich. III.* iii, 4] while present at a council 'to determine of the coronation' (*Hol.* iii, 721), is asked by Gloucester to send for some 'good strawberries' from his garden in Holborn (*Hol.* iii, 722). (iv, 3) it is announced that he 'is fled to Richmond' (*Hol.* iii, 741). (iv, 4) an adherent of Richmond.

'Morton' in Ff, 'Ely' in mod. edns. (text).

Moses. See MOYSES.

Moth (1). D.P. *L.L.L.* Page to Armado, i, 2] conversing with Ar., shows the quickness of his wit; instances great men who 'have been in love'; leads Costard 'to prison.' iii, 1] instructs his master in the art of love; releases Costard; quibbles about C.'s broken shin. v, 1] banters Holofernes. v, 2] (having been instructed how to act as the King's herald) attempts to recite an address to the Princess and her ladies, but breaks down; enacts the part of the infant Hercules.

The page's diminutive size is insisted on, and the name was probably pronounced 'mote,' of which 'moth' was a variant spelling. The fact that Mothe, or La Mothe, was 'a French Ambassador, who was long popular in London' (Lee, *Life of Sh.* p. 103 *n.*) may also be relevant. Fleay considers M. to stand for Thomas Nashe, the youthful pamphleteer. See DULL.

Moth (2). D.P. *M.N.D.* A fairy. iii, 1] attends on Bottom at Titania's bidding. iv, 1] *p.m.*

Mouldy, Ralph. D.P. *2 Hen. IV.* iii, 2] is taken as a recruit by Falstaff, but purchases his release.

Mountain. Name of a hound; *Temp.* iv, 1.

It has been pointed out (*Sh. Eng.* ii, 349) that the name appears among the trencher-fed pack in Surtees' *Handley Cross.*

Mountanto, Signior. Nonce-name, applied to Benedick by Beatrice; *M. Ado*, i, 1.

From 'montanto,' an upward thrust in fencing. *Cf.* Johnson, *Every Man in his Humour*, iv, 6.

Mountgomery. For 'Montgomery' in Ff.

Mowbray, John (1432–61). 3rd D. of Norfolk. He joined the Lancastrians, but reverted to the Yorkists in 1460, and fought at St Albans and Towton.

D.P. *3 Hen. VI.* i, 1] promises to support Richard, D. of York. ii, 2] *p.m.* (Acc. French, p. 189, confused with his son.)

Mowbray, Thomas (1). 6th Baron Mowbray, and 1st D. of Norfolk (*c.* 1366–99); Earl of Nottingham 1383; D. of Norfolk 1397; K.G.; Earl Marshal of England. (See SURREY, D. OF.) He was given the custody of the D. of Gloucester, and when called upon to produce him for trial, declared that Gl. had died in prison, at Calais.

Acc. *Hol.* iii, 489, however, Mowbray incurred the King's displeasure for having tried to save the Duke, whom he had been ordered to despatch 'with all expedition.'

D.P. *Rich. II.* i, 1] rebuts, before King Richard, Hereford's charges, but admits that he failed in his 'sworn duty' as regards Gloucester, and that he plotted against the life of John of Gaunt; defies his accuser; craves leave to defend his honour (*Hol.* iii, 493). i, 3] enters the lists at Coventry (*Hol.* iii, 494), to 'defend his loyalty and truth'; laments his 'heavy sentence' of lifelong banishment; reiterates his innocence, (iv, 1) dies at Venice (*Hol.* iii, 494).

Acc. *Hol.* iii, 494, the Duke died at Venice after leaving 'Almaine,' but Stow, *Annales* (1601), p. 525, states that it was on his return from Jerusalem.

Mowbray, Thomas (2). E.s. of the preceding; he was only fourteen years old at his father's death and did not succeed to the dukedom, but ranked as 7th Baron M., and 3rd E. of Nottingham. (He is correctly addressed as 'lord marshal' by the Abp., *2 Hen. IV*, i, 3.) He joined Scrope's rebellion (*Hol.* iii, 529), was captured at Shipton Moor, and executed without trial (*Hol.* iii, 530).

D.P. *2 Hen. IV.* i, 3] in council with Scrope and others. iv, 1] in Gualtree Forest; in reply to the envoy, Westmoreland, he recites his grievances against Henry. iv, 2] is treacherously seized while parleying with Prince John, and sent 'to the block of death.'

Moyses. An outlaw; mtd. *T.G.V.* v, 3.

'Moses,' Capell.

Much Ado About Nothing.
Composition. The play is not mentioned by Meres in his *Palladis Tamia* (1598) (unless, as has been conjectured, it is the 'Love labours wonne' of the list there given), and 1599 is generally accepted as the approximate date of its composition, a conclusion accordant with considerations of metre and style.

Publication. The play was entered in the Stationers' Registers on Aug. 4, 1600, as 'a booke to be staied'; but under the date Aug. 23 appears the entry: 'Andrew Wyse, William Aspley. Entered for their copies under the hands of the Wardens Two Bookes, the one called Muche a Doo about Nothinge [the other, 2 *Hen. IV*].'

The first edition (Q) appeared with the following title: 'Much adoe about Nothing. As it hath been sundrie times publikely acted by the right honourable, the Lord Chamberlaine his seruants. Written by William Shakespeare. London Printed by V. S. for Andrew Wise, and William Aspley, 1600.' The printer was Valentine Sims. There is no division into acts and scenes.

No other edition of the play is known until it appeared in the First Folio of 1623, printed from a copy of Q which had been corrected for the stage. Title: 'Much adoe about Nothing.' The acts, but not the scenes, are indicated.

Sources of the Plot. The main plot, dealing with the false accusation against Hero, is clearly identified with that of the 22nd tale of the *Novelle* of Matteo Bandello (publd. 1554–73); in this, Timbreo di Cardona and Girondo (both officers serving under Il Re Piero d'Aragona) are rivals for the hand of Fenicia, daughter of Lionato de' Lionati, a gentleman of Messina. Girondo, with the aid of a friend, excites Timbreo's suspicions of Fenicia's chastity, and contrives that T. shall see a man enter Lionato's house through a window. Timbreo thereupon denounces Fenicia to her father. The lady falls into a swoon which is mistaken for death, but recovers, and is concealed in the country. Girondo confesses his perfidy, and Timbreo, by way of atonement for his credulity agreeing to marry a wife of Lionato's choosing, is duly wedded to the resuscitated Fenicia.

Bandello's story appeared in French in François de Belleforest's *Histoires Tragiques*, but no English translation of this exists.

The incident of Hero's personation by the waiting-woman is paralleled by an episode in *The Faerie Queene* (II, iv, 25 ff.), which in its turn may be borrowed from the story of Ariodante and Genevra in Ariosto's *Orlando Furioso* (bk. v), translated by Sir J. Harington in 1591, a version of which (now lost) is known to have been acted before Queen Elizabeth in 1583.

The important underplot of Benedick and Beatrice, as well as the humours of Dogberry and Verges, are Sh.'s creations.

Mugs. Name by which the 'First Carrier' is addressed; *1 Hen. IV*, ii, 1.

Muliteus. A Moor, whose child, fair of complexion, Aaron directed to be changed for his own; *T. And.* iv, 2.

This reading is that of QqFf; the forms 'Muley' and 'Muli,' with changes of the text, were proposed by Steevens and Singer respectively.

Mulmutius. Legendary king of Britain, claimed by Cymbeline as his ancestor. 'Our ancestor was that M., which Ordain'd our laws ... Who was the first of Britain which did put His brows within a golden crown, and called Himself a king' (*Cymb.* iii, 1).

Acc. Holinshed, Britain was brought under the sway of Mulmucius Dunwallon, son of Cloton, King of Cornwall, 'in the yeere of the world 3529'; he 'made manie good lawes, which were long after used, ... turned out of the British speech into Latine by Gildas Priscus' (*c.* 516–70), and incorporated with Alfred's statutes. 'He ordeined him by the advise of his lords a crowne of gold, and caused himselfe to be crowned, according to the custom of the pagan lawes then in use,' whence, 'after the opinion of some writers, he is named the first king of Britaine' (*Hol.* i, 15).

[**Munda, Battle of.**] Alluded to; *Jul. C.* i, 1.

Murder. Personified. 'Wither'd m.' (*Macb.* ii, 1); 'Murder, as hating what himself hath done' (*John*, iv, 3); 'm.'s bloody axe' (*Rich. II*, i, 2); 'stern m.' (*ib. ib.*); 'treason and m. ... as two yoke-devils' (*Hen. V*, ii, 2); wakes, *Lucr.* 168.

Impersonated by Demetrius (*q.v.*) to influence Titus in his madness, *T. And.* v, 2 (5).

Murderers. *i.e.* unnamed, hired assassins. *Macbeth.* (*a*) Murderers of Banquo. iii, 1] 1st M. justifies his willingness to slay B.; 2nd M. is reckless what he does 'to spite the world.' iii, 3] they waylay B. and his son. iii, 4] 1st M. tells Macb. that he slew B.

In iii, 3, a 3rd M. unexpectedly joins the other two, and satisfies them that he is sent by Macb.; he shows knowledge of the locality and of the habits of the intended victims. It has been plausibly argued (*N. and Q.*, Sep.–Dec., 1869), that this is Macb. himself. See also P. Hookham, *Essays* (1914), pp. 109–117.

(*b*) Murderers of Macduff's son. iv, 2] (their number is not specified) one of them stabs the 'young fry of treachery.'

2 Hen. VI. Murderers of Humphrey, D. of Gloucester. iii, 2] 1st M. tells Suffolk that the deed is done; 2nd M. expresses remorse.

Rich. III. Murderers of Clarence. i, 3] are given their warrant and warned not to parley with their victim. i, 4] they present their commission to Brakenbury; 2nd M. is troubled by 'certain dregs of conscience'; they 'reason with' Clarence, who is eventually stabbed by 1st M.; 2nd M. 'repents him,' and refuses his reward.

Murdoch. See Mordake.

Murray, or **Moray, Thomas Dunbar, 2nd Earl of.** Made prisoner at Homildon (1402) (*Hol.* iii, 520). Mtd. *1 Hen. IV*, i, 1.

Muscovites. Ferdinand and his courtiers present themselves to the Princess of France 'like Muscovites or Russians' (*L.L.L.* v, 2). Rosaline describes their dress as 'shapeless gear,' so its fashion is doubtful. See Russian, and Love's Labour's Lost.

Muscovy. Russia. Rosaline suggests that Biron, looking pale, must be 'Sea-sick, I think, coming from M.' (*L.L.L.* v, 2).

Muses, The. Nine Roman divinities presiding over poetry and the arts and sciences. 'Those old nine, which rimers invocate' (*Son.* xxxviii); cf. *ib.* lxxxv.

'The thrice three M., mourning for the death Of learning late deceased in beggary' (*M.N.D.* v, 1) is by some commentators regarded as referring to Spenser's *Tears of the Muses* (1591); by others, to the miserable death of the poet Robert Greene (1592).

Musicians. As D.PP.

In *T.G.V.* iv, 2] perform beneath Silvia's window; one sings 'Who is Silvia?'

In *Rom. J.* iv, 5] in attendance at Capulet's house, to accompany Juliet's funeral; they bandy jests with Peter.

This scene is of the nature of an 'interlude,' and in any case, as Coleridge observed, the audience know that Juliet is not dead.

In *T. Nt.* i, 1] they play to Orsino (not indicated in st. dirs. Ff).

Music of the Spheres, The. A harmony produced, according to Pythagoras, by the movement of the heavenly bodies, but inaudible to mortal ears. Referred to by Plato, *Rep.* x, 14. *Cf.* Chaucer, *The Parliament of Fowls*, 1, 63; Cicero, *Somnium Scipionis*. 'There's not the slightest orb which thou behold'st But in his motion like an angel sings,' etc. (*M.V.* v, 1; *cf.* Job xxxviii, 7); 'music from the spheres' (*T. Nt.* iii, 1); 'We shall have shortly discord in the spheres' (*A. Y. L.* iii, 7); 'the tuned spheres' (*Ant. Cl.* v, 2); 'The music of the spheres' (*Per.* v, 1, l. 231).

Muskos. 'The M.s' regiment' (*All's Well*, iv, 1). Prob. for 'Muscovites.'

Mustard-seed. D.P. *M.N.D.* A fairy. iii, 1] attends on Bottom, at Titania's bidding. iv, 1] is ordered 'to help Cavalero Cobweb [? Pease-blossom] to scratch.'

Mutius. D.P. *T. And.* Son to Titus Andronicus. i, 2] attempts to bar the way against his father as he pursues Lavinia, and is slain by him; (in spite of the opposition of Titus he is buried with his brethren).

Myrmidons, The. Men of an Achaean race who accompanied Achilles to Troy. (Hence applied to unquestioning followers or agents.) The name is traditionally derived either from an ancestor Myrmidon, or from μύρμηκες (ants), changed into men in Aegina (Ovid, *Metam.* vii, 523–657).

'The M. are no bottle-ale houses' (*T. Nt.* ii, 3); possibly here the name of a tavern, if not a mere whimsy of Feste's.

'Mermidons,' Ff.

N

Naiads. Nymphs of fresh water (Ovid and Virgil). 'You nymphs call'd Naiads, of the windring brooks, With your sedged crowns and ever-harmless looks' (*Temp.* iv, 1).

'Nayades,' Ff; 'Nayads,' Pope.

Nan. Dim. of 'Anne': 'N., our maid' (*T.G.V.* iii, 3); 'another N.' (*M.W.W.* i, 4). As a forename: 'N. Page' (*M.W.W.* iv, 4, 6). For 'Anne Page': *ib.* iii, 4 (3); iv, 4 (2); v, 3.

Naples. City of Italy; formerly capital of the kingdom of Naples and of the Two Sicilies (*q.v.*).

Alonso (D.P. *Temp.*) is 'King of N.'; Ferdinand, believing his father to be dead, exclaims, 'myself am N.' (*Temp.* i, 2); mtd., *ib.* i, 2 (5), ii, 1 (6), 2, iii, 2, iv, 1 (3), Epil. René, Duke of Anjou, was titular King of N. (see Reignier). Mtd., *1 Hen. VI*, v, 3 (2), 4, 5; *2 Hen. VI*, i, 1; *3 Hen. VI*, i, 4. York calls Q. Margaret 'outcast of N.' (*2 Hen. VI*, v, 1), and 'Iron of N., hid with English gilt' (*3 Hen. VI*, ii, 2). The nasal twang of the people of N. is alluded to by the clown, *Oth.* iii, 1: 'Have your instruments been in N., that they speak i' th' nose thus?'

Naps, John. 'Old J.N. of Greece,' mtd. as an acquaintance of Sly's, *Tam. Sh.* Ind. 2, 'Greece' being probably an error for 'Greet,' a hamlet near Stratford-on-Avon.

Narbon, Gerard de. Father to Helena (D.P. *All's Well*), a learned physician. Mtd. *All's Well*, i, 1; ii, 1.

It is perhaps noteworthy that Girard de Rousillon was famous as a paladin in romance.

Narcissus. A beautiful youth condemned by Nemesis to become enamoured of his own image reflected in a fountain, till he pined away and became a flower (Ovid, *Metam.* iii, 407 ff.). 'Hadst thou N. in thy face, to me Thou would'st appear most ugly' (*Ant. Cl.* ii, 5); 'N... died to kiss his shadow in the brook' (*V.A.* 161); 'had N. seen her ... Self-love had never drowned him' (*Lucr.* 265).

Narrow Seas, The. See Channel, English.

[Nashfields.] Mtd. (*Hol.* iii, 730) as one of Richard's retainers who 'at lower end of the Hall, hurl'd up their caps,' etc. (*Rich. III*, iii, 7).

Naso. See Ovid.

Nathaniel (1). D.P. *L.L.L.* 'Sir N.' (iv, 2; v, 1); a curate. iv, 2] converses with Holofernes, whose pedantry he flatters; excuses Dull's ignorance; reads aloud Biron's sonnet, v, 1] converses with Hol. v, 2] represents Alexander in the masque of 'The Nine Worthies.'

In iv, 2, much confusion exists in early edns. between the speeches of 'Nat.' and 'Hol.' In iv, 2, the former is styled 'Master Person,' and it is possible that original pfxs. 'Per.' and 'Ped.' (Pedant) were inadvertently interchanged. In v, 1, the pfxs. 'Cura.' and 'Curat.' are exclusively used in Ff for N.

Nathaniel (2). D.P. *Tam. Sh.* One of Petruchio's servants. iv, 1] expresses surprise at his master's conduct.

Nature. Personified. 'Till forging N. be condemned of treason,' etc. (*V.A.* 729 ff.); 'Swear N.'s death for making thee so fair' (*ib.* 744); mtd., *ib.* 11, 953; 'N. hath framed strange fellows in her time' (*M.V.* i, 1); 'N., drawing of an antique, Made a foul blot' (*M. Ado*, iii, 1); 'O, thou goddess, Thou divine N.' (*Cymb.* iv, 2, l. 170); 'blots of N.'s hand' (*M.N.D.* v, 1, l. 416); 'N.'s bastards' (*Wint. T.*

iv, 4, l. 83); 'would beguile N. of her custom' (*ib.* v, 2, l. 108); 'By law and process of great N.' (*ib.* ii, 2, 1, 60); 'N. never lends The smallest scruple of her excellence' (*M. for M.* i, 1); 'Hear, N., hear; dear goddess, hear!' (*Lear*, i, 4, l. 297); 'N.'s hand' (2 *Hen. IV*, i, 1); 'N. and Fortune' (*John*, iii, 1, l. 52); 'N. seems dead' (*Macb.* ii, 1); 'N.'s mother,' etc. (*Rom. J.* ii, 3); 'N. thy friend' (*M.W.W.* iii, 3); 'N., sovereign mistress' (*Son.* cxxvi); mtd., *ib.* iv, xi, xx, lxvii.

For the passage in *Rom. J.* *cf.* Lucretius, *De Rerum Nat.* v, 260.

Navarre. An ancient Pyrenean kingdom, only mtd. in *Sh.* in connection with the fictitious 'Ferdinand, King of N.' (D.P.). *L.L.L.* i, 1 (2); ii, 1 (6).

Nazarite, The. Christ thus named by Shylock; *M. V.* i, 3.

'Nazarite' for 'Nazarene' is twice used in the Genevan version: Matt, ii, 23, Acts xxiv, 5 (New Testament, 1557).

Neapolitan. (*a*) *Subst.* 'A noble N., Gonzalo' (*Temp.* i, 2); 'two N.s 'scaped' (*ib.* ii, 2); 'Some N.' (*Tam. Sh.* i, 1). York addresses Margaret of Anjou as 'blood-bespotted N.' (2 *Hen. VI*, v, 1; in allusion to her father, Reignier, titular King of Naples).

(*b*) *Adj.* 'The N. prince, 'who 'doth nothing but talk of his horse' (*M.V.* i, 2). Neapolitan horses were esteemed in Sh.'s days.

G. Markham calls the Neapolitans 'the school-masters of all Christendom in the art of horsemanship' (*Sh. Eng.* ii, 409).

Nebuchadnezzar. King of Babylon 604–561 B.C.; in fulfilment of a prophecy 'he was driven from men and did eat grass as oxen' (Dan. iv, 33).

'I am no great N., sir; I have not much skill in grass' (*All's Well*, iv, 5). ('Nabuchadnezzar,' Ff.)

Ned. Dim. of 'Edward.' For 'Poins,' *1 Hen. IV*, i, 2, ii, 2, 4; *2 Hen. IV*, ii, 2, 4. For 'Edward, P. of Wales,' son to Hen. VI, *3 Hen. VI*, v, 4, 5. For the infant son of Edw. IV, afterward Edw. V, *3 Hen. VI*, v, 7.

Nedar. Father of Helena. *M.N.D.* i, 1; iv, 1.

The name seems an invention; Walker suggested 'Nestor.'

Nell. Dim. of Ellen, Helen, or Eleanor. Name of a kitchen-wench, *Com. Err.* iii, 2; name of a sister of Poins, *2 Hen. IV*, ii, 2; forename of Dame Quickly, *Hen. V*, ii, 1(2); for 'Eleanor, Duchess of Gloucester,' *2 Hen. VI*, i, 2 (2), ii, 4 (5); for 'Helen' (of Troy), *Tr. Cr.* iii, 1 (2); friend of a servant, *Rom. J.* i, 5. In error for 'Margaret' (of Anjou) (*q.v.*).

Nemean, *adj.* Pertaining to Nemea, a valley in Argolis, the haunt of a monstrous lion slain by Hercules. 'Thus dost thou hear the N. lion roar' (*L.L.L.* iv, 1); 'As hardy as the N. lion's nerve' (*Haml.* i, 4).

The word is accented on the first syllable in *Sh.* in accordance with the pronunciation then usual.

Nemesis. The goddess of retribution; avenging justice personified; 'common in the 17th cent.' (*N.E.D. s.v.*). 'Your kingdom's terror and black N.' (*1 Hen. VI*, iv, 7).

Neoptolemus. Also called Pyrrhus (*q.v.*), son of Achilles. In *Tr. Cr.* iv, 5, where alone in *Sh.* the name appears, since Ach. himself seems meant, some edrs. read 'N.'s sire.'

In *The Fall ... of Rebellion* (1573), by Wilfrid Holme, we find the same confusion: 'sending Polidamas to Neophtholemus, was vanquished.'

Neptune, Neptunus. Chief marine divinity of the Romans; by the poets identified with the Greek Poseidon; hence, the sea itself. One of N.'s common attributes is a trident.

'[Thunder and lightning] the most mighty N. Seem to besiege, and make his bold waves tremble, Yea, his dread trident shake' (*Temp.* i, 2); the elves 'Do chase the ebbing N., and do fly him When he comes back' (*ib.* v, 1); 'N.'s yellow sands' (*M.N.D.* ii, 1); at dawn, the Eastern gate is described as 'opening on N., with fair blessed beams' (*ib.* iii, 2); 'the green N. [became] a ram, and bleated' (*Wint. T.* iv, 4); (a strong sea) 'dreadful N.' (*ib.* v, 1); 'all great N.'s ocean' (*Macb.* ii, 2). Of England: 'N.'s arms, who clippeth thee about' (*John*, v, 2); (England) 'Whose rocky shore beats back the envious siege Of watery N.' (*Rich. II*, ii, 1). Of emergence of land: 'to see The beachy girdle of the ocean Too wide for N.'s hips' (2 *Hen. IV*, iii, 1). A wrecked boat 'made a toast for N.' (*Tr. Cr.* i, 3); the waterspout dizzies with 'clamour N.'s car' (*ib.* v, 2); 'rich conceit Taught thee to make vast N. weep for aye On thy low grave' (*Timon*, v, 3); Coriolanus 'would not flatter N. for his trident' (*Cor* iii, 1); Antony 'o'er green N.'s back With ships made cities' (*Ant. Cl.* iv, 14); England compared to 'N.'s park, ribb'd, and pal'd in With oaks unscalable' (*Cymb.* iii, 1); 'N.'s billow' (*Per.* iii, Gow.); 'mask'd N.' (*ib.* iii, 3); 'God N.'s feast' (*ib.* v, Gow.); 'N.'s triumphs' (*ib.* v, 1); the moon's influence on 'N.'s empire' (*Haml.* i, 1); 'N.'s salt wash' (*ib.* iii, 2). Referred to as 'God of this great vast' (*Per.* iii, 1).

In *Wint. T.* iv, 4, the allusion is to Theophane, whom Neptune transformed into a sheep. Becoming a ram himself, he begot the ram with the golden fleece (Ovid, *Metam.* vi, 117). The transformation is alluded to in *Pandosto*. *Cf.* Hygin. *Fab.* 188.

Nereides. Sea nymphs, the fifty daughters of Nereus and Doris (Ovid, *Metam.* ii, 269); Cleopatra's gentlewomen compared to the Nereides, *Ant. Cl.* ii, 2.

Nerissa. D.P. *M.V.* Waiting-maid to Portia. i, 2] converses with her mistress on the obligation Portia is under to wed the chooser of the right casket, and rehearses the names of the suitors. ii, 1] *p.m.* ii, 9] present. iii, 2] admits that she is affianced to Gratiano. iii, 4] is told by Portia that, to carry out a scheme shortly to be unfolded to her, they are both to be apparelled as young men. iv, 1] enters the Court of Justice as a lawyer's clerk and hands the Duke a letter. iv, 2] resolves to obtain, in her disguise, a ring from Gratiano which he had vowed 'to keep for ever'; accompanies him with this object. v, 1] returns to Belmont with Portia; accuses Gratiano of having given the ring to a woman; declares she will not be his wife until she sees it again; (the deception is explained); she hands Lorenzo Shylock's deed of gift.

'Nerrissa,' Qq, F1 (twice 'Nerissa'). Acc. T. Elze, *Sh. Jahrb.* xiii, 145, for the Italian 'Nericcia' (fr. 'Nero'), 'the black-haired.'

Nero. Roman Emperor (A.D. 54–68). Notorious for his crimes and follies. He caused his mother Agrippina to be put to death, and was popularly believed to have caused Rome to be set on fire, and to have chanted verses while viewing the conflagration. 'Like thee, Nero [omitted F1], Play on the lute, beholding the towns burn' (*1 Hen. VI*, i, 4); while Q. Margaret mourns, 'N. will be tainted with remorse' (*3 Hen. VI*, iii, 1); 'Frateretto ... tells me N. is an angler in the lake of darkness' (*Lear*, iii, 6); 'let not ever The soul of N. enter this firm bosom' (*Haml.* iii, 2). In the plural: 'You bloody Neroes, ripping up the womb Of your dear mother England' (*John*, v, 2).

In *Lear* there seems to be an allusion to Rabelais, *Pantagruel*, ii, 30, but there 'Trajan estoit pescheur de grenouilles,' and 'Neron estoit vielleux.' In the *Tr. R.* Philip threatens to treat his mother as N. treated Agrippina, if she will not divulge the truth.

Nervii. A warlike people of Gallia Belgica, 'the stoutest warriors of all the Belgae,' over whom Julius Caesar gained a complete victory after having rallied his men by a display of great personal valour (*Plut.* p. 61). Antony tells the citizens that the mantle covering Caesar's body was that which he put on in the evening of the day on which 'he overcame the N.' (*Jul. C.* iii, 2).

The battle was fought 57 BC, and Antony was not present at it.

Nessus. A centaur, slain by Hercules for an attempt on his wife Deianeira. The blood of Nessus was preserved by D., who believed that by its means she could retain her husband's love; but the blood had been poisoned by the arrow of Hercules, and, upon his donning a garment which had been dipped in it, it adhered to him, and caused him such agony that he immolated himself on a pyre (Ovid, *Metam.* ix, 101 ff.).

'For rapes and ravishments he parallels N.' (*All's Well*, iv, 3); 'The shirt of N. is upon me' (*Ant. Cl.* iv, 12). See LICHAS.

Nestor. King of Pylos; a leader of the Greeks at the siege of Troy, though then of a great age. He had ruled over three generations of men, and was renowned for his wisdom, justice, and eloquence.

Biron compares 'a scene of foolery' to N. playing 'at push-pin with the boys' (*L.L.L.* iv, 3); his gravity alluded to: 'Though N. swear the jest be laughable' (*M.V.* i, 1); Mortimer speaks of his own grey locks as 'Nestor-like aged' (*1 Hen. VI*, ii, 5); 'I'll play the orator as well as N.' (*3 Hen. VI*, iii, 2).

D.P. *Tr. Cr.* i, 3] argues that in adversity true valour shows itself; comments on the behaviour of Ajax and Achilles; would shed his 'three drops of blood' in combat with Hector, though he 'was a man When Hector's grandsire suck'd'; agrees that Hector's challenge is aimed solely at Achilles, but is convinced by Ulysses that Ajax should be induced to fight in Achilles' stead. (ii, 1) Thersites declares that Nestor's wit was mouldy ere Achilles' 'grandsires had nails on their toes.' (ii, 2) mtd. ii, 3] aids Ulysses in flattering Ajax, with the ulterior motive of arousing Achilles. iii, 3] with the other princes affects to treat Achilles with disdain. iv, 5] considers Cressida 'a woman of quick sense'; greets Hector, with whose grandsire he once fought, v, 1] *p.m.* (v, 4) is termed, by Thersites, a 'stale old mouse-eaten dry cheese.' v, 5] describes Hector's wondrous exploits. v, 10] in the field.

His oratory described, *Lucr.* 1401–21. 'The cunning Pylian orator; whose tongue pour'd forth a flood Of more than honey-sweet discourse: two ages were increas'd Of divers-languag'd men, all born in his time and deceas'd, In sacred Pylos' (Chapman, *Homer's Iliads*, bk. i).

Netherlands. Holland (*Fr.* Pays-Bas). The kitchen-wench having been compared to a globe, Ant. S. asks: 'where stood Belgia, the Netherlands?' but Dro. S. 'did not look so low' (*Com. Err.* iii, 2).

Prince Hal, in bantering Poins on the scantiness of his wardrobe, remarks: 'the rest of thy low. countries have made a shift to eat up thy holland' (*2 Hen. IV*, ii, 2). 'Holland,' as a country, does not otherwise appear in *Sh.*

Neville, Family of. 'The Nevils all Whose dreadful swords were never drawn in vain' (*2 Hen. VI*, iv, 1). Warwick is addressed by Henry IV as 'cousin Nevil' (*2 Hen. IV*, iii, 1; this is an error; see BEAUCHAMP, RICHARD). Warwick speaks of 'my father's badge, old Nevil's crest, The rampant bear chain'd to the ragged staff' (*2 Hen. VI*, v, 1); but this came to the Earl, through his wife, from the Beauchamps, the crest of the Nevilles being a bull's head. See Appendix 5.

Neville, Anne (1456–85). Daughter of Richard N., E. of Warwick and Salisbury, 'the King-maker'; betrothed (1470) to Edward, P. of Wales, but the marriage was prevented by his death; m. Richard, D. of Gloucester (1472), and became queen on his usurping the throne in 1483.

Acc. *Hol.* iii, 674, she was actually married to the Prince of Wales.

D.P. *Rich. III.* 'Lady Anne.' i, 2] accompanies the bier of Henry VI as chief mourner; laments over the body while the bearers rest; is confronted by Richard, D. of Gloucester (*q.v.*), upon whom she heaps maledictions, as well as on his wife, if 'ever he have one,' but is at last won over by his subtle and persistent wooing to accept from him a ring and to express her joy to see him 'become so penitent.' iv, 1] is summoned to Westminster, 'to be crowned Richard's royal queen'; bitterly recalls how she was 'captive to his honey words' and how she is now the subject of her own curse. (iv, 2) it is given out by Richard that she is 'like to die' (*Hol.* iii, 751). (iv, 3) her death announced. (iv, 4) mtd. (v, 3) her ghost appears to Richard at Bosworth.

The 'wooing,' of i, 2, is entirely fictitious; at the time, Anne was being kept in hiding by Clarence, for fear of Richard, in the guise of a cook-maid, acc. the continuation of the Chronicle of Croyland (*Script.* Rerum Angl. vol. i).

In *3 Hen. VI*, iii, 3,]. 247, she is wrongly called 'the eldest'; *cf.* also iv, 1.]. 118. The manner of Anne's death is doubtful. Holinshed (iii, 751) states that 'either by inward thought and pensiveness of heart, or by infection of poison (which is affirmed to be most likolie), within a few days after [hearing that Richard had spread a report of her death] the queen departed out of this transitorie life' (March 16, 1485).

With regard to the 'wooing scene' Gervinus observes: 'Vanity, self-complacency and weakness have all to be displayed at once; it is the part of the matron of Ephesus in the tragedy, though it is neither incredible nor forced. We must at the same time bear in view that the murder of her relatives admits of excuse as among the unavoidable evils of war and defence. We must take into account the extraordinary degree of dissimulation, which deceives even experienced men; and for this reason the artist who is to play Richard must woo rather as an actor than as a lover, but must yet go to the very limits of deception even as regards the initiated spectator.' (*Sh. Comm.* (1875), p. 272.)

Neville, Cicely (1415–95). Daughter of Ralph N., 1st E. of Westmoreland; known as 'the Rose of Raby'; m. Richard, 3rd D. of York, in 1438; she outlived all her sons, died at Berkhamsted, and was buried at Fotheringay. In *Rich. III*, iv, 1, her 'eighty odd years' were really 68. The slur cast by Richard on his mother's reputation (*ib.* iii, 5) was baseless.

D.P. *Rich. III.* 'Duchess of York.' ii, 2] overcome with grief at the death of her sons Clarence and Edward IV, replies distractedly to Cl.'s little son and daughter; Richard asks her to give counsel in 'weighty business' with regard to 'the young Prince' (Edw. V). ii, 4] resolves to join the Queen (Elizabeth) in sanctuary, iv, 1] tries to visit the Princes in the Tower. iv, 4] invokes a bitter curse on Richard, whose character as child and man she sums up.

Neville, George (1). 3rd Baron Abergavenny (*c* 1461–1535); g.s. of the 1st Baron; K.G. 1513; Warden of the Cinque Ports; m. Mary Stafford, d. of the 3rd D. of Buckingham.

D.P. *Hen. VIII*. i, 1] comments on Wolsey's pride and on the extravagance of the nobles at the Field of the Cloth of Gold; is committed to the Tower (*Hol.* iii, 863). (i, 2) mtd. as the D. of Buckingham's son-in-law.

'Aberga'ny' in the text; he was 'attached for concelement' (*Hol.* iii, 863).

Neville, George (2) (*c.* 1433–76). Son of Rich. Neville (1) (*q.v.*); Abp. of York, and owner of Middleham Castle. Edward IV given into his custody, *3 Hen. VI*, iv, 3, l. 53; *Hol.* iii, 673.

Neville, John (*ob.* 1471). Baron (1461) and Marq. of Montague (1470); 3rd s. of Richard, E. of Salisbury (D.P. *2 Hen. VI*), and brother to Warwick 'the King-maker'; he defeated the Lancastrians at Hexham (1464) but afterward joined that party, in anger that the earldom of Northumberland, which had been conferred on him, had been restored to the Percies; he allowed Edward IV to land in Yorkshire, but fought for the Lancastrians at Barnet, where he was slain in trying to rescue his brother (Hall, p. 296). He and Warwick were buried at Bisham Priory, Berks. 'Even as the marques was loth to consent to his [Warwick's] unhappie conspiracie, so with a faint hart he shewed himselfe an enimie unto King Edward; which double dissimulation was both the destruction of him and his brethren' (*Hol.* iii, 670). Again, at Barnet, Warwick 'wel knewe him not to be well mynded (but sore agaynste hys stomacke) to take part with these lordes' (Hall, p. 295).

D.P. *3 Hen. VI*. 'Marquis of Montague, of the Duke of York's party.' i, 1] shows his sword, stained, at St Albans, with 'the E. of Wiltshire's blood'; departs 'unto the sea from whence I came.' i, 2] is sent to London to win adherents. ii, 1, 2, 6] *p.m.*; in command of Yorkist forces. (iii, 3) sends letters to Warwick in France. iv, 1] deprecates King Edward's marriage with Lady Grey, but asseverates his loyalty. iv, 6] *p.m.*; with King Henry. iv, 8] at Henry's Court. v, 1] enters Coventry with forces, crying, 'Montague, Montague, for Lancaster.' (v, 2) slain at Barnet. (v, 4) Q. Margaret exclaims, 'M. our top-mast; what of him?' (v, 7) lamented by Edward as one of 'the two brave bears, Warwick and M.'

Neville, Ralph (1) (1364–1425). 1st E. of Westmoreland; 6th Baron Neville of Raby; cr. Earl of West. 1397, by Richard II, but was among the first nobles to join Bolingbroke. He was Bol.'s chief supporter against the rebellious Percies and was rewarded by being made K.G. and Earl Marshal. West. was one of the nobles before whom Bolingbroke swore that he claimed no more than his personal inheritance, and he accompanied B. to meet York; he is, however, not mentioned in *Rich. II*, but seems deliberately omitted, for the Bp. of Carlisle is represented (iv, 1) as arrested by Northumberland, instead of by West. as Holinshed states (*Hol.* iii, 512).

West. was not present at Agincourt, his duties as one of the council of the regent Bedford, and Warden of the Scotch Marches, keeping him in England. In the *Cron. Hist. of Henry the Fift* it is Warwick who desires more men (*Hen. V*, iv, 3), and not West., who is omitted from that play.

West.'s relationship to Henry V ('my cousin,' iv, 3) consists in his having married, as his second wife, Joan Beaufort, d. of John of Gaunt.

D.P. *1 Hen. IV*. i, 1] announces to Henry the defeat of Mortimer by Glendower, and the (then uncertain) issue of the Battle of Homildon (*Hol.* iii, 520). (iii, 2) sets out against Douglas. (iii, 3) Prince H. sends him a letter. (iv, 1) heads 7,000 men. iv, 2] thinks Falstaff's soldiers 'too beggarly.' (iv, 4) mtd. (v, 2) is sent, as a hostage, with a defiant message to the King from the Percies, v, 4] at the Battle of Shrewsbury. v, 5] *p.m.*; is sent to oppose Northumberland and Scrope.

D.P. *2 Hen. IV*. (i, 1, 2, 3) mtd. iv, 1] meets Scrope and Mowbray, and chides the Abp. for fomenting rebellion, though essentially a man of peace; declares that Mowbray has nothing 'to build an inch of grief on'; announces Prince John's offer of a parley (*Hol.* iii, 529); later, invites Scrope to meet the Prince midway between the armies (*Hol.* iii, 530). iv, 2] is present when a truce is agreed upon; pledges Scrope and Mowbray in wine (*Hol.* iii, 529); is sent to dismiss the Prince's troops; later, announces that they await the Prince's personal orders; hearing that Scrope's force has already dispersed, suddenly arrests the three rebel leaders (*ib. ib*). iv, 3] is ordered to stay the pursuit. iv, 4] announces to the King that 'there is not now a rebel's sword unsheathed.' v, 2] *p.m.*

D.P. *Hen. V*. i, 2] advises the King to attack Scotland before making war on France. ii, 2] comments on the innocent bearing of Cambridge and his fellow-conspirators. iv, 3] longs for more men at Agincourt, but is ready to fight even as the King's sole comrade. v, 2] is present when Katharine of Valois is affianced to Henry.

Neville, Ralph (2) (*ob.* 1484). 2nd E. of Westmoreland, g.s. of Ralph Neville (1); he married Elizabeth Percy, widow of Lord Clifford and d. of 'Hotspur.'

D.P. *3 Hen. VI*. i, 1] shows himself a keen supporter of Henry, but on the King's tamely submitting to York's conditions calls him 'faint-hearted and degenerate.'

This is unhistorical, since Neville held himself aloof from both parties.

Neville, Richard (1) (1400–60). 1st E. of Salisbury; e.s. of the 1st E. of Westmoreland; became E. of Salisbury on marrying Alice, heiress of Thomas Montacute (D.P. *1 Hen. VI*), the title being revived in his favour. At first attached to Henry VI, who conferred many honours upon him, he deserted the royal cause for that of the D. of York, and was one of his chief captains at the first Battle of St Albans. He was wounded and taken prisoner at Wakefield (1460) and put to death at Pontefract shortly after the battle. The circumstances of his death (*Hol.* iii, 659) and the removal of his head from York gate (*ib.* iii, 665) are not mtd. in *Sh.*, and the reference to Warwick's father having been brought 'untimely to his death' by the house of York (*3 Hen. VI*, iii, 3) is of course erroneous.

D.P. *2 Hen. VI.* 'Earl of Salisbury.' i, 1] protests against the cession of Anjou and Maine; resolves to bridle the pride of Suffolk and Card. Beaufort. i, 3] checks the arrogance of his son Warwick. ii, 2] discusses York's claim to the crown. ii, 3] is present at the combat between Horner and Peter, iii, 2] acts as spokesman of 'the commons' in demanding the execution or banishment of Suffolk, who calls him 'ambassador of tinkers.' iii, 3] is present at Beaufort's death. v, 1] declares himself adherent of York and argues that his oath of allegiance was 'sinful.' v, 3] (at St Albans) his gallantry praised; thrice rescued by Richard Plantagenet.

Neville, Richard (2) (1428–71). E. of Warwick and Salisbury; known after his death as 'the King-maker'; son of Richard Neville (1). He married Anne, d. of Richard Beauchamp, E. of Warwick, and succeeded to his father-in-law's title. Fought for York at St Albans 1455; victorious at Northampton 1460, and brought Henry VI captive to London; joined Edward of York (Edw. IV) and with him defeated the Lancastrians at Towton; was of great power and influence at the beginning of Edw. IV's reign, but disapproved of the King's marriage with Elizabeth Woodville; married his daughter to George, D. of Clarence, 1469; joined the Lancastrians, and proclaimed Henry VI king; Edward fled to Flanders, but, returning, defeated Warwick at Barnet, 1471, where the Earl was slain; *cf.* Hall, p. 296.

Of him Hall (pp. 231–2) writes: 'not onely a man of marvelous qualities and facundious facions but also from his youth, by a certayn practice or naturall inclinacion, so set them forward, with witte and gentle demeanour, to all persons of high and of lowe degre, that emong all sortes of people he obteyned great love, much favour, and more credence'; his hospitality, riches and noble birth gave him such influence 'that whiche waie he bowed, that waye ranne the streame, and what part he avaunced, that syde gat the superiorite.'

D.P. *2 Hen. VI.* 'Earl of Warwick, of the York faction.' i, 1] sheds tears on hearing of the loss of Anjou and Maine; vows to win the latter back from France. i, 3] displays his animosity against Somerset. ii, 2] listens to York's claim to the throne, and is convinced of its justice (*Hol.* iii, 657). iii, 2] is commanded to view the body of Gloucester, and then 'comment on his sudden death'; later, reports that he was undoubtedly murdered; is challenged by Suffolk, whom he calls 'bloodsucker of sleeping men'; later, is accused by Suf. of having set upon him 'with the men of Bury'; (the King has 'great matters' to impart to Warwick). iii, 3] present at Beaufort's death. (iv, 1) mtd. v, 1] is called by Henry, Salisbury's 'brain-sick son'; exchanges defiance with Clifford. v, 2] (at St Albans) 'is hoarse with calling' Clifford to arms; but York claims the combat. v, 3] rejoices in the victory 'won by famous York.'

In Warwick's exclamation 'Anjou and Maine, myself did win them both' (i, 1), he is clearly confused with another E. of Warwick, viz. Richard Beauchamp (*q.v.*).

W.'s claim to 'old Neville's crest, the rampant bear' (v, 1) was only based on his marriage with Anne, sister of Henry Beauchamp, D. of Warwick. The crest of the N.s was a bull's head.

D.P. *3 Hen. VI.* i, 1] hails Richard, D. of York, as rightful king, and leads him to the throne; takes part in the debate which ensues; summons armed men into the Parliament House; agrees to Henry's proposal to reign for life; determines to 'keep London' with his soldiers; mtd. as 'Chancellor and Lord of Calais' (historically, the latter only). (i, 2) mtd. ii, 1] announces the Yorkist defeat at St Albans, but proposes to attack the Queen and her adherents with fresh forces. ii, 2] is derided by the Queen as 'longtongued W.' who fled at St Albans. ii, 3] (at Towton) kills his horse to show he will not flee (*Hol.* iii, 664). ii, 4] *p.m.* (ii, 5) 'W. rages like a chafed bull.' ii, 6] orders Clifford's head to be substituted for York's over the city gates; proposes seeking Lady Bona's hand for Edward. (iii, 1) goes to France. iii, 3] on Edward's behalf, presents a proposal of marriage to the Lady Bona (*Hol.* iii, 667); wrangles with Oxford on the respective rights of Henry and Edw.; gains the goodwill of King Lewis in spite of Q. Margaret's expostulations; is amazed to learn that Edw. has married Lady Grey (*Hol.* iii, 668); renounces him, and resolves to adhere to Henry; gives his daughter in marriage to Prince Edw. (*Hol.* iii, 674); vows to be revenged on Edw. of York. (iv, 1) his action reported to K. Edw. iv, 2] plans the capture of K. Edw. iv, 3] seizes Edw. in his tent (*Hol.* iii, 673); upbraids him for disgracing him as envoy; removes his crown. (iv, 4) proceeds to London. (iv, 5) mtd. iv, 6] is made, by Henry, joint protector of the realm with Clarence (*Hol.* iii, 678); hears that Edw. has escaped to Burgundy. (iv, 7) mtd. iv, 8] devises means to resist Edward's forces. v, 1] (at Coventry) bids defiance to Edw. from the walls; welcomes reinforcements, but is disappointed at Clarence's defection; (his 'coal-black hair'). v, 2] (at Barnet) is mortally wounded, and made prisoner. (v, 4) Q. Margaret speaks of him as 'our anchor.' (v, 7) K. Edw. commemorates his valour.

In *Rich. III.* (i, 1) mtd. (i, 3) mtd. as Clarence's 'father'; C. speaks of him as 'my great father-in-law, renowned W.' (ii, 1) 'mighty W.' (iv, 1) mtd. by his d. Anne.

Warwick is 'The Last of the Barons' in Lytton's historical romance of that name: 'A man who stood colossal amidst the iron images of the age, – the greatest and last of the old Norman chivalry, – kinglier in pride, in state, in possessions, and in renown than the King himself.'

Newgate. One of the main gates of old London, N. of Ludgate; used as a prison from very early times. 'This gate hath of long time been a gaol ... as appeareth by records in the reign of king John' (Stow).

'*Fal.* Must we all march? *Bard.* Yea, two and two, N. fashion' (*1 Hen. IV*, iii, 3).

Cf. Dekker, *Satiromastix* (1601): 'Why, then, come, we'll walk arm in arm, as though we were leading one another to N.'

Nicander. Name of an attendant; *Per.* iii, 1.

The name, as that of the well-known physician and poet, occurs frequently in Pliny, *Nat. Hist.*

Nicanor. D.P. *Cor.* (not named in st. dirs. or pfxs.). A traitorous Roman. iv, 3] on his way to Antium meets Adrian (*q.v.*) and gives him important news from Rome.

The name occurs several times in Plut. *Phocion.*

Nicholas (1). As a forename. 'N. Gawsey,' 'N. Hopkins,' 'N. Vaux' (*qq.v.*)

Nicholas (2). D.P. *Tam. Sh.* One of Petruchio's servants. iv, 1] welcomes Grumio.

Nicholas, or **Nicolas, St.** Patron saint of the young, and especially of scholars. He was also the patron of merchants and travellers. The reason for robbers being called 'St N.'s clerks,' appears to be either that he was prayed to for protection by travellers, or that wandering scholars – who were licensed to beg – had gained a dubious reputation for honesty. Warburton made the improbable suggestion that a quibble between St N. and 'old Nick' is intended.

'*Speed*. Try me in thy paper. *Launce*. There; and St N. be thy speed' (*T.G.V.* iii, 1); 'If they meet not with St N.'s clerks, I'll give thee this neck. … I know thou worshippest St N. as truly as a man of falsehood may' (*1 Hen. IV*, ii, 1).

In *Coryat's Crudities*, Paneg. v, 'St N. knights' are men who have been hanged.

Nicke. Appears, as pfx., for 'Servant'; *Tam. Sh.* iii, 1, l. 80, F1, 2. Supposed by Steevens to stand for 'Nicholas Tooley' (*q.v.*).

Night. Personified. Mother of Dread and Fear, *Lucr.* 117; apostrophized by Lucrece, *ib.* 764 ff.; mtd., *Son.* xxvii, xxviii. 'Blackbrow'd n.' (*M.N.D.* iii, 2; *Rom. J.* iii, 2); 'heavy gait of n.' (*ib.* v, 1); 'scowl of n.' (*L.L.L.* iv, 3); 'n. doth play the runaway' (*M.V.* ii, 6); 'n. … with thy bloody and invisible hand' (*Macb.* iii, 2); 'n., whose black contagious breath' (*John*, v, 4); 'squires of the n.'s body' (*1 Hen. IV*, i, 2); 'Piercing the n.'s dull ear,' 'cripple, tardygaited n.' (*Hen. V*, iv, Chor.); 'horrid n., the child of hell' (*ib.* iv, 1); 'n. is fled, Whose pitchy mantle over-veil'd the earth' (*1 Hen. VI*, ii, 2); 'the jades That drag the tragic melancholy n.' (2 *Hen. VI*, iv, 1); 'n.'s black mantle' (*3 Hen. VI*, iv, 2); 'aged n.' (*Rich. III*, iv, 4); 'ugly n. comes breathing at his heels,' 'the dragon wing of n.' (*Tr. Cr.* v, 9); 'dragons of the n.' (*Cymb.* ii, 2); 'n.'s swift dragons' (*M.N.D.* iii, 2); 'the cheek of n.' (*Rom. J.* i, 5); 'wings of n.' (*ib.* iii, 2); 'N. kept chain'd below' (*Temp.* iv, 1).

Though there is classical authority for the chariot of Nox (*e.g.* Virg. *Aen.* v, 721), there is none for her dragons. These belonged to Ceres (Demeter).

Nightwork. Personal name. '*Shal.* And is Jane N. alive? … certain she's old; and had Robin N. by old N. before I came to Clement's Inn' (2 *Hen. IV*, iii, 2).

Nile. *Lat.* Nilus; river of Egypt. Cleopatra called 'serpent of old N.' (*Ant. Cl.* i, 5); 'Melt Egypt into N.; and kindly creatures Turn all to serpents' (*ib.* ii, 5); 'they take the flow of the N. By certain scales i' th' Pyramid' (*ib.* ii, 7); 'the flies and gnats of N.' (*ib.* iii, 13); 'slime … such as the aspick leaves Upon the caves of N.' (*ib.* v, 2); 'whose tongue Outvenoms all the worms of N.' (*Cymb.* iii, 4). Only once used with the article.

Nilus. 'The o'er-flowing N. presageth famine' (*Ant. Cl.* i, 2); 'the fire That quickens N.'s slime' (*ib.* i, 3); 'the higher N. swells, The more it promises; as it ebbs, the seedsman Upon the slime and ooze scatters his grain' (*ib.* ii, 7); 'rather on N. mud Lay me' (*ib.* v, 2); 'the pretty worm of N.' (*ib. ib.*); 'like N., it disdaineth bounds' (*T. And.* iii, 1).

Usually 'Nyle' and 'Nylus' in Ff.

Nine Worthies, The. Title of the masque presented by Holofernes and his associates before the King and Princess; *L.L.L.* v, 1, 2. The Worthies actually attempted are five in number, viz. Hector, Pompey, Alexander, Hercules, Judas Maccabaeus.

Falstaff is 'ten times better than the Nine Worthies' (2 *Hen. IV*, ii, 4).

Ritson, *Remarks*, etc. (1785), p. 38, gives the following list of 'IX Wurthy,' from a MS. *temp.* Edw. IV: 'Ector de Troye; Alisander; Julius Caesar; Josue; Davit; Judas Maccabeus; Arthour; Charles; Godefrey de Boleyn.' Steevens quotes MS. Harl. 2057, p. 31, to show that the nine consist of 3 Assaralits, 3 Infidels, and 3 Christians. The pageant of 'The Nine Worthies' is partly illustrated in the frontispiece of Halliwell's folio edition, vol. iv.

Ninny. Flute's perversion of 'Ninus'; *M.N.D.* iii, 1.

Ninus. Eponymous founder of Nineveh, husband of Semiramis (*q.v.*), who erected a magnificent tomb to his memory. 'Ninus' tomb' (*M.N.D.* iii, 1). See Thisbe.

Niobe. Daughter of Tantalus; her children having been slain by the arrows of Apollo and Diana, she was turned into a weeping rock (Ovid, *Metam.* vi, 182 ff., 301 ff.).

'Make wells and Niobes of the maids and wives' (*Tr. Cr.* v, 11); 'Like Niobe, all tears' (*Haml.* i, 2).

Noah. Patriarch. 'Since before N. was a sailor' (*T. Nt.* iii, 2); 'N.'s flood could not do it' (viz. cleanse the kitchen-maid's face) (*Com. Err.* iii, 2). Alluded to: 'another flood toward' (*A.Y.L.* v, 4).

Nob, Sir. 'I would not be sir N. in any case' (*John*, i, 1); perhaps derisively for 'Robert.' ('Nobbe,' Ff.)

Nobleman, A. D.P. *3 Hen. VI.* iii, 2] announces that Henry is a prisoner.

Probably Sir James Harrington, who was rewarded by Edw. IV for capturing Henry (Rymer's *Foedera*, July 29, 1465). 'Nobleman' was then applied to knights.

Noblemen, Four. 'Bearing a canopy, under which the Duchess of Norfolk, godmother, bearing the child,' at the christening of the Princess Elizabeth; *Hen. VIII*, v, 5 (st. dirs.). Acc. *Hol.* iii, 934, the noblemen were: 'the lord Rochford, the lord Husee, the lord William Howard and … lord Thomas Howard the elder.'

No-body. Name attached to a fanciful figure consisting only of head, arms, and legs, used as a shop sign, and forming the frontispiece to *No-body and Some-body*, a comedy (1606) (reproduced in Knight's *Pictorial Sh.*).

'*Trin.* This is the tune of our catch, played by the picture of No-body' (*Temp.* iii, 2).

Non Nobis. The opening words of Psalm cxv; sung as a thanksgiving anthem. After Agincourt Henry V caused 'his prelats and chapleins to sing … "In exitu Israel" [Ps. cxiv] … and commanded everie man to kneele downe … at this verse: Non nobis Domine … sed nomini tuo da gloriam' (*Hol.* iii, 555).

'Do we all holy rites; Let there be sung "Non nobis" and "Te Deum" ' (*Hen. V*, iv, 8; 'Nououes,' Q1).

Norbury, John. Sailed from Brittany with Bolingbroke (*Hol.* iii, 497); appointed Governor of Guisnes and Treasurer of the Exchequer by Henry IV. Mtd. as an adherent of Bol. ('Sir John Norbery'), *Rich. II*, ii, 1.

Norfolk, County of. Essex, N., Suffolk, and and Kent, Warwick's 'southern powers' (*3 Hen. VI*, i, 1); 'and I to N., with my followers' (*ib. ib.*). Clarence instructed to stir up his adherents in Suffolk, N., and Kent, *ib.* iv, 8.

Norfolk, Duchess of. See Tilney, Agnes.

Norfolk, Dukes of. *Mowbray Line:* 1st Duke, D.P. *Rich. II*; see Mowbray, Thomas (1). 3rd Duke, D.P. *3 Hen. VI*; see Mowbray, John.

Howard Line: 1st Duke, D.P. *Rich. III*; see Howard, John. 2nd Duke, D.P. *Rich. III* (Surrey), *Hen. VIII* (Norfolk); see Howard, Thomas (1). 3rd Duke, D.P. *Hen. VIII* (Surrey); see Howard, Thomas (2).

Norfolk, Earl of. See Bigot.

Norman. (*a*) *Subst.*, inhabitant of Normandy. Bourbon speaks of the English as 'Normans, but bastard Normans' (*Hen. V*, iii, 5); 'the false revolting Normans' (*2 Hen. VI*, iv, 1); Lamond, a Norman, mtd., *Haml.* iv, 7.

(*b*) *Adj.* 'Norman bastards' (*Hen. V*, iii, 5).

Normandy. District of N. France; conquered by Philip Augustus 1203; occupied temporarily by Edward III; conquered by Henry V 1415–19; retaken by the French 1450.

Mtd., *L.L.L.* ii, 1; the English nobles 'received deep scars in ... N.' (*2 Hen. VI*, i, 1); (Anjou and Maine) 'the keys of N.' (*ib. ib.*); Lord Say accused by Cade of giving up N., *2 Hen. VI*, iv, 7; (Lamond) 'a gentleman of N.' (*Haml.* iv, 7).

North. (*a*) The cold northern regions. 'The sharp wind of the N.' (*Temp.* i, 2); 'the N., Where shivering cold and sickness pines the clime' (*Rich. II*, v, 1); 'The grizzled N.' (*Per.* iii, Gow.); 'the frozen bosom of the N.' (*Rom. J.* i, 4). Metaph.: 'Sail'd into the N. of my lady's opinion' (*T. Nt.* iii, 2). Personified: 'Entreat the N. To make his black winds ... comfort me with cold' (*John*, v, 7).

(*b*) Northern part of England. 'Unwelcome news came from the N.' (*1 Hen. IV*, i, 1); 'Hotspur of the N.,' 'that same mad fellow of the N.' (*ib.* ii, 4); 'the Percies of the N.' (*1 Hen. VI*, ii, 5); 'At Berwick in the N.' (*2 Hen. VI*, ii, 1); 'horsemen of the N.' (*3 Hen. VI*, i, 1).

(*c*) North wind. 'The tyrannous breathing of the N.' (*Cymb.* i, 4); 'as liberal as the N.' (*Oth.* v, 2; doubtful).

(*d*) In a peculiar sense. '[Fiends] that are substitutes Under the lordly monarch of the N., Appear' (*1 Hen. VI*, v, 3).

'The monarch of the North was Zimimar, one of the four principal devils invoked by witches. The others were Amaimon king of the East, Gorson king of the South, and Goap king of the West... They are all enumerated, from Wier, *De praestigiis daemonum*, in Scot's *Discoverie of Witchcraft*, xv, 2, 3.' (Douce, *Ill. Sh.* ii, 5.)

Northampton. County town of N.-shire; also the county itself. Warwick bids Montague seek adherents in N. (shire), *3 Hen. VI*, iv, 8; Prince Edward at N., *Rich. III*, ii, 4; (see Stony Stratford).

Acc. Capell, the scene is laid at N. in *John*, i, 1; iv, 1, 2, 3; v, 1.

Northampton, Earl of. A title of the D. of Buckingham (*Hol.* iii, 865). The Duke is arrested as 'D. of Buckingham, and Earl of Hereford, Stafford, and N.' (*Hen. VIII*, i, 1).

The title is reminiscent of the Bohun family.

Northamptonshire. Philip Faulconbridge born in the county; *John*, i, 1.

Northumberland, Earls of. See Percy.

Northumberland, Lady. D.P. *2 Hen. IV.* ii, 3] advises her husband to fly to Scotland and await events.

Perhaps intended for Hotspur's mother, but, historically, would be the Earl's 2nd wife, Maud Lucy, widow of Gilbert de Umfreville.

Norway. (*a*) Country of N. 'Fortinbras of N.' (*Haml.* i, 1); 'in the skirts of N.' (*ib. ib.*); 'ambassadors from N.' (*ib.* ii, 2; doubtful). (*b*) For 'King of Norway.' 'N. himself' (*Macb.* i, 2); 'the ambitious N.' (*Haml.* i, 1); 'N., uncle of young Fortinbras' (*ib.* i, 2); 'greeting to old N.' (*ib. ib.*); 'our brother N.' (*ib.* ii, 2); 'rebuke from N.,' 'old N.' (*ib. ib.*); 'Whose powers are these? *Capt.* They are of N.' (*ib.* iv, 4); 'nephew to old N.,' 'now will it yield to N., or the Pole' (*ib. ib.*).

In 'Sweno, the Norweyes [Ff] king' (*Macb.* i, 2) the form is doubtful and has been rendered 'Norway's' and 'Norways'' by later edrs. Perhaps 'Norway' adjectively.

Norweyan, *adj.* Norwegian. 'The N. lord' (*Macb.* i, 2); 'N. banners' (*ib. ib.*); 'the stout N. ranks' (*ib.* i, 3).

Numa [Pompilius]. Second King of Rome (*Plut.* p. 1). 'Ancus Martius, N.'s daughter's son' (*Cor.* ii, 3).

Numbers, Book of. Cited: 'In the book of N. is it writ, When the man dies, let the inheritance Descend unto the daughter' (*Hen. V*, i, 2; cf. *Hol.* iii, 546).

The passage cited is Numb. xxvii, 8: 'If a man die, and have no son, then ye shall cause his inheritance to pass unto his daughter.'

Nuntius Emilius. For 'Aemilius'; *T. And.* iv, 4, st. dir.

Nurse (1). D.P. *T. And.* iv, 2] brings Aaron his child, to kill it, by Tamora's command; she is slain by A.

Nurse (2). D.P. *Rom. J.* i, 3] garrulously discourses on Juliet's infancy. i, 5] gives Romeo and J. information about each other. ii, 2] summons J. ii, 4] is offended at Mercutio's levity; acts as go-between for the lovers. ii, 5] with exasperating circumlocution bids J. betake herself to Friar Laurence's cell. iii, 2] announces Tybalt's death, at the hand of R., to Juliet. iii, 3] conveys messages between R. and J. iii, 5] rebukes her master for 'rating' J.; advises J. to marry Paris. iv, 2] in attendance. iv, 3] *p.m.* iv, 4] in attendance. iv, 5] finds J. seemingly dead, and raises the alarm.

In iv, 4, she is addressed as 'Angelica.' 'Let any man conjure up in his mind all the qualities and peculiarities that can possibly belong to a nurse, and he will find them in Sh.'s picture of the old woman: nothing is omitted. The effect is not produced by mere observation.' (Coleridge, Lecture VII.) 'The nearest of anything in Sh. to a direct borrowing from mere observation' (Id. *Notes on Romeo and Juliet*).

Nym. D.P. *M.W.W.* A follower of Falstaff; 'Corporal N.' i, 1] repudiates Slender's charge of having helped to rob him. i, 3] refuses to take Falstaff's letter to Mistress Ford (or Page) and schemes to betray him. ii, 1] tells Page that 'Falstaff loves his wife.' (ii, 2) mtd. (iv, 5) 'beguiled Slender of a chain.'

D.P. *Hen. V.* (Now a soldier in King Henry's army.) ii, 1] vows vengeance on Pistol for marrying Mistress Quickly; is pacified on P.'s promising to pay him a bet which he owes him. ii, 3] hears of Falstaff's death, and prepares to depart for France. iii, 2] (at the siege of Harfleur) opines that 'the knocks are too hot'; (characterized by the Boy). (iv, 4) hanged for theft. ('Nim,' Q1).

The name 'Nym' ('to filch') is punned upon by Pistol, *Hen. V*, ii, 1: 'I'll live by N., and N. shall live by me.'

Nymphs. D.PP. *Temp.* iv, 1] dance with Reapersin the visionary masque. ('Nimphes,' Ff).

O

O. Vowel. 'O shall end, I hope' (*T. Nt.* ii, 5, l. 125; acc. Johnson, 'a hempen collar,' but more probably merely a sigh); 'O that your face were not so full of O's' (*L.L.L.* v, 2, l. 45; referring to small-pox); 'within this wooden O' (*Hen. V*, i, Chor.; *i.e.* the Globe theatre); 'fiery oes' (*M.N.D.* iii, 2, l. 188; *i.e.* spangles).

Oberon. D.P. *M.N.D.* 'King of the Fairies' (Rowe). ii, 1] twits Titania, who speaks of Hippolyte as his 'buskin'd mistress,' with her 'love to Theseus'; after listening to the Queen's relation of the 'progeny of evils' wrought upon the land by their quarrels, renews his demand of 'a little changeling boy' from her, to be his henchman, and is refused; on Ti.'s departure summons Puck; explains to him the magic virtues of 'love-in-idleness' and their origin; bids Puck fetch the herb; resolves to apply it to Ti.; listens, invisible, to the 'conference' of Demetrius and Helena; receives the flower from Puck; describes the Queen's bower; bids Puck anoint with some of the magic juice the eyes of 'a disdainful youth' in Athenian garments. ii, 2] squeezes the juice on Titania's eyelids, and bids her 'Wake when some vile thing is near,' which she will infallibly take for her 'true-love.' (ii, 2) mtd. iii, 2] Puck reports his doings, and Ob. discovers, on the entrance of Dem., that Puck has mistaken his man; sends P. to fetch Helena; anoints the eyes of the sleeping Dem.; on Puck's return they are unobserved spectators of the four distracted lovers at cross-purposes; to P., who admits his error, Ob. gives directions for remedying its results. iv, 1] witnesses Titania's infatuation; pities her, and tells Puck that she has lately yielded him the changeling boy; awakes her with a counter-charm, and bids P. disenchant Bottom; joyfully trips away with his queen. v, 1] bids the fairies with dance and song bless the bridal chambers in the palace.

The name 'Oberon' is doubtless taken from *Huon of Bordeaux*, a transln. by Ld. Berners of an old French romance. This was dramatized in 1593, but the play is lost. The French form 'Auberon' is in turn derived from the *Teut.* 'Elberick,' or 'Alberick.' The Oberon of Huon has, however, little in common with Sh.'s. He is a misshapen dwarf, of angelic visage, the son of Julius Caesar by the grandmother of Alexander the Great. It is noteworthy, however, that the 'fairy' of Huon lives in the far East, while the Oberon of *M.N.D.* has 'come from the farthest steep of India'; the changeling, moreover, about whom the Fairy King and Queen fall out, was stolen from an 'Indian' King. 'Oberon, King of Fairies,' also appears in Greene's drama *The Scottish Historie of James IV*, *c.* 1590. It has been contended by Sir A. W. Ward (*Eng. Dram. Hist.* (1875), i, 380) that 'the idea of the entire machinery of Ob. and his fairy court was in all probability taken from' this play of Greene's. This opinion, however, is modified by the same critic (*ib.* p. 220) when he admits that though Greene's Oberon 'is the same personage as he who figures in the *M.N.D.*,' he is very differently drawn, 'if, indeed, he can be said to be drawn at all.' *Cf.* Furness, *Var.* p. 278.

Obidicut. Name of a fiend. 'Of lust, as O.' (*Lear*, iv, 1). Qq; omitted Ff.

Occident. The western regions of the sky, or of the world. 'His [the sun's] bright passage to the Oc.' (*Rich. II*, iii, 3); 'I may wander From east to oc.' (*Cymb.* iv, 2, l. 372).

Octavia. Younger daughter of C. Octavius (praetor 61 B.C.), by his 2nd wife Atia, and thus own sister of Octavius (Augustus). Married, first to C. Marcellus, and, secondly, to Mark Antony. Confused by Plutarch (p. 179) with her half-sister, who was d. of Ancharia, 1st wife of C. Octavius. Acc. *Plut.* she composed the strife between Ant. and her brother Oct. (p. 183); was left under her brother's care (p. 184); followed Ant. as far as Athens, but at his bidding returned to Rome (pp. 200–1); remained loyal to her faithless husband (p. 201).

D.P. *Ant. Cl.* (ii, 2) her marriage to Ant. arranged. ii, 3] expresses her devotion to Ant. (ii, 4) mtd. (ii, 5) wedded to Ant. (ii, 6) characterized. (iii, 3) described to Cl. iii, 2] bids her brother farewell. iii, 4] seeks to reconcile Ant. with him. iii, 6] returns (from Athens) and learns that Ant. has rejoined Cleopatra; laments that her heart is 'parted betwixt two friends, That do afflict each other!' (iv, 10) 'patient Oct.' (iv, 13) 'with her modest eyes.' (v, 2) 'the sober eye of dull Oct.'

The nobility of Oct. is manifested by the maternal care with which she brought up Antony's children by Cleopatra.

Octavius, Caius (63 B.C.–A.D. 14). Son of C. Octavius by Atia, niece of Jul. Caes.; on being adopted by his great-uncle, his name was changed to Julius Caesar Octavianus. After the murder of Jul. Caes., Oct. first joined the republican party and aided in the defeat of Ant. at Mutina; soon afterward he was reconciled to Ant. and became triumvir. In 42 B.C. Oct. and Ant. defeated Brutus and Cassius at Philippi. In the following year Fulvia, wife of Ant., having (with the aid of her brother-in-law Lucius Antonius) stirred up war in her husband's absence, Oct. attacked Perusia (into which L. Ant. had thrown himself), and captured it, 40 B.C. Ant. thereupon prepared for war, but a reconciliation between the triumvirs took place, and the empire was repartitioned. In 36 B.C. Oct. conquered Sext. Pompeius in Sicily, and Lepidus, on landing to aid his fellow triumvir, was stripped of his power by Oct. and sent to Rome. The Senate having declared war against Cleopatra, Oct. gained the naval victory of Actium (31 B.C.) over Ant. and the Egyptian Queen. Ant. and Cl. having put an end to their lives, Oct. became master of the Roman world, and accepted the title of *Augustus* (*q.v.*).

D.P. *Jul. C.* (iii, 1) Ant. instructs Oct.'s servant to warn his master that Rome is 'no Rome of safety' for him yet. (iii, 2) Oct. returns to Rome. iv, 1] assists in drawing up the lists of the proscribed (*Plut.* p. 169); considers Lepidus 'a tried and valiant soldier.' (iv, 3) thrice mtd. as 'young Oct.' by Brutus and Cassius. v, 1] refuses to obey Ant.'s orders at Philippi; bids defiance to the foe. (v, 2) Brutus perceives 'cold demeanour' in Oct.'s troops. (v, 3) the attack on his wing is reported successful. (v, 4) mtd. v, 5] orders the body of Brutus to be treated with due honour.

D.P. *Ant. Cl.* (i, 1) 'scarce-bearded'; his alleged power

over Ant. (i, 2) Charmian bids the soothsayer 'marry her with Oct. Caesar.' i, 4] censures Ant.'s dissolute conduct; hears of piratical attacks by the allies of Sext. Pompeius (*Plut.* p. 180); laments the absence of Ant., whose hardihood in former campaigns he recalls (*ib.* p. 167). (ii, 1) takes the field against Pomp. ii, 2] taxes Ant. with collusion in Fulvia's revolt, with ignoring his messages, and with breaking his oath; after hearing Ant.'s defence, falls in with the suggestion that Ant. should strengthen their alliance by marriage with his sister Octavia (*ib.* p. 179); discusses a plan of campaign against Pomp. ii, 3] attends his sister. (ii, 5) 'friends with' Ant. ii, 6] negotiates with Pomp. ii, 7] is present at Pompey's banquet (*ib.* p. 180); deprecates excess (*ib.* p. 232). (iii, 1) mtd. iii, 2] bids farewell to Octavia. (iii, 5) arrests Lepidus. iii, 6] complains to his courtiers of Ant.'s assumption of kingly rights in Egypt; justifies his deposition of Lep. (*ib.* pp. 201–2); welcomes Octavia on her return from Athens (*ib.* p. 201); and undeceives her as to Ant.'s conduct. (iii, 7) at Actium. iii, 8] (at Actium) gives the order: 'strike not by land.' (iii, 9) mtd. iii, 12] gives audience to Euphronius; despatches Thidias on a mission (*ib.* p. 218). iv, 1] derides Ant.'s challenge (*ib.* p. 219); prepares for battle on the morrow. (iv, 4) Cleopatra wishes he could meet Ant. 'in single fight.' (iv, 5) mtd. iv, 6] (before Alexandria) gives orders to Agrippa. (iv, 7, 9) mtd. iv, 10] leads his forces. (iv, 12) 'blossoming Caes.' (iv, 14) Ant. reflects on Caesar's triumph. v, 1] receives the sword of Ant., and laments over him dead (*ib.* p. 220); sends a soothing message to Cl. (*ib.* p. 222). v, 2] visits Cl. in the Monument, and protests that 'our care and pity is so much upon you, that we remain your friend' (*ib.* pp. 225–6).

In *Jul. C.* the name is 'Octavius' or 'Oct. Caesar' throughout ('Octavio,' v, 1, Ff), in *Ant. Cl.* 'Caesar' with one exception (i, 2). Macbeth says (*Macb.* iii, 1), 'Under him [Banquo] My Genius is rebuked, as it is said Mark Antony's was by Caesar' (*Plut.* p. 181).

'A passive instrument in the hands of fortune, tame and colourless, without one ray of poetry in his nature, Octavius both in history and in Shakespeare is an absolutely vapid and insipid person. To take him as the representative of an iron will, cold, patient, and certain of his aim, as some commentators have done ... is assuredly to do him too much honour.' (P. Stapfer, *Sh. and Clas. Ant.* (1880), p. 411.) J. Masefield, *W. Sh.*, regards him as an instance of 'a cool, resolute, astute soul who can and does take advantage of the blindness' of a noble nature, and as showing the basest ingratitude.

Officer (1). D.P. *Com. Err.* iv, 1] in charge of Ant. Eph. iv, 4] releases his prisoner.

Officer (2). D.P. *1 Hen. VI*, i, 3] Makes proclamation for the Mayor.

Officers of a Court of Judicature. D.PP. *Wint. T.*; added to the list by Theobald. Only one of them speaks ('Officer' in pfxs.). iii, 2] reads the indictment against Hermione; administers the oath to the bearers of the 'Oracle,' which he opens and reads.

Officers, Two (1). D.PP. *Cor.* ii, 2] they discuss the character of Cor., 1st Off. censuring his haughtiness, and 2nd Off. commending his 'noble carelessness' and high deserts.

Officers, Two (2). D.PP. *T. Nt.* iii, 4] arrest Antonio. v, 1] bring Ant. before the Duke.

Oldcastle, Sir John (*c.* 1378–1417). Known as Lord Cobham; a Lollard leader. He came of a Herefordshire family, and probably became acquainted with Prince Henry (Hen. V) when serving under Hen. IV in the Welsh Marches. He acquired the title of 'Lord Cobham' from his marriage with Joan, Lady C., in 1409. Becoming ardently attached to the doctrines of Wiclif, he was interrogated by Abp. Arundel, and, despite earnest efforts on the part of Hen. V to convert him, was condemned as a heretic – a sentence which was inevitable after he had denounced the Pope as Anti-Christ before a full court. Oldcastle escaped from the Tower during respite, and, after hiding in London and near Malvern, engaged in treasonable plots with the Scots. He was captured in 1417, and, being found guilty of treason as well as heresy, was cruelly put to death in St Giles' Fields. Execrated by his contemporaries, he was venerated as a martyr by Foxe and others in the following century.

The Shakesperean interest in Oldcastle resides in the fact that though the character of Falstaff (*q.v.*) originally bore his name, Sh. explicitly disclaims founding the dramatic on the historical personage: 'Oldcastle died a martyr, and this [Falstaff] is not the man' (*2 Hen. IV*, Epil.).

Three indications of the dramatic 'Oldcastle' remain in the text: (*a*) Prince Hal's apostrophe to Falstaff as 'my old lad of the castle' (*2 Hen. IV*, i, 2); (*b*) the occurrence, in the Quarto, of 'Old.' for 'Fal.' as a pfx. (*ib.* i, 2, l. 114); (*b*) the reference to Falstaff as a former 'page to Thomas Mowbray, Duke of Norfolk' (*ib.* iii, 2), an office which Oldcastle, as a boy, had filled.

It seems that the introduction of Oldcastle on the stage was protested against by his descendant, Henry Brooke, 8th Lord Cobham, whose father had shown, as Lord Chamberlam, puritanical prejudices against actors in general. (See BROOK.)

A play entitled *Sir John Oldcastle*, and intended to vindicate his memory, was produced in 1599, in two parts. It was groundlessly attributed to Sh. himself. See Lee, p. 244. In N. Field's *Amends for Ladies*, iv, 3 (1613), 'Oldcastle' is mentioned as 'the fat knight' who discoursed on 'honour' (*1 Hen. IV*, v, 1).

Old Man. (1). D.P. *Lear.* Tenant to Gloucester. iv, 1] begs Gl. not to trust himself to 'Mad Tom'; is sent to fetch apparel for Edgar.

Old Man (2). D.P. *Macb.* ii, 4] discusses with Ross the portents which preceded the murder of Duncan.

These portents are by Holinshed (ii, 151–2) associated with the murder of King Duff.

Oliver (1). *1 Hen. VI*, i, 2; see ROWLAND.

Oliver (2). As a forename. 'Ol. de Boys' (D.P. *A.Y.L.*); 'Ol. Martext' (D.P. *ib.*). The phrase 'O sweet Ol.,' here used by Touchstone, is the commencement of a ballad entered in the Stationers' Registers, Aug. 6, 1584. The phrase is used by Dekker and Jonson.

Oliver (3). D.P. *A.Y.L.* Not named in the text; 'Eldest son to Sir Rowland de Boys who had formerly been a Servant of the Duke' (Rowe). (i, 1) has persistently illtreated his youngest brother Orlando, who had been left in his care, and has withheld his patrimony. i, 1] has an altercation with Or., ending in a personal encounter; urges the wrestler Charles to kill Or. if he is matched against him on the morrow. iii, 1] is commanded by D. Frederick to seek Or. and bring him back 'dead or living.' iv, 3] reveals himself to Rosalind and Celia, and relates how he was rescued from a serpent and a lioness by Or. v, 2] tells Or. of his love for Celia, and settles his estate upon him. v, 4] (weds Celia) *p.m.*

The equivalent character in Lodge's *Rosalynde* is Saladyne. Lady Martin, *Sh.'s Fem. Char.* p. 281, observes: 'Making all allowance for the necessity of bringing the action of the play to a speedy conclusion, the readiness with which Celia succumbs to Oliver's suit is somewhat startling. Sh. perhaps felt this himself, and so does his best to take the edge off its apparent improbability.' The writer then quotes v, 1, ll. 31 ff.

Olivia. D.P. *T. Nt.* 'A Lady of great Beauty and Fortune, belov'd by the Duke' (Rowe). (i, 1) Orsino's love for her. (i, 2) her story told. i, 5] permits Feste to divert her by his jests, and rebukes Malvolio for his ill-natured comments; refuses to receive Orsino's messenger; censures Sir Toby's potations; accords 'Cesario' an interview; after some verbal fencing, consents to unveil and to hear Or.'s message; on hearing 'Cesario's' protestations of what he would do in his master's place, murmurs 'you might do much'; rejects Or.'s suit, but gives 'C.' an excuse for returning, and offers him a purse; soliloquizes on 'this youth's perfection'; sends Mal. after him with a ring which, she alleges, 'C.' left behind him. (ii, 2) her love for 'Cesario.' (ii, 4) mtd. iii, 1] refuses to listen to a renewal of Orsino's suit, but tells 'C.' that if he would undertake another suit 'I had rather hear you to solicit that, Than music from the spheres'; openly confesses to 'C.' her love for him, and, though treated by him scornfully, on hearing that 'no woman' has his heart, exclaims 'yet come again.' iii, 4] declares Malvolio's fantastical wooing to be 'very Midsummer madness'; meeting 'Cesario' in the garden, gives him a jewelled portrait of herself and bids him 'come again tomorrow.' iv, 1] discovers Sir Toby in the act of drawing on Sebastian (whom she mistakes for 'Cesario'), and dismisses her kinsman ignominiously; re-enters the house with Sebastian, whom she invites to accompany her. iv, 3] induces Seb. to consent to their betrothal before a priest. v, 1] encounters Or. and 'Cesario'; chides 'C.' for not keeping faith with her; treats Or.'s protestations with scorn; on learning that 'C.' intends to follow his master, passionately reminds him that he is her affianced husband, and causes the priest to be summoned to testify to the fact; orders the tipsy Sir Toby to be removed; on Sebastian's entrance, marvels at his resemblance to 'Cesario'; sends for Mal. and causes his letter to be read aloud; accepts the situation caused by the confusion of Seb. with 'C.' and begs Orsino to think of her 'as well a sister as a wife'; on Mal.'s entrance, disclaims having done him a wrong – pointing out that the letter was a forgery – but admits 'he hath been most notoriously abused.'

The name of the corresponding character in *Gl' Ingannati* is Isabella, in Bandello's story Catella, and in *Apolonius and Silla* Julina (a widow). See TWELFTH NIGHT. 'Olivia is in an unreal mood of mourning for her brother. Grief is a destroying passion. Olivia makes it a form of self-indulgence, or one sweet the more to attract flies to her.' (J. Masefield, *W. Sh.* p. 140.) For an elaborate study of the character, regarded as 'the central point of the whole action,' see Gervinus, *Sh. Comm.* (1875), pp. 434 ff.

Olympian, *adj.* Pertaining to the games held at Olympia in Elis every four years. 'I have seen thee ... take thy breath, When that a ring of Greeks have hemm'd thee in, Like an Olympian wrestling' (*Tr. Cr.* iv, 5).

Olympus. A range of mountains between Thessaly and Macedonia, regarded in Gk. mythol. as the abode of the gods. 'Great thunder-darter of Ol.' (*Tr. Cr.* ii, 3); 'as if Ol. to a molehill should Nod' (*Cor.* v, 3); 'Hence! Wilt thou lift up Ol.?' (*Jul. C.* iii, 1); 'as huge as high Ol.' (*ib.* iv, 3); 'Now climbeth Tamora Ol.'s top' (*T. And.* ii, 1); 'The skyish head of blue Ol.' (*Haml.* v, 1); 'hills of seas Olympus-high' (*Oth.* ii, 1).

[**Oonly, R.**] See BOLINGBROKE, ROGER.

Ophelia. D.P. *Haml.* Daughter of Polonius and sister to Laertes. i, 3] is warned by Laertes 'to keep within the rear of her affection' in respect of Hamlet; she trusts L. will practise the virtues he preaches; admits to her father that Haml. has wooed her, honourably, and is bidden to avoid the Prince's company. ii, 1] informs Pol. that Haml. has visited her in state of seeming madness. (ii, 2) shows Pol. a letter she has received from Haml. iii, 1] is ordered to be found reading alone when Haml. approaches, while Pol. and the King listen to the interview in hiding; is strangely questioned by Haml. and laments over the 'noble mind o'erthrown.' iii, 2] converses with Haml. during the performance of the play before the King. iv, 5] in a state of insanity is brought before the King and Queen; sings snatches of loose ditties; later, reappears when Laertes also is present. (iv, 7) is drowned. (v, 1) her burial.

The name is spelled 'Ofelia' in Q1. There is a discrepancy in connection with the account of O.'s death, for whereas the Queen (iv, 7) describes it as the result of an accident, the circumstances of her burial (v, 1) imply that it was a case of suicide. Yet the Priest tells Laertes that 'her death was doubtful.'

It has origin of the name has given rise to discussion.

The been regarded as equivalent to ὠφέλεια (assistance). Ruskin, *Munera Pulveris* (1872), p. 126, maintains that 'Ophelia, serviceableness, the true lost wife of Hamlet, is marked as having a Greek name by that of her brother Laertes,' and adds that its meaning is alluded to by him in the words 'a ministering angel' (*Haml.* v, 1).

But in the first quarto edn. of Sannazaro's *Arcadia* (*c.* 1504) Ofelia is the name of one of the love-sick swains, and is coupled with that of Montano (*q.v.*). This seems a modification of 'Ofella,' a known ? surname.

In *The Hystorie of Hamblet* (1608) the analogous character is unnamed, and appears merely as a fair woman employed by the courtiers to entrap H. and ascertain the truth as to his madness; but the plot fails, since she and H. are in truth lovers.

With regard to the arranged interview of iii, 1, Coleridge writes: 'Here it is evident that the penetrating Hamlet perceives, from the strange and forced manner of Oph. that the sweet girl was not acting a part of her own, but was a decoy. Such a discovery ... accounts for a certain harshness in him ... and particularly in his enumeration of the faults of the sex from which Oph. is so free, that the mere freedom therefrom constitutes her character.' (*Notes on Haml.*) 'Oph. is a character almost too exquisitely touching to be dwelt upon' (W. Hazlitt, *Char. of Sh. Plays*). 'Ophelia is a doll without intellect' (J. Masefield, *W. Sh.*). See Lady Martin's study of the character as acted by herself (*Sh.'s Fem. Char.* (1887)).

Opportunity. Personified; apostrophized by Lucrece, *Lucr.* 874 ff., 1023.

Oracle, Sir. A nonce-name. 'I am Sir Or., And when I ope my mouth let no dog bark' (*M.V.* i, 1, Qq). (In Ff, 'Sir an Oracle.')

Orient. The East (*q.v.*). Rumour flies 'from the Or. to the drooping West' (*2 Hen. IV*, Ind.); mtd., *Son.* vii.

Elsewhere used adjectively.

Orion. See Arion.

Orlando. D.P. *A.Y.L.* Youngest son of Sir Rowland de Bois. i, 1] describes his illtreatment by his eldest brother Oliver, who has denied him education and withheld his patrimony; has an altercation with Ol. ending in a personal encounter. i, 2] overthrows the wrestler Charles, after having been vainly dissuaded from the contest by Rosalind and Celia. (i, 3) mtd. ii, 3] is persuaded by the old steward, Adam, to seek refuge in flight from Oliver's vengeance. ii, 6] reaches the forest of Arden with Adam, who sinks exhausted. ii, 7] breaks in upon the Duke's 'banquet' and demands food at the point of the sword; is pacified, and bears in the fainting Adam. iii, 2] hangs verses, in praise of Ros., on trees in the forest, and carves her name in the bark; encounters Jaques, and, afterward, 'Ganymede' and 'Aliena,' whose disguise he does not penetrate; holds bantering conversation with the former and is persuaded to make feigned love to him under the name of 'Rosalind,' as a cure for his 'malady.' (iii, 4) discussed by Ros. and Celia. iv, 1] the mock courtship proceeds. (iv, 3) Or. is wounded by a lioness in rescuing his brother Ol. v, 2] consents to the marriage of Oliver and 'Aliena,' and is assured by 'Ganymede' that, by magical agency, he shall marry his Rosalind on the morrow. v, 4] admits that he has observed a resemblance between 'Ganymede' and Ros., and on the latter appearing in woman's attire, exclaims, 'If there be truth in sight, you are my Rosalind!'

The corresponding character in Lodge's *Rosalynde* is Rosader. 'Orlando' is the Italian form of his father's name 'Rowland.'

'As volatile as one of Alfred de Musset's heroes, he has, in all and through all, a firm ground of healthy English sense and truthfulness, which entitles him to serve as a type of those gallant youths who from so many a creek and inlet of Devonshire and Cornwall went forth in Sh.'s day to war against the Spaniard.' (C. E. Moberly, Introd. Rugby edn.)

Orleans. On the Loire, capital of the province of Orléanais, which was one of the few that acknowledged Charles VII at his succession. In Oct. 1428 it was besieged by the D. of Bedford and seemed doomed to fall, when in April 1429 Joan of Arc made her way into the town and with the help of Dunois (*q.v.*) and Alençon raised the siege in about ten days. Mtd. *Cymb.* i, 5, at a time when it would have been Civitas Aureliani.

The account given of the siege of Or., *1 Hen. VI*, i, ii, is largely unhistorical. It is reported lost by the English (i, 1), but it was not in their possession at the death of Henry V; the defeat of Talbot 'retiring from the siege of Or.' (i, 1) belongs to a later date; neither the Dauphin (Charles VII) nor Reignier was present at the siege, as stated (i, 2); the death of Salisbury (i, 4) took place some months before the appearance of Joan upon the scene; the recapture of Or. by Talbot (ii, 1) is imaginary.

Orleans, Bastard of. See Dunois.

Orleans, Charles, Duke of (1391–1465). Son of Lewis, D. of O. (brother to Charles VI), who was murdered (1407) by John, D. of Burgundy. Ch.'s first wife was Isabel, widow of Rich. II, whose d. Joan became wife of John, D. of Alençon (D.P. *1 Hen. VI*). Ch. was taken prisoner at Agincourt (*Hol.* iii, 555) and spent an easy captivity in England until 1440, to please the D. of Burgundy so long as the latter remained faithful to England (*Hol.* iii, 618; *1 Hen. VI*, iii, 3). While a prisoner he wrote poems of much merit (*cf.* Saintsbury, *French Lit.* p. 105). He was present at the espousals of Queen Margaret (*Hol.* iii, 625; *2 Hen. VI*, i, 1).

D.P. *Hen. V.* iii, 5] (at council of war) *p.m.* iii, 7] (the night before Agincourt) in bantering converse with the Constable and others, longs for the morrow, and scorns the English. iv, 2] (the morning of the battle) rallies his 'cousin' the Dauphin. iv, 5] fears that all is lost. (iv, 8) taken prisoner. (ii, 4) mtd.

Orleans, Henry, Duke of. Second son of Francis I (*Hol.* iii, 907); his marriage to Mary, d. of Henry VIII, mooted, *Hen. VIII*, ii, 4.

[**Ormonde, Earl of.**] See Wiltshire, Earl of.

Orpheus. Mythical Greek poet; with the lyre (or lute) given him by Apollo he enchanted wild beasts, trees, and rocks, and even put Cerberus to sleep; in revenge for his contempt, he was torn to pieces by Thracian Maenads during their Bacchanalian orgies (Ovid, *Metam.* xi).

'Or.'s lute' (*T.G.V.* iii, 2); 'Or. drew trees' (*M.V.* v, 1); 'Or. with his lute' (*Hen. VIII*, iii, 1). ('The riot of the tipsy Bacchanals, Tearing the Thracian singer in their rage' (*M.N.D.* v, 1); 'fell asleep, As Cerberus at the Thracian poet's feet' (*T. And.* ii, 5).)

'Moody Pluto winks while Or. plays' (*Lucr.* 553).

For taming tigers (*T.G.V.*) *cf.* Virg. *Geor.* iv, 510, 'mulcentem tigres.'

Orsino. D.P. *T. Nt.* 'Duke of Illyria' (Rowe). i, 1] rhapsodizes on Music and Love, and his own passion for Olivia, whose resolve to seclude herself from the world he now learns. (i, 2) discussed by Viola and the Sea-captain. i, 4] bids 'Cesario' (the disguised Viola) seek audience with Ol., take no denial of access, and unfold to her his master's passion. (i, 5) mtd. (ii, 1) his Court. ii, 4] calls for a song he lately heard; elicits that 'Cesario's eye' had already 'stay'd upon some favour that it loves,' and that the object of his affection was older than himself and of Orsino's own 'complexion'; bids 'Cesario' once more bear his vows to 'yond same sovereign cruelty'; denies that any woman's love can compare with his own in intensity; listens to 'Cesario's' parable of his 'father's daughter' who pined for love. (iii, 1) mtd. (iii, 4) mtd. v, 1] fees Feste to announce his presence to Olivia; identifies Antonio, who is brought in custody before him, and is bewildered by Ant.'s apparent recognition of 'Cesario'; he is treated scornfully by Ol. and is amazed by her claim that 'Cesario' (whom she confuses with Sebastian) is her affianced husband; in his wrath casts off 'Cesario' as a 'dissembling cub'; is disabused by the entrance of Seb.; assures Ol. that Seb. is of noble birth, and bids Viola assume her 'woman's weeds'; tells her that she shall 'from this time be her Master's mistress'; listens to Malvolio's protest; orders him to be followed and entreated 'to a peace'; remembers moreover that M. 'hath not told us of the Captain yet'; 'When that is known, and golden time convents, A solemn combination shall be made Of our dear souls.'

Virginio Orsino, Duke of Bracciano, and Ambassador to the English Court, was entertained by Elizabeth in the winter of 1600–1 (on Twelfth Night, among other occasions), and it has been suggested that this fact originated the name.

Or. is spoken of as 'Duke' in i, 2, 4, but elsewhere as 'Count' in the pfxs. always 'Duke'). This confusion of titles can be paralleled in other plays: *L.L.L.* ii, 1, 'duke' for 'king'; *T.G.V.* i, 3, 'emperor' for 'duke'; *T. And.* iii, 1, 'king' for 'emperor'; *Haml.* iii, 2, 'duke' for 'king.'

In *Gl' Ingannati* the equivalent character is Flaminio de Carandini; in Bandello's story Lattanzio; in *Apolonius and Silla* Apolonius. See TWELFTH NIGHT.

'It almost seems as if the Duke were more in love with his love than with his mistress; as if like Romeo with Rosaline he rather speculated in thought over his fruitless passion than felt it actually in his heart; as if his love were rather a production of his fancy than a genuine feeling.' (Gervinus, *Sh. Comm.* (1875), p. 430.)

Osric. D.P. *Haml.* A courtier. v, 2] is sent to inform Hamlet that the King has laid a wager on the result of a fencing-match between the Prince and Laertes; he attempts to deliver his message in highly affected terms, but is greatly disconcerted by Hamlet's derisive comments; later, hands the foils to Haml.; is appealed to as umpire during the fencing; the dying Laertes confesses to him his treachery; Osric announces the arrival of young Fortinbras.

He is styled 'young Os.' by a lord, and Hamlet declares 'he hath much land and fertile.' Much of Osric's court foppery is omitted in Ff. In Q1 (1603) he is designated only as 'a bragart gentleman.' Osrio is the name of the foster-brother of Amleth in Saxo Grammaticus' story. See HAMLET, PRINCE OF DENMARK.

Ossa. A mountain in Thessaly mtd. in the legend of the war of the giants against the gods; 'ter sunt conati imponere Pelio Ossam' (Virg. *Geor.* i, 281); see PELION.

Hamlet, outranting Laertes, would have 'millions of acres' thrown on the bodies of Ophelia and himself, and 'make Ossa like a wart' (*Haml.* v, 1).

'Oosell,' Q1.

Ostler, Robin. *1 Hen. IV*, ii, 1, Qq; see ROBIN (3). ('The Ostler,' Ff.)

Ostler, William. Mtd. as a 'principal actor' in F1.

Oswald. D.P. *Lear.* Steward to Goneril. i, 3] is ordered by Goneril to assume 'weary negligence' – 'you and your fellows' – to Lear. i, 4] behaves impudently to L., and is tripped up by Kent; later, is despatched by Goneril to Regan with a letter which he has written. ii, 2] on reaching Gloucester's castle is rated and beaten by Kent. ii, 4] *p.m.*; is ordered by Lear out of his sight. iii, 7] announces L.'s flight to Dover. iv, 2] informs Gon. of her husband's changed demeanour. iv, 5] refuses to give up to Regan Goneril's letter to Edmund; longs to kill Gloucester. iv, 6] prepares to murder him, but is killed by Edgar; with his dying words desires the letters to be given to Edm.

Oswald is regarded by Coleridge as 'the only character of utter irredeemable baseness in Sh.' His fidelity to his mistress seems, however, a redeeming point. Edgar depicts him in two words as a 'Serviceable villain' (iv, 6).

Always 'Steward' in st. dirs. and pfxs., QqFf. Only twice mtd. by name in the text (i, 4).

Otecake, or **Oatcake, Hugh.** Suggested as a 'desartless man to be constable' (*M. Ado*, iii, 3).

Othello. (In F1: 'The Tragedie of Othello, the Moore of Venice.' The acts and scenes are numbered.)

DATE OF PRODUCTION. For many years much uncertainty prevailed as to the year in which *Othello* first appeared upon the stage. The early critics attached importance to Othello's words to Desdemona (iii, 4), 'But our new Heraldry is hands, not hearts,' and seeing in this an allusion to the institution of the order of Baronets by James I, in 1611, considered that year to be the date of production. Malone, however, in 1821, remarked that 'we know it was acted in 1604,' without giving grounds for his statement. In 1842 P. Cunningham announced the discovery – in the Audit Office, Somerset House – of certain books of accounts kept by the Master of the Revels, showing the expenses incurred in the production of plays before royalty. In one of these *Revels' Books* appears the entry: '1605. By the King's Maties Plaiers Hallamas Day being the first of November A play in the Banketinge house at Whitehall called The Moor of Venis by Shaxberd.' (The context shows that '1605' is a clerical error for '1604.') Some years later the leaves of the *Revels' Books* containing references to Sh.'s plays were declared by experts to be forgeries, and the question of the date of the play once more fell into incertitude. In 1911, however, the authenticity of the MS. was, with general consent, re-established, and 'Nov. 1, 1604' is recognized as the true date. (There are good reasons for believing that Malone based his conviction on the same Audit Office records.)

PUBLICATION. In 1622 – only a few months therefore, before the publication of the First Folio – there appeared: 'The Tragœdy of Othello, The Moore of Venice. As it hath beene diverse times acted ... by his Majesties Seruants. Written by VVilliam Shakespeare. London, printed by N.O. for Thomas Walkley ... 1622.' This is known as the First Quarto, and shows ample evidence of having been derived from a source independent of the Folio. Walkley's property was assigned to successors, and two other editions of the Quarto were published, in 1630 and 1655 respectively. Their critical importance is small. The text of the play as it appears in the First Folio is the best available, and is regarded by Dyce as 'beyond all doubt printed from a transcript belonging to the theatre.'

SOURCE OF THE PLOT. The original of the story of *Othello* is to be found in the *Hecatommithi* of Giraldi Cinthio (Dec. iii, Nov. 7) publd. in 1565, of which no English translation existed in Sh.'s time. The only named character in the novel is 'Disdemona,' those corresponding to Othello, Iago, and Cassio being respectively 'un Capitano Moro,' 'un alfiero di bellissima presenza, ma della piu scelerata natura,' and 'un Capo di squadra.' Roderigo is of Sh.'s creation. (For Sh.'s innovations in the plot, see under the names of the characters.)

Othello. D.P. *Oth*. 'The Moore' (F1). (i, 1) Iago's hatred toward him becomes manifest; Oth. is clandestinely married to Desdemona. i, 2] Oth. is urgently summoned by the senators on business of state; is accused by Brabantio of having won his daughter's affections by magical practices. i, 3] Oth. defends himself before the senators against B.'s charge; he is acquitted, and sent to defend Cyprus against the Turks; he entrusts Desd., who is allowed to follow him, to the charge of Iago and his wife Emilia. ii, 1] arrives in Cyprus after Desd., having been delayed by a storm. (ii, 2) orders revels in celebration of the destruction of the Turkish fleet and his own nuptials. ii, 3] orders his lieutenant Cassio to look to the guard; finds Cas. intoxicated, and involved in a sanguinary brawl; dismisses him. (iii, 1) mtd. iii, 2] sends a message to Venice. iii, 3] finds Cas. in converse with Desd., and is entreated by her to reinstate Cas.; he procrastinates; Iago instils misgivings into Oth.'s mind with regard to Desd. and Cas.; Desd. finds him agitated; he rejects her offer of a handkerchief, and it falls to the ground; later, Oth. enters, in a frenzy of jealousy, and, prevailed upon by Iago, determines on her death. iii, 4] demands from Desd. the handkerchief he had given her, averring that 'there's magic in the web of it.' iv, 1] in further converse with Iago, is so agitated that he falls in an epileptic fit; on recovering he hears a conversation between Iago and Cas. concerning Bianca, which he supposes to refer to Desd.; resolves to kill her – 'but yet, the pity of it, Iago!'; is ordered home, Cas. being appointed as his deputy; in his fury he strikes Desd.; Lodovico thinks him mad. iv, 2] questions Emilia; alone with Desd., overwhelms her with vile accusations. iv, 3] bids Desd. retire to her chamber. v, 1] (*sol.*)! believing Cas. to be dead, mutters, 'Minion, your dear lies dead, And your unblest fate hies.' v, 2] murders Desd.; discovers Iago's plot; commits suicide.

Othello's colour has been much discussed. He is explicitly stated to be a Moor of high lineage – a fellow-countryman, in fact, of the Prince of Morocco in *M.V.* – and, since the complexion of Moors varies, it is legitimate, and perhaps expedient, to represent him on the stage as a merely swarthy personage, in accordance with the practice initiated by Kean.

Coleridge's comment that it is monstrous to conceive Desdemona 'falling in love with a veritable negro' seems irrelevant – a Moor, however dark, is not a negro. Yet there is a strong presumption that Sh. thought of Oth. as unequivocally black – following Cinthio's Novel, in which the Ensign tells the Moor (falsely) that Disdemona loathes his blackness (*nerezza*). Apart from the abusive exaggerations of his enemies, Oth. himself seems to supply conclusive evidence on the point, when he says (iii, 3), 'My name that was as fresh As Dian's visage, is now begrim'd and black As mine own face.'

With regard to the origin of the name nothing definite is known. Its occurence in nearly contemporary writings may be due to the play. The Moor in Cinthio's Novel is unnamed. It has been held that the 'Otelli del Moro' were noble Venetians, originally from the Morea, whose device was the mulberry – perverted in the play into a strawberry, upon the handkerchief. See F. A. Kemble, *Records of Later Life* (1884), p. 88.

Ottoman, *adj.* Turkish (strictly, pertaining to the descendants of Othman). Othello is ordered to proceed 'against the general enemy Ottoman' (*Oth*. i, 3).

'Ottaman,' Q1.

Ottomites. Turks; see OTTOMAN. Their fleet at Rhodes, *Oth*. i, 3; 'present wars against the Ottamites' (*ib. ib.*); mtd., *ib*. ii, 3.

'Ottamites,' or 'Ottamittes,' F1.

Outlaws. D.PP. *T.G.V.* iv, 1] (in a forest, near Mantua) they capture Valentine and Speed, and struck by the 'goodly shape' of the former, and the fact that he is a linguist, make him captain of the band (three of the outlaws are speaking characters, and relate the cause of their outlawry). v, 3] capture Silvia. v, 4] also capture the Duke and Thurio; they are pardoned by the former.

Two outlaws are named (v, 3), viz. Moyses and Valerius.

Overdone, Mistress. D.P. *M. for M.* A bawd. i, 2] discusses with Lucio the impending fate of Claudio, and the rumoured suppression of houses such as hers. (ii, 1) mtd. iii, 2] is committed to prison. (iv, 3) mtd.

Ovid. Publius Ovidius Naso, Roman poet (43 B.C.–A.D. 18). Banished, for an undetermined reason, to Tomi, a town on the Euxine, among the Getae (see GOTHS). Ovid's most famous poem, the *Metamorphoses* (*q.v.*), was translated into English verse by A. Golding (1565–7), whose version was undoubtedly used by Sh. In his *Lucrece* Sh. follows the story as told in Ovid's *Fasti*, ii, 728–852 (not then translated). A couplet from the *Amores*, I, xv, 35–6, forms a 'motto' to *Venus and Adonis; Heroides*, i, 33–4, is quoted in *Tam. Sh.* iii, 1, and *Metam.* i, 150, in *T. And.* iv,3; while *Her.* ii, 66, forms the dying ejaculation of young Rutland, *3 Hen. VI*, i, 3. *Trist.* III, ix, is alluded to, *2 Hen. VI*, v, 2; see ABSYRTUS. The *Ars Amat.* referred to, *Tam. Sh.* iv, 2.

'As the soule of Euphorbus was thought to live in Pythagoras, so the sweete wittie soule of Ovid lives in mellifluous and hony-tongued Shakespeare.' (F. Meres, 1598.)

The following are direct references to Ovid by name: 'I am here with thee and thy goats, as the most capricious poet, honest Ovid, was among the Goths' (*A.Y.L.* iii, 3); 'or so devote to Aristotle's checks As Ovid be an outcast quite abjured' (*Tam. Sh.* i, 1); 'Ovid's *Metamorphoses*' (*T. And.* iv, 1); 'Ovidius Naso was the man. And why indeed Naso, but for smelling out the odoriferous flowers of fancy?' (*L.L.L.* iv, 2).

The indebtedness of Sh. to Ovid as a source of mythology is amply illustrated by the references under various classical headings. Verbal coincidences show that Golding's translation was made use of in several instances rather than the original (*Temp.* v, 1, 1.33; *Oth.* ii, 1, II. 188 ff.; *M.N.D.* iv, 1, II. 107ff.; *M.W.W.* ii, 1, l. 122; *V.A.* 620 ff.).

The following translations were available for Sh.: *Metamorphoses*, by A. Golding (1567); *Heroides*, by G. Turbervile (1567); *Amores*, by Marlowe (*c.*1597); *Tristia*, by T. Churchyard (1572).

Owen. See GLENDOWER.

Oxford. A reading (for 'Spencer') in *Rich. II*, v, 6, l. 8, found in Qq; corrected in Ff. Cf. *Hol.* iii, 516.

Oxford, City of. It was planned by the Abbot of Westminster and his fellow-conspirators that 'a solemne justs' should be held at Oxford in the presence of Henry IV, and that 'when he should be most busilie marking the martiall pastime, he suddenly should be slaine' (*Hol.* iii, 514); but the plot becoming known to the King he was saved.

Aumerle intends to be present there at the 'justs and triumphs' (*Rich. II*, v, 2); Prince Hal would fain be at O., *ib.* v, 3; 'powers' sent thither, *ib. ib.*; the traitors at O., *ib.* v, 6.

Oxford, University of. Shallow's cousin William is still at O. 'to my cost' (2 *Hen. IV*, iii, 2); Christ Church (*q.v.*) founded by Wolsey, *Hen. VIII*, iv, 2.

Oxfordshire. 'And thou, brave Oxford, wondrous well belov'd, In Oxfordshire shalt muster up thy friends' (*3 Hen. VI*, iv, 8).

Oxford, Earls of. Vere, Aubrey de (*c.* 1340–1400); *Rich. III*, v, 6, Qq. Vere, John de (1) (*c.* 1408–62); *3 Hen. VI*, iii, 3, ll. 101 ff. Vere, John de (2) (1443–1513); D.P. *3 Hen. VI*, *Rich. III.*

P

Pabylon. Evans' pronunciation of 'Babylon' (*q.v.*); *M.W.W.* iii, 1. The snatch, 'When as I sat in B.,' is from William Whittingham's version of Ps. cxxxvii.

Pace, Richard (*c.* 1482–1536). Dean of St Paul's; engaged in important missions under Wolsey. Campeggio tells Wol. that 'one Doctor Pace ... a learned man' is believed to have incurred W.'s envy, so that he was kept continually abroad until 'he ran mad, and died' (*Hen. VIII*, ii, 2) (cf. *Hol.* iii, 907, where it is stated that P. 'fell out of his right wits,' from the cause alleged. Historically, he did not die until three years after the Queen's trial).

D.P. *Hen. VIII.* (Unnamed.) i, 1] appears as one of Wolsey's two secretaries. (ii, 2) mtd.

Acc. French, p. 269, the other sec. was William Burbank, Archdeacon of Carlisle.

Pacorus. Son of Orodes I, King of Parthia; he twice unsuccessfully invaded Syria, 40–38 B.C., and on the second occasion fell in battle. See VENTIDIUS. '*Ven.* Fortune does of Marcus Crassus' death Make me revenger. Bear the King's son's body Before our army; thy P. Orodes ['Orades,' Ff] Pays this for Marcus Crassus' (*Ant. Cl.* iii, 1; cf. *Plut.* p. 182).

Paddock. Name of an imp, or familiar. 'P. calls' (*Macb.* i, 1).

Dim. of 'pad' or 'paddle,' a toad or frog.

Padua. City of Italy; a centre of art and literature in the Middle Ages; its university, founded in the 13th cent., ranked among the most famous in Europe, especially for law and medicine. 'Signior Benedick of P.' (*M. Ado*, i, 1); the residence of the learned Doctor of Law, Bellario, *M.V.* iii, 4, iv, 1 (2), v, 1. The scene of *Tam. Sh.* is laid throughout in P., or in Petruchio's house in the vicinity; Lucentio speaks of it as 'fair P., nursery of arts' (*Tam. Sh.* i, 1); ' 'Tis death for any one in Mantua To come to P.' (*ib.* iv, 2). Mtd., *ib.* i, 1 (4), 2 (4); ii, 1; iii, 2 (2); iv, 2, 4 (3), 5; v, 1, 2.

In *M.V.* iii, 4, the error of 'Mantua,' for 'Padua,' was first corrected by Theobald.

Page (1). D.P. *All's Well.* i, 1] summons Parolles.

Page (2). D.P. *Rich. III.* iv, 2] tells Richard that Tyrrel can be bribed 'to anything'; later, returns with T. ('a secret page,' Hall, p. 375).

Page (3). D.P. *Tam. Sh.* Ind. See BARTHOLOMEW.

Page (4). D.P. *Timon.* ii, 2] has a verbal encounter with Apemantus.

Belongs to the same household as the Fool (*q.v.*).

Page to Falstaff. D.P. 2 *Hen. IV.* i, 2] (has been put in Fal.'s service by Prince Hal); reports to Fal. the results of certain errands. ii, 1] *p.m.* ii, 2] is rewarded by the Prince for his gibes at Bardolph. ii, 4] in attendance. v, 1, 3, 5] *p.m.* (See BOY; D.P. *Hen. V.*)

Page to Gardiner. D.P. *Hen. VIII.* v, 1] in attendance with a torch.

Page to Mercutio. D.P. *Rom. J.* iii, 1] *p.m.*; is sent for a surgeon.

Page to Paris. D.P. *Rom. J*, v, 3] seeing his master and Romeo fighting, runs for the watch; later, tells the Prince what he witnessed.

Page, Anne. D.P. *M.W.W.* 'Daughter to Mrs Page' (see NAN). i, 1] (Evans desires to arrange a match between Slender and Anne, who has brown hair, 'speaks small like a woman,' and, moreover, has 'seven hundred pounds and possibilities'); she brings in wine for the guests; later, tries in vain to overcome Slender's diffidence, and induce him to join the company at table. (i, 2) Quickly is urged by Evans to further the match. (i, 4) Q. consents, but afterward assures her master (Caius) that Anne loves him, and also gives a similar assurance to Fenton. (ii, 1) Q. pays her a visit. (ii, 3) mtd. (iii, 1) 'Sweet Anne Page !' is ever on Slender's lips. (iii, 2) of her three suitors her father approves of Sl. alone. iii, 4] Fenton, in converse with her, seeks to override Page's objections; she gives him hopes; she bids Sl. 'woo for himself' and learns that he fatuously leaves the courtship to her father and his uncle; she begs her mother not to marry her 'to yond fool'; but, on hearing that her mother destines her for Caius, declares that she 'had rather be set quick in the earth, And bowled to death with turnips.' (iv, 5) mtd. (iv, 6) her secret marriage with Fenton is arranged. v, 5] she enacts the part of the Fairy Queen in Windsor Forest (see QUICKLY); leads the band who torment Falstaff; steals away with Fenton; later, returns with him as her husband and is forgiven.

The name of Page occurs in the records of Stratford and Windsor in the 16th cent. (Halliwell).

Page, Master. D.P. *M.W.W.* A gentleman dwelling at Windsor; called 'George' (ii, 1 (2); v, 5), but 'Thomas' (i, 1) in Ff. i, 1] seeks to make peace between Falstaff (whom he is entertaining) and Shallow and Slender; invites them to dinner. (i, 3) mtd. ii, 1] is warned by Nym of Falstaff's designs on Mistress Page, but makes light of the matter. (ii, 2) his indulgence to his wife. ii, 3] present. iii, 1] helps to make peace between Caius and

Evans. iii, 2] objects to Fenton as his daughter Anne's suitor. iii, 3] rebukes Ford for baseless jealousy; invites the company to breakfast, on the morrow; 'after, we'll a-birding together.' iii, 4] favours Slender's suit; requests Fent. not to haunt his house, since Anne 'is disposed of.' iv, 2] witnesses Ford's second futile attempt to detect Falstaff, and deems his friend a lunatic. iv, 4] learns how the 'merry wives' have revenged themselves on Fal.; agrees to assist in his public discomfiture; plans Slender's marriage with Anne. v, 2] with Sl. in the park. v, 5] derides Fal., but bids him 'eat a posset' at his house that night; learns that Fent. has, after all, secured Anne.

Page, Mistress. D.P. *M.W.W.* Called 'Meg' by her husband (ii, 1), i, 1] *p.m.*; receives her husband's guests. (i, 3) Falstaff sends her a letter. ii, 1] she reads the letter; (*sol.*) vows to be revenged on Fal. for his impudence; finds that her friend Mrs Ford has received a similar missive; they agree feignedly to encourage Fal., though Mrs P. has never given her husband cause for jealousy. (ii, 2) she sends a message to Fal. by Quickly. iii, 2] converses with Fal.'s page, Robin. iii, 3] prepares, with Mrs Ford, for Fal.'s discomfiture; later, bursts into the room and tells Mrs F. that Ford is at hand; pretends to be scandalized to learn that Fal. is in the house; suggests his concealment in a buck-basket to be borne to Datchet Mead; helps to hide him; agrees to play a further trick upon him on the morrow; chides Ford for his jealousy. iii, 4] learns from Fenton that he loves her daughter Anne, and tells him she will be neutral in the matter. iv, 1] listens to the examination of her son William by Evans. iv, 2] in concert with Mrs Ford, again enters when Fal. is concealed in Ford's house, and this time they resolve to dress him in the gown of 'the old woman of Brentford'; later, leads in the supposed 'Mother Prat'; expresses some pity for Fal., who is cudgelled by Ford; the wives decide to tell Ford the truth. iv, 4] tells the tale of Herne the Hunter, and explains the device by which Fal. may be publicly shamed; resolves that Anne shall marry Dr Caius. v, 3] tells Dr C. that he will see A., dressed in green, in the park that night; sets out with Mrs Ford 'to the oak.' v, 5] they keep tryst with Fal., but on the approach of the 'fairies,' escape hurriedly; later, she derides Fal., and asks him, 'how like you Windsor wives?'; trusts that Anne is 'by this, Doctor Caius' wife'; on learning that Fent. has after all secured her, accepts the situation with good humour.

Page, William. D.P. *M.W.W.* A boy, son to Mr Page. iv, 1] is examined in Latin grammar by Evans.

Painter, A. D.P. *Timon.* i, 1] brings a painting for Timon's acceptance; exchanges compliments, and criticisms, with a Poet (*q.v.*); Timon thanks him for his work; with the Poet, is derided by Apemantus. v, 1] with the Poet, visits Timon in his cave; they are made hopeful of sharing his gold, but at last repulsed as 'rascal dogs.'

Paladour. The reading of Ff, *Cymb.* iii, 3, 1.95, for 'Polydore' (*q.v.*).

Probably a printer's error, but it has been defended by Steevens on the ground that 'Paladour was the ancient name of Shaftsbury'; cf. *A meeting Dialoguewise between Nature, the Phoenix, and the Turtle Dove*, by R. Chester (1601) (p. 27, ed. Grosart).

Palamedes. A Greek leader at Troy, according to post-Homeric legend, done to death by Ulysses, who hated him. He is referred to as 'sore hurt and bruised' in fight, *Tr. Cr.* v, 5.

Acc. Caxton's *Recuyell*, the Greek Palamydes, 'son of Kyng Naulus,' was killed by Paris with a poisoned arrow.

Palatine, The Count(y). A suitor of Portia. 'He doth nothing but frown' (*M.V.* i, 2).

Acc. Johnson, an allusion to a Polish Palatine, Albert a Lasco, who visited England in 1583. But this would be some seventeen years before the play was produced.

Palestine. The Holy Land. 'Richard ... fought the holy wars in P.' (*John*, ii, 1); 'a lady in Venice would have walk'd barefoot to P. for a touch of his nether lip' (*Oth.* iv, 3).

Alluded to: 'Those holy fields' (*1 Hen. IV*, i, 1).

Pallas. Goddess of wisdom, the Minerva (*q.v.*) of the Romans. Invoked by Marcus, *T. And.* iv, 1; Titus, in his madness, would send her a message on an arrow, *ib.* iv, 3.

Pandar. 'For Pandarus' (*q.v.*). *Tr. Cr.* i, 1 (3), 2; iii, 2 (2); v, 11.

Pandar, A. D.P. *Per.* iv, 3] thinks of giving up his trade; receives Marina, and hands her to his wife. iv, 6] wishes M. had never entered his house.

Pandarus. This name occurs in Hom. *Il.* ii, 824, etc., as that of a famous Lycian archer, and in Virg. *Aen.* ix, 672, 758, as that of a companion of Aeneas, but there is nothing, except the name, common to these personages and the Pandarus of late medieval romance. In 'Dares' and 'Dictys' he is merely a soldier, and he may be said first to appear *in propria persona* in the *Filostrato* of Boccaccio, as Pandaro, friend of Troilus. His character here is no way debased; as a chivalrous knight and faithful friend, he assists Tr. in his love affairs, but looks for no reward. In the *Troylus and Cryseyde* of Chaucer, however, he definitely assumes the vile *rôle* associated with the name in modern times.

Pistol indignantly exclaims: 'Shall I Sir Pandarus of Troy become?' (*M.W.W.* i, 3); 'I would play Lord Pand. of Phrygia, sir, to bring a Cressida to this Troilus' (*T. Nt.* iii, 1). Pand. is alluded to, *All's Well*, ii, 1, as 'Cressida's uncle.'

D.P. *Tr. Cr.* Uncle to Cressida. i, 1] in conversation with Troilus affects to depreciate the charms of his niece – 'let her to the Greeks,' after her father. i, 2] is bantered by a servant. iii, 1] sings to Helen and Paris. iii, 2] officiously contrives to fix a meeting between Tr. and Cr.; leaves the lovers together and returns to witness their mutual vows of fidelity. iv, 2] rallies Cr. loosely; learns that she is to be exchanged for Antenor; tells her the grave news. iv, 4] unctuously laments the lovers' fate. v, 3] gives Tr. a letter from Cr.; the former reviles him as a 'broker-lackey.' v, 11] Tr. repeats his invective – 'ignomy and shame Pursue thy life, and live aye with thy name!' Pand. speaks a short, cynical epilogue (which has been regarded as an interpolation).

'Worthless himself, and therefore willingly occupied for others, polite and cringing, foolish, like a member of Polonius's family, inquisitive, chattering, an adept in double meanings, habituated to lies, bragging, and perjury, he understands thoroughly how to arouse and goad the passions by turns with praise and jealousy, fanning the flame even when already burning clear enough, making the fool more foolish, and the wanton still more wanton.' (Gervinus, *Sh. Comm.* (1875), p. 682.)

Pandion. King of Athens; father of Philomela and Procne (*qq.v.*); *cf.* Ovid, *Metam.* vi, 426, 634. 'King Pandion he is dead' (*P.P.* xxi).

[**Pandosto.**] See LEONTES.

Pandulf. Papal legate. Bp. of Norwich 1216. Died at Rome (1226) and was buried in Norwich Cathedral. Has been mistakenly identified with the Cardinal Pandulfus de Masca. (*Cf.* French, p. 17; Clar. *John*, p. 113; *D.N.B. s.v.*)

The following is Holinshed's account of the relevant actions of Pandulf and Cardinal Gualo, with whom P. is partly confused in *John*.

In 1211 'the pope sent two legats into England, the one named Pandulph a lawier, and the other Durant a templer,' who, after threatening John without avail, 'left him accursed and the land interdicted, as they found it at their comming.' On the return of the legates to Rome, Innocent deposed John, and sent Pandulf and other ecclesiastics (including Langton) to France 'to exhort the French king to make warre upon' him (1212). Next year John had an interview with Pandulf at Dover, where, after listening to 'a sawcie speech of the proud Pandulph,' the King submitted, handed his crown to the legate and received it again after five days.

In 1216 the Pope sent Card. Gualo to France to dissuade Philip from taking up arms against John, and Gualo proceeded to England and had an interview with John at Gloucester. Peace was made with the invading Dauphin (Lewis) in 1217, Gualo being a negotiator (*Hol.* iii, 201) and a signatory of the treaty.

D.P. *John.* ('Pandolpho,' Ff.) iii, 1] (in France; but at Northampton acc. *Hol.* iii, 175) pronounces the papal ban against John for contumacy. iii, 4] rebukes Constance for her excess of grief concerning Arthur; explains to Lewis that John has made a fatal error in seizing Arthur, whose death would be to Lewis' own advantage. v, 1] receives the crown from John and hands it back to him by favour of the Pope. v, 2] informs Lewis that John 'hath reconciled Himself to Rome,' and urges the Dauphin to desist from invading England.

In *Tr. R.* Pandulf calls himself 'of Padua,' with which may be compared Holinshed's description of him as a lawyer. When sent to France, in 1212, Arthur had been dead for nine years. Lewis was advised to withdraw his expedition (by Gualo) three years after John's surrender of the crown.

Pannonians. People of a Roman province between the Danube and the Alps; mtd. *Cymb.* iii, 1, 7. See DALMATIANS.

Pansa. Roman Consul, 43 B.C., with Hirtius (*q.v.*). Defeated by Antony at Forum Gallorum and mortally wounded (*Plut.* pp. 167, 234). Mtd. *Ant. Cl.* i, 4; 'thou [Ant.] slew'st Hirtius and Pansa.'

[**Pantalaria, or Pantellaria.**] Island to the E. of Cape Bon (Tunis), held by T. Elze to be the scene of *Temp.* (*Sh. Jahrbuch*, xv, 251).

Pantheon. A temple in the Campus Martius, Rome; built by M. Agrippa, 27 B.C., and dedicated to Mars and Venus. (It is now used as a Christian church.) 'In the sacred Pantheon her [Lavinia] espouse' (*T. And.* i, 1; 'Pathan,' QF1); 'Ascend, fair queen [Tamora], Pantheon' (*ib. ib.*).

Panthino. D.P. *T.G.V.* 'Servant to Antonio' (F1). i, 3] conveys to Ant. the advice that he should send Proteus away to see the world, and suggests that Pr. should follow his friend Valentine to 'the Emperor's Court' at Milan; later, tells Pr. that his father calls for him. ii, 2] summons Pr. ii, 3] warns Launce that he will 'lose the tide' if he does not hasten after his master Pr.

'Panthion,' Ff, in 'Names of the Actors' and st. dir. i, 3. The misprint 'Panthmo,' i, 3, l. 76, F1, shows that the MS. had 'Panthino' (Camb. edrs.).

Paphlagonia. Country of Asia Minor. See PHILADELPHUS.

Paphos, or 'Old Paphos.' Town on the W. coast of Cyprus; the chief seat of the worship of Venus, who was said to have landed there after her birth on the sea.

'I met her deity [Venus] Cutting the clouds towards P.' (*Temp.* iv, 1); 'the dove of P.' (*Per.* iv, Gow.); 'her silver doves ... Holding their course to P.' (*V.A.* 1193).

Paracelsus. The assumed name of Theophrastus Bombastus von Hohenheim (1493–1541), afamous Swiss alchemist and physician. Classed with Galen: 'To be relinquished of the artists ... Both of Galen and P.' (*All's Well*, ii, 3).

Paradise. (*a*) The garden of Eden; (*b*) the abode of the righteous, before the Resurrection; (*c*) Heaven; (*d*) metaph., a place of felicity.

'Makes this place P.' (*Temp.* iv, 1, l. 124); 'a p. To what we fear of death' (*M. for M.* iii, 1); 'seem'd Athens like a p. to me' (*M.N.D.* i, 1); 'to lose an oath, to win a p.' (*L.L.L.* iv, 3, l. 73; *cf.* 1.143); 'although The air of P. did fan the house, And angels offic'd all' (*All's Well*, iii, 2); 'Adam that kept the P.' (*Com. Err.* iv, 3); 'whipp'd the offending Adam out of him, Leaving his body as a p., To ... contain celestial spirits' (*Hen. V*, i, 1); 'a fool's p.' (*Rom. J.* ii, 4); 'the spirit of a friend In mortal paradise' (*ib.* iii, 2); mtd., *L.C.* 91.

Parca. One of the Parcae, or Fates (*q.v.*). Used by Pistol as a personal name: 'To have me fold up P.'s fatal web' (*Hen. V*, v, 1).

Paris (1). 2nd son of Priam and Hecuba; his abduction of Helen, wife of Menelaus, caused the Trojan war. He fought with Men. before the walls of Troy, but was saved by Aphrodite (Homer, *Il.* iii, 380); he stubbornly refused to yield Helen to the Greeks (*ib.* vii, 347). 'Though Paris came, in hope to speed alone' (*Tam. Sh.* i, 2); Suffolk compares himself to 'the youthful Paris ... With hope to find the like event in love' (*1 Hen. VI*, v, 5).

D.P. *Tr. Cr.* (Prol.) 'Helen ... With wanton P. sleeps.' (i, 1) wounded by Menelaus. (i, 2) compared, by Pandarus, with Troilus. ii, 2] combats Hector's suggestion that Helen should be delivered to the Greeks. iii, 1] joins in bantering converse with Pandarus; bids Helen unarm Hector. iv, 1] presents Diomedes to Aeneas; discusses, with Dio., Helen's case. (iv, 2) mtd. iv, 3] pities Troilus, since 'I know what 'tis to love.' iv, 4] makes ready for the field. (iv, 5) mtd. v, 8] fights with Menelaus.

Before the birth of P., Hecuba dreamed that she was to be delivered of a torch; cf. *Tr. Cr.* ii, 2: 'our firebrand brother.'

Paris (2). D.P. *Rom. J.* A young nobleman, kinsman to the Prince of Verona. i, 2] is encouraged by Capulet in his suit to Juliet and bidden to a feast. (i, 3) his suit is mtd. to Juliet. (ii, 4) he is mtd. to Romeo by the Nurse. iii, 4] is told by Capulet that he may wed Jul. 'on Thursday.' (iii, 5) Jul. declares she will not be his bride; he is eulogized by the Nurse. iv, 1] he meets Jul. at Friar Laurence's cell, is rebuffed, and leaves her with a 'holy kiss.' (iv, 2, 4) mtd. iv, 5] on the wedding morning learns that Jul. has been claimed by Death; passionately laments her. v, 3] brings flowers to strew Juliet's sepulchre; is confronted by Romeo; they fight, and P. is slain.

Variously referred to as 'Sir Paris,' 'Country Paris,' and 'this noble earl.' First thus named by Bandello; 'A Count of Lodrone' in Da Porto's tale; 'Counte of Lodronne' in *Rhomeo and Julietta*. 'County Paris cliped was; an earle he had to syre' (*Romeus and Juliet*, l. 1883).

Paris, City of. The scene is laid in Paris in *All's Well*, i, 2; ii, 1, 3, 4, 5. Mtd., *ib.* i, 2, 3 (2). 'Paris balls' (*Hen. V*, ii, 4); loss of Paris reported, *1 Hen. VI*, i, 1; Henry VI at P., *ib.* iii, 2; 'governor of P.' (*ib.* iv, 1); mtd., *ib.* iv, 7, v, 2. The scene is laid in P. in *1 Hen. VI*, iii, 4, iv, 1; loss of P. mtd., *2 Hen. VI*, i, 1 (2), 3. Coronation of Hen. VI at P. mtd., *Rich. III*, ii, 3. Laertes and other Danes in P., *Haml.* ii, 1. 'Paris-ward': 'marching unto P. ward' (*1 Hen. VI*, iii, 3).

Paris Garden. On the bank-side in Southwark, where was an arena for bull- and bearbaiting. The noise of such 'bear-gardens' became proverbial. '*Porter*. You'll leave your noise anon, you rascals. Do you take the court for Paris ['Parish,' F1] Garden?' (*Hen. VIII*, V, 4).

Parisians. People of Paris. ' 'Tis said the stout Parisians do revolt' (*1 Hen. VI*, v, 3).

Parolles. D.P. *All's Well.* Follower of Count Bertram; his character is thus summed up by Helena (i, 1): 'I know him a notorious liar, Think him a great way fool, solely a coward.' i, 1] converses with Helena on the state of virginity, and is keenly bantered by her on his boasting to have been born under Mars. i, 2] (in attendance on Bertram) *p.m.* ii, 1] bids adieu vauntingly to the young lords proceeding to the Florentine war, and bids Ber. follow them, 'and take a more dilated farewell.' ii, 3] officiously interrupts Lafeu's comments on the King's cure; is disturbed at the entrance of Helena; has a hot altercation with Lafeu, who brands him as a coward and a knave; urges Ber. to leave France and go to the wars. ii, 4] conveys Ber.'s marital commands to Helena. ii, 5] (Ber. commends Parolles to Lafeu); L. nevertheless insists on P.'s worthlessness, to his face. (iii, 2) the Countess regrets that P. is her son's companion. iii, 5] (Mariana characterizes him as a dangerous knave); he is pointed out by her as 'that jack-an-apes with scarfs.' iii, 6] (French Lords make a design against him); he vows to recover a lost drum. iv, 1] (*sol.*) regrets that his 'tongue is too foolhardy'; is seized by apparent enemies, who speak in gibberish and bind and blindfold him; he offers to betray 'all the secrets of our camp' as the price of his liberty; he is taken away guarded. iv, 3] he is brought blindfolded before the Lords ('he has sat in the stocks all night, poor gallant knave!') and, in his eagerness to escape with his life, utters any slander that he thinks will please against the very nobles that are present; just as his sentence of death is pronounced he is unmuffled; he exclaims, 'Who cannot be crushed with a plot?' but concludes that henceforth he will 'live safest in shame.' v, 2] humiliates himself before Lafeu, who takes some pity on him and replies, 'though you are a fool and a knave, you shall eat.' v, 3] is examined as to his knowledge of the relations between Bertram and Diana; Lafeu bids him 'wait on me home, I'll make sport with thee.' See MILE END.

The character is of Sh.'s creation: there is no equivalent 'braggart' in the novel whence the main plot is derived. See ALL'S WELL THAT ENDS WELL. The name, of course, means that he is a man of 'words' only.

The purely comic character of P. has been taken very seriously by some commentators. 'He has been compared to Falstaff, but they ought rather to be contrasted; for Sir John is a man of genius, with real wit and power of fascination, and no ridicule can destroy him, but the exposure of Parolles makes him dwindle into his native pitifulness' (Dowden).

Parthia. Country of Asia, S.E. of the Caspian; it became an independent monarchy under the Arsacidae about 250 B.C. An invasion of Syria by the Parthians, 40–39 B.C., was defeated by Ventidius (*q.v.*), as was another the next year under Pacorus (*q.v.*), son of Orodes. Cf. *Plut.* pp. 180–2.

'In P. did I take thee [Pindarus] prisoner' (*Jul. C.* v, 3); Ventidius sent on an expedition thither, *Ant. Cl.* ii, 2, 3; 'darting P.' (*ib.* iii, 1); 'the ne'er-yet beaten horse of P.' (*ib.ib.*); given to Alexander, son of Antony, *ib.* iii, 6.

Parthian. (*a*) *Subst.*, native of Parthia; the P.s were a warlike race, and especially skilled as horse-archers. It was their practice to evade close combat by a rapid flight, during which they shot their arrows backward on their pursuers. 'Like the P., I shall flying fight' (*Cymb.* i, 7).

(*b*) *Adj.* 'Labienus hath with his P. force Extended Asia' (*Ant. Cl.* i, 2); 'while yet with P. blood thy [Ventidius'] sword is warm' (*ib.* iii, 1); 'the P. darts' (*ib.* iv, 14).

Partlet. From *O.F.* fem. name, 'Pertelote'; applied to a hen, as in Chaucer's *Nonne Prestis Tale*: 'the faireste hewed on hir throte Was cleped fayre damoysele Pertelote.'

Leontes declares that Antigonus is subservient to his wife, 'unroosted by thy dame Partlet here' (*Wint. T.* ii, 3); Falstaff to hostess: 'How now, Dame P. the hen!' (*1 Hen. IV*, iii, 3).

Passionate Pilgrim, The. A small volume bearing the title of 'The Passionate Pilgrim, by W. Shakespeare' was published by W. Jaggard in 1599. Of the twenty poems composing this little anthology only five are certainly by Sh., viz. I, II – which are the Sonnets cxxxviii and cxliv of the edition of 1609 – and III, V, XVI, which had already appeared in *L.L.L.*, with slight variations, A few of the other poems have been hesitatingly attributed to Sh. by some critics, viz. IV, VI, VII, IX, XII, XIX. A second edn. (now lost) appeared in 1606, and a third in 1612.

The last six poems bear the separate title of 'Sonnets to Sundry Notes of Musick.

'The nineteenth poem has a smack of his mind about it. If it be by him it must be his earliest extant work.' (J. Masefield, *W. Sh.* p. 244.)

[**Paston Letters, The.**] See FASTOLF, SIR JOHN.

Patay. Scene of a battle in which the English under Talbot were defeated by the French, June 18, 1429. 'A village in Beausse called Pataie' (*Hol.* iii, 601). See FASTOLFE. Mtd. *1 Hen. VI*, iv, 1,1.19 ('Poictiers' in Ff).

It is related in *Hol.* that after fighting for three hours Talbot was wounded and the English fied, losing twelve hundred slain and forty taken. Cf. *1 Hen. VI*, i, 1. The battle was fought six weeks after the English had raised the siege of Orleans.

Patience (1). D.P. *Hen. VIII.* 'Woman to Queen Katharine.' iv, 2] in attendance during the Queen's last illness, and receives from her instructions concerning her obsequies.

A. Strickland, *Lives of the Queens of England*, suggests that P. might have been one of the 'little maidens' to each of whom the Queen left ten pounds in her will. The names of her chief attendants are known.

Patience (2). The quality personified. 'P. herself would startle at this letter And play the swaggerer' (*A. Y. L.* iv, 3); 'P. herself, what goddess e'er she be' (*Tr. Cr.* i, 1); 'thou dost look Like P. gazing on king's graves, and smiling Extremity out of act' (*Per.* v, 1); 'P. on a monument, smiling at grief' (*T. Nt.* ii, 4). (Partial, or doubtful, personifications are numerous.)

Patrick, Friar. A confessor, near whose cell Silvia and Eglamour agree to meet. *T.G.V.* iv, 3; v, 1 (2).

Patrick, St. Patron Saint of Ireland. Hamlet asseverates 'by Saint P.' (*Haml.* i, 5); but the suggestion that there is an allusion here to 'St P.'s Purgatory' is not substantiated.

Patroclus. Friend of Achilles; when the latter withdrew from action before Troy P. followed his example (Hom. *Il.* ix, 190); later, equipped in the armour of Ach., he gallantly attacked the Trojans, but was slain by Hector (*ib.* xvi); Ach. thereupon resolved to avenge him (*ib.* xvii–xviii). In Caxton's *Recuyell* we are told that he 'louyd so moche Achylles that they were bothe of one Allyance.' He is not mtd. by Chaucer.

D.P. *Tr. Cr.* (i, 3) amuses Ach. by mimicry of the other Greek leaders. ii, 1] is termed 'Achilles' brach' by Thersites. ii, 3] is bantered by Ther.; bears messages to and from Ach. iii, 3] urges Ach. to bestir himself and save his reputation. iv, 5] salutes Cressida jestingly. v, 1] is reviled by Ther. (v, 2) mtd. (v, 5) is slain; his wounds rouse the 'drowsy blood' of Ach.

Paul, St. The apostle to the Gentiles. Mtd. in *Sh.* only in asseverations by Richard III. 'By Saint P.' (*Rich. III*, i, 1, 2; iii, 4); 'By holy P.' (*ib.* i, 3); 'by the Apostle P.' (*ib.* v, 3).

In i, 2, Ff give 'S. John.' 'By saint Paule' is given in *Hol.* iii, 723, as the oath used by Richard in declaring that he would not dine until Hastings was executed.

Paulina. D.P. *Wint. T.* 'Wife to Antigonus' (Ff). ii, 2] is denied audience with the imprisoned Hermione, but converses with the attendant Emilia, and undertakes to present the infant Perdita to the King. ii, 3] forces her way into Leontes' presence with the babe, to the discomfiture of Antigonus; is vituperated by the King, but stoutly holds her own against his threats and abuse, and retires, leaving Per. iii, 2] is present at the Queen's trial; later, announces her death; bitterly reproaches the King, but is touched by his remorse and asks forgiveness. (iii, 3) mtd. v, 1] protests against the advice given to Leon. to marry again, 'the crown will find an heir'; makes the King promise to let her 'choose a queen' for him; witnesses the arrival of Florizel and the unknown princess; chides Leon. for looking on the latter too tenderly. (v, 2) recognizes a handkerchief and rings formerly belonging to Antigonus. v, 3] shows Leon. 'the statue' of Hermione; affects to fear lest the fresh painting may be marred by a touch; bids the living Hermione descend from her pedestal; after witnessing the reunion of the King and Queen, prepares to lament her own lost husband in seclusion, but is bidden by Leontes to wed Camillo.

'She is a character strongly drawn from real and common life, – a clever, generous, strong-minded, warm-hearted woman, fearless in asserting the truth, firm in her sense of right, enthusiastic in all her affections; quick in thought, resolute in word, and energetic in action; but heedless, hot-tempered, impatient, loud, bold, voluble, and turbulent of tongue.' (Mrs Jameson, ii, 23.)

'For once, Mrs Jameson has failed to do justice; and Paulina's indignation at outrageous injustice and oppression has been mistaken for "hot temper" and "turbulence of tongue." ' (Furness, *Var.*)

Paul's. St Paul's Cathedral, London. The old cathedral fell into a state of dilapidation after a fire in 1561 (which destroyed the spire), and the underground portions of the halfruined church were used as cellars and workshops. The middle aisle, known as 'Paul's Walk' became the resort of traders and men of business as well as of mere idlers. Masters desiring servants 'set up their bills' there. Bobadil, in *Every Man in his Humour* was 'a Paul's man.'

Prince Hal declares that Falstaff 'is known as well as Paul's' (*1 Hen. IV*, ii, 4); Fal. 'bought' Bardolph 'in Paul's' (*2 Hen. IV*, i, 2); the body of Hen. VI lay at 'Paul's,' *Rich. III*, i, 2; the indictment of Lord Hastings to be 'read o'er in Paul's' (*ib.* iii, 6). Often written as pronounced by the Porter's man: 'We may as well push against Powle's, as stir 'em' (*Hen. VIII*, v, 4).

Paunch, Sir John. Nonce-name applied to Falstaff by Prince Hal; *1 Hen. IV*, ii, 2.

Peascod. Nonce-name for Peaseblossom's father; *M.N.D.* iii, 1.

Peaseblossom. D.P. *M.N.D.* A fairy. iii, 1] attends on Bottom at Titania's bidding. iv, 1] is ordered to scratch B.'s head.

Peck, Gilbert. A variant of 'Sir Gilbert Perke, priest,' Buckingham's chancellor, acc. *Hol.* iii, 863, and Hall, p. 623. But in the documents of the trial the Duke's chancellor is named 'Robert Gilbert.' Wright (Clar.) suggests that 'Perke' is a misreading of 'clerk.'

A warrant issued against him as Buckingham's 'chancellor,' *Hen. VIII*, i, 1; gives evidence against B. at his trial, *ib.* ii, 1.

Pecocke, Stephen. See MAYOR (D.P. *Hen. VIII*).

Pedant. D.P. *Tam. Sh.* iv, 2] (he is a Mantuan, and bound for Tripoli); is told that he risks his life in Padua, but that Tranio will save him if he personates Vincentio. iv, 4] posing as Vin., consents to the marriage of his 'son' to Baptista's daughter. v, 1] on the appearance of the real Vincentio, attempts to carry things with a high hand, but is unmasked, and takes to flight. v, 2] (at Lucentio's banquet) *p.m.*

For the 'Pedant' as a stock character in Italian comedy see HOLOFERNES. The corresponding character in *The Taming of A Shrew* is Phylotus, a merchant who personates Jerobel, and in *I Suppositi* an unnamed personator of Filogono.

Pedro, Don. D.P. *M. Ado.* 'Prince of Arragon.' i, 1] is welcomed at Messina by Leonato, after a victorious campaign; later, learns Claudio's passion for Hero and offers to woo her disguised as Cl. (i, 2, 3) mtd. ii, 1] converses, masked, with Hero; tells Cl. he has won her for him; resolves to make a match between Benedick and Beatrice. (ii, 2) mtd. ii, 3] discusses Beat.'s supposed love for Ben. in the hearing of the latter. iii, 2] banters Ben. on being in love; is staggered by Don John's charge against Hero. (iii, 3) mtd. iv, 1] bears witness to Hero's supposed unfaithfulness. v, 1] pities Leonato, but believes the accusation against his daughter 'very full of proof'; banters Ben.; learns Don John's treachery, and inveighs against him. (v, 2) mtd. v, 3] joins in the rites before Hero's monument. v, 4] present at Hero's reappearance; Ben. advises him to get a wife and cure his sadness.

In QFf the name appears as 'Don Peter' (i, 1). The corresponding character in Bandollo's *Novella* is Piero d' Aragona.

Peesel. Dame Quickly's perversion of 'Pistol'; *2 Hen. IV*, ii, 4.

Peg-a-Ramsey. 'Malvolio's a P.' (*T. Nt.* ii, 3). Ramsey is a town in Hunts. There are two old tunes under the name 'Peg-a-Ramsey' (W. Chappell, *Popular Music*, p. 218), but the point of Sir Toby's allusion is lost.

Pegasus (1). The winged horse, sprung from the blood of Medusa when slain by Perseus (Ovid, *Metam.* iv, 786). The Dauphin says of his horse, 'le cheval volant, the Pegasus ... It is a beast for Perseus' (*Hen. V*, iii, 7); 'to turn and wind a fiery Pegasus, And witch the world with noble horsemanship' (*1 Hen. IV*, iv, 1). See PERSEUS.

Pegasus (2). Name of an inn at Genoa; *Tam. Sh.* iv, 4.

The P. was a well-known inn in Cheapside in Sh.'s days, and is mentioned in *The Returne from Parnassus* (1602).

Pelion. Mountain-range in Thessaly, famous from the legend that the Giants tried to heap Ossa (*q.v.*) and Olympus on P. (or P. and Ossa on Olympus) in order to scale heaven. 'A mountain ... To o'ertop old P.' (*Haml.* v, 1).

Pella, Lucius. 'Brutus, upon complaint of the Sardians did condemn and note L. P. for a defamed person, that had been a Practor of the Romans and to whom Br. had given charge unto: for that he was accused and convicted of robbery and pilfery in his office' (*Plut.* p. 135).

Cassius complains that Br. had disregarded his appeal on behalf of L. P., *Jul. C.* iv, 3.

Peloponnesus. The S., or peninsular, part of Greece. Ant. and Cl. flee 'towards P.' after Actium, *Ant. Cl.* iii, 10 ('with full sail towards P.,' *Plut.* p. 212).

Pembroke. Formerly Penbroke; county town. Mtd. in connection with Richmond's landing at Milford Haven, *Rich. III*, iv, 5.

'The Penbrochians were readie to serve ... their naturall and immediat lord Iasper earle of Penbroke' (*Hol.* iii, 753).

Pembroke, Earl of (1). William Marshal (*ob.* 1219), son of John M.; obtained his title by marriage with Isabel de Clare, heiress of Richard 'Strongbow.' Historically, he remained uniformly loyal to King John, and was instrumental in clearing England of the French; his eldest son William, however, joined the Dauphin (*Hol.* iii, 191). It is possible that the son is intended in the play.

D.P. *John.* i, 1] *p.m.*; is ordered to provide safe conduct for the French envoy. iv, 2] deprecates John's second coronation, and begs that Arthur may be released; suspects foul play with regard to A., and, hearing of the Prince's death, with a stern warning leaves the King's presence. iv, 3] upon Ar.'s body being found, he is horror-stricken at the supposed murder, and vows vengeance. v, 2] *p.m.*; in the Dauphin's camp. v, 4] becomes aware of the Dauphin's intended treachery toward the English lords, and leaves him. v, 7] in attendance on the dying King.

In making Pembroke become disaffected to John, Sh. did but follow the *Tr. R.*

Pembroke, Earl of (2). Yorkist. D.P. *3 Hen. VI*; see HERBERT, SIR WILLIAM.

Pembroke, Earl of (3). Lancastrian. *Rich. III*, iv, 5; see TUDOR, JASPER.

Pembroke, Marchioness of. Title conferred on Anne Boleyn, Sept. 1, 1532. 'On the first of September being Sundaie, the K. being come to Windsor, created the ladie Anne Bullongne marchionesse of Penbroke, and gave to hir one thousand pounds land by the yeare' (*Hol.* iii, 928).

The Lord Chamberlain announces the honour, *Hen. VIII*, ii, 3; Wolsey exclaims against it, *ib.* iii, 2.

[**Pembrokeshire.**] An allusion to this county seems probable, *Hen. VIII*, ii, 3, where the 'Old Lady' remarks to Anne Boleyn, about to be made Marchioness of Pembroke, 'In faith, for little England You'ld venture an emballing.' Pembrokeshire was long known as 'little England beyond Wales,' from the fact that in the southern portion of it English alone is spoken. J. Taylor, 'the Water Poet,' mentions this in *A Short Relation of a Long Journey* (p. 19, Spenser Soc., reprint).

[**Penbroke.**] See PEMBROKE.

Pendragon. See UTHER.

Penelope. Wife of Ulysses; see ITHACA.

Penker, Friar. See SHAW, DR JOHN.

Pentapolis. ('Pantapoles,' '-is,' QqFf.) Name applied to any association of five cities, but specially to Cyrene, Berenice, Arsinoë, Ptolemais, and Apollonia in Cyrenaica, N. Africa. The place where Pericles was cast ashore after shipwreck. *Per.* ii, 1; iii, Gow.; v, 3 (3).

In Gower's *Conf. Amant.* 'Pentapolin.'

Pentecost. Whitsuntide (see WHITSUN). 'At P., When all our pageants of delight were played' (*T.G.V.* iv, 4); 'since P. the sum is due' (*Com. Err.* iv, 1); 'Come P. as quickly as it will' (*Rom. J.* i, 5).

Penthesilea, Penthesileia. Daughter of Mars, and Queen of the Amazons; fought for the Trojans against the Greeks (Ovid, *Heroid.* xxi, 118). The diminutive Maria jestingly called P. by Sir Toby, *T. Nt.* ii, 3.

Pepin. P. 'le Bref' (*ob.* 768); King of the Franks, son of Charles Martel. He became *Major domus* of Austrasia in 747, and, with the aid of the Pope, assumed the title of king in 751. 'An old saying, that was a man when King Pippin of France was a little boy' (*L.L.L.* iv, 1); 'a medicine ... whose simple touch Is powerful to araise King P.' (*All's Well*, ii, 1); alleged to have claimed the crown through female descent, *Hen. V*, i, 2 ('Pippin,' *Chr. Hist.*); 'you would swear ... their very noses had been counsellors to P.' (*Hen. VIII*, i, 3).

Percies. Family of Percy, Earls of Northumberland. 'The Percies of the North' (*1 Hen. VI*, ii, 5). See Appendix 6.

Percy, Henry (1) (1342–1408). 1st E. of Northumberland; made earl by Rich. II at his coronation, but joined Bolingbroke with a large force on his landing from exile; revolted from Hen. IV in 1403, with his son 'Hotspur' (*q.v.*), but after the defeat of the latter at Shrewsbury was pardoned, and again taken into favour by Henry (1404); plotted with Glendower and Mortimer; fled to Scotland, and in 1408 was defeated and slain in an unsuccessful attempt against England.

The following is a summary of Holinshed's account: N. is declared a traitor by Rich. II (*Hol.* iii, 499); receives Bolingbroke's oath that he makes no claim to the throne; joins Bol.'s forces (*ib.* 498); states to Rich. the terms of Bol.'s submission (*ib.* 500); is present at Richard's abdication (*ib.* 503–4); is 'especially grieved' because all the Scottish prisoners are claimed by Henry, and requires him to ransom Mortimer; enters into league with Glendower; seals, by deputy, an 'indenture' dividing the kingdom between the conspirators (*ib.* 521); is prevented by sickness from being present at the Battle of Shrewsbury (*ib.* 522); withdraws to Warkworth Castle, and submits to Henry (*ib.* 524); joins in Abp. Scrope's conspiracy (*ib.* 529); flees to Berwick and thence to Scotland (*ib.* 530); after visiting Wales, France, and Flanders, returns to Scotland; makes a descent upon Yorkshire; is defeated by the Sheriff of Yorkshire and slain (*ib.* 534).

D.P. *Rich. II.* ii, 1] announces John of Gaunt's death to the King; confers with the disaffected nobles on Richard's arbitrary conduct and the state of the realm; abruptly reveals that Bolingbroke has sailed from Brittany, and urges the nobles to hasten with him to Ravenspurgh, where Bol. will land. (ii, 2) proclaimed traitor. ii, 3] nears Berkeley with Bol., whom he flatters; learns that he has been proclaimed traitor; assures York that the nobles have sworn to aid Bol. to recover his own patrimony. iii, 1] (is given the custody of Bushy and Green) *p.m.* iii, 3] ('Before Flint Castle'; historically, at Conway) is rebuked by York for speaking disrespectfully of the King; assures Rich. that Bol. comes but to claim his 'lineal royalties' and 'to beg enfranchisement'; informs Bol. of the King's reply. iv, 1] (in Westminster Hall) arrests the Bp. of Carlisle 'of capital treason'; presents articles of accusation to Rich. and bluntly bids him read them. v, 1] informs Rich. that he is committed to Pomfret, and bids the Queen depart to France. v, 6] informs Bol. that he has sent the heads of four of his foes to London.

D.P. *1 Hen. IV.* (i, 1) mtd. i, 3] palliates to the King Hotspur's denial of prisoners; reproves his son's choler; declares that he heard Rich. II name Mortimer 'next of blood'; again tries to allay Hotspur's wrath; grudgingly consents to join in the revolt. (ii, 4) mtd. (iv, 3) his great services to Bolingbroke recounted. (iv, 4) reported sick. (v, 5) with Abp. Scrope.

D.P. *2 Hen. IV.* (Ind.) 'lies crafty-sick.' i, 1] hears that at Shrewsbury his party have gained a great victory, but is soon afterward disabused, and learns that they have suffered defeat and that his son is slain; ostensibly strives to throw off his sickness, and speaks of donning his armour. (i, 2) coupled with Abp. Scrope. (i, 3) his aid greatly needed. (ii, 1) the revolt mtd. ii, 3] is persuaded by his wife and daughter-in-law to flee to Scotland. (iii, 1) Richard's prophecy concerning him recalled. (iv, 1) writes to the Abp. refusing to join his party. (iv, 4) his defeat by the Sheriff of Yorks announced.

Percy, Henry (2). E.s. of H.P., 1st E. of Northumberland; 'surnamed, for his often pricking, Henrie Hotspur, as one that seldome times rested, if there were anie service to be doone abroad' (*Hol.* iii, 249); joined Bolingbroke, with his father, at Doncaster (*ib.* 498); was appointed 'generall, or rather ... master of the campe' under Bol. before Flint Castle (*ib.* 500) (for the quarrel of the Percies with Henry IV see previous article); hoping to be joined by Owen Glendower, raised 'an armie ... foorth of Cheshire and Wales' (*ib.* 552); in the absence of his father, from sickness, the command at Shrewsbury devolved on Hotspur and his uncle Worcester; notwithstanding the aid rendered by Scots and Welshmen to the rebels, the King was victorious after 'a sore battell' in which Hotspur was slain (*ib.* 523).

D.P. *Rich. II.* ii, 3] is presented to Bol. by his father, to whom he brings tidings of the E. of Worcester. iii, 1] (with Bol. at Bristol) *p.m.* iii, 3] before Flint Castle (*Hol.* iii, 500); informs Bol. that 'King Richard lies within.' iv, 1] (in Westminster Hall) gives the lie to Aumerle and challenges him. v, 3] brings Bol. news of his 'dissolute' and 'desperate' son, Prince Henry. v, 6] brings the Bp. of Carlisle before the King, for sentence.

In ii, 3, Hotspur speaks of himself as 'tender, raw and young,' while in *1 Hen. IV*, iii, 2, Bolingbroke, in rebuking Prince Henry, declares that the 'infant warrior,' the gallant Percy, is 'no more in debt to years than thou.' As a fact, however, Hotspur commanded at Otterbourne when Harry Monmouth was but a year old, and he was probably older than Bol. himself.

D.P. *1 Hen. IV.* i, 3] excuses himself to the King for not having delivered up the Scottish prisoners, on the ground that the messenger was a pestering 'popinjay'; defends 'the noble Mortimer' from the imputation of having willingly yielded to Glendower; on the King's departure storms against 'this canker'd Bolingbroke'; as for the prisoners, vows 'he shall not have a Scot of them'; he will give the King a starling taught to say nothing but 'Mortimer,' 'to keep his anger still in motion'; is at length sufficiently appeased to listen eagerly to Worcester's plot (cf. *Hol.* iii, 521). ii, 3] reads a letter from 'a frosty-spirited rogue' who declines to join in the plot (cf. *ib.* 522); pays no heed to his wife's reproaches at his not confiding in her, but after a bantering war of words promises that she shall follow him the next day. iii, 1] derides Glendower's claims to supernatural powers; wrangles over the map showing the tri-partite division of the realm; excuses himself to Mortimer for his impatience at Glendower's superstitious garrulity; indulges in further raillery with Lady Percy. iv, 1] hears that his father is prevented by sickness from joining in the revolt, but is not discouraged; on further learning that the King's forces are advancing, longs to cross swords with the Prince of Wales; hears that Glendower is delayed for a fortnight. iv, 3] replies indignantly to Blunt's recital of the King's terms, but decides to send Worcester as an envoy in the morning. v, 2] hears Worcester's false report of the King's answer; sends Douglas to bid defiance to Henry; longs to meet Harry Monmouth in combat; prepares for the battle. v, 3] tells Douglas that the man he has slain is not the King but Blunt. v, 4] is slain in combat by Prince Henry; (Falstaff stabs the corpse, declares he slew Hotspur, and bears off the body).

In *2 Hen. IV*, ii, 3, he is characterized and eulogized by his widow: 'he was the mark and glass, copy and book That fashion'd others.' 'Slain by an unknown hand' (*D.N.B.*).

Percy, Henry (3) (1394–1455). 2nd E. of Northumberland; only son of 'Hotspur'; killed at St Albans fighting against the D. of York (*Hol.* iii, 643). His death mtd. *3 Hen. VI*, i, 1; v, 7.

Percy, Henry (4) (1421–61). 3rd E. of Northumberland; g.s. of 'Hotspur'; defeated York at Wakefield, and Warwick at St Albans; led the van of the Lancastrians at Towton and fell fighting.

D.P. *3 Hen. VI*. i, 1] is reminded by Hen. VI that York slew his father; denounces the King for promising the crown after his death to York. i, 4] takes York prisoner at Wakefield; pities his fallen foe. (ii, 1) mtd. ii, 2] Richard holds him 'reverently.' (v, 7) Edward bears tribute to his bravery.

Percy, Lady (b. 1371). Eldest daughter of Edmund Mortimer, 3rd E. of March; wife of 'Hotspur'; though her name was Elizabeth, she is always called 'Kate' by her husband in *1 Hen. IV*.

D.P. *1 Hen. IV*. ii, 3] with playful threats entreats Hotspur to tell her what 'heavy business' he has in hand; he, half jestingly, refuses, and she 'must of force' acquiesce. iii, 1] joins in raillery with her husband concerning the Welsh Lady Mortimer.

D.P. *2 Hen. IV*. ii, 3] begs her father-in-law, the E. of Northumberland, not to go 'to these wars'; reminds him that he refused aid when her 'heart's dear Harry' needed him; laments and eulogizes her dead husband.

Percy, Thomas (*c.* 1344–1403). Earl of Worcester; Steward of the Household to Richard II; deserted the King for Bolingbroke 1399; joined the rebellion of his brother the E. of Northumberland 1403; captured at Shrewsbury and beheaded.

It is reported to Rich. that 'the E. of Worcester Hath broke his staff, resign'd his stewardship,' and fled to Bolingbroke (*Rich. II*, ii, 2); Northumberland introduces Hotspur to Bol. as 'sent from my brother Worcester' (*ib.* ii, 3).

Cf. *Hol.* iii. 499–500, where it is stated that some suppose W.'s defection was due to Richard's having proclaimed his brother a traitor.

D.P. *1 Hen. IV*. (i, 1) is alleged to have advised Hotspur not to yield up his prisoners. i, 3] dismissed by Henry from his presence, as being 'too bold and peremptory.' iii, 1] present at Glendower's meeting with Hotspur; chides his nephew for his haughtiness. iv, 1] (at Shrewsbury) deplores Northumberland's absence. iv, 3] urges delay. (iv, 4) mtd. v, 1] excuses his rebellion on the ground that Henry had broken faith with his supporters; is charged to convey the King's terms to the rebels. v, 2] is loth to let Hotspur know the King's liberal kind offer,' and tells him that Henry has no mercy for them, and that Prince Hal has challenged him 'to single fight.' v, 5] is taken prisoner and condemned to death.

His fate announced to Northumberland, *2 Hen. IV*, i, 1.

Holinshed does not explain (iii, 523) Worcester's suppression of the King's proposals; but Sh. suggests his motives, v, 2, ll. 4–23. Acc. *Hol.* iii, 524, his head was set on London Bridge.

Westmoreland describes Worc. to the King as 'Malevolent to you in all aspects' (*1 Hen. IV*, i, 1); *cf.* 'Thomas Persie ... whose studie was ever (as some write) to procure malice, and set things in a broile' (*Hol.* iii, 521).

Perdita. D.P. *Wint. T.* 'Daughter to Leontes and Hermione' (Ff). (ii, 2) is born in prison. ii, 3] is carried to Leon., who, in jealous frenzy, at first dooms the infant to perish by fire, but afterward entrusts it to Antigonus, to be left in 'some remote and desart place.' iii, 3] the infant is left on the seashore by Ant., and discovered by an old shepherd and his son, who take her to their home. (iv, Chor.) sixteen years later she is known as Perdita, and regarded as the shepherd's daughter. iv, 3] she is wooed by Florizel, son of Polixenes, King of Bohemia (Fl. being disguised as a shepherd), but dreads the anger of the King if he discovers his son's deception; she welcomes Pol. (who is also disguised) to the sheep-shearing festivities; discourses on the flowers that she loves; dances with Fl., and is called by the old courtier Camillo 'the queen of curds and cream'; is acknowledged by Fl. (before Polixenes) to be affianced to him; the King, in great wrath, declares that a cruel death shall be hers if she dares to meet Fl. again; when Pol. has departed, she declares that she 'was not much afeard,' but resolves 'to queen it no inch farther'; is persuaded by Fl. to flee with him to Sicily. v, 1] is presented by Fl. to her father as his wife, 'a Libyan princess.' (v, 2) her identity is revealed. v, 3] *p.m.*; is restored to her mother, Hermione.

Perdita is the 'Fawnia' of Green's novel *Pandosto*. Fawnia, daughter of King Pandosto, is set adrift in a boat and driven on the coast of Sicily: she is brought up by a shepherd and his wife as their daughter; Dorastus, the King's son, falls in love with her; they escape and land in Bohemia, where Pandosto imprisons Dorastus and himself becomes enamoured of Fawnia; the truth is revealed by the shepherd.

'She is one of the same company with Miranda and Marina, and the youthful sons of Cymbeline. The shepherdess-princess, "queen of curds and cream," is less a vision than Miranda, the child of wonder, but more perhaps a creature of this earth.' (Dowden.)

Pericles. D.P. *Per.* Prince of Tyre. i, 1] seeks the daughter of Antiochus in marriage, but, penetrating A.'s guilty secret, flees to save his life. i, 2] to save his country from A.'s vengeance, P. sets out to Tharsus. (i, 3) mtd. i, 4] reaches Tharsus, and relieves a famine there. (ii, Gow.) appears in Dumb Show. ii, 1] shipwrecked, and cast on the coast of Pentapolis; dons his lost suit of armour, recovered by fishermen. ii, 2] appears, unnamed, in the lists before King Simonides. ii, 3] at the royal banquet is given the crown of victory; acts with notable modesty, and reveals his name. (ii, 4) the people of Tyre agree to wait a year for his return. ii, 5] Simonides, after testing his courage, gives him his daughter Thaisa to wife. (iii, Gow.) P. learns that he must hasten back to Tyre if he would succeed to the throne. iii, 1] (on a ship at sea, during a storm) learns that a daughter has been born to him and that Thaisa is dead; resolves to make for Tharsus. (iii, 2) his scroll read by

Cerimon. iii, 3] leaves the infant Marina at Tharsus in the care of Cleon; vows that his hair shall remain 'unscissar'd' until Marina be married. (iii, 4) lamented as lost by Thaisa. (iv, Gow.) arrives at Tyre. (iv, 4) is bound for Tharsus; is shown in a Dumb Show visiting the supposed tomb of Marina. (v, Gow.) arrives off Mitylene. v, 1] lies speechless in a pavilion on deck; is aroused from his stupor by the song of Marina, who reveals herself to him, to his great joy; he falls into a slumber. v, 2] is bidden by Diana, in a vision, to hie to Ephesus. v, 3] reaches Eph. and makes himself known to his wife – 'Look, who kneels here! Flesh of thy flesh, Thaisa!'

The name 'Pericles' in all probability is due to a confusion of the Greek 'Pericles' with 'Pyrochles,' one of the heroes of Sidney's romance of *Arcadia*, whence Sh. had lately borrowed the by-plot of *Lear*. Richard Flecknoe, writing of the Shakespearean play in 1656, calls the hero 'Pyrochles' (Lee, p. 406*n*.). The hero of the original tale was Apollonius ('Appollinus' in the *Conf. Amant.*); see PERICLES, PRINCE OF TYRE.

Pericles, Prince of Tyre.

PUBLICATION. In the Stationers' Registers there occurs the entry: '1608. 20 Maij. Entred to Edw. Blount ... A booke called The booke of Pericles prynce of Tyre.' In 1609 there appeared 'The Late, and much admired Play, Called Pericles, Prince of Tyre. With the true Relation of the whole Historie ... of the said Prince: As also, The no lesse strange, and worthy accidents, in the Birth and Life, of his daughter Mariana ... By William Shakespeare.' This, however, was published not by Blount, but by Henry Gosson. The text abounds with errors. A second edn. was issued in the same year, and a third in 1611. In 1619 'Pericles' and 'The (Whole) Contention' (*q.v.*) appeared together in one vol. This was published by Thomas Pavier. *Per.* was excluded from the 1st and 2nd Folios, but appeared in the 3rd (1663), following the text of an edn. of 1635, with some alterations.

SOURCE OF THE PLOT. The story of 'Apollonius of Tyre,' the Latin version of a lost Greek original. Many MSS. of this are extant, and it was printed *c.* 1470. This romance had a widespread vogue in Europe. It appears in the *Gesta Romanorum*, in Belleforest's *Histoires Tragiques*, and in Gower's *Conf. Amant.* ('Appollinus, the Prince of Tyr'). It was also translated from the French by Robert Copeland and published by Wynkyn de Worde in 1510. In 1576 a translation by Lawrence Twine appeared, bearing the titel: 'The Patterne of painfull Adventures, containing the ... Historie of the strange accidents that befell unto Prince Apollonius, the Lady Lucina his wife and Tharsia his daughter,' etc. (Other edns. followed in 1595 and 1607.) Gower's *Conf. Amant.* is, however, the dramatist's chief source.

COMPOSITION AND PRODUCTION. The play was produced at the Globe in 1608, and had probably been just completed.

AUTHORSHIP. It is generally agreed that Sh. is responsible only for the story of Marina, and that the rest is by George Wilkins, who published in 1608 a novel, based on the play, entitled: 'The Painful Adventures of Pericles Prince of Tyre. Being the true History of the Play of Pericles, as it was lately presented by the worthy and ancient Poet John Gower.' George Rowley has also been suggested as a collaborator.

See *N.S.S.Tr.*, 1874, Pt. I, pp. 195 ff., for an elaborate discussion of the authorship of the play.

Perigenia. Apparently adapted from Plutarch's 'Perigouna.' 'Perigenia whom he ravished' (*M.N.D.* ii, 1).

'Sinnis had a goodly fair daughter called Perigouna which fled away when she saw her father slain'; she hid herself in a grove, 'but Theseus finding her, called her, and sware by his faith he would use her gently. ...Upon which she came out of the bush, and bare him a goodly boy, which was called Menalippus' (*Plut.* p. 279).

Perigort, Lord. Imaginary personage; his wedding mtd. *L.L.L.* ii, 1.

Perke. See PECK.

Perkes, Clement. 'Of the hill,' *i.e.* Stinchcombe Hill (*q.v.*); *2 Hen. IV*, v, 1. A family of the name dwelt there in the 16th cent. (Lee, p. 240).

Perseus. Famous Argive hero; he cut off the head of the Gorgon Medusa, from whose blood sprang the winged horse Pegasus (Ovid, *Metam.* iv, 786), which appears in the following passages to be regarded as Perseus' steed – perhaps by confusion of Perseus with Bellerophon.

The Dauphin declares that his horse, which he had compared with Pegasus, 'is a beast for Perseus: he is pure air and fire' (*Hen. V*, iii, 7); 'the strong-ribb'd bark ...Bounding between the two moist elements, Like Perseus' horse' (*Tr. Cr.* i, 3); 'I have seen thee, As hot as Perseus, spur thy Phrygian steed' (*ib.* iv, 5).

In the fable of 'The Hors, the Shepe and the Ghoos,' ptd. by Caxton (Univ. Lib. Camb. D. 5.42) we find: 'the stede of perseus was cleped pigase with swift wings' (Steevens).

By the flying horse that was engendered of the flood is understood that of her riches issuing of that realm Perseus made a ship named Pegase, and this ship was likened unto an horse flying' (*Troy Booke*).

Persia. Country of Asia. 'I am bound to Persia' (*Com. Err.* iv, 1).

Persian, *adj.* The Prince of Morocco 'slew ... a Persian prince' (*M.V.* ii, 1); 'I do not like the fashion of your garments. You will say they are Persian' (*Lear*, iii, 6).

A Persian embassy was sent to England early in the reign of James I; hence, perhaps, the allusion to Persian attire in *Lear* (C. E. Moberly, *Rugby Sh.*).

Peter (1). Servant to Horner (D.P. *2 Hen. VI*); see THUMP, PETER.

Peter. (2). D.P. *Tam. Sh.* A servant. iv, 1] comments on the 'taming.'

Peter (3). D.P. *Rom. J.* The Nurse's attendant. ii, 4] demurs to his mistress's charge of cowardice. ii, 5] in attendance. (iv, 4) mtd. iv, 5] banters the musicians, who will not play 'Heart's Ease' to him.

'Romeo's man' in *Romeus and Juliet*; 'Petre' in *Rhomeo and Julietta*; 'Pietro' in Bandello. In Da Porto, Pietro is a servant of Giulietta.

Peter (4). As a forename. 'P. Simple' (*M.W.W.* i, 4); 'P. Quince' (*M.N.D.* i, 2); iii, 1; iv, 1); 'P. Turf' (*Tam.Sh.* Ind. 2); 'if his name be George, I'll call him P.' (*John*, i, 1); 'P. Bullcalf' (*2 Hen. IV*, iii, 2).

Peter, Friar. D.P. *M. for M.* (iv, 3) is sent for by the Duke. iv, 5] is given confidential instructions by the Duke. iv, 6] escorts Mariana and Isabella to the Duke. v, 1] repels Lucio's slanders on 'Friar Lodowick.'

Peter of Pomfret. A hermit (of Pontefract or Wakefield), 'in great reputation with the common people' for his predictions, who foretold that John should be cast out of his kingdom at the Feast of the Ascension (1213) – offering 'to suffer death for it, if his prophecies prooved not true.' When the day came 'without any other notable damage unto King John,' Peter 'was drawn into the towne of Warham, and there hanged, together with his sonne.' Yet the people, taking note of the fact that John on the Vigil of Ascension Day did homage to the Pope for his kingdom, declared that P. had prophesied truly (*Hol.* iii, 180).

D.P. *John.* iv, 2] reiterates his prophecy before the King, who orders him to be hanged on Ascension Day. (v, 1) the truth, in a certain sense, of his prediction, is admitted by the King.

Peter, St. As the Janitor of Heaven. Mtd., *M. Ado*, ii, 1; 'You ... that have the office opposite to Saint Peter, And keep the gate of hell' (*Oth.* iv, 2); church dedicated to him (at Verona), *Rom. J.* iii, 5.

Petitioners, Three or Four. D.PP. *2 Hen. VI.* i, 3] their petitions, intended for the Protector, Gloucester, fall into the hands of the Queen and Suffolk.

Peto. D.P. *1 Hen. IV.* An associate of Falstaff's. (i, 2) mtd. ii, 2] takes part in the robbery of travellers near Gadshill. ii, 4] relates how Falstaff hacked his own sword. (iv, 2) lieutenant to F. in his 'charge of foot.'

D.P. *2 Hen. IV.* Now 'an attendant on Prince Henry.' ii, 4] tells the Prince that the King is at Westminster and that there are grave tidings from the north.

The family of Peto (Peito, or Peyto) was seated in Warwickshire from an early period; Sir Edw. P. was governor of Warwick Castle (French, p. 69).

Petrarch. Italian poet (1304–74). 'Now is he [Romeo] for the numbers that P. flowed in' (*Rom. J.* ii, 4).

Petruchio (1). A guest at Capulet's feast; *Rom. J.* i, 5.

Petruchio (2). D.P. *Tam. Sh.* A gentleman of Verona. i, 2] arrives at Padua to seek a wife; tells his friend Hortensio that he cares not for her beauty as long as she is wealthy; hears of Katharina, the shrewish daughter of Baptista Minola, and resolves to woo her, being quite undaunted by the ill report he hears of her. ii, 1] presents himself to Bapt. – an old friend of his father's – and introduces Hortensio in the guise of a musicmaster; ascertains K.'s dowry with accuracy, and regards his conquest as a matter of certainty; in his first encounter with her is given a full taste of her shrewishness, but vows that he finds her 'passing courteous'; tells Bapt., in her presence, that she is 'modest as the dove' and that their wedding-day is fixed; wholly disregards her expostulations. iii, 2] arrives mounted on a broken-down jade, 'for all the world caparisoned like his horse'; insists on being married forthwith, attired as he is; his mad behaviour at the wedding ceremony is described; later, will not stay to dinner, but sets out instantly, with Katharina and his servant Grumio. iv, 1] arrives at his country-house; rates the servants, declares the viands are ill cooked, and tells K. that 'for this night, we'll fast in company'; later, (*sol.*) describes his method of 'taming the shrew.' (iv, 2) mtd. iv, 3] compels K. to thank him for serving her with meat; rejects the garments furnished for K.'s use; suddenly declares his intention of returning with her to Padua. iv, 5] (on the way to Padua) comples K. to call the sun the moon, and Vincentio a young maiden. v, 1] exposes to V. the trick that is being played in personating him; K. shows her changed behaviour by kissing P. openly. v, 2] (at Lucentio's feast) P. proposes, as a test of their wives' obedience, that each of the newly married shall send for his wife; K. alone shows her submission and P. wins his wager.

The Italian name is properly 'Petrucio,' but, as Knight suggests, it is probably spelt 'Petruchio' to ensure its correct pronunciation by English actors. The equivalent character in *The Taming of A Shrew* is Ferando, whose general behaviour coincides with Petruchio's.

'Petruchio is a madman in his senses, a very honest fellow, who hardly speaks a word of truth, and succeeds in all his tricks and impostures. He acts his assumed character to the life, with the most fantastical extravagance, with complete presence of mind, with untired animal spirits, and without a particle of ill-humour from beginning to end.' (W. Hazlitt.)

Phaëton. or **Phaëthon.** Son of Phoebus and Clymene, wife of Merops. To prove his parentage he begged Phoebus to let him drive the chariot of the Sun for one day: since he could not rein the horses they left the track and almost set the earth on fire; whereupon Jove smote him with a thunderbolt, and he fell into the Eridanus (Ovid, *Metam.* ii, 1–324).

'Like glistering Ph. Wanting the manage of unruly steeds' (*Rich. II*, iii, 3); 'Why, Ph... Wilt thou aspire to guide the heavenly car, And ... burn the world?' (*T.G.V.* iii, 1); 'Now Ph. hath tumbled from his car' (*3 Hen. VI*, i, 4); 'Oh, Phoebus! hadst thou never given consent That Phaëton should check thy flery steeds, Thy burning car never had scorched the earth' (*ib.* ii, 6); 'such a waggoner As Ph. would whip you to the west' (*Rom. J.* iii, 2).

Pharamond. In Arthurian romance, the first king of France; the legendary period of his reign being A.D. 420–8. Claimed by the French to be the founder of the 'Salic Law,' *Hen. V*, i, 2. (Cf. *Hol.* iii, 545.)

Pharaoh. King of Egypt. His dream (Gen. xli, 2–4) referred to: 'if to be fat is to be hated, then P.'s lean kine are to be loved' (*1 Hen. IV*, ii, 4); a possible allusion to the destruction of his host in the Red Sea (Exod. xiv): 'Like P.'s soldiers in the reechy painting' (*M. Ado*, iii, 3).

Pharsalia. A district in Thessaly in which was fought the decisive battle between Jul. Caes. and Pompey the Great, 48 B.C. Antony's challenge to Octavius to fight him at Ph. (*Plut.* p. 208) referred to, *Ant. Cl.* iii, 7.

Phebe. As a verb. 'She Phebes me' (*A.Y.L.* iv, 3, l. 39). See PHOEBE.

Pheezar. A nonce-name devised by the Host to rime with 'Caesar'; *M.W.W.* i, 3.

If it has a meaning, it is as a derivative of 'pheese,' to beat, or worry.

Phibbus. Bottom's pronunciation of 'Phoebus'; *M.N.D.* i, 2.

Philadelphus. King of Paphlagonia (*Plut.* p. 207). Mtd. ('Philadelphos'), *Ant. Cl.* iii, 6.

Philario. D.P. *Cymb.* 'An Italian, friend to Posthumus' (Rowe). (i, 2) Post. resolves to visit him at Rome, since he had been his father's friend. i, 4] welcomes Post.; vainly endeavours to dissuade Post. and Iachimo from wagering on Imogen's fidelity. ii, 4] is discussing Britain's attitude to Rome when Iach. enters, and boasts of his alleged triumph over Imogen's virtue, on the departure of Posthumus he exclaims to Iach., 'You have won.'

When first mentioned, the name is given as 'Filorio' or 'Florio' in Ff.

Philarmonus. ('Philharmonus' Ff.) See SOOTHSAYER (3).

Philemon (1). The husband of Baucis; they hospitably entertained Jupiter and Mercury in their cottage (Ovid, *Metam.* viii, 623 ff.). '*D. Pedro.* My visor is Ph.'s roof; within the house is Jove ['Love,' Ff]' (*M. Ado*, ii, 1). The story is also alluded to in *A.Y.L.* iii, 3: 'ill-inhabited, worse than Jove in a thatched house!'

Philemon (2). D.P. *Per.* A servant. iii, 2] in attendance.

Philip (1). Name commonly applied to a sparrow, from its chirping note. Skelton's elegy on 'Philip Sparrowe,' Jane Scroope's pet bird, was well known. See *John*, i, 1, l. 231 (a disputed passage).

Philip (2). For 'Ph. Faulconbridge'; *John*, i, 1 (2).

Philip (3). King of Macedon. Mtd. by Fluellen as father of Alexander the Great, *Hen. V*, iv, 7.

Philip (4). For 'St Philip.' 'A year and a quarter old, come Philip and Jacob' (*M. for M.* iii, 2).

Philip (5). Name of a servant; *Tam. Sh.* iv, 1.

Philip II. 'Augustus,' King of France (1165–1223), son of Lewis VII, succ. 1180; married Isabel, d. of Baldwin, Count of Flanders. He joined Richard Coeur-de-lion in the 3rd Crusade, but, becoming jealous of him, returned to France and intrigued with John (Lackland) against him. He offered the Emperor Hen. VI a large sum to keep Rich. in captivity, and the latter, on being released, waged war on Philip and defeated him at Gisors. After Richard's death Ph. embraced the cause of Prince Arthur against John in the dispute as to the French possessions of the late King.

D.P. *John.* (i, 1) demands, by his envoy Chatillon, that England, Ireland, Poictiers, Anjou, Touraine, and Maine should be yielded to Arthur (there is no historical authority for this embassy, nor were Eng. and Ire. claimed for Arthur). ii, 1] is preparing to attack Angiers when he learns that the English are at hand; accuses John, to his face, of being a usurper; appeals to the men of Angiers to admit Arthur's claim, threatening the town with assault if they refuse; after an indecisive combat with the English, consents to join John in an assault on the 'peevish town' (Angiers); agrees to the suggestion that the Dauphin should wed John's niece Blanch of Castile. iii, 1] is persuaded by the papal legate to renounce his new alliance with John (*Hol.* iii, 175). iii, 4] admits his defeat; endeavours to console Constance in her despair.

The meeting of the Kings, described in ii, 1, actually took place between Boteavant and le Goulet (Normandy), and no agreement was come to (*Hol.* iii, 160).

Philip, St. The evangelist, who 'had four daughters, virgins, which did prophesy' (Acts xxi, 9). Charles declares that St Philip's daughters were not the equals of Joan of Arc, *1 Hen. VI*, i, 2.

Philippan. ('Phillippan,' Ff.) Doubtfully a proper name. The sword worn by Antony at Philippi thus mentioned by Cleopatra: 'I wore his sword Ph.' (*Ant. Cl.* ii, 5).

Philippe, or **Philippa.** Daughter of Lionel, D. of Clarence; married Edmund Mortimer, 3rd E. of March; mtd. *2 Hen. VI*, ii, 2 (2).

Philippi. City in Macedonia; scene of the victory gained by Octavius and Antony over Brutus and Cassius, 42 B.C.

Brutus and Cassius discuss the policy of accepting battle with their foes at Ph., *Jul. C.* iv, 3; the scene of Act V is laid at 'the plains of Ph.'; mtd., *ib.* v, 1 (2), 5; Caesar 'at Ph. the good Brutus ghosted' (*Ant. Cl.* ii, 6); mtd., *ib.* iii, 2, 11.

'Philippes' in *Plut.*; usually 'Phillippi' in Ff.

Phillida. Conventional name of a shepherdess. 'In the shape of Corin ... versing love To amorous Ph.' (*M.N.D.* ii, 1). See CORIN (2).

Phillips, Augustine (*ob.* 1605). Mtd. as a 'principal actor' in F1.

Philo. D.P. *Ant. Cl.* 'Friend and follower of Antony' (Rowe). i, 1] laments Ant.'s infatuation for Cleopatra.

Philomela, or **Philomel.** Daughter of King Pandion; changed into a nightingale. (For the story see TEREUS.)

(*a*) Philomel. 'Ph. with melody Sing in your sweet lullaby' (*M.N.D.* ii, 2); 'The tale of Tereus, here the leaf's turned down, Where Ph. gave up' (*Cymb.* ii, 2); 'His Ph. must lose her tongue today' (*T. And.* ii, 3); 'cut those pretty fingers off, That could have better sew'd than Ph.' (*ib.* ii, 5); 'the tragic tale of Ph.' (*ib.* iv, 1); 'Far worse than Ph. you used my daughter' (*ib.* v, 2); mtd., *Lucr.* 1079, 1128. For the nightingale: 'P. in Summer's front doth sing' (*Son.* cii).

(*b*) Philomela. 'Fair Ph., she but lost her tongue' (*T. And.* ii, 4); 'Ravish'd and wrong'd as Ph. was' (*ib.* iv, 1); mtd., *P.P.* xv.

Cf. Peele, *Arr. of Paris*, i, 2.

Philostrate. D.P. *M.N.D.* 'Master of the sports to the Duke' (Theobald). i, 1] *p.m.*; is sent by Theseus to arrange revels for the wedding-day. v, 1] presents a list of 'sports'; ridicules the clowns' 'Pyramus and Thisbe,' but, by command of Theseus, introduces the players.

In the last sc. Ff (against Qq) give 'Egeus' for 'Phil.'; one actor probably doubled the parts. The name occurs in Chaucer's *Knight's Tale*, and also, in the form 'Philostratus,' in *Plut.* p. 224.

Philoten. Only daughter of Cleon, Governor of Tarsus; her mother, becoming envious of Marina's superior accomplishments, plans to murder Marina, that Ph. 'Might stand peerless' (*Per.* iv, Gow.).

Philotis is a character in the *Hecyra* of Terence.

Philotus. D.P. *Timon.* Servant of one of Timon's creditors. iii, 4] presents himself at T.'s house to obtain payment.

Philotas is the name of a physician, *Plut.* pp. 176–7. The name only occurs in the parts of *Timon* which are regarded as non-Shakespearean by Fleury and others. 'Philo' in 'The Actors Names,' F1. See also PHYLOTUS.

Phoebe (1). ('Phebe,' Ff.) D.P. *A.Y.L.* 'A shepherdness' (Rowe). (ii, 4) is apostrophized by her lover. iii, 5] scornfully rejects the suit of the shepherd Silvius, and is there-upon sharply chided by 'Ganymede,' with whom, nevertheless she instantly falls in love; on 'G.'s' departure assumes a kindlier demeanour to Sil. and persuades him to convey 'a very taunting letter' to the 'pretty youth.' (iv, 3) her letter to 'Gan.' discussed by the latter and Sil. v, 2] rebukes 'Gan.' for showing Sil. The letter, and bids Sil. describe 'what it is to love.' v, 4] promises to marry Sil. in the inconceivable event of her refusing 'Gan.'; on Rosalind's revealing herself, Ph. keeps her word.

The name is that of the equivalent character in Lodge's *Rosalynde*. In two lines (iv, 3; v, 4) 'Phebe' appears to be a monosyllable, to be regarded as an affectionate abbreviation.

Phoebe (2). Surname of Diana, as goddess of the moon. 'Her [Phoebe's] silver visage' (*M.N.D.* i, 1); 'to Ph., to Luna, to the moon' (*L.L.L.* iv, 2); 'the stately Ph. 'mongst her nymphs' (*T. And.* i, 2).

Phoebus. A name of Apollo, regarded as the Sun-god; hence, the sun itself. The palace of the sun, bright with gold and carbuncles, and the glowing chariot of Phoebus with its wing-footed horses are described by Ovid (*Metam.* ii, 1–50), in relating the myth of Phaëthon.

'I shall think or Ph.'s steeds are founder'd Or Night kept chain'd below' (*Temp.* iv, 1); 'the wheels of Ph.' (*M. Ado*, v, 3); 'Where Ph.'s fire scarce thaws the icicles' (*M.V.* ii, 1); 'Bright Ph. in his strength' (*Wint. T.* iv, 4); 'With silken streamers the young Ph. fanning' (*Hen. V*, iii, Chor.); 'from the rise to set Sweats in the eye of Ph.' (*ib.* iv, 1); in connection with Phaëthon, *3 Hen. VI*, ii, 6; 'Modest as Morning when she coldly eyes The youthful Ph.' (*Tr. Cr.* i, 3); women's faces exposed to 'Ph.'s burning kisses' (*Cor.* ii, 1); Cleopatra 'with Ph.'s amorous pinches black' (*Ant. Cl.* i, 5); 'carbuncled Like holy Ph.'s car' (*ib.* iv, 8); 'golden Ph.' (*ib.* v, 2); 'Ph. 'gins arise, His steeds to water' (*Cymb.* ii, 3); 'a carbuncle of Ph.'s wheel' (*ib.* v, 5); 'radiant fire On flickering Ph.'s front' (*Lear*, ii, 2); 'Gallop apace, you fiery-footed steeds To Ph.'s lodging' (*Rom. J.* iii, 2); 'Ph.'s car' (*Haml.* iii, 2); 'Ph.'s lute' (*P.P.* viii).

'Ph., "he that wandering knight so fair" ' (*1 Hen. IV*, i, 2) is an allusion to 'The Knight of the Sun,' hero of the Spanish romance *El Donzel del Febo*, familiar in Eng. translns. (1585, etc.) and mtd. in *Don Quixote*.

Phoenicia, Phoenice. Country on the coast of Syria, inhabited by a Semitic people of great maritime enterprise. Under the Romans, part of the province of Syria. 'To Ptolemy he assigned … Ph. ['Phoenetia,' F1]' (*Ant. Cl.* iii, 6; *Plut.* p. 202).

Phoenicians. Antony is advised 'to let th' Egyptians And the Phoenicians go aducking,' but to fight on land himself (*Ant. Cl.* iii, 7).

Phoenix (1). Name of a ship, *T. Nt.* v, 1; name of a house, *Com. Err.* i, 2, ii, 2.

Phoenix (2). Quasi-proper name of a mythical bird, the sole one of its kind – 'unica semper avis' (Ovid, *Amores*, ii, 6, 54) – about which varying legends exist, all to the effect that after a life of several centuries it died, and was regenerated, or followed by a successor springing from its body or nest. It was supposed to live in Arabia, hence 'Arabian bird' (*Ant. Cl.* iii, 2); 'She is alone the A. bird' (*Cymb.* i, 6); 'in Arabia There is one tree, the phoenix' throne; one phoenix At this hour reigning there' (*Temp.* iii, 3). 'Rare as ph.' (*A.Y.L.* iv, 3); 'from their ashes shall be rear'd A ph. that shall make all France afeard' (*1 Hen. VI*, iv, 7); 'My ashes, as the ph., may bring forth A bird that will revenge upon you all' (*3 Hen. VI*, i, 4); 'When the bird of wonder dies, the maiden ph., Her ashes new create another heir' (*Hen. VIII*, v, 5); 'a naked gull, Which flashes now a ph.' (*Timon*, ii, 1). Mtd., *Son.* xix.

In *The Ph. and the Turtle* (*q.v.*) the ph. is fem. (as in *Hen. VIII*), and the dove masc. (l. 31).

Phoenix and the Turtle, The. A poem bearing this name, and attributed to Sh., appeared, with others, as a kind of appendix to a volume of verse by Robert Chester, entitled *Love's Martyr or Rosalin's Complaint*, etc., publd. 1601.

Recent criticism assigns the poem with much confidence to Sh. (Dowden dissents). 'In dark and noble verse it describes a spiritual marriage, suddenly ended by death. It is too strange to be the fruit of a human sorrow. It is the work of a great mind trying to express in unusual symbols a thought too subtle and too intense to be expressed in any other way.' (J. Masefield, *W. Sh.* p. 249.)

[**Phoenix Theatre.**] See Cockpit, The.

Photinus. An attendant of Cleopatra's, thus referred to by Enobarbus, speaking to Cl.: ' 'Tis said in Rome, That Photinus an eunuch and your maids Manage this war' *Ant. Cl.* iii, 7).

This is based on *Plut.* p. 206, where Octavius is said to have declared that Photinus, and others, 'were those that ruled all the affairs of Antonius' empire.' In the original Gk. the name is Pothinus, which is also that of an eunuch who was put to death by Jul. Caes., and who is referred to in *Plut.* pp. 85–6. The name 'Photinus' where it occurs in Beaumont and Fletcher's *False One* is accentuated on the penultimate.

Phrygia. Country of Asia Minor, of different extent at different times. 'Phrygian' was commonly used by the Latin poets in the sense of 'Trojan,' since at one time the Troad (in Mysia) belonged to Phrygia.

'Lord Pandarus of Phr.' (*T. Nt.* iii, 1); the Greek princes 'from the Athenian bay Put forth toward Phr.' (*Tr. Cr.* Prol.); 'his smiling becomes him [Troilus] better than any man in all Phr.' (*ib.* i, 2).

Phrygian, *adj.* Hector's 'Phr. steed' (*Tr. Cr.* iv, 5); 'every Phr. stone of Troy' (*ib. ib.*); 'our Phr. plains' (*ib.* v, 11); used at random by Pistol: 'base Phr. Turk' (*M.W.W.* i, 3); 'Phr. shepherds' (*Lucr.* 1502).

Phrynia. D.P. *Timon*. A mistress to Alcibiades. iv, 3] is reviled by Timon, and retorts; is given gold by him. (v, 1) mtd.

The name is probably adapted from 'Phryne,' the Athenian *hetaira*.

[**Phylotus.**] See Pedant.

Physician. D.P. *Lear*. iv, 4] ('Doctor,' Qq; 'Gentleman,' Ff) prescribes simples to procure repose for the King. iv, 7] watches the reawakening of Lear, and advises that his mind should be kept at rest.

In Ff the Physician's part is merged in that of 'Gentleman' (*q.v.*).

Pible. See Bible.

Picardy. A former government of N. France; it was a dependency of Flanders, but united to France under Louis XI. 'The regions of Artois, Walloon, and P., are friends to us' (*1 Hen. VI*, ii, 1); 'P. Hath slain their governors' (*2 Hen. VI*, iv, 1).

Pickbone, Francis. A former comrade of Shallow's; *2 Hen. IV*, iii, 2.

Pickt-hatch. District in London: a haunt of bad characters of all kinds, near the Charterhouse Wall in Goswell Road, where the 'hatches,' or half-doors, were apparently furnished with spikes as a defence. The name recently survived as 'Pickax Yard.'

(Fal to Pist.) 'To your manor of P., go' (*M.W.W.* ii, 2).

Frequently alluded to in the drama of the period; *cf.* 'Vestals of Pict-hatch' (*The Alchemist*, ii, 1).

[Piero d' Aragona.] See Pedro, Don.

Pigmy. See Pygmies.

Pigrogromitus. 'Thou wast in very gracious fooling last night, when thou spok'st of P., of the Vapians passing the Equinoctial of Queubus' (*T. Nt.* ii, 3).

These proper names, quoted by Aguecheek as having been used by Feste, have not been identified as distortions of any known equivalents. A Rabelaisian flavour has been discerned in the passage by some commentators. *Cf.* A.C. Swinburne, *A Study of Shakespeare* (1880), p. 155. Furness suggests a possible perversion of 'Tetragrammation.'

Pilate, Pontius. Roman procurator of Judaea, by whom Christ was tried and condemned. Twice mentioned in *Sh.* in allusion to his washing his hands before the people to assert his innocence of Christ's death (Matt. xxvii, 24).

'Some of you, with P., wash your hands' (*Rich. II*, iv, 1); 'How fain, like P., would I wash my hands Of this ... murther' (*Rich. III*, i, 4).

Pilch. Regarded as a personal name by mod. edrs., following Malone. 'What, ho, Pilch!' (*Per.* ii, 1; 'What, to pelch?' QqF3, 4, a meaningless phrase).

Pillycock. A name in a verse quoted by Edgar, *Lear*, iii, 4, as 'Pillicock sat on Pillicock-hill'; in *Gammer Gurton's Garland* (Ritson) it occurs as: 'Pillycock, Pillycock sat on a hill; If he's not gone, he sits there still.' Cotgrave has: '*Turelureau*. My pillicocke, my prettie knave.' Also used *sens. obsc.*; *cf.* Florio, *A Worlde of Wordes* (1598), *s.v.* 'Pugio.'

Pimpernell, Henry. Name alleged to have been mtd. by Sly; *Tam. Sh.* Ind. 2.

Pinch. D.P. *Com. Err.* iv, 4] at Adriana's request, endeavours to exorcize 'Satan, hous'd within' her husband; suggests that both Ant. E. and Dromio E., as madmen, should 'be bound and laid in some dark room'; helps to bind and bear away master and man. (v, 1) is described by Ant. E. as 'a mountebank, a threadbare juggler ... a living dead man.'

The equivalent character in the *Menaechmi*, Medicus, treats Menaechmus of Epidamnus in a similar manner. In st. dir. iv, 4, Ff, 'a Schoolmaster, call'd P.'

Pindarus. An enfranchised slave of Cassius, whom C. 'reserved ever for such a pinch,' viz. the slaying of his master when ordered to do so. He accordingly struck off the head of Cassius at Philippi, when C. thought the day was lost, and 'was never seen more' (*Plut.* pp. 143, 171). *Cf.* Dion Cass. xlvii, 46; Appian, *Bel. Civ.* iv, 113; Val. Max. vi, 8 (4).

D.P. *Jul. C.* iv, 2] *p.m.*; in attendance. v, 3] (at Philippi) urges Cassius to flee; announces that Titinius is captured; stabs C., as commanded; resolves to 'run Where never Roman shall take note of him.'

Pisa. City of Italy, on the Arno. Its university was founded *c.* 1343. P., 'renowned for grave citizens' (cf. *Tam. Sh.* iv, 2), is referred to as less eminent for learning than Padua, *ib.* i, 1 (3). Mtd., *ib.* ii, 1 (2); iii, 1; iv, 2 (3), 4, 5; v, 1 (2).

Pisanio. D.P. *Cymb.* 'Servant to Posthumus' (Rowe). i, 2] is placed at Imogen's command when his master is exiled; is sent to see Post. embark. i, 4] describes P.'s departure. i, 6] is given a box by the Queen (which she avers to contain a potent medicine) and is told that his merits will be rewarded; (*sol.*) when he proves untrue to his lord he 'will choke himself.' i, 7] announces Iachimo. ii, 3] is bidden to search for Imogen's bracelet. iii, 2] reads, with horror and amazement, a letter from Post. accusing Im. of faithlessness and ordering him to kill her; hands another letter to Im. bidding her set out for Milford; tells her she had 'best consider.' iii, 4] reveals Post.'s command to Im.; since its receipt he has not 'slept one wink'; advises her to attach herself to the train of the Roman ambassador and leave Britain; furnishes her with a suitable disguise; gives her the Queen's 'box of drugs.' iii, 5] (at the Court) in reply to Cloten's threatening inquiries concerning Im., hands him a deceptive letter; avers his willingness to serve Cl. and brings him a suit of Posthumus' clothes; (*sol.*) trusts that Cl.'s efforts will be fruitless. (iii, 6) mtd. iv, 3] is threatened with torture by Cymb. if he will not reveal what he knows of Im.; (*sol.*) is perplexed through lack of all news, but is resolved to fight for his country. (v, 1) is believed by Post. to have too compliantly killed Im. v, 5] on Post.'s striking 'Fidele,' springs to aid her, and reveals her identity; he exculpates himself when accused of having tried to poison her; explains how Cloten came to be attired in Posthumus' clothes when slain.

'Pisanio unites the cunning of the serpent with the harmlessness of the dove. His singular position is throughout that he is truest where he is most untrue. ...To serve his master with true obedience is more to him than life; yet he cannot kill the guiltless... By dissimulation he maintains his trust as an instrument for just action.' (Gervinus, *Sh. Comm.* (1875), pp. 673–4.)

Pistol. D.P. *2 Hen. IV.* ii, 4] is reviled by Doll Tearsheet, and, a brawl ensuing, he is turned out by Falstaff. v, 3] announces the death of Hen. IV, and welcomes 'these pleasant days.' v, 5] tells Fal. That Doll 'is in base durance'; witnesses Fal.'s rebuff by the King; is taken with the rest to the Fleet, exclaiming: 'Si fortuna me tormenta, spero me contenta.'

Piston, a bully and buffoon, appears in *Solimon and Perseda* (1599). Piston has but little resemblance to Pistol: he does not rant, but indulges in comical perversions such as 'O extempore, o flores!' (B2). See Basilisco. 'We find in the Addl. Charters in the Brit. Mus., Nos. 1021, 1022, that Wm. Pistail and R. Bardolf were among Canoniers serving in Normandy, Ao. 1435' (Knight).

D.P. *Hen. V.* ii, 1] quarrels with Nym about 'the quondam Quickly,' but is appeased by Bardolph; is summoned to the dying Fal. ii, 3] leaves his wife in charge of the house, and bids her 'let housewifery appear.' iii, 2] (before Harfleur) is driven to the attack by Fluellen; characterized by the Boy. iii, 6] begs Fl. to intercede for Bardolph, and on being refused insults him. v, 1] bids the King, whom he does not recognize, tell Fl. that he will 'knock his leek about his pate.' iv, 4] extorts a ransom from a Frenchman. v, 1] is cudgelled by Fl. and made to eat the leek; resolves to 'steal' to England and there 'steal.'

D.P. *M.W.W.* 'A follower of Falstaff.' i, 1] bombastically repels Slender's charge of picking his purse. i, 3] refuses to act as a go-between in Falstaff's love-affairs, and vows to unfold matters to Page (Ford, Q1). ii, 1] tells Ford that Fal. is in love with his wife. ii, 2] is refused a loan by Fal., and exclaims: 'Why, then the world's mine oyster, Which I with sword will open'; follows Quickly on her errand to Mrs Page. v, 5] takes part in the baiting of Fal. in Windsor forest.

The part allotted to P. in v, 5, seems out of keeping with his character. In Q (1602) he does not appear in this scene. (See QUICKLY.)

Pittie-ward. *M.W.W.* iii, 1, F1; perh. a thoroughfare in Windsor; *cf.* 'Pyttey Gate' in Bristol (Lee, ed.).

In F2, 3, 4, 'pitty-wary,' which is unintelligible. Without initial capital in each case.

Pius. Surname of Titus Andronicus, 'for many good and great deserts to Rome' (*T. And.* i, 1). ('Pious,' Ff.)

Placentio. An invited guest; *Rom. J.* i, 2.

Plantagenet. A surname, or rather nickname, applied to the descendants of Geoffrey, E. of Anjou, and especially to the kings of England from Henry II to Rich. III.

While the derivation of the name – *planta genista* (broom) – is clear, the reason for its adoption is doubtful. The title was not adopted by the family until *c.* 1450.

'Geffrey's son, Arthur P.' (*John*, i, 1); Philip Faulconbridge accepted as a P., *ib.* i, 1 (2). Percy and P. constrasted, *1 Hen. IV*, i, 1. Henry V speaks of himself as Henry P., *Hen. V*, v, 2. The E. of Salisbury a P., *1 Hen. VI*, i, 4; Richard P., *ib.* ii, 4 (5), 5 (2), iii, 1 (3). Cade claims that his mother was a P., *2 Hen. VI*, iv, 2.

Richard P., D. of York, *3 Hen. VI*, i, 1 (7), 3, 4 (2), ii, 1 (2); Edmund P., *ib.* ii, 2.

'These P.s' (*Rich. III*, i, 2); Gloucester calls himself P., *ib. ib.*; 'gallant-springing, brave P. [Prince Edw.]' (*ib.* i, 4); 'Famous P. [Richard]' (*ib.* iii, 7); Lady Margaret P., *ib.* iv, 1; Edward P., *ib.* iv, 4; 'little Ned P.' (*ib. ib.*).

Plantagenet, Edward (1). Edw. of Norwich (*c.* 1373–1415); e.s. of Edmund of Langley by Isabel of Castile; 2nd D. of York; E. of Rutland 1390; for his support of Rich. II was rewarded with the title of D. of Albemarle (Aumerle); acc. *Hol.*, became bail for Bolingbroke's appearance, and officiated as High Constable of England at the lists at Coventry (iii, 493–4); retired to King's Langley after the confiscation of Bol.'s inheritance (*ib.* 496); brought reinforcements to Rich. in Ireland, somewhat tardily (*ib.* 497); landed in Wales with Rich. (*ib.* 499), but soon deserted him (*ib.* 500); was accused of treason by Fitzwater (*ib.* 512); challenged the exiled Norfolk (*ib. ib.*); was deprived of his dukedom (*ib.* 513); joined the Abbot of Westminster's conspiracy against Hen. IV, but was detected by his father, and on full confession pardoned by the King; having become D. of York, he commanded the 'vaward' at Agincourt, and was slain in the battle (*ib.* 553–5). The story of his complicity in the conspiracy of 1399 is now not regarded as resting on trustworthy evidence.

D.P. *Rich. II.* 'Duke of Aumerle.' i, 3] officiates as High Constable at Coventry; bids farewell to Bol. and desires to hear from him. i, 4] assures Richard that he wishes Bol.'s banishment longer. ii, 1] *p.m.* (ii, 3) Bol. speaks of him as 'my noble cousin.' iii, 1] (with the King at Gaunt's death-bed) *p.m.* iii, 2] lands in Wales with Richard; considers Richard 'too remiss'; gives the King a few words of comfort. iii, 3] (at Flint Castle) deprecates armed resistance. iv, 1] Bagot and Fitzwater accuse him of having been accessory to Gloucester's death; he challenges them both and also Norfolk, who, he then hears, is dead (*Hol.* iii, 512); consents to confer secretly with the Abbot of Westminster and the Bp. of Carlisle. v, 2] has been deprived of his dukedom (*Hol.* iii, 513); his father snatches a paper from him, and sees that it is treasonable; 'Rutland' is urged by his mother to seize his father's horse and be himself the first to expose the plot to Henry. v, 3] reaches Henry first; his father and mother follow him closely, and the latter gains his pardon. (See YORK, DUCHESS OF.)

D.P. *Hen. V.* 'D. of York, cousin to the King.' iv, 3] is accorded the honour of leading the vaward. (iv, 8) his death upon the field announced (*Hol.* iii, 553–5).

Plantagenet, Margaret (1473–1541). Daughter of George, D. of Clarence. (Her later history, as the ill-fated Countess of Salisbury, is here irrelevant.)

D.P. *Rich. III.* 'A young daughter of Clarence.' ii, 2] laments her father's death. iv, 1] *p.m.*; called 'niece,' *i.e.* granddaughter, by the Duchess of York. (iv, 2) Richard intends to marry her to 'some mean poor gentleman,' and (iv, 3) announces that he has done so.

Perhaps confounded by the dramatist in the last two scenes with her cousin Cicely Plantagenet (*Hol.* iii, 752). Marg. was in fact only 12 years old at this time, and was ultimately married to Sir Rich. Pole.

Plantagenet, Richard. Earl of Cambridge; 2nd s. of Edm. of Langley. He married Anne, d. of Roger (VI) Mortimer, 4th E. of March (their son being the 'D. of York' of *1, 2, 3 Hen. VI*). Attainted, and beheaded at Southampton, Aug. 5, 1415, for conspiracy against Hen. V. Holinshed (iii, 549) states that C.'s true intent was 'to exalt to the crowne his brother in law, Edmund earle of March' – after whose death he 'was sure that the crowne should come to him by his wife' – and that he feigned to have been corrupted by the French King, to save the succession for his children.

D.P. *Hen. V.* (ii, Chor.) mtd. as having been bribed by France. ii, 2] adulates the King; counsels him not to pardon a prisoner who had 'railed' against him; is handed a paper disclosing Henry's knowledge of his guilt; submits himself to the King's mercy; declares that he was not seduced 'by gold of France'; is led to execution.

His son, Richard, declares that his father 'was attached but not attainted' (*1 Hen. VI*, ii, 4); his marriage to Anne mtd., *ib.* ii, 5.

Plashy, Pleshy. Between Chelmsford and Dunmow; seat of Thomas, D. of Gloucester, as Lord High Constable of England. (Prob. *Fr.* Plessis.) 'With all good speed at P. visit me' (*Rich. II*, i, 2); death of the Duchess of Gl. at P. announced, *ib.* ii, 2 (she actually died in Barking Abbey).

Plautus, Titus Maccius. Roman comic poet, 254–184 B.C.; his comedies were from early days renowned for their gaiety and good-humoured wit. 'Seneca cannot be too heavy, nor Pl. too light' (*Haml.* ii, 2). Mtd. in Preface to *Tr. Cr.* Q2.

For Sh.'s indebtedness to Pl. see COMEDY OF ERRORS.

Players (1). D.PP. *Haml.* ii, 2] (described as 'the tragedians of the city'; Polonius eulogizes them); they are welcomed by Hamlet; 1st P., at H.'s request, delivers a speech from 'Aeneas' tale to Dido'; they undertake to play *The Murder of Gonzago*, with an added speech. iii, 2] they receive advice on acting from H., and perform a part of the play before the King.

In ii, 2, ll. 330–51 are first found in F1; they contain a reference to 'an aery of children, little eyases' whose great popularity has ousted the 'tragedians' from the city – a passage which has given rise to much discussion, but which probably refers to companies of boy actors, recruited from the choristers of the Chapel Royal and St Paul's, who in 1600–1 became the rage,' to the detriment of adult players.

Players (2). D.PP. *Tam. Sh.* Ind. 1] are warned not to laugh at the strange lord. (Two players speak; see SOTO.)

In *The Taming of A Shrew* two players are named, Sander and Tom.

[**Pleiades.**] Alluded to as 'the seven stars.' '*Fal.* We that take purses go by the moon and the seven stars' (*1 Hen. IV*, i, 2); '*Fool.* The reason why the seven stars are no more than seven is a pretty reason' (*Lear*, i, 5).

[**Pliny, the Elder.**] C. Plinius Secundus (A.D. 23–79). His *Historia Naturalis* was translated by P. Holland, 1601. The following coincidences have been noted: Pliny, II, xcvii, 5, and *Oth.* iii, 3, ll. 454–7; Pliny, VII, Proeme, and *Lear*, iv, 6, ll. 183–5.

[**Plutarch.**] Πλούταρχος, a native of Chaeronea (*fl. c.* A.D. 100). His chief work is his *Parallel Lives* of forty-six famous Greeks and Romans, arranged in pairs.

A French transln. of the *Lives* by Jaques Amyot, Bp. of Auxerre, was published in 1559, and an English version of this, by Sir Thomas North, appeared in 1579, with the title 'The Lives of the Noble Grecians and Romanes, compared together by that grave learned Philosopher and Historiographer, Plutarke of Chaeronea; Translated out of Greeke into French by Iames Amyot ... and out of French into Englishe by Thomas North.'

A second edn. appeared in 1595, followed by another in 1603 (containing fifteen additional *Lives* from other sources), which was reprinted in 1612 and later.

W. W. Skeat's *Shakespeare's Plutarch*, to which page refs. are made in the present work, contains five relevant *Lives* from the edn. of 1612 (with extracts from two others), the spelling alone being modernized.

Pluto, Pluton. A surname of Hades, the god of the lower world (Virg. *Aen.* vii, 327). 'Pl.'s damned lake' (*2 Hen. IV*, ii, 4); 'by the dreadful Pl.' (*Tr. Cr.* iv, 4); 'by Pl.' (*ib.* v, 2); 'strong as Pl.'s gates' (*ib. ib.*; cf. 'the gates of hell,' Matt. xvi, 18); 'Pl. and hell' (*Cor.* i, 4); 'pierce the inmost centre of the earth; Then when you come to Pl.'s region ... deliver him this petition' (*T. And.* iv, 3); 'Pl. sends you word If you will have revenge from hell, you shall' (*ib. ib.*); 'Moody Pl. winks while Orpheus plays' (*Lucr.* 553).

See PLUTUS for confusion of names in Ff.

Plutus. The personification, rather than the god, of wealth. 'Almost every grain of Plutus' gold' (*Tr. Cr.* iii, 3; 'Plutoes,' F1); 'He [Timon] pours it out; Pl., the god of gold, Is but his steward' (*Timon*, i, 1); 'a heart Dearer than Plutus' mine, richer than gold' (*Jul. C.* iv, 3; 'Pluto,' Ff); 'Pl. himself, That knows the tinct and multiplying medicine' (*All's Well*, v, 3; 'Platus,' Ff).

In Lucian's 'Timon,' P. is sent by Jupiter to the misanthrope, to point out the hidden treasure.

Po. River in Italy. 'The Pyrenean and the river Po' (*John*, i, 1).

Poet (1). D.P. *Jul. C.* See MARCUS PHAONIUS.

Poet (2). D.P. *Timon.* i, 1] presents a poem to T. v, 1] vainly seeks to get a share of T.'s gold (see PAINTER).

Poictiers, Poitiers (*Lat.* Pictavium). For 'Poitou' (*q.v.*), of which it was the capital. Claimed for Arthur, *John*, i, 1; part of the dowry of Blanch of Castile, *ib.* ii, 2 (2); lost, *1 Hen. VI*, i, 1, iv, 3 (historically, P. was not an English possession in 1422). For 'Patay,' *1 Hen. VI*, iv, 1, Ff.

[**Poillot,** or **Poullot, Denis.**] French ambassador; mtd. *Hen. VIII*, i, 1, l. 97, as 'silenc'd,' in consequence of the attachment of English goods at Bordeaux.

Acc. Hall, p. 634, he 'was commanded to kepe his house in silence, and not come in presence till he was sent for.'

Poins, Edward. ('Poines,' 'Poynes,' Qq, and 'Points' sometimes in F1.) D.P. *1 Hen. IV.* i, 2] informs Prince Hal and Falstaff that rich booty may be obtained at Gadshill on the morrow; afterward unfolds to the Pr. his plan of discomfiting Fal. ii, 2] with the Pr., disguised, attacks Fal. and his comrades and seizes the booty. ii, 4] joins in playing a trick on Francis, the drawer; is accused by Fal. of running away at Gadshill; listens to Fal.'s tale of 'the men in buckram' (it is a moot point whether it is he or Peto that remains after the arrival of the sheriff). iii, 3] *p.m.* (om. QqFf).

P. is called 'Ned' by the Prince, and 'Yedward' by Fal.

D.P. *2 Hen. IV.* (In 'The Actors Names' (Ff) P. is one of the 'Irregular Humorists.') ii, 2] converses intimately with the Prince, who treats him familiarly, but with some contempt; reads Fal.'s letter aloud; suggests that the Pr. and he should observe Fal., in disguise. ii, 4] carries out the design, but Fal. soon detects them. (iv, 4) mtd. to the King as one of the Prince's 'continual followers.'

In *M.W.W.* iii, 2, P. is mentioned as a former companion of the Prince.

As this favourite companion of Prince Hal is evidently of more gentle blood than Gadshill or Bardolph ('the worst they can say of me is that I am a second brother,' *2 Hen. IV*, ii, 2), it is probable that Sh. intended him for a cadet of the family of Poyntz, one of high antiquity, in Gloucestershire. Nicholas de P., and his son Hugh de P., were among the barons in arms against King John. See French, p. 68.

[Poitou.] A former province of Western France, in early times ruled by Counts; passed to the English crown by the marriage of Elinor of Guienne to Henry of Anjou (Hen. II); conquered by Philip Augustus 1205; reverted to Edw. III 1360; retaken by Charles V 1369. See POICTIERS.

Polack. A native (or, the king) of Poland; *Pol.* Polak. 'He smote the sledded P.s on the ice' (*Haml.* i, 1); levies 'against the P.' (*ib.* ii, 2 (2)); 'the P. never will defend it' (*ib.* iv, 4); 'the P. wars' (*ib.* v, 2).

In i, 1, Ff have, variously, 'Pollax,' 'Polax,' and 'Poleaxe' – an error giving rise to unnecessary discussion.

Poland. A former kingdom of Europe; its ruler, 1587–1632, was Sigismund III; a Polish ambassador visited Elizabeth's Court in 1597.

The kitchen-wench's 'rags and the tallow in them' will 'burn a P. winter' (*Com. Err.* iii, 2); the Duke supposed to be in P., *M. for M.* i, 3; 'the main of P.' (*Haml.* iv, 4); 'Fortinbras, with conquest come from P.' (*ib.* v, 2).

Pole, The. The King of Poland. 'Nor will yield to Norway or the P.' (*Haml.* iv, 4).

Pole, Sir Henry, Baron Montague (or **Montacute**) (*c.* 1492–1538). G.s. of George, D. of Clarence; strongly opposed to the suppression of the monasteries; executed for treason on Tower Hill. 'The lord Montacute' (*Hol.* iii, 863).

A warrant for his attachment issued (*Hol.* iii, 863), *Hen. VIII*, i, 1. (This arrest, however, took place eighteen years before his execution. See Clar. p. 111.)

Pole, Michael de la (1394–1415). 3rd E. of Suffolk; served at the siege of Harfleur with his father, who died there. His death at Agincourt recorded, *Hen. V*, iv, 6; mtd., *ib.* iv, 8. Cf. *Hol.* iii, 555.

Pole, William de la (1396–1450). 4th E. and 1st D. of Suffolk; brother and successor of Michael de la Pole, 3rd Earl (*q.v.*); after seeing much service in France he became opponent of Humphrey, D. of Gloucester, and succeeded in bringing about the marriage of Hen. VI with Margaret of Anjou in spite of Gl.'s opposition; escorted Marg. to England 1444; on the death of Gl. and Card. Beaufort, became supreme as Henry's counsellor; incurred the enmity of Richard of York by getting him practically banished to Ireland; made Duke 1448; soon afterward became unpopular for having agreed to the cession of Anjou and Maine to France; was committed to the Tower and banished for five years; was slain at sea, off Dover, perhaps at the instigation of Richard of York.

D.P. *1 Hen. VI.* 'E. of Suffolk.' ii, 4] (in the Temple Gardens) at first evades controversy, but plucks a red rose to show his opposition to Rich. Plantagenet; angry words follow between him and Rich., who calls him 'proud Poole.' iii, 1] *p.m.* iv, 1] (at the King's coronation in Paris) *p.m.* (*Hol.* iii, 606). v, 3] (before Angiers) leads in Margaret of Anjou as his prisoner; struck by her beauty, he wavers between wooing her for himself, or offering her the crown as Henry's wife; craves a parley with her father Reignier; bargains with him concerning the projected match, and guarantees him Anjou and Maine (cf. *Hol.* iii, 624); in parting with Marg. exchanges kisses with her, but resolves to resist temptation, and affect loyalty to his King for ulterior purposes. v, 5] expatiates to Henry on Marg.'s charms and virtues; urges, in opposition to Gl. (*Hol.* iii, 624), that Marg. is daughter of a king, and that her lack of wealth is but a sordid consideration and of no weight; is sent to escort Marg. to England, and reflects that henceforth he 'will rule both her, the King, and realm.'

D.P. *2 Hen. VI.* 'D. of Suffolk.' i, 1] presents Marg., whom he has wedded 'as procurator,' to Henry (*Hol.* iii, 625); presents the 'articles of peace'; is made 'first D. of Suffolk' (*Hol.* iii, 627); (his ambition is animadverted upon by Gl. and other nobles). i, 3] gives confidential advice to Q. Margaret as to her treatment of the great nobles, and assures her that by his means the Duchess of Gl.'s pride will soon be brought low; opposes the appointment of York as regent in France. (i, 4) 'by water shall he die.' ii, 1] (at a royal hawking-party) joins in the bickering between the nobles. ii, 3] is present at the condemnation of the Dss. of Gl. iii, 1] (at Bury) accuses the Duke of Gl. of having instigated his wife's malpractices; advocates the putting to death of Gl.; undertakes to provide soldiers to quell the revolt in Ireland under York's command. iii, 2] learns from the murderers that Gl. has been despatched; later, announces that Gl. has been found dead in his bed; the King, on recovering from a swoon, regards Suffolk with horror and aversion; Suf. is accused by Warwick of being privy to the deed; they depart, to fight; later, Suf. returns, having been attacked by 'the men of Bury' under Warwick; he is banished by Henry (*Hol.* iii, 632); Q. Margaret and he bid each other a passionate farewell, as lovers. iv, 1] is captured at sea, and given as a prisoner to Walter Whitmore (*q.v.*); recalls a warning that he should die by 'water'; is reviled by his captors, and, disdaining to sue for mercy, dragged away and beheaded (cf. *Hol.* iii, 632).

The story of the guilty passion of Marg. and Suf. rests upon no historical basis, and seems founded merely on some phrases in *Hol.* and Hall implying that the Queen held him in high esteem as a friend and counsellor. He did not take M. Prisoner, and the marriage negotiations took place 14 years after the capture of Joan. He was thirty-four years older than Marg., and his wife, Alice Chaucer, accompanied him to France when he went thither as Henry's proxy. Acc. *Hol.* iii, 632, Suffolk's body was found on the sands, and buried at 'Wingfield College in Suffolke.' The prophecy regarding his death, as mtd. in the *Paston Letters*, i, 125 (Arber), was to the effect that he should beware of 'The Tower,' the fulfilment of this being that the ship that captured him was the 'Nicholas of the Tower' (*Hol.* iii, 632).

Polemon. King of Pontus, an ally of M. Antony (*Plut.* p. 207). Mtd. *Ant. Cl.* iii, 6 ('Polemen,' until corrd. by Theobald), the 'King of Pont' being, by an error, made a distinct personage.

Polixenes (1). D.P. *Wint. T.* 'King of Bohemia' (Ff). (i, 1) his affection for Leontes, King of Sicilia, dating from infancy, has been unbroken by separation. i, 2] after staying for nine months at L.'s Court, Pol. resists his earnest invitation to remain longer, but yields to Hermione's persuasion; is informed by Camillo that he has incurred the frenzied jealousy of L., and, to save his life, embarks forthwith secretly for Bohemia with Cam.

(ii, 1) Hermione is accused of adultery with him. (ii, 3) L.'s hatred of him. (iii, 2) his innocence declared by an oracle. iv, 1] (after the lapse of sixteen years) tells Cam. that his son, Prince Florizel, seems to be captivated by a shepherd's daughter (Perdita) and requests him to aid in probing the matter. iv, 4] is present in disguise, when a sheep-shearing festival is being celebrated; converses with Perd., is struck by her beauty, and thinks her 'too noble for this place'; obtains from Florizel an admission that he is about to wed Perd. without his father's leave; abruptly reveals himself, sternly rebukes Fl., and threatens the shepherd with death, and 'his daughter' with dire penalties if ever she permits Fl. to consort with her again. (v, 2) follows the lovers to Sicily; discovers that Perd. is Leontes' lost daughter. v, 3] is present at the reunion of Leontes and Hermione.

The corresponding character in Greene's *Pandosto* is Egistus, King of Sicily; in the novel E. gives Pandosto (Leontes) more cause for jealousy by his marked admiration of the Queen; after escaping from Bohemia his part in the tale is insignificant.

Polixenes (2). A Gk. warrior; mtd. as slain, *Tr. Cr.* v, 5. 'A noble duc' (Caxton, *Recuyell*). Also 'Polyxenes.'

Polonius. D.P. *Haml.* Lord Chamberlain. i, 2] begs the King to permit his son Laertes' departure. i, 3] gives L. counsel on conduct; warns Ophelia against trusting 'Lord Hamlet's vows.' ii, 1] instructs his servant to follow L. to Paris, and secretly to watch him; is led to believe that Haml. is really distraught with love for Oph., and regrets his suspicions. ii, 2] presents the ambassadors from Norway; relates to the King and Queen his discovery of the cause of Haml.'s madness; is bantered mercilessly by Haml.; later, announces the arrival of a troop of players. iii, 1] secretly observes, with the King, an interview of Haml. with Oph. iii, 2] in attendance when the play is presented; later, summons Haml. to the Queen and humours his supposed madness. iii, 3] resolves to overhear Haml.'s conversation with his mother. iii, 4] hides behind the arras, with the Queen's connivance; is slain by Haml. (iv, 1) the murder reported to the King; the disposal of his body. (iv, 2, 3, 5) the effect of his death on his son and daughter. See CORAMBIS.

Polydamas. A Trojan hero. Mtd. Homer, *Il.* xi, 57; xvi, 535; xvii, 40. 'Fierce P. Hath beat down Menon' (*Tr. Cr.* v, 5). 'Son of Anthenor' (Caxton, *Recuyell*).

'Polidamas,' Q; 'Poli(y)damus,' Ff; the right form restored by Pope.

Polydore. Name given to Guiderius, son of Cymbeline, by his supposed father Belarius. ('Polidore,' Ff.) In *Cymb.* (iii, 2) the name occurs once (in Ff) as 'Paladour' (*q.v.*) – an ancient name of Shaftesbury – and some critics have supposed that this should be the name throughout. On the other hand, 'Polydore [Vergil]' is so frequently quoted in the margin of *Hol.* that the name must have been familiar to Sh.

[**Polymestor.**] See HECUBA.

Polyxena. Daughter of Priam; acc. post-Homeric tradition, she was beloved by Achilles, who offered to bring about a peace if Priam would give him his daughter. Ulysses accuses Ach. of being in love with Polyxena, *Tr. Cr.* iii, 3.

Polyxenes. See POLIXENES (2).

Pomfret, Pontefract. A town in the W. Riding of Yorkshire. The Norman castle round which it seems to have arisen was founded *c.* 1076. The obscure origin of the name is discussed at length in *N. and Q.*, 1886–7.

Richard committed to P., *Rich. II*, v, 1; mtd., *ib.* v, 4; the murder of the King at P. Castle, *ib.* v, 5; 'the blood of ... Richard scrap'd from P. stones' (2 *Hen. IV*, i, 1); the murder referred to, 2 *Hen. VI*, ii, 2; Rivers and Grey committed to P., *Rich. III*, ii, 4; mtd., *ib.* iii, 1, 2; Rivers, Grey, and Vaughan led to execution at P. Castle, *ib.* iii, 3; mtd., *ib.* iii, 4, v, 3. (Cf. *Hol.* iii, 715.) Peter of P. (*q.v.*), *John*, iv, 2.

Pomgarnet. For 'Pomegranate'; name of a room in the (Boar's Head) Tavern, *1 Hen. IV*, ii, 4.

Pompeius, Cn. Son of Pompey the Great; sent by his father, 49 B.C., to Alexandria for reinforcements. 'Cleopatra ... guessing by the former access she had with ... Cn. Pompey (the son of Pompey the Great) only for her beauty, she began to have good hope that she might more easily win Antonius' (*Plut.* p. 174). Ant. reviles Cl. as 'a fragment of Cneius Pompey's' (*Ant. Cl.* iii, 13).

Pompeius, Sextus (75–35 B.C.). Younger son of Pompey the Great. Plutarch's account of him is very closely followed by Sh.

D.P. *Ant. Cl.* ii, 1] discusses with Menas and Menecrates the news that the triumvirs are joining forces (*Plut.* p. 179). ii, 6] confers with the triumvirs; alludes to his powerful fleet, and to his hospitality to Antony's mother (*ib.* p. 180); is allowed to hold Sicily and Sardinia on condition of ridding the sea of pirates (*ib. ib.*); invites the triumvirs to a feast on his galley (*ib. ib.*). ii, 7] during the banquet is urged by Menas (*q.v.*) to cut the cables, but refuses (*ib. ib.*). ('Pompey,' except in i, 2, 3; iii, 6.)

'The young Pompey, a frank but thoughtless soul, the image of political levity, opposed to the moderate Octavius, fights for the cause of freedom in company with pirates, foolishly brave, without friends... In the first words we hear him utter he shows himself less pious than the pirates, in the last action in which we see him, less impious than they.' (Gervinus, *Sh. Comm.* (1875), p. 744.)

Pompey. See CLOWN (3).

Pompey the Great. Cn. Pompeius Magnus, triumvir (106–48 B.C.). Slain after the Battle of Pharsalia by Egyptians acting under the orders of the ministers of Ptolemy XII. The murderers were put to death by Jul. Caes. 'Savage islanders murdered P.' (2 *Hen. VI*, iv, 1). Acc. Plutarch (North's transln. (1595), pp. 712–13), P. was slain by Septimius, Salvius, and Achillas, an Egyptian.

One of the 'Nine Worthies' (*q.v.*); represented by Costard, 'Because of his great limb or joint'; he performs the part with gusto, *L.L.L.* v, 1, 2, but calls him 'P. the big' (*ib.* v, 2, l. 553; cf. *Hen. V*, iv, 7, l. 14). See POMPION.

Pompion. A blunder of Costard's for 'Pompey'; *L.L.L.* v, 2. A pompion is a pumpkin.

Pont. For 'Pontus,' district in N.E. of Asia Minor (*Plut.* p. 207); mtd. *Ant. Cl.* iii, 6. See POLEMON.

Pontefract. See POMFRET.

Pontic Sea. See PROPONTIC.

[**Poole.**] See DORSETSHIRE.

Poole. See POLE.

Pope, Thomas (*ob.* 1603). Mtd. as a 'principal actor' in F1 ('Thomas Poope').

Popes. The following are mtd., or alluded to, in *Sh.*: Innocent III, Eugenius IV, Leo X, Clement VII (*qq.v.*).

The Pope who in 1570 issued the bull *Regnans in excelso*, excommunicating Queen Elizabeth, was Pius V, who is probably obliquely aimed at in *John*.

[**Porcia.**] See PORTIA (1).

Porpentine, The. Name of an inn. *Com. Err.* iii, 1, 2; iv, 1; v, 1.

Changed to 'Porcupine' by Rowe.

Port le Blanc. ('Port le Blan,' F1; 'le Port Blan,' Qq; 'Le Porte blanc,' *Hol.* iii, 497.) In Brittany, Dept. Côtes-du-Nord. Bolingbroke sails thence for England, *Rich. II*, ii, 1.

Porter (1). D.P. *2 Hen. IV.* i, 1] (at the gate of Warkworth Castle) tells Lord Bardolph where he may find Northumberland.

Porter (2). D.P. *Macb.* ii, 3] soliloquizes; admits Macduff and Lenox; confesses that he had been 'carousing till the second cock.'

The authenticity and dramatic propriety of the scene in which the Porter appears have been much disputed by commentators (Coleridge, *Notes and Lectures* (1849), i, 249; Heraud, *Sh.'s Inner Life* (1865), p. 513; De Quincey, 'The Knocking at the Gate, *Misc. Essays*).

Porter (3). Servitor of the Countess of Auvergne. D.P. *1 Hen. VI.* ii, 3] aids his mistress in attempting to make Talbot prisoner.

Porter and his Man. D.PP. *Hen. VIII.* v, 4] endeavour, with indifferent success, to control the crowds eager to see the christening procession of Elizabeth.

Portia (1). More correctly 'Porcia'; daughter of Cato Uticensis; married first to M. Bibulus and secondly to M. Brutus. She induced her husband to disclose to her the conspiracy against Caesar, and is said to have inflicted 'a great gash' (*Plut.* p. 115) in her thigh to show her courage. On the fatal Ides of March she swooned from anxiety, and Brutus was told that she was dead. After the death of B. at Philippi she put an end to her life by 'swallowing live coals' – suffocation by the fumes of charcoal being probably the actual means.

D.P. *Jul. C.* i, 2] *p.m.* ii, 1] entreats Brutus to confide in her, and tell her the cause of his ungentle looks, his moody silence she will not believe him when he curtly pleads ill health, and on her knees beseeches him to unfold his grief to his once-loved wife; she knows that mysterious men have had resort to him, and urges that she, 'Cato's daughter,' can be trusted with any secret; she discloses that she has wounded herself to make proof of her constancy; she is promised a disclosure shortly. ii, 4] in feverish agitation sends Lucius to the Capitol, to bring her tidings of anything unusual that may be occurring; converses with the Soothsayer (*q.v.*). (iv, 3) her death is announced by Brutus – 'she fell distract … and swallow'd fire.'

Portia (2). D.P. *M.V.* A rich heiress. i, 2] in converse with her maid Nerissa, repines at the galling conditions of her father's will, by which she is obliged to accept the suitor who chooses the right casket of three; she comments on her suitors as N. names them, and betrays a keen interest in a certain Venetian, Bassanio, who once visited her father; four of her suitors seek to take their leave, and a fifth is reported at hand. ii, 1] courteously receives the Prince of Morocco, whose trial is to be made after dinner. ii, 7] is present when the Pr. makes choice; he fails, and Portia remarks (*sol.*) 'a gentle riddance. Let all of his complexion choose me so.' ii, 9] witnesses the Pr. of Arragon's failure; hears that 'a young Venetian has arrived.' iii, 2] urges Bassanio to 'pause a day or two Before you hazard'; on his persisting in coming to the trial, she longs for his success; he chooses the right casket, and she commits herself to him with love and humility; on hearing of Antonio's grievous need, offers 'to pay the petty debt twenty times over' and urges Bas. to go forthwith to aid his friend. iii, 4] resolves to follow B., with Nerissa, and partly unfolds her ultimate design to the latter. iv, 1] in the guise of 'a young doctor of Rome' defends Antonio before the Magnificoes, and utterly discomfits Shylock; still in disguise, begs Bas. for a ring she had given him. iv, 2] he reluctantly sends it to her. v, 1] reaches Belmont at night; pretends to discover that Bas. has parted with the ring, and chides him sorely before divulging the merry deception.

For a very full analysis of the character, which she herself assumed, see Lady Martin's *Sh.'s Fem. Char.* (1887), pp. 25 ff.

Portugal, Bay of. 'My affection hath an unknown bottom, like the bay of P.' (*A.Y.L.* iv, 1).

Perh. the deep part of the sea off the coast of P. between Lisbon and Oporto. The term is used by Ralegh; see Edwards, *Life of R.* ii, 56 (Wright).

[**Pothinus.**] See PHOTINUS.

Poton de Xaintrailles. One of the greatest soldiers of the 15th cent. He became Marshal of France (see XAINTRAILLES). In 1431 at an action fought at Beauvais many Frenchmen were made prisoners, and 'amongst others of the cheefest prisoners, that valiant capteine, Pouton de Santrails was one; who without delaie was exchanged for the lord Talbot, before taken prisoner at the battell of Pataie' (*Hol.* iii, 606). As a fact, Talbot was not released until 1433, and Poton had been interned in London for about two years before the exchange was made.

'*Tal.* The Duke of Bedford had a prisoner Call'd the brave Ponton de Saintrailles; For him I was exchanged and ransomed' (*1 Hen. VI*, i, 4; 'Santrayle,' or '-ile,' Ff).

Historically, the Battle of Patay had not been fought when the events of the scene occurred.

Potpan. A servant; *Rom. J.* i, 5 (2).

Pots. Stabbed by Half-can; *M. for M.* iv, 3.

Poysam. 'Young Charbon the puritan, and old Poysam the papist, howsome'er their hearts are severed in religion, their heads are both one' (*All's Well*, i, 3).

According to Malone's conjecture, 'Poysam' is for 'poisson,' in allusion to the use of fish on fast-days, while 'Charbon' refors to the 'fiery zeal' of the Puritans. To eat fish was, in fact, reputed a badge of Popery; the saying, 'He's an honest man, and eats no fish,' implied that 'He's a protestant, and friend to the government.' Acc. another suggestion (Camb.), 'Ch.' may be for 'chair bonne' as opposed to Lenten fare. There is a Fr. proverb: 'Jeune chair et vicil poisson.'

Prague, Hermit of. 'The old hermit of Pr., that never saw pen and ink, very wittily said ... "that that is, is" ' (*T. Nt.* iv, 2). See GORBODUC.

Douce, taking Feste's nonsense seriously, held that this was not the well-known Jerome of Pr., but a certain hermit of Camaldoli, also born in Prague.

Prat, Mother. Falstaff, in disguise as 'my maid's aunt, the fat woman of Brentford,' is thus addressed by Mrs Page; *M.W.W.* iv, 2. See GILLIAN.

The name occurs in the Brentford registers for 1624 (Halliwell).

Prester John. Legendary Christian potentate of a vague region in the East, concerning whose wealth, vast armies, and conquests extravagant tales were current in the 12th–14th cents. Later, he was definitely located in Abyssinia.

Benedick, *M. Ado*, ii, 1, declares that he would rather 'bring you the length of Pr. J.'s foot' than converse with Beatrice.

'Benedick is not thinking so much of the danger of such an enterprise as of its remoteness, which would take him out of the reach of Beatrice' (Clar.).

Priam, Priamus. King of Troy at the time of the Trojan War. Acc. Homer (*Il.* xxiv, 495 ff.), he was the father of fifty sons, nineteen of whom were the children of Hecuba (*q.v.*). Acc. later poets, the aged King was slain at the altar of Jupiter by Pyrrhus (Virg. *Aen.* ii, 512 ff.).

'Was this [Helen] King P.'s joy?' (*All's Well*, i, 3); 'such a man ... drew P.'s curtain in the dead of night, And would have told him half his Troy was burnt; But P. found the fire ere he his tongue' (*2 Hen. IV*, i, 1); 'sad ... As P. was for all his valiant sons' (*3 Hen. VI*, ii, 5); 'five-and-twenty ... sons, half of the number that King P. had' (*T. And.* i, 1); 'King P.'s Troy' (*ib.* v, 3); slain by Pyrrhus, *Haml.* ii, 2. Latin: 'Hic steterat Priami regia celsa senis' (*Tam. Sh.* iii, 1; *cf.* Ovid, *Her.* i, 34).

D.P. *Tr. Cr.* ('Priamus,' ii, 2, and v, 3.) (Prol.) 'P.'s six-gated city.' (i, 1) 'P.'s royal table.' (i, 3) mtd. ii, 2] consults his sons as to whether Helen should be restored to the Greeks; rebukes Paris. (iii, 1) 'P.'s hall.' (iii, 3) mtd. (iv, 2) mtd. (iv, 4) 'as safe as P. is in Ilion.' (iv, 5) mtd. v, 3] tries to dissuade Hector from taking the field that day. (v, 8) mtd. (v, 11) Hector's death 'will P. turn to stone.'

Priam's death, at the hand of Pyrrhus, is depicted in the 'skilful painting' viewed by Lucrece, who moralizes on the fall of Troy and Priam's folly in believing Sinon, *Lucr.* 1365 ff.

Priapus. God of fertility. 'She's able to freeze the god P.' (*Per.* iv, 6).

Priest (1). D.P. *Haml.* v, 1] tells Laertes that it is only by 'great command' that Ophelia is buried in sanctified ground; is reviled by L.

Priest (2). D.P. *Rich. III.* See JOHN, SIR.

Priest (3). D.P. *T. Nt.* iv, 3] *p.m.* v, 1] testifies to the betrothal of Olivia and Sebastian.

Princess of France. D.P. *L.L.L.* Daughter of the King of France. (i, 1) visits Navarre 'in embassy' to negotiate the surrender of Aquitaine to her father. ii, 1] discusses the situation with Boyet, whom she sends to King Ferdinand; discovers that her ladies are in love with three of the courtiers; receives the King, and opens negotiation with him. iv, 1] visits the park to shoot deer, but deprecates the sport; listens to Armado's intercepted letter. v, 2] discusses with her ladies the letters and gifts they have received from their lovers; the King and his train appear, disguised as Russians, and the ladies being masked, the Princess is wooed by Biron in mistake for Rosaline; on the departure of the 'Muscovites' the Princess derides their 'poverty in wit'; on the reappearance of the King and courtiers in their proper attire she rebukes them for the contemplated breach of their vows, and refuses to visit the Court – 'Nor God, nor I, delights in perjured men'; she informs the King that she had penetrated their disguise, and that he had wooed the wrong lady; witnesses the pageant of 'The Nine Worthies'; receives news of her father's death; expresses her intention of immediately departing and of lamenting her father in solitude for a year; bids the King betake himself 'To some forlorn and naked hermitage' for a like period, at the end of which time, if his love bear the trial, she will marry him.

Priscian. A famous Roman grammarian (*fl. c.* A.D. 500), whose chief treatise, *Commentariorum Grammaticorum Libri xviii*, was in use as a text-book throughout the middle ages. One who violated the rules of Latin grammar was said 'to break P.'s head' – 'diminuis Prisciani caput.' 'P. a little scratched, 'twill serve' (*L.L.L.* v, 1).

Procrus. A perversion of 'Procris.' See SHAFALUS.

Proculeius, C. A Roman *eques*, friend of Augustus. ('Procleius' in Plutarch, not followed by North.)

D.P. *Ant. Cl.* (iv, 15) Ant. bids Cl. trust 'none about Caesar' but Pr. v, 1] is sent to take Cleopatra alive. v, 2] confers with her through barred gates; gains access to the Monument by a ladder; disarms Cl.; seeks to reassure her. (The narrative of *Plut.* pp. 222–3, is closely followed throughout.)

Promethean, *adj.* 'P. fire' (*L.L.L.* iv, 3); 'P. heat' (*Oth.* v, 2).

Prometheus. Son of the Titan Iapetus; according to one legend he stole fire from heaven, and was chained to Mt Caucasus to be tortured by an eagle. (Latin translns. of the *Prometheus Vinctus* of Aeschylus were published in 1555 and 1567.) 'P. tied to Caucasus' (*T. And.* ii, 1). (See TITYUS.)

Cf. Peele, *Arr. of Paris*, i, 2, l. 42; *Edw. I*, iv, 21.

[Promos and Cassandra.] See MEASURE FOR MEASURE.

Propontick, Propontis. *i.e.* the Sea of Marmora, so called from being 'before the Pontus,' or Euxine. 'The Pontic Sea, Whose icy current ... keeps due on To the Propontick and the Hellespont' (*Oth.* iii, 3).

This passage, omitted in Q1, is clearly based on Holland's *Pliny* (1601), ii, 97: 'And the sea Pontus evermore floweth and runneth out into Propontis, but the sea never retireth backe againe within Pontus.'

Proserpina, Proserpine. Dau. of Jupiter and Ceres (Demeter); acc. one legend, she was carried off by Pluto, while gathering flowers near Enna, and made queen of the underworld.

'O, Pr., For the flowers now, that, frighted, thou let'st fall From Dis's waggon!' (*Wint. T.* iv, 3; for this incident *cf.* Ovid, *Metam.* v, 399: 'Collecti flores tunicis cecidere remissis'); 'Thou art as full of envy at his greatness, as Cerberus at Pr.'s beauty' (*Tr. Cr.* ii, 1).

Prosper. See PROSPERO.

Prospero. D.P. *Temp.* ('Prosper,' ii, 1, 2 (2); iii, 3.) 'The right Duke of Millaine' (F1). i, 2] assures his daughter Miranda that no harm has befallen to any soul on board Alonso's vessel, which she has just seen driven ashore in the storm magically raised by Ariel; doffing his 'magic garment,' he relates the story of his life: how that, 'being transported and rapt in secret studies,' he handed over the government of Milan to his brother Antonio, who, treacherously calling in the aid of Alonso, King of Naples, expelled Pr., twelve years before the opening of the play, to be cast adrift in a rotten and unrigged boat, with his little daughter, and how they were cast on the desolate island where they now dwell. Pr. then summons Ariel, whom he entrusts with further commands, but chides for his impatient longing for liberty; incidentally relates the story of the sylph's deliverance; summons Caliban, and, in threatening and upbraiding him, throws light on the history and character of the 'deformed slave'; Ferdinand, son of Alonso, enters – led by Ariel's music – and immediately becomes enamoured of Miranda; Pr., though secretly rejoicing at the success of his design, feigns, 'lest too light winning make the prize light,' to regard the Prince as an impostor and a spy; threatens him with chains, and, casting a spell upon him, leads him away to perform a laborious task. (ii, 1) mtd. iii, 1] unseen by them, observes with approval the growth of love between Ferd. and Mir. (iii, 2) his murder plotted. iii, 3] 'invisible,' he is present when a magical and illusory banquet is offered by spirits to Alonso and his train, and the 'three men of sin' are denounced by Ar. iv, 1] admits to Ferd. that his harsh treatment was but a trial of his love, and yields him his daughter's hand, not without a warning – 'do not give dalliance too much the rein'; bids Ar. and his 'meaner fellows' present to the 'young couple,' as a 'vanity' of his magical art, a stately masque; suddenly recalls the plot contrived by Caliban and his companions against his life, and instructs Ar. how to checkmate it; watches the discomfiture of the conspirators. v, 1] assumes his magic robes, and instructs Ar. to bring before him Alonso and his train, who are spell-bound close at hand; on Ar.'s departure, recalls (*sol.*) the achievements of his magic art, but resolves to bury his staff, and, 'deeper than did ever plummet sound,' to drown his book; sternly rebukes the King and his companions for their villany, and dons the apparel he had worn as D. of Milan; pronounces his forgiveness of his late enemies, restores Ferd. to his father, and presents Miranda as the Prince's affianced bride; prepares to sail in the King's ship to Naples – thence to return to Milan, where 'every third thought shall be my grave.'

Prospero was the name of a character in Jonson's *Every Man in his Humour*, acted in 1595 or 1596 (in which Sh. played a part); also of a contemporary Italian riding-master in London. An illustration of Pr.'s 'saddle' is reproduced in *Sh. Eng.* ii, 419. For a comparison of Prospero with (Goethe's) Faust see Dr R. Garnett, *Irving Sh.* (1890), p. 185.

Proteus (1). (Gk. mythol.) The prophetic old man of the sea, who, in order to escape the necessity of prophesying, was wont to assume ever-varying shapes (Ovid, *Ars Am.* i, 761; *Fasti*, i, 369). Gloucester boasts: 'I can ... Change shapes with P., for advantages' (*3 Hen. VI*, iii, 2).

Proteus (2). ('Protheus,' F1.) D.P. *T.G.V.* One of 'the two Gentlemen.' i, 1] bids adieu to his friend Valentine, who is setting out for Milan; admits (*sol.*) that his love for Julia has 'metamorphosed him,' and makes him 'set the world at naught'; is given to understand that a letter from him has been delivered by Speed to J. (i, 2) is discussed by J. and Lucetta. i, 3] while reading a letter from J. is abruptly ordered by his father to betake himself to Milan. (ii, 1) mtd. ii, 2] bids J. farewell, and receives a ring from her. (ii, 3) sets out. ii, 4] (is eulogized by Val. to the Duke); reaches Milan; is presented to Silvia; is told by Val. that he is about to flee with Sil. at night; (*sol.*) admits that he has himself become violently enamoured of Silvia. ii, 6] (*sol.*) love has made him reckless, and he determines to reveal to the Duke his daughter's intended flight. (ii, 7) his faithlessness is lamented by Julia. iii, 1] with assumed unwillingness, betray's Val.'s secret to the Duke; later, informs the banished Val. that Silvia is imprisoned, but promises to convey Val.'s letter to her. iii, 2] undertakes to 'dispraise' Val. to Sil. and to promote Thurio's suit; advises Th. to serenade Sil. iv, 2] (*sol.*) admits that his treachery has brought him no reward; is joined by Th. and his musicians; is observed by Julia in her disguise; attempts to soften Silvia's heart, but in vain. iv, 4] takes 'Sebastian' (Julia) into his service; is dismayed to learn that Launce has lost the 'little jewel' of a dog he had destined for Silvia; bids Julia take a ring (her own) to Sil. v, 2] gives bantering replies to Th., who inquires how his suit prospers; learns that Sil. has fled, and resolves to follow her. v, 4] having rescued Sil. from a band of outlaws, in the forest, woos her roughly and is confronted by Val.; overcome by Val.'s reproaches, begs his forgiveness; discovers that 'Sebastian' is Julia, and all his former love for her returns.

'The name ... exactly describes the character of him who bears it. This is a sort of art which Sh. does not as a rule make use of, at least in the case of his leading persons.' (J. W. Hales, *N. S. S. Tr.*, 1874, Pt. I, p. 25.) Don Feliz in Montemayor's story.

Provincial. 'With two Pr. roses on my razed shoes' (*Haml.* iii, 2). Variously interpreted as roses of Provins, or of Provence, which according to Cotgrave are, respectively, 'the ordinarie double red Rose,' and 'the double Damaske Rose.'

Provost. D.P. *M. for M.* i, 3] excuses himself for conducting Claudio publicly to prison. ii, 1] is ordered to bring Cl. his confessor before execution. ii, 2] pities Cl., and trusts that he may be reprieved; is desired to witness Angelo's interview with Isabella and Lucio. ii, 3] grants 'Friar Lodowick' an interview with Julia, in prison. iii, 1] grants Cl. an interview with Isabella; later, permits 'Friar Lodowick' to confer alone with her. iii, 2] in attendance. iv, 2] procures Pompey as an assistant to the executioner; later, presents to Cl. his death-warrant; laments Angelo's severity; consents, on 'Friar Lodowick's earnest persuasion, and on being shown the Duke's seal, to have Barnardine substituted for Cl. iv, 3] suggests presenting the head of Ragozine, who has just died, to Ang. as Cl.'s; later, carries out his suggestion. v, 1] as ordered, arrests

'Friar Lodowick'; later, accompanies Ang. and Mariana to their compulsory wedding; later, returns with them; declares that Cl. was beheaded; the Duke demands his keys; later brings Barnardine and Cl. before the Duke, and is promised promotion for his 'care and secrecy.'

The word 'Provost,' which does not occur elsewhere in *Sh.*, has many meanings, and here seems equivalent to 'keeper of the prison'; *cf.* 'Seldom, when the steeled gaoler is the friend of man' (iv, 2).

Prudence, Sir. Nonce-name applied by Antonio to Gonzalo; *Temp.* ii, 1.

Psalmist, The. 'Death, as the Ps. saith, is certain to all' (2 *Hen. IV*, iii, 2). Apparently an allusion to Psalm xc, 10: 'the days of our age are threescore years and ten,' etc.

Ptolemy. Πτολεμαῖος, name of 13 kings of Egypt, *c.* 323–43 B.C. 'The Ptolemies' Pyramises' (*Ant. Cl.* ii, 7); 'the circle [crown] of the Pt.s' (*ib.* iii, 10).

Ptolemy (Philadelphus). Son of Mark Antony and Cleopatra; his life was spared by Augustus, but nothing more is recorded of him. 'To Pt. he assigned Syria, Cilicia and Phoenicia' (*Ant. Cl.* iii, 6). (Cf. *Plut.* p. 202.)

Ptolemy XII. King of Egypt, eldest son of Ptol. XI (Auletes); became joint ruler of Egypt with his sister and wife, Cleopatra (51 B.C.); defeated by Jul. Caes. and drowned in the Nile (47 B.C.). 'Queen of Pt.' (*Ant. Cl.* i, 4); 'bed of Pt.' (*ib. ib.*).

On the death of Pt., Cleo. was nominally married to another brother of the same name, who was put to death, as a mere child, 43 B.C.

Publicola, L. Gellius. Leader of the right wing of Antony's fleet at Actium (*Plut.* p. 210). Mtd. *Ant. Cl.* iii, 7.

Since he is not mentioned subsequently to the battle, it is supposed he perished in it.

Publicola, Valerius. Consul, as colleague of L. Junius Brutus, in the first year of the Republic. Subject of one of Plutarch's *Lives*. 'Valeria the noble sister of Publicola' (*Cor.* v, 3); cf. *Plut.* p. 34.

Publius (1). D.P. *Jul. C.* 'A senator.' ii, 2] greets Caesar on the morning of his assassination. iii, 1] after the murder, is 'quite confounded by this meeting.'

The character cannot be historically identified, but the same name is given to Mark Antony's sister's son, as one of the proscribed, *Jul. C.* iv, 1. This does not agree with Plutarch's account (p. 170), which names Lucius Caesar, Antony's uncle, as the victim.

Publius (2). Mtd. as an ancestor of Caius Marcius, 'of the same house Publius and Quintus were, That our best water brought by conduits hither' (*Cor.* ii, 3; cf. *Plut.* p. 1).

Publius (3). D.P. *T. And.* 'Son to Marcus the tribune.' iv, 3] humours the madness of his uncle Titus. v, 2] helps to bind Chiron and Demetrius.

Publius Cimber. Mtd. as brother to Metellus C.; the conspirators importune Caesar for his 'enfranchisement' immediately before they strike, *Jul. C.* iii, 1.

The name seems to be an invention of Sh.

Pucelle, La. Joan of Arc thus named. *1 Hen. VI*, i, 2, 4, 5; ii, 1; iii, 2 (4), 3 (2). 'Puzel' in Ff, except once, *ib.* iii, 2. Talbot puns upon the name, *ib.* i, 4.

Puck. D.P. *M.N.D.* 'Or Robin-good-fellow, a Fairy' (Rowe). ii, 1] warns a fairy attending on Titania to beware lest his mistress should be seen by 'jealous' Oberon; gaily admits that he is a 'shrewd and knavish sprite,' delighting in mischief, but ready to work for those that are civil to him; is sent by Ob. to fetch the flower 'love-in-idleness'; later, returns with it and is bidden to apply its juice to the eyes of a youth in 'Athenian garments.' ii, 3] administers the charm to the sleeping Lysander. iii, 1] interrupts the clowns' rehearsal of their interlude and provides Bottom with an ass's head; scatters the clowns, in terror, with strange sounds and appearances. iii, 2] reports his doings to Ob.; on the entrance of Dem. admits his blunder and is sent to fetch Helena; returns in joyful anticipation of forthcoming confusion; is ordered by Ob. to overcast the night with a fog, to lead the rivals astray by counterfeiting their voices, and eventually to apply a counter-charm to Lys.; carries out his orders faithfully. iv, 1] disenchants Bottom; warns Ob. that he hears 'the morning lark.' v, 1] is harbinger to the fairy train who enter the palace of Theseus at dead of night; speaks the Epilogue.

'Puck' is a generic term rather than a proper name, 'pouk,' 'pouke,' 'puke' in contemporary, or earlier, writers being used to denote what Rabelais calls 'un petit diabloteau.' It is to be observed that in the Epilogue P. speaks of himself as 'an honest P.' and 'the P.' Puck's identification of himself with Robin Goodfellow, or Hob-goblin, is an arbitrary link with current folk-lore for which Sh. is responsible. Thore is no satisfactory evidence that an alleged ballad entitled *The Merrie Puck, or Robin Goodfellow*, was anterior to *M.N.D.*

'He is, indeed, a most Epicurean little gentleman, dealing in quaint devices, and faring in dainty delights' (W. Hazlitt).

Pudding. As a personal name. 'Young Drop-heir that killed P.' (*M. for M.* iv, 3).

Puff. Name of a person apparently well known for his obesity. 'Thou [Falstaff] are now one of the greatest men of the realm. *Sil.* By'r lady, I think a be, but goodman P. of Barson' (2 *Hen. IV*, v, 3). See BARSON.

Pursuivant. D.P. *Rich. III.* iii, 2] is cheerfully greeted by Hastings on his way to the Tower. ('Hastin. a Purssuant,' Qq.)

This meeting is described at some length in *Hol.* p. 723, where it is stated that the P.'s name was also Hastings. A pursuivant was one of the third order of heraldic officers.

Pye Corner. At the N. end of Giltspur Street, acc. Stow, so called from an inn, The Pie; at this point the Great Fire stopped; mtd. 2 *Hen. IV*, ii, 2.

Pygmalion. A king of Cyprus who fell in love with the ivory image of a maiden, which he himself had made. At his prayer Aphrodite breathed life into the image and P. wedded the newly created being (Ovid, *Metam.* x, 243 ff.).

'Is there none of P.'s images, newly made woman, to be had now?' (*M. for M.* iii, 2).

Pygmies. 'In the edge and skirts of the mountains [of India] the Pigmaei Spythamei are reported to bee; called they are so, for that they are but a cubite of three shaftments (or spannes) high' (Holland's *Pliny*, vii, 2); in Mercator's *Atlas* (1602), there is inscribed on an island near the N. Pole: 'Pygmaei hic habitant 4 ad summum pedes longi, quemadmodum illi quos in Gronlandia Screlingers vocant' (Anders, *Sh.'s Books*, p. 237).

'*Bene.* I will ... do you any embassage to the Pigmies, rather than hold three words conference with this harpy' (*M. Ado*, ii, 1).

Pyramus. The part of Pyr. in the Interlude (*M.N.D.* v, 1) is played by Nick Bottom (*q.v.*). Mtd., i, 2 (7); iii, 1 (13), 2 (2); iv, 1, 2 (2); v, 1 (11). (In Ff usually, but not invariably, 'Piramus.') See THISBE.

'So pale did shine the moon on P., When he by night lay bath'd in maiden blood' (*T. And.* ii, 4).

Pyrenean. For 'Pyrenees,' following the *Lat.* 'Pyrenaei (*sc.* montes)'; *cf.* Holland's *Pliny*, iv, 17, 'the mountaine Pyrenaeus.' 'And talking of ... The Pyrencan and the river Po' (*John*, i, 1).

'Perennean' and 'Pyrrenean,' Ff.

Pyrrhus. Son of Achilles, otherwise known as Neoptolemus. At the taking of Troy he slew and beheaded Priam beside the altar of Jove (Virg. *Aen.* ii, 547 ff.), and sacrificed Polyxena to the spirit of his father. (Ovid, *Metam.* xiii, 448 ff.)

'It must grieve young Pyrrhus now at home' (to hear that Achilles loves Polyxena) (*Tr. Cr.* iii, 3); the slaying of Priam by Pyr. is magniloquently described in the declamations begun by Hamlet and continued by the First Player, *Haml.* ii, 2; mtd., *Lucr.* 1448, 1467.

Pythagoras. Of Samos; Greek philosopher chiefly famous, popularly, for his doctrine of the transmigration of souls. 'The opinion of P. concerning wild-fowl' (*T. Nt.* iv, 2); 'to hold opinion with P., that souls of animals infuse themselves into the trunks of men' (*M.V.* iv, 1); 'since P.'s time, that I was an Irish rat' (*A. Y. L.* iii, 2).

In Ovid, *Metam.* xv, 60 ff., Pythagoras is introduced expounding at large his doctrine of metempsychosis.

Q

Queen, Wife to Cymbeline. D.P. *Cymb.* (i, 2) having, as a widow, married the King, desires to see her son Cloten wedded to Imogen, Cymb.'s daughter. i, 2] permits Im. and Posthumus to have a brief farewell interview, but 'moves' the King 'to walk this way'; later, learns from Pisanio, to whom she is gracious, that Cl. and Post. have crossed swords. (i, 3) would confer with Im. i, 5] sends her ladies to gather flowers; receives poisonous drugs from Cornelius on the pretext that she needs them for experiment on animals; flatters Pisanio, and promises him 'preferment,' but, believing him faithful to his master, gives him the box of poison with the assurance that she knows not 'what is more cordial'; welcomes the flower-gatherers. (ii, 1) mtd. ii, 3] suggests to Cl. the best way of wooing Imogen. iii, 1] scornfully persuades Cymb. to reject the terms offered by Rome. (iii, 4) mtd. iii, 5] secretly rejoices that Im. has gone 'to death or to dishonour.' (iv, 2) mtd. (iv, 3) is reported to lie sick 'upon a desperate bed.' (v, 5) she dies 'with horror,' confessing that she had resolved to poison Cymb., whom she had never loved, that she had plotted also against Imogen, and that she 'repented' that the evils she had hatched 'were not effected'; such were her beauty and charm, that Cymb. declares 'It had been vicious To have mistrusted her.'

Queen to King Richard. D.P. *Rich. II.* ii, 1] is present at Gaunt's death-bed. ii, 2] is oppressed by dark forebodings; learns that Bolingbroke has landed, and that the Percies are in revolt. iii, 4] rejects the diversions proposed by her ladies; overhears a gardener discoursing on state affairs, and gathers from him Bolingbroke's triumph. v, 1] greets Richard on his way to the Tower; laments over his broken spirit; learns that she must 'away to France' and sorrowfully bids her husband farewell.

Richard's 1st wife, Anne of Bohemia, died in 1394; 'the Queen' of this play is therefore, historically, Isabella, d. of Charles VI of France, whom Richard married in 1396, and who, according to most authorities, was but 11 or 12 years old at his deposition. She became wife of Charles d' Angoulême, and died in 1410. (Holinshed merely alludes to her marriage with Richard.)

Queubus, Equinoctial of. See PIGROGROMITUS.

[**Quickly.**] The 'Vintner,' who appears as D.P., *1 Hen. IV*, ii, 4, and announces to Prince Hal the arrival of Falstaff, is presumably husband to the hostess, Mistress Q.

Quickly, Mistress (1). D.P. *1 Hen. IV.* 'Hostess of a tavern in Eastcheap' (Rowe). ii, 4] brings a message to 'my lord the Prince'; applauds Falstaff's personation of the King; announces the Sheriff. iii, 3] has a pungent altercation with Fal., who insists that his ring has been stolen in the tavern; reminds him of the money he owes her; appeals to Prince Hal, and accuses Fal. of slandering him; is ultimately 'forgiven.'

The references to her husband (iii, 3) show her to be a married woman.

D.P. *2 Hen. IV.* 'Hostess of a tavern in Eastcheap' (Ff); now a widow. ii, 1] endeavours to have Fal. arrested for debt; speaks of herself as 'a poor lone woman'; objurgates F. as 'a honey-seed, a manqueller'; with much circumlocution tries to state her case to the Lord Chief Justice; declares that Fal. promised her marriage; is cajoled by Fal. to withdraw her action and advance him a further loan. (ii, 2) mtd. as 'old mistress Q.' ii, 4] ministers to Doll, who has 'drunk too much canaries'; composes the 'discord' between D. and Fal.; demurs to the admission of the 'swaggerer' Pistol, but is civil to him; is dismayed at the brawl that ensues; in bidding Fal. farewell, mentions that she has known him 'twenty-nine years.' v, 4] is haled to prison, with Doll, in consequence of a fatal turmoil in the tavern.

D.P. *Hen. V.* Now wife to Pistol. ii, 1] begs Bardolph to compose the rising quarrel between Nym and her jealous husband; is summoned to attend Fal., who 'is very ill' – 'the King has killed his heart'; later, begs the 'sweet men' to 'come in quickly to Sir John.' ii, 3] describes the death of Fal. (v, 1) Pistol hears that she 'is dead i' the spital.'

In v, 1, Pistol speaks of her as 'Doll' (FfQq), whereas in ii, 1, she is 'Nell.' The former may be a term of endearment (Nicholson); Capell and most succeeding edrs. read 'Nell' in v, 1.

Quickly, Mistress (2). D.P. *M.W.W.* 'Servant to Dr Caius.' (i, 2) described by Evans as C.'s 'nurse, or his dry nurse, or his cook, or his laundry, his washer, and his wringer.' i, 4] questions Simple about his master, Slender; conceals him in a closet on C.'s return; soothes C. when he discovers the intruder; tells Simple that C. is in love with Anne Page; tells Fenton that she is sure Anne loves him. ii, 1] visits Anne. ii, 2] informs Falstaff that both Mrs Ford and Mrs Page are in love with him, and highly commends their virtue. (iii, 2) mtd. (iii, 3) termed by Mrs Ford 'that foolish carrion.' iii, 4] is ready to further the suit of any one of Anne's wooers: 'I will do what I can for them all three.' iii, 5] conveys a message to Fal. from Mrs Ford. iv, 1] interrupts Evans' examination of William in Latin. iv, 5] brings Fal. a letter. v, 1] promises to procure a chain and horns for Fal. v, 5] (acc. the st. dirs. of Q, she enacts the Queen of the Fairies in the park. In the st. dirs. of Ff the impersonator of the Queen is not specified, but speeches appropriate to the part are given to Quickly. In iv, 6, Ff, however, it is distinctly stated by Fenton that Anne Page is to present the Fairy Queen, and Knight – rightly as it would seem – gives the part to her).

It is generally held that the Hostess of the Histories is not identical with Caius' housekeeper in *M.W.W.* – the fact that the latter is, at first, unknown to Fal., would seem, indeed, conclusive on the point. And yet the simplicity of Quickly's nature, and the comicalities of her phraseology may well make the reader of the four plays feel that the same garrulous dame is presented to us throughout. In attempting, however, to construct a 'biography' of Mistress Quickly we may be attributing too much actuality to the offspring of imagination. The creatures of the dramatist have, in fact, a privilege not accorded to historical personages – the right, namely, of claiming *partial* identity, and an appeal to this privilege seems to meet the difficulties of the present case, without our having recourse to the suggested expedient of making the Quicklys 'sisters, or sisters-in-law.'

Quinapalus. An imaginary authority, feigned by Feste; *T. Nt.* i, 5.

Quince, Peter. D.P. *M.N.D.* A carpenter. i, 2] allots their parts to the players in the Interlude; persuades Bottom to remain content with the part of Pyramus. iii, 1] discusses objections made by the players; on the entrance of B. with an ass's head, flees in terror, declaring that B. is 'translated.' iv, 2] decides that the Interlude cannot 'go forward' in B.'s absence; is rejoiced by his return. v, 1] (acc. Ff) speaks the Prologue to the Interlude.

'Herr Peter Squentz' is the title of a farcical German play (1663), of unknown authorship, based on the clown scenes of *M.N.D.*

[**Quiney, Richard.**] See Bucklersbury.

Quintus (1). An alleged ancestor of Coriolanus; 'of the same house [the Martians] were Publius and Quintus, who brought to Rome their best water they had, by conduits' (*Plut.* p. 1). (But Publ. and Quint. belonged to a later generation than Coriolanus.) Plutarch's account is reproduced, *Cor.* ii, 3, 1.249.

Quintus (2). D.P. *T. And.* 'Son to Titus Andronicus.' i, 2] insists that Mutius shall be buried in the ancestral tomb. ii, 2] *p.m.* ii, 4] in endeavouring to rescue his brother from 'the loathsome pit,' where the body of Bassianus lies, falls into it himself; the brothers are accused of murdering Bas. iii, 1] *p.m.*; they are led to execution.

Quoint, Francis. See Coint.

R

R. Letter of the alphabet; referred to as 'the dog's name' (*Rom. J.* ii, 4).

Cf. 'litera canina' (Pers. *Sat.* i, 109).

Radcliffe. See Ratcliffe.

Ragozine. 'A most notorious pirate,' who died in prison, and whose head was foisted upon Angelo as that of the condemned Claudio. *M. for M.* iv, 3 (2); v, 1. Prob. *It.* 'Ragusino,' a Ragusan.

Ralph. A servant; mtd. *Tam. Sh.* iv, 1. A drawer; mtd. *1 Hen. IV*, ii, 4. As a forename: 'R. Mouldy' (*2 Hen. IV*, iii, 2).

Rambures. 'The lord Rambures, maister of the crosbowes' (*Hol.* iii, 552) at Agincourt; among the slain (*ib.* 554).

D.P. *Hen. V.* iii, 7] joins in raillery before the battle. iv, 2] jests. iv, 5] *p.m.* (iv, 8) among the slain.

'David, Seigneur de R.' (Boswell-Stone, *Sh. Hol.* Index).

Ramston, Sir Thomas. Sailed from Brittany with Bolingbroke (*Hol.* iii, 497).+ Warden of the Tower when Richard II was confined there; afterward Constable, and K.G.

Mtd. as 'Sir John R.,' *Rich. II*, ii, 1 ('Rainston,' Ff), where 'Thomas' would nevertheless be metrically preferable.

Rannius. Mtd. in the st. dir. of *Ant. Cl.* i, 2, but is not a speaking character. The nearest Roman name is 'Ranius,' a slave of Brutus (Cic. *Ad Att.* xii, 21).

Rape, or **Rapine.** Impersonated by Chiron (*q.v.*) to influence Titus in his madness; *T. And.* v, 2 (4).

Rash, Master. A debtor; *M. for M.* iv, 3.

Ratcliffe, or **Radcliffe, Sir Richard.** Counsellor of Rich. III; knighted by Edw. IV at Tewkesbury; carried out the execution of Earl Rivers and others at Pontefract, of which he was Governor, 1483 (*Hol.* iii, 725); K.G. 1484; slain at Bosworth (*Hol.* iii, 759). 'The Rat' of the well-known distich. Of him More wrote: 'having experience of the world and a shrewd wit, short and rude in speech, rough and boisterous of behaviour, bold in mischiefe, as far from pitie as from all feare of God' (*Hol.* iii, 725).

D.P. *Rich. III.* (ii, 1) mtd. Ff. iii, 3] conducts Rivers, Grey, and Vaughan to execution. iii, 4] is present at a council to fix a day for the coronation of Edw. V; is charged by Gloucester to see Hastings beheaded. iii, 5] *p.m.*; accompanied by Lovel, returns with H.'s head. iv, 4] tells Richard that a fleet, supposed to be Richmond's, is off the Western coast; is given contradictory instructions. v, 3] as ordered, rouses Richard before dawn on the day of battle, and bids him be of good cheer.

There is a confusion of 'Catesby' and 'Ratcliffe' in iii, 4, 5 (see Catesby); R. was at Pontefract on the very day when the council was held at the Tower. See French, p. 234, and Clar. p. 184.

Ravenspurgh. 'In Yorkshire ... betwixt Hull and Bridlington' (*Hol.* iii, 498). A seaport damaged by the sea in the 14th cent. and finally overwhelmed in the 16th cent. Landing-place of Bolingbroke. (Also 'Ravenspurn' and 'Ravenser.')

Mtd., *Rich. II*, ii, 1, 2, 3; *1 Hen. IV*, i, 3, iii, 2; 'the naked shore at R.' (*ib.* iv, 3); Edw. IV lands at R., *3 Hen. VI*, iv, 7.

Reading. County town of Berks; referred to by Evans as 'Readins,' *M.W.W.* iv, 5, 1.80.

Reapers. D.PP. *Temp.* iv, 1] dance with nymphs in the visionary masque.

Rebeck, Hugh. D.P. *Rom. J.* A musician. iv, 5] replies to Peter.

'Rebeck,' a kind of violin.

[Rebekah.] Mother of the patriarch Jacob. 'His wise mother' (*M.V.* i, 3).

Recorder. *Rich. III*, iii, 7; see Fitz william, Thomas.

Redeemer. Christ. '*K. Edw.* I every day expect an embassage From my Redeemer' (*Rich. III*, ii, 1); 'The precious image of our dear Redeemer' (*ib. ib.*; *cf.* Gen. i, 27).

Redemption, Mistris. An error, F4, in *Com. Err.* iv, 2, l. 46, for 'mistress, redemption.'

Regan. D.P. *Lear.* L.'s second daughter (i, 1); wife to the D. of Cornwall. i, 1] professes her filial love in extravagant terms, and is given a third of the kingdom; (acc. Qq, bids farewell to Cordelia with a sneer at her being received 'at fortune's alms' by France); discusses Lear's growing 'waywardness' with her sister. ii, 1] arrives with her husband at Gloucester's castle; declares that Edgar has been corrupted by the 'riotous knights' in L.'s train – if they come to sojourn at her house she'll 'not be there'; tells Gl., 'her good old friend,' that they seek his counsel on 'differences' concerning which they have had letters. ii, 2] suggests that Kent should be kept in the stocks 'all night' for assaulting Goneril's messenger. ii, 4] to Lear, when he dilates on Gon.'s unkindness, she coldly replies that her sister would not 'fail in her obligation,' and advises L. to seek her forgiveness; supposes that L. will curse her also 'when the rash mood is on'; pays no heed to his pathetic appeal; on Goneril's arrival, advises L. to return with her, even without a single attendant; on L.'s departure in the rising storm, says that she is ready to shelter him 'for his particular ... but not one follower' – let the doors be shut, lest his 'desperate train' should persuade him to violence. (iii, 4) mtd. iii, 7] urges that Gloucester should instantly be hanged; when he is being bound cries 'Hard, hard!' and plucks him by the beard; questions him as to L.'s whereabouts; when one of his eyes has been plucked out, cries 'th' other too!'; kills the servant who tries to protect Gl.; bids her men thrust Gl. out to 'smell his way to Dover'; leads out her wounded husband. iv, 5] in vain urges Oswald to give her the letter which he bears from Gon. to Edmund; tells him bluntly that Edm. is for her and not for his mistress; gives him a note for Edm. and bids him slay Gl. if he has the opportunity. v, 1] asks Edm. plainly if he is not her sister's lover; greets Albany and Gon. on their entrance and goes with Gon. to her tent. v, 3] (after the battle) insists that the victorious Edm. should be treated as 'a brother' by Albany; grows faint, and bids Edm. dispose of her forces and herself as their 'lord and master'; her sickness increasing, she is led away; (dies, having been poisoned by Goneril).

Spelt 'Ragan' in *Leir*, *A Mirour for Magistrates* (1586), and Percy's *Reliques*. In the ballad, and some of the early versions of the story, she is the eldest daughter; see W. Perrett, *Palaestra*, xxxv (Berlin, 1904).

Reignier. See Anjou, René, Duke of.

Religion. Personified. 'R. groans at it' (*Timon*, iii, 2); 'Religious love put out R.'s eye' (*L.C.* 250).

Remorse, Monsieur. Nonce-name applied to Falstaff by Prince Hal; *1 Hen. IV*, i, 2.

Report. Personified. 'If my gossip R. be an honest woman of her word' (*M.V.* iii, 1).

Reproach. Personified. 'Death, Reproach's debtor' (*Lucr.* 1155); 'R. and everlasting shame Sits mocking in our plumes' (*Hen. V*, iv, 5).

Revenge. Impersonated by Tamora (*q.v.*) to influence Titus in his madness; *T. And.* v, 2 (7).

Reynaldo. D.P. *Haml.* Servant to Polonius. ii, 1] is instructed by P. to follow Laertes to Paris, there to play the spy, and by laying 'light sullies' upon L., ascertain his conduct from his acquaintance.

'Montano,' Q1.

Rheims. Ancient city of France; scene of the coronation of the kings of France during seven centuries. Its former university dated from 1547 to 1793.

Lucentio presented as a 'young scholar, that hath been long studying at Rh.' (*Tam. Sh.* ii, 1; 'Rhemes,' FfQ); reported as lost to England, *1 Hen. VI*, i, 1; Charles crowned there, *ib. ib.*

Rh. was actually lost, and Ch. crowned there, in 1429, seven years after the death of Henry V.

Rhenish. (a) *Adj.*, pertaining to the Rhine. 'A deep glass of R. wine' (*M.V.* i, 2); 'there is more difference between … your bloods than there is between red wine and R.' (*ib.*iii, 1).

(*b*) *Subst.*, R. wine. 'He drains his draughts of R. down' (*Haml.* i, 4); 'a poured a flask of R. on my head once' (*ib.* v, 1).

Rhesus. A Thracian ally of the Trojans; his famous white horses were carried off by Ulysses and Diomedes, and he himself was slain in his sleep by Diom. (Hom. *Il.* x, 435, 495 ff.; Virg. *Aen.* i, 469).

The capture of the 'Thracian fatal steeds' is alluded to by Warwick, *3 Hen. VI*, iv, 2.

J. C. Collins has compared the dreams of Balthasar (*Rom. J.* v, 3), and of one of the grooms in *Macbeth* (ii, 2), with the warning dream of the charioteer in the *Rhesus* of Euripides (ll. 779–803) (*Studies in Sh.* p. 79).

Rhodes. Island of the Mediterranean; in 1523 finally captured by the Turks from the Knights Hospitallers of St John. (See Cyprus.) Iago refers to his having seen active service at Rh., *Oth.* i, 1; 'Cyprus more concerns the Turk than Rh.,' and is of more military advantage to him (*ib.* i, 3); 'the Ottamites … steering with due course towards the isle of Rh.' (*ib. ib.*).

Rhodope, Rhodopis. A famous Greek courtesan. The legend arose that she was the builder of the third pyramid (Pliny, *Nat. Hist.* XXXVI, xii, 1), and even queen of Egypt (probably from a confusion with the beautiful Queen Nitocris). See Memphis.

Charles declares that he will erect, in honour of Joan of Arc, 'a statelier pyramis … Than Rhodope's, or Memphis' (*1 Hen. VI*, i, 6).

And. Lang suggests that Sh. 'could get Rhodope, not from Pliny, but from B. R.'s lively translation (1584) of the first two books of Herodotus' (*The Valet's Tragedy*, etc. (1903), p. 342).

Rhys. See Rice.

Rialto, The. *Rivus altus*, one of the islands (Isola de Rialto) on which Venice was built; later, used to denote the Exchange, where merchants met. 'Upon the R.' (*M.V.* i, 3); 'what news on the R.?' 'in the R. you have rated me' (*ib. ib.*); 'dare scarce show his head on the R.' (*ib.* iii, 1).

Cf. 'with what a jolly presence he would pace round the Rialto' (Marston, *What You Will* (1607), B2).

Rice, or Rhys, ap Thomas (1449–1525). A Welsh supporter of the E. of Richmond, whom he joined 'with a goodly band of Welshmen' (*Hol.* iii, 753). He was afterward held in high esteem by Hen. VII, and made K.G. He and his 'valiant crew' mtd. *Rich. III*, iv, 5.

Fuller, *Worthies*, calls him 'Sir R. ap T. of Elmelin in Carmarthenshire … little less than a Prince in his Native Country,' and extols his valour at Bosworth Field.

Rice, John. Mtd. as a 'principal actor' in F1.

Rich, Lady Penelope (*c.* 1562–1607). Supposed by G. Massey to be alluded to in *Son.* cxxxv, l. 11: 'So thou, being rich in will, add to thy will One will of mine,' etc. She was the 'Stella' of Sir Philip Sidney.

Richard, 3rd Duke of York (1411–60). Only son of Richard, E. of Cambridge (*q.v.*); married Cicely Neville (*q.v.*), d. of Ralph N., E. of Westmoreland, and had by her four sons who survived their infancy: Edward (afterward Edw. IV); Edmund, E. of Rutland (killed by Clifford, cf. *3 Hen. VI*, i, 3); George, D. of Clarence (D.P. *3 Hen. VI*, *Rich. III*); and Richard (afterward Rich. III). Was the King's lieutenant in France (1440–5); practically exiled, as lieutenant in Ireland, 1447; returned to England and put himself at the head of an armed force 1450; elected Protector, in spite of the Queen's claim, 1454; on the King's recovery from an attack of insanity, was driven from power; defeated the royal forces at St Albans 1455; again made Protector 1455; the Queen's opposition led to his seeking refuge in Wales 1459; openly claimed the crown 1460, and was promised succession; besieged in Wakefield Castle and fell in battle Dec. 30, 1460.

D.P. *1 Hen. VI*. 'Richard Plantagenet,' and 'York.' ii, 4] (in the Temple Gardens) bids his supporters pluck a white rose; enters into an angry altercation with Somerset, who disdains him as a mere 'yeoman' in that his father was attainted; utters threats against his foes. ii, 5] visits the dying Mortimer (*q.v.*) in the Tower, learns from him the true cause of his father's execution, and receives prudent counsel. iii, 1] is 'restored to his blood' and created D. of York (*Hol.* iii, 595). iv, 1] is made regent in France; suspects the King's amity. iv, 3] (in France) refuses aid to Talbot, placing the blame on Somerset's traitorous delay. v, 3] fights hand to hand with La Pucelle and reviles her when she is made prisoner. v, 4] presides at the Maid's trial, and dooms her; receives tokens of fealty to England from Charles, and grudgingly confirms a truce.

D.P. *2 Hen. VI*. 'York.' i, 1] hears with dismay the terms of the marriage contract between Henry and Margaret; (*sol.*) inveighs against the cession of lands that are rightly his, and resolves to 'make him yield the crown, Whose bookish rule has pull'd fair England down.' i, 3] takes part in an acrimonious discussion regarding his fitness to be regent in France. i, 4] reads the necromancers' answers to the Duchess of Gloucester's queries. ii, 2] discusses, with Salisbury and Warwick, his title to the throne (*Hol.* iii, 627, 657). ii, 3] is present at judicial combat. iii, 1] (at Bury) accuses Gloucester of sundry crimes and misdemeanours; consents to be sent as regent to Ireland, instead of to France, but (*sol.*) resolves to make use of his 'mighty band' for his own purposes, and to instigate Cade to stir up revolt at home. v, 1] leads an army to Blackheath; being assured that Somerset is a prisoner, disbands his forces; on finding he has been deceived, inveighs fiercely against the King and Queen; boldly declares that he is the rightful king; summons Warwick and Salisbury to his aid, and bids defiance to the royal forces. v, 2] (at St Albans) kills Clifford in combat. v, 3] as victor, sets out for London.

Salisbury's reference (i, 1) to York's successful rule in Ireland (1499) anticipates the mission mtd. in iii, 1.

D.P. *3 Hen. VI.* i, 1] enters the Parliament House, with his adherents, and occupies 'the regal seat'; refuses to quit it on Henry's entrance, but after debate makes oath to yield the crown to Henry during his lifetime (*Hol.* iii, 658). i, 2] (at Sandal Castle) is persuaded by his sons to break his oath (cf. *Hol.* iii, 659); hears that 'the army of the Queen mean to besiege us.' i, 4] despairs of victory; is taken prisoner; is mocked by Margaret, and a paper crown is set on his head (*Hol.* iii, 659); after a fierce invective against the Queen, is stabbed to death, and his head is sent to be set on York Gates (*ib. ib*). (ii, 1) his fate related. (ii, 6) his head replaced by Clifford's.

In *3 Hen. VI*, i, 1, l. 78, Richard claims to be D. of York by 'inheritance.' But York's father, Richard, E. of Cambridge, was never Duke.

In *1 Hen. VI*, ii, 4, l. 83, 'grandfather' is an error for 'great-great-grandfather.' Richard's head was placed on Mickle-gate Bar, York.

Richard, Duke of York (1472–83). 2nd s. of Edw. IV; his mother sought sanctuary with him at Westminster, but was persuaded to give him up. The young Duke was murdered, with his brother, Edw. V, in the Tower by order of Richard III.

D.P. *Rich. III.* ii, 4] would not 'grow up so fast,' since he has heard that 'great weeds do grow apace'; has heard of his uncle Gloucester's precocity (*Hol.* iii, 712); the Queen, fearing danger, takes him to sanctuary (*Hol.* iii, 715). iii, 1] he greets his brother as king; converses vivaciously with his uncle Gl.; fears he shall not sleep in quiet in the Tower, by reason of his Uncle Clarence's 'angry ghost.' (iv, 2) his murder is planned and (iv, 3) perpetrated.

The discovery in the Tower of the supposed remains of Richard and his brother was made in 1674. The bones are interred in Henry VII's Chapel, Westminster Abbey.

Richard I, 'Coeur-de-lion' (1157–99). 3rd son of Henry II; Duke of Aquitaine 1169; King of England, D. of Normandy, and Count of Anjou 1189; joined Philip II of France in 3rd Crusade 1190. Returning from France, he was made prisoner by D. Leopold of Austria 1192; transferred to the Emp. Henry VI 1193; ransomed 1194; mortally wounded while besieging Chaluz-Chabrol, near Limoges, 1199. (See LYMOGES.) His intrigue with Lady Faulconbridge, *John*, i, 1; Arthur forgives 'Austria' his death, *ib.* ii, 1; his bequeathal of the crown to John, *ib. ib.* (cf. *Hol.* iii, 156); 'R. that robbed the lion of his heart' (*ib. ib.*); 'In this late-betrayed town [Rouen] Great Coeur-de-lion's heart was buried' (*1 Hen. VI*, iii, 2; cf. *Hol.* iii, 156, after Matth. Paris).

Acc. to one story, R. acquired his surname from having torn the heart out of a lion, when imprisoned in Germany, and to this Philip Faulc. alludes (*John*, i, 1) when he says: 'he that perforce robs lions of their hearts, May easily win a woman's.' But Hol. (iii, 156) attributes the name merely to his high courage.

Richard II (1367–1400). King of England; born at Bordeaux; son of Edward 'the Black Prince,' by his cousin Joan Holland, 'the Fair Maid of Kent'; succeeded to the throne of Edw. III in 1377. The play of *Rich. II* deals only with the last two years of the reign, at the commencement of which period the King had aroused great discontent by instituting forced loans, as well as by his favouritism and arbitrary rule. In 1397 Thomas of Woodstock, D. of Gloucester, the King's uncle, having been arrested on a charge of conspiracy, was sent to Calais, and died shortly afterward, having probably been murdered. This tragic event was intimately connected with the complications and ultimate catastrophe related in the play. In 1398 Richard banished for a time the D. of Hereford (afterward known as Bolingbroke), John of Gaunt's son, and on Gaunt's death refused to yield up to the exile his deceased father's possessions. During Richard's absence in Ireland for the purpose of quelling a revolt (May 1399) Hereford, now D. of Lancaster, landed in England with numerous adherents, and Richard, deserted by nearly all his subjects, submitted to him without a struggle. On Sept. 30, 1399, the King's abdication was recorded and confirmed by Parliament in Westminster Hall. Of Richard's ultimate fate there are various accounts: (i) that he was murdered at Pontefract; cf. *Rich. III*, iii, 3, l. 12; (ii) that he voluntarily starved himself to death; (iii) that he escaped to Scotland and died a lunatic. Sh., who closely follows Holinshed's account of the reign, assumes that he was murdered.

D.P. *Rich. II.* i, 1] inquires whether Hereford appeals Mowbray maliciously, or out of loyalty; commands the opponents to be brought before him; listens to their mutual accusations; asserts his impartiality; makes a vain attempt to compose the quarrel; appoints time and place for a judicial combat (*Hol.* iii, 493). i, 3] presides at the lists at Coventry; greets Hereford with the wish: 'as thy cause is right, So be thy fortune,' while in Mowbray he sees 'Virtue with valour couched in thine eye'; abruptly stays the combat (cf. *2 Hen. IV*, iv, 1); after taking counsel, declares that in the interests of civil peace Hereford shall be banished for ten years and Mowbray for life; exacts from each of them an oath never to become reconciled and never to plot against their king; in view of Gaunt's 'sad aspect' reduces Hereford's exile by four years, but reminds Gaunt that he himself assented, in council, to the original decree (*Hol.* iii, 494). i, 4] confides to Aumerle his distrust of Hereford's intentions, commenting on his 'courtship to the common people' before his exile; resolves to set out for Ireland, leaving 'blank charters' with his 'substitute,' wherewith to raise money for his pressing needs (*Hol.* iii, 495–6). ii, 1] visits Gaunt upon his death-bed, and in reply to the sick man's stern warnings and reproaches angrily replies that if the sick man were not his uncle his tongue 'Should run thy head from thy unreverent shoulders'; upon Gaunt's death, seizes, despite York's protestations, all his possessions; appoints Y. regent during his absence (*Hol.* iii, 496–7). iii, 2] returning from Ireland, lands in Wales (*Hol.* iii, 499); conjures the 'dear earth' itself of his kingdom to fight for him, yielding to his foe nettles and venomous reptiles, and the very stones proving 'armed soldiers' on his behalf; in reply to the Bp. of Carlisle's warning against neglecting the means granted by heaven, replies that Bolingbroke will be terror-stricken by the return of the King 'elected by the Lord,' for whom heaven and its angels fight; hears that the Welshmen have deserted him (*Hol.* iii, 499); after a moment of depression cheers himself with the thought of York's army; bids Scrope tell him the worst; learns that Bushy, Bagot, and Green have been executed; gives way to an outburst of despair – 'of comfort no man speak!' Bolingbroke is victor, Death is the lord of kings; is heartened by the Bp. of Carlisle, but on learning that 'York is joined with Bolingbroke' and that the revolt is widespread, resolves to take refuge in Flint Castle (*Monk of Evesham* (1729), p. 150; 'Conway,' *Hol.* iii, 499). iii, 3] sternly rebukes Northumberland for not bending the knee before him, and declares that heaven's vengeance will fall on the rebels and their children; after hearing N.'s reply, sends a gentle answer to Bol., but fears he has thereby debased himself; longs to die and to be buried where subjects' feet may hourly trample on their sovereign's head; descends to meet Bol. in 'the base court' (*Hol.* iii, 501); bids the kneeling Bolingbroke arise, openly admits that he is in his power, and proposes their setting out for London. iv, 1] (first given in the Q of 1608) is brought into Westminster Hall before Parliament; comments bitterly on the faithlessness of his former courtiers; resigns the crown to Bol.; expostulates with Northumberland, who bids him read the act of accusation; calls for a mirror, and dashes the 'flattering glass' to the ground after viewing in it 'the face That like the sun did make beholders wink'; begs 'leave to go,' and is conveyed to the Tower (cf. *Hol.* iii, 501; the committal is post-dated by Sh.). v, 1] on his way to the Tower meets the Queen, bids her look upon her former happiness as a dream, and advises her forthwith to 'cloister' herself in France and think of him as dead; warns Northumberland that he will ere long be feared by Bol. and incur his hatred (cf. *2 Hen. IV.* iii, 1); sorrowfully bids the Queen farewell. v, 5] (in ward at Pomfret) 'studies to compare' his prison with the world; a strain of music out of tune 'mads' him by its suggestions, 'Yet blessing on his heart that gives it me'; 'a poor groom of his stable' describes to him how 'roan Barbary' was ridden by Bolingbroke on coronation-day; Richard beats the keeper who refuses to taste the dish he brings, and is slain by Exton and his servants after a desperate resistance (*Hol.* iii, 517; cf. *2 Hen. IV*, iv, 1). (v, 6) the body is brought to Henry IV.

Of Richard's 'personage' Holinshed (iii, 507) writes: 'He was seemelie of shape and favor, and of nature good inough, if the wickednesse and naughtie demeanor of such as were about him had not altered it. ... He was prodigall, ambitious, and much given to the pleasure of the bodie.' There is a fine contemporary portrait of Richard in Westminster Abbey.

In *1 Hen. VI*, ii, 5, l. 64, R. is spoken of as 'nephew' of Henry IV; they were, of course, 1st cousins, as grandsons of Edw. III. Richard is referred to as murdered at Pomfret, *Rich. III*, iii, 4, l. 12. Abp. Scrope is said to have 'enlarged his rising with the blood of fair King R., scrap'd from Pomfret stones.'

For the play see pp. 206–7, **Richard the Second.**

Richard III (1452–85). King of England; 11th child of Richard, 3rd D. of York (*q.v.*); cr. D. of Gloucester, 1461 (cf. *2 Hen. VI*, ii, 6); led the vanguard at Tewkesbury, 1471; has been held responsible for the murder of Edward, P. of Wales (after Tewkesbury), and of Henry VI (in the Tower). Acc. *Hol.* iii, 688, 690, R. did not participate in the former crime, but personally committed the latter. Married Anne, younger d. of the E. of Warwick; quarrelled with his brother Clarence, and was suspected of having brought about his death (*Hol.* iii, 712); on the death of Edward IV became Protector, and, aided by Buckingham, proceeded to exterminate the Woodvilles and all the Queen-mother's party. Hastings and others of the council, becoming alarmed for the safety of the young King, Edward V, tried to remove him from R.'s power, but the latter caused Hastings and Edward's maternal uncles to be executed (see Rivers and Grey). R. then contrived to immure both Edward V and his brother the D. of York in the Tower (where they were soon afterward murdered). On June 22, 1483, Dr Shaw (*q.v.*) preached a sermon declaring the family of Edward IV illegitimate; R. was immediately hailed as king by an irregular parliament, and a few days later began his reign. Buckingham raised a rebellion the same year, but was executed. In 1485, Henry, E. of Richmond, invaded England, and defeated and slew Richard at Bosworth Field.

The following extracts from the chroniclers' account of Richard's character and personal appearance (*Hol.* iii, 712, 760) are illustrated in the plays: 'Little of stature, ill featured of limmes, crooke backed, his left shoulder much higher than his right' (cf. *3 Hen. VI*, iii, 2, ll. 153–62; *Rich. III*, i, 1, ll. 14–23); 'hard favoured of visage' (cf. *3 Hen. VI*, v, 5, l. 78); 'malicious, wrathful, envious'; it was further alleged that the manner of his birth was unusual, and that he was born 'not untoothed' (cf. *3 Hen. VI*, v, 6, Il. 49–54, 70–5; *Rich. III*, ii, 4, ll. 27–9, iv, 4, ll. 162–8). 'None evill capteine was he in the warre, as to which his disposition was more meetly than for peace.' He was lavish in gifts, but 'gat him unsteadfast freendship'; furthermore he was 'a deepe dissembler ... not letting to kisse whom he thought to kill [cf. *3 Hen. VI*, v, 7] ... he spared no man's death whose life withstood his purpose.' It was his habit, when musing, to 'bite and chaw busilie his nether lip' (cf. *Rich. III*, iv, 2, l. 27).

The apparitions which appeared to R. before Bosworth are thus limited by the chroniclers: 'The fame went that he had the same night a dreadfull and terrible dreame: for it seemed to him being asleepe, that he did see diverse images like terrible divels, which pulled and haled him, not suffering him to take anie quiet or rest' (*Hol.* iii, 755); indeed, ever after his nephews' murder, he 'rather slumbered than slept, troubled with fearfull dreames, suddenlie sometime start up, lept out of bed, and ran about the chamber' (*Hol.* iii, 735; cf. *Rich. III*, v, 3, ll. 159–60).

D.P. *2 Hen. VI.* v, 1] (at Dartford) comes, with his brother Edward, to his father's aid; Clifford reviles him as being 'crooked in thy manners as thy shape.' v, 2] (at St Albans) slays Somerset in single combat. v, 3] relates how he saved Salisbury's life in the battle.

The whole of R.'s dramatic action here is unhistorical. He was not born at the time of v, 1, and was only 3 years old at the time of v, 2, 3.

D.P. *3 Hen. VI.* i, 1] (at the Parliament House) produces Somerset's head; urges his father to 'tear the crown' from Henry's head. i, 2] (at Sandal Castle) persuades his father that his oath of loyalty to Henry is void. ii, 1] sees the portent of a triple sun; hears that his father is slain and that Warwick has been defeated at St Albans; prepares to march on London. ii, 2] in a verbal conflict before the Battle of Towton vows vengeance on Clifford and reviles Queen Margaret, who calls him 'a foul mis-shapen stigmatic.' ii, 3] (at Towton) urges Warwick to fresh efforts. ii, 4] fights with Clifford, who flees. (ii, 5) mtd. ii, 6] exults over Clifford's corpse; is made Duke of Gloucester. iii, 2] is present when Edward woos Lady Grey; (*sol.*) meditates on his own deformities and on the many obstacles that stand between him and the crown, but resolves to 'hew my way out with a bloody axe.' iv, 1] is reticent when asked his opinion with regard to Edward's marriage but 'thinks the more.' iv, 3] *p.m.*; flees when Edw. is captured. iv, 5] aids in Edward's escape from Middleham Castle. (iv, 6) mtd. iv, 7] (at York) persuades Edw. to proclaim himself king. iv, 8] present at Henry's capture. v, 1] with Edward before Coventry. v, 3] at Barnet. v, 4] (at Tewkesbury) *p.m.* v, 5] takes part in the murder of Prince Edward. v, 6] visits Henry in the Tower, and stabs him; (*sol.*) devises the death of Clarence. v, 7] feigns love for the Queen and her infant – 'so Judas kiss'd his master.'

The Battle of Wakefield was fought in 1460, and Mortimer's Cross as well as Barnet in 1461; Richard therefore was only 8–9 years old at the time, and his dramatic action in these scenes is unhistorical.

D.P. *Rich. III.* i, 1] (*sol.*) meditates on his personal deformity; since he 'cannot prove a lover' he will 'prove a villain'; resolves to cause hatred between his brother Clarence and the King; accosts Cl. on his way to the Tower; tells him that his arrest is due to 'Lady Grey,' and advises him to curry favour with her; promises to intercede for Cl.; (*sol.*) 'I do love thee so, That I will shortly send thy soul to heaven'; greets Hastings on his release from the Tower; hears of the King's illness; (*sol.*) looks forward to the time, now close at hand, when the death of Clarence and the King will 'leave the world for me to bustle in.' i, 2] meets 'Lady Anne' (*q.v.*) as she accompanies the corpse of Henry VI to burial; woos her, in spite of her detestation, not without success; (*sol.*) is amazed at his own victory – 'Was ever woman in this humour won?' i, 3] expostulates bitterly with the Queen (Elizabeth) for being accused of seeking to injure her or her 'faction'; scoffs at them and bids them tell the King if they will; treats with scorn the curses of Queen Margaret; (*sol.*) hugs himself on the success of his schemes; gives instructions for the murder of Clarence. (i, 4) mtd. ii, 1] visits the King in his illness; professes to be reconciled to the Queen and her adherents; announces the death of Clarence; hints to Buckingham and others that Cl.'s murder was due to the Queen. ii, 2] agrees to meet the young Prince (Edw. V) on his way to London. (ii, 3) mtd. (ii, 4) discussed by his mother and nephew York. iii, 1] welcomes young Edw., and suggests his reposing at the Tower; exchanges banter with little York; promises Buckingham advancement, 'when I am king.' iii, 4] attends the coronation council in what seems a most genial mood; later, returns in a rage; declares he has been bewitched by Elizabeth and Jane Shore; will not dine till Hastings has been beheaded. iii, 5] appears on the Tower walls, with Buckingham, 'in rotten armour,' as though under a spell; satisfies the Mayor of the justice of Hastings' death; orders Buckingham to declare publicly the illegitimacy of Edw.'s children. iii, 7] (at Baynard's Castle) receives a discouraging report from Buckingham; later, appears 'between two bishops'; listens to an impassioned appeal from Buckingham (in presence of the Mayor and Citizens) to accept the crown; with great apparent reluctance, consents. iv, 2] is enthroned; sounds Buckingham with regard to the removal of the young Princes by death; meeting with a cold response, sends for and instructs Tyrrel; is importuned by B. for the earldom of Hereford, but is 'not in the vein.' iv, 3] learns that the Princes are dead, that Ely 'is fled to Richmond,' and that Buckingham is in revolt. iv, 4] defends himself against the bitter reproaches of his mother and wife; hears that Richmond has landed, and that rebellion is everywhere rife. (v, 1) mtd. v, 3] (at Bosworth Field) prepares for the morrow; retires to his tent; in his sleep he is visited by apparitions of his victims; makes an oration to his army. v, 4] 'my kingdom for a horse!' (v, 5) his death announced.

R.'s appearance 'between two bishops' (iii, 7) is mtd. by Hall, p. 372, and not by Holinshed.

With reference to R.'s soliloquies, Julius Hare, *Guesses at Truth* (1871), pp. 418 ff., observes: 'Sh. has made his worse characters, Edmund, Iago, Richard, all more or less self-reflective... Even poets of considerable dramatic genius have at times erred grievously in this respect [in making their villains proclaim and boast of their villainy] especially during the immaturity of their genius... It is a common result of a natural malformation to awaken and irritate a morbid self-consciousness, by making a person continually and painfully sensible of his inferiority to his fellows... Still I cannot but think that Sh. would have made a somewhat different use even of this motive, if he had rewritten the play, like *King John*, in the maturity of his intellect. Would not Richard then, like Edmund and Iago, have palliated and excused his crimes to himself, and sophisticated and played tricks with his conscience!'

For the play see p. 207, **Richard the Third.**

Richard Conqueror. Sly's blunder for 'Wm. the C.'; *Tam. Sh.* Ind. 1.

Richard the Second. (In F1: 'The life and death of King Richard the Second.' The acts and scenes are indicated.)

Publication. First appeared, in quarto, in 1597, with the title 'The Tragedie of King Richard the second. As it hath beene publikely acted by the right Honourable the Lorde Chamberlaine his Servants. London. Printed by Valentine Simmes for Androw Wise,' etc. The author's name, 'William Shake-speare,' omitted here, appears in all succeeding editions.

A second quarto followed in 1598, and a third in 1608, 'With new additions of the Parliament Sceane, and the deposing of King Richard.' It seems probable that the new matter (viz. the abdication scene, iv, 1, ll. 154–318) was omitted from the earlier quartos for fear of giving offence to Queen Elizabeth at a time when her deposition was aimed at by the Pope. A fourth quarto appeared in 1615. The text in the First Folio follows that of Q3. The date of composition is probably 1593, immediately after that of *Rich. III.*

SOURCE. Almost the sole authority used by Sh. in *Rich. II* is Holinshed. Two other nearly contemporary plays on the subject seem to have been extant, but there is no reason to suppose that Sh. was indebted to them. A few details seem derived from Stow's *Annales* and unknown sources.

Richard the Third. (In F1: 'The Tragedy of Richard the Third: with the Landing of Earle Richmond, and the Battell at Bosworth Field.' The acts and scenes are numbered.)

PUBLICATION. First appeared, in quarto, in 1597, with the title 'The Tragedy of King Richard the third. Containing, His treacherous Plots against his brother Clarence: the pittiefull murther of his innocent nephewes; his tyrannicall vsurpation: with the whole course of his detested life, and most deserued death,' etc., published by Andrew Wise.

Six other quartos appeared, the last being dated 1630; they all follow the first closely. The claim of the third (1602) to be 'newly augmented' is baseless. Sh.'s name first appears on the title-page of the edn. of 1598.

The text in the First Folio contains 193 lines not found in the Qq, and at least 1200 small alterations and corrections. It is disputed whether F1 gives the text as corrected by Sh., or altered by an inferior hand from a copy so corrected. (See *N.S.S.Tr.*, 1875–6, pp. 1 ff.)

SOURCE. Holinshed's *Chronicles*, as derived from Hall and from Sir T. More's *The History of King Richard the thirde* (1513). *The True Tragedie of Richard III*, a play publd. in 1594, contains practically no parallels, except those due to the *Chronicles*.

DATE OF COMPOSITION. From considerations of style and metre, generally held to be 1593–4. The precise order of *John*, *Rich. II*, and *Rich. III* is, however, unascertained.

[Richardes, Griffin.] See GRIFFITHS.

Richmond, Earl of (1). A title promised to Arthur by John. 'For we'll create young Arthur Duke of Bretagne and Earl of R.' (*John*, ii, 1).

Arthur's grandfather, Conan le Petit, Duke of Brittany, and father of Constance, was the first who styled himself Earl of R. (Wright).

Richmond, Earl of (2). See HENRY VII.

Richmond and Derby, Countess of. See BEAUFORT, MARGARET.

Rinaldo. ('Steward,' in st. dirs.) D.P. *All's Well.* i, 3] informs the Countess that Helena loves the young Count Bertram. iii, 4] reads Helena's farewell message to the Countess, and is bidden immediately to inform Bertram by letter of his wife's flight.

'Rynaldo,' F1, 3, 4; 'Rynardo,' F2. Rinaldo is a prominent figure in medieval romance, as one of Charlemagne's paladins.

Ringwood. Name of a dog. 'Like Sir Actaeon he, with R. at thy heels' (*M.W.W.* ii, 1).

Golding translates 'Acutae vocis Hylactor' (Ovid, *Metam.* iii, 224) as 'Ringwood with a shyrle loud mouth.'

Rivers, Baron. See WOODVILLE, RICHARD.

Rivers, Earl. See WOODVILLE, ANTHONY.

Robert (1). As a forename. 'R. Shallow' (*M.W.W.* i, 1; 2 *Hen. IV*, iii, 2, iv, 3, v, 1, 3); 'R. Faulconbridge' (*John*, i, 1 (5)); 'R. Waterton' (*Rich. II*, ii, 1); 'R. Brackenbury' (*Rich. III*, v, 4).

Robert (2). D.P. *M.W.W.* iii, 3] helps to carry out Falstaff in the buck-basket. iv, 2] present.

Robin (1). D.P. *M.W.W.* Page to Falstaff. i, 3] *p.m.*; bears letters from his master to Mistresses Ford and Page. ii, 2] ushers in Mrs Quickly. iii, 2] accompanies Mrs Page to Ford's house. iii, 3] tells Mrs Ford that Fal. waits at her back-door, and assures Mistress P. that his master is unaware that she is within; is commended for his secrecy; later, ushers in Mrs P. as though she had just arrived; helps to conceal Fal. in the buckbasket.

Is termed 'skirted page' (i, 3); 'pretty weathercock,' 'little Jack-a-lent' (iii, 3).

Robin (2). For 'R. Goodfellow.' *M.N.D.* iii, 2; iv, 1; Epil.

Robin (3). An ostler. 'Never joyed since the price of oats rose; it was the death of him' (*1 Hen. IV*, ii, 1).

Robin (4). 'Hey, R., jolly R.,' snatch of a song; *T. Nt.* iv, 2.

Robin (5). A prentice; 2 *Hen. VI*, ii, 3.

Robin (6). 'Bonny sweet R.,' snatch of a song; *Haml.* iv, 5.

Robin (7). As a forename. 'R. Nightwork' (2 *Hen. IV*, iii, 2).

Robin Goodfellow. See PUCK.

Robin Hood. Traditionary hero of a group of old English ballads; a generous and gallant outlaw and robber, living a joyous life with his merry comrades, 'under the greenwood tree,' in more than one forest, but especially Sherwood. Attempts have been made to identify R. with an Earl of Huntingdon and various other personages – but he remains the elusive creation of popular imagination.

'Robin Hood's fat friar' (*T.G.V.* iv, 1); 'the old R.H. of England' (*A.Y.L.* i, 1); 'and R.H., Scarlet and John' (2 *Hen. IV*, v, 3, song).

Robinson, Richard. Mtd. as a 'principal actor' in F1.

Rochester. City in Kent. 'Gadshill lies tonight at R.' (*1 Hen. IV*, i, 2).

The scene of *1 Hen. IV*, ii, 1, is laid at R.

Rochford, Viscount. See BOLEYN, SIR THOMAS.

[Roderick.] See GERTRUDE.

Roderigo. D.P. *Oth.* 'A gull'd gentleman' (Ff); 'a foolish Gentleman in love with Desdemona' (Rowe). i, 1] blames Iago, to whom he has entrusted his purse, for not being open with him; at Iago's suggestion arouses Brabantio and tells him of Desdemona's elopement. i, 2] in Othello's presence, Iago affects to challenge him. i, 3] threatens to drown himself, in despair, but is dissuaded by Iago, who urges him to put money in his purse and persevere in his suit to Desdemona; resolves to 'sell all his land.' ii, 1] is told by Iago that Desdemona and Cassio are lovers, and is urged to pick a quarrel with the latter that night. ii, 3] Cassio, who has become tipsy, strikes Rod., who runs to cry 'a mutiny'; later, Rod. complains that he has been cudgelled and that his 'money is almost spent,' but Iago advises him to have patience. iv, 2] begins to suspect that Iago has retained the presents entrusted to him for Desdemona; Iago reassures him, and plans a combined attack on Cassio that night. v, 1] in assailing Cassio Rod. is wounded, and, later, is despatched by Iago in the darkness. (v, 2) letters relating to the plot are found in his pocket.

The name is spelled 'Rodorigo' in Ff. There is no corresponding character in Cinthio's *Novella*.

'R.'s suspicious credulity and impatient submission to the cheats which he sees practised upon him, and which by persuasion he suffers to be repeated, exhibit a strong picture of a weak mind betrayed by unlawful desires to a false friend' (Johnson).

Rodorigo. Name assumed by Sebastian on an unspecified occasion; *T. Nt.* ii, 1.

'Roderigo' in some mod. edns.

Roger. As a forename. 'R. Bolingbroke' (*2 Hen. VI*, i, 2); 'R. Earl of March' (*ib.* ii, 2); 'R. Mortimer' (*3 Hen. VI*, i, 1).

Rogero. D.P. *Wint. T.* A gentleman of Sicily ('Gent. 2' in pfxs.). v, 2] announces that 'the oracle is fulfill'd'; recalls Paulina's daily visits to the house where the supposed statue of Hermione was preserved.

Not given in 'The Names of the Actors' (Ff); first added as D.P. by Theobald. The name of a Saracen knight in Boiardo's *Orlando Innamorato* and Ariosto's *Or. Furioso*.

[**Rokeby, Sir Thomas.**] Sheriff of Yorkshire. Defeats the Earl of Northumberland, *2 Hen. IV*, iv, 4, l. 99.

'Sir Thomas, or (as other copies have) Rafe Rokesbie, shiriffe of Yorkeshire, assembled the forces of the countrie to resist the earle and his power... and finallie came forward vnto Bramham Moor,' where he defeated the Earl, Feb. 19, 1408 (*Hol.* iii, 534).

Roman. (*a*) *Subst.*, a citizen of Rome. (i) In the Histories. 'I will imitate the honourable R.s in brevity' (*2 Hen. IV*, ii, 2); 'the pristine wars of the R.s' (*Hen. V*, iii, 2). (ii) In the Tragedies. 'I am more an antique R. than a Dane' (*Haml.* v, 2); 'do you triumph, R.? do you triumph?' (*Oth.* iv, 1; Warburton and Collier propose 'rogue' and 'o'er me,' respectively). (iii) In the Roman plays and *Cymb.* frequent. Noteworthy instances are: 'like R.s, neither foolish in our stands nor cowardly in retire' (*Cor.* i, 6); 'a noble R. and well given' (Cassius; *Jul. C.* i, 2); 'the last of all the R.s' (Cassius; *ib.* v, 3); 'this was the noblest R. of them all' (Brutus; *ib.* v, 5); 'the firm R.' (Antony; *ib.* i, 5); 'a R. by a R. Valiantly vanquished' (*ib.* iv, 13).

(*b*) *Adj.* (i) In the Comedies. 'I think we do know the sweet R. hand [Olivia's]' (*T. Nt.* iii, 4); 'the face of an old R. coin' (*L.L.L.* v, 2); 'ancient R. honour' (*M.V.* iii, 2); 'like a R. conqueror' (*A.Y.L.* iv, 2); 'Roman Lucrece' (*Tam. Sh.* ii, 1). (ii) In the Histories. 'R. Brutus' (*Hen. V*, ii, 4); 'the R. disciplines' (*ib.* iii, 2); 'a R. sworder' (*2 Hen. VI*, iv, 1). (iii) In the Tragedies. 'Why should I play the R. fool, and die On my own sword?' (*Macb.* v, 7); 'gibber in the R. streets' (*Haml.* i, 1). (iv) In the Roman plays and *Cymb.* frequent. Noteworthy instances are: 'let's do it after the high R. fashion' (*Ant. Cl.* iv, 13); 'bear it as our R. actors do' (*Jul. C.* ii, 1); 'Jove's bird, the R. eagle' (*Cymb.* iv, 2); 'R. gentlemen' (*ib.* iv, 3); 'carved in R. letters' (*T. And.* v, 1).

Romano, Giulio (or **Julio**) (1492–1546). Painter and architect, a pupil of Raphael. His most famous works are the frescoes of the Sala di Constantino, in the Vatican, and 'The Fall of the Titans' at Mantua, where he built the Palazzo del T for Federico II.

In *The Winter's Tale* (v, 2), the supposed statue of Hermione is described as 'a piece many years in doing, and now newly performed, by that rare Italian master J.R., who (had he himself Eternity, and could put breath into his work) would beguile Nature of her custom, so perfectly is he her ape.'

This passage has produced much comment. Apart from the chronological inconsistency, which is characteristic of the play, two questions arise: (i) how came Sh. to select J. R. as the artist, and insist on his merits so aptly; and (ii) how came he to attribute a statue to a painter? In the first place, Vasari (1550) had dilated on J. R.'s 'truth to nature' and it is possible that Sh. was acquainted with V.'s work; and, secondly, since (*cf.* H. Green, *Sh. and the Emblem Writers* (1870), p. 111) there were in the time of Charles I sixteen works by J. R. in the Whitehall collection, the nucleus of which had been formed by Henry VIII, there may well have been some in Sh.'s days which he had seen. K. Elze (*Essays on Sh.* p. 284) regards the allusion as supporting his contention that Sh. visited Italy, and quotes from Romano's two epitaphs (as recorded by Vasari): 'videbat Jupiter corpora sculpta pictaque spirare,' and 'Romanus moriena secum tree Julius artes Abstulit.' It has furthermore been pointed out that it is not directly stated in the play that J. R. had originally made the statue – which had been 'many years in doing' – and that 'newly performed' may refer only to the painting of it. The dramatic setting of the passage must, moreover, be noted: the 'Third Gentleman' merely relates a hearsay description of a supposititious work of art, and the lifelike nature of 'the statue' would necessarily be insisted on by Paulina.

Rome. In the various meanings of the city (ancient and medieval), Imperium Romanum, and the Papacy.

The pronunciation 'Room' is illustrated by: 'Now is it Rome indeed and room enough' (*Jul. C.* i, 2); 'that I have room with Rome to curse awhile !' (*John*, iii, 1). This is confirmed by the rime of R. with 'doom' and 'groom' in *Lucrece*, 715, 1644. The play upon 'Rome' and 'roam' (*1 Hen. VI*, iii, 1) has been held to show that the latter word was also pronounced 'room' (Wright).

In the Comedies named only four times, viz. mtd., *M. for M.* iii, 2; a penance enjoined in R., *L.L.L.* v, 2; Balthasar 'a young doctor of R.' (*M.V.* iv, 1); mtd., *Tam. Sh.* iv, 2.

In the English Histories: Constance craves 'with R. to curse awhile!' (*John*, iii, 1); 'curse from (of) R.' (*ib.* iii, 1 (2)); Lewis scorns the peace made by John with R., *ib.* v, 2 (4); '[Jul. Caes.] the hook-nosed fellow of R.' (*2 Hen. IV*, iv, 3); 'nine sibyls of old R.' (*1 Hen. VI*, i, 2); 'R. shall remedy this' (*ib.* iii, 1); Q. Marg. wishes the cardinals would carry Henry to R., and make him Pope, *2 Hen. VI*, i, 3; 'R., the nurse of judgment' (*Hen. VIII*, ii, 2); 'court of R.' (*ib. ib.*); 'commission from R.,' 'whole consistory of R.,' 'tricks of R.' (*ib.* ii, 4); mtd., *ib.* iii, 2 (5).

In *Hamlet*: 'In the most high and palmy state of R.' (i, 1); 'When Roscius was an actor in R.' (ii, 2).

In *Cymbeline*: the scene of i, 5, ii, 4, 5, iii, 7, is laid in R.; Philario's house there, i, 1; 'gentleman of R.' (i, 7); 'ambassadors from R.' (ii, 3); Britain pays R. tribute, iii, 1; 'though R. be ... angry' (*ib.*); 'a leg of R.' (v, 3); mtd., iii, 5, iv, 2, v, 5 (2).

In *Coriolanus*: the scene of i, 1, 3, ii, iii, iv, 1, 2, 6, v, 1, 4, 5, is laid in R; the name occurs 83 times; 'senators of R.' (i, 1); 'renowned R.,' 'great R.' (iii, 1); (attrib.) 'R. gates' (iii, 3; iv, 5); insurrections in R., iv, 3; 'ungrateful R.' (iv, 5); 'nobility of R.' (iv, 7); 'the moon of R.' (v, 3).

In *Julius Caesar*: the scene of i, ii, iii, iv, 1, is laid in R.; the name occurs 34 times; 'streets of R.' (i, 1); 'a son of R.' (i, 2); 'what trash is R.' (i, 3); 'soul of R.' (ii, 1); 'great R.' (ii, 2); 'a mourning R.,' 'a dangerous R.,' 'No R. of safety' (iii, 1); 'the sun of R. is set' (v, 3).

In *Ant. Cl.*: the scene of i, 4, ii, 2, 3, 4, iii, 2, 6, is laid in R.; the name occurs 28 times; 'Let R. in Tiber melt' (i, 1); 'port gate of R.' (i, 3); 'despiteful R.' (ii, 6); 'great R.' (iv, 12); 'censuring R.' (v, 2).

In *T. And.*: the scene is laid in, or near, R. throughout; the name occurs 91 times; 'the imperial diadem of R.,' 'royal R.' (i, 1); 'ambitious R.,' 'the commonwealth of R.,' 'laws of R.,' 'the gods of R.' (i, 2); 'court of R.' (ii, 1); 'R. is but a wilderness of tigers' (iii, 1); 'the yoke of R.' (iv, 1); 'stately R.' (iv, 2); 'ungrateful R.' (iv, 3); 'great R.,' 'ingrateful R.' (v, 1); mtd., *Lucr.* 715, 1644, 1818, 1833, 1851.

Romeo. D.P. *Rom. J.* Son to Montague. i, 1] confides to Benvolio his hopeless love for Rosaline. i, 2] resolves to attend Capulet's feast in order to see R. i, 4] with the maskers on their way to the feast. i, 5] falls in love with Juliet, at first sight; Tybalt recognizes him. ii, 1] enters Capulet's garden. ii, 2] overhears Juliet's apostrophe to himself; he woos her; they plan their marriage. ii, 3] he enlists Friar Laurence as an ally. ii, 4] exchanges raillery with Mercutio; takes the Nurse into his confidence. ii, 6] meets Juliet at Friar Laurence's cell; (they are wedded). iii, 1] his intervention between Tybalt and Mercutio causes the latter to be mortally wounded; he fights with Tybalt, kills him, and flees. (iii, 2) his banishment announced to Juliet. iii, 3] falls into despair when Friar Laurence tells him he is exiled; threatens suicide; is advised by Friar L. to betake himself to Mantua. iii, 5] bids farewell to Juliet. (iv, 1, 3) mtd. v, 1] (at Mantua) hears that Juliet is dead; procures poison. (v, 2) Friar L. learns that his letter never reached R. v, 3] meeting Paris at the Capulets' Monument, fights with him and kills him; drinks the poison and dies just as Juliet recovers from the effect of her potion.

The name 'Romeo' originally meant one who had gone on pilgrimage to Rome. The spirit of Romeo, seneschal of Raymond Berenger IV, Count of Provence, is pointed out to Dante by the Emp. Justinian (*Par.* vi, 127–42), who describes him as 'persona umile e peregrina,' playing upon his name. See Toynbee, *Concise Dante Dict.* (1914), p. 464.

'Romeo is Hamlet in love. There is the same rich exuberance of passion and sentiment in the one, that there is of thought and sentiment in the other. Both are absent and self-involved, both live out of themselves in a world of imagination. Hamlet is abstracted from everything; Romeo is abstracted from everything but his love, and lost in it.' (W. Hazlitt.)

Romeo and Juliet. (In F1: 'The Tragedie of Romeo and Ivliet.' The acts and scenes, except i, 1, are not numbered.)

Publication. In 1597 there was published by John Danter, in quarto, 'An excellent conceited Tragedie of Romeo and Juliet. As it hath been often (with great applause) plaid publiquely, by the ... L. of Hunsdon his seruants.' This presents the play in a very imperfect form, and is doubtless based on shorthand notes.

'The most excellent and lamentable Tragedie of Romeo and Iuliet. Newly corrected, augmented, and amended,' etc., published by C. Burby, followed in 1599; a third quarto, further amended, appeared in 1609, as well as another undated.

Date of Composition. Uncertain, but the play, at least in its first draft, was probably written 1591–2. In i, 3, the Nurse refers to an earthquake which happened eleven years before; this would agree with one felt in England in 1580. A passage in v, 3 (ll. 74–120), contains reminiscences of Daniel's *Complainte of Rosamunde* (1592). Considerations of style would, in any case, give the play an early position in Sh.'s works.

Sources of the Plot. The story, in its main features, is an ancient one, and has been traced as far as the *Ephesiaca* of Xenophon of Ephesus (of uncertain date). It first appeared in Europe in the *Novellino* of Masuccio di Salerno (*c.* 1476); hence it was transferred by Bandello to his *Novelle* (1554), and was translated into French by François de Belleforest, or his collaborator Boaistuau, in the *Histoires Tragiques* (1559). A metrical version, from the French, by Arthur Broke (or Brooke) appeared in 1562, entitled *Romeus and Juliet*, and was followed by a prose rendering in Paynter's *Palace of Pleasure* (1567). Sh. was chiefly indebted to Broke, but there may have been an old English dramatic version, now lost.

It seems probable that *Rom. J.* had originally four choric speeches, of which only that prefixed to Act II remains. The Prologue is not found in Ff, but has been restored from Qq.

Ros, William de. 7th Baron Ros, of Hamlake; an adherent of Bolingbroke, who made him Lord Treasurer and K.G.; *ob.* 1414.

D.P. *Rich. II.* 'Lord Ross.' ii, 1] denounces Richard's exactions, and urges Northumberland to confide in Willoughby and himself; eagerly throws in his lot with Bolingbroke's party. ii, 3] 'fiery-red with haste,' joins Bol. near Berkeley (*Hol.* iii, 498). iii, 1] *p.m.*; with Bol. at Bristol.

[Rosader.] See Orlando.

Rosalind. D.P. *A.Y.L.* Daughter to the exiled Duke of Burgundy. (i, 1) is permitted to remain at Court, as a companion to her cousin Celia, the usurping Duke's daughter; 'from their cradles bred together... never two ladies loved as they do.' i, 2] converses with C. upon their situation; learns that a wrestling-match between the champion and the young Orlando is about to take place upon the lawn where they are seated; at the Duke's instigation tries to dissuade Or. from what seems so unequal a contest, but in vain; witnesses the overthrow of the champion; has been from the first favourably impressed by the 'excellent young man,' and after his victory, and the discovery that he is the son of her father's old friend, is strongly moved, and in parting gives him (iii, 2) her chain to wear. i, 3] converses with Celia on late events; is abruptly ordered by Duke Frederick to leave the Court within ten days, on pain of death – 'thou art thy father's daughter, there's enough'; agrees to C.'s suggestion that they should forthwith set out for the Forest of Arden, to seek the banished Duke; they determine to travel in disguise – R. in male attire as 'Ganymede,' a forester, and C. as 'Aliena,' his sister. ii, 4] reaches the forest with her two companions, and, though overcome with weariness, is unwilling 'to disgrace her man's apparel' and bids C. take courage; receives information from a shepherd which leads to the purchase, by C., of a cottage, with pasture and flocks. iii, 2] is astonished to find copies of verses addressed to 'Rosalind' in the forest, and the name carved on trees; is informed by C. that these love-tokens are due to Orlando; is at first dismayed at the thought of being discovered by her lover 'in doublet and hose,' but resolves to maintain the character; overhears Or.'s avowal to Jaques, that Rosalind is his 'love's name,' and enters 'like a saucy lackey' into conversation with him; tells him that the forest is haunted by a love-sick swain, and Or. admits that he is 'that unfortunate he'; 'Ganymede' thereupon avers that 'love is merely a madness,' which he once cured by treating the patient with such exasperating fickleness that he forswore the world; induces Or. to consent to visit the cottage and seek the remedy. iii, 4] is grieved and chagrined at Or.'s failure to keep his appointment, but gets cold comfort from Celia, who professes to doubt his constancy. iii, 5] interrupts, with C., the wooing of the scornful Phebe by Silvius, and after bitterly reproaching the vain beauty for despising so worthy a suitor, finds that, as 'Ganymede,' she has inspired Phebe with a passion for herself. iv, 1] is engaged in bantering conversation with Jaques when Or. enters and pleads that he comes 'within an hour' of his promise; retorts that she would 'as lief be wooed by a snail'; the mock love-making proceeds gaily, and, on Or.'s departure, R. exclaims, to C., 'O coz, ... that thou didst know how many fathom deep I am in love!' iv, 3] receives a versified love-letter from Phebe, at the hands of Silvius, and bids him tell the writer 'that if she love me, I charge her to love thee,' learns from Oliver de Bois that Orlando has been wounded in rescuing him from a lioness, and falls in a swoon on the exhibition by Oliver of 'a bloody napkin'; on recovering, insists that Or. shall be informed 'how well I counterfeit.' v, 2] becomes aware of Celia's betrothal to Oliver, and, as 'Ganymede,' mysteriously assures Orlando that by magic art he can bring it about that when Oliver marries 'Aliena,' Orlando himself shall be united to his Rosalind; on the entrance of Silvius and Phebe, again upbraids the latter, and after revelling in the lovers' cross-purposes, bids them all meet him on the morrow, when they shall be satisfied, although he himself 'loves no woman.' v, 4] appears, as 'Ganymede,' before the Duke, and reminds him of his promise to give his daughter to Orlando if she can be produced; later, the cousins enter in their proper attire, led by 'a person presenting Hymen' (acc. Capell), and are joyously welcomed by the Duke. (The Epilogue is spoken by Rosalind.)

The name is taken from Lodge's *Rosalynde*, the main source of the play. For a very full analysis of the character, by Lady Martin, who played the part, see *Sh.'s Fem. Char.* (1887), pp. 229 ff.

Rosalinda. For 'Rosalind'; *A. Y. L.* iii, 2, verses.

Rosaline (1). D.P. *L.L.L.* Lady attending on the Princess of France. ii, 1] characterizes Biron, with whom upon the entrance of the King and his Court, she exchanges raillery. iv, 1] holds her own in banter with Boyet. v, 2] plays 'a set of wit' with Katharine; receives a letter from Biron, 'whom I'll torture ere I go'; is masked, and on the entrance of Ferdinand and his courtiers, in disguise, poses as the Princess and is wooed by the King; on the re-entrance of the maskers, in their proper habits, informs Ferd. that the Princess had been visited by four Russians, who 'did not bless us with one happy word'; tells Biron that she penetrated the disguise, and informs the King of his error; imposes upon Biron a penance before their marriage – reminding him that 'a jest's prosperity lies in the ear of him that hears it,' she condemns him to visit the sick and converse with 'groaning wretches' for the space of a twelvemonth.

Rimes with 'thine,' iv, 3. Termed 'heir of Alençon,' ii, 1, but many commentators believe 'R.' here to be an error for 'Katharine.'

Rosaline (2). Niece to Capulet, of whom Romeo is enamoured. Rom. protests that 'the all-seeing sun Ne'er saw her match' (*Rom. J.* i, 2); Mercutio ironically enumerates her charms, *ib.* ii, 1; Rom. admits to Friar Laurence that he hath now 'forgot that name' (*ib.* ii, 3); Merc. terms her a 'pale hard-hearted wench' (*ib.* ii, 4).

'Rosaline was a mere creation of his fancy, and we should remark the boastful positiveness of Romeo in a love of his own making, which is never shown where love is really near the heart' (Coleridge, *Notes on R. and J.*).

Roscius, Quintus. A famous comic actor at Rome, friend and instructor of Cicero, who acquired great wealth by his profession. (Mtd. Plut. *Cic.*; Val. Max. viii, 7; Pliny, *Nat. Hist.* VII, xxxix, 5.)

'What scene of death hath R. now to act?' (*3 Hen. VI*, v, 6; 'Rossius,' Ff); 'When R. was an actor in Rome' (*Haml.* ii, 2).

Rose. For 'Rosalind'; *A. Y. L.* i, 2 (2).

Rose, Manor of the Red. A house belonging to the D. of Buckingham. The Duke's conversation with his surveyor, Knyvet, related *Hen. VIII*, ii, 1, took place 'at London in a place called the Rose, within the parish of Saint Laurence Poultrie in Canwike street Ward' (*Hol.* iii, 864). In 1561 the Merchant Tailors established in the house 'one notable grammar school' (Stow, p. 89, ed. Thoms).

Rosencrantz. D.P. *Haml.* A courtier, associated on all occasions with his friend Guildenstern. ii, 2] since they have been 'of so young days brought up with' Hamlet, the King commissions them to probe the cause of his transformation. iii, 1] they report their ill success. iii, 2] are present when the play is acted before the King (Gu. *p.m.*). iii, 3] they are ordered to proceed to England and to take Hamlet with them; they insist on the supreme importance of the King's safety. iv, 1] *pp.m.* iv, 2] they ask Haml. what he has done with the body of Polonius; Haml. jeers at R. as 'a sponge.' iv, 3] R. reports their failure; Gu. brings in Hamlet; they are ordered to 'tempt him with speed aboard.' iv, 4] present (not in Ff). (iv, 6) Haml. has 'much to tell of them.' (v, 2) Haml. relates how he sent them to their death in England.

Spelt 'Rosencrans,' Qq; 'Rosincrane,' F1; 'Rosincross(e),' F2, 3, 4; 'Guyldensterne,' Qq; 'Guildensterne,' F1; 'Guildenstare,' F2, 3, 4; also 'Rossencraft' and 'Gilderstone,' or 'Guilderstone,' in *The Tragicall Historie* (1603).

Rosse, Count. For 'Bertram'; st. dir. *All's Well*, ii, 1, Ff.

Rosse (Ross), Thane of. Acc. *Hol.* ii, 176, an adherent of Malcolm Canmore, on whose coronation he was made Earl of Rosse.

D.P. *Macb.* i, 2] brings tidings of Macbeth's victory over Sweno. i, 3] announces that Macb. has been made Thane of Cawdor. i, 4, 6] *p.m.* ii, 4] converses with an old man on the portents marking the night of Duncan's murder, and with Macduff on the subsequent events. iii, 1] *p.m.* iii, 4] begs Macb. to join his guests at table, and observes his agitation. iv, 2] excuses, to Lady Macduff, her husband's flight; speaks of his own danger. iv, 3] breaks the news of the murder of his family to Macduff. v, 7] tells Siward that his (S.'s) son 'has paid a soldier's debt.'

According to one account the title belonged to Macbeth himself, who had become Maormor of Ross on the death of his father. (The spelling 'Rosse' belongs properly to an Irish dignity (French, p. 293).)

Rossill. Name substituted in QqFf for 'Peto' in *1 Hen. IV*, i, 2, l. 182; probably, as Theobald suggested, the actor who performed the part. In Qq, moreover, 'Ross' appears (as a pfx.) for 'Gadshill' (Ff), *1 Hen. IV*, i, 2, ll. 193, 195, 199. See HARVEY.

Rotherham, Thomas (1423–1500). (Also known as Thos. Scot); Chancellor 1474; Abp. of York 1480; deprived of the chancellorship, and imprisoned, for adherence to Queen Elizabeth on the death of Edward IV.

D.P. *Rich. III.* ii, 4] on hearing that Elizabeth's brother and son have been imprisoned, resigns his seal, and conducts her with the young D. of York to the Sanctuary.

Acc. More, the interview with the Queen took place after she had taken sanctuary. Cf. *Hol.* iii, 715–16. See BOUCHIER, THOMAS. More's graphic description of the Queen's removal into sanctuary is quoted, Clar. p. 171.

Rouen. Former capital of Normandy. In possession of the English 1419 to 1449, when it was reoccupied by Charles VII. In 1431 Joan of Arc was burned as a witch in what is now the Place de la Pucelle. The surprise and recovery of R. described in *1 Hen. VI* are entirely fictitious. 'In a captive chariot into R. Bring him our prisoner' (*Hen. V*, iii, 5); 'Is R. yielded up?' (*1 Hen. VI*, i, 1; 'Rheimes,' Ff); the city taken by Talbot, *ib.* iii, 2; 'Nor grieve that R. is so recovered' (*ib.* iii, 3).

'Rone,' Qq, and 'Roan,' Ff. The imaginary capture of R. (*1 Hen. VI*, iii, 2), by soldiers disguised as peasants, is paralleled by an account (*Hol.* iii, 619) of the capture of the 'castell of Cornill.'

Rougemont. '*K. Rich.* Richmond! When last I was at Exeter, The Mayor in courtesy show'd me the castle, And call'd it Rougemont ['Ruge-mount,' Qq], at which name I started, Because a bard of Ireland told me once, I should not live long after I saw Richmond' (*Rich. III*, iv, 2; *Hol.* iii, 746).

For the history of the castle see E. A. Freeman, *Exeter* (1887).

Rousilion. Ancient government of France, bordering on Spain; almost the modern Dept. of Pyrénées-Orientales. A countship in the Middle Ages. The scene of *All's Well*, i, 1, 3; ii, 2; iii, 2, 4; iv, 5; v, 2, 3, is laid in R.

The capital of R. was Perpignan. Spelt 'Rosignoll,' 'Rossillion,' and 'Rosillion' (*All's Well*) in Ff.

Rousillon, Countess of. D.P. *All's Well.* i, 1] bids farewell to her son Bertram on his proceeding to Court; describes how Helena, daughter of a famous physician, became her ward; gives advice to her son. i, 3] permits her Fool to discourse facetiously about his marriage; sends him for Helena; learns from her steward that H. loves Bertram; converses freely with H. upon the subject, and approves of her visiting Paris and attempting to cure the King of his malady. ii, 2] entertains herself with the Fool, and sends him on an errand to Paris. iii, 2] learns that Bertram has married Helena only to desert her; condoles with H. and sends a cutting message to Bertram. iii, 4] learns that H. has set out as a pilgrim to 'St Jaques'; sends an urgent appeal to her son. iv, 5] hears of Bertram's arrival. v, 3] begs the King to forgive Bertram's conduct; recognizes the ring given by the King to Helena, and declares that the ring in Diana's possession was an heirloom handed down to Bertram, and that she must be his wife; (*p.m.* during the *dénouement*).

There is no equivalent character in Boccaccio's *Novella*.

Rousillon, Louis, Comte de. See BOURBON, LEWIS, BASTARD OF.

Roussi, or Roussy, Jean, Comte de. Killed at Agincourt; 'Erle of Roussie,' *Hol.* iii, 555. Mtd., *Hen. V*, iii, 5; among the slain, *ib.* iv, 8. ('Rosse,' *Chr. Hist.*)

[**Rowell, Thomas.**] See LOVELL, SIR T.

Rowland (1). Name of an officer; *M. for M.* iv, 5.

Rowland (2), or **Roland.** In medieval romance, Charlemagne's most famous paladin. He once fought for five days with another paladin, Oliver, without either gaining the advantage. 'England all Olivers and Rowlands bred During the time Edward the Third did reign' (*1 Hen. VI*, i, 2). The line 'Child Rowland to the dark tower came' (*Lear*, iii, 4) seems quoted by the assumed madman, Edgar, from a lost ballad. For the story of 'Childe R.' see Jamieson, *Illustr. of North Antiq.* p. 397, and F. J. Child, *Eng. and Scottish Ballads* (1857), i, 416.

Rowland, Sir. For 'Sir R. de Boys' (*q.v.*). 'Proud to be Sir R.'s son' (*A. Y. L.* i, 2); 'my father lov'd Sir R. as his soul' (*ib. ib.*); 'old Sir R.'s youngest son' (*ib.* i, 3); 'O you memory of old Sir R.' (*ib.* ii, 3); mtd., *ib.* ii, 7, v, 2, 4.

Rugby, John. D.P. *M.W.W.* 'Servant to Dr Caius.' i, 4] warns Mrs Quickly of his master's approach; in attendance on Caius when the latter discovers Simple in his closet; follows his master to the Court. ii, 3] accompanies C. to the scene of the intended duel; C. would fain illustrate upon R.'s person how he will kill Evans, but is interrupted. iii, 1, 2] *p.m.*

Neither Quickly's remark (i, 4) that R.'s 'worst fault is that he is given to prayer; he is something peevish that way,' nor the episode of ii, 3, occurs in the Qq.

Rumour. Personified; the st. dir. of the Induction to *2 Hen. IV* (acc. Q1) runs: 'Enter R., painted full of tongues,' which explains the sixth line of the Ind. spoken by R., 'Upon my tongues continual slanders ride.' 'R. doth double, like the voice and echo, The numbers of the feared' (*ib.* iii, 1).

Knight considers that a parallel to the description of Rumour in the Induction may be found in Virg. *Aen.* iv, 173 ff.

Russia. The long winter nights of the northern latitudes alluded to: 'this will last out a night in R.' (*M. for M.* ii, 1).

Russia, Emperor of. Indefinitely applied: 'Some say he is with the E. of R.' (*M. for M.* iii, 2); father of Hermione, *Wint. T.* iii, 2; 'a great king's daughter' (*ib. ib.*).

Russian. (*a*) *Subst.*, native of Russia. The appearance of the King and his courtiers before the Princess of France, apparelled 'like Muscovites or Russians' (*L.L.L.* v, 2), was probably suggested by the arrival in London of the Russian ambassador Pissemsky, and a large suite, with orders to bring back with him a relative of the Queen's to be the Czar's wife. The quaint ceremonial enacted on the occasion is related by Sir S. Lee, *Gent. Mag.* Oct. 1880.

(*b*) *Adj.* 'Russian bear' (*Macb.* iii, 4; *Hen. V*, iii, 7).

[Ruthall, or Rowthall, Thomas (*ob.* 1523).] Bp. of Durham, Keeper of Seal to Henry VIII.

His having inadvertently handed his private account book to the King (*Hol.* iii, 796) probably suggested a similar mischance attributed to Wolsey, *Hen. VIII*, iii, 2 (Steevens).

Rutland, Edmund, Earl of (1443–60). 3rd s. of Richard, D. of York. When not yet eighteen, he was murdered by Lord Clifford near Wakefield, on the ground that 'thy father slew myne, and so will I do thee' (Hall, p. 251); cf. *2 Hen. VI*, v, 2.

D.P. *3 Hen. VI.* i, 3] despite his pitiful entreaties, is slain by Clifford.

He is made to urge that C.'s father was slain before he himself was born; but he was 13 years old at the time. Hall makes him but 12 years old at his death, hence the terms 'brat' and 'child' applied to him in the scene. In *The True Tragedie* (i, 1) he accompanies his father to the Parliament House with a white rose in his hat. Many references to R.'s tragic fate occur, viz. *3 Hen. VI*, i, 4 (3), ii, 1, 2 (2), 4 (2), 6 (3); *Rich. III*, i, 2, 3, iv, 4 (2). In i, 3, l. 183, he is styled a 'babe.'

Rutland, Tutor to. D.P. *3 Hen. VI.* i, 3] pleads for the life of his charge at Wakefield and would die with him; 'his priesthood saves his life,' and he is dragged away.

Hall, p. 251, calls him 'Sir Robbert Aspall, chappelain and schole master.' ('Of Norfolk,' French, p. 200.)

S

Saba. The Queen of Sheba (1 Kings x). The Lat. form of Sheba, *cf.* Psalm lxxii, 10 (Pr. Bk. version). Properly the name of the capital of the Sabaei, in Arabia. Cranmer predicts of the infant Elizabeth: 'Saba was never More covetous of wisdom and fair virtue Than this pure soul shall be' (*Hen. VIII*, v, 5).

'Sheba' in some edns. after Rowe. *Cf.* also Marlowe, *Doctor Faustus*, Scene 5: 'Be she as chaste as was Penelope, As wise as Saba,' etc.

Sabbath. Jewish: 'By our holy S. have I sworn' (*M.V.* iv, 1). Sunday: '*Hast.* [to a priest]. Come the next S. and I will content thee' (*Rich. III*, iii, 2).

In *M.V.* Q2 has 'Sabaoth' and Q2 'Sabbaoth.' The confusion of the Heb. word meaning 'armies' with 'Sabbath' occurs even in Johnson's *Dictionary* (1st edn.), and is found in Bacon and Spenser.

Sack-and-Sugar, Sir John. Nonce-name applied to Falstaff by Poins; *1 Hen. IV*, i, 2.

The jest clearly implies that Sir J. used sugar in his sack, and that therefore the latter was a rough, or acid, wine, and not a sweet one as has been supposed by many. Cf. *ib.* ii, 4, l. 516.

Sackerson. A celebrated bear, kept for baiting, at Paris Garden (*q.v.*). Probably named after its keeper. 'I have seen S. loose twenty times, and have taken him by the chain' (*M.W.W.* i, 1).

Sir John Davies, *Epigrams* (*c.* 1596), mentions a law-student forsaking his books 'to see... Sacarson.' Other noted bears were 'George Stone,' 'Harry Hunks,' and 'Tom of Lincoln.' See *Sh. Eng.* ii, 432.

[Sadler, John.] See BUCKLERSBURY.

Sagittary, The (1). A centaur-like monster, an offspring of medieval imagination, that, according to Benoît de Sainte-More and his successors, aided the Trojans against the Greeks. Caxton's account is as follows: 'From beyond the royalme of Amasoune, came an ancient Kynge, wyse and discreete, named Epystrophus, abrought a thousand knyghtes, and a mervayllouse beste that was called Sagitayre, that behynde the myddes was an horse and to-fore, a man: this beste was heery like a horse, and had his eyen rede as a cole, and shotte well with a bowe: this beste made the Grekes sore aferde, and slewe many of them with his bowe.'

Lydgate, following Guido, expatiates on the monster's eyes, which 'were sparkling as bright as is a furnace with his red leven, or the lightning that falleth from the heaven'; but Benoit himself drew a yet grimmer picture, and declares that the 'gruesome devil' killed four men with one shot, that he touched his arrows with poisonous foam from his mouth, and that he killed more than twelve thousand Greeks in one day. 'Dares Phrygius,' Benoit's pseudo-classical source, does not even mention the creature.

Agamemnon exclaims: 'the dreadful S. Appals our numbers' (*Tr. Cr.* v, 5).

Sagittary, The (2). ('Sagitary,' F1; 'Sagittar,' Q1.) Apparently meant as the sign of an inn: either Sagittarius of the zodiac, or the medieval monster. 'Lead to the S. the raised search' (*Oth.* i, 1); 'send for the lady to the S.' (*ib.* i, 3).

Knight contended that this meant Othello's official residence at the Arsenal, and that 'the figure of an archer with his drawn bow, over the gates, still indicates the place.' But it has been pointed out that the figure here alluded to is merely that of an ordinary bowman, with bow undrawn, standing with other statues before the building, and that it does not appear that the Arsenal, or any part of it, was ever known as the Sagittary. On the other hand, in a list of Venetian Taverns 'contemporary with Othello,' given by Elze (*Shakespeare Jahrbuch* (1879), xiv, 147), the name does not appear.

St Albans, First Battle of. May 22, 1455. Defeat of the D. of Somerset by the D. of York. The battle described, *2 Hen. VI.*, v, 2, 3; cf. *Hol.* iii, 643, and the *Paston Letters*, i, 327 ff.

St Albans, Second Battle of. Feb. 17, 1461. Defeat of the Earl of Warwick by Queen Margaret.

Warwick gives an account of the battle, *3 Hen. VI*, ii, 1 (cf. *Hol.* iii, 661); mtd., *ib.* ii, 2, iii, 2; mtd. as 'Margaret's battle' (*Rich. III*, i, 3, l. 130). 'The King … look'd full gently on his warlike queen,' so his adherents left him (*3 Hen. VI*, ii, 1).

St Albans, Mayor of. D.P. *2 Hen. VI.* ii, 1] sends for the beadle to whip Simpcox (*q.v.*).

St Asaph, Bishop of. See Standish, H.

St Edmundsbury, Bury St Edmunds, or Bury. Town in Suffolk, burial-place of St Edmund, king and martyr (*ob.* 870), and seat of a great Benedictine abbey.

Acc. *Hol.* iii, 183, the disaffected barons made a 'cloked pilgrimage' to 'the abbaie of B.' (1214), and there made oath at the altar to obtain from John the ratification of the Great Charter. There is no historical ground for bringing Lewis the Dauphin to St E., this idea being wholly derived from *Tr. R.* Acc. *Hol.* iii, 627, 'a parlement was summoned to be kept at B.' (1247), at which the Duke of Gloucester was arrested. See Humphrey.

'*Sal.* Lord, I will meet him [Lewis] at Saint E.' (*John*, iv, 3); '*Bigot.* Away toward Bury, to the Dauphin there' (*ib. ib.*); '*Mel.* Thus hath he [Lewis] sworn … upon the altar at St E.' (*ib.* v, 4). '*Her.* I summon your grace [Gloucester] to his Majesty's Parliament, holden at Bury, the first of this next month' (2 *Hen. VI*, ii, 4); '*Suff.* The traitorous Warwick, with the men of B., Set all upon me' (*ib.* iii, 2).

The scene in 2 *Hen. VI*, iii, 1, 2, is laid at St E. (The scene in *John*, v, 2, 3, 4, 5, is also probably to be regarded as laid there.) The Parliament (2 *Hen. VI*, ii, 4) was actually opened Feb. 10, 1447 (*Rot. Parl.* v, 128).

St George's Fields. In Southwark, a muster-ground for London soldiers. 'Soldiers … meet me tomorrow in St G.'s field' (2 *Hen. VI*, v, 1); 'the windmill in St G.'s field' (2 *Hen. IV*, iii, 2).

The fields constituted a wide, open space through which the main road to Canterbury lay. Archery was practised there.

St Jaques le Grand. Probably the shrine of Santiago de Compostela, which 'was to Christians what the Ka'ba at Mecca was to Musulmans' (Dozy, *Spanish Islam* (1913), p. 517).

'*Wid.* God save you, pilgrim! Whither are you bound? *Hel.* To Saint Jaques le grand' (*All's Well*, iii, 5).

St Mary's Chapel, Angers. Here, acc. *John*, ii, 1, following the *Tr. R.*, the wedding of Lewis the Dauphin and Blanch of Castile took place. It has been conjecturally identified with the 'Church of Ronceray,' dedicated to Our Lady in 1028.

Saintrailles. See Poton de Xaintrailles.

Sala. Name of two rivers (mod. Saale), the one a tributary of the Main and the other of the Elbe, rising near one another in Thuringia, and giving their name to the Salian Franks. 'The land Salique is in Germany, Between the floods of Sala and of Elbe' (*Hen. V*, i, 2; rep.); 'Charles the Great … did seat the French Beyond the river S.' (*ib. ib.*).

'Sabeck,' Qq.

[Saladyne.] See Oliver (3).

Salanio. D.P. *M.V.* Friend to Antonio and Bassanio. i, 1] condoles with Ant. on his supposed anxiety about his argosies. ii, 4] is of opinion that a masque should be 'quaintly order'd' if undertaken at all. ii, 8] describes Shylock's anguish at the loss of his daughter and his ducats, and speaks of Antonio's kindness of heart. iii, 1] converses with Salarino on Ant.'s losses.

Capell, and Knight, named the character 'Solanio' to avoid confusion with Salarino, when abbreviated as pfxs. See Salerio.

Salarino. D.P. *M.V.* Friend to Antonio and Bassanio. i, 1] in his desire to find out the truth, attributes Antonio's sadness to various causes. ii, 4] prepares for a masque. ii, 8] converses with Salanio on the Jew's loss and Ant.'s danger. iii, 1] reports the loss of Ant.'s ship; converses with Shylock. iii, 3] meets Ant., who is under arrest.

Variously spelt 'Salaryno,' 'Salarino,' 'Solarino' (FfQq) in st. dirs., and 'Sal.,' 'Salar.' in pfxs., where it is often indistinguishable from 'Sal(anio).' See Salerio.

Salerio. D.P. *M.V.* (acc. Steevens). iii, 2] brings news to Belmont of Antonio's misfortunes. iv, 1] is present at the court of justice.

In iii, 2, 'Salerio' is given FfQq, but Rowe suggested 'Salanio,' Knight 'Solanio,' while Capell supposed the character to be identical with Salarino. In iii, 3, Q2, 3, have 'Salerio,' but F1, 2, 3, 'Solanio,' since the messenger to Belmont cannot be intended. In iv, 1, the speaker is 'Sal.,' Ff, but 'Salerio,' Q2. (As a distinct character, first introduced by Steevens, but the suggestion is by no means universally accepted.)

Salic, or Salique, Law. An ancient code of laws attributed to the Salian Franks; commonly applied to one of its provisions (*De Alodis*) by which women were precluded from certain kinds of inheritance. In the 14th cent. women were excluded from succession to the crown in France by an adaptation of this law.

Abp. Chichele argues before Henry V that this law applies only to 'the Salique land' (where this disqualification attached to the German women 'for some dishonest manners of their life'), and not in any case to France (*Hen. V*, i, 2; *Hol.* iii, 545).

Lat.: 'In terram Salicam mulieres ne succedant' (*Hen. V*, i, 2).

Salisbury, City of. Capital of Wiltshire. The D. of Norfolk urged to join forces with Richard at S., *Rich. III*, iv, 4; the captured Buckingham ordered to be taken thither, *ib. ib.*; intended assassination of Richard at S., *Hen. VIII*, i, 2, l. 196 (cf. *Hol.* iii, 864).

Salisbury, Earl of (1). (D.P. *John.*) See Longespée, William de.

Salisbury, Earl of (2). (D.P. *Rich. II.*) See Montacute, John de.

Salisbury, Earl of (3). (D.P. *Hen. V*, *1 Hen. VI.*) See Montacute, Thomas de.

Salisbury, Earl of (4). (D.P. *2 Hen. VI.*) See Neville, Richard.

Salisbury, or Salusbury, Sir John. A patron of poets, to whom Robert Chester (*q.v.*) dedicated his works. He married an illegitimate daughter of the 4th E. of Derby, who was a patron of Sh.'s dramatic company (Lee, *Life of Sh.* p. 270).

Some commendatory lines to Heminge and Condell, discovered by Sir I. Gollancz in 1921, are by him tentatively attributed to Sir Henry S., son to Sir John. See *Times Lit. Suppl.* Jan. 26, 1922.

Samingo. '*Sil.* [singing]. Do me right, and dub me knight; Samingo' (*2 Hen. IV*, v, 3).

Apparently for 'San Domingo.' Tollet (*Var.*) sees an allusion to the alleged gluttony of the Dominicans, and quotes Weever, *Funeral Monuments*, p. cxxxi, 'Sanctus Dominicus sit nobis semper amicus, cui canimus – siccatis ante lagenis – fratres qui non curant nisi ventres.' An old song, quoted in Nashe's *Summer's Last Will and Testament*, gives: 'Monsieur Mingo for quaffing doth surpass.'

Sampson. D.P. *Rom. J.* Servant to Capulet. i, 1] is drawn, somewhat unwillingly, into a brawl with Montague's men. As a forename: 'S. Stockfish' (*q.v.*).

Samson. Son of Manoah, a 'judge' of Israel; among his feats of strength were the carrying away of the gates of Gaza (Judges xvi, 3) and snapping the 'green withs' with which he had been bound at the instigation of the treacherous Delilah (*ib.* xvi, 6–9).

'He carried the town gates on his back ... and was in love' (*L.L.L.* i, 2); his love 'had a green wit,' 'S. was so tempted' (*ib. ib.*); 'Samsons and Goliasses' (*1 Hen. VI*, i, 2); 'I am not S. nor Sir Guy' (*Hen. VIII*, v, 4).

Sandal Castle. Near Wakefield; a stronghold of Richard Plantagenet, D. of York (*Hol.* iii, 659). Alluded to, *3 Hen. VI*, i, 1, by York: 'I'll to my castle'; the Duke welcomes his uncles 'to Sandal' (*ib.* i, 2).

Mtd. in modern st. dirs. to *3 Hen. VI*, i, 2, 3.

Sandys, or Sands, Sir William. Baron Sandys of 'the Vyne'; *ob.* 1540; took an active part at the Field of the Cloth of Gold; K.G. 1518; Baron 1523; Lord Chamberlain 1526.

D.P. *Hen. VIII.* i, 3] discusses with Sir T. Lovell and the Lord Chamberlain the French fashions in vogue among the courtiers, and the great supper about to be given to Wolsey. i, 4] (at the banquet) plays the gallant to the ladies before the King's arrival. ii, 1] *p.m.*; attends Buckingham on his way to execution ('Sir Walter,' Ff).

If the banquet of i, 4, had been held before Buckingham's trial, in 1521, Sands (as implied) would not have been Lord Chamberlain; but we gather from Cavendish that it took place on Jan. 3, 1527, and at that date Sands was himself Chamberlain, and superintended the festivities. *Cf.* Cavendish, *Life of Card, Wolsey* (1825), 2nd edn. p. 114.

Saracens. An indefinite term for any Moslems. 'Many a time hath banished Norfolk fought ... Against black pagans, Turks, and Saracens' (*Rich. II*, iv, 1).

Sardians. People of Sardis. 'You have ... noted Lucius Pella For taking bribes of the S.' (*Jul. C.* iv, 3).

Sardinia, Island of. Offered to Sextus Pompeius by Antony and Octavius, on condition that he should 'Rid all the sea of pirates' (*Ant. Cl.* ii, 6; cf. *Plut.* p. 180).

Sardis. Capital of Lydia. It was at S., acc. *Plut.* p. 134, that Brutus and Cassius joined forces before the Battle of Philippi, and a warning spirit appeared to Brutus (*ib.* p. 136). On the army leaving S., 'two eagles ... lighted upon two of the foremost ensigns and always followed the soldiers' (*ib.* p. 137), but flew away, and were succeeded by 'ravens, crows and kites' on reaching Philippi (*Jul. C.* v, 1).

The scene of *Jul. C.* iv, 2, 3, is laid at Sardis. Plutarch's narrative is followed, *ib.* iv, 2; v, 1, 2.

Sarum. An ancient city which stood about a mile to the N. of Salisbury (New Sarum). Hence 'Sarum Plain' (*Lear*, ii, 2). See CAMELOT.

Sathan. Satan, the Evil One; lit. 'the adversary.'

'As slanderous as S.' (*M.W.W.* v, 5); 'play at cherry-pit with S.' (*T. Nt.* iii, 4); 'fie, thou dishonest S.' (*ib.* iv, 2); 'talked of S. and of limbo' (*All's Well*, v, 3); 'S. avoid !' (*Com. Err.* iv, 3); 'I charge thee, S.' (*ib.* iv, 4); '[Falstaff] the old white-bearded S.' (*1 Hen. IV*, ii, 4).

In *Sh.* always 'Sathan' (except *1 Hen. IV*, ii, 4, Q7, 8), though this form does not occur in contemporary translations of the Bible. It 'appears to have been derived from the Miracle Plays' (W. A. Wright).

Saturday. '*Ros.* Yes, faith, will I [love thee] Fridays, S.s and all' (*A.Y.L.* iv, 1) mtd., *L.L.L.* iv, 1.

Saturn (1). Mythical king of Italy, identified by the Romans with the Greek Cronos, and deified as father of Jupiter, etc. Mtd. with Apollo, Pallas, and other deities, *T. And.* iv, 3.

In Ff 'Saturnine' is by a manifest printer's error substituted for 'Saturn.'

Saturn (2). Planet. 'Born under S.' (*M. Ado*, i, 3); 'S. and Venus in conjunction' (*2 Hen. IV*, ii, 4); 'S. is dominator' (*T. And.* ii, 3); 'might well have warmed old S.' (*Cymb.* ii, 5). In this last passage the planet seems personified; *cf.* 'frigida Saturni stella' (Virg. *Georg.* i, 336); *cf.* also 'heavy S. laughed and leaped with him [April]' (*Son.* xcviii).

Persons born 'under S.' were supposed to be of a morose and melancholy disposition, 'saturnine' being thus the very opposite of 'Saturnian.'

Saturninus. D.P. *T. And.* Son to the late Emperor of Rome. i, 1] claims the throne by right of primogeniture, but, on the appeal of Marcus Andronicus, agrees to submit his claim to the popular voice. i, 2] Titus having withdrawn his candidature, Sat. is elected Emperor by acclamation; he offers to make Lavinia his empress; on seeing Tamora, and on L. being claimed by Bassianus, Sat. scornfully makes Tamora his bride in her stead; later, at Tamora's entreaty, takes Titus into his favour and declares a general reconciliation. (ii, 1) mtd. ii, 2] takes part in 'our Roman hunting.' (ii, 3) mtd. ii, 4] is present at the discovery of the corpse of his brother Bassianus, and reads a letter implicating the sons of Titus in his murder. (iii, 1; iv, 3) mtd. iv, 4] resolves that T. shall be executed; hears that Lucius is leading the Goths against Rome; Tamora calms his fears. v, 3] attends Titus' banquet; kills T., and is instantly slain by Lucius.

'Saturnine' in i, 2 (10); ii, 1; iii, 1; iv, 1, 3 (2), 4. The name, as that of the famous demagogue, occurs in Plutarch's *Life of Marius*. *Cf.* SATURN (1).

Satyrs, Twelve Men Dressed as. D.PP. *Wint. T.* iv, 4] *pp.m.*; they dance.

In the text (F1) 'they cal themselves Saltiers' – either meaning 'vaulters,' or by a servant's blunder. On their entrance, F1 has: 'Heere a Dance of twelve Satyres.'

Saunder. As a forename. 'Saunder Simpcox' (*2 Hen. VI*, ii, 1).

Saviour (The). Christ. 'That season ... wherein our Saviour's birth is celebrated' (*Haml.* i, 1).

The common noun 'saviour' does not occur in *Sh.*

Savoy, The. A former palace in the Strand, of which the chapel still remains. Built (1245) by Peter, Count of Savoy and Earl of Richmond. It was rebuilt by Henry Plantagenet, 1st Duke of Lancaster. Within its walls John, King of France, was confined after Poictiers. Burnt to the ground in 1381, while in possession of John of Gaunt, by Wat Tyler. Partly rebuilt, as a hospital, by Henry VII. '*Cade*. Now go some and pull down the Savoy' (*2 Hen. VI*, iv, 7).

Jack Cade's suggestion is derived from the account of the earlier revolt, in *Hol.* iii, 431: 'the house of the S., to the which in beauty and stateliness of building ... there was not any other in the realm comparable ... they set on fire.' The scene of *Rich. II*, i, 2, is laid at 'The Duke of Lancaster's Palace.'

Saxons. Subdued by Charlemagne in a war lasting from 772 to 804. 'Charles the Great subdued the S. ... in the year Eight hundred five' (*Hen. V*, i, 2). Cf. *Hol.* iii, 545.

Saxony, Duke of. '*Ner.* How like you the young D. of S.'s nephew? *Por.* Very vilely in the morning, when he is sober, and most vilely in the afternoon, when he is drunk' (*M.V.* i, 2).

Johnson hazards the remark that in the enumeration of Portia's suitors there may be some covert allusion to those of Queen Elizabeth.

Say, Lord. See FIENNES.

Scales, Lord. See WOODVILLE, ANTHONY.

Scales, Thomas de, 7th Baron (*c.* 1399–1460). K.G.; a famous soldier; taken prisoner (at Patay); cf. *1 Hen. VI*, i, 1 and *Hol.* iii, 601; raised a force against the rebels under Cade (1450); was entrusted with the defence of the Tower, and commanded in the fight at London Bridge. Acc. *Hol.* iii, 634, 'Lord Scales promised them [the citizens] his aid, with shooting off the artillerie in the Tower.'

D.P. *2 Hen. VI*. iv, 5] advises the citizens to 'gather head' at Smithfield, since he is himself 'troubled' in the Tower. (See GOUGH, MATTHEW.)

Scarlet, Will. One of the companions of Robin Hood; also 'Scadlock' and 'Scathlock' in old Ballads. '*Fal.* [to Bardolph]. What say you, S. and John?' (*M.W.W.* i, 1); 'And Robin Hood, S., and John' (*2 Hen. IV*, v, 3, snatch of a song).

Scarus. ('Scarrus,' F1.) D.P. *Ant. Cl.* iii, 10] describes Cleopatra's flight at Actium. iv, 7] though wounded, is eager to pursue the foe. iv, 8] *p.m.*; is promised a suit of golden armour by Cl. iv, 12] relates that swallows have built in Cl.'s sails (cf. *Plut.* p. 207).

An invented name, perhaps adapted from 'Scaurus.' The officer given the armour is unnamed by Plutarch, who adds that he forthwith deserted to Octavius (*Plut.* p. 219).

Scicion. See SICYON.

Scogan. See SKOGAN.

Soone. On the Tay, N. of Perth; the ancient capital of Pictavia, and the coronation place of the Scottish kings from 1153 to 1488. The 'Stone of Destiny' was carried away by Edw. I in 1296, and placed in Westminster Abbey. See Urquhart, *Hist. of Sc.* (1884).

Macbeth hath 'gone to Sc. To be invested' (*Macb.* ii, 4); Malcolm invites the nobles 'to see us crown'd at Sc.' (*ib.* v, 8). Cf. *Hol.* ii, 176.

Scorn. Personified. 'When thou shalt be disposed to set me light, And place my merit in the eye of Scorn' (*Son.* lxxxviii).

Scot. Native of Scotland. 'That evervaliant and approved Scot [Douglas]' (*1 Hen. IV*, i, 1); 'ten thousand bold Scots' slain at Homildon (*ib. ib.*); mtd., *ib.* i, 3 (3); Hotspur 'kills me some six or seven dozen of S.s at a breakfast' (*ib.* ii, 4); 'the sprightly S. of Scots [Douglas]' (*ib. ib.*); 'my noble S.' (*ib.* iv, 1; Hotspur to Douglas); mtd., *ib.* iv, 3; 'thou haughty S.' (*ib.* v, 3; Blunt to Douglas); mtd., *ib. ib.*; 'vile S. [Douglas]' (*ib.* v, 4); 'hot and termagant S. [Hotspur]' (*ib. ib.*); 'noble S. [Douglas]' (*ib.* v, 5); 'That furious S., the bloody Douglas' (*2 Hen. IV*, i, 1); 'a great power of ... S.s' (*ib.* iv, 4); 'the Scot,' *i.e.* the people of Scotland as a whole (*Hen. V*, i, 2 (3)); 'King of S.s' (*ib. ib.*; *1 Hen. VI*, iv, 1).

Scotch, *adj.* 'A Scotch jig' (*M. Ado*, ii, 1); the only instance.

Scotland. In the fat kitchen-wench, regarded as a terrestrial globe, S. was found 'by the barrenness; hard in the palm of her hand' (*Com. Err.* iii, 2); 'King of S.' (*Macb.* i, 2; v, 7 (2)); 'stands S. where it did?' (*ib.* iv, 3); 'this fiend of S. [Macbeth]' (*ib. ib.*); mtd., *ib. ib.* (5); mtd., *1 Hen. IV*, i, 3 (2), iii, 1, 2, iv, 1; mtd., *2 Hen. IV*, ii, 3 (2), iv, 1; 'If that you France will win, Then with S. first begin' (*Hen. V*, i, 2); mtd., *3 Hen. VI*, iii, 1; Henry takes refuge in S., *ib.* iii, 3; Richard's victories in S., *Rich. III*, iii, 7.

Scots, *adj.* Scottish. 'The S. captain' (*Hen. V*, iii, 2).

Scottish. 'What think you of the S. lord' (*M.V.* i, 2; changed in F1 to 'other'); 'S. prisoners' (*1 Hen. IV*, i, 3); 'S. power' (*ib.* iii, 1).

Scripture. The Bible, or a text therefrom. 'The devil can cite S.' (*M.V.* i, 3); 'with a piece of S.' (*Rich. III*, i, 3); 'How dost thou understand the S.? The S. says Adam digged' (*Haml.* v, 1). Metaphorically: 'the scriptures of ... Leonatus all turned to heresy?' (*Cymb.* iii, 4).

Scrivener, A. D.P. *Rich. III*. iii, 6] comments on the fact that Hastings' 'indictment' was prepared before his death.

Cf. *Hol.* iii, 724: 'One that was schoolemaister of Powles ... comparing the shortnesse of the time with the length of the matter, said vnto them that stood about him: "Here is a gaie goodlie cast, foule cast awaie for hast." And a merchant answered him, that it was written by prophesie.'

Scroop. See SCROPE.

Scrope, Henry le. 3rd Baron S. of Masham (*c.* 1376–1415); e.s. of 'Sir Stephen S.' (*Rich. II*). He was trusted to the uttermost by Henry V (*Hol.* iii, 548), but on an embassy to France was corrupted by an immense bribe – 'For a million of golde, as I herde say' (Lydgate) – and induced the Earl of Cambridge and Sir Thos. Grey to conspire with him to murder the King. The plot was discovered and they were executed (1415).

D.P. *Hen. V*. 'Lord Scroop.' ii, 2] adulates the King; counsels him not to pardon an offender who had 'railed' on him; is handed a paper showing Henry's knowledge of his own treachery; his appeal for mercy is rejected by the King with relentless invective; he is led to execution. ('Thomas,' Ff.)

Scrope, Richard le (*c.* 1350–1405). Abp. of York; s. of Henry le S., 1st Baron S. of Masham. Joined Northumberland's rebellion (*Hol.* iii, 529); treacherously induced to surrender to Westmoreland at Skipton Moor (*ib.* iii, 530); executed at York.

D.P. *1 Hen. IV.* (i, 3) spoken of as resenting 'his brother's death at Bristol, the Lord S.' (this is an error; they were but distantly related). iv, 4] sends letters to the leaders of the rebellion, and discusses its probability of success. (Mtd. by Hotspur as 'my lord of York,' ii, 3.)

D.P. *2 Hen. IV.* (i, 1) 'turns insurrection to religion.' i, 3] confers with the rebel leaders, and inveighs against the fickleness of 'the vulgar heart.' iv, 1] (in Gualtree Forest) announces Northumberland's retirement; relates to the envoy Westmoreland the grievances which have made him, though a man of peace, take up arms; hands a schedule of them to W.; believes the King will show politic clemency. iv, 2] is deceived by Prince John of Lancaster, and arrested for treason. (iv, 4) he is 'brought to the correction of the law.'

'The gravitie of his age, his integritie of life, and incomparable learning, with the reverend aspect of his amiable personage, mooved all men to have him in no small estimation' (*Hol.* iii, 529).

Scrope, Stephen le. 2nd Baron Scrope of Masham; elder brother of William le Scrope, Earl of Wiltshire; Chamberain of Household to Richard II; succeeded to the barony 1391; distinguished as a soldier; died in Ireland 1408. Mtd. (as knight, though then baron), *Hol.* iii, 499, 501.

D.P. *Rich. II.* 'Sir Stephen Scroop.' iii, 2] breaks the news to Richard that 'young and old rebel,' that Bushy, Green, and the E. of Wiltshire are dead, and that the D. of York has joined Bolingbroke. iii, 3] (in attendance on Richard in Wales) *p.m.*

Scylla and Charybdis. Names of two rocks, formidable to ships, between Italy and Sicily, or of the legendary monsters that dwelt on them; Charybdis came also to mean a whirlpool. '*Launcelot*... when I shun Sc., your father, I fall into Ch., your mother' (*M.V.* iii, 5); *cf.* a proverbial line from Philip Gualtier (13th cent.): 'Incidis in Scyllam, cupiens vitare Charybdim.'

Steevens observes that Gualtier's *Alexandreis* had been a common school-book.

Scythia. The country of the nomadic Scythians. Acc. Herodotus, the S.E. parts of Europe, but by the later Roman writers used to denote the greater part of Asia between the Volga and India. '*Chi.* Was ever Scythia half as barbarous? *Demet.* Oppose not Sc. to ambitious Rome' (*T. And.* i, 2).

Scythian. (*a*) *Subst.*, an inhabitant of Scythia. 'The barbarous Sc., Or he that makes his generation messes To gorge his appetite' (*Lear*, i, 1).

Harrison in his *Description of Britain*, ch. iv, speaks of the Scots as 'a mixed people of Scithian and Spanish blood,' that came 'out of Ireland,' and quotes Diodorus and Strabo to show that they 'were given to the eating of man's flesh and therefore called Anthropophagi.'

(*b*) *Adj.* 'Scythian Thomyris' (*1 Hen. VI*, ii, 3).

Sea-captain (1). D.P. *T. Nt.* 'Friend to Viola' (Rowe). i, 2] comforts Viola with the confident hope that her brother is not drowned; relates the story of Olivia, and consents to aid Viola in her project of serving Orsino in disguise. (v, 1) 'he upon some action, Is now in durance at Malvolio's suit.'

Sea-captain (2). D.P. *2 Hen. VI.* iv, 1] having captured Suffolk, is inclined to take ransom for him, but, on discovering who his prisoner is, indulges in a tirade against his offences and sentences him to death.

Acc. *Hol.* iii, 632, the captain of the *Nicholas of the Tower*, a ship of war, 'with small fight' captured S., and in Dover-road, 'on the one side of a cock bote, caused his head to be striken off.'

Seacole, Francis. Is sent for, to 'bring his pen and inkhorn to the gaol' (*M. Ado*, iii, 5).

Seacole, George. D.P. *M. Ado.* (In pfxs. 'Sec. Watch.') iii, 3] is chosen as constable, because he 'can write and read.'

Changed to 'Francis S.' by Halliwell, on the plausible, but not necessary, assumption that he is identical with the preceding.

Sebastian (1). D.P. *Temp.* Brother to Alonso, King of Naples (associated throughout the play with Antonio (*q.v.*), whom he had aided in expelling Prospero from Milan). i, 1] reviles the boatswain. ii, 1] derides Gonzalo; is persuaded to join in Antonio's plot. iii, 3] is undismayed by the magical devices of Prospero and Ariel – 'But one fiend at a time, I'll fight their legions o'er.' v, 1] suggests that 'the devil speaks in' Prospero; jests at the plight of Stephano and his companions.

The name may have been derived from Eden's *History of Travaille* (1577), where 'Alonso,' 'Antonio,' 'Ferdinand,' 'Gonzalo,' and 'Setebos' also occur (Malone).

Sebastian (2). D.P. *T. Nt.* 'A young gentleman, brother to Viola' (Rowe). ii, 1] cast on the coast of Illyria, with Antonio, laments his sister Viola, whom he supposes to have been drowned; urging A. not to follow him, sets out for Orsino's Court. iii, 3] thanks A., who has, after all, followed him to the city, for his solicitude, and consents to become his purse-bearer for a while. iv, 1] is accosted by Feste, who mistakes him for 'Cesario' (*i.e.* Viola); is assailed by Aguecheek, who similarly mistakes him; beats A. and draws his sword upon Sir Toby; is checked by the entrance of Olivia, who, also deceived, begs him to accompany her to her house; follows Ol. in bewilderment. iv, 3] soliloquizes, in Olivia's garden, on the marvellous 'accident and flood of fortune' in which he is involved; on Olivia's entrance with a priest, consents to follow her to 'the chantry,' there to be betrothed to her. v, 1] apologizes to Olivia for having hurt Sir Toby; greets Antonio; is confronted with 'Cesario' and discovers him to be his 'drowned Viola'; consoles Ol. by the suggestion that when she mistook him for 'Cesario' 'Nature to her bias drew.'

The name of the corresponding character in *Gl' Ingannati* is Fabrizio, in Bandello's story Paolo, and in *Apolonius and Silla* Silvio.

Sebastian (3). Name assumed by Julia in disguise; *T.G.V.* iv, 4 (2).

Sebastian (4). Commander mtd. by Parolles; *All's Well*, iv, 3.

Secretaries, Two. (D.PP. *Hen. VIII.*) See Pace, Richard.

Secretary. D.P. *Hen. VIII.* i, 2] *p.m.*; Wolsey bids him publish 'the King's grace and pardon.'

If this is the Secrotary of State, he is Thos. Ruthall (*q.v.*).

Seely, Sir Bennet. Executed at Oxford for conspiracy against Henry IV (*Hol.* iii, 516; the name being given as 'Sir Benet Cilie'). His head sent to London, *Rich. II*, v, 6.

The name has been variously given by historians as Sir John Scheveley, Sir Benedict Sely, and Sir John Shelley.

[**Seimor, Sir Thomas.**] Acc. *Hol.* iii, 897, the Lord Mayor mtd. *Hen. VIII*, ii, 1, l. 151: 'He sent command to the Lord Mayor straight To stop the rumour [of the royal divorce].'

Seleucus. Plutarch relates that Cleopatra gave Octavius 'a brief and memorial of all the ready money and treasure she had. But by chance there stood one Seleucus by, one of her treasurers, who, to seem a good servant, came straight to Caesar to disprove Cleopatra, that she had not set in all, but kept many things back of purpose. Cleopatra was in such a rage with him, that she flew upon him, and took him by the hair of the head, and boxed him well-favouredly. Caesar fell a-laughing and parted the fray' (*Plut.* p. 225).

D.P. *Ant. Cl.* v, 2] refuses to confirm, before Octavius, the inventory of Cleopatra's possessions, and is reviled by his mistress.

A. Stahr, *Cleopatra*, p. 270, has propounded the ingenious theory that this action of Cleopatra's was merely part of a prearranged comedy, whereby Octavius might be induced to believe that, in Plutarch's words, 'she had yet a desire to save her life.' Cl.'s assault on Seleucus may be compared with that on the Messenger (ii, 5).

Semiramis. Legendary founder, with her husband Ninus (*q.v.*), of the empire of Nineveh. The beauty and voluptuousness of the great Queen were proverbial. *Cf.* Ovid, *Am.* i, 5, 11; Pliny, *Nat. Hist.* VIII, xlii, 1. Cf. *Locrine*, ii, 1.

'Softer and sweeter than the lustful bed On purpose trimmed up for S.' (*Tam. Sh.* Ind. 2); 'To wanton with this queen, This goddess, this S. [Tamora]' (*T. And.* ii, 1; 'Semerimis,' QqF1); 'Ay, come S., nay, barbarous Tamora' (*ib.* ii, 3). *Cf.* also Chaucer, ed. Skeat, Group B, l. 359.

Sempronius (1). D.P. *Timon.* 'A lord, and flatterer of T.' i, 2] *p.m.* (ii, 2) Timon sends to him for a loan. iii, 3] professes to be greatly offended at being the last to be applied to, and refuses the request. (iii, 4) invited to T.'s last banquet.

Sempronius (2). D.P. *T. And.* iv, 3] *p.m.*; is addressed by Titus.

The name occurs in Plut. *Galba.*

Senators, Two Roman. D.PP. *Cymb.* iii, 7] 1st Sen. announces that the Emperor has ordered a levy of gentlemen to be made, to proceed against the Britons.

Senators, Two Venetian. D.PP. *Oth.* Members of the court before which Othello and Desdemona appear. i, 3] both discuss the warlike news from Cyprus; 1st Sen. questions Oth.

Seneca, L. Annaeus. Roman philosopher, and author of tragedies, all of which had been translated into English by various scholars in Sh.'s days, having been collectively published in 1581. Seneca has been regarded as the father of 'the tragedy of horror' (Collins, *Studies in Sh.* p. 119). Seneca is twice quoted (imperfectly) in *Sh.*, viz. *Hippolytus*, 1180, 'per styga,' etc. (*T. And.* ii, 1), and *Hip.* 671–2, 'Magni dominator,' etc. (*ib.* iv, 1). Parallels have been suggested between *John*, iii, 4, l. 135, and *H. Fur.* 345; *Haml.* iii, 1, l. 79, and *H. Fur.* 869 ff.; *Macb.* i, 5, ll. 41–55, and *Medea*, i, 1 ff.

Contrasted with Plautus, *Haml.* ii, 2.

Senoys. For 'Siennese'; people of Siena. or Sienna. Painter's rendering (in *The Palace of Pleasure*) of Boccaccio's *Sanesi.* 'The Florentines and Senoys are by the ears' (*All's Well*, i, 2). *Cf.* Dante, *Inf.* xxix, 134.

Sentinel, A. D.P. *1 Hen. VI.* ii, 1] complains of his hard lot, 'When others sleep upon their quiet beds.'

Septentrion. The seven chief stars of the Great Bear; hence, the north. 'As opposite to every good ... as the south to the septentrion' (*3 Hen. VI*, i, 4). *Cf.* Chaucer, *Monk's Tale*, l. 477: 'Both Est and West, South and Septemtrioun.'

Sergeant, A. D.P. *Macb.* i, 2] is brought in wounded; describes Macbeth's victories.

'Sergeant' in the text, 'captaine' in pfxs. and st. dirs. (Ff). Perhaps suggested by 'a sergeant at armes' slain by rebels, *Hol.* ii, 168 (Steevens). B.'Nicholson suggests (*N.S.S. Tr.*, 1880–2, p. 81) that he had been promoted for rescuing Malcolm.

Sergeant, A French. D.P. *1 Hen. VI.* ii, 1] (at Orleans) warns the guard to be vigilant.

Sergeant-at-Arms. D.P. *Hen. VIII.* See Brandon.

Servants. The following are D.PP., with speaking parts:

All's Well: Bertram's. iv, 3] questioned.

Com. Err.: Ant. E.'s. v, 1] announces that 'My master and his man are both broke loose.'

M.V.: (*a*) Portia's. i, 2] in attendance. ii, 9] ditto. (*b*) Antonio's. iii, 1] conveys message.

M.W.W.: see John and Robert.

Tam. Sh.: (*a*) Lord's. Ind. 1] announces players; sent to prepare Page to perform his part. (*b*) Lord's three servants. Ind. 2] wait on Sly and expatiate on his recovery. (*c*) Baptista's. iii, 1] summons Bianca. (*d*) Petruchio's. See Nathaniel, Philip, Joseph, and Nicholas.

(In *The Taming of A Shrew* the servants in the Induction are Tom and Will.)

T. Nt.: Olivia's. iii, 4] announces 'Cesario.'

Tr. Cr.: (*a*) Troilus'. i, 2] in attendance. iii, 2] ditto. (*b*) Paris'. iii, 1] wittily parries Pandarus' inquiries. (*c*) Diomedes'. v, 5] takes Tr.'s horse to Cr.

Servilius. D.P. *Timon.* Servant to T. ii, 2] sent to borrow money from Lucius. iii, 2] applies to Lucius, ineffectually. iii, 4] offers excuses to T.'s creditors. See Flaminius.

Serving-men, of Gloucester and Winchester. In blue and tawny coats, respectively. D.PP. *1 Hen. VI.* i, 3] the two parties fight before the gateway of the Tower. (One speaks.)

Sestos, or Sestus. A town on the narrowest part of the Hellespont, opposite Abydos. See Hero (2).

Setebos. Diabolic being worshipped by Sycorax. *Temp.* i, 2; v, 1. According to Rich. Eden's *Historye of Trauaile* (1577) (in a passage translated from the Italian of M. Antonio Pigafetta, who accompanied Magellan in his great voyage), Setebos was a 'great devil' of the Patagonians.

After describing how Magellan captured by a stratagem two gigantic Patagonians, the narrator proceeds: 'when at last they sawe how they were deceaued, they rored like bulles, and cryed upon theyr great deuyll Setebos to helpe them.' Later, one of the 'giants,' on being shown a cross, 'suddeynly cried out Setebos, and declared by signes that if they made any more crosses, Setebos would enter into his body and make him brust.'

Severn, River. Mtd. *Hol.* iii, 521, as forming the proposed boundary between Glendower's and Mortimer's territories under the tripartite indenture' made at Bangor (1405).

The Roman Ambassador is ordered to be escorted 'Till he have cross'd the S.' (*Cymb.* iii, 5); Mortimer's fight with Glendower, 'on the gentle S.'s sedgy bank' described, and how they drank 'of swift S.'s flood' (*1 Hen. IV*, i, 3); the river personified, *ib. ib.*; 'sandy-bottom'd S.' (*ib.* iii, 1); mtd. in connection with the 'indentures,' *ib. ib.* (2).

Sexton, A. D.P. *M. Ado.* iv, 2] presides at the examination of Conrade and Borachio. v, 1] *p.m.*

In the st. dir. of QFf he is called 'the Towne clearke,' but 'Sexton' in the text and pfxs.

Seyton, or **Seiton.** A surname newly adopted by the bearer at the time of the coronation of Malcolm III (1057) (*Hol.* ii, 176).

D.P. *Macb.* 'An officer attending on Macbeth' (Rowe). v, 3] in attendance, as Macbeth's armour-bearer. v, 5] announces to Macb. the Queen's death.

'The name of Seyton, Seton, or Seaton, is one of the most distinguished in the annals of Scotland... The Setons of Touch were (and are still) hereditary armour-bearers to the kings of Scotland.' (French, p. 296.)

Seyward. See SIWARD (1).

[Sforza, Galeazzo M.] See BONA.

Shadow, Simon. D.P. *2 Hen. IV.* iii, 2] is taken as a recruit by Falstaff.

Shafalus. Bottom's blunder for 'Cephalus,' who, acc. Ovid (*Metam.* vii, 700 ff.), resisted the advances of the goddess Aurora through his fidelity to his wife Procris: 'ego Procrin amabam: Pectore Procris erat, Procris mihi semper in ore.'

'*Pir.* Not Shafalus to Procrus was so true. *This.* As Shafalus to Procrus, I to you' (*M.N.D.* v, 1).

Shakespeare, William (b. Apr. 22, or 23, 1564; *ob.* Apr. 23, 1616). Dramatist and poet. The poet's name thus spelt is appended to the dedications of *Venus and Adonis* and *Lucrece*; it also appears in the same form on the title-pages of the *Sonnets* and of twenty-two out of twenty-four quarto edns. of the plays, the exceptions being *L.L.L.*, 1598 ('Shakespere'), and *Lear*, 1608 (i) ('Shakspeare'). It is also the uniform spelling adopted in the First Folio (1623).

On the other hand, the six authentic signatures of Sh. which have been preserved (though abbreviated and not easily legible) seem to show that Sh. himself wrote 'Shakspere,' and this form had considerable vogue in the latter part of the 19th cent., in consequence of its adoption by the New Sh. Soc. under the influence of its Director, F. J. Furnivall. But of recent years 'Shakespeare' has once more become the usual literary form.

See Lee, *Life of Sh.* (1915), pp. 518 ff., and *Sh. Eng.* (1916), i, 297 ff., where the subject is fully discussed by Sir E. M. Thompson, with facsimiles. It may be added that few more protean names exist. The name of the poet's father is spelt in fourteen different ways in the Council books of Stratford-on-Avon.

The earliest mtn. of the name – 'Johannes Shakespere' – seems to occur in the Borough Records of Nottingham, Nov. 8, 1357 (E. Weekley, *Surnames*, p. 252).

'Mr George Wise has recently amused himself by drawing up a chart (Philadelphia, 1868), which exhibits 1906 ways of spelling the name' (Allibone, *Dict. Eng. Lit.* p. 2006 b).

Shallow, Robert. D.P. *2 Hen. IV.* 'A country justice.' iii, 2] greets his fellow justice, Silence; boasts of his youthful exploits, and laments the death of old acquaintances; is informed by Bardolph of Falstaff's approach; greets Fal., and produces the roll of recruits; pricks down the selected men; brags of old times at Clement's Inn, which, as Silence remarks, was 'fifty-five years ago'; later, discusses the recruits chosen by Fal., and talks of the days when he was 'Sir Dagonet in Arthur's show': Fal. remarks (*sol.*) 'I do see the bottom of Justice Shallow.' v, 1] presses Fal. to stay the night at his house; Fal. (*sol.*) resolves to make laughter for the Prince 'out of this Shallow.' v, 3] carouses in the garden with Fal. and Silence; learns from Pistol that the Prince has become Henry V. v, 5] awaits the royal procession with Falstaff (to whom he has lent a thousand pounds); on Fal.'s being denounced by Henry, Shallow asks in vain for even five hundred of his thousand, and realizes that his chance of advancement has vanished.

D.P. *M.W.W.* i, 1] declares that he will 'make a Star-Chamber matter' of the wrong-doings of Falstaff, who has 'beaten my men, killed my deer, and broke open my lodge'; tries to ascertain his nephew Slender's feelings with regard to his projected marriage with Anne Page. ii, 1] longs to witness the 'fray' between Evans and Caius; in former days 'I would have made you four tall fellows skip like rats.' ii, 3] as a justice, forbids Caius to fight Evans, though it goes against the grain with one who has 'some salt of his youth' in him to stop a duel. iii, 1] is present when the Host induces the two foes to be friends. iii, 2] on his way to dine at Page's. iii, 4] urges Slender to pay his addresses to Anne, and puts in a word on his behalf. iv, 2] deprecates Ford's jealousy. v, 2] awaits the 'fairies' in the castle-ditch. See LUCY, SIR THOMAS.

Shancke, John. Mtd. as a 'principal actor' in F1.

Shapes, Strange. D.PP. *Temp.* iii, 3] bring in an illusory banquet; later, dance, and bear out the table.

Gonzalo speaks of them as 'monstrous' but gentle.

Shaw, Sir Edmund. Goldsmith; Lord Mayor of London 1482; intimate with Edw. IV; Privy Councillor to Rich. III; brother to John Shaw (*q.v.*).

D.P. *Rich. III* (unnamed). iii, 1] welcomes Edw. V to London. iii, 5] is easily persuaded that Hastings was justly executed. iii, 7] on behalf of the citizens, begs Richard to assume the crown.

Cf. *Hol.* iii, 716, 731.

Shaw, Dr John (or **Ralph**). Richard, D. of Gloucester, employed as advocates of his right to the crown 'John Shaw, clarke, brother to the maior, and frier Penker, prouinciall to the Augustine friers; both doctors of divinitie, both great preachers, both of more learning than vertue, of more fame than learning' (*Hol.* iii, 725). Acc. Hall, 'Raffe Shaa,' and 'Pynkie.'

They are sent for to Baynard's Castle, by Richard, *Rich. III*, iii, 5.

According to instructions, Shaw at a sermon at Paul's Cross told the people that Edward IV and his children were illegitimate (*Hol.* iii, 725); *cf.* Richard's conversation with Buckingham, *Rich. III*, iii, 5, 7.

She, Doctor. A nonce-name for Helena; *All's Well*, ii, 1 (Grant White). (But 'doctor she,' Ff.)

Sheba. See SABA.

Sheffield. See FURNIVAL.

Shepherd, Old (1). Father to Joan la Pucelle. D.P. *1 Hen. VI.* v, 4] would fain die with his 'sweet daughter,' but on her repudiating him he casts her off as a 'cursed drab.'

Joan's father is described (*Hol.* iii, 600) as 'a sorie sheepheard, James of Are.' His denial by his daughter is the dramatist's invention.

Shepherd, Old (2). D.P. *Wint. T.* 'Reputed father of Perdita' (F1). iii, 3] discovers the infant (Perdita) upon the beach; listens to his son's account of the death of Antigonus; discovers treasure in the child's 'bearing-cloth.' iv, 3] chides Perdita for not welcoming the guests at the shearing-feast; tells the disguised Polixenes that 'Doricles' (Florizel) loves Perdita; joins the lovers' hands; is condemned to death by Polixenes, and curses Perdita as the cause; later, resolves to tell the King all; is terrified into entrusting Autolycus with his proofs. v, 2] (has been brought to Sicilia with Florizel); being now 'a gentleman born' (in reward for his revelation), graciously forgives Autolycus. (For his son, see CLOWN (7).)

The shepherd's name in *Pandosto* is Porrus; he discovers that 'Fawnia' is beloved by the King's son, and is about to tell the King, when he is kidnapped by Capnio; he is ultimately made a knight by Pandosto.

Sheriff. D.P. *John.* i, 1] *p.m.* In the *Tr. R.* the st. dir. is: 'Enter the Shrive, and whispers the Earl of Sals. in the ear.' Ff have simply 'Enter a Sheriffe,' but the context shows that he communicates with Salisbury or Essex. (See FITZPETER.)

The actual sheriff of Northants was Sir Simon de Pateshull, but acc. *Tr. R.* 'Thomas Newdigate.'

Shipmaster. D.P. *Temp.* i, 1] gives orders to the Boatswain. (v, 1) rejoices at the safety of his ship. v, 1] *p.m.*; is brought 'amazedly' to Prospero's cell.

In Dryden's version he is named Stephano.

Shirley, Sir Hugh. Master of the Hawks to Henry IV; slain at Shrewsbury. ('Shorlie,' *Hol.* iii, 523.) 'The spirits of valiant Shirley ... are in my arms' (*1 Hen. IV*, v, 4). ('Sherly,' Ff.)

Shooty, Master. *Quasi* 'Shoe-tye' ('Shootie,' F1), 'the great traveller' (*M. for M.* iv, 3), seems to be an allusion to Tom Coryate, who walked to Venice and back in one pair of shoes; but, if so, the passage must have been interpolated after 1608.

Shore, Jane. Wife of a London goldsmith; became mistress of Edward IV, and greatly influenced him by her wit and beauty. Later, she is said to have become, successively, mistress of Lord Hastings and Thos. Grey, 1st Marq. of Dorset. She was accused of sorcery by Richard III, imprisoned, and made to do penance. Died *c.* 1527.

Acc. Sir Thos. More, she exercised a benign influence over Edward, and 'where the king tooke displeasure, shee would mitigate and appease his mind,' and bring men out of favour 'in his grace' again.

Clarence and Gloucester discuss the power exercised over the King by her beauty and 'passing pleasing tongue' (*Rich. III*, i, 1); Gl. sends a mocking message to Hastings, to 'give Mistress S. one gentle kiss the more' (*ib.* iii, 1); Gl. declares that the Queen is in league with the 'harlot, strumpet Shore,' and that Hastings is the latter's protector, *ib.* iii, 4; the Mayor agrees that Hastings' ruin is due to his having consorted with her, *ib.* iii, 5.

Shortcake, Alice. An acquaintance of Slender's, to whom he lent the 'Book of Riddles'; *M.W.W.* i, 1.

Shrewsbury. County town of Shropshire: at Battlefield, about 3 m. N.E. of the town, Henry IV completely overthrew the rebellious Percies and their allies, July 21, 1403. Act V of *1 Hen. IV* is wholly concerned with the battle. 'There died in all upon the King's side sixteene hundred, and foure thousand were greevously wounded. On the contrarie side were slaine, besides the Lord Persie, the most part of the knights and esquires of the countie of Chester, to the number of two hundred, besides yeomen and footmen: in all of those who fought on the Persies side, about five thousand. This battell was fought on Marie Magdalene even, being saturdie' (*Hol.* iii, 523).

The rebel leaders prepare to set out for S., *1 Hen. IV*, iii, 1; their meeting at S. announced to the King, *ib.* iii, 2; Falstaff sets out for S., *ib.* iv, 2; mtd., *ib.* iv, 4; Falstaff claims to have fought with Hotspur 'a long hour by S. clock' (*ib.* v, 4); 'a bloody field by S.' (*2 Hen. IV*, Ind.); news from S. brought to Northumberland, *ib.* i, 1; Falstaff's 'good service at S.' mentioned to the Lord Chief Justice, *ib.* i, 2; Hotspur's alleged recklessness at S., *ib.* i, 3.

Shrewsbury, Earl of. See TALBOT, JOHN (1).

Shrovetide. See SHROVE TUESDAY.

Shrove Tuesday. The day before Ash Wednesday, so called from the custom of confessing, and being shriven, in preparation for Lent, on that day. 'Shrovetide' is the period of a few days before Lent. Sports and merrymaking were usual on the occasion. 'Welcome, merry Shrovetide' (*2 Hen. IV*, v, 3); 'as fit ... as a pancake for Shrove Tuesday' (*All's Well*, ii, 2).

Shylock. D.P. *M.V.* A Jew. i, 3] is asked by Bassanio for a loan of 3000 ducats, for three months, Antonio being surety; refers to the precarious nature of A.'s ventures; refuses B.'s invitation to dinner; on A.'s entrance, indicates (aside) that he chiefly hates him for lending money gratis; tells B. that he cannot instantly 'raise up' the sum, but adds, 'a wealthy Hebrew of my tribe will furnish me'; in discussing the ethics of usury, reminds A. of the device by which Jacob outwitted Laban in dividing their flocks, and declares that he makes his money breed as fast as sheep; recounts the insults heaped upon him by A. 'in the Rialto,' and asks bitterly whether he is to lend him money 'for these courtesies' – nevertheless he consents to lend A. the required sum, without interest, provided that the forfeit be a pound of the debtor's flesh; on B.'s protesting against such a bond, retorts that the 'hard dealings' of the Christians make them suspicious, and declares that he extends 'this friendship' to A. merely 'to buy his favour'; bids A. meet him at the notary's to seal 'this merry bond.' (ii, 2) is characterized by his servant Launcelot. (ii, 3) his daughter Jessica declares 'our house is hell.' ii, 5] discharges his servant; entrusts the keys of the house to his daughter, but has a premonition of 'some ill a-brewing,' and bids her lock the doors, and not look out of the windows during his absence at Bassanio's entertainment; trusts that Launcelot will help to waste the substance of Bassanio, into whose service he is entering. (ii, 8) his frantic outburst at the loss of his ducats and his daughter described. iii, 1] hearing that A. has suffered losses, declares that he will hold him to his bond; has A. not given him sufficient reason? – shall he not revenge as a Christian would? Tells his friend Tubal that Jessica has stolen from him a costly diamond and other jewels, and wishes her dead at his feet; is rejoiced to hear of A.'s multiplied losses, but is again exasperated by tidings of Jessica's extravagance at Genoa, and most of all because she had parted with a turquoise ring that he had of Leah when he was a bachelor; urges Tubal to bespeak him an officer a fortnight before the bond falls due. iii, 3] scorns A.'s expostulations – let him beware the fangs of the 'dog,' he will not relent 'to Christian intercessors.' iv, 1] (in the Court of Justice) in reply to the Duke's admonition, 'We all expect a gentle answer, Jew,' declares that he will have 'the due and forfeit' of his bond, and that he will vouchsafe no other reason than that he bears A. 'a lodged hate and certain loathing'; to Bassanio's expostulation he replies: 'Hates any man the thing he would not kill?' Refuses the offer of double the sum lent, and adds that if the pound of flesh, which he-has so dearly bought, is denied to him, 'There is no force in the decrees of Venice'; whetting his knife, he sneers at Gratiano's objurgations; to Portia's appeal, 'Then must the Jew be merciful,' replies, 'On what compulsion must I?' On hearing P. declare that 'there is no power in Venice Can alter a decree established,' exclaims that a Daniel has come to judgment; prepares to exact the penalty; refuses to supply a surgeon, since 'it is not in the bond'; exclaiming to Ant. 'A sentence! Come, prepare!' is suddenly checked by being warned that no drop of blood must be shed in exacting the penalty; would fain accept an offer of thrice the sum named in the bond – or even the bare principal – or, failing that, 'the devil give him good of it!'; learns that, since he has sought the life of a citizen of Venice, all his goods are confiscate; is adjured to sue for mercy, and exclaims, 'you take my life, When you do take the means whereby I live'; after hearing A.'s plea for leniency toward him, is constrained to sign a deed of gift, 'of all he dies possess'd,' to Jessica and her husband.

A nearly contemporary pamphlet, of which the exact date is doubtful, is entitled 'Caleb Shillocke, his Prophecie, or the Jewes Prediction,' and in Pepys' Coll. of Ballads is one entitled 'Calebbe Shillocke, his Prophecie: or the Jews prediction' (1607); the name was therefore not unknown. Sir S. Lee, in an article in the *Gent. Mag.* Feb. 1880, entitled 'The original of Shylock,' argues that 'the begetter' of S. was Roderigo Lopez, the Queen's physician, a Spanish Jew. Lopez was hanged in 1594 for plotting to poison Elizabeth and a Spanish refugee named Antonio Perez. See art. on Lopez in *D.N.B.* M. A. Lower (*N. and Q.* I, i, 184) draws attention to 'Richard Shylock of Hoo' as a holder of land in 1435.

'Shelah' (Salah), Gen. xi, 12 ff., has also been suggested as a source of the name. See GERNUTUS.

Sibylla, Sibyl. Used as a proper name; one of the sibyls – prophetic women usually given as ten, but sometimes as four, in number. The most famous Sibyl is the Cumaean, who conducted Aeneas to the lower world (Virg. *Aen.* vi). She is represented by Virgil (*Aen.* iii, 441 ff.) as writing fragmentary verses on leaves which are scattered far and wide by the winds. According to Ovid (*Metam.* xiv, 100 ff.) she obtained from Apollo as many years of life as there were grains in a heap of sand; but she omitted to ask for perpetual youth.

'If I live to be as old as Sibylla' (*M.V.* i, 2); 'As old as Sibyl' (*T. Sh.* i, 2; 'Sibel(1),' FfQ); 'A sibyl, that hath number'd in the world The sun to course two hundred compasses' (*Oth.* iii, 4); 'The wind Will blow these sands like Sibyls' leaves abroad' (*T. And.* iv, 1); 'the nine sibyls of old Rome' (*1 Hen. VI*, i, 2; 'nine' being not improbably a reminiscence of the 'nine Sibylline books'; *cf.* Pliny, *Nat. Hist.* XIII, xxviii, 1).

For 'Sibylla' *cf.* Bacon, *Col. of Good and Evil*, 10, and *Adv. of Learning*, ii, 23; and the argument to Phaer's *Virgil*, bk. vi.

Sicil. For 'Sicily.' 'In presence of the Kings of France and Sicil' (*2 Hen. VI*, i, 1).

Sicilia. Roman name of Sicily (*q.v.*); thus written in the 'articles of peace' (*2 Hen. VI*, i, 1); mtd., *Wint. T.* i, 1, iii, 2, iv, Chor., 1 (2), 4 (3), v, 1. For 'King of S.': *Wint. T.* i, 1, 2 (2).

Sicilian, *adj.* 'Your Sicilian shores' (*Wint. T.* v, 1).

Sicilius. ('Sicillius,' Ff.) Father of Posthumus Leonatus; he fought for Cassibelan, 'But had his titles by Tenantius' (*Cymb.* i, 1); the apparition of S. appears to Posthumus in a vision, and entreats Jove to aid his son, *ib.* v, 4.

A king of Britain named Sicilius is mtd. *Hol.* i, 19.

Sicils. The kingdom of 'the Two Sicilies,' consisting of Sicily and Naples (*i.e.* Southern Italy), so called at periods of union, as when under the Angevins. See REIGNIER.

'Thy father [René of Anjou] bears the type of King of Naples, Of both the Sicils' (*3 Hen. VI*, i, 4); 'Reignier ... to the King of France Hath pawn'd the Sicils' (*ib.* v, 7).

The mention of 'Naples' with 'both the Sicils,' is inaccurate. Acc. *Hol.* iii, 624, R. claimed to be 'king of Sicill, Naples and Jerusalem.'

Sicily, Island of. The scene of *Wint. T.* i; ii; iii, 1, 2; v. 'Let what is dear in S. be cheap' (*Wint. T.* i, 2); 'nor shall appear in S. ['Sicilia,' F1]' (*ib.* iv, 4); mtd., *Ant. Cl.* ii, 6 (3) ('Cicelie,' F1); mtd., *ib.* iii, 6 ('Cicilia,' Ff); 'now let hot Aetna cool in S.' (*T. And.* iii, 1).

Sicinius Vellutus. L. Sicinius Bellutus, leader of the plebeians in their secession to the Mons Sacer 464 B.C. Chosen one of the first tribunes (*Plut.* p. 6). Violently hostile to the patricians (*ib.* p. 13), he attacked the Senate on account of the high cost of food (Livy, ii, 32–3; iii, 54). Pronounced sentence of death on Coriolanus (*Plut.* p. 19).

D.P. *Cor.* i, 1] animadverts on the pride and insolence of Marcius. ii, 1] while awaiting the triumphal return of M.

(now Coriolanus), listens to Menenius' defence of the general; stands aside on Cor.'s entrance; discusses with his colleagues Cor.'s impending candidature for the consulship, and predicts that his 'soaring insolence' will inflame the people against him. ii, 2] is present when Cor. is nominated for the consulship, and assures him that the people will not 'bate one jot of ceremony.' ii, 3] admits that Cor. has 'discharged the custom,' and bids him proceed to the Senate-house; rebukes the citizens for not having extorted promises from Cor., and persuades them to repair to the Capitol and revoke their consent. iii, 1] stays Cor. on his way to the Senate-house, lest all should 'fall in broil'; threatens to let the people know Cor.'s harsh language concerning them; sends an Aedile to 'call the people'; Cor. lays hands on him, but he is rescued by the mob; S. urges them to cast Cor. from the Tarpeian rock; returning with the rabble after their repulse, bids them despatch 'the viperous traitor'; but finally accepts M.'s offer to bring Cor. to the Forum. iii, 3] orders an Aedile to summon the citizens and to instruct them how to act; formally demands whether Cor. submits to the popular decision; charges him with attempting to seize tyrannical power; declares that Cor. deserves death, but pronounces sentence on him of perpetual banishment. iv, 2] meeting Volumnia in the street, seeks to evade her. iv, 6] converses with Menenius and certain citizens on the peaceful times that have followed the expulsion of Cor.; hears reports that the Volscians have invaded Roman territories, led by Cor.; bids the citizens have no fear. v, 1] entreats Menenius to use his influence over Cor. and stop his advance. v, 4] hears that 'the ladies have prevail'd' and proposes to meet them 'and help the joy.'

Sicyon. Chief city of Sicyonia, in the N.E. of Peloponnesus. Fulvia, wife of Antony, died there (*Plut.* p. 179). The fact mtd. *Ant. Cl.* i, 2.

'Scicion' in Ff.

Sidnis. See CYDNUS.

Sienna. Siena, a city and district in N.W. Italy. Iachimo is spoken of as 'Syenna's brother' (*Cymb.* iv, 2, l. 341), S. standing for 'the Prince or ruler of S.' In Beaumont and Fletcher's *Women Pleased* there is a Duke of S., notwithstanding that S. was a republic (Dowden).

Sigeia. *Lat.* adj.; of Sigeum, a port and promontory in Troas; hence, *poet.* for 'Trojan.' 'Sigeia tellus' (Ovid, *Her.* i, 33); purposely mistranslated by Lucentio and Bianca, *Tam. Sh.* iii, 1.

[**Sigismund** (1361–1437).] Emperor, son of Charles IV; the last Emperor of the house of Luxemburg. On May 1, 1416, he 'came into England, to the intent that he might make an attonement between King Henrie and the French King' (*Hol.* iii, 556). His arrival is referred to, *Hen. V*, v, Chor. In 1435 the Emperor again sought to mediate between England and France. A letter from him to this intent is mtd. *1 Hen. VI*, v, 1, ll. 1–6.

Silence. D.P. *2 Hen. IV.* A country justice. iii, 2] briefly replies to the questions of his garrulous 'cousin,' Justice Shallow, on family matters and bygone days; remains taciturn during Falstaff's selection of recruits. v, 3] after supping with Shallow and Falstaff, he bursts into snatches of Bacchanalian ditties, and vows he has 'been merry twice and once ere now'; offends Pistol by comparing Falstaff with 'goodman Puff of Barson,' and is shortly afterward carried to bed.

'In his cousin Silence, the man of untameable mirth when he is tipsy, and of asinine dulness when he is abstinent, this great fool [Shallow] yet possesses an admirer' (Gervinus, *Sh. Comm.* (1875), p. 336).

[**Silenus.**] See BACCHUS.

Silius. ('Sillius,' F1, 2.) D.P. *Ant. Cl.* An officer under Ventidius. iii, 1] urges Ventidius to pursue the Parthians.

First mtd. in st. dirs. by Capell; 'Roman' in pfxs. until changed by Theobald. Not mtd. by Plutarch, but the name ('C. Silius, consul') occurs *Plut.* p. 275.

Silver. Name of a hound. *Tam. Sh.* Ind. 1; *Temp.* v, 1.

Silvia. D.P. *T.G.V.* Daughter of the D. of Milan, 'beloved of Valentine' (F1). ii, 1] is shown, by Val., a letter which at her request he has written to a 'secret nameless friend' of hers; wishes it had been 'writ more movingly'; suggests that he should write another – and take it for his labour. ii, 4] is entertained by 'a fine volley of words' between the rivals Val. and Thurio in her presence; welcomes Proteus to Milan and laughingly accepts him as her 'new servant.' (ii, 6) her charms extolled by Pr. (iii, 1) her intention to elope with Val. discovered by her father. (iii, 2) falls into melancholy. iv, 2] is serenaded by Thurio; is appealed to by Proteus and scorns him for his faithlessness, but promises him her picture in the morning, if he will send for it. iv, 3] confides to Eglamour her intention of following Val. to Mantua; enlists his sympathy and arranges a rendezvous. iv, 4] meets Julia, who is disguised as 'Sebastian,' a page; gives her the picture for Pr. but refuses to accept the ring he has sent, since she knows it was given him by the 'poor lady Julia'; inquires as to Julia's personal appearance; pities her sorrows and gives 'Sebastian' a purse. v, 1] joins Eglamour 'at friar Patrick's cell'; they set out together. (v, 2) her flight is discovered. v, 3] is captured by outlaws in the forest. v, 4] having been, to her chagrin, rescued by Proteus, resists his rough courtship with indignation; on Valentine's entrance, is released; she takes no part in the *éclaircissement*; (the Duke consents to her union with Valentine).

Celia in Montemayor's story. 'The auburn-haired Silvia, rash and reckless, steps somewhat beyond the sphere of a woman's nature ... she possesses that ready wit, with which Sh. has invested all his bolder prominent female characters' (Gervinus).

Silvius. D.P. *A.Y.L.* A shepherd. ii, 4] expatiates to Corin on his passion for Phoebe. iii, 5] endeavours to overcome P.'s indifference; rashly consents to bear a letter from her to 'Ganymede,' with whom she has fallen in love at first sight. iv, 3] delivers the letter, believing it to bear 'an angry tenor'; is undeceived by 'Ganymede,' who reads it aloud, and is dismissed by him with a message to the writer – 'if she love me, I charge her to love thee.' v, 2] appears with P. before 'Gan.' who assures him that he 'shall be married tomorrow.' v, 4] upon Rosalind's declaring herself, S. is somewhat grudgingly accepted by Phoebe.

The corresponding character in Lodge's *Rosalynde* is Montanus. 'Sylvius,' Rowe. 'The unrequited love of Silvius for Phebe shews the perversity of this passion in the commonest scenes of life, and the rubs and stops which nature throws in its way, where fortune has placed none' (Hazlitt).

Simois. A river flowing through the plain of Troy; mtd. in a passage from Ovid (*Her.* i, 33) quoted *Tam. Sh.* iii, 1. 'S.'s reedy banks' (*Lucr.* 1437, 1442).

Simon. As a forename. 'S. Shadow' (2 *Hen. IV*, iii, 2); 'S. Catling' (*Rom. J.* iv, 5); also (2 *Hen. VI*, ii, 1, l. 91) for 'Saunder' or 'Simpcox' of mod. edns., in Ff.

Simonides. D.P. *Per.* 'King of Pentapolis.' (ii, 1) 'the good King S.' ii, 2] the knights about to contend in the lists are presented to him. ii, 3] welcomes them at a banquet; observes Pericles, and drinks to him. ii, 5] informs the knights that his daughter Thaisa will not wed 'for this twelve-month'; tests P. by insulting him; eagerly assents to his marriage with Th.

The name seems chosen at random, but it may be worth while observing that S. the poet (of Samos) was the founder of a group of three cities.

Simpcox, Saunder, and his Wife. D.PP. 2 *Hen. VI.* ii, 1] S. pretends to have been miraculously cured by blindness at the shrine of St Alban; but the fraud is detected by Humphrey, D. of Gloucester, and S. is condemned, together with his wife who abets him, to be whipped through every market town to Berwick.

This story of an (unnamed) impostor was first related by Sir Thos. More, and has been quoted by other chroniclers; *cf.* Foxe, *Actes and Mon.* (1579), i, 679.

Simple, Peter. D.P. *M.W.W.* 'Servant to Slender.' i, 1] is rebuked by his master, and replies tartly. i, 2] is sent by Evans with a letter to Quickly. i, 4] describes his master to Quickly; is discovered in hiding, by Caius, and blurts out that Sl. is in love with Anne Page; Caius sends him with a challenge to the go-between, Evans. iii, 1] attends Evans to 'the place appointed' for the duel. iv, 5] seeks to consult 'the wise woman of Brentford' on Sl.'s behalf, and is oracularly answered by Falstaff.

'John' in Qq.

Sin. Personified. 'Foul S. may say, He learned to sin, and thou didst teach the way' (*Lucr.* 629); 'in thy shady cell ... Sits S., to seize the souls that wander by him' (*ib.* 882); 'S. ne'er gives a fee, He gratis comes' (*ib.* 913).

Sinel, or **Sinell.** Acc. *Hol.* ii, 168, Thane of Glamis and father of Macbeth. But acc. Fordun, *Scot. Chron.* iv, 49, Macbeth's father was Finele (Finlegh, Finlaagh), Thane of Ross. 'By S.'s death I know I am Thane of Glamis' (*Macb.* i, 3).

Sinklo, or **Sincklo.** In *Tam. Sh.* Ind. 1, F1Q, for 'A Player' (l. 86) 'Sincklo' appears ('Sin.,' F2; 'Sim.,' F3, 4); again, the st. dir. of 2 *Hen. IV*, v, 4, Q, reads 'Enter Sincklo and three or four officers,' the pfx. of l. 4 being also 'Sincklo'; finally, in 3 *Hen. VI*, iii, 1, the st. dir. of Ff is 'Enter Sincklo and Humfrey.' (S. also appears as an actor in the Induction to Marston's *The Malcontent.*)

S., who was clearly an actor, is not mtd. in the list of 'principal Actors' at the beginning of F1.

R. C. Rhodes, *Sh.'s First Folio* (1923), p. 89, points out that John Sincklo, or Sincler, was a member of the Lord Chamberlain's company.

'Humfrey' may be Humfrey Jeaffes (Malone), an actor mtd. in Henslowe's *Diary*.

Sinon. Acc. Virg., a kinsman of Ulysses, who made the Trojans believe that he had been ill-treated by the Greeks, and persuaded them to admit the wooden horse (*Aen.* ii, 57 ff.).

'Like a S., take another Troy' (3 *Hen. VI*, iii, 2); 'S.'s ['Synon,' Ff] weeping Did scandal many a holy tear' (*Cymb.* iii, 4); 'Tell us what S. hath bewitched our ears, Or who hath brought the fatal engine in' (*T. And.* v, 3); Tarquin compared to him by Lucrece, *Lucr.* 1521 ff.

Sirens. (Or, less correctly, 'Syrens.') Mythical beings with the power of magically charming all who heard their songs.

'This nymph, this siren [Tamora], that will charm Rome's Saturnine' (*T. And.* ii, 1); 'Sing, siren, for thyself, and I will dote' (*Com. Err.* iii, 2); 'What potions have I drunk of Siren tears' (*Son.* cxix; the allusion is obscure).

Siward (1). Earl of Northumberland (*ob.* 1055); assisted Edward the Confessor against the rebellious Earl Godwin and his sons; his sister married Duncan, King of Scots, and became mother of Malcolm Canmore.

Acc. *Hol.* ii, 175, he was sent by King Edward, with 10,000 men, to assist Malcolm against Macbeth. It is said that he rejoiced at the death of his son when told that his wound was in front (but acc. Henry of Huntingdon this relates to a previous invasion, *ib.* ii 192).

D.P. *Macb.* ('Seyward,' Ff.) v, 4] approaches Birnam Wood with his forces and orders an advance against Dunsinane. v, 6] undertakes to lead 'the first battle.' v, 7] declares that 'little is to do.' v, 8] leads the attack on the castle; comments on his son's death, as above.

Siward (2). Son of Siward (1). Holinshed does not give the name (Osberht, or Osberne) of this son of Earl S., and cites two somewhat discrepant accounts of his death (*Hol.* i, 192).

D.P. *Macb.* 'Young Siward' in st. dirs. and pfxs. v, 4] *p.m.* v, 7] challenges Macbeth to single combat, and is slain.

Skogan, or Scogan. The name of two persons who appear to have become confused with one another: (*a*) Henry Scogan, or Scoggin (*c.* 1361–1407), a poet and disciple of Chaucer, who was tutor to four sons of Henry IV; and (*b*) John Scogan (*fl.* 1480), fool at the Court of Edward IV, and perhaps M.A. of Oxford. In the 16th cent. a volume known as *Skogan's Jests* was compiled. No early edn. of this is extant, but in 1565–6 a licence for printing such a book was granted. The names of Skelton and the elder Scogan were frequently coupled, as poets, and on Skelton coupled with the younger Scogan jest-books were afterward fathered.

'Scogan' is mtd. in 2 *Hen. IV*, iii, 2, where Shallow recalls having seen Falstaff 'break Skogan's head at the court gate, when a was a crack, not thus high.' 'That's fifty-five years ago,' remarks Silence afterward, with regard to the same epoch, and this would make the date of the alleged battery about 1358. Hence it is clear that the name is used by Sh. mythically.

'Skoggins,' Qq; 'Scoggan's,' F1; 'Schoggans,' F2, 3, 4.

Slander. Personified. 'Sl., Whose edge is sharper than the sword, whose tongue Outvenoms all the worms of Nile, whose breath Rides on the posting winds' (*Cymb.* iii, 4); 'Sl.'s venom'd spear' (*Rich. II*, i, 1); also, acc. Theobald's conjecture, *Haml.* iv, 1, l. 40.

Slender, Abraham. D.P. *M.W.W.* 'Cousin to Shallow.' i, 1] is jealous for Shallow's dignity; accuses Falstaff's 'coney-catching rascals' of making him drunk and picking his pocket; resolves never to be drunk again 'but in honest, civil, godly company'; catches sight of Anne Page; longs for his books of songs and riddles; on being pressed, is willing to marry Anne if Shallow says 'marry her'; boasts to Anne of his courage, and is with difficulty induced to join the party at dinner. (i, 4) his servant describes him. ii, 3] present. iii, 1] does not open his lips except to ejaculate at intervals, 'O sweet Anne Page!' iii, 2] has father Page's good will. iii, 4] in attempting to 'speak for himself' to Anne, blunders into the confession that her father and his uncle can tell 'how things go better than' he can. (iv, 5) would fain consult 'the wise woman of Brentford.' v, 2] has arranged 'a nay-word' with Anne, 'how to know one another' in the park. v, 5] finds that his supposed bride is 'a postmaster's boy.'

'He is a very potent piece of imbecility. In him the pretensions of the worthy Gloucestershire family are well kept up, and immortalised. He and his friend Sackerson, and his book of songs, and his love for Anne Page, and his having nothing to say to her, can never be forgotten. It is the only first-rate character in the play: but it is in that class. Shakespear is the only writer who was as great in describing weakness as strength.' (Hazlitt.) 'An idiot' (J. Masefield, *W. Sh.* p. 124).

Sly, Christopher. D.P. *Tam. Sh.* 'A drunken tinker' (in *Taming of A Shrew* 'Slie' only). Ind. 1] after wrangling with the Hostess, and boasting that 'the Slys came in with Richard Conqueror,' he falls asleep before 'an alehouse on a heath'; a Lord, returning from hunting, resolves, as a jest, to persuade S. that he is himself a rich noble who has 'been lunatic,' and with this object has him borne gently 'to bed.' Ind. 2] S. awakes in a rich bed-chamber, and is with difficulty induced to believe that he has 'been in a dream' for fifteen years; he converses with his supposed wife (Bartholomew), and is told that 'a pleasant comedy' is to be performed, 'to frame his mind to mirth.' i, 2] at the end of the scene S. inquires if there is 'any more of it,' and wishes it were done.

The earliest story on the subject of a trick resembling that played on S. is 'The Sleeper Awakened' in the *Arabian Nights*. It next appears in *Heuterus de Rebus Burgundicis*, as a quotation from a letter of Ludovicus Vives. An English version of this is given in Goulart's *Admirable … Histories* (1607).

A family of this name resided at Stratford in Sh.'s days; 'Stephen S.' is mtd. as having joined in a riot in 1598, also as having been a labourer employed by William Combe in 1614 (Halliwell). 'Joan S.' was fined for sabbath-breaking in 1630.

William S. (*ob.* 1608) was joined with Sh. in the licence of 1603: he is supposed to have acted Osric in *Haml.*

Sly, Stephen. Mtd. by Christopher S.; *Tam. Sh.* Ind. 2.

Slye, William (*ob.* 1608). Mtd. as a 'principal actor' in F1.

Smalus. An alleged ruler of Libya; mtd. *Wint. T.* v, 1. (Perh. for 'Ismael.')

Smethwick, John. Published *Rom. J.* in 1609, and *Hamlet* in 1611; his name appears (as 'I. Smithweeke') in the colophon of the First Folio as one of the four at whose 'charges' it was printed.

Smile, Jane. An alleged sweetheart of Touchstone's; *A.Y.L.* ii, 4.

Smile, Sir. Nonce-name applied to a hypocrite. 'Sir S., his neighbour' (*Wint. T.* i, 2).

Smith, 'the Weaver.' D.P. *2 Hen. VI.* iv, 2] makes sarcastic comments (aside) during Cade's speech; identifies 'the clerk of Chatham.' iv, 7] again sneers at Cade.

Smithfield. Originally ground for jousts and tournaments, without the city walls. The name has been supposed to be a corruption of 'smooth-field.' Bartholomew Fair was long held there, and it was a market-place for horses and cattle in Sh.'s days. Smithfield was also a place of public execution before Tyburn. Bardolph goes to Sm. to buy Falstaff a horse, *2 Hen. IV*, i, 2; 'The witch in Sm. shall be burn'd to ashes' (*2 Hen. VI*, ii, 3); the citizens ordered to 'gather head' there to resist Cade, *ib.* iv, 5, 6.

Smolkin. ('Smulkin,' Ff; 'Snulbug,' Qq.) Name of a fiend. 'Peace, S.! peace, thou fiend!' (*Lear*, iii, 4).

The name of one 'of the punie spirits cast out of Trayford'; Harsnet, *Declaration*, etc., x, 54.

Smooth. 'Master S.'s the silkman' (*2 Hen. IV*, ii, 1).

Snare. D.P. *2 Hen. IV.* A sheriff's officer. ii, 1] attempts to arrest Falstaff at the suit of the Hostess, but fears 'he will stab.'

Sneak. Leader of a band of musicians. 'See if thou canst find out S.'s noise; mistress Tearsheet would fain have some music' (*2 Hen. IV*, ii, 4).

Snout, Tom. D.P. *M.N.D.* A tinker. i, 2] is allotted the part of 'Pyramus's father' in the Interlude. iii, 1] suggests that the ladies 'will be afeard of the lion.' iv, 2] *p.m.* v, 7] enacts the part of 'Wall' (Qq give this part to Flute).

Snug. D.P. *M.N.D.* A joiner. i, 2] is allotted 'the lion's part' in the Interlude, 'for it is nothing but roaring.' iii, 1] raises difficulties with regard to moonshine and the wall. iv, 2] reports that 'the Duke is coming from the temple.' v, 1] performs his part, revealing his identity to the audience.

Socrates. Famous Gk. philosopher; mtd. *Tam. Sh.* i, 2. See Xantippe.

Sol. The Sun, regarded as a planet. 'And therefore is the glorious planet Sol, In noble eminence enthroned and sphered Amidst the other' (*Tr. Cr.* i, 3). *Cf.* 'the golden sun … Gallops the zodiac in his glistering coach' (*T. And.* ii, 1).

Solanio. See Salanio.

Soldier. D.P. *2 Hen. VI.* iv, 6] is killed for naming Cade, and not calling him 'Lord Mortimer.'

Soldiers. D.PP. *All's Well.* iv, 1] No. 1 takes a leading part in terrifying Parolles; No. 2 also speaks. iv, 3] they bring in P.; No. 1 interrogates him at length.

Solinus. D.P. *Com. Err.* Duke of Ephesus. i, 1] warns Aegeon that since there is a mortal feud between Ephesus and Syracuse his life is forfeit for daring to land at the former place, unless he can pay a thousand marks as ransom; on hearing Aegeon's story, pities him, and gives him a day in which to make up the necessary sum. v, 1] causes it to be proclaimed that Aegeon shall not die 'if any friend will pay the sum for him'; hears Adriana's complaint against the abbess, and that of Ant. E. against

Adriana; thinks them 'all mated or stark mad'; grasps the situation, and pardons Aegeon.

The name 'Solinus' had been familiarized to English readers, shortly before the production of the play, by the publication of *The excellent and pleasant Worke of Julius Solinus Polyhistor ... translated out of Latin by Arthur Golding* (1587).

In error, 'Salinus,' F2, 3, 4.

Solomon. King of Israel. 'There is no evil angel but Love ... yet was S. so seduced, and he had a very good wit' (*L.L.L.* i, 2); 'to see ... profound S. tuning [or, 'to tune'] a jig' (*ib.* iv, 3).

'Salomon,' F1, 2. For S.'s wisdom, *cf.* 1 Kings iv, 29 ff.; for his frailties, cf. *ib.* xi, I ff.

Solyman, Sultan. 'A Persian prince That won thrice fields of Sultan S.' (*M.V.* ii, 1).

Perhaps in allusion to S. the Magnificent, who made war on Persia in 1535.

Somerset. D.P. *3 Hen. VI.* This character must be regarded as partly fictitious, or at any rate composite. In iv, 1, he 'follows Clarence' and would be, in this respect, Henry Beaufort, 3rd D. of Som., who deserted the Red for the White Rose, but rejoined the Lancastrians and was beheaded in 1464 after the Battle of Hexham. But the 'Somerset' of v, 1, is congruent with Henry's brother Edmund, who was always a Lancastrian.

Somerset, Charles. See CHAMBERLAIN, THE LORD.

Somerset, 1st Duke of. See BEAUFORT, JOHN (1).

Somerville, Sir John. D.P. *3 Hen. VI.* v, 1] (at Coventry) reports to Warwick the approach of Clarence's force. Thus first designated by Capell. Simply 'Summerfield' in *The True Tragedie*, and 'Somervile' in Ff. Conjectured by French (p. 199), to be Sir Thos. S. (*ob.* 1500) of Aston-Somerville, near Evesham.

Somme. River of Northern France. '*Fr. King.* 'Tis certain he hath passed the river S.' (*Hen. V*, iii, 5; cf. *Hol.* iii, 552: 'The French king, being at Rone, and hearing that king Henrie was passed the river Sone, was much displeased therewith').

Son that has killed his Father. D.P. *3 Hen. VI.* ii, 5] (at the Battle of Towton) discovers whom he has slain, and bitterly laments the deed, in the presence of King Henry, who bewails the 'piteous spectacle.' (See TOWTON.)

Sonnets. In 1609 there appeared a thin quarto bearing the title 'Shakespeare's Sonnets. Never before Imprinted. At London By G. Eld for T.T. and are to be solde by William Aspley. 1609.' In a part of the issue the title-page differs from this by the substitution of 'Iohn Wright, dwelling at Christ Church gate' for 'William Aspley.'

The sonnets in this volume are 154 in number and are followed by 'A Louers Complaint. By William Shakespeare' (*q.v.*). The text is very corrupt, being full of unintelligent blunders. Only eleven copies seem to be now extant.

No other edition of the *Sonnets* was published until 1640, when John Benson issued 'Poems written by Wil. Shakespeare Gent.' This contains 146 of the sonnets, together with all Jaggard's 'Passionate Pilgrim' of 1612 and other pieces. The order of the sonnets is quite different in this edition, and headings, or titles, are prefixed. No further issue of either edition appeared until 1740.

More has been written about the *Sonnets* than about any other of Sh.'s works, and many have seen in them a self-revelation which lovers of the poet have wished impossible. But the autobiographical importance of the *Sonnets* is largely to be discounted by three considerations: (*a*) that there was an astonishing 'sonnetteering vogue' in England just at the time when Sh. wrote these poems; (*b*) that extravagance in flattery, and in amorous 'conceits,' was a deliberate feature of the sonnets of the day; (*c*) that Sh.'s intensely dramatic genius enabled him to present imagined emotions and thoughts as though they were his own. (See, on the whole subject, Sir S. Lee's introduction to the facsimile of the 1609 edn., publd. by the Clarendon Press.)

Sooth, Signor. Nonce-name ('Master Flatterer') applied by Helicanus to a Lord; *Per.* i, 2.

Soothsayer (1). D.P. *Jul. C.* i, 2] bids Caesar 'Beware the Ides of March.' ii, 4] tells Portia that he fears harm may chance to Caesar; but hopes to warn him. iii, 1] reminds Caesar, who remarks that the Ides of March are come, that they are not past (*Plut.* p. 98).

Acc. Suetonius, *Caes.* 81, the name of the *haruspex* was Vestritius Spurinna. *Cf.* Val. Max. viii, 11.

Soothsayer (2). D.P. *Ant. Cl.* 'A soothsayer or astronomer of Egypt' (*Plut.* p. 181). i, 2] reads the hands of Charmian and Iras. ii, 3] warns Antony that his 'demon' or 'angel' is always overpowered by Caesar's when they are together, 'but, he away, 'tis noble' (cf. *Plut.* p. 181).

Cf. *Macb.* iii, 1: 'under him [Banquo] My genius is rebuk'd, as it is said Mark Anthonie's was by Caesar.'

Soothsayer (3). D.P. *Cymb.* **iv, 2]** interprets, auspiciously for Rome, a vision the gods had shown him. v, 5] interprets Posthumus' mystic 'label.'

He is addressed as 'Philharmonus' (v, 5).

Sophy, The. Title by which the Shah of Persia was usually known in the 16th and 17th centuries. (From the Safevi dynasty, founded by Shah Ismail, 1500.) The travels of the brothers Shirley, and their reception by the Shah, attracted English attention to Persia in 1600.

'*Fab.* I will not give my part of this sport for a pension of thousands to be paid from the S.' (*T. Nt.* ii, 5); '*To.* Why, man, he's a very devil; ... They say he has been fencer to the S.' (*ib.* iii, 4); 'this scimitar that slew the S.' (*M.V.* ii, 1).

'Soffi, and Sofito, an auncient word signifying a wise man, learned and skilfull in Magike Naturall. It is growen to be the common name of the Emperour of Persia' (*Hist. of the Warres between the Turkes and the Persians* ... by J. T. Minadoi, Eng. transln. 1595).

Sossius. For 'C. Sosius,' consul 66 B.C. 'Sossius, one of Antonius' lieutenants in Syria, did notable service' (*Plut.* p. 183). 'S. ... his lieutenant For quick accumulation of renown, ... lost his [A.'s] favour' (*Ant. Cl.* iii, 1).

Rowe substituted the classical form 'Sosius.'

Soto. Character in an unnamed play. 'A farmer's eldest son' who wooed a gentlewoman; mtd. *Tam. Sh.* Ind. 1.

It is very questionable whether Sh. alluded to a character of this name in Beaumont and Fletcher's *Women Pleased* (Knight).

South, The. The south wind, which was regarded as unhealthy. Cf. *Batman uppon Bartholome* (1582), xi, 3: 'Southerne winds vnbind humours, & moue them out of the inner parts outwards, & they cause heauinesse of wits & of feeling; they corrupt and destroye, they heat, and maketh men fall into sicknesse.' 'All the contagion of the s. light on you' (*Cor.* i, 4); 'the rotten diseases of the s.' (*Tr. Cr.* v. 1); 'like foggy s., puffing with wind and rain' (*A.Y.L.* iii, 5); 'tempest of commotion, like the s., Borne with black vapour' (*2 Hen. IV*, ii, 4).

In 'the sweet sound That breathes upon a bank of violets' (*T. Nt.* i, 1). Pope proposed 'south' for 'sound.' In no other instance is a laudatory epithet applied to this wind.

Soundpost, James. D.P. *Rom. J.* A singer. iv, 5] replies to Peter.

Southam. ('Sucham,' in Domesday.) A town about 7 m. S.E. of Leamington. Clarence's forces at S., *3 Hen. VI*, v, 1.

Southampton. Sea-port in Hants; Henry V thence embarked for France, *Hen. V*, ii, Chor.; mtd., *ib.* ii, 3. See also HAMPTON and BEVIS.

Southampton, Earls of. See WRIOTHESLEY.

South Sea. The Pacific Ocean, so called by its discoverer Balboa (1513), since it forms the southern shore of the Isthmus of Panama where he crossed it.

Rosalind exclaims to Celia, who is tantalizing her by withholding Orlando's name: 'One inch of delay more, is a South-Sea of discovery' (*A.Y.L.* iii, 2).

Drake returned from his voyage of circumnavigation in 1580. The precise force of Rosalind's phrase has led to much discussion. See Furness, *Var.* p. 159.

Southwark. District of London to the S. of London Bridge. (See PARIS GARDEN.) 'The rebels under Cade are in S.' (*2 Hen. VI*, iv, 4); the scene (*ib.* iv, 8) is laid in S., where the rebels submit to Buckingham and Clifford; cf. *Hol.* iii, 635.

Southwell, Thomas. 'Priest, and canon of S. Stephens at Westminster' (*Hol.* iii, 622), accused of joining in conspiracy to destroy the King by sorcery; died in the Tower before the date fixed for his execution (*ib.* iii, 623).

D.P. *2 Hen. VI.* 'Southwell.' i, 4] arrested while making conjurations before the Dss. of Gloucester. ii, 3] *p.m.*; condemned to be hanged.

Sowter. Name of a hound. 'S. will cry upon't ... though it be as rank as a fox' (*T. Nt.* ii, 5).

'S.' means a cobbler, but Furness plausibly suggests that the word stands for 'Shouter.'

Spain. 'A refined traveller of S.' (*L.L.L.* i, 1); 'many a knight from tawny S.' (*ib. ib.*); 'Where S.? ... I felt it hot in her breath' (*Com. Err.* iii, 2); 'the hot breath of S.' (*ib. ib.*); 'Lady Blanch of S.' (*John*, ii, 1); 'that daughter of S.' (*ib. ib.*); 'the fig of S.' (*Hen. V*, iii, 6); 'John of Gaunt, Which did subdue the greatest part of S.' (*3 Hen. VI*, iii, 3); '*Kath... Ferdinand my father, King of S... my friends in S.' (Hen. VIII*, ii, 4); '[Caesar] had the fever when he was in S.' (*Jul. C.* i, 2); 'a sword of S.' (*Oth.* v, 2).

Spaniard. 'A S. from the hip upward, no doublet' (*M. Ado*, iii, 2); 'A S.'s rapier' (*L.L.L.* i, 2); 'this Armado is a S.' (*ib.* iv, 1); 'fig me, like the bragging S.' (*2 Hen. IV*, v, 3); 'the S. tied by blood and favour to her' (*Hen. VIII*, ii, 2); 'a S.'s mouth so watered' (*Per.* iv, 3).

Spaniard, A. D.P. *Cymb.* (Ff). i, 4] *p.m.*

Spanish. (*a*) *Subst.*, Spanish language. 'The motto thus in S.' (*Per.* ii, 2). (*b*) *Adj.* 'S. sword' (*All's Well*, iv, 1); 'S. blades' (*Rom. J.* i, 4); 'S.-pouch' (*1 Hen. IV*, ii, 4).

Sparta. Chief city of Peloponnesus; Menelaus was King of S. 'If Helen be wife to Sparta's king' (*Tr. Cr.* ii, 2); 'a knight of S.' (*Per.* ii, 2); 'They bay'd the bear with hounds of S.' (*M.N.D.* iv, 1; rep.).

Spartan, *adj.* '*Thes.* My hounds are bred out of the S. kind' (*M.N.D.* iv, 1); *cf.* Golding's *Ovid*, iii: 'shaggie Rugge ... that had a sire of Crete and Dam of Sparta.'

Lodovico addresses Iago, who maintains obstinate silence, as 'S. dog' (*Oth.* v, 2), either with reference to the ferocity of the animal, or the proverbial silence of the Spartans under suffering.

Speed. D.P. *T.G.V.* 'A clownish servant to Valentine' (F1). i, 1] informs Proteus that he has delivered his letter to Julia (though he has actually handed it to her maid); complains that the lady gave him not so much as a ducat, and warns Pr. that she is 'as hard as steel'; hurries off to join his master who is setting out for Milan; (throughout the scene he indulges in the licensed banter of the conventional clown). ii, 1] expounds to Val. 'the special marks' of being in love, and declares that all can see that Pr. is enamoured of Silvia; is present at an interview between Val. and Sil., and is delighted to discover that the latter has induced his master to write a love-letter, in her name, to Val. himself; cannot 'feed on the air' like 'the cameleon Love.' ii, 4] warns Val. that Thurio 'frowns on him.' ii, 5] meeting Launce, they discuss their masters' love-affairs. iii, 1] is inveigled into a discussion on the faults and merits of L.'s sweetheart, learning at last to his dismay that Val. has been staying for him all the while. iv, 1] falls, with Val., into the hands of outlaws, and advises his master to join them.

Spencer. See DESPENSER, THOMAS LE.

Spenser, Edmund (*c.* 1552–99). Poet. 'Sp. to me, whose deep conceit is such As, passing all conceit, needs no defence' (*P.P.* viii; non-Shakespearean; publd. in the year of Spenser's death).

Sphinx. A she-monster who slew every one that could not solve a riddle she proposed. Biron declares that Love is 'subtle as S.' (*L.L.L.* iv, 3).

Spinii. 'The regiment of the S.' (*All's Well*, ii, 1). See SPURIO.

Spirit. Raised by Bolingbroke. D.P. *2 Hen. VI.* i, 4] prophesies concerning the King, Suffolk, and Somerset. (Not mtd. in *Hol.*)

Spirits, in the shape of hounds. D.PP. *Temp.* iv, 1] pursue Caliban and his companions.

Spring, Season of. (The capital initial is here used for distinction, but seldom occurs in the text.)

'S. come to you at the farthest In the very end of harvest!' (*Temp.* iv, 1); 'the roses of the S.' (*T. Nt.* iii, 1); 'the S., the Summer' (*M.N.D.* ii, 1); 'the S. is near when green geese are a-breeding,' 'the first-born infants of the S.' (*L.L.L.* i, 1); 'in the S. time, the only pretty ring time ... Sweet lovers love the S.' (*A.Y.L.* v, 3); 'flowers o' the S.' (*Wint. T.* iv, 4);

'Welcome ... as is the S. to the earth' (*ib.* v, 1); 'wanton Springs' (*Rich. II*, i, 3); 'this disorder'd S.' (*ib.* iii, 4); 'violets ... That strew the green lap of the new come S.,' 'this new S. of time' (*ib.* v, 2); Falstaff referred to as 'the latter S.' (*1 Hen. IV*, i, 2); 'in an early S. We see appearing buds; which, to prove fruit Hope gives not so much warrant, as despair That frosts will bite them' (*2 Hen. IV*, i, 3); 'Now 'tis the S., and weeds are shallow-rooted' (*2 Hen. VI*, iii, 1); 'our sunshine made thy S.' (*3 Hen. VI*, ii, 2); 'Short summers lightly have a forward S.' (*Rich. III*, iii, 1); 'Sun and showers there had made a lasting S.' (*Hen. VIII*, iii, 1); 'It is love's S.' (*Ant. Cl.* iii, 2); 'And in his S. became a harvest' (*Cymb.* i, 1); 'apparel'd like the S.' (*Per.* i, 1); 'wither'd in her S. of year' (*ib.* iv, 4); 'The canker galls the infants of the S.' (*Haml.* i, 3; see *L.L.L. supra*); 'gaudy S.' (*Son.* i); mtd., *ib.* liii, lxiii, cii, civ; mtd., *P.P.* x; 'tender S.' (*V.A.* 127, 656); 'gentle S.' (*ib.* 801); 'hasty S.' (*Lucr.* 49); 'tender S.' (*ib.* 869); mtd., *ib.* 331, 604.

Spurinna, Vestritius. See SOOTHSAYER (1).

Spurio. A captain 'in the regiment of the the Spinii,' whom Parolles claims to have wounded, *All's Well*, ii, 1; again mtd. by P., *ib.* iv, 3.

Squash, Mistress. Nonce-name for Peaseblossom's mother, *M.N.D.* iii, 1, meaning an unripe peascod; cf. *T. Nt.* i, 5, l. 166.

Squele, Will. 'A Cotswold man,' an old associate of Shallow in his student days; *2 Hen. IV*, iii, 2.

Stafford, Edmund. 5th E. of Stafford; slain at Shrewsbury while leading the 'foreward' of Henry IV's army (*Hol.* iii, 523); he had been made Constable of England on the field. Slain by Douglas, who mistakes him for the King, *1 Hen. IV*, v, 3; Prince Henry, attacking Douglas, exclaims that the spirits of 'Shirley, Stafford, Blunt are in my arms' (*ib.* v, 4).

Stafford, Edward (1478–1521). 3rd D. of Buckingham, having been restored to the dukedom by Henry VIII; e.s. of Henry S., 2nd D. (*q.v.*); attended Henry VIII at Gravelines; beheaded on a false charge of treason. Acc. *Hol.* iii, 860, the Duke was in attendance on Francis at the Field of the Cloth of Gold, but had grudged the expense (*ib.* iii, 855). His trial began on May 13, 1521, and he was executed on May 17.

D.P. *Hen. VIII.* i, 1] having been kept from 'the vale of Andren' by 'an untimely ague' seeks for news on the subject from the D. of Norfolk; comments on Wolsey's arrogance, and the expense the nobility had been put to on the occasion; as Wolsey passes by they look on one another disdainfully; declares that Wolsey sells the King's honour; is arrested for treason. (i, 2) his surveyor (Knyvet) bears witness against him (*Hol.* iii, 862–4). ii, 1] (his trial described) in passing to execution, addresses the populace, and avers his innocence; speaks of himself as 'Edward Bohun' (*q.v.*); he and his father both 'fell by their servants.' (iii, 2) Surrey speaks of him as 'my father-in-law.' (iv, 1) mtd.

His full title, as given at his arrest, was: 'D. of Buckingham, E. of Hereford, Stafford, and Northampton' (i, 1). 'Hertford' in Ff.

Stafford, Henry (*c.* 1454–83). 2nd D. of Buckingham; g.s. of Humphrey S. (*q.v.*); as High Steward, pronounced sentence on Clarence, 1478; joined Richard, D. of Gloucester, and officiated at his coronation; later, raised an army against him, but, his force being impeded by floods, he was captured and executed at Salisbury. (He married the Queen's sister, Katharine Woodville.)

D.P. *Rich. III.* i, 3] is present during a bitter altercation between Q. Margaret and Gloucester; is greeted as a friend by the former. ii, 1] at the King's request, embraces Q. Elizabeth in token of amity; hears of the death of Clarence. ii, 2] suggests that Edward V should be brought to London, 'with some little train' (*Hol.* iii, 714); invites Gl. 'to part the Queen's proud kin dred from the King.' (ii, 4) commits Rivers and Grey to prison. iii, 1] welcomes Edw. V to London; urges Abp. Rotherham to procure the young D. of York from sanctuary (*ib.* 718); consults with Catesby as to winning over Lord Hastings; is promised the earldom of Hereford by Gl., when he is king (*ib.* 721). iii, 2] accompanies Hastings to the Tower, in seeming friendliness. (iii, 3) mtd. iii, 4] present at coronation council; confers with Gl. iii, 5] with Gl., explains to the Mayor the reason of Hastings' execution; leaves for the Guildhall. iii, 7] describes how he persuaded the citizens that Gl. was rightful king (*ib.* 730); tells the Mayor that Gl. is 'meditating with two deep divines'; points out Gl. standing between two bishops; begs him in the name of the citizens to accept the crown; feigns to leave him in anger; returns to salute him as king (*ib.* 737). iv, 2] is told by Rich. III that he wishes the two Princes dead; hesitates to reply; Rich. resolves to be rid of him; later, he reminds Richard of his promised earldom; moved by R.'s replies, resolves to flee to Brecknock (*ib.* 736). (iv, 3) is in the field with a force of Welshmen (*ib.* 743). (iv, 4) his capture reported. v, 1] (at Salisbury) is led to execution (Hall, p. 395); reflects on Q. Margaret's curse. (v, 3) his ghost appears to Rich. at Bosworth Field.

Holinshed (iii, 721) declares that it is a moot point whether G. unfolded his full intentions to Buckingham until he had imprisoned the Queen's sons and kinsfolk. The capture of B. was by no means contemporaneous with Richmond's landing as stated (*Rich. III*, iv, 4), the dates being Oct. 1483 and Aug. 1485 respectively. For his betrayal see BANISTER; for his execution see LONG, H. His claim to the earldom of Hereford was based on his descent from Eleanor de Bohun; see BOHUN, EDMUND. Fuller, in his *Worthies* (Brecknockshire) states that Buckingham was seized as he was digging a ditch, in disguise.

Stafford, Humphrey (1) (*ob.* 1455). Earl of Stafford; son of H., 1st Duke of Buckingham; his death at the Battle of St Albans mtd. *3 Hen. VI*, i, 1 (*Hol.* iii, 643).

Stafford, Humphrey (2). Baron S. of Southwick, 'named but not created earle of Devonshire,' ordered to assist Pembroke against the northern rebels (*Hol.* iii, 672).

D.P. *3 Hen. VI.* iv, 1] *p.m.*; is ordered by Edw. V to 'Go, levy men, and make prepare for war.'

Stafford, Humphrey (3) (1402–60). 1st D. of Buckingham; s. of Edmund E. of Stafford (slain at Shrewsbury, cf. *1 Hen. IV*, v, 3); resolved to drive Humphrey, D. of Gloucester, from power (*Hol.* iii, 626); was present when Gl. was arrested (*ib.* iii, 627); sent to demand of York the reason of his advance; wounded at St Albans (*ib.* iii, 643); tried to reconcile Queen Margaret with the Yorkists; killed at Northampton.

D.P. *2 Hen. VI.* i, 1] declares 'or thou, or I, Somerset, will be protector.' i, 3] upbraids Gloucester for 'cruelty,' before the King. i, 4] arrests the Dss. of Gl. while she listens to incantations. ii, 1] announces her arrest to the King. (ii, 2) York winks at his ambition, to serve his own purpose. iii, 1] present at Gl.'s examination and arrest. iv, 4] urges Henry to escape from Cade. iv, 8] offers pardon to rebels who submit; sets a price on Cade's head. iv, 9] is sent to parley with York. v, 1] demands from York the meaning of his armed advance; tells him Somerset is a prisoner; accepts his submission.

Edward, Earl of March, claims to have slain or wounded Buckingham at St Albans, *3 Hen. VI*, i, 1; there is no authority for this in the chronicles.

Stafford, Sir Humphrey. Knight; with William his brother was sent to pursue Jack Cade, but both were 'slain at Senocke [Sevenoaks]' (*Hol.* iii, 634).

D.P. *2 Hen. VI.* iv, 2] at the head of an armed force, with William his brother, bids Cade's adherents lay down their weapons; scorns Cade's pretensions and declares his followers traitors. (iv, 3) the two Staffords are slain.

Stafford, William. See Stafford, Sir H.

Staffordshire. 'John Doit of S.' (*2 Hen. IV*, iii, 2).

Staines. Town in Middlesex. 'Let me bring [accompany] thee to S.' (*Hen. V*, ii, 3).

Stale, Bully. Nonce-name applied derisively by the Host to Dr Caius; *M.W.W.* ii, 3.

In allusion to professional uroscopy, *cf.* 'the stale of horses' (*Ant. Cl.* i, 4).

Stamford. Town in Lincs and Northants; 'How a good yoke of bullocks at S. fair?' (*2 Hen. IV*, iii, 2).

'Samforth,' Qq; 'Stratford,' Halliwell, conj.

Standish, Henry (*ob.* 1535). Bp. of St Asaph 1518–35. Mtd. in the st. dirs. as present at the court in Blackfriars, *Hen. VIII*, ii, 4. It appears (*Hol.* iii, 907) that he was one of the 'doctors of divinitie' chosen by the Queen to defend her cause.

Stanley, George (*ob.* 1504). Son of Thomas, Lord Stanley (*q.v.*). Richard III 'in no wise would suffer him [Lord Stanley] to depart before he had left as an hostage in the court George Stanleie lord Strange his first begotten sonne and heire' (*Hol.* iii, 751).

'Look your faith be firm, or else his [G.S.'s] head's assurance is but frail' (*Rich. III*, iv, 4); George is imprisoned, *ib.* iv, 5; the King orders Lord S. to bring his forces to Bosworth betimes, lest his son pay the penalty of death, *ib.* v, 3; the King orders G.'s execution, *ib. ib.*; G. reported 'safe in Leicester town' (*ib.* v, 5).

Stanley, Sir John. Brother of Sir Thos. 'Lord S.' (*q.v.*).

D.P. *2 Hen. VI.* ii, 4] is given the custody of the Duchess of Gloucester, and ordered to convey her to the Isle of Man.

The dramatist here follows Hall (p. 202), but acc. *Hol.* iii, 623, and other chroniclers, confirmed by *Proc. Priv. Co.* vi, 51, it was 'Sir Thos. S.' to whom the duchess was entrusted.

Stanley, Thomas, Lord (*c.* 1435–1504). Succeeded his father, Thos. S., as 2nd Baron S.; with Hen. VI at Northampton, but received into favour by Edw. IV; again Lancastrian in 1470; imprisoned for siding with Edw. V, but was released, and made K.G., by Rich. III; stood aloof at Bosworth from fear that his son George S., held as a hostage by Richard, might be executed, but crowned the victorious Richmond, and was by him created 1st Earl of Derby. Married, *c.* 1482, Margaret Beaufort, Countess of Richmond (*q.v.*); Richmond, *Rich. III*, v, 3, addresses him as his 'father-in-law' (*i.e.* stepfather).

D.P. *Rich. III.* ('Lord Stanley' and 'Derby' ('Darby,' Qq), indiscriminately, in QFf; the latter title is inaccurate, as he was not created Earl of D. until after the accession of Hen. VII.) i, 3] excuses his wife's attitude to Queen Elizabeth, on the plea of her 'wayward sickness'; Gloucester refers to him (*sol.*) as 'a simple gull.' ii, 1] craves pardon from Edw. IV for a servant of his (cf. *Hol.* iii, 703). ii, 2] *p.m.* iii, 2] sends a messenger to Hastings to relate that 'He dreamt tonight the boar had razed his helm' (*ib.* 723) and that he mistrusted the 'separated councils' (*ib.* 722); on entering reiterates his misgivings. iii, 4] present at a council in the Tower. iv, 1] summons Anne, Duchess of Gloucester, to be crowned queen; advises Dorset to flee immediately to Brittany. iv, 2] informs Richard of Dorset's flight, and is warned to beware lest his wife communicates with Richmond (*ib.* 746); iv, 4] informs Rich. III that Richmond has sailed for England; assures the King of his support, but is compelled to leave his son as a hostage (*ib.* 751). iv, 5] sends a message to Richmond to tell him how he is situated (*ib.* 754). v, 3] visits Richmond at night, before Bosworth; wishes him success, but cannot openly aid him (*ib.* 755); refuses help to Richard (*ib.* 760). v, 5] (after the battle) presents the crown to Richmond (*ib.* 760).

For a full discussion, by J. Spedding, of the confusion between 'Stanley' and 'Derby' (or 'Darby') in both the text and the st. dirs., see *N.S.S. Tr.*, 1875–6, pp. 65–8. By Theobald 'Stanley' was substituted for 'Derby' in every instance.

Stanley, Sir William (*ob.* 1495). Brother of Sir Thos. S., 'Lord S.' (*q.v.*), and of Sir John S. (D.P. *2 Hen. VI*).

D.P. *3 Hen. VI.* iv, 5] *p.m.*; aids in the escape of Edward IV from Middleham Castle; cf. *Hol.* iii, 673.

It was Sir W. S.'s succour, with 3000 'tall men,' that gave Richmond the victory at Bosworth (*Hol.* iii, 759); this fact is not referred to in *Rich. III*, but Sir W.S. is mtd. as an adherent of Richmond's (iv, 5).

Star-chamber. The name (of doubtful origin) of an apartment in the Palace of Westminster where was held a court of practically unlimited powers. It has been described as 'a criminal Court of Equity,' and among its particular functions was the infliction of punishment for provoking riots.

'*Shal.* I will make a Star-chamber matter of it ... it is a riot' (*M.W.W.* i, 1).

Starve-lackey. 'The rapier and dagger man' (*M. for M.* iv, 3).

Starveling, Robin. D.P. *M.N.D.* A tailor. i, 2] is allotted the part of 'Thisby's mother' in the Interlude. iii, 1] is present at rehearsal and opines that 'we must leave the killing out.' iv, 2] declares that Bottom is, out of doubt, 'transported.' v, 1] (presumably) enacts 'Moonshine.'

'S... does not start the objections himself but seconds them when made by others, as if he had not the spirit to express his fears without encouragement' (W. Hazlitt).

Statilius. A soldier sent by Brutus, at Philippi, to view the field at night, and to 'lift up a torch-light in the air' if all was well; this he did, but he was slain on his way back, and Brutus fell into despair (*Plut.* p. 150). 'S. show'd the torch-light, but, my lord, He came not back: he is or ta'en or slain' (*Jul. C.* v, 5).

'S. the Epicurian' is mtd. as a friend of Brutus (*Plut.* p. 114); *cf.* Plut. *Cat. Min.* 65–6, 73.

Stephano (1). D.P. *Temp.* 'A drunken butler' (F1). ii, 2] finds Caliban and Trinculo lying beneath the same cloak and, after solving the mystery of the four-legged monster, gives them drink from his bottle; relates how he escaped from the wreck upon a butt of sack, now hidden among the rocks (henceforth the trio are associated). iii, 2] accepts Cal.'s suggestion that they should murder Prospero in his sleep, and looks forward to being monarch of the island, with Miranda as his consort. iv, 1] on reaching P.'s cell, is chiefly concerned at the loss of his bottle; but begins 'to have bloody thoughts'; his attention is diverted by the 'glistering apparel' hung up by Ariel as a lure. Arrayed in this, he assumes kingly airs, until chased off by spirit hounds. v, 1] driven by Ariel into the presence of Alonso, ruefully admits 'I am not Stephano, but a cramp.' ('The shipmaster' in Dryden's version.)

Stephano (2). D.P. *M.V.* Servant to Portia. v, 1] announces that P. will shortly reach Belmont.

Here accented on the penultimate.

Stephan. As a forename. 'S. Sly,' 'S. Langton,' 'S. Scrope' (*qq.v.*).

Stephen, King. Mtd. in a song beginning, 'King S. was and-a worthy peer,' sung by Iago; *Oth.* ii, 2. Cf. *Temp.* iv, 1, l. 221.

'I tell thee sawcy skipjack, it was a good and blessed time heer in England when K. Stephen wore a pair of cloth breeches of a Noble a paire, and thought them passing costlye' (Greene, *A Quippe for an Upstart Courtier* (1592), xi, 234, ed. Grosart); also, 'his breeches were not so much worth as K. Stephen's, that cost but a poore noble' (Dekker, *The Gul's Hornbook* (1609), ii, 210, ed. Grosart). In Percy's MS. it is 'King Harry,' whose hose cost a crown.

Stephen, Saint. Mtd. by a quaint anachronism, in *T. And.* iv, 4: 'God and Saint Stephen give you good den.'

Steward (1). D.P. *Timon.* In mod. edns. 'Flavius' (*q.v.*).

'In ii, 2, there is a servant called Flavius, who talks very like the steward in iii, 4, iv, 2, and iv, 3, though not so like the steward of ii, 2, and v, 1. He has however been identified with the steward by the modern editors, and perhaps by the second writer [of the play, as argued by Fleay], but if so, it must have been by an afterthought, as in ii, 2, l. 194, he is summoned by Timon,' as Flavius. (Fleay, *N.S.S. Tr.*, 1874, Pt. I, p. 146.)

Steward (2). D.P. *All's Well.* See RINALDO.

Stewart, Murdoch. See FIFE, EARL OF.

Stewart, Walter, Earl of Atholl. Taken prisoner at Homildon; *1 Hen. IV*, i, 1.

At the date of the battle (1402) there was actually no Earl of A., a title which was not revived until 1408 in the person of Walter Stewart, 2nd s. of King Robert II (French, p. 73).

Stiberdigebit. The equivalent, in Qq, of 'Flibbertigibbet' (*Lear*, iv, 1). The latter was introduced by Theobald. The passage is omitted in Ff.

[Stinchcombe Hill.] Near Dursley; still locally known as 'The Hill.' 'Clement Perkes of the hill' (*2 Hen. IV*, v, 1).

Stockfish, Sampson. 'A fruiterer' with whom Justice Shallow in his student days had a fight; *2 Hen. IV*, iii, 2.

For the origin of the name cf. *Temp.* iii, 2, l. 81, and *1 Hen. IV*, ii, 4, l. 275.

Stokesly, or Stokesley, John (*c.* 1475–1539). Chaplain and almoner to Henry VIII; made Bp. of London 1530, being 'then ambassadour to the universities beyond the sea for the kings marriage' (*Hol.* iii, 909). Mtd. as present at Anne Boleyn's coronation (in which he helped to bear 'up the laps of the queenes robe' (*Hol.* iii, 933)), *Hen. VIII*, iv, 1. ('Stokeley,' F1, 2, 3.)

Stony Stratford. Town in Bucks, situated on the highroad from London to Chester. Edward V, in his progress to London, is represented as resting there, *Rich. III*, ii, 4; in Qq the passage runs: 'Last night, I hear, they lay at Northampton; at S.-S. will they be tonight'; but in Ff 'N.' and 'S.-S.' are interchanged, which is clearly an error, since the latter is some 14 m. nearer London than the former.

Strachy, Lady of the. (*T. Nt.* ii, 5), a phrase of unascertained meaning, S. being doubtfully a proper name, and probably a misprint.

Among suggested emendations are: 'Stratarch,' 'Satrape,' 'Trachy' (Thrace), 'Trachyne,' 'Saucery,' 'Strozzi,' 'Sophy,' 'Astrakhan,' 'Tragedy,' and 'Starchery.' Collier has suggested 'Straccia,' the name of a servant in *Gl' Inganni* – but the connection is not apparent. Cf. *T.L.S.* March 6, 1924.

Strangers, Three. D.PP. *Timon.* iii, 2] they tell Lucius that T.'s fortunes are failing, and that his friends deny him; they afterward inveigh against ingratitude.

This scene is regarded as non-Shakespearean by Fleay and others.

[Stranguilio.] See CLEON.

Strato, or **Straton.** Greek rhetorician, a friend of Brutus, who, according to one account, held the sword for Brutus to fall upon, after the Battle of Philippi. He was afterward treated with distinction by Octavius (*Plut.* p. 151).

D.P. *Jul. C.* v, 3] *p.m.* v, 5] falls asleep upon the field; holds the sword, as related above; is brought before Octavius, and taken as one of his followers.

Stygian, *adj.* Pertaining to Styx (*q.v.*). 'Like a strange soul upon the Stygian banks, Staying for waftage' (*Tr. Cr.* iii, 2).

Styx. River of the underworld, across which Charon (*q.v.*) ferries the shades of the dead, after the observance of funeral rites. 'Why suffer'st thou thy sons, unburied yet, To hover on the dreadful shore of St.?' (*T. And.* i, 2; 'Stigia,' QqF1, 2); 'Fly not, for should'st thou take the river Styx, I would swim after' (*Tr. Cr.* v, 4). As a Latin word (accus. 'Styga'): 'Per Styga, per manes vehor' (*T. And.* ii, 1; *cf.* Seneca, *Hippolytus*, 1180: 'Per Styga, per amnes igneos, amens sequar').

Sueno. See SWENO.

Suffolk, County of. Mtd. *3 Hen. VI*, i, 1.

Suffolk, Dukes of. See BRANDON, CHARLES, and POLE, WILLIAM DE LA.

Suffolk, Earl of. See POLE, MICHAEL DE LA.

Sugarsop. Name of a servant; *Tam. Sh.* iv, 1.

The name means a comfit or sugar-plum.

Summer, Season of. (The capital initial is here used for distinction, but seldom occurs in the text.)

Epithets: 'proud' (*L.L.L.* i, 1); 'costly' (*M.V.* ii, 9); 'fantastic' (*Rich. II*, i, 3); 'glorious' (*Rich. III*, i, 1); 'hot' (*Cymb.* iii, 4; *Hen. V*, v, 2); 'goodly' (*T. And.* v, 2); 'eternal' (*Son.* xviii).

Attrib.: 'S. air' (*L.L.L.* v, 2); 'S. smocks' (*ib. ib.*); 'S. songs' (*Wint. T.* iv, 2); 'S. leaves' (*Rich. II*, i, 2); 'S. corn' (*ib.* iii, 3); 'S. bird' (2 *Hen. IV*, iv, 4); 'S. flies' (*3 Hen. VI*, ii, 6; in Qq only); 'S. beauty' (*Rich. III*, iv, 3); 'S. fields' (*ib.* v, 2); 'S. birds' (*Timon*, iii, 6); 'S. butterflies' (*Cor.* iv, 6); 'S. news' (*Cymb.* iii, 4); 'S. days' (*Per.* iv, 1); 'S. air' (*Rom. J.* ii, 6); 'S. buds' (*M.N.D.* ii, 2).

As a measure of time: 'so many S.s' (*Wint. T.* v, 3); 'five S.s' (*Com. Err.* i, 1); 'twice five S.s' (*Rich. II*, i, 3); 'many S.s' (*Hen. VIII*, iii, 2); 'two more S.s' (*Rom. J.* i, 2); 'three S.s' (*Son.* civ).

Heat of Summer: 'so hot a S.' (*John*, v, 7); 'S.'s parching heat' (2 *Hen. VI*, i, 1); 'S.'s scalding heat' (*3 Hen. VI*, v, 7); 'S.'s drought' (*T. And.* iii, 1); 'hottest S.'s day' (*ib.* v, 1); 'S.'s heat' (*V.A.* 91).

Miscellaneous: Ariel flies after S., *Temp.* v, 1; 'let S. bear it out' (*T. Nt.* i, 5; meaning doubtful); 'since S. first was leavy' (*M. Ado*, ii, 3); 'in a S.'s day' (*i.e.* a long day)] (*M.N.D.* i, 2; *Hen. V*, iii, 6, iv, 8); 'the middle S.'s spring' (*M.N.D.* ii, 2); changes its winter livery, *ib. ib.*; 'the S. still doth tend upon my state' (*ib.* iii, 1); 'the time will bring on S.' (*All's Well*, iv, 4); the martlet 'a guest of S.' (*Macb.* i, 6); 'Allhallown S.' (*1 Hen. IV*, i, 2); 'St Martin's S.' (*1 Hen. VI*, i, 2); butterflies in the S., *Tr. Cr.* iii, 3; swallow follows S., *Timon*, iii, 6; 'S.'s ripening breath' (*Rom. J.* ii, 2); 'S.'s death' (*Wint. T.* iv, 3); 'middle S.' (*ib. ib.*); 'S.'s cloud' (*Macb.* iii, 4); 'S.'s dust' (*Rich. II*, iii, 3); 'a S.'s bower' (*1 Hen. IV*, iii, 1); 'Shadow will serve for S.' (2 *Hen. IV*, iii, 2); 'S.'s velvet buds' (*Hen. V*, i, 2); 'S.'s corn' (2 *Hen. VI*, iii, 2); 'short S.s' (*Rich. III*, iii, 1); 'Sweet as S.' (*Hen. VIII*, iv, 2); 'a S.'s evening' (*Jul. C.* iii, 2); 'fair day in S.' (*Per.* ii, 5); 'Verona's S.' (*Rom. J.* i, 3); 'a S.'s day' (*V.A.* 23); 'S.'s distillation' (*Son.* v, vi); 'S.'s green' (*ib.* xii); 'S.'s day,' 'S.'s lease' (*ib.* xviii); 'S.'s breath' (*ib.* liv); 'S.'s welcome' (*ib.* lvi); 'S.'s honey breath' (*ib.* lxv); 'S.'s flower' (*ib.* xciv); 'S.'s front' (*ib.* cii); youth compared to S., *P.P.* xii.

Mentioned: M.W.W. ii, 1; *M.V.* iii, 1; *Wint. T.* i, 1; 2 *Hen. VI*, ii, 4; *3 Hen. VI*, ii, 2; *Cymb.* iv, 2; *T. And.* ii, 3; *V.A.* 802; *Lucr.* 837; *Son.* lxviii, xcvii, xcviii.

Sunday. As a day of rest: 'Shipwrights whose sore task does not divide the S. from the week' (*Haml.* i, 1). As giving leisure for reflection: 'sigh away S.s' (*M. Ado*, i, 1). In allusion to S. attire: 'velvet-guards and S.-citizens' (*1 Hen. IV*, iii, 1); 'as fair on Friday as Helen is on S.' (*Tr. Cr.* i, 1). Wedding-day of both Kath. and Bianca, *Tam. Sh.* ii, 1 (5). See Sabbath.

Sun, The. See Hyperion, Phoebus, Sol, Titan.

Surecard. ('Soccard,' Qq.) Falstaff mistakes Silence for 'Master S.'; 2 *Hen. IV*, iii, 2.

'A colloquial term for a boon companion' (Lee); *cf.* 'as sure a card as ever won the set' (*T. And.* v, 1).

Surgeon, Dick. *i.e.* Dick the surgeon; *T. Nt.* v, 1.

Surrey. Name of horse. '*K. Rich.* Saddle white S. for the field [Bosworth] tomorrow' (*Rich. III*, v, 3).

Richard was 'mounted on a great white courser' when he entered Leicester (*Hol.* iii, 754).

Surrey, Duke of. Thomas Holland, 3rd E. of Kent (1374–1400); D. of S. 1397; an adherent of Rich. II; deprived by Hen. IV of his dukedom 1399; plotted against Hen. and escaped to Cirencester, where he was executed by the townsmen, Jan. 7, 1400 (*Chron. A. de Usk* (1876), pp. 40–1). (The title is unique.)

D.P. *Rich. II.* iv, 1] challenges Fitzwater, who had given him the lie (*Hol.* iii, 512). (v, 6) his head sent to London (here 'Kent').

'The Lord Marshal' (i, 3) was, in fact, Surrey, 'for that turn' (*Hol.* iii, 493), since Mowbray himself held that office, and therefore could not act personally.

Surrey, Earl of. D.P. *Hen. VIII*, iv, 1; see Fitz-Alan, William.

Surveyor to the Duke of Buckingham. D.P. *Hen. VIII*; see Knyvet.

Susan. Daughter of Juliet's Nurse. 'S. and she ... were of an age. Well, S. is with God; She was too good for me' (*Rom. J.* i, 3). As a forename: 'S. Grindstone' (*q.v.*).

[Susanna.] See Babylon and Daniel.

Suspicion. Personified. 'Bid S. doublelock the door' (*V.A.* 448).

Sutton Coldfield. Town in Warwickshire. Falstaff sends his recruits with Bardolph through Coventry: 'we'll to S. C. tonight' (*1 Hen. IV*, iv, 2).

'Sutton cophill,' Q2; 'Sutton-cop-hill,' Ff Q5, 6, 8; 'Sutton cop-hill,' the rest.

Sweetheart. Dog's name; *Lear*, iii, 6.

Sweno, or **Sueno.** 'King of Norway.' Acc. *Hol.* ii, 169–70, after the rebel Macdowald's defeat, S. arrived in Fife with a 'puissant armie' – the defending forces being under the command of Duncan, Macbeth, and Banquo. The Danes were defeated, after having been drugged with poisonous berries. Sweno escaped to Norway. This invasion is unhistorical. Sweyn, King of England and Denmark, with Canute his son, ravaged the north of England in 1013.

The defeat (but not the drugging) is described in *Macb.* i, 2, but Macbeth's refusal to allow Sweno 'burial of his men' is borrowed from Holinshed's account of a later Danish invasion (*Hol.* ii, 170). A runic monument, near Forres, traditionally commemorates Sw.'s defeat. See Inchcolm.

Swinsted (Ff), or **Swinstead.** Acc. *John*, v, 3, Ff, the place of John's death. The *Tr. R.* is followed, but the name is an error for 'Swineshead,' which is on the E. coast, and 'in the direct route from Lynn Regis to Sleaford, where John was taken ill, and Newark where he died' (French, p. 4). There was a Cistercian abbey at Swineshead.

In *Hol.* iii, 194, the name is, correctly, 'Swineshead' – showing that the old play rather than the Chronicle was followed. (But 'Swinstead' is found in Rastell and Stow.) The scene of *John*, v, 6, 7, is laid at S.

Swithold. See Withold, St.

Switzers. Swiss soldiers employed to guard the royal person. '*King.* Where are my S.? Let them guard the door' (*Haml.* iv, 5).

'Law, logicke, and the Switzers, may be hired to fight for anybody' (Nashe, *Christ's Teares over Jerusalem* (1594) (Malone).

Sword. Bloodshed, personified. 'At his [Henry V's] heels (Leash'd in, like hounds) should Famine, Sword and Fire Crouch for employment' (*Hen. V*, i, Chor.). See Fire.

Sycorax. A witch (*Temp.* i, 2; iii, 2), banished from Algiers 'for mischiefs manifold, and sorceries terrible to enter human hearing.' She was left on an uninhabited island, where she gave birth to Caliban, and died before

Prospero's arrival. 'For one thing she did, they [the Algerines] would not take her life' – an allusion that has not been satisfactorily explained. Lamb, however (*Works* (1870), iii, 260), finding in J. Ogilby's *Accurate Description of Africa* (1670), p. 230, an account of the deliverance of Algiers – when besieged by Charles V – through the agency of a witch, suggested that Sh. may have had an earlier version of this story in his mind. See CALIBAN and ARIEL.

Prospero (i, 2) terms Sycorax 'this blueeyed hag.' The epithet has led to much discussion. It has been held to describe 'the livid colour of the eyelid, and a blue eye in this sense was a sign of pregnancy' (W. A. Wright); 'that ... fish-like eye, which is often seen in hag-like women' (G. White, *Studies*, p. 324); the dull, bleared neutral white seen in the eyes of old crones (C. Clarke). It may be observed that what we call 'blue' eyes were 'grey' in Sh.'s days.

The following suggestions, among others, have been made as to the etymology of 'Sycorax'; 'Psychorrhagia is the death-struggle; and Psychorrax may be translated "heart-breaker," ψυχορρήξ' (Lloyd, *ap.* Singer, ed. ii, p. 103); 'compounded of the Greek σῦς (ὗς is a variant) [swine] and κόραξ (raven) ... The mere grossness of the one animal and the supposed malignity of the other may be referred to' (J. W. Hales, *Essays*. p. 113); Ruskin, in *Munera Pulveris*, also adopts 'swine-raven' as an equivalent. Clement (*Shakespeare's Sturm, historisch beleuchtet* (Leipzig, 1848), p. 81) actually derives the name from σῦκον (fig) and ῥάξ (venomous spider), and suggests that Queen Elizabeth is thereby symbolized, since she could be both sweet and dangerous.

In Dryden's version S. is also the name of Caliban's twin sister.

Sylla. For 'Sulla'; *2 Hen. VI*, iv, 1, l. 84.

Syracusa, Syracuse. Anciently the chief city of Sicily, on the S.E. coast, with two harbours. The mutual jealousies of Ephesus and S. were paralleled by the strained relations in commercial matters between England and the Netherlands in Elizabeth's reign, which caused much suffering to merchants on both sides. See also *Sh. Eng.* i, 315.

Aegeon admits that he was born at Syracuse, *Com. Err.* i, 1; 'seven years since, in Syracusa, boy, Thou know'st we parted' (*ib.* v, 1); '*Ant. S.* I came from Syracuse' (*ib. ib.*).

Syracusan. *Subst.*, inhabitant of S.: *Com. Err.* i, 1 (3); v, 1. *Adj.*: *ib.* i, 1, 2; v, 1.

Syria. A country of W. Asia, but the name has different meanings according to the context, and the period referred to. In 64 B.C. Syria became a province of the Roman republic.

Labienus 'his conqu'ring Banner shook, from S. to Lydia' (*Ant. Cl.* i, 2); 'Sossius in S.' (*ib.* iii, 1); 'to Ptolemy he assigned S.' (*ib.* iii, 6); 'lower S.' (*ib. ib.*); 'Caesar through S. intends his journey' (*ib.* v, 2); 'Antioch...the fairest city in all S.' (*Per.* i, Gow.).

T

Tailor. D.P. *Tam. Sh.* iv, 3] brings a gown for Katharina's approval; Petruchio will have none of it, in spite of the T.'s asseverations that he had made it after Grumio's directions; as T. departs, he is comforted by the whispered assurance that he will be duly paid.

A similar character appears in *The Taming of A Shrew*.

Talbot, Gilbert (*ob.* 1419). 5th Baron Talbot; K.G.; elder brother of John Talbot (*q.v.*), 1st E. of Shrewsbury. Mtd. as one of those who would become 'familiar as household words' (*Hen. V*, iv, 3).

Talbot, Sir Gilbert. 2nd s. of John T., 2nd E. of Shrewsbury; commanded the right wing of Richmond's forces at Bosworth. He is said to have brought with him 2000 men, 'the whole power of the young earle of Shrewesburie, then being in ward' (*Hol.* iii, 753). Mtd. *Rich. III*, iv, 5, among the persons 'of noble fame and worth' who had joined Richmond. He was rewarded 'with fair lands at Grafton, in Worcestershire, and made Governor of Calais' (Fuller, *Worthies*).

Talbot, John (1) (*c.* 1388–1453). 6th Baron T.; 1st Earl of Shrewsbury; as commander of the English forces in France he was present at the siege of Orleans, and met with almost unbroken success, until defeated and made prisoner by Joan of Arc at Patay (*q.v.*). This battle took place in 1429, but is mtd. (*1 Hen. VI*, i, 1) as though it occurred in 1422, that being the date of the funeral of Henry V. Talbot was kept prisoner for about two years, and was then exchanged for 'Lord Pouton [Poton] de Santrailles' (*q.v.*), the knight who had taken Talbot prisoner at Patay. Talbot was made E. of Shrewsbury (or, strictly, of Salop) in 1422, but in *1 Hen. VI*, iii, 4, the King is made to confer the honour upon him in 1431, at his coronation in Paris. Talbot took Bordeaux, but was defeated and killed, together with his son, Lord Lisle, at Castillon. This was 22 years after the execution of Joan of Arc; but the dramatist has made the death of the soldier precede that of the heroine. See LISLE, LORD.

D.P. *1 Hen. VI.* (i, 1) reported made prisoner in consequence of the cowardice of Sir J. Fastolfe (*q.v.*). (i, 2) 'T. is taken.' i, 4] (before Orleans) is welcomed on his return from captivity, and witnesses the death of Salisbury and Gargrave, whom he prepares to avenge. i, 5] crosses swords with La Pucelle, who evades the issue; is ashamed of his panic-stricken countrymen. ii, 1] enters Orleans by surprise; a soldier exclaims 'The cry of "Talbot" serves me for a sword!' ii, 2] rejoices that he has avenged Salisbury; accepts the invitation of the 'Countess of Auvergne' (unhistorical) to visit her. ii, 3] escapes from the trap she had laid for him. iii, 2] (before Rouen) utters invectives against Joan of Arc, who having entered the town by a ruse appears on the walls; vainly challenges the French knights to descend and fight; enters the town, and drives out Joan and the French; Rouen is 'Lost, and recover'd in a day again!' iii, 3] *p.m.* iii, 4] does homage to Hen. VI at Paris (*Hol.* iii, 623), having subdued 'fifty fortresses, twelve cities, and seven walled towns.' iv, 1] exposes Fastolfe's cowardice, and tears the garter from him; is ordered by the King to chastise Burgundy for his defection. iv, 2] (before Bordeaux) summons the town to surrender; learns that the Dauphin's forces are about to attack him in the rear. (iv, 3, 4) York and Somerset delay sending him succour. iv, 5] welcomes his son to the camp, but urges him to escape from his otherwise inevitable doom (*Hol.* iii, 640); they agree to die together. iv, 6] rescues his son, who is 'hemmed about'; glories in the young man's valour, but once more urges him to escape, and thus live to avenge his father's death and perpetuate the family. iv, 7] enters wounded, and after lamenting over the body of his son, dies; La Pucelle derides the 'silly stately style' of his dignities. (v, 2) mtd.

'This man was to the French people a very scorge and a daily terror; in so muche that as his person was fearfull and terrible to his adversaries present, so his name and fame was spitefull and dreadfull to the common people absent; in so much that women in Fraunce to feare their yong children, would crye, "the Talbot commeth, the Talbot commeth!" ' (Hall, p. 230; cf. *1 Hen. VI*, ii, 3). The Countess of Auvergne's sneer at him as a 'writhled shrimp' is unexplained. For his 'dignities' see R. Crompton, *Mansion of Magnanimitie* (1599) (Sig. E4) (B.-S. p. 233). Three of his hereditary titles (iv, 7) are thus accounted for: his maternal grandfather was Lord Strange of Blackmere (Salop); his father was Richard Talbot of Goodrich Castle 'in the March of Wales'; and he was Baron Wexford through his ancestress Joan de Valence. Further, he was summoned to Parliament as Lord Furnival, in right of his wife, Maud Neville, e.d. of the 5th Baron F.

Talbot, John (2). D.P. *1 Hen. VI*, son to Lord Talbot; see Lisle, Lord.

Talbotites. Nonce-word; followers, or adherents, of Talbot, *1 Hen. VI*, iii, 2. ('Talbonites,' Ff.)

Tale-porter, Mistress. A midwife referred to by Autolycus; *Wint. T.* iv, 4, l. 273.

Taming of A Shrew, The. In 1594 there was published *A Pleasant Conceited Historie, called The taming of a Shrew. As it was sundry times acted by the ... Earle of Pembrook his seruants.* This was printed by Peter Short, and sold by Cuthbert Burbie. Other editions, without any important alterations, appeared in 1596 and 1607. This play, which formed the ground-work of *Tam. Sh.*, has been attributed to Marlowe, Kyd, and Greene, as well as to Sh. himself. (When produced, at Newington Butts, June 11, 1594, it was described as an old piece.)

Taming of the Shrew, The.

Publication. No edition is known earlier than the Folio of 1623, with title as above. The acts, but not the scenes, are indicated, the Ind. being *Actus Primus, Scoena Prima.* A quarto edn. appeared in 1631.

Date of Composition. Uncertain: dates as far apart as 1594 and 1606 have been favoured.

Sources of the Plot. The Induction and the main plot of Katharine and Petruchio are based on an older play, *The Taming of A Shrew* (*q.v.*); the sub-plot of Bianca's wooing, on *The Supposes*, a play by G. Gascoigne derived from Ariosto's *Gli Suppositi.*

Authorship. The Bianca scenes are generally regarded as non-Shakespearean. (See *N.S.S.Tr.*, 1874.)

Tamora. D.P. *T. And.* Queen of the Goths. i, 2] is led captive to Rome by Titus; pleads fruitlessly for the life of her son Alarbus; Saturninus, the newly elected Emperor, comforts her, and, later, announces that he has chosen her as his empress; later, Tamora pleads for Titus, but (aside) vows to be revenged on him; she declares that 'This day all quarrels die.' (ii, 1) Aaron, the Moor, vows 'To mount aloft,' with T. as his 'imperial mistress.' ii, 3] her tryst with A. is interrupted by Bassianus and Lavinia, who threaten to inform the Emperor; Tam. tells her sons, who enter opportunely, that her life has been threatened, and incites them to take instant vengeance. ii, 4] throws suspicion on the sons of Titus of murdering Bassianus. (iii, 2; iv, 1, 2) mtd. iv, 4] pleads deceitfully for Titus; tells Saturninus that she will induce Titus 'To pluck proud Lucius from the warlike Goths.' (v, 1) her intrigue with Aaron discovered. v, 2] feigning to be Revenge in person, she visits Titus, supposed insane, and urges him, with deadly intent, to invite Lucius to a banquet. v, 3] she is stabbed by Titus.

Tamworth. Town in Staffordshire and Warwickshire; about 15m. from Bosworth Field; Richmond's forces halted there before the battle (*Hol.* iii, 754).

Richard is reported near Leicester; 'From Tamworth thither is but one day's march' (*Rich. III*, v, 2; the scene is 'the camp near T.').

Tantalus. A son of Jupiter; for some offence, which is variously related, he was condemned to suffer endless thirst and hunger, in the presence of water and fruits that always withdrew from him. (Ovid, *Metam.* iv, 457: 'tibi, Tantale, nullae Deprenduntur aquae; quaeque imminet, effugit arbos.') 'Worse than Tantalus' is her annoy' (*V.A.* 599); 'like still-pining T. he sits, And useless barns the harvest of his wits' (*Lucr.* 858–9).

Tapster, Thomas. (*i.e.* T. the tapster), a class name applied to Pompey (D.P.); *M. for M.* i, 2.

[**Tarbes, Bishop of.**] See Bayonne.

Tarentum. Taranto; a sea-port of Calabria. Octavius sails from T., *Ant. Cl.* iii, 7 (cf. *Plut.* pp. 183, 243).

Tarpeian Rock. A part of the Capitoline Hill in Rome, so named after Tarpeia, who treacherously opened a gate to the Sabines, but was crushed to death by their shields. Criminals condemned to death were hurled from its summit.

'Bear him [Coriolanus] to the rock Tarpeian, and from thence Into destruction cast him' (*Cor.* iii, 1; rep.); 'Let them pronounce the steep Tarpeian death' (*ib.* iii, 3; rep.). Cf. *Plut.* p. 19.

The cliff now popularly identified with the *Rupes Tarpeia* has no claim to be the original 'Rock.'

Tarquin (1). L. Tarquinius Superbus, the last King of Rome. Traditionally, his expulsion, with his sons, was due to the crime of Sextus (see Tarquin (2)). The story of the desperate attempts of the Tarquins to recover the throne (culminating in the Battle of Lake Regillus) is incidentally referred to in *Sh.* (see Coriolanus, and *Lucr.*, Argument).

'He [Marcius] received in the repulse of T. seven hurts'

(*Cor.* ii, 1); 'when T. made a head for Rome' (*ib.* ii, 2); 'T.'s self he met' (*ib. ib.*); 'a merrier day did never yet greet Rome, No, not the expulsion of the T.s' (*ib.* v, 4); '*Bru*...my ancestor did from the streets of Rome The Tarquin drive, when he was call'd a king' (*Jul. C.* ii, 1); 'make proud Saturnine and his empress Beg at the gates like T. and his queen' (*T. And.* iii, 1).

Acc. Livy, ii, 21, T. died in misery at Cumae.

Tarquin (2). Sextus Tarquinius, son of Tarquin (1). The story of his violation of Lucretia, wife of his relative Tarquinius Collatinus, is related in Sh.'s second poem (1594), *Lucrece*. Epithets: 'Lust-breathed,' (*Lucr.* 3); 'enchanted' (*ib.* 83); 'doting' (*ib.* 155); 'surfeit-taking' (*ib.* 698); 'false' (*ib.* 1197, 1743).

'Our T. thus Did softly press the rushes, ere he waken'd The chastity he wounded' (*Cymb.* ii, 2); 'With T.'s ravishing strides' (*Macb.* ii, 1); 'T. erst, that left the camp to sin in Lucrece' bed' (*T. And.* iv, 1).

In the passage from *Cymb.* 'our' implies the Italian nationality of the speaker.

Tarsus. ('Tharsus,' QqF3, 4.) Chief city of Cilicia, on the R. Cydnus, about 12 m. from its mouth. Only mtd. in *Sh.* in connection with the story of Pericles. (See THASOS.)

Pericles sets out from Tyre to T., *Per.* i, 2; Cleon, lamenting the famine, speaks of its late riches and splendour, *ib.* i, 4; mtd., *ib.* ii, Gow.; Thaisa committed to the sea near T., *ib.* iii, 1; Marina left at T., *ib.* iii, 3; mtd., *ib.* iv, Gow.; 'the pretty wrens of T.' (*ib.* iv, 3); Marina's escape from T. recalled, *ib.* v, 1; mtd., *ib.* v, 2.

Tartar (1). Tartarus; denoting Hades, or Hell. 'To the gates of T., thou most excellent devil of wit!' (*T. Nt.* ii, 5); 'that same demon ... might return to vasty T.' (*Hen. V*, ii, 2). Attrib.: 'he's in T. limbo, worse than hell' (*Com. Err.* iv, 2).

'Tartary' for 'Tartarus' occurs *Tr. R.* I, 12: 'the black tormentors of deep Tartary.'

Tartar (2). A native of Tartary (Central Asia); a Mongol, or any member of Jenghiz Khan's hordes which threatened Europe in the Middle Ages.

'*Puck.* Swifter than arrow from the T.'s bow' (*M.N.D.* iii, 2); 'Bearing a T.'s painted bow of lath' (*Rom. J.* i, 4; *cf.* Golding's *Ovid*, bk. x: 'And though that she Did fly as swift as arrow from a Turkye bowe'); Lysander calls the brunette Hermia 'a tawny T.' (*M.N.D.* iii, 2); the lips of a T. formed part of the ingredients of the witches' hellbroth, *Macb.* iv, 1; 'Stubborn Turks and T.s' (*M.V.* iv, 1); 'flinty T.'s bosom' (*All's Well*, iv, 4); Host speaks ironically of Simple as 'a Bohemian T.' (*M.W.W.* iv, 5).

Taurus (1). The Bull, second sign of the zodiac. 'One of T.'s horns' (*T. And.* iv, 3); ('the Bull being gall'd gave Aries such a knock,' *ib. ib.*); '*And.* Taurus? that's sides and heart. *Toby.* No, sir, it is legs and thighs' (*T. Nt.* i, 3).

In astrology, acc. some authorities, T. governs neck and throat, but acc. *Liber Novem Judicum* (1509), cited in *Sh. Eng.* i, 460, it governs 'crura et pedes, so Sir Toby would be nearly right.

Taurus (2). A mountain-chain in the S. of Asia Minor (Pliny, *Nat. Hist.* V, xxvii, 27). 'High Taurus snow' (*M.N.D.* iii, 2).

Taurus, Statilius. Roman general; commanded the land-force of Octavius at the Battle of Actium, 31 B.C. *Plut.* p. 210 ('Taurus'); *ib.* p. 245 ('Stat. T.').

D.P. *Ant. Cl.* ('Towrus,' Ff.) iii, 8] ordered by Oct. to withhold his attack. iii, 10] *p.m.*

Tavy. For 'David.' 'Saint Tavy's day' (*Hen. V*, iv, 7).

Tawyer. In Ff the st. dir. 'Tawyer with a Trumpet before them' precedes the entrance of the clowns; *M.N.D.* v, 1, l. 127.

Many conjectures as to the meaning of this word were made, but the matter was set at rest by Halliwell's discovery (*Outlines*, p. 500) that 'Tawyer' was the name of 'a subordinate in the pay of Hemmings' whose burial at St Saviour's in 1625 was recorded in the Sexton's notebook as that of 'William Tawier, Mr Heminges man.'

Taylor, Joseph. Mtd. as a 'principal actor' in F1. He seems to have succeeded Burbage (*q.v.*).

Tearsheet, Doll. D.P. 2 *Hen. IV.* (ii, 1) Falstaff would 'meet her at supper.' (ii, 2) described by the Page as 'a proper gentlewomen, ... and a kinswoman of my master's.' ii, 4] has 'drunk too much canaries,' and wrangles with Falstaff, yet would be friends with him, since he is 'going to the wars'; vituperates Pistol, and lauds the 'sweet little rogue,' Falstaff, for ejecting him; takes offence at a phrase applied to her by Fal., yet bids him a tearful farewell. v, 4] for being concerned in a brawl at the tavern is haled to prison, loudly reviling the 'beadles.' See DOROTHY (1).

In *Hen. V* (ii, 1) she is gibbeted by Pistol as a 'lazar kite of Cressid's kind.' The further allusion to 'my Doll' by P. (*ib.* v, 1) is generally held to be a mistake for 'Nell' (see QUICKLY, MISTRESS), yet the reference to 'the spital' in each case seems more than a coincidence.

'I am sometimes disposed to think that this respectable young lady's name is a very old corruption for Tear-street – street-walker, *terere stratam* (*viam*). Does not the Prince's question rather show this? – "This Doll T. should be some road?" ' (Coleridge).

Te Deum. Ancient hymn, sung at matins, and also separately as a service of thanks-giving on special occasions.

'*K. Hen.* [after Agincourt]. Do we all holy rites; Let there be sung "Non Nobis" and "Te Deum" ' (*Hen. V*, iv, 8; cf. *Hol.* iii, 555); at the coronation of Anne Boleyn, 'the choir, with all the choicest music of the kingdom, Together sung "Te Deum" ' (*Hen. VIII*, iv, 1; cf. *Hol.* iii, 933).

Telamon. For 'Ajax Telamonius' (*q.v.*). 'He is more mad than T. for his shield' (*Ant. Cl.* iv, 13).

Tellus. Roman personification of the earth (Ovid, *Fasti*, iv, 633); 'the goddess T.' (*Plut.* p. 120). 'Neptune's salt wash, and T.'s orbed ground' (*Haml.* iii, 2); 'I will rob T. of her weed [flowers]' (*Per.* iv, 1).

Temperance. Personified. 'T. was a delicate wench' (*Temp.* ii, 1, l. 42).

Tempest, The.

PUBLICATION. First printed in the Folio of 1623. The acts and scenes are numbered.

DATE OF COMPOSITION. The generally accepted date is 1610–11. The chief evidence for this is threefold: (*a*) considerations of style and metre, which rank it with Sh.'s latest plays; (*b*) obvious allusions to the casting away of

Sir George Somers on the Bermudas in 1609, described in several contemporary pamphlets, notably in Jourdain's *A Discovery of the Bermudas, otherwise called the Isle of Divels*, etc. (1610); (*c*) an entry in the Books of the Master of the Revels of a performance of *The Tempest* before the Court on Nov. 1, 1611 (this was long believed to be a forgery, but the researches of Mr Ernest Law, 1911–13, are generally admitted to have established its authenticity). A date as early as 1596 was attributed to the play by Joseph Hunter, while Knight, Dyce, and Staunton suggested 1602–3. The first-named critic believed *The Tempest* to be the 'Love's Labour's Won' of Meres' list.

Sources of the Plot. No play or novel can be indicated as the source of *The Tempest*. In minor details, however, hints are clearly traceable to (*a*) Jourdian's *Discovery*, already referred to; (*b*) Florio's translation of *Montaigne* (see Gonzalo); (*c*) Eden's *History of Travayle* (1577) (see Setebos); (*d*) the Earl of Sterling's *The Tragedie of Darius* (1603) (*Temp.* iv, 1, ll. 148–56). Some weight has, moreover, been attached to resemblances between *The Tempest* and an old German play, *Die Schöne Sidea* by Jakob Ayrer (*ob.* 1605). A literal translation of this is given in Furness' *Variorum* edn. of *The Tempest*, and the editor well remarks that 'it is only by reading the whole play, and not a mere synopsis, that English students can arrive at an intelligent conclusion concerning the claims that are so stoutly urged on its behalf.'

Temple Gardens, The. Formerly on the bank of the Thames, but now separated from the river by the Victoria Embankment. (Figured in Aggas's map of London, in the Guildhall.)

Here were plucked, according to the story related in *1 Hen. VI*, ii, 4, the white and red roses which formed the badges of York and Lancaster respectively during the Wars of the Roses. No historical basis for this scene is known.

The rent paid by Sir C. Hatton for the Gardens and neighbouring property included 'a red rose.'

Temple Hall, The. The Hall of the Middle Temple was built in 1572. *Twelfth Night* was there acted on Feb. 2, 1601 (2). Prince Hal bids Falstaff 'meet me tomorrow in the Temple Hall' (*1 Hen. IV*, iii, 3); the dispute carried on in the Gardens was begun there, *1 Hen. VI*, ii, 4.

Tenantius, or **Theomantius.** Father of Cymbeline, acc. *Hol.* i, 31–2 (where both forms occur). See Cymbeline, and Spenser, *F.Q.* II, x, 50. 'Sicilius ... had his titles by T., whom He served with glory' (*Cymb.* i, 1); '[the two young Leonati] were slain, Our fealty, and T.'s right, with honour to maintain' (*ib.* v, 4).

W. G. Boswell-Stone, *Sh. Hol.* p. 7*n.*, points out that Sh. seems to follow Fabian's conjecture (*Hol.* i, 31) that Tenantius was a son of Lud, since Cassibulan is referred to (*Cymb.* iii, 1, 1.5) as Cymbeline's uncle.

Tenedos. A small island off the coast of Troas, to which the Greeks withdrew in order to make the Trojans think they had departed for good (Virg. *Aen.* ii, 21 ff.). 'To T. they [the Greeks] come; And the deep-drawing barks do there disgorge Their warlike fraughtage' (*Tr. Cr.* Prol.).

Terence. P. Terentius Afer; Roman comic poet; *ob.* 159 B.C. Mtd. in Preface to *Tr. Cr.* (Q).

G. Colman in his transln. of Terence (1765) collected a considerable number of supposed Shakespearean parallels. R. Bernard's literal transln. of T.'s comedies appeared in 1598. Ter. *Eun.* i, l. 29, is qtd. imperfectly, *Tam. Sh.* i, 1, from Lyly's *Grammar*.

Tereus. King of Thrace. According to the story related by Ovid (*Metam.* vi, 412–676), he wedded Procne, daughter of Pandion, King of Athens, who bore him a son, Itys. At Procne's request, T. set out for Athens to fetch her sister Philomela, and on the way back violated her. To prevent her from revealing the crime, he cut out her tongue, abandoned her, and declared she was dead. But Philomela wove her story into a piece of cloth, and thus conveyed the truth to her sister. The latter, in a frenzy, slew her own son Itys, and served up his flesh to his unwitting father. Tereus, when told what had been done, was about to slay the two sisters, when all three were transformed into birds, Procne becoming a nightingale, Philomela a swallow, and Tereus a hoopoo (or, according to another version, Pr. became a swallow, Ph. a nightingale, and Te. a hawk (Hygin. *Fab.* 45)). See Philomela.

Lavinia is declared to be more unhappy than Philomela, 'a craftier Tereus hast thou met withal,' for Ph. 'but lost her tongue, And in a tedious sampler sew'd her mind,' but Lavinia, having lost her hands, could not do this (*T. And.* ii, 5); Lavinia directs attention to the story as told by Ovid, *ib.* iv, 1; 'She [Imogen] hath been reading late the tale of T.' (*Cymb.* ii, 2). Mtd., *Lucr.* 1134; *P.P.* xxi.

The story is also related in *A petite Pallace of Pettie his Pleasure* (1576), and Gower's *Confessio Amantis*, bk. v.

Termagant. *It.* Trivagante; a character in the mystery plays, supposed to represent a Saracenic deity. *Cf.* 'The Carle ... oftentimes by Turmagant and Mahound swore' (*Faerie Queene*, VI, vii, 47); 'Termagaunt' (Chaucer, *Canterbury Tales*, l. 15221).

Hamlet in his advice to the Players, says of a ranting actor: 'I would have such a fellow whipped for o'erdoing T.' (*Haml.* iii, 2).

Adj., boisterous: 'that hot termagant Scot' (*1 Hen. IV*, v, 4).

Terra. Another form of 'Tellus' (*q.v.*), a personification of the earth. 'Anon falleth like a crab on the face of T.' (*L.L.L.* iv, 2).

Tewksbury, or **Tewkesbury.** Town in Gloucestershire. The Battle of T., May 4, 1471, resulted in the victory of Edward IV over Queen Margaret and Prince Edward. The latter was slain after the battle, *3 Hen. VI*, v, 4, 5. T. is four times mtd. in *Rich. III* in connection with the stabbing of the young Prince (i, 2, 3, 4; v, 3).

'His wits as thick as T. mustard' (*2 Hen. IV*, ii, 4), says Falstaff of Poins. 'About Teuxbury they grind Mustard and make it into balls which are brought to London and other remote places as being the best that the world affords' (Wm. Coles, *Adam in Eden* (1675)).

Thaisa. D.P. *Per.* Daughter of Simonides, King of Pentapolis. ii, 2] she describes the 'devices' of the six knights who are presented to her in turn as they enter the lists. ii, 3] presents the wreath of victory to Pericles, of whom she becomes enamoured; at her father's bidding inquires his name and parentage. ii, 5] informing her father in a letter that she will wed Per., and, confirming her intention in person, they are married by the King's command. (iii, 1) believed to have died in child-birth, she is committed to the waves in a chest. iii, 2] is rescued, and revives at Ephesus. iii, 4] resolves to assume 'a vestal livery' at Diana's temple. (v, 1) Marina tells Pericles that her mother's name was Th. v, 3] while Th. is officiating as high priestess in Diana's temple, Per. and Mar. make themselves known to her, and the family are united.

Unnamed by Gower; Lucina in Twine's novel. 'Thaise' is Pericles' daughter in the *Conf. Amant.*

Thaliard. D.P. *Per.* Servant to Antiochus. i, 1] he is ordered to poison Pericles, and, on the flight of the latter, pursues him. i, 3] reaches Tyre, but finds that Pericles has departed; congratulates himself on the fact. (ii, Gow.) mtd.

Thaliarchus, or Taliarchus, in *The Patterne of Painfull Adventures* (1576).

Thames, River. The destination of Falstaff's buck-basket is 'the muddy ditch close to the T. side' (*M.W.W.* iii, 3); Fal. is 'thrown in the T.' (*ib.* iii, 5); 'he could wish himself in T. up to the neck' (*Hen. V*, iv, 1); 'throw them into the T.' (2 *Hen. VI*, iv, 8).

Thus the only direct references to T. are in connection with immersion in its waters. A portentous flowing of its waters is alluded to, 2 *Hen. IV*, iv, 4; cf. *Hol.* iii, 540.

Tharsus. See TARSUS.

Thasos. Island in the Aegean, off the coast of Thrace ('Thassos,' *Plut.* pp. 137, 144). The body of Cassius was sent thither for burial, *Jul. C.* v, 3.

'Tharsus' in Ff; an obvious error, corrected by Theobald.

Thassos. See THASOS.

Theban, *subst.* Lear, in his madness, calls Edgar 'this learned Th.,' in the sense of 'philosopher'; *Lear*, iii, 4.

If any relevancy is to be sought in Lear's phrase, it may be found in the legend that the use of letters was first intoduced into Boeotian Th. from Phoenicia. (Immediately afterward L. calls Edgar an 'Athenian.')

Thebes. Chief city in Boeotia. Acc. *Plut.* p. 288, Theseus helped Adrastus 'to recover the bodies of those that were slain in the battle before the city of Th.,' and Euripides relates that this was 'by force of arms'; hence Theseus (*M.N.D.* v, 1) speaks of the time 'when I from Th. came last a conqueror.'

Thersites. Son of Agrius, an ill-favoured and scurrilous Greek; described by Homer (*Il.* ii, 212 ff.) as having been chastised by Ulysses. He does not appear in the medieval romances, and as a character in *Tr. Cr.* seems taken from Chapman's *Iliads*. 'T.'s body is as good as Ajax,' when neither are alive' (*Cymb.* iv, 2, l. 325).

D.P. *Tr. Cr.* (i, 3) characterized by Agamemnon and Nestor. ii, 1] rails at Ajax and is beaten by him. ii, 3] (*sol.*) inveighs against the ignorance and folly of the Greeks; Achilles treats him as a licensed buffoon, 'a privileged man.' iii, 3] gives the other chiefs a biting account of Ajax. v, 1] brings Achilles a letter from Hecuba; reviles Patroclus. v, 4] (*sol.*) derides the Greeks; is terrified by Hector. v, 8] will not, as a brother bastard, fight Margarelon.

But he the filthiest fellow was of all that had deserts
In Troy's brave siege: he was squint-ey'd, and lame of
either foot;
... He most of all envied
Ulysses and Aeacides, whom still his spleen would chide.
Chapman

Walker considers Th. as the Fool, in the technical sense, of the play; *cf.* ii, 1, l. 89 ff. See also P. Stapfer, *Sh. and Clas. Ant.* p. 163.

Theseus. Son of Aegeus; the legendary hero of Attica. The only relevant incident of his adventurous life, as related by Plutarch, are his amours with Perigouna (*Plut.* p. 279), Ariadne (*ib.* p. 283), Aegle (*ib.* p. 284), and Antiopa the Amazon (*ib.* p. 286), and his marriage with Hippolyta (*ib.* p. 288).

'Ariadne, passioning For Th.'s perjury and unjust flight' (*T.G.V.* iv, 4; *cf.* Ovid, *Metam.* viii, 175, and *Her.* 10).

D.P. *M.N.D.* 'Duke of Athens' (Rowe). i, 1] reminds Hippolyta that he wooed her with his sword, but will wed her 'in another key'; commands revels to be prepared; hears Egeus' complaint against his daughter, and counsels Hermia to obey her father and thus avoid dire penalties; listens to the rival claims of Herm.'s two lovers, but again warns her. (ii, 1) his amours mtd. by Oberon. iv, 1] takes Hippolyta with him to the chase; lauds his hounds of Spartan breed; discovers the four lovers asleep in the wood; bids 'the huntsmen wake them with their horns'; after hearing the two young men, 'overbears' the will of Egeus, and declares that the two weddings shall be celebrated with his own. v, 1] discourses on imagination; welcomes the two couples; comments on a list of sports rife for the evening, and combats Hippolyta's objection to seeing 'wretchedness o'ercharged'; good-naturedly criticizes the Interlude, and decrees nightly revels for a fortnight's space.

The title 'Duke' for any great leader, is common in our early literature. 'Duke Theseus' occurs in Chaucer, *Knight's Tale.* He is termed a kinsman of Hercules, *M.N.D.* v, 1, l. 47; cf. *Plut.* p. 278.

Thessalian, *adj.* Of Thessaly. 'Crookkneed and dewlapt like Th. bulls' (*M.N.D.* iv, 1).

The bulls of the neighbouring Epirus are mtd., Ovid, *Metam.* viii, 283.

Thessaly. The largest division of ancient Greece, lying to the N.E. The hunting of the Calydonian boar (Ovid, *Metam.* viii, 279 ff.) took place in the adjacent country of Aetolia.

'The boar of Thessaly was never so emboss'd' (*Ant. Cl.* iv, 13); hunting in Th. alluded to, *M.N.D.* iv, 1.

Thetis. A marine divinity, daughter of Nereus. Hence, the sea, in post-Aug. prose. By Peleus she became the mother of Achilles.

In the inscription on Marina's monument (*Per.* iv, 4), Th. stands for the sea; as also in the following passage (*Tr. Cr.* i, 3): 'let the ruffian Boreas once engage the gentle Th.' 'Many Thetis' sons,' (*i.e.* many men as good as Achilles) (*ib. ib.*); 'great Thetis' son!' (*ib.* iii, 3); Antony addresses Cleopatra as 'my Th.,' apparently because about to aid him with a fleet, *Ant. Cl.* iii, 7.

Thidias. D.P. *Ant. Cl.* iii, 12] is despatched by Octavius on a mission to Cleopatra. iii, 13] delivers his message to Cl. and confers with her; just as she permits him to kiss her hand, Antony enters, and, in a rage, orders Th. to be dragged away by his servants and whipped; cf. *Plut.* p. 218. See THYREUS.

'Thidius' once (iii, 13) in Ff.

Thieves. In st. dir. *1 Hen. IV*, ii, 2, for 'Falstaff and his comrades.'

Thisbe. A Babylonian maiden beloved by Pyramus: since their parents forbade their marriage, the lovers, who lived in adjacent houses, were wont to converse through a chink in a wall. Once, when they had agreed to meet at the tomb of Ninus (*q.v.*), Thisbe, who had arrived first, fled at the aspect of a lioness which had just slain an ox; she dropped her cloak on the way, and the lioness, mauling it, stained it with blood. Pyramus, finding the garment, believed Th. had been killed, and slew himself beneath a mulberry, the fruit of which was henceforth red. This be returning, on seeing her lover's body, also put an end to her life. The tale as related by Ovid (*Metam.* iv) was universally familiar in the Middle Ages.

The part of Th. in the Interlude, *M.N.D.*, was performed by Flute (*q.v.*).

Thisby. A spelling of 'Thisbe' (*M.N.D.*) retained by Hanmer where the clowns are the speakers, and regarded as phonetically equivalent to 'This-bei.'

Thisne. Either a blunder of Bottom's for 'Thisbe,' or equivalent to 'in this way'; *M.N.D.* i, 2.

Thoas. 'King of Thoyle,' a Greek (Caxton, *Recuyell*). 'Thoas, deadly hurt' (*Tr. Cr.* v, 5). ('Thous,' QFf.)

Thomas. As a forename. 'T. Mowbray,' 'T. Erpingham,' 'T. Wart,' 'T. Grey,' T. Gargrave,' 'T. Horner,' 'T. Vaughan,' 'T. Lovel,' 'T. Boleyn,' 'T. More,' 'T. Cromwell' (*qq.v.*). (Acc. *Tr. R.* II, 6, the monk who murdered King John was named Th.)

Thomas, Duke of Clarence (*c.* 1388–1421). 2nd s. of Henry IV by Mary de Bohun. Holinshed (iii, 543) relates that, after Prince Henry had fallen into disgrace for having insulted the Lord Chief Justice, the King 'banisht him the court and made the duke of Clarence (his younger brother) president of councell in his steed.'

It seems, however, that the staid youth was not above indulging in riotous conduct (Stow, '1410,' p. 550). He was present at Troyes when Henry V married Katharine, and at the siege of Melun (*Hen. Quint.*, *Ang. Reg.*, *Gesta*, p. 144; Eng. Hist. Soc.). Acc. Rymer, *Foedera*, ix, 300, Clarence pronounced sentence on Cambridge and Scrope; cf. *Hen. V*, ii, 2.

D.P. *2 Hen. IV.* iv, 4] the King inquires why he is not in the company of his brother Henry, and declares that he neglects him; Clarence replies curtly to his father's questions; is present when the King swoons, and recalls a portent which has been lately repeated (see Edward III); retires, leaving Henry alone with his father; re-enters to find his brother gone, and the crown also. v, 2] advises the Lord Chief Justice to 'speak Sir John Falstaff fair.'

D.P. *Hen. V.* v, 2] (at Troyes) is addressed by Henry V. (Not included among the *dramatis personae* in any edn.)

Thomas, Friar. D.P. *M. for M.* i, 4] is informed by the Duke that he seeks concealment as a friar, in the monastery; at first mistakes his motive, which is further explained to him.

Johnson suggests that he is identical with Fr. Peter (iv, 5).

Thomas of Woodstock (1355–97). Youngest son. of Edw. III; E. of Buckingham 1377; D. of Gloucester 1385; m. Eleanor Bohun. He persistently opposed Rich. II, and was ultimately exiled to Calais, where he was probably murdered. Holinshed's references to him – closely followed by Sh. – may be thus summarized:

Gl., having conspired against the King, the latter ordered Mowbray 'to make the duke secretly awaie' (*Hol.* iii, 489). But M. declared, later, that he feared for his own life, 'by reason he had not put the duke to death' (*Hol.* iii, 511). In *Rich. II*, i, 1, Mowbray, when accused of the crime, replied that, on the contrary, he 'neglected his duty.' Gaunt and York, while sorrowful for their brother, were 'doubtfull of their own states' (*Hol.* iii, 489). Gl.'s widow urges Gaunt to avenge his brother (*Rich. II*, i, 2); and Gaunt, before his death, accuses the King of the murder (*Rich. II*, ii, 1). Aumerle, on being charged with the crime, indignantly denies it (*Hol.* iii, 511; *Rich. II*, iv, 1). Of Gl. Holinshed observes that he was 'fierce of nature, hastie, wilfull, and … ever repining against the king in all things,' but Gaunt speaks of him as a 'plain, well-meaning soul' (*Rich. II*, ii, 1, l. 128).

Thomyris. Tomyris, a queen of the Massagetae ('some say that this nation is Scythian,' Herod. i, 201). Cyrus the elder was slain in battle against her.

The Countess of Auvergne, in plotting the death of Talbot, says: 'I shall as famous be by this exploit As Scythian Th. by Cyrus' death' (*1 Hen. VI*, ii, 3). (A little later she calls Talbot 'bloodthirsty lord.')

'The Queene commaunded the head of Cyrus to be cut of, and throwen into a boll of mans bloud, casting him in the teeth in thys wise with his crueltie. Now fill thyself with bloud, which thou has ever thirsted' (Justin (*Trogus Pompeius*), A. Golding's transln. (1570), f. 5, *verso*). Orosius, *Hist.* ii, 7, § 6, also relates the story; whence Dante, *Purg.* xii, 55–7; *Mon.* ii, 9.

Thracian. Belonging to Thrace. 'Th. singer' (Orpheus) (*M.N.D.* v, 1); 'Th. poet' (Orpheus) (*T. And.* ii, 5); 'Th. fatal steeds' (horses of Rhesus) (*3 Hen. VI*, iv, 2); 'Th. tyrant' (Polymnestor) (*T. And.* i, 2); 'Th. King, Adallas' (*Ant. Cl.* iii, 6). (See these names.)

Three-pile. A mercer; *M. for M.* iv, 3.

Velvet with a rich nap; cf. *Wint. T.* iv, 3, l. 15; Autolycus in his time 'wore three-pile.'

Thump, Peter. D.P. *2 Hen. VI.* Servant to Horner (*q.v.*). i, 3] accuses his master of treason. ii, 3] kills him in a combat with sand-bags. Acc. *Hol.* iii, 626, he was ultimately hanged at Tyburn for felony.

Thurio. D.P. *T.G.V.* 'A foolish rival to Valentine' (F1). ii, 4] in an exchange of banter with Val., is worsted in Silvia's presence. (ii, 6) Proteus resolves to 'cross' him. iii, 1] *p.m.* iii, 2] complains that Silv. despises him more than ever since Val. has been exiled; is advised by Proteus to compose 'wailful sonnets to her' and to serenade her. iv, 2] provides music below S.'s window; is persuaded by Pro. that he will plead for him. v, 2] asks Pro. what S. thinks of him; will pursue her, rather to be revenged on Eglamour than for love of her. v, 4] encountering S. in the forest, claims her, but instantly resigns her on being threatened by Val.; is declared by the Duke to be 'degenerate and base.'

Thursday. The day fixed for Juliet's marriage to Paris. *Rom. J.* iii, 4 (5), 5 (3); iv, 1 (3), 2. Mtd., *1 Hen. IV*, ii, 4, iii, 2; *2 Hen. IV*, ii, 4.

[Thyamis.] A character in the *Aethiopica* of Heliodorus (transld. by Thos. Underdowne (*c.* 1569)). Th., a robber chieftain, having fallen in love with Chariclea, tries to kill her in order to save her from falling into the hands of his foes. Alluded to, *T. Nt.* v, 1: 'Why should I not, had I the heart to do it, Like to the Egyptian thief at point of death, Kill what I love?'

And. Lang, however, sees an allusion 'to Herodotus, ii, 121, the story of Rhampsinitus, translated by "B.R." and published in 1584' (*The Valet's Tragedy.* etc. (1903), p. 319).

Thyreus. The name substitued by Theobald, and all later editors, for 'Thidias' (D.P. *Ant. Cl.*), on the ground that the former is the envoy's name as given by Plutarch (*Plut.* p. 218). That Sh. deliberately changed the name is clear from its consistent use in the text and st. dirs. (Ff). See THIDIAS.

Tib. Fem. forename; dim. of 'Isabel'; hence, a loose woman. 'As fit ... as Tib's rush for Tom's forefinger' (*All's Well*, ii, 2); 'doorkeeper to every Coistrel that comes inquiring for his Tib' (*Per.* iv, 6).

'Tib' and 'Tom' were correlatives, as in 'tib-cat,' 'tom-cat.' For remarks on 'rush-ring marriages,' see *Sh. Eng.* ii, 145.

Tiber. River of Italy, flowing past Rome. 'A humorous patrician ... that loves a cup of hot wine with not a drop of allaying T. in't' (*Cor.* ii, 1); 'I would they [the plebeians] were in T.' (*ib.* iii, 1); 'T. banks' (*Jul. C.* i, 1); 'the waves of T.' (*ib.* i, 2); 'on this side T.' (*ib.* iii, 2); 'let Rome in T. melt' (*Ant. Cl.* i, 1). Feminine in *Sh.* when personified: 'T. trembled underneath her banks' (*Jul. C.* i, 1); 'the troubled T. chafing with her shores' (*ib.* i, 2).

This idiom is not unusual in English; *cf.* Drayton's *Polyolbion*, where nearly all the rivers are fem. The arbitrary personification of the rivers in *The Faerie Queene*, IV, ii, where they are mostly required as pages for Thames when he weds Medway, is scarcely relevant.

Tiberio, Son of. D.P. *Rom. J.* i, 5] *p.m.*

Tiger, The (1). Name of a ship. *T. Nt.* v, 1; *Macb.* i, 3; *cf.* Virg. *Aen.* x, 166: 'Massicus aerata princeps secat aequora Tigri.' A voyage by Ralph Fitch, in the *Tiger*, to Tripolis, and thence by caravan to Aleppo, in the year 1583, is described in Hakluyt, ii, 247, 251. Sir Kenelm Digby (*Journal* (1628), p. 45, Camden Society), mentions 'the *Tyger*, of London,' bound for Scanderoon. See ALEPPO.

Tiger, The (2). Name of an inn; *Com. Err.* iii, 1.

Tike, Sir. Nonce-name applied to Simple by Falstaff; *M.W.W.* iv, 5 (Steevens). ('Like,' Ff; 'I tike,' Qq.)

'Tike' means either a cur, or a rustie; *cf.* 'bobtail tike' (*Lear*, iii, 6); 'under tribut and taillage as tikes and cheorles' (*Piers Plowman* (C), xxii, 37).

Tilney, or **Tylney, Agnes.** Widow of Thomas Howard, 2nd D. of Norfolk. She bore the Queen's train at the coronation of Anne Boleyn, wearing 'a coronal of gold, wrought with flowers' (*Hen. VIII*, iv, 1); she was also godmother to the Princess Elizabeth (*ib.* v, 5), and at the christening bore the child richly habited 'in a mantell of purple veluet' (*ib. ib.*) and 'gave to hir a standing cup of gold, fretted with pearle' (*Hol.* iii, 934).

Timandra, or **Tymandra.** D.P. *Timon.* A mistress to Alcibiades. iv, 3] is reviled by Timon, but accepts gold from him. (v, 1) the gift becomes known. Acc. *Plut.* p. 304, it was a concubine of Alcibiades called T. who buried him. (The name is that of a daughter of Leda; Apollod. iii, 10.)

Time (1). Personified. 'T.'s the king of men ...' (*Per.* ii, 3); 'T. goes on crutches' (*M. Ado*, ii, 1); 'hasty-footed T.' (*M.N.D.* iii, 2); 'T.'s deformed hand' (*Com. Err.* v, 1); 'old T. the clock-setter, that bald sexton T.' (*John*, iii, 1); 'this bloody tyrant, T.' (*Son.* xvi); apostrophized, *Son.* xix, cxxiii; 'T.'s fell hand' (*ib.* lxiv); mtd., *ib.* c (3); 'T.'s fool' (*ib.* cxvi); mtd., *ib.* xii, xv, lx, lxiii, lxv, cxv, cxxv; mtd., *Lucr.* 995, 1765.

Time (2). D.P. *Wint. T.* Appears as 'Chorus,' between Acts III and IV; announces that sixteen years are supposed to have elapsed, and touches on the changes they have wrought.

The authenticity of the scene has been disputed by some commentators. It is noteworthy that the secondary title of Greene's *Pandosto* is *The Triumph of Time*.

Timon. D.P. *Timon.* A noble Athenian. i, 1] surrounded by flatterers and parasites; gladly consents to pay Ventidius' debt; enables Lucilius to marry; banters Apemantus; welcomes Alcibiades. i, 2] presides at a lavish banquet; refuses Ventidius' proffered return of the loan, declaring it to be a gift; in a speech to the company declares that 'we are born to do benefits'; witnesses a 'Masque of Amazons'; receives and distributes gifts. ii, 2] is importuned by his creditors' servants; later, the desperate state of his affairs is unfolded to him by his steward, Flavius; believes that his friends will rally to his assistance; sends messengers to solicit loans from his late guests and aid from the senators, whom Fl. has already fruitlessly approached; T. then remembers the loan to Ventidius, and sends a request for its repayment. (iii, 2) his poverty is discussed by Lucius and three strangers. (iii, 3) mtd. iii, 4] is infuriated by the clamour of his creditors; to the steward's amazement bids him invite all his false friends to another feast. iii, 6] welcomes his guests to the new feast; when they are seated the mockery of the banquet is displayed, he pours forth a torrent of objurgation upon the guests, and finally drives them forth, using the dishes as missiles. iv, 1] (without the walls of Athens) (*sol.*) curses Athens and all that dwell there. iv, 3] (in the woods) (*sol.*) rages against mankind; as he digs for roots he unearths a store of gold; resolves to make it 'do its right nature' in corrupting mankind; gives some to Alcibiades and his mistresses – the latter he curses, and the former he urges to spread devastation with the sword; (*sol.*) bids the earth produce 'new masters'; is visited by Apemantus, and they discuss with bitter gibes who is the better philosopher; A. in departing declares he will reveal T.'s wealth; T. gives gold to banditti and almost charms them 'from their profession'; Flavius visits his 'dearest master'; Timon is touched by the 'singly honest man,' but bids him flee lest he should curse him also. v, 1] after conversing ironically with Poet and Painter, drives out the 'rascal dogs.' v, 2] two senators beg T. to return to Athens and save her from Alcibiades by taking the captainship; with bitter scorn he rejects their offer. (v, 3) mtd. (v, 4) a soldier takes an impression of the inscription on his tomb. (v, 5) his epitaph read by Alcibiades.

For the origin of the character see TIMON OF ATHENS. The inconsistency of the epitaph is simply due to a combination of the two alternative versions given by Plutarch.

'Timon, the great-natured, truly generous man, whose mind is as beneficial as the sun, cannot be currish, nor stoop to the baseness of revenge. Finding men base he removes from them, and ministers with bitter contempt to the baseness that infects them.' (J. Masefield, *Wm. Sh.* p. 215.)

'In the extremity of his obdurate and immoderate hatred, the humane poet has not forgotten the original nature of the man, nor neglected to make the traces of his former goodness discernible through all his fury and curses' (Gervinus, *Sh. Comm.* (1875), p. 780).

Timon of Athens.

PUBLICATION. First published in the Folio of 1623, under the title of 'The Life of Tymon of Athens.' The acts and scenes are not numbered, with the exception of i, 1.

AUTHORSHIP. It is generally agreed that this play is not wholly the work of Sh. There are two main theories on the matter: (*a*) that Sh. partly rewrote, and expanded, the older work of another author; and (*b*) that the nucleus of the play is Sh.'s 'and that it was completed for the stage by a second and inferior hand' (*N.S.S. Tr.*, 1874, Pt. I, pp. 130–94, 242–51); the former theory is usually accepted. George Wilkins has been regarded as Sh.'s 'collaborator.'

DATE OF COMPOSITION. Sh.'s share of the play was probably written about 1607.

SOURCES OF THE PLOT. The story of Timon is found in two classical authors – Plutarch and Lucian. The former in his *Life of Antony* mentions Timon as one who had been driven by the thanklessness of false friends to become a savage misanthrope. He, however, courted the society of Alcibiades, because he knew that 'one day he shall do great mischief to the Athenians,' and he also consorted with Apemantus. The epitaph in its twofold form, as given in *Timon*, is copied from Plutarch. In Lucian's dialogue the discovery of gold in the woods, and the driving away of sycophantic friends with missiles occur (see PLUTUS). In 1575 the story of Timon appeared in Painter's *Palace of Pleasure*, but is only a weak adaptation of Plutarch. In 1841 an anonymous play, *Timon*, supposed to have been written about 1600, was edited by Dyce. This contains most of Lucian's details, and adds that T. pelted his guests at the final banquet with stones painted like artichokes; of this the last line of *Timon*, iii, 6, seems a reminiscence. The 'shadowy and irrelevant fable' (Lee) of the quarrel of Alcibiades with the Athenian Senate is but loosely connected with the main plot.

The slight reference to 'Critic Timon,' *L.L.L.* iv, 3, is the only allusion to the story of Timon in *Sh.* except in the play.

It seems probable that the play was printed in the Folio from a MS. and not from prompt-books.

Tisick, Master. 'The deputy,' *2 Hen. IV*, ii, 4; perhaps in allusion to his being short of breath.

Titan. A name of the Sun, frequent in Roman poets, especially Ovid, as being son of Hyperion (*q.v.*), one of the Titans.

'Didst thou never see T. kiss a dish of butter? pitiful-hearted T., that melted at the sweet tale of the sun's' (*1 Hen. IV*, ii, 4); 'Let T. rise as early as he dare' (*Tr. Cr.* v, 11); 'the greedy touch Of common-kissing T.' (*Cymb.* iii, 4); 'whose virtues will ... Reflect on Rome as T.'s rays on earth' (*T. And.* i, 2); 'thy cheeks look red as T.'s face Blushing to be encountered with a cloud' (*ib.* ii, 5); 'T.'s fiery wheels' (*Rom. J.* ii, 3); 'T., tired in the midday heat, With burning eye did hotly overlook them' (*V. A.* 177).

In *1 Hen. IV* Theobald very plausibly suggested 'pitiful-hearted butter.'

Titania. D.P. *M.N.D.* 'Queen of the Fairies' (Rowe). ii, 1] accuses Oberon, her lord, of having 'come from the farthest steep of India' for the sake of his 'buskin'd mistress,' Hippolyta; describes the evils that have fallen on 'human mortals' in consequence of their dissensions; gives reasons for refusal to give up her 'young squire' to Ob.; departs in wrath. ii, 2] bids her elves sing to her; she sleeps, and Ob. applies magic love-juice to her eyes. iii, 1] she awakes, and is 'on the first view' enamoured of Nick Bottom; bids the fairy attendants 'do him courtesies' and lead him to her bower. (iii, 2) Puck reports the circumstances. iv, 1] (has yielded up the Indian boy to Ob.); awakes, disenchanted, and loathes the sight of Bottom; joyously trips away with Ob., 'after the night's shade.' v, 2] bids the fairies join in blessing the sleeping Palace of Theseus.

'Titania' is used by Ovid (*Metam.* iii, 173), as a name, or epithet, of Diana, and in two other places of Latona and Circe. Sh. seems to have derived the name from the original, since it does not occur in Golding's translation.

Titchfield. Near Fareham (Hants); see WRIOTHESLEY, HENRY.

[**Tithonus.**] Beloved by Aurora, and rendered immortal but subject to old age. Supposed by Steevens to be alluded to, *M.N.D.* iii, 2: 'I [Oberon] with the morning's love have oft made sport.' See CEPHALUS.

Titinius. A centurion in the army of Cassius at Philippi; he was sent to see how Brutus fared, and, since he did not return immediately, Cassius thought all was lost, and put an end to his life. Thereupon T. killed himself (Val. Max. ix, 9; Appian, *B.C.* iv, 113). Spelt 'Titinnius,' *Plut.* p. 143.

D.P. *Jul. C.* (i, 2) waited on Caesar when he was ill. iv, 2] *p.m.* iv, 3] in attendance on Brutus. v, 1] (at Philippi) *p.m.* v, 3] is sent by Cassius to ascertain whether certain troops are friends or foes; Cassius believes he has been taken prisoner, and despairs; T. returning, finds the body of C., and kills himself with C.'s sword.

Titus (1). Nephew of Orsino; wounded in a sea-fight; mtd. *T. Nt.* v, 1.

Titus (2). D.P. *Timon.* Servant to one of Timon's creditors. iii, 4] speaks of the creditors' ingratitude; applies fruitlessly for payment.

Titus (3). See LARTIUS, TITUS.

Titus (4). See ANDRONICUS, TITUS.

Titus Andronicus. (In F1: 'The Lamentable Tragedy of Titus Andronicus.' The acts, but not the scenes, are numbered.)

DATE OF PUBLICATION. Two entries in the Registers of the Stationers' Company, of 1593 and 1602, mention, respectively, 'A noble Roman Historye of Tytus Andronicus' and 'a booke called Titus and Andronic,' but it is doubtful whether either entry refers to the play.

For many years a quarto volume (Q2) entitled 'The most lamentable Romaine Tragedie of Titus Andronicus ... Printed by I. R. for Edward White' (1600) was regarded as the earliest extant edition, but in 1905 a copy was discovered of an earlier edition (Q1) dated 1594, and it is known that the tragedy was acted in Jan. 1593–4, and was then described as a 'new' piece. A third quarto, dated 1611, closely follows Q2. The play as it appears in F1 was printed from Q2, with the addition of a new scene (iii, 2).

AUTHORSHIP. Much controversy has taken place as to the authorship of the tragedy. Francis Meres, in 1598, includes it in a list of Sh.'s plays with other dramas of unquestioned authenticity; the editors of the First Folio accepted it; from numerous contemporary references to it we gather 'that it was one of the most popular plays on the Elizabethan stage' (J. C. Collins, *Studies in Sh.* pp. 104–5). That Sh.'s name did not appear on the title-page of Qq is a fact of little weight, since the Qq of *Rich. II*, *1 Hen. IV*, and *Rom. J.* are also anonymous. Furthermore, critics who attribute *T. And.* to Sh. have been able to point out numerous parallel passages in undisputed plays and especially in the early poem of *Venus and Adonis* (see Collins, *ut supra*).

On the other hand, many critics, partly influenced by the revolting nature of its plot, and partly by the crudity of its construction, have refused to give Sh. any greater share in the play than that of having possibly added a touch to it, here and there, when acted by his company. Edward Ravenscroft, an unimportant dramatist, wrote in 1678 of *T. And.*: 'I have been told by some anciently conversant with the stage that it was not originally Sh.'s but brought by a private hand to be acted, and he only gave some master-touches to one or two of the principal parts or characters.' Sir S. Lee, *Life of W. Sh.* (1915), p. 129, considers that this 'assertion deserves acceptance' and that the play was probably written originally in 1591 by Thomas Kyd, perhaps aided by Greene or Peele, and improved by Sh. 'on its revival in 1594.' J. M. Robertson, *Did Sh. write Titus Andronicus?* (1905), refuses Sh. any share in the work.

SOURCE OF THE PLOT. The plot is, of course, wholly unhistorical. A lost play entitled 'Titus and Vespesian,' known to have been acted in 1591, seems to have been of a similar type. The influence of Ovid is manifest at several points of the tragedy.

'The play is certainly as unlike Sh.'s usual style as it is possible. ... In its kind it is full grown, and its features decided and overcharged. It is not like a first, imperfect essay, but shows a confirmed habit.' (W. Hazlitt.) 'I incline to think that both in this play and in Jeronymo Sh. wrote some passages, and that they are the earliest of his compositions.' (Coleridge.) 'Poets do not sin against their art unless they are in desperate want. Sh. certainly never touched this job for love.' (J. Masefield, *Wm. Sh.* p. 50.)

[**Tityus.**] A giant, cast into Tartarus, where vultures and snakes devoured and gnawed his liver (*Aen.* vi, 595 ff.; *Metam.* iv, 457). Tityus, or Prometheus, may be alluded to, *2 Hen. IV*, v, 3, l. 146; *M.W.W.* i, 3, l. 94; *Lear*, ii, 4, l. 137; *T. And.* v, 2, l. 31; *1 Hen. VI*, iv, 3, l. 47.

Toby. See BELCH, SIR TOBY.

Toledo. City in Spain. Wolsey was wrath with the Emperor 'For not bestowing on him, at his asking, The archbishopric of T.' (*Hen. VIII*, ii, 1); cf. *Hol.* iii, 906.

The Abp. of T. is Primate of Spain.

Tom (1). A prentice; *2 Hen. VI*, ii, 3.

Tom (2). An ostler; *1 Hen. IV*, ii, 1.

Tom (3). As a common name, correlative to 'Tib' (*q.v.*); coupled with 'Dick' and 'Francis,' *1 Hen. IV*, ii, 4; alone, *L.L.L.* v, 2. As a forename: 'T. Snout,' 'T. Drum' (*qq.v.*).

Tom-a-Bedlam. See EDGAR.

[**Tomyris.**] See THOMYRIS.

Tongue, Lady. Nonce-name applied by Benedick to Beatrice; *M. Ado*, ii, 1.

Tooley, Nicholas. Mtd. as a 'principal actor' in F1.

Topas, Sir. 'Sir T., the curate,' personated by Feste to deceive Malvolio; *T. Nt.* iv, 2. Mtd., *ib.* v, 1.

The name would be familiar from Chaucer's *Rime of Sir T.*

[**Torismond.**] See FREDERICK (1).

Toryne. 'A city of Albania' taken by Octavius (*Plut.* p. 208) τορύνη, a ladle). Mtd. *Ant. Cl.* iii, 7. ('Troine,' F1.)

Touchstone. D.P. *A.Y.L.* 'A clown attending on Celia and Rosalind' (Rowe). i, 2] exchanges raillery with C. and R. (i, 3) Celia relies on his faithful service. (ii, 3) he is missed from Court. ii, 4] shares his mistresses' hardships in Arden. (ii, 7) encounters Jaques in the forest. iii, 2] discusses a courtier's life with Corin; parodies Orlando's verses. iii, 3] is dissuaded by Jaques from being 'married under a bush, like a beggar.' v, 1] flouts his rustic rival. v, 3] criticizes the pages' song. v, 4] discourses before the Duke on quarrelling 'by the book.'

There is no equivalent character in Lodge's *Rosalynde.* Though T.'s name is thrice mtd. by other characters, he is, as D.P., referred to as 'Clown' simply. H. H. Furness (*New Var.* edn. pp. 308–9) has suggested that the Clown of i, 2, 'was not T., but a separate and very different character, and who should never have been called Touchstone'; the critic argues that the 'clownish fool' of Act I, 'with his bald jests of knights and pancakes, whom Rosalind threatens with the whip' cannot be the same character as the witty T. of Act V. It should be observed, however, that in Act I the Clown but jests perfunctorily, in his official capacity as a household fool; and Rosalind's light warning that he would 'be whipt for taxation one of these days' should be compared with the contemptuous rebuke, 'Peace, you dull fool!' addressed by her to the undoubted Touchstone (iii, 2).

'Perhaps Jaques, in his parody of Amiens' song, approaches the critical vein of Touchstone pretty closely, but he is inferior in that mixed vein of self-observation and self-knowledge, which approximates Touchstone at one time to Mr Pepys, and at another to Michel de Montaigne' (W. W. Lloyd, Singer's edn. (1854), p. 120).

Touraine. Former government of France, united in 1044 with Anjou (*q.v.*); conquered by Philip Augustus *c.* 1204. Claimed for Arthur, *John*, i, 1, ii, 1; part of the dowry of Blanch of Castile, *ib.* ii, 1 (2); la Pucelle at Touraine, *1 Hen. VI*, i, 2 (where T. seems to be regarded as a town; but 'Fierbois in T.' acc. *Hol.* iii, 600).

Tours. Capital of Touraine (*q.v.*). 'Won away' (*1 Hen. VI*, iv, 3); 'famous ancient city' (2 *Hen. VI*, i, 1); de la Pole (Suffolk) at Tours, *ib.* i, 3.

Tower of London, The. Formerly a royal palace, fortress, and State prison; its legendary foundation by Julius Caesar (see Stow, *Chron.* (1580) p. 34) is referred to, *Rich. III*, iii, 1; but, historically, it originated with William the Conqueror. The State prisoners were usually confined in the towers of the inner ward; of the palace, in the S.E. corner, scarcely a vestige remains.

Richard committed to the T. by Bolingbroke, after his abdication, *Rich. II*, iv, 1 (acc. *Hol.* iii, 501, he was 'had to the T. ... the next day after his coming to London'); the Queen awaits Richard on his 'way To Julius Caesar's ill-erected tower' (*ib.* v, 1), but Northumberland announces that he 'must to Pomfret, not unto the T.' (*ib. ib.*).

Duke Humphrey will 'to the T. ... to view the artillery and munition' (*1 Hen. VI*, i, 1); he is refused admission, and his adherents try to break in (the 'armour' in the T. mtd.), *ib.* i, 3 (cf. *Hol.* iii, 591); Humphrey accuses Henry Beaufort of laying a trap to take his life 'at the T.' (*ib.* iii, 1); help from the T. is called for against Cade's rebels, who have tried in vain to take it, 2 *Hen. VI*, iv, 5 (cf. *Hol.* iii, 634); Cade cries 'burn down the T. too' (2 *Hen. VI*, iv, 6); Henry threatens to send 'Duke Edmund and Somerset to the T.' (*ib.* iv, 9; cf. *Hol.* iii, 637); 'the Duke of Somerset is in the T.,' 'let him [York] to the T.' (*ib.* v, 1).

King Henry committed to the Tower, *3 Hen. VI*, iii, 2 (cf. *Hol.* iii, 667); also, on another occasion, *ib.* iv, 8 (*cf.* Hall, p. 294); mtd., *ib.* v, 1; 'the T.! the T.!' Richard has gone 'to make a bloody supper in the T.' (*ib.* v, 5); the murder of Henry by Gloucester in the T. described, *ib.* v, 6.

Clarence taken to the T., and Hastings delivered thence, *Rich. III*, i, 1 (4); mtd., *ib.* i, 3 (2), 4; Richard, D. of York, on being told that he is to be lodged in the T., exclaims 'I do not like the T., of any place. Did Julius Caesar build that place?' – moreover he fears that he will 'not sleep in quiet at the T.' for it is haunted by the ghost of Clarence, *ib.* iii, 1 (6); Hastings proceeds to the T., and recalls going thither as prisoner, *ib.* iii, 2 (3); meeting of coronation council at the T. (in the White Tower), *ib.* iii, 4; Q. Elizabeth, and ladies with her, denied entrance to the T., *ib.* iv, 1 (3); 'those bastards in the T.' (*ib.* iv, 2); the murder of the Princes in the T., *ib.* iv, 3; named by the ghosts of Henry and the Princes, *ib.* v, 3 (2).

Buckingham committed to the Tower, *Hen. VIII*, i, 1 (*Hol.* iii, 863); mtd., *ib.* i, 2; Henry hints to Cranmer that 'our T.' may be his abode, *ib.* v, 1; Cranmer committed to the T., but saved by Henry, *ib.* v, 3 (4).

The menagerie kept at the Tower may be alluded to in *T.G.V.* ii, 1: 'You were wont ... to walk like one of the lions.'

Tower Hill. N.W. of the Tower; where traitors were executed. 'The tribulation of T. hill' is mentioned as a disorderly element in playhouse audiences, *Hen. VIII*, v, 3; see LIMEHOUSE.

The suggestion (Johnson) that the 'Tribulation' was a puritanical meeting-house is unsupported.

Town Clerk. D.P. *M. Ado.* (St. dir. iv, 2, in QFf.) The 'Sexton' of mod. edns.

Towton, Battle of. March 29, 1461; total defeat of the Lancastrians under Hen. VI and Margaret, by the Yorkists under Edw. IV. The battle described, *3 Hen. VI*, ii, 3–6.

T. is a village in Yorkshire, about 12 m. N.E. of Leeds. The battle really began with a skirmish at Ferrybridge on March 28, in which the Lancastrians had the advantage; this combat referred to, *3 Hen. VI*, ii, 3.

'This conflict [Towton] was in a maner unnaturall, for in it the sonne fought agaynst the father, the brother agaynst the brother. ...' (Hall, p. 256): cf. '*K. Hen.* O piteous spectacle! O bloody times! Whiles lions war, and battle for their dens, Poor harmless lambs abide their enmity' (*3 Hen. VI*, ii, 5).

Tranio. D.P. *Tam. Sh.* Servant to Lucentio. i, 1] at Padua, urges his master to be no 'stoic,' and to study what he most affects; realizes that Luc. has fallen in love with Bianca; warns him that her sister Katharina must be wedded first; exchanges habits with L. and undertakes to pose as his master. i, 2] 'bravely apparelled,' he openly announces his intention of wooing Bianca; invites her other suitors to carouse with him. ii, 1] introduces himself, as Lucentio, to Baptista, Bianca's father, and proffers gifts for the ladies; later, outvies Gremio in his lavish offers of a dowry for Bi.; is warned by Bap. that he must obtain 'his father's assurance' ere the marriage can take place. (iii, 1) mtd. iii, 2] plans 'to get a man' who shall impersonate Vincentio, Lucentio's father. iv, 2] witnesses, with Hortensio, L.'s wooing of Bi.; assures Hort. that he will 'forswear Bi. and her love for ever'; instructs a Pedant how to play his part as Vincentio. iv, 4] introduces the false Vinc. to Baptista, whom he invites to his lodging, to 'pass the business privately and well' that night. v, 1] places the real Vinc. under arrest as a 'mad knave,' but takes to flight on Lucentio acknowledging his father. v, 2] at L.'s banquet admits that, like a greyhound, he ran for his master.

The name is that of a character in the *Mostellaria* of Plautus. The corresponding character in *The Taming of A Shrew* is Valeria, servant to Aurelius, whom he personates, and in *I Suppositi* Dulippo, servant to Erostrato, whom he personates.

Transylvanian, *subst.* Native of Transylvania. 'The poor Tr. is dead' (*Per.* iv, 2).

Travellers. D.PP. *1 Hen. IV.* ('Some eight or ten,' acc. Gadshill.) ii, 2] are set upon and robbed by Falstaff and his comrades.

Travers. D.P. 2 *Hen. IV.* A retainer of the Earl of Northumberland. i, 1] brings tidings that Hotspur has been slain at Shrewsbury. See MORTON.

Tray. Name of dog; *Lear*, iii, 6. (See TROILUS (2).)

Trebonius, Caius. A politician who long enjoyed the confidence and favour of Julius Caesar, and was made consul by him 45 B.C.; with base ingratitude, however, he assumed a leading part in the conspiracy against his benefactor; he was entrusted with keeping Antony outside the Senate-house while the murder of Caesar was perpetrated (*Plut.* p. 118; but a different account is given p. 100; see DECIUS BRUTUS).

D.P. *Jul. C.* (i, 3) among the conspirators. ii, 1] demurs to Cassius' proposal to kill Mark Antony. ii, 2] Caesar desires Tr. to be 'near him' that day; Tr. mutters that C.'s friends will wish he had been farther. (ii, 3) Artemidorus writes: 'trust not Tr.,' in his letter meant for C. iii, 1] leads Antony away from the Senate-house; after the assassination reports that Ant. has 'fled to his house amazed.'

When the conspirators doubted whether to make Ant. privy to the plot (ii, 1), acc. *Plut.* p. 164, 'all the rest liked of it, saving Tr. only.'

Trent, River. Discussed as an important boundary in the proposed division of the kingdom between Glendower, Mortimer, and Hotspur, *1 Hen. IV*, iii, 1; H. calls it 'the smug and silver Tr.,' and G. suggests having 'Tr. turned.' (Cf. *Hol.* iii, 521.)

Tressel. ('Tressill,' Qq.) D.P. *Rich. III.* 'Gentleman attending on the Lady Anne.' i, 2] *p.m.* (is addressed by Lady A.).

Possibly for 'Trussel'; Sir William Tr. was sheriff of Warwickshire, 16 Edw. IV. See French, p. 251.

Tribunes. D.PP. *Cymb.* iii, 7] receive commands from the Emperor to raise a force of gentlemen to proceed against the Britons.

Trigon. The junction of three signs of the zodiac, 'the fiery Trigon' consisting of the three 'dry' signs – Aries, Leo, and Sagittarius.

'*P. Hen.* Saturn and Venus this year in conjunction; what says the almanack to that? *Poins.* And, look, whether the fiery Trigon, his man, be not lisping to his master's old tables; his notebook, his counsel-keeper' (*2 Hen. IV*, ii, 4).

Trinculo. D.P. *Temp.* 'A jester' (F1). In the service (v, 1) of the King of Naples. ii, 2] when shipwrecked is separated from his companions; finds Caliban lying on the ground and creeps for shelter beneath his cloak; is discovered by Stephano, and henceforth the three are associated. iii, 2] derides Cal., but accepts a cuffing from Steph. without retaliating. iv, 1] is subservient to Steph., who assumes kingly airs. v, 1] admits to his master that he has been in such a pickle that he will 'not fear fly-blowing.' See STEPHANO.

The name seems adapted from It. *trincare*, to tipple.

Tripolis, Tripoli. Town in S. Africa, or in Syria. Mtd. *M.V.* i, 3, iii, 1, 2; *Tam. Sh.* iv, 2. The Syrian T. was the port of Aleppo (*q.v.*).

Triton. Son of Poseidon and Amphitrite; a divinity of the sea, represented as riding over the waves on horses, or sea-monsters (Ovid, *Her.* vii, 50: 'Caeruleis Triton per mare curret equis'). Also, in the plural, Poseidon's trumpeters. 'Hear you this Tr. of the minnows?' (*Cor.* iii, 1, l. 89; viz. Sicinius; his 'horn' is mtd. 1. 95; *cf.* Ovid, *Metam.* i, 333).

Troilus (1). Son of Priam and Hecuba. The only allusion to Tr. in Homer occurs in *Il.* xxiv, 257, where he is mentioned, among the slain, as a dashing charioteer (ἱππιοχάρμης). 'Dictys Cretensis' (iv, 9), represents him as strangled by order of Achilles. 'Dares Phrygius' makes him a somewhat more important personage; he advocates the prosecution of the war at Priam's council, and is so brave that Achilles durst not attack him face to face. As a hero of romance, however, Tr. owes his parentage entirely to Benoît de Sainte-More, and in the *Filostrato* of Boccaccio he becomes a protagonist, and is completely medievalized. The 'Troylus' of Chaucer gains his Criseyde (a widow) only by means of a treacherous plot, aided by Pandarus.

'*Clo.* I would play Lord Pandarus … to bring a Cressida to this Tr.' (*T. Nt.* iii, 1); 'T., the first employer of pandars' (*M. Ado*, v, 1); 'in such a night Tr. … mounted the Trojan walls And sigh'd his soul toward the Grecian tents' (*M.V.* v, 1; *cf.* Chaucer, *Troylus*, ll. 5, 648, 666); 'Tr. had his brains dash'd out with a Grecian club' (*A.Y.L.* iv, 1; this detail is an invention of Rosalind's); 'here Tr. swounds' (*Lucr.* 1486).

D.P. *Tr. Cr.* i, 1] tells Pandarus that he is 'mad in Cressida's love,' and believes P. adverse to his suit. i, 2] is discussed by P. and Cr. ('he ne'er saw three-and-twenty,' according to P.); as he passes by, P. dilates on his valour. ii, 2] (at Priam's council) urges the prosecution of the war and the retention of Helen; makes light of Cassandra's warnings. (iii, 1) mtd. iii, 2] awaits the coming of Cressida in Pandarus' orchard; P. is witness to their mutual vows. (iv, 1) mtd. iv, 2] the converse of the lovers is interrupted by Pandarus; later, Tr. learns that Cr. must be handed over to the Greeks. iv, 3] prepares to offer Cr. as at 'an altar.' iv, 4] warns Cr. against the wiles of 'the Grecian youths'; laments his own lack of accomplishments; gives Cr. a sleeve in exchange for her glove; warns Diomed, with a threat, to use her well. iv, 5] witnesses the combat between Hector and Ajax; is eulogized by Ulysses; asks U. to bring him to Menelaus' tent. v, 1] follows Diomed by night. v, 2] witnesses the interview between Cr. and D., and sees D. gain possession of his sleeve; in a passionate outburst of wrath and jealousy, vows to slay D. v, 3] chides Hector for giving quarter to the Greeks; insists on going to the field; derides Cassandra; receives a letter from Cressida. v, 4] fights with Diomed. (v, 5) his horse is sent to Cr. by D., who has 'chastised' Tr.; Ajax seeks him. v, 6] fights D. and Ajax; rushes to the aid of Aeneas. v, 11] laments the death of Hector.

In iii, 2, the name occurs in the plural: 'let all constant men be Troiluses.' In *Sh.* the name is always a dissyllable, 'Troylus.' The sending of T.'s horse to Cr. is mtd. by Lydgate.

Troilus (2). Name of a dog. 'My spaniel Tr.?' (*Tam. Sh.* iv, 1).

Probably as proverbial for faithfulness; *cf.* Tray (*treu*).

Troilus and Cressida. (In F1: 'The Tragedie of Troylus and Cressida.' Except i, 1, the acts and scenes are not indicated.)

PUBLICATION. In the Stationers' Registers, Feb. 7, 1602–3, a licence is recorded as granted to James Roberts for 'the booke of Troilus and Cresseda as yt is acted by my Lord Chamberlens men, to print when he hath gotten sufficient aucthoritye for it.' But apparently the authority was not forth-coming. In Jan. 1688–9, however, another licence was issued to R. Bonian and H. Walley for a book with a similar name, and a quarto appeared in 1609, entitled 'The Historie of Troylus and Cresseida. As it was acted – by the Kings Maiesties seruants at the Globe. Written by William Shakespeare.' Another quarto, identical as to its text with the first, appeared the same year. This bears a more pompous and elaborate title, and a long eulogistic preface, which claims that the play was a new one, 'never stal'd with the stage, never clapper-clawed with the palms of the vulger.' This is in all probability mere bravado, the text having been obtained surreptitiously from a prompter's copy.

The Folio text of 1623 is perhaps derived from some other source; *cf.* Lee, *Life of W. Sh.* pp. 369 ff., and R. C. Rhodes, *Sh.'s First Folio* (1923), pp. 21–6, 107–9.

DATE OF COMPOSITION AND PRODUCTION. This is undetermined, but generally placed, from internal evidence, about 1603. Some critics, however, have placed it as late as 1608–9. Of course, if we knew that Roberts' licence, mentioned above, referred to Sh.'s play, all would be clear, but Dekker and Chettle are known to have been at work upon a play on the subject in 1599.

SOURCE OF THE PLOT. The story of Troilus and Cressida is of medieval, not classical, origin. (Tr. is mentioned once in Homer, and Cr. not at all.) There are four channels by which the story may have descended to Sh.: (*a*) Chaucer's *Troylus and Criseyde*, following Boccaccio's *Il Filostrato*, derived, in its turn, from Guido delle Colonne's *Historia Trojana*; (*b*) from Lydgate's *Troy Booke* (also from Guido); (*c*) Caxton's *Recuyell of the Historyes of Troye* (1474), from a French epitome by Raoul Le Fevre of Guido's book; (*d*) to a slight extent from Chapman's *Iliads* (partly published by 1598).

Guido's work is an unacknowledged plagiarism from Benoît de Sainte-More's elaborate *Roman de Troie* (12th cent.), which is based on the pseudonymous works of 'Dictys Cretensis' (*De Bello Trojano*), and 'Dares Phrygius' (*De Excidio Trojae Historia*).

Trojan. (*a*) *Subst.*, a native of Troy. 'The false T.' (*M.N.D.* i, 1; *i.e.* Aeneas). Mtd. *Tr. Cr.* Prol.; i, 1; 3 (5); ii, 1, 2 (5), 3; iii, 3; iv, 1 (2); iv, 5 (4); v, 2 (2), 4, 5, 6, 9. 'The T.' (*1 Hen. VI*, v, 5; *i.e.* Paris). Used as a vague term of reproach: 'Hector was but a T. in respect of this' (*L.L.L.* v, 2); 'dost thou thirst, base T.?' (*Hen. V*, v, 1). In a commendatory sense: 'play the honest T.' (*L.L.L.* v, 2). For a boon companion: 'there are other T.s that thou dreamest not of' (*1 Hen. IV*, ii, 1); mtd., *Lucr.* 1551. See also TROY, GATES OF.

(*b*) *Adj.*, pertaining to Troy. 'In such a night Troilus ... mounted the T. walls, (*M.V.* v, 1); 'T. Greeks' (Pistol's rant; *2 Hen. IV*, ii, 4); 'like the T. horse, warstuff'd within' (*Per.* i, 4); 'T. blood' (*Tr. Cr.* i, 2; ii, 2); 'this is T.' (*ib.* iv, 5); 'a T. drab' (*ib.* v, 1); 'T. ass' (*ib.* v, 4); 'T. trumpets' (*ib.* v, 8); mtd., *Lucr.* 1431.

Trot. Apparently a nonce-name; Pompey thus addressed by Lucio, *M. for M.* iii, 2.

Troy, City of. Taken and destroyed by the Greeks after a ten years' siege. The story of the siege of Troy, as related by Homer, was practically unknown in the Middle Ages. The Virgilian legend, which glorified the Trojans at the expense of the Greeks, and taught that the former were the ancestors of the Romans, as a poem, held the field, but with regard to details of the siege, and the characters of the protagonists, implicit faith was placed in two spurious Latin works – professedly translations from Greek originals – the *De Excidio Trojae Historia* of 'Dares Phrygius,' and the *De Bello Trojano* of 'Dictys Cretensis.' Upon 'Dares' Benoît de Sainte-More based his *Roman de Troie*, a poem of nearly 30,000 lines, greatly expanding his original with fertile inventions of his own. On one of Benoît's episodes Boccaccio based his *Filostrato*; of this Chaucer's *Troylus and Criseyde* was a greatly expanded version, and Gower in his *Confessio Amantis* follows Chaucer.

Meanwhile Guido delle Colonne had translated Benoît's work into Latin, without acknowledgment; Raoul le Fevre produced an epitome of this in French, and a translation of this by Caxton appeared, in 1474, as the *Recuyell of the Historyes of Troye*.

Lydgate's *Troy Booke* (printed 1513) was derived directly from Guido's Latin. The old Homeric story was made available for English readers by Chapman's translation of the *Iliad* (bks. i, ii, vii, viii, ix, x, xi, xviii), which appeared in 1598. (See TROILUS AND CRESSIDA and ILIUM.)

'Sir Pandarus [*q.v.*] of T.' (*M.W.W.* i, 3); 'Hector [*q.v.*] of T.,' 'the worthy knight of T.' (*L.L.L.* v, 2); 'the virgin tribute paid by howling T. [see HESIONE]' (*M.V.* iii, 2); '[Helen] the cause ... Why the Grecians sacked T.' (*All's Well*, i, 3); 'the model where old T. did stand' (*Rich. II*, v, 1); 'would have told him half his T. was burnt [see PRIAM]' (*2 Hen. IV*, i, 1); 'Hector of T.' (*ib.* ii, 4); 'the time of night when T. was set on fire' (*2 Hen. VI*, i, 4); 'burning T. [see DIDO]' (*ib.* iii, 2); 'Hector, the hope of T.' (*3 Hen. VI*, ii, 1); 'like a Sinon [*q.v.*] take another T.' (*ib.* iii, 2); 'my Hector, and my T.'s true hope [Clarence]' (*ib.* iv, 8); rescue of Anchises 'from the flames of T.' (*Jul. C.* i, 2); 'arm'd the Queen of T. [Hecuba]' (*T. And.* i, 2); 'brought a fagot to bright-burning T.' (*ib.* iii, 1); 'how T. was burnt' (*ib.* iii, 2); 'Hecuba of T. ran mad through sorrow' (*ib.* iv, 1); 'that baleful burning night when subtle Greeks surpris'd Priam's T.,' 'our T., our Rome' (*ib.* v, 3).

In *Tr. Cr.* the scene is laid throughout in Troy, and the Grecian camp before it. Troy is named 53 times in the play: 'In T. there lies the scene,' 'their vow is made to ransack T.,' 'the sons of T.' (Prol.); 'walls of T.' (i, 1); mtd., i, 2; 'after seven years' siege, yet T. walls stand' (i, 3); mtd., *ib.* (9), ii, 1, 2, 3 (2); 'all the gallantry of T.' (iii, 1); mtd., iii, 3 (5), iv, 1 (3), 2 (3), 4 (3), 5 (4), v, 1 (2), 2, 3 (4), 4; 'now T. sink down' (v, 9); 'great T. is ours' (v, 10); mtd., v, 11 (4), and, masc., i, 3, l. 75, 'T., yet upon his basis.'

In *Lucrece*, 1366–561, occurs an elaborate description of the 'piece of skilful painting made for Priam's Troy.'

Troy, Gates of. 'The six gates of Troy' are thus named by 'Dares Phrygius,' *De Exc. Tro.* iv: 'Antenorea, Dardania, Ilia, Scaea, Thymbrea, Troiana.'

Acc. Caxton, *Recuyell*, f. 253: 'In this cyte were six pryncipall gates, of whome that one was named dardane, the second tymbria, the third helyas, the fourth chetas, the fifthe troyenne and the sixthe antenorides.'

In Lydgate's *Troy Booke* they appear thus: 'Dardanydes, Tymbria, Helyas, Cetheas, Trojana, Anthonydes.'

In *Tr. Cr.* Prol. F1: 'Priam's six-gated city, Dardan, and Timbria, Helias, Chetas, Troien, And Antenonidus.'

The sixth name seems reminiscent both of Caxton and Lydgate. (In mod. edns. 'Antenorides.')

[**Troyes.**] Town of France, on the Seine (Dept. Aube), where in 1420 a treaty was ratified between Henry V and Charles VI of France, and where Henry and Katharine were betrothed. It must therefore (although not named) be regarded as the scene of *Hen. V*, v, 2. Acc. *Hol.* iii, 527, the agreement had been made between the English ambassadors and the French Court before Henry arrived at Troyes.

Troylus. See TROILUS.

Truepenny. Doubtfully a proper name. Hamlet says to the ghost: 'Art thou there, truepenny?' (*Haml.* i, 5). Johnson explains the word as 'a familiar phrase for an honest fellow.' (No earlier instance is known.)

True Tragedie, The. Abbreviated title of the play on which *3 Hen. VI* was based; in full: 'The True Tragedie of Richard Duke of Yorke, and the death of good King Henrie the Sixt, with the whole contention betweene the two Houses Lancaster and Yorke, as it was sundrie times acted by the Right Honourable the Earle of Pem-brooke his servants'; published by T. Millington, 1595. See CONTENTION, THE.

In *3 Hen. VI*, about 1000 lines of the older play are retained unaltered, 900 are recast, and 1000 new lines are added. See Lee, *Life of Sh.* p. 120.

Truth. Personified. 'A palace for the crowned T. to dwell in' (*Per.* v, 1); 'you would think T. were a fool' (*All's Well*, iv, 3); mtd., *Lucr.* 911.

T.T. *i.e.* Thomas Thorpe (*c.* 1570–*c.* 1635), whose initials are appended to the Dedication in Shakespeare's *Sonnets* (1609) as their publisher. Thorpe had also published, or procured the publication of, Marlowe's *First Book of Lucan* in 1600, and was instrumental in issuing several plays by Chapman and Ben Jonson. His position in the trade was, however, always comparatively humble, and he usually seems to have acted as 'jackal' to the established publishers by providing them with MSS. piratically obtained. Except during 1608, the works in which his name appears were neither printed nor sold by himself. Thorpe's professional obscurity is germane to the interpretation of the much disputed 'Dedication.' See SONNETS and W. H., MR.

Tubal. A Jew, friend to Shylock. D.P. *M.V.* iii, 1] brings the welcome news to Shy. that Antonio has lost an argosy, but also tells him of his daughter's extravagance at Genoa. (Mtd., i, 3; iii, 2.)

The name of one of the sons of Japheth (Gen. x, 2).

[Tuck, Friar.] A vagabond monk; a character in the Robin Hood ballads, and in the morris-dance. Not named, but once alluded to, in *Sh.*: 'By the bare scalp of Robin Hood's fat friar' (*T.G.V.* iv, 1).

[Tudor, Edmund.] See BEAUFORT, MARGARET.

Tudor, Jasper (*c.* 1431–95). E. of Pembroke and D. of Bedford; 2nd s. of Owen Tudor, 'half brother to King Henrie VI' (*Hol.* iii, 660); defeated at Mortimer's Cross; joined his nephew Richmond (afterward Henry VII) in Brittany and landed with him at Milford Haven; fought at Bosworth, and held high offices under Henry VII.

'Redoubted Pembroke' mtd. as having joined Richmond's forces, *Rich. III*, iv, 5; before the Battle of Bosworth, 'the Earl of P. keeps his regiment' (*ib.* v, 3).

'The Pembrochians were readie to serve and give their attendance on their naturall and immediat lord Jasper earle of Pembroke' (*Hol.* iii, 753).

Tuesday. T. morning contrasted with Monday night, in illustrating a sudden change, *M. Ado*, v, 1; *1 Hen. IV*, i, 2. Mtd., *M. for M.* v, 1; *Macb.* ii, 4; *Oth.* iii, 3; *2 Hen. IV*, i, 1.

Tullus. For 'T. Aufidius' (*q.v.*). *Cor.* i, 1, 8; iv, 5; v, 5.

[Tully.] See CICERO.

Tunis. Roman city on the N. coast of Africa, near the site of ancient Carthage (*q.v.*). Mtd. in connection with 'Claribel, daughter of the King of Naples,' who has become 'Queen of T.,' and 'dwells ten leagues beyond man's life' (*Temp.* ii, 1); mtd., *ib.* v, 1.

Turf, Peter. Alleged to have been mtd. by Sly; *Tam. Sh.* Ind. 2.

Turk. An Osmanli; often used, rhetorically, to signify a savage fellow, a robber, or an infidel.

Pistol uses the word as a random term of abuse, 'base Phrygian Turk' (*M.W.W.* i, 3); Othello rebukes brawlers by exclaiming: 'Are we turn'd Turks?' (*Oth.* ii, 3). Their supposed ruthlessness is aimed at in: 'Stubborn T.s and Tartars, never train'd To offices of gentle courtesy' (*M.V.* iv, 1), and as renegades they are alluded to in 'Well, an you be not turn'd T.' (*M. Ado*, iii, 4), and 'if the rest of my fortunes turn T. with me' (*Haml.* iii, 2). Iago asseverates his veracity, 'or else I am a T.' (*Oth.* ii, 1); 'a malignant and a turban'd T.' (*ib.* v, 2). Often in the sense of 'the grand Turk,' the Sultan: 'A boy ... that shall go to Constantinople and take the T. by the beard' (*Hen. V*, v, 2); 'duer paid to the hearer than the T.'s tribute' (*2 Hen. IV*, iii, 2); 'the T. that two-and-fifty kingdoms hath' (*1 Hen. VI*, iv, 7); 'I would send them to the T.' (*All's Well*, ii, 3); 'in woman out-paramoured the T.' (*Lear*, iii, 4). As foes of the Crusaders: 'Why, she defies me, Like T. to Christian' (*A.Y.L.* iv, 3); Norfolk fought against 'black pagans, T.s and Saracens' (*Rich. II*, iv, 1); 'Think you we are T.s or infidels?' (*Rich. III*, iii, 5). 'The T.,' in the sense of the Turkish commander, or Government, *Oth.* i, 3 (4); mtd., *ib.* ii, 1 (2). 'Nose of T.' is one of the ingredients in the witches' hell-broth, *Macb.* iv, 1.

Turk Gregory. T.G. 'never did such deeds in arms as I [Falstaff] have done this day' (*1 Hen. IV*, v, 3).

Apparently an allusion to the militant Pope Gregory VII (Hildebrand), who brought the Emperor Henry IV to his knees. But this Pope was not personally a warrior.

Turkish. 'The desk that's cover'd o'er with T. tapestry' (*Com. Err.* iv, 1); Henry V, on his accession, reassures his brothers, who feared reprisals, in the words: 'This is the English, not the T. Court' (*2 Hen. IV*, v, 2; see AMURATH); 'Like T. mute, shall have a tongueless mouth' (*Hen. V*, i, 2); 'the T. preparation makes for Rhodes' (*Oth.* i, 3); 'T. fleet' (*ib.* i, 3; ii, 1, 2); 'T. loss' (*ib.* ii, 1).

Turlygood. Edgar speaks of himself as 'poor T., poor Tom' (*Lear*, ii, 3).

'Turlygod,' Ff. 'Turlupin' has been suggested, from It. *turlupino*, a madman, applied to the 'Beghards.' A corruption of 'thoroughly good' was regarded as possible by Collier.

Turnbull Street. 'The feats he hath done about T. street' (*2 Hen. IV*, iii, 2). Probably for Turnmill Street, Clerkenwell, formerly a haunt of bad characters.

'Turnball,' Ff.

Tuscan, *adj.* Pertaining to Tuscany. 'The T. service' (*All's Well*, i, 2); 'the T. wars' (*ib.* ii, 3).

Twelfth Night, or What you Will. (In F1: 'Twelfe Night, Or what you will.' The acts and scenes are numbered.)

DATE OF COMPOSITION. Direct external evidence exists fixing an inferior limit to the date of the production of the play. In the *Diary* of John Manningham, a student of the Middle Temple (Harl. MSS. No. 5353), printed by the Camden Society, there appears, under date Feb. 2, 1601–2, this entry: 'At our feast we had a play called "Twelve Night, or What you Will," much like the Commedy of Errores or Menechmi in Plautus, but most like and neere to that in Italian called *Inganni*,' and the writer goes on to describe the deceit practised on Malvolio and its consequences. Before the discovery of the *Diary* critics had attached undue importance to two or three supposed pieces of internal evidence pointing to a date as late as 1613–4 for the production of the play, but it is now generally agreed that it was probably first acted in 1599–1600. The comparison of Malvolio's affected smiles to the lines 'in the new map, with the augmentation of the Indies' (iii, 2) is corroborative, since the map which appeared in the 2nd edn. of Hakluyt's *Principal Navigations* (1598–1600) is covered with complicated rhumb-lines, to which Malvolio's puckers might aptly be compared. (See *Sh. Eng.* i, 174, for an illustration.)

TITLE. The main title is probably due to the known custom of presenting a new play before Queen Elizabeth each Twelfth Night, and the light alternative 'What you Will' may be compared to 'As you Like it.'

PUBLICATION. *Twelfth Night* was not published before 1623, when it appeared in the First Folio. In the Stationers' Registers, Nov. 8, 1623, it appears among the plays 'not formerly entred to other men.'

SOURCES OF THE PLOT. A play entitled *Gl' Ingannati* ('The Deceived') was produced at Siena in 1531, by an Italian Academy named 'Gl' Intronati,' and published in a volume entitled *Il Sacrificio*, which passed through several editions before 1554. In this play the complications consequent on the likeness to her brother of a girl disguised as a boy closely resemble the fortunes of Viola, Sebastian, Olivia, and Orsino. The plot of Matteo Bandello's romance of *Niculo*, included in his *Novelle* (1554) closely follows *Gl'Ingannati*. François de Belleforest published a French translation of Bandello in 1580. Cinthio had included the story in his *Hecatommithi* (1565) and Barnabe Riche in 1581 based on the same materials his tale of *Apolonius and Silla*. A Latin play entitled *Laelia*, on the same theme, was acted at Cambridge in 1590 and 1598. All these sources of the serious plot were therefore at Sh.'s disposal, but the great comic characters, Sir Toby, Aguecheek, Feste, and Maria, appear to be wholly his own creations.

'No comedy of Sh.'s unites such abounding mirth and fine satire, with the charm of a poetical romance. It is the summing up of the several admirable qualities which appear in the joyous comedies, of which it forms the last.' (Dowden.) 'This is justly considered as one of the most delightful of Sh.'s comedies. It is full of sweetness and pleasantry. It is perhaps too good-natured for comedy. It has little satire and no spleen. It makes us laugh at the follies of mankind, not despise them, and still less bear any ill-will towards them.' (W. Hazlitt.) 'Here is the right royal seal of Pantagruel, clean-cut and clearly stamped, and unincrusted by any flake of dirt from the dubious finger of Panurge' (Swinburne). 'One of the weakest plays that ever I saw on the stage' (S. Pepys, Jan. 20, 1668).

Two Gentlemen of Verona, The.

PUBLICATION. First appeared in the Folio of 1623, with title as above. The acts and scenes are numbered.

DATE OF COMPOSITION. Mentioned by F. Meres in his *Palladis Tamia* (1598). From considerations of style and metre it is usually dated about 1591.

SOURCES OF THE PLOT. A popular story, 'The Shepherdess Filismena,' forming part of George de Montemayor's *La Diana Enamorada*, was the basis of a lost play, *The History of Felix and Philiomena* [*sic*], acted in 1584. From this play Sh. probably gained the idea of the plot of *T.G.V.*, which, however, he complicated by the addition of Valentine, and enlivened by the comic characters Launce and Speed.

'Valentine's consenting to become a captain of robbers has been compared with a somewhat similar incident in Sidney's *Arcadia*, but the coincidences are slight and it may be doubted that Sh. had here any thought of the *Arcadia*' (Dowden, *Sh.* p. 69).

Tybalt. D.P. *Rom. J.* Nephew to Lady Capulet. i, 1] joins in a fray between adherents of the rival houses, and fights with Benvolio; the latter speaks of him as 'the fiery T.' (i, 2) invited to Capulet's feast. i, 5] recognizes Romeo amongst the maskers; hotly protests against his presence, but is checked by Capulet as 'a saucy boy.' (ii, 4) sends a challenge to Romeo; is characterized as 'the courageous captain of compliments' by Mercutio. iii, 1] deliberately picks a quarrel with M. and Romeo; fights with the former and mortally wounds him; later, 'the furious T.' returns, fights with Romeo and is himself killed. (iii, 2) his death is announced to his cousin Juliet. (iii, 3) Friar Laurence discusses the consequences with Romeo. (iii, 4) Capulet's formal grief at his death. (iii, 5) mtd. (iv, 1) Juliet appears to weep 'immoderately' for his death. (iv, 3) Juliet pictures his body in the vault. (v, 3) Romeo apostrophizes his corpse.

The name is a variant of 'Tybert,' the cat in the beast epic of *Reynard the Fox*: hence Mercutio's allusions: 'more than prince of cats' (ii, 1), and 'good king of cats,' one of whose 'nine lives' he means 'to make bold withal' (iii, 1): even when dying, M. declares he has been scratched to death by a cat, *ib.*

In *Rhomeo and Julietta* 'Thibault(e).'

Tyburn. Near Hyde Park; place of execution of London criminals. The triangular form of the gallows is alluded to in: 'Thou makest the Triumviry, the corner cap of society, The shape of Love's Tyburn, that hangs up simplicity' (*L.L.L.* iv, 3).

Tymbria. See TROY, GATES OF.

Typhon. A monster with a hundred heads, who sought to wrest the sovereignty from Jove, but was quelled by a thunderbolt. See ENCELADUS. 'With all his threatening band of T.'s brood' (*T. And.* iv, 2).

Golding in his transln. of Ovid's *Metamorphoses* puts 'Typhon' for 'Typhoeus' (bk. v, l. 321 of original).

Tyrant. Dog's name; *Temp.* iv, 1.

Tyre, Tyrus. Ancient Phoenician city. Pericles (D.P. *Per.*) is described as Prince of T.; the scene of *Per.* i, 2, 3, ii, 4; is laid at T. The name is mtd. only in *Per.* 'Tyre': i, 1 (2), 2, 3 (3), 4; ii, Gow., 3 (3), 5; iii, Gow. (3), 1; iv, Gow.; v, 1 (2), 3 (2). 'Tyrus': iii, Gow., 1, 3; iv, 4, Gow.

Tyrian, *adj.* 'T. tapestry' (*Tam. Sh.* ii, 1); 'T. ship' (*Per.* v, Gow.).

Tyrrel (also **Tyrrell** or **Tyrell**), **Sir James.** Master of the Horse to Rich. III; according to More's *Historie*, was instrumental in the murder of the Princes in the Tower. Executed 1502. Acc. More, T. was an able and ambitious man, who, being kept under by Catesby and Ratcliffe, resolved to gain Richard's favour without scruple as to the means (*Hol.* iii, 734–5).

D.P. *Rich. III.* iv, 2] consents, at Richard's request, to murder the Princes in the Tower. iv, 3] meditates on the horror of the deed which he has suborned Dighton and Forrest to do; tells Richard that the children are dead, but he knows not where they are buried.

Acc. More, he had the bodies buried at the stairfoot, but Richard ordered them to be removed to a secret place (*Hol.* iii, 735).

Tyrus. See Tyre.

U

Ullorxa. A name, probably due merely to a printer's error, which occurs (in F1 only) in *Timon*, iii, 4, l. 112. Timon, resolved to gather his false friends round him for the last time, exclaims to his steward (Flavius), 'Go, bid all my friends again, Lucius, Lucullus, and Sempronius Ullorxa: all. I'll once more feast the rascals.' The Second Folio, and subsequent editions, simply omit 'Ullorxa.' The strange aspect of the word has, however, given rise to an abundant crop of conjectural emendations. F. G. Fleay suggested that it is a mere mistake for 'Ventidius,' and points to other indications that the printer was deceived by a badly written MS. (*N.S.S. Tr.*, 1874, Pt. I, pp. 148–9). Collier suggested either 'Sempronius, all, look, sir,' or 'Sempronius – *Flav.* Alack, sir. *Tim.* All.' Keightley (*N. and Q.* II, ix, 159) proposed 'Sempronius, all on 'em, all,' and G. Joicey (*ib.* VIII, iii, 101) 'Villaine' for 'Ullorxa.' The Cambridge editors print 'Sempronius: All, sirrah, all.' The most ingenious, though scarcely the most probable suggestion, is due to T. Littledale (*Athenæum*, May 25, 1901), viz. 'VII or Xa,' meaning 'seven or ten others.'

This crux has recently attracted attention afresh, in the *Times Lit. Suppl.*, A. Macnaghten (Feb. 28, 1924) suggesting 'All hawks, all,' and H. Cunningham (March 13, 1924) 'All lords, ay, all.' No emendation yet made has been generally accepted.

Ulysses. Son of Laertes (*T. And.* i, 1); distinguished among the Greek leaders at the siege of Troy for his valour, prudence, and eloquence. He married Penelope (*q.v.*), and was restored to her, at Ithaca, after twenty years' wanderings. 'I'll … deceive more slily than U. could' (*3 Hen. VI*, iii, 2); he stole the 'fatal steeds' from Rhesus (*q.v.*), *ib.* iv, 2; his long absence from Ithaca, *Cor.* i, 3; mtd., *Lucr.* 1394, 1399.

D.P. *Tr. Cr.* i, 3] points out to the other chiefs that the Greeks are weakened by neglect of 'degree'; he describes how Achilles derides his peers and despises prudent counsel; devises, with Nestor, a plan whereby the arrogance of Achilles may be humbled. (ii, 1) mtd. ii, 3] reports that Ach. 'will not to the field tomorrow'; ironically flatters Ajax, for the purpose of arousing Achilles' jealousy. iii, 3] suggests that the other chiefs should pass by Ach. scornfully; afterward converses with Ach., and convinces him that by keeping himself in the background he will soon be forgotten, and Ajax will be exalted; tells him also that his love for Polyxena is well known. iv, 5] alone of the chiefs scorns to salute Cressida, whom he characterizes as a wanton; describes Troilus; converses courteously with Hector. v, 1] offers to accompany Tr. v, 2] with Tr. observes a meeting between Diomed and Cressida, and tries to restrain Tr.'s rage and grief. (v, 4) called a 'dog-fox' by Thersites. v, 5] announces that Achilles is arming.

Ulysses is mtd., *T. And.* i, 1 (l. 381), as pleading for the 'funerals' of the suicide Ajax. The only classical source for this incident seems to be the *Ajax* of Sophocles.

P. Stapfer (*Sh. and Clas. Antiq.* pp. 227 ff.) draws attention to the humorous side of U.'s character: 'We may find less amusement than Achilles did in Patroclus's imitation of Agamemnon and Nestor, but when Ulysses tells the latter of the way in which they are caricatured, for the purpose of enraging them, Ulysses being apparently full of indignation but all the time really laughing in his sleeve [i, 3, II. 145 ff.], it makes up a scene doubly and trebly comic. New words would have to be coined to describe the exquisite drollery of the compliment paid by Ulysses to Ajax: "I will not praise thy wisdom," etc. [ii, 3, II. 259 ff.].' G. Brandes, however (*William Shakespeare: A Critical Study* (1909), p. 526), makes the singular comment that 'Ulysses, who is represented as the sole statesman among the Greeks, degrades himself by low flattery of the idiotic Ajax, servilely referring to him as "this thrice worthy and right valiant lord" [ii, 3, l. 200] who should not soil the victory he has won by going as messenger to Achilles' tent.' But this view seems to ignore Nestor's appreciation of the wily chieftain's speech: 'O, this is well; he rubs the vein of him!' (*ib.* l. 210).

Umfrevile, Sir John. Variously spelt; doubtfully D.P. in *2 Hen. IV*; see Bardolph, Thomas. (i, 1) mtd. as sending tidings of the Battle of Shrewsbury to the E. of Northumberland. French (p. 92) points out that the families of Percy and Umfrevile were connected, for Robert Umphrevill, only son of the Earl's second countess by her first husband, married Margaret, daughter of Henry, Lord Percy.

In Qq he speaks l. 161.

Underwood, John. Mtd. as a 'principal actor' in F1.

Urchinfield. One of Talbot's titles was 'Lord Talbot of Goodrig and U.'; *1 Hen. VI*, iv, 7.

Ursa Major. Constellation. '*Edm*… my nativity was under Ursa Major' (*Lear*, i, 2). See Charles' Wain.

Ursa Minor. See Bear, The. [**Ursley.**] See Ursula (2).

Ursula (1). D.P. *T.G.V.* Servant to Silvia. iv, 4] *p.m.*; in attendance.

Ursula (2). D.P. *M. Ado.* Gentlewoman attending on Hero. ii, 1] tells Antonio saucily, at the masked dance, how she recognizes him. iii, 1] as instructed, converses with H. on the merits of Benedick and the disdainfulness of Beatrice, in the latter's hearing. iii, 4] is sent to summon Beat.; later, announces that the wedding *cortège* awaits Hero. v, 2] informs Beat. that the plot against Hero is laid bare. v, 4] *p.m.*

In the st. dir. and 1. 4 of iii, 1, 'Ursley,' Q.

Ursula (3). 'Old Mistress U., whom I [Falstaff] have weekly sworn to marry since I perceived the first white hair on my chin' (*2 Hen. IV*, i, 2).

Urswick, Christopher. Chaplain to Henry VII, and to the Countess of Richmond, who entrusted him with important negotiations. He held many preferments, and resigned the Deanery of Windsor (1502) to become rector of Hackney, where he died (Oct. 21, 1521) and was buried. 'An honest and wise priest,' who had all his life 'taken part with King Henrie the sixt' (*Hol.* iii, 742).

D.P. *Rich. III.* 'Sir Ch. U.' iv, 5] is sent to the Earl of Richmond by Lord Stanley, who learns from him the names of the Earl's chief adherents.

'In the meane ceason the countesse of Richemond toke into her service Christopher Vrswike an honest and a wise priest, and after an othe of hym for to be secret taken and sworne she vttred to him all her mynde & councell, adhibityng to him the more confidence and truth that he all his life had fauoured and taken part with kyng Henry the vi. and as a special iuell put to her service by sir Lewes her physician.' (Hall, *Richard III*, p. 392.)

Wright (Clar.) points out that the title 'Sir' which is here given him is out of place, since he was at the time LL.D. and Master of King's Hall, Cambridge (1483–8).

Uther, Pendragon. Legendary father of King Arthur and brother of Aurelius Ambrosianus. Of the latter it is related (*Hol.* ii, 99) that 'even sicke as he was, he caused himselfe to be carried forth in a litter; with whose presence his people were so incouraged, that, incountring with the Saxons, they wan the victorie.' But Geoffrey of Monmouth (viii, 22) tells the story of Uther himself.

Bedford, 'brought in sick in a chair' (*1 Hen. VI*, iii, 2), has read 'That stout Pendragon, in his litter, sick, Came to the field and vanquished his foes.'

'Pendragon' was not a proper name, but a title meaning 'over-king,' or 'generalissimo.' It has been suggested that Lear refers to this when he exclaims 'Come not between the dragon and his wrath' (*Lear*, i, 1, l. 120). In *Hol.* i, 87, another derivation is suggested: 'surnamed Pendragon, ... for that Merline the great prophet likened him to a dragons head, that at the time of his natiuite maruelouslie appeared in the firmament at the corner of a blazing star, as is reported. But others suppose he was so called of his wisdome and serpentine subtiltie, or for that he gave the dragons head in his banner.'

V

Valdes. A pirate. 'These roguing thieves serve the great pirate V.' (*Per.* iv, 1).

Valdes was the name of a chief admiral of the Spanish Armada, who was captured by Drake and imprisoned at Dartmouth. The career of Admiral Don Pedro de V. is fully set forth in R. Greene's novel *The Spanish Masquerado* (1589).

Valence. A French town on the Rhone (Dept. Drôme). In 1456 the Bps. of V. became vassals of the Dauphins. Joan de V. was an ancestress of John Talbot (*q.v.*), one of whose titles was Earl of V., *1 Hen. VI*, iv, 7.

Valentine (1). D.P. *T. Nt.* 'A gentleman attending on the Duke' (Rowe). i, 1] reports to Orsino Olivia's resolve to seclude herself. i, 4] tells Viola that, in her guise as 'Cesario,' she is in high favour with Orsino.

Valentine (2). D.P. *T.G.V.* One of 'the two Gentlemen' (F1). i, 1] wishes that his 'home-keeping' friend Proteus would accompany him to Milan, but recognizes that he is in love, and that it is waste of time to counsel one who is 'a votary of fond desire'; bids Pr. farewell, warning him that love and folly are akin. (i, 3) mtd. ii, 1] (at Milan) admits, to his servant Speed, that he is enamoured of the Duke's daughter, Silvia, who has enjoined him 'to write some lines to one she loves'; on Silvia's entrance shows her the letter, which he depreciates as 'writ at random,' since he knew not for whom it was intended; she somewhat scornfully reads it, and bids him write another 'more movingly' and take it for his labour; on S.'s departure Val. gives heed to Speed's suggestion that the lady had been making him write to himself, but does not openly assent. ii, 4] derides Thurio in Silvia's presence, and an active quarrel between them is imminent when the Duke enters; Val. warmly eulogizes Proteus to the Duke, and learns that his friend has arrived in Milan; as Val. renews his banter of Thurio, Pr. enters, and Val. begs Silvia entertain his friend as a 'fellow-servant'; when Val. and Pr. are alone Val. confesses that the mighty lord of Love has at last humbled him, and confides that Silvia is about to flee with him by the aid of a ropeladder. (ii, 6) Pr. plots against him. iii, 1] as Val. hurries by, with the rope beneath his cloak, he is intercepted by the Duke, who (having been prompted by Pr.) by an artifice obtains possession of his cloak, and discovers the ladder and a letter to Silvia; Val. is sentenced to instant banishment. (iii, 2) mtd. iv, 1] he falls into the hands of 'certain outlaws,' and becomes their leader. (iv, 2) alleged to be dead. (iv, 3) mtd. (v, 2, 3) mtd. v, 4] (in the forest) sees Pr., Sil., and Julia (as a boy) enter, and, on Pr. threatening to offer violence to Silvia, reveals himself and bitterly upbraids him; but, 'in a sudden flight of heroism' (Lamb), on seeing Pr. is overcome with remorse, and exclaims, 'All that was mine in Silvia I give thee!'; Julia's disguise is detected, and Pr. consequently resigns all pretensions to Sil.; the

Duke and Thurio enter, and the latter claims Sil.; Val. dares him even to breathe upon her, whereupon the D. applauds his spirit and confers his daughter's hand upon him; Val. secures the pardon of the outlaws.

What has been deemed Valentine's too ready renunciation of Silvia has given rise to much discussion; the lines expressing it have been transferred to Thurio and to Silvia herself, and Knight has plausibly argued that, by emphasizing the word 'was,' all that Val. implies is that he resigns the advantage he had gained and is ready to start afresh, with Proteus as his 'fellow-servant,' in 'a new career of generous rivalry.' It is, however, important to note that Tito (Boccaccio, *Decam.* x, 8) yields his lady to his friend Gesippo in a similar spirit of self-abnegation. 'Valentinus,' i, 3, l. 67, F1; 'Valentino,' F2, 3, 4; 'Valentinean,' ii, 4, l. 192, F2, 3, 4.

Valentine (3). D.P. *T. And.* A friend of Titus. v, 2] *p.m.*; seizes Tamora's sons.

Valentine (4). Brother to Mercutio; mtd. *Rom. J.* i, 2.

Valentine, St. A Christian martyr of the time of Claudius (*c.* A.D. 270); his festival, Feb. 14, seems to have been associated with the pairing-time of birds. *Cf.* Chaucer, *Parliament of Fowles*, 1. 310.

'Saint V. is past; Begin these wood-birds but to couple now?' (*M.N.D.* iv, 1); 'To-morrow is Saint V.'s day, ... And I a maid at your window To be your valentine' (*Haml.* iv, 5).

In the latter passage the secondary meaning of 'Valentine,' in the sense of a sweetheart, is illustrated. The term came later to denote a person (selected by lot, or otherwise) from whom a gift is due to another of the opposite sex on Feb. 14. *Cf.* Pepys, *Diary*, Feb. 14, 1666. (Hence, too, the gift itself.)

Valentinus (1). See VALENTINE (2).

Valentinus (2). An officer; mtd. *M. for M.* iv, 5.

Valentio. Cousin to Tybalt; mtd. *Rom. J.* i, 2.

Valeria. Sister of P. Valerius Publicola; advised the Roman matrons to ask the mother of Coriolanus to accompany them to the Volscian camp and entreat him to take pity upon his country (*Plut.* pp. 34–5).

D.P. *Cor.* 'Friend to Virgilia.' i, 3] visits Volumnia and Virginia; comments on the character of the child Marcius; twits Virginia with aping Penelope; brings news of the war. ii, 1] joins in welcoming Coriolanus. v, 3] *p.m.*; accompanies the matrons to the Volscian camp. v, 5] *p.m.*; is welcomed back to Rome.

Valerius. See OUTLAWS.

Valerius, Publius. Mtd. in the Argument of *Lucrece*, but not in the poem, as having accompanied Lucretius to Collatium after Sextus had 'wrought the deed of shame.' P. V. is mtd. in this connection in Livy, i, 57–9, and in Painter's *Palace of Pleasure*, but not in Chaucer's *Legend of Good Women*.

Valour, Sir. Nonce-name applied to Achilles by Ulysses; *Tr. Cr.* i, 3.

Vapians. See PIGROGROMITUS.

Varrius (1). D.P. *Ant. Cl.* 'Friend to Pompey' (Rowe). ii, 1] delivers a message to Pompey.

Not mtd. by Plutarch; L. Varius Cotyla was, how. ever, a boon companion of Antony's (*Plut.* p. 168).

Varrius (2). D.P. *M. for M.* A friend of the Duke's. iv, 5] *p.m.*

'[He] might be omitted, for he is only spoken to once, and says nothing' (Johnson). Omitted in 'Names of the Actors' (Ff).

Varro (1). A creditor of Timon's; two of his servants appear as D.PP. *Timon.* ii, 2] one applies fruitlessly for his master's money; bandies words with Apemantus and the Fool. iii, 4] both press their claim.

Both are addressed as 'Varro' by other servants. Knight compares the 'Lord Duke' and 'Sir Charles' of *High Life below Stairs*. See also Addison's *Spectator*, No. 88.

Varro (2). D.P. *Jul. C.* 'Servant to Brutus.' iv, 3] in attendance on Br.; is ordered to lie down in the tent.

The name occurs (*Plut.* p. 75) as that of one of Pompey's lieutenants. 'Varrus,' Ff.

Vaudemont, Earl of. A French noble slain at Agincourt. *Hen. V*, iii, 5; iv, 8.

'Ferri de Lorraine, Comte de' (B.-S., Index).

Vaughan, Sir Thomas. Son of Sir Roger V., of Tretower, Brecon. Sir T. V. was a personal attendant of Edw. IV, and Chamberlain to Edw., Prince of Wales, 1471; executed at Pontefract by Rich. III 1483 (*Hol.* iii, 715); buried in Westminster Abbey.

D.P. *Rich. III.* (i, 3) Gloucester would be revenged on him ('Dorset,' Ff). (ii, 4) a prisoner. (iii, 2) mtd. iii, 3] is led to execution; exclaims, 'You live that shall cry woe for this hereafter.' (v, 1) mtd. (v, 3) his ghost appears to Richard.

Always a dissyllable.

Vaumond. A military officer named by Parolles; *All's Well*, iv, 3.

Vaux, Sir Nicholas. Son of Sir Wm. V. (*q.v.*); made Governor of Guines by Henry VIII, and Lord V. of Harrowden shortly before his death (1523).

D.P. *Hen. VIII.* ii, 1] the D. of Buckingham, after sentence, is committed to his care.

Acc. *Hol.* iii, 865, V. received B. at the Tower.

Vaux, Sir William. Of Harrowden, killed at Tewkesbury 1471. For his adherence to Henry VI he was deprived of his possessions, but restitution was made to his son Nicholas (*q.v.*) by Henry VII.

D.P. 2 *Hen. VI.* 'Vaux.' iii, 2] announces that Card. Beaufort in the agony of death 'cries aloud for the King.'

Ven. The pfx. in *Ant. Cl.* iii, 7, l. 73, until altered to 'Can.' by Pope. It has been conjectured to stand for 'Vennard, an actor in the part of Canidius' (Collier), or for 'Ventidius' (Walker, *Crit.* ii, 185).

Venetia. See VINEGIA and VENICE.

Venetian. (*a*) *Subst.* 'A V. [Bassanio]' (*M.V.* i, 2); 'a young V. [ditto]' (*ib.* ii, 9); 'a supersubtle V.' (*Oth.* i, 3); 'certain V.s' (*ib.* iv, 1); 'a young V. [Roderigo]' (*ib.* v, 2); 'a turban'd Turk Beat a V.' (*ib. ib.*).

(*b*) *Adj.* 'Any tire of V. admittance' (*M.W.W.* iii, 3); 'my old V. friend' (*M.V.* iii, 2); 'the V. law' (*ib.* iv, 1); 'V. state' (*Oth.* v, 2).

Venice, City and State of. 'In the days of Sh., Venice, on account of its political position, its commerce, and its excellence in the fine arts, stood at the head, not only of

Italy, but of all the Romanic States ... It was the city of pleasure for all Europe' (K. Elze, *Essays on Sh.* (1874), pp. 264–5).

'If Cupid have not spent all his quiver in V., thou wilt quake for this shortly' (*M. Ado*, i, 1; in allusion to the gallantries for which it was famous); *cf.* Greene, *Never Too Late* (Works, ed. Grosart, viii, 221): 'this great Citie of V. is holden Loves Paradize.' The proverb 'Venetia, Venetia, Chi non ti vede, non ti pretia' quoted, *L.L.L.* iv, 2.

In *M.V.* the scene is laid in Venice except in i, 2; ii, 1, 7, 9; iii, 2, 4, 5; v, 1. Mtd., i, 1 (2), 3; ii, 8; iii, 1 (2), 2 (2).

'The commodity that strangers have with us in V.' (*ib.* iii, 3; *cf.* Thomas, *Historie of Italye* (1561), f. 85: 'The libertie of straungers' (in V.)); 'Unto the tranect, to the common ferry Which trades to V.' (*ib.* iii, 4; here K. Elze reads 'traghetto' for 'tranect'; see his *Essays on Sh.* (1874), p. 280); the laws of V. are cited on both sides in the trial scene, *ib.* iv, 1 (7).

Petruchio 'will into V., to buy apparel 'gainst the wedding-day' (*Tam. Sh.* ii, 1 (2)); 'valance of V. gold in needlework' (*ib. ib.*); 'your ships are stayed at V.' (*ib.* iv, 2); mtd., *ib.* iv, 4. Death-place of Mowbray (*q.v.*), *Rich. II*, iv, 1.

In *Oth.* the scene of Act I is laid in V.; 'what tell'st thou me of robbing? this is V.' (i, 1); mtd., ii, 1 (3), 3; 'in V. they do let heaven see the pranks They dare not show their husbands' (iii, 3); mtd., iii, 4, iv, 1 (3); 'cunning of V.' (iv, 2); mtd., iv, 3, v, 1.

Venice, Duke of (1). D.P. *M.V.* iv, 1] presides at the Court of Justice; warns Antonio that his adversary is 'an inhuman wretch'; tells Shylock that it is expected of him that he will but 'lead the fashion of his malice to the last hour of act,' and then relent; receives a letter from the 'learned doctor,' Bellario; welcomes his substitute, 'Balthasar' (*i.e.* Portia); after Shylock's discomfiture pardons him his life and decrees the division of his estate according to Antonio's suggestion; bids a courteous farewell to 'Balthasar.'

'Doge' might have been expected, but it is not recorded as an English word before 1645 (*N.E.D.*).

Venice, Duke of (2). D.P. *Oth.* i, 3] presides at meeting of the Senate; induces Brabantio to listen to reason; orders Othello to proceed to Cyprus. (See Venice, Duke of (1).)

Ventidius (1). Publius Ventidius Bassus was sent by Antony 'into Asia to stay the Parthians'; he defeated them, and also overcame Pacorus, son of Orodes, King of Parthia, but did not follow up his victory for fear of Antony's jealous displeasure; *Plut.* pp. 180–2.

D.P. *Ant. Cl.* ii, 2] *p.m.* ii, 3] receives orders from Antony ('Ventigius,' F1). iii, 1] orders the body of Pacorus to be borne before the army; refuses to pursue the Parthians – 'I could do more to do Antonius good, But 'twould offend him.'

Ventidius (2). D.P. *Timon.* (i, 1) Timon pays his debts, and liberates him from arrest. i, 2] having become rich, by inheritance, Ventidius offers to repay Timon's loan, but is assured that it was a gift. (ii, 2) is appealed to by Timon, in his need, for the sum in question. (iii, 3) refuses T.'s request.

'Ventigius' or 'Ventidgius,' in the 'Actors Names, i, 2, and iii, 3 (F1) – the latter being considered by Fleay non-Shakespearean.

Venus (1). Goddess of love, especially of sensual love, among the Romans. A remarkable reference to the birth of V. occurs in the Pref. to *Tr. Cr.* (Q): 'So much and such sauored salt of witte is in his [Sh.'s] Commedies, that they seeme (for their height of pleasure) to be borne in that sea that brought forth Venus.'

'More intemperate in your blood than V.' (*M. Ado*, iv, 1); 'Mars's hot minion' (*Temp.* iv, 1); 'smiles not in a house of tears' (*Rom. J.* iv, 1); 'with Mars' (*Ant. Cl.* i, 5); her doves (*cf.* Ovid, *Metam.* xv, 386), *Temp.* iv, 1, *M.N.D.* i, 1; her pigeons, *M.V.* ii, 6; 'by V.'s glove' (an 'untraded' oath) (*Tr. Cr.* iv, 5); picture of, *Ant. Cl.* ii, 2; mtd., *L.L.L.* ii, 1; mtd., *Tr. Cr.* iv, 1, 5, v, 2; mtd., *Cymb.* v, 5; mtd., *Rom. J.* ii, 1. See Cupid and Helen.

Venus (2). Planet. Brightness of, *M.N.D.* iii, 2 (2); *1 Hen. VI*, i, 2. Influence of, *T. And.* ii, 3. In conjunction with Saturn, *2 Hen. IV*, ii, 4. As 'Phosphorus': 'Aurora's harbinger' (*M.N.D.* iii, 2).

Venus and Adonis.

Publication. This poem, containing 199 stanzas of six lines each, was entered to Richard Field on April 18, 1593, in the Registers of the Stationers' Company, and was published the same year The title-page of the first edition runs as follows: 'Venus and Adonis. Vilia miretur vulgus; mihi flavus Apollo Pocula Castalia plena ministret aqua. London. Imprinted by Richard Field, and are to be sold at the signe of the white Greyhound in Paules Church-yard. 1593.' Other editions followed in 1594, 1596, 1599, 1600, 1602, and at later dates.

The Latin motto is taken from Ovid, *Amores*, I, xv, 35–6. A dedication to Henry Wriothesley (*q.v.*) is prefixed to the poem.

Sources of the Story. The passion of Venus for the youthful Adonis, and the killing of the latter by a wild boar, is briefly narrated by Ovid (*Metam.* x, 520 ff., 707 ff.). The youth's coyness in the presence of the goddess, a prominent feature in the poem, is not referred to by Ovid, and seems derived from the story of Salmacis and Hermaphroditus (*Metam.* iv), while the description of the boar is reminiscent of the Calydonian boar (*Metam.* viii). The shyness of Adonis had, however, been touched upon by Greene and Marlowe in their versions of the story – a very popular one in France and Italy during the second half of the 16th cent. Spenser's *Astrophel*, in a similar metre, and Lodge's *Scillaes Metamorphosis* both have passages strikingly similar to parts of Sh.'s poem.

Ver. *Lat.*, Spring. 'V., the Spring' (*L.L.L.* v, 2; rep.).

Verdun. One of Talbot's titles was 'Lord V. of Alton' (*1 Hen. VI*, iv, 7).

'Verdon,' F1, and in his epitaph in Richard Crompton's *Mansion of Magnanimitie*, 1599, sig. E 4 (B.-S. p. 233).

Vere, Aubrey de (1) (*c.* 1340–1400). 10th E. of Oxford; erroneously named as executed ('Oxford, Salisbury,' etc.), in Q1, 2, 3, 4 of *Rich. II*, v, 6, corrected in FfQ3 to 'Salisbury, Spencer,' etc.; as in *Hol.* iii, 516.

Vere, Aubrey de (2). E.s. of John, 12th E. of Oxford (*q.v.*). '*Oxf.* My elder brother, the lord Aubrey Vere Was done to death' (*3 Hen. VI*, iii, 3).

'The Earle of Oxford far stricken in age, and his son and heire the lord Awbreie Veer, either through malice of their enimies, or for that they had offended the king, were both ... attainted and put to execution; which caused John earle of Oxford ever after to rebell' (*Hol.* iii, 665).

Vere, John de (1). 12th E. of Oxford (*c.* 1408–62); executed on the charge of planning a Lancastrian rising (*Hol.* iii, 665) (see preceding article).

Vere, John de (2) (1443–1513). 13th E. of Oxford; son of the preceding; imprisoned as a Lancastrian 1468; escaped to France after the Battle of Barnet; prisoner in Hammes Castle (*q.v.*) 1474–84; accompanied Richmond to England, fought at Bosworth, and was rewarded with many honours.

The Earl was not, as represented in *3 Hen. VI*, v, 5, sent direct from the field of Barnet to Hammes, but not until a year later, after surrendering at St Michael's Mount, which he had seized.

D.P. *3 Hen. VI.* iii, 3] (in France) refuses to acknowledge Edward IV as king, who had condemned to death his father and elder brother, and vows to uphold the house of Lancaster. iv, 2] *p.m.* (with Warwick). iv, 3] suggests marching to London. iv, 6] in council. iv, 8] is urged to muster up his friends in Oxfordshire, where he is 'wondrous well belov'd.' v, 1] enters Coventry. v, 2] at Barnet. (v, 3) joins Queen Margaret. v, 4] (at Tewkesbury) encourages the Queen. v, 5] is sent as a captive to Hammes Castle (*Hol.* iii, 693).

D.P. *Rich. III.* (ii, 1) struck down Edward IV at Tewkesbury. (iv, 5) with Richmond (*Hol.* iii, 749). v, 2] with Richmond. v, 3] (at Bosworth) *p.m.*

The incident mtd. in ii, 1, is unhistorical. Oxford, moreover, was not present at Tewkesbury.

Verges. D.P. *M. Ado.* A headborough. iii, 3] assists Dogberry to 'charge' the watch. iii, 5] despite D.'s interruptions, manages to inform Leonato that the watch have arrested two 'arrant knaves.' iv, 2] is present at the examination of Borachio and Conrade; is called 'a coxcomb' by C. v, 1] is present when B. confesses his deceit.

'Verges' is a provincial pronunciation of 'verjuice.' the acid juice of crab-apples, etc. In iv, 2, Q and F have 'Couley,' or 'Cowley,' for 'Verges' in the pfxs., *i.e.* Richard C., an actor whose name is given in F1. Halliwell quotes (MS. Ashmole, 38): 'Here lyes father Varges Who died to save charges.'

Vernon (1). D.P. *1 Hen. VI.* ii, 4] suggests, in the Temple Gardens, that the verdict in the dispute between the Earl of Somerset and Richard Plantagenet should be decided by the respective numbers of white and red roses plucked by their supporters present; he himself plucks a white one. iii, 4] picks a quarrel with Basset, of the red rose faction, and strikes him. iv, 1] appears, with Basset, before the King; they crave permission to resort to combat, presumptuously making their patrons' dissension their own; they are bidden 'to forget this quarrel and the cause.'

The chronicles provide no source for these scenes. It has been suggested that Vernon was Sir Richard V., Speaker of the H. of C. in the Leicester Parliament, and Basset either Robert B. or Philip B., both heroes of Agincourt. *Cf.* French, pp. 142, 328.

Vernon (2). Mtd. as a 'cousin' of Sir Richard V. (*q.v.*); *1 Hen. IV*, iv, 3.

Vernon, Sir Richard. Of Shipbrook, Cheshire; joined the northern rebellion against Hen. IV, and was beheaded 'upon the mondaie folowing' the Battle of Shrewsbury (*Hol.* iii, 523).

D.P. *1 Hen. IV.* iv, 1] brings news to Hotspur of the approach of the royal forces (drawing a brilliant picture of Prince Henry), also of Glendower's delay. iv, 3] urges Hotspur to postpone the battle until the morrow. (iv, 4) mtd. v, 1] (with the E. of Worcester) *p.m.* v, 2] advises Worcester to inform Hotspur of the King's offer. v, 5] *p.m.*; a prisoner, and condemned to death.

Hotspur addresses him as 'cousin' (iv, 1).

Veroles. 'A French knight'; mtd. *Per.* iv, 3.

From the context, obviously *Fr.* 'Vérole'; probably meant as a nonce-name. (Malone's emendation for 'Verollus' of QqFf.)

Verona. Ancient city of N. Italy; it became of great importance during part of the 13th and 14th cents. under the Della Scala family.

The scene of *T.G.V.* i, ii, 2, 3, 7, is laid at V.; mtd., *T.G.V.* iv, 1 (2) (in iii, 1, and v, 4, it occurs in Ff, by an evident error, for 'Milan'). Petruchio comes from V. to Padua, *Tam. Sh.* i, 2 (3); 'old V.' (*ib. ib.*); Petruchio is 'a gentleman of V.' (*ib.* ii, 1). The scene of *Rom. J.*, with the exception of v, 1, is laid throughout at V.; 'fair V.' (Prol.; i, 2); 'V.'s ancient citizens' (i, 1); early marriages in V., i, 3; 'V.'s summer' (*ib.*); 'V. brags of him [Romeo]' (i, 5); 'V. streets' (iii, 1); 'V. walls' (iii, 3); Romeo banished thence, *ib.*; 'news from V.' (v, 1); Juliet's memory preserved 'whiles V. by that name is known' (v, 3).

Veronesa. A word of disputed form and meaning; *Oth.* ii, 1. The reading of F1 is: 'The Ship is heere put in: *A Verennessa, Michael Cassio* Lieutenant to the warlike Moore, *Othello* is come on Shore.' Qq read 'Veronessa'; F2, 3, 4, 'Veronesso.'

In the first place there is a doubt as to whether 'V.' refers to the ship or to Cassio. Either interpretation seems to involve a contradiction, since Cassio was a Florentine, and Verona an inland city. It has been replied (*a*) that Sh. simply made a slip; or (*b*) that, though the ship had previously been spoken of as 'a noble ship of Venice,' Verona was tributary to Venice and had fitted out the vessel. Steevens suggested as a plausible emendation, 'The Veronessa' – *i.e.* the name of the ship. Th. Elze proposes 'verrinessa, un perceflot'; but no such Italian word is known.

Vice, The. A buffoon in the old English moralities; often thus named, but sometimes acting the part of Iniquity (*q.v.*) or of some special vice. Perhaps the modern Harlequin is a descendant.

'Like to the old V... with dagger of lath' (*T. Nt.* iv, 2); 'the formal vice, Iniquity' (*Rich. III*, iii, 1); 'a Vice of Kings' (*Haml.* iii, 4); 'V.'s dagger' (2 *Hen. IV*, iii, 2).

[**Vico.**] See CLAUDIO (2).

Vienna, City of. The scene of *M. for M.* is laid in V. throughout. Mtd., *M. for M.* i, 1 (2); 'suburbs of V.' (*ib.* i, 2); mtd., *ib.* i, 4, ii, 1 (3), v, 1 (2). 'This play is the image of a murder done in V.' (*Haml.* iii, 2; in Q1 'guyana' – probably a misprint).

[**Villafranca.**] See FREETOWN.

Vincentio (1). D.P. *M. for M.* Duke of Vienna. i, 1] on his alleged departure from Vienna (for Poland, i, 4), appoints Angelo as his deputy, with full powers, and Escalus as his 'secondary'; disliking popular applause, he will 'privily away.' (i, 2) his supposed conference 'with the other dukes' mtd. i, 4] explains to Friar Thomas that he desires to assume a friar's garb, and to watch the 'sway' of Angelo, to whom as 'A man of stricture and firm abstinence' he has entrusted the revival of drastic laws too long fallen into abeyance. (i, 5) mtd. ii, 3] in disguise, as 'Friar Lodowick' (v, 1), visits Juliet in prison. iii, 1] visits the condemned Claudio, bids him prepare for death, and urges that it is preferable to life; later, tells Cl. that Ang. did but tempt his sister Isabella, to test her; unfolds to Is. a plan by which 'the corrupt deputy' shall be confounded. iii, 2] (as 'Fr. Lodowick') converses with Lucio on Angelo's severity, and hears an account of his own alleged delinquences; Escalus, however, praises him; *(sol.)* resolves to bring Ang. to shame. iv, 1] arranges details of the deception to be practised on Ang. iv, 2] orders the Provost, under 'the hand and seal of the Duke,' to present to A. the criminal Barnardine's head for Claudio's. iv, 3] learning that the pirate Ragozine has died, orders his head to be made use of; tells Is. that Cl. has been executed and that the Duke is at hand; Lucio can tell him 'pretty tales of the Duke,' and also inculpates himself. iv, 5] 'in his own habit,' instructs Friar Peter. (iv, 6) mtd. v, 1] enters the city with his train; at first affects to regard Isabella as mad, or a slanderer, in accusing Ang.; having heard Mariana's evidence, orders 'Friar Lodowick' to be sent for, and retires; later, enters as the Friar, and is examined by Escalus; on being committed to prison by Esc., reveals himself; orders Ang. immediately to marry Mariana, and then to be executed, in spite of Isabella's intercession; Claudio is produced, alive; the Duke pardons Angelo, suitably punishes Lucio, and chooses Isabella for his own wife.

The name Vincentio occurs nowhere in the text or pfxs. The equivalent character in *Promos and Cassandra* is the King of Hungary, and in Cinthio's *Novella* the Emperor Maximilian. Their action, however, is wholly behind the scenes.

Vincentio (2). D.P. *Tam. Sh.* 'An old gentleman of Pisa,' father to Lucentio. (i, 1) 'a merchant of great traffic through the world.' (iv, 2) a Pedant is instructed to personate him in Padua. iv, 5] meeting Petruchio on the road to Padua, is informed that his son is wedded to Bianca. v, 1] on presenting himself at Lucentio's abode, is accused by the Pedant of being an impostor, and is on the point of being haled to prison when Lucentio enters and greets him with 'Pardon, sweet father!'; vows vengeance for having been insulted. v, 2] present at Lucentio's banquet.

The equivalent character in *The Taming of A Shrew* is Jerobel, 'Duke of Cestus,' and in *I Suppositi* Filogono, a merchant of Catania.

Vinegia. Venice; *L.L.L.* iv, 2. In Ff printed as mere gibberish ('Vemchie,' 'Vencha,' 'Venachi,' 'Venachea'), and restored by Theobald to 'Vinegia, Vinegia ! qui non te vedi, ei non te pregia,' or, in the Camb. edn., 'Venetia, Venetia, Chi non ti vede, non ti pretia.' See Mantuanus.

Vintner. D.P. *1 Hen. VI*; see Quickly.

Viola. D.P. *T. Nt.* i, 2] having been shipwrecked off the coast of Illyria, is brought safe to land; is comforted by the Captain's assurance of her brother Sebastian's safety; hears the story of the Duke Orsino's love for Olivia; resolves to serve Or. in the garb of a page; enlists the Captain's aid. i, 4] assumes, in her new character, the name of 'Cesario'; rapidly grows in favour with the Duke, and is sent by him to unfold his passion to Ol.; in departing admits (aside), 'Who e'er I woo, myself would be his wife.' i, 5] having by importunity gained access to Ol., begins to address her in set phrases on Or.'s behalf, and, after getting rid of the waiting-maid, induces the Countess to unveil; is eloquent on the intensity of Orsino's passion, and on what 'he himself' would do, if in his master's place; refuses a purse offered by Ol., and departs with the words 'Farewell, fair cruelty.' ii, 2] is stopped in the street by Malvolio, who proffers a ring, which, he declares, was left with Ol. as a present from Or.; guesses that the Countess, believing her a man, has become enamoured of her; exclaims 'My state is desperate for my master's love.' ii, 4] ambiguously admits to Or. that she loves some one older than herself; listens to Feste's song; is charged with another mission to Ol.; relates the parable of her 'father's daughter,' who 'pined away for love'; is given a jewel to convey to Ol. iii, 1] exchanges repartee with Feste, whom she sends to Ol., to announce her presence; converses with Sir Toby and Aguecheek; attempts to deliver the Duke's message to Ol., but is checked by the latter, who openly admits her love for 'Cesario'; vows that she will give her heart to 'no woman.' iii, 4] is given a 'jewel' by Ol., but again rebuffs her wooing; is told by Sir Toby that a knight, whose skill Fabian extols, demands satisfaction; is confronted with Aguecheek, and unwillingly prepares to fight; the duel is interrupted by the entrance of Antonio; 'Cesario' disclaims all acquaintance with him, but protests against his charge of ingratitude; begins to suspect that she is mistaken for Sebastian. v, 1] in attendance on Or., listens to Antonio's tale; is claimed by Ol. as her betrothed husband, and is bid by Or., in his jealous wrath, to follow him as a lamb to the sacrifice; declares her willingness to suffer death to give her master ease; is detained by Ol., who brings the priest as witness to her betrothal with 'Cesario'; on the entrance of Seb. recognizes her brother, with some hesitation, and admits her disguise; learns from Or. that he loves his 'faithful page' in her true character; announces that Malvolio has arrested the Seacaptain.

(Viola is a woman's name in Gower's *Confessio Amantis*, v.) The name of the equivalent character in *Gl' Ingannati* is Lelia. Lelia's assumed name is 'Fabio.' In *Apolonius and Silla* her equivalent is Silla, with 'Silvio' as assumed name; in Bandello's story they are Nicuolo and 'Romolo' respectively. See Twelfth Night.

Violenta. D.P. *All's Well.* Friend of Diana's mother. iii, 5] *p.m.* (allotted the third speech by the Camb. edrs.).

Acc. Steevens, the name occurs in 'an old metrical history entitled *Didoco and Violenta*.'

[Virgil.] P. Virgilius Maro; Roman poet (70–19 B.C.). *Aen.* i, 11, 'Tantaene animis,' etc., is quoted, *2 Hen. VI*, ii, 1, l. 24; and perhaps *Aen.* vii, 446, is the source of *2 Hen. VI*, iv, 1, l. 117, though this may be from Ovid, *Metam.* iii, 40.

A transln. of the *Aen.* in a complete form, by T. Phaer and T. Twyne, appeared in 1573, and of bks. i–iv, by R. Stanyhurst, in 1583. The *Eclogues* and *Georgics* were translated in 1589 by A. Fleming.

Virgilia. Wife to Coriolanus, acc. Plutarch (but acc. Livy his wife's name was Volumnia); she accompanied her mother-in-law to the Volscian camp to intercede with Cor. (*Plut.* pp. 34–8).

D.P. *Cor.* i, 3] fears for her husband's safety in the wars, and, in spite of the deprecation of Volumnia and Valeria, resolves not to cross the threshold till he returns. ii, 1] hears of her husband's glorious deeds; welcomes him with tears of joy, and is addressed by him as 'my precious silence.' iv, 1] laments his banishment. iv, 2] makes a spirited retort to a tribune in defence of Cor. (this is by some edrs. given to Volumnia). v, 3] proceeds with the other ladies to the Volscian camp, and appeals to Cor. as the mother of his son. v, 5] *p.m.*; is welcomed back to Rome.

Virginity. Personified. 'V., like an old courtier, wears her cap out of fashion' (*All's Well*, i, 1).

Virginius, L. A Roman centurion who slew his daughter Virginia to prevent her falling into the hands of the decemvir Appius Claudius. It seems likely that in the passage quoted below Virginia is confused with Lucrece (*q.v.*).

'Was it well done of rash V., To slay his daughter ... because she was enforc'd?' (*T. And.* v, 3); then, having killed his daughter Lavinia, Titus Andronicus exclaims 'I am as woful as V. was' (*ib. ib.*).

Virgo. Constellation and sign of the zodiac. Titus, in his madness, sees an arrow fall 'in V.'s lap' (*T. And.* iv, 3).

Visor, William. 'Of Woncot'; according to Shallow, 'an arrant knave' (*2 Hen. IV*, v, 1). The Gloucestershire family of Visor, or Vizard, has flourished since the 16th cent., at Woodmancote, or 'Woncot' (*q.v.*). See Lee, p. 240.

Vitruvio. A Veronese gentleman. 'The lady widow of V.' (*Rom. J.* i, 2).

Volquessin. In N. France, country of the Velocasses (Caes. *B.G.* ii, 4), divided later into Vexin Normand (part of the depts. of Eure and Seine-Inférieure), and Vexin Francais (part of Oise and Seine-et-Oise). One of the five provinces offered by John as the dowry of Blanch of Spain, *John*, ii, 1. ('Veuxin,' or 'Veulquessine,' *Hol.* iii, 161.)

Volsce, A. D.P. *Cor.* iv, 3; see ADRIAN.

Volsces, or **Volscians.** The Volsci, warlike people of ancient Italy, inhabiting the region on both banks of the Liris (Garigliano); their capital was at first Suessa Pometia, and, later, Antium. They waged war with the Romans for two centuries and were not finally subdued, and created Roman citizens, until 338 B.C.

It is announced that 'the V.s are in arms' (*Cor.* i, 1); Marcius comments that they 'have much corn' (*ib. ib.*); mtd., *ib.* i, 3 (2); they make a sally from Corioli, *ib.* i, 4; mtd., *ib.* i, 6 (2); they rescue Aufidius, *ib.* i, 8; the camp of the V.s, *ib.* i, 10; mtd., *ib.* ii, 2, iii, 1 (2), iv, 5 (3), 6 (3), v, 3 (5), 4, 6; 'I flutter'd your V.s in Corioli' (*ib. ib.*). In the sing., 'a Volsce' (*ib.* i, 4, 10).

The spelling 'Volsces' is that adopted in *Plut.*; Ff have 'Volcies,' 'Volscies,' or 'Volces'; in later edns. 'Volscians' or 'Volcians' are usual forms.

Volscian, *adj.* 'V. state' (*Cor.* iv, 3, 7); 'V. breasts' (*ib.* v, 2); 'V. lords' (*ib.* v, 3.)

Voltimand. D.P. *Haml.* A courtier. i, 2] is sent on an embassage to the King of Norway. ii, 2] brings back a favourable message, and is thanked for his 'well-took labour.'

'Voltemar' in the Q of 1603.

Volumnia. Mother to Coriolanus, acc. Plutarch, but her name was Veturia acc. Livy. Was persuaded to visit the Volscian camp and to implore her son to lay aside his resolve to wreak his vengeance on his country; her entreaties prevailed (*Plut*, pp. 35–8).

D.P. *Cor.* i, 3] scorns the timidity of her daughter-in-law Virgilia, and urges her rather to exult in the warlike fame of Marcius than to fear for his safety. ii, 1] tells Menenius that letters have arrived from her son, announcing his return to Rome, wounded but victorious; welcomes Marcius and hails him by his new name 'Coriolanus'; hints that she now wishes to see him consul. iii, 2] persuades her son to dissemble with his nature, and by apparent submission to the plebeians to gain ultimate power over those whom she despises as much as he does. iv, 1] invokes 'the red pestilence' on the plebeians for rejecting Cor.; advises him to form a plan of action rather than trust to chance. iv, 2] meeting the tribunes, objurgates them for their treatment of Cor., and driving them from her presence cries, 'I would the gods had nothing else to do But to confirm my curses!' v, 3] at the Volscian camp, kneels before Cor. and expatiates on the plight of Virgilia and herself, torn between patriotism and love for him; points out that if he conquers Rome, his name will be 'to the ensuing age abhorr'd'; bitterly rebukes his stubborn silence; indicated the abject posture of his wife and son, and exclaims, 'Come, let us go! This fellow had a Volscian to his mother!'; he clasps her hand, and she knows that she has prevailed. (v, 4) her worth extolled by Menenius. v, 5] *p.m.*; she is welcomed back to Rome.

Volumnius, Publius. A philosopher who accompanied Brutus in his campaign against the triumvirs, and wrote an account of the prodigies which appeared before the death of Br. At Philippi, Br., speaking in Greek, asked his help in killing himself, but V. 'denied his request' (*Plut.* pp. 147, 150).

D.P. *Jul. C.* v, 3] *p.m.* v, 5] is asked by Brutus, since 'we two went to school together,' to hold his sword-hilts 'whilst I run upon it'; he refuses.

Vulcan. Roman god of fire, to whom all the stories relating to the Greek Hephaestus were transferred. He was the supreme artist in metals, his workshops being in some volcanic island (Virg. *Aen.* viii, 416 ff.). His wife was Venus, who proved faithless to him (Hom. *Od.* viii, 266 ff.). He was often represented as lame and dwarfish.

'As black as V. in the smoke of war' (*T. Nt.* v, 1); 'as foul as V.'s stithy' (*Haml.* iii, 2); a casque composed by V.'s skill' (*Tr. Cr.* v, 2); 'as like as V. and his wife' (*i.e.* very unlike) (*Tr. Cr.* i, 3); 'Do you play the flouting Jack, to tell us ... V. is a rare carpenter?' (*M. Ado*, i, 1); 'V.'s badge' (*i.e.* a cuckold's) (*T. And.* ii, 1).

W

Wakefield, Battle of. Fought Dec. 30, 1460; Queen Margaret's forces defeated the D. of York, who was slain. The battle described, *3 Hen. VI*, i, 2–4; 'the bloody fray at W. fought' (*ib.* ii, 1).

Dec. 29 and Dec. 31 are also given as dates of the battle in *Wilh. Worc. Ann. Rer. Ang.* (p. 485) and *Chron. Rich. II-Hen. VI* (p. 107) respectively. Cf. *Hol.* iii, 659; B.-S. p. 299.

Wales, Prince of. Thus styled: the Black Prince, *Rich. II*, ii, 1; *Hen. V*, ii, 4, iv, 7; *2 Hen. VI*, ii, 2. Afterward Henry V, *1 Hen. IV*, i, 3, ii, 4, iii, 2, iv, 1 ('madcap'), 4, v, 4; *2 Hen. IV*, ii, 1, iv, 4. Son to Henry VI, *Rich. III*, i, 3. Afterward Edward V, *Rich. III*, i, 3.

Wales, Province of. 'A post from W.' (*1 Hen. IV*, i, 1); 'he, of W. [*i.e.* Glendower]' (*ib.* ii, 4); 'the banks of ... W.,' 'W. beyond the Severn shore' (*ib.* iii, 1); Mortimer 'engag'd in W.' (*ib.* iv, 3); mtd., *2 Hen. IV*, i, 2, ii, 1, 4; Earl of Richmond in W., *Rich. III*, iv, 5; mtd., *Cymb.* iii, 2. The following scenes are laid in W.: *Rich. II*, ii, 4, iii, 3; *Cymb.* iii, 6, iv, 1, 4.

Wall. See Snout.

Walloon. A member of a race, descendants of the ancient Belgae, occupying parts of S. and S.E. Belgium and adjoining parts of France. They have been notable as good soldiers.

Talbot is represented as having been wounded in the back, while retiring from Orleans, 'by a base Walloon' (*1 Hen. VI*, i, 1), but in *Hol.* iii, 601 the man's nationality is not specified. W. is also used to signify 'the country of the Walloons' (*1 Hen. VI*, iii, 1), Talbot remarking that 'the regions of Artois, Walloon, and Picardy, are friends to us.'

Walter (1). A servant; *Tam. Sh.* iv, 1.

Walter (2). As a forename. 'Sir W. Blunt,' 'W. Whitmore,' 'Sir W. Herbert,' 'W., Lord Ferrers' (*qq.v.*). For the pronunciation see Whitmore.

War. Personified. 'Peace be to England, if that War return From France to England, there to live in peace' (*John*, ii, 1); 'O war, thou son of hell, whom angry heavens do make their minister' (*2 Hen. VI*, v, 2); 'Grim-visaged War hath smooth'd his wrinkled front ... He capers nimbly in a lady's chamber,' etc. (*Rich. III*, i, 1).

[**Wardon Abbey.**] In Bedfordshire; probably gave its name to 'Warden pears'; hence 'warden pies' (*Wint. T.* iv, 3, l. 48). Cf. *Archaeological Journal*, v, 301.

Ware. Town in Herts. 'The bed of W. in England' (*T. Nt.* iii, 2).

'The great bed of W.,' now at Rye House, is of carved oak and is some 12 ft. square. It is first mentioned in the *Itinerary* of Prince Ludwig of Anhalt-Köthen, who saw it in 1596. It bears the date 1460, but is of 16th-cent. origin.

Wars of the Roses. The conflict, lasting about thirty years, between the houses of York and Lancaster, distinguished by the white and red roses respectively adopted as their badges. The following are the chief battles, with their Shakespearean references:

St Albans (*I*), May 22, 1455. The D. of York defeats and slays Somerset. *2 Hen. VI*, v, 2, 3.

Northampton, July 10, 1460. Hen. VI captured by the Yorkists. Not mtd.

Wakefield, Dec. 30, 1460. York slain. *3 Hen. VI*, i, 3.

Mortimer's Cross, Feb. 2, 1461. Yorkist victory. *3 Hen. VI*, ii, 1.

St Albans (*II*), Feb. 17, 1461. Warwick defeated by Q. Margaret. *3 Hen. VI*, ii, 1.

Towton, March 29, 1461. Yorkist victory. *3 Hen. VI*, ii, 3–6.

Hedgeley Moor, Apr. 25, and *Hexham*, May 8, 1464. Yorkist victories. Not mtd.

Barnet, Apr. 14, 1471. Warwick defeated and slain by Edw. IV. *3 Hen. VI*, v, 1.

Tewkesbury, May 4, 1471. Margaret defeated by Edw. IV. *3 Hen. VI*, v, 5.

Bosworth, Aug. 22, 1485. Richard III defeated and slain by Richmond, who became Henry VII and united the two houses by marriage. *Rich. III*, v, 3–5.

Wart, Thomas. D.P. *2 Hen. IV*. iii, 2] is taken as a recruit by Falstaff.

Warwick, Edward, Earl of. See Edward.

Warwick, Richard, Earl of. See Beauchamp, Richard.

Warwickshire. Falstaff in W., *1 Hen. IV*, iv, 2; the E. of Warwick termed 'proud lord of W.' (*2 Hen. VI*, iii, 2); he declares that 'in W. I have true-hearted friends' (*3 Hen. VI*, iv, 8).

Wash, The. See Lincoln Washes.

Washford, Earl of. One of Talbot's titles; *1 Hen. VI*, iv, 7. Another name for Wexford.

Wat. Abbr. of 'Walter.' Familiar name of a hare: 'Poor Wat ... Stands on his hinder legs with listening ear' (*V.A.* 697).

Cf. 'I wold my master were a watt and my boke a wyld Catt' (*Babees Book*, E.E.T.S. p. 404).

Waterford. County and ancient city of Ireland, which received a charter from King John. One of Talbot's titles was 'Earl of W.' (*1 Hen. VI*, iv, 7).

Waterton, Sir Robert. Joined Bolingbroke's invading force ('R. W. esquire,' *Hol.* iii, 497); appointed Master of the Horse by Henry IV, and was the E. of Westmoreland's lieutenant against the Percies (not Prince John, as stated *2 Hen. IV*, i, 1) (*Hol.* iii, 524).

Mtd. *Rich. II*, ii, 1, as having sailed from Brittany with Bolingbroke.

Wednesday. 'W. the fourscore of April' (*Wint. T.* iv, 4); fixed for coronation of Hen. IV, *Rich. II*, iv, 1; 'he that died o' W.' (*1 Hen. IV*, v, 1); 'W. in wheeson week' (*2 Hen. IV*, ii, 1). Mtd., *Oth.* iii, 3; *M.V.* i, 3; *Com. Err.* i, 2; *1 Hen. IV*, i, 1, iii, 2; *2 Hen. IV*, ii, 4; *Cor.* i, 3; *Rom. J.* iii, 4 (2), iv, 1.

'Wensday,' *Oth.* iii, 3, l. 61; *Cor.* i, 3, l. 57, in F2.

Welkin. The sky, the region of clouds; personified. 'By thy favour, sweet W., I must sigh in thy face' (*L.L.L.* iii, 1). 'By W., and her star' (*M.W.W.* i, 3); 'W. and her fairies' (*ib.* i, 4, Qq).

The above are the most striking instances; but there is imperfect personification in almost every case where the word occurs.

[**Wellestreme Sands.**] See LINCOLN WASHES.

Welsh. (a) *Subst.*, Welsh language. 'No man speaks better W.'; 'Let me not understand you then; speak it in W.'; 'My wife can speak no English, I no W.'; 'that pretty W.'; 'thy tongue Makes W. as sweet as ditties highly penn'd'; 'now I perceive the devil understands W.'; 'hear the lady sing in W.' (*1 Hen. IV*, iii, 1).

(*b*) *Subst.*, people of Wales. Mtd. *2 Hen. IV*, i, 3 (2).

(*c*) *Adj.* 'W. priest' (*M.W.W.* ii, 1); 'French and W.' (*ib.* iii, 1); 'W. devil' (*ib.* v, 3); 'W. fairy,' 'W. goat,' 'W. flannel' (*ib.* v, 5); 'cross of a W. hook' (*1 Hen. IV*, ii, 4); 'W. Lady' (*ib.* iii, 1); 'I am W.,' 'W. plood' (*Hen. V*, iv, 7); 'a W. correction' (*ib.* v, 1).

Welshman. *Sing.*: 'I will rather trust ... the W. with my cheese' (*M.W.W.* ii, 2); 'thou trusty W.' (*Rich. II*, ii, 4); 'by the rude hands of that W. [Glendower]' (*1 Hen. IV*, i, 1); 'I am a W.,' 'There is much care and valour in this W. [Fluellen]' (*Hen. V*, iv, 1); 'You cannot guess wherefore the W. [Richmond] comes' (*Rich. III*, iv, 4).

Plu.: 'All the W... are ... dispers'd and fled' (*Rich. II*, iii, 2); 'the W. are dispers'd' (*ib.* iii, 3); 'the W. did goot service in a garden where leeks did grow [apparently Cressy, but without historical basis]' (*Hen. V*, iv, 7); 'the loving W.' (*3 Hen. VI*, ii, 1); 'Buckingham, back'd with the hardy W.' (*Rich. III*, iv, 3).

Welshwomen. Mutilation of the corpses of Mortimer's men by W.; *1 Hen. IV*, i, 1. An account of this 'shamfull villanie' is given, *Hol.* iii, 528.

[**West, Nicolas** (1461–1533).] Bp. of Ely. Appointed by Katharine as one of her counsel (*Hol.* iii, 907). Cf. *Hen. VIII*, ii, 2, ll. 111 ff.

West, The. The western region (*a*) of the sky, (*b*) of the world. (References to the cardinal point only, and the word used adjectively, are omitted.)

(*a*) 'The weary sun in the W.' (*Com. Err.* i, 2); 'the W. yet glimmers' (*Macb.* iii, 3); 'the lowly W.' (*Rich. II*, ii, 4); 'drooping W.' (*2 Hen. IV*, Ind.); 'shines here in the W.' (*Cymb.* v, 5); 'this part of the W.' (*ib.* iv, 2); mtd., *Son.* liii, cxxxii.

b) 'Throned by the W.' (*M.N.D.* ii, 2); 'utmost corner of the W.' (*John*, ii, 1); 'kingdoms of the W.' (*2 Hen. VI*, i, 1); 'serve their sovereign in the W.' (*Rich. III*, iv, 4).

Westminster Abbey. The scene of *1 Hen. VI*, i, 1; only once explicitly mtd. in the text: 'Methought I sat in seat of majesty In the cathedral church of W., And in that chair where kings and queens are crown'd' (*2 Hen. VI.* i, 2). *Cf.* 'Jack Cade ... vows to crown himself in W.' (*ib.* iv, 4). The scene of *2 Hen. IV*, v, 5, is 'a public place near W. A.' 'Come, madam [Anne], you must straight to W., There to be crowned Richard's royal queen' (*Rich. III*, iv, 1).

The present church, commenced by Henry III in honour of Edward the Confessor, was consecrated in 1269, and the building was carried on under successive kings. The Lady Chapel was built by Hen. VIII. For ten years, 1540–50, the church became a cathedral, Thomas Thirlby being the only bishop. For 'cathedral church,' as 'applied loosely to a collegiate or abbey church,' see *N.E.D. s.v.* 'cathedral,' *a.* and *sb.*

Westminster, Abbot of. D.P. *Rich. II.* iv, 1] is given the custody of the Bp. of Carlisle; hints to his prisoner and Aumerle that he has a plot against Henry IV to unfold to them (*Hol.* iii, 514). (v, 2) his conspiracy is discovered. (v, 3) Bolingbroke threatens his life. (v, 6) 'With clog of conscience and sour melancholy Hath yielded up his body to the grave.'

This abbot has been usually identified with 'William of Colchester,' who was a prisoner at Reigate in 1400, and does not seem to have died until 1420.

French (pp. 39–42), however, points out the improbability of 'the grand conspirator' (v, 6) remaining a mitred abbot, and cites evidence that the abbot of the play was his successor, Richard Harounden, or Harweden. Acc. *Holinshed* (iii, 516) 'the Abbot' died suddenly, soon after the plot was discovered.

Westminster Hall. The Great Hall of the palace of Westminster was first erected by Edward the Confessor, rebuilt by William Rufus, and again rebuilt, in its present form, by Richard II. The first Parliament held there recorded his deposition. The scene of *Rich. II*, iv, 1, is laid in W. H.

Westminster, Palace of. 'The King your father is at W.' (*2 Hen. IV*, ii, 4).

'The principal seat and Palace of all the kings of England since the conquest... A great part ... was once again burnt in the year 1512 ... since the which time it hath not been re-edified.' (Stow, *Survey*, ed. Thoms, pp. 172, 174.)

Westmoreland, Earls of. See NEVILLE, RALPH (1) and (2).

W. H., Mr. The unknown person to whom T. T. (*q.v.*) dedicated the first edition of Shakespeare's *Sonnets* in 1609, as being 'their onlie begetter.' A keen controversy has been waged, and is still undecided, as to the person intended by these initials. A detailed account would lie beyond the scope of this work; suffice it to say that the initials have been held to stand for: (*a*) William Herbert, the family name of the 3rd Earl of Pembroke (1580–1630), to whom the Folio of 1623 was dedicated, and who was a noted patron of literature. The objection to this theory is that 'Mr William Herbert' is an impossible appellation for this nobleman at any stage of his career (see Lee, *Life of Sh.* pp. 686 ff.); (*b*) an inversion of 'H. W.,' *i.e.* Henry Wriothesley (*q.v.*), but to him a similar objection applies; (*c*) William Hughes, a purely hypothetical friend of Sh.; this is based on *Son.* xx, l. 7, where in the original edn. 'hues' is spelt 'hews'; (*d*) William Hall, a printer and 'procurer' of MSS., assumed to be the personal friend of T. T.; weighty arguments in favour of this simple solution of the problem are given by Sir S. Lee (*op. cit.* pp. 672 ff.), the word 'begetter' being held to bear the meaning of 'procurer' or 'obtainer,' and the 'eternitie promised by our everlasting poet' to the object of his sonnets, being transferred with characteristic magniloquence by Thorpe to the dedicatee.

Wheeson. Quickly's perversion of 'Whitsun'; *2 Hen. IV*, ii, 1.

Whey-face. Nonce-name applied by Macbeth to a servant; *Macb.* v, 3.

Whitefriars. The friary of the Carmelites. On the dissolution of the monasteries the site was occupied by private buildings, and became notorious as 'Alsatia.' It was situated S. of Fleet Street, where the name is still perpetuated in 'W. Street.'

Gloucester orders the body of Henry VI to be taken to W., *Rich. III*, i, 2. But, acc. *Hol.* iii, 690, from St Paul's 'he was carried to the Blackfriers.'

Whitehall. A former royal palace, situated between Charing Cross and Westminster. In the 13th cent. it became the property of the Dominican monks (Black Friars) of Holborn, who, later, sold it to Walter de Gray, Abp. of York, who bequeathed it to the see, as the official London residence of the archbishops, and it became known as York House, or Place. On the fall of Wolsey it passed to the crown: 'Sir, You must no longer call it York Place, that's past; For, since the cardinal fell, that title's lost; 'Tis now the King's, and call'd Whitehall' (*Hen. VIII*, iv, 1).

No part of the original palace, as it existed in Sh.'s days, now remains. More than a hundred performances of Sh.'s plays must have taken place at W. during his lifetime. The great chamber, which served as a theatre, stood in the Horse Guards Avenue. (Wheatley.)

White Hart, The. Name of an inn in Southwark. 'The Kentish capteine [Cade], being advertised of the king's absence, came first into Southwark, and there lodged at the white hart' (*Hol.* iii, 634).

'*Cade.* Hath my sword therefore broke through London gates, that you should leave me at the White Hart in Southwark?' (2 *Hen. VI*, iv, 8).

Whitmore, Walter. D.P. 2 *Hen. VI.* iv, 1] is given the D. of Suffolk as his prize; he will take no ransom, and the Duke is startled at hearing the name of 'Walter,' since it has been predicted that by 'water' he must die; Whitmore leads Suffolk away, and returns with his dead body.

Nothing is known of Whitmore, who seems, nevertheless to be a historical character; he speaks of bearing arms, as a gentleman, and is reminded by Suffolk of the days when he was, in a humble capacity, the Duke's attendant. The Whitmores of Cheshire and Shropshire were a very ancient family. In *The Contention* the name is given as 'Water Whickmore.'

Whitsun, *adj.* Pertaining to Whitsuntide, the season of Pentecost, *i.e.* the week succeeding the seventh Sunday after Easter. Games and sports of all kinds, especially the morris-dance, were celebrated at this season.

Perdita says, 'Methinks I play as I have seen them do In Whitsun pastorals' (*Wint. T.* iv, 4); the Dauphin refers to England 'busied with a Whitsun morris-dance' (*Hen. V*, ii, 4); 'Wednesday in Whitsun week' (2 *Hen. IV*, ii, 1). (See Wheeson.)

Widow. D.P. *Tam. Sh.* (iv, 2) Hortensio declares that he will wed a rich widow, 'Ere three days pass.' (iv, 5) mtd. v, 2] (at Lucentio's banquet) flouts H., and is chided by Katharina for her frowardness.

The corresponding character in *The Taming of A Shrew* is Emelia, Alfonso's 3rd daughter.

Widow of Florence, An Old. D.P. *All's Well.* iii, 5] keeps the hostel of St Francis, and welcomes Helena as a pilgrim; complains of Bertram's importunate suit to her daughter Diana. iii, 7] though her estate is fallen, she was well born – in fact, a Capulet, for so her daughter signs her petition to the King (v, 3); accepts gifts from Helena for furthering her design of substituting herself for Diana. iv, 4] is thanked by Hel. v, 1] accompanies Hel. and Di. to Marseilles. v, 3] enters the royal presence with Diana; later, returns with Helena.

Will. Name of a prentice; 2 *Hen. VI*, ii, 3. As a forename: 'Will Squele' (2 *Hen. IV*, iii, 2). As Sh.'s own name: 'My name is W.' (*Son.* cxxxvi; also apparently punned upon in *Son.* cxxxv).

William (1). D.P. *A. Y. L.* 'A clown, in love with Audrey' (Rowe). v, 1] discovers Audrey in Touchstone's company, and, intimidated by the latter, submissively departs.

William (2). A relative of Shallow's, 'at Oxford'; 2 *Hen. IV*, iii, 2.

William. (3). Shallow's cook; 2 *Hen. IV*, v, 1.

William (4). As a forename. 'W. Page,' 'W. Visor,' 'Sir W. Stanley,' 'W., Lord Hastings,' 'Sir W. Stanley,' 'Sir W. Brandon,' 'Sir W. Blomer' (*qq.v.*).

William of Hatfield. 2nd son of Edward III; died in childhood. 'W. of H. died without an heir' (2 *Hen. VI*, ii, 2).

William of Windsor. 6th son of Edward III; died young; erroneously referred to as the 7th and last son, 2 *Hen. VI*, ii, 2, following *Hol.* iii, 657.

Williams, Michael. D.P. *Hen. V.* 'A soldier in the King's army.' iv, 1] disputes hotly, the night before Agincourt, with the King, whom he does not recognize; they exchange gloves, and W. vows to strike the man who claims the glove he will be wearing in his cap. iv, 7] is questioned by the King as to the glove he is displaying, and is sent on an errand; (the King gives Fluellen W.'s glove, telling him it is Alencon's, and that if any man challenge it he is 'a friend to A.'). iv, 8] meeting Fl., W. sees the glove and forthwith strikes him; Fl. cries out that he is a traitor; the King appears, and unfolds the jest, exhibiting the fellow glove; W. pleads his ignorance of Henry's identity, and urges that 'offences come from the heart'; he is rewarded with a gloveful of crowns, and is offered a shilling by Fluellen.

'The name of W. occurs frequently in the Stratford Corporation Records' (French, p. 328).

Willoughby, William de. 5th Baron Willoughby de Eresby, K.G. (*ob.* 1409). Became an adherent of Bolingbroke (*Hol.* iii, 498).

D.P. *Rich. II.* ii, 1] denounces Richard's exactions, and throws in his lot with the rebel nobles. (ii, 2) his defection announced to the Queen. ii, 3] joins Bolingbroke near Berkeley. iii, 1] *p.m.*; at Bristol.

Wilson, Jacke. The name, evidently that of the actor, given (Ff) for 'Musique' or 'Balthasar' in the st. dir. 'Enter Prince,' etc., *M. Ado*, ii, 3.

Wiltshire, Earl of (1). See Scrope, Stephen Le.

Wiltshire, Earl of (2). James Butler (1420–61), 5th E. of Ormonde; Lancastrian; created E. of Wiltshire 1449; Lord-Lieutenant of Ireland 1453–5; fought at Wakefield, Mortimer's Cross, and Towton; beheaded and attainted. Acc. *Hol.* iii, 643, at St Albans he 'left the king alone, and with a number fled awaie.' The Marq. Montague (John Neville), showing his sword after the Battle of St Albans, exclaims: 'Here is the Earl of Wiltshire's blood, whom I encountered as the battles joined' (*3 Hen. VI*, i, 1).

Wiltshire, Sheriff of. See LONG, HENRY.

Winchester. In the phrase 'W. goose,' or 'galled goose of W.' (*1 Hen. VI*, i, 3; *Tr. Cr.* v, 11).

Supposed to allude to the fact that the *lupanaria* of Southwark were in the 16th cent. under the jurisdiction of the Bp. of W. Hence, a person affected by venereal disease.

Winchester, Bishops of. Henry Beaufort, D.P. 1, 2 *Hen. VI*; Stephen Gardiner, D.P. *Hen. VIII* (*qq. v.*).

Wincot. Popular pronunciation of three villages in Warwickshire: Wilnecote, near Tamworth, famous for its ale in the 17th cent.; Wilmcote, the birthplace of Sh.'s mother, in the parish of Aston Cantlow, near Stratford; and Wincot, also near Stratford, where a contemporary family named Hacket (*q.v.*) dwelt (Lee, p. 237). 'Marian Hacket, the fat ale wife of W.' (*Tam. Sh.* Ind. 2).

Windsor. On the Thames. W. Castle was rebuilt by Edward III. St George's Chapel, the chapel of the Knights of the Order of the Garter, was begun by Edward IV and completed by Henry VIII. Windsor Forest was the favourite hunting-ground of the Court in the 16th cent., and is referred to as such by Surrey, *Tottel's Miscellany* (1557) (Arber, p. 14).

In *M.W.W.* the scene is laid in, or near, W. throughout. 'Never a woman in W. knows more of Anne's mind that I do' (i, 4); 'what tempest ... threw this whale [Falstaff] ashore at W.' (ii, 1); 'when the Court lay at W.' (ii, 2); mtd., *ib.* (2); 'all the officers in W.,' 'coming with half W. at his heels,' 'I would not have your distemper ... for the wealth of W. Castle' (iii, 3); 'W. forest,' 'mock him home to W.' (iv, 4); 'a W. stag,' 'W. chimneys,' 'W. Castle,' 'W. wives' (v, 5); mtd., *ib.* (2).

1 Hen. IV: 'our council we will hold at W.' (i, 1). *2 Hen. IV*: 'a singing-man of W.' (ii, 1); 'gone to hunt ... at W.,' 'why are thou not at W. with him?' (iv, 4).

1 Hen. VI: 'Henry, born at W., lose all' (iii, 1), so predicted by Henry V of his son, *Hol.* iii, 581. See also WILLIAM OF WINDSOR.

Windsor, Old. A village about 2 m. S.E. of Windsor. A royal residence of Saxon kings. Granted by Edward the Confessor to the monastery of St Peter's, Westminster. The site of the palace is unknown. The name 'Old Windsor' was first used in the reign of King John. 'Old W. way, and every way but the town way' (*M.W.W.* iii, 1).

Wingfield. In Derbyshire. One of Lord Talbot's titles was 'Lord Cromwell of W.' (*1 Hen. VI*, iv, 7).

Wingham. See BEST.

Winter, Season of. (As an adj., and when merely denoting passage of time, *e.g.* 'six winters,' the word is here excluded.) See HIEMS.

Characteristics of the season: 'Like w.'s drops from eaves of reeds' (*Temp.* v, 1); 'rough w.' (*T.G.V.* ii, 4); 'an open room and good for w.' (*M. for M.* ii, 1); 'human mortals want their w. here,' 'angry w.' (*M.N.D.* ii, 1); 'cooled by the same w.' (*M.V.* iii, 1); 'churlish chiding of the w.'s wind' (*A.Y.L.* ii, 1); 'a lusty w., Frosty but kindly' (*ib.* ii, 3); 'No enemy But w. and rough weather' (*ib.* ii, 5); 'together, As the w. to foul weather' (*ib.* v, 4); 'w. tames man, woman, and beast' (*Tam. Sh.* iv, 1); 'w. In storm perpetual' (*Wint. T.* iii, 2); 'the red blood reigns in the w.'s pale' (*ib.* iv, 3); 'rosemary and rue keep ... savour all the w.,' 'flower of w.,' 'trembling w.' (*ib.* iv, 4); 'a Poland w.' (*Com. Err.* iii, 2); 'sap-consuming w.' (*ib.* v, 1); 'as humorous as w.,' 'a summer bird Which ever in the haunch of w. sings' (2 *Hen. IV*, iv, 4); mtd., *Hen. V*, iii, 3; 'w.'s cold' (2 *Hen. VI*, i, 1); 'barren w.' (*ib.* ii, 4); 'that w. should cut off our spring-time' (*3 Hen. VI*, ii, 3); 'cold biting w.' (*ib.* iv, 8); 'w.'s powerful wind' (*ib.* v, 2); 'When great leaves fall, the w. is at hand' (*Rich. III*, ii, 3); 'nor more willingly [the swallow] leaves w.' (*Timon*, iii, 5); '[leaves] with one w.'s brush fell from their boughs' (*ib.* iv, 3); 'quake in the present w.'s state' (*Cymb.* ii, 4); 'furious w.' (*ib.* iv, 2); 'in w. with warm tears I'll melt the snow' (*T. And.* iii, 1); 'summer with your w. mixed' (*ib.* v, 2); 'w. kills the flies' (*Per.* iv, 4); 'w.'s not gone yet, if the wild geese fly that way,' the ant teaches that 'there's no labouring in the w.' (*Lear*, ii, 4); 'the w.'s flaw' (*Haml.* v, 1); 'poor as w.' (*Oth.* iii, 3); 'w. meads' (*Lucr.* 1218); 'rough w.' (*ib.* 1255); mtd., *P.P.* xii; mtd., *Son.* ii; 'hideous w.' (*ib.* v); 'w.'s ragged hand' (*ib.* vi); mtd., *ib.* ii, xiii, xviii, lvi, xcvii, xcviii, civ.

Winter personified: 'none of you will bid the w. come To thrust his icy fingers in my maw' (*John*, v, 7); 'churlish w.'s tyranny' (2 *Hen. IV*, i, 3); 'shrinking slaves of w.' (*Cymb.* iv, 4); 'April on the heel of limping w.' (*Rom. J.* i, 2). Represented on the stage: see HIEMS.

Tedium of winter: 'a sad tale's best for w.' (*Wint. T.* ii, 1); 'story, at a w.'s fire' (*Macb.* iii, 4); 'w.'s tedious nights' (*Rich. II*, v, 1); 'well could I curse away a w.'s night' (2 *Hen. VI*, iii, 2); 'Let Aesop fable in a w.'s night' (*3 Hen. VI*, v, 5); 'watch'd the w.'s night' (*ib.* v, 7).

Metaphorical: 'a nun of w.'s sisterhood' (*A.Y.L.* iii, 4); 'the w. of our discontent' (*Rich. III*, i, 1); 'death, that w.' (*Hen. VIII*, iii, 2); Achilles, kissing Cressida after Nestor, exclaims, 'I'll take that w. from your lips' (*Tr. Cr.* iv, 5); ''Tis deepest w. in Lord Timon's purse' (*Timon*, iii, 4); 'for his [Antony's] bounty, There was no w. in it' (*Ant. Cl.* v, 2); 'lust's w.' (*V.A.* 802).

Winter's Tale, The. (In F1: 'The Winters Tale.' The acts and scenes are numbered.)

PUBLICATION. First appeared in the Folio of 1623.

DATE OF COMPOSITION. Uncertain, but attributed to 1610–11 by the great majority of critics. Dr Forman notes in his *Booke of Plaies* a performance at the Globe on May 15, 1611.

SOURCE OF THE PLOT. Based on a novel by Robert Greene (1588) at first named *Pandosto* and later *Dorastus and Fawnia*. Autolycus is Sh.'s creation. In *Pandosto* Bellaria (Hermione) dies of grief.

'The progressive interest of the play, *malgré* the vast hiatus for which Sh. himself thought it necessary to apologise, is well sustained: but the catastrophe is hurried, and the Queen's reanimation beyond all human credibility. Yet it acts well, and the whole is pleasing and effective on the stage.' (Hartley

Coleridge, *Essays* (1851), ii, 148.) For Mrs Lennox's violent attack on the play see her *Sh. Ill.* (1753), ii, 75. 'One of the best-acting of our author's plays' (W. Hazlitt). 'It may be called the gentlest of Sh.'s plays' (J. Masefield). 'It is perhaps the last complete play that Sh. wrote' (E. Dowden).

Witches, Three. D.PP. *Macb.* i, 1] plan to meet Macbeth 'ere set of sun.' i, 3] devise revenge on a sea-captain; hail Macb. as Thane of Glamis and of Cawdor, and 'king hereafter'; Banquo they hail as ancestor of kings. iii, 5] are rebuked by Hecate for acting without her authority. iv, 1] brew a 'hell-broth,' and are joined by H.; exhibit to Macb. certain apparitions and vanish. See HECATE.

In *Holinshed*, ii, 170, the prophecy (i, 3) is made by 'three women of strange and wild apparell, resembling creatures of elder world... Afterwards the common opinion was that these women were either the weird sisters, that is ... the goddesses of destinie, or else some nymphs, or fairies.' The revenge on the sea-captain is paralleled (*Hol.* ii, 149) by the bewitchment of King Duff.

'The weird sisters are as true a creation of Sh.'s as his Ariel and Caliban, – fates, fairies and materializing witches being the elements. They are wholly different from any representations of witches in the contemporary writers, and yet presented a sufficient external resemblance to the creatures of vulgar prejudice to act immediately upon the audience.' (S. T. Coleridge, *Notes on Macbeth*.)

Withold, St. Theobald's emendation of 'Swithold' in *Lear*, iii, 4 (Ff; 'swithald,' Qq). Tyrwhitt suggests that St Vitalis is thus named. The name occurs in *Tr. R.* I, 11, ll. 5–6: 'Sweet Saint Withold of thy lenity, Defend us from extremity,' where the metre suggests the contracted form.

There are at least three saints named Vitalis, the earliest having been probably martyred under Nero.

Wittenberg. Town in Saxony; famous for its association with Luther and the early Reformation. Its university was founded in 1502. Hamlet resolves to go 'back to school in W.'; his mother dissuades him; Horatio has just returned thence, *Haml.* i, 2.

As the university is clearly implied by 'school,' an anachronism is obvious.

Wolsey, Thomas (*c.* 1475–1530). Cardinal and statesman; Abp. of York 1514; accompanied Hen. VIII to the Field of the Cloth of Gold 1520; supported Henry's claims to his divorce from Katharine of Arragon, but incurred Anne Boleyn's dislike in consequence of delay in the proceedings (due really to Card. Campeggio), and a bill of indictment was preferred against him; he was pardoned, and retired to Cawood Castle, where he was soon afterward arrested for treason, on false information, and died at Leicester on his way to London.

It is said that the Cardinal's father was one Robert Wulcy (or Wolsey), a butcher, of Ipswich, but Holinshed (iii, 917) quotes Edmund Campian's opinion that 'he was a man undoubtedly borne to honour: I thinke some princes bastard, no butchers sonne; exceeding wise; faire spoken; high minded; full of revenge; vitious of his bodie; lofty to his enemies, were they never so big; to those that accepted and sought his freendship wonderfull courteous; a ripe scholeman; thrall to affections; brought a bed with flatterie; insatiable to get, and more princelie in bestowing, as appeareth by his two colleges at Ipswich and Oxenford [*Hen. VIII*, iv, 2] ... a great preferrer of his servants, an advancer of learning, stout in everie quarell, never happie till this his overthrow. Wherein he shewed such moderation, and ended so perfectly, that the houre of his death did him more honor than all the pompe of his life passed.'

D.P. *Hen. VIII.* i, 1] prepares to examine the D. of Buckingham's surveyor (*Hol.* iii, 862); the Cardinal and the Duke eye one another disdainfully. i, 2] the Queen accuses W., in council, of having devised grievous exactions, productive of disloyalty; W. defends himself as having been only responsible as 'a single voice,' and urges that if statesmen are to be swayed by malevolent or ignorant critics, they might as well be 'state-statues'; (he privately tells his secretary to spread it abroad that the taxes are remitted through the Cardinal's intercession); takes part in the royal examination of the Duke's surveyor. (i, 3) his liberality noted. i, 4] receives the King at a sumptuous entertainment at York Place (*Hol.* iii, 921). (ii, 1) his hatred of the Emperor alleged (*Hol.* iii, 906). ii, 2] (the Dukes of Norfolk and Suffolk comment on his pride and ambition); W. presents Campeius to the King; later, presents Gardiner (*Hol.* iii, 907); is questioned by Campeius about Dr Pace (*q.v.*) ii, 4] is openly accused by Katharine of being her enemy, and repudiates the charge (*Hol.* iii, 908); appeals to Henry to exonerate him; the King declares that W. ever 'wish'd the sleeping of this business' (*Hol.* iii, 907). iii, 1] in company with Card. Campeius, urges Katharine to yield to the King's wishes. iii, 2] (letters from Wolsey to the Pope, urging reasons against the royal divorce, have fallen into Henry's hands; see RUTHALL); (*sol.*) W. declares that the King shall not marry Anne Boleyn (*Hol.* iii, 909); Henry reminds him of the honours and favours he has bestowed upon him, and, handing him papers, departs in anger; W. finds that the papers are his own letters to the Pope, and a private inventory of all his wealth; is ordered 'to render up the great seal' (*Hol.* iii, 909); listens to a rehearsal of the articles against him by the lords present (*Hol.* iii, 912); (*sol.*) 'bids farewell' to all his greatness; in an interview with Cromwell, confesses that ambition had been the true cause of his ruin, and wishes he had served God better (*Hol.* iii, 909). (iv, 1) mtd. (iv, 2) the circumstances of his death described (*Hol.* iii, 917); he is characterized by Griffith, following Campian's account (*vide supra*).

Woncot. Local pronunciation of 'Woodmancote,' a village in Gloucestershire; *2 Hen. IV*, v, 1. See VISOR.

Arbitrarily changed by Malone to 'Wincot' (*q.v.*); 'Woncote,' Q.

Woodstock. For 'Gloucester'; *Rich. II*, i, 2, Q1, 2, 3, 4.

Woodstock, Thomas of. See THOMAS OF WOODSTOCK.

Woodville, Anthony (*c.* 1442–83). Baron Scales and 2nd E. Rivers; son of Richard W. (*q.v.*); styled Lord S. (1462) through his marriage with Elizabeth, Baroness S. in her own right (*3 Hen. VI*, iv, 1); succeeded as E. Rivers in 1469; with Edw. IV in exile; made governor to Prince Edward; on the death of Edw. IV, he was executed, on a charge of treason, by the orders of Richard, D. of York, then Protector; 'a right honourable man, as valiant of hand as politike in counsell' (*Hol.* iii, 714).

D.P. *3 Hen. VI.* iv, 4] is told by his sister, Q. Elizabeth, that Edward IV is a prisoner, and is urged to flee (cf. *Hol.* iii, 675). (Historically, the King had been captured a year before.)

D.P. *Rich. III.* i, 3] is upbraided by Gloucester for thwarting him and bringing him into contempt. ii, 1] is reconciled to Hastings (in st. dirs., F1, the same as 'Rivers,' who is also named). ii, 2] urges that Prince Edward should be crowned; agrees to his 'little train.' (ii, 4) imprisoned at Pomfret (*Hol.* iii, 715). iii, 3] is taken to execution; recalls Q. Margaret's curse. (v, 1) mtd. (v, 3) his ghost appears to Richard before Bosworth.

After ii, 1, l. 67 (in Ff, but not in Qq), there follows: 'Of you, Lord Woodville and Lord Scales of you'; but these are merely other titles of Lord Rivers, already mtd.

Woodville, Elizabeth. See ELIZABETH (1).

Woodville, or Widvill, Richard. Constable of the Tower; by command of Henry Beaufort, Bp. of Winchester, refused to open the gates to the Duke of Gloucester (Hall, p. 130) (created Baron Rivers in 1448; his eldest daughter, Elizabeth, married Edward IV).

D.P. *1 Hen. VI.* (Styled 'Lieutenant of the Tower.') i, 3] resists Gloucester, as above.

Queen E.'s 'kindred' (*Rich. III*, i, 3, l. 67) were numerous; Richard W. had 13 children.

Worcester, City of. In the Lady Chapel of the cathedral King John was originally buried, and in the reign of Henry VIII his body was removed to the choir, where the tomb now stands.

'*Hen.* At W. must his body be interred, For so he willed it' (*John*, v. 7); 'there is more news: I learn'd in W. as I rode along [on the way to Shrewsbury]' (*1 Hen. IV*, iv, 1).

'Worster' in *John*, v, 7 F1, 2.

Worcester, Earl of. See PERCY, THOMAS.

Worm, Don. Nonce-name applied to Conscience by Benedick; *M. Ado*, v, 2.

Wriothesley, Henry. 3rd E. of Southampton (1573–1624). He proceeded to St John's College, Cambridge, at the age of twelve, and graduated as M.A. when he was sixteen; shortly afterward he was graciously received at Elizabeth's Court, and became a favourite of Essex. He early became a patron of literature; John Florio was his tutor in Italian, and the intimacy of his relations with Sh. – who was some years his senior – is beyond dispute. *Venus and Adonis* (1593) and *Lucrece* (1594) are both inscribed 'To the Right Honourable Henry Wriothesl(e)y, Earl of Southampton, and Baron of Tichfield,' and in the dedication of the latter Sh. declares: 'What I have done is yours; what I have to do is yours; being part in all I have, devoted yours.' With regard to the identification of 'the friend' of the *Sonnets* with Southampton see the article SONNETS.

In 1596 Southampton withdrew from Court, having become involved in an intrigue with one of the royal waiting-women, Elizabeth Vernon, whom he ultimately married. Out of favour with the Queen, he joined Essex in his conspiracy, and it is noteworthy that on the day before that fixed by Essex for a popular rising in London *Rich. II* was played at the Globe theatre to inflame the minds of the people by the exhibition of the deposition and murder of a king (see Lee, p. 254). For his share in the plot Southampton was condemned to death, but the sentence was commuted to imprisonment. On the accession of James I he was released (cf. *Son.* cvii) and received many marks of the monarch's favour.

The last syllable of the name is '-ley,' '-ly,' '-lie,' in the edns. of 1593, 1594, and 1596 respectively.

Wriothesley, Sir Thomas (1). *Ob.* 1534; appointed Garter King of Arms by Henry VIII.

D.P. *Hen. VIII.* (Unnamed.) iv, 1] appears in Anne's coronation procession.

[**Wriothesley, Sir Thomas** (2) (1505–50).] 1st Baron W. and Earl of Southampton; Lord Chancellor 1544, and therefore probably when Cranmer was brought before the Council, *Hen. VIII*, v, 3. 'It is probable that the dramatist supposed it was Sir Thomas More' (Clar.). It has also been suggested that Thos. Goodrick, Bp. of Ely, was Chancellor on the occasion.

Wye, River. Forms in its lower course the boundary between the counties of Monmouth and Gloucester. Glendower claims to have thrice driven back Henry IV from 'the banks of W.' (*1 Hen. IV*, iii, 1); 'it is called W. at Monmouth,' 'all the water in W. cannot wash your majesty's Welsh plood out of your pody' (*Hen. V*, iv, 7).

X, Y, Z

Xaintrailles, or Sainte-Traille. A commune in Dept. Lot-et-Garonne. In the 15th cent. the manor belonged to Poton de X. (*q.v.*).

Xantippe, or Xanthippe. Wife of Socrates; proverbial for her shrewish disposition; *cf.* Xenophon, *Mem.* ii, 2. 'As curst and shrewd as Socrates' X.' (*Tam. Sh.* i, 2). ('Zentippe,' 'Zantippe,' FfQ.)

A character in the morality *A Nice Wanton*, licensed 1560.

Yaughan. '[1st to 2nd grave-digger] Go, get thee to Y.: fetch me a stoup of liquor' (*Haml.* v, 1). This is the reading of Ff; those of Qq being 'get thee gone,' or 'get thee in,' simply.

It has been conjectured by Dr B. Nicholson that Y. is a corruption of 'Johan.' An alehouse stood near the Globe theatre; 'deaf John,' the keeper of such an alehouse, is mtd. in Jonson's *Alchemist*, i, 1; and 'a Jew, one Johan' in *Every Man out of his Humour*, v, 4. (Cf. *N. and Q.* IV, viii, 81.)

Yead. Colloquialism for 'Ned.' 'Yead Miller' (*M.W.W.* i, 1).

Yedward. For 'Edward'; Falstaff to Poins, *1 Hen. IV*, i, 2.

Yorick. The King of Denmark's jester; *Haml.* v, 1. 'A fellow of infinite jest'; Hamlet moralizes upon his skull, and recalls how he frolicked with Y. when a child.

The name has been conjectured to be a corruption of 'Rorick' (Roricus being Hamlet's maternal grandmother, acc. Saxo Grammaticus) (Douce and Magnusson), or adapted from 'Jørgen,' the Danish for 'George' (Ainger).

York. For 'house of Y.' in the phrase 'Y. and Lancaster.' *3 Hen. VI*, i, 1; *Rich. III*, i, 4, v, 5. 'House of York,' thus mtd.: *1 Hen. VI*, iii, 1; *2 Hen. VI*, iii, 1, iv, 1, v, 2; *3 Hen. VI*, i, 1 (3), ii, 6, iii, 2, 3, v, 1.

York, City of. The scene is laid at or near Y. in *1 Hen. IV*, iv, 4; *2 Hen. IV*, i, 3; *3 Hen. VI*, ii, 2, iv, 7. Mtd., *Rich. II*, v, 5; *1 Hen. IV*, v, 5; *2 Hen. IV*, i, 2, ii, 1; Colevile and his confederates executed at Y., 'in a place without the citie' (*ib.* iv, 3; *Hol.* iii, 530). '*Q. Mar.* Off with his [Richard, D. of York's] head, and set it on Y. gates; so Y. may overlook the town of Y.' (*3 Hen. VI*, i, 4; cf. *Hol.* iii, 659); 'on the gates of Y. they set the same' (*ib.* ii, 1); 'this brave town of Y.' (*ib.* ii, 2); 'from off the gates of Y. fetch down the head' (*ib.* ii, 6; cf. *Hol.* iii, 665); Edward IV arrives 'before the gates of Y.,' 'let's harbour here in Y.' (*ib.* iv, 7; *cf.* Hall, pp. 291–2); Wolsey arrested at Y., *Hen. VIII*, iv, 2 (actually arrested at Cawood Castle, Yorks).

York, Duchess of (1). D.P. *Rich. II.* v, 2] listens to York's description of Bolingbroke's entrance with Richard into London; attempts to conceal Aumerle's (Rutland's) treason from York; entreats the latter to have mercy; urges Au. to outride the Duke and seek Bolingbroke's pardon, promising to follow speedily. v, 3] throws herself at the King's feet, and will not rise until he has pardoned Au.

At the time of the action of the play the Duchess of Y. was Joan Holland (3rd d. of Thos. H., 2nd Earl of Kent), who was not Aumerle's mother, as supposed by Sh., and was a girl of about sixteen. The Duke's first wife, Isabella of Castile – Aumerle's mother – died in 1394. The 2nd Duchess was niece of Rich. II, a fact ignored in the play.

York, Duchess of (2). D.P. *Rich. III.* See NEVILLE, CICELY.

York, Dukes of. Edmund (1341–1402); D.P. *Rich. II.* See LANGLEY, EDMUND OF.

Edward (*c.* 1373–1415); D.P. *Hen. V.* See PLANTAGENET, EDWARD.

Richard (1411–60); D.P. 1, 2, *3 Hen. VI.* See RICHARD, 3RD DUKE OF YORK.

Richard, son of Edw. IV; D.P. *Rich. III.* See RICHARD, D. OF YORK.

Edward IV was D. of York, 1460–1. Cf. *3 Hen. VI.* ii, l. 90.

York, Lord Mayor of. D.P. *3 Hen. VI.* iv, 7] demurs to admitting Edw. IV into the city; but delivers the keys on its being pointed out that Edw. is D. of York, and that he and his companions are 'King Henry's friends.'

This personage was Thomas Beverley, Lord Mayor in 1460 and 1471. The title of 'Lord Mayor' was first granted in 1389. *The True Tragedie* gives him his correct title in the st. dirs., and he is addressed as 'My lord Maire,' instead of 'Master Mayor' as in *3 Hen. VI.* ('Two Aldermen,' Hall, pp. 291–2.)

Yorkshire, Sheriff of. See ROKEBY, SIR THOMAS.

Zenelophon. A perversion of 'Penelophon,' in Armado's letter to Jaquenetta; *L.L.L.* iv, 1. See COPHETUA.

It is not necessary to assume a misprint. Armado's earlier reference to the ballad, *L.L.L.* i, 2, implied but a vague acquaintance with it.

Zentippe. See XANTIPPE.

[Zimimar.] See NORTH.

BIBLIOGRAPHY

Jonathan Bate, with an Introduction by Simon Callow, The Genius of Shakespeare, Picador, 2016

Jonathan Bate and Dora Thornton with Becky Allen, Shakespeare's Britain, British Museum, 2012

Jonathan Bate, Soul of the Age: The Life, Mind and World of William Shakespeare, Penguin, 2008

Harold Bloom, Shakespeare: The Invention of the Human, Fourth Estate, 1999

Bill Bryson, Shakespeare: The World as a Stage, Harper Perennial, 2007

Hannah Crawforth and Elizabeth Scott-Baumann (eds), On Shakespeare's Sonnets, Bloomsbury Arden, 2016

Michael Davis, The Landscape of William Shakespeare, Webb & Bower, 1987

Frank Harris, The Man Shakespeare and his Tragic Life-Story, 1909, reprinted Wordsworth Editions, 2008

Frank Kermode, Shakespeare's Language, Penguin, 2001

John Kerrigan, Shakespeare's Binding Language, Oxford University Press, 2016

Hannah Manktelow, The Bard in Brief: Shakespeare in Quotations, British Library, 2016

L. L. M. Marsden, Shakespearian Quotations in Everyday Use, Witherby, 1927

James Shapiro, The Year of Lear: William Shakespeare in 1606, Faber & Faber, 2015

Emma Smith, Shakespeare's First Folio: Four Centuries of an Iconic Book, Oxford University Press, 2016

Helen Vendler, The Art of Shakespeare's Sonnets, Harvard University Press, 1997

APPENDIX 1
FAMILY OF BEAUFORT

John of Gaunt (1340–1399) = Catherine Swynford[1]

- John Beaufort, Earl of Somerset (*ob.* 1410) = Margaret Holland, daughter of Thomas Earl of Kent
  - Henry Beaufort, Earl of Somerset
  - John Beaufort[4], Duke of Somerset = Margaret Beauchamp
    - Margaret Beaufort = Edmund Tudor, Earl of Richmond (*ob.* 1456)
      - Henry VII
  - Edmund Beaufort[5], Duke of Somerset = Alianor Beauchamp
    - Henry Beaufort, Third Duke of Somerset (1436–1464)
    - Henry Beaufort[6], Fourth Duke of Somerset (*ob.* 1471)
- Henry Beaufort[2], Cardinal Bishop of Winchester (*ob.* 1447)
- Thomas Beaufort[3], Duke of Exeter (*ob.* 1427)

1 Her children were born to John of Gaunt before marriage but were afterwards legitimated.

2 D.P. *1, 2 Hen. VI*

3 D.P. *Hen. V, 1 Hen VI*

4 D.P. *1 Hen VI*

5 D.P. *2 Hen VI*

6 D.P. *3 Hen VI*

APPENDIX 2
HOUSE OF LANCASTER

BLANCHE OF LANCASTER[2] = JOHN OF GAUNT[1] = CATHERINE SWYNFORD
Duke of Lancaster (See Appendix 1.)
(1340–1399)

HENRY IV[3] = MARY BOHUN[4]
Henry of Bolingbroke (*ob.* 1394)
(1367–1413)

HENRY V[5] = KATHARINE[6]
(1387–1422) (1401–1437)

THOMAS[7]
Duke of Clarence
(*c.*1388–1421)

JOHN[8]
Duke of Bedford
(1389–1435)

HUMPHREY[9]
Duke of Gloucester
(1391–1447)

Henry VI[10] = Margaret of Anjou[11]
(1421–1471) (1430–1482)

EDWARD, Prince of Wales[12]
(1453–1471)

1 D.P. *Rich. II*; also married Constance of Castile
2 D.P. Daughter of Henry, Duke of Lancaster, who was great-grandson of Henry III
3 D.P. *Rich. II 1, 2 Hen. IV*
4 Second daughter of Humphrey, last Earl of Hereford
5 D.P. *1, 2 Hen IV*, *Hen. V*
6 Daughter of Charles VI of France; D.P. *Hen. V*
7 D.P. *2 Hen. IV*
8 D.P. *2 Hen. IV*, *Hen. V*, *1 Hen. VI*
9 D.P. *2 Hen. IV*, *Hen. V*, *1*, *2 Hen. VI*
10 D.P. *1*, *2*, *3 Hen. VI*
11 D.P. *1*, *2*, *3 Hen. VI*, *Rich. III*
12 D.P. *3 Hen. VI*

APPENDIX 3
HOUSE OF YORK

EDMUND OF LANGLEY[1] = ISABEL OF CASTILE[2]
First Duke of York (1341–1402) — (*ob.* 1394)

- EDWARD[3]
  Duke of York
  Earl of Rutland
  Duke of Albermarle
  (*c.*1373–1415)
- RICHARD[4] = ANNE MORTIMER[5]
  Earl of Cambridge
  (*ob.* 1415)
  - RICHARD[6] = CICELY NEVILLE[7]
    Duke of York
    (1411–1460)
    - EDWARD IV[8] (1442–1483) = ELIZABETH WOODVILLE[9] (*c.*1437–1492)
      - Edward V[13] (1470–1483)
      - Richard[14] Duke of York (1472–1483)
      - Elizabeth (1465–1503) = Henry VII
    - EDMUND[10] Earl of Rutland (1443–1460)
    - GEORGE[11] Duke of Clarence (1449–1478)
    - RICHARD III[12] (1452–1485)

1 D.P. *Rich. II*
2 Died before *Rich. II* opens.
3 D.P. *Rich. II* ('Aumerle'), *Hen. V*
4 D.P. *Hen. V*
5 See Appendix 4.
6 D.P. *1, 2, 3, Hen. VI*
7 D.P. *Rich. III*
8 D.P. *2 Hen. VI, 3 Hen. VI* ('Earl of March'), *Rich. III*
9 D.P. *Rich. III*
10 D.P. *3 Hen. VI*
11 D.P. *3 Hen. VI, Rich. III*
12 D.P. 2, *3, Hen. VI, Rich. III*
13 D.P. *Rich. III*
14 D.P. *Rich. III*

APPENDIX 4
FAMILY OF MORTIMER

Edmund Mortimer = Philippa Plantagenet[1]
Third Earl of March
(1351–1381)

- Roger Mortimer
  Fourth Earl of March
  (1374–1398)
  - Edmund Mortimer
    Fifth Earl of March
    (1391–1424)
  - Anne Mortimer[4] = Richard
    Earl of Cambridge
- Sir Edmund Mortimer[2]
  (1376–*c.*1409)
- Elizabeth Mortimer[3] = 'Hotspur'

1 Daughter of Lionel, second son of Edward III

2 Confused in *Sh.* with his nephew, the Fifth Earl of March.

3 D.P. *1, 2 Hen. IV*

4 See Appendix 3.

APPENDIX 5
FAMILY OF NEVILLE

Thomas de Montacute
Fourth Earl of Salisbury
(1388–1428)

Ralph Neville (of Raby)[1]
First Earl of Westmoreland
(1364–1425)

Alice de Montacute (heiress) = Richard Neville[2]
First Earl of Salisbury
(1400–1460)

Richard Beauchamp
Earl of Warwick
(1382–1439)

John Neville[3]
Marquis of Montague

Richard Neville[4]
Earl of Warwick
and Salisbury
= Anne Beauchamp (heiress)

Anne Neville[5] = Richard III

1 D.P. *1*, *2 Hen. IV*, *Hen. V*
2 D.P. *2 Hen. VI*
3 D.P. *3 Hen. VI*; slain at Barnet 1471.
4 The 'King Maker'; D.P. *2*, *3*, *Hen. VI*
5 D.P. *Rich. III* ('Lady Anne')

APPENDIX 6
FAMILY OF PERCY

HENRY PERCY = MARY PLANTAGENET[1]
Third Baron Percy
of Alnwick
(1322–1368)

HENRY PERCY[2] = MARGARET NEVILLE[3]
First Earl of
Northumberland

THOMAS PERCY[4]
Earl of Worcester
(*c.*1344–1403)

SIR HENRY PERCY[5] = ELIZABETH MORTIMER[6]
('Hotspur')
(1364–1403)
('Lady Percy')

HENRY PERCY[7] = ELEANOR NEVILLE[8]
Second Earl of Northumberland
(1394–1455)

HENRY PERCY[9]
Third Earl of Northumberland
(1421–1461)

1 Granddaughter of Edmund 'Crouchback', Earl of Lancaster
2 D.P. *Rich. II*, *1*, *2 Hen. IV*
3 Daughter of the second Lord Neville of Raby
4 D.P. *1 Hen. IV*
5 D.P. *Rich. II*, *1 Hen. IV*
6 Daughter of Edmund Mortimer, Third Earl of March; see Appendix 4.
7 Slain at St Albans
8 Daughter of Ralph Neville, First Earl of Westmoreland
9 D.P. 3 *Hen. VI*

APPENDIX 7
ACTORS

The names of the principal actors in all these plays
Reproduced from the First Folio, 1623

William Shakespeare
Richard Burbadge
John Hemmings
Augustine Phillips
William Kempt
Thomas Poope
George Bryan
Henry Condell
William Slye
Richard Cowly
John Lowine
Samuell Crosse
Alexander Cooke

Samuel Gilburne
Robert Armin
William Ostler
Nathan Field
John Underwood
Nicholas Tooley
William Ecclestone
Joseph Taylor
Robert Benfield
Robert Goughe
Richard Robinson
Iohn Shanke
Iohn Rice

APPENDIX 8

The following 'Catalogue' is reproduced from that prefixed to the First Folio, since in it the names of the plays differ in many respects from the titles given in the Folio itself and quoted in this work. It will be noticed that *Troilus and Cressida* is omitted, probably on account of a doubt as to how it should be classed.

A CATALOGVE
of the seuerall Comedies, Histories and Tragedies
contained in this Volume.